# Lecture Notes in Computer Science    13683

More information about this series at https://link.springer.com/bookseries/558

Shai Avidan · Gabriel Brostow ·
Moustapha Cissé · Giovanni Maria Farinella ·
Tal Hassner (Eds.)

# Computer Vision – ECCV 2022

17th European Conference
Tel Aviv, Israel, October 23–27, 2022
Proceedings, Part XXIII

Springer

*Editors*
Shai Avidan
Tel Aviv University
Tel Aviv, Israel

Gabriel Brostow
University College London
London, UK

Moustapha Cissé
Google AI
Accra, Ghana

Giovanni Maria Farinella
University of Catania
Catania, Italy

Tal Hassner
Facebook (United States)
Menlo Park, CA, USA

ISSN 0302-9743 ISSN 1611-3349 (electronic)
Lecture Notes in Computer Science
ISBN 978-3-031-20049-6 ISBN 978-3-031-20050-2 (eBook)
https://doi.org/10.1007/978-3-031-20050-2

This Springer imprint is published by the registered company Springer Nature Switzerland AG
The registered company address is: Gewerbestrasse 11, 6330 Cham, Switzerland

# Foreword

Organizing the European Conference on Computer Vision (ECCV 2022) in Tel-Aviv during a global pandemic was no easy feat. The uncertainty level was extremely high, and decisions had to be postponed to the last minute. Still, we managed to plan things just in time for ECCV 2022 to be held in person. Participation in physical events is crucial to stimulating collaborations and nurturing the culture of the Computer Vision community.

There were many people who worked hard to ensure attendees enjoyed the best science at the 16th edition of ECCV. We are grateful to the Program Chairs Gabriel Brostow and Tal Hassner, who went above and beyond to ensure the ECCV reviewing process ran smoothly. The scientific program includes dozens of workshops and tutorials in addition to the main conference and we would like to thank Leonid Karlinsky and Tomer Michaeli for their hard work. Finally, special thanks to the web chairs Lorenzo Baraldi and Kosta Derpanis, who put in extra hours to transfer information fast and efficiently to the ECCV community.

We would like to express gratitude to our generous sponsors and the Industry Chairs, Dimosthenis Karatzas and Chen Sagiv, who oversaw industry relations and proposed new ways for academia-industry collaboration and technology transfer. It's great to see so much industrial interest in what we're doing!

Authors' draft versions of the papers appeared online with open access on both the Computer Vision Foundation (CVF) and the European Computer Vision Association (ECVA) websites as with previous ECCVs. Springer, the publisher of the proceedings, has arranged for archival publication. The final version of the papers is hosted by SpringerLink, with active references and supplementary materials. It benefits all potential readers that we offer both a free and citeable version for all researchers, as well as an authoritative, citeable version for SpringerLink readers. Our thanks go to Ronan Nugent from Springer, who helped us negotiate this agreement. Last but not least, we wish to thank Eric Mortensen, our publication chair, whose expertise made the process smooth.

October 2022

Rita Cucchiara
Jiří Matas
Amnon Shashua
Lihi Zelnik-Manor

# Preface

Welcome to the proceedings of the European Conference on Computer Vision (ECCV 2022). This was a hybrid edition of ECCV as we made our way out of the COVID-19 pandemic. The conference received 5804 valid paper submissions, compared to 5150 submissions to ECCV 2020 (a 12.7% increase) and 2439 in ECCV 2018. 1645 submissions were accepted for publication (28%) and, of those, 157 (2.7% overall) as orals.

846 of the submissions were desk-rejected for various reasons. Many of them because they revealed author identity, thus violating the double-blind policy. This violation came in many forms: some had author names with the title, others added acknowledgments to specific grants, yet others had links to their github account where their name was visible. Tampering with the LaTeX template was another reason for automatic desk rejection.

ECCV 2022 used the traditional CMT system to manage the entire double-blind reviewing process. Authors did not know the names of the reviewers and vice versa. Each paper received at least 3 reviews (except 6 papers that received only 2 reviews), totalling more than 15,000 reviews.

Handling the review process at this scale was a significant challenge. To ensure that each submission received as fair and high-quality reviews as possible, we recruited more than 4719 reviewers (in the end, 4719 reviewers did at least one review). Similarly we recruited more than 276 area chairs (eventually, only 276 area chairs handled a batch of papers). The area chairs were selected based on their technical expertise and reputation, largely among people who served as area chairs in previous top computer vision and machine learning conferences (ECCV, ICCV, CVPR, NeurIPS, etc.).

Reviewers were similarly invited from previous conferences, and also from the pool of authors. We also encouraged experienced area chairs to suggest additional chairs and reviewers in the initial phase of recruiting. The median reviewer load was five papers per reviewer, while the average load was about four papers, because of the emergency reviewers. The area chair load was 35 papers, on average.

Conflicts of interest between authors, area chairs, and reviewers were handled largely automatically by the CMT platform, with some manual help from the Program Chairs. Reviewers were allowed to describe themselves as senior reviewer (load of 8 papers to review) or junior reviewers (load of 4 papers). Papers were matched to area chairs based on a subject-area affinity score computed in CMT and an affinity score computed by the Toronto Paper Matching System (TPMS). TPMS is based on the paper's full text. An area chair handling each submission would bid for preferred expert reviewers, and we balanced load and prevented conflicts.

The assignment of submissions to area chairs was relatively smooth, as was the assignment of submissions to reviewers. A small percentage of reviewers were not happy with their assignments in terms of subjects and self-reported expertise. This is an area for improvement, although it's interesting that many of these cases were reviewers hand-picked by AC's. We made a later round of reviewer recruiting, targeted at the list of authors of papers submitted to the conference, and had an excellent response which helped provide enough emergency reviewers. In the end, all but six papers received at least 3 reviews.

The challenges of the reviewing process are in line with past experiences at ECCV 2020. As the community grows, and the number of submissions increases, it becomes ever more challenging to recruit enough reviewers and ensure a high enough quality of reviews. Enlisting authors by default as reviewers might be one step to address this challenge.

Authors were given a week to rebut the initial reviews, and address reviewers' concerns. Each rebuttal was limited to a single pdf page with a fixed template.

The Area Chairs then led discussions with the reviewers on the merits of each submission. The goal was to reach consensus, but, ultimately, it was up to the Area Chair to make a decision. The decision was then discussed with a buddy Area Chair to make sure decisions were fair and informative. The entire process was conducted virtually with no in-person meetings taking place.

The Program Chairs were informed in cases where the Area Chairs overturned a decisive consensus reached by the reviewers, and pushed for the meta-reviews to contain details that explained the reasoning for such decisions. Obviously these were the most contentious cases, where reviewer inexperience was the most common reported factor.

Once the list of accepted papers was finalized and released, we went through the laborious process of plagiarism (including self-plagiarism) detection. A total of 4 accepted papers were rejected because of that.

Finally, we would like to thank our Technical Program Chair, Pavel Lifshits, who did tremendous work behind the scenes, and we thank the tireless CMT team.

October 2022

Gabriel Brostow
Giovanni Maria Farinella
Moustapha Cissé
Shai Avidan
Tal Hassner

# Organization

## General Chairs

Rita Cucchiara      University of Modena and Reggio Emilia, Italy
Jiří Matas      Czech Technical University in Prague, Czech Republic
Amnon Shashua      Hebrew University of Jerusalem, Israel
Lihi Zelnik-Manor      Technion – Israel Institute of Technology, Israel

## Program Chairs

Shai Avidan      Tel-Aviv University, Israel
Gabriel Brostow      University College London, UK
Moustapha Cissé      Google AI, Ghana
Giovanni Maria Farinella      University of Catania, Italy
Tal Hassner      Facebook AI, USA

## Program Technical Chair

Pavel Lifshits      Technion – Israel Institute of Technology, Israel

## Workshops Chairs

Leonid Karlinsky      IBM Research, Israel
Tomer Michaeli      Technion – Israel Institute of Technology, Israel
Ko Nishino      Kyoto University, Japan

## Tutorial Chairs

Thomas Pock      Graz University of Technology, Austria
Natalia Neverova      Facebook AI Research, UK

## Demo Chair

Bohyung Han      Seoul National University, Korea

## Social and Student Activities Chairs

Tatiana Tommasi                  Italian Institute of Technology, Italy
Sagie Benaim                     University of Copenhagen, Denmark

## Diversity and Inclusion Chairs

Xi Yin                           Facebook AI Research, USA
Bryan Russell                    Adobe, USA

## Communications Chairs

Lorenzo Baraldi                  University of Modena and Reggio Emilia, Italy
Kosta Derpanis                   York University & Samsung AI Centre Toronto,
                                 Canada

## Industrial Liaison Chairs

Dimosthenis Karatzas             Universitat Autònoma de Barcelona, Spain
Chen Sagiv                       SagivTech, Israel

## Finance Chair

Gerard Medioni                   University of Southern California & Amazon,
                                 USA

## Publication Chair

Eric Mortensen                   MiCROTEC, USA

## Area Chairs

Lourdes Agapito                  University College London, UK
Zeynep Akata                     University of Tübingen, Germany
Naveed Akhtar                    University of Western Australia, Australia
Karteek Alahari                  Inria Grenoble Rhône-Alpes, France
Alexandre Alahi                  École polytechnique fédérale de Lausanne,
                                 Switzerland
Pablo Arbelaez                   Universidad de Los Andes, Columbia
Antonis A. Argyros               University of Crete & Foundation for Research
                                 and Technology-Hellas, Crete
Yuki M. Asano                    University of Amsterdam, The Netherlands
Kalle Åström                     Lund University, Sweden
Hadar Averbuch-Elor              Cornell University, USA

| | |
|---|---|
| Hossein Azizpour | KTH Royal Institute of Technology, Sweden |
| Vineeth N. Balasubramanian | Indian Institute of Technology, Hyderabad, India |
| Lamberto Ballan | University of Padova, Italy |
| Adrien Bartoli | Université Clermont Auvergne, France |
| Horst Bischof | Graz University of Technology, Austria |
| Matthew B. Blaschko | KU Leuven, Belgium |
| Federica Bogo | Meta Reality Labs Research, Switzerland |
| Katherine Bouman | California Institute of Technology, USA |
| Edmond Boyer | Inria Grenoble Rhône-Alpes, France |
| Michael S. Brown | York University, Canada |
| Vittorio Caggiano | Meta AI Research, USA |
| Neill Campbell | University of Bath, UK |
| Octavia Camps | Northeastern University, USA |
| Duygu Ceylan | Adobe Research, USA |
| Ayan Chakrabarti | Google Research, USA |
| Tat-Jen Cham | Nanyang Technological University, Singapore |
| Antoni Chan | City University of Hong Kong, Hong Kong, China |
| Manmohan Chandraker | NEC Labs America, USA |
| Xinlei Chen | Facebook AI Research, USA |
| Xilin Chen | Institute of Computing Technology, Chinese Academy of Sciences, China |
| Dongdong Chen | Microsoft Cloud AI, USA |
| Chen Chen | University of Central Florida, USA |
| Ondrej Chum | Vision Recognition Group, Czech Technical University in Prague, Czech Republic |
| John Collomosse | Adobe Research & University of Surrey, UK |
| Camille Couprie | Facebook, France |
| David Crandall | Indiana University, USA |
| Daniel Cremers | Technical University of Munich, Germany |
| Marco Cristani | University of Verona, Italy |
| Canton Cristian | Facebook AI Research, USA |
| Dengxin Dai | ETH Zurich, Switzerland |
| Dima Damen | University of Bristol, UK |
| Kostas Daniilidis | University of Pennsylvania, USA |
| Trevor Darrell | University of California, Berkeley, USA |
| Andrew Davison | Imperial College London, UK |
| Tali Dekel | Weizmann Institute of Science, Israel |
| Alessio Del Bue | Istituto Italiano di Tecnologia, Italy |
| Weihong Deng | Beijing University of Posts and Telecommunications, China |
| Konstantinos Derpanis | Ryerson University, Canada |
| Carl Doersch | DeepMind, UK |

Matthijs Douze                  Facebook AI Research, USA
Mohamed Elhoseiny               King Abdullah University of Science and
                                  Technology, Saudi Arabia
Sergio Escalera                 University of Barcelona, Spain
Yi Fang                         New York University, USA
Ryan Farrell                    Brigham Young University, USA
Alireza Fathi                   Google, USA
Christoph Feichtenhofer         Facebook AI Research, USA
Basura Fernando                 Agency for Science, Technology and Research
                                  (A*STAR), Singapore
Vittorio Ferrari                Google Research, Switzerland
Andrew W. Fitzgibbon            Graphcore, UK
David J. Fleet                  University of Toronto, Canada
David Forsyth                   University of Illinois at Urbana-Champaign, USA
David Fouhey                    University of Michigan, USA
Katerina Fragkiadaki            Carnegie Mellon University, USA
Friedrich Fraundorfer           Graz University of Technology, Austria
Oren Freifeld                   Ben-Gurion University, Israel
Thomas Funkhouser               Google Research & Princeton University, USA
Yasutaka Furukawa               Simon Fraser University, Canada
Fabio Galasso                   Sapienza University of Rome, Italy
Jürgen Gall                     University of Bonn, Germany
Chuang Gan                      Massachusetts Institute of Technology, USA
Zhe Gan                         Microsoft, USA
Animesh Garg                    University of Toronto, Vector Institute, Nvidia,
                                  Canada
Efstratios Gavves               University of Amsterdam, The Netherlands
Peter Gehler                    Amazon, Germany
Theo Gevers                     University of Amsterdam, The Netherlands
Bernard Ghanem                  King Abdullah University of Science and
                                  Technology, Saudi Arabia
Ross B. Girshick                Facebook AI Research, USA
Georgia Gkioxari                Facebook AI Research, USA
Albert Gordo                    Facebook, USA
Stephen Gould                   Australian National University, Australia
Venu Madhav Govindu             Indian Institute of Science, India
Kristen Grauman                 Facebook AI Research & UT Austin, USA
Abhinav Gupta                   Carnegie Mellon University & Facebook AI
                                  Research, USA
Mohit Gupta                     University of Wisconsin-Madison, USA
Hu Han                          Institute of Computing Technology, Chinese
                                  Academy of Sciences, China

| | |
|---|---|
| Bohyung Han | Seoul National University, Korea |
| Tian Han | Stevens Institute of Technology, USA |
| Emily Hand | University of Nevada, Reno, USA |
| Bharath Hariharan | Cornell University, USA |
| Ran He | Institute of Automation, Chinese Academy of Sciences, China |
| Otmar Hilliges | ETH Zurich, Switzerland |
| Adrian Hilton | University of Surrey, UK |
| Minh Hoai | Stony Brook University, USA |
| Yedid Hoshen | Hebrew University of Jerusalem, Israel |
| Timothy Hospedales | University of Edinburgh, UK |
| Gang Hua | Wormpex AI Research, USA |
| Di Huang | Beihang University, China |
| Jing Huang | Facebook, USA |
| Jia-Bin Huang | Facebook, USA |
| Nathan Jacobs | Washington University in St. Louis, USA |
| C.V. Jawahar | International Institute of Information Technology, Hyderabad, India |
| Herve Jegou | Facebook AI Research, France |
| Neel Joshi | Microsoft Research, USA |
| Armand Joulin | Facebook AI Research, France |
| Frederic Jurie | University of Caen Normandie, France |
| Fredrik Kahl | Chalmers University of Technology, Sweden |
| Yannis Kalantidis | NAVER LABS Europe, France |
| Evangelos Kalogerakis | University of Massachusetts, Amherst, USA |
| Sing Bing Kang | Zillow Group, USA |
| Yosi Keller | Bar Ilan University, Israel |
| Margret Keuper | University of Mannheim, Germany |
| Tae-Kyun Kim | Imperial College London, UK |
| Benjamin Kimia | Brown University, USA |
| Alexander Kirillov | Facebook AI Research, USA |
| Kris Kitani | Carnegie Mellon University, USA |
| Iasonas Kokkinos | Snap Inc. & University College London, UK |
| Vladlen Koltun | Apple, USA |
| Nikos Komodakis | University of Crete, Crete |
| Piotr Koniusz | Australian National University, Australia |
| Philipp Kraehenbuehl | University of Texas at Austin, USA |
| Dilip Krishnan | Google, USA |
| Ajay Kumar | Hong Kong Polytechnic University, Hong Kong, China |
| Junseok Kwon | Chung-Ang University, Korea |
| Jean-Francois Lalonde | Université Laval, Canada |

| | |
|---|---|
| Ivan Laptev | Inria Paris, France |
| Laura Leal-Taixé | Technical University of Munich, Germany |
| Erik Learned-Miller | University of Massachusetts, Amherst, USA |
| Gim Hee Lee | National University of Singapore, Singapore |
| Seungyong Lee | Pohang University of Science and Technology, Korea |
| Zhen Lei | Institute of Automation, Chinese Academy of Sciences, China |
| Bastian Leibe | RWTH Aachen University, Germany |
| Hongdong Li | Australian National University, Australia |
| Fuxin Li | Oregon State University, USA |
| Bo Li | University of Illinois at Urbana-Champaign, USA |
| Yin Li | University of Wisconsin-Madison, USA |
| Ser-Nam Lim | Meta AI Research, USA |
| Joseph Lim | University of Southern California, USA |
| Stephen Lin | Microsoft Research Asia, China |
| Dahua Lin | The Chinese University of Hong Kong, Hong Kong, China |
| Si Liu | Beihang University, China |
| Xiaoming Liu | Michigan State University, USA |
| Ce Liu | Microsoft, USA |
| Zicheng Liu | Microsoft, USA |
| Yanxi Liu | Pennsylvania State University, USA |
| Feng Liu | Portland State University, USA |
| Yebin Liu | Tsinghua University, China |
| Chen Change Loy | Nanyang Technological University, Singapore |
| Huchuan Lu | Dalian University of Technology, China |
| Cewu Lu | Shanghai Jiao Tong University, China |
| Oisin Mac Aodha | University of Edinburgh, UK |
| Dhruv Mahajan | Facebook, USA |
| Subhransu Maji | University of Massachusetts, Amherst, USA |
| Atsuto Maki | KTH Royal Institute of Technology, Sweden |
| Arun Mallya | NVIDIA, USA |
| R. Manmatha | Amazon, USA |
| Iacopo Masi | Sapienza University of Rome, Italy |
| Dimitris N. Metaxas | Rutgers University, USA |
| Ajmal Mian | University of Western Australia, Australia |
| Christian Micheloni | University of Udine, Italy |
| Krystian Mikolajczyk | Imperial College London, UK |
| Anurag Mittal | Indian Institute of Technology, Madras, India |
| Philippos Mordohai | Stevens Institute of Technology, USA |
| Greg Mori | Simon Fraser University & Borealis AI, Canada |

| | |
|---|---|
| Vittorio Murino | Istituto Italiano di Tecnologia, Italy |
| P. J. Narayanan | International Institute of Information Technology, Hyderabad, India |
| Ram Nevatia | University of Southern California, USA |
| Natalia Neverova | Facebook AI Research, UK |
| Richard Newcombe | Facebook, USA |
| Cuong V. Nguyen | Florida International University, USA |
| Bingbing Ni | Shanghai Jiao Tong University, China |
| Juan Carlos Niebles | Salesforce & Stanford University, USA |
| Ko Nishino | Kyoto University, Japan |
| Jean-Marc Odobez | Idiap Research Institute, École polytechnique fédérale de Lausanne, Switzerland |
| Francesca Odone | University of Genova, Italy |
| Takayuki Okatani | Tohoku University & RIKEN Center for Advanced Intelligence Project, Japan |
| Manohar Paluri | Facebook, USA |
| Guan Pang | Facebook, USA |
| Maja Pantic | Imperial College London, UK |
| Sylvain Paris | Adobe Research, USA |
| Jaesik Park | Pohang University of Science and Technology, Korea |
| Hyun Soo Park | The University of Minnesota, USA |
| Omkar M. Parkhi | Facebook, USA |
| Deepak Pathak | Carnegie Mellon University, USA |
| Georgios Pavlakos | University of California, Berkeley, USA |
| Marcello Pelillo | University of Venice, Italy |
| Marc Pollefeys | ETH Zurich & Microsoft, Switzerland |
| Jean Ponce | Inria, France |
| Gerard Pons-Moll | University of Tübingen, Germany |
| Fatih Porikli | Qualcomm, USA |
| Victor Adrian Prisacariu | University of Oxford, UK |
| Petia Radeva | University of Barcelona, Spain |
| Ravi Ramamoorthi | University of California, San Diego, USA |
| Deva Ramanan | Carnegie Mellon University, USA |
| Vignesh Ramanathan | Facebook, USA |
| Nalini Ratha | State University of New York at Buffalo, USA |
| Tammy Riklin Raviv | Ben-Gurion University, Israel |
| Tobias Ritschel | University College London, UK |
| Emanuele Rodola | Sapienza University of Rome, Italy |
| Amit K. Roy-Chowdhury | University of California, Riverside, USA |
| Michael Rubinstein | Google, USA |
| Olga Russakovsky | Princeton University, USA |

| Mathieu Salzmann | École polytechnique fédérale de Lausanne, Switzerland |
| Dimitris Samaras | Stony Brook University, USA |
| Aswin Sankaranarayanan | Carnegie Mellon University, USA |
| Imari Sato | National Institute of Informatics, Japan |
| Yoichi Sato | University of Tokyo, Japan |
| Shin'ichi Satoh | National Institute of Informatics, Japan |
| Walter Scheirer | University of Notre Dame, USA |
| Bernt Schiele | Max Planck Institute for Informatics, Germany |
| Konrad Schindler | ETH Zurich, Switzerland |
| Cordelia Schmid | Inria & Google, France |
| Alexander Schwing | University of Illinois at Urbana-Champaign, USA |
| Nicu Sebe | University of Trento, Italy |
| Greg Shakhnarovich | Toyota Technological Institute at Chicago, USA |
| Eli Shechtman | Adobe Research, USA |
| Humphrey Shi | University of Oregon & University of Illinois at Urbana-Champaign & Picsart AI Research, USA |
| Jianbo Shi | University of Pennsylvania, USA |
| Roy Shilkrot | Massachusetts Institute of Technology, USA |
| Mike Zheng Shou | National University of Singapore, Singapore |
| Kaleem Siddiqi | McGill University, Canada |
| Richa Singh | Indian Institute of Technology Jodhpur, India |
| Greg Slabaugh | Queen Mary University of London, UK |
| Cees Snoek | University of Amsterdam, The Netherlands |
| Yale Song | Facebook AI Research, USA |
| Yi-Zhe Song | University of Surrey, UK |
| Bjorn Stenger | Rakuten Institute of Technology |
| Abby Stylianou | Saint Louis University, USA |
| Akihiro Sugimoto | National Institute of Informatics, Japan |
| Chen Sun | Brown University, USA |
| Deqing Sun | Google, USA |
| Kalyan Sunkavalli | Adobe Research, USA |
| Ying Tai | Tencent YouTu Lab, China |
| Ayellet Tal | Technion – Israel Institute of Technology, Israel |
| Ping Tan | Simon Fraser University, Canada |
| Siyu Tang | ETH Zurich, Switzerland |
| Chi-Keung Tang | Hong Kong University of Science and Technology, Hong Kong, China |
| Radu Timofte | University of Würzburg, Germany & ETH Zurich, Switzerland |
| Federico Tombari | Google, Switzerland & Technical University of Munich, Germany |

| | |
|---|---|
| James Tompkin | Brown University, USA |
| Lorenzo Torresani | Dartmouth College, USA |
| Alexander Toshev | Apple, USA |
| Du Tran | Facebook AI Research, USA |
| Anh T. Tran | VinAI, Vietnam |
| Zhuowen Tu | University of California, San Diego, USA |
| Georgios Tzimiropoulos | Queen Mary University of London, UK |
| Jasper Uijlings | Google Research, Switzerland |
| Jan C. van Gemert | Delft University of Technology, The Netherlands |
| Gul Varol | Ecole des Ponts ParisTech, France |
| Nuno Vasconcelos | University of California, San Diego, USA |
| Mayank Vatsa | Indian Institute of Technology Jodhpur, India |
| Ashok Veeraraghavan | Rice University, USA |
| Jakob Verbeek | Facebook AI Research, France |
| Carl Vondrick | Columbia University, USA |
| Ruiping Wang | Institute of Computing Technology, Chinese Academy of Sciences, China |
| Xinchao Wang | National University of Singapore, Singapore |
| Liwei Wang | The Chinese University of Hong Kong, Hong Kong, China |
| Chaohui Wang | Université Paris-Est, France |
| Xiaolong Wang | University of California, San Diego, USA |
| Christian Wolf | NAVER LABS Europe, France |
| Tao Xiang | University of Surrey, UK |
| Saining Xie | Facebook AI Research, USA |
| Cihang Xie | University of California, Santa Cruz, USA |
| Zeki Yalniz | Facebook, USA |
| Ming-Hsuan Yang | University of California, Merced, USA |
| Angela Yao | National University of Singapore, Singapore |
| Shaodi You | University of Amsterdam, The Netherlands |
| Stella X. Yu | University of California, Berkeley, USA |
| Junsong Yuan | State University of New York at Buffalo, USA |
| Stefanos Zafeiriou | Imperial College London, UK |
| Amir Zamir | École polytechnique fédérale de Lausanne, Switzerland |
| Lei Zhang | Alibaba & Hong Kong Polytechnic University, Hong Kong, China |
| Lei Zhang | International Digital Economy Academy (IDEA), China |
| Pengchuan Zhang | Meta AI, USA |
| Bolei Zhou | University of California, Los Angeles, USA |
| Yuke Zhu | University of Texas at Austin, USA |

Todd Zickler                          Harvard University, USA
Wangmeng Zuo                          Harbin Institute of Technology, China

## Technical Program Committee

Davide Abati
Soroush Abbasi
   Koohpayegani
Amos L. Abbott
Rameen Abdal
Rabab Abdelfattah
Sahar Abdelnabi
Hassan Abu Alhaija
Abulikemu Abuduweili
Ron Abutbul
Hanno Ackermann
Aikaterini Adam
Kamil Adamczewski
Ehsan Adeli
Vida Adeli
Donald Adjeroh
Arman Afrasiyabi
Akshay Agarwal
Sameer Agarwal
Abhinav Agarwalla
Vaibhav Aggarwal
Sara Aghajanzadeh
Susmit Agrawal
Antonio Agudo
Touqeer Ahmad
Sk Miraj Ahmed
Chaitanya Ahuja
Nilesh A. Ahuja
Abhishek Aich
Shubhra Aich
Noam Aigerman
Arash Akbarinia
Peri Akiva
Derya Akkaynak
Emre Aksan
Arjun R. Akula
Yuval Alaluf
Stephan Alaniz
Paul Albert
Cenek Albl

Filippo Aleotti
Konstantinos P.
   Alexandridis
Motasem Alfarra
Mohsen Ali
Thiemo Alldieck
Hadi Alzayer
Liang An
Shan An
Yi An
Zhulin An
Dongsheng An
Jie An
Xiang An
Saket Anand
Cosmin Ancuti
Juan Andrade-Cetto
Alexander Andreopoulos
Bjoern Andres
Jerone T. A. Andrews
Shivangi Aneja
Anelia Angelova
Dragomir Anguelov
Rushil Anirudh
Oron Anschel
Rao Muhammad Anwer
Djamila Aouada
Evlampios Apostolidis
Srikar Appalaraju
Nikita Araslanov
Andre Araujo
Eric Arazo
Dawit Mureja Argaw
Anurag Arnab
Aditya Arora
Chetan Arora
Sunpreet S. Arora
Alexey Artemov
Muhammad Asad
Kumar Ashutosh

Sinem Aslan
Vishal Asnani
Mahmoud Assran
Amir Atapour-Abarghouei
Nikos Athanasiou
Ali Athar
ShahRukh Athar
Sara Atito
Souhaib Attaiki
Matan Atzmon
Mathieu Aubry
Nicolas Audebert
Tristan T.
   Aumentado-Armstrong
Melinos Averkiou
Yannis Avrithis
Stephane Ayache
Mehmet Aygün
Seyed Mehdi
   Ayyoubzadeh
Hossein Azizpour
George Azzopardi
Mallikarjun B. R.
Yunhao Ba
Abhishek Badki
Seung-Hwan Bae
Seung-Hwan Baek
Seungryul Baek
Piyush Nitin Bagad
Shai Bagon
Gaetan Bahl
Shikhar Bahl
Sherwin Bahmani
Haoran Bai
Lei Bai
Jiawang Bai
Haoyue Bai
Jinbin Bai
Xiang Bai
Xuyang Bai

Yang Bai
Yuanchao Bai
Ziqian Bai
Sungyong Baik
Kevin Bailly
Max Bain
Federico Baldassarre
Wele Gedara Chaminda
    Bandara
Biplab Banerjee
Pratyay Banerjee
Sandipan Banerjee
Jihwan Bang
Antyanta Bangunharcana
Aayush Bansal
Ankan Bansal
Siddhant Bansal
Wentao Bao
Zhipeng Bao
Amir Bar
Manel Baradad Jurjo
Lorenzo Baraldi
Danny Barash
Daniel Barath
Connelly Barnes
Ioan Andrei Bârsan
Steven Basart
Dina Bashkirova
Chaim Baskin
Peyman Bateni
Anil Batra
Sebastiano Battiato
Ardhendu Behera
Harkirat Behl
Jens Behley
Vasileios Belagiannis
Boulbaba Ben Amor
Emanuel Ben Baruch
Abdessamad Ben Hamza
Gil Ben-Artzi
Assia Benbihi
Fabian Benitez-Quiroz
Guy Ben-Yosef
Philipp Benz
Alexander W. Bergman

Urs Bergmann
Jesus Bermudez-Cameo
Stefano Berretti
Gedas Bertasius
Zachary Bessinger
Petra Bevandić
Matthew Beveridge
Lucas Beyer
Yash Bhalgat
Suvaansh Bhambri
Samarth Bharadwaj
Gaurav Bharaj
Aparna Bharati
Bharat Lal Bhatnagar
Uttaran Bhattacharya
Apratim Bhattacharyya
Brojeshwar Bhowmick
Ankan Kumar Bhunia
Ayan Kumar Bhunia
Qi Bi
Sai Bi
Michael Bi Mi
Gui-Bin Bian
Jia-Wang Bian
Shaojun Bian
Pia Bideau
Mario Bijelic
Hakan Bilen
Guillaume-Alexandre
    Bilodeau
Alexander Binder
Tolga Birdal
Vighnesh N. Birodkar
Sandika Biswas
Andreas Blattmann
Janusz Bobulski
Giuseppe Boccignone
Vishnu Boddeti
Navaneeth Bodla
Moritz Böhle
Aleksei Bokhovkin
Sam Bond-Taylor
Vivek Boominathan
Shubhankar Borse
Mark Boss

Andrea Bottino
Adnane Boukhayma
Fadi Boutros
Nicolas C. Boutry
Richard S. Bowen
Ivaylo Boyadzhiev
Aidan Boyd
Yuri Boykov
Aljaz Bozic
Behzad Bozorgtabar
Eric Brachmann
Samarth Brahmbhatt
Gustav Bredell
Francois Bremond
Joel Brogan
Andrew Brown
Thomas Brox
Marcus A. Brubaker
Robert-Jan Bruintjes
Yuqi Bu
Anders G. Buch
Himanshu Buckchash
Mateusz Buda
Ignas Budvytis
José M. Buenaposada
Marcel C. Bühler
Tu Bui
Adrian Bulat
Hannah Bull
Evgeny Burnaev
Andrei Bursuc
Benjamin Busam
Sergey N. Buzykanov
Wonmin Byeon
Fabian Caba
Martin Cadik
Guanyu Cai
Minjie Cai
Qing Cai
Zhongang Cai
Qi Cai
Yancheng Cai
Shen Cai
Han Cai
Jiarui Cai

Bowen Cai
Mu Cai
Qin Cai
Ruojin Cai
Weidong Cai
Weiwei Cai
Yi Cai
Yujun Cai
Zhiping Cai
Akin Caliskan
Lilian Calvet
Baris Can Cam
Necati Cihan Camgoz
Tommaso Campari
Dylan Campbell
Ziang Cao
Ang Cao
Xu Cao
Zhiwen Cao
Shengcao Cao
Song Cao
Weipeng Cao
Xiangyong Cao
Xiaochun Cao
Yue Cao
Yunhao Cao
Zhangjie Cao
Jiale Cao
Yang Cao
Jiajiong Cao
Jie Cao
Jinkun Cao
Lele Cao
Yulong Cao
Zhiguo Cao
Chen Cao
Razvan Caramalau
Marlène Careil
Gustavo Carneiro
Joao Carreira
Dan Casas
Paola Cascante-Bonilla
Angela Castillo
Francisco M. Castro
Pedro Castro

Luca Cavalli
George J. Cazenavette
Oya Celiktutan
Hakan Cevikalp
Sri Harsha C. H.
Sungmin Cha
Geonho Cha
Menglei Chai
Lucy Chai
Yuning Chai
Zenghao Chai
Anirban Chakraborty
Deep Chakraborty
Rudrasis Chakraborty
Souradeep Chakraborty
Kelvin C. K. Chan
Chee Seng Chan
Paramanand Chandramouli
Arjun Chandrasekaran
Kenneth Chaney
Dongliang Chang
Huiwen Chang
Peng Chang
Xiaojun Chang
Jia-Ren Chang
Hyung Jin Chang
Hyun Sung Chang
Ju Yong Chang
Li-Jen Chang
Qi Chang
Wei-Yi Chang
Yi Chang
Nadine Chang
Hanqing Chao
Pradyumna Chari
Dibyadip Chatterjee
Chiranjoy Chattopadhyay
Siddhartha Chaudhuri
Zhengping Che
Gal Chechik
Lianggangxu Chen
Qi Alfred Chen
Brian Chen
Bor-Chun Chen
Bo-Hao Chen

Bohong Chen
Bin Chen
Ziliang Chen
Cheng Chen
Chen Chen
Chaofeng Chen
Xi Chen
Haoyu Chen
Xuanhong Chen
Wei Chen
Qiang Chen
Shi Chen
Xianyu Chen
Chang Chen
Changhuai Chen
Hao Chen
Jie Chen
Jianbo Chen
Jingjing Chen
Jun Chen
Kejiang Chen
Mingcai Chen
Nenglun Chen
Qifeng Chen
Ruoyu Chen
Shu-Yu Chen
Weidong Chen
Weijie Chen
Weikai Chen
Xiang Chen
Xiuyi Chen
Xingyu Chen
Yaofo Chen
Yueting Chen
Yu Chen
Yunjin Chen
Yuntao Chen
Yun Chen
Zhenfang Chen
Zhuangzhuang Chen
Chu-Song Chen
Xiangyu Chen
Zhuo Chen
Chaoqi Chen
Shizhe Chen

Xiaotong Chen
Xiaozhi Chen
Dian Chen
Defang Chen
Dingfan Chen
Ding-Jie Chen
Ee Heng Chen
Tao Chen
Yixin Chen
Wei-Ting Chen
Lin Chen
Guang Chen
Guangyi Chen
Guanying Chen
Guangyao Chen
Hwann-Tzong Chen
Junwen Chen
Jiacheng Chen
Jianxu Chen
Hui Chen
Kai Chen
Kan Chen
Kevin Chen
Kuan-Wen Chen
Weihua Chen
Zhang Chen
Liang-Chieh Chen
Lele Chen
Liang Chen
Fanglin Chen
Zehui Chen
Minghui Chen
Minghao Chen
Xiaokang Chen
Qian Chen
Jun-Cheng Chen
Qi Chen
Qingcai Chen
Richard J. Chen
Runnan Chen
Rui Chen
Shuo Chen
Sentao Chen
Shaoyu Chen
Shixing Chen

Shuai Chen
Shuya Chen
Sizhe Chen
Simin Chen
Shaoxiang Chen
Zitian Chen
Tianlong Chen
Tianshui Chen
Min-Hung Chen
Xiangning Chen
Xin Chen
Xinghao Chen
Xuejin Chen
Xu Chen
Xuxi Chen
Yunlu Chen
Yanbei Chen
Yuxiao Chen
Yun-Chun Chen
Yi-Ting Chen
Yi-Wen Chen
Yinbo Chen
Yiran Chen
Yuanhong Chen
Yubei Chen
Yuefeng Chen
Yuhua Chen
Yukang Chen
Zerui Chen
Zhaoyu Chen
Zhen Chen
Zhenyu Chen
Zhi Chen
Zhiwei Chen
Zhixiang Chen
Long Chen
Bowen Cheng
Jun Cheng
Yi Cheng
Jingchun Cheng
Lechao Cheng
Xi Cheng
Yuan Cheng
Ho Kei Cheng
Kevin Ho Man Cheng

Jiacheng Cheng
Kelvin B. Cheng
Li Cheng
Mengjun Cheng
Zhen Cheng
Qingrong Cheng
Tianheng Cheng
Harry Cheng
Yihua Cheng
Yu Cheng
Ziheng Cheng
Soon Yau Cheong
Anoop Cherian
Manuela Chessa
Zhixiang Chi
Naoki Chiba
Julian Chibane
Kashyap Chitta
Tai-Yin Chiu
Hsu-kuang Chiu
Wei-Chen Chiu
Sungmin Cho
Donghyeon Cho
Hyeon Cho
Yooshin Cho
Gyusang Cho
Jang Hyun Cho
Seungju Cho
Nam Ik Cho
Sunghyun Cho
Hanbyel Cho
Jaesung Choe
Jooyoung Choi
Chiho Choi
Changwoon Choi
Jongwon Choi
Myungsub Choi
Dooseop Choi
Jonghyun Choi
Jinwoo Choi
Jun Won Choi
Min-Kook Choi
Hongsuk Choi
Janghoon Choi
Yoon-Ho Choi

Yukyung Choi
Jaegul Choo
Ayush Chopra
Siddharth Choudhary
Subhabrata Choudhury
Vasileios Choutas
Ka-Ho Chow
Pinaki Nath Chowdhury
Sammy Christen
Anders Christensen
Grigorios Chrysos
Hang Chu
Wen-Hsuan Chu
Peng Chu
Qi Chu
Ruihang Chu
Wei-Ta Chu
Yung-Yu Chuang
Sanghyuk Chun
Se Young Chun
Antonio Cinà
Ramazan Gokberk Cinbis
Javier Civera
Albert Clapés
Ronald Clark
Brian S. Clipp
Felipe Codevilla
Daniel Coelho de Castro
Niv Cohen
Forrester Cole
Maxwell D. Collins
Robert T. Collins
Marc Comino Trinidad
Runmin Cong
Wenyan Cong
Maxime Cordy
Marcella Cornia
Enric Corona
Huseyin Coskun
Luca Cosmo
Dragos Costea
Davide Cozzolino
Arun C. S. Kumar
Aiyu Cui
Qiongjie Cui

Quan Cui
Shuhao Cui
Yiming Cui
Ying Cui
Zijun Cui
Jiali Cui
Jiequan Cui
Yawen Cui
Zhen Cui
Zhaopeng Cui
Jack Culpepper
Xiaodong Cun
Ross Cutler
Adam Czajka
Ali Dabouei
Konstantinos M. Dafnis
Manuel Dahnert
Tao Dai
Yuchao Dai
Bo Dai
Mengyu Dai
Hang Dai
Haixing Dai
Peng Dai
Pingyang Dai
Qi Dai
Qiyu Dai
Yutong Dai
Naser Damer
Zhiyuan Dang
Mohamed Daoudi
Ayan Das
Abir Das
Debasmit Das
Deepayan Das
Partha Das
Sagnik Das
Soumi Das
Srijan Das
Swagatam Das
Avijit Dasgupta
Jim Davis
Adrian K. Davison
Homa Davoudi
Laura Daza

Matthias De Lange
Shalini De Mello
Marco De Nadai
Christophe De
    Vleeschouwer
Alp Dener
Boyang Deng
Congyue Deng
Bailin Deng
Yong Deng
Ye Deng
Zhuo Deng
Zhijie Deng
Xiaoming Deng
Jiankang Deng
Jinhong Deng
Jingjing Deng
Liang-Jian Deng
Siqi Deng
Xiang Deng
Xueqing Deng
Zhongying Deng
Karan Desai
Jean-Emmanuel Deschaud
Aniket Anand Deshmukh
Neel Dey
Helisa Dhamo
Prithviraj Dhar
Amaya Dharmasiri
Yan Di
Xing Di
Ousmane A. Dia
Haiwen Diao
Xiaolei Diao
Gonçalo José Dias Pais
Abdallah Dib
Anastasios Dimou
Changxing Ding
Henghui Ding
Guodong Ding
Yaqing Ding
Shuangrui Ding
Yuhang Ding
Yikang Ding
Shouhong Ding

Haisong Ding
Hui Ding
Jiahao Ding
Jian Ding
Jian-Jiun Ding
Shuxiao Ding
Tianyu Ding
Wenhao Ding
Yuqi Ding
Yi Ding
Yuzhen Ding
Zhengming Ding
Tan Minh Dinh
Vu Dinh
Christos Diou
Mandar Dixit
Bao Gia Doan
Khoa D. Doan
Dzung Anh Doan
Debi Prosad Dogra
Nehal Doiphode
Chengdong Dong
Bowen Dong
Zhenxing Dong
Hang Dong
Xiaoyi Dong
Haoye Dong
Jiangxin Dong
Shichao Dong
Xuan Dong
Zhen Dong
Shuting Dong
Jing Dong
Li Dong
Ming Dong
Nanqing Dong
Qiulei Dong
Runpei Dong
Siyan Dong
Tian Dong
Wei Dong
Xiaomeng Dong
Xin Dong
Xingbo Dong
Yuan Dong

Samuel Dooley
Gianfranco Doretto
Michael Dorkenwald
Keval Doshi
Zhaopeng Dou
Xiaotian Dou
Hazel Doughty
Ahmad Droby
Iddo Drori
Jie Du
Yong Du
Dawei Du
Dong Du
Ruoyi Du
Yuntao Du
Xuefeng Du
Yilun Du
Yuming Du
Radhika Dua
Haodong Duan
Jiafei Duan
Kaiwen Duan
Peiqi Duan
Ye Duan
Haoran Duan
Jiali Duan
Amanda Duarte
Abhimanyu Dubey
Shiv Ram Dubey
Florian Dubost
Lukasz Dudziak
Shivam Duggal
Justin M. Dulay
Matteo Dunnhofer
Chi Nhan Duong
Thibaut Durand
Mihai Dusmanu
Ujjal Kr Dutta
Debidatta Dwibedi
Isht Dwivedi
Sai Kumar Dwivedi
Takeharu Eda
Mark Edmonds
Alexei A. Efros
Thibaud Ehret

Max Ehrlich
Mahsa Ehsanpour
Iván Eichhardt
Farshad Einabadi
Marvin Eisenberger
Hazim Kemal Ekenel
Mohamed El Banani
Ismail Elezi
Moshe Eliasof
Alaa El-Nouby
Ian Endres
Francis Engelmann
Deniz Engin
Chanho Eom
Dave Epstein
Maria C. Escobar
Victor A. Escorcia
Carlos Esteves
Sungmin Eum
Bernard J. E. Evans
Ivan Evtimov
Fevziye Irem Eyiokur
    Yaman
Matteo Fabbri
Sébastien Fabbro
Gabriele Facciolo
Masud Fahim
Bin Fan
Hehe Fan
Deng-Ping Fan
Aoxiang Fan
Chen-Chen Fan
Qi Fan
Zhaoxin Fan
Haoqi Fan
Heng Fan
Hongyi Fan
Linxi Fan
Baojie Fan
Jiayuan Fan
Lei Fan
Quanfu Fan
Yonghui Fan
Yingruo Fan
Zhiwen Fan

Zicong Fan
Sean Fanello
Jiansheng Fang
Chaowei Fang
Yuming Fang
Jianwu Fang
Jin Fang
Qi Fang
Shancheng Fang
Tian Fang
Xianyong Fang
Gongfan Fang
Zhen Fang
Hui Fang
Jiemin Fang
Le Fang
Pengfei Fang
Xiaolin Fang
Yuxin Fang
Zhaoyuan Fang
Ammarah Farooq
Azade Farshad
Zhengcong Fei
Michael Felsberg
Wei Feng
Chen Feng
Fan Feng
Andrew Feng
Xin Feng
Zheyun Feng
Ruicheng Feng
Mingtao Feng
Qianyu Feng
Shangbin Feng
Chun-Mei Feng
Zunlei Feng
Zhiyong Feng
Martin Fergie
Mustansar Fiaz
Marco Fiorucci
Michael Firman
Hamed Firooz
Volker Fischer
Corneliu O. Florea
Georgios Floros

Wolfgang Foerstner
Gianni Franchi
Jean-Sebastien Franco
Simone Frintrop
Anna Fruehstueck
Changhong Fu
Chaoyou Fu
Cheng-Yang Fu
Chi-Wing Fu
Deqing Fu
Huan Fu
Jun Fu
Kexue Fu
Ying Fu
Jianlong Fu
Jingjing Fu
Qichen Fu
Tsu-Jui Fu
Xueyang Fu
Yang Fu
Yanwei Fu
Yonggan Fu
Wolfgang Fuhl
Yasuhisa Fujii
Kent Fujiwara
Marco Fumero
Takuya Funatomi
Isabel Funke
Dario Fuoli
Antonino Furnari
Matheus A. Gadelha
Akshay Gadi Patil
Adrian Galdran
Guillermo Gallego
Silvano Galliani
Orazio Gallo
Leonardo Galteri
Matteo Gamba
Yiming Gan
Sujoy Ganguly
Harald Ganster
Boyan Gao
Changxin Gao
Daiheng Gao
Difei Gao

Chen Gao
Fei Gao
Lin Gao
Wei Gao
Yiming Gao
Junyu Gao
Guangyu Ryan Gao
Haichang Gao
Hongchang Gao
Jialin Gao
Jin Gao
Jun Gao
Katelyn Gao
Mingchen Gao
Mingfei Gao
Pan Gao
Shangqian Gao
Shanghua Gao
Xitong Gao
Yunhe Gao
Zhanning Gao
Elena Garces
Nuno Cruz Garcia
Noa Garcia
Guillermo
    Garcia-Hernando
Isha Garg
Rahul Garg
Sourav Garg
Quentin Garrido
Stefano Gasperini
Kent Gauen
Chandan Gautam
Shivam Gautam
Paul Gay
Chunjiang Ge
Shiming Ge
Wenhang Ge
Yanhao Ge
Zheng Ge
Songwei Ge
Weifeng Ge
Yixiao Ge
Yuying Ge
Shijie Geng

Zhengyang Geng
Kyle A. Genova
Georgios Georgakis
Markos Georgopoulos
Marcel Geppert
Shabnam Ghadar
Mina Ghadimi Atigh
Deepti Ghadiyaram
Maani Ghaffari Jadidi
Sedigh Ghamari
Zahra Gharaee
Michaël Gharbi
Golnaz Ghiasi
Reza Ghoddoosian
Soumya Suvra Ghosal
Adhiraj Ghosh
Arthita Ghosh
Pallabi Ghosh
Soumyadeep Ghosh
Andrew Gilbert
Igor Gilitschenski
Jhony H. Giraldo
Andreu Girbau Xalabarder
Rohit Girdhar
Sharath Girish
Xavier Giro-i-Nieto
Raja Giryes
Thomas Gittings
Nikolaos Gkanatsios
Ioannis Gkioulekas
Abhiram
Gnanasambandam
Aurele T. Gnanha
Clement L. J. C. Godard
Arushi Goel
Vidit Goel
Shubham Goel
Zan Gojcic
Aaron K. Gokaslan
Tejas Gokhale
S. Alireza Golestaneh
Thiago L. Gomes
Nuno Goncalves
Boqing Gong
Chen Gong

Yuanhao Gong
Guoqiang Gong
Jingyu Gong
Rui Gong
Yu Gong
Mingming Gong
Neil Zhenqiang Gong
Xun Gong
Yunye Gong
Yihong Gong
Cristina I. González
Nithin Gopalakrishnan
    Nair
Gaurav Goswami
Jianping Gou
Shreyank N. Gowda
Ankit Goyal
Helmut Grabner
Patrick L. Grady
Ben Graham
Eric Granger
Douglas R. Gray
Matej Grcić
David Griffiths
Jinjin Gu
Yun Gu
Shuyang Gu
Jianyang Gu
Fuqiang Gu
Jiatao Gu
Jindong Gu
Jiaqi Gu
Jinwei Gu
Jiaxin Gu
Geonmo Gu
Xiao Gu
Xinqian Gu
Xiuye Gu
Yuming Gu
Zhangxuan Gu
Dayan Guan
Junfeng Guan
Qingji Guan
Tianrui Guan
Shanyan Guan

Denis A. Gudovskiy
Ricardo Guerrero
Pierre-Louis Guhur
Jie Gui
Liangyan Gui
Liangke Gui
Benoit Guillard
Erhan Gundogdu
Manuel Günther
Jingcai Guo
Yuanfang Guo
Junfeng Guo
Chenqi Guo
Dan Guo
Hongji Guo
Jia Guo
Jie Guo
Minghao Guo
Shi Guo
Yanhui Guo
Yangyang Guo
Yuan-Chen Guo
Yilu Guo
Yiluan Guo
Yong Guo
Guangyu Guo
Haiyun Guo
Jinyang Guo
Jianyuan Guo
Pengsheng Guo
Pengfei Guo
Shuxuan Guo
Song Guo
Tianyu Guo
Qing Guo
Qiushan Guo
Wen Guo
Xiefan Guo
Xiaohu Guo
Xiaoqing Guo
Yufei Guo
Yuhui Guo
Yuliang Guo
Yunhui Guo
Yanwen Guo

Akshita Gupta
Ankush Gupta
Kamal Gupta
Kartik Gupta
Ritwik Gupta
Rohit Gupta
Siddharth Gururani
Fredrik K. Gustafsson
Abner Guzman Rivera
Vladimir Guzov
Matthew A. Gwilliam
Jung-Woo Ha
Marc Habermann
Isma Hadji
Christian Haene
Martin Hahner
Levente Hajder
Alexandros Haliassos
Emanuela Haller
Bumsub Ham
Abdullah J. Hamdi
Shreyas Hampali
Dongyoon Han
Chunrui Han
Dong-Jun Han
Dong-Sig Han
Guangxing Han
Zhizhong Han
Ruize Han
Jiaming Han
Jin Han
Ligong Han
Xian-Hua Han
Xiaoguang Han
Yizeng Han
Zhi Han
Zhenjun Han
Zhongyi Han
Jungong Han
Junlin Han
Kai Han
Kun Han
Sungwon Han
Songfang Han
Wei Han

Xiao Han
Xintong Han
Xinzhe Han
Yahong Han
Yan Han
Zongbo Han
Nicolai Hani
Rana Hanocka
Niklas Hansclmann
Nicklas A. Hansen
Hong Hanyu
Fusheng Hao
Yanbin Hao
Shijie Hao
Udith Haputhanthri
Mehrtash Harandi
Josh Harguess
Adam Harley
David M. Hart
Atsushi Hashimoto
Ali Hassani
Mohammed Hassanin
Yana Hasson
Joakim Bruslund Haurum
Bo He
Kun He
Chen He
Xin He
Fazhi He
Gaoqi He
Hao He
Haoyu He
Jiangpeng He
Hongliang He
Qian He
Xiangteng He
Xuming He
Yannan He
Yuhang He
Yang He
Xiangyu He
Nanjun He
Pan He
Sen He
Shengfeng He

Songtao He
Tao He
Tong He
Wei He
Xuehai He
Xiaoxiao He
Ying He
Yisheng He
Ziwen He
Peter Hedman
Felix Heide
Yacov Hel-Or
Paul Henderson
Philipp Henzler
Byeongho Heo
Jae-Pil Heo
Miran Heo
Sachini A. Herath
Stephane Herbin
Pedro Hermosilla Casajus
Monica Hernandez
Charles Herrmann
Roei Herzig
Mauricio Hess-Flores
Carlos Hinojosa
Tobias Hinz
Tsubasa Hirakawa
Chih-Hui Ho
Lam Si Tung Ho
Jennifer Hobbs
Derek Hoiem
Yannick Hold-Geoffroy
Aleksander Holynski
Cheeun Hong
Fa-Ting Hong
Hanbin Hong
Guan Zhe Hong
Danfeng Hong
Lanqing Hong
Xiaopeng Hong
Xin Hong
Jie Hong
Seungbum Hong
Cheng-Yao Hong
Seunghoon Hong

Yi Hong
Yuan Hong
Yuchen Hong
Anthony Hoogs
Maxwell C. Horton
Kazuhiro Hotta
Qibin Hou
Tingbo Hou
Junhui Hou
Ji Hou
Qiqi Hou
Rui Hou
Ruibing Hou
Zhi Hou
Henry Howard-Jenkins
Lukas Hoyer
Wei-Lin Hsiao
Chiou-Ting Hsu
Anthony Hu
Brian Hu
Yusong Hu
Hexiang Hu
Haoji Hu
Di Hu
Hengtong Hu
Haigen Hu
Lianyu Hu
Hanzhe Hu
Jie Hu
Junlin Hu
Shizhe Hu
Jian Hu
Zhiming Hu
Juhua Hu
Peng Hu
Ping Hu
Ronghang Hu
MengShun Hu
Tao Hu
Vincent Tao Hu
Xiaoling Hu
Xinting Hu
Xiaolin Hu
Xuefeng Hu
Xiaowei Hu

Yang Hu
Yueyu Hu
Zeyu Hu
Zhongyun Hu
Binh-Son Hua
Guoliang Hua
Yi Hua
Linzhi Huang
Qiusheng Huang
Bo Huang
Chen Huang
Hsin-Ping Huang
Ye Huang
Shuangping Huang
Zeng Huang
Buzhen Huang
Cong Huang
Heng Huang
Hao Huang
Qidong Huang
Huaibo Huang
Chaoqin Huang
Feihu Huang
Jiahui Huang
Jingjia Huang
Kun Huang
Lei Huang
Sheng Huang
Shuaiyi Huang
Siyu Huang
Xiaoshui Huang
Xiaoyang Huang
Yan Huang
Yihao Huang
Ying Huang
Ziling Huang
Xiaoke Huang
Yifei Huang
Haiyang Huang
Zhewei Huang
Jin Huang
Haibin Huang
Jiaxing Huang
Junjie Huang
Keli Huang

Lang Huang
Lin Huang
Luojie Huang
Mingzhen Huang
Shijia Huang
Shengyu Huang
Siyuan Huang
He Huang
Xiuyu Huang
Lianghua Huang
Yue Huang
Yaping Huang
Yuge Huang
Zehao Huang
Zeyi Huang
Zhiqi Huang
Zhongzhan Huang
Zilong Huang
Ziyuan Huang
Tianrui Hui
Zhuo Hui
Le Hui
Jing Huo
Junhwa Hur
Shehzeen S. Hussain
Chuong Minh Huynh
Seunghyun Hwang
Jaehui Hwang
Jyh-Jing Hwang
Sukjun Hwang
Soonmin Hwang
Wonjun Hwang
Rakib Hyder
Sangeek Hyun
Sarah Ibrahimi
Tomoki Ichikawa
Yerlan Idelbayev
A. S. M. Iftekhar
Masaaki Iiyama
Satoshi Ikehata
Sunghoon Im
Atul N. Ingle
Eldar Insafutdinov
Yani A. Ioannou
Radu Tudor Ionescu

Umar Iqbal
Go Irie
Muhammad Zubair Irshad
Ahmet Iscen
Berivan Isik
Ashraful Islam
Md Amirul Islam
Syed Islam
Mariko Isogawa
Vamsi Krishna K. Ithapu
Boris Ivanovic
Darshan Iyer
Sarah Jabbour
Ayush Jain
Nishant Jain
Samyak Jain
Vidit Jain
Vineet Jain
Priyank Jaini
Tomas Jakab
Mohammad A. A. K.
    Jalwana
Muhammad Abdullah
    Jamal
Hadi Jamali-Rad
Stuart James
Varun Jampani
Young Kyun Jang
YeongJun Jang
Yunseok Jang
Ronnachai Jaroensri
Bhavan Jasani
Krishna Murthy
    Jatavallabhula
Mojan Javaheripi
Syed A. Javed
Guillaume Jeanneret
Pranav Jeevan
Herve Jegou
Rohit Jena
Tomas Jenicek
Porter Jenkins
Simon Jenni
Hae-Gon Jeon
Sangryul Jeon

Boseung Jeong
Yoonwoo Jeong
Seong-Gyun Jeong
Jisoo Jeong
Allan D. Jepson
Ankit Jha
Sumit K. Jha
I-Hong Jhuo
Ge-Peng Ji
Chaonan Ji
Deyi Ji
Jingwei Ji
Wei Ji
Zhong Ji
Jiayi Ji
Pengliang Ji
Hui Ji
Mingi Ji
Xiaopeng Ji
Yuzhu Ji
Baoxiong Jia
Songhao Jia
Dan Jia
Shan Jia
Xiaojun Jia
Xiuyi Jia
Xu Jia
Menglin Jia
Wenqi Jia
Boyuan Jiang
Wenhao Jiang
Huaizu Jiang
Hanwen Jiang
Haiyong Jiang
Hao Jiang
Huajie Jiang
Huiqin Jiang
Haojun Jiang
Haobo Jiang
Junjun Jiang
Xingyu Jiang
Yangbangyan Jiang
Yu Jiang
Jianmin Jiang
Jiaxi Jiang

Jing Jiang
Kui Jiang
Li Jiang
Liming Jiang
Chiyu Jiang
Meirui Jiang
Chen Jiang
Peng Jiang
Tai-Xiang Jiang
Wen Jiang
Xinyang Jiang
Yifan Jiang
Yuming Jiang
Yingying Jiang
Zeren Jiang
ZhengKai Jiang
Zhenyu Jiang
Shuming Jiao
Jianbo Jiao
Licheng Jiao
Dongkwon Jin
Yeying Jin
Cheng Jin
Linyi Jin
Qing Jin
Taisong Jin
Xiao Jin
Xin Jin
Sheng Jin
Kyong Hwan Jin
Ruibing Jin
SouYoung Jin
Yueming Jin
Chenchen Jing
Longlong Jing
Taotao Jing
Yongcheng Jing
Younghyun Jo
Joakim Johnander
Jeff Johnson
Michael J. Jones
R. Kenny Jones
Rico Jonschkowski
Ameya Joshi
Sunghun Joung

Felix Juefei-Xu
Claudio R. Jung
Steffen Jung
Hari Chandana K.
Rahul Vigneswaran K.
Prajwal K. R.
Abhishek Kadian
Jhony Kaesemodel Pontes
Kumara Kahatapitiya
Anmol Kalia
Sinan Kalkan
Tarun Kalluri
Jaewon Kam
Sandesh Kamath
Meina Kan
Menelaos Kanakis
Takuhiro Kaneko
Di Kang
Guoliang Kang
Hao Kang
Jaeyeon Kang
Kyoungkook Kang
Li-Wei Kang
MinGuk Kang
Suk-Ju Kang
Zhao Kang
Yash Mukund Kant
Yueying Kao
Aupendu Kar
Konstantinos Karantzalos
Sezer Karaoglu
Navid Kardan
Sanjay Kariyappa
Leonid Karlinsky
Animesh Karnewar
Shyamgopal Karthik
Hirak J. Kashyap
Marc A. Kastner
Hirokatsu Kataoka
Angelos Katharopoulos
Hiroharu Kato
Kai Katsumata
Manuel Kaufmann
Chaitanya Kaul
Prakhar Kaushik

Yuki Kawana
Lei Ke
Lipeng Ke
Tsung-Wei Ke
Wei Ke
Petr Kellnhofer
Aniruddha Kembhavi
John Kender
Corentin Kervadec
Leonid Keselman
Daniel Keysers
Nima Khademi Kalantari
Taras Khakhulin
Samir Khaki
Muhammad Haris Khan
Qadeer Khan
Salman Khan
Subash Khanal
Vaishnavi M. Khindkar
Rawal Khirodkar
Saeed Khorram
Pirazh Khorramshahi
Kourosh Khoshelham
Ansh Khurana
Benjamin Kiefer
Jae Myung Kim
Junho Kim
Boah Kim
Hyeonseong Kim
Dong-Jin Kim
Dongwan Kim
Donghyun Kim
Doyeon Kim
Yonghyun Kim
Hyung-Il Kim
Hyunwoo Kim
Hyeongwoo Kim
Hyo Jin Kim
Hyunwoo J. Kim
Taehoon Kim
Jaeha Kim
Jiwon Kim
Jung Uk Kim
Kangyeol Kim
Eunji Kim

Daeha Kim
Dongwon Kim
Kunhee Kim
Kyungmin Kim
Junsik Kim
Min H. Kim
Namil Kim
Kookhoi Kim
Sanghyun Kim
Seongyeop Kim
Seungryong Kim
Saehoon Kim
Euyoung Kim
Guisik Kim
Sungyeon Kim
Sunnie S. Y. Kim
Taehun Kim
Tae Oh Kim
Won Hwa Kim
Seungwook Kim
YoungBin Kim
Youngeun Kim
Akisato Kimura
Furkan Osman Kınlı
Zsolt Kira
Hedvig Kjellström
Florian Kleber
Jan P. Klopp
Florian Kluger
Laurent Kneip
Byungsoo Ko
Muhammed Kocabas
A. Sophia Koepke
Kevin Koeser
Nick Kolkin
Nikos Kolotouros
Wai-Kin Adams Kong
Deying Kong
Caihua Kong
Youyong Kong
Shuyu Kong
Shu Kong
Tao Kong
Yajing Kong
Yu Kong

Zishang Kong
Theodora Kontogianni
Anton S. Konushin
Julian F. P. Kooij
Bruno Korbar
Giorgos Kordopatis-Zilos
Jari Korhonen
Adam Kortylewski
Denis Korzhenkov
Divya Kothandaraman
Suraj Kothawade
Iuliia Kotseruba
Satwik Kottur
Shashank Kotyan
Alexandros Kouris
Petros Koutras
Anna Kreshuk
Ranjay Krishna
Dilip Krishnan
Andrey Kuehlkamp
Hilde Kuehne
Jason Kuen
David Kügler
Arjan Kuijper
Anna Kukleva
Sumith Kulal
Viveka Kulharia
Akshay R. Kulkarni
Nilesh Kulkarni
Dominik Kulon
Abhinav Kumar
Akash Kumar
Suryansh Kumar
B. V. K. Vijaya Kumar
Pulkit Kumar
Ratnesh Kumar
Sateesh Kumar
Satish Kumar
Vijay Kumar B. G.
Nupur Kumari
Sudhakar Kumawat
Jogendra Nath Kundu
Hsien-Kai Kuo
Meng-Yu Jennifer Kuo
Vinod Kumar Kurmi

Yusuke Kurose
Keerthy Kusumam
Alina Kuznetsova
Henry Kvinge
Ho Man Kwan
Hyeokjun Kweon
Heeseung Kwon
Gihyun Kwon
Myung-Joon Kwon
Taesung Kwon
YoungJoong Kwon
Christos Kyrkou
Jorma Laaksonen
Yann Labbe
Zorah Laehner
Florent Lafarge
Hamid Laga
Manuel Lagunas
Shenqi Lai
Jian-Huang Lai
Zihang Lai
Mohamed I. Lakhal
Mohit Lamba
Meng Lan
Loic Landrieu
Zhiqiang Lang
Natalie Lang
Dong Lao
Yizhen Lao
Yingjie Lao
Issam Hadj Laradji
Gustav Larsson
Viktor Larsson
Zakaria Laskar
Stéphane Lathuilière
Chun Pong Lau
Rynson W. H. Lau
Hei Law
Justin Lazarow
Verica Lazova
Eric-Tuan Le
Hieu Le
Trung-Nghia Le
Mathias Lechner
Byeong-Uk Lee

Chen-Yu Lee
Che-Rung Lee
Chul Lee
Hong Joo Lee
Dongsoo Lee
Jiyoung Lee
Eugene Eu Tzuan Lee
Daeun Lee
Saehyung Lee
Jewook Lee
Hyungtae Lee
Hyunmin Lee
Jungbeom Lee
Joon-Young Lee
Jong-Seok Lee
Joonseok Lee
Junha Lee
Kibok Lee
Byung-Kwan Lee
Jangwon Lee
Jinho Lee
Jongmin Lee
Seunghyun Lee
Sohyun Lee
Minsik Lee
Dogyoon Lee
Seungmin Lee
Min Jun Lee
Sangho Lee
Sangmin Lee
Seungeun Lee
Seon-Ho Lee
Sungmin Lee
Sungho Lee
Sangyoun Lee
Vincent C. S. S. Lee
Jaeseong Lee
Yong Jae Lee
Chenyang Lei
Chenyi Lei
Jiahui Lei
Xinyu Lei
Yinjie Lei
Jiaxu Leng
Luziwei Leng

Jan E. Lenssen
Vincent Lepetit
Thomas Leung
María Leyva-Vallina
Xin Li
Yikang Li
Baoxin Li
Bin Li
Bing Li
Bowen Li
Changlin Li
Chao Li
Chongyi Li
Guanyue Li
Shuai Li
Jin Li
Dingquan Li
Dongxu Li
Yiting Li
Gang Li
Dian Li
Guohao Li
Haoang Li
Haoliang Li
Haoran Li
Hengduo Li
Huafeng Li
Xiaoming Li
Hanao Li
Hongwei Li
Ziqiang Li
Jisheng Li
Jiacheng Li
Jia Li
Jiachen Li
Jiahao Li
Jianwei Li
Jiazhi Li
Jie Li
Jing Li
Jingjing Li
Jingtao Li
Jun Li
Junxuan Li
Kai Li

Kailin Li
Kenneth Li
Kun Li
Kunpeng Li
Aoxue Li
Chenglong Li
Chenglin Li
Changsheng Li
Zhichao Li
Qiang Li
Yanyu Li
Zuoyue Li
Xiang Li
Xuelong Li
Fangda Li
Ailin Li
Liang Li
Chun-Guang Li
Daiqing Li
Dong Li
Guanbin Li
Guorong Li
Haifeng Li
Jianan Li
Jianing Li
Jiaxin Li
Ke Li
Lei Li
Lincheng Li
Liulei Li
Lujun Li
Linjie Li
Lin Li
Pengyu Li
Ping Li
Qiufu Li
Qingyong Li
Rui Li
Siyuan Li
Wei Li
Wenbin Li
Xiangyang Li
Xinyu Li
Xiujun Li
Xiu Li

Xu Li
Ya-Li Li
Yao Li
Yongjie Li
Yijun Li
Yiming Li
Yuezun Li
Yu Li
Yunheng Li
Yuqi Li
Zhe Li
Zeming Li
Zhen Li
Zhengqin Li
Zhimin Li
Jiefeng Li
Jinpeng Li
Chengze Li
Jianwu Li
Lerenhan Li
Shan Li
Suichan Li
Xiangtai Li
Yanjie Li
Yandong Li
Zhuoling Li
Zhenqiang Li
Manyi Li
Maosen Li
Ji Li
Minjun Li
Mingrui Li
Mengtian Li
Junyi Li
Nianyi Li
Bo Li
Xiao Li
Peihua Li
Peike Li
Peizhao Li
Peiliang Li
Qi Li
Ren Li
Runze Li
Shile Li

Sheng Li
Shigang Li
Shiyu Li
Shuang Li
Shasha Li
Shichao Li
Tianye Li
Yuexiang Li
Wei-Hong Li
Wanhua Li
Weihao Li
Weiming Li
Weixin Li
Wenbo Li
Wenshuo Li
Weijian Li
Yunan Li
Xirong Li
Xianhang Li
Xiaoyu Li
Xueqian Li
Xuanlin Li
Xianzhi Li
Yunqiang Li
Yanjing Li
Yansheng Li
Yawei Li
Yi Li
Yong Li
Yong-Lu Li
Yuhang Li
Yu-Jhe Li
Yuxi Li
Yunsheng Li
Yanwei Li
Zechao Li
Zejian Li
Zeju Li
Zekun Li
Zhaowen Li
Zheng Li
Zhenyu Li
Zhiheng Li
Zhi Li
Zhong Li

Zhuowei Li
Zhuowan Li
Zhuohang Li
Zizhang Li
Chen Li
Yuan-Fang Li
Dongze Lian
Xiaochen Lian
Zhouhui Lian
Long Lian
Qing Lian
Jin Lianbao
Jinxiu S. Liang
Dingkang Liang
Jiahao Liang
Jianming Liang
Jingyun Liang
Kevin J. Liang
Kaizhao Liang
Chen Liang
Jie Liang
Senwei Liang
Ding Liang
Jiajun Liang
Jian Liang
Kongming Liang
Siyuan Liang
Yuanzhi Liang
Zhengfa Liang
Mingfu Liang
Xiaodan Liang
Xuefeng Liang
Yuxuan Liang
Kang Liao
Liang Liao
Hong-Yuan Mark Liao
Wentong Liao
Haofu Liao
Yue Liao
Minghui Liao
Shengcai Liao
Ting-Hsuan Liao
Xin Liao
Yinghong Liao
Teck Yian Lim

Che-Tsung Lin
Chung-Ching Lin
Chen-Hsuan Lin
Cheng Lin
Chuming Lin
Chunyu Lin
Dahua Lin
Wei Lin
Zheng Lin
Huaijia Lin
Jason Lin
Jierui Lin
Jiaying Lin
Jie Lin
Kai-En Lin
Kevin Lin
Guangfeng Lin
Jiehong Lin
Feng Lin
Hang Lin
Kwan-Yee Lin
Ke Lin
Luojun Lin
Qinghong Lin
Xiangbo Lin
Yi Lin
Zudi Lin
Shijie Lin
Yiqun Lin
Tzu-Heng Lin
Ming Lin
Shaohui Lin
SongNan Lin
Ji Lin
Tsung-Yu Lin
Xudong Lin
Yancong Lin
Yen-Chen Lin
Yiming Lin
Yuewei Lin
Zhiqiu Lin
Zinan Lin
Zhe Lin
David B. Lindell
Zhixin Ling

Zhan Ling
Alexander Liniger
Venice Erin B. Liong
Joey Litalien
Or Litany
Roee Litman
Ron Litman
Jim Little
Dor Litvak
Shaoteng Liu
Shuaicheng Liu
Andrew Liu
Xian Liu
Shaohui Liu
Bei Liu
Bo Liu
Yong Liu
Ming Liu
Yanbin Liu
Chenxi Liu
Daqi Liu
Di Liu
Difan Liu
Dong Liu
Dongfang Liu
Daizong Liu
Xiao Liu
Fangyi Liu
Fengbei Liu
Fenglin Liu
Bin Liu
Yuang Liu
Ao Liu
Hong Liu
Hongfu Liu
Huidong Liu
Ziyi Liu
Feng Liu
Hao Liu
Jie Liu
Jialun Liu
Jiang Liu
Jing Liu
Jingya Liu
Jiaming Liu

Jun Liu
Juncheng Liu
Jiawei Liu
Hongyu Liu
Chuanbin Liu
Haotian Liu
Lingqiao Liu
Chang Liu
Han Liu
Liu Liu
Min Liu
Yingqi Liu
Aishan Liu
Bingyu Liu
Benlin Liu
Boxiao Liu
Chenchen Liu
Chuanjian Liu
Daqing Liu
Huan Liu
Haozhe Liu
Jiaheng Liu
Wei Liu
Jingzhou Liu
Jiyuan Liu
Lingbo Liu
Nian Liu
Peiye Liu
Qiankun Liu
Shenglan Liu
Shilong Liu
Wen Liu
Wenyu Liu
Weifeng Liu
Wu Liu
Xiaolong Liu
Yang Liu
Yanwei Liu
Yingcheng Liu
Yongfei Liu
Yihao Liu
Yu Liu
Yunze Liu
Ze Liu
Zhenhua Liu

Zhenguang Liu
Lin Liu
Lihao Liu
Pengju Liu
Xinhai Liu
Yunfei Liu
Meng Liu
Minghua Liu
Mingyuan Liu
Miao Liu
Peirong Liu
Ping Liu
Qingjie Liu
Ruoshi Liu
Risheng Liu
Songtao Liu
Xing Liu
Shikun Liu
Shuming Liu
Sheng Liu
Songhua Liu
Tongliang Liu
Weibo Liu
Weide Liu
Weizhe Liu
Wenxi Liu
Weiyang Liu
Xin Liu
Xiaobin Liu
Xudong Liu
Xiaoyi Liu
Xihui Liu
Xinchen Liu
Xingtong Liu
Xinpeng Liu
Xinyu Liu
Xianpeng Liu
Xu Liu
Xingyu Liu
Yongtuo Liu
Yahui Liu
Yangxin Liu
Yaoyao Liu
Yaojie Liu
Yuliang Liu

Yongcheng Liu
Yuan Liu
Yufan Liu
Yu-Lun Liu
Yun Liu
Yunfan Liu
Yuanzhong Liu
Zhuoran Liu
Zhen Liu
Zheng Liu
Zhijian Liu
Zhisong Liu
Ziquan Liu
Ziyu Liu
Zhihua Liu
Zechun Liu
Zhaoyang Liu
Zhengzhe Liu
Stephan Liwicki
Shao-Yuan Lo
Sylvain Lobry
Suhas Lohit
Vishnu Suresh Lokhande
Vincenzo Lomonaco
Chengjiang Long
Guodong Long
Fuchen Long
Shangbang Long
Yang Long
Zijun Long
Vasco Lopes
Antonio M. Lopez
Roberto Javier
    Lopez-Sastre
Tobias Lorenz
Javier Lorenzo-Navarro
Yujing Lou
Qian Lou
Xiankai Lu
Changsheng Lu
Huimin Lu
Yongxi Lu
Hao Lu
Hong Lu
Jiasen Lu

Juwei Lu
Fan Lu
Guangming Lu
Jiwen Lu
Shun Lu
Tao Lu
Xiaonan Lu
Yang Lu
Yao Lu
Yongchun Lu
Zhiwu Lu
Cheng Lu
Liying Lu
Guo Lu
Xuequan Lu
Yanye Lu
Yantao Lu
Yuhang Lu
Fujun Luan
Jonathon Luiten
Jovita Lukasik
Alan Lukezic
Jonathan Samuel Lumentut
Mayank Lunayach
Ao Luo
Canjie Luo
Chong Luo
Xu Luo
Grace Luo
Jun Luo
Katie Z. Luo
Tao Luo
Cheng Luo
Fangzhou Luo
Gen Luo
Lei Luo
Sihui Luo
Weixin Luo
Yan Luo
Xiaoyan Luo
Yong Luo
Yadan Luo
Hao Luo
Ruotian Luo
Mi Luo

Tiange Luo
Wenjie Luo
Wenhan Luo
Xiao Luo
Zhiming Luo
Zhipeng Luo
Zhengyi Luo
Diogo C. Luvizon
Zhaoyang Lv
Gengyu Lyu
Lingjuan Lyu
Jun Lyu
Yuanyuan Lyu
Youwei Lyu
Yueming Lyu
Bingpeng Ma
Chao Ma
Chongyang Ma
Congbo Ma
Chih-Yao Ma
Fan Ma
Lin Ma
Haoyu Ma
Hengbo Ma
Jianqi Ma
Jiawei Ma
Jiayi Ma
Kede Ma
Kai Ma
Lingni Ma
Lei Ma
Xu Ma
Ning Ma
Benteng Ma
Cheng Ma
Andy J. Ma
Long Ma
Zhanyu Ma
Zhiheng Ma
Qianli Ma
Shiqiang Ma
Sizhuo Ma
Shiqing Ma
Xiaolong Ma
Xinzhu Ma

Gautam B. Machiraju
Spandan Madan
Mathew Magimai-Doss
Luca Magri
Behrooz Mahasseni
Upal Mahbub
Siddharth Mahendran
Paridhi Maheshwari
Rishabh Maheshwary
Mohammed Mahmoud
Shishira R. R. Maiya
Sylwia Majchrowska
Arjun Majumdar
Puspita Majumdar
Orchid Majumder
Sagnik Majumder
Ilya Makarov
Farkhod F.
    Makhmudkhujaev
Yasushi Makihara
Ankur Mali
Mateusz Malinowski
Utkarsh Mall
Srikanth Malla
Clement Mallet
Dimitrios Mallis
Yunze Man
Dipu Manandhar
Massimiliano Mancini
Murari Mandal
Raunak Manekar
Karttikeya Mangalam
Puneet Mangla
Fabian Manhardt
Sivabalan Manivasagam
Fahim Mannan
Chengzhi Mao
Hanzi Mao
Jiayuan Mao
Junhua Mao
Zhiyuan Mao
Jiageng Mao
Yunyao Mao
Zhendong Mao
Alberto Marchisio

Diego Marcos
Riccardo Marin
Aram Markosyan
Renaud Marlet
Ricardo Marques
Miquel Martí i Rabadán
Diego Martin Arroyo
Niki Martinel
Brais Martinez
Julieta Martinez
Marc Masana
Tomohiro Mashita
Timothée Masquelier
Minesh Mathew
Tetsu Matsukawa
Marwan Mattar
Bruce A. Maxwell
Christoph Mayer
Mantas Mazeika
Pratik Mazumder
Scott McCloskey
Steven McDonagh
Ishit Mehta
Jie Mei
Kangfu Mei
Jieru Mei
Xiaoguang Mei
Givi Meishvili
Luke Melas-Kyriazi
Iaroslav Melekhov
Andres Mendez-Vazquez
Heydi Mendez-Vazquez
Matias Mendieta
Ricardo A. Mendoza-León
Chenlin Meng
Depu Meng
Rang Meng
Zibo Meng
Qingjie Meng
Qier Meng
Yanda Meng
Zihang Meng
Thomas Mensink
Fabian Mentzer
Christopher Metzler

Gregory P. Meyer
Vasileios Mezaris
Liang Mi
Lu Mi
Bo Miao
Changtao Miao
Zichen Miao
Qiguang Miao
Xin Miao
Zhongqi Miao
Frank Michel
Simone Milani
Ben Mildenhall
Roy V. Miles
Juhong Min
Kyle Min
Hyun-Seok Min
Weiqing Min
Yuecong Min
Zhixiang Min
Qi Ming
David Minnen
Aymen Mir
Deepak Mishra
Anand Mishra
Shlok K. Mishra
Niluthpol Mithun
Gaurav Mittal
Trisha Mittal
Daisuke Miyazaki
Kaichun Mo
Hong Mo
Zhipeng Mo
Davide Modolo
Abduallah A. Mohamed
Mohamed Afham
    Mohamed Aflal
Ron Mokady
Pavlo Molchanov
Davide Moltisanti
Liliane Momeni
Gianluca Monaci
Pascal Monasse
Ajoy Mondal
Tom Monnier

Aron Monszpart
Gyeongsik Moon
Suhong Moon
Taesup Moon
Sean Moran
Daniel Moreira
Pietro Morerio
Alexandre Morgand
Lia Morra
Ali Mosleh
Inbar Mosseri
Sayed Mohammad
    Mostafavi Isfahani
Saman Motamed
Ramy A. Mounir
Fangzhou Mu
Jiteng Mu
Norman Mu
Yasuhiro Mukaigawa
Ryan Mukherjee
Tanmoy Mukherjee
Yusuke Mukuta
Ravi Teja Mullapudi
Lea Müller
Matthias Müller
Martin Mundt
Nils Murrugarra-Llerena
Damien Muselet
Armin Mustafa
Muhammad Ferjad Naeem
Sauradip Nag
Hajime Nagahara
Pravin Nagar
Rajendra Nagar
Naveen Shankar Nagaraja
Varun Nagaraja
Tushar Nagarajan
Seungjun Nah
Gaku Nakano
Yuta Nakashima
Giljoo Nam
Seonghyeon Nam
Liangliang Nan
Yuesong Nan
Yeshwanth Napolean

Dinesh Reddy
    Narapureddy
Medhini Narasimhan
Supreeth
    Narasimhaswamy
Sriram Narayanan
Erickson R. Nascimento
Varun Nasery
K. L. Navaneet
Pablo Navarrete Michelini
Shant Navasardyan
Shah Nawaz
Nihal Nayak
Farhood Negin
Lukáš Neumann
Alejandro Newell
Evonne Ng
Kam Woh Ng
Tony Ng
Anh Nguyen
Tuan Anh Nguyen
Cuong Cao Nguyen
Ngoc Cuong Nguyen
Thanh Nguyen
Khoi Nguyen
Phi Le Nguyen
Phong Ha Nguyen
Tam Nguyen
Truong Nguyen
Anh Tuan Nguyen
Rang Nguyen
Thao Thi Phuong Nguyen
Van Nguyen Nguyen
Zhen-Liang Ni
Yao Ni
Shijie Nie
Xuecheng Nie
Yongwei Nie
Weizhi Nie
Ying Nie
Yinyu Nie
Kshitij N. Nikhal
Simon Niklaus
Xuefei Ning
Jifeng Ning

Yotam Nitzan
Di Niu
Shuaicheng Niu
Li Niu
Wei Niu
Yulei Niu
Zhenxing Niu
Albert No
Shohei Nobuhara
Nicoletta Noceti
Junhyug Noh
Sotiris Nousias
Slawomir Nowaczyk
Ewa M. Nowara
Valsamis Ntouskos
Gilberto Ochoa-Ruiz
Ferda Ofli
Jihyong Oh
Sangyun Oh
Youngtaek Oh
Hiroki Ohashi
Takahiro Okabe
Kemal Oksuz
Fumio Okura
Daniel Olmeda Reino
Matthew Olson
Carl Olsson
Roy Or-El
Alessandro Ortis
Guillermo Ortiz-Jimenez
Magnus Oskarsson
Ahmed A. A. Osman
Martin R. Oswald
Mayu Otani
Naima Otberdout
Cheng Ouyang
Jiahong Ouyang
Wanli Ouyang
Andrew Owens
Poojan B. Oza
Mete Ozay
A. Cengiz Oztireli
Gautam Pai
Tomas Pajdla
Umapada Pal

Simone Palazzo
Luca Palmieri
Bowen Pan
Hao Pan
Lili Pan
Tai-Yu Pan
Liang Pan
Chengwei Pan
Yingwei Pan
Xuran Pan
Jinshan Pan
Xinyu Pan
Liyuan Pan
Xingang Pan
Xingjia Pan
Zhihong Pan
Zizheng Pan
Priyadarshini Panda
Rameswar Panda
Rohit Pandey
Kaiyue Pang
Bo Pang
Guansong Pang
Jiangmiao Pang
Meng Pang
Tianyu Pang
Ziqi Pang
Omiros Pantazis
Andreas Panteli
Maja Pantic
Marina Paolanti
Joao P. Papa
Samuele Papa
Mike Papadakis
Dim P. Papadopoulos
George Papandreou
Constantin Pape
Toufiq Parag
Chethan Parameshwara
Shaifali Parashar
Alejandro Pardo
Rishubh Parihar
Sarah Parisot
JaeYoo Park
Gyeong-Moon Park

Hyojin Park
Hyoungseob Park
Jongchan Park
Jae Sung Park
Kiru Park
Chunghyun Park
Kwanyong Park
Sunghyun Park
Sungrae Park
Seongsik Park
Sanghyun Park
Sungjune Park
Taesung Park
Gaurav Parmar
Paritosh Parmar
Alvaro Parra
Despoina Paschalidou
Or Patashnik
Shivansh Patel
Pushpak Pati
Prashant W. Patil
Vaishakh Patil
Suvam Patra
Jay Patravali
Badri Narayana Patro
Angshuman Paul
Sudipta Paul
Rémi Pautrat
Nick E. Pears
Adithya Pediredla
Wenjie Pei
Shmuel Peleg
Latha Pemula
Bo Peng
Houwen Peng
Yue Peng
Liangzu Peng
Baoyun Peng
Jun Peng
Pai Peng
Sida Peng
Xi Peng
Yuxin Peng
Songyou Peng
Wei Peng

Weiqi Peng
Wen-Hsiao Peng
Pramuditha Perera
Juan C. Perez
Eduardo Pérez Pellitero
Juan-Manuel Perez-Rua
Federico Pernici
Marco Pesavento
Stavros Petridis
Ilya A. Petrov
Vladan Petrovic
Mathis Petrovich
Suzanne Petryk
Hieu Pham
Quang Pham
Khoi Pham
Tung Pham
Huy Phan
Stephen Phillips
Cheng Perng Phoo
David Picard
Marco Piccirilli
Georg Pichler
A. J. Piergiovanni
Vipin Pillai
Silvia L. Pintea
Giovanni Pintore
Robinson Piramuthu
Fiora Pirri
Theodoros Pissas
Fabio Pizzati
Benjamin Planche
Bryan Plummer
Matteo Poggi
Ashwini Pokle
Georgy E. Ponimatkin
Adrian Popescu
Stefan Popov
Nikola Popović
Ronald Poppe
Angelo Porrello
Michael Potter
Charalambos Poullis
Hadi Pouransari
Omid Poursaeed

Shraman Pramanick
Mantini Pranav
Dilip K. Prasad
Meghshyam Prasad
B. H. Pawan Prasad
Shitala Prasad
Prateek Prasanna
Ekta Prashnani
Derek S. Prijatelj
Luke Y. Prince
Véronique Prinet
Victor Adrian Prisacariu
James Pritts
Thomas Probst
Sergey Prokudin
Rita Pucci
Chi-Man Pun
Matthew Purri
Haozhi Qi
Lu Qi
Lei Qi
Xianbiao Qi
Yonggang Qi
Yuankai Qi
Siyuan Qi
Guocheng Qian
Hangwei Qian
Qi Qian
Deheng Qian
Shengsheng Qian
Wen Qian
Rui Qian
Yiming Qian
Shengju Qian
Shengyi Qian
Xuelin Qian
Zhenxing Qian
Nan Qiao
Xiaotian Qiao
Jing Qin
Can Qin
Siyang Qin
Hongwei Qin
Jie Qin
Minghai Qin

Yipeng Qin
Yongqiang Qin
Wenda Qin
Xuebin Qin
Yuzhe Qin
Yao Qin
Zhenyue Qin
Zhiwu Qing
Heqian Qiu
Jiayan Qiu
Jielin Qiu
Yue Qiu
Jiaxiong Qiu
Zhongxi Qiu
Shi Qiu
Zhaofan Qiu
Zhongnan Qu
Yanyun Qu
Kha Gia Quach
Yuhui Quan
Ruijie Quan
Mike Rabbat
Rahul Shekhar Rade
Filip Radenovic
Gorjan Radevski
Bogdan Raducanu
Francesco Ragusa
Shafin Rahman
Md Mahfuzur Rahman
   Siddiquee
Hossein Rahmani
Kiran Raja
Sivaramakrishnan
   Rajaraman
Jathushan Rajasegaran
Adnan Siraj Rakin
Michaël Ramamonjisoa
Chirag A. Raman
Shanmuganathan Raman
Vignesh Ramanathan
Vasili Ramanishka
Vikram V. Ramaswamy
Merey Ramazanova
Jason Rambach
Sai Saketh Rambhatla

Clément Rambour
Ashwin Ramesh Babu
Adín Ramírez Rivera
Arianna Rampini
Haoxi Ran
Aakanksha Rana
Aayush Jung Bahadur
   Rana
Kanchana N. Ranasinghe
Aneesh Rangnekar
Samrudhdhi B. Rangrej
Harsh Rangwani
Viresh Ranjan
Anyi Rao
Yongming Rao
Carolina Raposo
Michalis Raptis
Amir Rasouli
Vivek Rathod
Adepu Ravi Sankar
Avinash Ravichandran
Bharadwaj Ravichandran
Dripta S. Raychaudhuri
Adria Recasens
Simon Reiß
Davis Rempe
Daxuan Ren
Jiawei Ren
Jimmy Ren
Sucheng Ren
Dayong Ren
Zhile Ren
Dongwei Ren
Qibing Ren
Pengfei Ren
Zhenwen Ren
Xuqian Ren
Yixuan Ren
Zhongzheng Ren
Ambareesh Revanur
Hamed Rezazadegan
   Tavakoli
Rafael S. Rezende
Wonjong Rhee
Alexander Richard

Christian Richardt
Stephan R. Richter
Benjamin Riggan
Dominik Rivoir
Mamshad Nayeem Rizve
Joshua D. Robinson
Joseph Robinson
Chris Rockwell
Ranga Rodrigo
Andres C. Rodriguez
Carlos Rodriguez-Pardo
Marcus Rohrbach
Gemma Roig
Yu Rong
David A. Ross
Mohammad Rostami
Edward Rosten
Karsten Roth
Anirban Roy
Debaditya Roy
Shuvendu Roy
Ahana Roy Choudhury
Aruni Roy Chowdhury
Denys Rozumnyi
Shulan Ruan
Wenjie Ruan
Patrick Ruhkamp
Danila Rukhovich
Anian Ruoss
Chris Russell
Dan Ruta
Dawid Damian Rymarczyk
DongHun Ryu
Hyeonggon Ryu
Kwonyoung Ryu
Balasubramanian S.
Alexandre Sablayrolles
Mohammad Sabokrou
Arka Sadhu
Aniruddha Saha
Oindrila Saha
Pritish Sahu
Aneeshan Sain
Nirat Saini
Saurabh Saini

Takeshi Saitoh
Christos Sakaridis
Fumihiko Sakaue
Dimitrios Sakkos
Ken Sakurada
Parikshit V. Sakurikar
Rohit Saluja
Nermin Samet
Leo Sampaio Ferraz
    Ribeiro
Jorge Sanchez
Enrique Sanchez
Shengtian Sang
Anush Sankaran
Soubhik Sanyal
Nikolaos Sarafianos
Vishwanath Saragadam
István Sárándi
Saquib Sarfraz
Mert Bulent Sariyildiz
Anindya Sarkar
Pritam Sarkar
Paul-Edouard Sarlin
Hiroshi Sasaki
Takami Sato
Torsten Sattler
Ravi Kumar Satzoda
Axel Sauer
Stefano Savian
Artem Savkin
Manolis Savva
Gerald Schaefer
Simone Schaub-Meyer
Yoni Schirris
Samuel Schulter
Katja Schwarz
Jesse Scott
Sinisa Segvic
Constantin Marc Seibold
Lorenzo Seidenari
Matan Sela
Fadime Sener
Paul Hongsuck Seo
Kwanggyoon Seo
Hongje Seong

Dario Serez
Francesco Setti
Bryan Seybold
Mohamad Shahbazi
Shima Shahfar
Xinxin Shan
Caifeng Shan
Dandan Shan
Shawn Shan
Wei Shang
Jinghuan Shang
Jiaxiang Shang
Lei Shang
Sukrit Shankar
Ken Shao
Rui Shao
Jie Shao
Mingwen Shao
Aashish Sharma
Gaurav Sharma
Vivek Sharma
Abhishek Sharma
Yoli Shavit
Shashank Shekhar
Sumit Shekhar
Zhijie Shen
Fengyi Shen
Furao Shen
Jialie Shen
Jingjing Shen
Ziyi Shen
Linlin Shen
Guangyu Shen
Biluo Shen
Falong Shen
Jiajun Shen
Qiu Shen
Qiuhong Shen
Shuai Shen
Wang Shen
Yiqing Shen
Yunhang Shen
Siqi Shen
Bin Shen
Tianwei Shen

Xi Shen
Yilin Shen
Yuming Shen
Yucong Shen
Zhiqiang Shen
Lu Sheng
Yichen Sheng
Shivanand Venkanna
    Sheshappanavar
Shelly Sheynin
Baifeng Shi
Ruoxi Shi
Botian Shi
Hailin Shi
Jia Shi
Jing Shi
Shaoshuai Shi
Baoguang Shi
Boxin Shi
Hengcan Shi
Tianyang Shi
Xiaodan Shi
Yongjie Shi
Zhensheng Shi
Yinghuan Shi
Weiqi Shi
Wu Shi
Xuepeng Shi
Xiaoshuang Shi
Yujiao Shi
Zenglin Shi
Zhenmei Shi
Takashi Shibata
Meng-Li Shih
Yichang Shih
Hyunjung Shim
Dongseok Shim
Soshi Shimada
Inkyu Shin
Jinwoo Shin
Seungjoo Shin
Seungjae Shin
Koichi Shinoda
Suprosanna Shit

Palaiahnakote
    Shivakumara
Eli Shlizerman
Gaurav Shrivastava
Xiao Shu
Xiangbo Shu
Xiujun Shu
Yang Shu
Tianmin Shu
Jun Shu
Zhixin Shu
Bing Shuai
Maria Shugrina
Ivan Shugurov
Satya Narayan Shukla
Pranjay Shyam
Jianlou Si
Yawar Siddiqui
Alberto Signoroni
Pedro Silva
Jae-Young Sim
Oriane Siméoni
Martin Simon
Andrea Simonelli
Abhishek Singh
Ashish Singh
Dinesh Singh
Gurkirt Singh
Krishna Kumar Singh
Mannat Singh
Pravendra Singh
Rajat Vikram Singh
Utkarsh Singhal
Dipika Singhania
Vasu Singla
Harsh Sinha
Sudipta Sinha
Josef Sivic
Elena Sizikova
Geri Skenderi
Ivan Skorokhodov
Dmitriy Smirnov
Cameron Y. Smith
James S. Smith
Patrick Snape

Mattia Soldan
Hyeongseok Son
Sanghyun Son
Chuanbiao Song
Chen Song
Chunfeng Song
Dan Song
Dongjin Song
Hwanjun Song
Guoxian Song
Jiaming Song
Jie Song
Liangchen Song
Ran Song
Luchuan Song
Xibin Song
Li Song
Fenglong Song
Guoli Song
Guanglu Song
Zhenbo Song
Lin Song
Xinhang Song
Yang Song
Yibing Song
Rajiv Soundararajan
Hossein Souri
Cristovao Sousa
Riccardo Spezialetti
Leonidas Spinoulas
Michael W. Spratling
Deepak Sridhar
Srinath Sridhar
Gaurang Sriramanan
Vinkle Kumar Srivastav
Themos Stafylakis
Serban Stan
Anastasis Stathopoulos
Markus Steinberger
Jan Steinbrener
Sinisa Stekovic
Alexandros Stergiou
Gleb Sterkin
Rainer Stiefelhagen
Pierre Stock

Ombretta Strafforello
Julian Straub
Yannick Strümpler
Joerg Stueckler
Hang Su
Weijie Su
Jong-Chyi Su
Bing Su
Haisheng Su
Jinming Su
Yiyang Su
Yukun Su
Yuxin Su
Zhuo Su
Zhaoqi Su
Xiu Su
Yu-Chuan Su
Zhixun Su
Arulkumar Subramaniam
Akshayvarun Subramanya
A. Subramanyam
Swathikiran Sudhakaran
Yusuke Sugano
Masanori Suganuma
Yumin Suh
Yang Sui
Baochen Sun
Cheng Sun
Long Sun
Guolei Sun
Haoliang Sun
Haomiao Sun
He Sun
Hanqing Sun
Hao Sun
Lichao Sun
Jiachen Sun
Jiaming Sun
Jian Sun
Jin Sun
Jennifer J. Sun
Tiancheng Sun
Libo Sun
Peize Sun
Qianru Sun

Shanlin Sun
Yu Sun
Zhun Sun
Che Sun
Lin Sun
Tao Sun
Yiyou Sun
Chunyi Sun
Chong Sun
Weiwei Sun
Weixuan Sun
Xiuyu Sun
Yanan Sun
Zeren Sun
Zhaodong Sun
Zhiqing Sun
Minhyuk Sung
Jinli Suo
Simon Suo
Abhijit Suprem
Anshuman Suri
Saksham Suri
Joshua M. Susskind
Roman Suvorov
Gurumurthy Swaminathan
Robin Swanson
Paul Swoboda
Tabish A. Syed
Richard Szeliski
Fariborz Taherkhani
Yu-Wing Tai
Keita Takahashi
Walter Talbott
Gary Tam
Masato Tamura
Feitong Tan
Fuwen Tan
Shuhan Tan
Andong Tan
Bin Tan
Cheng Tan
Jianchao Tan
Lei Tan
Mingxing Tan
Xin Tan

Zichang Tan
Zhentao Tan
Kenichiro Tanaka
Masayuki Tanaka
Yushun Tang
Hao Tang
Jingqun Tang
Jinhui Tang
Kaihua Tang
Luming Tang
Lv Tang
Sheyang Tang
Shitao Tang
Siliang Tang
Shixiang Tang
Yansong Tang
Keke Tang
Chang Tang
Chenwei Tang
Jie Tang
Junshu Tang
Ming Tang
Peng Tang
Xu Tang
Yao Tang
Chen Tang
Fan Tang
Haoran Tang
Shengeng Tang
Yehui Tang
Zhipeng Tang
Ugo Tanielian
Chaofan Tao
Jiale Tao
Junli Tao
Renshuai Tao
An Tao
Guanhong Tao
Zhiqiang Tao
Makarand Tapaswi
Jean-Philippe G. Tarel
Juan J. Tarrio
Enzo Tartaglione
Keisuke Tateno
Zachary Teed

Ajinkya B. Tejankar
Bugra Tekin
Purva Tendulkar
Damien Teney
Minggui Teng
Chris Tensmeyer
Andrew Beng Jin Teoh
Philipp Terhörst
Kartik Thakral
Nupur Thakur
Kevin Thandiackal
Spyridon Thermos
Diego Thomas
William Thong
Yuesong Tian
Guanzhong Tian
Lin Tian
Shiqi Tian
Kai Tian
Meng Tian
Tai-Peng Tian
Zhuotao Tian
Shangxuan Tian
Tian Tian
Yapeng Tian
Yu Tian
Yuxin Tian
Leslie Ching Ow Tiong
Praveen Tirupattur
Garvita Tiwari
George Toderici
Antoine Toisoul
Aysim Toker
Tatiana Tommasi
Zhan Tong
Alessio Tonioni
Alessandro Torcinovich
Fabio Tosi
Matteo Toso
Hugo Touvron
Quan Hung Tran
Son Tran
Hung Tran
Ngoc-Trung Tran
Vinh Tran

Phong Tran
Giovanni Trappolini
Edith Tretschk
Subarna Tripathi
Shubhendu Trivedi
Eduard Trulls
Prune Truong
Thanh-Dat Truong
Tomasz Trzcinski
Sam Tsai
Yi-Hsuan Tsai
Ethan Tseng
Yu-Chee Tseng
Shahar Tsiper
Stavros Tsogkas
Shikui Tu
Zhigang Tu
Zhengzhong Tu
Richard Tucker
Sergey Tulyakov
Cigdem Turan
Daniyar Turmukhambetov
Victor G. Turrisi da Costa
Bartlomiej Twardowski
Christopher D. Twigg
Radim Tylecek
Mostofa Rafid Uddin
Md. Zasim Uddin
Kohei Uehara
Nicolas Ugrinovic
Youngjung Uh
Norimichi Ukita
Anwaar Ulhaq
Devesh Upadhyay
Paul Upchurch
Yoshitaka Ushiku
Yuzuko Utsumi
Mikaela Angelina Uy
Mohit Vaishnav
Pratik Vaishnavi
Jeya Maria Jose Valanarasu
Matias A. Valdenegro Toro
Diego Valsesia
Wouter Van Gansbeke
Nanne van Noord

Simon Vandenhende
Farshid Varno
Cristina Vasconcelos
Francisco Vasconcelos
Alex Vasilescu
Subeesh Vasu
Arun Balajee Vasudevan
Kanav Vats
Vaibhav S. Vavilala
Sagar Vaze
Javier Vazquez-Corral
Andrea Vedaldi
Olga Veksler
Andreas Velten
Sai H. Vemprala
Raviteja Vemulapalli
Shashanka
     Venkataramanan
Dor Verbin
Luisa Verdoliva
Manisha Verma
Yashaswi Verma
Constantin Vertan
Eli Verwimp
Deepak Vijaykeerthy
Pablo Villanueva
Ruben Villegas
Markus Vincze
Vibhav Vineet
Minh P. Vo
Huy V. Vo
Duc Minh Vo
Tomas Vojir
Igor Vozniak
Nicholas Vretos
Vibashan VS
Tuan-Anh Vu
Thang Vu
Mårten Wadenbäck
Neal Wadhwa
Aaron T. Walsman
Steven Walton
Jin Wan
Alvin Wan
Jia Wan

Jun Wan
Xiaoyue Wan
Fang Wan
Guowei Wan
Renjie Wan
Zhiqiang Wan
Ziyu Wan
Bastian Wandt
Dongdong Wang
Limin Wang
Haiyang Wang
Xiaobing Wang
Angtian Wang
Angelina Wang
Bing Wang
Bo Wang
Boyu Wang
Binghui Wang
Chen Wang
Chien-Yi Wang
Congli Wang
Qi Wang
Chengrui Wang
Rui Wang
Yiqun Wang
Cong Wang
Wenjing Wang
Dongkai Wang
Di Wang
Xiaogang Wang
Kai Wang
Zhizhong Wang
Fangjinhua Wang
Feng Wang
Hang Wang
Gaoang Wang
Guoqing Wang
Guangcong Wang
Guangzhi Wang
Hanqing Wang
Hao Wang
Haohan Wang
Haoran Wang
Hong Wang
Haotao Wang

Hu Wang
Huan Wang
Hua Wang
Hui-Po Wang
Hengli Wang
Hanyu Wang
Hongxing Wang
Jingwen Wang
Jialiang Wang
Jian Wang
Jianyi Wang
Jiashun Wang
Jiahao Wang
Tsun-Hsuan Wang
Xiaoqian Wang
Jinqiao Wang
Jun Wang
Jianzong Wang
Kaihong Wang
Ke Wang
Lei Wang
Lingjing Wang
Linnan Wang
Lin Wang
Liansheng Wang
Mengjiao Wang
Manning Wang
Nannan Wang
Peihao Wang
Jiayun Wang
Pu Wang
Qiang Wang
Qiufeng Wang
Qilong Wang
Qiangchang Wang
Qin Wang
Qing Wang
Ruocheng Wang
Ruibin Wang
Ruisheng Wang
Ruizhe Wang
Runqi Wang
Runzhong Wang
Wenxuan Wang
Sen Wang

Shangfei Wang
Shaofei Wang
Shijie Wang
Shiqi Wang
Zhibo Wang
Song Wang
Xinjiang Wang
Tai Wang
Tao Wang
Teng Wang
Xiang Wang
Tianren Wang
Tiantian Wang
Tianyi Wang
Fengjiao Wang
Wei Wang
Miaohui Wang
Suchen Wang
Siyue Wang
Yaoming Wang
Xiao Wang
Ze Wang
Biao Wang
Chaofei Wang
Dong Wang
Gu Wang
Guangrun Wang
Guangming Wang
Guo-Hua Wang
Haoqing Wang
Hesheng Wang
Huafeng Wang
Jinghua Wang
Jingdong Wang
Jingjing Wang
Jingya Wang
Jingkang Wang
Jiakai Wang
Junke Wang
Kuo Wang
Lichen Wang
Lizhi Wang
Longguang Wang
Mang Wang
Mei Wang

Min Wang
Peng-Shuai Wang
Run Wang
Shaoru Wang
Shuhui Wang
Tan Wang
Tiancai Wang
Tianqi Wang
Wenhai Wang
Wenzhe Wang
Xiaobo Wang
Xiudong Wang
Xu Wang
Yajie Wang
Yan Wang
Yuan-Gen Wang
Yingqian Wang
Yizhi Wang
Yulin Wang
Yu Wang
Yujie Wang
Yunhe Wang
Yuxi Wang
Yaowei Wang
Yiwei Wang
Zezheng Wang
Hongzhi Wang
Zhiqiang Wang
Ziteng Wang
Ziwei Wang
Zheng Wang
Zhenyu Wang
Binglu Wang
Zhongdao Wang
Ce Wang
Weining Wang
Weiyao Wang
Wenbin Wang
Wenguan Wang
Guangting Wang
Haolin Wang
Haiyan Wang
Huiyu Wang
Naiyan Wang
Jingbo Wang

Jinpeng Wang
Jiaqi Wang
Liyuan Wang
Lizhen Wang
Ning Wang
Wenqian Wang
Sheng-Yu Wang
Weimin Wang
Xiaohan Wang
Yifan Wang
Yi Wang
Yongtao Wang
Yizhou Wang
Zhuo Wang
Zhe Wang
Xudong Wang
Xiaofang Wang
Xinggang Wang
Xiaosen Wang
Xiaosong Wang
Xiaoyang Wang
Lijun Wang
Xinlong Wang
Xuan Wang
Xue Wang
Yangang Wang
Yaohui Wang
Yu-Chiang Frank Wang
Yida Wang
Yilin Wang
Yi Ru Wang
Yali Wang
Yinglong Wang
Yufu Wang
Yujiang Wang
Yuwang Wang
Yuting Wang
Yang Wang
Yu-Xiong Wang
Yixu Wang
Ziqi Wang
Zhicheng Wang
Zeyu Wang
Zhaowen Wang
Zhenyi Wang

Zhenzhi Wang
Zhijie Wang
Zhiyong Wang
Zhongling Wang
Zhuowei Wang
Zian Wang
Zifu Wang
Zihao Wang
Zirui Wang
Ziyan Wang
Wenxiao Wang
Zhen Wang
Zhepeng Wang
Zi Wang
Zihao W. Wang
Steven L. Waslander
Olivia Watkins
Daniel Watson
Silvan Weder
Dongyoon Wee
Dongming Wei
Tianyi Wei
Jia Wei
Dong Wei
Fangyun Wei
Longhui Wei
Mingqiang Wei
Xinyue Wei
Chen Wei
Donglai Wei
Pengxu Wei
Xing Wei
Xiu-Shen Wei
Wenqi Wei
Guoqiang Wei
Wei Wei
XingKui Wei
Xian Wei
Xingxing Wei
Yake Wei
Yuxiang Wei
Yi Wei
Luca Weihs
Michael Weinmann
Martin Weinmann

Congcong Wen
Chuan Wen
Jie Wen
Sijia Wen
Song Wen
Chao Wen
Xiang Wen
Zeyi Wen
Xin Wen
Yilin Wen
Yijia Weng
Shuchen Weng
Junwu Weng
Wenming Weng
Renliang Weng
Zhenyu Weng
Xinshuo Weng
Nicholas J. Westlake
Gordon Wetzstein
Lena M. Widin Klasén
Rick Wildes
Bryan M. Williams
Williem Williem
Ole Winther
Scott Wisdom
Alex Wong
Chau-Wai Wong
Kwan-Yee K. Wong
Yongkang Wong
Scott Workman
Marcel Worring
Michael Wray
Safwan Wshah
Xiang Wu
Aming Wu
Chongruo Wu
Cho-Ying Wu
Chunpeng Wu
Chenyan Wu
Ziyi Wu
Fuxiang Wu
Gang Wu
Haiping Wu
Huisi Wu
Jane Wu

Jialian Wu
Jing Wu
Jinjian Wu
Jianlong Wu
Xian Wu
Lifang Wu
Lifan Wu
Minye Wu
Qianyi Wu
Rongliang Wu
Rui Wu
Shiqian Wu
Shuzhe Wu
Shangzhe Wu
Tsung-Han Wu
Tz-Ying Wu
Ting-Wei Wu
Jiannan Wu
Zhiliang Wu
Yu Wu
Chenyun Wu
Dayan Wu
Dongxian Wu
Fei Wu
Hefeng Wu
Jianxin Wu
Weibin Wu
Wenxuan Wu
Wenhao Wu
Xiao Wu
Yicheng Wu
Yuanwei Wu
Yu-Huan Wu
Zhenxin Wu
Zhenyu Wu
Wei Wu
Peng Wu
Xiaohe Wu
Xindi Wu
Xinxing Wu
Xinyi Wu
Xingjiao Wu
Xiongwei Wu
Yangzheng Wu
Yanzhao Wu

Yawen Wu
Yong Wu
Yi Wu
Ying Nian Wu
Zhenyao Wu
Zhonghua Wu
Zongze Wu
Zuxuan Wu
Stefanie Wuhrer
Teng Xi
Jianing Xi
Fei Xia
Haifeng Xia
Menghan Xia
Yuanqing Xia
Zhihua Xia
Xiaobo Xia
Weihao Xia
Shihong Xia
Yan Xia
Yong Xia
Zhaoyang Xia
Zhihao Xia
Chuhua Xian
Yongqin Xian
Wangmeng Xiang
Fanbo Xiang
Tiange Xiang
Tao Xiang
Liuyu Xiang
Xiaoyu Xiang
Zhiyu Xiang
Aoran Xiao
Chunxia Xiao
Fanyi Xiao
Jimin Xiao
Jun Xiao
Taihong Xiao
Anqi Xiao
Junfei Xiao
Jing Xiao
Liang Xiao
Yang Xiao
Yuting Xiao
Yijun Xiao

Yao Xiao
Zeyu Xiao
Zhisheng Xiao
Zihao Xiao
Binhui Xie
Christopher Xie
Haozhe Xie
Jin Xie
Guo-Sen Xie
Hongtao Xie
Ming-Kun Xie
Tingting Xie
Chaohao Xie
Weicheng Xie
Xudong Xie
Jiyang Xie
Xiaohua Xie
Yuan Xie
Zhenyu Xie
Ning Xie
Xianghui Xie
Xiufeng Xie
You Xie
Yutong Xie
Fuyong Xing
Yifan Xing
Zhen Xing
Yuanjun Xiong
Jinhui Xiong
Weihua Xiong
Hongkai Xiong
Zhitong Xiong
Yuanhao Xiong
Yunyang Xiong
Yuwen Xiong
Zhiwei Xiong
Yuliang Xiu
An Xu
Chang Xu
Chenliang Xu
Chengming Xu
Chenshu Xu
Xiang Xu
Huijuan Xu
Zhe Xu

Jie Xu
Jingyi Xu
Jiarui Xu
Yinghao Xu
Kele Xu
Ke Xu
Li Xu
Linchuan Xu
Linning Xu
Mengde Xu
Mengmeng Frost Xu
Min Xu
Mingye Xu
Jun Xu
Ning Xu
Peng Xu
Runsheng Xu
Sheng Xu
Wenqiang Xu
Xiaogang Xu
Renzhe Xu
Kaidi Xu
Yi Xu
Chi Xu
Qiuling Xu
Baobei Xu
Feng Xu
Haohang Xu
Haofei Xu
Lan Xu
Mingze Xu
Songcen Xu
Weipeng Xu
Wenjia Xu
Wenju Xu
Xiangyu Xu
Xin Xu
Yinshuang Xu
Yixing Xu
Yuting Xu
Yanyu Xu
Zhenbo Xu
Zhiliang Xu
Zhiyuan Xu
Xiaohao Xu

Yanwu Xu
Yan Xu
Yiran Xu
Yifan Xu
Yufei Xu
Yong Xu
Zichuan Xu
Zenglin Xu
Zexiang Xu
Zhan Xu
Zheng Xu
Zhiwei Xu
Ziyue Xu
Shiyu Xuan
Hanyu Xuan
Fei Xue
Jianru Xue
Mingfu Xue
Qinghan Xue
Tianfan Xue
Chao Xue
Chuhui Xue
Nan Xue
Zhou Xue
Xiangyang Xue
Yuan Xue
Abhay Yadav
Ravindra Yadav
Kota Yamaguchi
Toshihiko Yamasaki
Kohei Yamashita
Chaochao Yan
Feng Yan
Kun Yan
Qingsen Yan
Qixin Yan
Rui Yan
Siming Yan
Xinchen Yan
Yaping Yan
Bin Yan
Qingan Yan
Shen Yan
Shipeng Yan
Xu Yan

Yan Yan
Yichao Yan
Zhaoyi Yan
Zike Yan
Zhiqiang Yan
Hongliang Yan
Zizheng Yan
Jiewen Yang
Anqi Joyce Yang
Shan Yang
Anqi Yang
Antoine Yang
Bo Yang
Baoyao Yang
Chenhongyi Yang
Dingkang Yang
De-Nian Yang
Dong Yang
David Yang
Fan Yang
Fengyu Yang
Fengting Yang
Fei Yang
Gengshan Yang
Heng Yang
Han Yang
Huan Yang
Yibo Yang
Jiancheng Yang
Jihan Yang
Jiawei Yang
Jiayu Yang
Jie Yang
Jinfa Yang
Jingkang Yang
Jinyu Yang
Cheng-Fu Yang
Ji Yang
Jianyu Yang
Kailun Yang
Tian Yang
Luyu Yang
Liang Yang
Li Yang
Michael Ying Yang

Yang Yang
Muli Yang
Le Yang
Qiushi Yang
Ren Yang
Ruihan Yang
Shuang Yang
Siyuan Yang
Su Yang
Shiqi Yang
Taojiannan Yang
Tianyu Yang
Lei Yang
Wanzhao Yang
Shuai Yang
William Yang
Wei Yang
Xiaofeng Yang
Xiaoshan Yang
Xin Yang
Xuan Yang
Xu Yang
Xingyi Yang
Xitong Yang
Jing Yang
Yanchao Yang
Wenming Yang
Yujiu Yang
Herb Yang
Jianfei Yang
Jinhui Yang
Chuanguang Yang
Guanglei Yang
Haitao Yang
Kewei Yang
Linlin Yang
Lijin Yang
Longrong Yang
Meng Yang
MingKun Yang
Sibei Yang
Shicai Yang
Tong Yang
Wen Yang
Xi Yang

Xiaolong Yang
Xue Yang
Yubin Yang
Ze Yang
Ziyi Yang
Yi Yang
Linjie Yang
Yuzhe Yang
Yiding Yang
Zhenpei Yang
Zhaohui Yang
Zhengyuan Yang
Zhibo Yang
Zongxin Yang
Hantao Yao
Mingde Yao
Rui Yao
Taiping Yao
Ting Yao
Cong Yao
Qingsong Yao
Quanming Yao
Xu Yao
Yuan Yao
Yao Yao
Yazhou Yao
Jiawen Yao
Shunyu Yao
Pew-Thian Yap
Sudhir Yarram
Rajeev Yasarla
Peng Ye
Botao Ye
Mao Ye
Fei Ye
Hanrong Ye
Jingwen Ye
Jinwei Ye
Jiarong Ye
Mang Ye
Meng Ye
Qi Ye
Qian Ye
Qixiang Ye
Junjie Ye

Sheng Ye
Nanyang Ye
Yufei Ye
Xiaoqing Ye
Ruolin Ye
Yousef Yeganeh
Chun-Hsiao Yeh
Raymond A. Yeh
Yu-Ying Yeh
Kai Yi
Chang Yi
Renjiao Yi
Xinping Yi
Peng Yi
Alper Yilmaz
Junho Yim
Hui Yin
Bangjie Yin
Jia-Li Yin
Miao Yin
Wenzhe Yin
Xuwang Yin
Ming Yin
Yu Yin
Aoxiong Yin
Kangxue Yin
Tianwei Yin
Wei Yin
Xianghua Ying
Rio Yokota
Tatsuya Yokota
Naoto Yokoya
Ryo Yonetani
Ki Yoon Yoo
Jinsu Yoo
Sunjae Yoon
Jae Shin Yoon
Jihun Yoon
Sung-Hoon Yoon
Ryota Yoshihashi
Yusuke Yoshiyasu
Chenyu You
Haoran You
Haoxuan You
Yang You

Quanzeng You
Tackgeun You
Kaichao You
Shan You
Xinge You
Yurong You
Baosheng Yu
Bei Yu
Haichao Yu
Hao Yu
Chaohui Yu
Fisher Yu
Jin-Gang Yu
Jiyang Yu
Jason J. Yu
Jiashuo Yu
Hong-Xing Yu
Lei Yu
Mulin Yu
Ning Yu
Peilin Yu
Qi Yu
Qian Yu
Rui Yu
Shuzhi Yu
Gang Yu
Tan Yu
Weijiang Yu
Xin Yu
Bingyao Yu
Ye Yu
Hanchao Yu
Yingchen Yu
Tao Yu
Xiaotian Yu
Qing Yu
Houjian Yu
Changqian Yu
Jing Yu
Jun Yu
Shujian Yu
Xiang Yu
Zhaofei Yu
Zhenbo Yu
Yinfeng Yu

Zhuoran Yu
Zitong Yu
Bo Yuan
Jiangbo Yuan
Liangzhe Yuan
Weihao Yuan
Jianbo Yuan
Xiaoyun Yuan
Ye Yuan
Li Yuan
Geng Yuan
Jialin Yuan
Maoxun Yuan
Peng Yuan
Xin Yuan
Yuan Yuan
Yuhui Yuan
Yixuan Yuan
Zheng Yuan
Mehmet Kerim Yücel
Kaiyu Yue
Haixiao Yue
Heeseung Yun
Sangdoo Yun
Tian Yun
Mahmut Yurt
Ekim Yurtsever
Ahmet Yüzügüler
Edouard Yvinec
Eloi Zablocki
Christopher Zach
Muhammad Zaigham
    Zaheer
Pierluigi Zama Ramirez
Yuhang Zang
Pietro Zanuttigh
Alexey Zaytsev
Bernhard Zeisl
Haitian Zeng
Pengpeng Zeng
Jiabei Zeng
Runhao Zeng
Wei Zeng
Yawen Zeng
Yi Zeng

Yiming Zeng
Tieyong Zeng
Huanqiang Zeng
Dan Zeng
Yu Zeng
Wei Zhai
Yuanhao Zhai
Fangneng Zhan
Kun Zhan
Xiong Zhang
Jingdong Zhang
Jiangning Zhang
Zhilu Zhang
Gengwei Zhang
Dongsu Zhang
Hui Zhang
Binjie Zhang
Bo Zhang
Tianhao Zhang
Cecilia Zhang
Jing Zhang
Chaoning Zhang
Chenxu Zhang
Chi Zhang
Chris Zhang
Yabin Zhang
Zhao Zhang
Rufeng Zhang
Chaoyi Zhang
Zheng Zhang
Da Zhang
Yi Zhang
Edward Zhang
Xin Zhang
Feifei Zhang
Feilong Zhang
Yuqi Zhang
GuiXuan Zhang
Hanlin Zhang
Hanwang Zhang
Hanzhen Zhang
Haotian Zhang
He Zhang
Haokui Zhang
Hongyuan Zhang

Hengrui Zhang
Hongming Zhang
Mingfang Zhang
Jianpeng Zhang
Jiaming Zhang
Jichao Zhang
Jie Zhang
Jingfeng Zhang
Jingyi Zhang
Jinnian Zhang
David Junhao Zhang
Junjie Zhang
Junzhe Zhang
Jiawan Zhang
Jingyang Zhang
Kai Zhang
Lei Zhang
Lihua Zhang
Lu Zhang
Miao Zhang
Minjia Zhang
Mingjin Zhang
Qi Zhang
Qian Zhang
Qilong Zhang
Qiming Zhang
Qiang Zhang
Richard Zhang
Ruimao Zhang
Ruisi Zhang
Ruixin Zhang
Runze Zhang
Qilin Zhang
Shan Zhang
Shanshan Zhang
Xi Sheryl Zhang
Song-Hai Zhang
Chongyang Zhang
Kaihao Zhang
Songyang Zhang
Shu Zhang
Siwei Zhang
Shujian Zhang
Tianyun Zhang
Tong Zhang

Tao Zhang
Wenwei Zhang
Wenqiang Zhang
Wen Zhang
Xiaolin Zhang
Xingchen Zhang
Xingxuan Zhang
Xiuming Zhang
Xiaoshuai Zhang
Xuanmeng Zhang
Xuanyang Zhang
Xucong Zhang
Xingxing Zhang
Xikun Zhang
Xiaohan Zhang
Yahui Zhang
Yunhua Zhang
Yan Zhang
Yanghao Zhang
Yifei Zhang
Yifan Zhang
Yi-Fan Zhang
Yihao Zhang
Yingliang Zhang
Youshan Zhang
Yulun Zhang
Yushu Zhang
Yixiao Zhang
Yide Zhang
Zhongwen Zhang
Bowen Zhang
Chen-Lin Zhang
Zehua Zhang
Zekun Zhang
Zeyu Zhang
Xiaowei Zhang
Yifeng Zhang
Cheng Zhang
Hongguang Zhang
Yuexi Zhang
Fa Zhang
Guofeng Zhang
Hao Zhang
Haofeng Zhang
Hongwen Zhang

Hua Zhang

Jiaxin Zhang

Zhenyu Zhang

Jian Zhang

Jianfeng Zhang

Jiao Zhang

Jiakai Zhang

Lefei Zhang

Le Zhang

Mi Zhang

Min Zhang

Ning Zhang

Pan Zhang

Pu Zhang

Qing Zhang

Renrui Zhang

Shifeng Zhang

Shuo Zhang

Shaoxiong Zhang

Weizhong Zhang

Xi Zhang

Xiaomei Zhang

Xinyu Zhang

Yin Zhang

Zicheng Zhang

Zihao Zhang

Ziqi Zhang

Zhaoxiang Zhang

Zhen Zhang

Zhipeng Zhang

Zhixing Zhang

Zhizheng Zhang

Jiawei Zhang

Zhong Zhang

Pingping Zhang

Yixin Zhang

Kui Zhang

Lingzhi Zhang

Huaiwen Zhang

Quanshi Zhang

Zhoutong Zhang

Yuhang Zhang

Yuting Zhang

Zhang Zhang

Ziming Zhang

Zhizhong Zhang

Qilong Zhangli

Bingyin Zhao

Bin Zhao

Chenglong Zhao

Lei Zhao

Feng Zhao

Gangming Zhao

Haiyan Zhao

Hao Zhao

Handong Zhao

Hengshuang Zhao

Yinan Zhao

Jiaojiao Zhao

Jiaqi Zhao

Jing Zhao

Kaili Zhao

Haojie Zhao

Yucheng Zhao

Longjiao Zhao

Long Zhao

Qingsong Zhao

Qingyu Zhao

Rui Zhao

Rui-Wei Zhao

Sicheng Zhao

Shuang Zhao

Siyan Zhao

Zelin Zhao

Shiyu Zhao

Wang Zhao

Tiesong Zhao

Qian Zhao

Wangbo Zhao

Xi-Le Zhao

Xu Zhao

Yajie Zhao

Yang Zhao

Ying Zhao

Yin Zhao

Yizhou Zhao

Yunhan Zhao

Yuyang Zhao

Yue Zhao

Yuzhi Zhao

Bowen Zhao

Pu Zhao

Bingchen Zhao

Borui Zhao

Fuqiang Zhao

Hanbin Zhao

Jian Zhao

Mingyang Zhao

Na Zhao

Rongchang Zhao

Ruiqi Zhao

Shuai Zhao

Wenda Zhao

Wenliang Zhao

Xiangyun Zhao

Yifan Zhao

Yaping Zhao

Zhou Zhao

He Zhao

Jie Zhao

Xibin Zhao

Xiaoqi Zhao

Zhengyu Zhao

Jin Zhe

Chuanxia Zheng

Huan Zheng

Hao Zheng

Jia Zheng

Jian-Qing Zheng

Shuai Zheng

Meng Zheng

Mingkai Zheng

Qian Zheng

Qi Zheng

Wu Zheng

Yinqiang Zheng

Yufeng Zheng

Yutong Zheng

Yalin Zheng

Yu Zheng

Feng Zheng

Zhaoheng Zheng

Haitian Zheng

Kang Zheng

Bolun Zheng

Haiyong Zheng
Mingwu Zheng
Sipeng Zheng
Tu Zheng
Wenzhao Zheng
Xiawu Zheng
Yinglin Zheng
Zhuo Zheng
Zilong Zheng
Kecheng Zheng
Zerong Zheng
Shuaifeng Zhi
Tiancheng Zhi
Jia-Xing Zhong
Yiwu Zhong
Fangwei Zhong
Zhihang Zhong
Yaoyao Zhong
Yiran Zhong
Zhun Zhong
Zichun Zhong
Bo Zhou
Boyao Zhou
Brady Zhou
Mo Zhou
Chunluan Zhou
Dingfu Zhou
Fan Zhou
Jingkai Zhou
Honglu Zhou
Jiaming Zhou
Jiahuan Zhou
Jun Zhou
Kaiyang Zhou
Keyang Zhou
Kuangqi Zhou
Lei Zhou
Lihua Zhou
Man Zhou
Mingyi Zhou
Mingyuan Zhou
Ning Zhou
Peng Zhou
Penghao Zhou
Qianyi Zhou

Shuigeng Zhou
Shangchen Zhou
Huayi Zhou
Zhize Zhou
Sanping Zhou
Qin Zhou
Tao Zhou
Wenbo Zhou
Xiangdong Zhou
Xiao-Yun Zhou
Xiao Zhou
Yang Zhou
Yipin Zhou
Zhenyu Zhou
Hao Zhou
Chu Zhou
Daquan Zhou
Da-Wei Zhou
Hang Zhou
Kang Zhou
Qianyu Zhou
Sheng Zhou
Wenhui Zhou
Xingyi Zhou
Yan-Jie Zhou
Yiyi Zhou
Yu Zhou
Yuan Zhou
Yuqian Zhou
Yuxuan Zhou
Zixiang Zhou
Wengang Zhou
Shuchang Zhou
Tianfei Zhou
Yichao Zhou
Alex Zhu
Chenchen Zhu
Deyao Zhu
Xiatian Zhu
Guibo Zhu
Haidong Zhu
Hao Zhu
Hongzi Zhu
Rui Zhu
Jing Zhu

Jianke Zhu
Junchen Zhu
Lei Zhu
Lingyu Zhu
Luyang Zhu
Menglong Zhu
Peihao Zhu
Hui Zhu
Xiaofeng Zhu
Tyler (Lixuan) Zhu
Wentao Zhu
Xiangyu Zhu
Xinqi Zhu
Xinxin Zhu
Xinliang Zhu
Yangguang Zhu
Yichen Zhu
Yixin Zhu
Yanjun Zhu
Yousong Zhu
Yuhao Zhu
Ye Zhu
Feng Zhu
Zhen Zhu
Fangrui Zhu
Jinjing Zhu
Linchao Zhu
Pengfei Zhu
Sijie Zhu
Xiaobin Zhu
Xiaoguang Zhu
Zezhou Zhu
Zhenyao Zhu
Kai Zhu
Pengkai Zhu
Bingbing Zhuang
Chengyuan Zhuang
Liansheng Zhuang
Peiye Zhuang
Yixin Zhuang
Yihong Zhuang
Junbao Zhuo
Andrea Ziani
Bartosz Zieliński
Primo Zingaretti

Nikolaos Zioulis
Andrew Zisserman
Yael Ziv
Liu Ziyin
Xingxing Zou
Danping Zou
Qi Zou

Shihao Zou
Xueyan Zou
Yang Zou
Yuliang Zou
Zihang Zou
Chuhang Zou
Dongqing Zou

Xu Zou
Zhiming Zou
Maria A. Zuluaga
Xinxin Zuo
Zhiwen Zuo
Reyer Zwiggelaar

# Contents – Part XXIII

# Accelerating Score-Based Generative Models with Preconditioned Diffusion Sampling

Hengyuan Ma[1], Li Zhang[1(✉)], Xiatian Zhu[2], and Jianfeng Feng[1]

[1] Fudan University, Shanghai, China
lizhangfd@fudan.edu.cn
[2] University of Surrey, Guildford, UK
https://github.com/fudan-zvg/PDS

**Abstract.** Score-based generative models (SGMs) have recently emerged as a promising class of generative models. However, a fundamental limitation is that their inference is very slow due to a need for many (*e.g.*, 2000) iterations of sequential computations. An intuitive acceleration method is to reduce the sampling iterations which however causes severe performance degradation. We investigate this problem by viewing the diffusion sampling process as a Metropolis adjusted Langevin algorithm, which helps reveal the underlying cause to be ill-conditioned curvature. Under this insight, we propose a model-agnostic *preconditioned diffusion sampling* (PDS) method that leverages matrix preconditioning to alleviate the aforementioned problem. Crucially, PDS is proven theoretically to converge to the original target distribution of a SGM, no need for retraining. Extensive experiments on three image datasets with a variety of resolutions and diversity validate that PDS consistently accelerates off-the-shelf SGMs whilst maintaining the synthesis quality. In particular, PDS can accelerate by up to 29× on more challenging high resolution (1024×1024) image generation.

**Keywords:** Image synthesis · Score-based generative model · Matrix preconditioning · Ill-conditioned curvature

## 1 Introduction

As an alternative framework to generative adversarial networks (GANs) [10], recent score-based generative models (SGMs) [30–33] have demonstrated

L. Zhang—School of Data Science, Fudan University.
H. Ma and J. Feng—Institute of Science and Technology for Brain-inspired Intelligence, Fudan University.
X. Zhu—Surrey Institute for People-Centred Artificial Intelligence, CVSSP, University of Surrey.

**Supplementary Information** The online version contains supplementary material available at https://doi.org/10.1007/978-3-031-20050-2_1.

**Fig. 1.** Facial images at a resolution of $1024 \times 1024$ generated by NCSN++ [33] under a variety of sampling iterations (top) without and (bottom) with our PDS. It is evident that NCSN++ decades quickly with increasingly reduced sampling iterations, which can be well solved with PDS. In terms of running speed for generating a batch of 8 images, PDS reduces the time cost from 2030 s (the sampling iterations $T = 2000$) to 71 s ($T = 66$) on one NVIDIA RTX 3090 GPU, which delivers 29× acceleration. Dataset: FFHQ [18]. More samples in supplementary material.

excellent abilities in data synthesis (especially in high resolution images) with easier optimization [31], richer diversity [36], and more solid theoretic foundation [5]. Starting from a sample initialized with a Gaussian distribution, a SGM produces a target sample by simulating a diffusion process, typically a Langevin dynamics. Compared to the state-of-the-art GANs [4,17,18], a significant drawback with existing SGMs is *drastically slower generation* due to the need of taking many iterations for a sequential diffusion process [23,33,36]. Formally, the discrete Langevin dynamic for sampling is typically formulated as

$$\mathbf{x}_t = \mathbf{x}_{t-1} + \frac{\epsilon_t^2}{2} \nabla_{\mathbf{x}} \log p^*(\mathbf{x}_{t-1}) + \epsilon_t \mathbf{z}_t, 1 \le t \le T \tag{1}$$

where $\epsilon_t$ is the step size (a positive real scalar), $\mathbf{z}_t$ is an independent standard Gaussian noise, and $T$ is the iteration number. Starting from a standard Gaussian sample $\mathbf{x}_0$, with a total of $T$ steps this sequential sampling process gradually transforms $\mathbf{x}_0$ to the sample $\mathbf{x}_T$ that obeys the target distribution $p^*$. Often, $T$ is at the scale of $1000$ s, and the entire sampling process is lengthy.

For accelerating the sampling process, a straightforward method is to reduce $T$ by a factor and proportionally expand $\epsilon_t$ simultaneously, so that the number of calculating the gradient $\nabla_{\mathbf{x}} \log p^*(\mathbf{x})$, which consumes the major time, decreases whilst keeping the total update magnitude. However, this often makes pretrained SGMs fail in image synthesis. In general, we observe two types of failure: insufficient detailed structures (left of Fig. 3 and Fig. 4), and dazzling with heavy noises (left of Fig. 1 and Fig. 5). Conceptually, the sampling process as defined in Eq. (1) can be considered as a special case of Metropolis adjusted Langevin algorithm (MALA) [9,27,35]. When the coordinates of a target sample (e.g., the pixel locations of a natural image) are strongly correlated, the isotropic Gaussian noises $\{\mathbf{z}_t\}$ would become *inefficient* for the variables $\mathbf{x}$, caused by the *ill-conditioned curvature* of the sampling process [9].

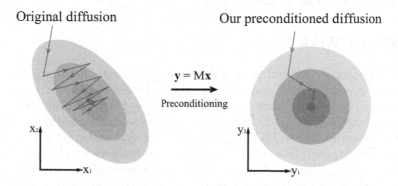

Original diffusion                                Our preconditioned diffusion

$\mathbf{y} = \mathbf{M}\mathbf{x}$

Preconditioning

**Fig. 2.** Illustration of the preconditioning method for accelerating sampling process.

In light of this insight as above, we propose an efficient, model-agnostic **preconditioned diffusion sampling** (PDS) method for accelerating existing pretrained SGMs without the need for model retraining. The key idea is to make the rates of curvature become more similar along all the directions [21,27] using a *matrix preconditioning*, hence solving the ill-conditioned curvature problem, as demonstrated in Fig. 2. Formally, we enrich the above Langevin dynamics (Eq. (1)) by imposing a preconditioning operation into the diffusion process as

$$\mathbf{x}_t = \mathbf{x}_{t-1} + \frac{\epsilon_t^2}{2} M M^{\mathsf{T}} \nabla_{\mathbf{x}} \log p^*(\mathbf{x}_{t-1}) + \epsilon_t M \mathbf{z}_t, \tag{2}$$

where $M$ is the newly introduced preconditioning matrix designed particularly for regulating the behavior of accelerated diffusion processes. This proposed reformulation equips the diffusion process with a novel ability to *enhance* or *restrain* the generation of detailed structures via controlling the different frequency components[1] of the noises [2]. Crucially, according to the theorems with Fokker-Planck equation [8] PDS can preserve the original SGM's target distribution. Further, structured priors available with a target distribution can be also accommodated, *e.g.*, the spatial structures of human faces. The computational cost of calculating $M$ is marginal when using Fast Fourier Transform (FFT) [3]. In this work, we make the following **contributions**: **(1)** We investigate the low inference efficiency problem of off-the-shelf SGMs for high-resolution image synthesis, which is critical yet under-studied in the literature. **(2)** For sampling acceleration, we introduce a novel preconditioned diffusion sampling (PDS) process. PDS preconditions the existing diffusion process additionally imposed for adaptively regulating the added noises, whilst keeping the original target distributions in convergence. **(3)** With PDS, a variety of pretrained SGMs can be accelerated significantly for image synthesis of various spatial resolutions, without model retraining. In particular, PDS delivers 29× reduction in wall-clock time for high-resolution image synthesis.

## 2   Related Work

Sohl-Dickstein et al. [28] first proposed to destroy the data distribution through a diffusion process slowly and learned the backward process to recover the data, inspired by non-equilibrium statistical physics. Later on, Song and Ermon [31] further explored SGMs by introducing the noise conditional score network (NCSN). Song and Ermon [32] proposed NCSNv2 that scaled NCSN for higher resolution image generation (*e.g.*, 256 × 256) by scaling noises and improving stability with moving average. Song et al. [33] summarized all the previous SGMs into a unified framework based on the stochastic differential equation (SDE) and proposed the NCSN++ model to generate high-resolution images via numerical SDE solvers for the first time. Bortoli et al. [5] provided the first quantitative convergence results for SGMs. Vahdat et al. [34] developed Latent Score-based Generative Model (LSGM) that trains SGMs in a latent space with the variational autoencoder framework. Another class of relevant generative models, mainly trained by reducing an evidence lower bound (ELBO) called denoising diffusion probabilistic models (DDPMs) [1,6,12,13,23,24,29], also demonstrate excellent performance on image synthesis. Commonly, all of the above works use isotropic Gaussian distributions for the diffusion sampling.

Recently there are some works proposed on accelerating SGMs. Dockhorn et al. [7] improved the SGMs with Hamiltonian Monte Carlo methods [22] and proposed critically-damped Langevin diffusion (CLD) based SGMs that achieves superior performance. Jolicoeur-Martineau et al. [16] utilized a numerical SDE solver with adaptive step sizes to accelerate SGMs. However, these methods are limited in the following aspects: **(1)** They tend to involve much extra computation. For example, CLD based SGMs expand the dimension of data by 2 times

---

[1] More theoretical explanation on why *directly* regulating the frequency domain of a diffusion process is possible is provided in Supplementary material .

for learning the velocity of the diffusion. Jolicoeur-Martineau et al. [16] added a high-order numerical solver that increases the number of calling the SGM, resulting in much more time. In comparison, with our PDS the only extra calculation relates the preconditioning matrix that can be efficiently implemented by Fast Fourier Transform. **(2)** They are restricted to a single specific SGM while our PDS is model agnostic. **(3)** Unlike this work, none of them has demonstrated a scalability to more challenging high-resolution image generation tasks (*e.g.*, FFHQ facial images).

## 3  Preliminary

**Scored-Based Generative Models (SGMs).** Score matching is developed for non-normalized statistical learning [15]. Given i.i.d. samples of an unknown distribution $p^*$, score matching allows the model to directly approximate the *score function* $\nabla_\mathbf{x} \log p^*(\mathbf{x})$. SGMs aim to generate samples from $p^*$ via score matching by simulating a Langevin dynamics initialized by Gaussian noise

$$d\mathbf{x} = \frac{g^2(t)}{2} \nabla_\mathbf{x} \log p^*(\mathbf{x})dt + g(t)d\mathbf{w}, \tag{3}$$

where $g : \mathbb{R}^+ \to \mathbb{R}^+$ controls the step size and $d\mathbf{w}$ represents a Wiener process. With this process, we transform a sample drawn from an initial Gaussian distribution to approach the desired distribution $p^*$. A classical SGM, noise conditional score network (NCSN) [31], is trained by learning how to reverse a process of gradually corrupting the samples from $p^*$, and aims to match the score function. After training, NCSN starts from a Gaussian distribution and travels to the target distribution $p^*$ by simulating an annealed Langevin dynamics.

**Recent Improvements.** Song and Ermon [32] presented NCSNv2 that improves the original NCSN by designing better noise scales, iteration number, and step size. This new variant is also more stable by using the moving average technique. Song et al. [33] further proposed NCSN++ that utilizes an existing numerical solver of stochastic differential equations to enhance both the speed of convergence and the stability of the sampling method. Importantly, NCSN++ can synthesize high-resolution images at high quality.

**Limitation Analysis.** Although SGMs have been able to generate images comparable to GANs [10], they are much slower due to the sequential computation during the sampling phase. For example, to produce 8 facial images at $1024 \times 1024$ resolution, a SGM spends more than 30 mins. To maximize the potential of SGMs, it is critical to solve this slow inference bottleneck.

## 4  Method

We aim to solve the slow inference problem with SGMs. For easier understanding, let us start from the most classical Langevin dynamics.

## 4.1   Steady-State Distribution Analysis

Consider the classical Langevin dynamics

$$dx = \frac{\epsilon^2}{2} \nabla_x \log p^*(\mathbf{x})dt + \epsilon d\mathbf{w}, \tag{4}$$

where $p^*$ is the target distribution, and $\epsilon > 0$ is the fixed step size. It is associated with a Fokker-Planck equation

$$\frac{\partial p}{\partial t} = -\frac{\epsilon^2}{2} \nabla_x \cdot (\nabla_x \log p^*(\mathbf{x})p) + \frac{\epsilon^2}{2} \Delta_x p, \tag{5}$$

where $p = p(\mathbf{x}, t)$ describes the distribution of $\mathbf{x}$ that evolves over time. The steady-state solution of Eq. (5) corresponds to the probabilistic density function of the steady-state distribution of Eq. (4), i.e., $p^*$

$$\nabla_x \cdot (\nabla_x \log p^*(\mathbf{x})p) = \Delta_x p. \tag{6}$$

The Fokker-Planck equation tells us how to preserve the steady-state distribution of the original process when we alter Eq. (4) for specific motivations. Concretely, we can impose an invertible linear operator $M$ to the noise term $d\mathbf{w}$ and conduct the associated operation on the gradient term so that the steady-state distribution can be preserved. This design is formulated as:

$$dx = \frac{\epsilon^2}{2}(MM^\mathsf{T} + S) \nabla_x \log p^*(\mathbf{x})dt + \epsilon M d\mathbf{w}, \tag{7}$$

where $S$ is a skew-symmetric linear operator. In fact, we have

**Theorem 1.** *The steady-state distribution of Eq. (4) and Eq. (7) are the same, as long as the linear operator $M$ is invertible and the linear operator $S$ is skew-symmetric.*

We can extend the above results to a more general case as follows.

**Theorem 2.** *Consider the diffusion process*

$$dx = \mathbf{f}(\mathbf{x}, t)dt + G(t)d\mathbf{w}, \tag{8}$$

*where $\mathbf{f} : \mathbb{R}^d \otimes \mathbb{R} \to \mathbb{R}^d$, $G : \mathbb{R} \to \mathbb{R}^{d \times d}$. $M$ is an invertible $d \times d$ matrix and $S$ is a skew-symmetric $d \times d$ matrix. Denote $p^*$ as the steady-state distribution of Eq. (8), then the process*

$$dx = MM^\mathsf{T}\mathbf{f}(\mathbf{x}, t)dt + S \nabla_x \log p^*(\mathbf{x})dt + MG(t)d\mathbf{w}, \tag{9}$$

*has the same steady-state distribution as Eq. (8), given $G(t)G(t)^\mathsf{T}$ and $M^\mathsf{T}$ are commutable $\forall t$.*

*Remark 1.* The conditions of this theorem are all satisfied for the diffusion process used in NCSN, NCSNv2, and NCSN++.

Theorem 2 motivates us to design a preconditioning matrix as Eq. (7) while keeping the steady-state distribution simultaneously. This is also because, pre-conditioning has been proved to be able to significantly accelerate the stochastic gradient descent algorithm (SGD) and Metropolis adjusted Langevin algorithms (MALA) [27]. Besides, SGD provides another view for interpreting our method, that is, SGMs sequentially reduce the energy $(-\log p^*(\mathbf{x}))$ of a sample $\mathbf{x}$ via stochastic gradient descent, with the randomness coming from the Gaussian noises added at every single step.

## 4.2  Preconditioned Diffusion Sampling

We study how to construct the preconditioning operator using $M$ to accelerate the sampling phase of SGMs, with $S = 0$ for Eq. (7). It is observed that when reducing the iteration number for the sampling process of a SGM and expand the step size proportionally for a consistent accumulative update, the images gener-ated tend to miss necessary detailed structures (see left of Fig. 3 and Fig. 4), or involve high-frequency noises (left of Fig. 1 and Fig. 5). These failure phenom-ena motivates us to leverage a preconditioning operator $M$ serving as a filter to regulate the frequency distribution of the samples.

1. Given an input vector $\mathbf{x}$, we first use Fast Fourier Transform (FFT) [3] to map it into the frequency domain $\hat{\mathbf{x}} = F[\mathbf{x}]$. For images, we adopt the 2D FFT that implements 1D FFT column-wise and row-wise successively.
2. Then we adjust the frequency signal using a mask $R$ in the same shape as $\mathbf{x}$: $R \odot \hat{\mathbf{x}}$, where $\odot$ means element-wise multiplication.
3. Lastly, we map the vector back to the original space by the inverse of Fast Fourier Transform: $F^{-1}[R \odot \hat{\mathbf{x}}]$.

For specific tasks (*e.g.*, human facial image generation), most samples might share a consistent structural characteristics. This prior knowledge however is unavailable with the noises added to each step in the diffusion process. To solve this problem, we further propose a space structure filter $A$ for ***space precon-ditioning***, constructed by statistical average of random samples. This can be used to regulate the noise via element-wise multiplication as: $A \odot [\cdot]$. Combining the both operations above, we define a preconditioning operator $M$ as

$$M[\cdot] = A \odot F^{-1}[R \odot F[\cdot]]. \tag{10}$$

To guarantee the invertibility of $M$, we set the elements of $R$ strictly positive. For the tasks without clear space structure priors, we simply do not apply the space preconditioning by setting all the elements of $A$ to 1. We operate $M$ on the noise term $d\mathbf{w}$ and adjust the gradient term to keep the steady-state distribution as shown in Eq. (7), utilizing Theorem 1.

Interestingly, we found that the proposed method above is likely to even cause further model degradation. This is because, if we implement a variable transformation as $\mathbf{y} = M^{-1}\mathbf{x}$, Eq. (7) can be rewritten as

$$dy = \frac{\epsilon^2}{2} \nabla_\mathbf{y} \log p^*(\mathbf{y})dt + \epsilon d\mathbf{w},$$

which returns to the same format as the original process. The diffusion process is made worse since, $M^{-1}$, the inverse of $M$, could impose the exactly opposite effect of $M$. To overcome this challenge, we further substitute $M$ with $M^{-1}$ in Eq. (7) in order to take the positive effect of $M$ as

$$dx = \frac{\epsilon^2}{2} M^{-1} M^{-\mathsf{T}} \nabla_{\mathbf{x}} \log p^*(\mathbf{x}) dt + \epsilon M^{-1} d\mathbf{w}. \tag{11}$$

Since in this case, we can rewrite Eq. (11) in the same format as the original process, after applying the variable transformation $\mathbf{y} = M\mathbf{x}$.

**A General Formulation.** or theory completeness, we further briefly discuss the possibility to construct preconditioning matrix using the matrix $S$ (Eq. (7)) as an accelerator of the diffusion process. This is motivated by the theories from [20, 25, 26] that the term $S \nabla_{\mathbf{x}} \log p^*(\mathbf{x}) dt$ drives a solenoidal flow that makes the system converge faster to the steady state. According to [14], under the regularity conditions, $|\mathbf{x}(t)|$ usually does not reach the infinity in a finite time, and the convergence of an *autonomous* (the right side of the equation does not contain time explicitly) diffusion process

$$d\mathbf{x} = \frac{\epsilon^2}{2} \nabla_{\mathbf{x}} \log p^*(\mathbf{x}) dt + \epsilon d\mathbf{w}$$

can be accelerated by introducing a vector field $C(\mathbf{x}) \in \mathbb{R}^d \to \mathbb{R}^d$

$$d\mathbf{x} = \frac{\epsilon^2}{2} \nabla_{\mathbf{x}} \log p^*(\mathbf{x}) dt + C(\mathbf{x}) dt + \epsilon d\mathbf{w},$$

where $C(\mathbf{x})$ should satisfy

$$\nabla_{\mathbf{x}} \cdot \left( \frac{C(\mathbf{x})}{p^*(\mathbf{x})} \right) = 0.$$

It is easy to show that $C(\mathbf{x}) = S \nabla_{\mathbf{x}} \log p^*(\mathbf{x})$ satisfies the above condition. However, the diffusion process of existing SGMs is typically *not autonomous*, due to the step size $\epsilon$ varies across time designed to guarantee numerical stability. Despite this, we consider it is still worth investigating the effect of $S$ for the sampling process for completeness (see evaluation in Sect. 5). As such, our investigation of preconditioning matrix is expanded from the invertible symmetric matrix in form of $MM^{\mathsf{T}}$, to more general cases where preconditioning matrices can be written as $MM^{\mathsf{T}} + S$.

### 4.3   Instantiation of Preconditioned Diffusion Sampling

We summarize our **preconditioned diffusion sampling** (PDS) method for accelerating the diffusion sampling process in Algorithm 1. For generality, we write the original diffusion process as

$$\mathbf{x}_t = \mathbf{h}(\mathbf{x}_{t-1}, t) + \phi(t) \mathbf{z}_t, \tag{12}$$

where $\mathbf{h}(\mathbf{x}_{t-1}, t)$ represents the drift term and $\phi(t)$ the function controlling the scale of the noise $\mathbf{z}_t$. We take the real part whilst dropping the imaginary part generated every step as it can not be utilized by the SGMs. Now we construct the space and frequency preconditioning filter. Given a target dataset image with distribution $p^*$, its space preconditioning filter $A$ is calculated as

$$A(c, w, h) = \log \left( \mathbb{E}_{\mathbf{x} \sim p^*(\mathbf{x})} [\mathbf{x}(c, w, h)] \right) + 1), \tag{13}$$

---

**Algorithm 1.** Preconditioned diffusion sampling

---

**Input:** The frequency $R$ and space $A$ preconditioning operators, the target sampling iterations $T$;

**Diffusion process:**
Drawing an initial sample $\mathbf{x}_0 \sim \mathcal{N}(0, I_{C \times H \times W})$
**for** $t = 1$ **to** $T$ **do**
    Drawing a noise $\mathbf{w}_t \sim \mathcal{N}(0, I_{C \times H \times W})$
    *Applying PDS:* $\eta_t \leftarrow F^{-1}[F[\mathbf{w}_t \bullet A] \bullet R]$         ▷ $\bullet$ means element-wise division
    Calculating the drift term $\mathbf{d}_t \leftarrow \mathbf{h}(\mathbf{x}_{t-1}, t, \epsilon_t)$
    *Applying PDS:* $\mathbf{d}_t \leftarrow F^{-1}[F[F^{-1}[F[\mathbf{d}_t] \bullet R] \bullet A^2] \bullet R]$
    Calculating the solenoidal term $S_t \leftarrow S \bigtriangledown_\mathbf{x} \log p^*(\mathbf{x}_{t-1})$
    Diffusion $\mathbf{x}_t \leftarrow Re[\mathbf{d}_t + S_t + \phi(t)\eta_t]$         ▷ $Re[\cdot]$ means taking the real part
**end for**

**Output:** $\mathbf{x}_T$

---

where $1 \le c \le C, 1 \le w \le W, 1 \le h \le H$ are the channel, width and height dimensions of image. There are two approaches for calculating the filter $R$. The first approach is to utilize the statistics of the dataset. Specifically, we first define the frequency statistics given a specific image dataset that we are aimed to synthesize as

$$R(c, w, h) = \log \left( \mathbb{E}_{\mathbf{x} \sim p^*(\mathbf{x})} \left[ F[\mathbf{x}] \odot \overline{F[\mathbf{x}]} \right] (c, w, h) + 1 \right) \tag{14}$$

where $F$ is Discrete Fourier Transform, $\odot$ is the element-wise multiplication. In practice, we normalize both space and frequency filter for stability; see supplementary material for more detail. Empirically, 200 images randomly sampled from the dataset is enough for estimating this statistics, therefore this involves marginal extra computation. We observe that this approach works well for accelerating NCSN++ [33], but has less effects on accelerating NCSN [31] and NCSNv2 [32]. The possible reason is that these two models are not sophisticated enough as NCSN++ to utilize the delicate information from the frequency statistics. To address this issue, we propose the second approach which constructs the filter $R$ simply using two parameters $\lambda$ and $r$. $\lambda$ specifies the ratio for shrinking or amplifying the coordinates located out of the circle $\{(h - 0.5\,H)^2 + (w - 0.5W)^2 \le 2r^2\}$, selected according to the failure behaviour of the vanilla SGM, and The radial range of the filter is controlled by $r$. See supplementary material for more details. This method works well on accelerating NCSN [31] and NCSNv2 [32].

*Remark 2.* For the computational complexity of PDS, the major overhead is from FFT and its inverse that only have the complexity of $O(CHW(\log H + \log W))$ [3], which is neglectable compared to the whole diffusion complexity.

## 5    Experiments

In our experiments, the objective is to show how off-the-shelf SGMs can be accelerated significantly with the assistance of the proposed PDS whilst keeping the image synthesis quality, without model retraining. See supplementary material for the detailed parameter settings and the implementation details.

**Datasets.** For image synthesis, we use MNIST, CIFAR-10 [19], LSUN (the tower, bedroom and church classes) [37], and FFHQ [18] datasets. Note, for all these datasets, the image height and width are identical, i.e., $H = W$.

**Baselines.** For evaluating the model agnostic property of our PDS, we test three recent SGMs including NCSN [31], NCSNv2 [32] and NCSN++ [33].

**Experiments on MNIST.** We use NCSN [31] as the SGM for the simplest digital image generation ($28 \times 28$). The results are shown in Fig. 3. We observe that when reducing the sampling iterations from 1000 to *20* for acceleration, the original sampling method tends to generate images that lack the digital structure (see the left part of Fig. 3). This suggests us to enlarge a band of frequency part of the diffusion process. Therefore, we set $(r, \lambda) = (0.2H, 1.6)$. It is observed that our PDS can produce digital images with the fine digital structure well preserved under the acceleration rate.

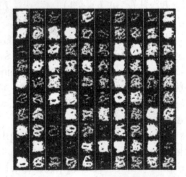 

**Fig. 3.** Sampling using NCSN [31] on MNIST ($28 \times 28$). **Left**: Results by the original sampling method with 20 sampling iterations. **Right**: Results by our PDS with 20 sampling iterations. More samples in supplementart material.

**Experiments on CIFAR-10.** Compared to DDPMs, SGMs have much worse performance when the number of sample iterations is relatively small. Our PDS can greatly alleviate this issue as shown in Table 1, where we evaluate NCSN++ for generating CIFAR-10 (32 × 32) by FID [11] score. We compare PDS with DDIM [29] and the Analytic-DDIM [1], two representative DDPMs. It is observed that NCSN++ with PDS achieves the best FID scores under different acceleration cases. We apply filter $R$ described by Eq. (14).

**Table 1.** FID scores of vanilla NCSN++ [33], NCSN++ with PDS, DDIM [29], and Analytic-DDIM [1] under different iterations on CIFAR-10.

| $T$ | NCSN++ | DDIM | Analytic-DDIM | NCSN++ W/ PDS |
|-----|--------|------|---------------|---------------|
| 100 | 29.39  | 6.08 | 3.55          | **3.26**      |
| 200 | 4.35   | 4.02 | 3.39          | **2.61**      |

**Experiments on LSUN** [37]. We first evaluate NCSNv2 [32] to generate church images at a resolution of 96 × 96 and tower at a resolution of 128 × 128. For both classes, when accelerated by reducing the iterations from original 3258 to *108* for tower and from original 3152 to *156* for church, we observe that the original sampling method tends to generate images *without sufficient detailed appearance*, similar as the situation on MNIST. Therefore, we also encourage the frequency part of the diffusion process that responsible for the details. The results are displayed in Fig. 4. It is evident that PDS can still generate rich fine details, even when the diffusion process is accelerated up to 20 ∼ 30 times.

Further, we evaluate NCSN++ [33] to generate bedroom and church images at a resolution of 256 × 256. In this case, we instead observe that the original sampling method tends to generate images *with overwhelming noises* once accelerated (left of Fig. 5). We hence set filter $R$ using Eq. (14) to regulate the frequency part of the diffusion process. As demonstrated in Fig. 5, our PDS is able to prevent the output images from being ruined by heavy noises. All these results suggest the ability of our PDS in regulating the different frequency components in the diffusion process of prior SGMs.

**Experiments on FFHQ** [18]. We use NCSN++ [33] to generate high-resolution facial images at a resolution of 1024 × 1024. Similar as on LSUN, we also find out that when accelerated, the original sampling method is vulnerable with heavy noises and fails to produce recognizable human faces. For example, when reducing the iteration from original 2000 to 100, the output images are full of noises and unrecognizable. Similarly, we address this issue with our PDS with filter $R$. We also apply the space preconditioning to utilize the structural characteristics shared across the whole dataset. It is shown in Fig. 1, PDS can maintain the image synthesis quality using only as less as *66* iterations. In summary, all the above experiments indicate that our method is highly scalable and generalizable across different visual content, SGMs, and acceleration rates.

**Evaluation on Running Speed.** Apart from the quality evaluation on image synthesis as above, we further compare the running speed between the vanilla and our PDS using NCSN++ [33]. In this test, we use one NVIDIA RTX 3090 GPU. We track the average wall-clock time of generating a batch of 8 images. As shown in Table 2, our PDS can significantly reduce the running time, particularly for high-resolution image generation on the FFHQ dataset.

**Fig. 4.** Sampling using NCSNv2 [32] on LSUN (church $96 \times 96$ and tower $128 \times 128$). **Left**: The original sampling method with 156 iterations for church and 108 iterations for tower. **Right**: PDS sampling method with 156 iterations for church and 108 iterations for tower. More samples in supplementary material.

**Fig. 5.** Sampling using NCSN++ [33] on LSUN (church and bedroom) ($256 \times 256$). **Left**: The original sampling method with 166 sampling iterations. **Right**: PDS sampling method with 166 sampling iterations. More examples in supplementary material.

**Parameter Analysis.** We investigate the effect of PDS's two parameters $r$ and $\lambda$ in mentioned Sect. 4.3. We use NCSN++ [33] with the sampling iterations $T = 166$ on LSUN (bedroom). It is observed in Fig. 6 that there exists a large good-performing range for each parameter. If $\lambda$ is too high or $r$ is too low, PDS will degrade to the vanilla sampling method, yielding corrupted images; Instead, if $\lambda$ is too low or $r$ is too high, which means over-suppressing high-frequency signals in this case, pale images with fewer shape details will be generated. For NCSN++ [33], since we directly use the statistics information to construct $R$, there is no need to worry about selecting $r$ and $\lambda$.

**Table 2.** Evaluating the wall-clock time of generating a batch of 8 images. *SGM: NCSN++* [33]. *Time unit:* Seconds.

| Dataset | LSUN | FFHQ |
|---|---|---|
| Vanilla | 1173 | 2030 |
| **PDS** | **90** | **71** |
| *Speedup times* | **13** | **29** |

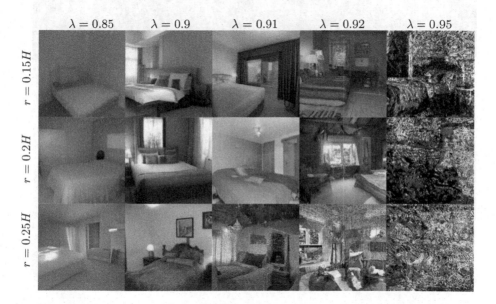

**Fig. 6. Parameter analysis.** Sampling produced by NCSN++ [33] w/ PDS on LSUN (bedroom) (256 × 256) with 166 sampling iterations. We set $(r, \lambda)$ to a variety of combination.

**Further Analysis.** In this section, we study the effect of the solenoidal term $S \bigtriangledown_{\mathbf{x}} \log p^*(\mathbf{x})^2$ to the diffusion process. As proved in Theorem 2, as long as $S$ is skew-symmetric, it will not change the steady-state distribution of the original process. To verify this claim, we generalize the original process as

$$d\mathbf{x} = \frac{\epsilon^2}{2}(M^{-1}M^{-\mathbf{T}} + \omega S) \bigtriangledown_{\mathbf{x}} \log p^*(\mathbf{x})dt + \epsilon M^{-1}d\mathbf{w},$$

---

² For NCSN++ [33], we use $\bigtriangledown_{\mathbf{x}} \log p_t(\mathbf{x})$, where $p_t$ is the distribution function of $\mathbf{x}$ at $t$, since $\bigtriangledown_{\mathbf{x}} \log p^*(\mathbf{x})$ is inaccessible in NCSN++.

where $\omega$ is the parameter that controls the scale of $S$. In Fig. 7, we set $S[\cdot] = Re[F[\cdot] - F^\mathsf{T}[\cdot]]$ which is obviously skew-symmetric. We change the scale of $\omega$ from 1 to 1000 for evaluating its impact on the output samples. It is observed that $\omega$ does not affect the quality of output images. This verifies that $S$ does not change the steady-state distribution of the original diffusion process. Additionally, we perform similar tests with different iterations and other different skew-symmetric operator $S$. We still observe no obvious acceleration effect from the solenoidal term (see supplementary material).

$\omega = 1$ $\qquad\qquad$ $\omega = 10$ $\qquad\qquad$ $\omega = 100$ $\qquad\qquad$ $\omega = 1000$

**Fig. 7.** Samples produced by NCSN++ [33] w/ PDS on FFHQ (1024x1024) with different solenoidal terms. Sampling iteration: 66. More samples in supplementary material.

## 6  Conclusion

In this work, we have proposed a novel preconditioned diffusion sampling (PDS) method for accelerating off-the-shelf score-based generative models (SGMs), without model retraining. Considering the diffusion process as a Metropolis adjusted Langevin algorithm, we reveal that existing sampling suffers from ill-conditioned curvature. To solve this, we reformulate the diffusion process with matrix preconditioning whilst preserving its steady-state distribution (the target distribution), leading to our PDS solution. Experimentally, we show that PDS significantly accelerates existing state-of-the-art SGMs while maintaining the generation quality.

**Acknowledgments.** This work was supported in part by National Natural Science Foundation of China (Grant No. 6210020439), Lingang Laboratory (Grant No. LG-QS-202202-07), Natural Science Foundation of Shanghai (Grant No. 22ZR1407500), Shanghai Municipal Science and Technology Major Project (Grant No. 2018SHZDZX01 and 2021SHZDZX0103), Science and Technology Innovation 2030 - Brain Science and Brain-Inspired Intelligence Project (Grant No. 2021ZD0200204).

# References

1. Bao, F., Li, C., Zhu, J., Zhang, B.: Analytic-dpm: an analytic estimate of the optimal reverse variance in diffusion probabilistic models. In: ICLR (2022)
2. Bovik, A.C.: The essential guide to image processing (2009)
3. Brigham, E.O.: The fast Fourier transform and its applications (1988)
4. Brock, A., Donahue, J., Simonyan, K.: Large scale GAN training for high fidelity natural image synthesis. In: ICLR (2019)
5. De Bortoli, V., Thornton, J., Heng, J., Doucet, A.: Diffusion schrödinger bridge with applications to score-based generative modeling. In: NeurIPS (2021)
6. Dhariwal, P., Nichol, A.: Diffusion models beat gans on image synthesis. In: NeurIPS (2021)
7. Dockhorn, T., Vahdat, A., Kreis, K.: Score-based generative modeling with critically-damped Langevin diffusion. In: ICLR (2022)
8. Gardiner, C.W., et al.: Handbook of stochastic methods (1985)
9. Girolami, M., Calderhead, B.: Riemann manifold langevin and hamiltonian monte carlo methods. J. Roy. Stat. Soc.: Ser. B (Stat. Methodol.) (2011)
10. Goodfellow, I., et al.: Generative adversarial nets. In: NeurIPS (2014)
11. Heusel, M., Ramsauer, H., Unterthiner, T., Nessler, B., Hochreiter, S.: Gans trained by a two time-scale update rule converge to a local nash equilibrium. In: NeurIPS (2017)
12. Ho, J., Jain, A., Abbeel, P.: Denoising diffusion probabilistic models. In: NeurIPS (2020)
13. Ho, J., Saharia, C., Chan, W., Fleet, D.J., Norouzi, M., Salimans, T.: Cascaded diffusion models for high fidelity image generation. arXiv preprint (2021)
14. Hwang, C.R., Hwang-Ma, S.Y., Sheu, S.J.: Accelerating diffusions. Ann. Appl. Probabil. (2005)
15. Hyvärinen, A., Dayan, P.: Estimation of non-normalized statistical models by score matching. JMLR **6**, 695–709 (2005)
16. Jolicoeur-Martineau, A., Li, K., Piché-Taillefer, R., Kachman, T., Mitliagkas, I.: Gotta go fast when generating data with score-based models. arXiv preprint arXiv (2021)
17. Karras, T., Aila, T., Laine, S., Lehtinen, J.: Progressive growing of gans for improved quality, stability, and variation. In: ICLR (2018)
18. Karras, T., Laine, S., Aila, T.: A style-based generator architecture for generative adversarial networks. In: CVPR (2019)
19. Krizhevsky, A., Hinton, G., et al.: Learning multiple layers of features from tiny images (2009)
20. Lelievre, T., Nier, F., Pavliotis, G.A.: Optimal non-reversible linear drift for the convergence to equilibrium of a diffusion. J. Stat. Phys. **152**, 237–274 (2013)
21. Li, C., Chen, C., Carlson, D., Carin, L.: Preconditioned stochastic gradient langevin dynamics for deep neural networks. In: AAAI (2016)

22. Neal, R.M., et al.: Mcmc using hamiltonian dynamics. In: Handbook of Markov Chain Monte Carlo (2011)
23. Nichol, A., et al.: Glide: towards photorealistic image generation and editing with text-guided diffusion models. arXiv preprint (2021)
24. Nichol, A.Q., Dhariwal, P.: Improved denoising diffusion probabilistic models. In: ICML (2021)
25. Ottobre, M.: Markov chain monte carlo and irreversibility. Rep. Math. Phys. **77**, 267–292 (2016)
26. Rey-Bellet, L., Spiliopoulos, K.: Irreversible langevin samplers and variance reduction: a large deviations approach. Nonlinearity **28**, 2081 (2015)
27. Roberts, G.O., Stramer, O.: Langevin diffusions and metropolis-hastings algorithms. Methodol. Comput. Appl. Probabil. **4**, 337–357 (2002)
28. Sohl-Dickstein, J., Weiss, E., Maheswaranathan, N., Ganguli, S.: Deep unsupervised learning using nonequilibrium thermodynamics. In: ICML (2015)
29. Song, J., Meng, C., Ermon, S.: Denoising diffusion implicit models. In: ICLR (2020)
30. Song, Y., Durkan, C., Murray, I., Ermon, S.: Maximum likelihood training of score-based diffusion models. In: NeurIPS (2021)
31. Song, Y., Ermon, S.: Generative modeling by estimating gradients of the data distribution. In: NeurIPS (2019)
32. Song, Y., Ermon, S.: Improved techniques for training score-based generative models. In: NeurIPS (2020)
33. Song, Y., Sohl-Dickstein, J., Kingma, D.P., Kumar, A., Ermon, S., Poole, B.: Score-based generative modeling through stochastic differential equations. In: ICLR (2021)
34. Vahdat, A., Kreis, K., Kautz, J.: Score-based generative modeling in latent space. In: NeurIPS (2021)
35. Welling, M., Teh, Y.W.: Bayesian learning via stochastic gradient langevin dynamics. In: ICML (2011)
36. Xiao, Z., Kreis, K., Vahdat, A.: Tackling the generative learning trilemma with denoising diffusion gans. In: ICLR (2022)
37. Yu, F., Seff, A., Zhang, Y., Song, S., Funkhouser, T., Xiao, J.: Lsun: construction of a large-scale image dataset using deep learning with humans in the loop. arXiv preprint (2015)

# Learning to Generate Realistic LiDAR Point Clouds

Vlas Zyrianov$^{(\boxtimes)}$, Xiyue Zhu, and Shenlong Wang

University of Illinois at Urbana-Champaign, Champaign, IL, USA
{vlasz2,xiyuez2,shenlong}@illinois.edu

**Abstract.** We present LiDARGen, a novel, effective, and controllable generative model that produces realistic LiDAR point cloud sensory readings. Our method leverages the powerful score-matching energy-based model and formulates the point cloud generation process as a stochastic denoising process in the equirectangular view. This model allows us to sample diverse and high-quality point cloud samples with guaranteed physical feasibility and controllability. We validate the effectiveness of our method on the challenging KITTI-360 and NuScenes datasets. The quantitative and qualitative results show that our approach produces more realistic samples than other generative models. Furthermore, LiDARGen can sample point clouds conditioned on inputs without retraining. We demonstrate that our proposed generative model could be directly used to densify LiDAR point clouds. Our code is available at: https://www.zyrianov.org/lidargen/.

**Keywords:** LiDAR generation · Self-driving · Diffusion models

## 1 Introduction

The past decade witnessed rapid progress in machine perception. Many embodied systems leverage various sensors and the power of deep learning to perceive the world better. LiDAR provides accurate 3D geometry of the surrounding environment, making it one of the most popular sensor choices for various autonomous systems, including self-driving cars [33,38,77], surveying drones [84], indoor robots [8], and planetary rovers [9].

Realistic and scalable LiDAR simulation suites are desirable for studying LiDAR-based perception for various reasons. First, LiDAR is an expensive sensor. A 64-beam spinning LiDAR costs over 50,000 USD [1]. Not everyone can afford one, prohibiting physical sensors from being a scalable and customizable solution for data collection in research. Furthermore, training and testing in safety-critical situations is crucial for autonomy safety. However, collecting data for extreme scenarios in the real world is costly, unsafe, and even unethical. Simulations allow overcoming the above limitations by generating realistic data for long-tail events and training and testing agents at low cost.

---

**Supplementary Information** The online version contains supplementary material available at https://doi.org/10.1007/978-3-031-20050-2_2.

S. Avidan et al. (Eds.): ECCV 2022, LNCS 13683, pp. 17–35, 2022.
https://doi.org/10.1007/978-3-031-20050-2_2

Nevertheless, generating highly realistic and scalable LiDAR data remains an unsolved challenge. Existing approaches are either unrealistic or not scalable. The primary paradigm for creating realistic LiDAR data is through model-based simulation. Early work on LiDAR simulation is purely physics-driven. The general idea is to mimic the time-of-flight (ToF) sensing process of LiDAR [14]. Specifically, the simulator casts rays in a 3D environment and simulates the receiver's returns by measuring the distance of the hitting surface to the sensor. The reality gap remains substantial because of the imperfect physical model and artist-designed assets. State-of-the-art simulation [44] combines physical modeling with learning components to compensate for complicated rendering artifacts. It produces high realism in both geometry and radiometric appearance. In addition, such a simulation method also gives complete controllability, allowing us to rearrange the scene layout and change viewpoint freely. However, the data-driven approach requires scanning the physical world in advance, which is expensive and not scalable. Recent approaches [5] investigated asset-free LiDAR generation using deep generative models to overcome such a limit. Nevertheless, neither controllability nor realism has yet been achieved.

In this paper, we present LiDARGen, a *realistic*, *controllable* and *asset-free* LiDAR point cloud generation framework. Following the imaging process of spinning LiDAR, we treat each LiDAR scan as an equirectangular view image, a 2.5D panoramic representation encoding information about ray angles, reflectance, and depth range. Generating LiDAR points under this representation guarantees physical feasibility. Inspired by the success of score-matching diffusion models in image generation [58], LiDARGen then learns a score function [25,67], modeling the log-likelihood gradient given a sample in the equirectangular image space. This score function is trained on real-world LiDAR datasets. In the sampling stage, our method gradually converts an initial Gaussian random noise point into a realistic point cloud by progressively applying the score function to remove the noise via Langevin dynamics [58,72]. Figure 1 depicts an overview of our approach.

LiDARGen can be applied to conditional generation, such as LiDAR densification, by sampling from a posterior distribution [61]. Specifically, we leverage Bayes' rule to calculate the prior gradient based on the score-matching generative model and the likelihood gradient reflecting the conditions. The generated results are both realistic and plausible with regard to the controlled input. Notably, we also enjoy the simplicity – such a controlled generation process does not require retraining new models.

We validate the effectiveness of our method on the KITTI-360 [38] and NuScenes [6] datasets. Results demonstrate superior performance compared to other competing methods in various metrics and visual quality. We further evaluate LiDAR densification performance, demonstrating LiDARGen's potential for downstream tasks.

## 2    Related Work

This work studies the problem of generating realistic 3D LiDAR point clouds. It closely relates to point cloud generation and 3D deep learning. We also draw upon various efforts in energy-based generative models and LiDAR simulation.

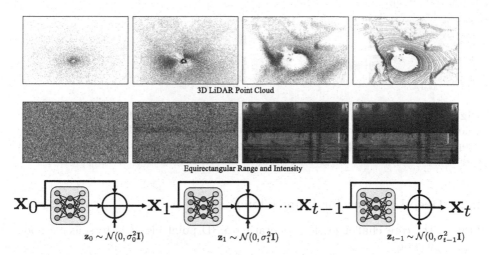

**Fig. 1.** Overview. We sample a LiDAR point cloud by progressively denoising the equirectangular view using a trained score function and Langevin dynamics.

## 2.1   Point Cloud Generation

Our task of generating LiDAR point clouds belongs to the broad category of 3D point cloud generation [2,15,17,55,64,66,82,83]. Various works successfully apply deep generative models to advance this task. Representative works include variational autoencoder [15,20,83], generative adversarial networks [2,35,55,66, 82], flow-based methods [64,78], and diffusion processes [7,43,79].

Most previous methods on point cloud generation treat point clouds as fixed-size data [2,15,55,66,82,83], restricting their practicability in handling real-world data, where the number of points varies significantly. Recent works [43,78] start to look into point cloud generation with a diverse size. However, to achieve this, these approaches require an additional resampling step from an implicit surface distribution or an expensive auto-regressive procedure. In our work, inspired by the physics of LiDAR sensing, we explicitly generate a mask from the range image, mimicking the ray-drop patterns of LiDAR. This masking operation allows us to generate point clouds with various sizes and guaranteed physical feasibility.

Most aforementioned point cloud generation methods are developed and evaluated on clean, synthetic object shapes, such as ShapeNet [10]. Due to several unique challenges, it remains unclear whether we can directly transfer this success to LiDAR point clouds. First, LiDAR scans are generated through a time-of-flight sensing process. An ideal generator should produce a point cloud following light transport physics. Additionally, LiDAR point clouds are partial observations of a large scene, making the data highly unstructured, sparse, and non-uniform. It is therefore much more challenging to generate realistic LiDAR point clouds. Several recent works explore this direction with moderate success [5,52]. The pioneering work [5] applies a variational autoencoder and generative adversarial network on LiDAR point clouds. Another line of work also leverages GANs but exploits a hybrid representation [52]. However, the level of realism is still limited.

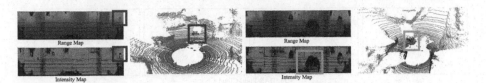

**Fig. 2.** LiDARGen sampling output. Left: equirectangular view. Right: 3D point cloud colored by intensity. Our method learns to generate cars with highly detailed structures, drop rays around transparent region, and produce reflectance intensity for specular objects.

## 2.2  Deep Learning for Point Clouds

One of the core challenges for generating a 3D point cloud is to select a good representation.

This subsection briefly categorizes them according to the representation.

**Voxelization** methods build a dense volumetric representation in the form of a 3D grid [12,18,41,42,49,77]. 3D convolution could then be directly applied to such representation. It is simple and straightforward. However, the dense voxel representation suffers from resolution loss and inefficient memory. Hence, researchers also improve the 3D voxel method with sparse convolutions [12,18], hierarchical structures [81] and hybrid representations [41,42].

Many neural networks directly learn to represent the **raw point cloud**. The pioneering work PointNet [39,48,50] leverages aggregation to collect context information. Other lines of research propose novel convolutional operators that can be directly applied on point clouds [24,36,45,56,62,65,69,74,76]. Graph-based methods explicitly create graph structures from the point cloud and exploit graph neural networks onto the structures [56,68,71,85].

Another popular line of research models 3D data by projecting it onto 2D perspectives [11,28,33,34,46,63,77]. One can then directly apply 2D deep learning algorithms for 3D tasks. In these works, the depth value is often encoded in the 2D map, providing partial yet compact information about 3D. **Bird's eye view representation** [33,77] is established through orthographically projecting the 3D point cloud along the vertical direction. **Perspective projection** obtains a 2D representation that resembles human vision. Several early works exploit perspective projection to produce images from multiple views and fuse the decision in 3D [11,63]. The most closely related representation to us is the **equirectangular view representation**, which encodes the polar coordinate into a 2.5D image [13,46,73]. It provides a panoramic view of the surrounding scene that closely resembles the imaging process of LiDAR.

## 2.3  LiDAR Simulation

LiDAR simulation aims to produce a realistic LiDAR point cloud by mimicking the physical process of its imaging [3,14,23,30,44,47,57,70,75,75]. Physical-based LiDAR simulation uses raycasting methods to simulate LiDAR. Ray intersections are calculated by shooting rays from the origin sensor position outwards onto a geometry surface of the environment. Most self-driving and robotics simulators (e.g., CARLA [14] and Gazebo [30]) typically use this approach. However, physical-based approaches can suffer from a lack of realism because it requires very high-quality 3D assets (e.g., car models with material reflectance information, detailed maps with realistic foliage, etc.), and many LiDAR effects are difficult to simulate (e.g., atmospheric noise or LiDAR ray drop, which occurs when a LiDAR ray reflects off a surface and never gets a reading back). To approach this problem, research has recently focused on building data-driven LiDAR simulations [3,23,44,70]. The representative work, LiDARSim [44] leverages machine learning models to learn ray-dropping patterns and exploits 3D assets that are built from modeling the urban environment. Many cut-and-paste data augmentation techniques could also be treated as a special form of LiDAR simulation, where objects are removed, inserted, or rearranged into a real LiDAR point cloud to create new ones. However, these methods build upon manipulating real-world point cloud data, restricting their scale and controllability. Furthermore, object insertion often aims to improve the performance of specific perception methods with little consideration for physical plausibility and realism [16,19,37].

## 3  Background

### 3.1  Energy-Based Models

Given a dataset $\{\mathbf{x}_1, ...\mathbf{x}_N\}$, where each data sample $\mathbf{x}_i$ is assumed to be independently sampled from an underlying distribution, energy-based generative models aim to find a probability model in the following form that best fits the dataset: $p(\mathbf{x}) = \frac{e^{-E_\theta(\mathbf{x})}}{Z_\theta}$ where the energy function $E_\theta(\mathbf{x}) : \mathbb{R}^D \to \mathbb{R}$ is a real-valued function and $\theta$ represents its learnable parameters. $Z_\theta$ is the normalization term $Z_\theta = \int e^{-E_\theta(\mathbf{x})} d\mathbf{x}$ that ensures the $p(\mathbf{x})$ to be a valid probability. Energy-based modeling is a family of expressive yet general probabilistic models that capture underlying dependencies among associated variables in high-dimensional space. Many generative models are instantiations of energy-based models, such as restricted Boltzmann machine [22], conditional random field [32], factor graphs [31] and recent deep energy-based generative models [58,60]. Nevertheless, learning a generic energy model by maximizing log-likelihood is difficult, since computing the partition function $Z_\theta$ or estimating its gradient $\nabla_\theta \log Z_\theta$ is computationally intractable due to the integration over a high-dimensional space.

### 3.2  Score-Based Energy Models

To alleviate this problem, researchers try to approximate the computation of the log-likelihood (or the gradient of the partition), with methods such as pseudolikelihood [4], variational inference [29], and contrastive divergence [22]. Other methods bypass it using other learning objectives to train energy-based models, such as structured loss minimization [21]. Among them, score matching [26] recently became a popular choice thanks to its simplicity. Formally speaking, the goal of score matching is to minimize the following objective:

$$\mathbb{E}_{p_{\text{data}}(\mathbf{x})} \left[ \text{tr}(\nabla_{\mathbf{x}}^2 \log p_\theta(\mathbf{x})) + \frac{1}{2} \| \nabla \log p_\theta(\mathbf{x}) \|_2^2 \right] \tag{1}$$

As shown in this equation, the objective only involves the first and second-order gradient w.r.t. the $\mathbf{x}$, both of which are independent of the partition function.

Based on this, Hyvarinen [26] proposes the score-based model. It directly models the gradient of log-likelihood $\log p(\mathbf{x})$ with a parametric score function $s_\theta(\mathbf{x}) = \nabla_{\mathbf{x}} \log p(\mathbf{x}) : \mathbb{R}^D \to \mathbb{R}^D$. However, minimizing the original score matching in Eq. 1 involves calculating the Hessian of log-likelihood (gradient of the score) $\nabla_\theta s_\theta(\mathbf{x})$, which is computationally expensive. Vincent et al. [67] further reformulates the score matching energy and shows that score-based models could be more efficiently trained with the following denoising objective:

$$\frac{1}{2} \mathbb{E}_{p_{\text{data}}(\mathbf{x})} \mathbb{E}_{\tilde{\mathbf{x}} \sim \mathcal{N}(\mathbf{x}, \sigma^2 I)} \left[ \left\| s(\tilde{\mathbf{x}}) + \frac{\tilde{\mathbf{x}} - \mathbf{x}}{\sigma^2} \right\|_2^2 \right] \tag{2}$$

where $\tilde{\mathbf{x}}$ is the Gaussian-noise perturbed sample and $\sigma$ is the standard deviation.

Sampling from a score-based model $s_\theta(\mathbf{x}) = \log_{\mathbf{x}} p_\theta(\mathbf{x})$ can be done with Langevin dynamics [72]. It is a Markov chain Monte Carlo (MCMC) process that can be interpreted as a noisy form of gradient ascent. For each step, Langevin dynamics sums the value of the previous step, the current gradient estimation based on the score function, and a Gaussian-distributed random noise:

$$\mathbf{x}_t = \mathbf{x}_{t-1} + \frac{\epsilon}{2} \nabla_{\mathbf{x}} \log p(\mathbf{x}_{t-1}) + \sqrt{\epsilon} z_t \tag{3}$$

where $z \sim \mathcal{N}(0, I)$ and $\epsilon$ is the learning rate, which is usually decreased (annealed) with a schedule [58]. When $\epsilon \to 0$ and $t \to +\infty$ Langevin dynamics is convergent to a true samples from the distribution $p(\mathbf{x})$ under certain mild conditions [58]. The denoising score-matching model and its variants have shown state-of-the-art performance in data generation [60, 79].

## 4  Method

Our goal is to model the underlying distribution of LiDAR point clouds in an urban driving scenario. We could then leverage such a generative model to sample new point clouds or use it for downstream MAP inference tasks. The challenge of LiDAR generation is to model the diverse structures that exist in the real world while still maintaining physical plausibility. Towards this goal, we leverage the denoising score-matching generative model [58] to model the gradient of its log-probability. Formally speaking, our training dataset consists of a list of raw LiDAR point clouds $\{(\mathbf{x}_1, r_1), ...(\mathbf{x}_N, r_N)\}$, where $\mathbf{x}_i \in \mathbb{R}^{D_i \times 3}$ represents the 3D location and $r_i \in \mathbb{R}$ is a scalar representing the reflectance intensity value for each point. Our method learns a score function $s_\theta(\mathbf{x})$ to approximate $\nabla_{\mathbf{x}} \log p(\mathbf{x})$ with score-matching [67]. Sampling can then be conducted with Langevin dynamics, which gradually denoises an initial random Gaussian point cloud and returns a clean and realistic point cloud. Inspired by LiDAR's imaging process, we leverage

Ground-Truth    LiDARGAN [5]    ProjectedGAN [53]    **Ours**

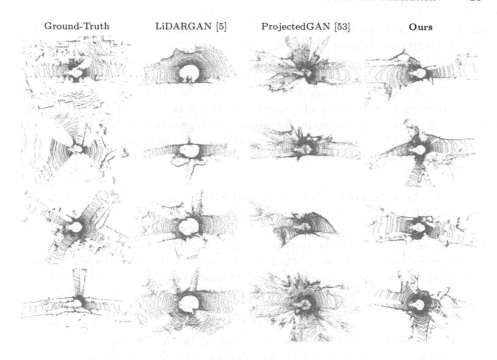

**Fig. 3.** Qualitative results for LiDAR point cloud generation on KITTI-360.

the equirectangular representation as our underlying representation to ensure physical feasibility and develop an encoder-decoder network on top of it as the score function. Fig. 1 gives an overview of our approach.

### 4.1 LiDAR Generation

**Input Representation.** Our model starts by converting the input parameterization from an unstructured point cloud sparsely distributed in euclidean space into a dense multi-channel equirectangular perspective image, with one channel representing depth and the other representing intensity. More specifically, we first convert each point from the Cartesian coordinate $\mathbf{x} = (x, y, z) \in \mathbb{R}^3$ into the spherical coordinate $\mathbf{z} \in (\theta, \phi, d)$: $d = \sqrt{x^2 + y^2 + z^2}, \theta = \arccos \frac{z}{\sqrt{x^2+y^2+z^2}}, \phi =$ atan2$(y, x)$, where $\theta$ is the inclination, $\phi$ is azimuth and $d$ is the depth range; atan2 is the standard 2-argument arctangent function taking into account the discontinuity across quadrant boundaries of atan$(y/x)$. Furthermore, we remap the depth range so that it is normalized from 0 to 1: The two-channel rectangular image is then produced through quantizing the two angles and rasterization. Concretely, for each point $\mathbf{z}_i = (\theta_i, \phi_i, d_i), r_i$: $\mathcal{I}(\lfloor \theta_i/s_\theta \rfloor, \lfloor \phi_j/s_\phi \rfloor) = \left( \frac{1}{6} \log_2(d_i + 1), \frac{1}{255} r_i \right)$. Both channels of the image are normalized to the range $(0, 1)$ and we use a logarithm mapping to esure nearby points have a higher geometry resolution. For simplicity, throughout the rest of section we will also use **x** to represent the point cloud in its equirectangular representation. Figure 2 demonstrates one example of the range view representation. Our input representation enjoys several benefits. Firstly, it encodes information into a dense and compact 2D map, allowing us to exploit efficient network architecture transferred from the 2D image generation domain. Secondly, due to the ray casting nature, most spinning LiDAR scans will only return the peak pulse for each beam[1]. In other words, encoding the point cloud into this representation will not lose any information, and the generated point cloud properly reflects the scanning and ray-casting nature of the sensor.

**Network Architecture.** Our score-based network $s_\theta$ uses a **U-Net** architecture [51] following its success in image generation [27,59]. Specifically, at each step, it takes a $W \times H \times 2$ input image and outputs a $W \times H \times 2$ score map at the same size. We also make important changes suitable for our LiDAR point cloud generation task. Firstly, standard 2D images have disconnected left and right boundaries. Hence zero-padding or symmetry padding is often sufficient for dense prediction. However, equirectangular images are inherently circular. Applying standard convolutions does not take into account such constraints. To alleviate this issue, **circular convolution** [54] treats left and right boundaries as connected neighbors in its topology. Inspired by this, we substitute all the convolution and pooling layers in our network with circular versions. Second, LiDAR point clouds collected from urban driving environments have a highly structured geometry. And this geometric structure is often viewpoint-aware. For instance, the depth range of the lower beam might have a strong bias due to the ground height; the depth range of the frontal facing positions tends to be larger since the car is mostly driving forward along a straight road. To better encode this prior, our model takes the **angular coordinate as an additional input** to the convolution, similarly to CoordConv [40].

**Training.** One of the difficulties for training denoising score matching models is the choice of a proper noise level for Eq. 2, which heavily influences the accuracy of score estimation. In practice, we find that having a noise-conditioned extension is crucial for its success. More specifically, we expand our score network $s_\theta(\mathbf{x}, \sigma_i)$ to be dependent on the current noise perturbation level $\sigma_i$. At the training stage, following the noise-conditioned score-matching model [58], we adopt a multi-scale loss function, with a re-weighting factor for the loss at each noise level:

$$\frac{1}{2L} \sum_{i=1}^{L} \sigma_i^2 \mathbb{E}_{p_{data}(\mathbf{x})} \mathbb{E}_{\tilde{\mathbf{x}} \sim \mathcal{N}(\mathbf{x}, \sigma_i^2 I)} \left[ \left\| s_\theta(\tilde{\mathbf{x}}, \sigma_i) + \frac{\tilde{\mathbf{x}} - \mathbf{x}}{\sigma_i^2} \right\| \right] \quad (4)$$

where $\tilde{\mathbf{x}}$ is the randomly perturbed noisy signal at each level, and $\sigma_i$ is the standard deviation of the noise distribution.

---

[1] some sensors return two beams for a small fraction of beams.

**Sampling.** We exploit annealed Langevin dynamics sampling [59] for our point generation task to increase sampling efficiency. Specifically, we start from the highest pretrained noise level and gradually reduce the noise level:

$$\mathbf{x}_t = \mathbf{x}_{t-1} + \gamma \frac{\sigma_i^2}{2\sigma_L^2} \nabla_\mathbf{x} \log s_\theta(\mathbf{x}_{t-1}, \sigma_i) + \gamma \frac{\sigma_i}{\sigma_L} \mathbf{z}_t \tag{5}$$

where $\gamma$ is the learning rate and $\sigma_L$ is the smallest noise level. The final step of Langevin dynamic sampling gives us a clean equirectangular range image. We unproject this resulting image back into 3D Cartesian space to recover the 3D point cloud. Please refer to Fig. 1 for the full sampling procedure.

## 4.2 Posterior Sampling

Learning the unconditional prior distribution $p(\mathbf{x})$ of LiDAR point clouds enables many applications. In particular, we often expect our generated LiDAR point cloud to satisfy a specific property or to be consistent with certain conditions. For instance, we might want to create a LiDAR point cloud that agrees with some partial observation; or we might generate a LiDAR point cloud conditioned on its semantic layout. Conventional methods, such as GANs, often require training different conditional generative models for each task. However, thanks to the gradient-based approach used in score-based models, we could efficiently conduct the tasks mentioned above with only the pretrained unconditional generation model $p(\mathbf{x})$. Next, we will show how to achieve this in LiDARGen.

Specifically, given a pretrained generation model $p(\mathbf{x})$ and an input condition $\mathbf{y}$, we formulate the agreement between the condition $\mathbf{y}$ and the LiDAR point cloud $\mathbf{x}$ as a likelihoood function $p(\mathbf{y}|\mathbf{x})$. Our goal is to sample new point cloud that reflect the input condition $p(\mathbf{x}|\mathbf{y})$. According to the Bayes' rule we have:

$$p(\mathbf{x}|\mathbf{y}) = p(\mathbf{y}|\mathbf{x})p(\mathbf{x})/p(\mathbf{y}), \nabla_\mathbf{x} \log p(\mathbf{x}|\mathbf{y}) = \nabla_\mathbf{x} p(\mathbf{y}|\mathbf{x}) + \nabla_\mathbf{x} p(\mathbf{x}) \tag{6}$$

where $\nabla_\mathbf{x} \log p(\mathbf{x})$ is our pretrained score function $s_\theta(\mathbf{x})$. In many situations, the likelihood model has an analytical gradient or is a neural network; hence calculating the gradient with respect to $\mathbf{x}$ is straightforward. We, therefore, leverage the following Langevin dynamics to sample from the posterior distribution:

$$\mathbf{x}_t = \mathbf{x}_{t-1} + \frac{\epsilon}{2} \left( \nabla_\mathbf{x} s_\theta(\mathbf{x}_{t-1}) + \nabla_\mathbf{x} \log p(\mathbf{y}|\mathbf{x}_{t-1}) \right) + \sqrt{\epsilon} \mathbf{z}_t. \tag{7}$$

Next, we will discuss three concrete applications of posterior sampling.

**LiDAR Densification.** Spinning LiDAR used on autonomy is expensive due to its complicated mechanical design. In particular, the price of LiDAR sensors grows exponentially as the number of beams increases. Therefore, there is a practical need to produce high-beam LiDAR readings with a low-beam model. Given a low-beam LiDAR point cloud $\mathbf{y}$, our goal is to recover its high-beam version **x**. Assuming that **m** is the visibility mask denoting pixels with a provided gt ray, the gradient of the posterior can be computed as follows:

$$\nabla_{\mathbf{x}} \log p(\mathbf{x}|\mathbf{y}) = \nabla_{\mathbf{x}} \left( \log p(\mathbf{x}) + \frac{\lambda}{2} \|(\mathbf{x} - \mathbf{y}) \odot \mathbf{m}\|^2 \right) = s_\theta(\mathbf{x}) + \lambda \left[ (\mathbf{x} - \mathbf{y}) \odot \mathbf{m} \right],$$

where $\odot$ is the Hadamard product. Intuitively, each Langevin dynamic step pushes the samples towards the direction of being both realistic and consistent with the partial observation **y**.

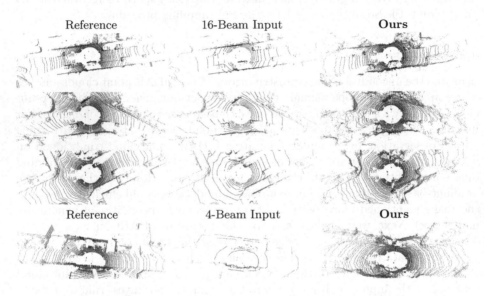

**Fig. 4.** Qualitative results for unsupervised LiDAR densification.

## 5    Experiments

### 5.1    Experimental Setup

**Datasets.** We train and test our model's performance on the challenging KITTI-360 [38] and **nuScenes** [6] datasets. KITTI-360 contains 81,106 LiDAR readings from 9 long sequences around the suburbs of Karlsruhe, Germany. The scenes KITTI-360 covers are diverse, consisting of driving on highways and through residential and commercial districts. We split the dataset into two parts, where the first two sequences (30,758 frames) are the testing set, and the rest are used for training and cross-validation. nuScenes contains 297,737 LiDAR sweeps in the training set and 52,423 LiDAR sweeps in the testing and cross-validation set. The LiDAR sweeps were collected in the cities of Boston and Singapore. The two datasets provide different sensors (64 and 32 beams), geographic regions (EU and NA), and content (suburbs and cities).

**Metrics.** Quantitatively measuring generative models is known to be difficult. In our work, we leverage three different metrics for evaluation. **Maximum Mean Discrepancy (MMD)** is a non-parametric distance between two sets of samples. It compares the distance between two sets of samples by measuring the mean squared difference of the statistics of the two. MMD could be measured through the kernel trick:

$$\text{MMD} = \frac{1}{N^2} \sum_i^N \sum_{i'}^N k(\mathbf{x}_i, \mathbf{x}_{i'}) - \frac{2}{NM} \sum_i^N \sum_j^M k(\mathbf{x}_i, \mathbf{x}_j) + \frac{1}{M^2} \sum_j^M \sum_{j'}^N k(\mathbf{x}_j, \mathbf{x}_{j'}).$$

For each point cloud we compute a $50 \times 50$ spatial histogram along the ground plane (x and y coordinates) then use a Gaussian kernel to measure the similarity between the two. Additionally, inspired by the FID score for image generation, we evaluate a new **Frechet Range Distance** (FRD score) on KITTI-360. It evaluates the squared Wasserstein metric between mean and the covariance of a LiDAR perception network's activations from the synthetic samples and true samples. We choose RangeNet++, which is a encoder-decoder based network for segmentation pretrained on KITTI-360. To trade-off between quality and preserve locality, we randomly choose 4,096 activation from the feature map of its bottleneck layer to fit the Gaussian distribution. Finally, we report the **Jensen-Shannon divergence** (JSD) between the empirical distributions of two sets of point clouds. We approximate the distribution through a birds-eye view 2D histogram at a resolution $100 \times 100$ for both reference sets and generated sets.

**Table 1.** Quantitative results on KITTI-360 [38].**Bold** is best; Blue is second.

| | $\text{MMD}_{\text{BEV}} \downarrow$ | $\text{FID}_{\text{range}} \downarrow$ | $\text{JSD}_{\text{BEV}} \downarrow$ |
|---|---|---|---|
| LiDAR GAN [5] | $3.06 \times 10^{-3}$ | 3003.8 | – |
| LiDAR VAE [5] | $1.00 \times 10^{-3}$ | 2261.5 | 0.161 |
| Projected GAN [53] | $\mathbf{3.47 \times 10^{-4}}$ | **2117.2** | **0.085** |
| Ours | $\mathbf{3.87 \times 10^{-4}}$ | **2040.1** | **0.067** |

**Baselines.** We have 3 baseline comparisons. The first baseline is the range-view based VAE-based LiDAR generation model proposed by Caccia et al. [5]. We have added additional layers and increased the generated range image size to $1024 \times 64$. We train the models for 165 epochs until convergence. The second baseline is the GAN-based model from Caccia et al. [5]. The GAN was pretrained at a resolution of $256 \times 40$ following the original paper[2], followed by a upsampling layer to $1024 \times 40$. The last baseline is Projected GAN [53], one of the state-of-art GAN models for image generation. We adapt ProjectedGAN into our setting and train it for 3,000 epochs. All the generated range image samples are converted to a 3D point cloud in Cartesian coordinates for quality comparison.

---

[2] we did not manage to make training converge in higher resolution.

**Implementation Details.** We use a UNet-like model for the score function. It takes in a $64 \times 1024 \times 2$ (KITTI) or $32 \times 1024 \times 2$ (Nuscenes) tensor as input and outputs the same size, denoting the gradient of log-prob. The U-Net comprises a stack of 6 down-sampling and a stack of 6 upsampling blocks, with skip connections in between. Each block has two convs. Each conv is preceded by InstanceNorm++ and an ELU activation. Number of channels is 32-64-64-64-128-128-128-128-64-64-64-32. Our model was trained with Adam optimizer with a learning rate of 1e-4. For sampling, we use a gradient update step of 2e-6 and 5 iterations per noise level. The initial $\sigma_0$ is 50, the final $\sigma_L$ is 0.01, and the number of levels is 232. To train Caccia et al.'s [5] models, we used a learning rate of 1e-4. All the models are trained and tested with an Nvidia RTX A4000 GPU.

**Table 2.** Human study results on KITTI-360

| Method | Percent prefer ours |
|---|---|
| Ours vs. VAE | 97% |
| Ours vs. GAN | 96.6% |
| Ours vs. ProjectedGAN | 100% |

## 5.2   KITTI-360 Evaluation

**Quantitative Results.** Table 1 shows quantitative results among all the competing algorithms. From the table we could see that our method produces superior performance on the FRD score compared against other methods. In terms of MMD our approach is also ranking high. It is slightly lower than projected GAN, however both match the histogram well with an MMD score smaller than 1e-4. As we mention in metric subsection, every metric is a partial evaluation of the sampling quality, and urge the readers to consider all quantitative metrics, the human study, and the qualitative results as a holistic evaluation.

**Qualitative Results.** Figure 3 demonstrates some randomly selected samples from all the competing algorithms. We also list the true point cloud samples from KITTI as a reference. From the figure, we could see our approach produces significantly higher quality samples than the competing algorithms. Specifically, LiDARGAN captures the overall layout, but fails in producing high-detailed structures, such as cars, trees, sidewalks, pedestrians, etc. Projected GAN generates reasonable, detailed structures at near range, but brings significant artifacts at far range. Ours excel in terms of both realism in layout and geometry details, as well as diversity in content. Additionally, we provide a zoom-in visualization of our 3D point cloud in Fig. 2, highlighting the high quality geometric details our method could offer.

**Human Study.** To evaluate the perceptual quality, we perform an A/B test on a team of students. Our test system shows a pair of randomly chosen images of two point cloud sampled from two different methods. Human judges then choose which one is more realistic. Participates also have access to real KITTI point clouds for reference. The raw results are shown in Table 2. In total, 5 participants labeled 600 image pairs. At a confidence level of 99% the two-sided test p-value is smaller than 1e–4, demonstrating statistical significance.

## 5.3  NuScenes Results

Figure 5 depicts the qualitative comparison results. From this figure, we can see that our method still achieves superior results compared to both VAE [5] and projected GAN [53]. An AB test on a group of four human subjects suggests that our method is significantly favored over other competing algorithms in 89% of cases. While achieving superior human study performance, we notice that our method tends to generate point clouds that concentrate their mass closer to the viewpoint. As a result, despite superior visual quality, our MMD score at BEV is worse than VAE and Projected GAN (2e–3 vs. 1.1e–3 and 6e–5). We will leave this shrinking effect for future investigation.

| Ground-Truth | VAE [5] | ProjectedGAN [53] | **Ours** |

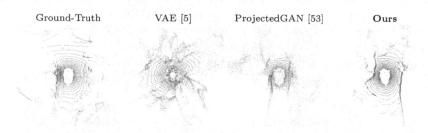

**Fig. 5.** Qualitative results on the nuScenes dataset.

**Table 3.** LiDAR densification.

|  | MAE ↓ |
| --- | --- |
| PUNet [80] | 6.88 |
| NN | 2.18 |
| Ours | **1.23** |

**Table 4.** Ablation study

| Coord-aware | CircConv | FRD | MMD |
| --- | --- | --- | --- |
| No | No | 2422.3 | $7.60 \times 10^{-4}$ |
| Yes | No | 2251.1 | $3.94 \times 10^{-4}$ |
| Yes | Yes | **2040.1** | $\mathbf{3.87 \times 10^{-4}}$ |

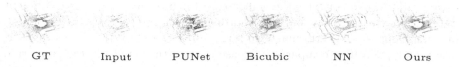

| GT | Input | PUNet | Bicubic | NN | Ours |

**Fig. 6.** Densification results.

## 5.4   Posterior Sampling

We also evaluate our LIDAR generation model on the task of LiDAR densifi-cation. More specifically, we simulate low-beam LiDAR sensor readings as our sparse input by selecting a subset of the beams from the raw 64-beam sensors. In this example, we create 4-beam and 16-beam input as shown in Fig. 4. Following the posterior sampling procedure described in Eq. 6 and Eq. 7. Figure 4 depicts the sparse input, a dense ground-truth reference and our qualitative posterior sampling results. As shown in the figure, the resulting point cloud is realistic and reflects the input guidance.

**Qualitative Comparison.** We compare PUNet [80], bicubic interpolation, and nearest neighbor interpolation with ours on KITTI-360. Quantitative results are shown in Table 3. Qualitative results are shown in Fig. 6. PUNet is B/W as it does not upsample intensity. Our results suggest that the proposed densification method is superior to both learned and interpolation approaches.

**Downstream Applications.** We run RangeNet++ semantic seg on densified point cloud without fine-tuning. (Fig. 7). Applying LiDARGen to densify a sparse (16 Beam) LiDAR helps RangeNet++ create cleaner results (e.g., the road) and recover lost details (e.g., the cars in the distance). Our method also achieves bet-ter quantitative results compared to nearest-neighbour up-sampling. Per-point accuracy is 0.546 (NN) and 0.608 (ours). IOU is 0.394 (NN) and 0.449 (ours).

True Reference          Nearest-Neighbor          Ours

**Fig. 7.** RangeNet++ segmentation on densified LiDAR.

## 5.5   Discussions

**Ablation Studies.** We conduct ablation studies to justify the design choice of our algorithms. We compare the same score function model in three different settings (w/o circular conv and w/o coordinate-encoding). As shown in Table 4, both help improve the performance in terms of FRD and MMD. For more infor-mation and qualitative comparison, please refer to the supplementary material.

**Limitations.** Despite producing superior performance and flexibility, LiDAR-Gen still has several limitations. First, sampling efficiency is one of the major drawback – LiDARGen takes approximately 12min to sample 36 LiDAR samples in a batch. We leave it as future work and anticipate that leveraging recent acceleration techniques for diffusion-based models is a promising direction to alleviate this issue. In addition, our approach cannot yet pass the Turing test for experienced LiDAR perception researchers. There are a few artifacts: our samples have degraded geometric details at far range and tended to have less straight walls than real samples. We plan to explore multi-modal networks (e.g. hybrid equirectangular view and bird's eye view) in the future.

## 6  Conclusion

We propose LiDARGen, a score-based approach for LiDAR point cloud generation. Our method samples a realistic point cloud by progressively denoising a noisy input. We demonstrate that our unconditional generation model could be directly applied for various conditional generation tasks through posterior sampling. A human study and perceptional similarity evaluation on the challenging KITTI-360 dataset validates the effectiveness of our method. We hope this approach will open up the research to provide easy access to realistic LiDAR sensory data directly from machine learning. We also expect to explore potential applications of LiDARGen in 3D environment generation and self-driving.

**Acknowledgement.** The authors thank Wei-Chiu Ma and Zhijian Liu for their feedback on early drafts and all the participants in the human perceptual quality study. The project is partially funded by the Illinois Smart Transportation Initiative STII-21-07. We also thank Nvidia for the Academic Hardware Grant.

## References

1. Google's waymo invests in lidar technology, cuts costs by 90 percent. https://arstechnica.com/cars/2017/01/googles-waymo-invests-in-lidar-technology-cuts-costs-by-90-percent/. Accessed 07 Mar 2012
2. Achlioptas, P., Diamanti, O., Mitliagkas, I., Guibas, L.: Learning representations and generative models for 3d point clouds. In: ICML (2018)
3. Amini, A., et al.: Vista 2.0: an open, data-driven simulator for multimodal sensing and policy learning for autonomous vehicles. arXiv preprint arXiv:2111.12083 (2021)
4. Besag, J.: Statistical analysis of non-lattice data. J. Roy. Stat. Soc.: Ser. D (Stat.) **24**(3), 179–195 (1975)
5. Caccia, L., van Hoof, H., Courville, A.C., Pineau, J.: Deep generative modeling of lidar data. In: IROS, pp. 5034–5040 (2019)
6. Caesar, H., et al.: nuscenes: a multimodal dataset for autonomous driving. arXiv preprint arXiv:1903.11027 (2019)
7. Cai, R., et al.: Learning gradient fields for shape generation. In: Vedaldi, A., Bischof, H., Brox, T., Frahm, J.-M. (eds.) ECCV 2020. LNCS, vol. 12348, pp. 364–381. Springer, Cham (2020). https://doi.org/10.1007/978-3-030-58580-8_22

8. Cao, C., Zhu, H., Choset, H., Zhang, J.: Tare: a hierarchical framework for efficiently exploring complex 3D environments. In: Robotics: Science and Systems Conference (RSS), Virtual (2021)

9. Carle, P.J., Furgale, P.T., Barfoot, T.D.: Long-range rover localization by matching lidar scans to orbital elevation maps. J. Field Rob. **27**(3), 344–370 (2010)

10. Chang, A.X., et al.: ShapeNet: an information-rich 3D model repository. Technical Report. arXiv:1512.03012 [cs.GR], Stanford University – Princeton University – Toyota Technological Institute at Chicago (2015)

11. Chen, X., Ma, H., Wan, J., Li, B., Xia, T.: Multi-view 3d object detection network for autonomous driving. In: CVPR (2017)

12. Choy, C.B., Xu, D., Gwak, J.Y., Chen, K., Savarese, S.: 3D-R2N2: a unified approach for single and multi-view 3D object reconstruction. In: Leibe, B., Matas, J., Sebe, N., Welling, M. (eds.) ECCV 2016. LNCS, vol. 9912, pp. 628–644. Springer, Cham (2016). https://doi.org/10.1007/978-3-319-46484-8_38

13. Cohen, T.S., Geiger, M., Köhler, J., Welling, M.: Spherical cnns. arXiv preprint arXiv:1801.10130 (2018)

14. Dosovitskiy, A., Ros, G., Codevilla, F., Lopez, A., Koltun, V.: CARLA: an open urban driving simulator. In: Proceedings of the 1st Annual Conference on Robot Learning, pp. 1–16 (2017)

15. Fan, H., Su, H., Guibas, L.J.: A point set generation network for 3D object reconstruction from a single image. In: CVPR (2017)

16. Fang, J.: Augmented lidar simulator for autonomous driving. IEEE Rob. Autom. Lett. **5**(2), 1931–1938 (2020)

17. Gadelha, M., Wang, R., Maji, S.: Multiresolution tree networks for 3d point cloud processing. In: Proceedings of the European Conference on Computer Vision (ECCV), pp. 103–118 (2018)

18. Graham, B., Engelcke, M., Van Der Maaten, L.: 3D semantic segmentation with submanifold sparse convolutional networks. In: CVPR (2018)

19. Gusmão, G.F., Barbosa, C.R.H., Raposo, A.B.: Development and validation of lidar sensor simulators based on parallel raycasting. Sensors **20**(24), 7186 (2020)

20. Han, Z., Wang, X., Liu, Y.S., Zwicker, M.: Multi-angle point cloud-vae: unsupervised feature learning for 3D point clouds from multiple angles by joint self-reconstruction and half-to-half prediction. In: 2019 IEEE/CVF International Conference on Computer Vision (ICCV), pp. 10441–10450. IEEE (2019)

21. Hazan, T., Keshet, J., McAllester, D.: Direct loss minimization for structured prediction. Adv. Neural Inf. Process. Syst. **23** (2010)

22. Hinton, G.E., Salakhutdinov, R.R.: Reducing the dimensionality of data with neural networks. Science **313**(5786), 504–507 (2006)

23. Hu, J.S., Waslander, S.L.: Pattern-aware data augmentation for lidar 3D object detection. In: 2021 IEEE International Intelligent Transportation Systems Conference (ITSC), pp. 2703–2710. IEEE (2021)

24. Hu, Q., et al.: Randla-net: efficient semantic segmentation of large-scale point clouds. In: CVPR (2020)

25. Hyvärinen, A.: Estimation of non-normalized statistical models by score matching. J. Mach. Learn. Res. **6**, 695–709 (2005)

26. Hyvärinen, A.: Estimation of non-normalized statistical models by score matching. J. Mach. Learn. Res. **6**(Apr), 695–709 (2005)

27. Isola, P., Zhu, J.Y., Zhou, T., Efros, A.A.: Image-to-image translation with conditional adversarial networks. In: Proceedings of the IEEE Conference on Computer Vision and Pattern Recognition, pp. 1125–1134 (2017)

28. Kanezaki, A., Matsushita, Y., Nishida, Y.: Rotationnet: joint object categorization and pose estimation using multiviews from unsupervised viewpoints. In: CVPR (2018)

29. Kingma, D.P., Welling, M.: Auto-encoding variational bayes. In: ICLR (2014)

30. Koenig, N., Howard, A.: Design and use paradigms for gazebo, an open-source multi-robot simulator. In: 2004 IEEE/RSJ International Conference on Intelligent Robots and Systems (IROS)(IEEE Cat. No. 04CH37566), vol. 3, pp. 2149–2154. IEEE (2004)

31. Kschischang, F.R., Frey, B.J., Loeliger, H.A.: Factor graphs and the sum-product algorithm. IEEE Trans. Inf. Theory **47**(2), 498–519 (2001)

32. Lafferty, J.D., McCallum, A., Pereira, F.C.: Conditional random fields: probabilistic models for segmenting and labeling sequence data. In: ICML (2001)

33. Lang, A.H., Vora, S., Caesar, H., Zhou, L., Yang, J., Beijbom, O.: Pointpillars: fast encoders for object detection from point clouds. In: CVPR (2019)

34. Li, B., Zhang, T., Xia, T.: Vehicle detection from 3D lidar using fully convolutional network. In: RSS (2016)

35. Li, C.L., Zaheer, M., Zhang, Y., Poczos, B., Salakhutdinov, R.: Point cloud gan. arXiv preprint arXiv:1810.05795 (2018)

36. Li, Y., Bu, R., Sun, M., Wu, W., Di, X., Chen, B.: Pointcnn: convolution on $\mathcal{X}$-transformed points. In: NIPS (2018)

37. Li, Y., Wen, C., Juefei-Xu, F., Feng, C.: Fooling lidar perception via adversarial trajectory perturbation. In: Proceedings of the IEEE/CVF International Conference on Computer Vision, pp. 7898–7907 (2021)

38. Liao, Y., Xie, J., Geiger, A.: KITTI-360: a novel dataset and benchmarks for urban scene understanding in 2D and 3D. arXiv preprint arXiv:2109.13410 (2021)

39. Lin, Z., et al.: A structured self-attentive sentence embedding. In: ICLR (2017)

40. Liu, R., et al.: An intriguing failing of convolutional neural networks and the coordconv solution. Adv. Neural Inf. Process. Syst. **31** (2018)

41. Liu, Z., Tang, H., Lin, Y., Han, S.: Point-voxel CNN for efficient 3D deep learning. CoRR abs/1907.03739 (2019)

42. Liu, Z., Tang, H., Zhao, S., Shao, K., Han, S.: Pvnas: 3D neural architecture search with point-voxel convolution. IEEE Trans. Pattern Anal. Mach. Intell. (2021)

43. Luo, S., Hu, W.: Diffusion probabilistic models for 3D point cloud generation. In: Proceedings of the IEEE/CVF Conference on Computer Vision and Pattern Recognition (CVPR) (2021)

44. Manivasagam, S., et al.: Lidarsim: realistic lidar simulation by leveraging the real world. In: Proceedings of the IEEE/CVF Conference on Computer Vision and Pattern Recognition, pp. 11167–11176 (2020)

45. Mao, J., Wang, X., Li, H.: Interpolated convolutional networks for 3D point cloud understanding. In: ICCV (2019)

46. Milioto, A., Vizzo, I., Behley, J., Stachniss, C.: Rangenet++: fast and accurate lidar semantic segmentation. In: 2019 IEEE/RSJ International Conference on Intelligent Robots and Systems (IROS), pp. 4213–4220. IEEE (2019)

47. Nakashima, K., Kurazume, R.: Learning to drop points for lidar scan synthesis. In: 2021 IEEE/RSJ International Conference on Intelligent Robots and Systems (IROS), pp. 222–229. IEEE (2021)

48. Qi, C.R., Su, H., Mo, K., Guibas, L.J.: Pointnet: deep learning on point sets for 3D classification and segmentation. In: CVPR (2017)

49. Qi, C.R., Su, H., Nießner, M., Dai, A., Yan, M., Guibas, L.: Volumetric and multiview cnns for object classification on 3D data. In: CVPR (2016)

50. Qi, C.R., Yi, L., Su, H., Guibas, L.J.: Pointnet++: deep hierarchical feature learning on point sets in a metric space. In: NeurIPS (2017)
51. Ronneberger, O., Fischer, P., Brox, T.: U-Net: convolutional networks for biomedical image segmentation. In: Navab, N., Hornegger, J., Wells, W.M., Frangi, A.F. (eds.) MICCAI 2015. LNCS, vol. 9351, pp. 234–241. Springer, Cham (2015). https://doi.org/10.1007/978-3-319-24574-4_28
52. Sallab, A.E., Sobh, I., Zahran, M., Essam, N.: Lidar sensor modeling and data augmentation with gans for autonomous driving. arXiv preprint arXiv:1905.07290 (2019)
53. Sauer, A., Chitta, K., Müller, J., Geiger, A.: Projected gans converge faster. In: Advances in Neural Information Processing Systems (NeurIPS) (2021)
54. Schubert, S., Neubert, P., Pöschmann, J., Protzel, P.: Circular convolutional neural networks for panoramic images and laser data. In: 2019 IEEE Intelligent Vehicles Symposium (IV), pp. 653–660 (2019)
55. Shu, D.W., Park, S.W., Kwon, J.: 3D point cloud generative adversarial network based on tree structured graph convolutions. In: Proceedings of the IEEE International Conference on Computer Vision, pp. 3859–3868 (2019)
56. Simonovsky, M., Komodakis, N.: Dynamic edge-conditioned filters in convolutional neural networks on graphs. In: CVPR (2017)
57. Sobczak, Ł, Filus, K., Domański, A., Domańska, J.: Lidar point cloud generation for slam algorithm evaluation. Sensors 21(10), 3313 (2021)
58. Song, Y., Ermon, S.: Generative modeling by estimating gradients of the data distribution. Adv. Neural Inf. Process. Syst. 32, 11895–11907 (2019)
59. Song, Y., Ermon, S.: Improved techniques for training score-based generative models. In: Advances in Neural Information Processing Systems (NeurIPS) (2020)
60. Song, Y., Garg, S., Shi, J., Ermon, S.: Sliced score matching: a scalable approach to density and score estimation. arXiv preprint arXiv:1905.07088 (2019)
61. Song, Y., Sohl-Dickstein, J., Kingma, D.P., Kumar, A., Ermon, S., Poole, B.: Score-based generative modeling through stochastic differential equations. In: 9th International Conference on Learning Representations (ICLR) (2021)
62. Su, H., et al.: Splatnet: sparse lattice networks for point cloud processing. In: CVPR (2018)
63. Su, H., Maji, S., Kalogerakis, E., Learned-Miller, E.G.: Multi-view convolutional neural networks for 3D shape recognition. In: ICCV (2015)
64. Sun, Y., Wang, Y., Liu, Z., Siegel, J.E., Sarma, S.E.: Pointgrow: autoregressively learned point cloud generation with self-attention. arXiv preprint arXiv:1810.05591 (2018)
65. Thomas, H., Qi, C.R., Deschaud, J.E., Marcotegui, B., Goulette, F., Guibas, L.J.: Kpconv: flexible and deformable convolution for point clouds. In: ICCV (2019)
66. Valsesia, D., Fracastoro, G., Magli, E.: Learning localized generative models for 3D point clouds via graph convolution (2018)
67. Vincent, P.: A connection between score matching and denoising autoencoders. Neural Comput. 23(7), 1661–1674 (2011)
68. Wang, C., Samari, B., Siddiqi, K.: Local spectral graph convolution for point set feature learning. In: Ferrari, V., Hebert, M., Sminchisescu, C., Weiss, Y. (eds.) ECCV 2018. LNCS, vol. 11208, pp. 56–71. Springer, Cham (2018). https://doi.org/10.1007/978-3-030-01225-0_4
69. Wang, S., Suo, S., Ma, W.C., Pokrovsky, A., Urtasun, R.: Deep parametric continuous convolutional neural networks. In: CVPR (2018)

70. Wang, T.H., Amini, A., Schwarting, W., Gilitschenski, I., Karaman, S., Rus, D.: Learning interactive driving policies via data-driven simulation. arXiv preprint arXiv:2111.12137 (2021)

71. Wang, Y., Sun, Y., Liu, Z., Sarma, S.E., Bronstein, M.M., Solomon, J.M.: Dynamic graph cnn for learning on point clouds. TOG **38**, 1–12 (2019)

72. Welling, M., Teh, Y.W.: Bayesian learning via stochastic gradient langevin dynamics. In: Proceedings of the 28th International Conference on Machine Learning (ICML-2011), pp. 681–688 (2011)

73. Wu, B., Wan, A., Yue, X., Keutzer, K.: Squeezeseg: convolutional neural nets with recurrent CRF for real-time road-object segmentation from 3d lidar point cloud. CoRR abs/1710.07368 (2017)

74. Wu, W., Qi, Z., Fuxin, L.: Pointconv: deep convolutional networks on 3D point clouds. In: CVPR (2019)

75. Xiao, A., Huang, J., Guan, D., Zhan, F., Lu, S.: Synlidar: learning from synthetic lidar sequential point cloud for semantic segmentation. arXiv preprint arXiv:2107.05399 (2021)

76. Xu, Y., Fan, T., Xu, M., Zeng, L., Qiao, Yu.: SpiderCNN: deep learning on point sets with parameterized convolutional filters. In: Ferrari, V., Hebert, M., Sminchisescu, C., Weiss, Y. (eds.) ECCV 2018. LNCS, vol. 11212, pp. 90–105. Springer, Cham (2018). https://doi.org/10.1007/978-3-030-01237-3_6

77. Yang, B., Luo, W., Urtasun, R.: Pixor: real-time 3D object detection from point clouds. In: Proceedings of the IEEE Conference on Computer Vision and Pattern Recognition, pp. 7652–7660 (2018)

78. Yang, G., Huang, X., Hao, Z., Liu, M.Y., Belongie, S., Hariharan, B.: Pointflow: 3D point cloud generation with continuous normalizing flows. In: Proceedings of the IEEE International Conference on Computer Vision, pp. 4541–4550 (2019)

79. Yang, M., Dai, B., Dai, H., Schuurmans, D.: Energy-based processes for exchangeable data. In: International Conference on Machine Learning, pp. 10681–10692. PMLR (2020)

80. Yu, L., Li, X., Fu, C.W., Cohen-Or, D., Heng, P.A.: Pu-net: point cloud upsampling network. In: CVPR (2018)

81. Yuan, Y., Wang, J.: Ocnet: object context network for scene parsing. arXiv:1809.00916 (2018)

82. Zamorski, M., Zieba, M., Nowak, R., Stokowiec, W., Trzcinski, T.: Adversarial autoencoders for generating 3D point clouds, vol. 2. arXiv preprint arXiv:1811.07605 (2018)

83. Zamorski, M., Zieba, M., Nowak, R., Stokowiec, W., Trzciński, T.: Adversarial autoencoders for generating 3D point clouds. arXiv preprint arXiv:1811.07605 (2018)

84. Zhang, J., Singh, S.: Loam: lidar odometry and mapping in real-time. In: Robotics: Science and Systems, Berkeley, CA, vol. 2, pp. 1–9 (2014)

85. Zhao, H., Jiang, L., Fu, C.W., Jia, J.: PointWeb: enhancing local neighborhood features for point cloud processing. In: CVPR (2019)

# RFNet-4D: Joint Object Reconstruction and Flow Estimation from 4D Point Clouds

Tuan-Anh Vu[1](✉)[iD], Duc Thanh Nguyen[2][iD], Binh-Son Hua[3][iD],
Quang-Hieu Pham[4][iD], and Sai-Kit Yeung[1][iD]

[1] Hong Kong University of Science and Technology, Hong Kong, China
tavu@connect.ust.hk
[2] Deakin University, Geelong, Australia
[3] VinAI Research, Hanoi, Vietnam
[4] Woven Planet North America, Level 5, Palo Alto, CA, USA

**Abstract.** Object reconstruction from 3D point clouds has achieved impressive progress in the computer vision and computer graphics research field. However, reconstruction from time-varying point clouds (a.k.a. 4D point clouds) is generally overlooked. In this paper, we propose a new network architecture, namely RFNet-4D, that jointly reconstruct objects and their motion flows from 4D point clouds. The key insight is that simultaneously performing both tasks via learning spatial and temporal features from a sequence of point clouds can leverage individual tasks, leading to improved overall performance. To prove this ability, we design a temporal vector field learning module using unsupervised learning approach for flow estimation, leveraged by supervised learning of spatial structures for object reconstruction. Extensive experiments and analyses on benchmark dataset validated the effectiveness and efficiency of our method. As shown in experimental results, our method achieves state-of-the-art performance on both flow estimation and object reconstruction while performing much faster than existing methods in both training and inference. Our code and data are available at https://github.com/hkust-vgd/RFNet-4D.

**Keywords:** Dynamic point clouds · 4D reconstruction · Flow estimation

## 1 Introduction

Literature has shown several breakthroughs in deep learning for reconstruction of 3D models from point clouds. Recently, the research community has seen great successes in neural representations using implicit fields [5,27,28,32], which pave an effective way on how 3D data can be represented by neural networks. Unlike traditional representations that are often realised in discrete forms (e.g., discrete grids of pixels in image representation, discrete grids of voxels in 3D

© The Author(s), under exclusive license to Springer Nature Switzerland AG 2022
S. Avidan et al. (Eds.): ECCV 2022, LNCS 13683, pp. 36–52, 2022.
https://doi.org/10.1007/978-3-031-20050-2_3

object representation), the neural implicit representation parameterises a signal as a continuous function via a neural network. This function maps a signal from its original domain, which can be queried at any resolution, to an output domain that captures some properties of the query. Most existing methods focus on neural representation of 3D data in static conditions. However, in reality, real-world objects exist in a dynamic environment that changes over time and space, and thus cannot be well modelled using implicit representations applied to static shapes. Approaches for 4D reconstruction (i.e., reconstruction of a 3D object over time) have been explored but they often need expensive multi-view settings [7, 22, 29, 30]. These settings rely on a template model (of the object) with fixed topology [1, 18, 40, 47], or require smooth spatio-temporal input [33, 42], and thus limiting their applicability in practice.

To enable object reconstruction directly from 4D data without predefined templates, OFlow [31], a pioneering method for 4D reconstruction, was developed to calculate motion fields of 3D points in a 3D point cloud in space and time to implicitly represent trajectories of all the points in dense correspondences between occupancy fields. To learn the motion fields in both space and time domain, OFlow made use of a spatial encoder to learn the spatial structure of the input point cloud and a temporal encoder to learn the temporal changes of the point cloud in time. Despite impressive reconstruction results, this paradigm has a number of drawbacks. First, its spatial encoder does not take geometric attributes from numerous frames into consideration, impairing the capacity to precisely reconstruct geometric surfaces. Neither does its temporal encoder take into account temporal correspondences, which are critical for accurately capturing temporal dynamics. Second, errors in prediction of temporal continuity and reconstructed geometries are accumulated by integral of estimated instantaneous findings. Third, OFlow is trained using supervised learning. This requires correspondence labelling for all 3D points across frames in training data, leading to high labelling cost and low scalability. Fourth, the method exhibits low computational efficiency in both training and inference phase. This is due to expensive computations required to sequentially determine trajectories of 3D points throughout time by solving complex ordinary differential equations.

To address the aforementioned challenges, we propose a network architecture, namely RFNet-4D, for 4D reconstruction and flow estimation of dynamic point clouds. Our key idea is to jointly perform two tasks: 4D reconstruction and flow estimation with an intention that each task can leverage the other one to improve the overall performance. Specifically, our network takes a sequence of 3D point clouds of an object over time as input, then encodes the point clouds into spatio-temporal representations using a compositional encoder. These spatio-temporal representations are formed inclusively. In particular, the spatio-temporal representation of a point cloud at a time step is calculated from the spatial layout of points in that point cloud and the temporal changes of the points in the point cloud throughout time. The spatio-temporal representations are then decoded by a joint decoder which jointly reconstructs the object and predicts a motion vector for each point in the reconstructed object throughout

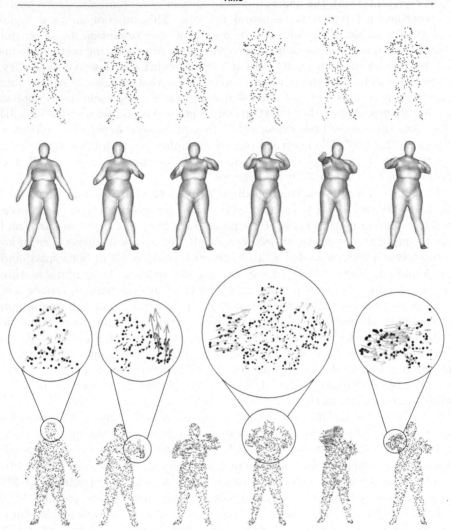

**Fig. 1. Summary of our method.** Given a sequence of time-varying 3D point clouds (first row), we jointly reconstruct corresponding 3D geometric shapes (second row) and estimate their motion fields for every point cloud (third row).

time. The entire network can be trained end-to-end, where the reconstruction and flow estimation task are trained with supervised and unsupervised learning, respectively. Our method also allows fast computations of spatial and temporal features as those computations can be performed in parallel. This is another advantage of our method, compared with OFlow which estimates the motion flows sequentially and thus often experiences time lags. We illustrate several results of our method in Fig. 1. In summary, the contributions of our work are as follows:

- RFNet-4D: a network architecture for joint object reconstruction and flow estimation from a sequence of time-varying 3D point clouds.
- A joint learning method for training the proposed RFNet-4D using both supervised and unsupervised learning, and in both forward and backward time direction. To the best of our knowledge, this learning mechanism is novel, and its benefit is verified throughout experiments.
- Extensive experiments and analyses that prove the effectiveness and efficiency of our proposed method on two tasks: 4D reconstruction and flow estimation.

## 2   Related Work

*3D Reconstruction.* Numerous studies have been conducted with the goal of reconstructing a continuous surface from a variety of input, including RGB images [19,39,46], point clouds [20]. Thanks to advances in deep learning, recent 3D object reconstruction approaches have resulted in significant progress. Early attempts represent reconstructed objects in regular grid of 3D voxels [11,45] or point clouds [10,35]. However, those representations cannot well capture surface details and suffer from low resolutions. Alternatively, there are methods, e.g., [17,23,44] reconstructing triangular meshes (including vertices and faces) of 3D objects. In these methods, an initial template with fixed topology is employed and the reconstruction is performed using regression. For surface representation, several methods focus on learning an implicit field function that allows more variable topology in reconstructed objects [4,6,9,16].

To extend the ability of implicit functions on representations other than traditional forms (i.e., voxels, points, meshes), occupancy maps [27,34] and distance fields [4,32] are proposed. An occupancy map of a 3D point cloud contains indicators that indicate being foreground of points in the 3D space. A distance field provides the distance from every point to its nearest surface. Since the implicit function models objects in a continuous manner, more information is preserved and more complicated shapes can be well described. For instance, Occupancy Network in [27] described a 3D object using continuous indicator functions that indicate which sub-sets of 3D space the object occupies, and an iso-surface retrieved by employing the Marching Cube algorithm [25].

*4D Reconstruction.* Despite being less studied compared with 3D reconstruction, literature has also shown recent attentions of the research community to 4D reconstruction, i.e., reconstruction of a sequence of 3D objects from time-varying point clouds [22,29,30]. In this section, we limit our review to only learning-based 4D reconstruction methods.

A crucial component in 4D reconstruction is motion capture and modelling. Niemeyer *et al.* [31] introduced a learning-based framework that calculates the integral of a motion field specified in space and time to implicitly represent the trajectory of a 3D point to generate dense correspondences between occupancy fields. Jiang *et al.* [15] proposed a compositional representation for 4D capture, i.e., a deformable representation that encloses a 3D shape and velocity of its 3D points over time. Such representation was composed of encoder-decoder architectures. Specifically, to simulate the motion in time-varying 3D data, a neural Ordinary Differential Equation was trained to update the starting state of motion based on a learnt motion representation, and a decoder was used to reconstruct a 3D model at each time step using a shape representation and the updated state. They also introduced an Identity Exchange Training technique to motivate their system to learn how to decouple each encoder-decoder successfully. Tang *et al.* [38] proposed a pipeline for determining the temporal evolution of the 3D shape of the human body using spatially continuous transformation functions between cross-frame occupancy fields. By explicitly learning continuous displacement motion fields from spatio-temporal shape representations, the pipeline aims to construct dense correspondences between projected occupancy fields at different time steps.

**Motion Transfer.** Traditional techniques for 3D pose transfer often use discrete deformation transfers. An example of mesh deformation is described in [43], where spatially adaptable instance normalisation [14] was used to modify 3D meshes. However, this method requires a dense triangular mesh of an object to be given in advance, while there is specific mechanism to depict continuous flows in both spatial and temporal domain.

3D motion transfer is another technique for creating 3D objects from a pair of source and target object sequences. It operates by causing the target object sequence to undergo the same temporal deformation in the source object sequence. This technique can be applied to model continuous transformation of an object's pose over time. For instance, OFlow [31] transmitted motion across sequences of source and target human models by applying motion field-based representations to the targets in a predetermined manner. However, since OFlow does not explicitly differentiate the representations of pose and shape, we found that it only produces reasonable motion transfer results when the identities and initial poses of both the source and target objects are similar.

**Shape Correspondence Modelling.** Modelling of point-to-point correspondences between two 3D shapes is a well-studied topic in computer vision and computer graphics [2]. The goal of modelling time-varying occupancy fields is strongly related to the goal of field-based deformation [26], which we have previously discussed. However, most of these works describe the motion fields only on object surfaces. To better describe the motion flow, we argue to model the correspondences between 3D shapes in the entire 3D space.

When modelling the growth of a signed distance field, Miroslava *et al.* [37] chose to implicitly provide the correspondences rather than explicitly yielding them. They optimised an energy function capturing the similarity between the Laplacian eigenfunction representations of the input and the target shape. However, we found that their method is sensitive to noise, probably due to lack of capability of providing correspondences accurately from signed distance fields.

In contrast, we learn the rich correspondences between time-varying occupancy fields based on a intuitive insight, that the occupancy values of points are always invariant during the temporal evolution of the occupation field.

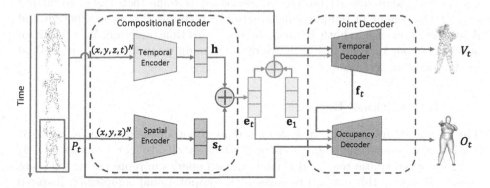

**Fig. 2. Overview of our method.** An input 3D point cloud sequence is fed into a spatio-temporal encoder to extract spatio-temporal representations. The representations are then passed via two distinct decoders, occupancy and motion decoders. In each data frame, the occupancy decoder aims to predict an occupancy field of the point cloud in the frame. Simultaneously, the motion decoder predicts the correspondences between points in the current frame and its preceding frame.

## 3   Our Method: RFNet-4D

### 3.1   Overview

Our network takes as input a sequence of sparse, incomplete, and noisy 3D point clouds $\{P_t | t = 1, ..., T\}$ where $T$ is the length of the sequence, and each point cloud $P_t$ is a set of 3D locations. Our aim is to simultaneously perform the following tasks:

- Reconstruct a sequence of occupancy maps $\{O_t | t = 1, ..., T\}$ where each $O_t$ is an occupancy map of a point cloud $P_t$, i.e., $O_t(\mathbf{p}) = 1$ if $\mathbf{p}$ is a 3D point on the reconstructed surface of $P_t$, and $O_t(\mathbf{p}) = 0$, otherwise;
- Estimate a sequence of vector fields $\{V_t | t = 1, ..., T\}$ where each $V_t$ is a 3D vector field capturing motion flows of reconstructed points of $P_t$, i.e., $V_t(\mathbf{p}) \in \mathbb{R}^3$ represents the motion flow of a reconstructed point $\mathbf{p}$ at time step $t$ given a point cloud $P_t$.

Both tasks benefit by a compositional encoder that learns spatio-temporal representations from time-varying point clouds. The temporal features contained in these spatio-temporal representations capture holistic motion information and are computed once on the entire input point cloud sequence. This allows fast computations in following operations as spatio-temporal data can be processed at any arbitrary frame. The spatio-temporal representations are processed by a joint decoder including two decoders, each of which extracts relevant information for its downstream task (i.e., reconstruction and flow estimation). These decoders do not operate independently but co-operate closely to fulfill their tasks. To further exploit the benefit of temporal information, we couple the reconstruction and flow estimation task in both forward and backward time direction. We present an overview of our method in Fig. 2. We describe main components of our method in the following sections.

## 3.2   Compositional Encoder

The compositional encoder includes a temporal encoder and a spatial encoder. There exist several manners to encode 4D point clouds. For instance, Liu *et al.* [24] applied spatio-temporal neighbourhood queries in representing 4D point clouds. However, this method requires high computational complexity. Inspired by the success and efficiency of the point cloud representation used in OFlow [31] and LPDC [38], we adopt the parallel ResNet [13] variant of PointNet [36] for both the spatial and temporal encoder (see Fig. 3). These encoders are basically similar in their architectures. The difference between them is that while the spatial encoder processes each point cloud $P_t$ individually at a time $t$ to generate a representation $\mathbf{s}_t$, the temporal encoder acquires the whole point cloud sequence to calculate a holistic temporal representation $\mathbf{h}$ once. These spatial and temporal representations are finally concatenated to form a spatio-temporal representation $\mathbf{e}_t$ that encodes the geometric information of a point cloud $P_t$ in space with regard to its temporal changes (see Fig. 2). Our encoders share similar structures with the encoders in LPDC [38]. However, instead of using a complicated fusion method, we empirically found that a simple concatenation of the spatial and temporal features is good enough to effectively create spatio-temporal representations.

Since $\mathbf{h}$ is computed once on the entire input point cloud sequence, $\mathbf{e}_t$ can be extracted at any arbitrary time step $t$ without time lags, as opposed to methods processing point clouds sequentially, e.g., OFlow [31]. Thanks to this advantage, the processing time RFNet-4D can be optimised by calculating spatio-temporal representations $\mathbf{e}_t$ in parallel.

## 3.3   Joint Decoder

The joint decoder takes a spatio-temporal representation $\mathbf{e}_t$ and the original point cloud sequence as input, then passes this input into two decoders (temporal decoder and occupancy decoder) to perform flow estimation and object reconstruction. Our temporal decoder and occupancy decoder are built upon the architecture from LPDC [38]. However, instead of decoupling the decoders as in [38], we hypothesized that jointly addressing two tasks by sharing information between corresponding decoders can leverage individual tasks. As a consequence, the close collaboration of flow estimation and object reconstruction allows some relaxation in the supervision need.

The temporal decoder operates as follows (see Fig. 4(a)). We first extract a spatio-temporal representation $e_1$ for the first point cloud $P_1$ from the input sequence, using the compositional encoder. For each following point cloud $P_t$, we compute its spatio-temporal representation $e_t$, then concatenate $e_t$ with $e_1$. This concatenated representation captures temporal changes of $P_t$ in relative to $P_1$, and is again concatenated with all points in $P_t$ to be processed by a series of five ResNet residual blocks [13]. Each block consists of two fully connected layers with skip connections and ReLU activation functions [12]. The outcome of these blocks is a feature map, namely $f_t$. This feature map is finally passed to a fully connected layer, returning a motion field $V_t$ describing the motion of $P_t$.

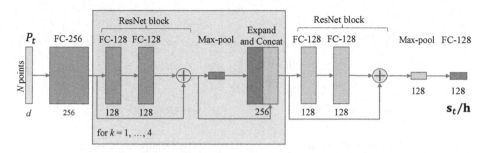

**Fig. 3. Architecture of the spatial/temporal encoder.** The input dimension $d$ is set accordingly to a corresponding encoder. In particular, $d = 3$ (i.e., $(x, y, z)$-coordinates) for the spatial encoder and $d = 4$ (i.e., $(x, y, z)$-coordinates and time variable) for the temporal encoder. $\oplus$ indicates a concatenation operation. Output of the spatial and temporal encoder are $s_t$ and $h$, respectively.

The occupancy decoder is slightly different from the temporal decoder (see Fig. 4(b)). Also different from all existing methods, our occupancy decoder works collaboratively with the temporal decoder. Particularly, input for the occupancy decoder to reconstruct the object at time step $t$ includes a point cloud $P_t$, a spatio-temporal representation $e_t$ (obtained from the compositional encoder), and a flow feature map $f_t$ (returned by the temporal decoder). The point cloud $P_t$ is first processed by a fully connected layer to extract a feature map. Similarly, the spatio-temporal representation $e_t$ is fed to two different fully connected layers to obtain feature maps $\beta$ and $\gamma$. These output feature maps (from $P_t$ and $e_t$) are passed to a series of five residual blocks, similar to those used in the temporal decoder. Following ONet [27], we apply Conditional Batch Normalization (CBN) introduced in [8,41] to $\beta$ and $\gamma$. Finally, the flow feature map $f_t$ is injected into the occupancy decoder to produce an occupancy map $O_t(\mathbf{p})$, where $O_t(\mathbf{p}) = 1$ if the point $\mathbf{p}$ belongs to the object at time step $t$, and $O_t(\mathbf{p}) = 0$ otherwise.

### 3.4   Joint Learning

Our RFNet-4D is trained by jointly performing two optimisation processes: unsupervision for flow estimation and supervision for object reconstruction. Existing works train flow estimation using supervised learning [10,15,27,31,38], requiring fully annotated point correspondences in training data. In this paper, we propose to learn point correspondences in a point cloud sequence via an unsupervised manner, thus opening ways to new applications and more training data. Specifically, let $V_t$ be a motion field (i.e., a set of 3D vectors) at $P_t$, $V_t$ is estimated using the temporal decoder. We measure the correspondences between points in $P_t$ and $P_{t+1}$ via the Chamfer distance between $P_{t+1}$ and a translated version of $P_t$ made by $V_t$ (i.e., $P_t + V_t$). We define our flow loss as follow,

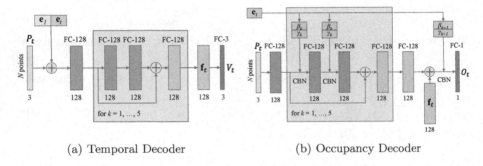

(a) Temporal Decoder          (b) Occupancy Decoder

**Fig. 4. Architecture of the temporal and occupancy decoder**; $\oplus$ indicates a concatenation operation. The temporal decoder returns both a motion field $V_t$ and a motion feature map $\mathbf{f}_t$, which is then inputted to the occupancy decoder.

$$\mathcal{L}_{flow} = \sum_t \max \left\{ \frac{1}{|P_t|} \sum_{\mathbf{p} \in P_t + V_t} \min_{\mathbf{p}' \in P_{t+1}} \|\mathbf{p} - \mathbf{p}'\|_2, \right.$$
$$\left. \frac{1}{|P_{t+1}|} \sum_{\mathbf{p}' \in P_{t+1}} \min_{\mathbf{p} \in P_t + V_t} \|\mathbf{p}' - \mathbf{p}\|_2 \right\} \tag{1}$$

Reconstruction task can be trained using supervised approach. We use conventional binary cross entropy (BCE) loss to measure the difference between predicted occupancy maps and corresponding ground truth maps. Specifically, we define our reconstruction loss as follow,

$$\mathcal{L}_{reconstruction} = \sum_t \sum_{\mathbf{p} \in P_t} \mathcal{L}_{BCE} \left( O_i(\mathbf{p}), O_i^{gt}(\mathbf{p}) \right) \tag{2}$$

where $O_i^{gt}$ represents the ground truth occupancy map of the point cloud $P_t$.

Finally, we use the following loss to train the entire RFNet-4D,

$$\mathcal{L} = \mathcal{L}_{flow} + \lambda\mathcal{L}_{reconstruction} \tag{3}$$

where $\lambda$ is a hyper-parameter.

To further exploit the benefit of temporal information, we train our RFNet-4D in both forward and backward direction in time. Particularly, we calculate the holistic temporal representation $\mathbf{h}$ for two sequences $\{P_1, ..., P_T\}$ (forward) and $\{P_T, ..., P_1\}$ (backward), and use $\mathbf{h}$ to encode the spatio-temporal representations $\mathbf{e}_t$ in both forward and backward time direction. As shown in our experiments, this training strategy improves the performance of our network in both object reconstruction and flow estimation task.

## 4   Experiments

### 4.1   Experimental Setup

***Dataset.*** We trained and evaluated our method on the pre-processed data of D-FAUST dataset [3], a benchmark dataset commonly used in state-of-the-art. D-FAUST dataset contains raw-scanned and registered meshes for 129 sequences of 10 human subjects (5 females and 5 males) with various motions such as "shake hips", "running on spot", or "one leg jump". We followed the train/test split used in [31]. Specifically, we divided all the sequences in D-FAUST dataset into three sets: training set (105 sequences), validation set (6 sequences), and test set (21 sequences). Since each sequence is relatively long (with more than 1,250 time steps) and in order to increase the size of the dataset, we sub-sampled each sequence into smaller sub-sequences of 17 to 50 time steps.

***Implementation Details.*** We implemented our method in Pytorch. We adopted Adam optimizer [21] where the learning rate $\gamma$ was set to $10^{-4}$ and decay was set to 5,000 iterations. We empirically set $\lambda$ to 0.1 in our experiments. Our RFNet-4D was trained with a batch size of 16, and on a single NVIDIA RTX 3090 GPU. We evaluated all the variants of our network (see Ablation study) on the validation set for every 2,000 iterations during the training process, and used the best model of each variant on the validation set for evaluation of the variant on the test set. The training process was completed once there were no further improvements achieved. For calculating the losses during training, we randomly sampled a fixed number of 512 points in 3D space and time interval for reconstruction loss, and uniformly sampled trajectories of 100 points for flow estimation loss. More details can be found in our supplied code.

We also followed the evaluation setup used in [31]. Specifically, for each evaluation, we carried out two case studies: seen individuals but unseen motions (i.e., test subjects were included in the training data but their motions were not given in the training set), and unseen individuals but seen motions (i.e., test subjects were found only in the test data but their motions were seen in the training set).

*Evaluation Metrics.* To measure the performance of 4D reconstruction, we applied the common volumetric IoU (Intersection over Union) and the Chamfer distance reflecting the coincidence of reconstructed data and ground-truth data. To evaluate flow estimation, we used $\ell_2$-distance to measure the correspondences between estimated flows and ground-truth flows.

## 4.2 Results

We report the performance of our RFNet-4D in two case studies in Table 1. As shown in experimental results, our method performed better in the seen individuals case study, for both object reconstruction and flow estimation. However, our method works consistently, and the differences in all performance metrics between the two case studies are marginal. For instance, the IoU difference between the two case studies is less than 4%, the differences in Chamfer distance and $\ell_2$ correspondence between these case studies are about $0.009 \times 10^{-3}$ and $0.03 \times 10^{-2}$ respectively.

**Table 1. Quantitative evaluation** of our method and existing methods on seen and unseen individuals test splits, in both reconstruction and flow estimation task. We report the volumetric IoU (higher is better), Chamfer distance (lower is better) and correspondence $\ell_2$ distance (lower is better). The notation '–' means no results, e.g., PSDN-4D does not perform reconstruction, ONet-4D and 4DCR do not predict point correspondences across time. For each evaluation metric, best performance is highlighted.

| Methods | Seen individuals Unseen motions | | | Unseen lSeen motions | | |
|---|---|---|---|---|---|---|
| | IoU↑ | Chamfer↓($\times10^{-3}$) | Corres.↓($\times10^{-2}$) | IoU↑ | Chamfer↓($\times10^{-3}$) | Corres.↓($\times10^{-2}$) |
| PSGN-4D [10] | – | 0.6189 | 1.1083 | – | 0.6877 | 1.3289 |
| ONet-4D [27] | 0.7712 | 0.5921 | – | 0.6827 | 0.7007 | – |
| OFlow [31] | 0.8172 | 0.1773 | 0.8699 | 0.7361 | 0.2741 | 1.0842 |
| LPDC [38] | 0.8511 | 0.1526 | **0.7803** | 0.7619 | 0.2188 | 0.9872 |
| 4DCR [15] | 0.8171 | 0.1667 | – | 0.6973 | 0.2220 | – |
| RFNet-4D | **0.8547** | **0.1504** | 0.8831 | **0.8157** | **0.1594** | **0.9155** |

In addition to evaluation of our method, we also compared it with existing methods including PSGN-4D [10], ONet-4D [27], OFlow [31], LPDC [38], and 4DCR [15]. For the previous works, we used their published pre-trained models which had also been trained on the same training data from D-FAUST dataset. Note that we also re-trained the previous models using their released source code. However, we were not able to achieve the same results as reported in their papers. We show comparison results in Table 1. It can be seen that RFNet-4D outperforms all existing works in 4D reconstruction using both IoU and Chamfer distance metrics. For flow estimation, RFNet-4D achieves comparable performance with state-of-the-art on seen individuals, e.g., there is a slight difference (about $0.1 \times 10^{-2}$) in $\ell_2$-distance from the first ranked method (i.e.,

LPDC). However, our RFNet-4D is trained using unsupervised fashion requiring no labels for learning point correspondences, while existing works follow supervised paradigm. Furthermore, as shown in Table 1, our method stands first in flow estimation on unseen individuals sequences, showing its robustness to novel object shapes.

We visualise several results of our methods and existing ones in Fig. 5. To illustrate these results, we apply the Multiresolution IsoSurface Extraction (MISE) algorithm [27] and Marching Cubes algorithm [25] on reconstructed occupancy maps to generate surface meshes. Compared with existing methods, our RFNet-4D achieves higher reconstruction quality with better geometry recovery, e.g., the reconstructed hands produced our method are more complete. In addition, by coupling both spatial and temporal information, the poses of body parts, e.g., the head, the lower arms, are well reserved by our method (in reference to corresponding ground truth meshes). The results also show that our method is better than existing works (e.g., OFlow, LPDC) in flow estimation, as clearly shown in the predicted flows in the two hands.

### 4.3   Ablation Studies

In this section, we present ablation studies to verify different aspects in the design of our model. In particular, we verified our joint learning of spatio-temporal representations for 4D point clouds reconstruction and flow estimation, compared with tackling these two tasks independently. We proved the improvement of learning flows in both forward and backward direction. We compared different distance metrics including the sliced Wasserstein distance (SWD) and the Hausdorff distance (HD), for the implementation of the flow loss in Eq. (1), and proved that our choice, i.e., the Chamfer distance, is the best. We experimented our model in both unsupervised and supervised fashion though it is intentionally designed for unsupervised learning, showing the flexibility our model.

We summarise results of our ablation studies in Table 2. Note that, in each ablation study, only one change was applied at a time while other settings remained unchanged. For settings using either temporal or spatial information (see the first two rows in Table 2), only the corresponding encoder and decoder (i.e., spatial/temporal encoder and decoder) were activated while the counterpart encoder and decoder were frozen. These settings correspond to solving the flow estimation and reconstruction task separately. To experiment our RFNet-4D with supervised learning for flow estimation, we followed the settings used in OFlow [31]. In particular, we used ground-truth point correspondences from the training data and $\ell_2$ distance for the motion loss, i.e., replacing the Chamfer distance in Eq. (1) by $\ell_2$ distance. Note that, D-FAUST dataset is fully annotated with point correspondences and thus also supports supervised learning. When training our model in unsupervised manner, those point correspondences were not used. Experimental results in Table 2 clearly confirm the design of our RFNet-4D in both object reconstruction and flow estimation.

## 4.4 Complexity Analysis

In this section, we provide a complexity analysis on the memory footprint and computational efficiency of our RFNet-4D and several existing models including OFlow [31] and LPDC [38] (current state-of-the-art). In this experiment, we trained all the models with a batch size of 16, using a sequence of 17 time steps with consistent intervals. All the models were run on a single NVIDIA RTX 3090. We report the memory footprint, training and inference time in Table 3. For the training time, we computed the average of batch training time throughout the first 100 k iterations of training (seconds per iteration). For the inference time, we reported the average time required to infer using a batch size of 1 for 1k test sequences (seconds per sequence). As shown in Table 3, despite our model takes larger memory footprint for training, its training time is approximately 3.5 times and 1.6 times faster than that of OFlow and LPDC respectively. Similarly, our model performs 1.9 times and 4 times faster than OFlow and LPDC in inference. We found that OFlow take much longer time for training since OFlow makes use of an ODE-solver requiring intensive computations and gradually increasing the number of iterations to fulfill error tolerance.

**Table 2. Ablation studies** on of various settings of our method. For each evaluation metric, best performance is highlighted.

| Variant | IoU ↑ | Chamfer ($\times 10^{-3}$) ↓ | Corr. ($\times 10^{-2}$) ↓ |
|---|---|---|---|
| RFNet-4D (only temporal flows) | – | – | 1.5519 |
| RFNet-4D (only spatial points) | 0.7712 | 0.5921 | – |
| RFNet-4D (only FW motion) | 0.4988 | 2.4887 | 3.5868 |
| RFNet-4D (SWD loss) | 0.4305 | 4.4621 | 4.0711 |
| RFNet-4D (HD loss) | 0.7953 | 0.2103 | 1.3017 |
| RFNet-4D (supervised) | **0.8656** | **0.0927** | **0.8125** |
| RFNet-4D (unsupervised) | 0.8547 | 0.1504 | 0.8831 |

**Table 3. Space and time complexity** of our method and existing ones.

| Method | Memory | Training (sec/iter) | Inference (sec/seq) |
|---|---|---|---|
| OFlow [31] | 3.96 GB | 4.65 s | 0.95 s |
| LPDC [38] | 11.90 GB | 2.09 s | 0.44 s |
| RFNet-4D | 14.20 GB | 1.33 s | 0.24 s |

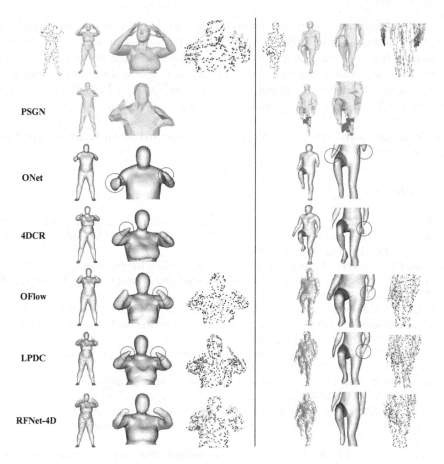

**Fig. 5. Qualitative evaluation** of our method and existing methods. The first row includes (from left to right): input point cloud, ground truth mesh of entire body, ground truth mesh of upper/lower body, and ground-truth flows (darker vectors show stronger motions). Each following row represents corresponding reconstruction and flow estimation results. Severe errors are highlighted.

## 5 Discussion and Conclusion

This paper proposes RFNet-4D, a network architecture for jointly reconstruction of objects and estimation of temporal flows from dynamic point clouds. The proposed network is built upon a compositional encoder effectively capturing informative spatio-temporal representations for 4D point clouds, and a joint learning paradigm leveraging sub-tasks to improve overall performance. We extensively evaluated our proposed RFNet-4D and compared it with existing works on benchmark dataset. Experimental results demonstrated the effectiveness and efficiency of our method in comparison with current state-of-the-art.

There is also room for future research. First, we found that existing 4D reconstruction methods often suffer from large displacements between data frames. Second, their reconstruction quality tends to drop over time due to accumulated errors. It is also worthwhile to study 4D reconstruction for different types of objects, and with more challenging input data types, e.g., LiDAR point clouds that are commonly used in autonomous driving applications.

**Acknowledgement.** This paper was partially supported by an internal grant from HKUST (R9429).

# References

1. Alldieck, T., Magnor, M., Xu, W., Theobalt, C., Pons-Moll, G.: Video based reconstruction of 3D people models. In: IEEE/CVF Conference on Computer Vision and Pattern Recognition (CVPR) (2018)
2. Biasotti, S., Cerri, A., Bronstein, A., Bronstein, M.: Recent trends, applications, and perspectives in 3D shape similarity assessment. Comput. Graph. Forum **35**, 87–119 (2016)
3. Bogo, F., Romero, J., Pons-Moll, G., Black, M.J.: Dynamic FAUST: registering human bodies in motion. In: IEEE/CVF Conference on Computer Vision and Pattern Recognition (CVPR) (2017)
4. Chabra, R., et al.: Deep local shapes: learning local SDF priors for detailed 3D reconstruction. In: Vedaldi, A., Bischof, H., Brox, T., Frahm, J.-M. (eds.) ECCV 2020. LNCS, vol. 12374, pp. 608–625. Springer, Cham (2020). https://doi.org/10. 1007/978-3-030-58526-6_36
5. Chen, Z., Zhang, H.: Learning implicit fields for generative shape modeling. In: IEEE/CVF Conference on Computer Vision and Pattern Recognition (CVPR) (2019)
6. Chibane, J., Alldieck, T., Pons-Moll, G.: Implicit functions in feature space for 3D shape reconstruction and completion. In: IEEE/CVF Conference on Computer Vision and Pattern Recognition (CVPR) (2020)
7. Coskun, H., Achilles, F., DiPietro, R., Navab, N., Tombari, F.: Long short-term memory kalman filters: Recurrent neural estimators for pose regularization. In: IEEE/CVF International Conference on Computer Vision (ICCV) (2017)
8. Dumoulin, V., et al.: Adversarially learned inference. In: International Conference on Learning Representations (ICLR) (2017)
9. Erler, P., Guerrero, P., Ohrhallinger, S., Mitra, N.J., Wimmer, M.: POINTS2SURF learning implicit surfaces from point clouds. In: Vedaldi, A., Bischof, H., Brox, T., Frahm, J.-M. (eds.) ECCV 2020. LNCS, vol. 12350, pp. 108–124. Springer, Cham (2020). https://doi.org/10.1007/978-3-030-58558-7_7
10. Fan, H., Su, H., Guibas, L.J.: A point set generation network for 3D object reconstruction from a single image. In: IEEE/CVF Conference on Computer Vision and Pattern Recognition (CVPR) (2017)
11. Girdhar, R., Fouhey, D.F., Rodriguez, M., Gupta, A.: Learning a predictable and generative vector representation for objects. In: Leibe, B., Matas, J., Sebe, N., Welling, M. (eds.) ECCV 2016. LNCS, vol. 9910, pp. 484–499. Springer, Cham (2016). https://doi.org/10.1007/978-3-319-46466-4_29
12. Glorot, X., Bordes, A., Bengio, Y.: Deep sparse rectifier neural networks. In: Proceedings of the Fourteenth International Conference on Artificial Intelligence and Statistics. Proceedings of Machine Learning Research, vol. 15 (2011)

13. He, K., Zhang, X., Ren, S., Sun, J.: Deep residual learning for image recognition. In: IEEE/CVF Conference on Computer Vision and Pattern Recognition (CVPR) (2016)
14. Huang, X., Belongie, S.J.: Arbitrary style transfer in real-time with adaptive instance normalization. In: IEEE/CVF International Conference on Computer Vision (ICCV) (2017)
15. Jiang, B., Zhang, Y., Wei, X., Xue, X., Fu, Y.: Learning compositional representation for 4D captures with neural ODE. In: IEEE/CVF Conference on Computer Vision and Pattern Recognition (CVPR) (2021)
16. Jiang, C.M., Sud, A., Makadia, A., Huang, J., Nießner, M., Funkhouser, T.: Local implicit grid representations for 3D scenes. In: IEEE/CVF Conference on Computer Vision and Pattern Recognition (CVPR) (2020)
17. Kanazawa, A., Tulsiani, S., Efros, A.A., Malik, J.: Learning category-specific mesh reconstruction from image collections. In: European Conference on Computer Vision (ECCV) (2018)
18. Kanazawa, A., Zhang, J.Y., Felsen, P., Malik, J.: Learning 3D human dynamics from video. In: IEEE/CVF Conference on Computer Vision and Pattern Recognition (CVPR) (2019)
19. Kato, H., Ushiku, Y., Harada, T.: Neural 3D mesh renderer. In: IEEE/CVF Conference on Computer Vision and Pattern Recognition (CVPR) (2018)
20. Kazhdan, M., Bolitho, M., Hoppe, H.: Poisson surface reconstruction. In: Symposium on Geometry Processing (2006)
21. Kingma, D.P., Ba, J.: Adam: a method for stochastic optimization. In: International Conference on Learning Representations (ICLR) (2015)
22. Leroy, V., Franco, J.S., Boyer, E.: Multi-view dynamic shape refinement using local temporal integration. In: IEEE/CVF International Conference on Computer Vision (ICCV) (2017)
23. Liao, Y., Donné, S., Geiger, A.: Deep marching cubes: learning explicit surface representations. In: IEEE/CVF Conference on Computer Vision and Pattern Recognition (CVPR) (2018)
24. Liu, X., Yan, M., Bohg, J.: MeteorNet: deep learning on dynamic 3D point cloud sequences. In: IEEE/CVF International Conference on Computer Vision (ICCV) (2019)
25. Lorensen, W.E., Cline, H.E.: Marching cubes: a high resolution 3D surface construction algorithm. In: SIGGRAPH Computer Graphics (1987)
26. Lüthi, M., Gerig, T., Jud, C., Vetter, T.: Gaussian process morphable models. IEEE Trans. Pattern Anal. Mach. Intell. **40**, 1860–1873 (2018)
27. Mescheder, L., Oechsle, M., Niemeyer, M., Nowozin, S., Geiger, A.: Occupancy networks: learning 3D reconstruction in function space. In: IEEE/CVF Conference on Computer Vision and Pattern Recognition (CVPR) (2019)
28. Michalkiewicz, M., Pontes, J.K., Jack, D., Baktashmotlagh, M., Eriksson, A.: Implicit surface representations as layers in neural networks. In: IEEE/CVF International Conference on Computer Vision (ICCV) (2019)
29. Mustafa, A., Kim, H., Guillemaut, J.Y., Hilton, A.: General dynamic scene reconstruction from multiple view video. In: IEEE/CVF International Conference on Computer Vision (ICCV) (2015)
30. Mustafa, A., Kim, H., Guillemaut, J.Y., Hilton, A.: Temporally coherent 4D reconstruction of complex dynamic scenes. In: IEEE/CVF Conference on Computer Vision and Pattern Recognition (CVPR) (2016)

31. Niemeyer, M., Mescheder, L.M., Oechsle, M., Geiger, A.: Occupancy flow: 4D reconstruction by learning particle dynamics. In: IEEE/CVF International Conference on Computer Vision (ICCV) (2019)
32. Park, J.J., Florence, P., Straub, J., Newcombe, R., Lovegrove, S.: Deepsdf: learning continuous signed distance functions for shape representation. In: IEEE/CVF Conference on Computer Vision and Pattern Recognition (CVPR) (2019)
33. Pekelny, Y., Gotsman, C.: Articulated object reconstruction and markerless motion capture from depth video. Comput. Graph. Forum **27**, 399–408 (2008)
34. Peng, S., Niemeyer, M., Mescheder, L., Pollefeys, M., Geiger, A.: Convolutional occupancy networks. In: Vedaldi, A., Bischof, H., Brox, T., Frahm, J.-M. (eds.) ECCV 2020. LNCS, vol. 12348, pp. 523–540. Springer, Cham (2020). https://doi.org/10.1007/978-3-030-58580-8_31
35. Qi, C.R., Liu, W., Wu, C., Su, H., Guibas, L.J.: Frustum pointnets for 3D object detection from RGB-D data. In: IEEE/CVF Conference on Computer Vision and Pattern Recognition (CVPR) (2018)
36. Qi, C.R., Su, H., Mo, K., Guibas, L.J.: PointNet: deep learning on point sets for 3D classification and segmentation. In: IEEE/CVF Conference on Computer Vision and Pattern Recognition (CVPR) (2017)
37. Slavcheva, M., Baust, M., Ilic, S.: Towards implicit correspondence in signed distance field evolution. In: IEEE/CVF International Conference on Computer Vision (ICCV) Workshops (2017)
38. Tang, J., Xu, D., Jia, K., Zhang, L.: Learning parallel dense correspondence from spatio-temporal descriptors for efficient and robust 4D reconstruction. In: IEEE/CVF Conference on Computer Vision and Pattern Recognition (CVPR) (2021)
39. Tatarchenko, M., Dosovitskiy, A., Brox, T.: Octree generating networks: efficient convolutional architectures for high-resolution 3D outputs. IEEE/CVF International Conference on Computer Vision (ICCV) (2017)
40. Tung, H.Y., Tung, H.W., Yumer, E., Fragkiadaki, K.: Self-supervised learning of motion capture. Adv. Neural Inf. Process. Syst. **30**, 1–11 (2017)
41. de Vries, H., Strub, F., Mary, J., Larochelle, H., Pietquin, O., Courville, A.C.: Modulating early visual processing by language. Adv. Neural Inf. Process. Syst. **30**, 1–11 (2017)
42. Wand, M., Jenke, P., Huang, Q., Bokeloh, M., Guibas, L., Schilling, A.: Reconstruction of deforming geometry from time-varying point clouds. In: Proceedings of the Fifth Eurographics Symposium on Geometry Processing (2007)
43. Wang, J., et al.: Neural pose transfer by spatially adaptive instance normalization. In: IEEE/CVF Conference on Computer Vision and Pattern Recognition (CVPR) (2020)
44. Wang, N., Zhang, Y., Li, Z., Fu, Y., Liu, W., Jiang, Y.G.: Pixel2Mesh: generating 3D mesh models from single rgb images. In: European Conference on Computer Vision (ECCV) (2018)
45. Wang, P.S., Liu, Y., Guo, Y.X., Sun, C.Y., Tong, X.: O-CNN: octree-based convolutional neural networks for 3D shape analysis. ACM Trans. Graph. (2017)
46. Wen, C., Zhang, Y., Li, Z., Fu, Y.: Pixel2Mesh++: multi-view 3D mesh generation via deformation. In: IEEE/CVF International Conference on Computer Vision (ICCV) (2019)
47. Zheng, Q., Fan, X., Gong, M., Sharf, A., Deussen, O., Huang, H.: 4D reconstruction of blooming flowers. Comput. Graph. Forum **36**, 405–417 (2017)

# Diverse Image Inpainting
# with Normalizing Flow

Cairong Wang[1], Yiming Zhu[1], and Chun Yuan[1,2(✉)]

[1] Tsinghua Shenzhen International Graduate School, Shenzhen, China
{wcr20,zym20}@mails.tsinghua.edu.cn, yuanc@sz.tsinghua.edu.cn
[2] Peng Cheng National Laboratory, Shenzhen, China

**Abstract.** Image Inpainting is an ill-posed problem since there are diverse possible counterparts for the missing areas. The challenge of inpainting is to keep the "corrupted region" content consistent with the background and generate a variety of reasonable texture details. However, existing one-stage methods that directly output the inpainting results have to make a trade-off between diversity and consistency. The two-stage methods as the current trend can circumvent such shortcomings. These methods predict diverse structural priors in the first stage and focus on rich texture details generation in the second stage. However, all two-stage methods require autoregressive models to predict the probability distribution of the structural priors, which significantly limits the inference speed. In addition, their discretization assumption of prior distribution reduces the diversity of the inpainting results. We propose Flow-Fill, a novel two-stage image inpainting framework that utilizes a conditional normalizing flow model to generate diverse structural priors in the first stage. Flow-Fill can directly estimate the joint probability density of the missing regions as a flow-based model without reasoning pixel by pixel. Hence it achieves real-time inference speed and eliminates discretization assumptions. In addition, as a reversible model, Flow-Fill can invert the latent variables for a specified region, which allows us to make the inference process as semantic image editing. Experiments on benchmark datasets validate that Flow-Fill achieves superior diversity and fidelity in image inpainting qualitatively and quantitatively.

**Keywords:** Diverse image inpainting · Normalizing flow

## 1 Introduction

Image inpainting aims to generate meaningful content to fill in a corrupted image's missing areas. Unfortunately, it is a fundamentally ill-posed problem. For a given corrupted image (masked image), theoretically, there exist

---

C. Wang and Y. Zhu—Equal contribution.

---

**Supplementary Information** The online version contains supplementary material available at https://doi.org/10.1007/978-3-031-20050-2_4.

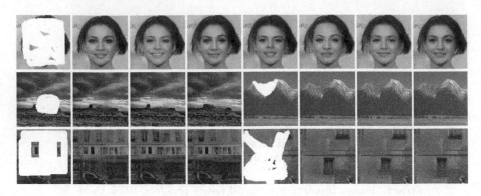

**Fig. 1.** Diverse free-form image completion results produced by our method.

infinitely many natural (i.e., visually realistic and semantically reasonable) repaired images. This poses a significant challenge to synthesize diverse natural contents that maintain consistency with contextual information of the known image regions.

With the advancement of generative networks (such as VAEs, GANs), deep learning based inpainting methods [12,18,19,23,24,27,34,36–39] typically utilize an encoder-decoder framework to synthesize the high-level semantic information consistent with the context. They treat Inpainting as an image reconstruction problem, filling in the corrupted areas by learning a one-to-one mapping to the ground truth. Although these methods yield a realistic result to fill the empty region, they cannot generate multiple possibilities. In contrast to deterministic Inpainting, many studies have recently emerged to challenge the ill-posed problem by addressing diverse Inpainting. For example, Zheng *et al.* [44] and Zhao *et al.* [42] use VAE-based networks to learn the prior distributions of missing parts conditional on the given corrupted image. Modulated GAN-based methods [20,43] modulate the deep features of random input noise from coarse to fine. Diffusion-based methods [22,28] restore images from random noise by iteration. However, these one-stage methods have to make a trade-off between diversity and consistency. In addition to these one-stage methods, some two-stage methods [25,32,40] predict diverse structural priors in the first stage and focus on rich texture details generation in the second stage. Although two-stage methods moderate the trade-off of diversity and fidelity, all of them require autoregressive models to predict the probability distribution of the structural priors[1], which significantly limits the inference speed. In addition, their discretization assumption of prior distribution reduces the diversity of the inpainting results (Fig. 1).

This paper follows the previous two-stage pipeline and develops Flow-Fill, a diverse image inpainting framework that utilizes a conditional normalizing flow network to naturally and accurately learn the distribution of structural priors

---

[1] Wan *et al.* [32] predicts the missing pixels one by one in an autoregressive form when inference. In addition, Wan *et al.* and Yu *et al.* [40] are based on Transformer, making the inference unbearably slow.

in the first stage. As a result, Flow-Fill can achieve real-time inference speed and eliminate discretization assumptions compared to the existing two-stage methods. Furthermore, compared to VAE and modulated GAN-based one-stage approaches mentioned above, Flow-Fill is reversible in the first stage and, therefore, can accurately learn the distribution of structural priors without suffering from mode-collapse and posterior collapse. In addition, as a flow-based model, Flow-Fill can map the input images to the corresponding latent variables and ensure exact reconstruction. Therefore, we can invert specific regions to the latent variable space for semantic Image Editing.

The main contributions in this work can be summarized as follows:

- We propose Flow-Fill, a flow-based two-stage diverse image inpainting framework. Flow-Fill is the first conditional normalizing flow network that completes large irregular corrupted areas with diverse results and achieves state-of-the-art image inpainting performance.
- As a flow-based model, Flow-Fill constructs a conditionally reversible bijective function, allowing inversion and inference about the content of a specific area. Therefore, Flow-Fill can be extended to region-specific semantic transfer tasks.
- Our Flow-Fill achieves a real-time inference speed that is approximately 87 times faster than autoregressive-based models and 142 times faster than diffusion-based models.
- Extensive experiments over multiple benchmark datasets demonstrate our proposed model's superiority in quality and diversity.

## 2    Related Work

As an ill-posed problem, image inpainting has multiple realistic and high-fidelity results. Based on the number of inpainting solutions, most existing image inpainting methods can be broadly classified into deterministic image inpainting and diverse image inpainting.

**Deterministic Image Inpainting.** Traditional image inpainting is mainly divided into diffusion-based methods [2,8] and patch-based methods [4,10]. Diffusion-based methods gradually spread the contextual pixel information to the damaged regions. Patch-based methods find the best matching patch in the visible area or a specified data library and then transfer it to the hole. With the advancement of generative networks, deep-learning based inpainting [12,18,19,23,24,27,34,36–39] often uses generative adversarial networks (GANs) to learn high-level semantic information consistent with the context. However, while these deep-learning-based methods generate realistic complementary results for the hole regions, they cannot generate diverse semantically meaningful results.

**Diverse Image Inpainting.** In order to obtain pluralistic image inpainting results, current methods can be broadly classified into four categories: 1) Some model the prior probability of the missing region based on a VAE paradigm [42,44]. Specifically, Zheng *et al.* [44] uses two coupled parallel VAEs to model the prior probability of the missing part. In contrast, Zhao *et al.* [42] uses two different encoders of VAEs to map the in-completed images and other additional reference images in the dataset to the same low-dimensional manifold. 2) Some gradually modulate a random noise to the repaired image [20,43]. For example, Liu *et al.* [20] first uses a pre-trained deterministic inpainting network to obtain an initially restored image and then inject it into the generator to modulate the generation process. Furthermore, Zhao *et al.* [43] further introduced the input noise of the GAN into the modulation process as well, proposing the co-modulation scheme. 3) Some [25,32,40] two-stage methods model the probability of coarse low-resolution structural priors in the first stage and use GAN in the second stage to generate rich texture details based on the previously obtained structural prior. Specifically, Peng *et al.* [25] uses VQ-VAE to separate and obtain discrete structural priors in the first stage. Wan *et al.* [32] uses a Transformer to model the probability distribution of masked tokens (i.e., missing pixels) by borrowing ideas from MLM (masked language model [5]). Yu *et al.* [40] combined the autoregressive model with MLM to further consider the dependencies between the missing pixels (masked tokens). 4) Some more recent diffusion-based methods [22,28] restore images from random noise by iteration. They have the same problem of slow inference as autoregressive-based methods.

**Normalizing Flow.** Normalizing flows have continuously made achievements in image generation tasks as they possess diverse generative capacity and exact likelihood computation. Normalizing flows are invertible generative models that learn a bijection function between the complex data distribution and simple predefined distribution. NICE [6], Real-NVP [7], Glow [16] are proposed in succession to promote the fitting ability of the flow models to the original data distribution. These efforts were later applied to audio generation [14,26,29,35], image modeling [3,9,21,31], and video prediction [17]. However, there is still a blank in employing a flow model in diverse image inpainting. The flexible nature of distribution mapping makes the flow-based model suitable for a diverse generation. Although VAEs and GANs-based methods work in diverse image generation tasks, they rely on deep-feature extraction and elaborate auxiliary modules to model the potential distribution of data. In addition, VAEs and GANs-based methods often suffer from mode collapse, posterior collapse, vanishing gradients, and instability. Based on the above analysis, we adopt a flow-based model to naturally model the distribution of coarse structural prior. As a result, the training process is more stable. In addition, conditional normalizing flow learns a conditionally reversible bijective function between a specific distribution and Gaussian distribution. Therefore, we can extend it to semantic transfer tasks.

# 3   Our Approach: Flow-Fill

Suppose we have an image $I_{gt}$ originally from a dataset, it degraded by a mask $M$ to become a masked image $I_m$ comprising the observed/visible pixels. Diverse image inpainting refers to generating multiple and diverse visually realistic and semantically reasonable completed/repaired images $\{I_c\}$. We formulate this task to learn the conditional probability distribution $p(I_c|I_m)$ over completed images, sampling from which could produce diverse inpainting results corresponding to a given $I_m$. As depicted in Fig. 2, we adopt the two-stage pipeline that generates diverse structural priors $I_s$ in the first stage and texture details in the second stage. Therefore $p(I_c|I_m)$ is decomposed into two parts $p(I_c|I_m) = p(I_c, I_s|I_m) = p(I_s|I_m) \cdot p(I_c|I_s, I_m)$, in which $p(I_s|I_m)$ is stochastic and $p(I_c|I_s, I_m)$ is deterministic. We adopt a conditional normalizing flow network $f$ to model $p(I_s|I_m)$, and a deterministic inpainting network $G$ to generate final results with rich textures: $I_c = G(I_s, I_m)$.

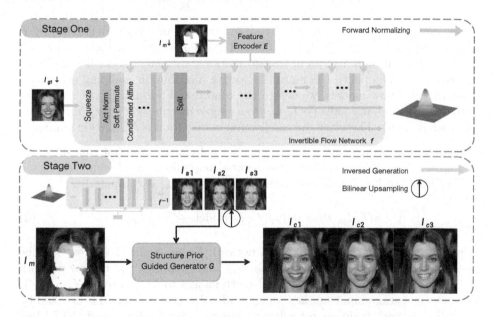

**Fig. 2. Pipeline overview.** Our method is a two-stage diverse inpainting model. In the first stage, we adopt a conditional normalizing flow network to transform the conditional structural priors distribution $p(I_s|I_m)$ to a Gaussian density $p_Z(\mathbf{z})$. Therefore in the second stage, we can use the reverse mapping of the flow network to transform the random latent variables $\mathbf{z}$ to stochastic structural priors and then use another generator $G$ to generate final texture-rich results guided by structural priors. $I_{gt}$: ground truth image, $I_m$: masked images, $\downarrow$: downscaled, $I_s$: structural prior, $I_c$: repaired image.

### 3.1 Normalizing the Conditonal Distribution of Structural Priors

Normalizing flows are invertible density estimation models that learn a bijection function $f_\theta$ between a complex data distribution $p_X$ and a simple pre-defined prior $p_Z$. Given a data sample $\mathbf{x} \in X$, the core idea of normalizing flow is that, according to the *change-of-variable formula*, the probability density $p(\mathbf{x})$ can be explicitly computed as:

$$p(\mathbf{x}, \theta) = p_Z(f_\theta(\mathbf{x})) \left| \det \frac{\partial f_\theta}{\partial \mathbf{x}} \right| \tag{1}$$

Here the second factor is the volume-scaling determinant of Jacobian $\frac{\partial f_\theta}{\partial \mathbf{x}}$. This allows the *exact* maximum likelihood estimation (MLE) for $p(\mathbf{x})$. Given the conditions $\mathbf{c}$, to learn the conditional distribution $p(\mathbf{x}|\mathbf{c})$ using normalizing flow, Eq. 1 is extended to a conditional scheme:

$$p(\mathbf{x}|\mathbf{c}, \theta) = p_Z(f_\theta(\mathbf{x}; \mathbf{c})) \left| \det \frac{\partial f_\theta}{\partial \mathbf{x}}(\mathbf{x}; \mathbf{c}) \right| \tag{2}$$

In our work, $f_\theta$ is implemented by an invertible neural network stacked by $T$ bijective layers $f_\theta = f_\theta^0 \circ f_\theta^1 \circ f_\theta^2 \circ ... \circ f_\theta^{T-1}$. The complex $\mathbf{x}$ is *normalized* to $\mathbf{z}$ as if it were a flow through a series of transformations, so such a model is called normalizing flow. Thanks to the natural bijective distribution mapping properties of normalizing flow models, we design the conditional normalizing flow network $f_\theta$ to directly map/normalize $p(I_s|I_m)$ to a simple distribution $p_Z(\mathbf{z})$ (e.g., Gaussian distribution). Therefore the conditional distribution $p(I_s|I_m, \theta)$ is implicitly defined by the reverse mapping: $p_Z(\mathbf{z}) \xrightarrow{f_\theta^{-1}} p(I_s|I_m, \theta)$. We can sample $I_s$ by sampling $\mathbf{z} \sim p_Z(\mathbf{z})$ and then use the reverse mapping to get $I_s = f_\theta^{-1}(\mathbf{z}, I_m)$.

According to Eq. 2, the probability density $p(I_s|I_m)$ is computed as:

$$p(I_s|I_m, \theta) = p_Z(f_\theta(I_s; I_m)) \left| \det \frac{\partial f_\theta}{\partial I_s}(I_s; I_m) \right| \tag{3}$$

In practice, we first use another CNN network $E_\theta$ as an encoder to extract the given masked image's features $ft = E_\theta(I_m)$, and then inject $ft$ to flow network $f_\theta$. We simply downsample the ground-truth images to $64 \times 64$ to get $I_s = I_{gt} \downarrow$. Thus the first stage input masked image is also down-sampled and is denoted by $I_m \downarrow$. For network training, we calculate the negative log-likelihood (NLL) loss to apply maximum likelihood estimation for $p(I_s|I_m \downarrow)$:

$$\begin{aligned} \mathcal{L}(\theta; I_s, I_m) &= -\log p(I_s|E_\theta(I_m \downarrow), \theta) \\ &= -\log P_Z(f_\theta(I_s; ft)) - \log \left| \det \frac{\partial f_\theta}{\partial I_s}(I_s; ft) \right| \end{aligned} \tag{4}$$

### 3.2 Flow Network Design

To calculate the NLL loss (Eq. 4) and to generate inpainting results using the reverse mapping, each layer of our flow network $f_\theta$ needs to be carefully designed to calculate both the Jacobian determinant and the inverse cheaply. Our work is based on the widely used un-conditional Glow [16] architecture and its conditional extension [1, 21]. Here we briefly view the flow layers we borrow in our network and then describe the overall stage one network architecture.

**Actnorm.** Since the performance of Batch Normalizing is known to degrade for small per-GPU minibatch size, Glow [16] proposed the Actnorm as a substitute for Batch Normalizing. The scaling and bias of Actnorm are data-independent (only the initialization is data-dependent) and learnable, removing the impact of a small minibatch size. Due to memory constraints, We choose Actnorm to enable small minibatch size training.

**Conditional Affine.** The coupling layer was first proposed by [6]. It divides the input into two parts and keeps one part unchanged to make the inverse and Jacobian cheaply calculated. This also captures the dependency between the two parts by using the information from the remaining part to transform the other part. We use the conditional form [1, 21] of the affine coupling layer to inject masked images' features as conditions into the flow network:

$$\mathbf{h}_1^{t+1} = \mathbf{h}_1^t, \quad \mathbf{h}_2^{t+1} = \exp(s_\theta^t(\mathbf{h}_1^t; ft)) \cdot \mathbf{h}_2^t + t_\theta^t(\mathbf{h}_1^t; ft) \tag{5}$$

where $(\mathbf{h}_1^t, \mathbf{h}_2^t) = \mathbf{h}^t$ is a partition of $t$-th layer's input activations. $s_\theta^t(\cdot)$ and $t_\theta^t(\cdot)$ are two arbitrary CNN networks that calculate the scaling and bias of $\mathbf{h}_2^t$. To further inject stronger conditional information, we use the affine injector layer proposed in [21] to apply the affine transformation on the full activations:

$$\mathbf{h}^{t+1} = \exp(s_\theta^{\prime t}(ft)) \cdot \mathbf{h}^t + t_\theta^{\prime t}(ft) \tag{6}$$

Here $s_\theta^{\prime t}(\cdot)$ and $t_\theta^{\prime t}(\cdot)$ are two other arbitrary networks. We implement Eq. 5 and Eq. 6 together to form our Conditional Affine layer.

**Squeeze.** We adopt the squeeze layer [16] as the downsampling operation. The squeeze layer reshapes every $2 \times 2$ adjacent pixel into the channel dimension. The flow network captures long-distance dependence by reducing the spatial resolution of activations.

**Soft Permutation.** Glow [16] proposed the invertible $1 \times 1$ convolution as the permutation operation on the channel dimension. It can be viewed as a linear transformation $\mathbf{h}^{t+1} = \mathbf{W}\mathbf{h}^t$, performed on each spatial position. Like [1], we set the weight matrix $\mathbf{W}$ as a fixed orthogonal matrix. This makes it easy to calculate both the Jacobian and the inverse of $\mathbf{W}$. Hence the training process is faster and more stable.

**Overall Network Architecture of the First Stage.** As depicted in Fig. 2, in the first stage, our Flow-Fill architecture consists of feature extraction network $E_\theta$ and flow network $f_\theta$. The flow network $f_\theta$ is composed of $L$ flow-blocks. Each flow block contains a Squeeze layer to reduce the spatial resolution of activations, followed by $K$ conditional flow steps. Each conditional flow step consists of an Actnorm, a Soft Permutation, and a Conditional Affine. Except for the last flow-block, each flow-block contains a Split layer [16] at the end, dividing the output into two parts, one as the final output $\{\mathbf{z}_i\}_{i=1}^L$ and one as input for the next flow-block. Our work uses the reimplemented generator proposed in [39] as the masked images' feature extraction network $E_\theta$. It is a coarse-to-fine inpainting generator with Gated Convolution. We select some intermediate feature maps of $E_\theta$ to concatenate together as the features $ft$ of the input masked images to inject into the flow network. See the Appendix for more details about $E_\theta$ and feature selection.

### 3.3 Guided Texture Generation

The structural priors $I_s$ obtained in the first stage are low-resolution and have no texture details. In the second stage, we upsample $I_s$ and concatenate it with $I_m$ as the input of another generator $G_\phi$ (parameterized by $\phi$). $G_\phi$ is a deterministic inpainting network that generates the final repaired image with rich textures under the guidance of $I_s$. Thus the overall two-stage inpainting process is:

$$\mathbf{z} \sim p_Z(\mathbf{z})$$
$$I_s = f_\theta^{-1}(\mathbf{z}; E_\theta(I_m \downarrow)) \tag{7}$$
$$I_c = G_\phi(I_s \uparrow, I_m)$$

Here $\downarrow$ indicates downsampling, and $\uparrow$ indicates upsampling. Follow [32], $G_\phi$ is composed of an encoder, decoder, and several residual blocks. The difference is that we replace all vanilla convolutions with gated convolution [39]. More details about the network architecture of $G_\phi$ are shown in the supplementary material.

For stage two training, we get $I_s$ by downsampling $I_{gt}$ and doing some degradation to maintain consistency with the results generated in the first stage. Specifically, we first calculate the latent variables $\mathbf{z} = f_\theta(I_{gt} \downarrow, I_m \downarrow)$ and replace some dimensions of $\mathbf{z}$ with random noise to get the slightly disturbed $\mathbf{z}'$. Then do the reconstruction by using the disturbed $\mathbf{z}'$: $I_s = f_\theta^{-1}(\mathbf{z}', I_m \downarrow)$. $G_\phi$ is optimized by adversarial training. Specifically, the adversarial loss is,

$$\mathcal{L}_{adv} = \mathbb{E}[\log 1 - D_\psi(I_c)] + \mathbb{E}[\log D_\psi(I_{gt})] \tag{8}$$

Here $D_\psi$ is the discriminator parameterized by $\psi$. Alone with the $L_1$ reconstruction loss,

$$\mathcal{L}_{rec} = \mathbb{E}(\|I_c - I_{gt}\|_1) \tag{9}$$

$G_\phi$ and $D_\psi$ are trained by solving the min-max optimization:

$$\min_G \max_D \mathcal{L}_{total} = \lambda_1 \mathcal{L}_{adv} + \lambda_2 \mathcal{L}_{rec} \tag{10}$$

In our experiments, $\lambda_1$ and $\lambda_2$ are empirically set at 0.1 and 1.0.

## 4    Experiments

### 4.1    Experimental Settings

*Implementation Details.* Our proposed method is implemented in PyTorch. We set the flow network architecture hyperparameters $L = 4$ and $K = 10$. The

**Fig. 3. Qualitative comparison with state-of-the-art methods on CelebA-HQ**. The completion results of our method are with better quality and diversity.

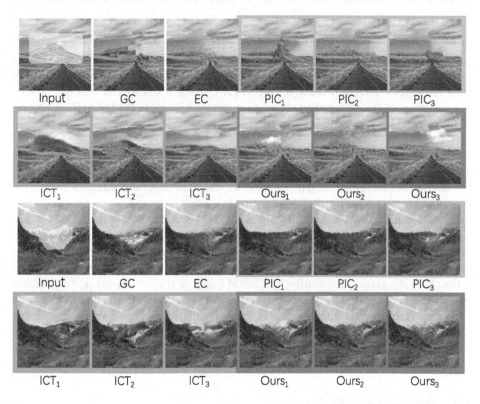

**Fig. 4. Qualitative comparison with state-of-the-art methods on Places2**. The completion results of our method are with better quality and diversity.

flow network $f_\theta$ and the feature extraction network $E_\theta$ were trained together for a total of 300k iterations with NLL loss (Eq. 4). For optimizer, we use Adam [15] with $\beta_1 = 0.9$ and $\beta_2 = 0.999$. The learning rate is initialized as $5 \cdot 10^{-4}$ and halved at 50%, 75%, 90%, and 95% of the training iterations. To train the

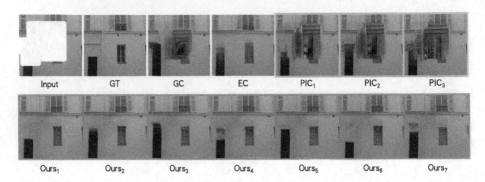

**Fig. 5. Qualitative comparison with state-of-the-art methods on Paris StreetView**. The completion results of our method are with better quality and diversity.

guided inpainting generator $G_\phi$ we use Adam [15] optimizer with fixed learning rate 1e-4, $\beta_1 = 0.0$ and $\beta_2 = 0.9$. The first stage of training takes about one day on a single NVIDIA(R) Tesla(R) V100 GPU with a minibatch size of 16. The second stage of training takes about four days on a single NVIDIA(R) Tesla(R) V100 GPU with a minibatch size of 8.

*Datasets and Evaluation Metrics.* We conduct our experiments on three datasets, including CelebA-HQ [13], Places2 [45], and Paris StreetView [24]. We follow the selection in [20] to produce the training, and validation sets for Places2. For CelebA-HQ and Paries StreetView, we keep the original training, validation, and testing split. All images are scaled to the resolution of $256 \times 256$ before inputting into the network. For non-square images in Pairs StreetView, random cropping is used. We train and evaluate our model with the irregular mask [18]. We adopt reconstruction-based metrics, including peak signal-to-noise ratio (PSNR), structural similarity (SSIM [33]), and mean $\ell_1$ error, to measure the low-level similarity between the inpainting result and ground truth. Our goal is to generate diverse, visually realistic, and semantically reasonable inpainting results that are unnecessarily similar to ground truth. Therefore, we further use Fréchet Inception Distance (FID [11]) as perceptual quality metrics, which are consistent with human judgment.

## 4.2   Performance Evaluation

We compare our method with the following state-of-the-art inpainting algorithms: GC [39], EC [23], PIC [44], ICT [32], and BAT [40]. GC and EC are single-solution methods. PIC, ICT, and BAT are multiple-solution methods. The performance of the compared methods was acquired by using the publicly available pre-trained models or implementation codes.

**Table 1. Quantitative comparison over CelebA-HQ and Places2 datasets.** For each metric, the best score is highlighted in **bold**, and the second-best score is highlighted in underline.

| Methods | Dataset | FID↓ | | | $\ell_1(\%)$↓ | | | PSNR↑ | | | SSIM↑ | | |
|---|---|---|---|---|---|---|---|---|---|---|---|---|---|
| | | 20-40% | 40-60% | Random | 20-40% | 40-60% | Random | 20-40% | 40-60% | Random | 20-40% | 40-60% | Random |
| EC [23] | CelebA-HQ [13] | 9.06 | 16.45 | 12.46 | 2.19 | 4.71 | 3.40 | 26.60 | 22.14 | 24.45 | <u>0.923</u> | 0.823 | 0.877 |
| GC [39] | | 14.12 | 22.80 | 18.10 | 2.70 | 5.19 | 3.88 | 25.17 | 21.21 | 23.32 | 0.907 | 0.805 | 0.858 |
| PIC [44] | | 10.21 | 18.92 | 14.12 | 2.50 | 5.65 | 4.00 | 25.92 | 20.82 | 23.46 | 0.919 | 0.780 | 0.852 |
| BAT [40] | | **6.32** | **12.50** | **9.33** | <u>1.91</u> | 4.57 | 3.18 | 27.82 | <u>22.40</u> | <u>25.21</u> | 0.944 | <u>0.834</u> | <u>0.890</u> |
| Ours | | <u>7.75</u> | <u>14.91</u> | <u>11.29</u> | 1.42 | 3.31 | 2.34 | 28.06 | 23.10 | 25.60 | 0.944 | 0.856 | 0.895 |
| EC [23] | Places2 [45] | 25.64 | 39.27 | 30.13 | 2.20 | 4.38 | 2.93 | 26.52 | <u>22.23</u> | 25.51 | 0.880 | <u>0.731</u> | 0.831 |
| GC [39] | | 24.76 | 39.02 | 29.98 | <u>2.15</u> | 4.40 | 2.80 | <u>26.53</u> | 21.19 | 25.69 | <u>0.881</u> | 0.729 | <u>0.834</u> |
| PIC [44] | | 26.39 | 49.09 | 33.47 | 2.36 | 5.07 | 3.15 | 26.10 | 21.50 | 25.04 | 0.865 | 0.680 | 0.806 |
| ICT [32] | | 21.60 | 33.85 | 25.42 | 2.44 | <u>4.31</u> | 2.67 | 26.50 | 22.22 | <u>25.79</u> | 0.880 | 0.724 | 0.832 |
| BAT [40] | | **17.78** | **32.55** | **22.16** | <u>2.15</u> | 4.64 | 2.84 | 26.47 | 21.74 | 25.69 | 0.879 | 0.704 | 0.826 |
| Ours | | <u>19.03</u> | <u>33.26</u> | <u>25.40</u> | 1.87 | 3.92 | 2.47 | 26.76 | 22.38 | 25.84 | 0.892 | 0.799 | 0.847 |

**Qualitative Comparisons.** We conduct qualitative comparisons over CelebA-HQ [13], Places2 [45] and Paris StreetView [24] datasets. For CelebA-HQ and Paris StreetView, our mthdod is compared with GC [39], EC [23], and PIC [44]. For Places2, our method is compared with GC, EC, PIC, and ICT [32]. All results are the direct output of the model without any post-processing.

Figure 3 shows the results on CelebA-HQ [13]. GC [39], and EC [23] generate generally reasonable content, but with some artifacts, they can only generate a single result. The results of PIC [44] have better fidelity than GC and EC but limited diversity. Compared to these methods, ours is superior in both photo-realism and diversity. Figure 5 shows the case of large missing areas on Paris StreetView [24]. This time GC and PIC generate incongruent content with the visible region. EC is much better but lacks sharp details. Again, ours have the best fidelity and diversity. Results on nature scenery images are shown in Fig. 4. EC's results have pronounced artifacts, while GC's are much better. The PIC's results look more realistic than ICT's [32], but the diversity is not as good as ICT's. Only ours look both natural and varied.

**Quantitative Comparisons.** We quantitatively compare our method with other deterministic and non-deterministic inpainting methods on ClebabA-HQ [13] and Places2 [45]. All tests use irregular masks [18], categorized according to the mask ratios. Here 'Random' indicates that the mask from this category has a mask ratio from 20% to 60%. Unlike PIC [44], which unitizes its discriminator to sort the results, our method uses all random samples without any selection to better evaluate our model's average performance. As shown in Table 1, Ours achieve the best reconstruction scores and have comparable perceptual quality.

### 4.3 Region-Specific Semantic Transfer

Given a masked region as a condition, Flow-Fill can build a bijection between semantic contents in this area and latent variable space. With this property, we can directly calculate the latent variables $z$ that contain the target image's semantic information and fill it in different source images by reverse inference

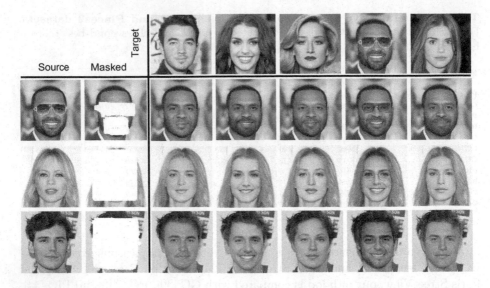

**Fig. 6. Specific-region semantic transfer results.** We use the target image to compute the latent variable in the first stage and thus obtain an inpainting result similar to the target style (eyes, eyebrows, mouth, glasses, etc.).

(no need to retrain the inpainting model). Note that in the semantic transfer task, we use $\mathbf{z}$ inverted from target images instead of randomly sampled.

Specifically, given a target image $I_t$ and a masked source image $I_m$ (masked with mask $M$), we first normalizing it to the latent variables $\mathbf{z} = f_\theta(I_t \downarrow; E_\theta((I_t \cdot M) \downarrow))$. Then we generate the structural prior $I_s$ by inversed generation: $I_s = f_\theta^{-1}(\mathbf{z}; E_\theta(I_m \downarrow))$. Finally, the result with rich texture is generated: $I_c = G_\phi(I_s \uparrow, I_m)$. Experimental results are shown in Fig. 6. By selecting the target image, we can control the hairstyle, lip color, whether to open the mouth, whether to wear glasses, etc., of the inpainting result.

**Table 2. Quantitative comparison on Paris StreetView dataset.** The best score is highlighted in **blod**.

| Method | Mask Ratio | PSNR ↑ | SSIM ↑ | $\ell_1$(%) ↓ | FID ↓ | LPIPS ↑ |
|---|---|---|---|---|---|---|
| PIC [44] | 20%–40% | 24.80 | 0.817 | 3.43 | 56.83 | 0.046 |
| BAT [40] | | 26.52 | 0.864 | 3.43 | 36.19 | 0.076 |
| Ours | | **26.87** | **0.897** | **1.95** | **33.98** | **0.078** |
| PIC [44] | 40%–60% | 20.12 | 0.570 | 7.47 | 90.91 | 0.127 |
| BAT [40] | | 21.89 | 0.678 | 5.83 | **64.20** | 0.147 |
| Ours | | **22.35** | **0.798** | **3.99** | 65.86 | **0.151** |
| PIC [44] | Random | 22.97 | 0.718 | 4.94 | 72.16 | 0.082 |
| BAT [40] | | 24.50 | 0.786 | 3.96 | **48.19** | 0.106 |
| Ours | | **24.58** | **0.849** | **2.90** | 50.18 | **0.109** |

## 4.4    Analysis

**Diversity.** Following [44,46], we utilize the LPIPS distance [41] to measure the diversity score. LPIPS is computed based on the in-depth features of the VGG [30] model pre-trained on ImageNet. Specifically, we randomly sampled five output pairs for each masked input image to calculate the average score. Because results with high variability are likely to be unreasonable, we measured PSNR, SSIM [33], mean $\ell_1$ error, and FID [11] simultaneously. Table 2 shows the results. Our model achieves the best diversity while maintaining high fidelity in all cases.

**Computational Time.** We randomly selected 200 images on the test set of Places2 [45] and calculated the average computational time per image. As shown in Table 3, our method achieves a real-time inference speed approximately 87 times faster than autoregressive-based models and 142 times faster than diffusion-based models. All tests were performed on an NVIDIA(R) GeForce RTX 3090 GPU.

| GT | Input | Output | GT | Input | Output |

**Fig. 7. Inpainting results of our method.** We achieve the first flow-based large missing region complementation.

**Ablation Study on First Stage Resolution.** We ablate the resolution for the first stage. As shown in Table 4, normalizing flow is difficult to generate high-quality images with high resolution. We use normalizing flow to complement a low-resolution (64×64) coarse result in the first stage and use GAN to generate a high-resolution visual pleasing result in the second stage. Thus we circumvent the difficulties of flow models in generation and achieve the first flow-based large missing region complementation. Some inpainting examples for large regions of missing images are shown in Fig. 7.

**Table 3. Comparison of inference speed.** Rows and columns correspond to different masked areas and methods respectively.

|         | BAT [40]   | ICT [32]  | Palette [28] | Ours       |
|---------|-----------|-----------|--------------|------------|
| 20–40%  | 11.33 s   | 9.40 s    | 27.01 s      | **0.18 s** |
| 40–60%  | 22.21 s   | 15.53 s   | 27.23 s      | **0.19 s** |
| Random  | 16.60 s   | 13.03 s   | 27.13 s      | **0.19 s** |

**Table 4. Ablation studies on CelebA-HQ.** The mask ratio is 20–60%. The best score is highlighted in **blod**.

| First stage resolution | FID↓    | $\ell_1(\%)$ ↓ | PSNR↑   | SSIM↑   |
|------------------------|---------|----------------|---------|---------|
| 32 × 32                | 12.44   | 2.54           | 25.04   | 0.888   |
| 48 × 48                | 11.86   | 2.40           | 25.46   | 0.892   |
| 64 × 64                | **11.29** | **2.34**     | **25.60** | **0.895** |
| 96 × 96                | 13.19   | 2.61           | 24.95   | 0.883   |
| 256 × 256              | 41.94   | 3.86           | 22.31   | 0.844   |

**Searching for Flow Network Structure Hyperparameters.** Our flow network consists of $L$ flow-blocks, and each flow-blocks consists of $K$ flow-steps. In general, the larger the $L$, $K$, the better the model performance. To reduce the model size while maintaining a good inpainting performance, we form this problem to a constrained optimization problem:

$$L^*, K^* = \arg\max_{L,K} \; \mathcal{Q}(L,K) + \lambda \mathcal{T}(L,K)$$

$$s.t. \; \& \; 12 \le L + K \le 15 \tag{11}$$

where $\mathcal{Q}$, $\mathcal{T}$ denotes the inpainting performance and network size function with respect to $L$, $K$. After a rough grid search, the best $L$ and $K$ are 4 and 10.

## 5   Conclusion

We propose a novelty two-stage image inpainting framework named Flow-Fill, which can directly estimate the joint probability density of the missing regions without reasoning pixel by pixel. Hence it achieves real-time inference speed and eliminates discretization assumptions. In addition, as a flow-based model, Flow-Fill can directly calculate the latent variables containing the specified semantic information, which allows us to control the reverse inpainting process to a certain extent. Experiments on benchmark datasets qualitatively and quantitatively verify that Flow-Fill achieves superior diversity and fidelity in image inpainting.

**Acknowledgement.** This work was supported by SZSTC Grant No. JCYJ20190809172201639 and WDZC20200820200655001, Shenzhen Key Laboratory. ZDSYS20210623092001004. We thank Yunpeng Bai for helpful discussion.

# References

1. Ardizzone, L., Lüth, C., Kruse, J., Rother, C., Köthe, U.: Guided image generation with conditional invertible neural networks. arXiv preprint arXiv:1907.02392 (2019)
2. Bertalmio, M., Sapiro, G., Caselles, V., Ballester, C.: Image inpainting. In: Proceedings of the 27th Annual Conference on Computer graphics and Interactive Techniques, pp. 417–424 (2000)
3. Chen, H.J., Hui, K.M., Wang, S.Y., Tsao, L.W., Shuai, H.H., Cheng, W.H.: Beautyglow: on-demand makeup transfer framework with reversible generative network. In: Proceedings of the IEEE/CVF Conference on Computer Vision and Pattern Recognition, pp. 10042–10050 (2019)
4. Darabi, S., Shechtman, E., Barnes, C., Goldman, D.B., Sen, P.: Image melding: combining inconsistent images using patch-based synthesis. ACM Transa. Graphi. **31**(4), 1–10 (2012)
5. Devlin, J., Chang, M.W., Lee, K., Toutanova, K.: BERT: pre-training of deep bidirectional transformers for language understanding. arXiv preprint arXiv:1810.04805 (2018)
6. Dinh, L., Krueger, D., Bengio, Y.: Nice: Non-linear independent components estimation. arXiv preprint arXiv:1410.8516 (2014)
7. Dinh, L., Sohl-Dickstein, J., Bengio, S.: Density estimation using real NVP. arXiv preprint arXiv:1605.08803 (2016)
8. Efros, A.A., Freeman, W.T.: Image quilting for texture synthesis and transfer. In: Proceedings of the 28th Annual Conference on Computer Graphics and Interactive Techniques, pp. 341–346 (2001)
9. Grover, A., Chute, C., Shu, R., Cao, Z., Ermon, S.: AlignFlow: cycle consistent learning from multiple domains via normalizing flows. In: Proceedings of the AAAI Conference on Artificial Intelligence, vol. 34, pp. 4028–4035 (2020)
10. Hays, J., Efros, A.A.: Scene completion using millions of photographs. ACM Trans. Graph. (ToG) **26**(3), 4-es (2007)
11. Heusel, M., Ramsauer, H., Unterthiner, T., Nessler, B., Hochreiter, S.: GANs trained by a two time-scale update rule converge to a local Nash equilibrium. In: 30th Proceedings of the International Conference on Advances in Neural Iinformation Processing Systems (2017)
12. Iizuka, S., Simo-Serra, E., Ishikawa, H.: Globally and locally consistent image completion. ACM Transa. Graph. **36**(4), 1–14 (2017)
13. Karras, T., Aila, T., Laine, S., Lehtinen, J.: Progressive growing of GANs for improved quality, stability, and variation. arXiv preprint arXiv:1710.10196 (2017)
14. Kim, S., Lee, S.g., Song, J., Kim, J., Yoon, S.: FlowaveNet: a generative flow for raw audio. arXiv preprint arXiv:1811.02155 (2018)
15. Kingma, D.P., Ba, J.: Adam: a method for stochastic optimization. arXiv preprint arXiv:1412.6980 (2014)
16. Kingma, D.P., Dhariwal, P.: Glow: Generative flow with invertible 1x1 convolutions. In: 31st Proceedings of the International Conference on Advances in Neural Information Processing Systems (2018)
17. Kumar, M., et al.: VideoFlow: a flow-based generative model for video. arXiv preprint arXiv:1903.01434 2(5) (2019)
18. Liu, G., Reda, F.A., Shih, K.J., Wang, T.-C., Tao, A., Catanzaro, B.: Image inpainting for irregular holes using partial convolutions. In: Ferrari, V., Hebert, M., Sminchisescu, C., Weiss, Y. (eds.) ECCV 2018. LNCS, vol. 11215, pp. 89–105. Springer, Cham (2018). https://doi.org/10.1007/978-3-030-01252-6_6

19. Liu, H., Jiang, B., Song, Y., Huang, W., Yang, C.: Rethinking image inpainting via a mutual encoder-decoder with feature equalizations. In: Vedaldi, A., Bischof, H., Brox, T., Frahm, J.-M. (eds.) ECCV 2020. LNCS, vol. 12347, pp. 725–741. Springer, Cham (2020). https://doi.org/10.1007/978-3-030-58536-5_43

20. Liu, H., Wan, Z., Huang, W., Song, Y., Han, X., Liao, J.: PD-GAN: Probabilistic diverse GAN for image inpainting. In: Proceedings of the IEEE/CVF Conference on Computer Vision and Pattern Recognition, pp. 9371–9381 (2021)

21. Lugmayr, A., Danelljan, M., Van Gool, L., Timofte, R.: SRFlow: learning the super-resolution space with normalizing flow. In: Vedaldi, A., Bischof, H., Brox, T., Frahm, J.-M. (eds.) ECCV 2020. LNCS, vol. 12350, pp. 715–732. Springer, Cham (2020). https://doi.org/10.1007/978-3-030-58558-7_42

22. Lugmayr, A., Danelljan, M., Romero, A., Yu, F., Timofte, R., Van Gool, L.: RePaint: Inpainting using denoising diffusion probabilistic models. In: Proceedings of the IEEE/CVF Conference on Computer Vision and Pattern Recognition, pp. 11461–11471 (2022)

23. Nazeri, K., Ng, E., Joseph, T., Qureshi, F.Z., Ebrahimi, M.: Edgeconnect: generative image inpainting with adversarial edge learning. arXiv preprint arXiv:1901.00212 (2019)

24. Pathak, D., Krahenbuhl, P., Donahue, J., Darrell, T., Efros, A.A.: Context encoders: Feature learning by inpainting. In: Proceedings of the IEEE Conference on Computer Vision and Pattern Recognition, pp. 2536–2544 (2016)

25. Peng, J., Liu, D., Xu, S., Li, H.: Generating diverse structure for image inpainting with hierarchical VQ-VAE. In: Proceedings of the IEEE/CVF Conference on Computer Vision and Pattern Recognition, pp. 10775–10784 (2021)

26. Prenger, R., Valle, R., Catanzaro, B.: Waveglow: a flow-based generative network for speech synthesis. In: ICASSP 2019–2019 IEEE International Conference on Acoustics, Speech and Signal Processing (ICASSP), pp. 3617–3621. IEEE (2019)

27. Ren, Y., et al.: StructureFlow: image inpainting via structure-aware appearance flow. In: Proceedings of the IEEE/CVF International Conference on Computer Vision, pp. 181–190 (2019)

28. Saharia, C., et al.: Palette: Image-to-image diffusion models. arXiv preprint arXiv:2111.05826 (2021)

29. Serrà, J., Pascual, S., Segura Perales, C.: Blow: a single-scale hyperconditioned flow for non-parallel raw-audio voice conversion. In: 32nd Proceedings of the International Conference on Advances in Neural Information Processing Systems (2019)

30. Simonyan, K., Zisserman, A.: Very deep convolutional networks for large-scale image recognition. arXiv preprint arXiv:1409.1556 (2014)

31. Sun, H., et al.: Dual-glow: conditional flow-based generative model for modality transfer. In: Proceedings of the IEEE/CVF International Conference on Computer Vision, pp. 10611–10620 (2019)

32. Wan, Z., Zhang, J., Chen, D., Liao, J.: High-fidelity pluralistic image completion with transformers. In: Proceedings of the IEEE/CVF International Conference on Computer Vision, pp. 4692–4701 (2021)

33. Wang, Z., Bovik, A.C., Sheikh, H.R., Simoncelli, E.P.: Image quality assessment: from error visibility to structural similarity. IEEE Trans. Image Process. **13**(4), 600–612 (2004)

34. Xu, S., Liu, D., Xiong, Z.: E2i: generative inpainting from edge to image. IEEE Trans. Circuits Syst. Video Technol. **31**(4), 1308–1322 (2020)

35. Yamaguchi, M., Koizumi, Y., Harada, N.: AdaFlow: domain-adaptive density estimator with application to anomaly detection and unpaired cross-domain transla-

tion. In: ICASSP 2019–2019 IEEE International Conference on Acoustics, Speech and Signal Processing (ICASSP), pp. 3647–3651. IEEE (2019)

36. Yan, Z., Li, X., Li, M., Zuo, W., Shan, S.: Shift-Net: image inpainting via deep feature rearrangement. In: Ferrari, V., Hebert, M., Sminchisescu, C., Weiss, Y. (eds.) Computer Vision – ECCV 2018. LNCS, vol. 11218, pp. 3–19. Springer, Cham (2018). https://doi.org/10.1007/978-3-030-01264-9_1

37. Yi, Z., Tang, Q., Azizi, S., Jang, D., Xu, Z.: Contextual residual aggregation for ultra high-resolution image inpainting. In: Proceedings of the IEEE/CVF Conference on Computer Vision and Pattern Recognition, pp. 7508–7517 (2020)

38. Yu, J., Lin, Z., Yang, J., Shen, X., Lu, X., Huang, T.S.: Generative image inpainting with contextual attention. In: Proceedings of the IEEE Conference on Computer Vision and Pattern Recognition, pp. 5505–5514 (2018)

39. Yu, J., Lin, Z., Yang, J., Shen, X., Lu, X., Huang, T.S.: Free-form image inpainting with gated convolution. In: Proceedings of the IEEE/CVF International Conference on Computer Vision, pp. 4471–4480 (2019)

40. Yu, Y., et al.: Diverse image inpainting with bidirectional and autoregressive transformers. In: Proceedings of the 29th ACM International Conference on Multimedia, pp. 69–78 (2021)

41. Zhang, R., Isola, P., Efros, A.A., Shechtman, E., Wang, O.: The unreasonable effectiveness of deep features as a perceptual metric. In: Proceedings of the IEEE Conference on Computer Vision and Pattern Rrecognition, pp. 586–595 (2018)

42. Zhao, L., et al.: UCTGAN: diverse image inpainting based on unsupervised cross-space translation. In: Proceedings of the IEEE/CVF Conference on Computer Vison and Pattern Recognition, pp. 5741–5750 (2020)

43. Zhao, S., et al.: Large scale image completion via co-modulated generative adversarial networks. arXiv preprint arXiv:2103.10428 (2021)

44. Zheng, C., Cham, T.J., Cai, J.: Pluralistic image completion. In: Proceedings of the IEEE/CVF Conference on Computer Vision and Pattern Recognition, pp. 1438–1447 (2019)

45. Zhou, B., Lapedriza, A., Khosla, A., Oliva, A., Torralba, A.: Places: a 10 million image database for scene recognition. IEEE Trans. Pattern Anal. Mach. Intell. **40**(6), 1452–1464 (2017)

46. Zhu, J.Y., et al.: Toward multimodal image-to-image translation. In: 30th Proceedings of the international Conference on Advances in Neural Information Processing Systems (2017)

# Improved Masked Image Generation with Token-Critic

José Lezama$^{(\boxtimes)}$, Huiwen Chang, Lu Jiang, and Irfan Essa

Google Research, Mountain View, USA
joselezama@google.com

**Abstract.** Non-autoregressive generative transformers recently demonstrated impressive image generation performance, and orders of magnitude faster sampling than their autoregressive counterparts. However, optimal parallel sampling from the true joint distribution of visual tokens remains an open challenge. In this paper we introduce Token-Critic, an auxiliary model to guide the sampling of a non-autoregressive generative transformer. Given a masked-and-reconstructed real image, the Token-Critic model is trained to distinguish which visual tokens belong to the original image and which were sampled by the generative transformer. During non-autoregressive iterative sampling, Token-Critic is used to select which tokens to accept and which to reject and resample. Coupled with Token-Critic, a state-of-the-art generative transformer significantly improves its performance, and outperforms recent diffusion models and GANs in terms of the trade-off between generated image quality and diversity, in the challenging class-conditional ImageNet generation.

**Keywords:** Generative models · Vision transformer · Diffusion process · Image generation

## 1 Introduction

Class-conditional image synthesis is a challenging task, requiring the generation of varied and semantically meaningful images with realistic details and few or none visual artifacts. The field has seen impressive progress in the hand of mainly three techniques: large Generative Adversarial Networks (GANs) [3], diffusion models [9,19], and transformer-based models over a vector-quantized (VQ) latent space [5,12]. Each of these techniques presents different advantages trading-off model size, computational cost of sampling, image quality and diversity.

Building upon the transformers [39] for the natural language generation tasks [4], generative vision transformers achieved impressive image generation performance. While early works applied an autoregressive transformer in the VQ latent space [12,29], recently the state-of-the-art on the common ImageNet

---

**Supplementary Information** The online version contains supplementary material available at https://doi.org/10.1007/978-3-031-20050-2_5.

benchmark was further advanced by a new model called MaskGIT [5] using mask-and-predict training inspired by BERT [8] and non-autoregressive sampling adapted from neural machine translation [13, 26].

To be more specific, during inference, MaskGIT [5] starts from a blank canvas with all the tokens masked out. In each step, it predicts all tokens in parallel but only keeps the ones with the highest prediction scores. The remaining tokens are masked out and will be re-predicted (resampled) in the next iteration until all tokens are generated with a few iterations of refinement. The non-autoregressive nature of MaskGIT allows orders-of-magnitude faster sampling, generating an image typically in 8–16 steps as opposed to hundreds of steps in autoregressive transformers [12] and diffusion models [9, 19].

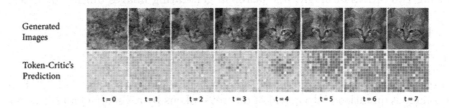

**Fig. 1.** Overview of the sampling procedure using Token-Critic. At each sampling iteration, Token-Critic predicts a high score for the tokens that are more likely sampled together under the joint distribution. Tokens with lower score are masked and resampled at the next iteration.

One of the central challenges of iterative non-autoregressive generation is knowing how many and which tokens to keep and which to resample at each sampling step. For instance, MaskGIT [5] uses a predefined masking schedule and keeps the predicted tokens for which the model's prediction is more confident. However, this procedure presents three notable drawbacks. First, to select tokens to resample, it relies on the generator's predicted confidences which can be sensitive to modeling errors. Secondly, the decision to reject or accept is made independently for each token, which impedes capturing rich correlations between tokens. In addition, the sampling procedure is greedy and "non-regrettable", which does not allow to correct previously sampled tokens, even if they become less likely given the latest context.

In this work, we propose *Token-Critic*, a second transformer that takes as input the output of the generative transformer (or generator for short). Intuitively, the Token-Critic is trained to recognize configurations of tokens likely under the real distribution, and those that were sampled from the generator. During the iterative sampling process, the scores predicted by Token-Critic are used to select which token predictions are kept, and which are masked and resampled in the next iteration (*c.f.* Fig. 1).

With Token-Critic we tackle the three aforementioned limitations: 1) the masking of tokens is delegated to the Token-Critic model, trained to distinguish which tokens are unlikely under the true distribution. 2) Token-Critic looks at the entire set of sampled tokens collectively, thus is capable of capturing (spatial or semantic) correlations between tokens. 3) The proposed sampling procedure allows to correct previously sampled tokens during the iterative decoding.

When using Token-Critic, the state-of-the-art non-autoregressive generative transformer MaskGIT [5] significantly improves its performance on ImageNet $256 \times 256$ and $512 \times 512$ class-conditional generation, while achieving a better trade-off between image quality and diversity. Furthermore, the gain obtained by using Token-Critic is complementary to the gain obtain by a pretrained ResNet classifier for rejection sampling. When coupled with classifier-based rejection sampling [31], Token-Critic parallels or surpasses the state-of-the-art continuous diffusion models with classifier guidance [9] in image synthesis quality while offering two orders of magnitude faster in generating images during inference.

## 2   Background

### 2.1   Non-autoregressive Generative Image Transformer

Generally, transformer-based models generate images in two stages [12, 30]. First, the image is quantized into a grid of discrete tokens by a Vector-Quantized (VQ) autoencoder built upon VAE [29, 31], GAN [12], or vision transformer backbones [40], in which each token is represented as an integer index in a codebook. In the second stage, an autoregressive transformer decoder [6] is learned on the flattened token sequence to generate image tokens sequentially based on the previously generated result (*i.e.* autoregressive decoding). In the end, the generated codes are mapped to pixel space using the decoder obtained from the first stage.

Non-autoregressive transformers [13, 15, 26], which were originally proposed for machine translation, are, very recently, extended to improve the second stage of autoregressive decoding [25]. For example, MaskGIT [5] demonstrates highly-competitive fidelity and diversity of conditional image synthesis on the ImageNet benchmark as well as faster inference than the autoregressive transformer [12] in addition to the diffusion models [9, 28]. To be specific, MaskGIT is trained on the masked language modeling (MLM) proxy task proposed in BERT [8]. During inference, the model adopts a non-autoregressive decoding method to synthesize an image in a constant number of steps (typically 8–16 steps) [15]. Starting with all the tokens masked out, in each inference step, MaskGIT predicts all tokens simultaneously in parallel and only keeps the ones with the highest prediction scores. The remaining tokens are masked out and will be re-predicted in the next iteration. The mask ratio is made decreasing, according to a cosine function, until all tokens are generated. In the following, Sects. 2.2 and 2.3 describe limitations in the training and sampling of the MaskGIT model. Then, in Sect. 3 we introduce the Token-Critic as a solution to mitigate these limitations.

### 2.2   Challenges in Training Non-autoregressive Transformers

Ideally, one would like the masked generative transformer to learn the joint distribution of unobserved tokens $\mathbf{x} = [x_1, \ldots x_N]$ given the observed tokens $\mathbf{o}$.

Both $\mathbf{x}$ and $\mathbf{o}$ are sequences of $N$ tokens where $N$ (*e.g.*, $16 \times 16$) indicates the latent size of the VQ autoencoder obtained in the first stage. Each $x_j \in \mathcal{V} = \{1, \cdots, K\}$ is an integer token in the codebook of size $K$. Notice the element in $\mathbf{o}$ can take the value of a special mask token, *i.e.* $o_j \in \mathcal{V} \cup \{[\text{MASK}]\}$. We shall refer to their true joint distribution as $q(x_1, \ldots, x_N | \mathbf{o})$.

Current non-autoregressive generative transformers [5,13] are trained to optimize the sum of *the marginal* cross-entropies for each unobserved token:

$$\mathcal{L}_i = -\sum_{j=1}^{N} \sum_{k=1}^{K} \tilde{q}(x_j = k | \mathbf{o}) \log p_\theta(x_j = k | \mathbf{o}), \tag{1}$$

where $\tilde{q}$ represents an approximation to the true marginal given by considering one random real sample.

A limitation is that optimizing over the marginals hinders capturing the richness of the underlying joint distribution of unobserved tokens. Essentially, this training scheme is equivalent to minimizing the Kullback-Leibler (KL) divergence between the data and model distributions, both approximated as fully factorizable distributions.

### 2.3   Challenges in Sampling from Non-autoregressive Transformers

During sampling, one is interested in sampling from the full joint distribution of unobserved tokens $q(x_1, \ldots x_N | \mathbf{o})$. However, even if the transformer representations are distributed, the output for each token models its sampling distribution independently. More precisely, for a given unobserved token $x_t$, a value is sampled from $p_\theta(x_t | \mathbf{z}, \mathbf{o}) = p_\theta(x_t | \mathbf{z})$, where $\mathbf{z}$ is the latent embedding visible by all output tokens (*i.e.* the activations of the last attention layer). Sampling from the true distribution would require coordinating the values of all sampled tokens, which is not possible with the current architecture (unless the sampling is made deterministic, which harms the diversity of the generated images). Thus, non-autoregressive vision transformers still need to resort to iterative ancestor sampling. Typically, in each step of the sampling process, a growing subset of the tokens is accepted and the rest is rejected and resampled.

Aiming at better approximating the true joint distribution, the question of how to select which sampled tokens to keep and which to resample is the main focus of this work. We propose to do this using an auxiliary model that we term the Token-Critic. The Token-Critic is a second transformer trained to individually identify which tokens in a sampled vector-quantized image are plausible under the true joint distribution and which are not. During the iterative non-autoregressive sampling procedure, the Token-Critic is used in each iteration to reject the tokens that are less likely given the context.

## 3   Method

The goal of Token-Critic is to guide the iterative sampling process of a non-autoregressive transformer-based generator. Given the tokenized image outputted by the generative transformer, Token-Critic is designed as a second transformer that provides a score for each token, indicating whether the token is likely under the real distribution, given its context.

In Sect. 3.1, we first introduce the procedure for training the Token-Critic and in Sect. 3.2 we describe how it is used during sampling. At all times we assume a pre-trained non-autoregressive transformer generator is available. Finally, in Sect. 3.3 we explain the role of the Token-Critic by drawing a connection to discrete diffusion processes.

## 3.1   Training the Token-Critic

The training procedure for Token-Critic is straightforward. Given a masked image and its corresponding completion by the generative non-autoregressive transformer, the Token-Critic is trained to distinguish which of the tokens in the resulting image were originally masked.

More specifically, consider a real vector-quantized image $\mathbf{x}_0$, a random binary mask $\mathbf{m}_t$ and the resulting masked image $\mathbf{x}_t = \mathbf{x}_0 \odot \mathbf{m}_t$. The subindex $t$ indicates the masking ratio, as will be detailed shortly. First, the generative transformer $G_\theta$, parameterized by $\theta$, is used to predict the masked tokens, namely sampling $\tilde{\mathbf{x}}_0$ from $p_\theta(\hat{\mathbf{x}}_0|\mathbf{x}_t, c)$, in which to condition on the class index $c$, we prepend a class token to the flattened set of visual tokens. The unmasked tokens in $\mathbf{x}_t$ are copied into the output to form $\hat{\mathbf{x}}_0 = \tilde{\mathbf{x}}_0 \odot \mathbf{m}_t + \mathbf{x}_0 \odot (1 - \mathbf{m}_t)$.

The Token-Critic transformer, parameterized by $\phi$, takes as input $\hat{\mathbf{x}}_0$ and outputs a predicted binary mask for $\mathbf{m}_t$. During training, the parameters $\phi$ are optimized to minimize the following objective:

$$\mathcal{L}_i = \mathop{\mathbb{E}}_{q(\mathbf{x}_0, c)q(t)q(\mathbf{m}_t|t)p_\theta(\hat{\mathbf{x}}_0|\mathbf{m}_t \odot \mathbf{x}_0, c)} \left[ \sum_{j=1}^{N} BCE\left( \mathbf{m}_t^{(j)},\ p_\phi(\mathbf{m}_t^{(j)}|\hat{\mathbf{x}}_0, c) \right) \right], \quad (2)$$

where $q(\mathbf{x}_0, c)$, $q(t)$, $q(\mathbf{m}_t|t)$ are the distributions of real unmasked images, timesteps, and binary masks, respectively, and BCE denotes the binary cross-entropy loss. The sampling distribution $p_\theta(\hat{\mathbf{x}}_0|\mathbf{m}_t \odot \mathbf{x}_0)$ induced by the generator $G_\theta$ is held fixed during the training of the Token-Critic model.

The training algorithm is summarized as pseudocode in Algorithm 1. Notice that $\gamma(t) \in (0, 1)$ in Step 4 is the cosine mask scheduling function. Given a uniform random number $t$ sampled from $q(t) = \mathcal{U}(0, 1)$, the number of masked tokens in $\mathbf{m}_t$ is computed as $r = \lceil N \cdot \gamma(t) \rceil$, where $N$ is the total number of tokens within an image.

## 3.2   Sampling with Token-Critic

During inference, we are interested in progressively replacing masked tokens with an actual code in the vocabulary. Starting from a fully masked image $\mathbf{x}_T$ and the class condition $c$, we iteratively sample from $p(\mathbf{x}_{t-1}|\mathbf{x}_t, c)$, which may be approximated by:

$$p(\mathbf{x}_{t-1}|\mathbf{x}_t, c) = \sum_{\mathbf{x}_0} p_\phi(\mathbf{x}_{t-1}|\mathbf{x}_0, c) p_\theta(\mathbf{x}_0|\mathbf{x}_t, c) \tag{3}$$

$$= \mathop{\mathbb{E}}_{\mathbf{x}_0 \sim p_\theta(\mathbf{x}_0|\mathbf{x}_t, c)} \Big[ p_\phi(\mathbf{x}_{t-1}|\mathbf{x}_0, c) \Big] \tag{4}$$

$$\approx p_\phi(\mathbf{x}_{t-1}|\hat{\mathbf{x}}_0, c), \ \hat{\mathbf{x}}_0 \sim p_\theta(\mathbf{x}_0|\mathbf{x}_t, c). \tag{5}$$

In (4), we assume that $\mathbf{x}_{t-1}$ is conditionally independent of $\mathbf{x}_t$ given $\mathbf{x}_0$. We will get back to this assumption shortly. In (5), the expectation is empirically approximated using a single sample Monte Carlo for $p_\theta(\mathbf{x}_0|\mathbf{x}_t, c)$, which is obtained from the output of the generative transformer $G_\theta$. The next step is to sample from $p_\phi(\mathbf{x}_{t-1}|\hat{\mathbf{x}}_0, c)$. Recall that $\mathbf{x}_{t-1}$ is a masked version of $\hat{\mathbf{x}}_0$, rendering it solely determined by $\hat{\mathbf{x}}_0$ and a mask $\mathbf{m}_{t-1}$. Thus, we can sample $\mathbf{x}_{t-1}$ in (5) using Token-Critic to predict a mask $\mathbf{m}_{t-1}$ given $\hat{\mathbf{x}}_0$.

Note that the mask computation of MaskGIT [5] only relies on the prediction score $p_\theta(\mathbf{x}_0|\mathbf{x}_t, c)$, in which tokens with the lowest predictions are masked. The mask sampling is independent for each token and moreover greedy which means previously unmasked tokens will be kept unmasked forever. In contrast, the proposed mask sampling is learned by the Token-Critic model $\phi$ to approximate sampling from the joint distribution by taking into account the correlation among tokens. This notably improves the sampling leading to better generation quality. Secondly, Token-Critic makes generation regrettable, allowing to revoke prior decisions based on the most recent generation.

The sampling process is given as pseudocode in Algorithm 2 and represented schematically in Fig. 1. The rate of masking in each step is given by the scheduling function $\gamma(t)$, with $t = T - 1 \ldots 0$, where higher values of $t$ correspond to more masking. After predicting $\mathbf{m}_t$ in each step, we mask the $R = \lceil \gamma(t/T) \cdot N \rceil$ tokens with the lowest Token-Critic score. Following [5], to introduce randomness in the first steps, we add a small "selection noise" $\mathbf{n}(t)$ to the Token-Critic scores before ranking them. This selection noise is annealed according to $\mathbf{n}(t) = K \cdot \mathbf{u} \cdot (t/T)$, where $K$ is a hyperparameter and $\mathbf{u} \in [-0.5, 0.5]^N$ is a random uniform vector. Furthermore, the sampling temperature for each token is also annealed according to a linear schedule $T(t) = a \cdot (t/T) + b$.

Finally, we get back to the assumption in (4) that $\mathbf{x}_{t-1}$ is made independent of $\mathbf{x}_t$ given $\mathbf{x}_0$. This assumption can be dropped by simply adapting the Token-Critic's input by concatenating the previous mask $\mathbf{m}_t$ to $\hat{\mathbf{x}}_0$. However, in practice, we find this does not yield a better result. In fact, by ignoring the previous mask, Token-Critic has the ability to correct previously sampled tokens that are no longer as likely given the latest context, which addresses the greedy mask selection in the MaskGIT model [5].

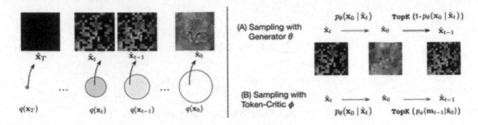

**Fig. 2.** Token-Critic in the lens of a discrete stochastic process that gradually masks a real image $\mathbf{x}_0$ from $t = 0 \ldots T$, where $\mathbf{x}_T$ is fully masked. The circles represent the distributions of real vector-quantized images under different masking rates. During the reverse process, a masked image estimate $\hat{\mathbf{x}}_t$ is refined by first using the generator to predict a clean image $\hat{\mathbf{x}}_0$, and then predicting the mask for the next timestep. While prior works (A) use the confidence of the generator $G_\theta$, we use the predictions of Token-Critic (B) to select which tokens to mask.

---

**Algorithm 1.** Token-Critic Training

**Input:** Pre-trained generator $G_\theta$, scheduling function $\gamma(t)$, learning rate $\eta$
**Output:** Token-Critic parameters $\phi$

1: **repeat**
2: $\quad \mathbf{x}_0, c \leftarrow$ i.i.d. sampled VQ image
3: $\quad t \sim \mathcal{U}_{(0,1)}$
4: $\quad \mathbf{m}_t \leftarrow$ random mask($\lceil \gamma(t) \cdot N \rceil$)
5: $\quad \mathbf{x}_t \leftarrow \mathbf{x}_0 \odot \mathbf{m}_t$
6: $\quad \hat{\mathbf{x}}_0 \leftarrow G_\theta(\mathbf{x}_t, c)$
7: $\quad \phi \leftarrow \phi - \eta \nabla_\phi BCE(\mathbf{m}_t, p_\phi(\mathbf{m}_t | \hat{\mathbf{x}}_0, c))$
8: **until** convergence

**Algorithm 2.** Token-Critic Sampling

1: $\mathbf{x}_T \leftarrow [\texttt{[MASK]}]_N$
2: **for** $t = T \ldots 1$ **do**
3: $\quad k = \lceil \gamma((t-1)/T) \cdot N \rceil$
4: $\quad \hat{\mathbf{x}}_0 = G_\theta(\mathbf{x}_t, c)$
5: $\quad \{p_i\}_{i=1\ldots,N} \leftarrow p_\phi(\mathbf{m}_{t-1}^{(i)} | \hat{\mathbf{x}}_0, c) + n(t)$
6: $\quad \tau \leftarrow \text{rank}_k(\{p_i\})$
7: $\quad \{\mathbf{m}_{t-1}^{(i)}\} \leftarrow 1$ if $p_i > \tau$, else $0$
8: $\quad \mathbf{x}_{t-1} = \hat{\mathbf{x}}_0 \odot \mathbf{m}_{t-1}$
9: **end for**

---

### 3.3 Relation to Discrete Diffusion Processes

The role of Token-Critic can also be understood under the perspective of discrete diffusion processes [1,11,16,20], where it is assumed that there exists a stochastic process that gradually destroys information by masking. In this setting, the reverse process aims to progressively replace masked tokens with elements from the VQ codebook following the true distribution. In our case, this is what the generator transformer $G_\theta$ does in each step of the sampling procedure. Ideally, each intermediate result should lie within the distribution of partially masked real images, since this is the distribution used to train $G_\theta$. The role of Token-Critic is to guide the intermediate samples towards these regions.

Figure 2 represents a schematic representation of the reverse sampling process. Given a current estimate of a masked image $\hat{\mathbf{x}}_t$, we use the generator to produce an estimate clean image $\hat{\mathbf{x}}_0$. Note that due to the aforementioned modeling limitations, this estimate typically falls far from the distribution of real images. Token-Critic is then used to predict a less corrupted image $\hat{\mathbf{x}}_{t-1}$ from $\hat{\mathbf{x}}_0$. Since it was trained to distinguish incompatible tokens, the improved prediction is achieved by masking the least "plausible-looking" tokens.

In the diffusion processes literature, a similar sampling strategy relying on an estimate of the clean image was used in [37] for the continuous case and [1,16,20] for the discrete case. The difference in our approach is that we implicitly use a learned forward model instead of a fixed one obtained beforehand (*e.g.*, the Gaussian prior). On the other hand, previous discrete diffusion models for image generation [1,11,16,20] typically assume a stochastic process that is independent for each token, and give a fixed form Markov chain that defines the probabilities of each token being masked, converted randomly or staying the same. Even under the independence assumption, if the number of token categories is large, the computation of the $n$-step Markov transition matrix required to obtain the posterior can be impractical. These design differences in part explain the diffusion models' low-efficiency when synthesizing high-resolution images. Instead, Token-Critic trades-off the analytical interpretability and tractability of these assumptions for a more efficient, learned forward process $p_\phi(\mathbf{x}_t|\hat{\mathbf{x}}_0)$.

Finally, we can derive the training objective of Token-Critic from the KL divergence between the distributions of real partially masked images $q(\mathbf{x}_{t-1})$, and the distribution of partially masked images obtained in the intermediate steps by the proposed sampling scheme $p_{\theta,\phi}(\mathbf{x}_t)$. We refer to the appendix for the derivation.

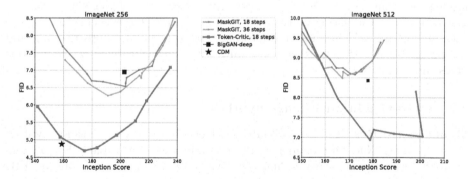

**Fig. 3.** FID-vs-IS curves on ImageNet $256 \times 256$ and $512 \times 512$ (bottom right is better). The trade-off between diversity and quality is traversed by varying the sampling temperature. Compared to the baseline [5], sampling using Token-Critic produces a significant improvement in performance, and outperforms BigGAN-deep [3] and CDM [19], achieving a new state-of-the-art for methods that do not rely on an external classifier.

## 4    Experiments

In this section we evaluate the proposed approach on class-conditional image generation tasks on ImageNet [7] $256 \times 256$ and $512 \times 512$. We compare over classical metrics to examine the trade-off between quality and variablity, notably FID [18] vs. Inception Score [33] and Precision vs. Recall [27]. We observed that the highly-competitive baseline is significantly improved when using Token-Critic, and that the proposed method obtains an advantageous quality-diversity trade-off, compared to state-of-the-art GANs and continuous diffusion models.

### 4.1    Experimental Setup

We use a pre-trained MaskGIT [5] model as the generator, and use the Token-Critic to guide the sampling, as described in Sect. 3.2. We adopt the VQ encoder-decoder of [12] and [5], with a codebook with 1024 tokens, trained at $256 \times 256$ resolution in the same datasets. The VQ encoding compresses the image by a factor of 16, so that a $256 \times 256$ ($512 \times 512$) image is represented as a grid of $16 \times 16$ ($32 \times 32$) integers. The generator is a transformer with 24 layers and 16 heads. For the Token-Critic, we use a relatively smaller transformer with 20 layers and 12 heads, but otherwise of identical architecture. Both transformers use embeddings of dimension 768 and a hidden dimension of 3,072, learnable positional embedding [39], LayerNorm [2], and truncated normal initialization (stddev = 0.02). The following training hyperparameters were used for both MaskGIT and Token-Critic: dropout rate = 0.1, Adam optimizer [22] with $\beta_1 =$ 0.9 and $\beta_2 = 0.96$. We use RandomResizeAndCrop for data augmentation. All models are trained on $8 \times 8$ TPU devices with a batch size of 256. The MaskGIT generators and the Token-Critic models were trained for 600 epochs. We use the same cosine schedule for the masking rate as in [5], for both training and sampling. We use 18 steps when sampling with Token-Critic, as we found this gives the best results.

### 4.2    Class-Conditional Image Synthesis

**Quantitative Results.** We evaluate our method on class-conditional synthesis using ImageNet. Our main results are summarized in Table 1. For a more comprehensive quantitative comparison, we compare Inception Score vs. FID in Fig. 3. These represent the trade-off between image quality, associated to Inception Score, and diversity or coverage, associated to FID. To traverse the quality-diversity trade-off for the baseline and Token-Critic, we modify the sampling temperature and selection noise parameter $K$ (Sect. 3.2). Higher selection noise and temperature produce higher variability but lower quality.

We compare the proposed approach to the MaskGIT baseline which uses the generator's prediction confidence to select which tokens to reject in each step of the iterative sampling. To account for the fact that the proposed method requires two forward passes for each sampling step, in Fig. 3 we compare the proposed approach to the MaskGIT baseline for double the number of sampling steps.

**Table 1.** Comparison between methods that do not leverage an external classifier. We report the sampling configurations that obtain the best FID score for each method, and refer to Fig. 3 for the more comprehensive trade-off between FID and Inception Score. All methods are evaluated on ImageNet training set. Results for [3] are as reproduced by [34].

| Model | Steps | ImageNet 256 × 256 | | | | ImageNet 512 × 512 | | | |
|---|---|---|---|---|---|---|---|---|---|
| | | FID ↓ | IS ↑ | Prec | Rec | FID ↓ | IS ↑ | Prec | Rec |
| BigGAN-deep [3] | 1 | 6.95 | 202.65 | **0.86** | 0.24 | 8.43 | 177.9 | **0.85** | 0.25 |
| ADM [9] | 250 | 10.94 | 101.0 | 0.69 | **0.63** | 23.24 | 58.06 | 0.73 | **0.60** |
| CDM [19] | 100 | 4.88 | 158.7 | n/a | n/a | n/a | n/a | n/a | n/a |
| MaskGIT [5] | 18 | 6.56 | **203.6** | 0.79 | 0.48 | 8.48 | 167.1 | 0.78 | 0.46 |
| MaskGIT+Token-Critic | 18(x2) | **4.69** | 174.5 | 0.76 | 0.53 | **6.80** | **182.1** | 0.73 | 0.50 |

We also compare to state-of-the-art GAN architectures BigGAN-deep [3], and continuous Cascaded Diffusion Model (CDM) [19] and Ablated Diffusion Model (ADM) [9] without external classifier guidance.

Of all the methods that do not rely on an external classifier, the proposed approach achieves the lowest FID, while providing an advantageous FID/Inception Score balance. Compared to the MaskGIT baseline, it achieves a significant improvement in terms of FID and Inception Score.

**Table 2.** Comparison between methods that use an external classifier during training or sampling. We report the sampling configurations that obtain the best FID score for each method. We refer to Fig. 4 to better appreciate the improvement obtained by Token-Critic in the trade-off between image quality and sample diversity. Sampling with Token-Critic and a classifier rejection scheme significantly improves the baseline and obtains the best Inception Score of all compared methods.

| Model | ImageNet 256 × 256 | | | | ImageNet 512 × 512 | | | |
|---|---|---|---|---|---|---|---|---|
| | FID ↓ | IS ↑ | Prec | Rec | FID ↓ | IS ↑ | Prec | Rec |
| ADM+Guid. [9] | 4.59 | 186.7 | 0.82 | 0.52 | 7.72 | 172.7 | **0.87** | 0.42 |
| ADM+Guid.+Upsamp. [9] | 3.94 | 215.8 | **0.83** | 0.53 | 3.85 | 221.7 | 0.84 | **0.53** |
| StyleGAN-XL ($\Psi = 1.0$ ) [34] | **3.26** | 225.6 | 0.74 | 0.45 | **3.58** | 219.8 | 0.73 | 0.43 |
| MaskGIT [5] (a.r. 20%) | 4.70 | 266 | 0.80 | 0.48 | 5.13 | 250.7 | 0.79 | 0.47 |
| [5]+Token-Critic (a.r. 20%) | 3.75 | **287.0** | 0.75 | **0.55** | 4.03 | **305.2** | 0.73 | 0.50 |

**Leveraging an External Classifier.** Classifier-guidance is a commonly adopted technique in diffusion models to improve class-conditional generation [12,31], consisting on using the gradient of an external classifier to improve the class score of the sampled image, and thus render it more semantically meaningful. We show that the improvement obtained by leveraging an external pretrained classifier is independent of the improvement brought by the Token-Critic. Moreover, the combination of both further improves the quantitative performance, achieving the highest reported Inception Score, and FID scores competitive with the most advanced GANs and Diffusion Models that use an external classifier.

Since classifier guidance is not directly transferable to the VQ latent space, here we adopt a classifier-based rejection sampling scheme [31]. Given the conditioning class, we generate multiple image candidates and keep only the one with the highest classifier score for the class. For the external classifier we use a ResNet [17] with 50 layers. We experiment with acceptance rates of 10% and 20% (meaning we keep one out of 10 and one out of 5 images with the highest scores). Results are summarized in Table 2 and the FID vs. Inception Score curves are plotted in Fig. 4. We include a comparison with concurrent work StyleGAN-XL [34]. Whilst StyleGAN-XL achieves better FID score, Token-Critic is superior with repsect to Inception Score, Precision and Recall.

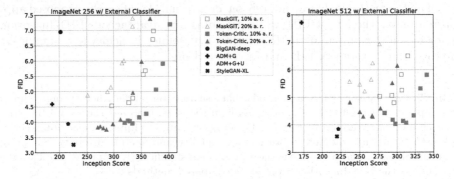

**Fig. 4.** FID-vs-Inception Score trade-off for methods that leverage an external classifier (bottom right is better). We use an external ResNet classifier for rejection sampling at acceptance rates 10% and 20%. Points in the graph indicate different sampling temperatures to balance quality and diversity, the remaining hyperparameters being equal. Token-Critic improves significantly upon [5], and also obtains a superior trade-off to diffusion models with upsampling [9]. The trade-off is also comparable to the concurrent work StyleGAN-XL [34], which obtains the best FID but with much lower Inception Score.

**Qualitative Results.** Figure 5 shows a qualitative comparison on ImageNet class-conditional generation between the baseline MaskGIT's original sampling procedure [5] and the proposed sampling using Token-Critic. We demonstrate the models without classifier-based rejection to better isolate the difference in image quality and diversity obtained by the proposed approach. Notably, sampling with the proposed approach achieves better structural consistency, showing the ability of the Token-Critic to capture long range dependencies. We refer to the supplementary material for further results and comparisons.

### 4.3  VQ Image Refinement

To demonstrate the ability of Token-Critic to identify unlikely visual tokens, we apply it to refine the output of the baseline model. Given a generated VQ-encoded image by a MaskGIT generator, we compute the Token-Critic scores on the generated tokens, and proceed to resample the tokens that have low scores. We start by rejecting and replacing 60% of the original tokens in the first step, and then progressively reject and replace fewer tokens, following again a cosine schedule for $T = 9$ steps. The result of this procedure can be regarded as a visual quality improvement of the original images, see Fig. 6. By applying this refinement procedure we improve the FID score of the baseline generator form 6.56 to 5.73 in $256 \times 256$ and from 8.48 to 7.64 in $512 \times 512$.

## 5  Related Work

While there exist other types of generative models such as VAEs [24,38] and Flow-based models [32], we briefly review the works closely relevant to ours.

*Generative Adversarial Networks (GANs)* are capable of synthesizing high-fidelity images at blazing speeds. GAN based methods demonstrate impressive capability in yielding high-fidelity samples [3,14,21]. They suffer from, however, well known issues including training instability and mode collapse which causes a lack of sample diversity. Addressing these issues still remains an active research problem. Note that MaskGIT and Token-Critic are not affected by adversarial training instability, as the Token-Critic is trained asynchronously over a pre-trained MaskGIT.

*Generative Image Transformers.* Inspired by the success of the transformer in the NLP field [4,8], vision transformers [10] have been applied to various vision tasks. In particular, the generative image transformer (GIT) [6] is inspired by the generative pre-trained transformer or GPT [4]. Generally, modern GITs consist of two stages [30]: image quantization and autoregressive decoding, where the former is to compress an image into tokens of a reasonable length whereas the latter, borrowed from neural machine translation [39], generate image tokens as if they were "visual words". Most recent contributions are on improving the first stage, *e.g.*, using vector-quantized models of various architectures and losses [12,30,40]. Very recently, [5,41] proposed to use bi-directional transformers to synthesize images, which significantly accelerate the decoding time. Our work builds upon the MaskGIT model [5] and improves its mask sampling in non-autoregressive decoding.

*Denoising Diffusion Models.* [36] define a parameterized Markov chain trained to reverse a forward process of corrupting a training image into pure noise. While many works have focused on continuous (Gaussian) diffusion processes [23],

Baseline [5] + Token-Critic (FID 6.80).

Baseline [5] (FID 8.48).

**Fig. 5.** Samples from ImageNet $512 \times 512$ models for classes Toucan (96), German Shepherd (235), Ladybug (301), Beagle (162) and Lion (291). All models ran for 18 steps.

**Fig. 6.** Refinement of previously generated vector-quantized images by [5] with an ImageNet $512 \times 512$ model. **Top:** Original samples (FID/IS 8.48/167). **Bottom:** After refining 60% of the tokens with lowest Token-Critic score (FID/IS 7.64/182.4). The semantics of the original image is maintained, but it is given a more realistic aspect.

closely related to ours are diffusion models with *discrete* state spaces [35]. For example, Austin *et al.* [1] proposed a discrete diffusion (D3) model corrupting data by transition matrices that embed structure knowledge. Song *et al.* [37] introduced implicit diffusion models of non-Markovian diffusion processes. Hoogeboom *et al.* [20] modeled the categorical data through a fixed multinomial diffusion for image segmentation, which was improved in Image-BART [11] by combing with the autoregressive formulation.

The majority of diffusion models is characterized by a forward process with tractable known expressions according to [1], which is essential for permitting not only efficient forward sampling but also computation of the posterior. From this perspective, our method, similar to MaskGIT [5], is not a traditional diffusion model because it parameterizes the forward process by a transformer that does not have a tractable expression. Since the direct computation of the forward process is intractable in our case, we resort to learning a non-Markov transformer that can teleport to any forward state. This is achieved by the proposed second transformer (Token-Critic). Empirically, we found this strategy to be effective needing considerably fewer number of decoding steps (typically 8–16 steps) while producing competitive quality.

# 6   Conclusion

In this work, we proposed a novel method for sampling from a non-autoregressive generative vision transformer. It is based on using a second transformer, the Token-Critic, to select which tokens are accepted and which are rejected and resampled during the iterative generative process. Given a reconstructed masked image, the Token-Critic is trained to distinguish which visual tokens belong to the original image and which are predictions of the generative transformer. Coupled with the Token-Critic, an already powerful non-autoregressive transformer significantly improves its performance, and outperforms the state-of-the-art in terms of the trade-off between generated image quality and variety, in the challenging task of class-conditional ImageNet generation.

# References

1. Austin, J., Johnson, D., Ho, J., Tarlow, D., van den Berg, R.: Structured denoising diffusion models in discrete state-spaces. In: 34th Proceedings of the International Conference on Advances in Neural Information Processing Systems 34 (2021)
2. Ba, J.L., Kiros, J.R., Hinton, G.E.: Layer normalization. arXiv preprint arXiv:1607.06450 (2016)
3. Brock, A., Donahue, J., Simonyan, K.: Large scale GAN training for high fidelity natural image synthesis. arXiv preprint arXiv:1809.11096 (2018)
4. Brown, T., et al.: Language models are few-shot learners. In: NeurIPS (2020)
5. Chang, H., Zhang, H., Jiang, L., Liu, C., Freeman, W.T.: MasKGIT: masked generative image transformer. arXiv preprint arXiv:2202.04200 (2022)
6. Chen, M., Radford, A., Child, R., Wu, J., Jun, H., Luan, D., SutsKever, I.: generative pretraining from pixels. In: International Conference on Machine Learning, pp. 1691–1703. PMLR (2020)
7. Deng, J., et al.: ImageUet: a large-scale hierarchical image database. In: 2009 IEEE Conference on Computer Vision and Pattern Recognition, pp. 248–255. IEEE (2009)
8. Devlin, J., Chang, M.W., Lee, K., Toutanova, K.: BERT: pre-training of deep bidirectional transformers for language understanding. arXiv preprint arXiv:1810.04805 (2018)
9. Dhariwal, P., Nichol, A.: Diffusion models beat GANs on image synthesis. In: 34th Proceedings of the International Conference on Advances in Neural Information Processing Systems (2021)
10. Dosovitskiy, A., et al.: An image is worth 16x16 words: transformers for image recognition at scale. In: ICLR (2021)
11. Esser, P., Rombach, R., Blattmann, A., Ommer, B.: Imagebart: Bidirectional context with multinomial diffusion for autoregressive image synthesis. In: 34th Proceedings of the International Conference on Advances in Neural Information Processing Systems (2021)
12. Esser, P., Rombach, R., Ommer, B.: Taming transformers for high-resolution image synthesis. In: Proceedings of the IEEE/CVF Conference on Computer Vision and Pattern Recognition, pp. 12873–12883 (2021)
13. Ghazvininejad, M., Levy, O., Liu, Y., Zettlemoyer, L.: Mask-predict: parallel decoding of conditional masked language models. In: EMNLP-IJCNLP (2019)
14. Goodfellow, I., et al.: Generative adversarial nets. In: NeurIPS (2014)
15. Gu, J., Kong, X.: Fully non-autoregressive neural machine translation: tricks of the trade. In: Findings of ACL-IJCNLP (2021)
16. Gu, S., et al.: Vector quantized diffusion model for text-to-image synthesis. arXiv preprint arXiv:2111.14822 (2021)
17. He, K., Zhang, X., Ren, S., Sun, J.: Deep residual learning for image recognition. In: Proceedings of the IEEE Conference on Computer Vision and Pattern Recognition, pp. 770–778 (2016)
18. Heusel, M., Ramsauer, H., Unterthiner, T., Nessler, B., Hochreiter, S.: GANs trained by a two time-scale update rule converge to a local Nash equilibrium. In: 30th Proceedings of the International Conference on Advances in Neural Information Processing Systems (2017)

19. Ho, J., Saharia, C., Chan, W., Fleet, D.J., Norouzi, M., Salimans, T.: Cascaded diffusion models for high fidelity image generation. J. Mach. Learn. Res. **23**(47), 1–33 (2022)
20. Hoogeboom, E., Nielsen, D., Jaini, P., Forré, P., Welling, M.: Argmax flows and multinomial diffusion: Learning categorical distributions. In: Thirty-Fifth Conference on Neural Information Processing Systems (2021)
21. Karras, T., Laine, S., Aittala, M., Hellsten, J., Lehtinen, J., Aila, T.: Analyzing and improving the image quality of StyleGAN. In: CVPR (2020)
22. Kingma, D.P., Ba, J.: Adam: a method for stochastic optimization. arXiv preprint arXiv:1412.6980 (2014)
23. Kingma, D.P., Salimans, T., Poole, B., Ho, J.: Variational diffusion models. arXiv preprint arXiv:2107.00630 (2021)
24. Kingma, D.P., Welling, M.: Auto-encoding variational bayes. arXiv preprint arXiv:1312.6114 (2013)
25. Kong, X., Jiang, L., Chang, H., Zhang, H., Hao, Y., Gong, H., Essa, I.: BLT: bidirectional layout transformer for controllable layout generation. arXiv preprint arXiv:2112.05112 (2021)
26. Kong, X., Zhang, Z., Hovy, E.: Incorporating a local translation mechanism into non-autoregressive translation. arXiv preprint arXiv:2011.06132 (2020)
27. Kynkäänniemi, T., Karras, T., Laine, S., Lehtinen, J., Aila, T.: Improved precision and recall metric for assessing generative models. In: 32nd Proceedings of the International Conference on Advances in Neural Information Processing Systems 32 (2019)
28. Nichol, A., Dhariwal, P.: Improved denoising diffusion probabilistic models. arXiv preprint arXiv:2102.09672 (2021)
29. van den Oord, A., Vinyals, O., Kavukcuoglu, K.: Neural discrete representation learning. In: Guyon, I., von Luxburg, U., Bengio, S., Wallach, H.M., Fergus, R., Vishwanathan, S.V.N., Garnett, R. (eds.) NeurIPS (2017)
30. Ramesh, A., et al.: Zero-shot text-to-image generation. In: Meila, M., Zhang, T. (eds.) ICML (2021)
31. Razavi, A., Van den Oord, A., Vinyals, O.: Generating diverse high-fidelity images with VQ-VAE-2. In: 32nd Proceedings of the International Conference on Advances in Neural Information Processing Systems (2019)
32. Rezende, D., Mohamed, S.: Variational inference with normalizing flows. In: International Conference on Machine Learning, pp. 1530–1538 (2015)
33. Salimans, T., Goodfellow, I., Zaremba, W., Cheung, V., Radford, A., Chen, X.: Improved techniques for training GANs. In: 29th Proceedings of the International Conference on Advances in Neural Information Processing Systems (2016)
34. Sauer, A., Schwarz, K., Geiger, A.: Stylegan-xl: Scaling styleGan to large diverse datasets. arXiv preprint arXiv:2202.00273 (2022)
35. Seff, A., Zhou, W., Damani, F., Doyle, A., Adams, R.P.: Discrete object generation with reversible inductive construction. In: 32nd Proceedings of the International Conference on Advances in Neural Information Processing Systems (2019)
36. Sohl-Dickstein, J., Weiss, E., Maheswaranathan, N., Ganguli, S.: Deep unsupervised learning using nonequilibrium thermodynamics. In: International Conference on Machine Learning, pp. 2256–2265. PMLR (2015)
37. Song, J., Meng, C., Ermon, S.: Denoising diffusion implicit models. arXiv preprint arXiv:2010.02502 (2020)
38. Vahdat, A., Kautz, J.: Nvae: a deep hierarchical variational autoencoder. In: Proceedings of the International Conference on Advances in Neural Information Processing Systems (2020)

39. Vaswani, A., et al.: Attention is all you need. In: 30tth Proceedings of the International Conference on Advances in Neural Information Processing systems (2017)
40. Yu, J., et al.: Vector-quantized image modeling with improved VQGAN. arXiv preprint arXiv:2110.04627 (2021)
41. Zhang, Z., et al.: M6-UFC: unifying multi-modal controls for conditional image synthesis. arXiv preprint arXiv:2105.14211 (2021)

# TREND: Truncated Generalized Normal Density Estimation of Inception Embeddings for GAN Evaluation

Junghyuk Lee[iD] and Jong-Seok Lee[(✉)][iD]

School of Integrated Technology, Yonsei University, Seoul, Republic of Korea
{junghyuklee,jong-seok.lee}@yonsei.ac.kr

**Abstract.** Evaluating image generation models such as generative adversarial networks (GANs) is a challenging problem. A common approach is to compare the distributions of the set of ground truth images and the set of generated test images. The Frechét Inception distance is one of the most widely used metrics for evaluation of GANs, which assumes that the features from a trained Inception model for a set of images follow a normal distribution. In this paper, we argue that this is an over-simplified assumption, which may lead to unreliable evaluation results, and more accurate density estimation can be achieved using a truncated generalized normal distribution. Based on this, we propose a novel metric for accurate evaluation of GANs, named TREND (TRuncated gEneralized Normal Density estimation of inception embeddings). We demonstrate that our approach significantly reduces errors of density estimation, which consequently eliminates the risk of faulty evaluation results. Furthermore, the proposed metric significantly improves robustness of evaluation results against variation of the number of image samples.

**Keywords:** Generative adversarial networks · Image generation · Image quality · Performance evaluation metrics

## 1 Introduction

Generative models for realistic image generation is one of the most active research topics in recent days. The objective of the generative models is to find a mapping from random noise to real images by estimating probability density $P_g$ from target distribution $P_r$. Among different types of generative models, generative adversarial networks (GANs) are particularly popular, which learn the target distribution by solving the objective equation $P_g = P_r$ as a min-max game of a generator and a discriminator [7]. Recent state-of-the-art GANs [3,12,24] can generate highly realistic images such as faces, animals, structures, etc.

---

**Supplementary Information** The online version contains supplementary material available at https://doi.org/10.1007/978-3-031-20050-2_6.

Evaluation of GAN models is crucial for developing models and improving their performance. Assessing the quality of generated images via subjective tests is inadequate due to the issues of excessive time and cost. Accordingly, performance evaluation is usually based on measuring the likelihood of the learned probability density $P_g$ with respect to the ground truth $P_r$. However, since $P_g$ defined by GANs is implicit, it is difficult to directly measure the likelihood. Therefore, evaluation of GANs is usually based on sample statistics to estimate $P_g$ and $P_r$ for comparison.

Building the distribution from generated or real image samples is a challenging part in GAN evaluation. In early literature, there exist attempts to directly measure likelihood using a kernel density estimation method. However, due to high dimensionality of pixel-domain images, this method requires a substantial number of samples. Moreover, it is noted that the measured likelihood is sometimes unrelated to the quality of generated images [26].

In order to address the high dimensionality and sample quality issues, the Inception score (IS) [23] proposes to use an Inception model that is trained for image classification [25]. It measures the Kullback-Leibler divergence (KLD) of the conditional label distribution for generated images and the marginal distribution of the pre-trained model. Although IS performs well, it has major drawbacks as well. It measures correctness of generated images compared to the classification model, instead of considering the target distribution of GANs, which causes inability to detect overfitting and mode collapse [27].

The Fréchet Inception distance (FID) [9] also uses a pre-trained Inception model but in a different way from IS. It uses the output of a specific layer of the Inception model, called Inception feature, to embed sampled images to an informative domain. Then, the Fréchet distance, also known as earth mover's distance, is measured between the Inception features of generated test samples and those of target real samples. Showing better performance than other metrics, FID is one of the most frequently used metrics for evaluation of GANs nowadays.

Despite its widespread usage, we argue that FID has several drawbacks. As a major drawback, we find out that FID incorrectly estimates the distribution of Inception features. FID assumes that Inception features follow a normal distribution, which is not accurate for real data. First, the distribution of Inception features is truncated at zero due to the rectified linear unit (ReLU) applied to obtain the features, which is also noted in [2]. Second, the shape of the distribution is significantly different from the normal distribution, having a sharper peak. In addition, FID has a high bias in terms of the number of samples. Although a method reducing the bias is proposed in [4], it is still based on FID under the normality assumption.

In this paper, we propose a novel method for accurate GAN evaluation, which is named TREND (TRuncated gEneralized Normal Density estimation of inception embeddings). In order to address the aforementioned issues, we thoroughly analyze Inception features with respect to their distributional properties. We find that the truncated generalized normal distribution can effectively model the probability density of Inception features of real-world images, based on which we design the proposed TREND metric. Our main contributions are as follows:

- We analyse Inception features and show that density estimation using the normal distribution is inaccurate in conventional evaluation methods. We conduct thorough and complete analysis regarding the distribution of Inception embeddings.
- Based on the analysis, we propose to model the distribution of Inception features with the truncated generalized normal distribution and measure the Jensen-Shannon divergence between the estimated distributions of generated and real images.
- We demonstrate that the proposed method can accurately evaluate various generative models including not only GANs but also variational autoencoders (VAEs) and diffusion models compared to existing metrics. Furthermore, we show that the proposed method removes the bias caused by the variation of the number of samples.

## 2   Related Work

### 2.1   GANs

Generative models aim to capture the probability distribution of target real image data, $P_r$. After training, one can generate new data according to the learned probability density $P_g$. Among generative models, GANs [7] train a generator ($G$) and a discriminator ($D$) playing a min-max game to find a Nash equilibrium:

$$\min_G \max_D \mathbb{E}_{x^r \sim P_r}[\log D(x^r)] + \mathbb{E}_{z \sim P_z}[\log(1 - D(G(z)))], \tag{1}$$

where $x^r$ is a sample from the target distribution $P_r$ and $z$ is a latent vector drawn from the latent distribution $P_z$ that is usually set to be a normal or uniform distribution.

Plenty of studies on image generation using GANs have been conducted with variations such as modification of the loss function [1], model architecture [21,28], normalization strategy [17], and up-scaling approach [3,10–12] in order to improve stability of learning and to enhance the quality and resolution of generated images. Popular GAN models include DCGAN [21], ProGAN [10], StyleGAN [11], StyleGAN2 [12], and BigGAN [3].

### 2.2   Evaluation Metrics for GANs

A common procedure for GAN evaluation is composed of the following steps. The first step is to prepare a set of generated images from the test GAN model and a set of real images from the target dataset (e.g., ImageNet). Second, an embedding function is applied to extract low-dimensional informative features from the images (e.g., Inception feature embedding). Then, the probability density of each set of features is estimated for comparison. Finally, difference of the two distributions is measured using a proper metric, where a smaller difference indicates better performance of the GAN.

IS [23] uses the pre-trained Inception model for both embedding and density estimation. Given test images, it measures the KLD of the conditional probability $p(y|x)$ from the marginal distribution $p(y)$ using the softmax output of the Inception model:

$$IS = \exp\left(\mathbb{E}_{x^g}[KLD(p(y|x^g)\|p(y))]\right), \tag{2}$$

where $x^g$ is a test data (i.e., generated image) and $y$ is the predicted class label. Since IS does not consider the target distribution and only uses the conditional probability estimated by the Inception model for the generated images, its adequacy has been controversial [27]. For example, it favors highly classifiable images instead of high quality images.

FID [9] also uses the Inception model for image embedding. Assuming that the distribution of embedded features is Gaussian, it measures the Fréchet distance between the Gaussian distributions for the generated and real data, i.e.,

$$FID = \|\mu^g - \mu^r\|_2^2 + \mathrm{Trace}\left(\Sigma^g + \Sigma^r - 2\left(\Sigma^g \Sigma^r\right)^{1/2}\right), \tag{3}$$

where $\|\cdot\|_2^2$ denotes the $l2$-norm operator and $(\mu^g, \Sigma^g)$ and $(\mu^r, \Sigma^r)$ are the mean and the covariance of the generated and real data, respectively. Having a straightforward approach and formula, it is commonly used for GAN evaluation in recent days. However, it has been argued that FID is biased [4,18] and the normality is not guaranteed [2]. In order to address the bias problem, extrapolating FID with respect to the number of samples is proposed in [4]. Nonetheless, the issue of inaccurate normal density estimation still remains. In addition, FID is unexpectedly susceptible to low-level preprocessing such as resizing and compression [20].

The Kernel Inception distance (KID) [2] measures the maximum mean discrepancy of the two distributions after transforming the Inception features using a kernel function. While KID estimates feature distributions without normality assumption, the choice of a proper kernel function has not been well studied.

Measuring different aspects (e.g., fidelity and diversity) of generated images separately has been also considered [14,19,22]. For instance, the improved precision and recall method [14] applies the precision and recall approach in machine learning to real and generated images for GAN evaluation. Although such an approach can be effective for a diagnostic purpose, using a single-valued metric facilitates more efficient and convenient evaluation and comparison of GAN models, and thus has been more popular.

## 3  Analysis of Inception Features

The Inception model pre-trained using the ImageNet dataset [5] is widely used as an image embedding function in most state-of-the-art GAN evaluation metrics [2,

4, 9, 23]. The 2048-dimensional Inception feature is the output of the last pooling layer before the fully connected layer of the model. In this section, we thoroughly analyze the distribution and characteristics of the Inception features.

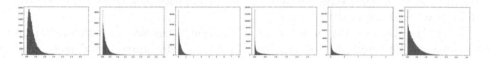

**Fig. 1.** Histograms of the Inception features from the ImageNet validation dataset for selected dimensions. In each figure, the x-axis and y-axis are the feature value and the frequency, respectively.

In Fig. 1, histograms of the Inception features from the validation split of the ImageNet dataset are shown. Some representative feature dimensions are chosen out of the 2048 dimensions. From the figure, we find the following observations.

First, the distribution of the Inception feature is left-truncated. This is because the Inception model uses the ReLU as the activation function, by which the negative values are set to zero.

Second, the shapes of the distributions differ from normal distributions. The distributions in Fig. 1 have sharper peaks than normal distributions, i.e., they are leptokurtic. When the truncation at zero is excluded, the kurtosis value of the Inception features for the ImageNet dataset is measured as 28.6 on average across dimensions, which is larger than that of the normal distribution (which is 3). Furthermore, the measured kurtosis ranges from 1.3 to 592.2 with a median of 8.5, implying that the sharpness significantly varies according to the dimension.

Third, the Inception feature dimensions are nearly independent with each other. We measure the Pearson correlation coefficient (PCC) value between each pair of dimensions. The average PCC is 0.055 with a standard deviation of 0.046. While FID uses a multivariate normal distribution, the independence allows us to separately estimate the dimension-wise distributions. This can significantly reduce the number of parameters to be estimated. More details of the independence are presented in the Supplemental Materials.

FID does not consider these characteristics, which consequently may lead to unreliable and inaccurate evaluation results. In order to address this issue, we propose a new method with more accurate modeling of the distributions of the Inception features in the following section.

## 4    Proposed Method

A brief summary of the proposed method called TREND is as follows. First, we extract the $d$-dimensional Inception feature $x \in \mathbb{R}^d$ from an image (i.e., $d = 2048$). Next, we model the probability density of the Inception feature as

$$f(x) = \text{TGN}(x|M, S, B), \tag{4}$$

where TGN is a multivariate truncated generalized normal distribution with mean $M$, covariance $S$, and shape parameter $B$. This is much more flexible than the normal distribution, allowing us to model the truncation at zero and peak sharpness varying with respect to the feature dimension. Finally, we use the Jensen-Shannon divergence (JSD) as a dissimilarity metric between the estimated test and target distributions.

Based on the observation in Sect. 3, we assume independence between feature dimensions. Therefore, we can replace the multivariate probability density with a product of dimension-wise distributions:

$$f(x) = \prod_{i=1}^{d} f_i(x_i), \tag{5}$$

where $x_i$ is the $i$th dimension of $x$ and $f_i(x_i)$ is a one-dimensional truncated generalized normal distribution for the $i$th dimension:

$$f_i(x_i) = \frac{\beta}{\sigma G} e^{-\left|\frac{x_i - \mu}{\sigma}\right|^{\beta}}, \tag{6}$$

where $\mu$, $\sigma$, and $\beta$ are the mean, standard deviation, and shape parameter, respectively[1]. Note that $\beta < 2$ for leptokurtic distributions. $G$ is a scale factor for normalization due to truncation, which is defined as

$$G = \gamma\left(\frac{1}{\beta}, \left|\frac{A_1 - \mu}{\sigma}\right|^{\beta}\right) + \gamma\left(\frac{1}{\beta}, \left|\frac{A_2 - \mu}{\sigma}\right|^{\beta}\right), \tag{7}$$

where $A_1$ and $A_2$ are the lower and upper truncation points, respectively. $\gamma(u, v)$ is the lower incomplete gamma function with upper limit $v$ of integral, i.e.,

$$\gamma(u, v) = \int_0^v t^{u-1} e^{-t}\, dt.$$

We set lower and upper truncation points (i.e., $A_1$ and $A_2$) to zero and positive infinity, respectively. Then, (7) becomes

$$G = \gamma\left(\frac{1}{\beta}, \left|\frac{\mu}{\sigma}\right|^{\beta}\right) + \Gamma\left(\frac{1}{\beta}\right). \tag{8}$$

The parameters $(\mu, \sigma, \beta)$ are estimated by maximizing the likelihood of $n$ samples from the distribution. When we denote the $i$th feature dimension of the $j$th sample as $x_i^j$ ($j = 1, \ldots, n$), the likelihood $L$ is written as

$$L = \left(\frac{\beta}{\sigma G}\right)^n \prod_{j=1}^{n} e^{-\left|\frac{x_i^j - \mu}{\sigma}\right|^{\beta}}. \tag{9}$$

---

[1] We omit subscript $i$ for $\mu$, $\sigma$, $\beta$, and $G$ for simplicity.

By taking logarithm, we get log-likelihood as follows:

$$\log L = n \log \beta - n \log \sigma - n \log G - \sum_{j=1}^{n} \left| \frac{x_i^j - \mu}{\sigma} \right|^{\beta}. \tag{10}$$

Since it is intractable to formulate an analytic solution for the parameters $(\mu, \sigma, \beta)$ maximizing (10), a numerical approach should be adopted to estimate the parameters. We use a trust-region minimization method [15]. For the density estimation, we omit the feature values at zero occurring by truncation.

Finally, we measure the JSD between the estimated probability density of the Inception features for the generated images $f^g$ and that for the target real images $f^r$ as

$$TREND = JSD(f^g, f^r). \tag{11}$$

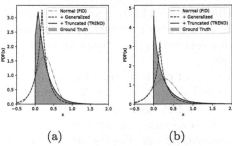

(a)        (b)

**Fig. 2.** Ground truth histograms and estimated densities of the Inception features in (a) the 120th dimension and (b) the 504th dimension. The estimated parameters $(\mu, \sigma, \beta)$ by TREND are $(0.08, 0.25, 1.03)$ and $(-1.9 \times 10^{-11}, 0.19, 0.82)$, respectively.

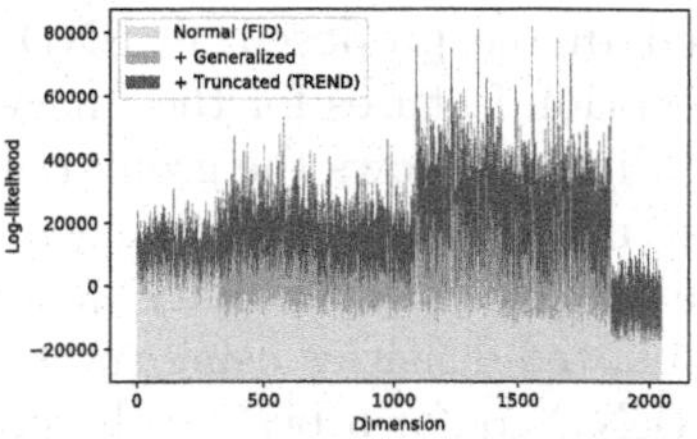

**Fig. 3.** Log-likelihoods from the estimated densities for each dimension of the Inception features.

JSD measures the divergence of each distribution from their average distribution using KLD and is defined by $JSD(p, q) = \frac{1}{2} \left( KLD(p\|m) + KLD(q\|m) \right)$, where $m = (p + q)/2$. Since we assume independence between feature dimensions, (11) can be written as the average of the dimension-wise JSDs:

$$TREND(f^g, f^r) = \frac{1}{d} \sum_{i=1}^{d} JSD(f_i^g, f_i^r). \tag{12}$$

There are two reasons of using JSD instead of the Frechét distance used in FID to compare distributions. First, it is too complex to calculate the Frechét distance between general distributions other than Gaussian distributions. Furthermore, JSD is bounded within $[0, 1]$ and thus more intuitive to interpret the result of performance comparison than the Frechét distance that has only the lower bound of 0. TREND reaches its minimum value of 0 when the test and target distributions are identical, which can be achieved for an ideal GAN. Conversely, when the distributions are completely different from each other, TREND yields its maximum value of 1.

## 5  Experiments

In this section, we conduct various experiments to demonstrate that the proposed method enables accurate and effective performance evaluation of GANs. Details of the experimental setup can be found in the Supplemental Materials.

### 5.1  Choice of Distribution

In order to demonstrate that TREND can effectively estimate distributions of Inception features, we perform an ablation study with respect to the choice of distribution. We compare the normal distribution (as in FID), generalized normal distribution without truncation, and truncated generalized normal distribution used in the proposed TREND method for estimating the distribution of the Inception features for the ImageNet dataset.

Figure 2 shows the ground truth histograms of the Inception features at specific dimensions for all images as blue-colored bars. And, each line represents the estimated probability density using one of the distributions. Overall, the estimated densities using the truncated generalized normal distribution used in TREND conform best to the ground truth distributions. On the other hand, in the cases of the normal distribution, the estimated densities significantly deviate from the ground truth on both left and right sides. Not only the shapes, but also the peak locations are far different from those of the ground truth. For the generalized normal distribution, in Fig. 2a, the sharpness of the peak is estimated better than the normal distribution. However, due to the truncated region, it fails to estimate the peak location. In Fig. 2b, inaccuracy of the generalized normal distribution is more prominent since truncation removes all the left tail and even some of the right tail near the peak.

For quantitative analysis, Fig. 3 shows log-likelihoods of the Inception features from the estimated densities using the three fitting distributions. The average log-likelihoods are -9463, 879, and 23867 for the normal distribution (FID), generalized normal distribution, and the truncated generalized normal distribution (TREND), respectively. As shown in Fig. 3, TREND performs best with the highest likelihood values than the others in all feature dimensions. We also conduct one-tailed $t$-tests under the null hypothesis that the average log-likelihoods are the same between the truncated generalized normal distribution and one of the other two, which confirm the significance of the differences: $t(2047) = 110$, $p < 5 \times 10^{-16}$ for truncated generalized normal vs. normal; $t(2047) = 69$, $p < 5 \times 10^{-16}$ for truncated generalized normal vs. generalized normal. In conclusion, the distribution used in TREND is more appropriate to estimate the density of the Inception features than the other ones.

## 5.2   Comparing Metrics Using Toy Datasets

In the previous experiments, the accuracies of density estimation using different distributions were compared. In this section, we investigate how the estimation accuracy affects the result of performance evaluation of GANs. In order to effectively demonstrate this, we build toy datasets using continuous distributions as if they are probability densities of the Inception features. We present two scenarios where FID fails to accurately determine the difference of distributions, while TREND does not.

In the first scenario, we set a hypothetical density for ground truth images to a truncated generalized normal distribution. Two hypothetical GAN models (model 1 and model 2) are evaluated against the ground truth distribution, which are also modeled as truncated generalized normal distributions. The three distributions have the same $\mu$ but different $\sigma$ and $\beta < 2$. 50000 random samples are drawn from each distribution, which correspond to the Inception features. The samples from model 1 and model 2 are evaluated against 50000 samples from the ground truth distribution using FID and TREND. When the distributions are compared in Fig. 4, an accurate metric will determine that model 2 is a better approximation of the ground truth than model 1. However, FID yields almost the same scores and even favors model 1 against model 2. On the contrary, the result of TREND is consistent with the expectation.

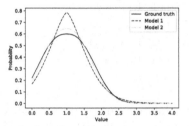

**Fig. 4.** Probability densities for the first toy scenario. FIDs are **0.0017** (model 1) and 0.0018 (model 2), and TRENDs are 0.0086 (model 1) and **0.0022** (model 2).

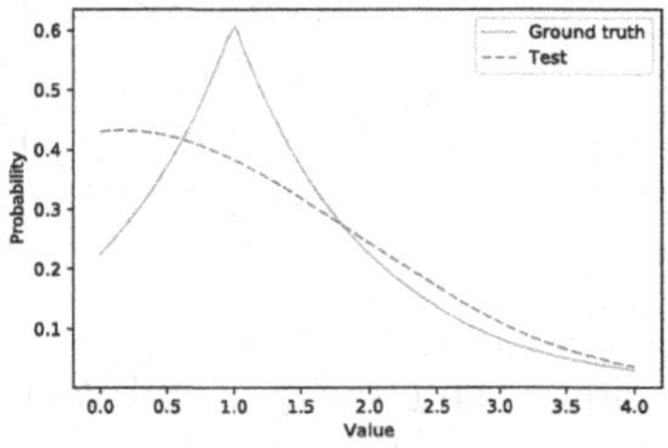

**Fig. 5.** Probability densities for the second toy scenario.

The second scenario considers a case where a GAN model fails to learn the ground truth distribution, as shown in Fig. 5. Again, truncated generalized normal distributions are used for the ground truth distribution and the learned distribution by the GAN, from each of which 50000 samples are drawn. For TREND, the difference between the distributions is well captured with a score of 0.015. However, FID yields a score of $1.4 \times 10^{-4}$, determining that the difference is insignificant.

In both scenarios, the failure of FID is due to inaccurate density estimation of non-Gaussian distributions using normal distributions. On the other hand, TREND provides more accurate density estimation and thus more accurate evaluation results.

## 5.3    Density Estimation of Real-World Datasets

In this section, we examine the distributions of Inception features of real-world image datasets. We estimate the parameters of the truncated generalized normal distribution as in TREND in each dimension of the Inception features and compare them for various datasets. We consider sets of generated images by DCGAN, ProGAN, BigGAN, StyleGAN, and StyleGAN2, and the original datasets (CIFAR10 [13], CelebA [16], ImageNet [5], and FFHQ [11]) used to train the models. Table 1 shows the average values of the estimated parameters along with their standard deviations. Histograms of the estimated parameters are provided in the Supplemental Materials.

**Table 1.** Estimated parameters for various datasets. In each case, the mean and standard deviation are shown.

| Dataset | $\mu$ | $\sigma$ | $\beta$ |
|---------|-------|----------|---------|
| CIFAR10 | 0.07±0.18 | 0.28±0.25 | 0.94±0.38 |
| DCGAN | 0.08±0.19 | 0.30±0.26 | 1.01±0.40 |
| ImageNet | 0.02±0.04 | 0.13±0.12 | 0.68±0.25 |
| BigGAN | 0.02±0.04 | 0.14±0.12 | 0.71±0.27 |
| CelebA | 0.10±0.20 | 0.26±0.24 | 1.04±0.45 |
| ProGAN | 0.14±0.22 | 0.25±0.21 | 1.11±0.43 |
| FFHQ | 0.09±0.16 | 0.28±0.23 | 1.04±0.39 |
| StyleGAN | 0.10±0.17 | 0.28±0.22 | 1.06±0.39 |
| StyleGAN2 | 0.09±0.17 | 0.28±0.23 | 1.05±0.41 |

Since the images of different datasets have different characteristics, the estimated parameters are also different for each dataset. In the perspective of GAN evaluation, the estimated parameters for the images generated by BigGAN are similar to those for ImageNet. On the other hand, the estimated parameters of DCGAN images are slightly different from those of the CIFAR10 dataset, which explains the well-known performance inferiority of DCGAN to BigGAN.

In terms of the shapes of the distributions, the average of shape parameter $\beta$ is smaller than 2 for all datasets, which indicates that the distributions are sharper than the normal distribution. Especially in the case of the ImageNet dataset, the distributions in all dimensions are sharper than the normal distribution. For the other datasets, only small numbers of dimensions have $\beta$ larger than 2.

In terms of the location of the distribution, $\mu$ is slightly greater than zero on average. Nonetheless, 23.8%, 22.6%, 40.0%, and 20.1% of the feature dimensions have $\mu < 0$ for CIFAR10, CelebA, ImageNet, and FFHQ, respectively, for which more than a half of a (non-truncated) generalized normal distribution is cut off. In these cases, the discrepancy from normal distributions becomes large as shown in Fig. 2b, thus density estimation and subsequent evaluation results would be particularly unreliable.

## 5.4    Effectiveness for Image Disturbance

For a metric performing GAN evaluation, it is important to be able to identify unnatural images that are from different distributions from those of natural images. In this section, we demonstrate that TREND can effectively capture the differences. We apply disturbances such as noise, where the difference can be easily determined by human judgement. For the experiment, two sets of images are used, where one consists of the original images and the other consists of images with disturbance. Then, we measure the differences between two sets using FID and IS as well as TREND for comparison.

We use 50000 images from the ImageNet validation dataset. For image disturbance, Gaussian noise with variance $\sigma_{gn}^2$, Gaussian blur with width $\sigma_{gb}$, and random erasing with erasing ratio $r$ are applied to the images. We set three levels of disturbances: $\sigma_{gn}^2 \in \{0.05, 0.10, 0.15\}$, $\sigma_{gb} \in \{1, 2, 3\}$, and $r \in \{0.25, 0.50, 0.75\}$. In general, the larger the disturbance level is, the larger the image differences are, and the larger the perceptual differences are. An example of disturbed images is shown in the Supplemental Materials.

**Table 2.** Evaluation results of disturbed images

| Evaluation metric | Disturbance level | Gaussian noise | Gaussian blur | Random erasing |
|---|---|---|---|---|
| IS | 1 | 189.5 | 139.5 | 66.3 |
|  | 2 | 145.7 | 54.0 | 11.3 |
|  | 3 | 106.9 | 22.0 | 3.1 |
| FID | 1 | 7.95 | 7.81 | 44.27 |
|  | 2 | 21.34 | 23.13 | 96.47 |
|  | 3 | 41.09 | 40.67 | 127.24 |
| TREND | 1 | 0.0058 | 0.0057 | 0.0369 |
|  | 2 | 0.0120 | 0.0127 | 0.0670 |
|  | 3 | 0.0208 | 0.0211 | 0.0827 |

The results are shown in Table 2. In all cases, TREND becomes larger when the disturbance level increases, which demonstrates that TREND can effectively capture the deviations in distribution for the disturbed images. FID behaves similarly to TREND. In the case of IS, the random erasing with level 1 is determined to be better than the Gaussian blur with level 2 (66.3 vs. 54.0), which is not consistent with human judgment.

## 5.5    Evaluating Generative Models

In this section, we evaluate the performance of TREND for evaluation of state-of-the-art GANs. Various types of GANs have been proposed so far, and their training datasets are also diverse, such as objects, structures, animals, and human faces. A metric for GANs should work well across the variety of training datasets of GANs. Thus, we examine evaluation results of GANs that are trained on different datasets. For comparison, we use not only IS, FID, and KID but also the improved precision and recall [14], which is a two-dimensional metric. We employ four GANs: DCGAN, BigGAN, StyleGAN, and StyleGAN2 and use 50000 generated images for each model to evaluate performance of the models. We also evaluate other generative models based on VAE and diffusion models (i.e., E-VDVAE [8] and ADM [6], respectively).

DCGAN is an early model having a rather simple structure compared to the other models, thus its performance is generally considered to be worse than the others. In the case of BigGAN, a smaller threshold value for the truncation trick yields a lower level of diversity of the generated images, which usually imposes a penalty on evaluation. StyleGAN2 has modified some layers of StyleGAN to improve the quality of generated images and to resolve blob artifacts of generated images. Recently, ADM has shown remarkable performance with accessible likelihood measures, which is even better than GANs. Although E-VDVAE can also measure the likelihood, generated images are often blurred. Appropriate evaluation metrics should be able to identify these characteristics of the models.

**Table 3.** Evaluation results of generative models using various metrics

| Model | Dataset | Precision($\uparrow$) | Recall($\uparrow$) | IS($\uparrow$) | FID($\downarrow$) | KID($\downarrow$) | TREND($\downarrow$) |
|-------|---------|-----------|---------|------|------|------|-------|
| DCGAN | CIFAR10 | 0.875 | 0.164 | 3.0 | 45.44 | 0.0316 | 0.0181 |
| E-VDVAE | ImageNet | 0.568 | 0.439 | 6.9 | 46.98 | 0.0407 | 0.0275 |
| BigGAN (0.2) | ImageNet | 0.958 | 0.007 | 330.4 | 24.97 | 0.0118 | 0.0165 |
| BigGAN (0.4) | ImageNet | 0.960 | 0.025 | 321.2 | 20.20 | 0.0106 | 0.0139 |
| BigGAN (0.6) | ImageNet | 0.962 | 0.097 | 292.5 | 15.45 | 0.0078 | 0.0106 |
| BigGAN (0.8) | ImageNet | 0.954 | 0.159 | 250.5 | 11.09 | 0.0048 | 0.0069 |
| BigGAN ($\infty$) | ImageNet | 0.916 | 0.294 | 144.6 | 6.24 | 0.0009 | 0.0032 |
| ADM-C | ImageNet | 0.872 | 0.669 | 61.8 | 8.91 | 0.0076 | 0.0043 |
| ADM-U | ImageNet | 0.890 | 0.705 | 208.6 | 4.94 | 0.0015 | 0.0026 |
| E-VDVAE | FFHQ | 0.865 | 0.199 | 2.4 | 33.83 | 0.0230 | 0.0213 |
| StyleGAN | FFHQ | 0.795 | 0.491 | 4.7 | 4.58 | 0.0011 | 0.0014 |
| StyleGAN2 | FFHQ | 0.768 | 0.585 | 4.8 | 3.09 | 0.0006 | 0.0012 |

In Table 3, the evaluation results are shown. In the case of IS, DCGAN, StyleGAN, and StyleGAN2 show extremely low scores compared to BigGAN, which indicates that IS is inadequate to evaluate GANs trained on datasets other than ImageNet. Moreover, as the truncation threshold of BigGAN increases, IS rather decreases because IS does not consider the diversity of generated images. In the case of the two-dimensional metric, precision yields inaccurate results, showing fluctuating scores with respect to the increase of the truncation threshold and judging that superiority of StyleGAN over StyleGAN2. KID underrates the performance of diffusion models, by favoring BigGAN ($\infty$) over ADM-U. Both TREND and FID show sensible evaluation results, while FID has weakness related to the number of test samples, which will be discussed in the next section.

## 5.6   Robustness to the Number of Samples

Since performance evaluation of GANs are based on sample statistics, robustness of an evaluation metric against the number of test data is highly desirable. Otherwise, the result of performance evaluation and comparison would change depending on the number of test data. Thus, when a robust metric is used, it is not restricted to generate as many images as in the original target dataset. Furthermore, a robust metric enables performance comparison across different studies that use different numbers of samples. In this section, we demonstrate the robustness of the proposed method against the number of test data.

For the experiment, we randomly drop some of the generated image data to keep a certain proportion (i.e., 1, 1/5, 1/10, and 1/50), while the ground truth datasets remain the same. The generated images used in Sect. 5.5 are used.

The results are shown in Fig. 6. FID in Fig. 6a significantly varies with respect to the number of samples. In particular, it always decreases by increasing the number of samples. Thus, using more samples may be wrongly interpreted as being better in image generation when FID is used. On the other hand, TREND is hardly affected by the number of samples, resulting in consistent scores across different numbers of test data for all models in Fig. 6b.

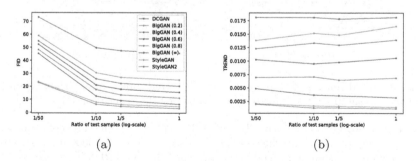

(a)                                          (b)

**Fig. 6.** Evaluation of DCGAN, BigGAN, StyleGAN, and StyleGAN2 with respect to the number of test samples using (a) FID and (b) TREND. The values in parentheses of BigGAN are the threshold values for the truncation trick and '$\infty$' means that the trick is not used.

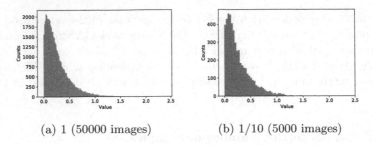

(a) 1 (50000 images)    (b) 1/10 (5000 images)

**Fig. 7.** Histograms of the Inception features for the 120th dimension with (a) 50000 and (b) 5000 images.

FID is sensitive to the number of samples because its density estimation is inaccurate. As shown in Fig. 7, the distributions of the Inception features appear similar for different numbers of samples[2]. Thus, accurate estimation of these distributions in TREND does not change much. In the case of FID, however, we observe that although the first term accounting for difference of $\mu$ in (3) remains almost the same for different numbers of test data, the second term for difference of $\Sigma$ in (3) increases when the number of data is reduced.

Due to the bias caused by the number of samples, evaluation of GANs using FID may be misleading. In Fig. 8, generated images using BigGAN with different threshold values are shown. Overall, the quality of the generated images for both

(a) *threshold*=0.4    (b) *threshold*=0.6

**Fig. 8.** Generated images of 'Tibetan terrier' (left) and 'breakwater' (right) from Big-GAN with threshold values of (a) 0.4 and (b) 0.6 for the truncation trick.

**Table 4.** Evaluation results using FID and TREND for different threshold values and numbers of samples. For a threshold of 0.6, we repeat sampling of 5000 images 10 times and the minimum, mean, and maximum values of FID and TREND are shown.

| Threshold (# images) | FID | TREND |
|---|---|---|
| 0.4 (50000) | **20.2** | 0.0139 |
| 0.6 (5000) | 20.7/21.1/21.5 | **0.0091/0.0094/0.0098** |

[2] The Mann-Whitney U test fails to reject the null hypothesis that the two distributions are statistically identical for 1992 (97.3%) out of 2048 dimensions.

threshold values is similar. However, the images for the larger threshold value are more diverse (Fig. 8b), while the pose and background are almost identical in Fig. 8a due to the smaller threshold value. As a result, the model with a threshold of 0.6 is preferable to that with a threshold of 0.4. The evaluation results in Table 4 show that TREND is consistent with this observation, whereas FID is not due to the undesirable influence of the number of samples (Fig. 6a).

## 6  Conclusion

We proposed a novel metric called TREND for evaluation of GANs. We performed in-depth analysis of the Inception feature and showed the invalidity of the normality assumption used in the existing metrics. We used the truncated generalized normal distribution for more accurate density estimation of the Inception feature, based on which the proposed TREND was designed. The experimental results demonstrated that TREND is reliable in density estimation, effective for GAN evaluation, and robust against the number of samples. In the future, we expect that TREND can be applied to various domains such as audio, motion pictures, or multimodal data, with proper selection of feature spaces.

**Acknowledgements.** This work was supported in part by the Artificial Intelligence Graduate School Program, Yonsei University under Grant 2020-0-01361, and in part by the Ministry of Trade, Industry and Energy (MOTIE) under Grant P0014268.

## References

1. Arjovsky, M., Chintala, S., Bottou, L.: Wasserstein generative adversarial networks. In: Proceedings of the International Conference on Machine Learning, pp. 214–223, August 2017
2. Bińkowski, M., Sutherland, D.J., Arbel, M., Gretton, A.: Demystifying MMD GANs. In: Proceedings of the International Conference on Learning Representations (2018)
3. Brock, A., Donahue, J., Simonyan, K.: Large scale GAN training for high fidelity natural image synthesis. In: Proceedings of the International Conference on Learning Representations (2019)
4. Chong, M.J., Forsyth, D.: Effectively unbiased FID and Inception score and where to find them. In: Proceedings of the IEEE Conference on Computer Vision and Pattern Recognition, pp. 6070–6079 (2020)
5. Deng, J., Dong, W., Socher, R., Li, L.J., Kai Li, Li Fei-Fei: Imagenet: a large-scale hierarchical image database. In: Proceedings of the IEEE Conference on Computer Vision and Pattern Recognition, pp. 248–255 (2009)
6. Dhariwal, P., Nichol, A.Q.: Diffusion models beat GANs on image synthesis. In: Advances in Neural Information Processing Systems (2021)
7. Goodfellow, I.J., et al.: Generative adversarial nets. In: Advances in Neural Information Processing Systems, vol. 27, pp. 2672–2680 (2014)
8. Hazami, L., Mama, R., Thurairatnam, R.: Efficient-VDVAE: less is more (2022). arXiv preprint arXiv:2203.13751

9. Heusel, M., Ramsauer, H., Unterthiner, T., Nessler, B., Hochreiter, S.: GANs trained by a two time-scale update rule converge to a local Nash equilibrium. In: Advances in Neural Information Processing Systems. pp. 6629–6640 (2017)
10. Karras, T., Aila, T., Laine, S., Lehtinen, J.: Progressive growing of GANs for improved quality, stability, and variation. In: Proceedings of the International Conference on Learning Representations (2018)
11. Karras, T., Laine, S., Aila, T.: A style-based generator architecture for generative adversarial networks. In: Proceedings of the IEEE Conference on Computer Vision and Pattern Recognition, June 2019
12. Karras, T., Laine, S., Aittala, M., Hellsten, J., Lehtinen, J., Aila, T.: Analyzing and improving the image quality of StyleGAN. In: Proceedings of the IEEE Conference on Computer Vision and Pattern Recognition, June 2020
13. Krizhevsky, A., et al.: Learning multiple layers of features from tiny images. Technical report (2009)
14. Kynkäänniemi, T., Karras, T., Laine, S., Lehtinen, J., Aila, T.: Improved precision and recall metric for assessing generative models. In: Advances in Neural Information Processing Systems, vol. 32 (2019)
15. Lalee, M., Nocedal, J., Plantenga, T.: On the implementation of an algorithm for large-scale equality constrained optimization. SIAM J. Optim. $8(3)$, 682–706 (1998)
16. Liu, Z., Luo, P., Wang, X., Tang, X.: Deep learning face attributes in the wild. In: Proceedings of the International Conference on Computer Vision, pp. 3730–3738, December 2015
17. Miyato, T., Kataoka, T., Koyama, M., Yoshida, Y.: Spectral normalization for generative adversarial networks. In: Proceedings of the International Conference on Learning Representations (2018)
18. Morozov, S., Voynov, A., Babenko, A.: On self-supervised image representations for GAN evaluation. In: Proceedings of the International Conference on Learning Representations (2021)
19. Naeem, M.F., Oh, S.J., Uh, Y., Choi, Y., Yoo, J.: Reliable fidelity and diversity metrics for generative models. In: Advances in Neural Information Processing Systems, vol. 119, pp. 7176–7185, July 2020
20. Parmar, G., Zhang, R., Zhu, J.Y.: On aliased resizing and surprising subtleties in GAN evaluation. In: Proceedings of the IEEE Conference on Computer Vision and Pattern Recognition, pp. 11410–11420 (2022)
21. Radford, A., Metz, L., Chintala, S.: Unsupervised representation learning with deep convolutional generative adversarial networks. In: Proceedings of the International Conference on Learning Representations (2016)
22. Sajjadi, M.S.M., Bachem, O., Lucic, M., Bousquet, O., Gelly, S.: Assessing generative models via precision and recall. In: Advances in Neural Information Processing Systems, pp. 5234–5243 (2018)
23. Salimans, T., Goodfellow, I., Zaremba, W., Cheung, V., Radford, A., Chen, X., Chen, X.: Improved techniques for training GANs. In: Advances in Neural Information Processing Systems, pp. 2234–2242 (2016)
24. Sauer, A., Chitta, K., Müller, J., Geiger, A.: Projected GANs converge faster. In: Advances in Neural Information Processing Systems (2021)
25. Szegedy, C., Vanhoucke, V., Ioffe, S., Shlens, J., Wojna, Z.: Rethinking the inception architecture for computer vision. In: Proceedings of the IEEE Conference on Computer Vision and Pattern Recognition, pp. 2818–2826 (2016)

26. Theis, L., van den Oord, A., Bethge, M.: A note on the evaluation of generative models. In: Proceedings of the International Conference on Learning Representations, April 2016
27. Xu, Q., et al.: An empirical study on evaluation metrics of generative adversarial networks. arXiv preprint (2018). arXiv:1806.07755
28. Zhang, H., Goodfellow, I., Metaxas, D., Odena, A.: Self-attention generative adversarial networks. In: Proceedings of the International Conference on Machine Learning, pp. 7354–7363, June 2019

# Exploring Gradient-Based Multi-directional Controls in GANs

Zikun Chen[1][✉], Ruowei Jiang[1], Brendan Duke[1,2], Han Zhao[3], and Parham Aarabi[1,2]

[1] ModiFace Inc., Toronto, Canada
{zikun,irene,brendan,parham}@modiface.com
[2] University of Toronto, Toronto, Canada
[3] University of Illinois at Urbana-Champaign, Champaign, USA
hanzhao@illinois.edu

**Abstract.** Generative Adversarial Networks (GANs) have been widely applied in modeling diverse image distributions. However, despite its impressive applications, the structure of the latent space in GANs largely remains as a black-box, leaving its controllable generation an open problem, especially when spurious correlations between different semantic attributes exist in the image distributions. To address this problem, previous methods typically learn linear directions or individual channels that control semantic attributes in the image space. However, they often suffer from imperfect disentanglement, or are unable to obtain multi-directional controls. In this work, in light of the above challenges, we propose a novel approach that discovers nonlinear controls, which enables multi-directional manipulation as well as effective disentanglement, based on gradient information in the learned GAN latent space. More specifically, we first learn interpolation directions by following the gradients from classification networks trained separately on the attributes, and then navigate the latent space by exclusively controlling channels activated for the target attribute in the learned directions. Empirically, with small training data, our approach is able to gain fine-grained controls over a diverse set of bi-directional and multi-directional attributes, and we showcase its ability to achieve disentanglement significantly better than state-of-the-art methods both qualitatively and quantitatively. The source code is available at https://github.com/zikuncshelly/GradCtrl.

**Keywords:** GAN · Gradient information · Latent space · Disentanglement · Multi-directional

## 1 Introduction

Generative adversarial networks (GANs) [9] are implicit generative models from which it is straightforward to sample data from the learned distributions. GANs

**Supplementary Information** The online version contains supplementary material available at https://doi.org/10.1007/978-3-031-20050-2_7.

S. Avidan et al. (Eds.): ECCV 2022, LNCS 13683, pp. 104–119, 2022.
https://doi.org/10.1007/978-3-031-20050-2_7

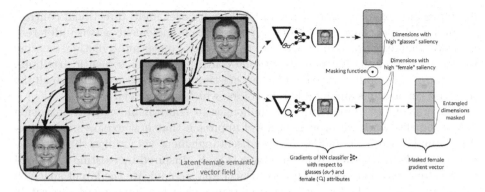

**Fig. 1.** Our method's semantic interpolation in a nonlinear vector field. Directions corresponding to the "female" semantic in GAN latent space (left) are determined by differentiating a simple neural network classifier (middle). Disentanglement is achieved by masking channels of the "female" semantic gradient vector that are highly salient for non-target attributes such as glasses (right).

work by learning to generate data from random noise sampled from natural distributions such as isotropic Gaussians. Due to the flexibility of neural networks in modeling complex transformations, GANs and the follow-up variants [3,13, 17,26] have been widely applied in modeling image distributions. Furthermore, the remarkable success of GANs' ability to generate realistically looking images has powered many real-world applications, including image inpainting [30,32], super-resolution [5,14], and image-to-image translations [11,33].

However, despite the impressive existing applications, the structure of the latent space in GANs largely remains as a black box. For example, is there a correspondence between interpolation directions in the latent space and visual factors in the generated images? If yes, how can we generate images in a controllable way? Furthermore, are different interpolation directions independent of each other? If not, is it possible to disentangle them in an interpretable fashion?

To answer the above important but challenging questions, existing works have studied the learned latent space by identifying and linearly interpolating along directions that correspond to certain semantic factors in the generated images [10, 18,21,24,28]. For example, on facial image data, early works [18,24] use simple linear arithmetic operations in the latent space to control the age of the generated persons. Recent works [21,29] further studied the interpolation directions by learning a linear binary classifier, and illustrated the effects of linearly interpolating different channels in a supervised or unsupervised manner [10,28].

On the other hand, existing works aim to identify directions that correspond to unique semantic factors, and to control generation based on a single factor. However, semantic factors in images, such as age and eyeglasses, are often highly correlated with each other. As a result, artifacts often appear when applying controllable generation to one factor. Another issue arises due to spurious correlations in the training image data. These cause undesirable changes to the generated image to appear even if controllable generation is applied to an independent semantic factor.

Furthermore, existing approaches still fail to discover multi-directional controls in the latent space and suffer from imperfect disentanglement between different interpolation directions. In fact, due to the nature of linear interpolation, existing works can only apply linear bi-directional controls over each semantic attribute. For example, to modify the color of a car, existing approaches need to learn all the pairwise connections among different colors, which is nontrivial [10,28].

In light of the aforementioned challenges in controllable generations using GANs, in this work we propose a novel approach that first explores the multi-directional controls and addresses the disentanglement via gradient-based information in the learned GAN latent space (Fig. 1). Inspired by existing visualization techniques on classification networks [4,20], we navigate the latent space by using gradient-based information learned from a classification network separately trained on the factors and attributes of interest. Using the latent vectors from a pre-trained GAN network [13] as inputs, we train classification networks over all attributes. To disentangle the controllable generation of different attributes, we separate the manipulation into two steps. First, we identify the direction using the gradient on the target attribute of interest. Then, we exclusively control the channels that only affect the probability of the target attribute, based on gradient-weighted attribute activations.

To demonstrate the effectiveness of our approach, we present our method's ability to obtain nonlinear multi-directional controls as well as disentangled manipulations on multiple benchmark datasets. Furthermore, we show that our classification network can gain proper controls by using a tiny dataset of 30 images per class. We also compare our results to the state-of-the-art models both qualitatively and quantitatively. Finally, we present real image manipulation results on several attributes by inverting the image back to a latent code. To our knowledge, this work provides the first nonlinear multi-directional controls that achieve disentanglement successfully. Overall, our contributions are:

- We propose a novel approach to navigate the GAN latent space by gradient-based information that allows nonlinear multi-directional controls.
- We disentangle the controls of different attributes by gradient-based channel selection to exclusively control a single attribute without affecting the others.
- Empirically, we show that our method discovers disentangled controls with small amounts of data, widening the range of applications of our method.

## 2    Related Work

**Conditional Manipulations on GANs.** GANs have been widely applied to a variety of tasks that allow conditional manipulations, including image editing [7, 11,15–17,19,21,26,33], image inpainting [30,32], and super-resolution [5,14], just to name a few. Early works [11,33] explored image translations between two domains by using unpaired and paired training images. Some more recent works focused on improving diversity by translating in multiple domains [7,8] while other works tried to improve the quality of the manipulation by effectively propagating the conditional information [17]. However, these methods often require a huge amount of paired data for training, which limits their applications in settings where it is expensive to manually label these pairs.

**Understanding GAN Latent Space.** Many attempts have been made to understand and visualize the latent representations of GANs [1,2,10,18,21,24, 28,29]. Bau et al. [1,2] used semantic segmentation models to detect and quantify the existence and absence of certain objects at both the individual and population levels. Previous work [18,24] empirically studied linear vector arithmetic in the latent representations. To gain direct controls along attribute manipulations, later works [21,29] further explored linear interpolation in the latent space by finding semantically meaningful directions with explicit binary classifiers. Inter-FaceGAN [21] hypothesized and showed the existence of a hyperplane serving as a linear separation boundary in the StyleGAN [12] latent space for some binary semantic relationships. In addition, they attempted to solve the entanglement issue on interpolated images via subspace projections between entangled attributes. However, identity change is often observed in simple linear interpolations settings, and the disentangled direction sometimes fails to manipulate the target attribute. A more recent work [28] analyzed StyleGAN's style space and proposed a method to obtain valid semantic controls by identifying highly localized channels that only affect a specific region, which achieves well-disentangled changes on some attributes. However, this approach lacks the ability to control globally aligned features such as age.

Another line of works aim to identify semantic controls in a self-supervised or unsupervised manner [6,10,25]. For example, GANSpace [10] identifies important latent directions by applying principal component analysis (PCA) to vectors in GAN latent space or feature space. Voynov et al. [25] discover interpretable directions in the GAN latent space by jointly optimizing the directions and a reconstructor that recovers these directions and manipulation strengths from images generated based on the manipulated GAN latent codes. These types of methods usually involve extensive manual examinations of different manipulation directions as well as the identification of meaningful controls. More importantly, in contrast to our approach, controlling over a target semantic is not always guaranteed and attributes are often observed as entangled due to the potential correlations in the training image distribution.

**Gradient-Based Network Understanding.** Gradient-based interpretation methods [4,20,22,23] have been widely explored on discriminative models. Grad-CAM [4,20] used gradient information from the classification outputs to obtain localization maps that visualize evidence in images. In contrast to local sensitivity, Integrated Gradients [23] estimated the global importance of each pixel to address gradient saturation. Integrated Gradients generated so-called gradient-based sensitivity maps, which were further sharpened by SmoothGrad [22].

The generative model LOGAN [27] increased the stability of the training dynamics of GANs by adding an extra step before optimizing the generator and discriminator jointly. In LOGAN, the latent code is first optimized towards regions regarded as more real by the discriminator, and the direction is obtained by calculating the gradient with respect to the latent codes. Intuitively, the gradient points in a direction that obtains a better score from the discriminator. We observed that when using LOGAN the discriminator gradient direction corresponds to meaningful transformations in GAN-synthesized images, for example, removal of artifacts, change in gender, and so on. This observation inspired us to use auxiliary classifier gradients to obtain controls over GAN output semantics. To the best of our knowledge, we are the first to take this approach.

## 3   Methods

In this section, we describe our proposed method to obtain disentangled controls in the GAN latent space. Our method first finds semantically meaningful directions by calculating gradients of multi-class classifiers that score different semantics given latent code inputs. Next, by selecting the channels in the latent code that correspond to these directions, our technique achieves attribute disentanglement during manipulation through masking (Fig. 2).

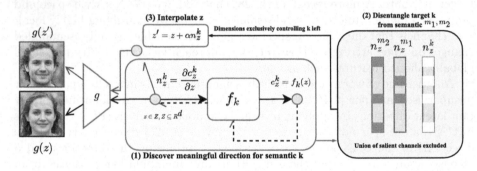

**Fig. 2.** Overview of our method. We first obtain the control for a semantic attribute $k$, e.g., gender, by calculating the gradient direction $n_z^k$ from the mapping function $f_k$ in (1). To disentangle direction $n_z^k$ from attributes $m_1, m_2$, e.g., smile and age, the union of salient dimensions in control directions $n_z^{m_1}, n_z^{m_2}$ for the corresponding semantics are masked to 0 in $n_z^k$, as shown in (2). We then interpolate the latent code following the direction computed at each step in (3).

### 3.1   Discovery of Semantically Meaningful Directions

**Learning Semantics in GAN Latent Space.** GANs learn a mapping $g :$ $Z \to X$ from a latent code $z$ in its latent space $Z \subseteq \mathbb{R}^d$ to an image $x = g(z)$ in the image space $X \subseteq \mathbb{R}^{H \times W \times 3}$, where $H \times W$ is the spatial resolution. Human-interpretable semantics such as age of a person exist in the image space. Given a series of scoring functions $(s_1, \ldots, s_K)$ for $K$ semantics, we can obtain $K$ mappings from the GAN latent space $Z$ to the semantic spaces $C_1, \ldots, C_K$ respectively, where

$$c_z^k = s_k(g(z)) \in C_k. \tag{1}$$

Here $c_z^k$ denotes the $k$th semantic score of the image generated based on the latent code $z$, and $C_k \in \mathbb{R}^{d_k}$, where $d_k$ denotes the number of classes the $k$th semantic has, e.g., for binary semantics, $d_k = 1$. We parametrize each mapping function $s_k(g(z))$ with a neural network $f_k$ trained on paired samples of GAN latent codes and corresponding semantic labels. The labels are generated by pre-trained image classifiers or human supervision. With $(f_1, \ldots, f_k)$, we are able to estimate human-interpretable semantics based on GAN latent codes, without inferring from the image space.

**Manipulating Semantics in GAN Latent Space.** Provided the accuracy of $(f_1, \ldots, f_k)$, it is expected that when controlling the $k$th semantic by interpolating $z$ along meaningful directions, its score $c_z^k$ changes accordingly. We hypothesize that such changes correspond to the changes in image space semantics. Inspired by LOGAN [27], which hypothesizes that the gradient from a GAN discriminator points in the direction of better samples, as the discriminator can be seen as a scoring function for "realness", we propose to control the $k$ semantics using the Jacobians of $(f_1, \ldots, f_k)$. In particular, our method controls $c_z^k$ by interpolating the latent code following gradient directions that are rows of the Jacobian of $f_k$ with respect to $z$:

$$n_z^k = \nabla f_k(z) = \frac{\mathrm{d} f_k(z)}{z} \in \mathbb{R}^{d_k \times d}, \tag{2}$$

where the matrix $n_z^k$ denotes the Jacobian of the $k$th latent-semantic mapping $c_z^k$ at $z$. Note that for binary attributes, $d_k = 1$ and we use $n_z^k = n_z^k[0]$ to denote a gradient vector. For multi-class attributes, when optimizing towards the $j$th class for semantic $k$, we take the corresponding row in the Jacobian and $n_z^k = n_z^k[j]$. For notational simplicity, $n_z^k[j]$ is abbreviated as $n_z^k$ in the following sections, so that $n_z^k$ always refers to a gradient vector.

Intuitively, for each target semantic, interpolating the latent code following the gradient from its scoring function changes the semantic score, then the semantic is manipulated accordingly. More specifically, to manipulate the semantic $k$ with respect to its $i$th class once, we update $z$ with

$$z' = z + \alpha n_z^k, \tag{3}$$

where $\alpha$ is a hyperparameter that controls the interpolation step size and sign of change in the target semantic value. In contrast to works that discovered linear semantically meaningful directions applicable to all coordinates in GAN latent space [21], our method finds unique local and data-dependent directions for each coordinate due to the nonlinear nature of the latent-semantic mapping (Eq. 1).

## 3.2 Disentanglement of Attributes During Manipulation

Entanglements such as changing the gender affecting one's age can emerge during latent code interpolation following the gradient of the latent-semantic mapping (Eq. 3). In this section, we propose a technique to minimize this effect.

---

**Algorithm 1.** Disentangle attributes

---

1: Target attribute $k$ is entangled with attributes $m_1, \ldots, m_j$ in direction $n_z^k$
2: Scoring function $f_{m_1}, \ldots, f_{m_j}$, numbers of top channels excluded $\{c_1, \ldots, c_j\}, j \neq k$
3: Excluded set of dimensions $E = \{\}$
4: For each $(m, f_m, c) \in (\{m_1, \ldots, m_j\}, \{f_{m_1}, \ldots, f_{m_j}\}, \{c_1, \ldots, c_j\})$:
5:      $n_z^m = \nabla f_m(z) = \frac{\mathrm{d}f_m(z)}{\mathrm{d}z}, L_i^m = |(n_z^m)_i|$
6:      $t = sorted(L^m)[-c], e = \{i\}$ where $L_i^m \geq t$
7:      $E = E \cup e$
8: $(n_z^k)_i = 0$ for $i \in E$
9: Return $n_z^k$

---

**Target-Specific Dimensions in Direction Vectors.** In early experiments, we observed that interpolation along the gradient direction alters non-target semantics, but disentanglement is occasionally achieved by randomly excluding dimensions in the direction vector used for interpolation. Therefore, we hypothesize that within the $d$-dimensional direction vector discovered, only some dimensions are responsible for the change in the target semantic. Conversely, the remaining channels denote bias learned from the training data. For example, when interpolating in the direction that increases a person's age, eyeglasses appear since eyeglasses and age are correlated in the dataset.

**Filtering Dimensions to Control Target Attributes Exclusively.** To construct disentangled controls, we propose to filter out dimensions based on gradient magnitudes from the semantic scoring function in a technique inspired by Grad-CAM [20]. Grad-CAM measures the importance of neurons by

$$a_k^c = \frac{1}{Z} \sum_i \sum_j \frac{\partial y^c}{\partial A_{ij}^k}, \tag{4}$$

where the derivative of the score $y^c$ for class $c$ with respect to the activation map $A$ is average pooled over spatial dimensions. The final heatmap is then

$$L_{\mathrm{Grad-CAM}}^c = \mathrm{ReLU}\left(\sum_k a_k^c A^k\right). \tag{5}$$

For our approach, gradient $n_z^k$ is regarded as the only activation map, and the saliency of the $i$th dimension is calculated by

$$L_i^k = |(n_z^k)_i|, \tag{6}$$

where $|(n_z^k)_i|$ denotes the absolute value of the $i$th element of the gradient vector. Contrary to the original classification setting for Grad-CAM where ReLU is chosen as the activation, here the absolute value is used because in our classification setting dimensions with negative influence on the semantic score also contain meaningful information.

By definition, the value of gradient $n_z^k$ at its $i$th dimension indicates the rate of change in $c_z^k$ induced by a small change in latent vector $z$ along dimension $i$.

Intuitively, dimensions in $n_z^k$ with greater saliency $L_i^k$ are more relevant and have more impact on $c_z^k$, whereas less relevant dimensions for $c_z^k$ could have high saliency in another semantic $m$'s gradient $n_z^m, m \neq k$. Hence even small changes in these dimensions while optimizing for the $k$th semantic could affect $c_z^m$ significantly, causing attribute entanglement. Note that such effects could be either positive or negative, hence we use the absolute values as the saliency. To alleviate this issue, we exclude the top-$k$ salient dimensions for predicting an entangled attribute from the target direction, with $k$ in {50, 100, 150, 200, 250}. Algorithm 1 describes the full process to calculate the new direction with disentangled attributes before interpolating the latent code (Eq. 3).

## 4    Experiments

In this section, we apply our method to learned latent representations by state-of-the-art GAN models, and compare it with existing state-of-the-art latent code interpolation methods both qualitatively and quantitatively. In particular, we analyze the ability to achieve disentangled controls using each method.

### 4.1    Qualitative Results

**Image Bank.** We perform our experiments on StyleGAN2 [13] pretrained on FFHQ [12], LSUN Car [31], LSUN Cat [31], and StyleGAN [12] pretrained on LSUN Bedroom [31]. To prepare an image bank, we synthesize images by randomly sampling the latent codes and obtain labelled pairs for each attribute value, via pre-trained classifiers or human supervision.

**Training the Classifier.** We train a simple classifier with only 30 examples for each attribute value. The network consists of two fully connected layers, followed by the corresponding prediction head: sigmoid for binary classification and softmax for multi-class classification. In the Appendix, we also demonstrate the effects of using different numbers of training samples.

**Interpolating in the Latent Space.** We interpolate the latent codes following the gradient directions of our trained classifiers by a fixed step size of 0.6. We perform layer-wise edits by applying the learned directions to certain layers in **W**+ space in StyleGAN/StyleGAN2. More implementation details can be found in the Appendix.

**Disentangled Attribute Manipulation.** In this section, we evaluate our method on StyleGAN2 models pretrained on the FFHQ [12], LSUN-Cars [31], LSUN-Cats datasets [31] and the StyleGAN model [12] pretrained on the LSUN-Bedroom dataset [31]. We demonstrate that our approach obtains multi-directional controls over GAN-generated images in a disentangled manner. We show a qualitative comparison among key attributes in the FFHQ dataset [12]: smile, gender, age, and eyeglasses (Fig. 3). For the age and gender attributes, not only is our approach able to generate realistic localized target effects such as wrinkles or acne for age, but it is also capable of editing the image on a global

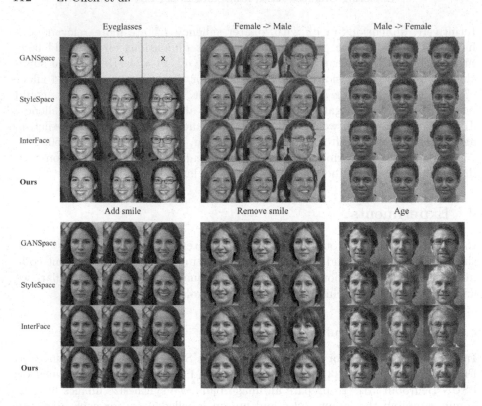

**Fig. 3.** Comparison with state-of-the-art methods on StyleGAN2 [13] pretrained on FFHQ [12]. For each group of images, left: source; middle, right: small and large step size. Our method edits eyeglasses and smiles naturally, and for gloabl-level attributes, ours is able to produce more visually distinguishable editing results compared to StyleSpace [28] and GANSpace, and achieves more disentangled control than Inter-FaceGAN [21].

level while preserving the person's identity and irrelevant attributes disentangled, such as keeping the person's smile when changing from female to male.

We further show that our method works on a variety of attributes on multiple datasets with qualitative results on LSUN car and LSUN bedroom [31] (Fig. 4).

**Multiclass Manipulation.** In this section, we showcase our method's ability to manipulate multiclass attributes. Based on the latent-semantic Jacobian (Eq. 2), regardless of the original state of the image, we identify the control direction and the activated channels with respect to the target class. Using only one classifier, our method performs manipulations in any direction (Fig. 5).

**Real Image Manipulation.** We present real image editing results to verify that the semantic controls learned by our method can be applied to real images. We first invert real human face images into the $W$ space of StyleGAN2 [13]

**Fig. 4.** LSUN-Cars and LSUN-Bedroom [31] editing results only trained on 30 pairs of examples. For each group of 4 images, left: source, right: modified.

trained on FFHQ [12] via an optimization-based framework [13]. We then interpolate the latent codes along directions learned by our method. In the resulting manipulations (Fig. 6), our method manipulates all attributes successfully.

### 4.2    Quantitative Evaluation

We compare our method with the related works [10,21,28] by measuring the accuracy and the level of attribute entanglement. We test on StyleGAN2 [13] pretrained on the FFHQ [12] dataset. We generate a test image bank with 500k samples using the StyleGAN2 model and score 4 attributes (age, gender, smile and eyeglasses) with the corresponding pre-trained CelebA classifiers [12]. From our test image bank, we sample 3k images with logits around the decision boundaries for 4 attributes, and for each image, we sample a target attribute $k$ uniformly from the 4 to optimize until the modified attribute logit crosses the boundary, and we include the details regarding the algorithm in the Appendix.

In a nutshell, we manipulate the latent code until the target attribute classification changes. We stop after crossing the boundary as for attributes like smile and eyeglasses, further optimization results in regions in the latent space irrelevant to the original target, e.g., removing eyeglasses from a person not wearing eyeglasses generally makes the person younger.

**Attribute Manipulation Accuracy.** We measure whether the attributes of an optimized image match the intended targets, i.e., change in the target attribute label and unchanged labels for the rest (Table 1). High accuracy corresponds to a low level of attribute entanglement and high success rate, i.e., target attribute being present. Our approach achieves the best results among all.

Fur color                    Car color                    Hood style

(a) Multi-class manipulation results for LSUN cats and cars [31] . For each group of images, left: source, right: modified. Regardless of the original color of the car/cat, our proposed method can independently identify any target control direction.

Source    Rotation ──────────────────→    Source    Rotation ──────────────────→

(b) Multi-class manipulation results for LSUN cars rotation. To avoid 3D-unaware changes, starting from the initial angle class, the latent code is optimized towards increments of 45 degrees which correspond to different classes.

**Fig. 5.** Multi-class manipulation for LSUN cats and LSUN cars [31]. Our method can easily apply multi-directional changes without learning each direction between each pair of classes.

**Attribute Disentanglement.** Attribute Dependency (AD) [28] measures the level of entanglements for semantic controls in GAN latent space, and here we follow a similar paradigm. On a high level, for images with target attribute $k \in A$ being manipulated, where $A$ stands for all attributes, we group the modified images by $x = \frac{\Delta l_k}{\sigma_k}$. We then compute mean-AD with $E(\frac{1}{|A|-1}\Sigma_{i\in A\setminus k}\frac{\Delta l_i}{\sigma l_i})$ for each group. The full algorithm can be found in the appendix.

Figure 7a plots the mean AD for each target attribute, where methods with extremely low accuracy are excluded, including StyleSpace for gender and age and GANSpace for eyeglasses as it doesn't offer such control. For attributes that only require localized changes, including eyeglasses and smile, our method performs similarly to StyleSpace and GANSpace. Our eyeglasses control shows higher AD than StyleSpace, as StyleSpace only modifies channels responsible for the eye area, yet for ours, the image is edited on a global level, and the pre-trained classifiers might be sensitive to some subtle changes. Nevertheless, our method significantly outperforms the rest when editing gender and age, as

**Fig. 6.** Manipulating real faces by first inverting them into $W$ space.

**Table 1.** Attribute manipulation accuracy in a disentangled manner. A resulting image is considered a true positive if only the target attribute is successfully changed. Among all, our method achieves the highest scores for all 4 attributes, corresponding to fewer changes in attributes other than the target during manipulation, and higher success rates, i.e., target attribute being edited successfully.

| Accuracy | Gender | Smile | Eyeglasses | Age |
|---|---|---|---|---|
| InterFaceGAN | 0.5859 | 0.9033 | 0.5946 | 0.5620 |
| GANSpace | 0.2770 | 0.6146 | x | 0.0063 |
| StyleSpace | 0.0812 | 0.7390 | 0.3510 | 0.0034 |
| **Ours** | **0.6937** | **0.9254** | **0.6626** | **0.6139** |

the amount of change in the target increases. As we traverse longer distances in the latent space to increase a person's age, the linear directions learned by the SVMs become inaccurate with lots of entanglement with gender and eyeglasses, whereas our non-linear method continues to disentangle the target direction from the others.

To provide further insights for AD, we visualize the change in smile logits when changing from non-smiling male to female in (Fig. 7b), and big negative slopes indicate entanglement between smile and gender, i.e., smile being added after optimization. InterFaceGAN suffers from the entanglement issue with a lot of big negative slopes, whereas GANSpace and StyleSpace have a lot of failure cases (the green points lying on the left of the blue vertical threshold line after interpolation in (Fig. 7b)), indicating manipulation in the wrong/unclear semantic direction. Our method has much less entanglement (slopes are more similar to the flat pink arrow) with fewer failure cases, and for those that failed, the direction is mostly correct as the gender logits are still moving towards the blue dash line.

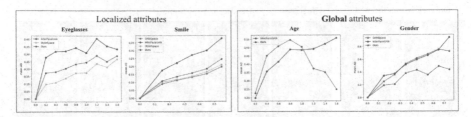

(a) X-axis: Change in logits of the target attribute. Y-axis: Mean AD. Lower AD indicates better disentanglement. Our method (green) is significantly less entangled than InterFaceGAN and GANSpace for gender, which involves global-level changes, and achieves similar levels of disentanglement for editing smile compared to StyleSpace and GANSpace. Note that unnatural looking and identity change will not affect this calculation.

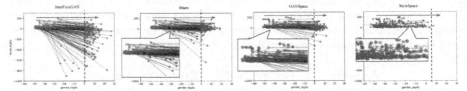

(b) Disentanglement visualization for gender and smile. X-axis: gender logits; Y-axis: smile logits. Red crosses: original logits; Green dots: logits after modification. Pink arrow: change in logits when attributes are perfectly disentangled. Blue dash line: success threshold. Flatter lines indicate less disentanglement. More green dots lying to the right of the blue dash line indicate a higher success rate. Ours exhibits the best disentanglement with a high success rate.

**Fig. 7.** Disentanglement analysis (Color figure online)

### 4.3    Ablation Studies: Attribute Disentanglement

In this section, we demonstrate how controls over different target attributes computed by our method can be disentangled using gradient information from each entangled attribute. We first demonstrate how our method enables disentanglement from multiple attributes for StyleGAN2 [13] pre-trained on the FFHQ [12] dataset in (Fig. 8a), where the original gender direction is entangled with smile, eyeglasses and age. By filtering out activated channels for the entangled attribute(s) calculated from the gradient weights in our classification network, we achieve different levels of disentanglement. We further present disentanglement results for StyleGAN2 [13] pretrained on the LSUN-Cars [31] dataset and StyleGAN [12] pretrained on the LSUN-Bedrooms dataset [31] in (Fig. 8b).

Next, we study the **robustness** of attribute disentanglement with respect to the number of top-$k$ channels selected. When setting $k$ to 100 for all attributes as shown in (Fig. 8c), our method produces disentangled results, and the level of disentanglement for editing each attribute can be further improved by manually adjusting based on the results on a small meta-validation set of 30 examples with $k$ in {50, 100, 150, 200, 250}.

Female->male optimization direction

(a) Disentangle gender from other attributes one by one. The upper left row shows entanglement with eyeglasses, smile and age. At the bottom right row, by excluding the union of the activated channels for all entangled attributes, we successfully achieve disentanglement, where only the gender attribute is changed.

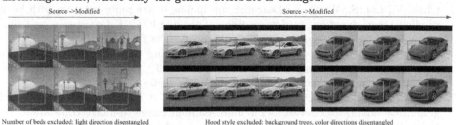

(b) Disentanglement results for LSUN-Cars and LSUN-Bedrooms [31]. The first row and second row shows original direction and disentangled direction respectively.

(c) Effect of number of channels excluded for smile, age, eyeglasses when editing gender. Tweaked: results shown in (Fig. 3).

**Fig. 8.** Ablation studies on disentanglement.

## 5    Discussion

**Limitations.** Despite the overall success of our method, we also notice some failures which lack 3D understanding (e.g. car rotation) or result in identity change. Examples and discussions can be found in the Appendix.

**Conclusions.** In this work, we propose a simple but powerful approach based on gradients to obtain multi-directional controls and disentangle one attribute from the others. Our findings show that attributes' controls can be separated even with strongly correlated training datasets via gradient information. This work shows considerable potential to discover rich controls in the learned latent space via gradient-based information, as well as its effectiveness in small data regimes.

# References

1. Bau, D., et al.: Gan dissection: visualizing and understanding generative adversarial networks. In: Proceedings of the International Conference on Learning Representations (ICLR) (2019)
2. Bau, D., et al.: Seeing what a GAN cannot generate. In: Proceedings of the IEEE/CVF International Conference on Computer Vision, pp. 4502–4511 (2019)
3. Brock, A., Donahue, J., Simonyan, K.: Large scale GAN training for high fidelity natural image synthesis. In: International Conference on Learning Representations (2019). https://openreview.net/forum?id=B1xsqj09Fm
4. Chattopadhay, A., Sarkar, A., Howlader, P., Balasubramanian, V.N.: Grad-CAM++: generalized gradient-based visual explanations for deep convolutional networks. In: 2018 IEEE Winter Conference on Applications of Computer Vision (WACV), pp. 839–847. IEEE (2018)
5. Chen, Y., Liu, S., Wang, X.: Learning continuous image representation with local implicit image function. In: Proceedings of the IEEE/CVF Conference on Computer Vision and Pattern Recognition, pp. 8628–8638 (2021)
6. Cherepkov, A., Voynov, A., Babenko, A.: Navigating the GAN parameter space for semantic image editing. In: Proceedings of the IEEE/CVF Conference on Computer Vision and Pattern Recognition, pp. 3671–3680 (2021)
7. Choi, Y., Choi, M., Kim, M., Ha, J.W., Kim, S., Choo, J.: StarGAN: unified generative adversarial networks for multi-domain image-to-image translation. In: Proceedings of the IEEE Conference on Computer Vision and Pattern Recognition, pp. 8789–8797 (2018)
8. Choi, Y., Uh, Y., Yoo, J., Ha, J.W.: StarGAN V2: diverse image synthesis for multiple domains. In: Proceedings of the IEEE/CVF Conference on Computer Vision and Pattern Recognition, pp. 8188–8197 (2020)
9. Goodfellow, I., et al.: Generative adversarial nets. In: Advances in Neural Information Processing Systems, vol. 27 (2014)
10. Härkönen, E., Hertzmann, A., Lehtinen, J., Paris, S.: GANspace: discovering interpretable GAN controls. In: Advances in Neural Information Processing Systems, vol. 33, pp. 9841–9850 (2020)
11. Isola, P., Zhu, J.Y., Zhou, T., Efros, A.A.: Image-to-image translation with conditional adversarial networks. In: Proceedings of the IEEE Conference on Computer Vision and Pattern Recognition (CVPR), July 2017
12. Karras, T., Laine, S., Aila, T.: A style-based generator architecture for generative adversarial networks. In: Proceedings of the IEEE/CVF Conference on Computer Vision and Pattern Recognition, pp. 4401–4410 (2019)
13. Karras, T., Laine, S., Aittala, M., Hellsten, J., Lehtinen, J., Aila, T.: Analyzing and improving the image quality of StyleGAN. In: Proceedings of the IEEE/CVF Conference on Computer Vision and Pattern Recognition, pp. 8110–8119 (2020)
14. Ledig, C., et al.: Photo-realistic single image super-resolution using a generative adversarial network. In: Proceedings of the IEEE Conference on Computer Vision and Pattern Recognition, pp. 4681–4690 (2017)
15. Li, Z., Jiang, R., Aarabi, P.: Continuous face aging via self-estimated residual age embedding. In: Proceedings of the IEEE/CVF Conference on Computer Vision and Pattern Recognition, pp. 15008–15017 (2021)
16. Liu, M., et al.: STGAN: a unified selective transfer network for arbitrary image attribute editing. In: Proceedings of the IEEE Conference on Computer Vision and Pattern Recognition, pp. 3673–3682 (2019)

17. Park, T., Liu, M.Y., Wang, T.C., Zhu, J.Y.: Semantic image synthesis with spatially-adaptive normalization. In: Proceedings of the IEEE/CVF Conference on Computer Vision and Pattern Recognition, pp. 2337–2346 (2019)
18. Radford, A., Metz, L., Chintala, S.: Unsupervised representation learning with deep convolutional generative adversarial networks (2016)
19. Saha, R., Duke, B., Shkurti, F., Taylor, G., Aarabi, P.: LOHO: latent optimization of hairstyles via orthogonalization. In: CVPR (2021)
20. Selvaraju, R.R., Cogswell, M., Das, A., Vedantam, R., Parikh, D., Batra, D.: Grad-Cam: visual explanations from deep networks via gradient-based localization. In: Proceedings of the IEEE International Conference on Computer Vision, pp. 618–626 (2017)
21. Shen, Y., Yang, C., Tang, X., Zhou, B.: InterFaceGAN: interpreting the disentangled face representation learned by GANs. IEEE Trans. Pattern Anal. Mach. Intell. (2020)
22. Smilkov, D., Thorat, N., Kim, B., Viégas, F., Wattenberg, M.: SmoothGrad: removing noise by adding noise. arXiv preprint arXiv:1706.03825 (2017)
23. Sundararajan, M., Taly, A., Yan, Q.: Axiomatic attribution for deep networks. In: International Conference on Machine Learning, pp. 3319–3328. PMLR (2017)
24. Upchurch, P., et al.: Deep feature interpolation for image content changes. In: Proceedings of the IEEE Conference on Computer Vision and Pattern Recognition, pp. 7064–7073 (2017)
25. Voynov, A., Babenko, A.: Unsupervised discovery of interpretable directions in the GAN latent space. In: International Conference on Machine Learning, pp. 9786–9796. PMLR (2020)
26. Wang, T.C., Liu, M.Y., Zhu, J.Y., Tao, A., Kautz, J., Catanzaro, B.: High-resolution image synthesis and semantic manipulation with conditional GANs. In: Proceedings of the IEEE Conference on Computer Vision and Pattern Recognition, pp. 8798–8807 (2018)
27. Wu, Y., Donahue, J., Balduzzi, D., Simonyan, K., Lillicrap, T.: LOGAN: latent optimisation for generative adversarial networks. arXiv preprint arXiv:1912.00953 (2019)
28. Wu, Z., Lischinski, D., Shechtman, E.: StyleSpace analysis: disentangled controls for StyleGAN image generation. In: Proceedings of the IEEE/CVF Conference on Computer Vision and Pattern Recognition, pp. 12863–12872 (2021)
29. Yang, C., Shen, Y., Zhou, B.: Semantic hierarchy emerges in deep generative representations for scene synthesis. Int. J. Comput. Vision 129(5), 1451–1466 (2021)
30. Yeh, R.A., Chen, C., Yian Lim, T., Schwing, A.G., Hasegawa-Johnson, M., Do, M.N.: Semantic image inpainting with deep generative models. In: Proceedings of the IEEE Conference on Computer Vision and Pattern Recognition, pp. 5485–5493 (2017)
31. Yu, F., Seff, A., Zhang, Y., Song, S., Funkhouser, T., Xiao, J.: LSUN: construction of a large-scale image dataset using deep learning with humans in the loop. arXiv preprint arXiv:1506.03365 (2015)
32. Yu, J., Lin, Z., Yang, J., Shen, X., Lu, X., Huang, T.S.: Free-form image inpainting with gated convolution. In: Proceedings of the IEEE/CVF International Conference on Computer Vision, pp. 4471–4480 (2019)
33. Zhu, J.Y., Park, T., Isola, P., Efros, A.A.: Unpaired image-to-image translation using cycle-consistent adversarial networks. In: Proceedings of the IEEE International Conference on Computer Vision, pp. 2223–2232 (2017)

# Spatially Invariant Unsupervised 3D Object-Centric Learning and Scene Decomposition

Tianyu Wang[✉] [ID], Miaomiao Liu[ID], and Kee Siong Ng[ID]

Australian National University, Canberra, ACT 2601, Australia
{Tianyu.Wang2,miaomiao.liu,KeeSiong.ng}@anu.edu.au

**Abstract.** We tackle the problem of object-centric learning on point clouds, which is crucial for high-level relational reasoning and scalable machine intelligence. In particular, we introduce a framework, **SPAIR3D**, to factorize a 3D point cloud into a spatial mixture model where each component corresponds to one object. To model the spatial mixture model on point clouds, we derive the *Chamfer Mixture Loss*, which fits naturally into our variational training pipeline. Moreover, we adopt an object-specification scheme that describes each object's location relative to its local voxel grid cell. Such a scheme allows **SPAIR3D** to model scenes with an arbitrary number of objects. We evaluate our method on the task of unsupervised scene decomposition. Experimental results demonstrate that **SPAIR3D** has strong scalability and is capable of detecting and segmenting an unknown number of objects from a point cloud in an unsupervised manner.

**Keywords:** Deep generative model · Variational inference · Unsupervised scene understanding

## 1 Introduction

3D scenes can exhibit complex and combinatorially large observation spaces even when there are only a few basic elements. Motivated in part by cognitive psychology studies [26] that suggest human brains organize observations at an object level, recent advances in physical prediction [8], and the superior robustness demonstrated by object-oriented reinforcement learning agent [12,27], we tackle in this paper the problem of deep object-centric learning on point clouds, which is crucial for high-level relational reasoning and scalable machine intelligence.

There is a good body of existing literature on unsupervised object-centric generative models for images and videos. The spatial mixture models are widely adopted to model observations in an object-oriented way [5,10,14,16,30]. These approaches effectively define objectness as a region with strong appearance correlations, and Variational Autoencoders (VAE) [19,28] play a critical role in

---

**Supplementary Information** The online version contains supplementary material available at https://doi.org/10.1007/978-3-031-20050-2_8.

S. Avidan et al. (Eds.): ECCV 2022, LNCS 13683, pp. 120–135, 2022.
https://doi.org/10.1007/978-3-031-20050-2_8

exploiting such correlations. More precisely, the encoder-decoder structure of VAE effectively creates an information bottleneck [2,6,36] limiting the amount of information passing through. To reconstruct the observation under a limited information budget, highly correlated information must be encoded together. Thus, objectness emerges from the encoding strategy. The above-mentioned papers mainly exploit appearance correlations on objects that are colored uniformly. In this paper, we show that this paradigm is also applicable to structural correlations conveyed by point clouds without appearance information, as long as we can overcome some irregularities in point cloud data as described in Sect. 3. Specifically, inspired by SPAIR [10], we propose in this paper a VAE-based model named **Sp**atially Invariant **A**ttend, **I**nfer, **R**epeat in **3D** (SPAIR3D), a model that generates spatial mixture distributions on point clouds to discover 3D objects in static scenes. Here we summarize the key contributions:

- We propose, to the best of our knowledge, the first unsupervised object-centric learning pipeline for point cloud data, named SPAIR3D.
- We also propose a new *Chamfer Mixture Loss* function tailored for learning mixture models over point cloud data with a novel graph neural network that can be used to model and generate a variable number of 3D points.
- We provide qualitative and quantitative results to show that SPAIR3D learns meaningful object-centric representation and decomposes point clouds scene with an arbitrary number of objects in an object-oriented manner.

## 2 Related Work

**Generative Unsupervised Object-Centric Learning.** Unsupervised object-centric learning based on generative models has attracted increasing attention in recent times. Such approaches focus on joint object representation-learning and scene decomposition based on single or multiple views [5,9,10,13,16,29,30,35]. A spatial Gaussian mixture model is typically defined on 2D images consisting of $K$ mixture components that correspond to $K$ objects. Each component spans the entire image and places an isotropic Gaussian on the RGB value of all pixels with a predicted mean and a constant covariance. Each component also assigns each pixel a non-negative mixing weight that sums to one across all components. The definition can be easily extended to voxel and neural radiance fields.

Under the spatial mixture model formulation, different inference methods are proposed. IODINE [16] employs iterative amortized inference to refine latent variable posteriors for all components in parallel. GENESIS [13] and MONET [5] sequentially infer the latent representation, one component at a time. Slot attention [31] and Neural Expectation Maximization (NEM) [17] can be regarded as differentiable clustering algorithms.

Instead of treating each component of the mixture model as a full-scale observation, **A**ttend, **I**nfer, **R**epeat (AIR) [14] confines the extent of each component to a local region. In AIR, one network is trained to propose a set of candidate object regions in the form of 2D bounding boxes. Each region is then cropped out and processed by a VAE. The final reconstruction is obtained by placing the reconstructed patches back in the inferred locations. Pixels that are not covered by any patches are deemed background. While AIR fails in scenes of dense objects, SPAIR [10] addresses the challenge with a grid spatial attention mechanism with which bounding boxes are proposed locally from each grid cell. This extension is also proven effective in object-tracking tasks [11]. By confining the extent of each component, constraints on maximum object sizes are imposed. SPACE [30] employs MONET to model background components that are normally much larger than foreground objects.

**Graph Neural Network for Point Cloud Generation.** Generative models such as VAEs [15] and generative adversarial networks [1] have been successfully used for point cloud generation but with a pre-defined number of points per-object. It is shown that a point cloud generation process can be modeled as a latent variable conditioned Markov chain [32]. PointFlow [38] is a normalizing flow-based approach that models object shapes as continuous distributions and allows the generation of a variable number of points. It could not be naturally integrated into our framework due to the need for an ODE solver.

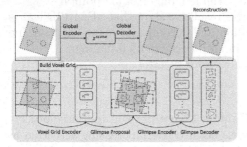

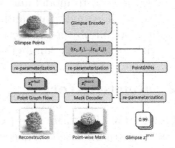

(a) Structure of SPAIR3D                    (b) Structure of Glimpse VAE

**Fig. 1.** (a) Structure of SPAIR3D. For clarity, we adopt 2D abstraction and use colors to highlight important correspondence. (b) Structure of Glimpse VAE. Glimpse encoder encodes foreground glimpses and produce $\mathbf{z}_i^{what}$, $\mathbf{z}_i^{mask}$ and $z_i^{pres}$ for each glimpse. Point Graph Decoder takes $\mathbf{z}_i^{what}$ and reconstructs input points (left branch). Mask Decoder takes $\mathbf{z}_i^{mask}$ and generates masks for each point (middle branch). The dashed line represents the dependency on the coordinates of the intermediate points in the hierarchy and $\mathcal{G}_i$. Multi-layer PointGNN enable message passing between $(\mathbf{c}_i, \mathbf{f}_i)$ and produces $z_i^{pres}$ (right branch).

## 3    SPAIR3D

While the application of generative-model-based object-centric learning on image [5,16], voxel [18], and mesh [18] shows encouraging results, its application on point cloud has not been explored up till now. Unlike point cloud data, the reconstructions of images, and voxels are all coordinate-dependent. For each mixture component, given a coordinate, a mixing weight (defining mask) and a feature vector (RGB value) are generated at that coordinate to form a well-defined mixture model. For image data, the coordinate dependency can be implicitly embedded in the network structure since the input and output are of fixed sizes [21]. The coordinate thus provides the correspondence between input and reconstruction, inducing a natural likelihood function.

However, a point cloud takes the form of an unordered set with irregular structures. Each point cloud may have a varying number of points. More importantly, the point coordinates carrying structural information becomes the reconstruction target, and there is usually no natural correspondence between the input and the reconstruction. While *Chamfer Distance* commonly serves as a loss function for point cloud reconstruction, it does not support mixture model formulation directly. Such data irregularity makes defining a mixture model over point cloud a non-trivial task.

To overcome the issues outlined above, we extend the SPAIR framework and introduce **SPAIR3D**, a deep generative model for 3D object-centric learning and 3D scene decomposition via object-centric point-cloud generation. There are two main reasons for choosing the SPAIR framework over others. Firstly, as a consequence of the lack of correspondence between input and reconstruction, the likelihood computation commonly involves a bi-directional matching between the generated point cloud and the ground truth, leading to quadratic time complexity. The local object proposal and reconstruction mechanism allow us to confine the matching computation in each local region, which significantly reduces the algorithm's time complexity (see Supp. Sec. 1 for further analysis).

Secondly, 3D point cloud reconstruction commonly requires the target object to be centered [32,38]. While it is straightforward to center objects in single-object reconstruction tasks, it is difficult to center all objects in the same coordinate system in the 3D scene reconstruction setup. In contrast, thanks to the local object proposal mechanism proposed in this paper, each object can be naturally centered in a local coordinate system.

Below we first introduce our generative model formulation over key latent variables (Sect. 3.1). Then we detail the inference model implementation (Sect. 3.3). We discuss the particular challenges arising in handling a varying number of points with a novel *Chamfer Mixture Loss* (Sect. 3.2) and *Point Graph Decoder* (Sect. 3.3).

## 3.1   Local Object Proposal and Generative Model

As shown in Fig. 1a, SPAIR3D first divides a 3D scene into a spatial attention voxel grid with possible empty voxel cells covering no points. We discard empty cells and associate a bounding box with each non-empty voxel cell. The set of input points captured by a bounding box is termed an *object glimpse*. Besides object glimpses, SPAIR3D also defines a *scene glimpse* covering all points in an input scene. Later, we show that we encode and reconstruct each glimpse and generate a mixing weight on each point to form a probability mixture model.

Similar to SPAIR, each grid cell generates posterior distributions over a set of latent variables defined as $\mathbf{z}_i^{cell} = \{\mathbf{z}_i^{where}, \mathbf{z}_i^{apothem}\}$, where $\mathbf{z}_i^{where} \in \mathbb{R}^3$ encodes the relative position of the center of the $i^{th}$ bounding box to the center of the $i^{th}$ cell, $\mathbf{z}_i^{apothem} \in \mathbb{R}^3$ encodes the apothem of the bounding box. Thus, each $\mathbf{z}_i^{cell}$ induces one object glimpse associated with the $i^{th}$ cell. Each object glimpse is then associated with posterior distributions over latent variables specified as $\mathbf{z}_i^{object} = \{\mathbf{z}_i^{what}, \mathbf{z}_i^{mask}, z_i^{pres}\}$, where $\mathbf{z}_i^{what} \in \mathbb{R}^A$ encodes the structure information of the corresponding object glimpse, $\mathbf{z}_i^{mask} \in \mathbb{R}^B$ encodes the mask for each point in the glimpse, $z_i^{pres} \in \{0, 1\}$ is a binary variable indicating whether the proposed object should exist ($z_i^{pres} = 1$) or not ($z_i^{pres} = 0$). The scene glimpse is associated with only one latent variable $\mathbf{z}^{scene} = \{\mathbf{z}_0^{what}\}$. We assume $z_i^{pres}$ follows a Bernoulli distribution. The posteriors and priors of other latent variables are all set to isotropic Gaussian distributions.

Given latent representations of objects and the scene, the complete likelihood for a point cloud $\mathcal{X}$ is $p(\mathcal{X}) = \int_{\mathbf{z}} p(\mathbf{z}) p(\mathcal{X}|\mathbf{z}) d\mathbf{z}$, where $\mathbf{z} = (\bigcup_i \mathbf{z}_i^{cell}) \cup (\bigcup_i \mathbf{z}_i^{object}) \cup \mathbf{z}^{scene}$. As maximizing the objective $p(\mathcal{X})$ is intractable, we resort to the variational inference to maximize its evidence lower bound (ELBO).

## 3.2 Chamfer Mixture Loss

Unlike generative model-based unsupervised 2D segmentation methods that reconstruct the pixel-wise appearance conditioning on its spatial coordinate, the reconstruction of a point cloud lost its point-wise correspondence to the original point cloud. *Chamfer distance* is commonly adopted to measure the discrepancy between the generated point cloud ($\hat{\mathcal{X}}$) and the input point cloud ($\mathcal{X}$). Formally, *Chamfer distance* is defined by $d_{CD}(\mathcal{X}, \hat{\mathcal{X}}) = \sum_{x \in \mathcal{X}} \min_{\hat{x} \in \hat{\mathcal{X}}} \|x - \hat{x}\|_2^2 + \sum_{\hat{x} \in \hat{\mathcal{X}}} \min_{x \in \mathcal{X}} \|x - \hat{x}\|_2^2$. We refer to the first and the second term as the forward loss and the backward loss, respectively.

Unfortunately, the *Chamfer distance* does not fit naturally into the mixture model framework. To get around that, we propose a *Chamfer Mixture Loss* (CML) tailored for training probability mixture models defined on point clouds. The *Chamfer Mixture Loss* is composed of a *forward likelihood* and a *backward regularization* corresponding to the forward and backward loss, respectively.

Denote the $i^{th}$ glimpse as $\mathcal{G}_i$, $i \in \{0, \ldots, n\}$ and its reconstruction as $\hat{\mathcal{G}}_i$, $i \in \{0, \ldots, n\}$. Specifically, we treat the scene glimpse as the $0^{th}$ glimpse that contains all input points, that is, $\mathcal{G}_0 = \mathcal{X}$. Note that one input point can be a member of multiple glimpses. Below we use $\mathcal{N}(x|\mu, \sigma)$ to denote the probability density value of point $x$ evaluated at a Gaussian distribution of mean $\mu$ and variance $\sigma$. For each input point $x$ in the $i^{th}$ glimpse, the glimpse-wise forward likelihood of that point is defined as $\mathcal{L}_i^F(x) = \frac{1}{u_i} \max_{\hat{x} \in \hat{\mathcal{G}}_i} \mathcal{N}(x|\hat{x}, \sigma_c)$, where $u_i = \int_{x \in \mathcal{X}} \max_{\hat{x} \in \hat{\mathcal{G}}_i} \mathcal{N}(x|\hat{x}, \sigma_c) dx$ is the normalizer and $\sigma_c$ is a hyperparameter. For each glimpse $\mathcal{G}_i$, $i \in \{0, \ldots, n\}$, $\alpha_i^x \in [0, 1]$ defines a mixing weight for point $x$ in the glimpse and $\sum_{i=0}^n \alpha_i^x = 1$. In particular, $\alpha_i^x$, $i \in \{1, \ldots, n\}$, is determined by $\alpha_i^x = \frac{z_i^{pres} \pi_i^x}{\sum_{j=1}^n z_j^{pres} \pi_j^x} z_i^{pres} \pi_i^x$, where $\pi_i^x$ is the predicted mask value and $\pi_i^x = 0$ if $x \notin \mathcal{G}_i$. The mixing weight for the scene layout points completes the distribution through $\alpha_0^x = 1 - \sum_{i=1}^n \alpha_i^x$ for $x \in \mathcal{G}_0$. Thus, the final mixture model for an input point $x$ is $\mathcal{L}^F(x) = \sum_{i=0}^{n} \alpha_i^x \mathcal{L}_i^F(x)$. The total forward likelihood of $\mathcal{X}$ is then defined as $\mathcal{L}^F(\mathcal{X}) = \prod_{x \in \mathcal{X}} \mathcal{L}^F(x)$.

The forward likelihood alone leads to a trivial sub-optimal solution with $\hat{\mathcal{X}}$ distributed densely and uniformly in the space. To enforce a high-quality reconstruction, we define a backward regularization term. For each predicted point $\hat{x}$, the point-wise backward regularization is $\mathcal{L}^B(\hat{x}) = \max_{x \in \mathcal{G}_{i(\hat{x})}} \mathcal{N}(\hat{x}|x, \sigma_c)$, where $i(\hat{x})$ returns the glimpse index of $\hat{x}$. We denote $x(\hat{x}) = \arg\max_{x \in \mathcal{G}_{i(\hat{x})}} \mathcal{N}(\hat{x}|x, \sigma_c)$ and $\hat{\mathcal{X}} = \bigcup_{i=0}^{n} \hat{\mathcal{G}}_i$. The backward regularization is then defined as $\mathcal{L}^B(\hat{\mathcal{X}}) = \prod_{i=0}^{n} \prod_{\hat{x} \in \hat{\mathcal{G}}_i} \mathcal{L}^B(\hat{x})^{\alpha_i^{x(\hat{x})}}$. The exponential weighting, i.e. $\alpha_i^{x(\hat{x})} \in [0,1]$, is crucial. As each predicted point $\hat{x} \in \hat{\mathcal{X}}$ belongs to one and only one glimpse, it is difficult to impose a mixture model interpretation on the backward regularization. The exponential weighting encourages the generated points in object glimpse to be close to input points with a high probability belonging to $\mathcal{G}_i$. Combining the forward likelihood and the backward regularization together, we define *Chamfer Mixture Loss* as $\mathcal{L}_{\mathcal{CD}}(\mathcal{X}, \hat{\mathcal{X}}) = \mathcal{L}^F(\mathcal{X}) \cdot \mathcal{L}^B(\hat{\mathcal{X}})$. During inference, the segmentation label for each point $x$ is naturally obtained by $\arg\max_i \alpha_i^x$.

The overall loss function is $\mathcal{L} = -\log \mathcal{L}_{\mathcal{CD}}(\mathcal{X}, \hat{\mathcal{X}}) + \mathcal{L}_{KL}(\mathbf{z}^{cell}, \mathbf{z}^{object}, \mathbf{z}^{scene})$, where $\mathcal{L}_{KL}$ is the KL divergence between the prior and posterior of the latent variables (Supp. Sec. 2 for details). In general, one cannot find a closed-form solution for the normalizer in Chamfer Mixture Loss. However, the experiments below show that we can safely ignore it during optimization.

### 3.3   Model Structure

We next introduce the encoder and decoder network structure for SPAIR3D. The building blocks are based on graph neural networks and point convolution operations (See Sect. 4 in the Supp. for details).

**Encoder Network.** We design an encoder network $q_\phi(\mathbf{z}|x)$ to obtain the latent representations $\{\mathbf{z}_i^{cell}\}_{i=1}^n$ and $\{\mathbf{z}_i^{object}\}_{i=1}^n$ from a point cloud. To achieve the spatially invariant property, we group one PointConv [37] layer and one Point-GNN [34] layer into pairs for message passing and information aggregation among points and between cells.

**(a) Voxel Grid Encoding.** The voxel-grid encoder takes a point cloud as input and generates for each spatial attention voxel cell $\mathcal{C}_i$ two latent variables $\mathbf{z}_i^{where} \in \mathbb{R}^3$ and $\mathbf{z}_i^{apothem} \in \mathbb{R}^3$ to propose a glimpse $\mathcal{G}_i$ potentially occupied by an object. To better capture the point cloud information in $\mathcal{C}_i$, we build a voxel pyramid within each cell $\mathcal{C}_i$ with the bottom level corresponding to the finest voxel grid. We aggregate information hierarchically using PointConv-PointGNN pairs from bottom to top through each level of the pyramid. For each layer of the pyramid, we aggregate the features of all points and assign them to the point spawned at the center of mass of the voxel cell. Then PointGNN is employed to perform message passing on the radius graph built on all spawned points. The output of the final aggregation block produces $\mathbf{z}_i^{where}$ and $\mathbf{z}_i^{apothem}$ via the re-parametrization trick [28].

We obtain the offset distance of a glimpse center from its corresponding grid cell center using $\Delta g_i = \tanh(\mathbf{z}_i^{where}) \cdot L$, where $L$ is the maximum offset distance. The apothems of the glimpse in the $x, y, z$ direction is given by $\Delta \mathbf{g}_i^{apo} = T(\mathbf{z}_i^{apothem})(\mathbf{r}^{max} - \mathbf{r}^{min}) + \mathbf{r}^{min}$, where $T(\cdot)$ is the sigmoid function and $[\mathbf{r}^{min}, \mathbf{r}^{max}]$ defines the range of apothem.

**(b) Glimpse Encoding.** The predicted glimpse center offset and the apothems uniquely determine one glimpse for each spatial attention voxel cell. We adopt the same encoder structure to encode each glimpse $\mathcal{G}_i$ into one point $\mathbf{a}_i = (\mathbf{c}_i, \mathbf{f}_i)$, where $\mathbf{c}_i$ is the glimpse center coordinate and $\mathbf{f}_i$ is the glimpse feature vector. We then generate $\mathbf{z}_i^{what}$ and $\mathbf{z}_i^{mask}$ from $\mathbf{a}_i$ via the re-parameterization trick.

The variable $z_i^{pres}$ governs the glimpse rejection process and is crucial to the final decomposition quality. Unlike previous work [10, 30], SPAIR3D generates $z^{pres}$ from glimpse features instead of cell features based on our observation that message passing across glimpses provides more benefits in the glimpse-rejection process. To this end, a radius graph is first built on the point set $\{(\mathbf{c}_i, \mathbf{f}_i)\}_{i=1}^n$ to connect nearby glimpse centers, which is followed by multiple PointGNN layers with decreasing output channels to perform local message passing. The $z_i^{pres}$ of each glimpse is then obtained via the re-parameterization trick. Information exchange between nearby glimpses can help avoid over-segmentation that would otherwise occur because of the high dimensionality of point cloud data.

**(c) Global Encoding.** The global encoding module adopts the same encoder as the object glimpse encoder to encode scene glimpse $\mathcal{G}_0$. The learned latent representation is $\mathbf{z}_0^{what}$ with $z_0^{pres} = 1$.

**Decoder Network.** We now introduce the decoders used for point-cloud and mask generation.

**(a) Point Graph Decoder (PGD).** Given the $\mathbf{z}_i^{object}$ of each glimpse, the decoder is used for point-cloud reconstruction as well as segmentation-mask generation. In reconstruction, the number of generated points has a direct effect on the magnitudes of the forward and backward terms in the Chamfer Mixture Loss. An unbalanced number of reconstruction points can lead to under- or over-segmentation. To balance the forward likelihood and the backward regularization, the number of predictions for each glimpse should be approximately the same as the number of input points. We propose a graph network based point decoder to allow setting the size of $\hat{\mathcal{X}}$ in run time.

PGD treats the point cloud reconstruction as a point diffusion process [32]. The input to the PGD is a set of 3D points with coordinates sampled from a zero-centered Gaussian distribution, with the population determined by the number of points in the current glimpse. Features of the input points are set uniformly to the latent variable $\mathbf{z}_i^{what}$. PGD is composed of several PointGNN layers, each of which is preceded by a radius graph operation. The output of each PointGNN layer is of dimension $f + 3$, with the first $f$ dimensions interpreted as the updated features and the last 3 dimensions interpreted as the updated 3D coordinates for estimated points. Since we only focus on point coordinates prediction, we set $f = 0$ for the last PointGNN layer.

(b) **Mask Decoder.** The Mask Decoder decodes $(\mathbf{c}_i, \mathbf{z}_i^{mask})$ to the mask value, $\pi_i^x \in [0,1]$, of each point within a glimpse $\mathcal{G}_i$. The decoding process follows the exact inverse pyramid structure of the Glimpse Encoder. To be more precise, the mask decoder can access the spatial coordinates of the intermediate aggregation points of the Glimpse Encoder as well as the point coordinates of $\mathcal{G}_i$. During decoding, PointConv is used as deconvolution operation.

**Glimpse VAE and Global VAE.** The complete Glimpse VAE structure is presented in Fig. 1b. The Glimpse VAE is composed of a Glimpse Encoder, Point Graph Decoder, Mask Decoder and a multi-layer PointGNN network. The Glimpse Encoder takes all glimpses as input and encodes each glimpse $\mathcal{G}_i$ individually and in parallel into feature points $(\mathbf{c}_i, \mathbf{f}_i)$. Via the re-parameterization trick, $\mathbf{z}_i^{what}$ and $\mathbf{z}_i^{mask}$ are then obtained from $\mathbf{f}_i$. From there, we use the Point Graph Decoder to decode $\mathbf{z}_i^{what}$ to reconstruct the input points, and we use the Mask Decoder to decode $\mathbf{z}_i^{mask}$ to assign a mask value for each input point within $\mathcal{G}_i$. Finally, $\mathbf{z}_i^{pres}$ is generated via message passing among neighbour glimpses. All glimpses are processed in parallel. The Global VAE consisting of the Global Encoder and a PGD outputs the reconstructed scene layout.

### 3.4 Soft Boundary

The prior of $\mathbf{z}^{apothem}$ is set to encourage apothem to shrink so that the size of the glimpses will not be overly large. However, if one point is excluded from one glimpse, its gradient is disconnected from the size and location of the glimpse anymore, and this can lead to over-segmentation. To solve this problem, we introduce a soft boundary weight $b_i^x \in [0,1]$ which decreases as a point $x \in \mathcal{G}_i$ moves away from the bounding box of $\mathcal{G}_i$. Taking $b_i^x$ into the computation of $\alpha$, we obtain an updated mixing weight $\overline{\alpha}_i^x = \frac{z_i^{pres}\pi_i^x b_i^x}{\sum_{j=1}^n z_j^{pres}\pi_j^x b_j^x} z_i^{pres}\pi_i^x b_i^x$. By employing such a boundary loss, the gradual exclusion of points from glimpses will be reflected in gradients to counter over-segmentation.

## 4 Experiments

### 4.1 Simulated Datasets

**Dataset Generation.** While many benchmark datasets have been established [23,25] for unsupervised object-centric learning, they do not come in the form of a point cloud. Thus, we introduce two new point-cloud datasets *Unity Object Room* and *Unity Object Table* built on the *Unity* platform [24]. The Unity Object Room (UOR) dataset is built to approximate the Object Room [25] dataset but with increased scope and complexity. In each scene, objects sampled from a list of 8 regular geometries are randomly placed on a square floor. The Unity Object Table (UOT) dataset approximates the Robotic Object Grasping scenario where multiple objects are placed on a round table. We populate each scene with objects from a pool of 9 objects with challenging irregular structures. For both datasets, the number of objects placed in each scene varies from 2 to 5 with equal probabilities. During the scene generation, the size and orientation of the objects are varied randomly within a pre-defined range.

We capture the depth, RGB, normal frames, and pixel-wise semantics as well as instance labels for each scene from 10 different viewpoints. This setup aims to approximate the scenario where a robot equipped with depth and RGB sensors navigates around target objects. The point cloud data for each scene is then constructed by merging these 10 depth maps. For each dataset, we collect $50K$ training scenes, $10K$ validation scenes and $5K$ testing scenes.

**Baseline.** Due to the sparse literature on unsupervised 3D point cloud object-centric learning, we could not find a generative baseline to compare with. Thus, we compare SPAIR3D with PointGroup (PG) [22], a recent supervised 3D point cloud segmentation model. PointGroup is trained with ground-truth semantic labels and instance labels and performs semantic prediction and instance predictions on a point cloud. To ensure a fair comparison, we assign each point the same color (white). The PointGroup network is fine-tuned on the validation set to achieve the best performance.

**Performance Metric.** For UOR and UOT datasets, we use the Adjust Rand Index (ARI) [20] to measure the segmentation performance against the ground truth instance labels. We also employ foreground Segmentation Covering (SC) and foreground unweighted mean Segmentation Covering (mSC) [13] for performance measurements as ARI does not penalize object over-segmentation [13].

**Table 1.** 3D point cloud segmentation results on UOR (blue) and UOT (red).

| UOR<br>UOT | PG | Ours | voxel size 0.75$l$<br>voxel size 1.25$l$ | 6 − 12 objects | object matrix |
|---|---|---|---|---|---|
| ARI↑ | 0.976 | 0.915 ± 0.03 | 0.932 | 0.912 | 0.872 |
| | 0.923 | 0.901 ± 0.02 | 0.922 | 0.892 | 0.879 |
| SC↑ | 0.907 | 0.832 ± 0.04 | 0.853 | 0.846 | 0.856 |
| | 0.917 | 0.835 ± 0.03 | 0.857 | 0.843 | 0.877 |
| mSC↑ | 0.900 | 0.836 ± 0.04 | 0.850 | 0.842 | 0.861 |
| | 0.907 | 0.831 ± 0.03 | 0.861 | 0.834 | 0.886 |

**Evaluation.** Table 1 shows that SPAIR3D achieves comparable performance to the supervised baseline on both UOT and UOR datasets. As demonstrated in Fig. 4, each foreground object is proposed by one and only one glimpse. The scene layout is separated from objects and accurately modelled by the global VAE. It is worth noting that the segmentation errors mainly happen at the bottom of objects. Without appearance information, points at the bottom of objects are also correlated to the ground. In Fig. 2, we sort the test data based on their performance in ascending order and plot the performance distributions. As expected, the supervised baseline (Orange) performs better but SPAIR3D manages to achieve high-quality segmentation (SC score > 0.8) on around 80% of the scenes without supervision. The reported quantitative (Table 1) and qualitative results (Fig. 5(a)–(d)) show that our method achieves stable performance for those challenging scenes.

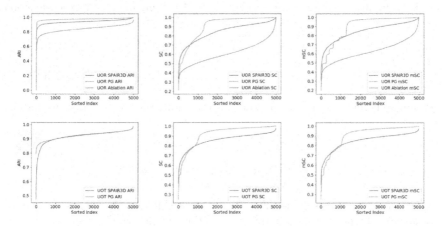

**Fig. 2.** Performance distributions on UOR (row one) and UOT (row two).

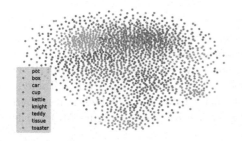

**Fig. 3.** t-SNE visualization of $z^{what}$ on UOT

**Object Centric Representation.** One advantage of our model is simultaneous segmentation and representation learning. To show that our model learns meaningful representations, we collect the $z^{what}$ of 200 instances per-type and visualize them with the t-SNE algorithm [33]. Figure 3 shows the $z^{what}$ of different object types occupy different regions. Note the embeddings of *pot* and *box* instances occupy the same area since they have almost identical spatial structure.

**Voxel Size Robustness and Scalability.** In the literature, the cell voxel size, an important hyperparameter, is chosen to match the object size in the scene [10,30]. To evaluate the robustness of our method w.r.t voxel size, we train our model on the UOR dataset with voxel size set to 0.75 $l$ and 1.25 $l$ with $l$ being the average size of the objects. Results in Table 1 show that our method achieves stable performance w.r.t the voxel size. To demonstrate scalability, we evaluate our pre-trained model on 1000 scenes containing 6–12 randomly selected objects and report performance in Table 1. Due to the spatial invariance property, SPAIR3D suffers no performance drop on 6–12 object scenes.

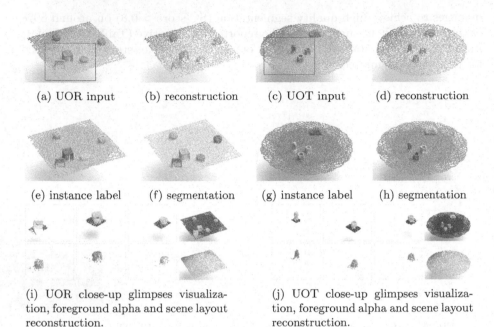

(a) UOR input    (b) reconstruction    (c) UOT input    (d) reconstruction

(e) instance label    (f) segmentation    (g) instance label    (h) segmentation

(i) UOR close-up glimpses visualization, foreground alpha and scene layout reconstruction.

(j) UOT close-up glimpses visualization, foreground alpha and scene layout reconstruction.

**Fig. 4.** Visualization of segmentation results on UOR and UOT dataset.

We also evaluated our approach on scenes termed as *Object Matrix*, which consists of 16 objects placed in a matrix form. We fixed the position of all 16 objects but set their size and rotation randomly. For each dataset, SPAIR3D is evaluated on 100 *Object Matrix* scenes. The results are reported in Table 1. Note that our model is trained on scenes with 2 to 5 objects which is less than one-third of the number of objects in *Object Matrix* scenes. Figure 5(c)–(d) is illustrative of the results.

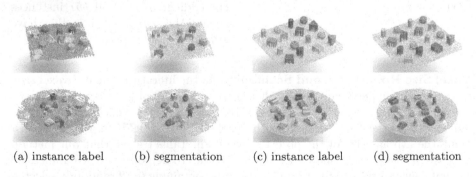

(a) instance label    (b) segmentation    (c) instance label    (d) segmentation

**Fig. 5.** Segmentation on 6–12 object scenes (a, b) and object matrix (c, d)

## 4.2   Real Dataset

To demonstrate the performance of our approach on real data, we apply our model to the S3DIS [3] dataset, which contains point clouds of 6 large-scale indoor areas with 271 rooms (scenes).

**Data Preprocessing.** While the dataset contains objects from 13 semantic categories, we focus on objects with regular structures, including chairs, tables, and sofas. As our approach focuses on object-centric learning, we thus manually inspect the dataset and remove rooms that are too empty (such as hallways), containing clutter (such as storage rooms), and connected objects (such as lecture theater with connected chairs). Finally, we kept 174 scenes in total. We then downsample the dense point cloud of each scene for computational efficiency.

**Baseline.** Besides Point Group [22] as a supervised baseline, we use Mean-shift as a rule-based as well as an unsupervised baseline. Floors are removed before applying Mean-shift and the bandwidth parameter is determined by grid-search.

**Performance Metric.** Due to the scene diversity, instead of reporting the average per-scene ARI, SC, or mSC, we report the per-class mIoU on test sets. For our model and Point Group, we perform 6-fold cross-validation on the 6 areas and report the average.

**Table 2.** Segmentation results on S3DIS. 'S' and 'U' denote the corresponding models are trained in supervised and unsupervised manner, respectively.

|  |  | Chair ↑ | Table ↑ | Sofa ↑ | macro-avg ↑ |
|---|---|---|---|---|---|
| PG | S | 0.61 | 0.69 | 0.52 | 0.60 |
| MS 0.06 | U | 0.75 | 0.34 | 0.36 | 0.48 |
| MS 0.15 | U | 0.33 | 0.46 | 0.38 | 0.39 |
| Ours | U | 0.59 | 0.43 | 0.49 | 0.50 |

**Evaluation.** Per-class mIoU are reported in Table 2. Since the number of objects of different types varies greatly, we thus additionally report macro-average to show the overall performance of different models. Not surprisingly, Point Group (PG) achieves the highest mIoU across all categories. Similar to our model, Point Group misclassifies object points that are close to the floor as floor category (row 1 Fig. 6). Mean-shift (MS) does not share the same vulnerability since floors are manually detected and removed. However, Mean-shift is sensitive to the bandwidth value. The bandwidth reflects the prior object sizes. With the bandwidth tuned for Chair (MS 0.06) whose sizes are small on average, tables and sofas are largely over-segmented. With the bandwidth tuned for Table (MS 0.15), chairs tend to be under-segmented.

As demonstrated in row 3 Fig. 6, chairs are successfully segmented by our model even when multiple chairs are clustered together. The segmentation of tables presents a challenge for our model since their sizes are commonly larger than our maximum glimpses sizes. However, SPAIR3D still tries to expand the glimpses sizes to better model larger objects while keeping the total number of glimpses low (row 2 Fig. 6). The experimental results in Table 2 demonstrate the potential of applying a generative model to more complicated scenarios.

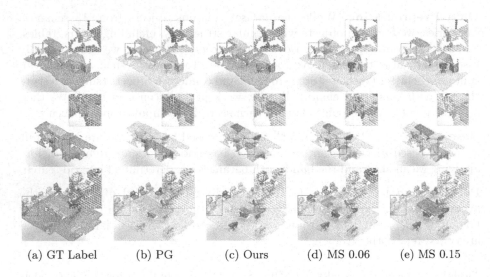

(a) GT Label      (b) PG      (c) Ours      (d) MS 0.06      (e) MS 0.15

**Fig. 6.** S3DIS segmentation results.

## 4.3   Ablation Study of Multi-layer PointGNN

To evaluate the importance of multi-layer PointGNN in $\mathbf{z}_i^{pres}$ generation (right branch in Fig. 1b), we remove the multi-layer PointGNN and generate $\mathbf{z}_i^{pres}$ directly from $\mathbf{f}_i$. The ablated model on the UOR dataset achieves **ARI:0.841**, **SC:0.610**, and **mSC:0.627**, which is significantly worse than the full SPAIR3D model. The performance distribution of ablated SPAIR3D (Fig. 2, first row) indicates that removing the multi-layer PointGNN has a negative influence on the entire dataset. Figure 7 shows that the multi-layer PointGNN is crucial to preventing over-segmentation.

## 4.4   Empirical Evaluation of PGD

3D objects of the same category can be modeled by a varying number of points. The generation quality of the point cloud largely depends on the robustness of our model against the number of points representing each object. To demonstrate that PGD can reconstruct each object with a dynamic number of points, we train the global VAE on the ShapeNet dataset [7], where each object is composed of roughly 2000 points, and reconstruct the object with a varying number of points. For reference input point clouds of size $N$, we force PGD to reconstruct a point cloud of size $1.5\,N$, $1.25\,N$, $N$, $0.75\,N$, and $0.5\,N$, respectively. As shown in Fig. 8, while with fewer details compared to the input, the reconstructions capture the overall object structure in all 5 settings.

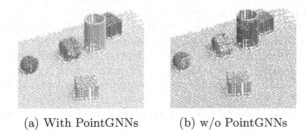

(a) With PointGNNs          (b) w/o PointGNNs

**Fig. 7.** The comparison between models with (left) and without (right) multi-layer PointGNNs. It shows that objects are over-segmented severely without multi-layer PointGNNs.

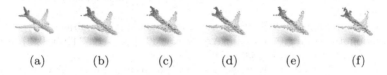

(a)          (b)          (c)          (d)          (e)          (f)

**Fig. 8.** PGD trained on ShapeNet. (a) Input point cloud with $N$ points. Reconstruction with (b) $1.5N$, (c) $1.25N$, (d) $N$, (e) $0.75N$, and (f) $0.5N$ points.

## 5  Limitations

Similar to SPAIR, the good scalability in SPAIR3D stems from the local attention and reconstruction mechanisms. By design, each voxel cell can only propose one object. Thus, it is difficult to detect multiple objects that exist in the same voxel cell. If one object is much larger than the size of the voxel cells, no voxel cells can accurately infer complete object information from its local perceptive field. One can alleviate the problem with overlapping voxel cells and make the mixture model hierarchical, which we leave as future work.

## 6  Conclusion and Future Work

Our proposed *SPAIR3D* algorithm is, to the best of our knowledge, the first generative unsupervised object-centric learning model on point cloud with applications to 3D object segmentation task. The experimental results demonstrate that SPAIR3D can generalize well to previously unseen scenes with a large number of objects without performance degeneration. The spatial mixture interpretation of SPAIR3D opens up the possibility to other extensions including memory mechanism [4] or iterative refinement [16], which is left as our future work.

# References

1. Achlioptas, P., Diamanti, O., Mitliagkas, I., Guibas, L.: Learning representations and generative models for 3D point clouds. In: ICML, pp. 40–49. PMLR (2018)
2. Alemi, A., Fischer, I., Dillon, J., Murphy, K.: Deep variational information bottleneck. In: ICLR (2017). https://arxiv.org/abs/1612.00410
3. Armeni, I., Sax, A., Zamir, A.R., Savarese, S.: Joint 2D–3D-Semantic Data for Indoor Scene Understanding. arXiv e-prints, February 2017
4. Bornschein, J., Mnih, A., Zoran, D., Rezende, D.J.: Variational memory addressing in generative models. In: NIPS (2017)
5. Burgess, C., et al.: Monet: unsupervised scene decomposition and representation. arXiv abs/1901.11390 (2019). https://arxiv.org/abs/1901.11390
6. Burgess, C.P., et al.: Understanding disentangling in $\beta$-VAE. arXiv abs/1804.03599 (2018)
7. Chang, A.X., et al.: ShapeNet: an information-rich 3D model repository. Technical report, arXiv:1512.03012 [cs.GR], Stanford University – Princeton University – Toyota Technological Institute at Chicago (2015)
8. Chang, B.M., Ullman, T., Torralba, A., Tenenbaum, B.J.: A compositional object-based approach to learning physical dynamics. In: ICLR (2017)
9. Chen, C., Deng, F., Ahn, S.: Roots: object-centric representation and rendering of 3D scenes (2021)
10. Crawford, E., Pineau, J.: Spatially invariant unsupervised object detection with convolutional neural networks. In: AAAI, vol. 33, pp. 3412–3420 (2019). https://doi.org/10.1609/aaai.v33i01.33013412
11. Crawford, E., Pineau, J.: Exploiting spatial invariance for scalable unsupervised object tracking. In: AAAI, vol. 34, pp. 3684–3692 (2020). https://doi.org/10.1609/aaai.v34i04.5777
12. Diuk, C., Cohen, A., Littman, M.L.: An object-oriented representation for efficient reinforcement learning. In: ICML, ICML 2008, pp. 240–247. Association for Computing Machinery, New York (2008). https://doi.org/10.1145/1390156.1390187
13. Engelcke, M., Kosiorek, A.R., Jones, O.P., Posner, I.: Genesis: generative scene inference and sampling with object-centric latent representations. In: ICLR (2020). https://openreview.net/forum?id=BkxfaTVFwH
14. Eslami, S.M.A., et al.: Attend, infer, repeat: Fast scene understanding with generative models. In: Proceedings of the 30th International Conference on Neural Information Processing Systems, NIPS 2016, pp. 3233–3241. Curran Associates Inc., Red Hook (2016)
15. Gadelha, M., Wang, R., Maji, S.: Multiresolution tree networks for 3D point cloud processing. In: ECCV, pp. 103–118 (2018)
16. Greff, K., et al.: Multi-object representation learning with iterative variational inference. In: ICML (2019)
17. Greff, K., van Steenkiste, S., Schmidhuber, J.: Neural expectation maximization. In: NeurIPS, NIPS 2017, pp. 6694–6704. Curran Associates Inc., Red Hook (2017)
18. Henderson, P., Lampert, C.H.: Unsupervised object-centric video generation and decomposition in 3D. In: NeurIPS (2020)
19. Higgins, I., et al.: $\beta$-VAE: learning basic visual concepts with a constrained variational framework. In: ICLR (2017)
20. Hubert, L., Arabie, P.: Comparing partitions. J. Classif. **2**, 193–218 (1985)
21. Islam, M.A., Jia, S., Bruce, N.D.B.: How much position information do convolutional neural networks encode? In: International Conference on Learning Representations (2020). https://openreview.net/forum?id=rJeB36NKvB

22. Jiang, L., Zhao, H., Shi, S., Liu, S., Fu, C.W., Jia, J.: Pointgroup: dual-set point grouping for 3D instance segmentation. In: CVPR (2020)
23. Johnson, J., Hariharan, B., van der Maaten, L., Fei-Fei, L., Zitnick, C., Girshick, R.: CLEVR: a diagnostic dataset for compositional language and elementary visual reasoning, pp. 1988–1997 (2017). https://doi.org/10.1109/CVPR.2017.215
24. Juliani, A., et al.: Unity: a general platform for intelligent agents. arXiv abs/1809.02627 (2020)
25. Kabra, R., et al.: Multi-object datasets (2019). https://github.com/deepmind/multi-object-datasets/
26. Kahneman, D., Treisman, A., Gibbs, B.J.: The reviewing of object files: object-specific integration of information. Cogn. Psychol. **24**(2), 175–219 (1992). https://doi.org/10.1016/0010-0285(92)90007-O. https://www.sciencedirect.com/science/article/pii/001002859290007O
27. Kansky, K., et al.: Schema networks: zero-shot transfer with a generative causal model of intuitive physics. arXiv abs/1706.04317 (2017)
28. Kingma, D.P., Welling, M.: Auto-encoding variational Bayes. In: 2nd International Conference on Learning Representations, ICLR 2014, Banff, AB, Canada, 14–16 April 2014, Conference Track Proceedings (2014)
29. Li, N., Eastwood, C., Fisher, R.: Learning object-centric representations of multi-object scenes from multiple views. In: Larochelle, H., Ranzato, M., Hadsell, R., Balcan, M.F., Lin, H. (eds.) Advances in Neural Information Processing Systems, vol. 33, pp. 5656–5666. Curran Associates, Inc. (2020). https://proceedings.neurips.cc/paper/2020/file/3d9dabe52805a1ea21864b09f3397593-Paper.pdf
30. Lin, Z., et al.: Space: unsupervised object-oriented scene representation via spatial attention and decomposition. In: ICLR (2020). https://openreview.net/forum?id=rkl03ySYDH
31. Locatello, F., et al.: Object-centric learning with slot attention. In: NeurIPS (2020)
32. Luo, S., Hu, W.: Diffusion probabilistic models for 3D point cloud generation. In: Proceedings of the IEEE/CVF Conference on Computer Vision and Pattern Recognition (CVPR), June 2021
33. van der Maaten, L., Hinton, G.: Visualizing data using t-SNE. J. Mach. Learn. Res. **9**, 2579–2605 (2008). https://www.jmlr.org/papers/v9/vandermaaten08a.html
34. Shi, W., Rajkumar, R.: Point-GNN: graph neural network for 3D object detection in a point cloud. In: CVPR, pp. 1708–1716 (2020)
35. Stelzner, K., Kersting, K., Kosiorek, A.R.: Decomposing 3D scenes into objects via unsupervised volume segmentation (2021)
36. Tishby, N., Pereira, F.C., Bialek, W.: The information bottleneck method. In: Proceedings of the 37th Annual Allerton Conference on Communication, Control and Computing, pp. 368–377 (1999). https://arxiv.org/abs/physics/0004057
37. Wu, W., Qi, Z., Li, F.: Pointconv: deep convolutional networks on 3D point clouds. In: CVPR, pp. 9613–9622 (2019). https://doi.org/10.1109/CVPR.2019.00985
38. Yang, G., Huang, X., Hao, Z., Liu, M.Y., Belongie, S., Hariharan, B.: Pointflow: 3D point cloud generation with continuous normalizing flows, pp. 4540–4549 (2019). https://doi.org/10.1109/ICCV.2019.00464

# Neural Scene Decoration from a Single Photograph

Hong-Wing Pang[1]([✉]), Yingshu Chen[1], Phuoc-Hieu Le[2], Binh-Son Hua[2],
Duc Thanh Nguyen[3], and Sai-Kit Yeung[1]

[1] Hong Kong University of Science and Technology, Hong Kong, China
hwpang@connect.ust.hk
[2] VinAI Research, Hanoi, Vietnam
[3] Deakin University, Geelong, Australia

**Abstract.** Furnishing and rendering indoor scenes has been a long-standing task for interior design, where artists create a conceptual design for the space, build a 3D model of the space, decorate, and then perform rendering. Although the task is important, it is tedious and requires tremendous effort. In this paper, we introduce a new problem of domain-specific indoor scene image synthesis, namely neural scene decoration. Given a photograph of an empty indoor space and a list of decorations with layout determined by user, we aim to synthesize a new image of the same space with desired furnishing and decorations. Neural scene decoration can be applied to create conceptual interior designs in a simple yet effective manner. Our attempt to this research problem is a novel scene generation architecture that transforms an empty scene and an object layout into a realistic furnished scene photograph. We demonstrate the performance of our proposed method by comparing it with conditional image synthesis baselines built upon prevailing image translation approaches both qualitatively and quantitatively. We conduct extensive experiments to further validate the plausibility and aesthetics of our generated scenes. Our implementation is available at https://github.com/hkust-vgd/neural_scene_decoration.

**Keywords:** GANs · Image synthesis · Indoor scenes rendering

## 1 Introduction

Furnishing and rendering indoor scenes is a common task for interior design. This is typically performed by professional designers who carefully craft a conceptual design and furniture placement, followed by extensive modeling via CAD/CAM software to finally create a realistic image using a powerful rendering engine. Such a task often requires extensive background knowledge and experience in

**Supplementary Information** The online version contains supplementary material available at https://doi.org/10.1007/978-3-031-20050-2_9.

the field of interior design, as well as high-end professional software. This makes it difficult for lay users to design their own scenes from scratch.

On the other hand, different image synthesis methods have been developed and become popular in the field. Various types of deep neural networks - typically in the form of auto-encoders [20] and generative adversarial networks [5] - have shown their capability of synthesizing images from a variety of inputs, e.g., semantic maps, text description.

Deep neural networks have also been explored in the generation of indoor scenes. Specifically, an indoor scene can be generated from a collection of objects placed in specific arrangements in 3D space or 2D forms such as top-down coordinates of objects or a floor plane.

In this paper, we combine both research directions: image synthesis and scene generation, into a new task, namely *neural scene decoration*. To solve this task, we propose a scene generation architecture that accepts an empty scene and an object layout as input and produces images of the scene decorated with furniture provided in the object layout (see Fig. 2). Although several existing image synthesis techniques could be applied to create scenes from simple input, e.g., object bounding boxes, the problem of scene generation from an empty background has not yet been adequately explored. Our goal is to generate images of decorated scenes with improved visual quality, e.g., the placement of objects should be coherent.

An immediate application of neural scene decoration is creating conceptual designs of interior space. In particular, based on a few example images of a scene, a conceptual design of the scene can be made prior to texturing and rendering objects in the scene. Despite the availability of computer-aided design software, creating interior designs is still a challenging task as it requires close collaborations between artists and customers, and may involve third parties. The entire process of making interior designs is also expensive as it requires manual operations, and thus could take several days to complete one design. In this paper, we aim to make neural scene decoration simple and effective in creating realistic furnished scenes. To this end, we have made the following contributions in our work.

- A new task on scene synthesis and modeling that we name as *neural scene decoration*: synthesize a realistic image with furnished decorations from an empty background image of a scene and an object layout.
- A neural network architecture that enables neural scene decoration in a simple and effective manner.
- Extensive experiments that demonstrate the performance of our proposed method and its potential for future research. Quantitative evaluation results show that our method outperforms previous image translation works. Qualitative results also confirm the ability of our method in generating realistic-looking scenes.

## 2   Related Work

### 2.1   Image Synthesis

Prior to the resurgence of deep learning, editing a single photograph has often been done by building a physical model of the scene in the photo for object composition and rendering [3, 17–19]. Such an approach requires tremendous effort as it involves huge manual manipulations.

Deep neural networks, well-known for their learning and generalization capabilities, have been used recently for image synthesis. Technically, network architectures used in existing image synthesis methods fall within two categories: autoencoders (AEs) [20] and generative adversarial networks (GANs) [5]. Conditional GAN (cGAN) [29] is a variant of GANs where generated results are conditioned on input data. A seminal work of cGAN for image synthesis is the image translation method (a.k.a pix2pix) in [10], where a cGAN was used to translate an image from one domain to another domain. Much effort has been made to extend the approach in various directions such as generation of high-resolution images [42], greater appearance diversity [51], and from arbitrary viewpoints [38]. CycleGAN proposed by Zhu et al. [50] extended the image translation to unpaired data (i.e., there are no pairs of images in different domains in training data) by adopting a cycle-consistency loss. Bau et al. [1] allowed users to edit the latent layer in the generator to control the generated content. Recently, Park et al. [33] proposed spatially-adaptive normalization (SPADE) to modulate intermediate activations, opposed to feeding input data directly into the generator, to strengthen semantic information during the generation process.

Recent developments in GANs led to the generation of high-resolution images [11] with different styles [12, 14, 16] and fewer aliasing [13] in the family of StyleGANs [15] especially for human faces. For natural and indoor scenes, GANs have also been applied to 2D layout generation. For example, in LayoutGAN [22], a layout was treated as an image and generated in a GAN-style manner. In HiGAN [43], latent layers capturing semantic information such as layout, category and lighting were used for scene synthesis. In HouseGAN [30], planar apartment room layout and furniture layout were generated. A class of conditional image synthesis methods focuses on the problem of translating layout to images [6, 24, 25, 35]. In these methods, Li et al. [24] combined salient object layout and background hallucination GAN (BachGAN) [24] for image generation. LostGANs [35] explored the reconfigurability of the layouts, but their results mainly have objects on a simple background, which is structurally different from indoor scenes where objects and background must be geometrically aligned. Recent works focus on improving the image generation quality by further using context [6] and locality [25]. Compared to these works, our method is a conditional image synthesis focused on indoor scenes while the previous works are often tested with images in the wild like those in MS-COCO [27] and Visual Genome dataset [21]. The most related work to ours is perhaps BachGAN, where the generation of indoor scene images from layouts are demonstrated but with random backgrounds.

## 2.2   Scene Modeling

The problem of neural scene decoration is also relevant to the topic of image-based and 3D scene modeling. Earlier works include the spatial arrangement of objects into a 3D scene with spatial constraints, which is often modeled into objective functions that can be solved using optimization techniques [4,44]. Additional constraints can also be used to model object relations in a scene. For example, Henderson et al. [7] modeled the relationships among object placement, room type, room shape, and other high-end factors using graphical models. Recently, Li et al. [23] defined object relations in a scene in a hierarchical structure. Ritchie et al. [34] proposed to iteratively insert objects into a scene from a top-down view by four different convolutional neural networks (CNNs) capturing the category, location, orientation, and dimension of objects. Wang et al. [40] proposed PlanIT, a framework that defines a high-level hierarchical structure of objects before learning to place objects into a scene. Zhang et al. [48] proposed a GAN-like architecture to model the distribution of position and orientation of indoor furniture, and to jointly optimize discriminators in both 3D and 2D (i.e., rendered scene images). Several works utilized spatial constraints as priors, e.g., relation graph prior [9,30,40], convolution prior [41], and performed well on spatial organization.

Our solution for neural scene decoration shares some ideas with scene unfurnishing [46] and scene furnishing [26,45,47]. Instead of utilizing RGBD as input [46], our method takes only a single input photograph of an empty scene and an object layout. Both ClutterPalette [45] and MageAdd [47] make 3D scenes by letting users select objects from a synthetic object database. In contrast, our method generates 2D scenes by automatically learning object appearance from training data. DecorIn [26] only predicts decoration locations on walls, while our method really decorates a scene image from a given background and object layout.

## 3    Proposed Method

### 3.1    Problem Formulation

Our goal is to develop a neural scene decoration (NSD) system that produces a decorated scene image $\hat{Y} \in \mathbb{R}^{3 \times W \times H}$, given a background image $X \in \mathbb{R}^{3 \times W \times H}$, and an object layout $L$ for a list of objects to be added in the scene (see Fig. 2). Note that both the generated image $\hat{Y}$ and the background image $X$ are captured from the same scene. Ideally, the NSD system should be able to make $\hat{Y}$ realistically decorated with objects specified in $L$, and also assimilate $\hat{Y}$ to the provided background image $X$.

The format of the object layout $L$ is crucial in determining how easy and effective the NSD system is. In SPADE [33], synthesized objects are labeled using a pixel-wise fashion. This manner, however, requires detailed labeling which is not effective in describing complicated objects and also takes considerable effort. In our work, we propose to represent $L$ using simple yet effective formats: *box label* and *point label*. Specifically, let $O = \{o_1, ..., o_N\}$ be a set of objects added to $X$; these objects belong to $K$ different classes, e.g., chair, desk, lamp, etc. Each object $o_i$ is associated with a class vector $I_i \in \{0,1\}^{K \times 1}$ and a layout map $f_i \in \mathbb{R}^{1 \times W \times H}$. The class vector $I_i$ is designed such as $I_i(k) = 1$ if $k$ is the class

ID of $o_i$, and $I_i(k) = 0$, otherwise. We define the object layout $L$ as a 3D tensor: $L \in \mathbb{R}^{K \times W \times H}$ as follow:

$$L = \sum_{i=1}^{N} I_i f_i \tag{1}$$

*Box Label.* Like BachGAN [24], a box label indicates the presence of an object by its bounding box. For each object $o_i$, the layout map $f_i$ is constructed by simply filling the entire area of the bounding box of $o_i$ with 1s, and elsewhere with 0s. Mathematically, we define:

$$f_i(1, x, y) = \begin{cases} 1, & \text{if } (x, y) \in \text{bounding\_box}(o_i) \\ 0, & \text{otherwise} \end{cases} \tag{2}$$

Box label format has the advantage of indicating the boundary where objects should be inserted and allowing finer control over the rough shape of objects.

*Point Label.* We devise another representation for $f_i$, where each $o_i$ is specified by its center $\mathbf{c}_i = (c_{i,x}, c_{i,y})$ and its size $s_i$ (i.e., a rough estimate of the area of $o_i$). $f_i$ is defined as a heat-map of $\mathbf{c}_i$ and $s_i$ as follow:

$$f_i(1, x, y) = \exp\left( -\frac{\|(x, y) - (c_{i,x}, c_{i,y})\|_2^2}{s_i} \right) \tag{3}$$

We find this format interesting to explore, as it allows the user to place decorated objects by simply specifying a rough location and size. The exact forms of decorated objects are automatically inferred based on observed training data.

## 3.2    Architecture Design

Our generator $G(X, L)$ is designed to take a pair of a background image $X$ and an object layout $L$, and generate a decorated scene image $\hat{Y} = G(X, L)$. We also train a discriminator $D(\hat{Y}, L)$ to classify the image $\hat{Y}$ (as synthesized image vs. real image) and to validate if $\hat{Y}$ conforms to the object layout $L$.

**Generator.** The generator $G(X, L)$ is depicted in Fig. 1, and includes multiple generator blocks varying from low to high resolutions. For example, the "GeneratorBlock $4 \rightarrow 8$" generates a feature map of spatial dimension $8 \times 8$ from $4 \times 4$.

Each generator block takes input from a feature map produced by its preceding generator (except the first one), an object layout and a background image at a corresponding resolution, and results in a feature map at a higher resolution. Each generator employs a SPADE block [33] to learn an object layout feature map (used to condition generated content), then up-samples the feature map

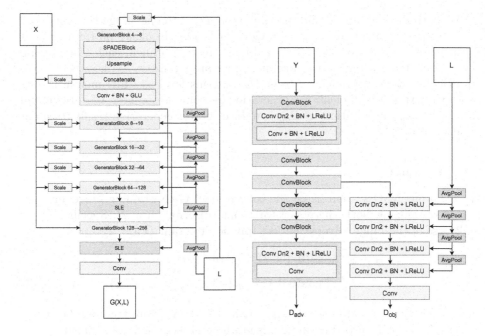

**Fig. 1.** Overview of our generator (left) and discriminator (right). Convolution layers labeled with Dn2 halve the spatial dimensions of input feature maps using stride 2.

(by a factor of 2), concatenates it with a down-scaled version of the background image, and finally performs a convolution (Conv) with batch normalization (BN) and GLU. We follow [28] using skip-layer excitations (SLE) that modulates the output of the last two generator blocks with that of the first two blocks. The resulting feature map is passed through a final convolution layer to produce the synthesized image $\hat{Y}$.

To enforce the integration of object layout in the generation process, we insert $L$ into every generator block in a bottom-up manner. Specifically, down-scaled versions of $L$ are created by consecutive average pooling layers and then fused with corresponding feature maps at different resolutions. Likewise, to constrain the consistency in the background of the synthesized image $\hat{Y}$ and the input image $X$, we make $X$ in different scales and insert these scaled images into every generator block. We refer readers to the supplementary material for further details of our architecture.

**Discriminator.** The discriminator $D(Y, L)$ consists of an adversarial discriminator $D_{adv}(Y)$ and an object layout discriminator $D_{obj}(Y, L)$. We show our discriminator in Fig. 1.

The adversarial discriminator $D_{adv}$ takes in only the generated image $\hat{Y} = G(X, L)$ as input, and is solely responsible for fitting it towards the target image distribution. In our implementation, $D_{adv}$ is a feedforward network and associated with a global adversarial loss.

We introduce an additional discriminator, $D_{obj}$, to encourage the generated image to follow the object layout provided in $L$. $D_{obj}$ branches off from $D_{adv}$ at the feature map of size $32 \times 32$ (see Fig. 1). In this branch, each feature map is concatenated with an object layout $L_i$ in a proper size $s_i \in \{4, 8, 16, 32\}$. We empirically chose to branch off from $D_{adv}$ at this level as experimental results show that this is sufficient for generating reasonable images. We also found the use of $D_{obj}$ in addition to $D_{adv}$ produces better generation results (see our ablation study).

### 3.3 Training

We train our NSD system using the conventional GAN training procedure, i.e., jointly optimizing both the generator $G$ and discriminator $D$. Specifically, we make use of the hinge adversarial loss function to train $D$ as:

$$\mathcal{L}_D = \mathbb{E}_Y[\max(0, 1 + D_{adv}(Y))]$$
$$+ \mathbb{E}_{\hat{Y},L}[\max(0, 1 - D_{adv}(\hat{Y}) - \lambda_{obj} D_{obj}(\hat{Y}, L)] \tag{4}$$

where $Y$ is the decorated scene image paired with $X$ (from training data) and $\hat{Y} = G(X, L)$. $Y$ is also the source image where objects in $L$ are defined.

The generator $G$ is updated to push the discriminator's output towards the real image direction:

$$\mathcal{L}_G = \mathbb{E}_{X,L}[D(G(X, L))] \tag{5}$$

In our implementation, we optimize both $\min_D \mathcal{L}_D$ and $\min_G \mathcal{L}_G$ simultaneously and iteratively. We observed that setting $\lambda_{obj}$ to small values is sufficient for generating plausible results. We set $\lambda_{obj} = 0.01$, which empirically works well in our experiments. We trained the discriminator and generator with Adam optimizer. We set the learning rate and batch size to 0.0001 and 32, respectively, and updated the gradients every four iterations. An exponential moving average of the generator weights was applied. The training was conducted on a single RTX 3090 GPU and within 400,000 iterations, which took approximately 44 h. For inference, the generator performed at 0.760 s per image on average.

## 4    Experiments

### 4.1    Dataset

We chose to conduct experiments on the Structured3D dataset [49], as it is, to the best of our knowledge, the only publicly available dataset with pre-rendered image pairs of empty and decorated scenes. The Structured3D dataset consists of 78, 463 pairs of decorated and empty indoor images, rendered from a total of 3, 500 distinct 3D scenes. Following the recommendation of the dataset authors, we use 3,000 scenes for training and the remaining scenes for validation.

The Structured3D dataset consists of a variety of indoor scenes, including bedrooms, living rooms, and non-residential locations. However, we carried out experiments on bedrooms and living rooms scenes as those scenes contain sufficient samples for training and testing.

## 4.2  Baselines

Since we propose a new problem formulation, it is hard to find existing baselines that exactly address the same problem setting. However, our research problem and conditional image synthesis somewhat share a common objective, which is to generate an image conditioned on some given input. Therefore, some image synthesis methods could be adapted and modified to build baselines for comparison. Particularly, we adopted three state-of-the-art image synthesis methods, namely SPADE [33], BachGAN [24], and context-aware layout to image generation [6] for our baselines. Those methods were selected for several reasons. First, they follow conditional image generation setting, i.e., generated contents are conformed to input conditions, e.g., semantic maps in SPADE [33] and BachGAN [24], and layout structures in [6, 25, 36]. Second, their input conditions can be customised with minimal modifications to be comparable with ours. We present these modifications below.

SPADE [33] is a generative architecture conditioned on pixel-wise semantic maps. We concatenate the background image and object layout into each SPADE layer, in place of pixel-wise semantic maps. We also concatenate this tensor to the generated image before passing it to the discriminator.

BachGAN [24] is built upon the SPADE's generator and synthesizes a scene image from foreground object bounding boxes. It uses a *background hallucination module* to make generated background match with the object layout. To conform BachGAN to our problem setting, we directly feed the input background image $X$ into the background hallucination module, instead of pooling features from multiple background image candidates.

We also compare to the context-aware layout to image generation method by He et al. [6], which is state-of-the-art in layout-based image generation for general scenes. Their method is reportedly better than LostGANs v2 [36] in terms of quantitative evaluation, and the implementation is publicly available. We modified their implementation by inserting the background into every block in their generator.

In the supplementary material, we provide an additional comparisons to GLIDE [31], a text-guided image synthesis method, which also use coarse layout descriptions similar to ours, unlike fine-grained semantic maps. Please refer to the supplementary material for this result.

## 4.3  Quantitative Evaluation

We quantitatively evaluate the image synthesis ability of our method using the Frechet Inception Distance (FID) [8] and the Kernel Inception Distance

**Table 1.** Quantitative assessment of our method against various baselines. Lower FID/KID values indicate better performance.

| Method | Bedroom | | | | Living room | | | |
|---|---|---|---|---|---|---|---|---|
| | Box label | | Point label | | Box label | | Point label | |
| | FID ↓ | KID×10³ ↓ | FID ↓ | KID×10³ ↓ | FID ↓ | KID×10³ ↓ | FID ↓ | KID×10³ ↓ |
| SPADE [33] | 23.780 | 12.622 | 20.345 | 9.850 | 21.527 | 12.594 | 19.471 | 10.412 |
| BachGAN [24] | 21.319 | 10.054 | 18.829 | 7.932 | 20.463 | 11.961 | 18.997 | 9.446 |
| He et al. [6] | 21.311 | **9.869** | 18.899 | 7.958 | 19.732 | 10.828 | 18.762 | 9.656 |
| Ours | **20.596** | 11.609 | **15.108** | **6.797** | **18.478** | **10.113** | **17.986** | **9.421** |

**Table 2.** Comparison of the use of $D_{adv}$ only, and the combination of $D_{adv}$ and $D_{obj}$ as in our design.

| Descriptor | Bedroom | | | | Living room | | | |
|---|---|---|---|---|---|---|---|---|
| | Boxes | | Points | | Boxes | | Points | |
| | FID ↓ | KID×10³ ↓ | FID ↓ | KID×10³ ↓ | FID ↓ | KID×10³ ↓ | FID ↓ | KID×10³ ↓ |
| $D_{adv}$ | 22.341 | 13.245 | 21.069 | 11.231 | 25.051 | 15.950 | 24.786 | 14.562 |
| $D_{adv} + D_{obj}$ | **20.596** | **11.609** | **15.108** | **6.797** | **18.478** | **10.113** | **17.986** | **9.421** |

(KID) [2]. Both FID and KID measure the dissimilarity between inception representations [37] of a synthesized output and its real version. Wasserstein distance and polynomial kernel are used in FID and KID respectively as dissimilarity metrics [32].

For quantitative evaluation purpose, we used pairs of background and decorated images from ground-truth. We also extracted bounding boxes and object masks of decorated objects from the ground-truth to construct box labels and point labels. We report the performance of our method and other baselines in Table 1. As shown in the results, our method outperforms all the baselines on both bedroom and living room test sets, with both box label and point label format in FID metric. The same observation is true for the KID metric, with the only exception that He et al.'s method [6] is ranked best with box label format for bedroom scenes.

Our method also has a computational advantage. Specifically, the BachGAN baseline took roughly the same amount of training time as our method but required four GPUs. In contrast, our method can produce even better results using less computational resources.

Table 1 also shows that point label scheme slightly outperforms box label scheme. However, as discussed in the next section, each scheme is favored to specific types of objects. For example, from a usage perspective, box label format has a strong focus on user's desire on how a decorated object appears, while point label format offers more flexibility and autonomy to the NSD system.

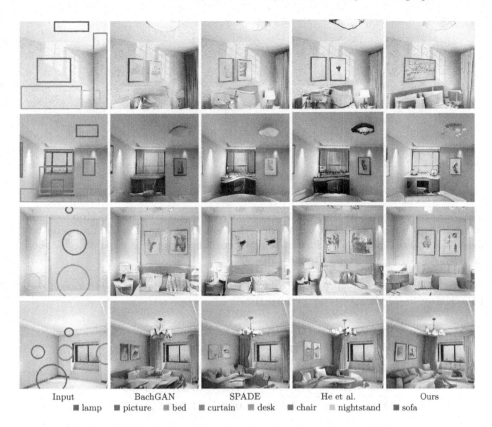

Input          BachGAN          SPADE          He et al.          Ours
■ lamp     ■ picture     ■ bed     ■ curtain     ■ desk     ■ chair     ■ nightstand     ■ sofa

**Fig. 2.** Generation results of our method and other baselines, using box label format (the first two rows) and point label format (the last two rows). For point label format, the center and radius of each circle represent the location $\mathbf{c}_i$ and size $s_i$ of an object (see Eq. (3)). Best view with zoom.

### 4.4   Ablation Study

In this experiment, we prove the role of the additional discriminator $D_{obj}$. Recall that $D_{obj}$ is branched off from $D_{adv}$ and combines $L$ at various scales (see Fig. 1). To validate the role of $D_{obj}$, we amended the architecture of the discriminator $D$ by directly concatenating the object layout $L$ with the decorated image $Y$ to make the input for $D$, like the designs in [33] and [24]. Experimental results are in Table 2, which clearly confirms the superiority of our design for the discriminator (i.e., using both $D_{adv}$ and $D_{obj}$) over the use of $D_{adv}$ only.

### 4.5   Qualitative Evaluation

*Generation Quality.* We qualitatively compare our method with the baselines, on both box label and point label format in Fig. 2. As shown in these results, our method is able to generate details in foreground objects. We hypothesize

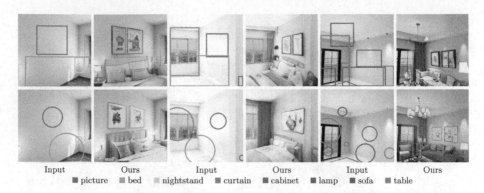

Input          Ours          Input          Ours          Input          Ours
■ picture   ■ bed   ■ nightstand   ■ curtain   ■ cabinet   ■ lamp   ■ sofa   ■ table

**Fig. 3.** Generation results (from the same input) using box label format (top row) and point label format (bottom row). While box label format suits small and relatively fixed-size objects, point label format is more flexible to describe large objects whose dimensions can be adjusted automatically.

**Table 3.** Performance of our method and the baselines using default object sizes. Lower FID/KID values indicate better performance.

| Method | Bedroom | | Living room | |
|---|---|---|---|---|
| | FID | KID$_{\times 10^3}$ | FID | KID$_{\times 10^3}$ |
| SPADE [33] | 22.985 | 10.993 | 23.630 | 13.620 |
| BachGAN [24] | 19.914 | 8.119 | 23.391 | 13.006 |
| Ours | **17.489** | **8.007** | **21.019** | **11.277** |

that our method successfully incorporates the layout information in early layers in the generator as each pixel in a down-scaled object layout encourages object generation within a specific local region in the output image.

*Box Label vs. Point Label.* Figure 3 visualizes some generation results using box label and point label format on the same input background. In this experiment, on each scene, box labels and point labels were derived from the same set of objects. We observed that some object classes are better suited to a particular label format. For example, small objects and those whose aspect ratio can be varied (e.g., pictures can appear in either portrait or landscape shape) should be described using box label format. On the other hand, objects that often occupy large areas in a scene, such as beds and sofas, tend to have less distortion and clearer details when represented with point label format.

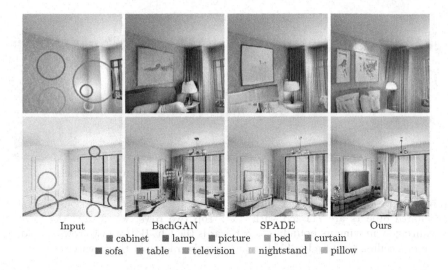

Input            BachGAN            SPADE            Ours

■ cabinet   ■ lamp   ■ picture   ■ bed   ■ curtain
■ sofa   ■ table   ■ television   ▨ nightstand   ■ pillow

**Fig. 4.** Generation results using default values for object size.

**Table 4.** Performance using different object sizes methods. (*) indicate the default setting used in our experiments.

| Method | Bedroom | | Living room | |
|---|---|---|---|---|
| | FID | KID$_{\times 10^3}$ | FID | KID$_{\times 10^3}$ |
| Class mean | 20.145 | 10.457 | 27.365 | 14.639 |
| Class median | 17.489 | 8.007 | 21.019 | 11.277 |
| $m = 4.0$ | 24.045 | 14.701 | 28.128 | 15.979 |
| $m = 2.5(*)$ | **15.108** | **6.797** | **17.986** | **9.421** |
| $m = 1.0$ | 20.201 | 9.105 | 19.114 | 11.797 |

## 4.6   Setting Object Sizes

In the quantitative assessment, the sizes of decorated objects in the point label format (i.e., $s_i$ in Eq. (3)) were retrieved from ground-truth. However, in reality, this information is provided by the user. In this experiment, we investigate a simpler input for the point label format where the object sizes are set by default values rather than given by either the ground-truth or user. In particular, for each decorated object $o_i$, we set the size $s_i$ to the median size of all the objects having the same object class with $o_i$ in the training data. Particularly, the ground truth value of $s_i$ of each object is given by $s_i = m\sqrt{A_i}$, where $m$ is a fixed constant and $A_i$ is the area (i.e., the no. of pixels) of the object mask of $o_i$. Here we set $m = 2.5$ for our experiments.

We applied this setting to all the baselines and reported their performance in Table 3. We observed that compared with using ground-truth values for the object sizes (see Table 1), setting the object sizes to default values degrades the

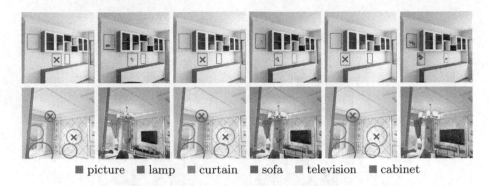

■ picture   ■ lamp   ■ curtain   ■ sofa   ■ television   ■ cabinet

**Fig. 5.** Generation results under different settings for objects' locations and sizes. Manipulated objects are marked with "X". Top two rows: we change the location of a painting by moving its bounding box towards the left. Bottom two rows: we adjust the size of a ceiling light and a TV by changing the radius at their centers.

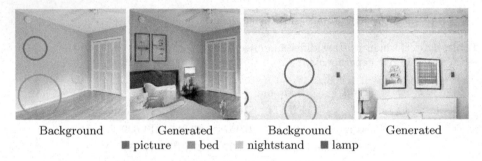

Background        Generated        Background        Generated
■ picture   ■ bed   ■ nightstand   ■ lamp

**Fig. 6.** Generation results on real-world scenes.

performance of all the competitors. However, our method still consistently outperforms all the baselines on all the test sets, using both FID and KID metrics. We illustrate several results of this setting in Fig. 4. In Table 4, we further compare different variants of point label format, including the use of mean value and median value to compute $s_i$. We show the results of using alternate values for $m$ in Table 4, which clearly confirms our choice for $m$ for the best performance.

## 4.7   Layout Manipulation

We demonstrate in Fig. 5 how our method performs under various settings for decorated objects' positions and sizes. For box label format, these settings can be done by changing the location and dimensions of objects' bounding boxes. For point label format, we adjust the center position and radius of objects. As shown in Fig. 5, our method can generate contents adaptively to different settings, proving its applicability in creating conceptual designs of interior space.

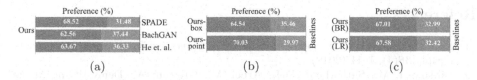

**Fig. 7.** User study's results: Preference with (a) different methods, (b) box labels vs point labels, and (c) different room types. (BR = bedroom, LR = living room)

Please also refer to our supplementary material for additional discussions on the diversity of the generation results, the impact of the background to furniture, and iterative decoration, where the furniture can be added one by one.

### 4.8   Generalization to Real-World Data

To validate the universality of our method, we experimented with it on several real-world scenes not included in the Structured3D dataset. We present several results of this experiment in Fig. 6. Interestingly, we discovered that paintings and furniture are generated in different artistic styles but still in line with the entire decoration and background style.

### 4.9   User Study

In addition to quantitative evaluation, we conducted a user study on the generation quality of our method and other baselines. We collected responses from 26 participants and summarized these results in Fig. 7. I general, our model is often preferred in generating images with point label format, especially in the bedroom test case with fewer objects and clutter. When using box label format, our method still produces results around the same level of quality compared with the baselines. More details of our user study is in the supplementary material.

## 5   Conclusion

We introduced a new task called neural scene decoration. The task aims to render an empty indoor space with furniture and decorations specified in a layout map. To realize this task, we propose an architecture conditioned on a background image and an object layout map where decorated objects are described via either bounding boxes or rough locations and sizes. We demonstrate the capability of our method in scene design over previous works on the Structured3D dataset. Neural scene decoration is henceforth a step toward building the next generation of user-friendly interior design and rendering applications. Future work may include better support of sequential object generation [39], interactive scene decoration, and integration of more advanced network architecture.

**Acknowledgment.** This paper was partially supported by an internal grant from HKUST (R9429) and the HKUST-WeBank Joint Lab.

# References

1. Bau, D.: Semantic photo manipulation with a generative image prior. ACM Trans. Graph. **38**(4), 1–11 (2019)
2. Bińkowski, M., Sutherland, D.J., Arbel, M., Gretton, A.: Demystifying MMD GANs. In: Proceedings of the International Conference on Learning Representations (2018)
3. Fisher, M., Ritchie, D., Savva, M., Funkhouser, T.A., Hanrahan, P.: Example-based synthesis of 3d object arrangements. ACM Trans. Graph. **31**(6), 1–11 (2012)
4. Germer, T., Schwarz, M.: Procedural arrangement of furniture for real-time walk-throughs. Comput. Graph. Forum **28**(8), 2068–2078 (2009)
5. Goodfellow, I., et al.: Generative adversarial nets. In: Proceedings of the Advances in Neural Information Processing Systems (2014)
6. He, S., et al.: Context-aware layout to image generation with enhanced object appearance. In: CVPR (2021)
7. Henderson, P., Subr, K., Ferrari, V.: Automatic generation of constrained furniture layouts. arXiv preprint arXiv:1711.10939 (2017)
8. Heusel, M., Ramsauer, H., Unterthiner, T., Nessler, B., Hochreiter, S.: GANs trained by a two time-scale update rule converge to a local nash equilibrium. In: Proceedings of the Advances in Neural Information Processing Systems (2017)
9. Hu, R., Huang, Z., Tang, Y., van Kaick, O., Zhang, H., Huang, H.: Graph2Plan: learning floorplan generation from layout graphs. ACM Trans. Graph. **39**(4), 118–128 (2020)
10. Isola, P., Zhu, J.Y., Zhou, T., Efros, A.A.: Image-to-image translation with conditional adversarial networks. In: Proceedings of the IEEE Conference on Computer Vision and Pattern Recognition (2017)
11. Karras, T., Aila, T., Laine, S., Lehtinen, J.: Progressive growing of GANs for improved quality, stability, and variation. In: Proceedings of the International Conference on Learning Representations (2018)
12. Karras, T., Aittala, M., Hellsten, J., Laine, S., Lehtinen, J., Aila, T.: Training generative adversarial networks with limited data. In: Proceedings of the Advances in Neural Information Processing Systems (2020)
13. Karras, T., et al.: Alias-free generative adversarial networks. arXiv preprint arXiv:2106.12423 (2021)
14. Karras, T., Laine, S., Aila, T.: A style-based generator architecture for generative adversarial networks. In: Proceedings of the IEEE Conference on Computer Vision and Pattern Recognition (2019)
15. Karras, T., Laine, S., Aila, T.: A style-based generator architecture for generative adversarial networks. IEEE Trans. Pattern Anal. Mach. Intell. **43**(12), 4217–4228 (2021)
16. Karras, T., Laine, S., Aittala, M., Hellsten, J., Lehtinen, J., Aila, T.: Analyzing and improving the image quality of StyleGAN. In: Proceedings of the IEEE Conference on Computer Vision and Pattern Recognition (2020)
17. Karsch, K.: Inverse Rendering Techniques for Physically Grounded Image Editing. Ph.D. thesis, University of Illinois at Urbana-Champaign (2015)
18. Karsch, K., Hedau, V., Forsyth, D., Hoiem, D.: Rendering synthetic objects into legacy photographs. ACM Trans. Graph. **30**(6), 1–14 (2011)
19. Karsch, K., et al.: Automatic scene inference for 3D object compositing. ACM Trans. Graph. **33**(3), 1–15 (2014)

20. Kingma, D.P., Welling, M.: Auto-encoding variational Bayes. In: Proceedings of the International Conference on Learning Representations (2014)
21. Krishna, R., et al.: Visual genome: Connecting language and vision using crowd-sourced dense image annotations. Int. J. Comput. Vis. **123**, 32–73 (2017)
22. Li, J., Yang, J., Hertzmann, A., Zhang, J., Xu, T.: LayoutGAN: generating graphic layouts with wireframe discriminators. In: Proceedings of the International Conference on Learning Representations (2019)
23. Li, M., et al.: GRAINS: generative recursive autoencoders for indoor scenes. ACM Trans. Graph. **38**(2), 1–16 (2019)
24. Li, Y., Cheng, Y., Gan, Z., Yu, L., Wang, L., Liu, J.: BachGAN: high-resolution image synthesis from salient object layout. In: Proceedings of the IEEE Conference on Computer Vision and Pattern Recognition (2020)
25. Li, Z., Wu, J., Koh, I., Tang, Y., Sun, L.: Image synthesis from layout with locality-aware mask adaption. In: ICCV (2021)
26. Liang, Y., Fan, L., Ren, P., Xie, X., Hua, X.S.: Decorin: an automatic method for plane-based decorating. IEEE Trans. Vis. Comput. Graph. **27**, 3438–3450 (2021)
27. Lin, T.-Y., et al.: Microsoft COCO: common objects in context. In: Fleet, D., Pajdla, T., Schiele, B., Tuytelaars, T. (eds.) ECCV 2014. LNCS, vol. 8693, pp. 740–755. Springer, Cham (2014). https://doi.org/10.1007/978-3-319-10602-1_48
28. Liu, B., Zhu, Y., Song, K., Elgammal, A.: Towards faster and stabilized GAN training for high-fidelity few-shot image synthesis. In: Proceedings of the International Conference on Learning Representations (2021)
29. Mirza, M., Osindero, S.: Conditional generative adversarial nets. arXiv preprint arXiv:1411.1784 (2014)
30. Nauata, N., Chang, K.-H., Cheng, C.-Y., Mori, G., Furukawa, Y.: House-GAN: relational generative adversarial networks for graph-constrained house layout generation. In: Vedaldi, A., Bischof, H., Brox, T., Frahm, J.-M. (eds.) ECCV 2020. LNCS, vol. 12346, pp. 162–177. Springer, Cham (2020). https://doi.org/10.1007/978-3-030-58452-8_10
31. Nichol, A., et al.: GLIDE: towards photorealistic image generation and editing with text-guided diffusion models. arXiv preprint 2112.10741 (2021)
32. Obukhov, A., Seitzer, M., Wu, P.W., Zhydenko, S., Kyl, J., Lin, E.Y.J.: High-fidelity performance metrics for generative models in pytorch (2020)
33. Park, T., Liu, M.Y., Wang, T.C., Zhu, J.Y.: Semantic image synthesis with spatially-adaptive normalization. In: Proceedings of the IEEE Conference on Computer Vision and Pattern Recognition (2019)
34. Ritchie, D., Wang, K., Lin, Y.A.: Fast and flexible indoor scene synthesis via deep convolutional generative models. In: Proceedings of the IEEE Conference on Computer Vision and Pattern Recognition (2019)
35. Sun, W., Wu, T.: Image synthesis from reconfigurable layout and style. In: ICCV (2019)
36. Sun, W., Wu, T.: Learning layout and style reconfigurable gans for controllable image synthesis. IEEE Trans. Pattern Anal. Mach. Intel. (PAMI) **44**, 5070–5087 (2021)
37. Szegedy, C., et al.: Going deeper with convolutions. In: Proceedings of the IEEE Conference on Computer Vision and Pattern Recognition (2015)
38. Tang, H., Xu, D., Sebe, N., Wang, Y., Corso, J.J., Yan, Y.: Multi-channel attention selection GAN with cascaded semantic guidance for cross-view image translation. In: Proceedings of the IEEE Conference on Computer Vision and Pattern Recognition (2019)

39. Turkoglu, M.O., Thong, W., Spreeuwers, L., Kicanaoglu, B.: A layer-based sequential framework for scene generation with gans. In: AAAI Conference on Artificial Intelligence (2019)
40. Wang, K., Lin, Y.A., Weissmann, B., Savva, M., Chang, A.X., Ritchie, D.: Planit: planning and instantiating indoor scenes with relation graph and spatial prior networks. ACM Trans. Graph. **38**(4), 1–15 (2019)
41. Wang, K., Savva, M., Chang, A.X., Ritchie, D.: Deep convolutional priors for indoor scene synthesis. ACM Trans. Graph. **37**(4), 1–14 (2018)
42. Wang, T.C., Liu, M.Y., Zhu, J.Y., Tao, A., Kautz, J., Catanzaro, B.: High-resolution image synthesis and semantic manipulation with conditional GANs. In: Proceedings of the IEEE Conference on Computer Vision and Pattern Recognition (2018)
43. Yang, C., Shen, Y., Zhou, B.: Semantic hierarchy emerges in deep generative representations for scene synthesis. Int. J. Comput. Vision **129**(5), 1451–1466 (2020)
44. Yu, L.F., Yeung, S.K., Tang, C.K., Terzopoulos, D., Chan, T.F., Osher, S.J.: Make it home: automatic optimization of furniture arrangement. ACM Trans. Graph. **30**(4), 1–11 (2011)
45. Yu, L.F., Yeung, S.K., Terzopoulos, D.: The clutterpalette: an interactive tool for detailing indoor scenes. IEEE Trans. Vis. Comput. Graph. **22**, 1138–1148 (2015)
46. Zhang, E., Cohen, M.F., Curless, B.: Emptying, refurnishing, and relighting indoor spaces. ACM Trans. Graph. **35**(6), 1–14 (2016)
47. Zhang, S.K., Li, Y.X., He, Y., Yang, Y.L., Zhang, S.H.: Mageadd: real-time interaction simulation for scene synthesis. In: ACM International Conference on Multimedia (2021)
48. Zhang, Z., et al.: Deep generative modeling for scene synthesis via hybrid representations. ACM Trans. Graph. **39**(2), 1–21 (2020)
49. Zheng, J., Zhang, J., Li, J., Tang, R., Gao, S., Zhou, Z.: Structured3D: a large photo-realistic dataset for structured 3D modeling. In: Proceedings of the European Conference on Computer Vision (2020)
50. Zhu, J.Y., Park, T., Isola, P., Efros, A.A.: Unpaired image-to-image translation using cycle-consistent adversarial networks. In: Proceedings of the IEEE International Conference on Computer Vision (2017)
51. Zhu, J.Y., et al.: Toward multimodal image-to-image translation. In: Proceedings of the Advances in Neural Information Processing Systems (2017)

# Outpainting by Queries

Kai Yao[1,2], Penglei Gao[1,2], Xi Yang[1], Jie Sun[1], Rui Zhang[1],
and Kaizhu Huang[3(✉)]

[1] Xi'an Jiaotong Liverpool University, Suzhou, China
{kai.yao19,penglei.gao19}@student.xjtlu.edu.cn,
{xi.yang01,jie.sun,rui.zhang02}@xjtlu.edu.cn
[2] University of Liverpool, Liverpool, England
[3] Duke Kunshan University, Suzhou, China
kaizhu.huang@dukekunshan.edu.cn

**Abstract.** Image outpainting, which is well studied with Convolution
Neural Network (CNN) based framework, has recently drawn more
attention in computer vision. However, CNNs rely on inherent inductive biases to achieve effective sample learning, which may degrade
the performance ceiling. In this paper, motivated by the flexible self-
attention mechanism with minimal inductive biases in transformer
architecture, we reframe the generalised image outpainting problem
as a patch-wise sequence-to-sequence autoregression problem, enabling
query-based image outpainting. Specifically, we propose a novel hybrid
vision-transformer-based encoder-decoder framework, named **Query
O**utpainting **TR**ansformer (**QueryOTR**), for extrapolating visual context all-side around a given image. Patch-wise mode's global modeling capacity allows us to extrapolate images from the attention mechanism's query standpoint. A novel Query Expansion Module (QEM) is
designed to integrate information from the predicted queries based on the
encoder's output, hence accelerating the convergence of the pure transformer even with a relatively small dataset. To further enhance connectivity between each patch, the proposed Patch Smoothing Module (PSM)
re-allocates and averages the overlapped regions, thus providing seamless predicted images. We experimentally show that QueryOTR could
generate visually appealing results smoothly and realistically against
the state-of-the-art image outpainting approaches. Code is available at
https://github.com/Kaiseem/QueryOTR.

**Keywords:** Image outpainting · Transformer · Query expanding

## 1 Introduction

Image outpainting, usually known as image extrapolation, is a challenging task
that requires extending image boundaries by generating new visually harmo-

---

K. Yao and P. Gao—Equal Contribution.

---

**Supplementary Information** The online version contains supplementary material
available at https://doi.org/10.1007/978-3-031-20050-2_10.

S. Avidan et al. (Eds.): ECCV 2022, LNCS 13683, pp. 153–169, 2022.
https://doi.org/10.1007/978-3-031-20050-2_10

nious contents with semantically meaningful structure from a restricted input image. It could be widely applied in the real world to enrich humans' social lives based on limited visual content, such as automatic creative image, virtual reality, and video generation [31]. Different from image inpainting [2,3,35,45], which could take advantage of visual contexts surrounding an inpainting area, generalised image outpainting should extrapolate the unknown regions in all directions around the sub-image. As the unknown pixels farther from the image borders are less constrained, they have a greater chance of accumulating expanded-errors or generating repetitive patterns than those closer to the borders. Consequently, the challenges of this task include: (a) determining where the missing features should be located relative to the output's spatial locations for both nearby and faraway features; (b) guaranteeing that the extrapolated image has a realistic appearance with reasonable content and a consistent structural layout with the conditional sub-image; and (c) the borders between extrapolated regions and the original sub-image should be smooth and seamless.

Convolutional architectures have been proven successful for computer vision tasks nowadays. Existing image outpainting methods utilize kinds of variants of CNN-based methods to conduct image extrapolation. CNNs rely on inherent inductive biases to achieve effective sample learning, which may degrade the performance ceiling. Although the existing CNN-based outpainting methods achieve solid performance [22,31,40,43,44], they still suffer from blunt structures and abrupt colours when extrapolating the unknown regions of the images. The potential reason might be that the inductive biases of convolution in such CNN-based architectures are hard-coded in the form of two strong constraints on the weights: locality and weight sharing [10]. These constraints may degrade the model's ability to represent global features and capture long-range dependencies.

Transformer architectures have competitive performance in areas such as image and video recognition. The transformer dispenses with the convolutional inductive bias by performing self-attention across embeddings of patches of pixels, which breaks through the limitation of capturing long-range dependencies. However, in the pure transformer, the model converges very slowly with a relatively small dataset [10]. On the ImageNet benchmark, Dosovitskiy et al. [8] developed the Vision Transformer (ViT) interpreting a picture as a sequence of tokens, which can achieve comparable image classification accuracy while requiring less computational budgets. ViT relies on globally-contextualized representation, in which each patch is attended to all patches of the same image, as opposed to local-connectivity in CNNs. ViT and its variants have shown promising superiority in modeling non-local contextual relationships as well as good efficiency and scalability, though they are still in their infancy. In light of the global interaction and the generation of distant features with conditional sub-image, these benefits could enhance image extrapolation in a beneficial fashion.

To better cope with image long-range dependencies and spatial relationships between predicted regions and conditional sub-images, we reconsider the outpainting problem as a patch-wise sequence-to-sequence autoregression problem inspired by the original transformer [41] in natural language processing. We develop a novel hybrid query-based encoder-decoder transformer framework, named **Query Outpainting TRansformer (QueryOTR)**, to extrapolate visual

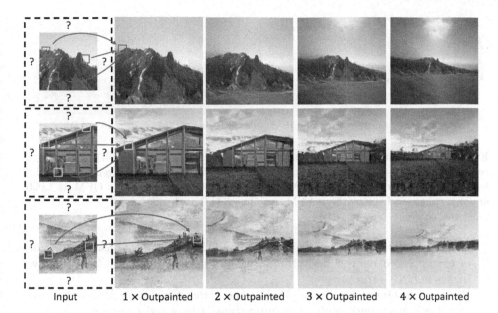

Input        1 × Outpainted    2 × Outpainted    3 × Outpainted    4 × Outpainted

**Fig. 1.** Demonstration of recursive outpainting by our QueryOTR. Our method generates a sequence of extrapolated image patches by querying the sequence of input image patches, enabling a remarkable perceptual consistency.

context all-side around a given image taking advantages of both ViT [8] and pure transformer [41] in the image outpainting task, as shown in Fig. 1. Specifically, we design two special modules, Query Expansion Module (QEM) and Patch Smoothing Module (PSM), to conduct feature forecasting from the perspective of the query in the attention mechanism. In contrast to the query learning in pure transformer, our designed query in QEM is predicted by the stacked CNN-based blocks based on the output of the transformer encoder. The predicted query is easy to learn and has better flexibility by drawing on the advantages of CNNs' inductive biases to accelerate query prediction converge in pure transformer for approximately three times faster than that without QEM in training, which is shown in Fig. 2(a). The developed PSM re-allocates the predicted patches around the conditional sub-image and averages the overlapping parts to make the generated image smoothly and seamlessly. Also, PSM contributes to alleviate the problem of checkerboard artifact caused by the independent procession among the output image patches. In this way, the model could focus more on the connections between each patch and enhance the representing ability as shown in Fig. 2(b) and (c). Our **QueryOTR** is the first hybrid transformer as a sequence-to-sequence modeling, which is able to extend image borders seamlessly and generate unseen images smoothly and realistically.

The main contributions of this work are three-fold:

- We rephrase the image outpainting problem as a patch-wise sequence-to-sequence autoregression problem and develop a novel hybrid transformer

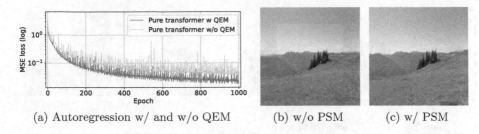

(a) Autoregression w/ and w/o QEM    (b) w/o PSM    (c) w/ PSM

**Fig. 2.** (a) Training a pure transformer encoder-decoder with and without QEM to regress unseen image patches. QEM significantly speeds up the convergence (about 3.3 times faster than that without QEM: w/ QEM at 300 epoch v.s. w/o QEM at 1,000 epoch). (b) QueryOTR without PSM. (c) QueryOTR with PSM.

encoder-decoder framework, named **QueryOTR**, for query-based prediction of extrapolated images, and minimization of degradation from the inductive biases in CNN-structures.
– We propose *Query Expansion Module* and *Patch Smoothing Module* to solve the slow convergence problem in pure transformers and to generate realistic extrapolated images smoothly and seamlessly.
– Experimental results show that the proposed method achieves state-of-the-art one-step and multi-step outpainting performance as compared to recent image outpainting methods.

## 2    Related Work

### 2.1    Image Outpainting

Generative Adversarial Networks (GANs) [12] have been widely applied in many research fields, such as image super-resolution, image synthesis, and image denoising [4,14,15,25,32]. Efforts have been made for image generation with GAN under certain conditions. Image extrapolation aims to generate the surrounding regions from the visual content, which can be considered as an image-conditioned generation task [16]. Sabini and Rusak [36] brought the image outpainting task into public attention with a deep neural network framework inspired by the image inpainting methods. This effort focused on enhancing the quality of generated images smoothly by using GANs and the post-processing methods to perform horizontal outpainting. Van et al. [40] designed a CNN-based encoder-to-decoder framework by using GAN for image outpainting. Wang et al. [43] proposed a Semantic Regeneration Network to directly learn the semantic features from the conditional sub-image. Han et al. [28] developed a 3-stage deep learning model with an edge-guided generative network to produce semantically consistent output from a small image input. Although these methods avoid the bias in the general padding and up-sampling pattern, they still suffer from blunt structures and abrupt colours issues, which tend to ignore the spatial and semantic consistency. To tackle these issues, Yang et al. [44] proposed a

Recurrent Content Transfer (RCT) block for temporal content prediction with Long Short Term Memory (LSTM) networks as the bottleneck. To increase the contextual information, Lu et al. [30] and Kim et al. [22] rearranged the boundary region by switching the outer area of the image into its inner area. These latest models are based on convolutional neural networks. As global information is not well captured, they all have limitations in explicitly modelling long-range dependency.

## 2.2 Transformer

Recently, transformer has attracted much attention in computer vision. Transformer was first proposed to solve NLP tasks by replacing the traditional CNN and Recurrent Neural Network (RNN) structures [41]. The Self-Attention mechanism helps the model learn the global representation from the input which could improve the performance for basic visual feature extraction [41]. Jacob et al. [7] introduced a very deep network to pretrain deep bidirectional representations from unlabeled text by jointly conditioning on both left and right context in all layers. It can be fine-tuned with just one additional output layer for better performance. ViT [8] is a convolution-free Transformer that conducts image classification over a sequence of image patches. The superiority of the Transformer architecture is presented in ViT fully utilizing the advantage of pretraining on large-scale datasets compared with the CNN-based methods. Many ViT-based variants also demonstrated the success in computer vision tasks [13,19,47], such as object detection [5], video recognition [1], and image synthesis [26]. Moreover, Liu et al. [29] proposed Swin Transformer to extend vision tasks for object detection and semantic segmentation. Gao et al. [11] designed a transformer-based framework for image outpainting with an encoder-decoder architecture. They used Swin Transformer which involved shifted window attention to bridge the windows of the preceding layer, which significantly enhanced modelling power as well as achieved lower latency.

## 3 Methodology

### 3.1 Problem Statement

Given an image $x \in \mathbb{R}^{H \times W \times 3}$, we aim to extrapolate outside contents beyond the image boundary with extra $M$-pixels. The generator will produce a visually convincing image $\hat{x} \in \mathbb{R}^{(H+2M) \times (W+2M) \times 3}$. Different from previous work which is almost based on convolutional operations, we rephrase the problem as a patch-wise sequence-to-sequence autoregression problem. In particular, we partition the image $x$ into regular non-overlapping patches with the patch size $P \times P$ ($P$ is typically empirically set to 16), resulting in a sequence of patch tokens $\{x_p^1, x_p^2, \cdots, x_p^L\}$, where $x_p^i \in \mathbb{R}^{(P^2 \cdot 3)}$ and the sequence length is $L = \frac{H \times W}{P^2}$. Our goal is to predict the extra sequence $\{x_p^{L+1}, x_p^{L+2}, \cdots, x_p^{L+R}\}$ representing the extrapolated regions, where $x_p^i \in \mathbb{R}^{(P^2 \cdot 3)}$ and the expanded

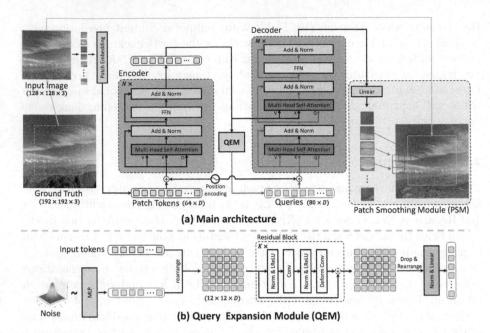

**Fig. 3.** (a) Main architecture of hybrid transformer generator in QueryOTR consists of transformer encoder and decoder, QEM and PSM. (b) Structure of query expansion module.

sequence length is $R = \frac{(H+2M) \times (W+2M) - H \times W}{P^2}$. The extrapolated image $\hat{x}$ can be obtained by reshaping the new sequence of patch tokens into image patches, and then rearranging the image patches around the input image, leading to $\hat{\mathbf{x}} = \mathcal{F}(x, \{x_p^{L+1}, x_p^{L+2}, \cdots, x_p^{L+R}\})$.

### 3.2   Hybrid Transformer Autoencoder

The architecture of the proposed QueryOTR generator is presented in Fig. 3, which is a hybrid transformer autoencoder. The overall architecture is composed of four major components: a transformer encoder extracting patch tokens' representation, a CNN-based Query Expansion Module (QEM) predicting the expanded queries, a transformer decoder processing the expanded queries, and a Patch Smoothing Module (PSM) generating the expanded patches and rearranging them around the original images.

**Transformer Encoder.** Our encoder is a standard ViT [8]. Inspired from ViT, the input image is first converted to several non-overlapping patches represented as a sequence of patch tokens $\mathbf{X}_p$. The encoder module embeds the patch tokens through a linear projection $\mathbf{E}$ with the added positional embeddings $\mathbf{E}_{pos}$. Then the encoder processes the set of patch tokens via a series of Transformer Blocks with a length of $N$. The transformer-based encoder can be described as follows:

$$\mathrm{h}_0 = [\mathrm{x}_p^1 \mathbf{E}; \mathrm{x}_p^2 \mathbf{E}; ...; \mathrm{x}_p^L \mathbf{E}] + \mathbf{E}_{pos}, \qquad \mathbf{E} \in \mathbb{R}^{(P^2 \cdot 3) \times D}, \mathbf{E}_{pos} \in \mathbb{R}^{L \times D} \qquad (1)$$

$$\mathrm{h}_n' = \mathrm{MSA}(\mathrm{LN}(\mathrm{h}_{n-1})) + \mathrm{h}_{n-1}, \qquad n = 1, ..., N \qquad (2)$$

$$\mathrm{h}_n = \mathrm{FFN}(\mathrm{LN}(\mathrm{h}_n')) + \mathrm{h}_n', \qquad n = 1, ..., N \qquad (3)$$

$$\mathrm{h}_{enc} = \mathrm{LN}(\mathrm{h}_N), \qquad (4)$$

where $D$ is the hidden dimension of transformer block, FFN is a feed forward network, LN denotes layer normalization, $\mathrm{h}_n$ are the intermediate tokens' representations, $\mathrm{h}_{enc}$ denotes the output patch tokens of the transformer encoder, and MSA represents the multi-headed self-attention.

Given the learnable matrices $\mathbf{W}_q$, $\mathbf{W}_k$, $\mathbf{W}_v$ corresponding to query, key, and value representations, a single self-attention head (indexed with $h$) is computed:

$$\mathrm{Attention}_h(\mathbf{X}, \mathbf{Y}) = \mathrm{softmax}(\mathbf{Q}\mathbf{K}^\top / \sqrt{d_h})\mathbf{V}, \qquad (5)$$

where $\mathbf{Q} = \mathbf{X}\mathbf{W}_q$, $\mathbf{K} = \mathbf{Y}\mathbf{W}_k$, $\mathbf{V} = \mathbf{Y}\mathbf{W}_v$. Multi-headed self-attention aggregates information with linear projection operation on the concatenation of the $H$ self-attention heads:

$$\mathrm{MSA}(\mathbf{X}) = \mathrm{concat}_{h=1}^{H}[\mathrm{Attention}_h(\mathbf{X}, \mathbf{X})]\mathbf{W} + \mathbf{b}, \qquad (6)$$

where $\mathbf{W}$ and $\mathbf{b}$ are learnable matrices for the aggregated features.

**Query Expansion Module.** The proposed QEM is designed to speed up the convergence of pure transformer by generating the expanded queries for the transformer decoder. We predict the decoders' queries conditioned on encoders' features, and take advantage of CNN's inductive bias to accelerate the convergence. As shown in Fig. 3(b), the input tokens $\mathrm{h}_{enc}$ are first reshaped to the feature map with the size of $\frac{H}{P} \times \frac{W}{P} \times D$. Then the reshaped feature maps are extrapolated with extra $\frac{M}{P}$ pixels along width and height, where the padded tokens are generated by Multi-layer Perceptual (MLP) with input of Gaussian noise. After that, we utilize stacked residual blocks [18] equipped with deformable convolutional layers [48] to process the queries, which is commonly practiced to capture local and long-term dependencies. Finally, the expanded queries are extracted and transformed as sequence, followed by one Normalization Layer and one Linear Layer. This process can be described as:

$$\mathrm{q}_{expand} = \mathrm{QEM}(\mathrm{h}_{enc}, z), \qquad z \sim \mathcal{N}(0, 1). \qquad (7)$$

**Transformer Decoder.** Inspired from the original transformer [41], the decoder equips one extra sub-layer which performs the multi-head cross attention (MCA) similar to the encoder with two sub-layers. Specifically, in MCA the queries come from the previous decoder layer and the keys and values come from the output of the encoder. This allows each position in the decoder to attend over all positions in the input sequence, leading to significant improvements of the generating performance. The process can be described as follows:

$$q_0 = q_{expand} + \mathbf{E}'_{pos}, \qquad\qquad \mathbf{E}'_{pos} \in \mathbb{R}^{R \times D} \qquad (8)$$

$$q'_m = \text{MSA}(\text{LN}(q_{m-1})) + q_{m-1}, \qquad m = 1, ..., M \qquad (9)$$

$$q''_m = \text{MCA}(\text{LN}(q'_m), h_{enc}) + q'_m, \qquad m = 1, ..., M \qquad (10)$$

$$q_m = \text{FFN}(\text{LN}(q''_m)) + q''_m, \qquad m = 1, ..., M \qquad (11)$$

The multi-headed cross-attention in Eq. 10 aggregates information from $H$ cross attention heads, as follows:

$$\text{MCA}(\mathbf{X}, \mathbf{Y}) = \text{concat}_{h=1}^{H}[\text{Attention}_h(\mathbf{X}, \mathbf{Y})]\mathbf{W} + \mathbf{b}. \qquad (12)$$

**Patch Smoothing Module.** The linear module is prone to generate artifacts if predicting output patches using predefined patch size of $P \times P$. The reason is that the output tokens are processed independently without explicit constraints. These arbitrary grid partitions could make the image contents discontinuous across the border edge of each patch. In order to mitigate this issue, we allow some overlaps among image patches. For each border edge of one patch, we extend it by $o$ pixels generating the output image patch size as $(P+2o) \times (P+2o)$. This operation involves the decoder with the neighboring patches' content having a better sense of locality in the transformer architecture, thus enabling the output sequence to have same length but less effect as the predefined grids. PSM can be described as:

$$\hat{x} = \mathcal{S}(x, q_M \mathbf{W}_{proj}), \qquad\qquad \mathbf{W}_{proj} \in \mathbb{R}^{D \times ((P+2o)^2 \cdot 3)}, \qquad (13)$$

where $\mathcal{S}$ is a function to place the extrapolated overlapped patches around the input image, and average the pixel values in the overlapped areas.

### 3.3 Loss Functions

Our loss function consists of three parts: a patch-wise reconstruction loss, a perceptual loss, and an adversarial loss. The reconstruction loss is responsible for capturing the overall structure of predicted patches, whilst the perceptual loss and adversarial loss are coupled to maintain good perceptual quality and promote more realistic prediction.

**Patch-wise Reconstruction Loss.** We utilize an L2 distance between the sequence of ground truth image patches $\{y_p^{L+1}, y_p^{L+2}, \cdots, y_p^{L+R}\}$ and the sequence of predicted image patches $\{x_p^{L+1}, x_p^{L+2}, \cdots, x_p^{L+R}\}$:

$$\mathcal{L}_{rec} = \frac{1}{R} \sum_{i=L+1}^{L+R} \|y_p^i - x_p^i\|_2^2, \qquad (14)$$

where the patch size is $(P+2o) \times (P+2o)$. We engage a per-patch normalization to enhance the patch contrast locally, where the mean and std of the image patches are pre-computed.

**Perceptual Loss.** Perceptual loss provides a supervision on the intermediate features that can help retain more semantic information. Following previous work [9, 21, 24], we extract the features from a VGG-19 [38] network pretrained on ImageNet [6], which is denoted as $\phi$. The perceptual loss is devised as follows:

$$\mathcal{L}_{perceptual} = \frac{1}{5} \sum_{j=1}^{5} (w^j \times (\phi^j(\hat{x}) - \phi^j(y))), \tag{15}$$

where the superscript $j$ is the index of feature map scales from $\phi$, and $w^j$ is set to $1/32, 1/16, 1/8, 1/4, 1$ as the scale decreases.

**Adversarial Loss.** We utilize the same multi-scale PatchGAN discriminator $D$ used in pix2pixHD [42] except that we replace the least squared loss term [32] with the hinge loss term [27]. Since the PatchGAN discriminator has a fixed receptive field of patch, we take the whole generated images instead of image patches to train the GAN. The extrapolated images generated by our QueryOTR should be indistinguishable from real images by the discriminator. Given the extrapolated images $\hat{x} \sim \mathbb{P}_g$ generated by QueryOTR and real images $y \sim \mathbb{P}_y$, the adversarial loss for the discriminator is

$$\mathcal{L}_{adv}^{D} = \min_{D} \mathbb{E}_{\hat{x} \sim \mathbb{P}_g}(min(1 + D(\hat{x}))) + \mathbb{E}_{y \sim \mathbb{P}_y}(min(1 - D(y))). \tag{16}$$

Additionally, the adversarial loss for the generator is

$$\mathcal{L}_{adv}^{G} = \min_{G} -\mathbb{E}_{\hat{x} \sim \mathbb{P}_g} D(\hat{x}). \tag{17}$$

We jointly train the hybrid transformer generator and CNN discriminators and optimize the final objective as a weighted sum of the above mentioned loss terms:

$$\min_{G} \max_{D} \mathcal{L}_{adv} + \lambda_{rec}\mathcal{L}_{rec} + \lambda_{perceptual}\mathcal{L}_{perceptual}, \tag{18}$$

where $\lambda_{rec}, \lambda_{perceptual}$ are weights controlling the importance of loss terms. In our experiments, we set $\lambda_{rec} = 5$, and $\lambda_{perceptual} = 10$.

## 4 Experiments

### 4.1 Datasets, Implementation and Training Details

We use three datasets with {Scenery [44], Building Facades [11], and WikiArt [39]} for the experiments. Details about the three datasets could be found in the supplementary materials.

We implement our framework with PyTorch [34] equipped with a NVIDIA GeForce RTX 3090 GPU 1.9.0. Hybrid transformer generator contains 12 stacked transformer encoder layers and 4 stacked transformer decoder layers. We initialise the weights of generator encoder by utilizing the pre-trained ViT [17]. Adam [23] is used as the optimizer to minimize the objective function with the mini-batch of 64, $\beta_1 = 0.0$, $\beta_2 = 0.99$, and weight decay of 0.0001. The $o$ is

**Table 1.** Quantitative results of one-step and multi-step outpainting. Best and second best results are **boldface** and <u>underlined</u>. 1× represents one step outpainting, while 2× and 3× denote two- and three-step outpainting respectively.

| | Methods | Scenery | | | Building facades | | | WikiArt | | |
|---|---|---|---|---|---|---|---|---|---|---|
| | | FID↓ | IS↑ | PSNR↑ | FID↓ | IS↑ | PSNR↑ | FID↓ | IS↑ | PSNR↑ |
| 1× | SRN | 47.781 | 2.981 | 22.440 | 38.644 | 3.862 | 18.588 | 76.749 | 3.629 | <u>20.072</u> |
| | NSIPO | 25.977 | 3.059 | 21.089 | 30.465 | 4.153 | 18.314 | 22.242 | 5.600 | 18.592 |
| | IOH | 32.107 | 2.886 | 22.286 | 49.481 | 3.924 | 18.431 | 40.184 | 4.835 | 19.403 |
| | Uformer | <u>20.575</u> | <u>3.249</u> | <u>23.007</u> | <u>30.542</u> | <u>4.189</u> | <u>18.828</u> | <u>15.904</u> | <u>6.567</u> | 19.610 |
| | QueryOTR | **20.366** | **3.955** | **23.604** | **22.378** | **4.978** | **19.680** | **14.955** | **7.896** | **20.388** |
| 2× | SRN | 83.772 | 2.349 | 18.403 | 74.304 | 3.651 | 15.355 | 137.997 | 3.039 | <u>16.646</u> |
| | NSIPO | 45.989 | 2.606 | 17.733 | <u>58.341</u> | 3.669 | 15.262 | 51.668 | 4.591 | 15.679 |
| | IOH | 44.742 | 2.655 | 18.739 | 76.476 | 3.456 | 15.443 | 75.070 | 4.289 | 16.056 |
| | Uformer | <u>39.801</u> | <u>2.920</u> | <u>18.920</u> | 63.915 | <u>3.798</u> | <u>15.612</u> | **41.107** | <u>5.900</u> | 15.947 |
| | QueryOTR | **39.237** | **3.431** | **19.358** | **41.273** | **4.547** | **16.213** | <u>43.757</u> | **6.341** | **17.074** |
| 3× | SRN | 115.193 | 2.087 | 16.123 | 110.036 | 2.938 | 13.693 | 181.533 | 2.504 | <u>14.609</u> |
| | NSIPO | 64.457 | 2.405 | 15.606 | <u>81.301</u> | <u>3.431</u> | 13.791 | 75.785 | 4.225 | 14.257 |
| | IOH | **58.629** | 2.432 | 16.307 | 95.068 | 2.790 | 13.894 | 108.328 | 3.728 | 13.919 |
| | Uformer | <u>60.497</u> | <u>2.638</u> | <u>16.379</u> | 93.888 | 3.388 | <u>14.051</u> | <u>72.923</u> | **5.904** | 13.464 |
| | QueryOTR | 60.977 | **3.114** | **16.864** | **64.926** | **4.612** | **14.316** | **69.951** | <u>5.683</u> | **15.294** |

set to 8 considering the complexity and precision. Our QueryOTR is trained for 300, 200 and 120 epochs on Scenery, Building Facades, and WikiArt datasets respectively with the learning rate of 0.0001. The warm-up trick [18] is utilized in the first 10 epochs with the reconstruction loss only. For discriminator regularization, DiffAug [46] and spectral normalization [33] are used to stabilise the training dynamics.

We conduct generalised image outpainting for experimental comparison following the previous work. In the training stage, the original images are resized to the size 192 × 192 as the ground truth images. Then the input images with the size 128 × 128 are obtained by the center cropping operation. In the testing stage, all images are resized to 192 × 192 as the ground truth, and then the input images are obtained by center cropping to the sizes 128 × 128, 86 × 86, and 56 × 56 for 1×, 2×, and 3× outpainting respectively. Excepted for horizontal flip and image normalization, no other data augmentation is used for ease of setup. The total output sizes are 2.25, 5, and 11.7 times of the input in terms of 1×, 2×, and 3× outpainting, indicating that over half of all pixels will be generated.

## 4.2  Experimental Results

We make comparisons with three SOTA CNN-based image outpainting methods, NSIPO [44], SRN [43], and IOH [40], and one transformer-based method Uformer [11] to demonstrate the effectiveness of QueryOTR. For all the experiments, we set the input and output sizes as 128 × 128 and 192 × 192.

We use Inception Score (IS) [37], Fréchet Inception Distance (FID) [20], and peak signal-to-noise ratio (PSNR) to measure the generative quality objectively. The upper-bounds of IS are 4.091, 5.660 and 8.779 for Scenery, Building Facades and WikiArt, respectively, which are calculated by real images in test set.

**Quantitative Result.** Table 1 shows quantitative results. Our QueryOTR outperforms the competition on almost all metrics on 1-step and multi-step outpainting. In particular, QueryOTR shows obvious superiority in all entries compared with CNN-based methods, e.g., SRN, NSIPO, and IOH. These results show that transformer structure succeeds in capturing global dependencies for image outpainting compared with CNN's inductive biases. Meanwhile, our QueryOTR outperforms the very competitive Swin-based Uformer which uses an image-to-image translation approach for image extrapolation, mainly because our query-based method allows to generate image patches attended to all the visual locations, yielding a better perceptual consistency. It is noted that our results for 1× outpainting are very close to the IS upper-bound for all the datasets, indicating realistic image generation and good perceptual consistency. Extra results of replacing the center region with input sub-images are in the supplementary.

**Qualitative Result.** Some examples of visual results on all the datasets are shown in Fig. 4. Our QueryOTR effectively extrapolates the images by querying the global semantic-similar image patches. Seen from the 1× outpainting results, our QueryOTR could generate more realistic images with vivid details and enrich the contents of the generated regions marked in white box. Furthermore, our method could weaken the sense of edges between the generated regions and input sub-image. Compared with other baselines, our QueryOTR could generate water containing more realistic ripples in the $3^{rd}$ row and intact trees in the $5^{th}$ row of Fig. 4, which could be seen in the white dotted box. In the $7^{th}$ row of Fig. 4, the whole skyscraper generated by QueryOTR indicates the success of our query-based method which predicts the detailed contents with global information by queries. In the $9^{th}$ row, our method could capture the global information of the green background on the corner marked in the white box. More visual results could be seen in the supplementary material.

## 4.3  Ablation Study

We ablate several critical factors in QueryOTR by progressively adjusting each factor here. It can be seen that each factor contributes to the final success of QueryOTR. We conducted all the ablation experiments on the Scenery dataset.

**Transformer Encoder and Decoder.** We compare the impact of the pre-trained ViT-based encoder and the number of transformer decoder layers $M$. As shown in Table 2(a), utilizing a pretrained ViT encoder contributes to the improvements of FID and IS by 2.418 and 0.204, respectively. The main reason is that the small datasets might not be sufficient to train the model for performance saturation. The pretrained ViT encoder is capable of capturing the long-term dependencies, which may benefit the patch prediction. Additionally,

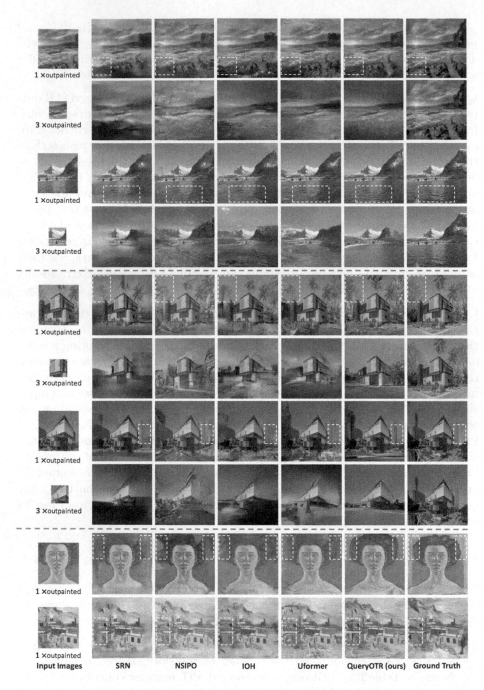

**Fig. 4.** Comparisons on 1-step and multi-step outpainting with the state-of-the-art methods. Our QueryOTR achieves the best image quality. (Color figure online)

**Table 2.** Ablation studies validated on Scenery dataset.

| Pretrained *Enc.* | M | FID↓ | IS↑ |
|---|---|---|---|
| – | 4 | 22.784 | 3.751 |
| ✓ | 2 | 20.731 | 3.931 |
| ✓ | 4 | **20.366** | **3.955** |
| ✓ | 8 | 20.373 | 3.852 |

(a) Ablation of the pretrained ViT-base encoder and the number of transformer decoder layers M.

| | FID↓ | IS↑ |
|---|---|---|
| w/o $\mathcal{L}_{rec}$ & $\mathcal{L}_{perceptual}$ | 38.009 | 3.433 |
| w/o $\mathcal{L}_{rec}$ | 31.282 | 3.744 |
| w/o $\mathcal{L}_{perceptual}$ | 33.380 | 3.510 |
| QueryOTR (baseline) | **20.366** | **3.955** |

(b) Impact of $\mathcal{L}_{rec}$ and $\mathcal{L}_{perceptual}$ contribute to the overall performance. The model is default trained with three losses.

| | FID↓ | IS↑ |
|---|---|---|
| w/o QEM | 36.967 | 3.642 |
| QEM w/o Noise | 23.444 | 3.728 |
| QEM w/o DC [48] | 23.530 | **3.775** |
| w QEM | **22.784** | 3.751 |

(c) Impact of proposed Query Expansion Module (QEM) and its key internal components.

| PSM | Per-Patch *Norm.* | FID↓ | IS↑ |
|---|---|---|---|
| – | – | 51.945 | 3.801 |
| – | ✓ | 31.073 | 3.753 |
| ✓ | – | 22.501 | 3.707 |
| ✓ | ✓ | **20.366** | **3.955** |

(d) Effect of the proposed Patch Smoothing Module (PSM) and per-patch image normalization.

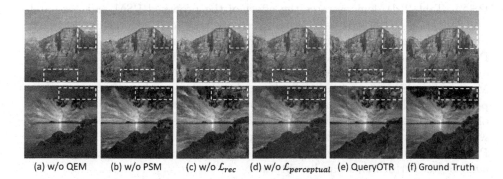

(a) w/o QEM    (b) w/o PSM    (c) w/o $\mathcal{L}_{rec}$    (d) w/o $\mathcal{L}_{perceptual}$    (e) QueryOTR    (f) Ground Truth

**Fig. 5.** Visualisation of ablation study.

our QueryOTR performs optimally in both FID and IS when the number of decoder layers is set to 4. Further increasing the depth of decoder indefinitely will not improve the performance of our QueryOTR.

**Loss Terms.** We investigate the impact of patch-wise reconstruction loss $\mathcal{L}_{rec}$ and perceptual loss $\mathcal{L}_{perceptual}$ in Table 2(b). We first train the model with only adversarial loss, which is equivalent to training the model unpaired, resulting in a FID of 38.009 and IS of 3.433. On the basis of adversarial training, using either $\mathcal{L}_{rec}$ or $\mathcal{L}_{perceptual}$ could improve the overall performance. Figure 5(c) and (d) show that high-frequency checkerboard artifacts occur when trained without $\mathcal{L}_{rec}$, and the details cannot be generated without $\mathcal{L}_{perceptual}$.

**QEM.** We ablate the impact of QEM and its internal key components. In the experiments, we do not use a pretrained encoder to avoid reducing the difficulty of training learnable queries. Since training pure transformer may require larger datasets and longer time, it is hard for learnable queries to converge well on Scenery dataset, resulting in a high FID (see Table 2(c)) and blurry image patches (see Fig. 5(a)). On the other hand, the proposed QEM generates queries conditioned on input images, significantly improving FID by 14.227. Meanwhile, generating queries with noise slightly improves the patch diversity, and deformable convolution enables an active long distance modeling for query generation.

To further investigate how QEM affect the convergence speed of pure transformer, we train the pure transformer with and without QEM module for 1000 epochs. As shown in Fig. 2(a), the convergence rate of the pure transformer with QEM is about 3.3 times faster than that without QEM on a relatively small dataset indicating the superiority of QEM in accelerating the model convergence. On the other hand, the loss declines slowly without QEM, which might be caused by the insufficient training data. The reason leading to this phenomenon is that the pure transformer will process almost 4 billion possibilities if the $16 \times 16$ pixel patch is treated as a word, which needs larger semantic space for attention processing. When dealing with a small dataset, the amount of data is not enough to regress the extrapolated patches resulting in model degradation.

**PSM.** Table 2(d) demonstrates the effect of the proposed PSM and per-patch normalization. Although using a single linear layer can generate vivid image patches, the connections between patches are unnatural, as shown in Fig. 5(b). Per-patch normalization could improve the reconstruction of high-frequency by enhancing the local contrast of patches, leading an improvement of FID 20.872. Meanwhile, PSM significantly alleviates the checkerboard artifacts caused by per-patch prediction, and improves the overall perceptual quality of the extrapolated images. PSM alleviates checkerboard artifacts via explicit constraints, while perceptual loss penalizes image discontinuity from a semantic perspective. PSM appears more effective and direct than perceptual loss. If both are applied, even better performance can be obtained.

## 5    Conclusion

In this paper, we have proposed a novel hybrid query-based encoder-decoder transformer framework, **QueryOTR**, to extrapolate visual context all-side around a given image. The transformer structure breaks through the limitation of capturing image long-rang dependencies and intrinsic locality. The special designed module QEM helps to accelerate the transformer model convergence on small datasets and PSM contributes to generate seamless extrapolated images realistically and smoothly. Extensive experiments on Scenery, Building and WikiArt datasets proved the superiority of our query-based method.

**Acknowledgments.** The work was partially supported by the following: National Natural Science Foundation of China under no.61876155; Jiangsu Science and Technology Programme under no. BE2020006-4; Key Program Special Fund in XJTLU under no. KSF-T-06 and no. KSF-E-37; Research Development Fund in XJTLU under no. RDF-19-01-21.

# References

1. Arnab, A., Dehghani, M., Heigold, G., Sun, C., Lučić, M., Schmid, C.: ViViT: a video vision transformer. In: Proceedings of the IEEE/CVF International Conference on Computer Vision, pp. 6836–6846 (2021)
2. Barnes, C., Shechtman, E., Finkelstein, A., Goldman, D.B.: PatchMatch: a randomized correspondence algorithm for structural image editing. ACM Trans. Graph. **28**(3), 24 (2009)
3. Bertalmio, M., Sapiro, G., Caselles, V., Ballester, C.: Image inpainting. In: Proceedings of the 27th Annual Conference on Computer Graphics and Interactive Techniques, pp. 417–424 (2000)
4. Brock, A., Donahue, J., Simonyan, K.: Large scale GAN training for high fidelity natural image synthesis. In: Proceedings of the International Conference on Learning Representations (2019)
5. Carion, N., Massa, F., Synnaeve, G., Usunier, N., Kirillov, A., Zagoruyko, S.: End-to-end object detection with transformers. In: Vedaldi, A., Bischof, H., Brox, T., Frahm, J.-M. (eds.) ECCV 2020. LNCS, vol. 12346, pp. 213–229. Springer, Cham (2020). https://doi.org/10.1007/978-3-030-58452-8_13
6. Deng, J., Dong, W., Socher, R., Li, L.J., Li, K., Fei-Fei, L.: ImageNet: a large-scale hierarchical image database. In: Proceedings of the IEEE/CVF Conference on Computer Vision and Pattern Recognition, pp. 248–255 (2009)
7. Devlin, J., Chang, M.W., Lee, K., Toutanova, K.: BERT: pre-training of deep bidirectional transformers for language understanding. In: Annual Conference of the North American Chapter of the Association for Computational Linguistics: Human Language Technologies (2019)
8. Dosovitskiy, A., et al.: An image is worth 16x16 words: transformers for image recognition at scale. In: Proceedings of the International Conference on Learning Representations (2021)
9. Dosovitskiy, A., Brox, T.: Generating images with perceptual similarity metrics based on deep networks. In: Advances in Annual Conference on Neural Information Processing Systems, vol. 29 (2016)
10. D'Ascoli, S., Touvron, H., Leavitt, M.L., Morcos, A.S., Biroli, G., Sagun, L.: ConViT: improving vision transformers with soft convolutional inductive biases. In: Proceedings of the International Conference on Machine Learning, pp. 2286–2296. PMLR (2021)
11. Gao, P., Yang, X., Zhang, R., Huang, K., Geng, Y.: Generalised image outpainting with U-Transformer. arXiv preprint arXiv:2201.11403 (2022)
12. Goodfellow, I., et al.: Generative adversarial nets. In: Advances in Annual Conference on Neural Information Processing Systems, vol. 27 (2014)
13. Graham, B., et al.: LeViT: a vision transformer in convnet's clothing for faster inference. In: Proceedings of the IEEE/CVF International Conference on Computer Vision, pp. 12259–12269 (2021)

14. Gu, J., Shen, Y., Zhou, B.: Image processing using multi-code GAN prior. In: Proceedings of the IEEE/CVF Conference on Computer Vision and Pattern Recognition, pp. 3012–3021 (2020)
15. Gulrajani, I., Ahmed, F., Arjovsky, M., Dumoulin, V., Courville, A.C.: Improved training of Wasserstein GANs. In: Advances in Annual Conference on Neural Information Processing Systems, vol. 30 (2017)
16. Guo, D., et al.: Spiral generative network for image extrapolation. In: Vedaldi, A., Bischof, H., Brox, T., Frahm, J.-M. (eds.) ECCV 2020. LNCS, vol. 12364, pp. 701–717. Springer, Cham (2020). https://doi.org/10.1007/978-3-030-58529-7_41
17. He, K., Chen, X., Xie, S., Li, Y., Dollár, P., Girshick, R.: Masked autoencoders are scalable vision learners. arXiv preprint arXiv:2111.06377 (2021)
18. He, K., Zhang, X., Ren, S., Sun, J.: Deep residual learning for image recognition. In: Proceedings of the IEEE/CVF Conference on Computer Vision and Pattern Recognition, pp. 770–778 (2016)
19. Heo, B., Yun, S., Han, D., Chun, S., Choe, J., Oh, S.J.: Rethinking spatial dimensions of vision transformers. In: Proceedings of the IEEE/CVF International Conference on Computer Vision, pp. 11936–11945 (2021)
20. Heusel, M., Ramsauer, H., Unterthiner, T., Nessler, B., Hochreiter, S.: GANs trained by a two time-scale update rule converge to a local Nash equilibrium. In: Advances in Annual Conference on Neural Information Processing Systems, vol. 30 (2017)
21. Johnson, J., Alahi, A., Fei-Fei, L.: Perceptual losses for real-time style transfer and super-resolution. In: Leibe, B., Matas, J., Sebe, N., Welling, M. (eds.) ECCV 2016. LNCS, vol. 9906, pp. 694–711. Springer, Cham (2016). https://doi.org/10.1007/978-3-319-46475-6_43
22. Kim, K., Yun, Y., Kang, K.W., Kong, K., Lee, S., Kang, S.J.: Painting outside as inside: Edge guided image outpainting via bidirectional rearrangement with progressive step learning. In: Proceedings of the IEEE/CVF Winter Conference on Applications of Computer Vision, pp. 2122–2130 (2021)
23. Kingma, D.P., Ba, J.: Adam: a method for stochastic optimization. arXiv preprint arXiv:1412.6980 (2014)
24. Larsen, A.B.L., Sønderby, S.K., Larochelle, H., Winther, O.: Autoencoding beyond pixels using a learned similarity metric. In: Proceedings of the International Conference on Machine Learning, pp. 1558–1566. PMLR (2016)
25. Ledig, C., et al.: Photo-realistic single image super-resolution using a generative adversarial network. In: Proceedings of the IEEE/CVF Conference on Computer Vision and Pattern Recognition, pp. 4681–4690 (2017)
26. Lee, K., Chang, H., Jiang, L., Zhang, H., Tu, Z., Liu, C.: ViTGAN: training GANs with vision transformers. arXiv preprint arXiv:2107.04589 (2021)
27. Lim, J.H., Ye, J.C.: Geometric GAN. arXiv preprint arXiv:1705.02894 (2017)
28. Lin, H., Pagnucco, M., Song, Y.: Edge guided progressively generative image outpainting. In: Proceedings of the IEEE/CVF Conference on Computer Vision and Pattern Recognition, pp. 806–815 (2021)
29. Liu, Z., et al.: Swin transformer: hierarchical vision transformer using shifted windows. In: Proceedings of the IEEE/CVF International Conference on Computer Vision, pp. 10012–10022 (2021)
30. Lu, C.N., Chang, Y.C., Chiu, W.C.: Bridging the visual gap: wide-range image blending. In: Proceedings of the IEEE/CVF Conference on Computer Vision and Pattern Recognition, pp. 843–851 (2021)
31. Ma, Y., et al.: Boosting image outpainting with semantic layout prediction. arXiv preprint arXiv:2110.09267 (2021)

32. Mao, X., Li, Q., Xie, H., Lau, R.Y., Wang, Z., Paul Smolley, S.: Least squares generative adversarial networks. In: Proceedings of the IEEE International Conference on Computer Vision, pp. 2794–2802 (2017)
33. Miyato, T., Kataoka, T., Koyama, M., Yoshida, Y.: Spectral normalization for generative adversarial networks. In: Proceedings of the International Conference on Learning Representations (2018)
34. Paszke, A., et al.: PyTorch: an imperative style, high-performance deep learning library. In: Advances in Annual Conference on Neural Information Processing Systems, vol. 32 (2019)
35. Pathak, D., Krahenbuhl, P., Donahue, J., Darrell, T., Efros, A.A.: Context encoders: feature learning by inpainting. In: Proceedings of the IEEE/CVF Conference on Computer Vision and Pattern Recognition, pp. 2536–2544 (2016)
36. Sabini, M., Rusak, G.: Painting outside the box: Image outpainting with GANs. arXiv preprint arXiv:1808.08483 (2018)
37. Salimans, T., Goodfellow, I., Zaremba, W., Cheung, V., Radford, A., Chen, X.: Improved techniques for training GANs. In: Advances in Annual Conference on Neural Information Processing Systems, vol. 29 (2016)
38. Simonyan, K., Zisserman, A.: Very deep convolutional networks for large-scale image recognition. In: Proceedings of the International Conference on Learning Representations (2015)
39. Tan, W.R., Chan, C.S., Aguirre, H.E., Tanaka, K.: Ceci n'est pas une pipe: a deep convolutional network for fine-art paintings classification. In: Proceedings of the IEEE International Conference on Image Processing, pp. 3703–3707. IEEE (2016)
40. Van Hoorick, B.: Image outpainting and harmonization using generative adversarial networks. arXiv preprint arXiv:1912.10960 (2019)
41. Vaswani, A., et al.: Attention is all you need. In: Advances in Annual Conference on Neural Information Processing Systems, vol. 30 (2017)
42. Wang, T.C., Liu, M.Y., Zhu, J.Y., Tao, A., Kautz, J., Catanzaro, B.: High-resolution image synthesis and semantic manipulation with conditional GANs. In: Proceedings of the IEEE/CVF Conference on Computer Vision and Pattern Recognition, pp. 8798–8807 (2018)
43. Wang, Y., Tao, X., Shen, X., Jia, J.: Wide-context semantic image extrapolation. In: Proceedings of the IEEE/CVF Conference on Computer Vision and Pattern Recognition, pp. 1399–1408 (2019)
44. Yang, Z., Dong, J., Liu, P., Yang, Y., Yan, S.: Very long natural scenery image prediction by outpainting. In: Proceedings of the IEEE/CVF International Conference on Computer Vision. pp. 10561–10570 (2019)
45. Yu, J., Lin, Z., Yang, J., Shen, X., Lu, X., Huang, T.S.: Generative image inpainting with contextual attention. In: Proceedings of the IEEE/CVF Conference on Computer Vision and Pattern Recognition, pp. 5505–5514 (2018)
46. Zhao, S., Liu, Z., Lin, J., Zhu, J.Y., Han, S.: Differentiable augmentation for data-efficient GAN training. In: Advances in Annual Conference on Neural Information Processing Systems, vol. 33, pp. 7559–7570 (2020)
47. Zhou, D., et al.: DeepViT: towards deeper vision transformer. arXiv preprint arXiv:2103.11886 (2021)
48. Zhu, X., Hu, H., Lin, S., Dai, J.: Deformable convnets V2: more deformable, better results. In: Proceedings of the IEEE/CVF Conference on Computer Vision and Pattern Recognition, pp. 9308–9316 (2019)

# Unleashing Transformers: Parallel Token Prediction with Discrete Absorbing Diffusion for Fast High-Resolution Image Generation from Vector-Quantized Codes

Sam Bond-Taylor[1]([✉]) [ID], Peter Hessey[1] [ID], Hiroshi Sasaki[1] [ID],
Toby P. Breckon[1,2] [ID], and Chris G. Willcocks[1] [ID]

[1] Department of Computer Science, Durham University, Durham, UK
{samuel.e.bond-taylor,peter.hessey,hiroshi.sasaki,toby.breckon,
christopher.g.willcocks}@durham.ac.uk
[2] Department of Engineering, Durham University, Durham, UK

**Abstract.** Whilst diffusion probabilistic models can generate high quality image content, key limitations remain in terms of both generating high-resolution imagery and their associated high computational requirements. Recent Vector-Quantized image models have overcome this limitation of image resolution but are prohibitively slow and unidirectional as they generate tokens via element-wise autoregressive sampling from the prior. By contrast, in this paper we propose a novel discrete diffusion probabilistic model prior which enables parallel prediction of Vector-Quantized tokens by using an unconstrained Transformer architecture as the backbone. During training, tokens are randomly masked in an order-agnostic manner and the Transformer learns to predict the original tokens. This parallelism of Vector-Quantized token prediction in turn facilitates unconditional generation of globally consistent high-resolution and diverse imagery at a fraction of the computational expense. In this manner, we can generate image resolutions exceeding that of the original training set samples whilst additionally provisioning per-image likelihood estimates (in a departure from generative adversarial approaches). Our approach achieves state-of-the-art results in terms of the manifold overlap metrics Coverage (LSUN Bedroom: 0.83; LSUN Churches: 0.73; FFHQ: 0.80) and Density (LSUN Bedroom: 1.51; LSUN Churches: 1.12; FFHQ: 1.20), and performs competitively on FID (LSUN Bedroom: 3.27; LSUN Churches: 4.07; FFHQ: 6.11) whilst offering advantages in terms of both computation and reduced training set requirements.

**Keywords:** Generative model · Diffusion · High-resolution image synthesis

S. Bond-Taylor and P. Hessey—Authors contributed equally. Source code for this work is available at https://github.com/samb-t/unleashing-transformers

**Supplementary Information** The online version contains supplementary material available at https://doi.org/10.1007/978-3-031-20050-2_11.

**Fig. 1.** Our approach uses a discrete diffusion to quickly generate high quality images optionally larger than the training data (right).

# 1   Introduction

Artificially generating plausible photo-realistic images, at ever higher resolutions, has long been a goal when designing deep generative models. Recent advancements have benefited fields such as medical image synthesis [23], computer graphics [11,91], image editing [52], image translation [77], and super-resolution [33].

These methods can be divided into five main classes [5], each making different trade-offs to scale to high resolutions. Techniques to scale Generative Adversarial Networks (GANs) [25] include progressive growing [42], large batches [8], and regularisation [53,56]. Variational Autoencoders (VAEs) [49] can be scaled by building complex priors [12,63,84] and correcting samples [89]. Autoregressive approaches can make independence assumptions [69] or partition dimensions [55]. Normalizing Flows use multi-scale architectures [50], while diffusion models can be scaled using SDEs [81] and cascades [33]. Each of these have their own drawbacks, such as unstable training, slow sampling, and lack of global context.

Of particular interest to this work is the popular Transformer architecture [86] which models long distance relationships using a powerful parallelisable attention mechanism. By constraining the Transformer architecture to attend a fixed unidirectional ordering of tokens, they can be used to parameterise a generative autoregressive model [13,64]. However, image data does not conform to such a structure and hence this bias limits the representation ability and unnecessarily restricts the sampling process to be sequential and slow.

Addressing these issues, our main contributions are:

- We propose a parallel token prediction approach for generating Vector-Quantized images allowing much faster sampling than autoregressive models.
- Our approach is able to generate globally consistent images at resolutions exceeding that of the original training data by aggregating multiple context windows, allowing for much larger context regions (Fig. 1).
- Our approach demonstrates state-of-the art performance on three benchmark datasets in terms of Density (LSUN Bedroom: 1.51; LSUN Churches: 1.12;

FFHQ: 1.20) and Coverage (Bedroom: 0.83; Churches: 0.73; FFHQ: 0.80), and is competitive on FID (Bedroom: 3.64; Churches: 4.07; FFHQ: 6.11).

## 2   Prior Work

Extensive work in deep generative modelling [5] and self-supervised learning [20] laid the foundations for this research, which we review here in terms of both existing models (Sects. 2.1–2.4) and Transformer architectures (Sect. 2.5).

### 2.1   Autoregressive Models

Autoregressive models are a family of powerful generative models capable of directly maximising the likelihood of the data on which they are trained. These models have achieved impressive image generation results, however, their sequential nature limits them to relatively low dimensional data [14,41,62,71,76,85].

The training and inference process for autoregressive models is based on the chain rule. By decomposing inputs into components $x = \{x_1, ..., x_n\}$, an autoregressive model with parameters $\theta$ can generate new latent samples sequentially:

$$p_\theta(x) = p_\theta(x_1, x_2, ..., x_n) = \prod_{i=1}^{n} p_\theta(x_i|x_1, ..., x_{i-1}). \tag{1}$$

For many tasks, appropriate input orderings are not obvious; since the receptive field is limited to previous tokens, this can significantly affect sample quality.

### 2.2   Vector-Quantized Image Models

To scale autoregressive models to high-resolution data, Vector-Quantized image models can be used. These learn a highly compressed discrete representation taking advantage of an information rich codebook [63]. A convolutional encoder downsamples images $x$ to a smaller spatial resolution, $E(x) = \{e_1, e_2, ..., e_L\} \in \mathbb{R}^{L \times D}$. A simple quantisation approach is to use the argmax operation which maps continuous encodings to their closest elements in a finite codebook of vectors [63]. Specifically, for a codebook $\mathcal{C} \in \mathbb{R}^{K \times D}$, where $K$ is the number of discrete codes in the codebook and $D$ is the dimension of each code, each $e_i$ is mapped via a nearest-neighbour lookup onto a discrete codebook value, $c_j \in \mathcal{C}$:

$$z_q = \{q_1, q_2, ..., q_L\} , \text{ where } q_i = \min_{c_j \in \mathcal{C}} \|e_i - c_j\|. \tag{2}$$

As this operation is non-differentiable, the straight-through gradient estimator [3] is used to approximate gradients resulting in bias. The quantized latents are fed through a decoder $\hat{x} = G(z_q)$ to reconstruct the input based on a perceptual reconstruction loss [22,92]; this process is trained by minimising the loss $\mathcal{L}_{VQ}$,

$$\mathcal{L}_{VQ} = \mathcal{L}_{rec} + \|sg[E(x)] - z_q\|_2^2 + \beta\|sg[z_q] - E(x)\|_2^2. \tag{3}$$

## 2.3  Discrete Energy-Based Models

Since the causal nature of autoregressive models limits their representation ability, other approaches with less constrained architectures have begun to outperform them even on likelihood [48]. Energy-based models (EBMs) are an enticing method for representing discrete data as they permit unconstrained architectures with global context. Implicit EBMs define an unnormalised distribution over data that is typically learned through contrastive divergence [19,31]. Unfortunately, sampling EBMs using Gibbs sampling is impractical for high dimensional discrete data. However, incorporating gradients can reduce mixing times [27].

Similar to autoregressive models, masked language models (MLMs) such as BERT [15] model the conditional probability of the data. However, these are trained bidirectionally by randomly masking a subset of tokens from the input sequence, allowing a much richer context than autoregressive approaches. Some attempts have been made to define an implicit energy function using the conditional probabilities [87], however, obtaining true samples leads to very long sample times and we found them to be ineffective at modelling longer sequences [26].

## 2.4  Discrete Denoising Diffusion Models

Diffusion models [32,80] define a Markov chain $q(\boldsymbol{x}_{1:T}|\boldsymbol{x}_0) = \prod_{t=1}^{T} q(\boldsymbol{x}_t|\boldsymbol{x}_{t-1})$ that gradually destroys data $\boldsymbol{x}_0$ by adding noise over a fixed number of steps $T$ so that $\boldsymbol{x}_T$ contains little to no information about $\boldsymbol{x}_0$ and can be easily sampled. The reverse procedure is a generative model that gradually denoises towards the data distribution $p_\theta(\boldsymbol{x}_{0:T}) = p_\theta(\boldsymbol{x}_T) \prod_{t=1}^{T} p_\theta(\boldsymbol{x}_{t-1}|\boldsymbol{x}_t)$, learned by optimising the variational upper bound on negative log-likelihood, with $t^{\text{th}}$ term

$$\mathbb{E}_{q(\boldsymbol{x}_{t+1}|\boldsymbol{x}_0)} \left[ D_{KL}(q(\boldsymbol{x}_t|\boldsymbol{x}_{t+1},\boldsymbol{x}_0) \,\|\, p_\theta(\boldsymbol{x}_t|\boldsymbol{x}_{t+1})) \right], \tag{4}$$

where sampling from the reverse process is not required during training. In continuous spaces, distributions are typically parameterised as Normal distributions.

Discrete diffusion models [1,36,80] constrain the state space so that $\boldsymbol{x}_t$ is a discrete random variable falling into one of $K$ categories. As such, the forward process can be represented as categorical distributions $q(\boldsymbol{x}_t|\boldsymbol{x}_{t-1}) = \mathrm{Cat}(\boldsymbol{x}_t; \boldsymbol{p} = \boldsymbol{x}_{t-1}\boldsymbol{Q}_t)$ for one-hot $\boldsymbol{x}_{t-1}$ where $\boldsymbol{Q}_t$ is a matrix denoting the probabilities of moving to each successive state. $q(\boldsymbol{x}_t|\boldsymbol{x}_0)$ can be expressed as $q(\boldsymbol{x}_t|\boldsymbol{x}_0) = \mathrm{Cat}(\boldsymbol{x}_t; \boldsymbol{p} = \overline{\boldsymbol{Q}}_t)$ where $\overline{\boldsymbol{Q}}_t = \boldsymbol{x}_0\boldsymbol{Q}_1\boldsymbol{Q}_2\cdots\boldsymbol{Q}_t$, therefore scaling is simple if $\overline{\boldsymbol{Q}}_t$ can be expressed in closed form. Transition processes include moving states with some low uniform probability [36], moving to nearby states with some probability based on similarity or distance, and of particular interest to this work, masking inputs similar to generative MLMs.

## 2.5  Transformers

Transformers [86] have made a huge impact across many fields [30] due to their power and flexibility. They are based on self-attention, a function which allows

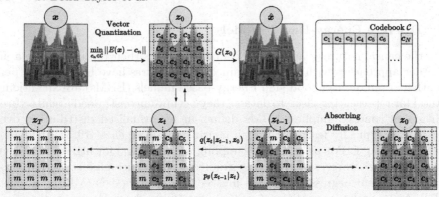

**Fig. 2.** Our approach uses a discrete absorbing diffusion model to represent Vector-Quantized images allowing fast high-resolution image generation. Specifically, after compressing images to an information-rich discrete space, elements are randomly masked and an unconstrained Transformer is trained to denoise the data, using global context to ensure samples are consistent and high quality.

interactions with strong gradients between all inputs, irrespective of their spatial relationships. This procedure (Eq. 5) encodes inputs as key-value pairs, where values $V$ represent embedded inputs and keys $K$ act as an indexing method, subsequently, a set of queries $Q$ are used to select which values to observe:

$$\mathrm{Attn}(Q, K, V) = \mathrm{softmax}\left(\frac{QK^T}{\sqrt{d_k}}\right)V. \tag{5}$$

While this allows long distance dependencies to be learned, complexity increases with sequence length quadratically, making scaling difficult. Approaches to mitigate this include independence assumptions [69], sparsity [13], and low rank [46].

## 3   Method

Modelling Vector-Quantized image representations with autoregressive models has a number of downsides, namely the slow sequential nature of sampling and the requirement to choose an input ordering which ignores the 2D structure of images thereby restricting modelling ability. To address these problems, we propose using a discrete diffusion model to represent Vector-Quantized image representations; this is visualised in Fig. 2. We hypothesise that by removing the autoregressive constraint, allowing bidirectional context when generating samples, not only will it be possible to speed up sampling, but an improved feature representation will be learned, enabling higher quality image generation.

## 3.1   Sampling Globally Coherent Latents

Once the training data is encoded as discrete, integer-valued latents $z \in \mathbb{Z}^D$, a discrete diffusion model can be used to learn the distribution over this highly compressed space. Specifically, we use the absorbing state diffusion [1] where in each forward time step $t$, each discrete latent at coordinate $i$, $[z]_i$, is independently either kept the same or masked out entirely with with probability $\beta_t = \frac{1}{T-t+1}$; the reverse process gradually unveils these masks. In this formulation, the transition matrix is defined as $Q_t = (1 - \beta_t)I + \beta_t 1 e_m^T$ where $e_m$ is a vector with a one on mask states $m$ and zeros elsewhere. Rather than directly approximating $p_\theta(z_{t-1}|z_t)$, training stochasticity is reduced by predicting $p_\theta(z_0|z_t)$ [32]. In this case, the variational bound reduces to

$$\mathbb{E}_{q(z_0)} \left[ \sum_{t=1}^{T} \frac{1}{t} \mathbb{E}_{q(z_t|z_0)} \left[ \sum_{[z_t]_i=m} \log p_\theta([z_0]_i|z_t) \right] \right]. \tag{6}$$

With $p_\theta$ modelled using multinomial distributions, a temperature $\tau < 1$ can be applied to the logits to improve sample quality at the expense of diversity.

Unlike, uniform diffusion, absorbing diffusion is an effective strategy for Vector-Quantized image modelling as noisy elements are removed entirely rather than being changed to a different value which in the discrete case may be unrelated but are much less easy to identify. Gaussian and token distance transitions which change states based on embedding distances are similarly ineffective as Vector-Quantized latents are not ordinal meaning that state changes can significantly change tokens' semantics. This effectiveness is further evidenced by the success of BERT [15] which similarly learns to denoise randomly masked data.

**Architecture.** Esser et al. [22] demonstrated that in the autoregressive case, Transformers [86] are better suited for modelling Vector-Quantized images than convolutional approaches due to the importance of long-distance relationships in this compressed form. As such, we use transformers to model the prior, but without the architectural restrictions imposed by autoregressive approaches.

**Fast Sampling.** Because the diffusion model is trained to predict $p(z_0|z_t)$, it is possible to sample skipping an arbitrary number of time steps $k$, $p_\theta(z_{t-k}|z_t)$, allowing sampling in significantly fewer steps than autoregressive approaches.

## 3.2   Addressing Gradient Variance

When inputs are very noisy (at time steps close to $T$), denoising is difficult and the stochastic training results in gradients with high variance. As such, in practice continuous diffusion models are trained to estimate the noise rather than directly predict the denoised data, significantly reducing the variance. Unfortunately, no relevant reparameterisation currently exists for discrete distributions [36]. Instead, we address this problem by reweighting the ELBO based on the information available at time $t$, $\frac{T-t+1}{T}$ [1], so that components of the loss at time steps closer to $T$ are weighted less than earlier steps. This effectively alters the learning rate based on gradient variance, improving convergence,

$$\mathbb{E}_{q(z_0)}\left[\sum_{t=1}^{T}\frac{T-t+1}{T}\mathbb{E}_{q(z_t|z_0)}\left[\sum_{[z_t]_i=m}\log p_\theta([z_0]_i|z_t)\right]\right]. \tag{7}$$

This is equivalent to the loss obtained by assuming the posterior does not have access to $z_t$, i.e. if the $t-1^{th}$ loss term is $D_{KL}(q(z_{t-1}|z_0) \| p_\theta(z_{t-1}|z_t))$ (proof in Appendix B). Since we predict $z_0$ this assumption does not harm the training.

### 3.3   Generating High-Resolution Images

Using convolutions to build Vector-Quantized image models encourages latents to be highly spatially correlated with generated images. It is therefore possible to construct essentially arbitrarily sized images by generating latents with the required shape. We propose an approach that allows globally consistent images substantially larger than those in the training data to be generated.

First, a large $a$ by $b$ array of mask tokens, $\bar{z}_T = m^{a \times b}$, is initialised that corresponds to the size of image we wish to generate. In order to capture the maximum context when approximating $\bar{z}_0$ we apply the denoising network to all subsets of $\bar{z}_t$ with the same spatial size as the usual inputs of the network, aggregating estimates at each location. Specifically, using $c_j(\bar{z}_t)$ to represent local subsets, we approximate the denoising distribution as a mixture,

$$p([\bar{z}_0]_i|\bar{z}_t) \approx \frac{1}{Z}\sum_{j} p([\bar{z}_0]_i|c_j(\bar{z}_t)), \tag{8}$$

where the sum is over subsets $c_j$ that contain the $i^{th}$ latent and $Z$ is the normalising constant. For extremely large images, this can require a very large number of function evaluations, however, the sum can be approximated by striding over latents with a step $> 1$ or by randomly selecting positions.

### 3.4   Improving Code Representations

There are various options to obtain high-quality image representations including using large numbers of latents and codes [67] or building a hierarchy of latent variables [68]. We use the adversarial framework proposed by Esser et al. [22] to achieve higher compression rates with high-quality codes using only a single GPU, without tying our approach to the characteristics typically associated with generative adversarial models. Additionally, we apply differentiable augmentations $T$, such as translations and colour jitter, to all discriminator inputs; this has proven to be effective at improving sample quality across methods [41,93]. The overall loss $\mathcal{L}$ is a linear combination of $\mathcal{L}_{VQ}$, the Vector-Quantized loss, and $\mathcal{L}_G$ which uses a discriminator $D$ to assess realism based on an adaptive weight $\lambda$. On some datasets, $\lambda$ can grow to extremely large values hindering training. We find simply clamping $\lambda$ at a maximum value $\lambda_{max} = 1$ an effective solution that stabilises training,

$$\mathcal{L} = \min_{E,G,\mathcal{C}} \max_{D} \mathbb{E}_{p_d} \left[ \mathcal{L}_{\text{VQ}} + \lambda\, \mathcal{L}_{\text{G}} \right], \quad (9a) \qquad \lambda = \min \left( \frac{\nabla_{G_L}[\mathcal{L}_{\text{rec}}]}{\nabla_{G_L}[\mathcal{L}_{\text{G}}] + \delta}, \lambda_{\max} \right), \quad (9b)$$

$$\mathcal{L}_{\text{G}} = \log D(T(\boldsymbol{x})) + \log(1 - D(T(\hat{\boldsymbol{x}}))). \quad (9c)$$

The argmax quantisation approach can result in codebook collapse, where some codes are never used; while other quantisation methods can reduce this [17,40, 54,67], we found argmax to yield the highest reconstruction quality.

**Fig. 3.** Samples from our models trained on $256 \times 256$ datasets: LSUN Churches, FFHQ, and LSUN Bedroom.

## 4  Evaluation

We evaluate our approach on three high-resolution $256 \times 256$ datasets: LSUN Bedroom, LSUN Churches [90], and FFHQ [44]. Section 4.1 evaluates the quality of samples from our proposed model. Section 4.2 demonstrates the representation abilities of absorbing diffusion models applied to the learned discrete latent spaces, including how sampling can be sped up, improvements over equivalent autoregressive models, and the effect of our reweighted ELBO. Finally, Sect. 4.3 evaluates our Vector-Quantized image model.

In all experiments, our absorbing diffusion model parameterised with an 80M parameter Transformer Encoder [86] is applied to $16 \times 16$ latents discretised to a codebook with 1024 entries and optimised using the Adam optimiser [47]. While, as noted by Esser et al. [22], a GPT2-medium [66] architecture (307M parameters) fits onto a GPU with 12GB of VRAM, in practice this requires small batch sizes and learning rates making training in reasonable times impractical. More details can be found in Appendix A. Source code is available here.

### 4.1  Sample Quality

In this section we evaluate our model quantitatively and qualitatively. In contrast to other multi-step methods, our approach allows sampling in the fewest steps. Samples can be found in Figs. 3 and 5 which are high quality and diverse.

**Limitations of the FID Metric.** FID is a popular choice for evaluating sample quality, it has been found to correlate well with image quality and is efficient to calculate. However, it unrealistically approximates the data distribution as Gaussian in embedding space and is insensitive to the global structure of the data distribution [83]. For likelihood models, calculating NLL is possible instead; by fine tuning our approach to model pixels as Gaussians, likelihood can be estimated as $p(x) \geq p(x|z)p(z)$ [63], giving 2.72BPD on 5-bit FFHQ. However, likelihood does not correlate well with quality [82]. Other approaches that address these issues [6] include PPL [44], which assesses sample consistency through latent interpolations; IMD [83], which uses all moments making it sensitive to global structure; and MTD [2], which compares image manifolds.

**Table 1.** Precision (P), Recall (R), Density (D), and Coverage (C) [51,57,75] for approaches trained on LSUN Churches, LSUN Bedroom, and FFHQ.

| Model | LSUN Churches | | | | LSUN Bedroom | | | | FFHQ | | | |
|---|---|---|---|---|---|---|---|---|---|---|---|---|
| | P ↑ | R ↑ | D ↑ | C ↑ | P ↑ | R ↑ | D ↑ | C ↑ | P ↑ | R ↑ | D ↑ | C ↑ |
| DCT [58] | 0.60 | 0.48 | – | – | 0.44 | **0.56** | – | – | 0.51 | 0.40 | – | – |
| TT [22] | 0.67 | 0.29 | 1.08 | 0.60 | 0.61 | 0.33 | 1.15 | 0.75 | 0.64 | 0.29 | 0.89 | 0.5 |
| VDVAE [12] | – | – | – | – | – | – | – | – | 0.59 | 0.20 | 0.80 | 0.50 |
| PGGAN [42] | 0.61 | 0.38 | 0.83 | 0.63 | 0.43 | 0.40 | 0.70 | 0.64 | – | – | – | – |
| StyleGAN [44] | – | – | – | – | 0.55 | 0.48 | 0.96 | 0.80 | – | – | – | – |
| StyleGAN2 [45] | 0.60 | 0.43 | 0.83 | 0.68 | – | – | – | - | 0.69 | 0.40 | 1.12 | 0.80 |
| ProjGAN [78] | 0.56 | **0.53** | 0.65 | 0.64 | 0.55 | 0.46 | 0.90 | 0.79 | 0.66 | 0.46 | 0.98 | 0.77 |
| **Ours** ($\tau = 1.0$) | 0.70 | 0.42 | **1.12** | 0.73 | 0.64 | 0.38 | 1.27 | 0.81 | 0.69 | 0.48 | 1.06 | 0.77 |
| **Ours** ($\tau = 0.9$) | **0.71** | 0.45 | 1.07 | **0.74** | **0.67** | 0.38 | **1.51** | **0.83** | **0.73** | 0.48 | **1.20** | **0.80** |

**PRDC.** In this work, we evaluate using Precision (P) and Recall (R) [75] approaches (Table 1) which, unlike FID, evaluate sample quality and diversity separately by quantifying the overlap between the data and sample distributions, and have been used in similar recent work assessing high-resolution image generation [38,45,58,68]. Precision is the expected likelihood of fake samples lying on the data manifold and recall vice versa. These metrics are computed by approximating the data and sample manifolds as hyper-spheres around data and sample points respectively; manifold $\mathrm{m}(X_1, \ldots, X_N) = \bigcup_{i=1}^{N} B(X_i, \mathrm{NND}_k(X_i))$, where $B(x, r)$ is a hypersphere around $x$ with radius $r$ and $\mathrm{NND}_k$ is $k^{\mathrm{th}}$ nearest neighbour distance [51]. While modelling manifolds as hyperspheres is a flawed assumption, it is beneficial to evaluate on multiple metrics to obtain a more accurate representation of performance. We also calculate Density (D) and Coverage (C) which are modifications to Precision and Recall respectively that address manifold overestimation [57]. Formally, these metrics can be defined as,

$$P = \frac{1}{M} \sum_{j=1}^{M} 1_{Y_j \in \mathrm{m}(X_1,\ldots,X_N)}, \quad (10a) \quad D = \frac{1}{kM} \sum_{j=1}^{M} \sum_{i=1}^{N} 1_{Y_j \in B(X_i, \mathrm{NND}_k(X_i))}, \quad (10b)$$

$$R = \frac{1}{N} \sum_{i=1}^{N} 1_{X_i \in m(Y_1,...,Y_M)}, \quad (10c) \qquad C = \frac{1}{N} \sum_{i=1}^{N} 1_{\exists j s.t Y_j \in B(X_i, \mathrm{NND}_k(X_i))}. \quad (10d)$$

Due to limited computing resources, we are unable to provide Density and Coverage scores for DCT [58] and PRDC scores for StyleGAN2 on LSUN Bedroom since training on a standard GPU would take more than 30 days, much more than the 10 days to train our models. On LSUN our approach achieves the highest Precision, Density, and Coverage; indicating that the data and sample manifolds have the most overlap. On FFHQ our approach achieves the highest Precision and Recall. When sampling with lower temperatures to improve FID, generative models generally trade precision and recall [45,68]; since we also calculate FID with $\tau = 0.9$, we evaluate the effect on PRDC. In almost all cases this improves scores, indicating that more samples in data regions, increasing overlap.

**Fig. 4.** Our method allows unconditional images larger than those seen during training to be generated by applying the denoising network to all subsets of the image, aggregating probabilities to encourage global continuity.

**FID.** In Table 2 we calculate the Fréchet Inception Distance (FID) of samples from our models using torch-fidelity [61]. Using a fraction of the parameters of other Vector-Quantized image models, our approach achieves much lower FID.

**Higher Resolution.** Figure 4 shows samples generated at higher resolutions (up to $768 \times 256$) than the observed training data using the method described in Sect. 3.3 with $\tau = 0.8$. Even at larger scales we observe high-quality, diverse, and consistent samples.

**Table 2.** FID comparison on FFHQ, LSUN Bedroom and Churches (lower is better).

| Method | Params | Bed | Church | FFHQ |
|---|---|---|---|---|
| DDPM [32] | 114M | 6.36 | 7.89 | – |
| DCT [58] | 448M | 6.40 | 7.56 | – |
| VDVAE [12] | 115M | – | – | 28.5 |
| TT [21,22] | 600M | 6.35 | 7.81 | 9.6 |
| I-BART [21] | 2.1B | 5.51 | 7.32 | 9.57 |
| PGGAN [42] | 47M | 8.34 | 6.42 | – |
| SGAN2 [45] | 60M | 2.35 | 3.86 | 3.8 |
| ADM [16] | 552M | 1.90 | – | – |
| ProjGAN [78] | 106M | 1.52 | 1.59 | 3.39 |
| **Ours** ($\tau = 1.0$) | 145M | 5.07 | 5.58 | 7.12 |
| **Ours** ($\tau = 0.9$) | 145M | 3.27 | 4.07 | 6.11 |

## 4.2   Absorbing Diffusion

In this section we analyse the usage of absorbing diffusion for high-resolution image generation, determining how many sampling steps are required to obtain high-quality samples and ablating the components of our approach.

**Sampling Speed.** Our approach applies a diffusion process to a highly compressed image representation, meaning it is already 18× faster to sample from than DDPM (ours: 3.8 s, DDPM: 70 s per image on a NVIDIA RTX 2080 Ti). However, since the absorbing diffusion model is trained to approximate $p(z_0|z_t)$ it is possible to speed the sampling process up further by skipping arbitrary numbers of time steps, unmasking multiple latents at once. In Table 3 we explore how sample quality is affected using a simple step skipping scheme: evenly skipping a constant number of steps so that the total number of steps meets some fixed computational budget. As expected, FID increases with fewer sampling steps.

(a) Non-cherry picked, $\tau = 0.9$, 256×256 LSUN Churches samples.

(b) Non-cherry picked, $\tau = 0.85$, 256×256 FFHQ samples.

(c) Non-cherry picked, $\tau = 0.9$, 256×256 LSUN Bedroom samples.

**Fig. 5.** Samples from our approach are diverse and high quality.

However, the increase in FID is minor relative to the improvement in sampling speed: our approach achieves similar FID to the equivalent autoregressive model using half the number of steps. With 50 sampling steps, our approach is 88× faster than DDPMs. Using a more sophisticated step selection scheme such as dynamic programming [88], FID could potentially be reduced further.

**Autoregressive vs Absorbing DDPM.** Table 4 compares the representation ability of our absorbing diffusion model with an autoregressive model, both utilising exactly the same Transformer architecture, but with the Transformer unconstrained in the diffusion case. On both datasets diffusion achieves lower FID, which is calculated in the image space. Validation NLL is evaluated in latent space (i.e. $-\log p(z)$) and again the diffusion model outperforms the autoregressive model despite being trained on a harder task with the same number of parameters, indicating that the diffusion models better approximate the prior distribution. Following previous works, early stopping was used to prevent autoregressive models from overfitting [21,41]; increasing weight decay and dropout in some cases slightly improved validation NLL but caused FID to increase.

**Table 3.** Our approach allows sampling in much fewer steps with only minor FID increase.

| Steps | 50 | 100 | 150 | 200 | 256 |
|---|---|---|---|---|---|
| Church | 6.86 | 6.09 | 5.81 | 5.68 | 5.58 |
| Church ($\tau = 0.9$) | 4.90 | 4.40 | 4.22 | 4.19 | 4.07 |
| FFHQ | 9.60 | 7.90 | 7.53 | 7.52 | 7.12 |
| FFHQ ($\tau = 0.9$) | 6.87 | 6.24 | 6.16 | 6.14 | 6.11 |

**Table 4.** FID and validation latent NLL (in bpd) using the same Transformer. *=Default VQGAN

| Method | Churches | | FFHQ | |
|---|---|---|---|---|
| | FID ↓ | NLL ↓ | FID ↓ | NLL ↓ |
| *AR | 13.23 | 6.67 | 9.47 | 6.65 |
| *Absorbing | 11.84 | 6.41 | 8.52 | 6.48 |
| AR | 5.93 | 6.24 | 8.15 | 6.18 |
| Absorbing | **5.58** | **6.01** | **7.12** | **5.96** |

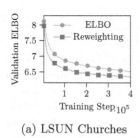

(a) LSUN Churches

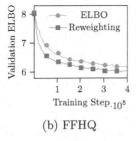

(b) FFHQ

**Fig. 6.** Models trained with reweighting converge faster than models trained on ELBO.

**Table 5.** Effect of proposed VQGAN changes on FID.

| Modifications | Churches | FFHQ |
|---|---|---|
| Default | 5.25 | 3.37 |
| $\lambda_{max} = 1$ | 8.67 | 4.72 |
| DiffAug | 5.16 | 6.57 |
| Both | **2.70** | **3.12** |

**Reweighted ELBO.** In Sect. 3.2 we proposed using a reweighted ELBO when training the diffusion model to reduce gradient variance. We evaluate this in Fig. 6 by comparing validation ELBO (calculated with Eq. 6) during training for models trained directly on ELBO and our reweighting. The models trained on reweighted ELBO converge substantially faster, demonstrating that our reweighting is valid and simplifies optimisation.

### 4.3    Reconstruction Quality

In Table 5 we evaluate the effect of DiffAug [93] and $\lambda$ limiting on Vector-Quantized image models. While each technique individually can lead to worse FID due to imbalance between the generator and discriminator, we found combining techniques offered the most stability and improved FID across all datasets.

Temperature

(a) Impact of sampling temperature on diversity. For small temperature changes it is unclear how bias changes.

(b) Our bidirectional approach allows local image editing by targeting regions to be changed (highlighted in grey).

**Fig. 7.** Evaluation of practical use cases of our proposed generative model.

### 4.4    Sample Diversity

To improve sample quality, many generative models are sampled using a reduced temperature or by truncating distributions. This is problematic, as these methods amplify any biases in the dataset. We visualise the impact of temperature on sampling from a model trained on FFHQ in Fig. 7a. For very low temperatures the bias the obvious: samples are mostly front-facing white men with brown hair on solid white/black backgrounds. Exactly how the bias changes for more subtle temperature changes is less clear, which is problematic. Practitioners should be aware of this effect and it emphasises the importance of dataset balancing.

### 4.5    Image Editing

An additional advantage of using a bidirectional diffusion model to model the latent space is that image inpainting is possible. Since autoregressive models are conditioned only on the upper left region of the image, they are unable to edit internal masked image regions in a consistent manner. Diffusion models, on the other hand, allow masked regions to be placed at arbitrary locations. After a region has been highlighted, we mask corresponding latents, identify the starting time step by counting the number of masked latents, then continue the denoising process from that point. Examples of this process can be found in Fig. 7b.

## 4.6 Limitations

In our experiments we only tested our approach on $256 \times 256$ datasets; directly scaling to higher resolutions would require more GPU resources. However, future work using more efficient Transformer architectures [39] may alleviate this. Our method outperforms all approaches tested on FID except StyleGAN2 [45]; we find that the primary bottleneck is the Vector-Quantized image model, therefore more research is necessary to improve these discrete representations. Whilst our approach is trained for significantly less time than other approaches such as StyleGAN2, the stochastic training procedure means that more training steps are required compared to autoregressive approaches. Although when generating extra-large images the large context window made possible by the diffusion model encourages consistency, a reduced temperature is required, reducing diversity.

## 5  Discussion

While other classes of discrete generative model exist, they are less suitable for Vector-Quantized image modelling than discrete diffusion models: VAEs introduce prior assumptions about the latent space that can be limiting, in particular, continuous spaces may not be appropriate when modelling discrete data [7]; GAN training requires sampling from the generator meaning that gradients must be backpropagated through a discretistion procedure [60]; discrete normalising flows require functions to be invertible, significantly restricting function space [4,37].

Another approach for modelling latent spaces using diffusion models is LSGMs [84], which model continuous latents with SDEs. However, our approach trains more than 15× faster thanks to the efficiency discrete approaches allow. There also exists a variety of different discrete diffusion methods [1,35,79]: ImageBART [21], developed concurrently with this work, models discrete latents using multinomial diffusion with separate autoregressive Transformers per diffusion step leading to slower training, inference, and substantially more parameters than our method. Other concurrent works [10,29,70] which apply diffusion processes to VQGANs are discussed in Appendix D. Also of interest are non-autoregressive discrete methods for translation [24,28,72] and alignment [9,73].

There are a number of avenues that would make for interesting future work based upon the models proposed in this paper: methods that scale diffusion models such as momentum [18], noise schedules [59], cascaded models [34,74] and classifier guidance [16] may yield improved performance. Or, to improve discrete image representations, networks invariant to translation and rotation [43] or other more powerful generative models could be used. Finally, by conditioning on both text and discrete image representations, absorbing diffusion models could allow text-to-image generation and image captioning to be accomplished using a single model with faster run-time than independent approaches [65, 67].

## 6   Conclusion

In this work we proposed a discrete diffusion probabilistic model prior capable of predicting Vector-Quantized image representations in parallel, overcoming the high sampling times, unidirectional nature and overfitting challenges associated with autoregressive priors. Our approach makes no assumptions about the inherent ordering of latents by utilising an unconstrained Transformer architecture. Experimental results demonstrate the ability of our approach to generate diverse, high-quality images, optionally at resolutions exceeding the training samples. Additional work is needed to reduce training times and to efficiently scale our approach to even higher resolutions.

## References

1. Austin, J., Johnson, D., Ho, J., Tarlow, D., van den Berg, R.: Structured Denoising Diffusion Models in Discrete State-Spaces. arXiv preprint arXiv:2107.03006 (2021)
2. Barannikov, S., et al.: Manifold topology divergence: a framework for comparing data manifolds. arXiv preprint arXiv:2106.04024 (2021)
3. Bengio, Y.: Estimating or propagating gradients through stochastic neurons (2013)
4. van den Berg, R., Gritsenko, A.A., Dehghani, M., Sønderby, C.K., Salimans, T.: IDF++: analyzing and improving integer discrete flows for lossless compression. In: International Conference on Learning Representations (2021)
5. Bond-Taylor, S., Leach, A., Long, Y., Willcocks, C.G.: Deep generative modelling: a comparative review of VAEs, GANs, normalizing flows, energy-based and autoregressive models. IEEE Trans. Pattern Anal. Mach. Intell. (2021). https://doi.org/10.1109/TPAMI.2021.3116668
6. Borji, A.: Pros and Cons of GAN Evaluation Measures: New Developments. arXiv preprint arXiv:2103.09396 (2021)
7. Bowman, S.R., Vilnis, L., Vinyals, O., Dai, A.M., Jozefowicz, R., Bengio, S.: Generating Sentences from a Continuous Space. arXiv:1511.06349 (2016)
8. Brock, A., Donahue, J., Simonyan, K.: Large scale GAN training for high fidelity natural image synthesis. In: International Conference on Learning Representations (2019)
9. Chan, W., Saharia, C., Hinton, G., Norouzi, M., Jaitly, N.: Imputer: sequence modelling via imputation and dynamic programming. In: International Conference on Machine Learning, pp. 1403–1413. PMLR (2020)
10. Chang, H., Zhang, H., Jiang, L., Liu, C., Freeman, W.T.: MaskGIT: masked generative image transformer. In: Proceedings of the IEEE/CVF Conference on Computer Vision and Pattern Recognition, pp. 11315–11325 (2022)
11. Chen, X., Cohen-Or, D., Chen, B., Mitra, N.J.: Towards a neural graphics pipeline for controllable image generation. In: Computer Graphics Forum, vol. 40, pp. 127–140. Wiley Online Library (2021)

12. Child, R.: Very deep VAEs generalize autoregressive models and can outperform them on images. In: International Conference on Learning Representations (2021)
13. Child, R., Gray, S., Radford, A., Sutskever, I.: Generating Long Sequences with Sparse Transformers. arXiv preprint arXiv:1904.10509 (2019)
14. Child, R., Gray, S., Radford, A., Sutskever, I.: Generating long sequences with sparse transformers. arXiv:1904.10509 (2019)
15. Devlin, J., Chang, M.W., Lee, K., Toutanova, K.: BERT: pre-training of deep bidirectional transformers for language understanding. In: NAACL-HLT (2019)
16. Dhariwal, P., Nichol, A.: Diffusion models beat GANs on image synthesis. In: Advances in Neural Information Processing Systems 34 (2021)
17. Dieleman, S., Oord, A.v.d., Simonyan, K.: The challenge of realistic music generation: modelling raw audio at scale. In: Advances in Neural Information Processing Systems, vol. 31 (2018)
18. Dockhorn, T., Vahdat, A., Kreis, K.: Score-based generative modeling with critically-damped langevin diffusion. In: International Conference on Learning Representations (2022)
19. Du, Y., Mordatch, I.: Implicit generation and generalization in energy-based models. In: Advances in Neural Information Processing Systems, vol. 33 (2019)
20. Ericsson, L., Gouk, H., Hospedales, T.M.: How well do self-supervised models transfer? In: Proceedings of the IEEE/CVF Conference on Computer Vision and Pattern Recognition, pp. 5414–5423 (2021)
21. Esser, P., Rombach, R., Blattmann, A., Ommer, B.: Imagebart: bidirectional context with multinomial diffusion for autoregressive image synthesis. arXiv preprint arXiv:2108.08827 (2021)
22. Esser, P., Rombach, R., Ommer, B.: Taming Transformers for High-Resolution Image Synthesis. arXiv:2012.09841 (2021)
23. Fetty, L., et al.: Latent space manipulation for high-resolution medical image synthesis via the StyleGAN. Z. Med. Phys. 30(4), 305–314 (2020)
24. Ghazvininejad, M., Levy, O., Liu, Y., Zettlemoyer, L.: Mask-predict: parallel decoding of conditional masked language models. arXiv preprint arXiv:1904.09324 (2019)
25. Goodfellow, I., et al.: Generative adversarial nets. In: Advances in Neural Information Processing Systems, vol. 27 (2014)
26. Goyal, K., Dyer, C., Berg-Kirkpatrick, T.: Exposing the implicit energy networks behind masked language models via metropolis-hastings. arXiv preprint arXiv:2106.02736 (2021)
27. Grathwohl, W., Swersky, K., Hashemi, M., Duvenaud, D., Maddison, C.J.: Oops I took a gradient: scalable sampling for discrete distributions. In: International Conference on Machine Learning (2021)
28. Gu, J., Wang, C., Zhao, J.: Levenshtein transformer. In: Advances in Neural Information Processing Systems 32 (2019)
29. Gu, S., et al.: Vector quantized diffusion model for text-to-image synthesis. In: Proceedings of the IEEE/CVF Conference on Computer Vision and Pattern Recognition, pp. 10696–10706 (2022)
30. Han, K., et al.: A survey on visual transformer. arXiv preprint arXiv:2012.12556 (2020)
31. Hinton, G.E.: Training products of experts by minimizing contrastive divergence. Neural Comput. 14(8), 1771–1800 (2002). https://doi.org/10.1162/089976602760128018
32. Ho, J., Jain, A., Abbeel, P.: Denoising diffusion probabilistic models. In: Advances in Neural Information Processing Systems, vol. 33 (2020)

33. Ho, J., Saharia, C., Chan, W., Fleet, D.J., Norouzi, M., Salimans, T.: Cascaded diffusion models for high fidelity image generation. arXiv preprint arXiv:2106.15282 (2021)
34. Ho, J., Saharia, C., Chan, W., Fleet, D.J., Norouzi, M., Salimans, T.: Cascaded diffusion models for high fidelity image generation. J. Mach. Learn. Res. **23**(47), 1–33 (2022)
35. Hoogeboom, E., Gritsenko, A.A., Bastings, J., Poole, B., van den Berg, R., Salimans, T.: Autoregressive diffusion models. In: International Conference on Learning Representations (2022)
36. Hoogeboom, E., Nielsen, D., Jaini, P., Forré, P., Welling, M.: Argmax flows and multinomial diffusion: towards non-autoregressive language models. arXiv preprint arXiv:2102.05379 (2021)
37. Hoogeboom, E., Peters, J., van den Berg, R., Welling, M.: Integer discrete flows and lossless compression. In: Advances in Neural Information Processing Systems, vol. 32 (2019)
38. Hudson, D.A., Zitnick, C.L.: Generative adversarial transformers. In: Proceedings of the 38th International Conference on Machine Learning, ICML (2021)
39. Jaegle, A., et al.: Perceiver IO: a general architecture for structured inputs & outputs. arXiv preprint arXiv:2107.14795 (2021)
40. Jang, E., Gu, S., Poole, B.: Categorical reparameterization with gumbel-softmax. In: International Conference on Learning Representations (2017)
41. Jun, H., et al.: Distribution augmentation for generative modeling. In: ICML (2020)
42. Karras, T., Aila, T., Laine, S., Lehtinen, J.: Progressive growing of GANs for improved quality, stability, and variation. In: International Conference on Learning Representations (2018)
43. Karras, T., et al.: Alias-Free Generative Adversarial Networks. arXiv preprint arXiv:2106.12423 (2021)
44. Karras, T., Laine, S., Aila, T.: A style-based generator architecture for generative adversarial networks. In: Proceedings of the IEEE/CVF Conference on Computer Vision and Pattern Recognition, pp. 4401–4410 (2019)
45. Karras, T., Laine, S., Aittala, M., Hellsten, J., Lehtinen, J., Aila, T.: Analyzing and improving the image quality of StyleGAN. In: Proceedings of the IEEE/CVF Conference on Computer Vision and Pattern Recognition (2020)
46. Katharopoulos, A., Vyas, A., Pappas, N., Fleuret, F.: Transformers are RNNs: fast autoregressive transformers with linear attention. In: International Conference on Machine Learning (2020)
47. Kingma, D.P., Ba, J.: Adam: A Method for Stochastic Optimization. arXiv preprint arXiv:1412.6980 (2014)
48. Kingma, D.P., Salimans, T., Poole, B., Ho, J.: Variational Diffusion Models. arXiv preprint arXiv:2107.00630 (2021)
49. Kingma, D.P., Welling, M.: Auto-encoding variational bayes. In: International Conference on Learning Representations (2014)
50. Kingma, D.P., Dhariwal, P.: Glow: generative flow with invertible 1x1 convolutions. In: Advances in Neural Information Processing Systems, vol. 31 (2018)
51. Kynkäänniemi, T., Karras, T., Laine, S., Lehtinen, J., Aila, T.: Improved precision and recall metric for assessing generative models. In: Wallach, H., Larochelle, H., Beygelzimer, A., d' Alché-Buc, F., Fox, E., Garnett, R. (eds.) Advances in Neural Information Processing Systems, vol. 32 (2019)
52. Lin, J., Zhang, R., Ganz, F., Han, S., Zhu, J.Y.: Anycost GANs for interactive image synthesis and editing. In: Proceedings of the IEEE/CVF Conference on Computer Vision and Pattern Recognition, pp. 14986–14996 (2021)

53. Liu, B., Zhu, Y., Song, K., Elgammal, A.: Towards faster and stabilized GAN training for high-fidelity few-shot image synthesis. In: International Conference on Learning Representations (2021)
54. Maddison, C.J., Mnih, A., Teh, Y.W.: The concrete distribution: a continuous relaxation of discrete random variables. In: International Conference on Learning Representations (2017)
55. Menick, J., Kalchbrenner, N.: Generating high fidelity images with subscale pixel networks and multidimensional upscaling. In: International Conference on Learning Representations (2019)
56. Miyato, T., Kataoka, T., Koyama, M., Yoshida, Y.: Spectral normalization for generative adversarial networks. In: International Conference on Learning Representations (2018)
57. Naeem, M.F., Oh, S.J., Uh, Y., Choi, Y., Yoo, J.: Reliable fidelity and diversity metrics for generative models. In: International Conference on Machine Learning, pp. 7176–7185 (2020)
58. Nash, C., Menick, J., Dieleman, S., Battaglia, P.W.: Generating images with sparse representations. arXiv preprint arXiv:2103.03841 (2021)
59. Nichol, A.Q., Dhariwal, P.: Improved denoising diffusion probabilistic models. In: International Conference on Machine Learning, pp. 8162–8171. PMLR (2021)
60. Nie, W., Narodytska, N., Patel, A.: RelGAN: relational generative adversarial networks for text generation. In: International Conference on Learning Representations (2019)
61. Obukhov, A., Seitzer, M., Wu, P.W., Zhydenko, S., Kyl, J., Lin, E.Y.J.: High-fidelity performance metrics for generative models in pytorch (2020)
62. van den Oord, A., Kalchbrenner, N., Espeholt, L., kavukcuoglu, k., Vinyals, O., Graves, A.: Conditional Image Generation with PixelCNN Decoders. NeurIPS 29 (2016)
63. van den Oord, A., Vinyals, O., Kavukcuoglu, K.: Neural discrete representation learning. NeurIPS 30 (2017)
64. Parmar, N., et al.: Image transformer. In: ICML (2018)
65. Radford, A., et al.: Learning transferable visual models from natural language supervision. arXiv preprint arXiv:2103.00020 (2021)
66. Radford, A., Wu, J., Child, R., Luan, D., Amodei, D., Sutskever, I.: Language models are unsupervised multitask learners (2019)
67. Ramesh, A., e al.: Zero-shot text-to-image generation. arXiv preprint arXiv:2102.12092 (2021)
68. Razavi, A., van den Oord, A., Vinyals, O.: Generating diverse high-fidelity images with VQ-VAE-2. NeurIPS 32 (2019)
69. Reed, S., et al.: Parallel multiscale autoregressive density estimation. In: International Conference on Machine Learning (2017)
70. Rombach, R., Blattmann, A., Lorenz, D., Esser, P., Ommer, B.: High-resolution image synthesis with latent diffusion models. In: Proceedings of the IEEE/CVF Conference on Computer Vision and Pattern Recognition, pp. 10684–10695 (2022)
71. Roy, A., Saffar, M., Vaswani, A., Grangier, D.: Efficient content-based sparse attention with routing transformers. Trans. Assoc. Comput. Ling. 9, 53–68 (2021)
72. Ruis, L., Stern, M., Proskurnia, J., Chan, W.: Insertion-deletion transformer. arXiv preprint arXiv:2001.05540 (2020)
73. Saharia, C., Chan, W., Saxena, S., Norouzi, M.: Non-autoregressive machine translation with latent alignments. arXiv preprint arXiv:2004.07437 (2020)
74. Saharia, C., Ho, J., Chan, W., Salimans, T., Fleet, D.J., Norouzi, M.: Image super-resolution via iterative refinement. arXiv preprint arXiv:2104.07636 (2021)

75. Sajjadi, M.S., Bachem, O., Lucic, M., Bousquet, O., Gelly, S.: Assessing generative models via precision and recall. In: Advances in Neural Information Processing Systems, vol. 31 (2018)
76. Salimans, T., Karpathy, A., Chen, X., Kingma, D.P.: PixelCNN++: improving the PixelCNN with discretized logistic mixture likelihood and other modifications. ICLR (2017)
77. Sasaki, H., Willcocks, C.G., Breckon, T.P.: UNIT-DDPM: UNpaired image translation with denoising diffusion probabilistic models. arXiv preprint arXiv:2104.05358 (2021)
78. Sauer, A., Chitta, K., Müller, J., Geiger, A.: Projected GANs converge faster. Adv. Neural. Inf. Process. Syst. **34**, 17480–17492 (2021)
79. Savinov, N., Chung, J., Binkowski, M., Elsen, E., van den Oord, A.: Step-unrolled denoising autoencoders for text generation. In: International Conference on Learning Representations (2022)
80. Sohl-Dickstein, J., Weiss, E.A., Maheswaranathan, N., Ganguli, S.: Deep unsupervised learning using nonequilibrium thermodynamics. In: International Conference on Machine Learning (2015)
81. Song, Y., Sohl-Dickstein, J., Kingma, D.P., Kumar, A., Ermon, S., Poole, B.: Score-based generative modeling through stochastic differential equations. In: International Conference on Learning Representations (2021)
82. Theis, L., Oord, A.v.d., Bethge, M.: A note on the evaluation of generative models. arXiv:1511.01844 (2016)
83. Tsitsulin, A., et al.: The shape of data: intrinsic distance for data distributions. In: International Conference on Learning Representations (2020)
84. Vahdat, A., Kreis, K., Kautz, J.: Score-based generative modeling in latent space. In: Advances in Neural Information Processing Systems 34 (2021)
85. Van Den Oord, A., Kalchbrenner, N., Kavukcuoglu, K.: Pixel recurrent neural networks. In: ICML (2016)
86. Vaswani, A., et al.: Attention is all you need. In: Advances in Neural Information Processing Systems, vol. 30 (2017)
87. Wang, A., Cho, K.: BERT has a mouth, and it must speak: BERT as a Markov random field language model. In: NeuralGen (2019)
88. Watson, D., Ho, J., Norouzi, M., Chan, W.: Learning to efficiently sample from diffusion probabilistic models. arXiv preprint arXiv:2106.03802 (2021)
89. Xiao, Z., Kreis, K., Kautz, J., Vahdat, A.: VAEBM: a symbiosis between variational autoencoders and energy-based models. In: International Conference on Learning Representations (2021)
90. Yu, F., Zhang, Y., Song, S., Seff, A., Xiao, J.: Lsun: construction of a large-scale image dataset using deep learning with humans in the loop. arXiv preprint arXiv:1506.03365 (2015)
91. Yu, N., Barnes, C., Shechtman, E., Amirghodsi, S., Lukac, M.: Texture mixer: a network for controllable synthesis and interpolation of texture. In: Proceedings of the IEEE/CVF Conference on Computer Vision and Pattern Recognition, pp. 12164–12173 (2019)
92. Zhang, R., Isola, P., Efros, A.A., Shechtman, E., Wang, O.: The unreasonable effectiveness of deep features as a perceptual metric. In: Proceedings of the IEEE Conference on Computer Vision and Pattern Recognition, pp. 586–595 (2018)
93. Zhao, S., Liu, Z., Lin, J., Zhu, J.Y., Han, S.: Differentiable augmentation for data-efficient GAN training. In: Advances in Neural Information Processing Systems, vol. 33 (2020)

# ChunkyGAN: Real Image Inversion
# via Segments

Adéla Šubrtová[1], David Futschik[1], Jan Čech[1], Michal Lukáč[2], Eli Shechtman[2],
and Daniel Sýkora[1(✉)]

[1] Faculty of Electrical Engineering, Czech Technical University in Prague,
Prague, Czech Republic
{subrtade,futscdav,cechj,sykorad}@fel.cvut.cz
[2] Adobe Research, San Jose, USA
{lukac,elishe}@adobe.com

**Abstract.** We present ChunkyGAN—a novel paradigm for modeling
and editing images using generative adversarial networks. Unlike previous techniques seeking a global latent representation of the input image,
our approach subdivides the input image into a set of smaller components
(chunks) specified either manually or automatically using a pre-trained
segmentation network. For each chunk, the latent code of a generative
network is estimated locally with greater accuracy thanks to a smaller
number of constraints. Moreover, during the optimization of latent codes,
segmentation can further be refined to improve matching quality. This
process enables high-quality projection of the original image with spatial disentanglement that previous methods would find challenging to
achieve. To demonstrate the advantage of our approach, we evaluated it
quantitatively and also qualitatively in various image editing scenarios
that benefit from the higher reconstruction quality and local nature of
the approach. Our method is flexible enough to manipulate even out-of-
domain images that would be hard to reconstruct using global techniques.

**Keywords:** StyleGAN · Image inversion · Segmentation · Latent
editing

## 1 Introduction

The increasing ability of GANs to generate images virtually indistinguishable
from real photographs [12,14], has created a new paradigm for image editing. In
this paradigm, one first estimates a latent code for the network that best reconstructs the input image [13,23], and then manipulates this latent code in specific

---

A. Šubrtová and D. Futschik—Joint first authors.

---

**Supplementary Information** The online version contains supplementary material
available at https://doi.org/10.1007/978-3-031-20050-2_12.

S. Avidan et al. (Eds.): ECCV 2022, LNCS 13683, pp. 189–204, 2022.
https://doi.org/10.1007/978-3-031-20050-2_12

**Fig. 1.** Real image manipulation examples created interactively using our method. The left-most images are the original photographs, the remaining columns show following edits: changing gaze direction, opening mouth, growing a beard and aging. *Source images: Shutterstock*

ways to create particular variations of the input image. With a knowledge of which directions in latent space of a particular generator encode which properties of the output image, it is possible to perform high-level semantic editing of the appearance of the input photo while retaining the original visual features, e.g., adding more hair to a bald person while retaining their identity [18,22].

Due to the nature of adversarial training, a well-trained generator transforms any latent code drawn from the trained distribution into a plausible output, but mapping of an arbitrary in-domain image to a latent code might be difficult or even not possible. Existing methods address this by instead projecting into deeper spaces which makes accurate reconstruction easier, but weakens the original guarantee that every code maps to a plausible output, meaning that manipulated results may be out of domain and visually appear broken. This means there is an inherent trade-off between ease and accuracy of reconstruction, and quality of edited outputs [22], and existing methods perform on the spectrum of this trade-off. For example in StyleGAN2 [14], the original input code $z \in \mathbb{R}^{512}$ is transformed into a latent vector $\mathcal{W} \in \mathbb{R}^{512}$ which is easy to edit but difficult to reconstruct, whereas Abdal et al. [1] use $\mathcal{W}^+ \in \mathbb{R}^{18 \times 512}$ that has enough degrees of freedom to provide good reconstruction, but is more difficult to manipulate.

This issue becomes much more apparent when we examine examples that are in-domain, but far from typical. For example in the case of StyleGAN trained on a dataset of faces, we may consider human faces with unique features or accessories that do not appear in training datasets such as CelebA [15] or FFHQ [13], such as bindis, unusual glasses, heavy occlusions, etc. In these cases even techniques that have greater flexibility such as $\mathcal{S}$-space [23] usually fail.

The source of much of these difficulties are two underlying assumptions: that there exists a single latent code that exactly or almost exactly reconstructs the target image, and that the manifold of representative images is nearly convex with respect to finding such a latent code. But because the number of output pixels is much higher than the number of degrees of freedom in the latent space, we may view the reconstruction problem as overdetermined, and although the aggregated reconstruction loss has local minima that can be found, a minimum for the entire image is not necessarily a minimum for all its regions. In practice, this means that the code retrieval problem is difficult and the solutions we arrive at are in effect suboptimal. In this paper we propose to resolve this difficulty by relaxing exactly these assumptions. We search not for a single latent code to represent the entire image, but rather a vector of latent codes, each corresponding to a segment of the image, such that when assembled they resemble the original image as closely as possible (see Fig. 2).

Since each latent code is then estimated for a much lower dimensional target, each of the regional subproblems become less overdetermined, which makes for an easier optimization problem. This in turn means that we can achieve much lower total error and thus more accurate reconstruction of the original. Besides superior accuracy and greater ability to generalize to the out-of-domain features, the segment-based nature of our method also allows for strictly localized edits, either based on segmentation generated automatically as a by-product of our method, or based on user-specified segments. Thanks to that property, visual content in different segments remains intact and thus helps retain the fidelity of the original photo. This leads to an interesting novel interactive scenario where the user adaptively applies individual local modifications in sequence to achieve a desired output that would normally be difficult to obtain using global manipulation techniques (see examples in Fig. 1). We demonstrate the power of our approach in various use cases that would be difficult to achieve using current state of the art. Moreover, a great advantage of our approach is that it does not replace previous methods but rather serves as a complementary part that, when plugged in, enables even better results than those produced by the technique applied in isolation.

## 2    Related Work

State-of-the-art approaches to finding suitable latent codes for the input image can be broadly split into two major categories: direct optimization and encoder-based techniques.

The first category takes into account the fact that the generator network is differentiable function on its own and thus gradient descent can be used to move from a real image into its latent code [10,11,17,24]. This typically leads to an inversion which is close to the original, however, since constraining the optimization to search across the manifold of naturally looking latent codes is nontrivial, the resulting projection is usually difficult to manipulate.

The other category relies on training an encoder which predicts the specific latent code given an image, using generated samples as training data [5,29].

Tov et al. [22] show that the encoder can learn to embed the real image into the natural manifold much closer than optimization methods, it does, however, often come at the cost of overall reconstruction quality, even considering multi-pass iterative techniques [3] or a modulation of StyleGAN weights [4,7].

Both of these approaches, therefore, are characterized by an important trade-off between faithfulness to the original image and the ability to perform editing operations on the projected latent code. Hybrid approach has also been proposed, such as the one by Zhu et al. [28], in which the direct optimization method is initialized by latent code proposed by a trained encoder, striking a better balance on the trade-off chart, however, the final result is far from ideal in either axis.

The trade-off itself is also not one dimensional. As the representation of the latent code turns into the final image via operations inside the generator network, it becomes easier to invert images into intermediate representations, at the cost of increased dimensionality, making editing more difficult. Recent work [11,25,30] tries to exploit this knowledge by imposing constraints like segmentation on relatively high-level, spatial representations, leading to solutions that can create high-quality inversions at the cost of restricting the set of possible edits.

Ling et al. [16] presented EditGAN that enables to edit images by altering their segmentation masks. In contrast to our technique EditGAN can only change shape and relative position of selected regions. There is no control over the content generated inside the edited area, and it is also challenging to perform global edits. Moreover, EditGAN uses only a single latent code with lower expressive power while relying on a pre-trained DatasetGAN model [27] that jointly generates images and their corresponding semantic segmentations. In our approach, each region have its own latent code, can be added on the fly at arbitrary locations and subsequently edited.

In StyleFlow, Abdal et al. [2] use continuous normalizing flows in the latent space that are conditioned by various attribute features. This enables edit disentanglement comparable to our approach that is, however, redeemed by lower reconstruction quality. Moreover, StyleFlow also requires pre-trained classifiers to find the disentangled attributes along which the edits are performed.

Roich et al. [21] propose that it is possible to fine-tune the generator network itself to improve the reconstruction quality while retaining the editability offered by a natural latent code. While their technique provides a well-rounded solution to both inversion accuracy and latent code editability, it requires fitting and storing per-image generator network, making it more resource-intensive and less suitable for downstream tasks.

In the earlier version of our method [9], segmentation-based inversion was developed for user-assisted local editing. In this extended version, we introduce joint optimization framework that enables automatic projection of the entire image while refining the shape of individual segments.

## 3   Our Approach

Our method accepts a real image $I$ and reconstructs it as a vector of segmentation masks $S = \{S_i\}_{i=1}^n$, where pixel values range continuously from 0 to represent fully outside and 1 fully inside, and a vector of corresponding per-segment latent codes $X^I = \{X^I_i\}^n_{i=1}$. The masks are constrained so that they per-pixel sum up to 1. These latent codes are interpreted as images using a shared image generator $G^I$ and the output image is obtained by pixelwise linear blending, visualised in Fig. 2:

$$O(X^I, S) = \sum_{i=1}^{n} G^I(X^I_i) \cdot S_i. \tag{1}$$

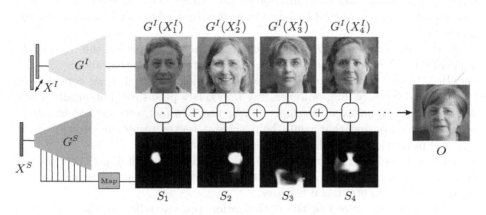

**Fig. 2.** ChunkyGAN flowchart—the output image $O$ computed as a weighted combination of $n$ images generated by a network $G^I$ given a set of $n$ latent codes $X^I$. Weights are specified by a set of $n$ segmentation masks $S$ that can be specified manually or generated automatically by a segmentation network $G^S$ using a latent code $X^S$. *Source image:* Raimond Spekking/CC BY-SA 4.0 (via Wikimedia Commons)

This expression is trivially differentiable with respect to both $S$ and $X$, and is optimized with respect to some dissimilarity measure between $I$ and the composite $O$ just like in a single-segment reconstruction scenario. Unless otherwise specified, in this paper we optimise with respect to the perceptual loss $\mathcal{L}_{\text{LPIPS}}$ of Zhang et al. [26].

Because the semantic segmentation is not universal and can vary dramatically between individual faces, it is necessary to optimize the masks as well. Optimizing them on a per-pixel basis would be memory intensive and would not take advantage of the domain knowledge we have for the problem. Therefore, we use a mask generator $G^S$ to generate them from a segment latent code $X^S$, i.e., $S_i = G^S(X^S)_i$. In this work, we use a segment generator network based on DatasetGAN [27]. It consists of StyleGAN2 generator and a mapping network trained on a modest dataset (a few tens of images) of randomly generated Style-GAN2 images annotated by example based synthesis [8], using a single manually annotated image as exemplar.

To this end, the canonical form of our optimization problem is as follows:

$$\min_{X^S, X^I} \mathcal{L}_{\text{LPIPS}}\left(I, \sum_{i=1}^{n} G^I(X_i^I) \cdot G^S(X^S)_i\right) + \lambda_{reg} \sum_{i=1}^{n} \|X_i^I - X_\mu^I\|_2^2, \qquad (2)$$

where the first term measures reconstruction loss and the second term penalizes dispersion among the latent codes, measured as sum of squared deviations from the mean code $X_\mu^I$. Such regularization helps avoid mutually distant latent codes that do not produce realistic images. This is not typically a problem in the projection step, but during manipulation distant codes may diverge in appearance more quickly. This is caused by limitations in visual coherence in the pre-trained editing directions.

Our approach is orthogonal to the choice of the latent space of the $X$ codes. In general it can be any combination of common latent spaces that allows compact encoding of the input image. In the case of StyleGAN [13,14], we consider $\mathcal{W}$, $\mathcal{W}^+$ [1], and $\mathcal{S}$-space [23], however, any previously published, potentially newly developed or a mixture of methods can be used. In fact, our method is a complementary extension that could help achieve better results regardless of the selected projection method.

In Fig. 3, we show an example of the optimization (per Eq. 2) progression, starting from mean latent codes until convergence. Note that the segments tend to align with semantic facial features.

The processing speed of the optimization process relies on the number of segments and the number of optimization steps. When a joint multi-segment optimization with the DatasetGAN is performed the projection can take several minutes. However, during the interactive editing (as seen in our supplementary video), where segments are specified by the user one-by-one, the method runs at interactive rates on the GPU (a few seconds).

**Fig. 3.** Progression of the optimization. Images and color-coded segmentation maps for iterations 1, 5, 9, 15, 23, 37, 500. *Source image: Adobe Stock*

## 4    Evaluation

To validate our approach we performed two quantitatively and qualitatively evaluated experiments. In the first experiment we validate whether the projections produced by our method can reproduce target photos with greater fidelity when compared to standard projection techniques. In the second experiment we demonstrate the ability of our approach to edit projected images by manipulating estimated latent codes and compare the fidelity of the resulting edits with standard techniques. Finally, we compare our approach with current optimization-based and encoder-based projection techniques.

## 4.1 Fidelity of Projected Images

To quantitatively evaluate fidelity of projected images we took the first 100 images from CelebA dataset [15] excluding blurred images and those with people wearing additional props such as hats or glasses. We then projected all those images globally into $\mathcal{W}$, $\mathcal{W}^+$, $\mathcal{S}$-space, and also locally using our method. When using $\mathcal{W}^+$, we show both cases, with ($\lambda_{reg} = 1$) and without ($\lambda_{reg} = 0$) the regularization. For all projections we measured the LPIPS, identity (measured as cosine distance between ArcFace descriptors [6]), and $L_2$ loss with respect to the original target photos.

**Table 1.** Projection fidelity. Losses were measured between the projected and the original image for each of the projection methods. Each cell reports the loss averaged over the CelebA subset along with the standard deviation. Our method significantly outperforms the baseline methods in all latent spaces for all losses.

| Projection | LPIPS | Identity | $L_2$ |
|---|---|---|---|
| $\mathcal{W}$ | 0.4190 ± 0.0363 | 0.1745 ± 0.1328 | 0.0725 ± 0.0699 |
| Ours in $\mathcal{W}$ | 0.3697 ± 0.0396 | 0.1384 ± 0.1117 | 0.0481 ± 0.0289 |
| $\mathcal{W}^+$ | 0.3675 ± 0.0387 | 0.1195 ± 0.1047 | 0.0436 ± 0.0623 |
| Ours in $\mathcal{W}^+$ | **0.3194 ± 0.0365** | 0.0937 ± 0.0855 | **0.0207 ± 0.0151** |
| Ours in $\mathcal{W}^+$ reg. | 0.3330 ± 0.0350 | **0.0894 ± 0.074** | 0.0217 ± 0.0130 |
| $\mathcal{S}$ | 0.3577 ± 0.0397 | 0.1070 ± 0.0965 | 0.0328 ± 0.0188 |
| Ours in $\mathcal{S}$ | 0.3572 ± 0.0401 | 0.1053 ± 0.0928 | 0.0319 ± 0.0187 |

The resulting numbers are shown in Table 1 which shows losses averaged over all 100 images with corresponding standard deviations. Those confirm that on average our method outperforms global projection methods significantly. This fact is visually apparent from scatter plots shown in Fig. 4 where each point corresponds to an image and its coordinates encode the LPIPS losses for the global and the segmented projection respectively. Red line depicts the margin where losses for both projection methods are equal.

Since the best projection is achieved by our method in $\mathcal{W}^+$, we select $\mathcal{W}^+$ as the default space for our method. The regularization slightly decreases the projection fidelity in terms of LPIPS, but improves the identity and editability, which is discussed in Sect. 4.2.

Because differences between the evaluated methods are difficult to observe in a typical case, we have for the purposes of qualitative evaluation of projection fidelity deliberately pre-selected a subset of hard-to-project images. Specifically, these were images that contain features uncommon in the standard datasets, e.g. bindis, face masks, asymmetric glasses, or occluded faces. For those examples all compared methods were initialized equally (using mean latent vector) and the corresponding projection results are presented in Fig. 5. It is apparent that thanks to greater flexibility of our approach, more realistic projections can be achieved when compared to standard techniques. Moreover, a workable inversion can be obtained even on out-of-domain images as shown in Fig. 5 (two bottom rows).

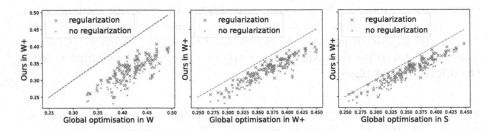

**Fig. 4.** Projection fidelity – scatter plots. Our method is compared with global projections ($\mathcal{W}, \mathcal{W}^+, \mathcal{S}$-space). X and Y axis represent the LPIPS loss between the original image and the image projected globally and projected by our method in $\mathcal{W}^+$ respectively. Each point corresponds to one image from the CelebA subset, in blue and in orange with and without the regularization respectively. The red line delineates the equal LPIPS losses. Our method improves projection for all images in all tested latent spaces. The regularization slightly decreases the projection fidelity, but remains still better than global methods. (Color figure online)

## 4.2   Editability of Projected Images

Quantitative evaluation of editability was performed on the same set of CelebA images used for evaluation of projection fidelity. We pre-selected 4 semantic directions (gender, smile, age, and beard), changed all latent codes $X$ in the same direction with the same magnitude, and finally measured the effect of the edits on identity.

Since the effect of unit strength manipulation along a pre-trained semantic direction can differ among latent spaces and the use of global/local projection, we calibrate the changes to make sure the effect on the manipulated image is equal. To do that we use an image classifier for each semantic direction. For each space and method, we measure image classifier responses while spanning the latent edit strength along a semantic direction for the entire dataset. We use linear regression to find the rate of change of the classifier response to the edit strength, and adjust the edit strength to be equal for all tested methods.

| Real Image | Ours in $\mathcal{W}^+$ with reg | $\mathcal{W}$ | $\mathcal{W}^+$ | $\mathcal{S}$ |

**Fig. 5.** Qualitative assessment of projection fidelity on hard examples. All images were projected with regularization. For more examples refer to the supplementary material. *Source images: Adobe Stock*

**Table 2.** Identity preservation during editing. Identity loss was computed between the projected and the edited images (a), and between the original and the edited images (b). Our method with regularization outperforms all other methods.

| | (a) | | | | (b) | | | |
|---|---|---|---|---|---|---|---|---|
| | Gender | Smile | Age | Beard | Gender | Smile | Age | Beard |
| $\mathcal{W}$ | 0.169 | 0.022 | 0.07 | 0.279 | 0.249 | 0.18 | 0.191 | 0.328 |
| $\mathcal{W}^+$ | 0.209 | 0.02 | 0.095 | 0.296 | 0.256 | 0.128 | 0.171 | 0.325 |
| Ours in $\mathcal{W}^+$ | 0.298 | 0.049 | 0.151 | 0.312 | 0.325 | 0.125 | 0.203 | 0.333 |
| Ours in $\mathcal{W}^+$ reg. | **0.126** | **0.018** | **0.069** | **0.091** | **0.169** | **0.099** | **0.129** | **0.144** |

Table 2 shows a quantitative evaluation of the identity loss between the projected and edited images. It is apparent that the identity losses are the best for our method with the regularization engaged since regularization pushes the codes of all segment images towards latent areas where the linear latent manipulation works better. The results confirm that our method keeps the identity consistent during editing.

Regarding the reconstruction-editability trade-off [22], latent code regularization is essential in order to perform realistic edits. While our method without regularization achieves better results in projection fidelity it performs poorly during editing. By adding the regularization term, projection fidelity slightly deteriorates, but the identity preservation during edits improves by a large margin. The editability can be observed during the classifier-based calibration; methods without regularization need much stronger edits in order to achieve the same editing effect.

For the qualitative evaluation we pre-selected images and directions (age and yaw) that would cause difficulties to standard techniques, i.e., the identity is not well preserved during editing. During the yaw manipulation using our method the segmentation masks were edited as well (the segmentation latent code was manipulated automatically in the same way as the images) to adjust the segments geometrically. Results are presented in Fig. 6 and 7. It is clearly visible that our method keeps the identity better. Figure 7, a man wearing a mask is especially challenging. The global techniques are unable to project the image properly. Our method projects the image faithfully and moreover, the global edits still work. Note that these results were achieved fully automatically, neither manual adjustment of the segmentation partitioning nor any post-processing were applied for images in Fig. 6 and 7.

### 4.3   Comparison with Current State-of-the-Art

To demonstrate how our approach compares to current state-of-the-art in the optimization-based and encoder-based techniques we performed various qualitative experiments seen in Figs. 7 and 8. When compared to current best approaches based on optimization (Pivotal Tuning [21] and StyleFlow [2]), our

Original    Ours in $\mathcal{W}^+$ reg    Ours in $\mathcal{W}^+$    $\mathcal{W}$    $\mathcal{W}^+$

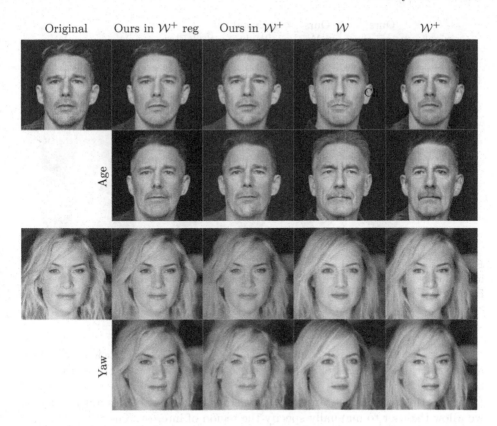

**Fig. 6.** Global edits with the same effective strength. For our methods the latent codes of all segments were manipulated equally. *Source images:* Mingle Media TV *(Kate Winslet),* Neil Grabowsky/Montclair Film *(Ethan Hawke)*

method achieves better or comparable projection quality while still being able to deliver compelling edits (c.f. Fig. 7). Our method also outperforms encoder-based techniques (HyperStyle [4], ReStyle [3], pSp [20], and e4e [22]) with respect to the projection fidelity namely thanks to its ability to reproduce small details that are usually omitted by encoders (c.f. Fig. 8).

## 5    Applications

Aside from the fully automatic solution proposed in Sect. 3 our framework can also be extended to allow for interactive step-by-step manipulation in a few different ways. To facilitate this, we define the notion of a static mask $S^X$ which defines an area of the image which is not changed during the optimisation. In terms of our objective function, this creates a mixed composite:

$$O(X^I, S, S^X, I) = S^X \cdot I + (1 - S^X) \cdot \sum_{i=1}^{n} G^I(X_i^I) \cdot S_i \qquad (3)$$

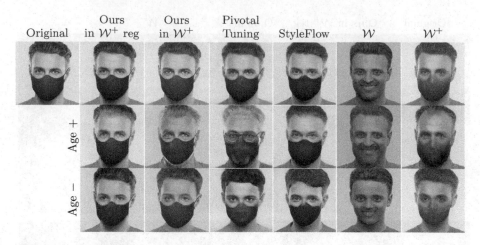

**Fig. 7.** Challenging global edits. The first row depicts the original and the projected images using our approach with and without regularization, Pivotal Tuning [21], Style-Flow [2], $\mathcal{W}$ and $\mathcal{W}^+$ [1]. The remaining two rows show resulting global edits of age. *Source image:* BlochWorld

In practice, for edits with small spatial extent it is often sufficient to reduce the number of segments being optimized to one, in which case there is no need to optimize $S_i$.

Using this static mask, instead of generating segment masks automatically, we allow the user to manually specify the region of interest. The user then runs the projection, edits the latent code, and produces an intermediate composite $O$ which can then become a new $I$ for next iteration. This user-driven iterative scheme is shown in Fig. 9. Such a workflow is intuitive for users as they can specify what they want to change, overview the resulting composition, and then possibly go back and revise their requirements by making additional changes in different regions.

When making the composite $O$ from edited image, even when edits of $X$ are consistent, continuity around boundaries may no longer be guaranteed. Small discrepancies are suppressed automatically thanks to blending with soft masks. When the edit produces more notable global color shift we use Poisson image editing [19] to alleviate them. In most challenging scenario segment boundaries may start to interfere with newly synthesized salient features. In this case continuity can be enforced using a slightly modified version of our segmentation-based approach that will act as semantically meaningful hole-filling as illustrated in Fig. 10.

Suppose we have a photo of a person (Fig. 10a) and the aim is to add glasses. We select a loose region $S_1$ around eyes (Fig. 10b) and run the local projection to get latent code $X_1$ that reproduces the original image within $S_1$ (Fig. 10b). Then we manipulate $X_1$ to add glasses, however, as visible in Fig. 10c the shape of $S_1$ is insufficient to encompass newly added content. To fix this discrepancy we let the user specify correction mask $S_2$ with two connected components (Fig. 10d) and refine $X_1$ to obtain a new code $X_2$ that will match the content within $S_2$ (green region). From the image generated by $X_2$ we then use the dark part that lies inside $S_2$ to make the final composite (Fig. 10e). The $X_2$ code in fact generates a semantically meaningful hole-filling that completes the missing part of glasses.

## 6   Limitations

While the multi-segment reconstruction is remarkably robust, and segmented editing produces superior results for spatially limited edits, we can experience incoherence between segments for global edits (e.g. age, yaw) with high strength. The reason for this is that the editing directions are local linear approximations of the property of interest on the latent manifold, and for higher edit strength this linearity assumption no longer applies. This issue is present also in single-code editing, where it may cause loss of identity which may be in some scenarios more tolerable. With multiple segments however, this is highlighted as a greater change resulting in individual segments to lose identity in different ways and therefore gives rise to incoherence. It only occurs in editing and not in reconstruction because in reconstruction the input image provides effective supervision to maintain coherence between segments.

**Fig. 8.** Projection fidelity of our method with respect to the current state-of-the-art in encoder-based techniques: HyperStyle [4], ReStyle [3], pSp [20], and e4e [22]. *Source images:* Ayush Kejriwal *(bindi)*, BlochWorld *(face mask)*

The incoherence does not usually occur for easy-to-invert images and moderate edits, as seen in Fig. 6, but can be spotted in harder examples with a challenging global edit, as e.g., in Fig. 7 in Age+ of our method with regularization. Nevertheless, the small artifact on the mask shape, can be interactively removed by the hole-filling method demonstrated in Fig. 10.

As another option, this issue could be addressed by formulating and imposing an explicit segment coherence measure during editing, which can be done either

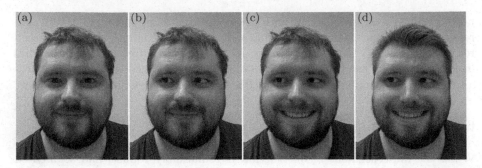

**Fig. 9.** Examples of local layered edits applied subsequently on a real photograph (a): changing gaze direction (b), adding smile (c), changing haircut and nose shape (d).

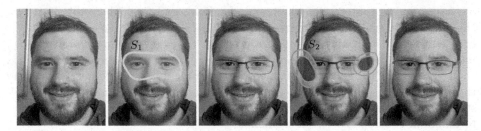

**Fig. 10.** Enforcing continuity of inconsistent edits—a photo of a person to which we would like to add glasses (a), user-specified segmentation mask $S_1$ with a projection $X_1$ matching the original image (b), manipulating $X_1$ generates glasses that do not fit the shape of $S_1$ (c), a new mask $S_2$ is marked encompassing two discontinuous parts (d), a composite with a projected region $S_2$ where the new latent code $X_2$ is refined from $X_1$ to produce the dark region inside $S_2$ (e).

locally, by measuring agreement between segments in their regions of overlap, or globally by e.g. an adversarial loss. Alternatively, instead of linear directions, one might train a separate model to explicitly encode a higher-order approximation of identity-preserving edit direction, which has the potential to also benefit vanilla methods under high edit strength.

# 7   Conclusion

We presented a new technique for image reconstruction and editing based on generative adversarial networks that subdivides the input image into a set of segments for which the corresponding latent vectors are retrieved separately. By so decomposing the problem, we facilitate more accurate reconstructions that better preserve the identity and visual appearance of facial images, especially in more challenging cases that are difficult to handle using state-of-the-art techniques.

We demonstrated the utility of this technique for both the base project-and-edit scenario as well as novel interactive sequential editing applications. As our approach provides measurable improvements while being easily combined with other techniques, we anticipate it will find a place in modern image editing tools.

**Acknowledgments.** We thank the anonymous reviewers for their valuable feedback and insightful comments. We are also grateful to Jakub Javora for creating some of the interactive editing examples. This research was supported by Adobe, the Grant Agency of the Czech Technical University in Prague, grants No. SGS19/179/OHK3/3T/13 and No. SGS20/171/OHK3/3T/13, and by the Research Center for Informatics, grant No. CZ.02.1.01/0.0/0.0/16_019/0000765.

# References

1. Abdal, R., Qin, Y., Wonka, P.: Image2StyleGAN: how to embed images into the StyleGAN latent space? In: Proceedings of IEEE International Conference on Computer Vision (2019)
2. Abdal, R., Zhu, P., Mitra, N.J., Wonka, P.: StyleFlow: attribute-conditioned exploration of styleGAN-generated images using conditional continuous normalizing flows. ACM Trans. Graph. **40**(3), 21 (2021)
3. Alaluf, Y., Patashnik, O., Cohen-Or, D.: ReStyle: a residual-based StyleGAN encoder via iterative refinement. In: Proceedings of IEEE International Conference on Computer Vision, pp. 6711–6720 (2021)
4. Alaluf, Y., Tov, O., Mokady, R., Gal, R., Bermano, A.H.: HyperStyle: StyleGAN inversion with hypernetworks for real image editing. In: Proceedings of IEEE Conference on Computer Vision and Pattern Recognition, pp. 18511–18521 (2022)
5. Bau, D., et al.: Seeing what a GAN cannot generate. In: Proceedings of IEEE International Conference on Computer Vision, pp. 4501–4510 (2019)
6. Deng, J., Guo, J., Zafeiriou, S.: ArcFace: additive angular margin loss for deep face recognition. In: Proceedings of IEEE Conference on Computer Vision and Pattern Recognition, pp. 4685–4694 (2019)
7. Dinh, T.M., Tran, A.T., Nguyen, R., Hua, B.S.: HyperInverter: improving style-GAN inversion via hypernetwork. In: Proceedings of IEEE Conference on Computer Vision and Pattern Recognition, pp. 11389–11398 (2022)
8. Fišer, J., et al.: Example-based synthesis of stylized facial animations. ACM Trans. Graph. **36**(4), 155 (2017)
9. Futschik, D., Lukáč, M., Shechtman, E., Sýkora, D.: Real image inversion via segments. In: arXiv. No. 2110.06269 (2021)
10. Huh, M., Zhang, R., Zhu, J.Y., Paris, S., Hertzmann, A.: Transforming and projecting images into class-conditional generative networks. In: Proceedings of IEEE Conference on Computer Vision and Pattern Recognition, pp. 17–34 (2020)
11. Kang, K., Kim, S., Cho, S.: GAN inversion for out-of-range images with geometric transformations. In: Proceedings of IEEE International Conference on Computer Vision, pp. 13941–13949 (2021)
12. Karras, T., et al.: Alias-free generative adversarial networks. In: Proceedings of Conference on Neural Information Processing Systems (2021)
13. Karras, T., Laine, S., Aila, T.: A style-based generator architecture for generative adversarial networks. In: Proceedings of IEEE Conference on Computer Vision and Pattern Recognition, pp. 4401–4410 (2019)
14. Karras, T., Laine, S., Aittala, M., Hellsten, J., Lehtinen, J., Aila, T.: Analyzing and improving the image quality of StyleGAN. In: Proceedings of IEEE Conference on Computer Vision and Pattern Recognition, pp. 8107–8116 (2020)

15. Lee, C.H., Liu, Z., Wu, L., Luo, P.: MaskGAN: towards diverse and interactive facial image manipulation. In: Proceedings of IEEE Conference on Computer Vision and Pattern Recognition, pp. 5549–5558 (2020)
16. Ling, H., Kreis, K., Li, D., Kim, S.W., Torralba, A., Fidler, S.: EditGAN: high-precision semantic image editing. In: Proceedings of Conference on Neural Information Processing Systems (2021)
17. Lipton, Z.C., Tripathi, S.: Precise recovery of latent vectors from generative adversarial networks. In: Proceedings of International Conference on Learning Representations (2017)
18. Patashnik, O., Wu, Z., Shechtman, E., Cohen-Or, D., Lischinski, D.: StyleCLIP: text-driven manipulation of StyleGAN imagery. In: Proceedings of IEEE International Conference on Computer Vision, pp. 2085–2094 (2021)
19. Pérez, P., Gangnet, M., Blake, A.: Poisson image editing. ACM Trans. Graph. **22**(3), 313–318 (2003)
20. Richardson, E., et al.: Encoding in style: a styleGAN encoder for image-to-image translation. In: Proceedings of IEEE Conference on Computer Vision and Pattern Recognition, pp. 2288–2296 (2021)
21. Roich, D., Mokady, R., Bermano, A.H., Cohen-Or, D.: Pivotal tuning for latent-based editing of real images. In: arXiv. No. 2106.05744 (2021)
22. Tov, O., Alaluf, Y., Nitzan, Y., Patashnik, O., Cohen-Or, D.: Designing an encoder for StyleGAN image manipulation. ACM Trans. Graph. **40**(4), 133 (2021)
23. Wu, Z., Lischinski, D., Shechtman, E.: StyleSpace analysis: disentangled controls for StyleGAN image generation. In: Proceedings of IEEE Conference on Computer Vision and Pattern Recognition, pp. 12863–12872 (2021)
24. Xu, Y., Du, Y., Xiao, W., Xu, X., He, S.: From continuity to editability: inverting GANs with consecutive images. In: Proceedings of IEEE International Conference on Computer Vision, pp. 13910–13918 (2021)
25. Yao, X., Newson, A., Gousseau, Y., Hellier, P.: Feature-style encoder for style-based GAN inversion. In: arXiv. No. 2202.02183 (2022)
26. Zhang, R., Isola, P., Efros, A.A., Shechtman, E., Wang, O.: The unreasonable effectiveness of deep features as a perceptual metric. In: Proceedings of IEEE Conference on Computer Vision and Pattern Recognition, pp. 586–595 (2018)
27. Zhang, Y., et al.: DatasetGAN: efficient labeled data factory with minimal human effort. In: Proceedings of IEEE Conference on Computer Vision and Pattern Recognition, pp. 10145–10155 (2021)
28. Zhu, J., Shen, Y., Zhao, D., Zhou, B.: In-domain GAN inversion for real image editing. In: Vedaldi, A., Bischof, H., Brox, T., Frahm, J.-M. (eds.) ECCV 2020. LNCS, vol. 12362, pp. 592–608. Springer, Cham (2020). https://doi.org/10.1007/978-3-030-58520-4_35
29. Zhu, J.-Y., Krähenbühl, P., Shechtman, E., Efros, A.A.: Generative visual manipulation on the natural image manifold. In: Leibe, B., Matas, J., Sebe, N., Welling, M. (eds.) ECCV 2016. LNCS, vol. 9909, pp. 597–613. Springer, Cham (2016). https://doi.org/10.1007/978-3-319-46454-1_36
30. Zhu, P., Abdal, R., Femiani, J., Wonka, P.: Barbershop: GAN-based image compositing using segmentation masks. ACM Trans. Graph. **40**(6), 215 (2021)

# GAN Cocktail: Mixing GANs Without Dataset Access

Omri Avrahami[1]([⊠]), Dani Lischinski[1], and Ohad Fried[2]

[1] The Hebrew University of Jerusalem, Jerusalem, Israel
`omri.avrahami@mail.huji.ac.il`
[2] Reichman University, Herzliya, Israel

**Abstract.** Today's generative models are capable of synthesizing high-fidelity images, but each model specializes on a specific target domain. This raises the need for model merging: combining two or more pre-trained generative models into a single unified one. In this work we tackle the problem of model merging, given two constraints that often come up in the real world: (1) no access to the original training data, and (2) without increasing the network size. To the best of our knowledge, model merging under these constraints has not been studied thus far. We propose a novel, two-stage solution. In the first stage, we transform the weights of all the models to the same parameter space by a technique we term model rooting. In the second stage, we merge the rooted models by averaging their weights and fine-tuning them for each specific domain, using only data generated by the original trained models. We demonstrate that our approach is superior to baseline methods and to existing transfer learning techniques, and investigate several applications. (Code is available at: https://omriavrahami.com/GAN-cocktail-page/).

**Keywords:** Generative adversarial networks · Model merging

## 1 Introduction

Generative adversarial networks (GANs) [9] have achieved impressive results in neural image synthesis [5, 13–15]. However, these generative models typically specialize on a specific image domain, such as human faces, kitchens, or landscapes. This is in contrary to traditional computer graphics, where a general purpose representation (e.g., textured meshes) and a general purpose renderer can produce images of diverse object types and scenes. In order to extend the applicability and versatility of neural image synthesis, in this work we explore *model merging* — the process of combining two or more generative models into a single conditional model. There are several concrete benefits to model merging:

1. It is well suited for decentralized workflows. Different entities can collect their own datasets and train their own models, which may later be merged.

**Supplementary Information** The online version contains supplementary material available at https://doi.org/10.1007/978-3-031-20050-2_13.

2. If performed properly, merged models can reduce memory and computation requirements, enabling their use on edge devices with limited resources.
3. Merged models enable semantic editing across domains, as described next.

GANs often produce a semantically meaningful latent space. Several embedding techniques [1, 2, 29] have been proposed to map real input images to latent codes of a pre-trained GAN generator, which enables semantic manipulation. Images can be interpolated and transformed using semantic vectors in the embedding space [11, 34], effectively using it as a strong regularizer. A problem arises when one wants to use several pre-trained generators for semantic manipulations (e.g., interpolating between images from GAN $A$ and GAN $B$) — the different models do not share the same latent representation, and hence do not "speak the same language". Model merging places several GANs in a shared latent space, allowing such cross-domain semantic manipulations.

We tackle the problem of merging several GAN models into a single one under the following real-world constraints:

1. **No access to training data.** Many GAN models are being released without the data that they were trained on. This can occur because datasets are too large [6, 30, 31] or due to privacy/copyright issues. Hence, we assume that no training data is available, and only rely on data generated by the pre-trained models.
2. **Limited computing power.** A naïve approach to merging several GAN models is to sample from them separately (e.g., by multinomial sampling functions [40]). With this approach, the model size and inference time grow linearly with the number of GAN models, which may not be practical due to lack of computing power (e.g., edge devices). In addition, this approach does not result in a shared latent space, so it does not support cross-domain semantic manipulations as described earlier. Our goal is to maintain a constant network size, regardless of the number of GANs being merged.

To the best of our knowledge, performing model merging under these constraints has not been studied yet. This is a challenging task: pre-trained GANs typically do not model the entire real image distribution [4]; hence, learning from the outputs of pre-trained models will be sub-optimal. In addition, the constraint on the model size may reduce its capacity.

We start by adapting existing solutions from the field of transfer-learning as baselines (Sect. 3). Next, we present our novel two-stage solution for model merging. We first transfer the weights of the input models to a joint semantic space using a technique we term model rooting (Sect. 4.1). We then merge the rooted models via averaging and fine-tuning (Sect. 4.2). We find that model rooting introduces an inductive bias that helps the merged model achieve superior results compared to baselines and to existing transfer-learning methods (Sect. 5).

To summarize, this paper has the following contributions:

– We introduce the real-world problem of merging several GAN models without access to their training data and with no increase in model size or inference time.

– We adapt several transfer-learning techniques to the GAN merging problem.
– We introduce a novel two-stage approach for GAN merging and evaluate its performance.

## 2    Related Work

**Generative Adversarial Networks:** GANs [9] consist of a generator $G$ and a discriminator $D$ that compete in a two-player minimax game: the discriminator tries to distinguish real training data from generated data, and the generator tries to fool the discriminator. Training GANs is difficult, due to mode collapse and training instability, and several methods focus on addressing these problems [10,20,21,23,32], while another line of research aims to improve the architectures to generate higher quality images [5,13–15]. Karras et al. [14,15] introduced the StyleGAN architecture that leads to an automatically learned, unsupervised separation of high-level attributes and stochastic variation in the generated images and enables intuitive, scale-specific control over the synthesis. For our experiments we use the StyleGAN2 framework. It is important to note that our approach, as well as the baselines, are model-agnostic and there is no dependency on any StyleGAN-specific capabilities. We demonstrate mixing between models of different architectures in Supp. Section 2.1.

**Transfer Learning:** Learning how to transfer knowledge from a source domain to a target domain is a well-studied problem in machine learning [3,7,17,25,27,28, 38], mainly in the discriminative case. It is important to note that the transfer-learning literature focuses on the case where there is a training dataset for the target domain, which is not the case in our scenario. Recent works that are more related to our problem by Shu et al. [36] and Geyer et al. [8] demonstrate the ability to perform transfer learning from several source models into a single target model. However they are not applicable to our setting because: (1) neither method tackles generative models, as we do; (2) both of these methods assume that all the source models share the same architecture, whereas our problem formulation specifically focuses on the general case with arbitrary architectures (which is the real-world scenario, especially for generative models); (3) both methods assume access to training data, while we assume that the training data is unavailable; (4) T-IMM method [8] assumes that the user trains the *source models* incrementally, which is different from our setting, where the source models training is not under the user control. To conclude, the current literature mainly focuses on the discriminative case and assumes access to the training data.

As shown by Wang et al. [41], the principles of transfer learning can be applied to image generation with GANs. Later, Noguchi and Harada [26] proposed to constrain the training process to only update the normalization parameters instead of all of the model's trainable parameters. This shrinks the model capacity, which mitigates the overfitting problem and enables fine-tuning with an extremely small dataset. However, limiting the capacity of the model enables to only change the style of the objects but not their shape, which isn't applicable to our setting, where the merged image domains may exhibit objects of completely different shapes.

Another approach for GAN transfer learning consists of adding a layer that steers the generated distribution towards the target distribution, which is also applicable for sampling from several models [40]. However, this approach stitches the source models together, and thus the model size and the inference time grow linearly in the number of source models. In addition, the models in this approach do not share the same latent space which limits their applicability.

**Continual Learning:** Continual Learning, also known as lifelong learning, is a setting where a model learns a large number of tasks sequentially without forgetting knowledge obtained from the preceding tasks, even though their training data is no longer available while training newer ones. Continual learning mainly deals with the "catastrophic forgetting" phenomenon, i.e., learning consecutive tasks without forgetting how to perform previously trained ones. Most previous efforts focused on classification tasks [16,19,45], and were later also adapted to the generative case [33].

Again, the literature focuses on the case where the new dataset is available, while the old dataset is not, which is not the case in our scenario, but we can adapt it to our setting, and do so in Sect. 3.4. Also, approaches that rely on designated architectures (e.g., lifelong GANs [46]) cannot be adapted to our setting.

Another approach addressing the catastrophic forgetting problem that was proposed by Wu et al. [42] is a memory-replay mechanism that uses the old generative model as a proxy to the old data. Our adaptation of the method of Wang et al. [41] to our setting in Sect. 3.3 may be viewed also as adapting the approach of Wu et al. [42].

## 3    Problem Formulation and Baselines

Our goal is to merge several GANs without access to their original training data. For example, given two trained GAN models, one that generates images of cats and another that generates images of dogs, we want to train a new single GAN model that produces images from both domains, without increasing the model size. Below, we first formulate the problem, present several baselines, and then introduce our approach to solving this task in Sect. 4.

### 3.1    Problem Formulation

We are given $N$ GANs: $\{GAN_i = (G_i, D_i)\}_{i=1}^{N}$, where $GAN_i$ is pretrained on dataset $data_i$ and consists of a generator $G_i$ and a discriminator $D_i$. We denote the distribution of images that are produced by the generator $G_i$ by $P_{G_i}(z)$ and the real data distribution as $P_{data_i}(x)$.

Our goal is to create a "union GAN", $\text{UNIONGAN} = (G_u, D_u)$, which is a conditional GAN [22], with the condition $c$ indicating which of the $N$ domains the generated sample should come from: $\forall_{c \in [N]} P_{G_u}(z, c) = P_{data_c}(x)$ and $P_{D_u}(x, c)$ is the probability that $x$ came from $data_c$, rather than $P_{G_u}$. Note that the datasets $data_i$ are not provided. Furthermore, the $N$ pretrained GAN models may have different architectures. Below, we adapt some current techniques from the transfer learning literature to address this problem.

**Table 1.** Comparison between FID scores of models that were trained on real and generated images

| Dataset | Trained on | |
|---------|------|-----------|
|         | Real | Generated |
| FFHQ     | **5.58**  | 8.84  |
| LSUN cat | **17.37** | 21.78 |
| LSUN dog | **20.48** | 24.31 |
| LSUN car | **7.12**  | 12.79 |

## 3.2   Baseline A: Training from Scratch

Arguably, the simplest approach would be to train UNIONGAN from scratch, by using the samples generated by the pretrained input GANs as the only training data. The objective function of a two-player minimax game that we aim to solve in this case is:

$$\min_G \max_D V(D, G) = \mathbb{E}_{c \in [N], z \sim p_z(z), x \sim P_{G_c}(z)}[\log D(x, c)] + \\ \mathbb{E}_{c \in [N], z \sim p_z(z)}[\log(1 - D(G(z, c), c))] \tag{1}$$

Note that this formulation differs from a standard GAN in two ways: the discriminator is trained on the outputs of the given generators instead of on real data, and UNIONGAN is conditioned on both the class and the latent code $z$. Thus, we simply treat the pre-trained generators as procedural sources of training data. We convert the unconditional model into a conditional one by adding a class embedding layer to the generator and concatenate its output the latent code $z$. An embedding layer is also added to the discriminator. See the supplementary material for more details.

Although the number of generated images that can be produced by a generator is unlimited (in contrast to a real training dataset), we found that training using the real dataset produces better results. This is likely caused by the fact that the pretrained GANs generate only a subset of the training data manifold. To validate that the issue is not due to limited capacity, we train UNIONGAN on the degenerate case of $N = 1$, using different pretrained GANs, and observe a consistent increase in the resulting FID score, as reported in Table 1. In general, the best results can be achieved using the original real training data.

## 3.3   Baseline B: TransferGAN

The above method uses only the outputs of the pretrained models, thereby using them as black boxes. Below we improve this method by using not only the generated data, but also the weights of the trained models.

Specifically, we adapt TransferGAN [41] to our problem as follows: we initialize the UNIONGAN with the $i$-th source model, and then train it on the outputs of all the GAN models (as described in the previous section) until convergence. Thus, we treat one of the models as both an initializer and a data source, and the remaining models as training data sources.

Compared to training from scratch, such initialization lowers the total FID score (for the union of the datasets), as reported in Table 3. Furthermore, Table 4 shows that the FID score is lowered not only for the $i$-th dataset, but for the other datasets as well.

### 3.4    Baseline C: Elastic Weight Consolidation

We observe that although the TransferGAN approach improves the final FID score, if we focus on the source model, we can see that its FID score (on the source class) is initially high and is degraded over the training process (the FID score of the original dataset class increases while the FIDs for the other classes decrease). This occurs due to catastrophic forgetting [16] and can be mitigated by Elastic Weight Consolidation (EWC) [16,18], applied to TransferGAN.

In order to assess the importance of the model parameters to its accuracy, we use Fisher information, which formulates how well we estimate the model parameters given the observations. In order to compute the empirical Fisher information given a pretrained model for a parameter $\theta_i$, we generate a certain amount of data $X$ and compute: $F_i = \mathbb{E}[(\frac{\partial}{\partial \theta_i}\mathcal{L}(x|\theta_i))^2]$ where $\mathcal{L}(x|\theta_i)$ is the log-likelihood. In the generative case, we can equivalently compute the binary cross-entropy loss using the outputs of the discriminator that is fed by the outputs of the generator.

Thus, feeding the discriminator with the generator's outputs, we generate a large number of random samples, compute the binary cross-entropy loss on them and compute the derivative via back-propagation. We can add to our loss term the Elastic Weight Consolidation (EWC) penalty: $\mathcal{L}_{EWC} = \mathcal{L}_{adv} + \lambda \sum_i F_i(\theta_i - \theta_{S,i})$ where $\theta_S$ represents the weights learned from the source domain, $i$ is the index of each parameter of the model and $\lambda$ is the regularization weight to balance different losses.

Unfortunately, as can be seen in Table 4, this procedure mitigates the catastrophic forgetting phenomena at the expense of degrading performance on the other classes. We also experimented with a more naïve approach of applying a L2 loss on the source model weights, but, as we expected, the results were much worse for all but the source class.

## 4    Our Approach: GAN Cocktail

The main limitation of the transfer-learning approach is that it only uses the weights of one of the pre-trained GAN models ($GAN_i$, the source model). In order to leverage the weights of all models, we propose a two-stage approach: At the first stage we perform *model rooting* for all the input GAN models and in the second stage we perform *model merging* by averaging the weights of the rooted models and then fine-tuning them using only data generated by the original models to obtain the merged UNIONGAN.

$GAN_i$      $GAN_j$      Average          $GAN_i$      $GAN_{i \rightarrow j}$      Average

**Fig. 1. Left:** Averaging of two models $GAN_i$ and $GAN_j$ with the same architecture, but without a common root. *Average* is a model in which each weight is the arithmetic mean of the corresponding weights in the original two models. Each row corresponds to the same input $z$. Note that the resulting images exhibit no obvious semantic structure. **Right:** Averaging of two models which have a common root model. The resulting networks (before any fine-tuning) produce images which are a semantically meaningful mix of the two object categories.

### 4.1 First Stage: Model Rooting

Our goal is to merge the GAN models while maintaining as much information and generative performance as possible from the original models. In order to do so we need to somehow combine the weights of these models.

One way to combine several neural networks is by performing some arithmetic operations on their parameters. For example, Exponential Moving Average (EMA) is a technique for averaging the model weights during the training process in order to merge several versions of the same model (from different checkpoints during the training process). EMA may be used for both discriminative [37] and generative tasks [13–15].

In order to average the weights of several models, the weights must have the same dimensions. However, this condition is not sufficient for achieving meaningful results. For example, Fig. 1 (left) demonstrates that if we simply average the weights of two generators with the same architecture, which were trained on two different datasets, the resulting images have no apparent semantic structure.

A key feature in the EMA case is that the averaging is performed on the same model from different training stages. Thus, we can say that the averaging is done on models that share the same *common ancestor* model, and we hypothesize that this property is key to the success of the merging procedure.

Thus, given $N$ source GANs, $\{GAN_i = (G_i, D_i)\}_{i=1}^{N}$, we (a) convert them to the same architecture (if their original architectures differ), and (b) create a

**Table 2.** Rooted vs. not-rooted distance. The distance between the weights of the rooted model is much closer than that of the not-rooted model

| Merged Datasets | $d(A, B)$ | $d(A, A \to B)$ |
|---|---|---|
| Cat + Dog | 418.55 | **232.21** |
| FFHQ + Cat | 433.87 | **252.34** |
| Cat + Car | 454.23 | **264.31** |

common ancestor for all the models. To meet these conditions we propose the model rooting technique: we choose one of the models arbitrarily (see Sect. 5.1 for details) to be our root model $GAN_r$; next, for each $i \in [N] \backslash r$ we train a model that is initialized by $GAN_r$ on the outputs of $GAN_i$, with the implicit task of performing catastrophic forgetting [16] of the source dataset $r$. We denote each one of the resulting models as $GAN_{r \to i}$. Now, models $GAN_r$ and $GAN_{r \to i}$ not only share the same architecture but also share a common ancestor. Hence, averaging their weights will yield more semantically meaningful results, as demonstrated in Fig. 1 (right).

In order to quantify the distance between two models $GAN_A$ and $GAN_B$ we can measure the $L_2$ distance between their weights, i.e.: $d(A, B) = \frac{1}{L} \sum_i \|\theta_{A,i} - \theta_{B,i}\|_2$ where $\theta_{A,i}$ is the $i$ layer of model $A$, $\theta_{B,i}$ is the $i$ layer of model $B$, and $L$ is the number of layers. Figure 1 (right) implies that the weights of $GAN_A$ are more aligned with those of $GAN_{A \to B}$ than with the weights of $GAN_B$. In order to verify this quantitatively, we report the distances $d(A, B)$ and $d(A, A \to B)$ in Table 2. Indeed, the rooted models $GAN_{A \to B}$ are much closer to the root, despite being trained on other datasets until convergence. Note that semantically closer datasets (e.g., cats and dogs) yield a smaller distance.

To conclude, the model rooting step transfers all the models to the same architecture and aligns their weights such that they can be averaged. Next, inspired by EMA, we will show that the averaging of the models introduces an inductive-bias to the training procedure that yields better results.

## 4.2    Second Stage: Model Merging

We now have $N$ rooted models, averaging whose weights yields somewhat semantically meaningful results. However, images generated by the averaged models are typically somewhere in between all the training classes (Fig. 1, rightmost column). We want the model to learn to reuse filters that are applicable for all datasets, and differentiate the class-specific filters. For that, we continue with an adversarial training of the averaged model using the original GAN models as the data sources.

Specifically, given the $N$ rooted models from the previous stage: $GAN_r$ and $\{GAN_{r \to i}\}_{i \in [N] \backslash r}$ we create an average model: $GAN_a = (G_a, D_a)$, s.t. $\theta_a = \frac{1}{N}(\theta_r + \sum_{i \in [N] \backslash r} \theta_{r \to i})$ where $\theta_i$ are the parameters of model $i$. We also experimented with more sophisticated weighted average initialization based on the diagonal of the Fisher information matrix [16] but it did not improve the results over a simple averaging. We then fine-tune $GAN_a$ using the outputs of the original $GAN_i$ models to obtain the desired UNIONGAN.

## 5    Results

Our main evaluation metric is the commonly-used Fréchet Inception Distance (FID) [12] which measures the Fréchet distance in the embedding space of the inception network between the real images and the generated images. The embedded data is assumed to follow a multivariate normal distribution, which is estimated by computing their mean and covariance. We measure quality by computing FID between 50k generated images and all of the available training images, as recommended by Heusel et al. [12].

All the FID scores that are reported in this paper were computed against the original training data. Note that this is for evaluation purposes only, and our models did not have access to the original data during training.

We evaluate our model on several representative cases using LSUN [44] and FFHQ [14] datasets. We specifically chose to compare between domains that are semantically close (cats and dogs), as well as domains that are more semantically distant (cats and cars). In addition, we compare aligned and unaligned datasets:

- **Aligned and unaligned images:** we used LSUN cat dataset which contains images of cats in different poses and sizes, and FFHQ dataset which contains images of human faces that are strictly aligned. The FID between these two datasets is 196.59.
- **Unaligned imaged from related classes:** we used LSUN cat and LSUN dog classes. The FID between the two datasets is 72.2.
- **Unaligned imaged from unrelated classes:** we used LSUN cat and LSUN car classes. The FID between the two datasets is 161.62.

The FID distances reported above provide an indication of the semantic proximity between each pair of datasets. Not surprisingly, cat images are semantically closer to dog images than to images of humans (FFHQ) or of cars.

We compare our method against the following methods: training from scratch (Sect. 3.2), TransferGAN (Sect. 3.3), Elastic Weight Consolidation (Sect. 3.4) and the recently proposed Freeze Discriminator method [24] which aims to improve transfer learning in GANs by freezing the highest-resolution layers of the discriminator during transfer.

In Table 3 we calculate the FID score between the union of all classes and the union of 50K samples of each class of the generated images. Our method outperforms other methods on all the datasets we experimented with.

In addition, we evaluated the FID score on each class separately in order to measure the effect of each method on each class. As can be seen in Table 4, when the classes are semantically close, such as in the case of cat + dog, our method achieves better results than all the baselines. When the classes are semantically distant, such as in the case of cat + FFHQ or cat + car, we can see that EWC

**Table 3.** Comparison of FID score w.r.t. the union of all the datasets, for several dataset combinations. Cat, dog, and car datasets are taken from LSUN [44]

| Datasets | FFHQ cat | Cat dog | Cat car | FFHQ cat dog | FFHQ cat dog car |
|---|---|---|---|---|---|
| From scratch | 19.61 | 27.58 | 20.52 | 23.22 | 24.88 |
| TransferGAN [41] | 18.63 | 22.17 | 17.77 | 20.64 | 19.34 |
| EWC [16] | 19.45 | 22.17 | 17.65 | 19.47 | 19.14 |
| Freeze-D [24] | 18.17 | 21.92 | 17.52 | 19.71 | 19.41 |
| Our | **16.44** | **20.77** | **16.85** | **18.98** | **18.44** |
| Upper bound (real data training) | 11.86 | 17.68 | 14.28 | 15.93 | 16.45 |

**Table 4.** FID scores per-class over different dataset combinations

| Dataset | LSUN cat+dog | | LSUN cat+car | | LSUN cat+FFHQ | |
|---|---|---|---|---|---|---|
| | Cat | Dog | Cat | Car | FFHQ | Cat |
| Scratch | 30.37 | 33.21 | 32.21 | 14.43 | 13.35 | 31.64 |
| TransferGAN [41] | 23.32 | 28.84 | 30.06 | 11.49 | 11.16 | 32.08 |
| EWC [16] | 23.04 | 30.11 | 30.65 | **10.54** | **9.85** | 35.36 |
| Freeze-D [24] | 23.36 | 28.40 | 29.78 | 11.44 | 10.64 | 31.57 |
| Our | **22.08** | **26.52** | **27.78** | 11.59 | 10.60 | **27.82** |
| Upper bound (real data training) | 16.49 | 24.75 | 23.23 | 9.5 | 8.49 | 19.19 |

achieves better results on the class with respect to which it minimizes its weights distances, but this comes at the expense of the other class. This is the reason for the better overall performance of our method, reported in Table 3.

As mentioned at the outset, the premise of this work is that the original training data is not available (which is the case with many real-world models). If the original training data is available to the merging process, the best merging results may unsurprisingly be achieved by simply training the new class-conditioned model on the union of the original training datasets. Results achieved in this manner are an upper bound for the results that can be achieved without access to the training data. Table 3 and Table 4 show the gap between our merging approach (without training data) and the aforementioned upper bound.

## 5.1 Choosing the Root Model

At the first stage of our approach we arbitrarily choose one of the models to serve as the root model. This raises the question of whether the choice of the root model matters. Table 5 shows that our method outperforms the baselines regardless of the model that is chosen as the root model. On the other hand, it does not mean that the choice of the root model is insignificant for the overall performance of the final merged model. As we can see from Table 5, when merging LSUN cat and LSUN dog models, the better overall result is achieved when LSUN dog is

**Table 5.** Our method outperforms the baselines, in terms of FID score, regardless of the model that is chosen as the root model.

| Root model | LSUN cat + LSUN dog | | LSUN cat + FFHQ | |
|---|---|---|---|---|
| | LSUN cat | LSUN dog | FFHQ | LSUN cat |
| Scratch | 27.58 | 27.58 | 19.61 | 19.61 |
| TransferGAN [41] | 22.17 | 21.11 | 18.63 | 16.40 |
| EWC [16] | 22.17 | 25.16 | 19.45 | 16.52 |
| Freeze-D [24] | 21.92 | 25.03 | 18.17 | 16.87 |
| Our | **20.77** | **20.03** | **16.44** | **15.60** |

chosen as the root, while when merging the LSUN cat and FFHQ models, the better result is achieved by choosing LSUN cat to be the root model.

We hypothesized that a better candidate for the root model would be the generator that is more diverse, i.e., whose generated images are semantically far from each other. To test our hypothesis we calculated the diversity by measuring pairwise LPIPS scores between the generated images of each model. However, we found that it is not always the case that the more diverse generator is the better root model.

## 5.2  Applications

The output of our model is a single conditional GAN with a common latent space for all the classes. Hence, the merged model supports a variety of GAN applications from the literature. To name a few:

**Latent space interpolation** is used for demonstrating the smoothness of the latent space of a GAN. It can also be used for creating smooth transition sequences between objects of different classes. In Fig. 2 we demonstrate a transition between a cat and a dog by interpolating between their two $w$ latent vectors in the merged model from two different classes.

**Style mixing**, introduced by Karras et al. [14], is the ability the mix between generated images on different semantic levels (e.g., gender, hairstyle, pose, etc.) by feeding a different latent vector $w$ to different generation layers. Given a shared latent space for different classes enables us to use the style mixing mechanism to mix attributes from images belonging to these different classes, e.g., change the pose of a cat to that of a dog, while retaining the appearance of the cat. A few such examples are shown in Fig. 3. Note how both the pose and the general shape are taken from the source class (e.g., the shape of the ears in column 1 is taken from the dog images, rather than from the cat images).

**Fig. 2.** Interpolation in the merged model's latent space of between images of different classes.

**Semantic editing** is the ability to perform image editing operations on images by manipulating their latent space [11,34,39]. One advantage of our framework is the ability to edit images from different domains using the same latent direction because of the shared latent space. For example, given a model that merges FFHQ and LSUN cat generators, we can leverage an off-the-shelf pose classifier, which is available for humans but not for cats, in order to classify poses as "positive" (pose from left to right) or "negative" (pose from right to left). Applying this classifier only to images of humans generated by the merged model, we obtain a direction in the shared latent space that corresponds to a pose change, as the hyperplane normal of a linear SVM trained on the latent vectors of the human faces. Figure 4 demonstrates that the same latent direction (that was calculated on humans only) can be applied for both humans and cats. So, using our model merging solution we can leverage off-the-shelf classifiers on one class to operate on all of the classes.

## 6    Limitations and Future Work

Due to our self-imposed constraint on model size, we have found that our solution (and the baselines) are sensitive to the number of source models and their properties: merging more models or merging models with semantically distant distributions produces higher FID scores, as may be seen in Table 6. For example, merging LSUN cat and LSUN dog produced better FID scores on the cat dataset on all the baselines in comparison to merging LSUN cat and LSUN car. We conjecture that this happens because more filters can be reused among the semantically similar datasets. Additionally, we can see that merging four of the datasets produces the worst result on our method. Notice that merging FFHQ + cat + dog produced a better result than cat + car and FFHQ + cat because of the semantical closeness of cat and dog.

Yet another disadvantage of our method is that the training time is longer due to the two-stage approach. The baselines converge faster to their local minima, but result in a higher FID score than our method.

Future work can be to relax the capacity constraint and allow a minimal capacity and run-time increase to enable merging more models or models from semantically distant distributions with better results in terms of FID score.

**Fig. 3.** Style mixing between images of two different domains: taking the pose and shape from the dog image and the appearance from the cat image.

## 7    Broader Impact

One major barrier when developing a machine learning model is the lack of training data. Many small organizations and individuals find it hard to compete with larger entities due to the lack of training data. This is especially true in fields where curating and annotating the training data is time-consuming and expensive (e.g., medical data). It was shown that GANs can be used in order to augment and anonymize sensitive training data [35,43]. Our method can be used to alleviate the problem of scarce training data, by allowing entities with small budgets to use pre-trained GANs in two ways: use them as training data, and reuse some of the knowledge incorporated in their weights.

On the other hand, our method may amplify the copyright issues that arise when training a model on synthetic data. The legal implications of training a model using another model that was trained on a private or copyrighted dataset are currently unclear. We would like to encourage the research community to work with governments and legal scholars to establish new laws and regulations in lockstep with the rapid advancement of synthetic media.

(-) Pose                    Neutral                    (+) Pose

**Fig. 4.** We determine the pose direction in the latent space of the merged model of FFHQ and LSUN cat using images of the FFHQ class only. Applying this direction to images from both classes reveals that the semantics stay the same.

**Table 6.** Comparison of FID scores of cat class only, when merging LSUN cat with different datasets. Semantically closer datasets (e.g., cats and dogs) lead to better scores compared to far datasets (e.g., cats and cars). Merging 4 datasets produces the worst result

| Datasets | Cat dog | Cat car | FFHQ cat | FFHQ cat dog | FFHQ cat dog car |
|---|---|---|---|---|---|
| From scratch | 30.37 | 32.21 | 31.64 | 34.75 | 45.02 |
| TransferGAN [41] | 23.32 | 30.06 | 32.08 | 29.06 | 30.50 |
| EWC [16] | 23.04 | 30.65 | 35.36 | 25.70 | 27.98 |
| Freeze-D [24] | 23.36 | 29.78 | 31.57 | 28.68 | 30.95 |
| Our | 22.08 | 27.78 | 27.82 | 26.80 | 30.17 |

## 8    Conclusions

In this paper, we introduced the problem of merging several generative adversarial networks without having access to the training data. We adapted current methods for transfer-learning and continual-learning and set them as our baselines. We then introduced our novel two-stage solution to the GAN mixing problem: model rooting and model merging. Later, we compared our method to the baselines and demonstrated its superiority on various datasets. Finally, we presented some applications of our model merging technique.

**Acknowledgments.** This work was supported in part by Lightricks Ltd and by the Israel Science Foundation (grants No. 2492/20, 1574/21, and 2611/21).

# References

1. Abdal, R., Qin, Y., Wonka, P.: Image2stylegan: how to embed images into the StyleGAN latent space? In: Proceedings of the IEEE/CVF International Conference on Computer Vision, pp. 4432–4441 (2019)
2. Abdal, R., Qin, Y., Wonka, P.: Image2stylegan++: how to edit the embedded images? In: Proceedings of the IEEE/CVF Conference on Computer Vision and Pattern Recognition, pp. 8296–8305 (2020)
3. Bao, Y., et al.: An information-theoretic approach to transferability in task transfer learning. In: 2019 IEEE International Conference on Image Processing (ICIP), pp. 2309–2313. IEEE (2019)
4. Bau, D., et al.: Seeing what a GAN cannot generate. In: Proceedings of the IEEE/CVF International Conference on Computer Vision, pp. 4502–4511 (2019)
5. Brock, A., Donahue, J., Simonyan, K.: Large scale GAN training for high fidelity natural image synthesis. In: International Conference on Learning Representations (2018)
6. Chen, M., et al.: Generative pretraining from pixels. In: International Conference on Machine Learning, pp. 1691–1703. PMLR (2020)
7. Donahue, J., et al.: Decaf: a deep convolutional activation feature for generic visual recognition. In: International Conference on Machine Learning, pp. 647–655. PMLR (2014)
8. Geyer, R., Corinzia, L., Wegmayr, V.: Transfer learning by adaptive merging of multiple models. In: International Conference on Medical Imaging with Deep Learning, pp. 185–196. PMLR (2019)
9. Goodfellow, I., et al.: Generative adversarial nets. In: Ghahramani, Z., Welling, M., Cortes, C., Lawrence, N., Weinberger, K.Q. (eds.) Advances in Neural Information Processing Systems, vol. 27. Curran Associates, Inc. (2014). https://proceedings.neurips.cc/paper/2014/file/5ca3e9b122f61f8f06494c97b1afccf3-Paper.pdf'
10. Gulrajani, I., Ahmed, F., Arjovsky, M., Dumoulin, V., Courville, A.C.: Improved training of Wasserstein GANs. In: NIPS (2017)
11. Härkönen, E., Hertzmann, A., Lehtinen, J., Paris, S.: GANSpace: discovering interpretable GAN controls. Advances in Neural Information Process. Syst. **33**, 9841–9850 (2020)
12. Heusel, M., Ramsauer, H., Unterthiner, T., Nessler, B., Hochreiter, S.: GANs trained by a two time-scale update rule converge to a local Nash equilibrium. In: Guyon, I., Luxburg, U.V. (eds.) Advances in Neural Information Processing Systems. vol. 30. Curran Associates, Inc. (2017). https://proceedings.neurips.cc/paper/2017/file/8a1d694707eb0fefe65871369074926d-Paper.pdf
13. Karras, T., Aila, T., Laine, S., Lehtinen, J.: Progressive growing of GANs for improved quality, stability, and variation. arXiv preprint arXiv:1710.10196 (2017)
14. Karras, T., Laine, S., Aila, T.: A style-based generator architecture for generative adversarial networks. In: Proceedings of the IEEE/CVF Conference on Computer Vision and Pattern Recognition, pp. 4401–4410 (2019)
15. Karras, T., Laine, S., Aittala, M., Hellsten, J., Lehtinen, J., Aila, T.: Analyzing and improving the image quality of StyleGAN. In: Proceedings of the IEEE/CVF Conference on Computer Vision and Pattern Recognition, pp. 8110–8119 (2020)
16. Kirkpatrick, J., et al.: Overcoming catastrophic forgetting in neural networks. Proc. Nat. Acad. Sci. **114**(13), 3521–3526 (2017)
17. Kornblith, S., Shlens, J., Le, Q.V.: Do better imagenet models transfer better? In: Proceedings of the IEEE/CVF Conference on Computer Vision and Pattern Recognition, pp. 2661–2671 (2019)

18. Li, Y., Zhang, R., Lu, J.C., Shechtman, E.: Few-shot image generation with elastic weight consolidation. In: Larochelle, H., Ranzato, M., Hadsell, R., Balcan, M.F., Lin, H. (eds.) Advances in Neural Information Processing Systems, vol. 33, pp. 15885–15896. Curran Associates, Inc. (2020). https://proceedings.neurips.cc/paper/2020/file/b6d767d2f8ed5d21a44b0e5886680cb9-Paper.pdf

19. Li, Z., Hoiem, D.: Learning without forgetting. IEEE Trans. Pattern Anal. Mach. Intell. **40**(12), 2935–2947 (2017)

20. Mao, X., Li, Q., Xie, H., Lau, R.Y., Wang, Z., Paul Smolley, S.: Least squares generative adversarial networks. In: Proceedings of the IEEE International Conference on Computer Vision, pp. 2794–2802 (2017)

21. Mescheder, L., Geiger, A., Nowozin, S.: Which training methods for GANs do actually converge? In: International Conference on Machine Learning, pp. 3481–3490. PMLR (2018)

22. Mirza, M., Osindero, S.: Conditional generative adversarial nets. arXiv preprint arXiv:1411.1784 (2014)

23. Miyato, T., Kataoka, T., Koyama, M., Yoshida, Y.: Spectral normalization for generative adversarial networks. arXiv preprint arXiv:1802.05957 (2018)

24. Mo, S., Cho, M., Shin, J.: Freeze discriminator: a simple baseline for fine-tuning GANs. arXiv preprint arXiv:2002.10964 (2020)

25. Nguyen, C., Hassner, T., Seeger, M., Archambeau, C.: Leep: a new measure to evaluate transferability of learned representations. In: International Conference on Machine Learning, pp. 7294–7305. PMLR (2020)

26. Noguchi, A., Harada, T.: Image generation from small datasets via batch statistics adaptation. In: Proceedings of the IEEE/CVF International Conference on Computer Vision, pp. 2750–2758 (2019)

27. Oquab, M., Bottou, L., Laptev, I., Sivic, J.: Learning and transferring mid-level image representations using convolutional neural networks. In: Proceedings of the IEEE Conference on Computer Vision and Pattern Recognition, pp. 1717–1724 (2014)

28. Pan, S.J., Yang, Q.: A survey on transfer learning. IEEE Trans. Knowl. Data Eng. **22**(10), 1345–1359 (2009)

29. Pidhorskyi, S., Adjeroh, D.A., Doretto, G.: Adversarial latent autoencoders. In: Proceedings of the IEEE/CVF Conference on Computer Vision and Pattern Recognition, pp. 14104–14113 (2020)

30. Radford, A., et al.: Learning transferable visual models from natural language supervision. arXiv preprint arXiv:2103.00020 (2021)

31. Ramesh, A., et al.: Zero-shot text-to-image generation. arXiv preprint arXiv:2102.12092 (2021)

32. Salimans, T., Goodfellow, I., Zaremba, W., Cheung, V., Radford, A., Chen, X.: Improved techniques for training GANs. arXiv preprint arXiv:1606.03498 (2016)

33. Seff, A., Beatson, A., Suo, D., Liu, H.: Continual learning in generative adversarial nets. arXiv preprint arXiv:1705.08395 (2017)

34. Shen, Y., Gu, J., Tang, X., Zhou, B.: Interpreting the latent space of GANs for semantic face editing. In: Proceedings of the IEEE/CVF Conference on Computer Vision and Pattern Recognition, pp. 9243–9252 (2020)

35. Shin, H.-C., et al.: Medical image synthesis for data augmentation and anonymization using generative adversarial networks. In: Gooya, A., Goksel, O., Oguz, I., Burgos, N. (eds.) SASHIMI 2018. LNCS, vol. 11037, pp. 1–11. Springer, Cham (2018). https://doi.org/10.1007/978-3-030-00536-8_1

36. Shu, Y., Kou, Z., Cao, Z., Wang, J., Long, M.: Zoo-tuning: adaptive transfer from a zoo of models. In: International Conference on Machine Learning, pp. 9626–9637. PMLR (2021)
37. Tarvainen, A., Valpola, H.: Mean teachers are better role models: weight-averaged consistency targets improve semi-supervised deep learning results. In: Guyon, I., et al. (eds.) Advances in Neural Information Processing Systems. vol. 30. Curran Associates, Inc. (2017). https://proceedings.neurips.cc/paper/2017/file/68053af2923e00204c3ca7c6a3150cf7-Paper.pdf
38. Tran, A.T., Nguyen, C.V., Hassner, T.: Transferability and hardness of supervised classification tasks. In: Proceedings of the IEEE/CVF International Conference on Computer Vision, pp. 1395–1405 (2019)
39. Viazovetskyi, Y., Ivashkin, V., Kashin, E.: StyleGAN2 distillation for feed-forward image manipulation. In: Vedaldi, A., Bischof, H., Brox, T., Frahm, J.-M. (eds.) ECCV 2020. LNCS, vol. 12367, pp. 170–186. Springer, Cham (2020). https://doi.org/10.1007/978-3-030-58542-6_11
40. Wang, Y., Gonzalez-Garcia, A., Berga, D., Herranz, L., Khan, F.S., Weijer, J.V.D.: Minegan: effective knowledge transfer from GANs to target domains with few images. In: Proceedings of the IEEE/CVF Conference on Computer Vision and Pattern Recognition, pp. 9332–9341 (2020)
41. Wang, Y., Wu, C., Herranz, L., van de Weijer, J., Gonzalez-Garcia, A., Raducanu, B.: Transferring GANs: generating images from limited data. In: Proceedings of the European Conference on Computer Vision (ECCV), pp. 218–234 (2018)
42. Wu, C., Herranz, L., Liu, X., van de Weijer, J., Raducanu, B., et al.: Memory replay GANs: learning to generate new categories without forgetting. Adv. Neural Inf. Process. Syst. **31**, 5962–5972 (2018)
43. Yoon, J., Drumright, L.N., Van Der Schaar, M.: Anonymization through data synthesis using generative adversarial networks (ADS-GAN). IEEE J. Biomed. Health Inf. **24**(8), 2378–2388 (2020)
44. Yu, F., Seff, A., Zhang, Y., Song, S., Funkhouser, T., Xiao, J.: LSUN: construction of a large-scale image dataset using deep learning with humans in the loop. arXiv preprint arXiv:1506.03365 (2015)
45. Zenke, F., Poole, B., Ganguli, S.: Continual learning through synaptic intelligence. In: International Conference on Machine Learning, pp. 3987–3995. PMLR (2017)
46. Zhai, M., Chen, L., Tung, F., He, J., Nawhal, M., Mori, G.: Lifelong GAN: continual learning for conditional image generation. In: Proceedings of the IEEE/CVF International Conference on Computer Vision, pp. 2759–2768 (2019)

# Geometry-Guided Progressive NeRF for Generalizable and Efficient Neural Human Rendering

Mingfei Chen[1,2], Jianfeng Zhang[3], Xiangyu Xu[1(✉)], Lijuan Liu[1], Yujun Cai[1],
Jiashi Feng[1], and Shuicheng Yan[1]

[1] Sea AI Lab, Shanghai, China
xuxy@sea.com
[2] University of Washington, Seattle, USA
[3] National University of Singapore, Singapore, Singapore

**Abstract.** In this work we develop a *generalizable* and *efficient* Neural Radiance Field (NeRF) pipeline for high-fidelity free-viewpoint human body synthesis under settings with *sparse* camera views. Though existing NeRF-based methods can synthesize rather realistic details for human body, they tend to produce poor results when the input has self-occlusion, especially for unseen humans under sparse views. Moreover, these methods often require a large number of sampling points for rendering, which leads to low efficiency and limits their real-world applicability. To address these challenges, we propose a Geometry-guided Progressive NeRF (GP-NeRF). In particular, to better tackle self-occlusion, we devise a geometry-guided multi-view feature integration approach that utilizes the estimated geometry prior to integrate the incomplete information from input views and construct a complete geometry volume for the target human body. Meanwhile, for achieving higher rendering efficiency, we introduce a progressive rendering pipeline through geometry guidance, which leverages the geometric feature volume and the predicted density values to progressively reduce the number of sampling points and speed up the rendering process. Experiments on the ZJU-MoCap and THUman datasets show that our method outperforms the state-of-the-arts significantly across multiple generalization settings, while the time cost is reduced $> 70\%$ via applying our efficient progressive rendering pipeline.

## 1 Introduction

High-fidelity free-viewpoint synthesis of human body is important for many applications such as virtual reality, telepresence and games. Some recent works [12,22,25,36] deploy a Neural Radiance Fields (NeRF) [18] pipeline, which

**Supplementary Information** The online version contains supplementary material available at https://doi.org/10.1007/978-3-031-20050-2_14.

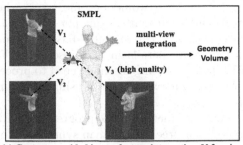

(a) Geometry-guided image feature integration: V for view.

| | Previous | Ours |
|---|---|---|
| # Density Points (↓) | 4.03M | 0.95M (-76%) |
| Density MLP T (↓) | 109ms | 28ms (-74%) |
| # Color Points (↓) | 4.03M | 0.24M (-94%) |
| Color MLP T (↓) | 145ms | 10ms (-93%) |
| Memory (↓) | 20.7GB | 9.9GB (-52%) |

(c) Efficiency Comparison

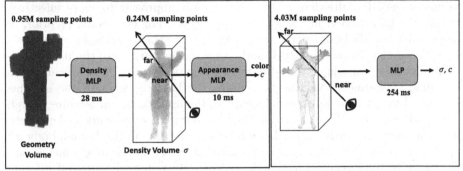

(b) Rendering pipeline: our efficient geometry-guided progressive pipeline (left) vs. previous (right). The amount of sampling points and forward time in blue are measured on the same data and model parameters.

**Fig. 1.** Our method can better handle self-occlusion (a) and high computational cost (b) issues than previous methods [10,24]. In (a), our multi-view integration can extract high-quality geometry information from $V_3$ for the red SMPL vertex. In (b), our progressive rendering pipeline leverages the geometric volume and the predicted density values to progressively reduce the number of sampling points and speed up the rendering, while previous methods [10,24] wastes large amount of computations at redundant empty regions. The efficiency comparison shown in (c) further verifies our high efficiency.

achieved fairly realistic synthesis of human body. However, these works usually require dense-view capturing of human body, and have to train a separate model for each person to render new views. The limited generalization ability as well as demand for cost computation severely hinder their application in the real-world scenarios.

In this work, we aim at boosting high-fidelity free-viewpoint human body synthesis with a generalizable and efficient NeRF framework based on only single-frame images from sparse camera views. To pursue such a high-standard framework, there are mainly two challenges that need to be tackled. First, the human body is highly non-rigid and commonly has self-occlusions over body parts, which may lead to ambiguous results with only sparse-view captures. This ambiguity could drastically degrade the rendering quality without proper regularizations, which cannot be easily solved by simply sampling features from multi-view images as in [26,33,35]. This problem would become worse when using one model to synthesize unseen scenarios without specific per-scene training. Second, the high computation and memory cost of NeRF-based methods severely hinder human synthesis with accurate details in high-resolution. For example, when rendering one $512 \times 512$ image, existing methods need to process millions of sampling points through the neural network, even if using the bound of the geometry prior to remove empty regions.

To address these challenges, we propose a geometry-guided progressive NeRF, called GP-NeRF, for generalizable and efficient free-view human synthesis. More specifically, to regularize the learned 3D human representation, we propose a geometry-guided multi-view feature integration approach to more effectively exploit the information in the sparse input views. For the geometry prior, we adopt a coarse 3D body model, $i.e.$, SMPL [17], which serves as a base estimate of our algorithm. We attach multi-view image features to the base geometry model using an adaptive multi-view aggregation layer. Then we can obtain an enhanced geometry volume by refining the base model with the attached image features, which substantially reduces the ambiguities in learning a high-fidelity 3D neural field. It is worth noting that our multi-view enhanced geometry prior differs significantly from related methods that also utilize human body priors [10,14,23,24]. NB [24] learns a per-scene geometry embedding, which is hard to generalize to unseen human bodies; NHP [10] relies on temporal information to complement the base geometry model, which is less effective for regions occluded throughout the input video. In contrast, our approach can adaptively combine the geometry prior and multi-view features to enhance the 3D estimation, and thus can better handle the self-occlusion problem and acquire lifted generalization capacity even without using videos (see Fig. 1 (a)). By integrating the multi-view information and form a complete geometry volume adapting to the target human body, we can also compensate some limitations of the geometry prior (e.g., inaccurate body shape or lacks cloth information as in [14,23]), and support our following efficiency progressive pipeline.

Furthermore, to tackle the high computation and memory cost, we introduce a geometry-guided progressive rendering pipeline. As shown in Fig. 1 (b), different from previous methods [10,24], our pipeline decouples the density and color prediction process, leveraging the geometry volume as well as the predicted density values to reduce the number of sampling points for rendering progressively. By simply deploying our progressive rendering pipeline with the same data and model parameters, we can remove 76.4% points for density prediction (with Density MLP in Fig. 1 (b)) and 94% points for color prediction (with Appearance MLP in Fig. 1 (b)), reducing the total forwarding time of this part for all points by 85%. Later experiments verify that our progressive pipeline causes no performance decline while requiring shorter training time, which is credited to focusing on the density and appearance learning separately.

Our main contributions are in three folds:

- We propose a novel geometry-guided progressive NeRF (GP-NeRF) for generalizable and efficient human body rendering, which reduces the computational cost of rendering significantly and also gains higher generalization capacity simply based on the single-frame sparse views.

- We propose an effective geometry-guided multi-view feature integration approach, where we let each view compensate the low-quality occluded information for other views with the guidance of the geometry prior.
- Our GP-NeRF has achieved state-of-the-art performance on the ZJU-MoCap dataset, taking only 175 ms on RTX 3090 and reducing time for rendering per image by over 70%, which well verifies effectiveness and efficiency of our framework.

## 2    Related Work

*Human Performance Capture.* Previous works [2,5,8,20] apply traditional modeling and rendering pipelines for novel view synthesis of human performance, relying on either dense camera setup [4,8] or depth sensors [2,5,31] to ensure photo-realistic reconstruction. Follow-up improvements are made by introducing neural networks to the rendering pipeline to alleviate geometric artifacts. To enable human performance capture in a sparse multi-view setup, template-based methods [1,3,6,30] adopt pre-scanned human models to track human motion. However, these approaches require per-scene optimization and the pre-scanned human models are hard to collect in practice, which hinders them from real-world applications. Instead of performing per-scene optimization, recent methods [19,27,28,37] adopt neural networks to learn human priors from ground-truth 3D data, and hence can reconstruct detailed 3D human geometry and texture from a single image. However, due to the limited diversity of training data, it is difficult for them to generate photo-realistic view synthesis or generalize to human poses and appearances that are very different from the training ones. And some other methods [11,38] sample points from the generated 3D feature space, and then decide the human body opacity for later rendering, but they might generate results that violate the normal human body structures without involving human body geometry constraints.

*Neural 3D Representations.* Recently, researchers propose implicit function-based approaches [13,15,21,29] to learn a fully-connected network to translate a 3D positional feature into local feature representation. A very recent work NeRF [18] achieves high fidelity novel view synthesis by learning implicit fields of color and density along with a volume rendering technique. Later, several works extend NeRF to dynamic scenes modeling [12,22,25,36] by optimization NeRF and dynamic deformation fields jointly. Despite impressive performance, it is an extremely under-constrained problem to learn both NeRF and dynamic deformation fields together. NB [24] combines NeRF with a parametric human body model SMPL [17] to regularize the training process. It requires a lengthy optimization for each scene and hardly generalizes to unseen scenarios. To avoid such expensive per-scene optimization, Generalizable NeRFs [10,26,33,35] condition the network on the pixel-aligned image features. However, directly extending such methods to complex and dynamic 3D human modeling is highly non-trivial due to self-occlusion, especially when modeling unseen humans under sparse views. Besides, these approaches suffer low efficiency since they need to process a large number of sampling points for volumetric rendering, harming their real-world applicability. Different from existing methods, we carefully design a multi-view information aggregation approach and a progressive rendering technique to improve model robustness and generalization to unseen scenarios under sparse views and also speed up the rendering.

## 3    Methodology

Given a set of $M$ sparse source views $\{\mathbf{I}_m | m = 1, 2, ..., M\}$ of an arbitrary human model, which are captured by $M$ pre-calibrated cameras respectively, we aim to synthesize the novel view $\mathbf{I}_t$ of the human model from an arbitrary target camera.

To this end, we propose a geometry-guided progressive NeRF (GP-NeRF) framework for efficient and generalizable free-view human synthesis under very sparse views (e.g., $M = 3$). Figure 2 illustrates the overview of our framework. Firstly, a CNN backbone is used to extract image features $\mathbf{F}_m$ for each of the views $\mathbf{I}_m$. Then our GP-NeRF framework integrates these multi-view features to synthesize the novel-view image through three modules progressively, leveraging the geometry prior from SMPL [17] as guidance. The three modules are 1) geometry-guided multi-view feature integration (GMI) module (Sect. 3.1); 2) density network (Sect. 3.2); and 3) appearance network (Sect. 3.3). Details of the whole progressive human rendering pipeline are elaborated in Sect. 3.4, and the training method is described in Sect. 3.5.

### 3.1    Geometry-Guided Multi-view Integration

The geometry-guided multi-view feature integration module, shown in Fig. 2 (a), enhances the coarse geometry prior with multi-view image features by adaptively aggregating these features via a geometry-guided attention module. Then it constructs a complete geometry feature volume that adapts to the target human body.

Firstly, we use the SMPL model [17] as the geometry prior, and get the pixel-aligned image features for each of the 6890 SMPL vertices $v_l$ from each source image $\mathbf{I}_m$. Specifically, we multiply the coordinate of $v_l$ with each source camera pose $[\mathbf{R}_m | \mathbf{t}_m]$ to transform the original $v_l$ to $v_{lm}$ into the source camera coordinate system, and then utilize the intrinsic matrix $\mathbf{K}_m$ to obtain the projected coordinate $\pi(v_{lm})$ in the corresponding image plane. We denote the pixel-aligned features from the image features $\mathbf{F}_m$ that corresponds to the pixel location of $\pi(v_{lm})$ as $\mathbf{F}_m(\pi(v_{lm}))$. We use bilinear interpolation to obtain the corresponding features if the projected location is fractional.

After obtaining $\mathbf{F}_m(\pi(v_{lm}))$ from $M$ source views, we integrate them to represent the geometry information at vertex $v_l$ through a geometry-guided attention module. Concretely, we learn an embedding $\mathbf{Q}_l$ for each $v_l$, and then take

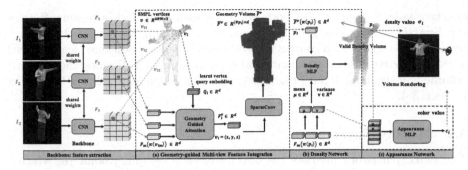

**Fig. 2. Overview of our proposed framework.** Our progressive pipeline mainly contains three parts. **(a) Geometry-guided multi-view feature integration.** We first learn query embedding $Q_l$ for each SMPL vertex to adaptively integrate the multi-view pixel-aligned image features $\mathbf{F}_m(\pi(v_{lm}))$ through the geometry-guided attention module. Based on this, we utilize the SparseConvNet to construct a denser geometry feature volume $\tilde{\mathbf{F}}^v$. **(b) Density Network.** For point $p_i$ within $\tilde{\mathbf{F}}^v$, we concatenate its geometry feature $\tilde{\mathbf{F}}^v_i$ with the mean ($\boldsymbol{\mu}$) and variance ($\mathbf{v}$) of its pixel-aligned image features $\mathbf{F}_m(\pi(p_i))$, and predict its density value $\sigma_i$ through the density MLP. $p_i$ with a positive $\sigma_i$ form the valid density volume. **(c) Appearance Network.** For point $p_i$ within the valid density volume, we utilize $\mathbf{F}_m(\pi(p_i))$ to predict its color value $c_i$ through the appearance MLP. Finally, we conduct the volume rendering to render the target image.

$\mathbf{Q}_l$ as a query embedding to calculate the correspondence score $s_{lm}$ with each $\mathbf{F}_m(\pi(v_{lm}))$ respectively:

$$s^v_{lm} = \frac{(\boldsymbol{W}_1\mathbf{Q}_l + b_1)(\boldsymbol{W}_{2m}\mathbf{F}^v_{lm} + b_{2m})^\top}{\sqrt{d}}, \tag{1}$$

where we denote $\mathbf{F}_m(\pi(v_{lm}))$ as $\mathbf{F}^v_{lm}$ for simplicity. $d$ is the channel dimension of $\mathbf{F}^v_{lm}$. $\boldsymbol{W}$ represents linear projection layers. After that, we weighted sum the $M$ pixel-aligned feature embeddings $\mathbf{F}_m(\pi(v_{lm}))$ based on the scores $s_{lm}$ to obtain the aggregated geometry related feature $\mathbf{F}^v_l$ for vertex $v_l$:

$$\mathbf{F}^v_l = \sum_{m=1}^{M} s^v_{lm}\mathbf{F}^v_{lm}. \tag{2}$$

Considering the $6,890$ SMPL vertices with their corresponding features are not dense enough to represent the whole human body volume, we further learn to extend and fill the holes of the sparse geometry feature volume $\mathbf{F}^v = \{\mathbf{F}^v_l, l = 1, 2, ..., 6890\}$ through the SparseConvNet [7] and thus obtain a denser geometry feature volume, denoted as $\tilde{\mathbf{F}}^v$. In our method, we take the geometry volume $\tilde{\mathbf{F}}^v$ as a more reliable basis to indicate occupancy of the human body in the whole space volume. More advanced than the coarse model SMPL, $\tilde{\mathbf{F}}^v$ leverages the multi-view image-conditioned features to enhance the coarse geometry prior, which adapts to the shape of the target human body. $\tilde{\mathbf{F}}^v$ only preserves the effective volume regions with body contents, including clothes regions. Because the SparseConvNet can gain experience from training to extend the features towards the regions with contents, based on the image-conditioned features with some instructive context information at each feature point. Besides, the geometry volume will also benefit our progressive rendering pipeline, which will be detailed in Sect. 3.4.

## 3.2  Density Network

The density network predicts the opacity of each sampling point $\mathbf{p}_i$, which is highly related to the geometry of human body, like postures and shapes. Through the geometry-guided multi-view integration module in Sect. 3.1, we can construct a geometry feature volume $\tilde{\mathbf{F}}^v$ which can provide sufficient reliable geometry information of the target human body. As shown in Fig. 2 (b), for each sampling point $\mathbf{p}_i$, we obtain its corresponding geometry related feature $\tilde{\mathbf{F}}_i^v$ from $\tilde{\mathbf{F}}^v$ based on its coordinate. Though the feature volume can provide the geometry information of human body, such geometry-related features are coarse and may lose some fine image-conditioned features that benefit the high-fidelity rendering. To compensate the information loss, we combine these two kinds of features at each sampling point to predict its density value more accurately. Therefore, we concatenate $\tilde{\mathbf{F}}_i^v$ with the mean ($\boldsymbol{\mu}$) and variance ($\mathbf{v}$) feature embedding of its corresponding pixel-aligned image features $\{\mathbf{F}_m(\pi(v_{lm})), m = 1, 2, ..., M\}$ that contain more detailed information, and process the concatenated feature through a density MLP to predict the density value at this point.

## 3.3  Appearance Network

The appearance network aims to predict the RGB color value for each sampling point $\mathbf{p}_i$. Since the RGB value is more related to the appearance details of human body, we utilize the image-conditioned features as the input to the appearance network for more detailed information. As shown in Fig. 2 (c), we first aggregate the pixel-aligned image features from input views for each color sampling point $\mathbf{p}_i^c$. Specifically, similar to obtaining the pixel-aligned image features for each SMPL vertex, we project the coordinate of $\mathbf{p}_i$ to the image plane of each source view, and obtain the pixel-aligned feature embedding, denoted as $\mathbf{F}_m(\pi(\mathbf{p}_i))$. We then concatenate $\mathbf{F}_m(\pi(\mathbf{p}_i))$ from $M$ source views with their mean ($\boldsymbol{\mu}$) and variance ($\mathbf{v}$) feature embeddings together. Afterwards, based on the concatenated feature embeddings, an appearance MLP is deployed to predict the RGB value $\hat{\mathbf{c}}_i = (\hat{r}_i, \hat{g}_i, \hat{b}_i)$ for the corresponding point $\mathbf{p}_i$.

## 3.4  Geometry-Guided Progressive Rendering

We render the human body in the target view through the volumetric rendering following previous NeRF-based methods [10,18,24]. Instead of sampling many redundant points for rendering, we introduce an efficient geometry-guided progressive rendering pipeline for the inference process. Our pipeline leverages the geometry volume in Sect. 3.1 as well as the predicted density values in Sect. 3.2 to reduce the number of points progressively.

Specifically, we first preserve the sampling points that occupy the geometry volume $\tilde{\mathbf{F}}^v$ as valid density sampling points $\mathbf{p}_i^d$. Compared to the smallest pillar that contains the human body that is used by previous methods [10,24], the geometry volume is closer to the human body shape and contains much fewer redundant void sampling points. Then we predict the density values for $\mathbf{p}_i^d$ through the density network, and the sampling points that have positive density values form a valid density volume. As shown in Fig. 2, the valid density volume is very close to the 3D mesh of the target human body and we further remove many empty regions compared to the geometry volume. We take the sampling points in the valid density volume as the new valid sampling points $\mathbf{p}_i^c$, and further predict their color values through the appearance network in Sect. 3.3.

We conduct volume rendering based on the density and color predictions to synthesize the target view $\mathbf{I}_t$. Traditional volume rendering methods often march rays $\mathbf{r}$ from the target camera to the pixels of the target view image, and then sample $N$ points on each $\mathbf{r}$. Denoting the distance of two adjacent sampling points on $\mathbf{r}$ as $\delta$, we can formulate the color rendering process for each $\mathbf{r}$ as:

$$\hat{C}(\mathbf{r}) = \sum_{i=1}^{N} T_i \left(1 - \exp\left(-\sigma_i \delta_i\right)\right) \hat{\mathbf{c}}_i,$$

$$\text{where } T_i = \exp\left(-\sum_{j=1}^{i-1} \sigma_j \delta_j\right). \tag{3}$$

For our progressive rendering pipeline, we use projection to bind the sampling points to $\mathbf{r}$. Concretely, we project the points within the geometry volume to the target view, take the nearest four pixels of the projected points as valid pixels to march a ray, and then uniformly sample $N$ points between its near and far bounds as [10,24]. We only process the sampling points within the valid volume regions and then conduct volume rendering based on the rays $\mathbf{r}$.

Experiments in Sect. 4.4 verify that our geometry-guided progressive rendering pipeline reduces the memory and time consumption during rendering significantly, and our performance can be even lifted by removing noisy unnecessary sampling points.

## 3.5    Training

During training, we do not deploy the progressive rendering pipeline in Sect. 3.4, because it is useful only when our density network is reliable. Instead, we march rays from the target camera to pixels randomly sampled on the image while ensuring no fewer than half of the pixels are on the human body. We uniformly sample points on the rays to predict the corresponding density and color values. By performing the volume rendering in Eq. (3), we obtain the predicted color $\hat{C}(\mathbf{r})$ for each $\mathbf{r}$. To supervise the network, we calculate the Mean Square Error loss between $\hat{C}(\mathbf{r})$ and the corresponding ground truth $C(\mathbf{r})$ color value as our training loss $\mathcal{L}_{rgb}$.

# 4 Experiments

We study four questions in experiments. 1) Is GP-NeRF able to improve the fitting and generalization performance of human synthesis on the seen and unseen scenarios (Sect. 4.3)? 2) Is GP-NeRF effective at reducing the time and memory cost for rendering (Sect. 4.4)? 3) How does each individual design choice affect model performance (Sect. 4.5) 4) Can GP-NeRF provide promising results, both for human rendering and 3D reconstruction (Sect. 4.6)? We describe the datasets and evaluation metrics in Sect. 4.1, and our default implementation setting in Sect. 4.2.

## 4.1 Datasets and Metrics

We train and evaluate our method on the ZJU-MoCap dataset [24] and THUman 1.0 dataset [37]. ZJU-MoCap contains 10 sequences with 21 synchronized cameras. We split the 10 sequences into a training set with 7 sequences and a test set with the remaining 3 sequences, following [10] for a fair comparison. THUman contains 202 human body 3D scans. 80% of the scans are taken as the training set, and the remaining are the test set. We render images for each scan from 24 virtual cameras, which are uniformly set on the horizontal plane.

To evaluate the rendering performance, we choose two metrics: peak signal-to-noise ratio (PSNR) and structural similarity index (SSIM) following [18,24]. For the 3D reconstruction, we only provide the qualitative results since the corresponding ground truth is not available.

## 4.2 Implementation Details

In our implementation, we perform training and inference with an image size of $512 \times 512$ under $M = 3$ camera views, where the horizontal angle interval is around $120°$ (Uniform). We utilize a U-Net like architecture [33] as our backbone to extract the image features $\mathbf{F}$ in Sect. 3 with a dimension of 32. We sample $N = 64$ points uniformly between the near and far bound on each ray. For training, we utilize the Adam optimizer [9], and the learning rate decays exponentially from $1e - 4$ for 180k steps. We use one RTX 3090 GPU with a batch size of 1 for both training and inference.

## 4.3 Synthesis Performance Analysis

In Table 1, we compare our human rendering results to previous state-of-the-art methods. To evaluate the capacity of fitting and generalization on different levels, we train our framework on the first 300 frames of 7 training video sequences of ZJU-MoCap (ZJU-7), and test on 1) the training frames, 2) unseen frames of

**Table 1. Synthesis performance comparison.** Our proposed method outperforms existing methods on all the settings.

| Method | Dataset Train | Test | Per-scene training | Unseen Pose | Body | Results PSNR (↑) | SSIM (↑) |
|---|---|---|---|---|---|---|---|
| Performance on training frames | | | | | | | |
| NT [32] | ZJU-7 | ZJU-7 | ✓ | ✗ | ✗ | 23.86 | 0.896 |
| NHR [34] | ZJU-7 | ZJU-7 | ✓ | ✗ | ✗ | 23.95 | 0.897 |
| NB [24] | ZJU-7 | ZJU-7 | ✓ | ✗ | ✗ | 28.51 | **0.947** |
| NHP [10] | ZJU-7 | ZJU-7 | ✗ | ✗ | ✗ | 28.73 | 0.936 |
| GP-NeRF (Ours) | ZJU-7 | ZJU-7 | ✗ | ✗ | ✗ | **28.91** | 0.944 |
| Performance on unseen frames from training data | | | | | | | |
| NV [16] | ZJU-7 | ZJU-7 | ✓ | ✓ | ✗ | 22.00 | 0.818 |
| NT [32] | ZJU-7 | ZJU-7 | ✓ | ✓ | ✗ | 22.28 | 0.872 |
| NHR [34] | ZJU-7 | ZJU-7 | ✓ | ✓ | ✗ | 22.31 | 0.871 |
| NB [24] | ZJU-7 | ZJU-7 | ✓ | ✓ | ✗ | 23.79 | 0.887 |
| NHP [10] | ZJU-7 | ZJU-7 | ✗ | ✓ | ✗ | 26.94 | 0.929 |
| GP-NeRF (Ours) | ZJU-7 | ZJU-7 | ✗ | ✓ | ✗ | **27.92** | **0.934** |
| Performance on test frames from test data | | | | | | | |
| NV [16] | ZJU-3 | ZJU-3 | ✓ | ✓ | ✗ | 20.84 | 0.827 |
| NT [32] | ZJU-3 | ZJU-3 | ✓ | ✓ | ✗ | 21.92 | 0.873 |
| NHR [34] | ZJU-3 | ZJU-3 | ✓ | ✓ | ✗ | 22.03 | 0.875 |
| NB [24] | ZJU-3 | ZJU-3 | ✓ | ✓ | ✗ | 22.88 | 0.880 |
| PVA [26] | ZJU-7 | ZJU-3 | ✗ | ✓ | ✓ | 23.15 | 0.866 |
| Pixel-NeRF [35] | ZJU-7 | ZJU-3 | ✗ | ✓ | ✓ | 23.17 | 0.869 |
| NHP [10] | ZJU-7 | ZJU-3 | ✗ | ✓ | ✓ | 24.75 | 0.906 |
| GP-NeRF (Ours) | ZJU-7 | ZJU-3 | ✗ | ✓ | ✓ | **25.96** | **0.921** |
| Generalization performance across datasets | | | | | | | |
| NHP [10] | AIST | ZJU-3 | ✗ | ✓ | ✓ | 17.05 | 0.771 |
| GP-NeRF (Ours) | THUman-7 | ZJU-3 | ✗ | ✓ | ✓ | 24.74 | 0.907 |
| GP-NeRF (Ours) | THUman-all | ZJU-3 | ✗ | ✓ | ✓ | **25.60** | **0.917** |

ZJU-7, and 3) test frames from the 3 test sequences (ZJU-3), respectively. The results in Table 1 verify our advanced generalization capacity on the unseen scenarios. We also achieve competitive fitting performance on the training frames, even comparable to the per-scene optimization methods [24,32,34].

Notably, our method outperforms the state-of-the-art NHP [10] which utilizes the geometry prior with features of multi-view videos. Specifically, for the unseen poses and the unseen bodies, we outperform NHP by 0.98 and 1.21 dB on PSNR, and also by 0.5% and 1.5% on SSIM respectively, using only single-frame input. We also conduct generalization experiments across two datasets with different domains. We train our model on 7 random human bodies from the THUman dataset (THUman-7) and all 202 human bodies (THUman-all) separately, and test the synthesis performance on the test frames of ZJU-3. From Table 1, we observe our method outperforms NHP by a large margin under cross-dataset evaluation setup, i.e., around 7.7 dB and 13.6% improvements on PSNR and SSIM respectively. All these results demonstrate the effectiveness of our geometry-guided multi-view information integration approach.

### 4.4  Efficiency Analysis

In Table 2, we analyze the efficiency improvements[1] gained from our progressive pipeline on the first 300 frames of the 315 (Taichi) sequence in ZJU-MoCap dataset.

**Table 2. Computation and memory cost comparison.** GP-NeRF[†] has the same structure as our GP-NeRF but adopts vanilla rendering technique. $\times N$ indicates the sampling points are split into $N$ chunks to be processed. #$\mathbf{r}$ means the number of sampling rays; #$\mathbf{p}^d$ and #$\mathbf{p}^c$ mean sampling points through the density network and appearance network, respectively. $T^d$-total indicates the total time cost from backbone output to the density volume, including $T^d$-MLP which means the forwarding time of the density MLP. $T^c$-total means the time from density volume to the color prediction, and $T^c$-MLP is the time for the appearance MLP.

| Method | #$\mathbf{r}$ (M) ($\downarrow$) | #$\mathbf{p}^d$ (M) ($\downarrow$) | #$\mathbf{p}^c$ (M) ($\downarrow$) | Time (ms) ($\downarrow$) | Mem (GB) ($\downarrow$) |
|---|---|---|---|---|---|
| NHP [10] | 0.063 | 4.03 | 4.03 | 1160 | 14.20 |
| NHR [34] | 0.063 | 4.03 | 4.03 | 636 | 10.20 |
| NB [24] | 0.063 | 4.03 | 4.03 | 611 | 21.80 |
| GP-NeRF[†] 3× | 0.063 (−0.0%) | 4.03 (−0.0%) | 4.03 (−0.0%) | 589 (−3.6%) | 14.53 (−33.3%) |
| GP-NeRF[†] 2× | 0.063 (−0.0%) | 4.03 (−0.0%) | 4.03 (−0.0%) | 567 (−7.2%) | 20.74 (−4.9%) |
| GP-NeRF 2× | **0.039 (−38.1%)** | **0.95 (−76.4%)** | **0.24 (−94.0%)** | 243 (−60.2%) | **9.88 (−54.7%)** |
| GP-NeRF 1× | **0.039 (−38.1%)** | **0.95 (−76.4%)** | **0.24 (−94.0%)** | **175 (−71.4%)** | 14.25 (−34.6%) |

| Method | $T^d$-MLP (ms) ($\downarrow$) | $T^d$-total (ms) ($\downarrow$) | $T^c$-MLP (ms) ($\downarrow$) | $T^c$-total (ms) ($\downarrow$) | PSNR ($\uparrow$) |
|---|---|---|---|---|---|
| GP-NeRF[†] 2× | 108.58 | 226.56 | 145.38 | 146.39 | 26.56 |
| GP-NeRF 2× | 28.08 (−74.1%) | 83.65 (−63.1%) | 10.02 (−93.1%) | 11.4 (−92.2%) | **26.67 (+0.4%)** |
| GP-NeRF 1× | **23.55 (−78.3%)** | **74.07 (−67.3%)** | **9.50 (−93.5%)** | **10.27 (−93.0%)** | **26.67 (+0.4%)** |

Considering the limited GPU memory, our final GP-NeRF can process all the sampling points in one run, but GP-NeRF[†] and NB [24] requires at least twice. As shown in the upper panel of Table 2, compared to NB, NHR and NHP which also use the SMPL bounds to remove redundant marched rays, our GP-NeRF can further remove 38.1% rays and 76.4% #$\mathbf{p}^d$ by referring to the constructed geometry volume, and remove 94.0% #$\mathbf{p}^c$ based on the valid density volume. Comparing to NB, NHR and NHP, our GP-NeRF 2× costs 60% − 79% less time with lower memory. For fair comparison to GP-NeRF[†] 2×, we also test the

---

[1] We count averaged per-sample inference time in milliseconds. For all methods, the time is counted on NVIDIA GeForce RTX 3090 and CPU Intel i7-11700 @ 2.50 GHz, PyTorch 1.8, CUDA 11.4.

speed on GP-NeRF for 2 chunks, and our progressive pipeline still reduces the time cost by 57% and the memory cost by 52.4%, which verifies the significant efficiency improvement from the proposed rendering pipeline.

In the bottom panel of Table 2, we compare the time cost of each component in GP-NeRF to GP-NeRF[†] without progressive points reduction. The results show that we can reduce over 74% and 63% time cost for density MLP forwarding and the total density related time $T^d$-total respectively, by simply using our progressive rendering pipeline on the same network structures. Our pipeline can also reduce over 92% time cost for the appearance MLP forwarding. Moreover, our progressive pipeline improves the efficiency significantly while even improving the PSNR metric by 0.4%, as it can ignore some noisy sampling points during rendering that might degrade the performance.

**Table 3. Ablations: feature integration.** G, Q, P are different approaches to obtain input features for the shared density and appearance network. G: geometry feature volume; Q: integrate multi-view information at each geometry vertex; P: pixel-aligned image features.

| Variants | G | Q | P | PSNR (↑) | SSIM (↑) |
|----------|---|---|---|----------|----------|
| G | ✓ | ✗ | ✗ | 23.47 | 0.880 |
| QG | ✓ | ✓ | ✗ | 23.68 | 0.885 |
| P | ✗ | ✗ | ✓ | 26.09 | 0.915 |
| QG+P | ✓ | ✓ | ✓ | **26.69** | **0.924** |

**Table 4. Ablations: progressive structure.** G, Q, P have the same meanings as Table 3. Disentangle indicates whether the density and appearance networks are in a progressive pipeline. Steps mean the number of training steps. The columns of Density and Appearance demonstrate components of the input features.

| Disentangle | Density | Appearance | Steps | PSNR (↑) | SSIM (↑) |
|-------------|---------|------------|-------|----------|----------|
| ✗ | QG+P | QG+P | 5000 | 26.05 | 0.912 |
| ✓ | QG+P | QG+P | 5000 | 26.13 | 0.917 |
| ✓ | QG+P | P | 5000 | 26.16 | 0.920 |
| ✓ | QG | P | 5000 | 25.71 | 0.904 |
| ✗ | QG+P | QG+P | 35000 | 26.69 | 0.924 |
| ✓ | QG+P | QG+P | 35000 | 26.65 | 0.925 |
| ✓ | QG+P | P | 35000 | 26.67 | 0.923 |
| ✓ | QG | P | 35000 | 26.40 | 0.918 |

## 4.5   Ablation Studies

We conduct ablation studies under the *uniform camera setting* in Sect. 4.2 to verify effectiveness of our main designed components on generalization capacity. We train our model on 7 training sequences of the ZJU-MoCap dataset for 35k steps and validate it on remaining 3 sequences.

**Feature Integration.** In Table 3, we explore the effectiveness of the proposed geometry-guided feature integration mechanism on the baseline GP-NeRF, i.e., GP-NeRF without adopting progressive rendering pipeline. As shown in Table 3, adaptively aggregating multi-view image features with the guidance of the geometry prior to construct the geometry feature volume ($QG$) achieves better performance (i.e., 0.21 dB and 0.5% improvements on PSNR and SSIM respectively) than baseline that simply uses the mean of multi-view image features ($G$), as the proposed geometry-guided attention module helps focus more on the views corresponding to the geometry prior. We also observe baseline using only pixel-aligned image features ($P$) gains 2.41 dB PSNR and 3% SSIM over baseline using only geometry feature ($G$), as it captures more detailed appearance features from images for high-fidelity rendering. Moreover, by combining the geometry feature and its corresponding detailed image features ($QG+P$), we can improve upon $P$ by 0.6 dB PSNR and 0.9% SSIM respectively. This indicates that both the geometry and the pixel-aligned image features can compensate each other for better generalization performance on unseen scenarios.

**Progressive Structure.** Our progressive rendering pipeline in Sect. 3.4 requires a progressive structure of the density and appearance network. Based on the same experimental settings, we further decouple the density and appearance networks to form a progressive pipeline as in Fig. 2 and evaluate the performance. As shown in Table 4, the progressive structure does not harm the performance and even reaches relatively high performance faster. This is because it allows these two networks to lean their different focus, thus improving the performance more quickly during training. For the density network, involving more detailed image features $P$ can enhance the relatively coarse geometry feature $QG$, and bring around 0.5% improvements on SSIM. The results also show that the geometry feature $QG$ is much more impactful on the geometry-related density prediction than on the appearance-related color value prediction.

## 4.6   Visualization

We visualize our human rendering results under three uniform camera views in different experimental settings (Fig. 3). As Fig. 3 (a), (b) and (c) show, compared with other approaches, our method achieves better quality on unseen poses or bodies by synthesizing more high-fidelity details like the clothes wrinkles and reconstructing the body shape more accurately. From Fig. 3 (d), we demonstrate some rendering results on the unseen bodies of the THUman dataset after training on it. Our method generalizes well on the same THUman dataset and can synthesize accurate details.

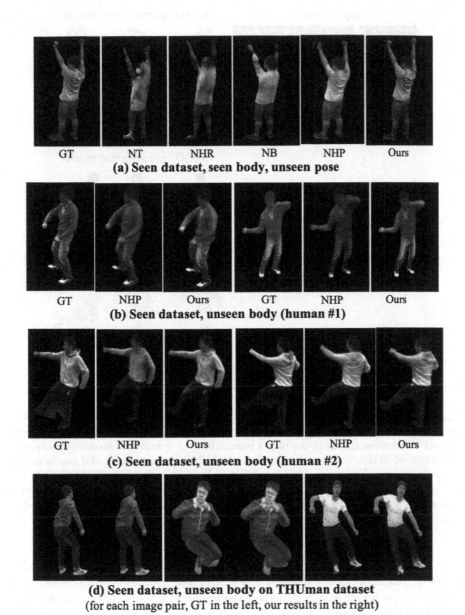

(a) Seen dataset, seen body, unseen pose

(b) Seen dataset, unseen body (human #1)

(c) Seen dataset, unseen body (human #2)

(d) Seen dataset, unseen body on THUman dataset
(for each image pair, GT in the left, our results in the right)

**Fig. 3. Visualization comparisons on human rendering.** Comparing to other methods, ours can synthesize more high-fidelity details like the clothes wrinkles and reconstructing the body shape more accurately. Our synthesis can stick to the normal human body geometry better than methods without geometry priors like NT and NHR. We can also recover more accurate lighting conditions than the previous video-based generalizable method NHP on unseen bodies (as (b) and (c)).

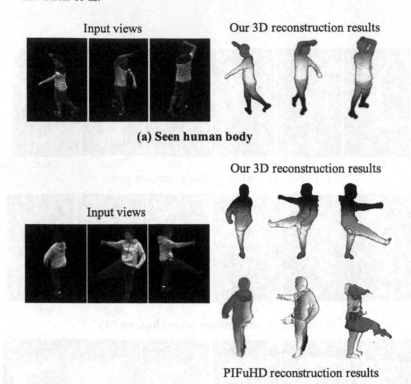

(a) Seen human body

(b) Unseen human body

**Fig. 4. Visualization of our 3D reconstruction results.** The color in the mesh is only for clearer visualization. By integrating multi-view information to form a complete geometry volume adapting to the target human body, our method can compensate some limitations of SMPL (e.g., not accurate or lack cloth information), and can generally reconstruct very close human body shape and even clothes details like hoods and folds on unseen human bodies (as (b)). We can generalize better on the unseen human bodies than previous image based 3D construction method like PIFuHD, which predicts incomplete or redundant body parts in its reconstruction results (as (b)).

In Fig. 4, we visualize the density volume from the density MLP in Sect. 3.2 as the mesh results of our 3D reconstruction. Different from previous methods that densely sample points within bounds of the geometry prior to determine the inside points through the density network for mesh construction, our progressive pipeline directly determines the sampling points from the geometry volume in Sect. 3.1, which contains much fewer redundant points and thus is more efficient for 3D reconstruction. Then we construct the mesh based on the points with higher density values. As Fig. 4 (b) shows, on the unseen human bodies, previous image based 3D construction method like PIFuHD [28] can not generalize well. Besides their lower efficiency on making predictions for a lot of redundant sampling points, they are more likely to predict body parts that do not conform to a normal human body structure, because they can not integrate and adapt the given geometry information as well as we do. As shown in Fig. 4, by integrating multi-view information to form a complete geometry volume adapting to the target human body, our method can generally reconstruct very close human body shape and even clothes details like folds on even unseen human bodies (Fig. 4 (b)).

## 5    Conclusion

We propose a geometry-guided progressive NeRF model for generalizable and efficient free-viewpoint human rendering under sparse camera settings. Using our geometry-guided multi-view feature aggregation approach, the geometry prior can be effectively enhanced with the integrated multi-view information and form a complete geometry volume adapting to the target human body. The geometry feature volume combined with the detailed image-conditioned features can benefit the generalization performance on unseen scenarios. We also introduce a progressive rendering pipeline for higher efficiency, which reduces over 70% rendering time cost without performance degradation. Experimental results on two datasets verify our model can outperform previous methods significantly on generalization capacity and efficiency.

## References

1. Carranza, J., Theobalt, C., Magnor, M.A., Seidel, H.P.: Free-viewpoint video of human actors. ACM Trans. Graph. **22**(3), 569–577 (2003)
2. Collet, A., et al.: High-quality streamable free-viewpoint video. ACM Trans. Graph. **34**(4), 1–13 (2015)
3. De Aguiar, E., Stoll, C., Theobalt, C., Ahmed, N., Seidel, H.P., Thrun, S.: Performance capture from sparse multi-view video. In: ACM Trans Graphics (2008)
4. Debevec, P., Hawkins, T., Tchou, C., Duiker, H.P., Sarokin, W., Sagar, M.: Acquiring the reflectance field of a human face. In: Proceedings of the 27th Annual Conference on Computer Graphics and Interactive Techniques (2000)
5. Dou, M., et al.: Fusion4d: real-time performance capture of challenging scenes. ACM Trans. Graph. **35**(4), 1–13 (2016)
6. Gall, J., Stoll, C., De Aguiar, E., Theobalt, C., Rosenhahn, B., Seidel, H.P.: Motion capture using joint skeleton tracking and surface estimation. In: CVPR (2009)
7. Graham, B., Engelcke, M., Van Der Maaten, L.: 3d semantic segmentation with submanifold sparse convolutional networks. In: CVPR (2018)
8. Guo, K., et al.: The relightables: volumetric performance capture of humans with realistic relighting. ACM Trans. Graph. **38**(6), 1–19 (2019)
9. Kingma, D.P., Ba, J.: Adam: a method for stochastic optimization. In: ICCV (2015)
10. Kwon, Y., Kim, D., Ceylan, D., Fuchs, H.: Neural human performer: learning generalizable radiance fields for human performance rendering. In: NeurIPS (2021)
11. Li, R., Xiu, Y., Saito, S., Huang, Z., Olszewski, K., Li, H.: Monocular real-time volumetric performance capture. In: ECCV (2020)
12. Li, T., et al.: Neural 3d video synthesis. arXiv (2021)
13. Liu, L., Gu, J., Lin, K.Z., Chua, T.S., Theobalt, C.: Neural sparse voxel fields. arXiv (2020)

14. Liu, L., Habermann, M., Rudnev, V., Sarkar, K., Gu, J., Theobalt, C.: Neural actor: neural free-view synthesis of human actors with pose control. ACM Trans. Graph. **40**(6), 1–16 (2021)
15. Liu, S., Zhang, Y., Peng, S., Shi, B., Pollefeys, M., Cui, Z.: Dist: rendering deep implicit signed distance function with differentiable sphere tracing. In: CVPR (2020)
16. Lombardi, S., Simon, T., Saragih, J., Schwartz, G., Lehrmann, A., Sheikh, Y.: Neural volumes: Learning dynamic renderable volumes from images. In: ACM Transactions on Graphics (2019)
17. Loper, M., Mahmood, N., Romero, J., Pons-Moll, G., Black, M.J.: SMPL: a skinned multi-person linear model. ACM Trans. Graph. **34**(6), 1–16 (2015)
18. Mildenhall, B., Srinivasan, P.P., Tancik, M., Barron, J.T., Ramamoorthi, R., Ng, R.: NeRF: representing scenes as neural radiance fields for view synthesis. In: ECCV (2020)
19. Natsume, R., et al.: SiCloPe: silhouette-based clothed people. In: CVPR (2019)
20. Newcombe, R.A., Fox, D., Seitz, S.M.: Dynamicfusion: reconstruction and tracking of non-rigid scenes in real-time. In: CVPR (2015)
21. Niemeyer, M., Mescheder, L., Oechsle, M., Geiger, A.: Differentiable volumetric rendering: Learning implicit 3d representations without 3d supervision. In: CVPR (2020)
22. Park, K., et al.: Deformable neural radiance fields. arXiv (2020)
23. Peng, S., et al.: Animatable neural implicit surfaces for creating avatars from videos (2022)
24. Peng, S., et al.: Neural body: implicit neural representations with structured latent codes for novel view synthesis of dynamic humans. In: CVPR (2021)
25. Pumarola, A., Corona, E., Pons-Moll, G., Moreno-Noguer, F.: D-nerf: neural radiance fields for dynamic scenes. In: CVPR (2021)
26. Raj, A., et al.: Pva: pixel-aligned volumetric avatars. arXiv (2021)
27. Saito, S., Huang, Z., Natsume, R., Morishima, S., Kanazawa, A., Li, H.: Pifu: pixel-aligned implicit function for high-resolution clothed human digitization. In: ICCV (2019)
28. Saito, S., Simon, T., Saragih, J., Joo, H.: Pifuhd: multi-level pixel-aligned implicit function for high-resolution 3d human digitization. In: CVPR (2020)
29. Sitzmann, V., Zollhöfer, M., Wetzstein, G.: Scene representation networks: Continuous 3d-structure-aware neural scene representations. arXiv (2019)
30. Stoll, C., Gall, J., De Aguiar, E., Thrun, S., Theobalt, C.: Video-based reconstruction of animatable human characters. ACM Trans. Graph. **29**(6), 1–10. (2010)
31. Su, Z., Xu, L., Zheng, Z., Yu, T., Liu, Y., Fang, L.: Robustfusion: human volumetric capture with data-driven visual cues using a RGBD camera. In: ECCV (2020)
32. Thies, J., Zollhöfer, M., Nießner, M.: Deferred neural rendering: image synthesis using neural textures. ACM Trans. Graph. **38**(4), 1–12 (2019)
33. Wang, Q., et al.: IBRNet: learning multi-view image-based rendering. In: CVPR (2021)
34. Wu, M., Wang, Y., Hu, Q., Yu, J.: Multi-view neural human rendering. In: CVPR (2020)
35. Yu, A., Ye, V., Tancik, M., Kanazawa, A.: pixelNeRF: neural radiance fields from one or few images. arXiv (2020)
36. Yuan, W., Lv, Z., Schmidt, T., Lovegrove, S.: Star: self-supervised tracking and reconstruction of rigid objects in motion with neural rendering. In: CVPR (2021)

37. Zheng, Z., Yu, T., Wei, Y., Dai, Q., Liu, Y.: Deephuman: 3d human reconstruction from a single image. In: ICCV (2019)
38. Zins, P., Xu, Y., Boyer, E., Wuhrer, S., Tung, T.: Data-driven 3d reconstruction of dressed humans from sparse views. In: 2021 International Conference on 3D Vision (3DV), pp. 494–504 (2021)

# Controllable Shadow Generation Using Pixel Height Maps

Yichen Sheng[1(✉)], Yifan Liu[2], Jianming Zhang[3], Wei Yin[2],
A. Cengiz Oztireli[4], He Zhang[3], Zhe Lin[3], Eli Shechtman[3], and Bedrich Benes[1]

[1] Purdue University, West Lafayette, USA
sheng30@purdue.edu
[2] University of Adelaide, Adelaide, Australia
[3] Adobe Research, San Jose, USA
[4] University of Cambridge, Cambridge, UK

**Abstract.** Shadows are essential for realistic image compositing from 2D image cutouts. Physics-based shadow rendering methods require 3D geometries, which are not always available. Deep learning-based shadow synthesis methods learn a mapping from the light information to an object's shadow without explicitly modeling the shadow geometry. Still, they lack control and are prone to visual artifacts. We introduce "Pixel Height", a novel geometry representation that encodes the correlations between objects, ground, and camera pose. The Pixel Height can be calculated from 3D geometries, manually annotated on 2D images, and can also be predicted from a single-view RGB image by a supervised approach. It can be used to calculate hard shadows in a 2D image based on the projective geometry, providing precise control of the shadows' direction and shape. Furthermore, we propose a data-driven soft shadow generator to apply softness to a hard shadow based on a softness input parameter. Qualitative and quantitative evaluations demonstrate that the proposed Pixel Height significantly improves the quality of the shadow generation while allowing for controllability.

## 1 Introduction

Shadow generation is an important step for image compositing that enhances photo realism and adds positional and directional cues for the composed objects. Advanced image editing techniques enable composing objects into a new background with accurate segmentation and matting [23] and harmonization of color styles [17]. However, the composited objects are not realistic if no matching shadows are synthesized (see the 1st and 3rd images in the second row in Fig. 1). Manually creating a perceptually plausible shadow for a 2D object is tedious, even for an experienced artist, especially for extended (linear or area) light sources.

Y. Sheng and Y. Liu—Contributed equally.

**Supplementary Information** The online version contains supplementary material available at https://doi.org/10.1007/978-3-031-20050-2_15.

Mature techniques that calculate soft shadows for 3D scenes exist [6,26]. However, 3D shape information is often unavailable when we composite objects from real images. Recent deep learning advancements brought significant progress to shadow generation in 2D images. A series of methods [14,21,45] based on generative adversarial networks (GANs) have been proposed to automatically generate shadows by training with pairs of shadow and shadow-free images. These methods mainly focus on generating hard shadows, and the final results are not editable. Moreover, these methods require the background scene to implicitly provide light information, while in many application scenarios, objects are either composited on abstract or pure color background. Also, shadow editing needs to be applied on separate image layers with background images missing or incomplete at the time of editing. Therefore, shadow generation for object cutouts with user control is more suited for professional image editing workflows. Recently, Sheng et al. [36] proposed to learn a mapping from a 2D cutout of the object to the corresponding soft shadows based on a controllable lightmap and achieved promising results. However, due to the lack of geometry guidance, this method cannot generalize well for varying scenes and may lead to visible artifacts in the generated shadows.

**Fig. 1.** Controllable shadow generation with the proposed method. **First row**: With the help of our new introduced *Pixel Height* of an object, users can control the position and the softness of the generated shadows. **Second row**: The composited images with our generated shadows (2nd and 4th) are much more natural than the direct composites (1st and 3rd).

We introduce a controllable and editable shadow generation method for 2D object cutouts. We introduce *Pixel Height*, a new 2.5D shape representation for an image to provide geometry guidance. The Pixel Height is defined as the pixel distance between a point on an object and its *footpoint*, namely its vertical projection on the ground in the image (see Fig. 2-(a)). Based on Pixel Height, we can explicitly compute the shadow point based on projective geometry. The Pixel Height could be measured and annotated on a 2D image or calculated from synthetic data with 3D object models. Similar to monocular depth estimation, Pixel Height can also be estimated from a single RGB image by a data-driven method. We collect synthetic and real annotated data (see Fig. 2-(b) and (c)) to train a Pixel Height map prediction model for object cutouts.

Given the annotated or predicted Pixel Height map of an object, we render a hard shadow based on the position of the horizon and the point light in the 2D image space with a proposed *hard shadow renderer*. To add softness to the shadow, we learn an efficient and controllable mapping from the hard shadow to the soft shadows based on a softness parameter using *a soft shadow generator*. As shown in Fig. 1, our system can generate varying shadow maps controlled by the light source position and the softness control. Our method explicitly models the shadow geometry that is more controllable and robust than methods that directly predict shadows based on an image background or a light map.

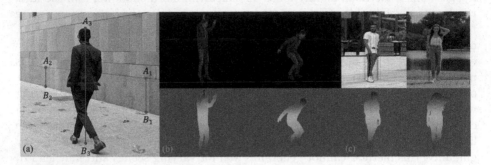

**Fig. 2. Pixel Height.** (a). The number of pixels between point $A_i$ and $B_i$ is the Pixel Height for point $A_i$. We collected two datasets with Pixel Height annotation: Synthetic60K and Real1500. (b) shows the sample data with various poses from 3D models. (c) shows samples of the sparsely labeled data and the interpolated Pixel Height map. Note that every Pixel Height map is divided by its max-height value for visualization.

We conduct extensive experiments to show that the Pixel Height map improves the controllability of shadow generation. Realistic shadows are synthesized by easy and intuitive user control given the RGB image and an object segmentation mask. Qualitative and quantitative results demonstrate that our method generates higher quality shadows than previous interactive and automatic shadow generation algorithms in 2D images. Our main contributions are:

- A formulation of hard shadow rendering in images based on a novel geometry representation, Pixel Height, which can be manually labeled or predicted by a model from a single image.
- A controllable shadow generation framework, where users control the position and softness of an object shadow. The framework consists of a Pixel Height estimation, a hard shadow renderer and a soft shadow generator.
- Extensive evaluation and analysis, showing improved quality and controllability of our proposed Pixel Height based shadow synthesis method.

## 2    Related Work

**Shadow Rendering in Graphics.** Shadow rendering based on 3D geometries is a well-studied technique in computer graphics. In real-time rendering, shadow volume [2,34] and shadow map based rendering techniques are mainstream approaches [7,28,35,41]. The soft shadow is approximated either by blurring the hard shadow boundaries [1,4,8,11,12,38] or weighted sum of a set of hard shadows sampling on an area or volume light source [6]. Many works [9,24,26] have been proposed to speed up this sampling process by adjusting the density and the weight. Besides, some simplified geometries [10,30] or light representations [13] are proposed to render shadows in real-time. Global illumination algorithms [5,18,25,37,40] render soft shadows implicitly. Such methods can render realistic shadows for complicated objects given accurate 3D object models. However, 3D models are not always available for objects in real images, especially in image compositing tasks in computer vision.

**Shadow Synthesis with Deep Learning.** In recent years, generative adversarial networks (GANs) have achieved significant improvements on image translation tasks [16,22]. A series of works [14,15,21,39,45] have been introduced for generating shadows directly from a composited shadow-free image based on the object mask guidance. ARShadowGan [21] renders a dataset by inserting 3D objects into real background images with augmented reality. Hong *et al.* [14] generate the shadow-free images by removing the shadow region from the real-world images. These methods try to predict the style and the color of the final shadow by a data-driven method, but they cannot provide controllability for the user.

Sheng *et al.* [36] propose an interactive soft shadow generation network based on a user-provided lightmap. Physics-based methods on 3D object models render their training data. The network is trained to learn the mapping from the 2D object cutout and environment lightmap to the soft shadow maps. Contrary to the previous works, we generate soft shadows by first generating a hard shadow and converting it to a soft shadow using a softness input parameter. This hard-to-soft transformation is much easier to learn. The hard shadow can be obtained with our proposed pixel-height map by calculating the occlusion directly in the 2D projection space with a simple shadow projection model.

**Geometry Representation.** Similar to monocular depth estimation [33], recovering Pixel Height map from a single image is an ill-posed problem. Numerous methods [20,43,44] exist to estimate depth from a single view image by supervised methods. As the depth is a 2.5D representation, the intrinsic camera parameters are required for recovering the 3D shape of the object. The 3D point cloud [29] is another geometry representation for 3D objects' shape. They can be captured by special scanners, recovered from multi-view images, but cannot be labeled directly just from a monocular image. Furthermore, methods [31,32] have been proposed to directly recover the 3D shape, especially for humans from a monocular image. The proposed Pixel Height map is a new geometry representation, which reflects the correlation among the object, shadow receiver, and camera pose. It is easier to interpret and annotate, and it is useful for applications that require explicit occluder-receiver constraints such as shadow generation.

## 3   Method

We propose a new approach to generate perceptually plausible soft shadows on 2D images without 3D object models. The key idea of our approach is to render the object's hard shadow from a point light in the image plane following a simplified projective geometry constraint (see Sec. 3.1), and then synthesize the corresponding soft shadow based on the hard shadow using a data-driven approach (see Sec. 3.3).

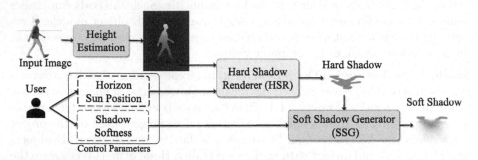

**Fig. 3.** Given a 2D foreground image and its Pixel Height map, a user can control the position and the softness of the generated shadow by the user-defined light information or the existing image-based light information. The Pixel Height map can be manually annotated on images or predicted from a single image by training a model.

We need to know the shape of the object and its relationship with the shadow receiver and the camera to render a hard shadow on the image plane. A new geometry representation Pixel Height is proposed to represent the object shape in 2D images, which is essential to rendering the hard shadow. We verify that this representation can be estimated by a data-driven approach (see Sec. 3.2).

As shown in Fig. 3, given the foreground object image and its mask, we can annotate or estimate its Pixel Height map. The hard shadow's position and shape can be determined by the controllable light information (the sun position) and the ground (the horizon line). Finally, based on the hard shadow, the soft shadow generator can produce a perceptually pleasing soft shadow according to the softness control parameter. The user could provide all the controllable variables with a simple GUI (see the supplementary videos), but they can also be potentially estimated from the background image.

## 3.1   Hard Shadow Renderer in 2D Image

This section introduces our novel hard shadow rendering method based on the following assumptions: (1) images are upright, and the vertical lines are parallel. This corresponds to the one-point perspective or the two-point perspective, which is very common, and (2) the light source is a point light and is always above ground. Note that if the first assumption does not exactly hold, the generated hard shadow will be slightly distorted, but still a good approximation.

A simple example of the projective geometry following our assumptions is shown in Fig. 4. Given an object $A'B'$ that stands vertically on the ground and a point light source $P'$, the object's shadow is then cast to $B'C'$. Given an image

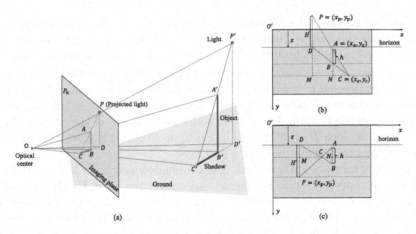

**Fig. 4. Hard shadow renderer using Pixel Height representation.** (a) shows the camera model, where $A'B'$ is the object standing upright on the ground, $P'$ is the point light source and $C'$ is the shadow point of $A'$. (b) and (c) shows two typical cases of the projection of the light, the object, and its shadow on the image plane. $D$ is the perpendicular feet of $P$. The intersection point $C$ of $DB$ and $PA$ is a projection of the shadow point $C'$. The 3D collinear property in the shadow geometry is preserved after being projected to the image plane.

plane, the light source, the object, and the shadow are projected to $P$, $AB$, and $BC$, respectively. The point $D'$ is the perpendicular footpoint of the light, which is projected to $D$. Note that $P'$, $A'$ and $C'$ are always collinear; and $C'$, $B'$ and $D'$ are always co-linear. Thus, the projections of these points are also collinear in the image plane. For a non-planar shadow receiver, *e.g.* a wall, a similar collinear condition still holds except that the shadow point $C'$ will be above the ground, and it will have its footpoint. For simplicity, we study the special case where the shadow receiver is the ground plane in the following. A more general formulation can be found in the supplementary material.

Figure 4 (b) and (c) show the image plane and the relevant variables. We define the upper left corner of the image as the origin of the coordinate system. The light $P$ and its projected perpendicular footpoint $D$ are located at $(x_p, y_p)$ and $(x_p, y_p + H)$ respectively, where $H$ is the pixel distance between $P$ and its footpoint, and we call it the *Pixel Height* of the light. Similarly, the object point $A$, its footpoint $B$ and its shadow point $C$ are located at $(x_a, y_a)$, $(x_a, y_a + h)$ and $(x_c, y_c)$, where $h$ is the Pixel Height of $A$.

According to the triangle similarity in Fig. 4-(b) and Fig. 4-(c), we have

$$\frac{h}{H} = \frac{CN}{CM} = \frac{x_c - x_a}{x_c - x_p} = \frac{AN}{PM} = \frac{y_c - y_a}{y_c - y_p}. \tag{1}$$

The shadow point $C$ can be derived from $(x_a, y_a, h)$ and $(x_p, y_p, H)$ by

$$C = [x_c, y_c] = \frac{1}{H - h} [Hx_a - hx_p, Hy_a - hy_p]. \tag{2}$$

Note that $H$ may take a positive or a negative value. A negative value of $H$ indicates that the light is behind the camera, and the shadow will be cast away from the camera (see Fig. 4-(c)). Note that the derived $C$ may not exist. For example, when $h > H > 0$, the ray $\overrightarrow{PA}$ will not intersect with the ground. In this case, the derived $C$ is actually the ground intersection point in the opposite direction of the ray. There is a special case when the light is infinity, and its footpoint is on the horizon. Let $Z$ denote the y coordinate of the horizon. In this case, we can replace $H$ with $Z - y_p$ in Eq. 2, and control the perspective of the shadow using the horizon line (see Fig. 9).

The above formulation describes how the shadow geometry is derived for our Pixel Height representation. For generic scenarios, the Pixel Height map of the shadow receiver needs to be provided, and the shadow map can be calculated by checking the collinear conditions similar to the ones mentioned above. We implemented the rendering algorithm for generic shadow receivers using CUDA. Please refer to supplementary materials for details. The visibility of the pixels on the shadow receiver can be computed in 20 ms for a $512 \times 512$ image.

## 3.2 Pixel Height Map Estimation

A Pixel Height map is a 2.5D representation similar to a depth map. Different from the depth map, the Pixel Height map uses the ground plane as a world frame reference to locate the object. It captures the object-ground relation so that the contact points and the uprightness of the object are explicitly enforced. In addition, Pixel Height map is measurable in the image space and can be annotated manually. In contrast, traditional 2.5D representations like depth are challenging to annotate from a single image. Objects reconstructed from a depth map can also be tilted if the camera intrinsic parameters are unknown.

The proposed Pixel Height representation is essential to the hard shadow rendering in a 2D image, and can be useful in other applications as well. In this section, we propose several methods to obtain the Pixel Height map.

**Calculated from 3D Geometries.** Given a 3D geometry and camera parameters, the Pixel Height map can be computed by calculating the projection of the distance between each projected point and its footpoint. Figure 2-(b) illustrates the rendererd RGB image and its Pixel Height map. With an accurate Pixel Height map, the proposed approach can render realistic soft shadows in real-time and generate visually comparable results with the renderings from a physics-based renderer (see Fig. 7).

**Labeled from 2D Images.** The Pixel Height could also be annotated from a real RGB image by experienced annotators. Annotators are required to label sparse points on the object masks. For each point, its perpendicular footpoint on the ground is annotated. Thus, the Pixel Height could be calculated by the distance along the y-axis. Bi-linear interpolation is employed to get the dense Pixel Height map for the object of interest. Although the interpolation method is not physically correct, the generated hard shadows with the interpolated dense Pixel Height maps are perceptually pleasing. Figure 2-(c) illustrates the sparsely labeled RGB images and interpolated Pixel Height maps.

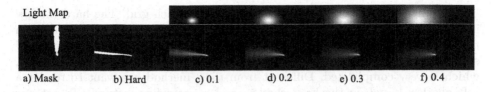

Light Map

a) Mask          b) Hard          c) 0.1          d) 0.2          e) 0.3          f) 0.4

**Fig. 5.** The training set for the soft shadow generator. a) the mask of the object. b) the hard shadow of the object. Figures c)-f) show the soft shadows and visualized light maps at different levels of softness. Softness models the size of the light source.

**Estimated from 2D Images.** Similar to the monocular depth estimation [33], estimating the Pixel Height from a single view image is an ill-posed problem. We verify that the Pixel Height could be estimated from a single view image. We propose a neural network for estimating humans' Pixel Height. The input to the network is the concatenation of the foreground image, the object mask, and a Y-Coordinate Map (YCM). We normalize the YCM by setting the lowest point in the object mask to be zero. Pixel Height map estimation is a high-level prediction problem, and the network should encode global information to get a better understanding of the geometry of the object. We employ an off-the-shelf transformer backbone, Mix Transformer encoder (MiT) [42]. A simple decoder merges features from different scales. The network's output is a one-channel Pixel Height map. For the training, We minimize the mean square error for each pixel inside the object mask between the prediction and the ground truth Pixel Height map. A total variation loss is used to regularize the prediction.

We use a synthetic dataset consisting of $60K$ renderings of 3D human models with various poses. We name this dataset *Synthetic60K*. To improve the model's generalization on real images, $1,500$ real images are collected and sparsely annotated to build a benchmark named *Real1500*. We used $1,000$ ($500$) images as the training (validation set). The ground truth Pixel Height of Synthetic60K and Real1500 are generated based on the methods described earlier in this section. We merge the *Synthetic60K* and the *Real1500* training set to train a Pixel Height Estimation Network (HENet). Each mini-batch is evenly sampled from the two datasets. More implementation details about the training are in the supplementary materials.

### 3.3   Soft Shadow Generator

With the Pixel Height map and the proposed hard shadow renderer, a hard shadow map can be generated given a point light position in the image. To add softness to the shadow, we train a soft shadow generator to create the effect of an area light and control the softness based on user input.

**Data Generation.** The soft shadows are generated following the pipeline in the Soft Shadow Network (SSN) [36]. They divided the location of the light into grids, and then randomly sampled an environment light map based on a 2D Gaussian distribution at one random grid. Soft shadow bases are generated by merging the hard shadows of a local patch for each grid. The hard shadow is generated by a GPU-based render with 3D models. Soft shadow based on the environment lightmap will be the weighted sum for the shadow bases. SSN enforces the network to learn a mapping from the lightmap and the soft shadow, which is very complicated. Different from their method, we want to render a soft shadow based on the hard shadow and a pre-define softness. To get our training samples, for each soft shadow and its paired environment lightmap, we find the corresponding hard shadow and the softness from the lightmap. The hard shadow is rendered with a given point light, which locates at the center of the area light. The softness is defined as the size of the Gaussian which is used to generate the lightmap. Figure 5 illustrates that an environment lightmap can be represented as a hard shadow and a softness value. Finally, we get our training triplet (hard shadow, soft shadow, and softness) on the fly during training.

**Network Structure.** The soft shadow generator (SSG) is a variant of the U-Net. Similar to the shadow render in SSN [36], the encoder of the network is composed of a series of $3 \times 3$ convolution layers. Skip connections are employed to capture the low-level features. SSN [36] estimates the soft shadow based on the object mask and the environment lightmap. It requires the network to learn a complex mapping between the object shadow and the light source. In contrast, we use a physical model to render the hard shadow in 2D space (described in Sect. 3.1). The input of the encoder network is the concatenation of the mask and the hard shadow. To inject a softness control into the network, we uniformly discretize the continuous softness into multiple bins in the log space and then sampled a soft Gaussian distribution on these bins following [3,44]. Thus, a softness value can be represented by an embedding with a fixed dimension. Following [19], the adaptive instance normalization is then employed in the decoder to take the softness embedding for the softness control. The training details follow [36].

## 4    Experiments and Evaluation

Our system consists of several key components: the Height Estimation Network (HENet), the Hard Shadow Renderer (HSR), and the Soft Shadow Generator (SSG). We first validate the effectiveness of HENet on human images and then the soft shadow quality from SSG. Finally, a user study and qualitative comparisons are conducted to evaluate our full system on real images.

HENet is trained to predict the Pixel Height for human images in our current implementation. In the following experiments, unless otherwise specified, the Pixel Height  maps for humans are predicted by our HENet. The Pixel Height  maps for other general objects are manually labeled. The average labeling time for one object is about two minutes.

### 4.1    Evaluation of HENet

We conduct ablation studies on the proposed components to estimate the Pixel Height map. The network is trained on the merged dataset of Synthetic60K and

**Table 1.** Effectiveness of each components in predicting the Pixel Height. YCM: using normalized Y-coordinate Map as input. Real: training on the real and synthetic data. $\ell_{tv}$: training with the total variation loss. The metrics are evaluated on the sparse points labelled by annotators on natural images. Base: Employing Y-Coordinate Map as the Pixel Height.

|      | YCM | Real | $\ell_{tv}$ | Abs ↓ | rel ↓ |
|------|-----|------|-------------|-------|-------|
| Base |     |      |             | 10.84 | 3.64  |
| a    | ✓   | ✓    |             | 6.12  | 2.01  |
| b    |     | ✓    | ✓           | 6.04  | 1.98  |
| c    | ✓   |      | ✓           | 7.05  | 2.34  |
| d    | ✓   | ✓    | ✓           | 5.92  | 1.94  |

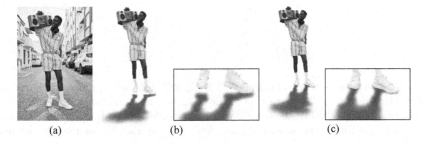

(a)　　　　　　　　(b)　　　　　　　　(c)

**Fig. 6.** For the input image without shadow (a) we use the Y-Coordinate Map to replace the Pixel Height map in our system (b). It can not handle the foot contact with the ground properly. Based on our predicted Pixel Height map, the shadow in the foot contact area is more realistic (c).

the Real1500 training set. The results are evaluated on the sparse points labeled by annotators of the Real1500 validation set. In Table 1, the evaluation results show that adding the Y-Coordinate Map (YCM) and using the total variation loss ($\ell_{tv}$) can both reduce the error. Moreover, training on the merged dataset can significantly improve the model's generalization ability, reducing the relative error from 2.34% to 1.82%. We also list the evaluation results of the baseline to verify that HENet does not just learn a trivial identity mapping of the YCM. As shown in Fig. 6, using the YCM instead of the Pixel Height map can not generate the correct shadow in the foot contact area.

### 4.2　Evaluation of SSG

Instead of implicitly learning a mapping from the light source to a shadow [36], our SSG only focuses on adding softness to the hard shadow based on a controllable input scalar. We build an evaluation benchmark to evaluate the model. We used 20 new assets of 3D models that have no overlap with the training set, and they are collected from the Internet. For each new asset, we uniformly sample $4 \times 66$ positions of the light source and divide them into three groups on average

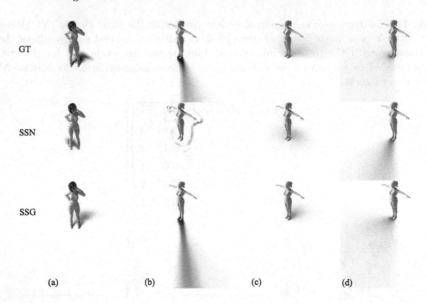

**Fig. 7.** Comparison between our proposed SSG, SSN [36] and synthetic ground truth based on 3D models. (a) The direction of the shadow is more accurate as a hard shadow is given. (b) SSN may fail to generate a long hard shadow. (c-d) Both methods perform well on soft shadows. The shadows from SSG are comparable to the physics-based renderer.

based on the length of the generated shadows, named as 'Short', 'Medium', and 'Long'. For each position, 9 types of softness are sampled. The evaluation benchmark is also divided into 'Soft', 'Medium', and 'Hard' based on the softness. The ground truth shadows are rendered with Mitsuba with 3D models. The evaluation metrics include the average of the pixel-level absolute error (Abs) and the zero normalized cross-correlation (ZNCC). The first one evaluates the pixel-level error, and the second one considers the similarity of the shape.

**Results.** The evaluation results are shown in Table 2. On average, the proposed SSG outperforms SSN on both evaluation metrics, improving Abs and ZNCC by 27% and 112%, respectively. For hard shadows, the proposed SSG reduces the Abs error of SSN from 0.039 to 0.025, and increases the ZNCC from 0.198 to 0.761. The SSN performs slightly better on 'Short' shadows according to the Abs, indicating that directly learning the mapping has some advantage in those cases. Still, it gets unstable for generating long and hard shadows due to the lack of model capacity in long-distance geometric modeling. Samples of visualization results are shown in Fig. 7. SSN may produce inaccurate direction of the shadow based on the given lightmap as shown in Fig. 7-(a). The errors on harder shadows are more apparent, and people are less sensitive to the difference in soft shadows.

**Table 2. Quantitative evaluation.** Abs: pixel-level absolute error. ZNCC: zero normalized cross-correlation. The ground truth shadows are rendered with Mitsuba given 3D shapes. On average, our proposed SSG outperforms SSN [36]. The quality of the 'Long' shadow and the 'Hard' shadow is improved with a larger margin.

| | Mean abs | | | Mean ZNCC | | |
|---|---|---|---|---|---|---|
| SSN [36] | 0.033 | | | 0.370 | | |
| Ours | 0.024 | | | 0.788 | | |
| | Abs ↓ | | | ZNCC ↑ | | |
| Length | Long | Medium | Short | Long | Medium | Short |
| SSN [36] | 0.041 | 0.029 | **0.031** | 0.330 | 0.311 | 0.437 |
| Ours | **0.028** | **0.012** | 0.033 | **0.743** | **0.883** | **0.725** |
| Softness | Hard | Medium | Soft | Hard | Medium | Soft |
| SSN [36] | 0.039 | 0.034 | 0.024 | 0.198 | 0.336 | 0.606 |
| Ours | **0.025** | **0.028** | **0.017** | **0.761** | **0.779** | **0.834** |

**Table 3. User study on natural images.** In a 2AFC study the users chose the more realistic image from a pair. The results indicate that 74% of users perceived the shadows generated by our algorithm as more realistic.

| Rate | Length | | | Softness | | | Mean |
|---|---|---|---|---|---|---|---|
| | Long | Medium | Short | Hard | Medium | Soft | |
| SSN | 0.27 | 0.22 | 0.35 | 0.20 | 0.29 | 0.31 | 0.26 |
| SSG | **0.73** | **0.78** | **0.65** | **0.80** | **0.71** | **0.69** | **0.74** |

### 4.3 Full System Evaluation

We qualitatively evaluated our entire system on natural images. Specifically, we performed a user study, where we asked human subjects to compare the perceived visual quality of the generated shadows from our method and SNN.

We conducted a user study on the shadows generated for 2D natural images. For SSN, the shadow is rendered with the cutout of the object and an interactive light source. For our method, the shadow is rendered with an interactive interface with shadow position and softness controls (see the video demo in our supplementary materials). We prepared 24 shadow pairs mimicking the effect of different lengths and softness. We have shown pairs of images in random order and random position (left-right) to 50 users (80% males and 20% females) and asked the participants which of the two images looks more realistic. Table 3 shows that 74% of the users perceived the shadows rendered with our method as more realistic, especially for long and hard shadows (see Fig. 8).

## 5 Discussions

**Controllability.** Our system based on Pixel Height improves the controllability of the shadow synthesis. A demo video of our simple GUI is in the *supplementary*

**Fig. 8. Samples images from our user study.** Our results have clearer shapes on hard shadows and less artifact on long shadows compared with SSN [36].

**Fig. 9. Controllability.** We can mimic the shadow effect for different camera poses by changing the horizon line.

*materials*, enabling users to change the direction of the shadow by a simple click on the preferred position, similar to the method presented in [27]. Our method also allows the control of the shadow shape using the horizon line, mimicking the perspective effect from a camera (see Fig. 9). The softness is controlled by a slider. Figure 10 shows some example results generated from our GUI using height maps obtained from different approaches. Figure 11 shows a case where the object's shadow is cast on a complex shadow receiver with a floating effect. Our method can also be applied on animated objects. Please check out our supplementary materials for more examples.

**Potential Applications of the Pixel Height Map.** Pixel Height map can also be used to generate reflection effects. A slightly modified checking condition is used to compute the correspondence between a point and its reflection on the ground. We demonstrate this in the supplementary material.

Synthetic                    Manually Annotated                    Predicted

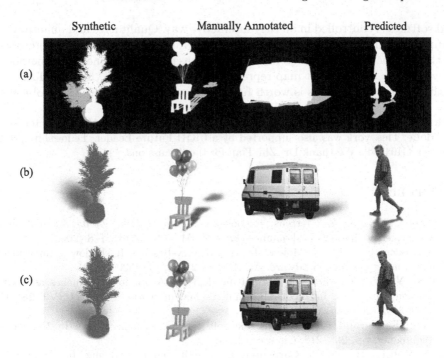

(a)

(b)

(c)

**Fig. 10.** Given a Pixel Height map, our method can produce realistic shadows with desired position and softness. The Pixel Height map can be calculated from 3D models, manually annotated or predicted by HENet. (a) Hard shadow mask. (b) Softness is 0.05. (c) Softness is 0.4.

(a)                        (b)                        (c)                        (d)

**Fig. 11.** Shadow generation for a floating object and a complex shadow receiver. (a) and (c) show that hard shadows can be cast on a non-planar shadow receiver using the Pixel Height map of background as input. Our hard shadow renderer can also render shadows for floating objects by simply adding a shift value to the Pixel Height map of the object. (b) and (d) show the corresponding soft shadow generated by SSG.

## 6  Conclusion

We proposed an approach for generating controllable perceptually plausible shadows based on the Pixel Height map. The new geometry representation, Pixel Height map, encodes the correlations among objects shape, camera pose, and the ground. It can be directly labeled or estimated from 2D images. The position and softness is controlled in an easy interactive way. Qualitative and quantitative comparisons demonstrate the results and generalization ability of the proposed method outperforms previous deep learning-based shadow generation methods. However, our Pixel Height map representation only considers the frontal surface of the object. A thickness is worth future exploration to address the problem.

**Acknowledgment.** Most of the work was done during Yifan and Yichen's internship at Adobe. This work was also supported by a UKRI Future Leaders Fellowship [grant number G104084]. We thank Dr. Zhi Tian for the discussions.

# References

1. Annen, T., Dong, Z., Mertens, T., Bekaert, P., Seidel, H.P., Kautz, J.: Real-time, all-frequency shadows in dynamic scenes. ACM TOG **27**(3), 1–8 (2008)
2. Assarsson, U., Akenine-Möller, T.: A geometry-based soft shadow volume algorithm using graphics hardware. ACM TOG **22**(3), 511–520 (2003)
3. Cao, Y., Wu, Z., Shen, C.: Estimating depth from monocular images as classification using deep fully convolutional residual networks. IEEE TCSVT **28**(11), 3174–3182 (2017)
4. Chan, E., Durand, F.: Rendering fake soft shadows with smoothies. In: Rendering Techniques, pp. 208–218. Citeseer (2003)
5. Cook, R.L., Porter, T., Carpenter, L.: Distributed ray tracing. In: ACM SIGGRAPH, pp. 137–145 (1984)
6. Crow, F.C.: Shadow algorithms for computer graphics. ACM SIGGRAPH **11**(2), 242–248 (1977)
7. Donnelly, W., Lauritzen, A.: Variance shadow maps. In: Proceedings of the 2006 Symposium on Interactive 3D Graphics and Games, pp. 161–165 (2006)
8. Fernando, R.: Percentage-closer soft shadows. In: ACM SIGGRAPH, pp. 35-es (2005)
9. Franke, T.A.: Delta voxel cone tracing. In: 2014 IEEE International Symposium on Mixed and Augmented Reality (ISMAR), pp. 39–44. IEEE (2014)
10. Fuchs, H., et al.: Fast spheres, shadows, textures, transparencies, and Images enhancements in pixel-planes. ACM SIGGRAPH **19**(3), 111–120 (1985)
11. Guennebaud, G., Barthe, L., Paulin, M.: Real-time soft shadow mapping by back-projection. In: Rendering Techniques, pp. 227–234 (2006)
12. Guennebaud, G., Barthe, L., Paulin, M.: High-quality adaptive soft shadow mapping. In: Computer Graphics Forum, vol. 26, pp. 525–533. Wiley Online Library (2007)
13. Heitz, E., Dupuy, J., Hill, S., Neubelt, D.: Real-time polygonal-light shading with linearly transformed cosines. ACM TOG **35**(4), 1–8 (2016)
14. Hong, Y., Niu, L., Zhang, J., Zhang, L.: Shadow generation for composite image in real-world scenes. arXiv preprint arXiv:2104.10338 (2021)
15. Hu, X., Jiang, Y., Fu, C.W., Heng, P.A.: Mask-ShadowGAN: learning to remove shadows from unpaired data. In: ICCV, pp. 2472–2481 (2019)
16. Isola, P., Zhu, J.Y., Zhou, T., Efros, A.A.: Image-to-image translation with conditional adversarial networks. In: CVPR, pp. 1125–1134 (2017)
17. Jiang, Y., et al.: SSH: a self-supervised framework for image harmonization. In: ICCV, pp. 4832–4841 (2021)
18. Kajiya, J.T.: The rendering equation. In: ACM SIGGRAPH, pp. 143–150 (1986)

19. Karras, T., Laine, S., Aila, T.: A style-based generator architecture for generative adversarial networks. In: CVPR, pp. 4401–4410 (2019)
20. Li, Z., Snavely, N.: MegaDepth: learning single-view depth prediction from internet photos. In: CVPR, pp. 2041–2050 (2018)
21. Liu, D., Long, C., Zhang, H., Yu, H., Dong, X., Xiao, C.: ARShadowGAN: shadow generative adversarial network for augmented reality in single light scenes. In: CVPR, pp. 8139–8148 (2020)
22. Liu, Y., Qin, Z., Wan, T., Luo, Z.: Auto-painter: cartoon image generation from sketch by using conditional wasserstein generative adversarial networks. Neurocomputing **311**, 78–87 (2018)
23. Lu, H., Dai, Y., Shen, C., Xu, S.: Indices matter: learning to index for deep image matting. In: ICCV, pp. 3266–3275 (2019)
24. Mehta, S.U., Wang, B., Ramamoorthi, R.: Axis-aligned filtering for interactive sampled soft shadows. ACM TOG **31**(6), 1–10 (2012)
25. Ng, R., Ramamoorthi, R., Hanrahan, P.: All-frequency shadows using non-linear wavelet lighting approximation. In: ACM SIGGRAPH, pp. 376–381 (2003)
26. Öztireli, A.C.: Integration with stochastic point processes. ACM TOG **35**(5), 1–16 (2016)
27. Pellacini, F., Tole, P., Greenberg, D.P.: A user interface for interactive cinematic shadow design. ACM TOG **21**(3), 563–566 (2002)
28. Reeves, W.T., Salesin, D.H., Cook, R.L.: Rendering antialiased shadows with depth maps. In: ACM SIGGRAPH, pp. 283–291 (1987)
29. Remondino, F.: From point cloud to surface: the modeling and visualization problem. Int. Arch. Photogrammetry Remote Sens. Spat. Inf. Sci. **34** (2003)
30. Ren, Z., et al.: Real-time soft shadows in dynamic scenes using spherical harmonic exponentiation. In: ACM SIGGRAPH, pp. 977–986 (2006)
31. Saito, S., Huang, Z., Natsume, R., Morishima, S., Kanazawa, A., Li, H.: PIFu: pixel-aligned implicit function for high-resolution clothed human digitization. In: ICCV (2019)
32. Saito, S., Simon, T., Saragih, J., Joo, H.: PIFuHD: multi-level pixel-aligned implicit function for high-resolution 3d human digitization. In: CVPR, June 2020
33. Saxena, A., Chung, S.H., Ng, A.Y., et al.: Learning depth from single monocular images. In: NeurIPS, vol. 18, pp. 1–8 (2005)
34. Schwarz, M., Stamminger, M.: Bitmask soft shadows. In: Computer Graphics Forum, vol. 26, pp. 515–524. Wiley Online Library (2007)
35. Sen, P., Cammarano, M., Hanrahan, P.: Shadow silhouette maps. ACM TOG **22**(3), 521–526 (2003)
36. Sheng, Y., Zhang, J., Benes, B.: SSN: soft shadow network for image compositing. In: CVPR, pp. 4380–4390 (2021)
37. Sillion, F.X., Arvo, J.R., Westin, S.H., Greenberg, D.P.: A global illumination solution for general reflectance distributions. In: ACM SIGGRAPH, pp. 187–196 (1991)
38. Soler, C., Sillion, F.X.: Fast calculation of soft shadow textures using convolution. In: ACM SIGGRAPH, pp. 321–332 (1998)
39. Wang, Y., Curless, B.L., Seitz, S.M.: People as scene probes. In: Vedaldi, A., Bischof, H., Brox, T., Frahm, J.-M. (eds.) ECCV 2020. LNCS, vol. 12355, pp. 438–454. Springer, Cham (2020). https://doi.org/10.1007/978-3-030-58607-2_26
40. Westin, S.H., Arvo, J.R., Torrance, K.E.: Predicting reflectance functions from complex surfaces. In: ACM SIGGRAPH, pp. 255–264 (1992)
41. Williams, L.: Casting curved shadows on curved surfaces. In: ACM SIGGRAPH, pp. 270–274 (1978)

42. Xie, E., Wang, W., Yu, Z., Anandkumar, A., Alvarez, J.M., Luo, P.: SegFormer: simple and efficient design for semantic segmentation with transformers. In: NeurIPS (2021)
43. Yin, W., Liu, Y., Shen, C.: Virtual normal: enforcing geometric constraints for accurate and robust depth prediction. IEEE TPAMI **44**, 7282–7295 (2021)
44. Yin, W., Liu, Y., Shen, C., Yan, Y.: Enforcing geometric constraints of virtual normal for depth prediction. In: ICCV, pp. 5684–5693 (2019)
45. Zhang, S., Liang, R., Wang, M.: ShadowGAN: shadow synthesis for virtual objects with conditional adversarial networks. Comput. Vis. Media **5**(1), 105–115 (2019). https://doi.org/10.1007/s41095-019-0136-1

# Learning Where to Look – Generative NAS is Surprisingly Efficient

Jovita Lukasik[1,2]($\boxtimes$)(ID), Steffen Jung[2](ID), and Margret Keuper[2,3](ID)

[1] University of Mannheim, Mannheim, Germany
jovita@uni-mannheim.de
[2] Max Planck Institute for Informatics, Saarland Informatics Campus,
Saarbrücken, Germany
[3] University of Siegen, Siegen, Germany

**Abstract.** The efficient, automated search for well-performing neural architectures (NAS) has drawn increasing attention in the recent past. Thereby, the predominant research objective is to reduce the necessity of costly evaluations of neural architectures while efficiently exploring large search spaces. To this aim, surrogate models embed architectures in a latent space and predict their performance, while generative models for neural architectures enable optimization-based search within the latent space the generator draws from. Both, surrogate and generative models, have the aim of facilitating query-efficient search in a well-structured latent space. In this paper, we further improve the trade-off between query-efficiency and promising architecture generation by leveraging advantages from both, efficient surrogate models and generative design. To this end, we propose a generative model, paired with a surrogate predictor, that iteratively learns to generate samples from increasingly promising latent subspaces. This approach leads to very effective and efficient architecture search, while keeping the query amount low. In addition, our approach allows in a straightforward manner to jointly optimize for multiple objectives such as accuracy and hardware latency. We show the benefit of this approach not only w.r.t. the optimization of architectures for highest classification accuracy but also in the context of hardware constraints and outperform state-of-the-art methods on several NAS benchmarks for single and multiple objectives. We also achieve state-of-the-art performance on ImageNet. The code is available at https://github.com/jovitalukasik/AG-Net.

**Keywords:** Neural architecture search · Generative model

---

J. Lukasik and S. Jung—Authors contributed equally.

---

**Supplementary Information** The online version contains supplementary material available at https://doi.org/10.1007/978-3-031-20050-2_16.

S. Avidan et al. (Eds.): ECCV 2022, LNCS 13683, pp. 257–273, 2022.
https://doi.org/10.1007/978-3-031-20050-2_16

# 1    Introduction

The first image classification network [20] applied to the large-scale visual recognition challenge ImageNet [8] achieved unprecedented results. Since then, the main driver of improvement on this challenge are new architecture designs [14, 38, 40, 41] that, ultimately, lead to architectures surpassing human performance [13]. Since manual architecture design requires good intuition and a huge amount of trial-and-error, the automated approach of neural architecture search (NAS) receives growing interest [10, 18, 21, 32, 54, 58]. Well-performing architectures can be found by applying common search practices like random search [2], evolutionary search [31, 32], Bayesian optimization (BO) [16, 35, 45], or local search [46] on discrete architecture search spaces, such as NAS-Bench-101, NAS-Bench-201, DARTS and NAS-Bench-NLP [10, 18, 25, 54]. However, these methods are inefficient because they require to evaluate thousands of architectures, resulting in impracticable search times. Recent approaches avoid this problem of immense computation costs by either training surrogate models to approximate the performance of an architecture [3, 25] or by generating architectures based on learned architecture representation spaces [26, 56]. Both methods aim to improve the query efficiency, which is crucial in NAS, since every query implies a full training and evaluation of the neural architecture on the underlying target dataset.

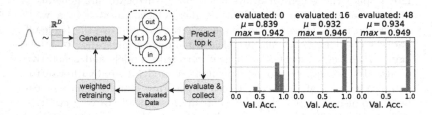

**Fig. 1.** (**left**) Our search method generates architectures from points in an architecture representation space that is iteratively optimized. (**right**) The architecture representation space is biased towards better-performing architectures with each search iteration. After only 48 evaluated architectures, our generator produces state-of-the-art performing architectures on NAS-Bench-101.

This trade-off between query efficiency and resulting high-scoring architectures is an active research field. Yet, no attempts were made so far to leverage the advantages of both search paradigms. Therefore, we propose a model that incorporates the focus of promising architectures already in the architecture generation process by optimizing the latent space *directly*: We let the generator learn in which areas of the data distribution to look for promising architectures. This way, we reduce the query amount even further, resulting in a query efficient and very effective NAS method. Our proposed method is inspired by a latent space optimization (LSO) technique [42], originally used in the context of variational autoencoders [17] to optimize generated images or arithmetic expressions using BO. We adapt this concept to NAS and pair it with an architecture performance predictor in an end-to-end learning setting, so that it allows us to iteratively reshape the architecture representation space. Thereby, we promote desired properties of generated architectures in a highly query-efficient way, i.e. by learning expert generators for promising architectures. Since we couple the generation process with a surrogate model to predict desired properties such as high accuracy or low latency of generated architectures, there is no need in our method for BO in the generated latent space, making our method even more efficient.

In practice, we pretrain, on a target space of neural architectures, a GNN-based generator network, which does not rely on any architecture evaluation and is therefore fast and query-free. The generator is trained in a novel generative setting that directly compares generated architectures to randomly sampled architectures using a reconstruction loss without the need of a discriminator network as in generative adversarial networks (GANs) [12] or an encoder as in variational autoencoders (VAEs) [17]. We use an MLP as a surrogate to rank performances and hardware properties of generated architectures. In contrast, previous generative methods either rely on training and evaluating supernets [15], which are expensive to train and dataset specific, or pretrain a latent space and search within this space directly using BO [26,53,56], reinforcement learning (RL) [33] or gradient based methods [27]. These methods incorporate either GANs, which can be hard to train or VAEs, which are biased by the regularization, whereas our plain generative model is easy to train. In addition we enable backpropagation from the performance predictor to the generator. Thereby, the generator can efficiently learn which part of the architecture search space is promising with only few evaluated architectures.

By extensive experiments on common NAS benchmarks [10,18,21,37,54] as well as ImageNet [8], we show that our method is effective and sample-efficient. It reinforces the generator network to produce architectures with improving validation accuracy (see Fig. 1), as well as in improving on hardware-dependent latency constraints (see Fig. 4) while keeping the number of architecture evaluations small. In summary, we make the following contributions:

- We propose a simple model that learns to focus on promising regions of the architecture space. It can thus learn to generate high-scoring architectures from only a few queries.
- We learn architecture representation spaces via a *novel generative design* that is able to generate architectures stochastically while being trained with a simple reconstruction loss. Unlike VAEs [17] or GANs [12], no encoder network nor discriminator network is necessary.
- Our model allows sample-efficient search and achieves state-of-the-art results on several NAS benchmarks as well as on ImageNet. It allows joint optimization w.r.t. hardware properties in a straightforward way.

## 2   Related Work

*Neural Architecture Search.* Intrinsically, Neural Architecture Search (NAS) is a discrete optimization problem seeking the optimal configuration of operations (such as convolutions, poolings and skip connections) in a constrained *search space* of computational graphs. To enable benchmarking within the NAS community, different search spaces have been proposed. The tabular benchmarks NAS-Bench-101 [54] and NAS-Bench-201 [10] provide both an exhaustive covering of metrics and performances. NAS-bench-NLP [18] provides a search space for natural language processing. In addition to these tabular benchmarks NAS-Bench-301 [37] provides a surrogate benchmark, which allows for fast evaluation of NAS methods on the DARTS [25] search space by querying the validation accuracy. NAS-Bench-x11 [52] is another surrogate benchmark. It outputs full training information for each architecture in all four mentioned benchmarks. NAS-Bench-Suite [28] facilitates reproducible search on these NAS benchmarks.

Early NAS approaches are based on discrete encodings of search spaces, such as in the form of adjacency matrices, and can be distinguished by their *search strategy*. Examples are random search [2,22], reinforcement learning (RL) [23, 57], evolutionary methods [31,32], local search [46], and Bayesian optimization (BO) [16,35]. Recent NAS methods shift from discrete optimization to faster weight-sharing approaches, resulting in differentiable optimization methods [1,3, 25,30,49,55]. Several approaches map the discrete search space into a continuous architecture representation space [26,27,53,56] and search or optimize within this space using for example BO (e.g. [53]) or gradient-based point operation [27]. In this paper, we also learn continuous architecture representation spaces. However, in contrast to former works, we propose to optimize the representation space, instead of performing point optimization within a fixed space such as e.g. [27]. A survey of different strategies can be found in [11].

All NAS approaches are dependent on *performance estimation* of intermediate architectures. To avoid the computation heavy training and evaluation of queries on the target dataset, methods to approximate the performance have been explored [47]. Common approaches include neural predictors that take path encodings [45] or graph embeddings learned by GNNs [36,43] as input. Weak-NAS [48] proposes to progressively evaluate the search space towards finding high-performing architectures using a set of weak predictors. In our method, we integrate a weak expert predictor with a generator to yield an efficient interplay between predicting for high-performing architectures and generating them.

*Graph Generative Models.* Most graph generation models in NAS employ variational autoencoders (VAE) [17]. [27] uses an LSTM-based VAE, coupled with performance prediction for gradient-based architecture optimization. Note that [27] optimizes the latent point in a fixed latent space while our approach optimizes the latent space itself. [56] use GNNs with asynchronous message-passing to train a VAE for BO. [15] combines a generator with a supernet and searches for neural architectures for different device information. [53] facilitates [50] with an MLP decoder. [26] proposes smooth variational graph embeddings (SVGe) using two-sided GNNs to capture the information flow within a neural architecture.

Our proposed model's generator is inspired by SVGe with the aim to inherit its flexible applicability to various search spaces. Yet, similar to [53], due to the intrinsic discretization and training setting, SVGe does not allow for backpropagation. Recently, [33] facilitates GNNs in a GAN [12] setting, where the backpropagation issue is circumvented using reinforcement learning. In contrast, our

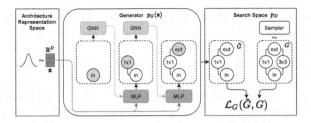

**Fig. 2.** Representation of the training procedure for our generator in AG-Net. The input is a randomly sampled latent vector $\mathbf{z} \in \mathbb{R}^d$. First, the input node is generated, initialized and input to a GNN to generate a partial graph representation. The learning process iteratively generates node scores and edge scores using $\mathbf{z}$ and the partial graph representation until the output node is generated. The target for this generated graph is a randomly sampled architecture.

proposed GNN generator circumvents the intermediate architecture discretization and can therefore be trained by a single reconstruction loss using backpropagation. Its iterative optimization is inspired by [42], who proposes to use a VAE with weighted retraining w.r.t. a target function to adapt the latent space for the optimization of images and arithmetic functions using BO. Our model transfers the idea of weighted retraining to NAS. It uses our plain generator and improves sample efficiency by employing a differentiable surrogate model on the target function such that, in contrast to [42], no further black-box optimization step is needed. Next, we describe the proposed generator network.

## 3   Architecture Generative Model

*Preliminaries.* We aim to generate neural networks represented as directed acyclic graphs (DAG). This representation is in line with the cell-based architecture search spaces commonly used as tabular benchmarks [10,54]. Each cell is a DAG $G = (V, E)$, with nodes $v \in V$ and edges $e \in E$. The graph representations differ between the various benchmarks in terms of their labeling of operations. For example in NAS-Bench-101 [54] each node is associated with an operation, whereas in NAS-Bench-201 [10] each edge is associated with an operation.

**Generative Network.** Commonly used graph generative networks are based on variational autoencoders (VAE) [17]. In contrast, our proposed network is a *purely generative* network, $p_G$ (see Fig. 2). To generate valid graphs, we build our model similar to the graph decoder from the VAE approach SVGe [26]. The generator takes a randomly sampled variable $\mathbf{z} \sim \mathcal{N}(0, 1)$ as input and reconstructs a randomly sampled graph from the cell-based search space. The model iteratively builds the graph: it starts with generating the input node $v_0$, followed by adding subsequent nodes $v_i$ and their labels and connecting them with edges $e_{(j,i)}, j < i$, until the end node $v_T$ with the label *output* is generated. Additionally, we want to learn a surrogate for performance prediction on the generated data and allow for end-to-end training of both. To allow for backpropagation, we need to adapt several details of the generator model. We initialize the node-attributes for each node by one-hot encoded vectors, which are initialized during training using a 2-layer MLP to replace the learnable look-up table proposed in SVGe. The output of our generator is a vector graph representation consisting of a concatenation of generated node scores and edge scores. It is important to note that the iterative generation process is independent of the ground truth data, which are only used as a target for the reconstruction loss. Note that the end-to-end trainability of the proposed generator is a prerequisite for our model: It allows to pair the generator with a learnable performance predictor such that information on the expected architectures' accuracy can be learned by the generator. This enables a stronger coupling with the predictor's target for the generation process and higher query efficiency (see Subsect. 4.4). In contrast, previous models such as [15, 26, 53] are not fully differentiable and do not allow such optimization. Our generative model is pretrained on the task of reconstructing neural architectures, where for each randomly drawn latent space sample, we evaluate the reconstruction loss to a randomly drawn architecture. This simple procedure is facilitated by the heavily constrained search spaces of neural architectures, making it easy for the model to learn to generate valid architectures without being supported by a discriminator model as in generative adversarial networks (GANs) [12]. An evaluation of the generation ability of our model and implementation details are provided in the supp. mat. section D.

**Performance Predictor.** This generative model is coupled with a simple surrogate model, a 4-layer MLP with ReLU non-linearities, for target predictions $C$. These targets can be validation or test accuracy of the generated graph, or the latency with respect to a certain hardware. For comparison, we also include a tree-based method, XGBoost (XGB) [4] as an alternative prediction model. XGB [4] is used as a surrogate model in NAS-Bench-301 [37] and shows high prediction abilities. The input to XGB is the vector representation of the architectures. Since this method is non-differentiable, we additionally include a gradient estimation for rank-based metrics [34]. This way, we are able to include gradient information to the generator. Yet, it is important to note, that this approach is not fully differentiable. This comparison will allow us to measure the trade-off between using supposedly stronger predictors over the capability to allow for full end-to-end learning.

**Training Objectives.** The generative model $p_G$ learns to reconstruct a randomly sampled architecture $G$ from search space $p_D$ given a randomly sampled latent vector $\mathbf{z} \sim \mathcal{N}(0, 1)$. The objective function for this generation process can be formulated as the sum of node-level loss $\mathcal{L}_V$ and edge-level loss $\mathcal{L}_E$:

$$\mathcal{L}_G(\tilde{G}, G) = \mathcal{L}_V + \mathcal{L}_E; \ \tilde{G} \sim p_G(\mathbf{z}); \ G \sim p_D, \tag{1}$$

where $\mathcal{L}_V$ is the Cross-Entropy loss between the predicted and the ground truth nodes and $\mathcal{L}_E$ is the Binary-Cross Entropy loss between the predicted and ground truth edges of the generated graph $\tilde{G}$. This training step is *completely unsupervised*. Figure 2 presents an overview of the training process. To include the training of the surrogate model, the objective function is reformulated to:

$$\mathcal{L}(\tilde{G}, G) = (1 - \alpha)\mathcal{L}_G(\tilde{G}, G) + \alpha\mathcal{L}_C(\tilde{G}, G), \tag{2}$$

where $\alpha$ is a hyperparameter to trade-off generator loss $\mathcal{L}_G$ and prediction loss $\mathcal{L}_C$ for the prediction targets $C$ of graph $G$. We set the predictor loss as an MSE. Furthermore, each loss is optimized using mini-batch gradient descent.

**Generative Latent Space Optimization (LSO).** To facilitate the generation process, we optimize the architecture representation space via weighted retraining [42], resulting in a sample efficient search algorithm. The intuition of this approach is to place more probability mass on high-scoring latent points, (e.g. high performing or low latency architectures) and less mass on low-scoring points. Thus, this strategy does not discard low-scoring architectures completely, which would be inadequate for proper learning. The generative model is therefore trained on a data distribution that systematically increases the probability of high-scoring latent points. This can be done by simply assigning a weight $w_i$ to each data point $G_i \sim p_D$, indicating its likelihood to occur during batch-wise training. In addition, the training objective is weighted via a weighted empirical mean $\sum_{G_i \sim p_D} w_i \mathcal{L}$ for each data point. As for the weights itself, [42] proposed a rank-based weight function

$$w(G; p_D, k) \propto \frac{1}{kN + \text{rank}_{f,p_D}(G)}$$

$$\text{rank}_{f,p_D}(x) = |\{G_i : f(G_i) > f(G), G_i \sim p_D\}|,$$

(3)

where $f(\cdot)$ is the evaluation function of the architecture $G_i$; for NAS-Bench-101 [54] and NAS-Bench-201 [10] it is the tabular benchmark entry, for NAS-Bench-301 [37] and NAS-Bench-NLP [18] it is the surrogate benchmark prediction. Similar to [42], we set $k = 10e - 3$. The retraining procedure itself then consists of finetuning the pretrained generative model coupled with the surrogate model, where loss functions and data points are both weighted by $w(G; p_D, k)$.

## 4 Experiments

We evaluate the proposed simple architecture generative network (AG-Net) on the two commonly used tabular benchmarks NAS-Bench-101 [54] and NAS-Bench-201 [10], the surrogate benchmarks NAS-Bench-301 [37] evaluated on the DARTS search space [25], NAS-Bench-NLP [18] and the first hardware device induced benchmark [21]. Additionally we perform experiments on the ImageNet [8] classification task and show state-of-the-art performance on the DARTS search space. In our experiments in Subsect. 4.3 for the Hardware-Aware Benchmark we consider the latency information on the NAS-Bench-201 search space. Details about all hyperparameters are given in the supp. mat. section E.

### 4.1 Experiments on Tabular Benchmarks

*NAS-Bench-101.* For our experiments on NAS-Bench-101, we first pretrain our generator for generating valid graphs on the NAS-Bench-101 search space. This step does not require information about the performance of architectures and is therefore inexpensive. The pretrained generator is then used for all experiments on NAS-Bench-101. Our NAS algorithm is initialized by randomly sampling 16 architectures from the search space, which are then weighted by the weighting function $\mathcal{W} = w(G)_{G \sim p_D}$. Then, latent space optimized architecture search is performed by iteratively retraining the generator coupled with the MLP surrogate model for 15 epochs and generating 100 architectures of which the top 16 (according to their accuracy prediction) are evaluated and added to the training data. This step is repeated until the desired number of queries is reached. When generating architectures , we sample from a grid, containing the 99%-quantiles from $\mathcal{N}(0, 1)$ uniformly distributed. This way, we sample more distributed latent variables for better latent space coverage. We compare our method to the VAE-based search method Arch2vec [53] and predictor based model WeakNAS [48], as well as state-of-the-art methods, such as NAO [27][3], random search [22], local search [46], Bayesian optimization [39], regularized evolution [31] and BANANAS [45][2]. Additionally, we compare the proposed AG-Net to the model using an XGBoost Predictor (see section C)). The results of this comparison are listed in Table 1. Here, we report the mean over 10 runs. Results including the standard deviation can be found in the supp. mat. Note, we search for the architecture with the best validation accuracy and report the corresponding test accuracy. Furthermore, we plot the search progress in Fig. 3 (bottom left). As we can see, our model AG-Net improves over all state-of-the-art methods, not only at the last query of 300 data points, reaching a top 1 test accuracy of 94.2%, but is also almost any time better during the search process.

A direct comparison to the recently proposed GANAS [33] on NAS-Bench-101 is difficult, since GANAS searches on NAS-Bench-101 until they find the best architecture in terms of validation accuracy, whereas we limit our search to a maximal amount of 192 queries and are able to find high-performing architectures already in this small query setting. The comparison of AG-Net to the generator paired with an XGBoost [4] predictor shows that our end-to-end learnable approach is favorable even over potentially stronger predictors.

*NAS-Bench-201.* This benchmark contains three different image classification tasks: CIFAR-10, CIFAR-100 [19] and ImageNet16-120 [7]. For the experiments on NAS-Bench-201 [10] we retrain AG-Net in the weighted manner for 30 epochs. In this setting, we also compare AG-Net to two recent generative models [15,33]. SGNAS [15] trains a supernet by uniform sampling, following SETN [9]. Additionally a CNN based architecture generator is trained to search architectures on the supernet. When comparing with [53], we also adopt their evaluation scheme of adding only the best-performing architecture (top-1) to the training data instead of top-16 as in our other experiments.

We report the search results for different numbers of queries for the NAS-Bench-201 dataset in Table 2. In addition, we plot the search progress in terms of queries in Fig. 3 (top). Our method provides state-of-the-art results on all

---

[3] We reran this experiment using the implementation from [47].

[2] We reran these experiments using the official implementation from [44–46], with the same initial training data and amount of top k architectures as for AG-Net.

datasets for a varying number of queries. Most importantly, AG-Net shows strong performance in the few-query regime compared to [53] with the exception of CIFAR-100, proving its high query efficiency.

**Table 1.** Results on NAS-Bench-101 for the search of the best architecture in terms of validation accuracy on CIFAR-10 to state-of-the-art methods (mean over 10 trials).

| NAS method | Val. Acc. (%) | Test Acc. (%) | Queries |
|---|---|---|---|
| Optimum* | 95.06 | 94.32 | |
| Arch2vec + RL [53] | – | 94.10 | 400 |
| Arch2vec + BO [53] | – | 94.05 | 400 |
| NAO [‡] [27] | 94.66 | 93.49 | 192 |
| BANANAS[†] [45] | 94.73 | 94.09 | 192 |
| Bayesian optimization[†] [39] | 94.57 | 93.96 | 192 |
| Local search[†] [46] | 94.57 | 93.97 | 192 |
| Random search[†] [22] | 94.31 | 93.61 | 192 |
| Regularized evolution[†] [31] | 94.47 | 93.89 | 192 |
| WeakNAS [48] | – | **94.18** | 200 |
| XGB (ours) | 94.61 | 94.13 | 192 |
| XGB + ranking (ours) | 94.60 | 94.14 | 192 |
| AG-Net (ours) | **94.90** | **94.18** | 192 |

### 4.2   Experiments on Surrogate Benchmarks

We furthermore apply our search method on larger search spaces as DARTS [25] and NAS-Bench-NLP [18] without ground truth evaluations for the whole search space, making use of surrogate benchmarks as NAS-Bench-301 [37], NAS-Bench-X11 [52] and NAS-Bench-Suite [28].

*NAS-Bench-301.* Here, we report experiments on the cell-based DARTS [25] search space using the surrogate benchmark NAS-Bench-301 [37] for the CIFAR-10 [19] image classification task. The exact search procedure using the cells individually is described in the supp. mat. subsection C.5. The results are described in Table 3 (left) and visualized in Fig. 3 (bottom middle). Our method is comparable to other state-of-the-art methods in this search space.

*NAS-Bench-NLP.* Next, we evaluate AG-Net on NAS-Bench-NLP [18] for the language modeling task on Penn TreeBank [29]. We retrain AG-Net coupled with the surrogate model for 30 epochs to predict the validation perplexity. Note, since the search space considered in NAS-Bench-NLP is too large for a full tabular benchmark evaluation, we make use of the surrogate benchmark NAS-Bench-X11 [52] and NAS-Bench-Suite [28] instead of tabular entries.

   For fair comparison we compare our methods to the same state-of-the-art methods as in previous experiments. The results are reported in Fig. 3 (right) and visualized in Fig. 3 (bottom right). Our AG-Net improves over all state-of-the-art methods by a substantial margin and using XGB as a predictor even improves the search further.

**ImageNet Experiments.** The previous experiment on NAS-Bench-301 [37] shows the ability of our generator to generate valid architectures and to perform well in the DARTS [25] search space. This allows for searching a well-performing architecture on ImageNet [8]. Yet evaluating up to 300 different found architectures on ImageNet is extremely expensive. Our first approach is to retrain the best found architectures on the CIFAR-10 [19] image classification task from the previous experiment on NAS-Bench-301 (AG-Net and the XGBoost adaptions) on ImageNet [8]. Our second approach is based on a training-free neural architecture search approach. The recently proposed TE-NAS [5] provides a training-free neural architecture search approach, by ranking architectures by analysing the neural tangent kernel (NTK) and the number of linear regions (NLR) of

**Table 2.** Architecture Search on NAS-Bench-201. We report the mean over 10 trials for the search of the architecture with the highest validation accuracy.

| NAS method | CIFAR-10 | | CIFAR-100 | | ImageNet16-120 | | Queries | Search method |
|---|---|---|---|---|---|---|---|---|
| | Val. Acc | Test Acc | Val. Acc. | Test Acc. | Val. Acc | Test Acc. | | |
| Optimum* | 91.61 | 94.37 | 73.49 | 73.51 | 46.77 | 47.31 | | |
| SGNAS [15] | 90.18 | 93.53 | 70.28 | 70.31 | 44.65 | 44.98 | | Supernet |
| Arch2vec + BO [53] | 91.41 | 94.18 | **73.35** | **73.37** | 46.34 | 46.27 | 100 | Bayesian optimization |
| AG-Net (ours) | **91.55** | **94.24** | 73.2 | 73.12 | 46.31 | 46.2 | 96 | Generative LSO |
| AG-Net (ours, topk = 1) | 91.41 | 94.16 | 73.14 | 73.15 | **46.42** | **46.43** | 100 | Generative LSO |
| BANANAS[†] [45] | 91.56 | 94.3 | **73.49*** | 73.50 | **46.65** | **46.51** | 192 | Bayesian optimization |
| BO[†] [39] | 91.54 | 94.22 | 73.26 | 73.22 | 46.43 | 46.40 | 192 | Bayesian optimization |
| RS [†] [22] | 91.12 | 93.89 | 72.08 | 72.07 | 45.87 | 45.98 | 192 | Random |
| XGB (ours) | 91.54 | 94.34 | 73.10 | 72.93 | 46.48 | 46.08 | 192 | Generative LSO |
| XGB + Ranking (ours) | 91.48 | 94.25 | 73.20 | 73.24 | 46.40 | 46.16 | 192 | Generative LSO |
| AG-Net (ours) | **91.60** | **94.37*** | **73.49*** | **73.51*** | 46.64 | 46.43 | 192 | Generative LSO |
| GANAS [33] | – | 94.34 | – | 73.28 | – | **46.80** | 444 | Generative reinforcement learning |
| AG-Net (ours) | **91.61*** | **94.37*** | **73.49*** | **73.51*** | **46.73** | 46.42 | 400 | Generative LSO |

**Table 3.** Results on: (**left**) NAS-Bench-301 (mean validation accuracy over 50 trials). (**right**) NAS-Bench-NLP (mean validation perplexity over 100 trials).

| NAS method | NAS-Bench-301 | | NAS-Bench-NLP | |
|---|---|---|---|---|
| | Val. Acc (%) | Queries | Val. Perplexity (%) | Queries |
| BANANAS[†] [45] | 94.77 | 192 | 95.68 | 304 |
| Bayesian optimization[†] [39] | 94.71 | 192 | – | – |
| Local search[†] [46] | **95.02** | 192 | 95.69 | 304 |
| Random search[†] [22] | 94.31 | 192 | 95.64 | 304 |
| Regularized evolution[†] [31] | 94.75 | 192 | 95.66 | 304 |
| XGB (ours) | 94.79 | 192 | **95.95** | 304 |
| XGB + Ranking (ours) | 94.76 | 192 | 95.92 | 304 |
| AG-Net (ours) | 94.79 | 192 | 95.86 | 304 |

each architecture. These two measurements are training free and do not need any labels. The intuition between those two measurements is their implication towards trainability and expressivity of a neural architecture and also their correlation with the neural architecture's accuracy; NTK is negatively correlated and NLR positively correlated with the architecture's test accuracy. We adapt this idea for our search on ImageNet and search architectures in terms of their NTK value and their number of linear regions instead of their validation accuracy. We describe the detailed search process in the supp. mat. subsection C.5.

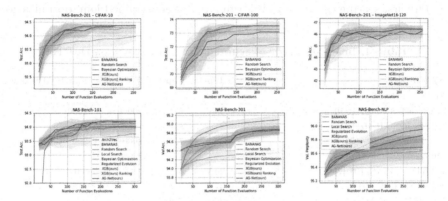

**Fig. 3.** Architecture search evaluations on NAS-Bench-201, NAS-Bench-101, NAS-Bench-301 and NAS-Bench-NLP for different search methods.

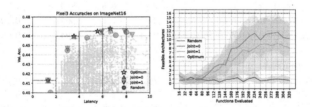

**Fig. 4.** (**left**) Exemplary searches on HW-NAS-Bench for image classification on ImageNet16 with 192 queries on Pixel 3 and latency conditions $L \in \{2, 4, 6, 8, 10\}$ (y-axis zoomed for visibility). (**right**) Amount of architectures generated and selected in each search iteration (at most 16) that satisfy the latency constraint. In this example we searched on Edge GPU with $L = 2$.

Table 4 shows the results. Note that our latter described search method on ImageNet is **training-free** (as TE-NAS [5]) and the amount of queries displays the amount of data we evaluated for the zero cost measurements. Other query information include the amount of (partly) trained architectures. Furthermore, the displayed differentiable methods are based on training supernets which can lead to expensive training times. The best found architectures on NAS-Bench-301 [37] (CIFAR-10) result in comparable error rates on ImageNet to former approaches. As a result, our search method approach is highly efficient and outperforms previous methods in terms of needed GPU days. The result in terms of top-1 and top-5 error rates are even improving over the one from previous approaches when using the training free approach.

### 4.3  Experiments on Hardware-Aware Benchmark

Next, we apply AG-Net to the Hardware-Aware NAS-Benchmark [21]. We demonstrate in two settings that AG-Net can be used for multi-objective learning. The first setting (*Joint = 1*) is formulated as constrained joint optimization:

**Table 4.** ImageNet **error** of neural architecture search on DARTS.

| NAS method | Top-1↓ | Top-5↓ | # Queries | Search GPU days |
|---|---|---|---|---|
| *Mixed methods* | | | | |
| NASNET-A (CIFAR-10) [58] | 26.0 | 8.4 | 20000 | 2000 |
| PNAS (CIFAR-10) [24] | 25.8 | 8.1 | 1160 | 225 |
| NAO (CIFAR-10) [27] | 24.5 | 7.8 | 1000 | 200 |
| *Differentiable methods* | | | | |
| DARTS (CIFAR-10) [25] | 26.7 | 8.7 | – | 4.0 |
| SNAS (CIFAR-10) [49] | 27.3 | 9.2 | – | 1.5 |
| PDARTS (CIFAR-10) [6] | **24.4** | **7.4** | – | 0.3 |
| PC-DARTS (CIFAR-10) [51] | 25.1 | 7.8 | – | **0.1** |
| PC-DARTS (ImageNet) [51] | **24.2** | **7.3** | – | 3.8 |
| *Predictor based methods* | | | | |
| WeakNAS (ImageNet) [48] | **23.5** | **6.8** | 800 | 2.5 |
| XGB (NB-301)(CIFAR-10) (ours) | 24.1 | 7.4 | 304 | **0.02** |
| XGB + Ranking (NB-301)(CIFAR-10) (ours) | 24.1 | 7.2 | 304 | **0.02** |
| AG-Net (NB-301)(CIFAR-10) (ours) | 24.3 | 7.3 | 304 | 0.21 |
| *Training-free methods* | | | | |
| TE-NAS (CIFAR-10) [5] | 26.2 | 8.3 | – | 0.05 |
| TE-NAS (ImageNet) [5] | 24.5 | 7.5 | – | 0.17 |
| AG-Net (CIFAR-10) (ours) | **23.5** | 7.1 | 208 | **0.02** |
| AG-Net (ImageNet) (ours) | **23.5** | 6.9 | 208 | **0.09** |

$$\max_{G \sim p_D} f(G) \wedge \min_{G \sim p_D,} g_h(G) \qquad \text{s.t. } g_h(G) \leq L, \exists\, h \in H, \qquad (4)$$

where $f(\cdot)$ evaluates architecture $G$ for accuracy and $g_h(\cdot)$ evaluates for latency given a hardware $h \in H$ and a user-defined latency constraint $L$. The second setting (*Joint = 0*) is formulated as constraint objective:

$$\max_{G \sim p_D} f(G) \qquad \text{s.t. } g_h(G) \leq L, \exists\, h \in H, \qquad (5)$$

where we drop the optimization on latency and only optimize accuracy given the latency constraint. The loss function to train our generator in these settings is updated from Eq. 2 to:

$$\mathcal{L}(\tilde{G}, G) = (1 - \alpha)\mathcal{L}_G(\tilde{G}, G) + \alpha \big[\lambda \mathcal{L}_{C_1}(\tilde{G}, G) + (1 - \lambda)\mathcal{L}_{C_2}(\tilde{G}, G)\big], \qquad (6)$$

where $\alpha$ is a hyperparameter trading off generation and prediction loss, and $\lambda$ is a hyperparameter trading off both prediction targets $C_1$ (accuracy) and $C_2$ (latency).

To perform LSO in the joint objective setting from Eq. 4, we rank the training data $D$ for both accuracy and latency jointly by summing both individual rankings. To fulfill the optimization constraint, we further penalize the ranks via a multiplicative penalty if the latency does not fulfill the constraint. This overall ranking is then used for the weight calculation in Eq. 3. The LSO for the constraint objective setting from Eq. 5 only ranks architectures by accuracy and penalizes architectures with infeasible latency property. We choose random search as a baseline in this setting as it is generally regarded as a strong base-

**Table 5.** Results for searches with at most 200 queries on HW-NAS-Bench [21] with varying devices and latency (Lat.) constraints in two multi-objective settings: *Joint = 0* optimizes accuracy under latency constraint, while *Joint = 1* optimizes for accuracy and latency jointly. We report the best found architecture out of 10 runs with their corresponding latency, as well as the mean of these runs. We compare to random search as a strong baseline [22]. Feasibility (Feas.) is the proportion of evaluated architectures during the search that satisfy the latency constraint (larger is better). The optimal architecture (*) is the architecture with the highest accuracy satisfying the latency constraint.

| Settings | | Best out of 10 runs | | | | | | Mean | | | | | | | |
|---|---|---|---|---|---|---|---|---|---|---|---|---|---|---|---|
| Constraint | | Joint = 0 | | Joint = 1 | | Random | | Joint = 0 | | Joint = 1 | | Random | | Optimum* | |
| Device | Lat.↓ | Acc.↑ | Lat.↓ | Acc.↑ | Lat.↓ | Acc.↑ | Lat.↓ | Acc.↑ | Feas.↑ | Acc.↑ | Feas.↑ | Acc.↑ | Feas.↑ | Acc.↑ | Lat.↓ |
| Edge GPU | 2 | **0.406*** | 1.90 | **0.406*** | 1.90 | 0.397 | 1.78 | **0.397** | 0.29 | *0.391* | 0.31 | 0.372 | 0.05 | 0.406 | 1.90 |
| Edge GPU | 4 | **0.448*** | 3.49 | **0.448*** | 3.49 | 0.437 | 3.35 | *0.428* | 0.29 | **0.433** | 0.43 | 0.417 | 0.22 | 0.448 | 3.49 |
| Edge GPU | 6 | *0.458* | 5.29 | **0.464*** | 5.96 | *0.458* | 5.29 | **0.453** | 0.64 | *0.450* | 0.79 | 0.449 | 0.72 | 0.464 | 5.96 |
| Edge GPU | 8 | *0.465* | 6.81 | **0.468*** | 6.81 | 0.464 | 7.44 | **0.463** | 0.98 | *0.462* | 0.99 | 0.457 | 1.00 | 0.468 | 6.81 |
| Raspi 4 | 2 | **0.355*** | 1.58 | **0.355*** | 1.58 | 0.348 | 1.60 | *0.346* | 0.28 | **0.347** | 0.30 | 0.339 | 0.08 | 0.355 | 1.58 |
| Raspi 4 | 4 | *0.431* | 3.83 | **0.436*** | 3.79 | 0.427 | 3.85 | *0.420* | 0.47 | **0.428** | 0.50 | 0.419 | 0.37 | 0.436 | 3.79 |
| Raspi 4 | 6 | *0.449* | 5.95 | **0.452*** | 5.29 | 0.445 | 5.95 | *0.440* | 0.56 | **0.441** | 0.57 | 0.432 | 0.55 | 0.452 | 5.95 |
| Raspi 4 | 8 | *0.456* | 6.33 | 0.455 | 7.96 | **0.457** | 7.97 | 0.451 | 0.69 | *0.449* | 0.79 | 0.447 | 0.76 | 0.465 | 7.43 |
| Raspi 4 | 10 | 0.466 | 8.66 | *0.465* | 8.62 | 0.464 | 8.72 | **0.464** | 0.77 | *0.454* | 0.94 | *0.454* | 0.90 | 0.468 | 8.83 |
| Raspi 4 | 12 | **0.468*** | 8.83 | 0.463 | 9.05 | *0.464* | 8.72 | **0.465** | 0.91 | *0.457* | 0.98 | 0.456 | 0.96 | 0.468 | 8.83 |
| Edge TPU | 1 | **0.468*** | 0.96 | *0.466* | 0.97 | 0.464 | 1.00 | **0.464** | 0.74 | *0.457* | 0.82 | 0.454 | 0.79 | 0.468 | 0.96 |
| Pixel 3 | 2 | **0.413*** | 1.30 | **0.413*** | 1.30 | 0.400 | 1.50 | **0.409** | 0.48 | *0.405* | 0.59 | 0.388 | 0.30 | 0.413 | 1.30 |
| Pixel 3 | 4 | **0.460*** | 3.55 | 0.446 | 3.01 | *0.447* | 3.23 | **0.453** | 0.69 | *0.441* | 0.77 | 0.438 | 0.64 | 0.460 | 3.55 |
| Pixel 3 | 6 | *0.464* | 5.92 | **0.465*** | 5.95 | 0.458 | 4.68 | **0.457** | 0.77 | *0.452* | 0.94 | 0.451 | 0.88 | 0.465 | 5.57 |
| Pixel 3 | 8 | **0.468*** | 6.65 | *0.465* | 7.88 | 0.461 | 7.13 | **0.464** | 0.87 | *0.457* | 0.99 | 0.454 | 0.97 | 0.468 | 6.65 |
| Pixel 3 | 10 | 0.466 | 6.70 | 0.461 | 8.48 | *0.464* | 8.01 | **0.464** | 0.96 | 0.455 | 1.00 | *0.456* | 0.99 | 0.468 | 6.65 |
| Eyeriss | 1 | **0.452*** | 0.98 | *0.449* | 0.98 | 0.447 | 0.98 | **0.445** | 0.49 | *0.436* | 0.53 | 0.433 | 0.23 | 0.452 | 0.98 |
| Eyeriss | 2 | 0.465 | 1.65 | 0.465 | 1.65 | 0.464 | 1.65 | **0.463** | 0.87 | *0.457* | 0.99 | *0.457* | 0.95 | 0.468 | 1.65 |
| FPGA | 1 | 0.440 | 1.00 | 0.440 | 0.97 | 0.438 | 0.97 | **0.433** | 0.65 | **0.433** | 0.80 | 0.429 | 0.58 | 0.444 | 1.00 |
| FPGA | 2 | **0.465*** | 1.60 | 0.460 | 1.60 | *0.463* | 1.97 | **0.462** | 0.82 | 0.451 | 0.99 | *0.453* | 0.97 | 0.465 | 1.60 |

line in NAS [22]. Figure 4 depicts searches with our model in both optimization settings on Pixel 3 with different latency conditions. More results on different hardware and latency constraints are shown in Table 5. We observe that either optimization setting outperforms the random search baseline in almost all tasks. Additionally, our method is able to find the optimal architecture for a task regularly (in 15 out of 20 tasks), which random search was not able to provide. When considering mean accuracy and feasibility of the best architectures of all runs, we see that $Joint = 1$ is able to improve the ratio of feasible architectures found during the search substantially. This is to be expected given that the latent space is explicitly optimized for latency in this setting. Consequently, $Joint = 1$ is able to find better-performing architectures compared to $Joint = 0$ if the constraint restricts the space of feasible architectures strongly (see results on Raspi 4). The feasibility ratio of random search is an indicator on how restricted the space is. In most cases, the latency penalization seems to be sufficient to find enough well-performing and feasible architectures, as can be seen by the feasibility of $Joint = 0$ which is greatly improved compared to random search. We show the development of feasibility over time from Table 5 in Fig. 4.

**Table 6.** Ablation: search results on NAS-Bench-101 and NAS-Bench-201 using AG-Net (mean over 10 trials with a maximal query amount of 192).

| | NAS-Bench-101 | | NAS-Bench-201 | | | | | |
|---|---|---|---|---|---|---|---|---|
| | CIFAR-10 | | CIFAR-10 | | CIFAR-100 | | ImageNet16-120 | |
| | Val. Acc. | Test Acc. | Val. Acc. | Test Acc. | Val. Acc. | Test Acc. | Val. Acc. | Test Acc. |
| Optimum* | 95.06 | 94.32 | 91.61 | 94.37 | 73.49 | 73.51 | 46.77 | 47.31 |
| AG-Net (ours) w/o LSO | 94.38 | 93.78 | 91.15 | 93.84 | 71.72 | 71.83 | 45.33 | 45.04 |
| AG-Net (ours) w/o backprop | 94.71 | 94.12 | **91.60** | 94.30 | 73.38 | 73.22 | 46.62 | 46.13 |
| AG-Net (ours) | **94.90** | **94.18** | **91.60** | **94.37*** | **73.49*** | **73.51*** | **46.64** | **46.43** |

### 4.4   Ablation Studies

In this section we analyse the impact of the LSO technique and the backpropagation ability to the search efficiency. Therefore, we compare our AG-Net with the latter named adaptions on the tabular benchmarks NAS-Bench-101 [54] and NAS-Bench-201 [10]. The results of our ablation study are reported in Table 6. As we can see, the lack of weighted retraining decreases the search substantially. In addition the results without backpropagation support that the coupling of the predictor's target and the generation process enables a more efficient architecture search over different search spaces. Thus, the combination of LSO and a fully differentiable approach improves the effectiveness of the search.

## 5   Conclusion

We propose a simple architecture generative network (AG-Net), which allows us to directly generate architectures without any additional encoder or discriminator. AG-Net is fully differentiable, allowing to couple it with surrogate models for different target predictions. In contrast to former works, it enables to backpropagate the target information from the surrogate predictor into the generator. By iteratively optimizing the latent space of the generator, our model learns to focus on promising regions of the architecture space, so that it can generate high-scoring architectures directly in a query and sample-efficient manner. Extensive experiments on common NAS benchmarks demonstrate that our model outperforms state-of-the-art methods at almost any time during architecture search and achieves state-of-the-art performance on ImageNet. It also allows for multi-objective optimization on the Hardware-Aware NAS-Benchmark.

**Acknowledgment.** JL and MK acknowledge the German Federal Ministry of Education and Research Foundation via the project DeToL.

# References

1. Bender, G., Kindermans, P., Zoph, B., Vasudevan, V., Le, Q.V.: Understanding and simplifying one-shot architecture search. In: ICML (2018)
2. Bergstra, J., Bengio, Y.: Random search for hyper-parameter optimization. J. Mach. Learn. Res. **13**(10), 281–305 (2012)
3. Cai, H., Zhu, L., Han, S.: ProxylessNAS: direct neural architecture search on target task and hardware. In: ICLR (2019)
4. Chen, T., Guestrin, C.: XGBoost: a scalable tree boosting system. In: Proceedings of the 22nd ACM SIGKDD International Conference on Knowledge Discovery and Data Mining (2016)
5. Chen, W., Gong, X., Wang, Z.: Neural architecture search on ImageNet in four GPU hours: a theoretically inspired perspective. In: ICLR (2021)
6. Chen, X., Xie, L., Wu, J., Tian, Q.: Progressive differentiable architecture search: bridging the depth gap between search and evaluation. In: ICCV (2019)
7. Chrabaszcz, P., Loshchilov, I., Hutter, F.: A downsampled variant of ImageNet as an alternative to the CIFAR datasets. CoRR abs/1707.08819 (2017)
8. Deng, J., Dong, W., Socher, R., Li, L.J., Li, K., Fei-Fei, L.: ImageNet: a large-scale hierarchical image database. In: CVPR (2009)
9. Dong, X., Yang, Y.: One-shot neural architecture search via self-evaluated template network. In: ICCV (2019)
10. Dong, X., Yang, Y.: Nas-bench-201: extending the scope of reproducible neural architecture search. In: ICLR (2020)
11. Elsken, T., Metzen, J.H., Hutter, F.: Neural architecture search: a survey. J. Mach. Learn. Res. **20**(1), 1997–2017 (2019)
12. Goodfellow, I.J., et al.: Generative adversarial networks. arXiv preprint arXiv:1406.2661 (2014)
13. He, K., Zhang, X., Ren, S., Sun, J.: Delving deep into rectifiers: surpassing human-level performance on ImageNet classification. In: ICCV (2015)
14. He, K., Zhang, X., Ren, S., Sun, J.: Deep residual learning for image recognition. In: CVPR (2016)
15. Huang, S., Chu, W.: Searching by generating: flexible and efficient one-shot NAS with architecture generator. In: CVPR (2021)
16. Kandasamy, K., Neiswanger, W., Schneider, J., Póczos, B., Xing, E.P.: Neural architecture search with bayesian optimisation and optimal transport. In: NIPS (2018)

17. Kingma, D.P., Welling, M.: Auto-encoding variational bayes. In: ICLR (2014)
18. Klyuchnikov, N., Trofimov, I., Artemova, E., Salnikov, M., Fedorov, M., Burnaev, E.: NAS-Bench-NLP: neural architecture search benchmark for natural language processing. CoRR abs/2006.07116 (2020)
19. Krizhevsky, A.: Learning multiple layers of features from tiny images (2009)
20. Krizhevsky, A., Sutskever, I., Hinton, G.E.: ImageNet classification with deep convolutional neural networks. In: NIPS (2012)
21. Li, C., et al.: HW-NAS-Bench: hardware-aware neural architecture search benchmark. In: ICLR (2021)
22. Li, L., Talwalkar, A.: Random search and reproducibility for neural architecture search. In: UAI (2019)
23. Li, Y., Vinyals, O., Dyer, C., Pascanu, R., Battaglia, P.W.: Learning deep generative models of graphs. CoRR abs/1803.03324 (2018)
24. Liu, C., et al.: Progressive neural architecture search. In: ECCV (2018)
25. Liu, H., Simonyan, K., Yang, Y.: DARTS: differentiable architecture search (2019)
26. Lukasik, J., Friede, D., Zela, A., Hutter, F., Keuper, M.: Smooth variational graph embeddings for efficient neural architecture search. In: IJCNN (2021)
27. Luo, R., Tian, F., Qin, T., Chen, E., Liu, T.: Neural architecture optimization. In: NeurIPS (2018)
28. Mehta, Y., et al.: NAS-bench-suite: NAS evaluation is (now) surprisingly easy. CoRR abs/2201.13396 (2022)
29. Mikolov, T., Karafiát, M., Burget, L., Cernocký, J., Khudanpur, S.: Recurrent neural network based language model. In: Kobayashi, T., Hirose, K., Nakamura, S. (eds.) INTERSPEECH 2010, 11th Annual Conference of the International Speech Communication Association, Makuhari, Chiba, Japan, 26–30 September 2010 (2010)
30. Pham, H., Guan, M.Y., Zoph, B., Le, Q.V., Dean, J.: Efficient neural architecture search via parameter sharing. In: ICML (2018)
31. Real, E., Aggarwal, A., Huang, Y., Le, Q.V.: Regularized evolution for image classifier architecture search. In: AAAI (2019)
32. Real, E., et al.: Large-scale evolution of image classifiers. In: ICML (2017)
33. Rezaei, S.S.C., et al.: Generative adversarial neural architecture search. In: IJCAI (2021)
34. Rolínek, M., Musil, V., Paulus, A., P., M.V., Michaelis, C., Martius, G.: Optimizing rank-based metrics with blackbox differentiation. In: CVPR (2020)
35. Ru, B., Wan, X., Dong, X., Osborne, M.: Interpretable neural architecture search via bayesian optimisation with Weisfeiler-Lehman kernels (2021)
36. Shi, H., Pi, R., Xu, H., Li, Z., Kwok, J.T., Zhang, T.: Multi-objective neural architecture search via predictive network performance optimization. CoRR abs/1911.09336 (2019)
37. Siems, J., Zimmer, L., Zela, A., Lukasik, J., Keuper, M., Hutter, F.: Nas-bench-301 and the case for surrogate benchmarks for neural architecture search. CoRR abs/2008.09777 (2020)
38. Simonyan, K., Zisserman, A.: Very deep convolutional networks for large-scale image recognition. In: ICLR (2014)
39. Snoek, J., et al.: Scalable bayesian optimization using deep neural networks. In: ICML (2015)
40. Szegedy, C., et al.: Going deeper with convolutions. In: CVPR (2015)
41. Szegedy, C., Vanhoucke, V., Ioffe, S., Shlens, J., Wojna, Z.: Rethinking the Inception architecture for Computer Vision. In: CVPR (2016)

42. Tripp, A., Daxberger, E., Hernández-Lobato, J.M.: Sample-efficient optimization in the latent space of deep generative models via weighted retraining. In: NeurIPS (2020)
43. Wen, W., Liu, H., Chen, Y., Li, H.H., Bender, G., Kindermans, P.: Neural predictor for neural architecture search. In: ECCV (2020)
44. White, C., Neiswanger, W., Nolen, S., Savani, Y.: A study on encodings for neural architecture search. In: NeurIPS (2020)
45. White, C., Neiswanger, W., Savani, Y.: Bananas: bayesian optimization with neural architectures for neural architecture search. In: AAAI (2021)
46. White, C., Nolen, S., Savani, Y.: Exploring the loss landscape in neural architecture search (2021)
47. White, C., Zela, A., Ru, B., Liu, Y., Hutter, F.: How powerful are performance predictors in neural architecture search? (2021)
48. Wu, J., et al.: Stronger NAS with weaker predictors. In: NeurIPS (2021)
49. Xie, S., Zheng, H., Liu, C., Lin, L.: SNAS: stochastic neural architecture search. In: ICLR (2019)
50. Xu, K., Hu, W., Leskovec, J., Jegelka, S.: How powerful are graph neural networks? In: ICLR (2019)
51. Xu, Y., et al.: PC-DARTS: partial channel connections for memory-efficient architecture search. In: ICLR (2020)
52. Yan, S., White, C., Savani, Y., Hutter, F.: NAS-bench-x11 and the power of learning curves (2021)
53. Yan, S., Zheng, Y., Ao, W., Zeng, X., Zhang, M.: Does unsupervised architecture representation learning help neural architecture search? In: NeurIPS (2020)
54. Ying, C., Klein, A., Christiansen, E., Real, E., Murphy, K., Hutter, F.: NAS-bench-101: towards reproducible neural architecture search. In: ICML (2019)
55. Zela, A., Elsken, T., Saikia, T., Marrakchi, Y., Brox, T., Hutter, F.: Understanding and robustifying differentiable architecture search. In: ICLR (2020)
56. Zhang, M., Jiang, S., Cui, Z., Garnett, R., Chen, Y.: D-VAE: a variational autoencoder for directed acyclic graphs. In: NIPS (2019)
57. Zoph, B., Le, Q.V.: Neural architecture search with reinforcement learning. In: ICLR (2017)
58. Zoph, B., Vasudevan, V., Shlens, J., Le, Q.V.: Learning transferable architectures for scalable image recognition. In: CVPR (2018)

# Subspace Diffusion Generative Models

Bowen Jing$^{(\boxtimes)}$, Gabriele Corso, Renato Berlinghieri, and Tommi Jaakkola

Massachusetts Institute of Technology, Cambridge, USA
{bjing,gcorso,renb}@mit.edu, tommi@csail.mit.edu

**Abstract.** Score-based models generate samples by mapping noise to data (and vice versa) via a high-dimensional diffusion process. We question whether it is necessary to run this entire process at high dimensionality and incur all the inconveniences thereof. Instead, we restrict the diffusion via projections onto *subspaces* as the data distribution evolves toward noise. When applied to state-of-the-art models, our framework simultaneously *improves* sample quality—reaching an FID of 2.17 on unconditional CIFAR-10—and *reduces* the computational cost of inference for the same number of denoising steps. Our framework is fully compatible with continuous-time diffusion and retains its flexible capabilities, including exact log-likelihoods and controllable generation. Code is available at https://github.com/bjing2016/subspace-diffusion.

**Keywords:** Generative models · Diffusion models · Score matching

## 1 Introduction

Score-based models are a class of generative models that learn the score of the data distribution as it evolves under a diffusion process in order to generate data via the reverse process [6,20]. These models—also known as diffusion models—can generate high-quality and diverse samples, evaluate exact log-likelihoods, and are easily adapted to conditional and controlled generation tasks [20]. On the CIFAR-10 image dataset, they have recently achieved state-of-the-art performance in sample generation and likelihood evaluation [9,21].

Despite these strengths, in this work we focus on and aim to address a drawback in the current formulation of score-based models: the forward diffusion occurs in the full ambient space of the data distribution, destroying its structure but retaining its high dimensionality. However, it does not seem parsimonious to represent increasingly noisy latent variables—which approach zero mutual information with the original data—in a space with such high dimensionality. The practical implications of this high latent dimensionality are twofold:

---

B. Jing and G. Corso—Equal contribution.

**Supplementary Information** The online version contains supplementary material available at https://doi.org/10.1007/978-3-031-20050-2_17.

S. Avidan et al. (Eds.): ECCV 2022, LNCS 13683, pp. 274–289, 2022.
https://doi.org/10.1007/978-3-031-20050-2_17

*High-dimensional Extrapolation.* The network must learn the score function over the entire support of the high-dimensional latent variable, even in areas very far (relative to the scale of the data) from the data manifold. Due to the curse of dimensionality, much of this support may never be visited during training, and the accuracy of the score model in these regions is called into question by the uncertain extrapolation abilities of neural networks [23]. Learning to match a lower-dimensional score function may lead to refined training coverage and further improved performance.

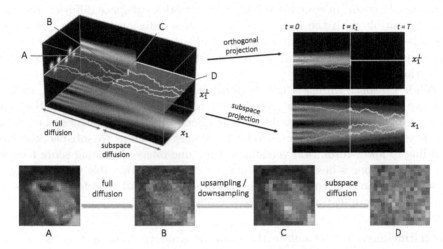

**Fig. 1.** Visual schematic of subspace diffusion with one projection step. *Top left*: The starting data distribution $\mathbf{x}_0(0)$ lies near a subspace (light blue line). As the data evolves, the distribution of the orthogonal component $\mathbf{x}_1^\perp(t)$ approaches a Gaussian faster than the subspace component $\mathbf{x}_1(t)$. At time $t_1$ we project onto the subspace and restrict the remaining diffusion to the subspace. To generate data, we use the full and subspace score models to reverse the full and subspace diffusion steps, and sample $\mathbf{x}_1^\perp(t_1)$ from a Gaussian to reverse the projection step. *Top right*: The diffusion of the subspace component $\mathbf{x}_1(t)$ is unaffected by the projection step and restriction to the subspace; while the orthogonal component is diffused until $t_1$ and discarded afterwards. *Bottom*: CIFAR-10 images corresponding to points along the trajectory, where the subspaces correspond to lower-resolution images and projection is equivalent to downsampling.

*Computational Cost.* Hundreds or even thousands of evaluations of the high-dimensional score model are required to generate an image, making inference with score-based models much slower than GANs and VAEs [6,20]. A number of recent works aim to address this challenge by reducing the number of steps required for inference [2,3,8,10,11,13,16–18,22]. However, these methods trade-off inference runtime with sample quality. Moreover, the dimensionality of the score function—and thereby the computational cost of a single score evaluation—is an independent and equally important factor to the overall runtime, but this factor has received less attention in existing works.

*Subspace diffusion models* aim to address these challenges. In many real-world domains, target data lie near a linear subspace, such that under isotropic forward diffusion, the components of the data orthogonal to the subspace become Gaussian significantly before the components in the subspace. We propose to use a full-dimensional network to model the score only at lower noise levels, when all components are sufficiently non-Gaussian. At higher noise levels, we use smaller networks to model in the subspace only those components of the score which remain non-Gaussian. As this reduces both the number and domain of queries to the full-dimensional network, subspace diffusion addresses both of our motivating concerns. Moreover, in contrast to many prior works, subspace diffusion remains fully compatible with the underlying continuous diffusion framework [20], and therefore preserves all the capabilities available to continuous score-based models, such as likelihood evaluation, probability flow sampling, and controllable generation.

While subspace diffusion can be formulated in fully general terms, in this work we focus on generative modeling of natural images. Because the global structure of images is dominated by low-frequency visual components—i.e., adjacent pixels values are highly correlated—images lie close to subspaces corresponding to lower-resolution versions of the same image. Learning score models over these subspaces has the advantage of remaining compatible with the translation equivariance of convolutional neural networks, and therefore requires no architectural modifications to the score model.

**Contributions.** We formulate the diffusion process, training procedure, and sampling procedure in subspaces; to our knowledge, this represents the first investigation of dimensionality reduction in a score-based model framework. We develop a method, the *orthogonal Fisher divergence*, for choosing among candidate subspaces and the parameters of the subspace diffusion. Experimentally, we train and evaluate lower-dimensional subspace models in conjunction with state-of-the-art pretrained full-dimensional models from [20]. We improve over those models in sample quality and runtime, achieving an FID of 2.17 and a IS of 9.99 on CIFAR-10 generation. Finally, we demonstrate probability flow sampling and likelihood evaluation with subspace models.

## 2   Background and Related Work

**Score-Based Models.** In score-based models, one considers the data distribution $\mathbf{x}(0) \in \mathbb{R}^d$ to be the starting distribution for a continuous diffusion process, defined by an Ito stochastic differential equation (SDE)

$$d\mathbf{x} = \mathbf{f}(\mathbf{x}, t)\, dt + \mathbf{G}(\mathbf{x}, t)\, d\mathbf{w} \quad t \in (0, T) \tag{1}$$

known as the *forward process*, which transforms $\mathbf{x}(0)$ into (approximately) a simple Gaussian $\mathbf{x}(T)$. By convention, we typically set $T = 1$. A neural network is then trained to model the score $\nabla_{\mathbf{x}} \log p_t(\mathbf{x})$ conditioned on $t$. Solving the reverse stochastic differential equation

$$d\mathbf{x} = \mathbf{f}(\mathbf{x}, t)\, dt - \mathbf{G}(\mathbf{x}, t)\mathbf{G}(\mathbf{x}, t)^T \nabla_{\mathbf{x}} \log p(\mathbf{x}, t)\, dt + \mathbf{G}(t)\, d\bar{\mathbf{w}} \tag{2}$$

starting with samples from the simple Gaussian distribution $\mathbf{x}(T)$ yields samples from the data distribution $\mathbf{x}(0)$ [1,20]. Score-based models were originally formulated separately in terms of denoising score matching at multiple noise scales [19]; and of reversing a discrete-time Markov chain of diffusion steps [6]. Due to the latter formulation (associated with the term *diffusion model*), $\mathbf{x}(t)$ for $t > 0$ are often referred to as *latents* of $\mathbf{x}(0)$, and the simple Gaussian $\mathbf{x}$ as the *prior*. The two views are unified by the observation that the variational approximation to the reverse Markov chain matches the score of the diffused data [20].

The score model $s_\theta(\mathbf{x}, t)$ can be trained via denoising score matching [19] using the perturbation kernels $p(\mathbf{x}(t) \mid \mathbf{x}(0))$, which are analytically determined by $\mathbf{f}(\mathbf{x}, t), \mathbf{G}(t)$ at each time $t$. The learned score can be readily adjusted with fixed terms for controlled generation tasks in the same manner as energy-based models [5]. Finally, the reverse stochastic differential equation produces the same marginals $\mathbf{x}$ as the *ordinary* differential equation (ODE)

$$d\mathbf{x} = \mathbf{f}(\mathbf{x}, t) \, dt - \frac{1}{2}\mathbf{G}(\mathbf{x}, t)\mathbf{G}(\mathbf{x}, t)^T \nabla_\mathbf{x} \log p(\mathbf{x}, t) \, dt \tag{3}$$

which enables evaluation of exact log-likelihoods, but empirically results in degraded quality when used for sampling [20].

**Accelerating Score-Based Models.** Due to the fine discretization required to solve (2) to high accuracy, score-based models suffer from slow inference. Several recent works aim to address this. Denoising diffusion implicit models (DDIM) [18] can be viewed as solving the equivalent ODE with a reduced number of steps. Progressive distillation [16] proposes a student-teacher framework for learning sampling networks requiring logarithmically fewer steps. [8] derives an adaptive step-size solver for the reverse SDE. Other works [2,3,10,11,13,17,22] focus on reducing the number of steps in the discrete-time Markov chain formulation. However, these approaches generally result in degraded sample quality compared to the best continuous-time models.

Taking a different approach, latent score-based generative models (LSGM) [21] use a score-based model as the prior of a deep VAE, resulting in more Gaussian scores, improved sample quality, and fewer model evaluations. In a similar vein, critically-damped Langevin diffusion (CLD-SGM) [4] augments the data dimensions with momentum dimensions and diffuses only in momentum space, resulting in more Gaussian scores and fewer evaluations for comparable quality. However, both these methods significantly modify the original formulation of score-based models, such that exact likelihood evaluation and controllable generation become considerably more difficult.[1]

Unlike these previous works, subspace diffusion simultaneously improves sample quality and inference runtime while also preserving all the capabilities of the original formulation. Compared with LSGM and CLD-SGM, subspace diffusion also has the advantage of being compatible with existing trained score models, incurring only the overhead required to train the smaller subspace score models.

---

[1] In CLD-SGM, one must marginalize over the momentum variables; and in LSGM one must marginalize over the latent variable of VAE.

**Cascading Generative Models.** Subspace diffusion bears some similarity to cascading generative models consisting of one low-dimensional model followed by one or more super-resolution models [12,14]. Cascading score-based models have yielded strong results on high-resolution class-conditional ImageNet generation [3,7,15]. These models formulate each super-resolution step as a full diffusion process conditioned on the lower-resolution image. Subspace diffusion, on the other hand, models a single diffusion process punctuated by projection steps. This leads to a more general theoretical framework that is useful even in domains where the concept of super-resolution does not apply (see for example the synthetic experiments in the supplementary material). Chaining conditional diffusion processes also complicates the application of other capabilities of score-based models—for example, evaluating log-likelihoods would require marginalizing over the intermediate lower-resolution images. Our subspace diffusion framework is a modification of a single diffusion and does not incur these difficulties.

# 3   Subspace Diffusion

A concrete formulation of a score-based model requires a choice of forward diffusion process, specified by $\mathbf{f}(\mathbf{x}, t)$, $\mathbf{G}(\mathbf{x}, t)$. Almost always, these are chosen to be *isotropic*, i.e., of the form

$$\mathbf{f}(\mathbf{x}, t) = f(t)\,\mathbf{x} \quad \mathbf{G}(\mathbf{x}, t) = g(t)\,\mathbf{I}_d \tag{4}$$

where $d$ is the data dimensionality. For example, the variance exploding (VE) SDE has $f(t) = 0$ and $g(t) = \sqrt{d\sigma^2/dt}$ where $\sigma^2(t)$ is the variance of the perturbation kernel at time $t$ [20]. The sole exception is the Langevin diffusion in CLD-SGM [4], but this required new forms of score-matching and specialised SDE solvers for numerical stability. We aim to keep the simplicity and convenience of form (4) while addressing its limitations discussed in Sect. 1. We thus propose that at every point in time, the diffusion is restricted *to some subspace*, but is otherwise isotropic *in that subspace*. Specifically, the forward diffusion begins in the full space, but is projected and restricted to increasingly smaller subspaces as time goes on. Any isotropic forward diffusion can therefore be converted into a subspace diffusion.

For any diffusion with the form (4), define the corresponding subspace diffusion as follows. Divide $(0, T)$ into $K + 1$ subintervals, $(t_0, t_1), \ldots, (t_K, t_{K+1})$ where for notational convenience $t_0 = 0, t_{K+1} = T$. Then define:

$$\mathbf{G}(\mathbf{x}, t) = g(t)\mathbf{U}_k\mathbf{U}_k^T \tag{5}$$

for each interval $t_k < t < t_{k+1}$, where $\mathbf{U}_k \in \mathbb{R}^{d \times n_k}$ is the matrix whose $n_k \leq d$ orthonormal columns span a subspace of $\mathbb{R}^d$. We refer to this subspace as the $k$th subspace and to the columns of $\mathbf{U}_k$ as its basis. For notational convenience, $\mathbf{U}_0 = \mathbf{I}_d$. We choose $n_k$ such that $d = n_0 > n_1 > \ldots > n_K$. We also require the $k$th subspace to be a subspace of the $j$th subspace for any $j < k$, which can be written as $\mathbf{U}_j\mathbf{U}_j^T\mathbf{U}_k = \mathbf{U}_k$. Together, these definitions state that diffusion is coupled or constrained to occur in progressively smaller subspaces defined by $\mathbf{U}_k$ in the interval $(t_k, t_{k+1})$.

Turning to $\mathbf{f}(\mathbf{x}, t)$, define

$$\mathbf{f}(\mathbf{x}, t) = f(t)\mathbf{x} + \sum_{k=1}^{K} \delta(t - t_k)(\mathbf{U}_k \mathbf{U}_k^T - \mathbf{I}_d)\mathbf{x} \tag{6}$$

where $\delta$ is the Dirac delta. This states that at time $t_k$, $\mathbf{x}$ is projected onto the $k$th subspace. Figure 1 illustrates the high-level idea of subspace diffusion, along with some of its properties discussed in more detail below.

**Notation.** For the rest of the exposition, we define:

- $\mathbf{U}_{k|j} = \mathbf{U}_j^T \mathbf{U}_k \in \mathbb{R}^{n_j \times n_k}$ for $j \leq k$ defines the $k$th subspace written in the basis of the $j$th subspace. In particular, $\mathbf{U}_{k|0} = \mathbf{U}_k$ and $\mathbf{U}_{k|k} = \mathbf{I}_{n_k}$.
- $\mathbf{P}_{k|j} = \mathbf{U}_{k|j}\mathbf{U}_{k|j}^T \in \mathbb{R}^{n_j \times n_j}$ for $j \leq k$ is the projection operator onto the $k$th subspace, written in the basis of the $j$th subspace.
- $\mathbf{P}_{k|j}^{\perp} = \mathbf{I}_{n_j} - \mathbf{P}_{k|j} \in \mathbb{R}^{n_j \times n_j}$ for $j < k$ is the projection operator onto the complement of the $k$th subspace, written in the basis of the $j$th subspace.
- $\mathbf{x}_k = \mathbf{U}_k^T \mathbf{x} \in \mathbb{R}^{n_k}$ is the component of $\mathbf{x}$ in the $k$th subspace, written in that basis. In particular, $\mathbf{x}_0 = \mathbf{x}$.
- $\mathbf{x}_{k|j}^{\perp} = \mathbf{P}_{k|j}^{\perp}\mathbf{x}_j \in \mathbb{R}^{n_j}$ for $j < k$ is the component of $\mathbf{x}_j$ orthogonal to the $k$th subspace, written in the basis of the $j$th subspace.

## 3.1   Score Matching

To generate data, we need to learn the score $\nabla_{\mathbf{x}} \log p(\mathbf{x}, t)$ as usual. However, for times $t_k < t < t_{k+1}$, the support of $p(\mathbf{x}, t)$ is only in the $k$th subspace. This means that if we learn a separate score model $\mathbf{s}_k(\mathbf{x}, t) \approx \nabla_{\mathbf{x}} \log p(\mathbf{x}, t)$ for each interval $t \in (t_k, t_{k+1})$, then the model $\mathbf{s}_k$ *only needs to have dimensionality* $n_k$. In particular, we use models smaller than $n_0 = d$ for all times $t > t_1$.

To learn these lower-dimensional models, we leverage the fact that the subspace components $\mathbf{x}_k$ of the data diffuse under an SDE with the same $f(t), g(t)$ as the full data, independent of the orthogonal components. This is due to the fact that the original diffusion is isotropic. To see this, consider (for simplicity) the case $K = 1$, i.e., we only use one proper subspace. Then since $d\mathbf{x}_1 = \mathbf{U}_1^T d\mathbf{x}$,

$$\begin{aligned} d\mathbf{x}_1 = {} & f(t)\mathbf{U}_1^T \mathbf{x}\, dt + \delta(t - t_1)\mathbf{U}_1^T(\mathbf{U}_1\mathbf{U}_1^T - \mathbf{I}_d)\mathbf{x}\, dt \\ & + g(t)\left(\mathbf{U}_1^T\left(\mathbb{1}_{t<t_1}\mathbf{I}_d + \mathbb{1}_{t>t_1}\mathbf{U}_1\mathbf{U}_1^T\right)\right)\, d\mathbf{w} \end{aligned} \tag{7}$$

However, because $\mathbf{U}_1^T\mathbf{U}_1 = \mathbf{I}_d$, the above simplifies as

$$d\mathbf{x}_1 = f(t)\mathbf{x}_1\, dt + g(t)\, d\mathbf{w}_1 \tag{8}$$

where, because the columns of $\mathbf{U}_1$ are orthonormal, $d\mathbf{w}_1 := \mathbf{U}_1^T\, d\mathbf{w}$ is a Brownian diffusion in $\mathbb{R}^{n_1}$. As a result, the perturbation kernels $p(\mathbf{x}_1(t) \mid \mathbf{x}_1(0))$ in the subspace have the same form as in the full space. This allows us to train a model to match the scores $\nabla_{\mathbf{x}_1} \log p(\mathbf{x}_1, t)$ via precisely the same procedure as in [20], except we treat $\mathbf{x}_1(0)$ as the original undiffused data. These scores are related to the full-dimensional scores $\nabla_{\mathbf{x}} \log p(\mathbf{x}, t)$ via $\mathbf{U}_1$, but since $\mathbf{x} = \mathbf{U}_1 \mathbf{x}_1$ for times $t > t_1$, we can directly work with data points $\mathbf{x}_1$ and score models $\nabla_{\mathbf{x}_1} \log p(\mathbf{x}_1, t)$ with no loss of information for times $t > t_1$. Thus, in the general case, we train $K + 1$ different score models $\mathbf{s}_k(\mathbf{x}_k, t) \approx \nabla_{\mathbf{x}_k} \log p(\mathbf{x}_k, t)$, where we consider $\mathbf{x}_k$ to have diffused under the original $f(t), g(t)$ for the full time scale $(0, T)$.

## 3.2   Sampling

To generate a sample, we use each score model $\mathbf{s}_k(\mathbf{x}_k, t)$ in the corresponding interval $(t_k, t_{k+1})$ to solve the reverse diffusion of $\mathbf{x}_k$. However, we cannot use the score to reverse the projection steps at the boundaries times $t_k$. Thus, to impute $\mathbf{x}_{k-1}(t_k)$ from $\mathbf{x}_k(t_k)$, we sample $\mathbf{x}^{\perp}_{k|k-1}(t_k)$ by injecting isotropic Gaussian noise orthogonal to the $k$th subspace. The variance $\Sigma^{\perp}_{k|k-1}$ of the injected noise is chosen to match the marginal variance of $\mathbf{x}^{\perp}_{k|k-1}$ at time $t_k$, which is the sum of the original variance of $\mathbf{x}^{\perp}_{k|k-1}$ in the data and the variance of the perturbation kernel:

$$\Sigma^{\perp}_{k|k-1}(t_k) := \frac{\alpha^2(t_k)}{n_{k-1} - n_k} \mathbb{E}\left[\|\mathbf{x}^{\perp}_{k|k-1}(0)\|^2_2\right] + \sigma^2(t_k) \tag{9}$$

where $\alpha(t)$ and $\sigma^2(t)$ are the scale and variance of the perturbation kernels.

Sampling $\mathbf{x}^{\perp}_{k|k-1}$ in this manner assumes that (at time $t_k$) it is independent of $\mathbf{x}_k$ and roughly an isotropic Gaussian. The final sample quality will depend on the validity of this assumption. Intuitively, however, we specifically choose subspaces and times such that the original magnitude of $\mathbf{x}^{\perp}_{k|k-1}$ (the first term in (9)) is very small compared to the diffusion noise (the second term), which is indeed isotropic and independent of the data. We also find that a few conditional Langevin dynamics steps with $s_k(\mathbf{x}_k, t_{k+1})$ to correct for the approximations of noise injection help sampling quality. The complete sampling procedure is outlined in Algorithm 1.

So far we have presented subspace diffusion as an explicit modification to the forward diffusion involving projection and confined diffusion, which best matches how we implement unconditional sample generation. However, an alternate view is more suitable for controlled generation, where a full-dimensional score model is required; or in ODE-based likelihood evaluation or probability flow sampling, where the adaptive, non-monotonic evaluations make working with discrete projection steps inconvenient. In these settings, we regard subspace diffusion at time $t \in (t_k, t_{k+1})$ as *explicitly* modeling the score component in $k$th subspace with $\mathbf{s}_k(\mathbf{x}_k, t)$, and *implicitly* modeling all orthogonal components with Gaussians. Specifically, for $t \in (t_k, t_{k+1})$ we decompose $\mathbf{x}$ as

$$\mathbf{x} = \sum_{j=0}^{k-1} \mathbf{U}_j \mathbf{x}^{\perp}_{j+1|j} + \mathbf{U}_k \mathbf{x}_k \tag{10}$$

---

**Algorithm 1:** Unconditional sampling with subspace diffusion

---

**Input**: subspaces $\mathbf{U}_k$, projection times $t_k$, score models $\mathbf{s}_k(\mathbf{x}_k, t)$, $k = 0 \ldots K$

**Output**: approximate sample $\mathbf{x}_0$ from $p(\mathbf{x}_0, 0) = p_{\text{data}}(\mathbf{x})$

$\mathbf{x}_K \leftarrow$ sample from prior $p(\mathbf{x}_K, T) \in \mathbb{R}^{n_K}$;

**for** $k \leftarrow K$ **to** $0$ **do**

    $\mathbf{x}_k \leftarrow$ solve reverse SDE with $\mathbf{s}_k(\mathbf{x}_k, t)$ from $t_{k+1}$ to $t_k$ starting from $\mathbf{x}_k$;

    **if** $k > 0$ **then**

        $\mathbf{x}_{k|k-1}^{\perp} \leftarrow$ sample from $\mathcal{N}(0, \Sigma_{k|k-1}^{\perp}(t_k) \, \mathbf{I}) \in \mathbb{R}^{n_{k-1}}$;

        $\mathbf{x}_{k|k-1}^{\perp} \leftarrow \mathbf{P}_{k|k-1}^{\perp} \mathbf{x}_{k|k-1}^{\perp}$;

        $\mathbf{x}_{k-1} \leftarrow \mathbf{U}_{k|k-1} \mathbf{x}_k + \mathbf{x}_{k|k-1}^{\perp}$;

        **for** $i \leftarrow 1$ **to** $n$ **do**        // n is a hyperpameter

            $\mathbf{x}_{k-1} \leftarrow$ LangevinStep($\mathbf{x}_{k-1}, t_k$);

---

where the sum corresponds to the components that are "Gaussianized" out by each projection step. We thus model each $\mathbf{x}_{j+1|j}^{\perp}$ implicitly as isotropic Gaussian with variance $\Sigma_{j+1|j}^{\perp}$, and model $\mathbf{x}_k$ explicitly with score model $\mathbf{s}_k(\mathbf{x}_k, t)$, giving the full score:

$$\nabla_{\mathbf{x}} \log p_t(\mathbf{x}, t) \approx \mathbf{U}_k \mathbf{s}_k(\mathbf{U}_k^T \mathbf{x}, t) - \sum_{j=0}^{k-1} \left( \mathbf{P}_{j|0} - \mathbf{P}_{j+1|0} \right) \frac{\mathbf{x}}{\Sigma_{j+1|j}^{\perp}(t)} \quad (11)$$

where, for clarity, we write all components in terms of $\mathbf{x}$ in the original basis.

### 3.3   Image Subspaces

We now restrict our attention to generative modeling of natural images.[2] Motivated by the observation that adjacent pixels tend to be *similar* in color, we choose subspaces that correspond to images where adjacent groups of pixels are *equal* in color—i.e., downsampled versions of the image. Henceforth, we refer to such *downsampling subspaces* in terms of their resolution (e.g., the $16 \times 16$ subspace), refer to projection onto subspaces at times $t_k$ as *downsampling*, and to the reverse action as *upsampling*.[3]

To more precisely formulate these subspaces, suppose we have a full-resolution image $\mathbf{X} \in \mathbb{R}^{(n \times n \times 3)}$. In particular, we will work with $n$ that are integer powers of 2. Then we define a downsampling operator $\mathcal{D} : \mathbb{R}^{(n \times n \times 3)} \rightarrow \mathbb{R}^{(n/2 \times n/2 \times 3)}$ such that if $\mathbf{X}_{k+1} = \mathcal{D}\mathbf{X}_k$, then

$$\mathbf{X}_{k+1}[a, b, c] = \frac{1}{2} \sum_{(i,j) \in \{0,1\}^2} \mathbf{X}_k[2a + i, 2b + j, c] \quad (12)$$

---

[2] See the supplementary material for experiments on more generic synthetic data.

[3] It is via this choice of subspace that subspace diffusion superficially resembles the cascading models discussed in Sect. 2.

which states that $\mathbf{X}_{k+1}^{(t)}$ is simply $\mathbf{X}_k^{(t)}$ after mean-pooling $2 \times 2$ patches, multiplied by 2. We can use $\mathcal{D}$ to implicitly define $\mathbf{U}_k$:

$$\mathbf{U}_k^T \mathbf{x} = \mathcal{D}^k \mathbf{x} \quad \text{or} \quad \mathbf{U}_k^T \mathbf{x} = \mathcal{D} \mathbf{U}_{k-1}^T \mathbf{x} \tag{13}$$

where here we consider $\mathbf{x}$ to be the column vector representation of the array $\mathbf{X}$. The choice of $\mathcal{D}$ corresponds to orthonormal $\mathbf{U}_k$, as each column of $\mathbf{U}_k$ has $2^{2k}$ nonzero entries, each with magnitude $1/2^k$. Thus, all of the general results from the preceding section apply. In particular, we can consider the same forward diffusion process defined by $f(t), g(t)$ to be occurring for each downsampled image $\mathcal{D}^k \mathbf{x}$, such that the subspace score models $\mathbf{s}_k(\mathbf{x}_k, t)$ correspond to the same score model trained over a lower-resolution version of the same dataset.

It is natural to consider whether there may exist more optimal subspaces for natural images. In Table 1 we compare the downsampling subspaces to the optimal subspaces of equivalent dimensionality[4] found by principle components analysis (PCA) in terms of root mean square distance (RMSD) of the data from the subspace. Generally, the downsampling subspaces can be seen to be suboptimal. However, if we were to use the optimal PCA subspaces, the coordinates would not take the form of an image-structured latent with translation equivariance, and thus would be incompatible with the convolutional neural networks in the score model. Therefore, a more appropriate comparison is with the subspace found via PCA of the distribution of all *patches* of pixels of the appropriate size, which we call Patch-PCA (see supplementary information for details). These subspaces offer only minor improvements over the downsampling subspaces, so we did not explore them further.

It is also possible that for any given dimensionality $n < d$, the $n$-dimensional substructure that best approximates the data distribution is a nonlinear manifold rather than a subspace. However, leveraging such manifolds to reduce the dimensionality of diffusion would require substantial modifications to the present framework. While potentially promising, we leave such extensions to nonlinear manifolds to future work.

## 3.4   Orthogonal Fisher Divergence

We now propose a principled manner to choose among the candidate subspaces for a given image dataset, as well as the downsampling times $t_k$.

For any fixed choice of proper subspaces $\mathbf{U}_1 \dots \mathbf{U}_k$, the optimal values of each $t_k$ must balance two factors: smaller $t_k$ reduces the number of reverse diffusion steps occurring at higher dimensionality $n_{k-1}$, whereas larger $t_k$ makes the Gaussian approximation of the orthogonal components $\mathbf{x}_{k|k-1}^\perp$ more accurate when we sample at time $t_k$. This suggests that we should choose the minimum times that keep the error of the Gaussian approximation below some tolerance threshold. However, we cannot quantify the true error as we do not have access to the underlying distribution of $\mathbf{x}_{k|k-1}^\perp$. Thus, we instead examine how much the

---

[4] That is, an $N \times N$ subspace has dimensionality $3N^2$.

**Table 1.** Comparison of downsampling subspaces with optimal subspaces of equivalent dimensionality found by PCA and Patch-PCA. RMSD per dim refers to $RMSD/\sqrt{d-n}$, where $d, n$ are the original and subspace dimensionalities. PCA and Patch-PCA were run on a subset of CelebA and LSUN.

| Dataset | Subspace dim. | RMSD per dim. | | |
|---|---|---|---|---|
| | | PCA | Patch-PCA | Downsampling |
| CIFAR-10 | $16 \times 16$ | 0.024 | 0.064 | 0.075 |
| $(32 \times 32)$ | $8 \times 8$ | 0.061 | 0.093 | 0.110 |
| CelebA-HQ | $128 \times 128$ | — | 0.034 | 0.034 |
| $(256 \times 256)$ | $32 \times 32$ | 0.041 | 0.063 | 0.073 |
| | $8 \times 8$ | 0.083 | 0.117 | 0.141 |
| LSUN Church | $128 \times 128$ | — | 0.058 | 0.070 |
| $(256 \times 256)$ | $32 \times 32$ | 0.082 | 0.099 | 0.109 |
| | $8 \times 8$ | 0.126 | 0.146 | 0.158 |

*learned* full-dimensional score model $s_0(\mathbf{x}, t)$ diverges from the Gaussian approximation on $\mathbf{x}^{\perp}_{k|k-1}$ as $t$ is varied. To quantify this divergence, for any $j < k$ we introduce the *orthogonal Fisher divergence* of $\mathbf{U}_{k|j}$ as:

$$D_F(\mathbf{U}_{k|j}; t) = \frac{\Sigma^{\perp}_{k|j}(t)}{n_j - n_k} \mathbb{E}_{\mathbf{x}(t)} \left[ \left\| \mathbf{P}^{\perp}_{k|j} \mathbf{U}^T_j s_0(\mathbf{x}, t) + \frac{\mathbf{x}^{\perp}_{k|j}}{\Sigma^{\perp}_{k|j}(t)} \right\|^2 \right] \tag{14}$$

The first term is the component of the score orthogonal to $\mathbf{U}_{k|j}$, and the second term is the score of the Gaussian approximation of $\mathbf{x}^{\perp}_{k|j}$. The divergence is normalized by the (approximate) expected norm of the Gaussian score, which enables values for different $t, j, k$ to be compared. The expectation over $\mathbf{x}(t)$ can then be approximated using the training data. The divergence $D(\mathbf{U}_{k|k-1}; t)$ then corresponds to the error that would be introduced by the upsampling step at time $t$.

Given a sequence of subspaces, the divergence threshold becomes the sole hyperparameter of the sampling process, as we can compute (14) to determine the upsampling times $t_k$ for any threshold. Once the $t_k$ are known, we can estimate the runtime improvement over the full-dimensional score model. Thus, we can choose the subspaces sequence to minimize the estimated runtime. Additionally, it is more convenient to consider $D_F(\mathbf{U}_{k|0}; t)$ as opposed to $D(\mathbf{U}_{k|k-1}; t)$, which corresponds to assuming that at time $t_k$, $\mathbf{x}^{\perp}_{k|k-1}$ is sampled with variance $\Sigma^{\perp}_{k|0}$ rather than $\Sigma^{\perp}_{k|k-1}$.[5] The benefit of this approximation is that we can speak of the divergence purely as a property of the subspace, independent of the preceding subspace (if any). Thus, we can simultaneously plot the orthogonal

---

[5] The difference is minimal as the variance of the perturbation kernel dominates either term for reasonable divergence thresholds.

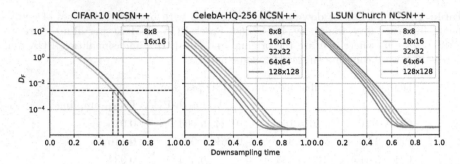

**Fig. 2.** Orthogonal Fisher divergence plots computed with respect to the pretrained NCSN++ full-dimensional score models from [20]. Similar plots can be generated for other models. Given a divergence threshold, the optimal downsampling times $t_k$ for any subspace sequence are the times at which the corresponding divergences attain that threshold. For example, on CIFAR-10 with a target $D_F = 3 \times 10^{-3}$ and the sequence $32 \rightarrow 16 \rightarrow 8$, the downsampling times are $t_1 = 0.516, t_2 = 0.558$. In this case, the intermediate $16 \times 16$ subspace would be used for only 4.2% of the diffusion. As the plot shows, this imbalance would characterise any sequence of more than one proper subspace.

Fisher divergence for each downsampling subspace, as illustrated in Fig. 2. The choice of intervals for any subspace sequence and divergence threshold can then be directly read off the plot.

As Fig. 2 shows, for standard image datasets there appears to be little utility to using more than one proper subspace, as the diffusion in intermediate dimensions would be very brief. On the other hand, training additional models is computationally expensive and adds to the sum of the model sizes required for inference. Thus, our experiments focus on subspace diffusions consisting of only one proper downsampling subspace. In particular, for CIFAR-10, we consider the $8 \times 8$ and $16 \times 16$ subspaces separately, while for CelebA-HQ and LSUN Church we consider only the $64 \times 64$ subspace, which offers the best potential runtime improvement.

## 4 Experiments

We demonstrate the utility and versatility of our method by improving upon and accelerating state-of-the-art continuous score-based models. Specifically, we take the pretrained models on CIFAR-10, CelebA-256-HQ, and LSUN Church from [20] as full-dimensional score models, train additional subspace score models of the same architecture, and use them together in the subspace diffusion framework. All lower-dimensional models are trained with the same hyperparameters and training procedure as the original model. During inference, we use the unmodified reverse SDE solvers and the same number and spacing of denoising steps. We investigate results for a range of divergence thresholds, corresponding

**Table 2.** CIFAR-10 sample quality for 50k images. *Left*: the best performance of previous methods to accelerate score-based models. *Right*: the original full diffusion from [20] and the respective best subspace diffusion (all $16 \times 16$), with the corresponding divergence threshold, downsampling time $t_1$, and empirical runtime relative to the full model.

| Model | FID ↓ |
|---|---|
| DDIM [18] | 4.04 |
| FastDPM [10] | 2.86 |
| Bilateral DPM [11] | 2.38 |
| Analytic DPM [2] | 3.04 |
| Prog. Distillation [16] | 2.57 |
| CLD-SGM [4] | 2.23 |
| LSGM [21] | 2.10 |
| Adaptive solver [8] | 2.44 |

| Model | | FID ↓ | IS ↑ | Thresh. | $t_1$ | Run. |
|---|---|---|---|---|---|---|
| NCSN++ | Full | 2.38 | 9.83 | | | |
| | Subspace | 2.29 | **9.99** | 3e-3 | 0.52 | 0.66 |
| NSCN++ (deep) | Full | 2.20 | 9.89 | | | |
| | subspace | **2.17** | 9.94 | 1e-3 | 0.56 | 0.69 |
| DDPM++ | Full | 2.61 | 9.56 | | | |
| | Subspace | 2.60 | 9.54 | 3e-5 | 0.62 | 0.73 |
| DDPM++ (deep) | Full | 2.41 | 9.57 | | | |
| | Subspace | 2.40 | 9.66 | 1e-4 | 0.56 | 0.69 |

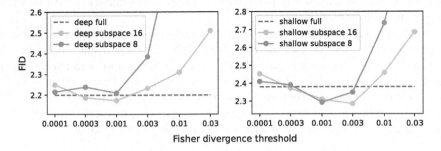

**Fig. 3.** CIFAR-10 sample quality from NCSN++ subspace diffusion (shallow and deep models) with different subspaces and divergence thresholds.

to different durations of diffusion in the subspace. For all experiments, further results and additional samples may be found in the supplementary material.

**Unconditional Sampling.** We evaluate subspace diffusion on unconditional CIFAR-10 generation with the Inception score (IS) and Frechet Inception distance (FID) as metrics. We examine both the NCSN++ and DDPM++ models from [20], which correspond to different forward diffusion processes, as well as the deep versions of these models, for a total of 4 full-dimensional models. For each model, we separately construct subspace diffusion with $8 \times 8$ and $16 \times 16$ subspaces. As in [20], we choose the best checkpoint by FID.

In Fig. 3, we show the performance of the NCSN++ subspace diffusion models for different choices of the Fisher divergence threshold $D_F$. In all cases, the models display U-shaped performance curves as the threshold is varied. When the threshold is small, most of the diffusion is done at full dimensionality, and the performance is close to that of the full model alone. As the threshold increases and more diffusion is done in the subspace, the models *improve* over the full model until reaching the best performances between $D_F = 1 \times 10^{-3}$

and $D_F = 3 \times 10^{-3}$. This improvement offers support for the hypothesis, discussed in the introduction, that restricting the dimensionality (or support) of the score to be matched can help the subspace model learn and extrapolate more accurately than the full-dimensional model. Finally, for large thresholds the performance deteriorates as the Gaussian approximation of the orthogonal component becomes too inaccurate.

Table 2 compares the performance of the best subspace diffusion models with the original full-dimensional models from [20] and with prior methods for accelerating score-based models. Subspace diffusion and LSGM [21] are the only methods where the improved runtime does not come at the cost of decreased performance (relative to [20]). The runtime improvement over the full-dimensional baseline varies with the choice of divergence threshold; for those leading to the best sample qualities, the improvements are typically around 30%. Since the concept of subspace diffusion is orthogonal to the techniques used by most previous work (see Sect. 2), it can potentially be used in combination with them for further runtime improvement.

Next, we show the applicability of our method to larger resolution datasets by generating samples on CelebA-HQ-256 with NCSN++ subspace diffusion. As discussed in Sect. 3.4, we use only the $64 \times 64$ subspaces and perform no hyperparameter tuning or checkpoint selection. In Fig. 4, we show random samples from CelebA-HQ for different amounts of diffusion in the subspace, along with the corresponding Fisher divergence. Qualitatively, we can restrict up to 60–70% of the diffusion to the subspace without significant loss of quality.

**ODE Sampling and Likelihood.** Subspace diffusion retains the flexible capabilities of the continuous-time SDE framework. In particular, the corresponding probability flow ODE (3) can be used to evaluate exact log-likelihoods and generate samples, as described in [20]. In Table 3, we show results for these tasks on CIFAR-10 for subspace diffusion in combination with the DDPM++ (deep) model. We use the alternate subspace score formulation (11) with the original ODE solvers, and use the last checkpoint of each training run. Subspace diffusion has little to no impact on the log-likelihoods obtained and slightly hurts sample quality.

**Table 3.** ODE sampling and NLL evaluation on CIFAR-10 from DDPM++ (deep) with subspace diffusion.

| Subspace | Thresh. | NLL ↓ | FID ↓ |
|---|---|---|---|
| None | — | 2.995 | 2.95 |
| $8 \times 8$ | $1 \times 10^{-4}$ | 2.998 | 3.02 |
| | $3 \times 10^{-4}$ | 2.999 | 3.12 |
| | $1 \times 10^{-3}$ | 2.998 | 3.53 |
| $16 \times 16$ | $1 \times 10^{-4}$ | 2.997 | 2.95 |
| | $3 \times 10^{-4}$ | 2.997 | 3.00 |
| | $1 \times 10^{-3}$ | 2.997 | 3.17 |

**Inpainting.** Subspace diffusion can also be used for controllable generation tasks, an example of which is image inpainting. Indeed, by using the alternate formulation (11), the subspace model appears as a full-dimensional model and integrates seamlessly with the existing inpainting procedures described in [20].

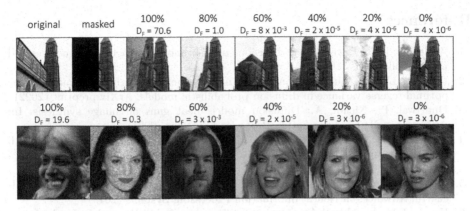

**Fig. 4.** Random high resolution samples with $64 \times 64$ subspace diffusion. *Top:* Inpainting on the $256 \times 256$ LSUN Church dataset. *Bottom:* Unconditional generation of samples for CelebA-HQ-256. From right to left, the fraction of the diffusion in the subspace increases in intervals of 20%, with the corresponding orthogonal Fisher divergence shown. As expected from the divergence analysis in Fig. 2, there is little deterioration in quality for images generated with up to 60% of the diffusion in the subspace.

In Fig. 4, we show inpainting results on LSUN Church with $64 \times 64$ subspace diffusion in conjunction with the pretrained NCSN++ model. As with the unconditional samples, quality does not significantly deteriorate with up to 60% of the diffusion occurring in the subspace.

## 5   Conclusion

We presented a novel method for more efficient generative modeling with score-based models. *Subspace diffusion models* restrict part of the diffusion to lower-dimensional subspaces such that the score of the projected distribution is faster to compute and easier to learn. Empirically on image datasets, our method provides inference speed-ups while preserving or improving the performance and capabilities of state-of-the-art models. Potential avenues of future work include applying subspace diffusion to other data domains and combining it with step-size based methods for accelerating inference. More generally, we hope that our work opens up further research on dimensionality reduction in diffusion processes, particularly to nonlinear manifolds and/or learned substructures, as a means of both simplifying and improving score-based generative models.

**Acknowledgements.** We thank Yilun Du, Xiang Fu, Jason Yim, Shangyuan Tong, Yilun Xu, Felix Faltings, and Saro Passaro for helpful feedback and discussions. Bowen Jing acknowledges support from the Department of Energy Computational Science Graduate Fellowship.

# References

1. Anderson, B.D.: Reverse-time diffusion equation models. Stochastic Processes and their Applications (1982)
2. Bao, F., Li, C., Zhu, J., Zhang, B.: Analytic-dpm: an analytic estimate of the optimal reverse variance in diffusion probabilistic models. ArXiv preprint (2022)
3. Dhariwal, P., Nichol, A.: Diffusion models beat gans on image synthesis. In: Advances in Neural Information Processing Systems (2021)
4. Dockhorn, T., Vahdat, A., Kreis, K.: Score-based generative modeling with critically-damped langevin diffusion. In: International Conference on Learning Representations (2022)
5. Du, Y., Mordatch, I.: Implicit generation and generalization in energy-based models. In: Advances in Neural Information Processing Systems (2019)
6. Ho, J., Jain, A., Abbeel, P.: Denoising diffusion probabilistic models. In: Advances in Neural Information Processing Systems (2020)
7. Ho, J., Saharia, C., Chan, W., Fleet, D.J., Norouzi, M., Salimans, T.: Cascaded diffusion models for high fidelity image generation. ArXiv preprint (2021)
8. Jolicoeur-Martineau, A., Li, K., Piché-Taillefer, R., Kachman, T., Mitliagkas, I.: Gotta go fast when generating data with score-based models. ArXiv preprint (2021)
9. Kingma, D.P., Salimans, T., Poole, B., Ho, J.: Variational diffusion models. In: Advances in Neural Information Processing Systems (2021)
10. Kong, Z., Ping, W.: On fast sampling of diffusion probabilistic models. In: ICML Workshop on Invertible Neural Networks, Normalizing Flows, and Explicit Likelihood Models (2021)
11. Lam, M.W., Wang, J., Su, D., Yu, D.: Bddm: Bilateral denoising diffusion models for fast and high-quality speech synthesis. In: International Conference on Learning Representations (2021)
12. Menick, J., Kalchbrenner, N.: Generating high fidelity images with subscale pixel networks and multidimensional upscaling. In: International Conference on Learning Representations (2019)
13. Nichol, A., Dhariwal, P.: Improved denoising diffusion probabilistic models. In: International Conference on Machine Learning (2021)
14. Razavi, A., van den Oord, A., Vinyals, O.: Generating diverse high-fidelity images with vq-vae-2. In: Advances in Neural Information Processing Systems (2019)
15. Saharia, C., Ho, J., Chan, W., Salimans, T., Fleet, D.J., Norouzi, M.: Image super-resolution via iterative refinement. ArXiv preprint (2021)
16. Salimans, T., Ho, J.: Progressive distillation for fast sampling of diffusion models. In: International Conference on Learning Representations (2022)
17. San-Roman, R., Nachmani, E., Wolf, L.: Noise estimation for generative diffusion models. ArXiv preprint (2021)
18. Song, J., Meng, C., Ermon, S.: Denoising diffusion implicit models. In: International Conference on Learning Representations (2021)
19. Song, Y., Ermon, S.: Generative modeling by estimating gradients of the data distribution. In: Advances in Neural Information Processing Systems (2019)
20. Song, Y., Sohl-Dickstein, J., Kingma, D.P., Kumar, A., Ermon, S., Poole, B.: Score-based generative modeling through stochastic differential equations. In: International Conference on Learning Representations (2021)
21. Vahdat, A., Kreis, K., Kautz, J.: Score-based generative modeling in latent space. In: Advances in Neural Information Processing Systems (2021)

22. Watson, D., Ho, J., Norouzi, M., Chan, W.: Learning to efficiently sample from diffusion probabilistic models. ArXiv preprint (2021)
23. Xu, K., Zhang, M., Li, J., Du, S.S., Kawarabayashi, K.i., Jegelka, S.: How neural networks extrapolate: From feedforward to graph neural networks. In: International Conference on Learning Representations (2021)

# DuelGAN: A Duel Between Two Discriminators Stabilizes the GAN Training

Jiaheng Wei, Minghao Liu, Jiahao Luo, Andrew Zhu, James Davis,
and Yang Liu$^{(\boxtimes)}$

University of California, Santa Cruz, Santa Cruz CA 95060, USA
yangliu@ucsc.edu

**Abstract.** In this paper, we introduce DuelGAN, a generative adversarial network (GAN) solution to improve the stability of the generated samples and to mitigate mode collapse. Built upon the Vanilla GAN's two-player game between the discriminator $D_1$ and the generator $G$, we introduce a peer discriminator $D_2$ to the min-max game. Similar to previous work using two discriminators, the first role of both $D_1$, $D_2$ is to distinguish between generated samples and real ones, while the generator tries to generate high-quality samples which are able to fool both discriminators. Different from existing methods, we introduce a duel between $D_1$ and $D_2$ to discourage their agreement and therefore increase the level of diversity of the generated samples. This property alleviates the issue of early mode collapse by preventing $D_1$ and $D_2$ from converging too fast. We provide theoretical analysis for the equilibrium of the min-max game formed among $G, D_1, D_2$. We offer convergence behavior of DuelGAN as well as stability of the min-max game. It's worth mentioning that DuelGAN operates in the unsupervised setting, and the duel between $D_1$ and $D_2$ does not need any label supervision. Experiments results on a synthetic dataset and on real-world image datasets (MNIST, Fashion MNIST, CIFAR-10, STL-10, CelebA, VGG) demonstrate that DuelGAN outperforms competitive baseline work in generating diverse and high-quality samples, while only introduces negligible computation cost. Our code is publicly available at https://github.com/UCSC-REAL/DuelGAN.

**Keywords:** GAN · Image generation · Peer discriminator · Stability

## 1 Introduction

Vanilla GAN (Generative Adversarial Nets [16]) proposed a data generating framework through an adversarial process which has achieved great success in image generation [4,6,12,15,16,18,23,38,47,49,51,63], image translation

---

J. Wei and M. Liu—Equal contributions.

**Supplementary Information** The online version contains supplementary material available at https://doi.org/10.1007/978-3-031-20050-2_18.

[11,54,62,64], and other real-life applications [3,22,29,31,35,42,43,48,53,58,61]. However, training Vanilla GAN is usually accompanied with a number of common problems, for example, vanishing gradients, mode collapse and failure to converge. Unfortunately, none of these issues have been completely addressed. There is a large amount of follow up work on Vanilla GAN. Due to space limitations, we only discuss the two most related lines of works.

**Stable and Diverse GAN Training.** Several stabilization techniques have been implemented in GAN variants. Modifying architectures is the most extensively explored category. Radford et al. [45] make use of convolutional and convolutional-transpose layer in training the discriminator and generator. Karras et al. [23] adopt a hierarchical architecture and trains the discriminator and generator with progressively increasing size. Huang et al. [21] proposed a generative model which consists of a top-down stack of GANs. Chen et al. [8] split the generator into the noise prior and also latent variables. The optimization task includes maximizing the mutual information between latent variables and the observation. Designing suitable loss functions is another favored technique. Successful designs include $f$-divergence based GAN [36,41] (these two approaches replace loss functions of GAN by estimated variational $f$-divergence or least-square loss respectively), introducing auxiliary terms in the loss function [37] and integral probability metric based GAN [5,18,26,44]. A detailed survey of methods for stabilizing GANs exists [57].

**Multi-player GANs.** Multi-player GANs explore the situation where there are multiple generators or multiple discriminators. The first published work to introduce multiple discriminators to GANs is multi-adversarial networks, in which discriminators can range from an unfavorable adversary to a forgiving teacher [13]. Nguyen et al. [40] formulate D2GAN, a three-player min-max game which utilizes a combination of Kullback-Leibler (KL) and reverse KL divergences in the objective function and is the most closely related to our work. Albuquerque et al. [1] show that training GAN variants with multiple discriminators is a practical approach even though extra capacity and computational cost are needed. Employing multiple generators and one discriminator to overcome the mode collapse issue and encourages diverse images has also been proposed [14,20].

In contrast to the above existing work, we demonstrate the possibility of improving GAN training with a computationally light modification by adding only one competing discriminator. We introduce a duel game among two discriminators and demonstrate the benefits of doing so in stabilizing and diversifying the training. Our main contributions summarize as follows:

- We introduce a duel between two discriminators to encourage diverse predictions and avoid early failure. The intuition is that predictions with high consensus will be discouraged, and effectively both discriminators are rewarded for having diverse predictions. The introduced game between the two discriminators results in a different convergence pattern for the generator.

- Theoretically, we derive the equilibrium for discriminators and the generator. We show how DuelGAN alleviates the vanishing gradient issue and mode collapse intuitively and empirically. We derive evidence for how the peer discriminator helps the dynamics of the learning. In addition, we demonstrate that if the peer discriminator is better than a random guess classifier, the intermediate game and the objective function in DuelGAN are stable/robust to a bad peer discriminator.
- Experimental results on a synthetic dataset validate that DuelGAN addresses mode collapse. Results on real datasets demonstrate that DuelGAN generates high-quality image samples compared with baseline works. Besides, the introduced duel-game could also be viewed as a regularizer which complements well with existing methods and further improves the performance.

## 2   Background

We first review Vanilla GAN and D2GAN, which are the most relevant to understanding our proposed DuelGAN.

**Vanilla GAN** [16]. Let $\{x_i\}_{i=1}^n \subseteq \mathcal{X}$ denote the given training dataset drawn from the unknown distribution $p_{\text{data}}$. Traditional GAN formulates a two-player game: a discriminator $D$ and a generator $G$. To learn the generator $G$'s distribution over $\mathcal{X}$, $G$ maps a prior noise distribution $p_z(z)$ to the data space. $\forall x \in \mathcal{X}$, $D(x)$ returns the probability that $x$ belongs to $p_{\text{data}}$ rather than $p_g$, where $p_g$ denotes the distribution of $G(z)$ implicitly defined by $G$. GAN trains $D$ to maximize the probability of assigning the correct label to both training samples and those from the generator $G$. Meanwhile, GAN trains $G$ to minimize $\log(1 - D(G(z)))$.

$$\min_G \max_D V(D, G) = \mathbb{E}_{x \sim p_{\text{data}}}[\log D(x)] + \mathbb{E}_{z \sim p_z}\Big[\log\Big(1 - D\big(G(z)\big)\Big)\Big]. \quad (1)$$

**D2GAN** [40]. D2GAN is the most closely related method to DuelGAN. This three-player game aims to solve the mode collapse issue and the optimization task is equivalent to minimize both KL divergence and Reverse-KL divergence between $p_{\text{data}}$ and $p_g$. The formulation of D2GAN comes as follows:

$$\min_G \max_{D_1, D_2} V(D_1, D_2, G) = \alpha \cdot \mathbb{E}_{x \sim p_{\text{data}}}[\log D_1(x)] + \mathbb{E}_{z \sim p_z}\big[-D_1\big(G(z)\big)\big]$$

$$+ \mathbb{E}_{x \sim p_{\text{data}}}[-D_2(x)] + \beta \cdot \mathbb{E}_{z \sim p_z}\big[\log D_2\big(G(z)\big)\big], \quad (2)$$

with $0 \leq \alpha, \beta \leq 1$. Given a sample $x$ in data space, $D_1(x)$ rewards a high score if $x$ is drawn from $p_{\text{data}}$, and gives a low score if generated from the generator distribution $p_g$. In contrast, $D_2(x)$ returns a high score for $x$ generated from $p_g$ and gives a low score for a sample drawn from $p_{\text{data}}$. A large $\alpha$ induces multiple modes of $p_g$, but may include undesirable samples, while a large $\beta$ induces the single mode. However, it is non-trivial to make a balance of these two terms in practice; if $D_i$ fails/crashes (unstable), the overall training is influenced. And $D_i$ won't be corrected since there is no interaction between discriminators!

Our work is similar to D2GAN in containing a pair of discriminators, instead of discriminators with different goals, we use identical discriminators and introduce a duel/competition between them.

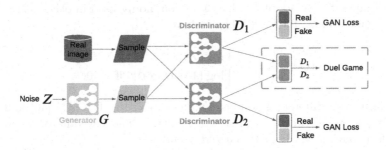

**Fig. 1.** Illustration of the proposed DuelGAN. Compared with Vanilla GAN, DuelGAN has one more identical discriminator and a Duel Game between two discriminators. The introduced Duel Game induces diversified generated samples by discouraging the agreement between $D_1$ and $D_2$. In D2GAN, although both discriminators are trained with different loss functions, they do not interfere with each other in the training.

## 3    DuelGAN: A Duel Between Two Discriminators

In this section, we first give the formulation and intuition of DuelGAN. Then we will present the equilibrium strategy of the generator and the discriminators.

### 3.1    Formulation

Similar to related works, we assume that the data follows the distribution $p_{\text{data}}$, our ultimate goal is to achieve $p_g = p_{\text{data}}$ where $p_g$ is the generator's distribution. DuelGAN formulates a three-player game which consists of two discriminators $D_1$, $D_2$ and one generator $G$. Denote by $p_{\text{duel}}$ an equal mixture of $p_{\text{data}}$, $p_g$, $\forall x$: $p_{\text{duel}}(x) = [p_{\text{data}}(x) + p_g(x)]/2$. Recall that $p_z$ denotes the prior noise distribution, now we are ready to formulate the min-max game of DuelGAN as follows:

$$\min_{G} \max_{D_1,D_2} \mathcal{L}(D_1, D_2, G)$$

$$= \min_{G} \max_{D_1,D_2} \mathbb{E}_{x \sim p_{\text{data}}} [\log D_1(x)] + \mathbb{E}_{x \sim p_{\text{data}}} [\log D_2(x)]$$

$$+ \beta \cdot \text{Duel-D} + \mathbb{E}_{z \sim p_z} [\log (1 - D_1(G(z)))] + \mathbb{E}_{z \sim p_z} [\log (1 - D_2(G(z)))], \quad (3)$$

where Duel-D introduces the duel (a peer competition game) among $D_1, D_2$, defined as:

$$\text{Duel-D} = \mathbb{E}_{x \sim p_{\text{duel}}} \left[ \underbrace{\ell\Big(D_1(x), \mathbb{1}\big(D_2(x) > \tfrac{1}{2}\big)\Big)}_{\text{Term 1a}} - \alpha \cdot \underbrace{\ell\Big(D_1(x_{p_1}), \mathbb{1}\big(D_2(x_{p_2}) > \tfrac{1}{2}\big)\Big)}_{\text{Term 1b}} \right]$$

$$+ \mathbb{E}_{x \sim p_{\text{duel}}} \left[ \underbrace{\ell\Big(D_2(x), \mathbb{1}\big(D_1(x) > \tfrac{1}{2}\big)\Big)}_{\text{Term 2a}} - \alpha \cdot \underbrace{\ell\Big(D_2(x_{p_1}), \mathbb{1}\big(D_1(x_{p_2}) > \tfrac{1}{2}\big)\Big)}_{\text{Term 2b}} \right]. \quad (4)$$

In Duel-D, $x_{p_1}$ and $x_{p_2}$ are drawn randomly from $p_{\text{duel}}$ and that $\underline{x, x_{p_1} \text{ and } x_{p_2}}$ $\underline{\text{are independent with each other}}$. $\mathbb{1}(\cdot)$ is the indicator function, $\alpha, \beta \in [0, 1]$ are hyper-parameters controlling the disagreement level and the weight of the competition game between two discriminators, respectively. $\ell$ is an evaluation function, for simplicity, we adopt $\ell = \log(\cdot)$, as commonly used in other terms in the min-max game. Thus, for $i \in \{0, 1\}$, we have:

$$\ell(D_i(x), y) = \begin{cases} \log\big(D_i(x)\big) & \text{if y=1;} \\ \log\big(1 - D_i(x)\big) & \text{if y=0.} \end{cases} \tag{5}$$

To clarify the differences among Vanilla GAN [16], D2GAN [40] and Duel-GAN, we use an workflow to illustrate in Fig. 1. The key differences in Duel-GAN's formulation can be summarized as follows:

- Compared with Vanilla GAN (see Eq.(1)), DuelGAN (see Eq.(3)) introduces a peer discriminator $D_2$ which has the same objective function as $D$ appeared in Eq.(1). An intermediate duel game Duel-D is added which will be explained below.
- The differences between D2GAN (see Eq.(2)) and DuelGAN are highlighted with the underscores in red. Primarily, there is no interaction between discriminators in D2GAN, while our Duel-D term introduces another duel game between the discriminators, which we explain below. In addition to Duel-D, the objective function in DuelGAN encourages both discriminators to fit perfectly on both training samples and generated samples. While in D2GAN, one discriminator fits overly on training samples, the other fits overly on generated samples.

**Competition Introduced by Duel-D.** Duel-D bridges $D_1$ and $D_2$ by introducing 4 terms specified in Eq.(4). Since we do not expect arbitrarily different discriminators, and both $D_i$s should play against the generator $G$, Term 1a and Term 2a encourage agreements between $D_1$ and $D_2$. With only these two terms, $D_1$ and $D_2$ will eventually be encouraged to converge to agree with each other. Mode collapse issue remains a possibility. DuelGAN introduces Term 1b and Term 2b to the objective function which punish $D_1$ and $D_2$ from over-agreeing with each other (where the duel happens), especially at the early phase of training. Particularly, the Term 1b and 2b are evaluating the agreements of $D_1$ and $D_2$ on two entirely independent samples $x_{p_1}, x_{p_2}$. Because of the independence, the two discriminators' predictions should not match with high probability. Note that the calculation of Duel-D does not need label supervisions, which distinguishes our work from other works that introduces multiple discriminators but would require additional label supervisions [11].

We provide more details of our intuition as well as theoretical evidences of this property in Sect. 4.

## 3.2 The Max Game of Discriminators

Denote the true label of $x$ as $y = 1$ if $x$ comes from $p_{\text{data}}$, otherwise, $y = 0$. For any given generator $G$, let us first analyze the best responding/optimal discriminator $D_{i,G}^*(x)$, $i \in 1, 2$. We define the following quantities:

$$r_{i,G}(x) := \mathbb{P}_{x \sim p_{\text{duel}}}\left(\mathbb{1}\left(D_i(x) > \frac{1}{2}\right) = 1\right), \quad p_{i,G} := \mathbb{E}_{x \sim p_{\text{duel}}}[r_{i,G}(x)], \quad (6)$$

where $r_{i,G}(x)$ represents the probability/confidence of $x$ being categorized as the real data by $D_i$ and $p_{i,G}$ is the expectation of $r_{i,G}(x)$ for $x \sim p_{\text{duel}}$. Let $\hat{r}_{i,G}^*(x) := r_{i,G}(x) - \alpha \cdot p_{i,G}$. Given discriminator $D_i$, when there is no confusion, <u>we use $D_j$ to denote the peer discriminator without telling $j \neq i$ in later sections.</u>

**Proposition 1.** *For $G$ fixed, denote by $w := \beta \cdot (1 - \alpha)$, the optimal discriminators $D_1, D_2$ are given by:*

$$D_{i,G}^*(x) = \frac{p_{data}(x) + \beta \cdot \hat{r}_{j,G}^*(x) \cdot p_{duel}(x)}{p_{data}(x) + p_g(x) + w \cdot p_{duel}(x)}, \quad i = 1, 2. \quad (7)$$

## 3.3 The Min Game of the Generator

Remember that the training objective for $D_i$ can be interpreted as maximizing the log-likelihood for estimating the conditional probability $\mathbb{P}(Y = y|x)$ where $Y$ indicates whether $x$ comes from $p_{\text{data}}$ (with $y = 1$) or from $p_g$ (with $y = 0$). With the introduce of Duel Game, the distributions $p_{\text{data}}$ and $p_g$ in the Vanilla GAN got changed due to the appearance of $p_{\text{duel}}$. Thus, we define the corresponding updated distributions in DuelGAN w.r.t. discriminator $D_i$ as $p_{\text{data}_i}$ and $p_{g_i}$, respectively. For a clean presentation, we defer the exact form of $p_{\text{data}_i}$, $p_{g_i}$ in Appendix (Eq.(22)).

Denote $C(G) := \max_D \mathcal{L}(G, D_1, D_2)$, the inner-max game ($C(G)$) can be rewritten as (straightforward in the proof of Proposition 1 which is available in the Appendix B.1):

$$C(G) = \mathbb{E}_{x \sim p_{\text{data}_1}}[\log D_{1,G}^*(x)] + \mathbb{E}_{x \sim p_{g_1}}\left[\log\left(1 - D_{1,G}^*(x)\right)\right]$$
$$+ \mathbb{E}_{x \sim p_{\text{data}_2}}[\log D_{2,G}^*(x)] + \mathbb{E}_{x \sim p_{g_2}}\left[\log\left(1 - D_{2,G}^*(x)\right)\right]. \quad (8)$$

**Theorem 1.** *When $\alpha = 0, r_{j,G}(x) = 1/2$, the global minimum of the virtual training criterion $C(G)$ is achieved if and only if $p_{data} = p_g$. At this point, $C(G)$ achieves the value of $-\log 16$.*

**When $r_{j,G}(x) = 1/2$?** Note that $r_{j,G}(x)$ is merely representing the probability that $D_j$ classifies $x$ to be real samples, $p_{j,G}$ is the probability that $D_j$ classifies a random sample as the real one. Without loss of generality, we assume real and generated samples are of uniform/equal prior. At the very beginning of the training process, the discriminator can do well in distinguishing real or generated samples, since the generator at this time generates low-quality samples. In this case, $r_{j,G}(x)$ is supposed to approach its max/min value, for example, $r_{j,G}(x) \to 0$ if $x$ is from generated samples, and otherwise, $r_{j,G}(x) \to 1$. During the training process, the generator progressively tries to mislead the predictions made by discriminators, which means the discriminator can not decide whether the sample is being fake or real. Thus, $r_{j,G}(x) \to 1/2$. At this time, for $\alpha = 0, i = 1, 2$, we have:

$$D_{i,G}^*(x) = \frac{p_{\text{data}}(x) + \beta \cdot \hat{r}_{j,G}^*(x) \cdot p_{\text{duel}}(x)}{p_{\text{data}}(x) + p_g(x) + \beta \cdot p_{\text{duel}}(x)} \to \frac{p_{\text{data}}(x) + \frac{\beta}{2} \cdot p_{\text{duel}}(x)}{p_{\text{data}}(x) + p_g(x) + \beta \cdot p_{\text{duel}}(x)}.$$

$$(9)$$

This allows us to rewrite $C(G)/2$ as: $\mathbb{E}_{x \sim p_{\text{data}_i}} \left[ \log \frac{p_{\text{data}}(x) + \frac{\beta}{2} \cdot p_{\text{duel}}(x)}{p_{\text{data}}(x) + p_g(x) + \beta \cdot p_{\text{duel}}(x)} \right] +$
$\mathbb{E}_{x \sim p_{g_i}} \left[ \log \frac{p_g(x) + \frac{\beta}{2} \cdot p_{\text{duel}}(x)}{p_{\text{data}}(x) + p_g(x) + \beta \cdot p_{\text{duel}}(x)} \right]$. Our subsequent proof is then based on the above reformulation. Due to space limits, we defer the formal statement of Duel-GAN algorithm to the beginning of Appendix.

## 4    Properties of DuelGAN

In this section, we first illustrate how DuelGAN alleviates common issues in GAN training, for example, the vanishing gradients issue and the mode collapse issue. Then we present properties of DuelGAN including its stability guarantee and converging behavior.

### 4.1    DuelGAN and Common Issues in GAN Training

**Vanishing Gradients Issue.** In training GAN, discriminators might be too good for the generator to fool with and to improve progressively. When training with neural networks with back-propagation or gradient-based learning approaches, a vanishing small gradient only results in minor changes even with a large weight. As a result, the generator training may fail due to the vanishing gradients issue.

**Mode Collapse Issue.** Mode collapse refers to the phenomenon that the generator will rotate through a small set of output types. For the given fixed discriminator, the generator over-optimizes in each iteration. Thus, the corresponding discriminator fails to learn its way out of the trap.

**How DuelGAN Alleviates the Vanish Gradient and Mode Collapse.** DuelGAN alleviates the above two issues by preventing discriminators from "colluding" on its discrimination ability. In DuelGAN, for either discriminator $D_i$, recall that $x_{p_1}$ and $x_{p_2}$ are randomly drawn from $p_{\text{duel}}$ which are independent from each other. Then the max game of $D_i$, given its peer discriminator $D_j$, is to perform the following task:

$$\max_{D_i} \mathcal{L}(D_i, G)|_{D_j}$$

$$\overbrace{\phantom{= \max_{D_i} \mathbb{E}_{x \sim p_{\text{data}}}[\log D_i(x)] + \mathbb{E}_{z \sim p_z}\left[\log\left(1 - D_i(G(z))\right)\right]}}^{\text{Term ⓐ}}$$

$$= \max_{D_i} \mathbb{E}_{x \sim p_{\text{data}}}[\log D_i(x)] + \mathbb{E}_{z \sim p_z}\left[\log\left(1 - D_i(G(z))\right)\right]$$

$$+ \beta \cdot \mathbb{E}_{x \sim p_{\text{duel}}}\Big[\underbrace{\ell\Big(D_i(x), \mathbb{1}\big(D_j(x) > \tfrac{1}{2}\big)\Big)}_{\text{Term ⓑ}} \underbrace{- \alpha \cdot \ell\Big(D_i(x_{p_1}), \mathbb{1}\big(D_j(x_{p_2}) > \tfrac{1}{2}\big)\Big)}_{\text{Term ⓒ}}\Big].$$

$$(10)$$

Term ⓐ maximizes the probability of assigning the correct label to both real samples and generated samples. Term ⓑ maximizes the probability of matching predicted label with peer discriminator predicted ones. In other words, Term ⓑ controls the agreement level of $D_i$ with respect to its peer discriminator $D_j$. However, note that Term ⓒ checks on the predictions of $D_j$ on two different tasks $x_{p_1}, x_{p_2}$. When $D_i$ agrees/fits overly on $D_j$, Term ⓒ returns a lower value if $D_j$'s predictions on these two different tasks are matching, mathematically, $\mathbb{1}\big(D_j(x_{p_1}) > 1/2\big) = \mathbb{1}(D_j(x_{p_2}) > 1/2)$. And Term ⓒ will return a high value if $D_j$'s predictions on these two different tasks are indeed different $\mathbb{1}\big(D_j(x_{p_1}) > 1/2\big) \neq \mathbb{1}\big(D_j(x_{p_2}) > 1/2\big)$. The weight $\alpha$ controls this disagreement level compared with Term ⓑ by referring to the fact that a larger $\alpha$ encourages more disagreement/diverse predictions from discriminators.

Based on the above intuitions, when two discriminators are of a high disagreement level, there exists a set $S_{\text{dis}}$ such that $\mathbb{1}(D_i(x) > 1/2) \neq \mathbb{1}(D_j(x) > 1/2)$ for $x \in S_{\text{dis}}$ and $S_{\text{dis}}$ is non-negligible. Therefore, there exists at least one discriminator $D_i$ that can't perfectly predict labels (real/generated) of given data samples. The generator will then be provided with sufficient information, e.g., information or features that can be extracted from $S_{\text{dis}}$, to progress. This property helps us address the vanishing gradients issue. As for the mode collapse issue, suppose the over-optimized generator is able to find plausible outputs for both discriminators in the next generation. However, note that optimization is implemented on mini-batches in practice, the randomly selected samples $x_{p_1}, x_{p_2}$ in Duel-D as well as the dynamically changing weights $\alpha, \beta$ can bring a certain degree of randomness in the next generation. Thus, rotating through this subset of the generator's output types could not force Term ⓒ to remain unchanged, so that the discriminators won't maintain a constant disagreement level and they unlikely get stuck in a local optimum.

To theoretically demonstrate how DuelGAN alleviates the mode collapse issue, we borrow from [32] and formalize the mode collapse issue as:

**Definition 1.** *Data distribution $p_{data}$ and a generator $p_g$ in vanilla GAN exhibit $(\epsilon, \delta)$-mode collapse for some $0 \leq \epsilon < \delta \leq 1$ if $\exists$ a set $S \subseteq \mathcal{X}$ such that $p_{data}(S) \geq \delta$ and $p_g(S) \leq \epsilon$.*

A generator with a small $\delta$ or a large $\epsilon$ indicates a mild mode collapse issue (the better mode coverage). For $D_i$ in DuelGAN, we could replace the distribution $p_{\text{data}}, p_{\text{g}}$ by $p_{\text{data},i} := c_{i,1} \cdot p_{\text{data}} + (1 - c_{i,1}) \cdot p_{\text{g}}$ and $p_{\text{g},i} :=$

$(1 - c_{i,2}) \cdot p_{\text{data}} + c_{i,2} \cdot p_{\text{g}}$, respectively, for some distributions $c_{i,1}(x), c_{i,2}(x)$ $(\geq \frac{1}{2})$, which implicitly encode the information of $\beta, \hat{r}_{j,G}^*$ (appeared in Eq. (7)). We have:

**Theorem 2.** *Suppose $\exists S \subseteq \mathcal{X}$ such that the Vanilla GAN has the $(\epsilon, \delta)$-mode collapse, DuelGAN has $(\epsilon_d, \delta_d)$-mode collapse given $S$, where:*

$$\delta_d := \mathbb{E}_{x \in S}[c_{i,1}(x)] \cdot \mathbb{E}_{x \in S}[p_{data}(x)] + \mathbb{E}_{x \in S}[(1 - c_{i,1}(x))] \cdot \mathbb{E}_{x \in S}[p_g(x)] + Cov(c_{i,1}, p_{data} - p_g),$$
$$\epsilon_d := \mathbb{E}_{x \in S}[c_{i,2}(x)] \cdot \mathbb{E}_{x \in S}[p_g(x)] + \mathbb{E}_{x \in S}[(1 - c_{i,2}(x))] \cdot \mathbb{E}_{x \in S}[p_{data}(x)] + Cov(c_{i,2}, p_g - p_{data}).$$

In the mode collapse scenario where $D_j$ is fooled by $G$ easily, we have $c_{i,1}, c_{i,2} \rightarrow (1 + \frac{1}{2})/2 = \frac{3}{4}$ and Covariance terms become 0. Note that $0 \leq \mathbb{E}_{x \in S}[p_{\text{g}}(x)] \leq \epsilon < \delta \leq \mathbb{E}_{x \in S}[p_{\text{data}}(x)] \leq 1$, we then have: $\delta_d < \delta$ and $\epsilon_d > \epsilon$, the mode collapse issue is alleviated with the introduce of duel game.

In Sect. 5.1, we use synthetic experiments to show that DuelGAN addresses mode collapse issues. And we include more empirical observations of the competition introduced by Duel-D in the Appendix C.5, i.e., the stability of the DuelGAN training, and the visualization of agreement levels between $D_1$ and $D_2$ due to the introduce of the duel game.

## 4.2  Stability and Convergence Behavior

In Sect. 4.1, we discussed the significant role of the introduced intermediate duel game. Now we discuss the potential downsides of introducing a second discriminator. Particularly, we are interested in understanding if the introduce of a peer discriminator $D_j$ will disrupt the training and make the competition game with $D_i$ unstable. Suppose $D_j$ diverges from the optimum in the max game, in other words, the diverged peer discriminator $\widetilde{D}_j$ fails to provide qualified verification label $Y_j^*$ (given by $D_{j,G}^*$), and provides $\widetilde{Y}_j$ instead. Denote by:

$$e_{\text{data},j} := \mathbb{P}(\widetilde{Y}_j = 0 | Y_j^* = 1), \quad e_{g,j} := \mathbb{P}(\widetilde{Y}_j = 1 | Y_j^* = 0). \tag{11}$$

For any peer discriminator $D_j$, $D_j$ may be a diverged peer discriminator $\widetilde{D}_j$ or an optimal one $D_{j,G}^*$, we denote the Duel Game of $D_i$ given $D_j$ as:

$$\text{Duel}(D_i)|_{D_j} := \mathbb{E}_{x \sim p_{\text{duel}}}\left[\ell\left(D_i(x), \mathbb{1}\left(D_j(x) > \frac{1}{2}\right)\right) - \alpha \cdot \ell\left(D_i(x_{p_1}), \mathbb{1}\left(D_j(x_{p_2}) > \frac{1}{2}\right)\right)\right]. \tag{12}$$

Theorem 3 explains the condition of stability (for $D_i$) when its peer discriminator in DuelGAN diverges from the corresponding optimum.

**Theorem 3.** *Given $G$, suppose $D_i$ has enough capacity, and at one step of Algorithm 1 (Appendix), if $e_{\text{data},j} + e_{g,j} < 1$, $\alpha = 1$, the duel term of discriminator $D_i$ is stable/robust with diverged peer discriminator $\widetilde{D}_j$. Mathematically,*

$$\max_{D_i} \text{Duel}(D_i)|_{\widetilde{D}_j} \quad \text{is equivalent with} \quad \max_{D_i} \text{Duel}(D_i)|_{D_{j,G}^*}. \tag{13}$$

The above theorem implies that a diverging and degrading peer discriminator $D_j$ will not disrupt the training of $D_i$.

*Remark 1.* Note that assuming uniform prior of real and generated samples, the condition to be stable is merely requiring that the proportion of false/wrong $D_j$'s prediction is less than a half (random guessing). This condition can be easily satisfied in practice. Thus, Theorem 3 provides the stability/robustness guarantee when the peer discriminator diverged from its optimum.

Build upon Theorem 1, with sufficiently small updates, Theorem 4 presents when $p_g$ converges to $p_{\text{data}}$.

**Theorem 4.** *If $G$ and $D_i$s have enough capacity, and at each step of Algorithm 1, $D_i$s are allowed to reach its optimum given $G$, $D_i$ is updated so as to improve the criterion in Eq.(10), and $p_g$ is updated so as to improve:*

$$C(G) = \mathbb{E}_{x \sim p_{data_1}} [\log D_{1,G}^*(x)] + \mathbb{E}_{x \sim p_{g_1}} \left[ \log \left( 1 - D_{1,G}^*(x) \right) \right]$$
$$+ \mathbb{E}_{x \sim p_{data_2}} [\log D_{2,G}^*(x)] + \mathbb{E}_{x \sim p_{g_2}} \left[ \log \left( 1 - D_{2,G}^*(x) \right) \right]. \tag{14}$$

*If $\beta = 0$ (remove the duel game to end the training and lead to convergence), we have $D_{1,G}^* = D_{2,G}^*$, $p_g$ converges to $p_{\text{data}}$.*

## 5    Experiments

In this section, we empirically validate the properties of DuelGAN through a set of datasets, including a synthetic task and several real world datasets ranging from hand-written digits to human faces.

### 5.1    Experiment Results on Synthetic Data

We apply the experiment and model structures proposed in UnrolledGAN [37] to investigate whether the DuelGAN design can prevent mode collapse. This experiment aims to generate eight 2D Gaussian distributions with a covariance matrix $0.02I$, arranged around the same centroid with radius 2.0. Vanilla GAN fails on this example. D2GAN has been shown to outperform UnrolledGAN, so we include it as an alternate method which performs well.

Figure 2 shows symmetric KL-divergence, Wasserstein distance, and a visualization of results with Vanilla GAN, D2GAN, and DuelGAN. Knowing the target distribution $p_{\text{data}}$, we can employ symmetric KL divergence and Wasserstein distance, which calculate the distance between the true $p_{\text{data}}$ and the normalized histogram of 10,000 generated points. On the left of Fig. 2, the plots for symmetric KL-divergence and Wasserstein distance show that DuelGAN has a much better score than Vanilla GAN and slightly better than D2GAN.

On the right side of Fig. 2 is a visualization of 512 generated blue samples points, together with red data points drawn from the true distribution. Vanilla GAN generates data points around only a single valid mode of the data distribution. D2GAN and DuelGAN distribute data around all eight mixture components, demonstrating the ability to resolve modal collapse in this case.

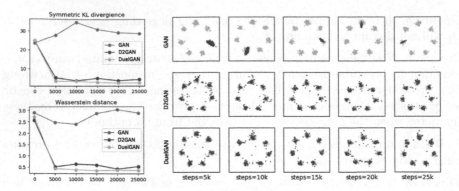

**Fig. 2.** Comparison of Vanilla GAN, D2GAN, and proposed DuelGAN on 2D synthe-sized data. The top-left graph shows the symmetric KL divergence over the training iterations, while the bottom left graph shows the Wasserstein distance. Both metrics compare the generated data points to data points drawn from the true target distribution. DuelGAN has the best performance. The right side visualizes generated blue data points and true red $p_{data}$ data points. Note that Vanilla GAN has a clear mode collapse which both D2GAN and DuelGAN avoid. (Color figure online)

### 5.2 Experiments on Real Image Datasets

We tested the proposed DuelGAN and baseline methods on MNIST [28], FashionMNIST [59], CIFAR-10 [27], STL-10 [10], CelebA [34] and VGGFace2 [7]. For quantitative evaluation, we adopt Fréchet Inception Distance (FID) [19] and Inception score(IS) [46] as the evaluation metric. FID summarizes the distance between the Inception features of the generated images and the real images. A lower FID indicates both better accuracy and higher diversity, so that a batch of generated images with good accuracy but identical to each other will have a poor FID score. A higher IS score indicates a higher generated image quality.

**Baseline Methods.** We reproduce/report the performance of a list of existing baseline methods, including: DCGAN [45], D2GAN [40], WGAN [18], DRAGAN [26], LSGAN [44], MicroBatchGAN [39], Dist-GAN [50], PresGAN [12], and QSNGAN [17]. We used the same generator and discriminator backbone for all the comparison methods in each dataset unless specified by the original author. We recorded the best performing checkpoints when evaluating each method.

**Grey-Scale Images.** MNIST [28] and FashionMNIST [59] are small grey-scale image datasets including 60,000 training and 10,000 testing $28 \times 28$ gray-scale images of hand-written digits and clothing. Since they are of small-scale, we adopt the shallow version of the generator and discriminators to generate the grey-scale images. We include a comprehensive comparison via FID score in Table 1. And the first two columns in Table 1 show our method has the best FID score among all tested methods. Figure 3 (left) shows FashionMNIST image results.

**Table 1.** Experiment FID score results of grey-scale image dataset: MNIST and FashionMNIST; natural scene image dataset: CIFAR-10 and STL-10; human face image dataset: CelebA and VGGFace2. Baseline results denoted with (*) were extracted from the original paper report, not independently run in our experiments.

|  | MNIST | FasionMNIST | CIFAR10 | STL-10 | CelebA | VGG |
|---|---|---|---|---|---|---|
| DCGAN [45] | 19.86 | 24.78 | 27.45 | 59.79 | 17.38 | 49.99 |
| WGAN* [18] | 14.07 | 28.24 | 35.37 | 60.21 | 15.23 | 39.24 |
| DRAGAN [26] | 66.96 | 62.64 | 36.49 | 91.07 | 14.57 | 50.20 |
| D2GAN [40] | 22.20 | 29.33 | 27.38 | 54.12 | 17.30 | 20.67 |
| Dist-GAN* [50] | – | – | 22.95 | **36.19** | 23.70 | – |
| PresGAN* [12] | 42.02 | – | 52.20 | – | – | – |
| LSGAN [44] | 23.80 | 43.00 | 51.42 | 70.37 | 15.35 | 55.96 |
| MicroBatchGAN* [39] | 17.10 | – | 77.70 | – | 34.50 | – |
| QSNGAN* [17] | – | – | 31.97 | 59.61 | – | – |
| **DuelGAN (ours)** | **7.87** | **21.73** | **21.55** | 51.37 | **13.95** | **19.05** |

**Natural Scene Images.** CIFAR-10 [27] and STL-10 [10] are natural scene RGB image datasets. CIFAR-10 includes 50K training and 10K testing $32 \times 32$ images with ten unique categories: airplane, automobile, bird, cat, deer, dog, frog, horse, ship, and truck. STL-10 is sub-sampled from ImageNet, and has more diverse samples than CIFAR-10, containing about 100K $96 \times 96$ images. We adopt the deep version of the generator and discriminator to generate $32 \times 32$ RGB images. Table 1 middle two columns show FID score results. Note that the introduce of competitive Duel Game in two discriminator GAN setup, brings performance boost in all the experiments. Figure 3 (middle) shows STL-10 image results.

**Fig. 3.** Image results generated by proposed DuelGAN. Left: FashionMNIST, greyscale clothing images; Middle: STL-10, natural scene images; Right: CelebA, large-scale celebrate face images.

**Human Face Images.** CelebA [34] and VGGFace2 [7] are large-scale face datasets. CelebA includes 162,770 training and 19,962 testing images of celebrity faces. VGGFace2 contains more than 3.3 million face images of celebrities caught in the 'wild'. There are different lighting conditions, emotions, and viewing angles. We randomly choose 200 categories from VGGFace2 and trained on the reduced dataset. We adopt the deep version of the generator and discriminators to generate $32 \times 32$ RGB images on CelebA and $64 \times 64$ RGB images on VGGFace2. Table 1 last two columns show our method has the best FID score among tested methods. Figure 3 (right) shows CelebA image results.

**Implementation Details.** Our model architecture adopts the same generator and discriminator backbone as DCGAN [45]. In DuelGAN, the newly introduced discriminator is a duplicate of the first one. DuelGAN achieves low FID scores and high IS scores when $\alpha$ and $\beta$ are simply set to constant values. However we found that we could obtain an approximately 10% improvement through dynamic tuning. The parameter $\beta$ controls the overall weight of Duel-D, while $\alpha$ punishes the condition when $D_1$ over-agrees with $D_2$. In the early training phase, when we have an unstable generator and discriminator, we set $\alpha$ and $\beta$ to 0. As training progresses, we gradually increase these parameters to a max value, which helps with vanishing gradients. After the midpoint of training we decrease these parameters to help the discriminators converge, until the parameters reach approximately 0 at the end of the training process. We adopt 0.3, 0.5 as the max value for $\alpha$ and $\beta$, respectively.

## 5.3  Duel Game as a Regularizer

Intuitively, the introduced duel game could be well applied to a large family of GAN variants defined w.r.t a single discriminator $D_1$ and a generator $G$. This is due to the fact that Eq.(3) could be denoted by:

$$\min_{G} \max_{D_1,D_2} \mathcal{L}(D_1, D_2, G) = \min_{G} \max_{D_1,D_2} [\text{GAN}(D_1) + \beta \cdot \text{Duel-D} + \text{GAN}(D_2)],$$

(15)

where $\text{GAN}(D_i) := \mathbb{E}_{x \sim p_{\text{data}}} [\log D_i(x)] + \mathbb{E}_{z \sim p_z} [\log (1 - D_i (G(z)))]$. Thus, if we substitute the GAN loss $\text{GAN}(D_i)$ by a state-of-the-art GAN variant, i.e., StyleGAN-ADA [24], one could view the duel game Duel-D as a regularizer.

We take the higher resolution version ($256 \times 256$ RGB images) of CelebA [34] for illustration. Clearly in Table 2, StyleGAN-ADA reaches the state-of-the-art result on this task. And the introduced Duel-D regularizer could further improve its performance. Figure 4 shows the corresponding generated images.

We train StyleGAN-ADA with and w/o Dual-D regularizer on three datasets. Table 3 shows StyleGAN-ADA has higher recall score by introducing the Dual-D regularizer. This indicates the duel game regularizer could alleviate mode collapse issue and have a better mode coverage.

**More Experiment Results.** Due to space limits, we defer more experiment results to the Appendix C, including: an ablation study of hyper-parameters tuning; experiment validations about the stability of training; the visualization of the duel game between $D_1$ and $D_2$.

**Table 2.** Experiment FID score results of CelebA (256×256 RGB images). Baseline results denoted with (*) were obtained from the original paper report.

| Method | GLF* [60] | MSP* [30] | NCP-VAE* [2] | LSGM* [52] | StyleGAN-ADA [24] | StyleGAN-ADA+Duel-D |
|--------|-----------|-----------|--------------|------------|-------------------|---------------------|
| FID | 41.80 | 35.00 | 24.79 | 7.22 | 4.85 | **4.32** |

**Table 3.** Comparisons of recall (↑) on 3 datasets (StyleGAN-ADA w/o a duel game).

| Methods | FFHQ | CelebA | CIFAR-10 |
|---------|------|--------|----------|
| StyleGAN-ADA | 0.61 | 0.75 | 0.49 |
| StyleGAN-ADA + Dual GAME | **0.67** | **0.83** | **0.60** |

**Fig. 4.** Image results generated by proposed DuelGAN. (Trained on CelebA 256×256 RGB images. More generated images are deferred to the Appendix C.)

## 6 Conclusion

We propose DuelGAN which introduces a peer discriminator to Vanilla GAN. The role of the peer discriminator is to allow an intermediate game (duel game) between discriminators. Theoretical analysis demonstrates that the introduced duel game incentivizes incremental improvement, addresses vanishing gradients and mode collapse issues, punishes over-agreements among discriminators and is stable with diverged peer discriminator. Experimental results on a synthetic dataset and multiple real world datasets validate that DuelGAN produces high quality images, with lower error than competing techniques.

**Acknowledgements.** JHW and YL are partially supported by the National Science Foundation (NSF) under grants IIS-2007951, IIS-2143895, and CCF-2023495. MHL, JHL, and JD are supported in part by WISEautomotive through a ATC+ Program award from the Korean Ministry of Trade, Industry and Energy (MOTIE).

# Appendix

The appendix is organized as follows:

- Sect. A gives the detailed algorithm of DuelGAN.
- Sect. B includes the omitted proofs for all theoretical conclusions in the main paper.
- Sect. C includes experiment details and additional experiment results.

## A   The DuelGAN Algorithm

Our introduced duel game between two discriminators is inspired by peer prediction mechanism which has shown successful applications in designing robust loss functions [9,33,55,56]. To give a more detailed and practical implementation of the duel game, we summarize the overall DuelGAN algorithm in Algorithm 1. In experiments, we train $G$ to minimize $\log(1 - D_i(G(z)))$ which is equivalent to maximizing $\log D_i(G(z))$.

---

**Algorithm 1.** DuelGAN

---

1: **Input**: two discriminators $D_1, D_2$, generator $G$, training samples $\{x_i\}_{i=1}^n$, weights $\alpha, \beta$.

2: **For** number of training iterations **do**

   **For** 1 to $k$ steps **do**

   - Sample mini-batch of $m$ noise samples $Z = \{z_1, ..., z_m\}$ from noise prior $p_z$.
   - Sample mini-batch of $m$ samples $X = \{x_1, ..., x_m\}$ from data generating distribution $p_{\text{data}}(x)$.
   - Combine two subsets $T := X \cup Z$, and denote by $T = \{t_1, ..., t_{2m}\}$.
   - Update discriminator $D_i (i \in \{1, 2\})$ by ascending the stochastic gradient:

$$\nabla_{\theta_{d_i}} \frac{1}{m} \sum_{i=1}^m \left[ \log D_i(x_i) + \log \left(1 - D_i(G(z_i))\right) \right]$$

$$+ \frac{\beta}{2m} \sum_{j=1}^{2m} \left[ -\ell_{\text{CE}}\left(D_i(t_j), \mathbb{1}\left(D_j(t_j) > \frac{1}{2}\right)\right) + \alpha \cdot \ell_{\text{CE}}\left(D_i(t_{p_1}), \mathbb{1}\left(D_j(t_{p_2}) > \frac{1}{2}\right)\right) \right], \quad (16)$$

   where $t_{p_1}, t_{p_2}$ are randomly selected (with replacement) samples from $T$.
   - Update $G$ by descending its stochastic gradient:

$$\nabla_{\theta_g} \frac{1}{m} \sum_{i=1}^m \left[ \log \left(1 - D_1(G(z_i))\right) + \log \left(1 - D_2(G(z_i))\right) \right]. \quad (17)$$

---

# B    Omitted Proofs

## B.1    Proof of Proposition 1

We firstly introduce Lemma 1 which helps with the proof of Proposition 1.

**Lemma 1.** *For any $(a,b) \in \mathbb{R}^2 \setminus \{0,0\}$, the function $y \to a\log(y) + b\log(1-y)$ achieves its maximum in $[0,1]$ at $\frac{a}{a+b}$.*

*Proof.* Denote by $f(y) := a\log(y) + b\log(1-y)$, clearly, when $y = 0$ or $y = 1$, $f(y) = -\infty$. For $y \in (0,1)$, we have:

$$f'(y) = 0 \iff \frac{a}{y} - \frac{b}{1-y} = 0 \iff y = \frac{a}{a+b}. \tag{18}$$

Note that $f'(y) > 0$ if $0 < y < \frac{a}{a+b}$ and $f'(y) < 0$ if $1 > y > \frac{a}{a+b}$. Thus, the maximum of $f(y)$ should be $\max(f(a), f(\frac{a}{a+b}), f(b)) = f(\frac{a}{a+b})$. And $f(y)$ achieves its maximum in $[0,1]$ at $\frac{a}{a+b}$.

Now we proceed to prove Proposition 1.

*Proof of Proposition* 1

*Proof.* The trainer criterion for the discriminator $D_i$, given any generator $G$, is to maximize the quantity $\mathcal{L}(D_1, D_2, G)$. Remember that:

$$\mathcal{L}(D_1, D_2, G)$$
$$= \mathbb{E}_{x \sim p_{\text{data}}} \left[\log D_1(x)\right] + \mathbb{E}_{x \sim p_{\text{data}}} \left[\log D_2(x)\right]$$
$$+ \mathbb{E}_{z \sim p_z} \left[\log\left(1 - D_1\left(G(z)\right)\right)\right] + \mathbb{E}_{z \sim p_z} \left[\log\left(1 - D_2\left(G(z)\right)\right)\right]$$
$$+ \beta \cdot \mathbb{E}_{x \sim p_{\text{duel}}} \left[\ell\left(D_1(x), \mathbb{1}\left(D_2(x) > \frac{1}{2}\right)\right) - \alpha \cdot \ell\left(D_1(x_{p_1}), \mathbb{1}\left(D_2(x_{p_2}) > \frac{1}{2}\right)\right)\right]$$
$$+ \beta \cdot \mathbb{E}_{x \sim p_{\text{duel}}} \left[\ell\left(D_2(x), \mathbb{1}\left(D_1(x) > \frac{1}{2}\right)\right) - \alpha \cdot \ell\left(D_2(x_{p_1}), \mathbb{1}\left(D_1(x_{p_2}) > \frac{1}{2}\right)\right)\right].$$
$$\tag{19}$$

We then have:

$$
\begin{aligned}
\text{Eqn.(19)} &= \int_x p_{\text{data}}(x)\big[\log\big(D_1(x)\big) + \log\big(D_2(x)\big)\big]dx \\
&+ \int_z p_z(z)\Big[\log\big(1 - D_1\big(G(z)\big)\big) + \log\big(1 - D_2\big(G(z)\big)\big)\Big]dz \\
&+ \beta \cdot \int_x p_{\text{duel}}(x)\big(r_{2,G}(x) - \alpha \cdot p_{2,G}\big) \cdot \log\big(D_1(x)\big)dx \\
&+ \beta \cdot \int_x p_{\text{duel}}(x)\big(r_{1,G}(x) - \alpha \cdot p_{1,G}\big) \cdot \log\big(D_2(x)\big)\big]dx \\
&+ \beta \cdot \int_x p_{\text{duel}}(x)\big(1 - \alpha - r_{2,G}(x) + \alpha \cdot p_{2,G}\big) \cdot \log\big(1 - D_1(x)\big)dx \\
&+ \beta \cdot \int_x p_{\text{duel}}(x)\big(1 - \alpha - r_{1,G}(x) + \alpha \cdot p_{1,G}\big) \cdot \log\big(1 - D_2(x)\big)dx \\
&= \int_x p_{\text{data}}(x)\big[\log\big(D_1(x)\big) + \log\big(D_2(x)\big)\big]dx \\
&+ \int_x p_g(x)\big[\log\big(1 - D_1(x)\big) + \log\big(1 - D_2(x)\big)\big]dx \\
&+ \beta \cdot \int_x p_{\text{duel}}(x)\big(r_{2,G}(x) - \alpha \cdot p_{2,G}\big) \cdot \log\big(D_1(x)\big)dx \\
&+ \beta \cdot \int_x p_{\text{duel}}(x)\big(r_{1,G}(x) - \alpha \cdot p_{1,G}\big) \cdot \log\big(D_2(x)\big)dx \\
&+ \beta \cdot \int_x p_{\text{duel}}(x)\big(1 - \alpha - r_{2,G}(x) + \alpha \cdot p_{2,G}\big) \cdot \log\big(1 - D_1(x)\big)dx \\
&+ \beta \cdot \int_x p_{\text{duel}}(x)\big(1 - \alpha - r_{1,G}(x) + \alpha \cdot p_{1,G}\big) \cdot \log\big(1 - D_2(x)\big)dx \\
&= \int_x \big[p_{\text{data}}(x) + \beta \cdot \big(r_{2,G}(x) - \alpha \cdot p_{2,G}\big) \cdot p_{\text{duel}}(x)\big] \cdot \log\big(D_1(x)\big)dx \\
&+ \int_x \big[p_g(x) + \beta \cdot \big(1 - \alpha - r_{2,G}(x) + \alpha \cdot p_{2,G}\big) \cdot p_{\text{duel}}(x)\big] \cdot \log(1 - D_1(x))dx \\
&+ \int_x \big[p_{\text{data}}(x) + \beta \cdot \big(r_{1,G}(x) - \alpha \cdot p_{1,G}\big) \cdot p_{\text{duel}}(x)\big] \cdot \log\big(D_2(x)\big)dx \\
&+ \int_x \big[p_g(x) + \beta \cdot \big(1 - \alpha - r_{1,G}(x) + \alpha \cdot p_{1,G}\big) \cdot p_{\text{duel}}(x)\big] \cdot \log\big(1 - D_2(x)\big)dx.
\end{aligned}
\tag{20}
$$

For $D_1, D_2$, according to Lemma 1, the above objective function respectively achieves its maximum in $[0,1], [0,1]$ at:

$$
D_{i,G}^*(x) = \frac{p_{\text{data}}(x) + \beta \cdot (r_{j,G}(x) - \alpha \cdot p_{j,G}) \cdot p_{\text{duel}}(x)}{p_{\text{data}}(x) + p_g(x) + \beta \cdot (1 - \alpha) \cdot p_{\text{duel}}(x)}, \qquad i \neq j. \tag{21}
$$

With the introduce of Duel Game, the distributions $p_{\text{data}}$ and $p_g$ in the Vanilla GAN got changed due to the appearance of $p_{\text{duel}}$. Thus, we define the corresponding updated distributions in DuelGAN w.r.t. discriminator $D_i$ as $p_{\text{data}_i}$

and $p_{g_i}$, respectively:

$$p_{\text{data}_i}(x) := \frac{p_{\text{data}}(x) + \beta \cdot \hat{r}^*_{j,G}(x) \cdot p_{\text{duel}}(x)}{\int_x p_{\text{data}}(x) + \beta \cdot \hat{r}^*_{j,G}(x) \cdot p_{\text{duel}}(x)dx}, \tag{22}$$

$$p_{g_i}(x) := \frac{p_g(x) + \beta \cdot \left(1 - \hat{r}^*_{j,G}(x)\right) \cdot p_{\text{duel}}(x)}{\int_x p_g(x) + \beta \cdot \left(1 - \hat{r}^*_{j,G}(x)\right) \cdot p_{\text{duel}}(x)dx}. \tag{23}$$

## B.2   Proof of Theorem 1

*Proof.* When $\alpha = 0, r_{j,G}(x) = 1/2$, for $\alpha = 0, i = 1, 2$, we have:

$$D^*_{i,G}(x) = \frac{p_{\text{data}}(x) + \beta \cdot \hat{r}^*_{j,G}(x) \cdot p_{\text{duel}}(x)}{p_{\text{data}}(x) + p_g(x) + \beta \cdot p_{\text{duel}}(x)} \rightarrow \frac{p_{\text{data}}(x) + \frac{\beta}{2} \cdot p_{\text{duel}}(x)}{p_{\text{data}}(x) + p_g(x) + \beta \cdot p_{\text{duel}}(x)}. \tag{24}$$

This allows us to rewrite $C(G)/2$ as:

$$\frac{C(G)}{2} = \mathbb{E}_{x \sim p_{\text{data}_i}} \left[ \log \frac{p_{\text{data}}(x) + \frac{\beta}{2} \cdot p_{\text{duel}}(x)}{p_{\text{data}}(x) + p_g(x) + \beta \cdot p_{\text{duel}}(x)} \right]$$
$$+ \mathbb{E}_{x \sim p_{g_i}} \left[ \log \frac{p_g(x) + \frac{\beta}{2} \cdot p_{\text{duel}}(x)}{p_{\text{data}}(x) + p_g(x) + \beta \cdot p_{\text{duel}}(x)} \right]. \tag{25}$$

$\implies$ Note that $2 \cdot \left( \mathbb{E}_{x \sim p_{\text{data}_i}}[- \log 2] + \mathbb{E}_{x \sim p_{g_i}}[- \log 2] \right) = - \log 16$, by subtracting this expression from $C(G)$, we have:

$$C(G) = - \log 16 + 2 \cdot KL\left( p_g + \frac{\beta}{2} \cdot p_{\text{duel}} \middle\| \frac{p_{\text{data}} + p_g + \beta \cdot p_{\text{duel}}}{2} \right)$$
$$+ 2 \cdot KL\left( p_{\text{data}} + \frac{\beta}{2} \cdot p_{\text{duel}} \middle\| \frac{p_{\text{data}} + p_g + \beta \cdot p_{\text{duel}}}{2} \right), \tag{26}$$

where KL is the Kullback-Leibler divergence. Note that:

$$C(G) = - \log 16 + 2 \cdot JSD\left( p_{\text{data}} + \frac{\beta}{2} \cdot p_{\text{duel}} \middle\| p_g + \frac{\beta}{2} \cdot p_{\text{duel}} \right), \tag{27}$$

and the Jensen-Shannon divergence between two distributions is always non-negative and zero only when they are equal, we have shown that $C(G)^* = - \log 16$ is the global minimum of $C(G)$. Thus, we need

$$p_{\text{data}} + \frac{\beta}{2} \cdot p_{\text{duel}} = p_g + \frac{\beta}{2} \cdot p_{\text{duel}} \Leftrightarrow p_{\text{data}} = p_g.$$

$\Longleftarrow$ Given that $p_{\text{data}} = p_g$, we have:

$$C(G) = \max_D \mathcal{L}(G, D_1, D_2)$$

$$= 2 \cdot \mathbb{E}_{x \sim p_{\text{data}_i}} \left[ \log \frac{p_{\text{data}}(x) + \dfrac{\beta}{2} \cdot p_{\text{duel}}(x)}{p_{\text{data}}(x) + p_g(x) + \beta \cdot p_{\text{duel}}(x)} \right]$$

$$+ 2 \cdot \mathbb{E}_{x \sim p_{g_i}} \left[ \log \frac{p_g(x) + \dfrac{\beta}{2} \cdot p_{\text{duel}}(x)}{p_{\text{data}}(x) + p_g(x) + \beta \cdot p_{\text{duel}}(x)} \right]$$

$$= 2 \cdot \left( \log \frac{1}{2} + \log \frac{1}{2} \right) = -\log 16. \tag{28}$$

## B.3   Proof of Theorem 4

*Proof.* Since for the Vanilla GAN, there exists a set $S$ in the instance domain $\mathcal{X}$ such that $p_{\text{data}}(S) \geq \delta$, $p_g(S) \leq \epsilon$. For the set $S$ given by the $(\epsilon, \delta)$-mode collapse of Vanilla GAN, we have:

$$1 \geq \mathbb{E}_{x \in S} \left[ p_{\text{data}}(x) \right] \geq \delta, \qquad 0 \leq \mathbb{E}_{x \in S} \left[ p_g(x) \right] \leq \epsilon.$$

For either discriminator $D_i$ in the DuelGAN, we have:

$$p_{\text{data}_i}(x) := \frac{p_{\text{data}}(x) + \beta \cdot \hat{r}_{j,G}^*(x) \cdot p_{\text{duel}}(x)}{\int_x p_{\text{data}}(x) + \beta \cdot \hat{r}_{j,G}^*(x) \cdot p_{\text{duel}}(x) dx},$$

$$p_{g_i}(x) := \frac{p_g(x) + \beta \cdot (1 - \hat{r}_{j,G}^*(x)) \cdot p_{\text{duel}}(x)}{\int_x p_g(x) + \beta \cdot (1 - \hat{r}_{j,G}^*(x)) \cdot p_{\text{duel}}(x) dx}.$$

We then have:

$$\mathbb{E}_{x \in S} \left[ p_{\text{data}_i}(x) \right] = \mathbb{E}_{x \in S} \left[ c_{i,1}(x) \cdot p_{\text{data}}(x) \right] + \mathbb{E}_{x \in S} \left[ (1 - c_{i,1}(x)) \cdot p_g(x) \right]$$

$$= \mathbb{E}_{x \in S} \left[ c_{i,1}(x) \right] \cdot \mathbb{E}_{x \in S} \left[ p_{\text{data}}(x) \right] + \text{Cov}(c_{i,1}, p_{\text{data}})$$

$$\quad + \mathbb{E}_{x \in S} \left[ (1 - c_{i,1}(x)) \right] \cdot \mathbb{E}_{x \in S} \left[ p_g(x) \right] - \text{Cov}(c_{i,1}, p_g)$$

$$= \mathbb{E}_{x \in S} \left[ c_{i,1}(x) \right] \cdot \mathbb{E}_{x \in S} \left[ p_{\text{data}}(x) \right] + \mathbb{E}_{x \in S} \left[ (1 - c_{i,1}(x)) \right] \cdot \mathbb{E}_{x \in S} \left[ p_g(x) \right] + \text{Cov}(c_{i,1}, p_{\text{data}} - p_g)$$

$$> \mathbb{E}_{x \in S} \left[ c_{i,1}(x) \right] \cdot \delta + \mathbb{E}_{x \in S} \left[ (1 - c_{i,1}(x)) \right] \cdot \mathbb{E}_{x \in S} \left[ p_g(x) \right] + \text{Cov}(c_{i,1}, p_{\text{data}} - p_g).$$

And:

$$\mathbb{E}_{x \in S} \left[ p_{g_i}(x) \right] = \mathbb{E}_{x \in S} \left[ c_{i,2}(x) \cdot p_g(x) \right] + \mathbb{E}_{x \in S} \left[ (1 - c_{i,2}(x)) \cdot p_{\text{data}}(x) \right]$$

$$= \mathbb{E}_{x \in S} \left[ c_{i,2}(x) \right] \cdot \mathbb{E}_{x \in S} \left[ p_g(x) \right] + \mathbb{E}_{x \in S} \left[ (1 - c_{i,2}(x)) \right] \cdot \mathbb{E}_{x \in S} \left[ p_{\text{data}}(x) \right] + \text{Cov}(c_{i,2}, p_g - p_{\text{data}})$$

$$< \mathbb{E}_{x \in S} \left[ c_{i,2}(x) \right] \cdot \epsilon + \mathbb{E}_{x \in S} \left[ (1 - c_{i,2}(x)) \right] \cdot \mathbb{E}_{x \in S} \left[ p_{\text{data}}(x) \right] + \text{Cov}(c_{i,2}, p_g - p_{\text{data}}).$$

## B.4  Proof of Theorem 3

*Proof.* Ignoring the weight $\beta$, the duel term of discriminator $D_i$ w.r.t. its diverged peer discriminator $\widetilde{D}_j$ becomes:

$$
\begin{aligned}
\text{Duel}(D_i)|_{\widetilde{D}_j} &:= \mathbb{E}_{x\sim p_{\text{duel}}}\left[\ell\Big(D_i(x), \mathbf{1}\big(\widetilde{D}_j(x) > \tfrac{1}{2}\big)\Big) - \alpha \cdot \ell\Big(D_i(x_{p_1}), \mathbf{1}\big(\widetilde{D}_j(x_{p_2}) > \tfrac{1}{2}\big)\Big)\right] \\
&= \mathbb{E}_{x\sim p_{\text{duel}}, Y_j^*=1}\left[\mathbb{P}(\widetilde{Y}_j = 1 | Y_j^* = 1) \cdot \ell(D_i(x), 1) + \mathbb{P}(\widetilde{Y}_j = 0 | Y_j^* = 1) \cdot \ell(D_i(x), 0)\right] \\
&\quad + \mathbb{E}_{x\sim p_{\text{duel}}, Y_j^*=0}\left[\mathbb{P}(\widetilde{Y}_j = 1 | Y_j^* = 0) \cdot \ell(D_i(x), 1) + \mathbb{P}(\widetilde{Y}_j = 0 | Y_j^* = 0) \cdot \ell(D_i(x), 0)\right] \\
&\quad - \alpha \cdot \mathbb{E}_{x_{p_1}\sim p_{\text{duel}}}\left[\mathbb{P}(\widetilde{Y}_j = 1) \cdot \ell(D_i(x_{p_1}), 1) + \mathbb{P}(\widetilde{Y}_j = 0) \cdot \ell(D_i(x_{p_1}), 0)\right] \\
&= \mathbb{E}_{x\sim p_{\text{duel}}, Y_j^*=1}\left[(1 - e_{\text{data},j}) \cdot \ell(D_i(x), 1) + e_{\text{data},j} \cdot \ell(D_i(x), 0)\right] \\
&\quad + \mathbb{E}_{x\sim p_{\text{duel}}, Y_j^*=0}\left[e_{g,j} \cdot \ell(D_i(x), 1) + (1 - e_{g,j}) \cdot \ell(D_i(x), 0)\right] \\
&\quad - \alpha \cdot \mathbb{E}_{x_{p_1}\sim p_{\text{duel}}}\left[\big[\mathbb{P}(Y_j^* = 1) \cdot (1 - e_{\text{data},j}) + \mathbb{P}(Y_j^* = 0) \cdot e_{g,j}\big] \cdot \ell(D_i(x_{p_1}), 1)\right] \\
&\quad - \alpha \cdot \mathbb{E}_{x_{p_1}\sim p_{\text{duel}}}\left[\big[\mathbb{P}(Y_j^* = 1) \cdot e_{\text{data},j} + \mathbb{P}(Y_j^* = 0) \cdot (1 - e_{g,j})\big] \cdot \ell(D_i(x_{p_1}), 0)\right] \\
&= \mathbb{E}_{x\sim p_{\text{duel}}, Y_j^*=1}\left[(1 - e_{\text{data},j} - e_{g,j}) \cdot \ell(D_i(x), 1) + e_{\text{data},j} \cdot \ell(D_i(x), 0) + e_{g,j} \cdot \ell(D_i(x), 1)\right] \\
&\quad + \mathbb{E}_{x\sim p_{\text{duel}}, Y_j^*=0}\left[(1 - e_{\text{data},j} - e_{g,j}) \cdot \ell(D_i(x), 0) + e_{\text{data},j} \cdot \ell(D_i(x), 0) + e_{g,j} \cdot \ell(D_i(x), 1)\right] \\
&\quad - \alpha \cdot \mathbb{E}_{x_{p_1}\sim p_{\text{duel}}}\left[c_1 \cdot \ell(D_i(x_{p_1}), 1)\right] - \alpha \cdot \mathbb{E}_{x_{p_1}\sim p_{\text{duel}}}\left[c_2 \cdot \ell(D_i(x_{p_1}), 0)\right],
\end{aligned}
$$

where we define:

$$
c_1 := \mathbb{P}(Y_j^* = 1) \cdot (1 - e_{\text{data},j} - e_{g,j}) + \mathbb{P}(Y_j^* = 0) \cdot e_{g,j} + \mathbb{P}(Y_j^* = 1) \cdot e_{g,j},
$$
$$
c_2 := \mathbb{P}(Y_j^* = 0) \cdot (1 - e_{\text{data},j} - e_{g,j}) + \mathbb{P}(Y_j^* = 1) \cdot e_{\text{data},j} + \mathbb{P}(Y_j^* = 0) \cdot e_{\text{data},j},
$$

for a clear presentation. Proceeding the previous deduction, we then have:

$$
\begin{aligned}
\text{Duel}(D_i)|_{\widetilde{D}_j} &= (1 - e_{\text{data},j} - e_{g,j}) \cdot \mathbb{E}_{x\sim p_{\text{duel}}}\left[\ell\big(D_i(x), Y_j^*\big)\right] \\
&\quad + \mathbb{E}_{x\sim p_{\text{duel}}}\left[e_{\text{data},j} \cdot \ell\big(D_i(x), 0\big) + e_{g,j} \cdot \ell\big(D_i(x), 1\big)\right] \\
&\quad - \alpha \cdot (1 - e_{\text{data},j} - e_{g,j}) \cdot \mathbb{E}_{x\sim p_{\text{duel}}}\left[\ell\big(D_i(x_{p_1}), Y_j^*\big)\right] \\
&\quad - \alpha \cdot \mathbb{E}_{x\sim p_{\text{duel}}}\left[e_{\text{data},j} \cdot \ell\big(D_i(x), 0\big) + e_{g,j} \cdot \ell\big(D_i(x), 1\big)\right]. \quad (29)
\end{aligned}
$$

Thus,

$$
\begin{aligned}
\text{Duel}(D_i)|_{\widetilde{D}_j} &= (1 - e_{\text{data},j} - e_{g,j}) \cdot \text{Duel}(D_i)|_{D_{j,G}^*} \\
&\quad + \underbrace{(1 - \alpha) \cdot \mathbb{E}_{x\sim p_{\text{duel}}}\left[e_{\text{data},j} \cdot \ell\big(D_i(x), 0\big) + e_{g,j} \cdot \ell\big(D_i(x), 1\big)\right]}_{\textbf{Bias}}. \quad (30)
\end{aligned}
$$

Note that:

$$
\textbf{Bias} = (1 - \alpha) \cdot \mathbb{E}_{x\sim p_{\text{duel}}}\left[e_{\text{data},j} \cdot \log\big(1 - D_i(x)\big) + e_{g,j} \cdot \log\big(D_i(x)\big)\right]. \quad (31)
$$

Thus, given $\alpha = 1$, the **Bias** term is cancelled out. When $e_{\text{data},j} + e_{g,j} < 1$, we have:

$$\text{Duel}(D_i)|_{\tilde{D}_j} = (1 - e_{\text{data},j} - e_{g,j}) \cdot \text{Duel}(D_i)|_{D_{j,G}^*}, \tag{32}$$

and we further have:

$$\max_{D_i} \text{Duel}(D_i)|_{\tilde{D}_j} = \max_{D_i} \text{Duel}(D_i)|_{D_{j,G}^*}. \tag{33}$$

## B.5   Proof of Theorem 4

*Proof.* When $\beta = 0$, the overall min-max game becomes:

$$\min_{G} \max_{D_1, D_2} \mathcal{L}(D_1, D_2, G)$$
$$= \min_{G} \max_{D_1, D_2} \mathbb{E}_{x \sim p_{\text{data}}} \big[ \log D_1(x) \big] + \mathbb{E}_{z \sim p_z} \Big[ \log \big( 1 - D_1(G(z)) \big) \Big]$$
$$+ \mathbb{E}_{x \sim p_{\text{data}}} \big[ \log D_2(x) \big] + \mathbb{E}_{z \sim p_z} \Big[ \log \big( 1 - D_2(G(z)) \big) \Big]. \tag{34}$$

Since we assume enough capacity, the inner max game is achieved if and only if: $D_1(x) = D_2(x) = \frac{p_{\text{data}}(x)}{p_{\text{data}}(x) + p_g(x)}$. To prove $p_g$ converges to $p_{\text{data}}$, only need to reproduce the proof of proposition 2 in [16]. We omit the details here.

# C   Experiment Details and Additional Results

**Model Architectures.** For the small-scale datasets, we used a shallow version of generator and discriminator: three convolution layers in the generator and four layers in the discriminators. We use a deep version of generator and discriminator for natural scene and human face image generation, which have three convolution layers in the generator and seven layers in the discriminators. The deep version is the original design of DCGAN [45]. The peer discriminator uses the duplicate version of the first one.

## C.1   Architecture Comparison Between GAN, D2GAN and DuelGAN

Fig. 5 shows the architecture designs of single discriminator, dual discriminator, and our proposed DuelGAN. Compared with Vanilla GAN, DuelGAN has one more identical discriminator and a competitive Duel Game between two discriminators. The introduced Duel Game induces diversified generated samples by discouraging the agreement between $D_1$ and $D_2$. In D2GAN, although both discriminators are trained with different loss functions, they do not interfere with each other in the training.

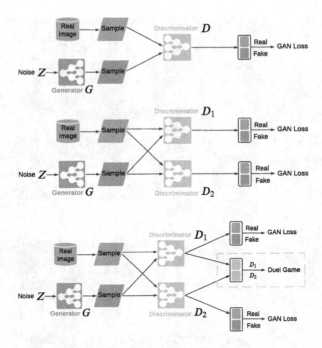

**Fig. 5.** Architecture comparisons between GAN based method (first row), dual discriminators GAN based method (second row) and DuelGAN (third row).

## C.2    Additional Experiment Results

StyleGAN-ADA [24] is the state-of-the-art method in image generation. We applied our duel game to StyleGAN-ADA and further improves its performance. On CelebA [34] dataset, we improved FID from 4.85 to 4.52, and FFHQ-10k [25] dataset improved FID from 7.24 to 6.01. We show the generated image results (trained on CelebA) in Fig. 6.

## C.3    Additional Experiment Details

**Model Architectures.** For the small-scale datasets, we used a shallow version of generator and discriminator: three convolution layers in the generator and four layers in the discriminators. We use a deep version of generator and discriminator for natural scene and human face image generation, which have three convolution layers in the generator and seven layers in the discriminators. The deep version is the original design of DCGAN [45]. The peer discriminator uses the duplicate version of the first one.

**Hyper-parameters.** DuelGAN achieves low FID scores when $\alpha$ and $\beta$ are simply set to constant values. However we found that we could obtain an approximately 10% improvement through dynamic tuning. The parameter $\beta$ controls

**Fig. 6.** More CelebA image generation results of applying duel game on StyleGAN-ADA.

the overall weight of Duel-D, while $\alpha$ punishes the condition when $D_1$ over-agrees with $D_2$. In the early training phase when we have an unstable generator and discriminator, we set $\alpha$ and $\beta$ to 0. As training progresses, we gradually increase these parameters to a max value, which helps with vanishing gradients. After the midpoint of training we decrease these parameters to help the discriminators converge, until the parameters reach approximately 0 at the end of the training process. We adopt 0.3, 0.5 as the max value for $\alpha$ and $\beta$, respectively.

## C.4  Ablation Study of DuelGAN

During training, We initialize the $\alpha$ and $\beta$ as 0, and gradually increase to the set maximum value. We experimentally discover $\alpha = 0.3$ and $\beta = 0.5$ can achieve the best FID score in the datasets we tested on. Table 3 shows an thorough ablation of different hyper-parameter setting on STL-10 dataset. The bold text are the best $\alpha$ setting when beta is fixed.

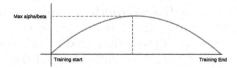

**Fig. 7.** The trend of $\alpha, \beta$ in the training.

**Table 4.** Ablation study of max $\alpha$ and max $\beta$ value tuning on STL-10 dataset (evaluate with FID score).

|  | $\alpha = 0.1$ | $\alpha = 0.3$ | $\alpha = 0.5$ | $\alpha = 0.7$ | $\alpha = 0.9$ |
|---|---|---|---|---|---|
| $\beta = 0.25$ | 60.88 | 56.01 | **51.86** | 58.17 | 60.91 |
| $\beta = 0.50$ | 58.77 | **51.37** | 58.45 | 55.16 | 57.75 |
| $\beta = 0.75$ | **55.07** | 59.58 | 58.58 | 58.22 | 57.75 |

## C.5 Stability of Training

Now we empirically show the stability of DuelGAN training procedure. We adopt STL-10 dataset and $\beta = 0.25$ for illustration. In Fig. 8 and 9, we visualize the loss of two discriminators during the training procedure of STL-10 dataset. The red lines indicate the smoothed trend of the loss evaluated on the generated images and real images. Real losses are represented by the shaded red lines. Although there exists certain unstable episodes (the difference between smoothed loss and the real loss is large) for both discriminators, the overall trend of both discriminators are stable. What is more, we do observe that $D_1$ and $D_2$ hardly experience unstable episodes at the same time. This phenomenon further validates our conclusion in Theorem 2: an unstable/diverged discriminator hardly disrupts the training of its peer discriminator!

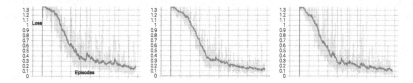

**Fig. 8.** The loss of $D_1$ in DuelGAN with $\beta = 0.25$ on STL-10 dataset, left: $\alpha = 0.3$; middle: 0.5; right: $\alpha = 0.7$.

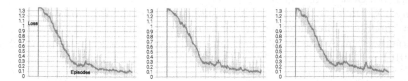

**Fig. 9.** The loss of $D_2$ in DuelGAN with $\beta = 0.25$ on STL-10 dataset, left: $\alpha = 0.3$; middle: 0.5; right: $\alpha = 0.7$.

*Agreements Between Two Discriminators.* We also empirically estimate the agreement level between two discriminators while training. In Fig. 10, the $y$−axis denotes the percentage of predictions that reach a consensus by $D_1$ and $D_2$. The smoothed curve depicts the overall change of the agreement level. At the initial stage, $D_i$ is not encouraged to agree overly on its peer discriminator $D_j$. As the training progresses, the agreement level gradually increases to a high value to help the convergence. The shaded red line means that the practical agreement level fluctuates around the smoothed line, incurs a certain degree of randomness and prevents discriminators from getting stuck in a local optimum.

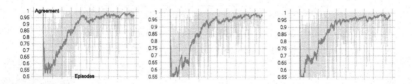

**Fig. 10.** The agreement level between $D_1$ and $D_2$ in DuelGAN with $\beta = 0.25$ on STL-10 dataset, left: $\alpha = 0.3$; middle: 0.5; right: $\alpha = 0.7$.

# References

1. Albuquerque, I., Monteiro, J., Doan, T., Considine, B., Falk, T., Mitliagkas, I.: Multi-objective training of generative adversarial networks with multiple discriminators. arXiv preprint arXiv:1901.08680 (2019)
2. Aneja, J., Schwing, A., Kautz, J., Vahdat, A.: A contrastive learning approach for training variational autoencoder priors. In: Advances in Neural Information Processing Systems vol. 34 (2021)
3. Antipov, G., Baccouche, M., Dugelay, J.L.: Face aging with conditional generative adversarial networks. In: 2017 IEEE international conference on image processing (ICIP), pp. 2089–2093. IEEE (2017)
4. Arbel, M., Sutherland, D., Bińkowski, M., Gretton, A.: On gradient regularizers for mmd gans. In: Advances in neural information processing systems, pp. 6700–6710 (2018)
5. Arjovsky, M., Chintala, S., Bottou, L.: Wasserstein gan. arXiv preprint arXiv:1701.07875 (2017)
6. Brock, A., Donahue, J., Simonyan, K.: Large scale gan training for high fidelity natural image synthesis. arXiv preprint arXiv:1809.11096 (2018)
7. Cao, Q., Shen, L., Xie, W., Parkhi, O.M., Zisserman, A.: Vggface2: A dataset for recognising faces across pose and age. In: International Conference on Automatic Face and Gesture Recognition (2018)
8. Chen, X., Duan, Y., Houthooft, R., Schulman, J., Sutskever, I., Abbeel, P.: Infogan: Interpretable representation learning by information maximizing generative adversarial nets. In: Advances in neural information processing systems, pp. 2172–2180 (2016)

9. Cheng, H., Zhu, Z., Li, X., Gong, Y., Sun, X., Liu, Y.: Learning with instance-dependent label noise: A sample sieve approach. In: International Conference on Learning Representations (2021), https://openreview.net/forum?id=2VXyy9mIyU3

10. Coates, A., Ng, A., Lee, H.: An Analysis of Single Layer Networks in Unsupervised Feature Learning. In: AISTATS (2011). https://cs.stanford.edu/acoates/papers/coatesleeng_aistats_011.pdf

11. Dash, A., Gamboa, J.C.B., Ahmed, S., Liwicki, M., Afzal, M.Z.: Tac-gan-text conditioned auxiliary classifier generative adversarial network. arXiv preprint arXiv:1703.06412 (2017)

12. Dieng, A.B., Ruiz, F.J., Blei, D.M., Titsias, M.K.: Prescribed generative adversarial networks. arXiv preprint arXiv:1910.04302 (2019)

13. Durugkar, I., Gemp, I., Mahadevan, S.: Generative multi-adversarial networks. arXiv preprint arXiv:1611.01673 (2016)

14. Ghosh, A., Kulharia, V., Namboodiri, V.P., Torr, P.H., Dokania, P.K.: Multi-agent diverse generative adversarial networks. In: Proceedings of the IEEE Conference on Computer Vision and Pattern Recognition, pp. 8513–8521 (2018)

15. Gong, X., Chang, S., Jiang, Y., Wang, Z.: Autogan: Neural architecture search for generative adversarial networks. In: Proceedings of the IEEE International Conference on Computer Vision, pp. 3224–3234 (2019)

16. Goodfellow, I., et al.: Generative adversarial nets. In: Advances in neural information processing systems, pp. 2672–2680 (2014)

17. Grassucci, E., Cicero, E., Comminiello, D.: Quaternion generative adversarial networks. arXiv preprint arXiv:2104.09630 (2021)

18. Gulrajani, I., Ahmed, F., Arjovsky, M., Dumoulin, V., Courville, A.C.: Improved training of wasserstein gans. In: Advances in neural information processing systems, pp. 5767–5777 (2017)

19. Heusel, M., Ramsauer, H., Unterthiner, T., Nessler, B., Hochreiter, S.: Gans trained by a two time-scale update rule converge to a local nash equilibrium. In: Advances in neural information processing systems, pp. 6626–6637 (2017)

20. Hoang, Q., Nguyen, T.D., Le, T., Phung, D.: Multi-generator generative adversarial nets. arXiv preprint arXiv:1708.02556 (2017)

21. Huang, X., Li, Y., Poursaeed, O., Hopcroft, J., Belongie, S.: Stacked generative adversarial networks. In: Proceedings of the IEEE Conference on Computer Vision and Pattern Recognition, pp. 5077–5086 (2017)

22. Jin, Y., Zhang, J., Li, M., Tian, Y., Zhu, H., Fang, Z.: Towards the automatic anime characters creation with generative adversarial networks. arXiv preprint arXiv:1708.05509 (2017)

23. Karras, T., Aila, T., Laine, S., Lehtinen, J.: Progressive growing of gans for improved quality, stability, and variation. arXiv preprint arXiv:1710.10196 (2017)

24. Karras, T., Aittala, M., Hellsten, J., Laine, S., Lehtinen, J., Aila, T.: Training generative adversarial networks with limited data. Adv. Neural. Inf. Process. Syst. **33**, 12104–12114 (2020)

25. Karras, T., Laine, S., Aila, T.: A style-based generator architecture for generative adversarial networks. In: Proceedings of the IEEE/CVF Conference on Computer Vision and Pattern Recognition, pp. 4401–4410 (2019)

26. Kodali, N., Abernethy, J., Hays, J., Kira, Z.: On convergence and stability of gans. arXiv preprint arXiv:1705.07215 (2017)

27. Krizhevsky, A., Hinton, G.: Convolutional deep belief networks on cifar-10. Unpublished Manuscript **40**(7), 1–9 (2010)

28. LeCun, Y., Cortes, C.: MNIST handwritten digit database (2010). http://yann.lecun.com/exdb/mnist/
29. Ledig, C., et al.: Photo-realistic single image super-resolution using a generative adversarial network. In: Proceedings of the IEEE Conference on Computer Vision and Pattern Recognition, pp. 4681–4690 (2017)
30. Li, X., Lin, C., Li, R., Wang, C., Guerin, F.: Latent space factorisation and manipulation via matrix subspace projection. In: International Conference on Machine Learning, pp. 5916–5926. PMLR (2020)
31. Li, Y., Liu, S., Yang, J., Yang, M.H.: Generative face completion. In: Proceedings of the IEEE Conference on Computer Vision and Pattern Recognition, pp. 3911–3919 (2017)
32. Lin, Z., Khetan, A., Fanti, G., Oh, S.P.: The power of two samples in generative adversarial networks. arxiv 2017. arXiv preprint arXiv:1712.04086
33. Liu, Y., Guo, H.: Peer loss functions: Learning from noisy labels without knowing noise rates. In: International Conference on Machine learning, pp. 6226–6236. PMLR (2020)
34. Liu, Z., Luo, P., Wang, X., Tang, X.: Large-scale celebfaces attributes (celeba) dataset. Retrieved 11 August (2018)
35. Ma, L., Jia, X., Sun, Q., Schiele, B., Tuytelaars, T., Van Gool, L.: Pose guided person image generation. In: Advances in Neural Information Processing Systems, pp. 406–416 (2017)
36. Mao, X., Li, Q., Xie, H., Lau, R.Y., Wang, Z., Paul Smolley, S.: Least squares generative adversarial networks. In: Proceedings of the IEEE International Conference on Computer Vision, pp. 2794–2802 (2017)
37. Metz, L., Poole, B., Pfau, D., Sohl-Dickstein, J.: Unrolled generative adversarial networks. arXiv preprint arXiv:1611.02163 (2016)
38. Miyato, T., Kataoka, T., Koyama, M., Yoshida, Y.: Spectral normalization for generative adversarial networks. arXiv preprint arXiv:1802.05957 (2018)
39. Mordido, G., Yang, H., Meinel, C.: microbatchgan: Stimulating diversity with multi-adversarial discrimination. In: Proceedings of the IEEE/CVF Winter Conference on Applications of Computer Vision, pp. 3061–3070 (2020)
40. Nguyen, T., Le, T., Vu, H., Phung, D.: Dual discriminator generative adversarial nets. In: Advances in Neural Information Processing Systems, pp. 2670–2680 (2017)
41. Nowozin, S., Cseke, B., Tomioka, R.: f-gan: Training generative neural samplers using variational divergence minimization. In: Advances in neural information processing systems, pp. 271–279 (2016)
42. Pathak, D., Krahenbuhl, P., Donahue, J., Darrell, T., Efros, A.A.: Context encoders: Feature learning by inpainting. In: Proceedings of the IEEE Conference on Computer Vision and Pattern Recognition, pp. 2536–2544 (2016)
43. Perarnau, G., Van De Weijer, J., Raducanu, B., Álvarez, J.M.: Invertible conditional gans for image editing. arXiv preprint arXiv:1611.06355 (2016)
44. Qi, G.J.: Loss-sensitive generative adversarial networks on lipschitz densities. Int. J. Comput. Vision 128(5), 1118–1140 (2020)
45. Radford, A., Metz, L., Chintala, S.: Unsupervised representation learning with deep convolutional generative adversarial networks. arXiv preprint arXiv:1511.06434 (2015)
46. Salimans, T., Goodfellow, I., Zaremba, W., Cheung, V., Radford, A., Chen, X.: Improved techniques for training gans. arXiv preprint arXiv:1606.03498 (2016)
47. Song, Y., Ermon, S.: Generative modeling by estimating gradients of the data distribution. In: Advances in Neural Information Processing Systems, pp. 11918–11930 (2019)

48. Taigman, Y., Polyak, A., Wolf, L.: Unsupervised cross-domain image generation. arXiv preprint arXiv:1611.02200 (2016)
49. Tran, N.-T., Bui, T.-A., Cheung, N.-M.: Dist-GAN: an improved GAN using distance constraints. In: Ferrari, V., Hebert, M., Sminchisescu, C., Weiss, Y. (eds.) Computer Vision – ECCV 2018. LNCS, vol. 11218, pp. 387–401. Springer, Cham (2018). https://doi.org/10.1007/978-3-030-01264-9_23
50. Tran, N.T., Bui, T.A., Cheung, N.M.: Dist-gan: An improved gan using distance constraints. In: Proceedings of the European Conference on Computer Vision (ECCV). pp. 370–385 (2018)
51. Tran, N.T., Tran, V.H., Nguyen, B.N., Yang, L., Cheung, N.M.M.: Self-supervised gan: analysis and improvement with multi-class minimax game. Adv. Neural. Inf. Process. Syst. **32**, 13253–13264 (2019)
52. Vahdat, A., Kreis, K., Kautz, J.: Score-based generative modeling in latent space. In: Advances in Neural Information Processing Systems, vol. 34 (2021)
53. Vondrick, C., Pirsiavash, H., Torralba, A.: Generating videos with scene dynamics. In: Advances in neural information processing systems, pp. 613–621 (2016)
54. Wang, T.C., Liu, M.Y., Zhu, J.Y., Tao, A., Kautz, J., Catanzaro, B.: High-resolution image synthesis and semantic manipulation with conditional gans. In: Proceedings of the IEEE Conference on Computer Vision and Pattern Recognition, pp. 8798–8807 (2018)
55. Wei, J., Liu, H., Liu, T., Niu, G., Liu, Y.: Understanding generalized label smoothing when learning with noisy labels. arXiv preprint arXiv:2106.04149 (2021)
56. Wei, J., Liu, Y.: When optimizing $f$-divergence is robust with label noise. arXiv preprint arXiv:2011.03687 (2020)
57. Wiatrak, M., Albrecht, S.V., Nystrom, A.: Stabilizing generative adversarial networks: A survey. arXiv preprint arXiv:1910.00927 (2019)
58. Wu, H., Zheng, S., Zhang, J., Huang, K.: Gp-gan: Towards realistic high-resolution image blending. In: Proceedings of the 27th ACM International Conference on Multimedia, pp. 2487–2495 (2019)
59. Xiao, H., Rasul, K., Vollgraf, R.: Fashion-mnist: a novel image dataset for benchmarking machine learning algorithms. arXiv preprint arXiv:1708.07747 (2017)
60. Xiao, Z., Yan, Q., Amit, Y.: Generative latent flow. arXiv preprint arXiv:1905.10485 (2019)
61. Yeh, R.A., Chen, C., Yian Lim, T., Schwing, A.G., Hasegawa-Johnson, M., Do, M.N.: Semantic image inpainting with deep generative models. In: Proceedings of the IEEE Conference on Computer Vision and Pattern Recognition, pp. 5485–5493 (2017)
62. Zhang, H., et al.: Stackgan: Text to photo-realistic image synthesis with stacked generative adversarial networks. In: Proceedings of the IEEE International Conference on Computer Vision, pp. 5907–5915 (2017)
63. Zhang, H., Zhang, Z., Odena, A., Lee, H.: Consistency regularization for generative adversarial networks. arXiv preprint arXiv:1910.12027 (2019)
64. Zhu, J.Y., Park, T., Isola, P., Efros, A.A.: Unpaired image-to-image translation using cycle-consistent adversarial networks. In: Proceedings of the IEEE International Conference on Computer Vision, pp. 2223–2232 (2017)

# MINER: Multiscale Implicit Neural Representation

Vishwanath Saragadam$^{(\boxtimes)}$, Jasper Tan, Guha Balakrishnan,
Richard G. Baraniuk, and Ashok Veeraraghavan

Rice University, Houston, TX 77005, USA
vishwanath.saragadam@rice.edu

**Abstract.** We introduce a new neural signal model designed for efficient high-resolution representation of large-scale signals. The key innovation in our *multiscale implicit neural representation* (MINER) is an internal representation via a Laplacian pyramid, which provides a sparse multiscale decomposition of the signal that captures orthogonal parts of the signal across scales. We leverage the advantages of the Laplacian pyramid by representing small disjoint patches of the pyramid at each scale with a small MLP. This enables the capacity of the network to adaptively increase from coarse to fine scales, and only represent parts of the signal with strong signal energy. The parameters of each MLP are optimized from coarse-to-fine scale which results in faster approximations at coarser scales, thereby ultimately an extremely fast training process. We apply MINER to a range of large-scale signal representation tasks, including gigapixel images and very large point clouds, and demonstrate that it requires fewer than 25% of the parameters, 33% of the memory footprint, and 10% of the computation time of competing techniques such as ACORN to reach the same representation accuracy. A fast implementation of MINER for images and 3D volumes is accessible from https://vishwa91.github.io/miner.

## 1 Introduction

Neural implicit representations have emerged as a promising paradigm for signal representation and interpolation with pervasive applications in 3D view synthesis [9,16,19,23], images [3], video [2], and linear inverse problems [3,25]. At the core of such neural representations is one or several multi layer perceptrons (MLPs) that produce a continuous mapping from signal coordinates to the values of the signal at those coordinates.

The success of neural implicit representations relies on the ability to fit models accurately (high representation accuracy), rapidly (short training time), and in a concise manner (small number of parameters). However, most state-of-the-art implicit representations require training a single large MLP (parameters in

---

**Supplementary Information** The online version contains supplementary material available at https://doi.org/10.1007/978-3-031-20050-2_19.

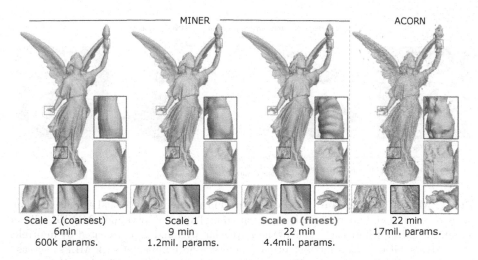

Fig. 1. **Multiscale Implicit Representations.** We present a novel implicit representation framework called MINER for large visual signals such as images, videos, and 3D volumes. We leverage the self-similarity of visual signals across scales to iteratively represent models from coarse to fine scales, resulting in a dramatic decrease in inference and training time, while requiring fewer parameters and less memory than state-of-the-art representations. This figure demonstrates fitting of the Lucy 3D mesh over three scales with scale 2 being the coarsest and 0 being the finest. MINER achieves high quality results across all scales with high IoU value and achieves an IoU of 0.999 at the finest scale in less than 30 min. In comparison, the state-of-the-art approach (ACORN) results in an IoU of 0.97 in that time, while requiring far more parameters.

millions) that suffers from high computational cost, requiring large memory footprints and long training times. While there have been several modifications to the network architecture [13,20,22] and inference [31], neural implicit representations are not yet practical for handling extremely high dimensional signals such as gigapixel images or 3D point clouds with several billion data points.

We introduce a multiscale implicit neural representation (MINER) that is well-suited for representing very high dimensional signals in a concise manner. Our key observation is that Laplacian pyramids of visual signals offer a sparse and multiscale decomposition that naturally separates a signal's frequency content across spatial scales. We leverage the multiscale decomposition by representing each spatial scale of the Laplacian pyramid with different MLPs. Instead of using a single MLP at each scale, we represent a small disjoint image/volume patch of fixed size with a small MLP, resulting in both a multiscale and multipatch decomposition. Such a multipatch decomposition is well-suited for sparse signals as most patches will have near-zero intensity, thereby not requiring an explicit MLP for that patch. MINER enables a fast and flexible multi-resolution analysis, as representing the signal at lower resolution requires training $2\times$ fewer MLPs along each spatial dimension (due to fewer patches), An example on fitting a 3D volume across three spatial scales on one billion points is shown in

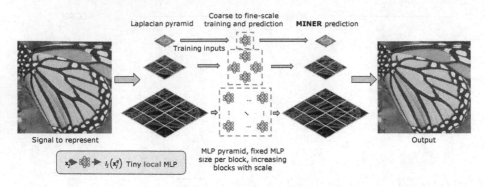

**Fig. 2. MINER trains and predicts Laplacian pyramids.** Visual signals are similar across scales and are compactly represented by Laplacian pyramids. MINER follows a similar scheme where each scale of the Laplacian pyramid is represented by multiple, local MLPs with a small number of parameters. The number of such MLPs increase by a factor of 2 from coarse to fine scale, thereby representing a fixed spatial size at each scale. This multi-scale representation naturally lends itself to a sequential, coarse-to-fine scale training process that is fast and memory efficient.

Fig. 1. MINER provides a visually pleasing result even at the coarsest spatial scale in six minutes with as few as 600k parameters. The finest scale converges in 22 min. In contrast, for the same amount of training time, state-of-the-art approaches such as ACORN result in many artifacts while also requiring 4× more parameters. An overview of the MINER signal model is shown in Fig. 2.

The multiscale, multi-MLP architecture lends itself to a fast and memory efficient training procedure. At each spatial scale, the parameters of the MLPs are trained for the corresponding Laplacian pyramid scale. We then *sequentially* train MLPs from coarsest scale to the finest scale. The near-orthogonality of the Laplacian transform across scales ensures that new information is added at every scale, thereby resulting in an iterative refinement framework. We leverage the sparsity of the Laplacian transform by comparing the upsampled signal from the fine block and the target signal at that fine block – if the error in representation (or variance of signal) is smaller than a threshold, we prune out the blocks before training starts. This leads to fewer blocks to train at finer resolutions.

MINER is 10× or more faster compared to state-of-the-art implicit representations in terms of training process for a comparable number of parameters and target accuracy. MINER can represent gigapixel images with greater than 38 dB accuracy in less than three hours, compared to more than a day with techniques such as ACORN [13]. For 3D point clouds, MINER achieves an intersection over union (IoU) of 0.999 or higher in less than three minutes, resulting in two orders of magnitude speed up over ACORN. Due to the multiscale representation, MINER can be used for streaming reconstruction of images, as with JPEG2000 [21], or efficiently sampling for rendering purposes with octrees [31] – making neural representations ready for extremely large scale visual signals.

## 2    Prior Work

MINER draws inspiration from classical multiscale techniques and more recent neural representations. We outline some of the salient works here to set context.

*Implicit Neural Representations.* Implicit neural representations learn a continuous mapping from local coordinates to the signal value such as intensity for images and videos, and occupancy value for 3D volumes. The learned models are then used for a myriad of tasks including image representations [3], multi-view rendering [16], and linear inverse problems solving [25]. Recent advances in the choice of coordinate representation [27] and non-linearity [22] have resulted in training processes that have high fitting accuracy. Salient works related to implicit representations include the NeRF representations [16] and its many derivatives that seek to learn the 3D geometry from a set of multi-view images. Despite the interest and success of these implicit representations, current approaches often require disproportionately large number of parameters compared to the signal dimension. This culminates in a large memory footprint and training times, precluding representation of very high-dimensional signals.

*Architectural Changes for Faster Learning.* Several interesting modifications have been proposed to increase training or inference speed. KiloNeRF [20] and deep local shapes [1] replaced the large MLP with multiple small MLPS that fit only a small, disjoint part of the 3D space. Such approaches dramatically speed up the inference time (often by 60×) and in some cases enable better generalization [15], but they have little to no effect on the training process itself. ACORN [13] utilized an adaptive coordinate decomposition to efficiently fit various signals. By utilizing a combination of integer programming and interpolation, ACORN reduced training time for fitting of images and 3D point clouds by one to two orders of magnitude compared to techniques like SIREN [22] and the convolutional occupancy network [19]. However, ACORN does not leverage the cross-scale similarity of visual signals, and this often leads to long convergence times for very large signals. Moreover, the adaptive optimized blocks requires several hundreds of thousands of gradient steps which can be prohibitively expensive.

*Multi-scale Representations.* Visual signals are similar across scales, and this has been exploited for a wide variety of applications. In computer vision and image processing, the wavelet transform and Laplacian pyramids are often used to efficiently perform tasks such as image registration [28], optical flow computation [29], and feature extraction [11]. Multi-scale representations such as octrees [4,14] and mip-mapping are used to speed up the rendering pipeline. This has also inspired neural mipmapping techniques [9] that utilize neural networks to represent texture at each scale. Along the same lines, spatially adaptive progressive encoding [6] enables a coarse-to-fine training approach that gradually learns higher spatial frequencies. Multi-scale representations are also utilized for several linear inverse problems such as multi-scale dictionary learning for denoising [24], compressive sensing [17], and sparse approximation [12]. Some recent works have focused on a level-of-detail approach to neural representations [26] (NGLOD) where the multiple scales are *jointly* learned. The implicit displacement fields (IDF) approach [30] similarly learns a smooth approximation of the surface, along with a high frequency displacement at each spatial point to represent the shape. While efficient in rendering, NGLOD and IDF have no advantage in the training phase, as it relies on training all levels of detail at the same time. MINER also results in an LOD representation, but the underlying approach is significantly different. MINER relies on a block-wise representation at each scale with sequential training from coarse to fine scales, which enables more compact representation with faster training times.

## 3    MINER

MINER combines Laplacian pyramid with a block decomposition of the signal. We now describe the MINER signal model and the training process.

### 3.1    Signal Model

Let $\mathbf{x}$ be the coordinate and $I(\mathbf{x})$ be the target. We will assume that the coordinates lie in $[-1, 1]$. Let $\mathcal{D}_j$ be the domain specific operator that downsamples the signal by $j$ times, and $\mathcal{U}_j$ be the domain-specific operator that upsamples the signal by $j$ times. We will leverage $J$ implicit representations, $I_j(\mathbf{x}) \approx N_j$ for $j \in [0, J - 1]$, where $N_j$ is the MLP at the $j^{\text{th}}$ level of a Laplacian pyramid, a multiscale representation which separates the input signal into scales capturing unique spatial frequency bands. Two desirable properties of such a bandpass pyramid is that signals across scales are approximately orthogonal to one another [5] and are sparse. We found in our experiments that these properties dramatically reduce the training and inference times compared to a lowpass pyramid such as the Gaussian pyramid (see Fig. 3a).

Letting $R_j$ denote the MLP modeling the residual signal at scale $j$, our Laplacian pyramid representation may be written as:

$$I_{J-1}(\mathbf{x}) = \mathcal{D}_{J-1}(I)(\mathbf{x}) \approx N_{J-1}(\mathbf{x}) \tag{1}$$

$$I_{J-2}(\mathbf{x}) = \mathcal{D}_{J-2}(I)(\mathbf{x}) \approx R_{J-2}(\mathbf{x}) + \mathcal{U}_2(N_{J-1}(\mathbf{x}/2)) \tag{2}$$

$$\vdots$$

$$I(\mathbf{x}) \approx R_0(\mathbf{x}) + \mathcal{U}_2(N_1(\mathbf{x}/2)) \tag{3}$$

$$\approx N_0(\mathbf{x}) + \mathcal{U}_2(N_1(\mathbf{x}/2)) + \cdots + \mathcal{U}_{2^{J-1}}(N_{J-1}(\mathbf{x}/2^{J-1})), \tag{4}$$

where Eq. (1) is the coarsest representation of the signal. At finer scales (as in Eq. (2)), we write the signal to be approximated as a sum of the upsampled version of the previous scale and a residual term. This results in a recursive multi-resolution representation that naturally shares information across scales.

We make two observations about MINER:

- Signals at coarser resolutions are low-dimensional, and therefore require smaller MLPs. These MLPs are faster for inference, which is beneficial for tasks such as mipmapping and LOD-based rendering.
- The parameters of the MLPs up to scale $j$ only rely on the signal at scales $q = j, j+1, \cdots, J-1$. This implies the MLPs can be trained *sequentially* from coarsest to finest scale. We will see next that this offers a dramatic reduction in training time without sacrificing quality.

**Using Multiple MLPs per Scale.** Equation (4) implies that obtaining a value at a spatial point $\mathbf{x}$ requires evaluating a total of $J$ MLPs across scales. Such joint evaluation has no computational benefit compared to a single scale approach like SIREN [22] with comparable number of parameters. Further, the residual signals at finer scales are often low-amplitude, a consequence of visual signals being composed of several smooth areas. To leverage this fact and make inference faster, we split the signal into equal sized blocks at each scale. We create an MLP for each block that requires significantly fewer parameters than a single full MLP at that scale. Moreover, blocks with small residual energy can be represented as a zero signal, and do not even need to be represented with an MLP.

We now combine the Laplacian representation with the multi-MLP approach stated above. Let $\widetilde{\mathbf{x}}$ be a local coordinate at the finest scale in a block with coordinate $(m, n)$, where $m \in 1, 2, \cdots M$ is the number of vertical blocks, and $n \in 1, 2, \cdots, N$ is the number of horizontal blocks. To evaluate the signal at $\mathbf{x}$,

$$I(\mathbf{x}) = I\left(\widetilde{\mathbf{x}} + \left[\frac{mH}{M}, \frac{nW}{N}\right]\right) = \mathcal{R}_0^{(m,n)}\left(\widetilde{\mathbf{x}} + \left[\frac{mH}{M}, \frac{nW}{N}\right]\right) + \cdots$$

$$+ \cdots \mathcal{U}_2\left(\mathcal{N}_1^{(\lfloor m/2\rfloor, \lfloor n/2\rfloor)}\left(\widetilde{\mathbf{x}} + \left[\left\lfloor\frac{mH}{2M}\right\rfloor, \left\lfloor\frac{nW}{2N}\right\rfloor\right]\right)\right), \tag{5}$$

where $\lfloor\cdot\rfloor$ is the floor operator, and $\mathcal{N}_j^{(m,n)}$ is the MLP for block at $(m, n)$ and at scale $j$. With this formulation, we require evaluation of at most $J$ *small* MLPs instead of large MLPs, thereby dramatically reducing inference time.

## 3.2   Training MINER

MINER requires estimation of parameters at each scale and each block. We now present an efficient *sequential* training procedure that starts at the coarsest scale and trains up to the finest scale.

*Training at Coarsest Sscale.* The training process starts by fitting $I_{J-1}(\mathbf{x})$, the image at the coarsest scale. We estimate the parameters of each of the MLPs $\mathcal{N}_{J-1}^{(m,n)}$ by solving the objective function,

$$\min_{\mathcal{N}_{J-1}^{(m,n)}} \left\| I_{J-1}\left(\widetilde{\mathbf{x}} + \left(\frac{mH}{2^{J-1}M}, \frac{nW}{2^{J-1}N}\right)\right) - \mathcal{N}_{J-1}^{(m,n)}(\widetilde{\mathbf{x}})\right\|^2. \tag{6}$$

Let $\widehat{I}_{J-1}(\mathbf{x}_{J-1})$ be the estimate of the image at this stage.

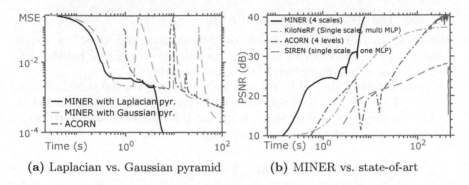

(a) Laplacian vs. Gaussian pyramid          (b) MINER vs. state-of-art

**Fig. 3. Laplacian pyramid enables faster convergence.** The plot in (a) shows training error across time for a 2048 × 2048 image of Pluto. MINER when combined with a Laplacian pyramid offers a significantly faster convergence as the MLPs at finer scale capture orthogonal information. This also results in small jumps in training accuracy that is strongly present when MINER is trained with a Gaussian pyramid, or ACORN. (b) shows PSNR as a function of time for various approaches for a one megapixel Pluto image. MINER achieves higher accuracy at all times, and converges significantly faster than competing approaches. Moreover, the drop in accuracy when changing from coarse to fine scale is less severe for MINER compared to when ACORN re-estimates coordinate decomposition.

*Pruning at Convergence.* As the training proceeds, some MLPs, particularly for blocks with limited variations, will converge to a target mean squared error (MSE) earlier than the more complex blocks. We remove those MLPs that have converged from the optimization process and continue with the remaining blocks.

*Training at Finer Scales.* As with the coarsest scale, we continue to fit small MLPs to blocks at each finer scale. For scale $J - 2$, the target signal is given by

$$R_{J-2}(\mathbf{x}) = I_{J-2}(\mathbf{x}) - \mathcal{U}_2(\widehat{I}_{J-1})(\mathbf{x}/2). \tag{7}$$

We leverage the fact that blocks within each scale occupy disjoint regions and can optimize each MLP independently of one another:

$$\min_{\mathcal{R}_{J-2}^{(m,n)}} \left\| R_{J-2}\left(\widetilde{\mathbf{x}} + \left(\frac{mH}{2^{J-2}M}, \frac{nW}{2^{J-2}N}\right)\right) - \mathcal{R}_{J-2}^{(m,n)}(\widetilde{\mathbf{x}}) \right\|^2. \tag{8}$$

*Pruning Before Optimization.* Due to the sparseness of gradients of visual signals, we expect a large number of spatial regions to have little to no signal. Nominally, the number of blocks and MLPs double along each dimension at finer scales. However, some blocks may already be adequately represented by the corresponding MLP at the coarser scale. In such a case, we do not assign an MLP to that block and set the estimate of the residue to all zeros. Depending on the frequency content in the image, this decision dramatically reduces the number of total MLP parameters, and thereby the overall training and inference times. In cases where *a priori* information about residual energy is not available (such as view synthesis from images), we can rely on each block's variance. Blocks with low variance likely converge at the coarser scale and hence can be pruned from training.

## 4   Experimental Results

*Baselines.* For fitting to images and 3D volumes, we compared MINER against SIREN [22], KiloNeRF [20], and ACORN [13]. We also compared MINER against convolutional occuppancy networks [19] for 3D volumes. We used code from the respective authors and optimized the training parameters for a fair comparison.

*Training Details.* We implemented MINER with the PyTorch [18] framework. Multiple MLPs were trained efficiently using the block matrix multiplication function (`torch.bmm`) and hence, we required no complex coding outside of stock PyTorch implementations. All our models were trained on a system unit equipped with Intel Xeon 8260 running at 2.4 Ghz, 128 GB RAM, and NVIDIA GeForce RTX 2080 Ti with 12 GB memory. For all experiments, we excluded any time taken by logging activities such as saving models, images, meshes, and computing intermittent metrics such as PSNR and IoU.

*Fitting Images.* We split up RGB images into $32 \times 32 \times 3$ patches at all spatial scales. For each patch and at each scale, we trained a single MLP with two hidden layers and sinusoidal activation function [22]. We fixed the number of features to be 20 for each layer. We did not add any further positional encoding. We used the ADAM [8] optimizer with a learning rate of $5 \times 10^{-4}$ and an exponential decay with $\gamma = 0.999$. At each scale, we trained either for 500 epochs, or until the change in loss function was greater than $2 \times 10^{-7}$. We used an $\ell_2$ loss function at all scales with no additional prior. We pruned a block from the training pipeline if the block MSE was smaller than $10^{-4}$. Similarly, a block was not added at the starting of the training process if the block MSE was smaller than $10^{-4}$. The effect of block-stopping threshold is analyzed in the supplementary material.

Figure 3a shows training error for a 4 megapixel (MP) image of Pluto across epochs for MINER by representing a Laplacian pyramid, a Gaussian pyramid, and ACORN. MINER converges rapidly to an error of $10^{-4}$ compared to other approaches. Moreover, the periodic and abrupt increase in error are more prevalent in Gaussian representation, and ACORN, which further hamper their performance, but not with Laplacian pyramid due to near-orthogonality of signal across scales. Figure 3b shows training error for a 1 MP image for various approaches with a fixed number of parameters (900k). MINER with four scales is nearly two orders of magnitude faster than all approaches. Figure 4 shows the fitting result for a 64 megapixel Pluto image across training iterations. The times correspond to the instances when MINER converged at a given scale. MINER maintains high quality reconstruction at all instances due to the multiscale training scheme and rapidly converges to a PSNR of 40 dB within 50 s. In contrast, ACORN achieves

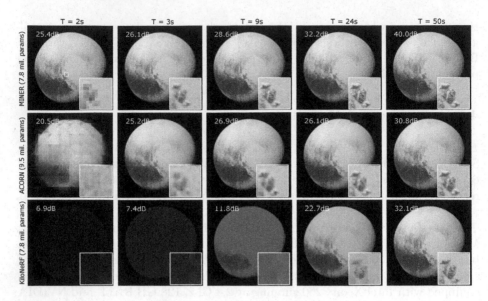

**Fig. 4. Image fit over time.** The figure compares fitting of the 16 megapixel pluto image at various times during the training process. A distinct advantage of MINER is that the signal is similar to the final output (albeit downsampled) from the starting itself which enables an easy visual debug of the fitting process.

qualitatively good results after 10 s and achieves a PSNR of 30.8 dB after 50 s, and KiloNeRF achieves a qualitatively good result only after 50 s. SIREN Results are not shown in the plot as the first epoch was completed after 4 min. Results with analysis on effect of parameters such as number of scales and patch size is included in supplementary.

Figure 3b shows a plot of PSNR as a function of time for various approaches. We also note that ACORN curve shows significant drop in accuracy as a result of re-computation of coordinate blocks. In contrast, the drop in accuracy for the MINER curve due to scale change is significantly smaller than ACORN. Figure 5 shows results on training a 2 megapixel image with active blocks at all scales. The blocks are concentrated around the high frequency areas (such as the antennae of the grasshopper) as the scale increases from coarse to fine. MINER took less than 10 s to converge to 40 dB fitting accuracy. In contrast, KiloNeRF took 6 minutes to converge and ACORN took 7 min to converge to 40 dB with approximately equal number of parameters.

Figure 6 compares MINER, KiloNeRF, and ACORN in terms of time taken to achieve 36 dB and GPU memory for fitting a 16 MP image of Pluto. For Fig. 6 (a), we used author's implementation of ACORN with default batch size and number of layers and only varied the number of hidden features. For Fig. 6 (b), we set batch size such that up to all pixels were trained simultaneously. Similarly, we set the batchsize for MINER to train all pixels simultaneously to keep comparisons fair. MINER consistently achieves 36 dB faster than competing

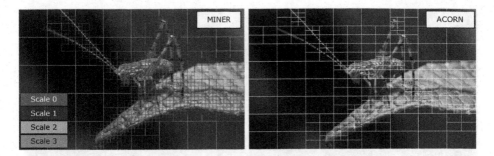

**Fig. 5. MINER adaptively selects window sizes.** MINER adaptively selects the appropriate scale for each local area resulting in patch sizes that are chosen according to texture variations within the window. The figure above shows a macro photograph of a grasshopper fit by MINER (left image). Large parts of the image such as background have very smooth texture implying that they can be fit accurately at a coarser scale– which translates to large spatial size for low frequency areas. In contrast, area around the antennae are made of high spatial frequencies, which required fitting at finer scales. ACORN provides a similar decomposition (right image) but represents image at only a single image, thereby not being amenable to multiscale analysis.

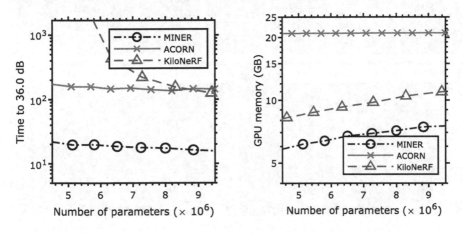

**Fig. 6. MINER requires shorter training time and memory footprint.** The plot shows the time taken to achieve 36 dB and the GPU memory utilization to fit a 16MP image (Pluto) with ACORN and MINER for varying number of parameters. MINER is an order of magnitude faster than ACORN and requires less than one third of the GPU memory as ACORN–implying MINER is well-suited to train very large models.

methods and requires significantly smaller memory footprint while being able to train on the whole signal at a time, making it highly scalable for large-sized problems.

MINER scales up graciously for extremely large signals. We trained ACORN on a gigapixel image shown in Fig. 7 over 7 scales. We set the number of features

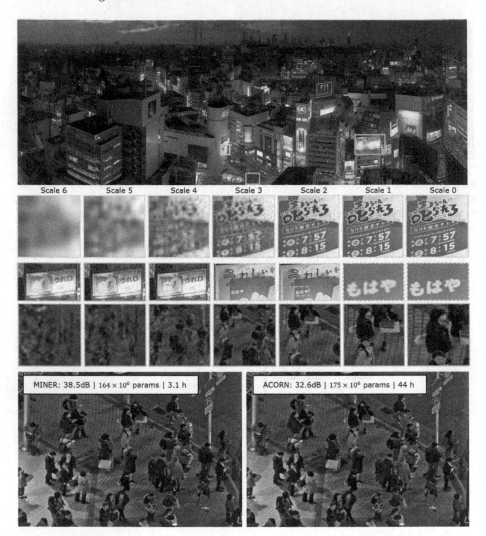

**Fig. 7. Fitting gigapixel images.** The figure shows the results on fitting a gigapixel image $(20,480 \times 56,420)$ with MINER and ACORN. MINER required 188 million parameters and converged to 38.5 dB in 3.1 h. In contrast, even after 44 h of training, ACORN, which required 175 million parameters, achieved only 32.6 dB.

per each block to be 9, and used a patch size of $32 \times 32$. MINER converged to a PSNR of 38.5 dB in 3.1 h and required a total of 164 million parameters. In contrast, after 44 h of training, ACORN converged to only 32.6 dB while using a total of 175 million parameters. We trained both ACORN and MINER on an 11 GB NVIDIA RTX 2080 Ti GPU, which required us to decrease the maximum number of patches for ACORN to 3072 from the original authors' implementation they ran on a 48 GB GPU. MINER also enables compression of

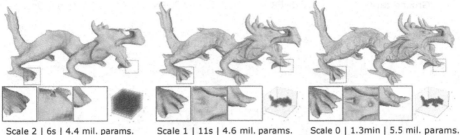

Scale 2 | 6s | 4.4 mil. params.    Scale 1 | 11s | 4.6 mil. params.    Scale 0 | 1.3min | 5.5 mil. params.

**Fig. 8. Active blocks reduce with increasing scale.** The figure shows MINER results at the end of training at each scale and the active blocks at each scale. As the iterations progress, only the blocks on the surface of the object remain, which leads to a dramatic reduction in non-zero blocks, and hence the total number of parameters.

the image. Storing the image image as 16-bit `tiff` format required 2.4 GB of disk space. In contrast, MINER required 650 MB with 32 bit precision, implying MINER enables very high compression for images with high dynamic range.

*Fitting 3D Point Clouds.* cnspired by Convolutional occupancy networks [19], we utilized signed density function where the value was 1 inside the mesh and 0 outside. We sampled a total of one billion points, resulting in a $1024 \times 1024 \times 1024$ occupancy volume. We then optimized MINER over four scales for a maximum of 2000 iterations at each scale. We experimented with logistic loss and MSE and found the MSE resulting in signficantly faster convergence. We divided the volume into disjoint blocks of size $16 \times 16 \times 16$. The learning rate was set to $10^{-3}$. We set the number of features to 16 and the number of hidden layers to 2 for MLP for each block at all scales. As with images, we set the per-block MSE stopping threshold to be $10^{-4}$, and did not include positional encoding for the inputs. We then constructed meshes from the resultant occupancy volumes using marching cubes [10]. We compared our results against ACORN and convolutional occupancy networks for accuracy and timing comparisons. For ACORN, we used the implementation and the hyperparameters provided by the original authors. For convolutional occupancy networks, we used 200,000 randomly sampled points from the volume as input. Comparisons against screened Poisson surface reconstruction (SPSR) [7], which does not utilize neural networks but requires local normals, is included in the supplementary.

Figure 1 shows reconstructed meshes for the Lucy 3D model at each scale. MINER converges in 22 min to an Intersection over Union (IoU) of 0.999. In the same time, ACORN achieved an IoU of 0.97 with worse results than MINER. ACORN took greater than 7 h to converge to an IoU of 0.999, clearly demonstrating the advantages of MINER for 3D volumes. We also note that MINER required less than a third of the number of parameters as ACORN – this is a direct consequence of using a block-based representation – most blocks outside the mesh and inside the mesh converge rapidly within the first few scales, requiring far fewer representations than a single scale representation. An example of

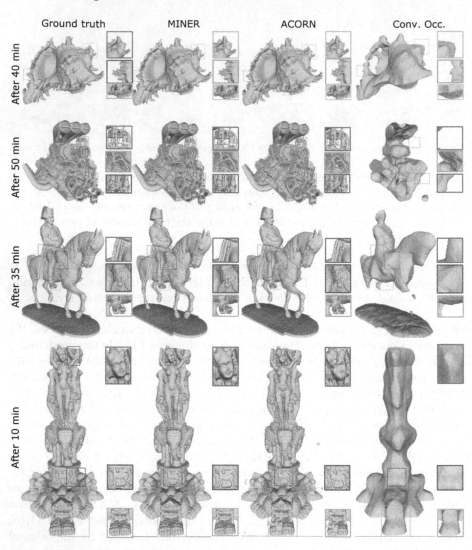

**Fig. 9. Comparisons against state-of-the-art for 3D volume fitting.** We 3D occupancy fitting for a **fixed duration** with MINER, ACORN, and Convolutional occupancy [19]. The number of parameters of MINER was chosen adaptively according to model complexity. MINER achieves high accuracy in a short duration for arbitrarily complex shapes, which is not possible with prior works, even though some models such as the engine (second row) require significantly more parameters.

active blocks at each scale is shown in Fig. 8. As iterations progress, the number of active blocks after pruning reduce, which in turn results in more compact representation, and fewer parameters. Figure 9 visualizes the meshes fit with various reconstruction approaches for a fixed duration. The time for each experiment

**Table 1. Comparison on the Thai Statue 3D Point Cloud.** For all experiments, we fixed the batch size to the equivalent of 1024 $16 \times 16 \times 16$ blocks. MINER requires lower training and testing times, similar GPU memory, fewer parameters, and smaller size on disk compared to state-of-the-art techniques. MINER also occupies smaller disk space compared to storing the mesh as a ply file, thereby enabling compression.

|  | IOU | GPU Mem. | #Params. | Test time | Storage |
|---|---|---|---|---|---|
| MINER - scale 3 | 0.95 (17 s) | 1.8 GB | 900k | 0.02 s | 3.5 MB |
| scale 2 | 0.97 (42 s) | 2.5 GB | 1.3 million | 0.04 s | 4.8 MB |
| scale 1 | 0.98 (1.9 min) | 5.0 GB | 2.8 million | 0.16 s | 10.6 MB |
| scale 0 | 0.99 (6 min) | 6.6 GB | 9.9 million | 0.8 s | 37.9 MB |
| ACORN [13] | 0.99 (53 min) | 8.0 GB | 17 million | 18.1 s | 68 MB |
| Conv. Occ [19] | 0.82 | 5.8 GB | 160k | – | 64 KB |
| ply file | – | – | – | – | 180 MB |

was chosen to be when MINER achieved an IoU of 0.999. MINER has superior reconstruction quality compared to ACORN and convolutional occupancy networks [19]. Table 1 compares IoU after a fixed time, GPU memory for training, number of parameters, testing (inference) time, and disk space for MINER at various scales, and competing approaches. The memory usage of ACORN increased from 3.9 GB at the start (with no further splitting) to 8 GB, which we reported. MINER achieves high accuracy (IoU) within 17 s at the coarsest scale where GPU utilization, number of parameters (and hence size on disk) are low. At the finest scale, MINER achieves very high accuracy, and requires fewer parameters, thereby enabling training on very large meshes. Moreover, MINER occupies a third of the size on disk compared to a standard ply file, thereby enabling mesh compression.

## 5   Conclusions

We have proposed a novel multi-scale neural representation that trains faster, requires same or fewer parameters, and has lower memory footprint than state-of-the-art approaches. We demonstrated that the advantages of a Laplacian pyramid including multiscale and sparse representation enable computational efficiency. We showed that leveraging self-similarity across scales is beneficial in reducing training time drastically while not affecting the training accuracy. MINER naturally lends itself to rendering where level-of-detail is of importance including representation and mipmapping for texture mapping. MINER can be combined with fast, multiscale rendering approaches [31] to achieve real time neural graphics. With the low computational complexity and fast training and inference time, MINER opens avenues for rendering extremely large and complex geometric shapes that was previously impractical.

**Acknowledgements.** This work was supported by NSF grants CCF-1911094, EEC-1648451, IIS-1838177, IIS-1652633, and IIS-1730574; ONR grants N00014-18-12571, N00014-20-1-2534, and MURI N00014-20-1-2787; AFOSR grant FA9550-22-1-0060; and a Vannevar Bush Faculty Fellowship, ONR grant N00014-18-1-2047.

# References

1. Chabra, R., et al.: Deep local shapes: learning local SDF priors for detailed 3D reconstruction. In: Vedaldi, A., Bischof, H., Brox, T., Frahm, J.-M. (eds.) ECCV 2020. LNCS, vol. 12374, pp. 608–625. Springer, Cham (2020). https://doi.org/10.1007/978-3-030-58526-6_36
2. Chen, H., He, B., Wang, H., Ren, Y., Lim, S.N., Shrivastava, A.: Nerv: Neural Representations for Videos. Adv. Neural Info, Processing Systems (2021)
3. Chen, Y., Liu, S., Wang, X.: Learning continuous image representation with local implicit image function. In: IEEE Computer Vision and Pattern Recognition (CVPR) (2021)
4. Chien, C.H., Aggarwal, J.K.: Volume/surface octrees for the representation of three-dimensional objects. Comput. Vision Graph. Image Process. **36**(1), 100–113 (1986)
5. Do, M.N., Vetterli, M.: Framing pyramids. IEEE Trans. Signal Process. **51**(9), 2329–2342 (2003)
6. Hertz, A., Perel, O., Giryes, R., Sorkine-Hornung, O., Cohen-Or, D.: Sape: spatially-adaptive progressive encoding for neural optimization. Adv. Neural Info. Process. Syst. **34**, 8820–8832 (2021)
7. Kazhdan, M., Hoppe, H.: Screened poisson surface reconstruction. ACM Trans. Graph. **32**(3), 1–13 (2013)
8. Kingma, D.P., Ba, J.: Adam: A method for stochastic optimization. In: International Conference Learning Representations (2015)
9. Kuznetsov, A., Mullia, K., Xu, Z., Hašan, M., Ramamoorthi, R.: NeuMIP: Multi-resolution neural materials. ACM Trans. Graphics **40**(4), 1–13 (2021)
10. Lorensen, W.E., Cline, H.E.: Marching cubes: a high resolution 3D surface construction algorithm. ACM SIGGRAPH **21**(4), 163–169 (1987)
11. Lowe, D.G.: Distinctive image features from scale-invariant keypoints. Intl. J. Comput. Vision **60**(2), 91–110 (2004)
12. Mairal, J., Sapiro, G., Elad, M.: Multiscale sparse image representation with learned dictionaries. In: IEEE International Conference Image Processing (ICIP), vol. 3, pp. III-105 (2007)
13. Martel, J.N., Lindell, D.B., Lin, C.Z., Chan, E.R., Monteiro, M., Wetzstein, G.: Acorn: Adaptive coordinate networks for neural scene representation. arXiv preprint arXiv:2105.02788 (2021)
14. Meagher, D.: Geometric modeling using octree encoding. Comput. Graph. Image Process. **19**(2), 129–147 (1982)
15. Mehta, I., Gharbi, M., Barnes, C., Shechtman, E., Ramamoorthi, R., Chandraker, M.: Modulated periodic activations for generalizable local functional representations. In: IEEE International Conference Computer Vision (ICCV) (2021)
16. Mildenhall, B., Srinivasan, P.P., Tancik, M., Barron, J.T., Ramamoorthi, R., Ng, R.: Nerf: Representing scenes as neural radiance fields for view synthesis. In: IEEE European Conf. Computer Vision (ECCV) (2020)
17. Park, J.Y., Wakin, M.B.: A multiscale framework for compressive sensing of video. In: Picture Coding Symposium (2009)

18. Paszke, A., et al.: Pytorch: An imperative style, high-performance deep learning library. In: Advance Neural Information Processing Systems (2019)

19. Peng, S., Niemeyer, M., Mescheder, L., Pollefeys, M., Geiger, A.: Convolutional occupancy networks. In: Vedaldi, A., Bischof, H., Brox, T., Frahm, J.-M. (eds.) ECCV 2020. LNCS, vol. 12348, pp. 523–540. Springer, Cham (2020). https://doi. org/10.1007/978-3-030-58580-8_31

20. Reiser, C., Peng, S., Liao, Y., Geiger, A.: Kilonerf: Speeding up neural radiance fields with thousands of tiny mlps. arXiv preprint arXiv:2103.13744 (2021)

21. Shapiro, J.M.: Embedded image coding using zerotrees of wavelet coefficients. In: Fundamental Papers in Wavelet Theory, pp. 861–878 (2009)

22. Sitzmann, V., Martel, J., Bergman, A., Lindell, D., Wetzstein, G.: Implicit neural representations with periodic activation functions. Adv. Neural Info, Processing Systems (2020)

23. Srinivasan, P.P., Deng, B., Zhang, X., Tancik, M., Mildenhall, B., Barron, J.T.: Nerv: Neural reflectance and visibility fields for relighting and view synthesis. In: IEEE Computer Vision and Pattern Recognition (CVPR) (2021)

24. Sulam, J., Ophir, B., Elad, M.: Image denoising through multi-scale learnt dictionaries. In: IEEE International Conference Image Processing (ICIP) (2014)

25. Sun, Y., Liu, J., Xie, M., Wohlberg, B., Kamilov, U.S.: Coil: Coordinate-based internal learning for imaging inverse problems. arXiv preprint arXiv:2102.05181 (2021)

26. Takikawa, T., et al.: Neural geometric level of detail: Real-time rendering with implicit 3d shapes. In: IEEE Computer Vision and Pattern Recognition (CVPR) (2021)

27. Tancik, M.: Fourier features let networks learn high frequency functions in low dimensional domains. Adv. Neural Info, Processing Systems (2020)

28. Thévenaz, P., Unser, M.: Optimization of mutual information for multiresolution image registration. IEEE Trans. Image Processing 9(12), 2083–2099 (2000)

29. Weber, J., Malik, J.: Robust computation of optical flow in a multi-scale differential framework. Intl. J. Comput. Vision 14(1), 67–81 (1995)

30. Yifan, W., Rahmann, L., Sorkine-Hornung, O.: Geometry-consistent neural shape representation with implicit displacement fields. arXiv preprint arXiv:2106.05187 (2021)

31. Yu, A., Li, R., Tancik, M., Li, H., Ng, R., Kanazawa, A.: Plenoctrees for real-time rendering of neural radiance fields. arXiv preprint arXiv:2103.14024 (2021)

# An Embedded Feature Whitening Approach to Deep Neural Network Optimization

Hongwei Yong and Lei Zhang$^{(\boxtimes)}$

The Hong Kong Polytechnic University, Hong Kong, China
{cshyong,cslzhang}@comp.polyu.edu.hk

**Abstract.** Compared with the feature normalization methods that are widely used in deep neural network (DNN) training, feature whitening methods take the correlation of features into consideration, which can help to learn more effective features. However, existing feature whitening methods have several limitations, such as the large computation and memory cost, inapplicable to pre-trained DNN models, the introduction of additional parameters, etc., making them impractical to use in optimizing DNNs. To overcome these drawbacks, we propose a novel Embedded Feature Whitening (EFW) approach to DNN optimization. EFW only adjusts the gradient of weight by using the whitening matrix without changing any part of the network so that it can be easily adopted to optimize pre-trained and well-defined DNN architectures. The momentum, adaptive dampening and gradient norm recovery techniques associated with EFW are consequently developed to make its implementation efficient with acceptable extra computation and memory cost. We apply EFW to two commonly used DNN optimizers, *i.e.*, SGDM and Adam (or AdamW), and name the obtained optimizers as W-SGDM and W-Adam. Extensive experimental results on various vision tasks, including image classification, object detection, segmentation and person ReID, demonstrate the superiority of W-SGDM and W-Adam to state-of-the-art DNN optimizers. The code are publicly available at https://github.com/Yonghongwei/W-SGDM-and-W-Adam.

**Keywords:** DNN optimization · Feature whitening · Deep learning

## 1 Introduction

The remarkable success of Deep Neural Networks (DNNs) on various vision tasks, including image classification [7], object detection [5,29], segmentation [5], image retrieval [22,46], etc., largely owes to the development of DNN optimization techniques. The main goal of DNN optimization is to find a favorable local minimum

**Supplementary Information** The online version contains supplementary material available at https://doi.org/10.1007/978-3-031-20050-2_20.

of the objective function by using the given training data and ensure good generalization performance of the trained model to testing data. Meanwhile, it is anticipated that we can accelerate the converge speed and reduce the training cost. To achieve these goals, a variety of DNN optimization techniques have been proposed, such as weight initialization strategies [4,6], efficient active functions (*e.g.*, ReLU [25]), batch normalization (BN) [13], gradient clipping [26,27], adaptive learning rate optimizers [3,14,47], and so on. All these techniques facilitate the training of very deep and effective DNN models.

Among the above techniques, normalization methods have been widely used as a basic module to train a variety of DNN architectures [7,9]. The most representative method is BN [13]. Similar to BN, instance normalization (IN) [12,36], layer normalization (LN) [16] and group normalization (GN) [37] have also been proposed to perform Z-score standardization on other dimensions. It has been shown that normalization methods can both speed up the training speed and improve the generalization performance [32,35,41,43]. However, normalization methods do not take the correlation of features into consideration. Therefore, feature whitening or feature decorrelation methods have been developed to solve this problem. For instance, decorrelated batch normalization (DBN) [10] was proposed to perform ZCA-whitening on each mini-batch with a ZCA transformation matrix obtained by eigen-decomposition. IterNorm [11] aims at a more efficient approximation of the ZCA transformation matrix with Newton's iteration. Network deconvolution (ND) [39] extends the ZCA-whitening transformation on a patch of features. The DNN models trained with whitening methods can achieve certain performance gains over normalization methods.

Nevertheless, the existing feature whitening methods have several obvious weaknesses, which make them hard to be widely used in practical applications. The major disadvantage of feature whitening lies in its large computational cost. In each iteration, the ZCA transformation matrix has to be computed by eigen-decomposition, which is computationally expensive when the dimension of features is high. Although some works [11,39] adopt Newton's iteration to speed up the computation of ZCA transformation, the training cost is still unacceptable compared with BN. Meanwhile, the inference time of the network will increase largely when feature whitening is used. Moreover, feature whitening methods are very memory-consuming in training because more intermediate features need to be stored, especially for the iterative whitening methods. Last but not the least, the existing feature whitening methods cannot be directly applied to optimize pre-trained and well-defined DNN models. One needs to add a feature whitening module into the proper layer and redefine the forward propagation. For instance, if we want to adopt the ResNet50 [7] model pre-trained on ImageNet to downstream tasks, we must redefine the ResNet50 with these whitening methods and train it again on ImageNet. All these drawbacks largely limit the practical usage of feature whitening methods in DNN training.

To address these problems, we propose a novel approach, namely Embedded Feature Whitening (EFW), to DNN optimization by adjusting the gradient of weight with the ZCA transformation matrix. There are several advantages of our proposed approach. First, EFW inherits the advantages of feature whitening, *i.e.*, accelerating the training process and improving the generalization performance. Second, compared with existing feature whitening methods, EFW does not introduce any module into the DNN model to be trained. As a result, it can be directly adopted to optimize most of the existing DNN models without increasing the inference time. Third, its computation and memory cost is acceptable because EFW only computes the ZCA transformation matrix once for many iterations (*e.g.*, 500) and it does not store any additional intermediate features. In this paper, we adopt EFW into two widely used DNN optimizers: SGD with momentum (SGDM) [14,28] and Adam (or AdanW) [14,21], and name the obtained optimizers as W-SGDM and W-Adam. Extensive experiments are conducted to validate the effectiveness of EFW on various vision tasks.

**Notation System.** In the following development of this paper, we denote by $W$ the weight matrix, whose dimension is $C_{out} \times C_{in}$ for fully connected layers (FC layers) and $C_{out} \times C_{in} \times k_1 \times k_2$ for convolutional layers (Conv layers), where $C_{in}$ is the number of input channels, $C_{out}$ is the number of output channels, and $k_1, k_2$ are the kernel size of convolutional layers. We denote by $A = [A_n]_{n=1}^N$ and $X = [X_n]_{n=1}^N$ the input and output features of the $N$ samples in one layer. For FC layers, $A \in \mathbb{R}^{C_{out} \times N}$, $X \in \mathbb{R}^{C_{in} \times N}$ and $A = WX$. For Conv layers, $A \in \mathbb{R}^{C_{out} \times h \times w \times N}$, $X \in \mathbb{R}^{C_{in} \times h \times w \times N}$ and $A = W * X$, where $h$ and $w$ are the height and width of a feature map and "$*$" is the convolution operator. Let $\mathcal{L}$ be the objective function, and $\frac{\partial \mathcal{L}}{\partial A}$ and $\frac{\partial \mathcal{L}}{\partial W}$ be its gradients on activation and weight, respectively. $\mathcal{U}_1(\cdot)$ denotes the mode 1 unfold operation of a tensor. For example, for a convolution based weight matrix $W \in \mathbb{R}^{C_{out} \times C_{in} \times k_1 \times k_2}$, $\mathcal{U}_1(W) \in \mathbb{R}^{C_{out} \times C_{in} k_1 k_2}$. $vec(\cdot)$ denotes the vectorization function.

## 2 Related Work

**DNN Optimizers.** The first-order optimization algorithms have been widely adopted in training a DNN. For example, SGD with Momentum (SGDM) [28] makes use of the momentum of gradient to avoid oscillations and strengthen the relevant gradient direction. Adagrad [3] adapts adaptive learning rates to different parameters, performing larger/smaller gradient steps for infrequent/frequent ones. RMSprop and Adadelta [42] use a similar mechanism to Adagrad, and Adam [14] further introduces the momentum of gradient into adaptive learning rate methods. Based on Adam, Adabelief [47] considers the belief of observed gradient to adjust the adaptive learning rates.

For the second-order optimizers, AdaHessian [38] simplifies the Hessian matrix with the diagonal elements through Hessian-free techniques. Similar to AdaHessian, Apollo [23] simplifies the BFGS algorithm with only diagonal elements. Meanwhile, Kronecker Factored Approximation Curvature (KFAC) [24] uses the Kronecker Factor decomposition to approximate the natural gradient layer-wisely. However, in many computer vision tasks, the generalization performance of these second-order methods does not outperform SGDM.

---

**Algorithm 1:** Overview of Batch Feature Whitening

**Input:** Mini-batch input $\boldsymbol{X} \in \mathbb{R}^{C_{out} \times N}$
**Output:** Output $\boldsymbol{Y} \in \mathbb{R}^{C_{out} \times N}$

1 **if** *Training* **then**
2 $\quad$ Centralization: $\hat{\boldsymbol{X}} = \Phi_1(\boldsymbol{X}|\mu_{\mathcal{B}})$, $\mu_{\mathcal{B}} = \frac{1}{N}\boldsymbol{X}\boldsymbol{1}$;
3 $\quad$ Standardization or decorrelation: $\boldsymbol{Y} = \Phi_2(\hat{\boldsymbol{X}}|\Sigma_{\mathcal{B}})$, $\Sigma_{\mathcal{B}} = \frac{1}{N}\hat{\boldsymbol{X}}\hat{\boldsymbol{X}}^T + \epsilon\boldsymbol{I}$;
4 $\quad$ Update the population statistics $\mu$ and $\Sigma$;
5 **else**
6 $\quad$ Calculate output $\boldsymbol{Y} = \Phi_3(\boldsymbol{X}|\mu, \Sigma)$;
7 **end**
8 Recovery Operation $\hat{\boldsymbol{Y}} = \Phi_4(\boldsymbol{Y})$

---

**Feature Whitening.** Feature whitening methods remove the linear correlation among different channel features to perform gradient descent more efficiently. Beyond standardization, DBN [10] was proposed to perform ZCA-whitening by eigen-decomposition and backpropagating the transformation. IterNorm [11] aims at a more efficient approximation of the ZCA-whitening matrix in DBN with Newton's iteration. Network deconvolution (ND) [39] adopts deconvolution filters to remove pixel-wise and channel-wise correlations. It has been shown that feature whitening methods can boost both the optimization and the generalization of DNNs [11,39]. However, they usually need a lot of extra computation and memory, making them impractical in real-world applications.

## 3 Embedded Feature Whitening

### 3.1 Overview of Batch Feature Whitening

We briefly summarize the batch whitening process in Algorithm 1. In training, batch feature whitening [11,39] usually involves two main steps, *i.e.*, centralization $\Phi_1(\boldsymbol{X})$ and decorrelation $\Phi_2(\boldsymbol{X})$, which are defined as follows:

$$\Phi_1(\boldsymbol{X}|\mu) = \boldsymbol{X} - \mu\boldsymbol{1}^T, \ \mu = \frac{1}{N}\boldsymbol{X}\boldsymbol{1},$$
$$\Phi_2(\boldsymbol{X}|\Sigma) = \boldsymbol{T}\boldsymbol{X}, \ \Sigma = \frac{1}{N}\boldsymbol{X}\boldsymbol{X}^T + \epsilon\boldsymbol{I}, \tag{1}$$

where $\boldsymbol{T}$ is the whitening matrix, which is related to $\Sigma$. For different whitening methods, $\boldsymbol{T}$ has different formulations [10,11,33,39]. All the whitening matrices should meet that $\frac{1}{N}\Phi_2(\boldsymbol{X})\Phi_2(\boldsymbol{X})^T = \boldsymbol{I}$. Among those whitening transformations, PCA and ZCA whitening are widely used, whose whitening matrices are $\boldsymbol{T} = \boldsymbol{D}^{-\frac{1}{2}}\boldsymbol{U}^T$ and $\boldsymbol{T} = \boldsymbol{U}\boldsymbol{D}^{-\frac{1}{2}}\boldsymbol{U}^T$, respectively, where $\Sigma = \boldsymbol{U}\boldsymbol{D}\boldsymbol{U}^T$ is the eigen-decomposition of $\Sigma = \boldsymbol{X}\boldsymbol{X}^T/N + \epsilon\boldsymbol{I}$.

In the training step, the batch statistics $\mu_{\mathcal{B}}$ and $\Sigma_{\mathcal{B}}$ are used to perform whitening. Meanwhile, the population statistics $\mu$ and $\Sigma$ are updated by exponential moving average [11,39]. In the inference step, the population statistics are used to replace batch statistics, $i.e.$, $\Phi_3(X|\mu, \Sigma) = \Phi_2(\Phi_1(X|\mu), \Sigma)$. After the whitening operation, an additional recovery operation $\Phi_4(\cdot)$ is used to keep the representation capability of the network. The recovery operation is usually a linear operation, such as affine transformation [11] and coloring operation [33], which introduces extra parameters in training.

During the DNN training process, due to the variation of input feature statistics, the whitening matrix also changes. As a consequence, whitening may change the intermediate features acutely, making the following layers hard to learn. It has been shown that ZCA whitening can avoid such a Stochastic Axis Swapping (SAS) problem, leading to better feature learning performance [10]. Actually, we can show that the solution of the following objective function

$$\min_T ||X - \Phi(X)||_2^2, \quad s.t. \quad \Phi(X) = TX, \quad \frac{1}{N}\Phi(X)\Phi(X)^T = I \quad (2)$$

is $T = (XX^T/N)^{-\frac{1}{2}}$, which is just the ZCA whitening formulation. (The proof can be found in the **supplementary file**). This ensures that the ZCA whitened feature $\Phi(X)$ is close to the original data $X$ and hence dilutes the SAS issue.

### 3.2 Drawbacks of Feature Whitening

Although many works have shown that feature whitening can both speed up training and gain generalization performance, it has some obvious drawbacks that largely limit its applications to DNN training. First, it needs to perform eigen-decomposition or use Newton's iteration to compute the whitening matrix, both of which will significantly increase the computation and memory cost. Second, existing feature whitening methods cannot be directly adopted to optimize pre-trained DNN models ($e.g.$, ImageNet pre-trained models). We have to redefine the forward propagation of DNNs by introducing a whitening module and retrain the models. Third, the batch feature whitening methods are very sensitive to the training batch size. When batch size is small, the statistics will become inaccurate, leading to a large performance drop. Fourth, most of the current whitening methods will introduce additional parameters into the recovery operation step to keep the representation capability of the DNNs, which increases the number of parameters to be optimized.

Due to the above limitations, though having many attractive properties, feature whitening methods have not been widely used to optimize DNNs yet. To overcome the above drawbacks of feature whitening while inheriting its advantages, we should not change the forward propagation of DNN or introduce new modules ($e.g.$, whitening layer) in DNN, and should reduce its extra computation cost. To achieve these goals, we propose a novel approach to embed the feature whitening operation into the optimization algorithms.

### 3.3 Removal of Recovery and Centralization Operations

Most batch whitening methods employ a recovery operation to keep the representation capability of DNNs. Actually, the recovery operation may not be necessary. According to their locations in DNN layers, whitening methods can be divided into pre-whitening and post-whitening ones.

When the whitening layer is placed before the convolutional layer, it is a pre-whitening layer, otherwise, it is a post-whitening layer. Traditional normalization layers and whitening layers usually introduce an additional recovery transformation, such as affine transformation [11] or coloring operation [33], to keep the feature representation performance. When post-whitening is adopted, the recovery transformation must be introduced after the whitening operation to keep the performance.

When pre-whitening is adopted, however, the recovery transformation can be removed without harming the representation power of DNNs, because it can be assimilated by the following Conv layer. For instance, supposing that $W_r * X$ is the recovery transformation (affine and coloring transformation can be viewed as a sparse convolutional operation), where $W_r$ is the extra parameters to be learned, $W * W_r * X$ will be the output feature of Conv layer. We can let $W' = W * W_r$ and hence only optimize the Conv layer with parameter $W'$. This property of pre-whitening inspires us to embed the whitening layer into the optimization algorithm without changing any module of the DNN.

Meanwhile, in the traditional whitening methods, there are two main operations: centralization and decorrelation. In forward propagation, we need to introduce these two operations into the whitening layer before optimization. However, for a well-defined DNN, the mean of input feature to a Conv or FC layer is usually not zero since there is no centralization operation before them. A practical way to achieve feature centralization is to introduce an extra bias that is related to the mean of input activation. However, since the normalization layers are usually located after the Conv layer in many popular DNNs (*e.g.*, ResNet), the bias in the Conv layer will have no function. Moreover, since our goal is to optimize a well-defined DNN without changing its forward propagation and introducing any extra parameters, we omit the centralization operation and only take the decorrelation into consideration.

### 3.4 Formulation of Embedded Feature Whitening

For a FC layer $Y = WX$, where $W$ denotes the parameters to learn, suppose there is a virtual whitening layer before FC layer, which is $\hat{X} = TX$, where $T$ is defined in Eq. (1). We can reformulate this FC layer with a whitening transformation as $Y = W'TX$, where $W'$ is the new parameters to be optimized. In this way, we can optimize the loss function w.r.t. $W'$, and let $W = W'T$ once the training is finished. According to the backpropagation algorithm, the gradient of $W'$ can be easily obtained by $\frac{\partial \mathcal{L}}{\partial W'} = \frac{\partial \mathcal{L}}{\partial W}T$. However, the above approach has several serious problems. First, the whitening matrix $T$ will change during the training process because of the update of weights in the previous layers. As a consequence, the relationship between $W$ and $W'$ is not fixed. Second, in the training process, $T$ will contain a certain amount of noise due to the random batch sampling, so it is hard to get an accurate $T$. Therefore, it is difficult to obtain an accurate $W$ from the optimization of $W'$.

To maintain the benefits of batch feature whitening on optimization, we propose to use a modified gradient $\frac{\partial \mathcal{L}}{\partial W}T$ to replace the original weight gradient $\frac{\partial \mathcal{L}}{\partial W}$, and name the method Embedded Feature Whitening (EFW), which embeds the information of feature whitening into the weight gradient. EFW can be introduced into the FC layer, convolutional layer, and Norm layer. Compared with the weight updating formula of SGD $W^{t+1} = W^t - \eta\frac{\partial \mathcal{L}}{\partial W^t}$, the updating formula of SGD with EFW is

$$W^{t+1} = W^t - \eta\frac{\partial \mathcal{L}}{\partial W^t}T^t. \tag{3}$$

**Table 1.** The updating formulas and whitening matrices of FC, Conv and Norm layers in SGD with the proposed EFW.

| Layer | Updating formula | Whitening matrix |
|---|---|---|
| FC layer | $W^{t+1} = W^t - \eta\frac{\partial \mathcal{L}}{\partial W^t}T^t$ | $T^t = \left(X^t X^{tT}\right)^{-\frac{1}{2}}$ |
| Conv layer | $\mathcal{U}_1(W^{t+1}) = \mathcal{U}_1(W^t) - \eta\mathcal{U}_1(\frac{\partial \mathcal{L}}{\partial W^t})T^t$ | $T^t = \left(\mathfrak{X}^t \mathfrak{X}^{tT}\right)^{-\frac{1}{2}}$ |
| Norm layer | $\begin{bmatrix} \gamma^{t+1} \\ \beta^{t+1} \end{bmatrix} = \begin{bmatrix} \gamma^t \\ \beta^t \end{bmatrix} - \eta T^t \begin{bmatrix} \frac{\partial \mathcal{L}}{\partial \gamma^t} \\ \frac{\partial \mathcal{L}}{\partial \beta^t} \end{bmatrix}$ | $T^t = \left(\begin{bmatrix} vec(X^t)^T \\ \mathbf{1}^T \end{bmatrix}[vec(X^t), \mathbf{1}]\right)^{-\frac{1}{2}}$ |

The detailed updating formulas are summarized in Table 1. We ignore the factor $1/N$ in the second-order statistic because of the gradient norm recovery operation, which will be explained in Sect. 3.5.

For the FC layer, we need to calculate the second-order statistic of input activation, $i.e.$, $X^t X^{tT}$, and the whitening matrix $T^t$, which can be obtained by SVD decomposition of $X^t X^{tT}$. For the Conv layer, the difference from the FC layer lies in that we need to unfold the convolution operation to matrix multiplication first. The convolution operation can be formulated as a matrix multiplication with the $im2col$ operation [39,44], and then the Conv layer can be viewed as an FC layer. The updating formula of weights for the Conv layer is listed in Table 1, where $\mathcal{U}_1(\cdot)$ is the mode 1 unfold operation of a tensor and $\mathfrak{X}$ is the matrix of $X^t$ after $im2col$ operation. The normalization layers usually have a channel-wise affine transformation, which is also a linear operation. Suppose that the normalized features are $X^t$ and the parameters of affine transformation are $\gamma$ and $\beta$ for one channel, we can obtain the updating rules for $\gamma, \beta$ as shown in the bottom row of Table 1. If the mean and variance of $X^t$ are zero and one, the second-order statistics will be a diagonal $2 \times 2$ matrix. For example, when BN [13] and IN [12,36] are used, the update rules for $(\gamma, \beta)$ degrade to the case of SGD. However, for other normalization methods such as GN [37] and LN [16], the mean and variance of each channel may not be zero and one.

In practice, to avoid that the condition number of the statistic matrix $X^t X^{tT}$ is too large, we need to add an additional term $\epsilon I$ to the statistic matrix, where $I$ is an identity matrix and $\epsilon$ is the dampening parameter. We will discuss how to choose a proper $\epsilon$ in the next section.

---

**Algorithm 2:** Algorithm of EFW

---

**Input:** $T_{xx}$, $T_{svd}$, $\alpha$, $M_{xx}^{t-1}$, $T^{t-1}$, $\epsilon$, input activation $X^t$, gradient $\nabla_{W^t}\mathcal{L}$
**Output:** $\widetilde{G}^t$

1   $G^t = \nabla_{W^t}\mathcal{L}$;
2   **if** $t\%T_{xx} = 0$ **then**
3     |   $M_{xx}^t = \alpha M_{xx}^{t-1} + (1-\alpha)X^t X^{t^T}$    % *Momentum step*
4   **else**
5     |   $M_{xx}^t = M_{xx}^{t-1}$
6   **end**
7   **if** $t\%T_{svd} = 0$ **then**
8     |   $UDU^T = M_{xx}^t$          % *SVD decomposition*
9     |   $T^t = U(D + \epsilon d_{max}I)^{-1/2}U^T$    % *Whitening matrix with dampening*
10 **else**
11   |   $T^t = T^{t-1}$
12 **end**
13 $\widehat{G}^t = G^t T^t$              % *Adjust gradient with whitening matrix*
14 $\widetilde{G}^t = \widehat{G}^t \frac{\|G^t\|_2}{\|\widehat{G}^t\|_2}$;        % *Gradient norm recovery*

---

### 3.5   Implementation of EFW

**Momentum.** The estimation of the second-order statistics of $X$ is very important for the whitening methods. The original batch whitening method can only use the current batch statistics for computation, and hence they are very sensitive to the training batch size. When the training batch size is small, the batch statistics will have large noise so that the training will be unstable. In contrast, our proposed EFW method works directly on the final weight updating stage, and it does not change the forward propagation and backward propagation during training. Therefore, EFW can adopt the statistics from more batches to achieve a more accurate estimation of feature statistics. Specifically, we compute the momentum of the batch statistics as follows:

$$M_{xx}^t = \alpha M_{xx}^{t-1} + (1-\alpha)X^t X^{t^T}, \tag{4}$$

where $M_{xx}^t$ is the momentum of statistics $XX^T$ in iteration $t$ and $\alpha$ is the momentum parameter. As an approximation to the population of feature statistics, momentum can significantly reduce the noise caused by random batch sampling.

**Statistics Computation.** Feature whitening methods need to compute the second-order statistics and then compute the whitening matrix for feature learning. The previous batch whitening methods need to perform these computations in each iteration for each batch because the batch statistics and whitening matrix are involved in forward and backward propagations. This however introduces a large amount of computational burden.

Different from the previous batch whitening methods, in our proposed EFW there is no need to compute the second-order statistics and the whitening matrix in each iteration. We only need to compute them once for many iterations. Two hyperparameters, $T_{xx}$ and $T_{svd}$, are introduced to control the interval for updating the statistics matrix and the whitening matrix, respectively. For the whitening matrix, the updating interval should be set larger because its computation involves SVD decomposition, which is more computationally expensive. In our experiments, we set $T_{xx} = 50$ and $T_{svd} = 500$ and we find that they work effectively to improve the DNN optimization performance without introducing much additional computational cost. Meanwhile, we also implement a cross-GPU synchronization method to facilitate the computation of more reliable feature statistics when using multiple GPUs.

**Adaptive Dampening.** The dimension of $M_{xx}^t$ is very high and it is usually a very singular matrix. When the condition number of $M_{xx}^t$ is too large, it will be unstable to compute the inverse square root of it. To avoid such a case, in practice we need to add an additional term $\epsilon I$ to the statistic matrix, where $I$ is an identity matrix and $\epsilon$ is a dampening parameter.

A too-small dampening may not improve the condition number of $M_{xx}^t$, while a too strong dampening may reduce the accuracy of statistics. Therefore, it is important to choose a proper dampening parameter $\epsilon$. For different layers in a DNN, the statistics $M_{xx}^t$ may have different magnitude. Thus, it is improper to use a uniform dampening scheme for all layers. By taking the magnitude of different features into consideration, we choose an adaptive dampening parameter $\epsilon d_{max}$, where $d_{max}$ is the max singular value of $M_{xx}^t$. It is easy to show that the condition number of $M_{xx}^t + \epsilon d_{max} I$ is $\frac{d_{max} + \epsilon d_{max}}{d_{min} + \epsilon d_{max}} < \frac{1+\epsilon}{\epsilon}$. In practice, we can first compute the SVD decomposition of $M_{xx}^t$, i.e., $UDU^T = M_{xx}^t$, and then obtain the whitening matrix by $T^t = U(D + \epsilon d_{max} I)^{-1/2} U^T$. The computation cost of adaptive dampening is the same as fixed dampening.

**Gradient Norm Recovery.** SGDM and Adam are among the most commonly used optimizers in training DNNs. Their hyperparameters, including learning rate and weight decay, have been well-tuned by researchers on many specific tasks. For example, in objection detection, SGDM with a learning rate 0.02 and weight decay 0.0001 is widely adopted. A natural question is can we hold these well-tuned hyperparameters in the proposed method to ease the tedious work of hyperparameter tuning? If this can be done, EFW can be easily used for solving various vision tasks without further hyperparameter tuning.

In the proposed EFW, the scale of adjusted gradient $\hat{G}^t = G^t T^t$ might be changed. This implies that the optimal setting of hyperparameters should be changed for the adopted optimizer, limiting the application of the proposed method. Fortunately, this problem of gradient scale changing can be easily addressed by recovering the gradient norm, which is

$$\tilde{G}^t = \hat{G}^t \frac{||G^t||_2}{||\hat{G}^t||_2}, \tag{5}$$

It is easy to see that $\tilde{G}^t$ and $G^t$ have the same $L_2$ norm. With the gradient norm recovery operation, $\tilde{G}^t$ can be readily used in the employed optimizers (*e.g.*, SGDM and Adam) to achieve favorable performance without additional hyperparameter tuning. Of course, one may further improve the performance by tuning fine-grained hyperparameters around their default settings.

**Algorithm of EFW.** The complexity of EFW is $T(O(\frac{C_{in}^3}{T_{svd}}) + O(\frac{C_{in}^2 N}{T_{xx}}) + O(C_{in}^2 C_{out}))$ for a FC layer, and $T(O(\frac{C_{in}^3 k_1^3 k_2^3}{T_{svd}}) + O(\frac{C_{in}^2 k_1^2 k_2^2 N}{T_{xx}}) + O(C_{in}^2 k_1^2 k_2^2 C_{out}))$ for a Conv layer, where $T$ is the total number of iterations. Since $T_{xx}$ and $T_{svd}$ can be set as large numbers in our implementation (50 and 500, respectively), the complexity is acceptable. The algorithm of EFW is summarized in Algorithm 2. In the experiments, we apply EFW to the two commonly used DNN optimizers, *i.e.*, SGDM and Adam (or AdamW), and name the obtained new optimizers as W-SGDM and W-Adam accordingly. We found that EFW only introduces 10%–20% extra memory consumption in our experiments.

**Table 2.** Testing accuracies (%) on CIFAR100/CIFAR10. The best and second best results are highlighted in bold and italic fonts, respectively. The numbers in red color indicate the improvement of W-SGDM/W-Adam over SGDM/AdamW, respectively. "-" means that the result is not available due to the problem of "out of memory".

| | | | | | CIFAR100 | | | | |
|---|---|---|---|---|---|---|---|---|---|
| Model | SGDM | AdamW [21] | RAdam [19] | Ranger | Adabelief [47] | AdaHessian [38] | Apollo [23] | W-SGDM | W-Adam |
| R18 | 77.20±.30 | 77.23±.10 | 77.05±.15 | 76.75±.11 | 77.43±.36 | 76.73±.23 | 77.65±.11 | **79.28±.27** (↑2.08) | 78.75±.16 (↑1.52) |
| R50 | 77.78±.43 | 78.10±.17 | 78.20±.15 | 78.13±.12 | 79.08±.23 | 78.48±.22 | 79.25±.26 | **80.90±.23** (↑3.12) | *80.15±.22* (↑2.05) |
| V11 | 70.80±.29 | 71.20±.29 | 71.08±.24 | 70.58±.14 | 72.43±.16 | 67.78±.34 | 72.35±.33 | **73.42±.28** (↑2.62) | 72.92±.14 (↑1.72) |
| D121 | 79.53±.19 | 78.05±.26 | 78.65±.05 | 78.28±.08 | 79.88±.08 | - | 79.83±.16 | **81.23±.10** (↑1.70) | *80.10±.25* (↑2.05) |
| MobileNet | 68.03±.37 | 70.07±.19 | 69.55±.32 | 69.35±.15 | *71.40±.12* | 69.45±.30 | 70.75±.22 | 70.35±.21 (↑2.32) | **71.92±.16** (↑1.85) |
| | | | | | CIFAR10 | | | | |
| R18 | 95.10±.07 | 94.80±.10 | 94.70±.18 | 94.75±.18 | 95.12±.14 | 94.70±.15 | 95.20±.12 | **95.43±.08** (↑0.33) | *95.20±.10*(↑0.40) |
| R50 | 94.75±.30 | 94.72±.10 | 94.72±.10 | 95.27±.12 | 95.35±.05 | 95.35±.11 | 95.37±.10 | **95.80±.15** (↑1.05) | *95.70±.07*(↑0.98) |
| V11 | 92.17±.19 | 92.02±.08 | 92.00±.18 | 92.10±.07 | 92.45±.18 | 91.85±.16 | 92.58±.04 | **92.95±.20** (↑0.78) | *92.88±.19*(↑0.86) |
| D121 | 95.37±.17 | 94.80±.07 | 95.02±.08 | 95.45±.11 | 95.37±.04 | - | 95.23±.10 | **95.72±.14** (↑0.35) | *95.47±.12*(↑0.67) |
| MobileNet | 90.90±.14 | 92.08±.10 | 92.08±.25 | 92.05±.08 | *92.33±.19* | 91.25±.12 | 92.03±16 | 91.30±.12(↑0.40) | **92.45±.18**(↑0.37) |

## 4 Experiment Results

### 4.1 Experiment Setup

We evaluate the proposed W-SGDM and W-Adam on various vision tasks, including image classification (on CIFAR100/CIFAR10 [15] and ImageNet [31]), object detection and segmentation (on COCO [18]), and Person Re-identification (Person ReID, on Market1501 [46] and DukeMTMC-ReID [30]). The compared methods include the representative and state-of-the-art DNN optimizers, including SGDM, AdamW [21], RAdam [19], Ranger [19,40,45] and Adabelief [47], AdaHessian[1] [38] and Apollo [23]. For the competing methods, we use the default

---

[1] Since AdaHessian is very memory expensive, we can only give partial results in the following experiments.

settings for most of their hyper-parameters, and tune their learning rates and weight decays to report their best results.

We first testify W-SGDM and W-Adam with different DNN models on CIFAR100/CIFAR10, including VGG11 [34], ResNet18, ResNet50 [7], DenseNet-121 [9] and MobileNet [8]. Then we perform experiments on ImageNet to validate their performance on the large-scale datasets. After that, we test W-SGDM on COCO for detection and segmentation, and test W-Adam on Market1501 [46] and DukeMTMC-ReID for Person ReID to demonstrate that EFW can be easily adopted to finetune pre-trained models. All experiments are conducted under the Pytorch 1.7 framework with NVIDIA GeForce RTX 2080Ti and eight 3090Ti GPUs. For the hyper-parameters of EFW, we set $\alpha = 0.95$, $T_{xx} = 50$ and $T_{svd} = 500$, $\epsilon = 0.001$ throughout the experiments if not specified. Ablation studies on hyperparameter selection are also provided.

## 4.2  Image Classification

**Results on CIFAR100 and CIFAR10:** CIFAR100 and CIFAR10 [15] are two popular datasets to testify DNN optimizers. They include 50K training images and 10K testing images from 100 categories and 10 categories, respectively, and the resolution of the input image is $32 \times 32$. We conduct experiments on these two relatively small-scale datasets to illustrate the effectiveness of W-SGDM and W-Adam with different DNN backbone models, including VGG11 (V11), ResNet18 (R18), ResNet50 (R50), DenseNet121 (D121) and MobileNet[2]. All the DNN models are trained for 200 epochs with batch size 128 on one 2080Ti GPU. The learning rate is multiplied by 0.1 for every 60 epochs. We tune the learning rate in $\{1e^{-4}, 5e^{-4}, 1e^{-3}, 5e^{-3}, 1e^{-2}, 5e^{-2}, 0.1, 0.15\}$ and weight decay in $\{1e^{-4}, 5e^{-4}, 1e^{-3}, 5e^{-3}, 1e^{-2}, 5e^{-2}, 0.1, 0.5, 1\}$, and choose the best combination of them for all methods. The detailed settings can be found in the **supplementary material**. We use the default settings for other hyperparameters.

The experiments are repeated 4 times and the results are reported in Table 2 in mean ± std format. We can see that W-SGDM and W-Adam achieve the best and second-best testing accuracies for all the used DNN models. More specifically, W-SGDM improves SGDM from 1.7% to 3.12% on CIFAR100, and from 0.33% to 1.05% on CIFAR10, while W-Adam improves AdamW from 1.52% to 2.05% on CIFAR100, and from 0.37% to 0.98% on CIFAR10. Among the adaptive learning rate methods, Adam, AdamW, RAdam and Ranger perform worse than SGDM. Only Adabelief outperforms SGDM but it is still much worse than W-SGDM and W-Adam. It can be seen that W-SGDM and W-Adam significantly surpass other optimizers in generalization performance, validating the effectiveness of our proposed EFW scheme.

**Results on ImageNet:** We then evaluate W-SGDM and W-Adam on the large-scale image classification dataset ImageNet [31], which consists of 1.28 million

---

[2] These models for CIFAR100/10 can be downloaded at the repository https://github. com/weiaicunzai/pytorch-cifar100.

**Table 3.** Top 1 accuracy (%) on the validation set of ImageNet. The numbers in red color indicate the improvement of W-SGDM/W-Adam over SGDM/AdamW, respectively. "-" means that the result is not available due to the problem of "out of memory".

| Model | SGDM | AdamW [21] | RAdam [19] | Ranger | Adabelief [47] | AdaHessian [38] | Apollo [23] | W-SGDM | W-Adam |
|-------|------|-----------|-----------|--------|---------------|----------------|------------|--------|--------|
| R18 | 70.47 | 70.01 | 69.92 | 69.35 | 70.08 | 70.08 | 70.39 | 71.43(↑0.96) | **71.59**(↑1.58) |
| R50 | 76.31 | 76.02 | 76.12 | 75.95 | 76.22 | - | 76.32 | **77.48**(↑1.17) | 76.83(↑0.81) |

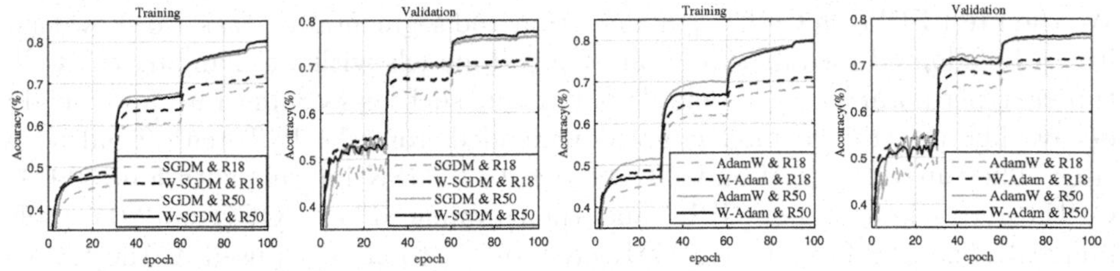

**Fig. 1.** Training and validation accuracy curves of SGDM, W-SGDM, AdamW and W-Adam on ImageNet with ResNet18 and ResNet50.

training images and 50K validation images from 1000 categories. ResNet18 and ResNet50 are employed as the backbone models with training batch size 256 on four 2080Ti GPUs. The standard settings in [1] are used, where the models are trained for 100 epochs. We refer to the strategies in [47] to set the learning rate and weight decay. The detailed settings for different optimizers can be found in the **supplementary material**. The top 1 accuracies of competing optimizers on the validation set are reported in Table 3. We can see that W-SGDM and W-Adam are the top 2 performers. Specifically, W-SGDM outperforms SGDM by 0.96% and 1.17%, and W-Adam outperforms AdamW by 1.58% and 0.81% for ResNet18 and ResNet50, respectively. The training and validation accuracy curves of SGDM vs. W-SGDM and AdamW vs. W-Adam are plotted in Fig. 1. For ResNet18, the learning rate and weight decays of W-SGDM and W-Adam are the same as SGDM and AdamW, respectively. While for ResNet50, the weight decays of W-SGDM and W-Adam are set larger than SGDM and AdamW. It can

**Table 4.** Detection results of Faster-RCNN on COCO. $\Delta$ means the gain of W-SGDM over SGDM.

| Backbone | Algorithm | AP | AP.5 | AP.75 | APs | APm | APl |
|----------|-----------|-----|------|-------|-----|-----|-----|
| R50 | SGDM | 37.4 | 58.1 | 40.4 | 21.2 | 41.0 | 48.1 |
|  | W-SGDM | 39.4 | 60.6 | 43.1 | 23.1 | 42.9 | 50.7 |
|  | $\Delta$ | ↑2.0 | ↑2.5 | ↑2.7 | ↑1.9 | ↑1.9 | ↑2.6 |
| R101 | SGDM | 39.4 | 60.1 | 43.1 | 22.4 | 43.7 | 51.1 |
|  | W-SGDM | 41.1 | 61.6 | 45.1 | 24.0 | 45.2 | 54.3 |
|  | $\Delta$ | ↑1.7 | ↑1.5 | ↑2.0 | ↑1.6 | ↑1.5 | ↑3.2 |

**Table 5.** Detection and segmentation results of Mask-RCNN on COCO. $\Delta$ means the gain of W-SGDM over SGDM.

| Backbone | Algorithm | $AP^b$ | $AP^b_{.5}$ | $AP^b_{.75}$ | $AP^m$ | $AP^m_{.5}$ | $AP^m_{.75}$ |
|----------|-----------|--------|-------------|--------------|--------|-------------|--------------|
| R50 | SGDM | 38.2 | 58.8 | 41.4 | 34.7 | 55.7 | 37.2 |
|  | W-SGDM | 39.8 | 60.8 | 43.4 | 36.4 | 57.6 | 38.9 |
|  | $\Delta$ | ↑1.6 | ↑2.0 | ↑2.0 | ↑1.7 | ↑1.9 | ↑1.7 |
| R101 | SGDM | 40.0 | 60.5 | 44.0 | 36.1 | 57.5 | 38.6 |
|  | W-SGDM | 41.7 | 62.5 | 45.5 | 37.9 | 59.4 | 40.8 |
|  | $\Delta$ | ↑1.7 | ↑2.0 | ↑1.5 | ↑1.8 | ↑1.9 | ↑2.2 |
| Swin-T | AdamW | 42.7 | 65.2 | 46.8 | 39.3 | 62.2 | 42.2 |
|  | W-Adam | 43.4 | 65.7 | 47.5 | 40.1 | 63.0 | 43.2 |
|  | $\Delta$ | ↑0.7 | ↑0.5 | ↑0.7 | ↑0.8 | ↑0.8 | ↑1.0 |

be seen that W-SGDM and W-Adam achieve both higher training accuracy and validation accuracy than SGDM and AdamW. This indicates that EFW can not only boost the generalization performance but also speed up the training process of DNN models on large-scale datasets.

### 4.3   Object Detection and Segmentation

We then test EFW on COCO [18] detection and segmentation tasks to show that it can be adopted for fine-tuning pre-trained models without changing the well-tuned hyper-parameters of default optimizer, such as learning rate and weight decay. The pre-trained models are downloaded from the PyTorch official websites. They are fine-tuned on COCO $train2017$ (118K images) with four 3090Ti GPUs and 4 images per GPU, and then evaluated on COCO $val2017$ (40K images). The latest version of MMDetection [2] toolbox[3] is used as the framework. We adopt the official implementations and settings for all experiments here. The backbone networks include ResNet50 (R50), ResNet101 (R101) and Swin-T vision transformer [20]. The Feature Pyramid Network (FPN) [17] is also used. The learning rate schedule is 1X for both Faster-RCNN [29] and Mask-RCNN [5].

As we discussed in Sect. 3.5, with the gradient norm recovery operation in EFW, we can directly adopt the hyperparameters of SGDM into W-SGDM, and the hyperparameters of AdamW into W-Adam. Table 4 lists the Average Precision (AP) of object detection by Faster-RCNN. One can see that the models trained by W-SGDM achieve a clear performance boost of 2.0% for ResNet50 and 1.7% for ResNet101. Table 5 reports the $AP^b$ of detection and $AP^m$ of segmentation by Mask-RCNN. W-SGDM gains $AP^b$ by 1.6% and 1.7% on object detection and 1.7% and 1.8% on segmentation for ResNet50 and ResNet101, respectively. W-Adam achieves 0.7% $AP^b$ gain and 0.8% $AP^m$ gain on Swin-T backbone, showing that EFW can work well on the self-attention layer and transformer backbones. Figure 2 shows the training loss curves of Faster-RCNN and Mask-RCNN with ResNet50 backbone. One can see that W-SGDM accelerates the training process and achieves a more favorable local minimum than SGDM. This experiment clearly validates that EFW can be readily embedded into existing optimizers without extra hyper-parameter tuning.

### 4.4   Person Re-identification

We then use two widely used Person ReID benchmarks, Market1501 [46] and DukeMTMC-ReID [30], to show that W-Adam can also be easily adopted into pre-trained models without extra hyperparameter tuning. In this task, the Adam with $L_2$ regularization weight decay usually outperforms other optimizers and its hyperparameters have been well-tuned. The person ReID baselines in [22] are used[4]. The default hyperparameters of Adam, such as learning rate and weight

---

[3] https://github.com/open-mmlab/mmdetection.
[4] https://github.com/michuanhaohao/reid-strong-baseline.

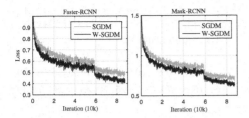

**Fig. 2.** Training loss curves on COCO by ResNet50.

**Table 6.** Rank1(%) and mAP(%) on Market1501 and DukeMTMC-reID. $\Delta$ means the gain of W-Adam over Adam.

| Dataset | | Market1501 | | DukeMTMC | |
|---|---|---|---|---|---|
| Backbone | Algorithm | Rank1 | mAP | Rank1 | mAP |
| R18 | Adam | 91.7 | 77.8 | 82.5 | 68.8 |
| | W-Adam | 91.8 | 79.2 | 83.5 | 70.4 |
| | $\Delta$ | ↑0.1 | ↑1.4 | ↑1.0 | ↑1.6 |
| R50 | Adam | 94.5 | 85.9 | 86.4 | 76.4 |
| | W-Adam | 94.5 | 86.5 | 87.5 | 77.2 |
| | $\Delta$ | ↑0.0 | ↑0.6 | ↑1.1 | ↑0.8 |
| R101 | Adam | 94.5 | 87.1 | 87.6 | 77.6 |
| | W-Adam | 95.0 | 87.9 | 88.2 | 78.3 |
| | $\Delta$ | ↑0.5 | ↑0.8 | ↑0.6 | ↑0.7 |

decay, are directly applied to W-Adam. The experiments are repeated 4 times, and the average results are reported. Table 6 shows the Rank1 and mAP on Market1501 and DukeMTMC-ReID with ResNet18, ResNet50 and ResNet101 backbones. It is clear that W-Adam outperforms Adam, especially in mAP. This experiment again demonstrates the advantages of EFW as a general DNN optimization technique.

### 4.5 Ablation Study

**Hyper-Parameter Tuning:** We first tune the dampening parameter $\epsilon$ and momentum parameter $\alpha$. A too small $\epsilon$ cannot improve the condition number of the statistic matrix, while a too large $\epsilon$ will suppress the useful information in the second order statistics. The results of ResNet18 trained by W-SGDM on CIFAR100 with different $\epsilon$ and $\alpha$ are shown in Table 7 and Table 8. We choose the settings with $\epsilon = 1e^{-3}$ and $\alpha = 0.95$ as our default settings. We then tune $T_{xx}$ and $T_{svd}$ to balance the performance and efficiency. Because of the high computational cost of SVD decomposition, $T_{svd}$ should be set larger than $T_{xx}$. We test six combinations of $T_{xx}$ and $T_{svd}$, and report their testing accuracies and training time per epoch (sec/epoch) in Table 9. The baseline methods are SGDM and AdamW. We can see that EFW costs less than 30% additional training time over the original SGDM/AdamW but achieves convincing performance gain over them. The combination of $T_{xx} = 50$ and $T_{svd} = 500$ can balance the performance and efficiency well, and it is chosen as our default setting.

**Training Efficiency:** We further compare EFW with another two representative whitening methods, *i.e.*, ND [39] and IterNorm [11], with the SGDM optimizer. ND and IterNorm need to redefine the forward propagation of DNN models by replacing the normalization layers with whitening layers. Table 10 shows the testing accuracy (%) and training efficiency (sec/epoch) of different whitening methods on CIFAR100/CIFAR10. One can see that the proposed W-SGDM clearly outperforms ND and IterNorm in both accuracy and efficiency.

**Table 7.** Testing accuracies (%) of ResNet18 by W-SGDM on CIFAR100 w.r.t. dampening $\epsilon$.

| $\epsilon$ | $1e^{-4}$ | $5e^{-4}$ | $\mathbf{1e^{-3}}$ | $5e^{-3}$ | $1e^{-2}$ |
|---|---|---|---|---|---|
| Acc | 79.05 | 79.18 | **79.28** | 79.12 | 78.88 |

**Table 8.** Testing accuracy (%) of ResNet18 by W-SGDM on CIFAR100 w.r.t. momentum $\alpha$.

| $\alpha$ | 0.5 | 0.8 | 0.9 | **0.95** | 0.99 | 0.999 |
|---|---|---|---|---|---|---|
| Acc | 79.08 | 79.15 | 79.25 | **79.28** | 78.88 | 78.50 |

**Table 9.** Testing accuracy (%) and training efficiency of ResNet18 by W-SGDM and W-Adam on CIFAR100 w.r.t. $T_{xx}$ and $T_{svd}$.

| Algorithm | $T_{xx}$ | 5 | 10 | 20 | **50** | 100 | 200 | baseline |
|---|---|---|---|---|---|---|---|---|
|  | $T_{svd}$ | 50 | 100 | 200 | **500** | 1000 | 2000 |  |
| W-SGDM | Acc | 79.40 | 79.33 | 79.23 | **79.28** | 79.11 | 79.02 | 77.20 |
|  | Sec/epoch | 85.50 | 58.32 | 38.93 | **29.78** | 26.03 | 24.25 | 23.45 |
| W-Adam | Acc | 78.84 | 78.79 | 78.76 | **78.75** | 78.67 | 78.40 | 77.23 |
|  | Sec/epoch | 90.17 | 60.1 | 40.9 | **30.18** | 27.14 | 25.55 | 24.21 |

**Table 10.** Testing accuracy (%) and training efficiency of whitening methods on CIFAR100/CIFAR10.

| Method | Dataset | CIFAR100 | | | CIFAR10 | | |
|---|---|---|---|---|---|---|---|
|  | Model | R18 | R50 | V11 | R18 | R50 | V11 |
| SGDM-IterNorm | Acc | 77.15 | 79.65 | 72.30 | 95.30 | 95.52 | 92.45 |
|  | sec/epoch | 109.27 | 388.08 | 98.85 | 103.12 | 367.73 | 96.49 |
| SGDM-ND | Acc | 78.65 | 80.20 | 72.70 | 95.37 | 95.73 | 93.03 |
|  | sec/epoch | 65.37 | 218.34 | 32.18 | 64.12 | 213.45 | 30.39 |
| W-SGDM | Acc | 79.28 | 80.90 | 73.42 | 95.43 | 95.80 | 92.95 |
|  | sec/epoch | 29.78 | 95.05 | 13.98 | 29.02 | 92.12 | 13.51 |

ND and IterNorm cost more than two times the training time of EFW. Clearly, EFW is much more efficient to perform feature whitening and achieves a more favorable performance boost than conventional whitening methods. It overcomes the major drawbacks of whitening methods and inherits their advantages.

## 5 Conclusion

In this work, we proposed a novel DNN optimization technique, namely Embedded Feature Whitening (EFW), to address the drawbacks of conventional feature whitening methods, such as large computation cost, extra parameter introduction, inapplicable to pre-trained DNN models, and so on. Different from the existing feature whitening methods, which usually perform a whitening operation on features during forward propagation, EFW only adjusts the gradient of weight with the whitening matrix without changing the forward and backward propagation processes of DNN model training. Meanwhile, we developed the associated momentum, statistics matrix computation, adaptive dampening and gradient norm recovery techniques to make EFW effective and efficient to use. By adopting EFW to the popular SGDM and Adam optimizers, the resulting W-SGDM and W-Adam methods demonstrated their superiority to other leading DNN optimizers in various vision tasks with acceptable extra computation, including image classification, detection, segmentation and person ReID.

# References

1. Chen, J., Zhou, D., Tang, Y., Yang, Z., Cao, Y., Gu, Q.: Closing the generalization gap of adaptive gradient methods in training deep neural networks. arXiv preprint arXiv:1806.06763 (2018)
2. Chen, K., et al.: MMDetection: open MMLab detection toolbox and benchmark. arXiv preprint arXiv:1906.07155 (2019)
3. Duchi, J., Hazan, E., Singer, Y.: Adaptive subgradient methods for online learning and stochastic optimization. J. Mach. Learn. Res. 12(Jul), 2121–2159 (2011)
4. Glorot, X., Bengio, Y.: Understanding the difficulty of training deep feedforward neural networks. In: Proceedings of the Thirteenth International Conference on Artificial Intelligence and Statistics, pp. 249–256 (2010)
5. He, K., Gkioxari, G., Dollár, P., Girshick, R.: Mask R-CNN. In: Proceedings of the IEEE International Conference on Computer Vision, pp. 2961–2969 (2017)
6. He, K., Zhang, X., Ren, S., Sun, J.: Delving deep into rectifiers: surpassing human-level performance on imagenet classification. In: Proceedings of the IEEE International Conference on Computer Vision, pp. 1026–1034 (2015)
7. He, K., Zhang, X., Ren, S., Sun, J.: Deep residual learning for image recognition. In: Proceedings of the IEEE Conference on Computer Vision and Pattern Recognition, pp. 770–778 (2016)
8. Howard, A.G., et al.: Mobilenets: efficient convolutional neural networks for mobile vision applications. arXiv preprint arXiv:1704.04861 (2017)
9. Huang, G., Liu, Z., Van Der Maaten, L., Weinberger, K.Q.: Densely connected convolutional networks. In: Proceedings of the IEEE Conference on Computer Vision and Pattern Recognition, pp. 4700–4708 (2017)
10. Huang, L., Yang, D., Lang, B., Deng, J.: Decorrelated batch normalization. In: Proceedings of the IEEE Conference on Computer Vision and Pattern Recognition, pp. 791–800 (2018)
11. Huang, L., Zhou, Y., Zhu, F., Liu, L., Shao, L.: Iterative normalization: beyond standardization towards efficient whitening. In: Proceedings of the IEEE/CVF Conference on Computer Vision and Pattern Recognition, pp. 4874–4883 (2019)
12. Huang, X., Belongie, S.: Arbitrary style transfer in real-time with adaptive instance normalization. In: Proceedings of the IEEE International Conference on Computer Vision, pp. 1501–1510 (2017)
13. Ioffe, S., Szegedy, C.: Batch normalization: accelerating deep network training by reducing internal covariate shift. arXiv preprint arXiv:1502.03167 (2015)
14. Kingma, D.P., Ba, J.: Adam: a method for stochastic optimization. arXiv preprint arXiv:1412.6980 (2014)
15. Krizhevsky, A., Hinton, G.: Learning multiple layers of features from tiny images. Technical report, Citeseer (2009)
16. Lei Ba, J., Kiros, J.R., Hinton, G.E.: Layer normalization. arXiv preprint arXiv:1607.06450 (2016)
17. Lin, T.Y., Dollár, P., Girshick, R., He, K., Hariharan, B., Belongie, S.: Feature pyramid networks for object detection. In: Proceedings of the IEEE Conference on Computer Vision and Pattern Recognition, pp. 2117–2125 (2017)
18. Lin, T.-Y., et al.: Microsoft COCO: common objects in context. In: Fleet, D., Pajdla, T., Schiele, B., Tuytelaars, T. (eds.) ECCV 2014. LNCS, vol. 8693, pp. 740–755. Springer, Cham (2014). https://doi.org/10.1007/978-3-319-10602-1_48
19. Liu, L., et al.: On the variance of the adaptive learning rate and beyond. arXiv preprint arXiv:1908.03265 (2019)

20. Liu, Z., et al.: Swin transformer: hierarchical vision transformer using shifted windows. In: Proceedings of the IEEE/CVF International Conference on Computer Vision, pp. 10012–10022 (2021)
21. Loshchilov, I., Hutter, F.: Decoupled weight decay regularization. arXiv preprint arXiv:1711.05101 (2017)
22. Luo, H., Gu, Y., Liao, X., Lai, S., Jiang, W.: Bag of tricks and a strong baseline for deep person re-identification. In: Proceedings of the IEEE/CVF Conference on Computer Vision and Pattern Recognition Workshops (2019)
23. Ma, X.: Apollo: an adaptive parameter-wise diagonal quasi-newton method for nonconvex stochastic optimization. arXiv preprint arXiv:2009.13586 (2020)
24. Martens, J., Grosse, R.: Optimizing neural networks with kronecker-factored approximate curvature. In: International Conference on Machine Learning, pp. 2408–2417. PMLR (2015)
25. Nair, V., Hinton, G.E.: Rectified linear units improve restricted boltzmann machines. In: Proceedings of the 27th International Conference on Machine Learning (ICML 2010), pp. 807–814 (2010)
26. Pascanu, R., Mikolov, T., Bengio, Y.: Understanding the exploding gradient problem. CoRR, abs/1211.5063, vol. 2 (2012)
27. Pascanu, R., Mikolov, T., Bengio, Y.: On the difficulty of training recurrent neural networks. In: International Conference on Machine Learning, pp. 1310–1318 (2013)
28. Qian, N.: On the momentum term in gradient descent learning algorithms. Neural Netw. 12(1), 145–151 (1999)
29. Ren, S., He, K., Girshick, R., Sun, J.: Faster R-CNN: towards real-time object detection with region proposal networks. In: Advances in Neural Information Processing Systems, pp. 91–99 (2015)
30. Ristani, E., Solera, F., Zou, R., Cucchiara, R., Tomasi, C.: Performance measures and a data set for multi-target, multi-camera tracking. In: Hua, G., Jégou, H. (eds.) ECCV 2016. LNCS, vol. 9914, pp. 17–35. Springer, Cham (2016). https://doi.org/10.1007/978-3-319-48881-3_2
31. Russakovsky, O., et al.: Imagenet large scale visual recognition challenge. Int. J. Comput. Vision 115(3), 211–252 (2015)
32. Santurkar, S., Tsipras, D., Ilyas, A., Madry, A.: How does batch normalization help optimization? In: Advances in Neural Information Processing Systems, vol. 31 (2018)
33. Siarohin, A., Sangineto, E., Sebe, N.: Whitening and coloring batch transform for gans. arXiv preprint arXiv:1806.00420 (2018)
34. Simonyan, K., Zisserman, A.: Very deep convolutional networks for large-scale image recognition. arXiv preprint arXiv:1409.1556 (2014)
35. Teye, M., Azizpour, H., Smith, K.: Bayesian uncertainty estimation for batch normalized deep networks. arXiv preprint arXiv:1802.06455 (2018)
36. Ulyanov, D., Vedaldi, A., Lempitsky, V.: Instance normalization: the missing ingredient for fast stylization. arXiv preprint arXiv:1607.08022 (2016)
37. Wu, Y., He, K.: Group normalization. In: Ferrari, V., Hebert, M., Sminchisescu, C., Weiss, Y. (eds.) ECCV 2018. LNCS, vol. 11217, pp. 3–19. Springer, Cham (2018). https://doi.org/10.1007/978-3-030-01261-8_1
38. Yao, Z., Gholami, A., Shen, S., Mustafa, M., Keutzer, K., Mahoney, M.W.: Adahessian: an adaptive second order optimizer for machine learning. arXiv preprint arXiv:2006.00719 (2020)
39. Ye, C., et al.: Network deconvolution. arXiv preprint arXiv:1905.11926 (2019)

40. Yong, H., Huang, J., Hua, X., Zhang, L.: Gradient centralization: a new optimization technique for deep neural networks. In: Vedaldi, A., Bischof, H., Brox, T., Frahm, J.-M. (eds.) ECCV 2020. LNCS, vol. 12346, pp. 635–652. Springer, Cham (2020). https://doi.org/10.1007/978-3-030-58452-8_37

41. Yong, H., Huang, J., Meng, D., Hua, X., Zhang, L.: Momentum batch normalization for deep learning with small batch size. In: Vedaldi, A., Bischof, H., Brox, T., Frahm, J.-M. (eds.) ECCV 2020. LNCS, vol. 12357, pp. 224–240. Springer, Cham (2020). https://doi.org/10.1007/978-3-030-58610-2_14

42. Zeiler, M.D.: Adadelta: an adaptive learning rate method. arXiv preprint arXiv:1212.5701 (2012)

43. Zhang, C., Bengio, S., Hardt, M., Recht, B., Vinyals, O.: Understanding deep learning requires rethinking generalization. arXiv preprint arXiv:1611.03530 (2016)

44. Zhang, H., Chen, W., Liu, T.Y.: Train feedfoward neural network with layer-wise adaptive rate via approximating back-matching propagation. arXiv preprint arXiv:1802.09750 (2018)

45. Zhang, M.R., Lucas, J., Hinton, G., Ba, J.: Lookahead optimizer: k steps forward, 1 step back. arXiv preprint arXiv:1907.08610 (2019)

46. Zheng, L., Shen, L., Tian, L., Wang, S., Wang, J., Tian, Q.: Scalable person re-identification: a benchmark. In: Proceedings of the IEEE International Conference on Computer Vision, pp. 1116–1124 (2015)

47. Zhuang, J., et al.: Adabelief optimizer: adapting stepsizes by the belief in observed gradients. arXiv preprint arXiv:2010.07468 (2020)

# Q-FW: A Hybrid Classical-Quantum Frank-Wolfe for Quadratic Binary Optimization

Alp Yurtsever[1], Tolga Birdal[2], and Vladislav Golyanik[3](✉)

[1] Umeå University, Umeå, Sweden
[2] Imperial College London, London, UK
[3] MPI Saarbrücken, Saarbrücken, Germany
golyanik@mpi-inf.mpg.de

**Abstract.** We present a hybrid classical-quantum framework based on the Frank-Wolfe algorithm, Q-FW, for solving quadratic, linearly-constrained, binary optimization problems on quantum annealers (QA). The computational premise of quantum computers has cultivated the re-design of various existing vision problems into quantum-friendly forms. Experimental QA realisations can solve a particular non-convex problem known as the quadratic unconstrained binary optimization (QUBO). Yet a naive-QUBO cannot take into account the restrictions on the parameters. To introduce additional structure in the parameter space, researchers have crafted ad-hoc solutions incorporating (linear) constraints in the form of regularizers. However, this comes at the expense of a hyper-parameter, balancing the impact of regularization. To date, a true constrained solver of quadratic binary optimization (QBO) problems has lacked. Q-FW first reformulates constrained-QBO as a copositive program (CP), then employs Frank-Wolfe iterations to solve CP while satisfying linear (in)equality constraints. This procedure unrolls the original constrained-QBO into a set of unconstrained QUBOs all of which are solved, in a sequel, on a QA. We use D-Wave Advantage QA to conduct synthetic and real experiments on two important computer vision problems, graph matching and permutation synchronization, which demonstrate that our approach is effective in alleviating the need for an explicit regularization coefficient.

## 1   Introduction

Combinatorial optimization is at the heart of computer vision (CV). In a variety of applications such as structure-from-motion (SfM) [66], SLAM [56], 3D reconstruction [21], camera re-localization [65], image retrieval [51] and 3D scan stitching [24,40], correspondences serve as a powerful proxy to visual perception. In many problems, correspondences are defined over two or multiple point

**Supplementary Information** The online version contains supplementary material available at https://doi.org/10.1007/978-3-031-20050-2_21.

sets and can be encoded as *permutation matrices* that are binary assignment operators. Recovering permutations from observations involve solving NP-hard combinatorial problems. As a remedy, scholars have opted to *relax* those problems to arrive at tractable albeit suboptimal solutions [8,14,43,70]. However, recent advances in computer hardware urges us to re-visit our approaches.

Quantum computers (QCs) harness the collective properties of quantum states, such as superposition, interference and entanglement to perform calculations [60]. Thanks to the use of a more advanced physics, QCs can offer theoretical improvements in the face of complexity classes that are challenging to handle today [68]. With the experimental realization of quantum supremacy [4], we are now more confident that practical quantum computing is right around the corner, *i.e.* the numer of usable Qubits now reach 5000 (DWave Advantage) and are expected to exceed beyond 7000 (DWave Advantage 2) [69].

A particular quantum computational model, known as *Adiabatic Quantum Computing* (AQC), is based on the adiabatic theorem of quantum mechanics [12]. Closely related to it is *Quantum Annealing* (QA), which is a quantum optimization method (AQC-type) that implements a qubit-based quantum system described by the Ising model [42]. Albeit restricted, experimental realisations of QA, such as DWave [22], can solve non-convex, *quadratic unconstrained binary optimization* (QUBO) problems, without resorting to continuous relaxations. This premise of AQC and QA has led to the emergence of *quantum computer vision* (QCV), where researchers started to port existing computer vision problems into forms amenable to quantum computation [7,32,36,50,67,75].

Even though employing QA to solve CV problems has shown benefit[1], a large body of computer vision algorithms rely on some form of (in)equality constraints to be incorporated. For example, estimating correspondences require solving QBOs for permutations and not for arbitrary binary vectors. To this end, the state-of-the-art QCV methods either use a regularization with cherry-picked coefficients [7] or resort to heuristics for auto-controlling the impact of the constraints [67,75]. Unfortunately, none of these approaches are optimal and jeopardize the solution quality guarantees of quantum computers.

In this paper, we address the above issue of incorporating (in)equality constraints and introduce Quantum-Frank Wolfe (Q-FW), a Frank-Wolfe framework for satisfying linear (in)equality constraints in a QBO problem. Q-FW is based on an equivalent *copositive programming* formulation of constrained QBO and involves iteratively solving a sequence of classical, unconstrained QUBOs. At its core, on a classical computer, Q-FW employs one of the two variants of FW tailored for solving CP problems; FW with augmented Lagrangian (FWAL) [72] or FW with quadratic penalty (FWQP) [73]. At every iteration, these methods identify an update direction by minimizing a linear approximation of a penalized proxy of the objective function. Q-FW formulates this linear minimization as a QUBO and obtains the update direction via QA. We then take a small step in

---

[1] Quantum computers are still in early stages. However, a diverse set of CV experiments present optimistic predictions regarding the future.

this update direction. In addition, FWAL maintains a dual variable, updated by a small gradient step for improved numerical performance.

Thanks to the convexity inherent in CP, Q-FW converges to the global minimum regardless the choice of its algorithm parameters. By virtue of the exact copositive-reformulation, our solutions are oftentimes near the true global minimum, obtained via an exhaustive search in small problems. We deploy Q-FW on multiple computer vision tasks of permutation synchronization and graph matching, which both have wide applicability. Our contributions are:

- We introduce Q-FW, an adaptation of the classical FW algorithm for solving copositive programs on a hybrid classical-quantum computing system.
- We solve the challenging QUBO sub-problems using an actual experimental realisation of a quantum annealer (QA), DWave Advantage 4.1 [22,62].
- We tackle both graph matching and permutation synchronization problems and obtain excellent results on both synthetic and real benchmarks.

Our evaluations confirm the theoretical advantages of Q-FW: Q-FW is robust, can solve larger problems than brute-force search, can exactly satisfy (in)equality constraints and enjoys a tight copositive relaxation. Our MATLAB implementation as well as scripts required to run D-Wave are available under: github.com/QuantumComputerVision/QuantumFrankWolfe.

## 2   Related Work

Our approach relates to different methods both in classical optimization and quantum computer vision. In this section, we review the most related works in QCV, copositive programming and FW.

**Quantum Computer Vision (QCV).** QCV encompasses hybrid classical-quantum methods with parts solved on a gate-based quantum computer or a quantum annealer. This young field seeks to identify how challenging problems can be formulated for and benefit from quantum hardware. While it remained predominantly theoretical at early stages [17,58], QCV methods from various domains were evaluated on real quantum hardware during the recent few years, including image classification [16,57,59], object detection [50], graph matching [67], mesh alignment [5], robust fitting [25] and permutation synchronisation [7].

Some of the proposed algorithms require additional constraints formulated as weighted linear terms (Lagrange multipliers) [7,67,75]. Such conditions rectify the original unconstrained objective and preserve the QUBO form consumable by modern QA. However, since the linear constraints modify the problem's energy landscape, the corresponding weights have to be chosen with care; too high or too low weights can significantly decrease the probability of measuring optimal solutions after the sampling. Birdal et al. [7] select the weights with a time-consuming grid search (for small problem instances). Benkner et al. [67] derive lower bounds on the rectification weights for the quadratic assignment problem.

Both policies have a common limitation: The determined weights are problem-specific and do not generalise to other problems. Moreover, even problems of the same type and size can demand new multipliers.

In contrast to existing methods, our unified policy does not require selecting the weights of linear terms in advance. Similar to Q-Match [5], our method is iterative: a sequence of optimisation tasks are solved on QPU; in each iteration, the control is returned to CPU to define a follow-up QUBO until convergence. Q-Match [5] update its solutions via a series of permutation-ness-preserving directions (collections of 2-cycles). Its policy does not generalise to other problems, arbitrary solution encodings and weighted linear constraints, as our method does.

**Copositive Programming (CP).** CP is a subfield of convex optimization concerned with optimizing a linear objective under affine constraints over the cone of copositive matrices, or its dual cone, the cone of completely positive matrices. By definition, a matrix $\mathbf{X} \in \mathbb{R}^{n \times n}$ is said to be copositive if its quadratic form is nonnegative on the first orthant (*i.e.*, $\mathbf{z}^{\top} \mathbf{X} \mathbf{z} \geq 0$ for all $\mathbf{z} \in \mathbb{R}_{+}^{n}$) and completely positive if $\mathbf{X} \in \text{conv}\{\mathbf{x}\mathbf{x}^{\top} : \mathbf{x} \in \mathbb{R}_{+}^{n}\}$. Compared to semidefinite programming, CP provides a tighter relaxation of quadratic problems [63]. However, despite its convexity, solving a CP problem is NP-Hard [10]. Several NP-Hard problems in quadratic and combinatorial optimization are subsets of CP, including the binary quadratic problems [13], problems of finding stability and chromatic numbers of a graph [23,26], quadratic assignment problem [61], and training of vector-output RELU networks [64]. We refer to the excellent surveys [27,28] and references therein for more details.

**Frank Wolfe (FW).** FW (also known as conditional gradient method or CGM) is a classical method in convex optimization dating back to 1956 [30]. Initially, the method is proposed for minimizing a convex quadratic loss function over a polytope. The analysis is extended in [49] to minimize a generic smooth and convex objective over an arbitrary convex and compact set. The eccentric feature of FW is that it does not require a projection step, which is in stark contrast with most other methods for constrained optimization, and it makes FW efficacious for problems where projection is computationally prohibitive. FW is demonstrated as an effective method for optimization over simplex [19] or spactrahedron domains [35]. We refer to [41] for convergence analysis of FW and a detailed discussion on its applications, and to [11] for a review on recent advances in FW.

The original form of FW is not suitable to tackle affine equality constraints present in our CP formulation. Instead, we consider two design variants of FW: FWQP [73], which equips FW with a quadratic penalty strategy for affine constraints; and FWAL [72], which extends FWQP for an augmented Lagrangian penalty. Our choice is inspired by [74] using FWAL for solving semidefinite programs. We adopt a similar approach for solving CPs.

In what follows, we first formulate QBO as an instance of the more general copositive program class Sect. 3. We then provide our Q-FW framework for solving copositive programs in a generic way (Sect. 4). Finally, we cast graph matching (Sect. 5.1) and permutation synchronization (Sect. 5.2) tasks as instances of QBOs with equality constraints, which Q-FW could solve effectively.

## 3    Problem Formulation

This section presents our model problem, a quadratic binary optimization (QBO) with affine (in)equality constraints[2], and an equivalent copositive program outlined in [13].

We assume that the problems are presented in the following form:

$$\min_{\mathbf{x} \in \mathbb{Z}_2^n} \ \mathbf{x}^\top \mathbf{Q} \mathbf{x} + 2\mathbf{s}^\top \mathbf{x} \quad \text{subject to} \quad \mathbf{a}_i^\top \mathbf{x} = b_i, \quad i = 1, 2, \ldots, m, \tag{1}$$

where $\mathbf{x} \in \mathbb{Z}_2^n$ is the binary valued decision variable, $\mathbf{Q} \in \mathbb{R}^{n \times n}$ and $\mathbf{s} \in \mathbb{R}^n$ are the quadratic and linear cost coefficients, and $\{(\mathbf{a}_i, b_i) \in \mathbb{R}^n \times \mathbb{R}\}$ are the constraint coefficients. We assume $b_i \geq 0$ without loss of generality. Throughout, we treat $\mathbf{Q}$ as a symmetric matrix since (1) is invariant under symmetrization of $\mathbf{Q}$:

$$\mathbf{x}^\top \mathbf{Q} \mathbf{x} = \tfrac{1}{2} \mathbf{x}^\top \mathbf{Q} \mathbf{x} + \tfrac{1}{2} (\mathbf{x}^\top \mathbf{Q} \mathbf{x})^\top = \mathbf{x}^\top (\tfrac{1}{2}\mathbf{Q} + \tfrac{1}{2}\mathbf{Q}^\top) \mathbf{x}. \tag{2}$$

One can also drop the linear term $\mathbf{s}^\top \mathbf{x}$ from the objective, because we can translate it into the quadratic term: Given that $\mathbf{x}$ is binary valued, $\mathbf{s}^\top \mathbf{x} = \mathbf{x}^\top \mathrm{Diag}(\mathbf{s})\, \mathbf{x}$.

To reformulate this problem, consider the rank-one completely positive matrix $\mathbf{X} = \mathbf{x}\mathbf{x}^\top \in \mathbb{Z}_2^{n \times n}$. Since $\mathbf{x}$ is binary valued, we have $\mathrm{diag}(\mathbf{X}) = \mathbf{x}$. Then, the quadratic objective in (1) can be cast as a linear function of $\mathbf{X}$:

$$\mathbf{x}^\top \mathbf{Q} \mathbf{x} = \mathrm{Tr}(\mathbf{x}^\top \mathbf{Q} \mathbf{x}) = \mathrm{Tr}(\mathbf{Q} \mathbf{x}\mathbf{x}^\top) = \mathrm{Tr}(\mathbf{Q}\mathbf{X}). \tag{3}$$

Similarly, we rewrite affine constraints from problem (1) by using

$$\begin{aligned} \mathbf{a}_i^\top \mathbf{x} = b_i \iff (\mathbf{a}_i^\top \mathbf{x})^2 = b_i^2 \\ \iff \mathrm{Tr}(\mathbf{A}_i \mathbf{X}) = b_i^2, \quad \text{where} \quad \mathbf{A}_i := \mathbf{a}_i \mathbf{a}_i^\top, \end{aligned} \tag{4}$$

which holds true since $(\mathbf{a}_i^\top \mathbf{x})^2 = \mathbf{x}^\top \mathbf{a}_i \mathbf{a}_i^\top \mathbf{x} = \mathrm{Tr}(\mathbf{x}^\top \mathbf{a}_i \mathbf{a}_i^\top \mathbf{x}) = \mathrm{Tr}(\mathbf{a}_i \mathbf{a}_i^\top \mathbf{x}\mathbf{x}^\top)$.

Now, we reformulate problem (1) as follows:

$$\min_{\mathbf{x}, \mathbf{X}} \ \mathrm{Tr}(\mathbf{Q}\mathbf{X}) + 2\mathbf{s}^\top \mathbf{x} \quad \text{subject to} \quad \mathbf{a}_i^\top \mathbf{x} = b_i, \quad i = 1, 2, \ldots, m,$$

$$\mathrm{Tr}(\mathbf{A}_i \mathbf{X}) = b_i^2, \quad i = 1, 2, \ldots, m, \tag{5}$$

$$\mathbf{X} = \mathbf{x}\mathbf{x}^\top, \quad \text{and} \quad \mathbf{x} \in \mathbb{Z}_2^n.$$

By replacing the nonconvex nonlinear constraint $\{\mathbf{X} = \mathbf{x}\mathbf{x}^\top, \mathbf{x} \in \mathbb{Z}_2^n\}$ with

$$\mathrm{diag}(\mathbf{X}) = \mathbf{x}, \quad \text{and} \quad \begin{bmatrix} 1 & \mathbf{x}^\top \\ \mathbf{x} & \mathbf{X} \end{bmatrix} \in \Delta^{n+1} \text{ where } \Delta^n := \mathrm{conv}\{\mathbf{x}\mathbf{x}^\top : \mathbf{x} \in \mathbb{Z}_2^n\}, \tag{6}$$

---

[2] Throughout the paper we concentrate on the equality constraints and provide a simple modification to satisfy inequality constraints in our supplementary material.

we get a CP problem:

$$\min_{\mathbf{x},\mathbf{X}} \ \text{Tr}(\mathbf{Q}\mathbf{X}) \quad \text{subject to} \quad \mathbf{a}_i^\top \mathbf{x} = b_i, \quad i = 1, 2, \ldots, m,$$

$$\text{Tr}(\mathbf{A}_i\mathbf{X}) = b_i^2, \quad i = 1, 2, \ldots, m, \tag{7}$$

$$\text{diag}(\mathbf{X}) = \mathbf{x}, \text{ and } \begin{bmatrix} 1 & \mathbf{x}^\top \\ \mathbf{x} & \mathbf{X} \end{bmatrix} \in \Delta^{n+1}.$$

This reformulation is tight, see Theorem 2.6 in [13] for the technical derivation. Our numerical experiments demonstrate the tightness of this reformulation empirically for the graph matching and permutation synchronization problems.

**Compact Notation.** We introduce a compact notation for problem (7) for convenience. Let $p = n + 1$, denote the new decision variable by $\mathbf{W} \in \Delta^p$, and introduce a new cost matrix $\mathbf{C} = \begin{bmatrix} 0 & \mathbf{s}^\top \\ \mathbf{s} & \mathbf{Q} \end{bmatrix}$. Further, let $d = 2m + n + 1$ and introduce a linear map $\mathcal{A} : \mathbb{R}^{p\times p} \to \mathbb{R}^d$ and vector $\mathbf{v} \in \mathbb{R}^d$ combining all affine constraints in problem (7), including $\{\mathbf{a}_i^\top \mathbf{x} = b_i\}$, $\{\text{Tr}(\mathbf{A}_i\mathbf{X}) = b_i^2\}$, $\text{diag}(\mathbf{X}) = \mathbf{x}$, and $W_{1,1} = 1$.

In this notation, problem (7) becomes

$$\min_{\mathbf{W}\in\Delta^p} \ \text{Tr}(\mathbf{C}\mathbf{W}) \quad \text{subject to} \quad \mathcal{A}\mathbf{W} = \mathbf{v}. \tag{8}$$

This is a convex optimization problem, but it is NP-Hard because of the complete positivity constraint.

## 4  Quantum Frank-Wolfe (Q-FW)

In the light of the copositive reformulation above, we now develop the main algorithm for solving a constrained-QBO. We describe the algorithm with FWAL. FWQP is covered as a special case by removing the dual steps of FWAL.

First, we construct the augmented Lagrangian of problem (8) by introducing a dual variable $\mathbf{y} \in \mathbb{R}^d$ and a penalty parameter $\beta > 0$:

$$L_\beta(\mathbf{W};\mathbf{y}) = \text{Tr}(\mathbf{C}\mathbf{W}) + \mathbf{y}^\top(\mathcal{A}\mathbf{W} - \mathbf{v}) + \frac{\beta}{2}\|\mathcal{A}\mathbf{W} - \mathbf{v}\|^2 \quad \text{for } \mathbf{W} \in \Delta^p. \tag{9}$$

The goal is to minimize $L_\beta(\mathbf{W};\mathbf{y})$ with respect to the primal variable $\mathbf{W}$ and maximize with respect to the dual variable $\mathbf{y}$:

$$\min_{\mathbf{W}\in\Delta^p} \ \max_{\mathbf{y}\in\mathbb{R}^d} \ \text{Tr}(\mathbf{C}\mathbf{W}) + \mathbf{y}^\top(\mathcal{A}\mathbf{W} - \mathbf{v}) + \frac{\beta}{2}\|\mathcal{A}\mathbf{W} - \mathbf{v}\|^2. \tag{10}$$

Note, the inner maximization gives an indicator function for $\mathcal{A}\mathbf{W} = \mathbf{v}$:

$$\max_{y\in\mathbb{R}^m} \ \mathbf{y}^\top(\mathcal{A}\mathbf{W} - \mathbf{v}) = \begin{cases} 0 & \text{if } \mathcal{A}\mathbf{W} = \mathbf{v} \\ +\infty & \text{otherwise} \end{cases} \tag{11}$$

Hence, the saddle point problem (10) is equivalent to our model problem (8).

The FWAL iteration employs a simple optimization strategy with two main steps, performed on the augmented Lagrangian loss function $L_\beta(\mathbf{W}; \mathbf{y})$:
(1) A primal step to update $\mathbf{W}$, inspired by the FW algorithm, and
(2) A dual gradient ascent step to update $\mathbf{y}$.
The penalty parameter, $\beta$, is increased at a specific rate to ensure convergence of $\mathbf{W}$ to a feasible solution. Next, we describe the algorithm steps in detail.

**Initialization.** Choose an initial penalty parameter $\beta_0 > 0$, and initial primal and dual estimates $\mathbf{W}_0 \in \Delta^p$ and $\mathbf{y}_0 \in \mathbb{R}^d$. In practice, we let $\beta_0 = 1$, and we choose $\mathbf{W}$ and $\mathbf{y}$ as the matrix/vector of zeros.

At iteration $t = 1, 2, \ldots$, we increase the penalty parameter $\beta_t = \beta_0 \sqrt{t+1}$ and perform the following updates:

**Primal Step.** For primal step, we fix the dual variable $\mathbf{y}_t$ and take a FW step on the primal variable $\mathbf{W}_t$ with respect to the augmented Lagrangian loss (9). First, we compute the partial derivative of $L_{\beta_t}$ with respect to $\mathbf{W}$:

$$\mathbf{G}_t = \mathbf{C} + \mathcal{A}^\top \mathbf{y}_t + \beta_t \mathcal{A}^\top (\mathcal{A}\mathbf{W}_t - \mathbf{v}). \tag{12}$$

Then, we find an update direction $\mathbf{H}_t \in \Delta^p$ by minimizing the first-order Taylor expansion of $L_{\beta_t}$:

$$\mathbf{H}_t \in \arg\min_{\mathbf{W} \in \Delta^p} L_{\beta_t}(\mathbf{W}_t; \mathbf{y}_t) + \mathrm{Tr}(\mathbf{G}_t(\mathbf{W} - \mathbf{W}_t)) \equiv \arg\min_{\mathbf{W} \in \Delta^p} \mathrm{Tr}(\mathbf{G}_t\mathbf{W}). \tag{13}$$

This step can be written as a standard, unconstrained QUBO. Specifically,

$$\text{if} \quad \mathbf{w}_t \in \arg\min_{\mathbf{w} \in \mathbb{Z}_2^p} \mathbf{w}^\top \mathbf{G}_t \mathbf{w}, \quad \text{then} \quad \mathbf{H}_t := \mathbf{w}_t \mathbf{w}_t^\top \in \arg\min_{\mathbf{W} \in \Delta^p} \mathrm{Tr}(\mathbf{G}_t\mathbf{W}). \tag{14}$$

Therefore, we can **implement and solve this step effectively on an AQC.** This is a key observation for our framework.

Finally, we update the primal variable $\mathbf{W}_t$ by taking a step towards $\mathbf{H}_t$:

$$\mathbf{W}_{t+1} = (1 - \eta_t)\mathbf{W}_t + \eta_t \mathbf{H}_t, \quad \text{with step-size } \eta_t = \frac{2}{t+1}. \tag{15}$$

**Dual Step.** For dual step, we fix $\mathbf{W}_{t+1}$ and take a gradient ascent step on the dual variable with respect to the augmented Lagrangian loss (9). The partial derivative of $L_{\beta_t}$ with respect to $\mathbf{y}$ is

$$\mathbf{g}_t = \mathcal{A}\mathbf{W}_{t+1} - \mathbf{v}. \tag{16}$$

Then we take a gradient step in this direction

$$\mathbf{y}_{t+1} = \mathbf{y}_t + \gamma_t \mathbf{g}_t, \quad \text{with step-size } \gamma_t \geq 0. \tag{17}$$

There are two different strategies for the dual step-size $\gamma_t$, for more details we refer to Sect. 3.1 in [72]. In practice, we choose a constant step-size $\gamma_t = \beta_0$.

This completes one FWAL iteration. The following proposition, a simple adaptation from [72, Theorem 3.1], establishes the convergence rate of FWAL for our model problem (8).

**Proposition 1.** *Consider FWAL for problem* (8). *Choose an initial penalty parameter* $\beta_0 > 0$. *Assume that the solution set is nonempty, strong duality holds*[3]*, and the effective dual domain is bounded (i.e. , there exists* $D < +\infty$ *such that* $\|y_t\| \leq D$ *at every iteration). Then, the primal sequence* $\mathbf{W}_t \in \Delta^p$ *converges to a solution* $\mathbf{W}_\star$ *with the following bounds on the error:*

$$\mathrm{Tr}(\mathbf{C}\mathbf{W}_t) - \mathrm{Tr}(\mathbf{C}\mathbf{W}_\star) \leq \frac{1}{\sqrt{t}} \left( 6\beta_0 p^2 \|\mathcal{A}\|^2 + \frac{D^2}{2\beta_0} \right) \quad \textit{(objective suboptimality)}$$

$$\tag{18}$$

$$\|\mathcal{A}\mathbf{W}_t - \mathbf{v}\| \leq \frac{1}{\sqrt{t}} \left( 2\sqrt{3}p\|\mathcal{A}\| + \frac{4D}{\beta_0} \right) \quad \textit{(infeasibility error)} \quad (19)$$

*where* $\|\mathcal{A}\| := \sup\{\|\mathcal{A}\mathbf{X}\| : \|\mathbf{X}\|_F \leq 1\}$ *is the operator norm of* $\mathcal{A}$.

*Remark 1.* We recover FWQP from FWAL by choosing $\mathbf{y}_0 = \mathbf{0}$ and $\gamma_t = 0$, in other words, by removing the dual steps. These two methods have similar guarantees with the same rate of convergence up to a constant factor, but FWAL is reported to perform better for most instances in practice [72].

**Rounding.** We can immediately extract a solution for the original QBO problem (1) from a solution $\mathbf{W}_\star$ of CP reformulation (8). However, in practice, with finite time and computation, we get only an approximate solution $\hat{\mathbf{W}}$. A naive estimate that we extract from $\hat{\mathbf{W}}$ can be infeasible for (1). To this end, we implement the following rounding procedure: First, we get $\hat{\mathbf{X}}$ by removing the first row and first column of $\hat{\mathbf{W}}$. Next, we compute the best rank-one approximation $\hat{\mathbf{x}}\hat{\mathbf{x}}^\top$ of $\hat{\mathbf{X}}$ with respect to the Frobenius norm.[4] Finally, as an optional step, we project $\hat{\mathbf{x}}$ onto the feasible set of (1). The set of permutation matrices is the feasible set in our numerical experiments. We use Hungarian algorithm [46] for projection.

**Quantum Annealing (QA).** QA converts a QUBO objective to the equivalent Ising problem that is then solved by a meta-heuristic governed by quantum fluctuations [29]. Since this analogue optimisation process is prone to different physical disturbances (e.g., state decoherence and cosmic radiation)—and is, hence, non-deterministic—multiple repetitions are required to obtain an optimal solution with high probability. Furthermore, the current experimental QA realisations do not easily allow defining high-level constraints; the latter must be integrated so that the QUBO structure is preserved. In practice, constraints are formulated as weighted linear terms adjusting qubit couplings and biases [7,67]. Finding optimal weights (e.g., by a grid search) is a tedious procedure that does not guarantee the generalisation of the selected multipliers across the problems. We provide further details on quantum annealing in our supplementary material.

**On Computational Complexity.** The convergence of FW is sub-linear and hence may require significant number of iterations, *e.g.* 200–1000. At each iteration, Q-FW attempts to solve an NP-Hard QUBO problem whose computational

---

[3] Strong duality is a standard assumption for primal-dual methods in optimization.

[4] This amounts to computing the top singular vector of $\hat{\mathbf{X}}$ [54].

complexity class is $FP^{NP}$-complete[5] [71]. Thanks to the exploitation of quantum phenomena, QA can bring a quadratic improvement reducing the theoretical complexity from $O(e^N)$ to $O(e^{\sqrt{N}})$, in a similar vein to Grover algorithm [1,34]. Though, it is not straightforward to get a problem-specific, realistic estimate of the time complexity of the QA process. Nevertheless, fixing a constant annealing time and a constant number of repetitions, as we do for our small problems, can lead to an optimistic, polynomial time algorithm [3].

## 5    Experimental Evaluation

The proposed approach (Q-FWAL) is general and not tailored towards a specific problem. Hence, we assess its validity in realizing quantum versions two different problems, *graph matching* and *permutation synchronization*, both requiring equality constraints to be accounted for.[6] We use problem-specific synthetic and real datasets to showcase the effectiveness of our approach.

**Implementation Details.** In both of the experiments we use the DWave Advantage 4.1 system [53] which has at least 5,000 qubits and ~35,000 couplers. Except the ablation studies, we use 50 or 250 annealing cycles of $20\,\mu s$ in each iteration with an annealing schedule of $100\,\mu s$ breaks. We set the chain strength $\xi$ according to the *maximum chain strength criterion*: We inspect the minor embedding calculated by Cai *et al.* [15] and set $\xi = s_{\max} + \omega$, with $s_{\max}$ being the maximum chain length in the minor embedding and $\omega = 0.5$ is the strengthening weight. If we observe frequent chain breaks for larger problems, we increase $\omega$ to 3.0. We access DWave at each iteration through the *Leap2* API [20]. We investigate three modes of Q-FW: (i) with intermediary exhaustive solution instead of DWave (FWAL), (ii) without Hungarian rounding (Q-FWAL relaxed) and (iii) the full configuration (Q-FWAL). Note that vanilla FWAL (i) cannot be applied to large problems due to the combinatorial explosion. In all of our problems, we are interested in linear permutation constraints, as those are the most common in CV problems. Hence, we use *Hungarian algorithm* [46] as the projector onto the constraint set (*cf. Rounding* in Sect. 4) and formulate permutation-ness into linear constraints as in [7,67] (*cf.*supplementary material).

### 5.1    Quantum Graph Matching (QGM)

In general, 3D vision problems relate two abstract shape/image manifolds $\mathcal{M}_1$ and $\mathcal{M}_2$. In many applications, these manifolds can be sampled by two point clouds (e.g. keypoints) $\mathcal{X}_1 \in \mathbb{R}^{N_1 \times n}$ and $\mathcal{X}_2 \in \mathbb{R}^{N_2 \times n}$ where $n$ is the dimensionality of the problem domain, *e.g.* two for images, three for meshes and etc. We further

---

[5] A binary relation $P(x, y)$, is in $FP^{NP}$ if and only if there is a deterministic polynomial time algorithm that can determine whether $P(x, y)$ holds given both $x$ and $y$.

[6] While still providing a way to handle inequalities in our supplementary material, we leave it as a future work to study problems with inequality constraints.

**Table 1.** Evaluations of graph matching on random problem instances with different sizes [67]. We report mean normalized energies over ten instances (the lower the better). Last five columns correspond to the variants of our method.

| N | [67] ins. | [67] row. | [6] DS* | [44] SA | FWAL | Q-FWAL relaxed (50) | Q-FWAL (50) | Q-FWAL relaxed (250) | Q-FWAL (250) |
|---|---|---|---|---|---|---|---|---|---|
| 3 | 1.49 | 2.12 | 0.85 | 0.82 | **7e-4** | 1.72 | 0.093 | 1.72 | **7e-4** |
| 4 | 5.68 | 7.37 | 0.43 | 2.43 | **1.3e-3** | 3.41 | 1.82 | 0.23 | **1.43e-3** |

assume a distance function $\phi(.)$ defined over the points of these point clouds. The quadratic assignment problem (QAP) then takes the form:

$$\max_{\Pi} \ \text{vec}(\Pi)^\top \mathbf{Q}_{\text{QGM}} \text{vec}(\Pi) \quad \text{subject to} \quad \Pi \in \mathcal{P} \tag{20}$$

where $\mathcal{P}$ denotes the set of (partial) permutations and $\text{vec}(\cdot)$ acts as a vectorizer. Assuming $N := N_1 = N_2$, *i.e.* *total* permutations (TP), $\mathbf{Q}_{\text{QGM}} \in \mathbb{R}^{N^2 \times N^2}$ denotes a *ground cost* matrix or the quadratic energy measuring the gain of matching $\mathcal{M}_1$ and $\mathcal{M}_2$ by a sub-permutation $\Pi$, computed using the distance $\phi(\cdot)$.

**Baselines & Dataset.** We benchmark QGM against the exhaustive solution, obtained by searching over all possible permutations, as well as against the first AQC approach which was proposed by Benkner *et al.* [67] who used multiple strategies (*e.g.* *inserted, row-wise*) to inject soft-permutation constraints into QUBO. This required tuning of a parameter $\lambda \in \mathbb{R}$, whose large values are found to cause problems [7,67,75]. As a heuristic, [67] suggested a *spectral-gap*[7] analysis to bound the regularization coefficient $\lambda$. We also include: (i) the result obtained by running *simulated annealing* (SA) [44] on a CPU (the implementation from the Ocean tools [20]); (ii) a state of the art classical graph matching algorithm [6].

To assess, we use two sets of ten random problem instances with $N = 3$ and $N = 4$ as in Sect. 5.1 of [67]. The ground-truth permutations are calculated by brute force and compared qualitatively with the expected outcomes on real data. The number or qubits in the minor embeddings equals to 14 ($N = 3$) and 40 ($N = 4$).

**Results.** We report the *mean normalized energies over ten instances* in Table 1. This quantity is obtained by first shifting all energies by the minimum energy (of the ground-truth solution) and then averaging them. Clearly, FWAL and Q-FWAL perform the best on this experiment. However, FWAL cannot be scaled to large problems, and as we will see later in Sect. 5.2, Q-FWAL is able to handle much larger problems thanks to the advances in AQCs. DS* is a powerful classical algorithm, yet it cannot match the errors we achieve. SA is good for small problems, but its solution quality quickly drops with the problem size. Finally, it is visible that 50 cycles might be insufficient to get high quality results. Note, in practical scenarios where the number of keypoints across two images/scenes

---

[7] The difference between the lowest and second-lowest energy state/eigen-value.

**Fig. 1.** Willow Dataset [18]. (**left**) Manual annotations of keypoints. (**right**) Ground truth multi-image matches.

are different (*e.g.* $N_1 \neq N_2$), we will have to adopt *partial* permutations as non-square matrices yielding *inequality* constraints. We provided how inequality constraints can be factored into our framework, theoretically (*cf.* supp. Sect. 1.5).

### 5.2  Quantum Permutation Synchronization (QPS)

Many multi-shape/view/instance computer vision problems can be solved by synchronization, including shape (point set) alignment [31,37], structure from motion [9,33], multi-view matching [8,52] and motion segmentation [2,38].

A specific branch, *permutation synchronization* seeks to find globally consistent image/shape matches from a set of relative matches over a collection. In particular, consider a *collection* of K point sets $\mathcal{X}_1, \ldots, \mathcal{X}_K$[8] of N points each such that there exists a bijective map for each pair $(\mathcal{X}_i, \mathcal{X}_j)$. We assume the availability of a set of noisy *relative* permutations $\{\mathbf{P}_{ij} : \mathcal{X}_i \rightarrow \mathcal{X}_j\}_{ij}$ estimated in *isolation, i.e.* independently. Our goal is then to solve this multi-graph matching problem even when a significant fraction of the pairwise matches are incorrect. To this end, a large body works minimize a *cycle-consistency loss*, that is shown to be equivalent to a QUBO (*cf.* [7] for a proof):

$$\arg\min_{\{\mathbf{X}_i \in \mathcal{P}_n\}} \sum_{(i,j) \in \mathcal{E}} \|\mathbf{P}_{ij} - \mathbf{X}_i \mathbf{X}_j^\top\|_F^2 = \arg\min_{\{\mathbf{X}_i \in \mathcal{P}_n\}} \mathbf{x}^\top \mathbf{Q}_{QPS} \mathbf{x}. \tag{21}$$

Here, $\mathbf{x} = [\cdots \mathbf{x}_i^\top \cdots]^\top$ and $\mathbf{x}_i = \mathrm{vec}(\mathbf{X}_i)$ depict the *canonical ordering* of points. The first AQC approach to this problem is proposed by Birdal *et al.* [7], who, similar to [67], regularize $\mathbf{Q}_{QPS}$ to incorporate permutation-ness as a soft constraint. Note that, this whole problem has a gauge freedom, where we can freely choose $\mathbf{X}_0$ *e.g.* , as an identity matrix (*cf.* supplementary material).

**Datasets.** As a real dataset, we follow [7] and use the kindly provided subset of the Willow Object Classes [18] composed of four categories (*duck, car, winebottle, motorbike*) with 40 RGB images each, acquired *in the wild* (*cf.* Fig. 1). This subset contains multiple sets of four points sampled out of ten annotations. This leads to 35 small problems per category each of which is a fully connected graph of all four consecutive frames. Initial permutations are obtained via a Hungarian algorithm [55] applied to matching costs obtained by Alexnet [45] features. As the data is manually annotated, the ground-truth relative maps are known.

---

[8] Such sets are easy to obtain by keypoint detection or sampling either on images or on shapes, *e.g.* by detecting $N$ landmarks per image, in a $M$-view image collection.

**Table 2.** Evaluations on Willow Dataset.

| | Car | Duck | Motorbike | Winebottle | Average |
|---|---|---|---|---|---|
| MatchEIG [52] | 0.81 ± 0.083 | 0.86 ± 0.102 | 0.77 ± 0.059 | 0.87 ± 0.107 | 0.83 ± 0.088 |
| MatchALSS [76] | 0.84 ± 0.095 | 0.90 ± 0.102 | 0.81 ± 0.078 | 0.94 ± 0.092 | 0.87 ± 0.092 |
| MatchLIFT [39] | 0.84 ± 0.102 | 0.90 ± 0.103 | 0.81 ± 0.078 | 0.94 ± 0.092 | 0.87 ± 0.094 |
| MatchBirkhoff [8] | 0.84 ± 0.094 | 0.90 ± 0.107 | 0.81 ± 0.079 | 0.94 ± 0.093 | 0.87 ± 0.093 |
| QuantumSync [7] | 0.84 ± 0.104 | 0.90 ± 0.104 | 0.81 ± 0.080 | 0.93 ± 0.095 | 0.87 ± 0.096 |
| [7]-search | 0.84 ± 0.104 | 0.91 ± 0.115 | 0.82 ± 0.10 | 0.95 ± 0.096 | 0.88 ± 0.104 |
| Q-FWAL (ours) | **0.92 ± 0.094** | **0.97 ± 0.072** | **0.89 ± 0.093** | **0.99 ± 0.044** | **0.94 ± 0.076** |

**Baselines.** We compare Q-FWAL against the classical algorithms of MatchEIG [52], MatchALS [76], MatchLift [39], MatchBirkhoff [8] as well as the first Quantum approach, QuantumSync [7]. QuantumSync uses $\lambda = 2.5$ in all experiments. The *exhaustive* solution is obtained by enumerating all possible permutations. Note that due to the limitations in the available DWave time, we had to implement an *early-stopping* heuristic whose details are provided in the supplementary document. The number or qubits in the minor embeddings in this experiment (for $\mathbf{Q} \in \mathbb{R}^{64 \times 64}$) was $\approx$270, and the chain length did not exceed eight.

**Results.** We follow the protocol of Birdal *et al.* [7] and report in Table 2, the portion of correct bits *i.e. accuracy*. Our approach consistently and significantly outperforms both the classical algorithms and the state-of-the-art quantum approach, QuantumSync [7]. [7]-*search* denotes the softly-constrained search detailed in [7]. Overall, Q-FW is more applicable to problems of growing size.

### 5.3 Ablation Studies

**Tightness of the Copositive Relaxation.** To assess the tightness of our algorithm, we randomly generate fully connected, synthetic synchronization problems with $N = 3$ and $K = 3$ with different noise levels $\sigma \in \{0, 0.2\}$. For this small problem we could use an exact QUBO solver and monitor the convergence of the relaxed problem to the ground truth (GT): $\varepsilon_{CC} = |\mathrm{Tr}(\mathbf{QX}_t) - \mathrm{Tr}(\mathbf{QX}_t^{gt})|$ where $\mathbf{X}^{gt}$ is obtained by lifting the GT permutations. As shown on the right, $\varepsilon_{CC}$ decreases monotonically for all methods, even in the case of noise. Moreover, our D-Wave implementation strictly matches FWAL.

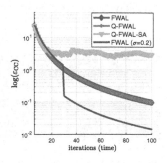

**Monitoring Convergence.** As heuristic fearly stopping criteria are harmful for the convergence guarantees we provide, it is of interest to see how our algorithm behaves as iterations progress. In Fig. 2 we plot minimization curves for different

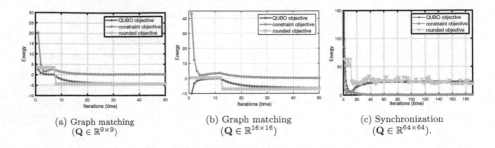

(a) Graph matching
$(\mathbf{Q} \in \mathbb{R}^{9 \times 9})$

(b) Graph matching
$(\mathbf{Q} \in \mathbb{R}^{16 \times 16})$

(c) Synchronization
$(\mathbf{Q} \in \mathbb{R}^{64 \times 64})$.

**Fig. 2.** Solving two graph matching and one synchronization problem using Q-FWAL. The problem gets more complex from left to right. Thus, the required number of iterations to converge increases.

problems we consider: two graph matching (a,b) and one synchronization (c). For each problem, we plot the QUBO objective, infeasibility eror (constraint objective) and the error attained after Hungarian rounding. It is visible that simplicity of the problem has a positive impact on finding good solutions early on. For larger problems, settling on a good solution can take > 200 iterations, when early stopping is not used. We also note that the QUBO objective converges to the rounded objective, indicating the tightness of our relaxation.

**On the Evolution of Sub-problems and Sparsity.** We now visually compare the sub-problems emerging in solving the noiseless, synthetic synchronization problem (detailed in the previous experiment and in our supplementary material), for exact method and for the D-Wave implementation. As seen in Fig. 3, there is no noticeable difference between the two evolutions, confirming that D-Wave could solve the sub-QUBO-problems reliably. Moreover, over iterations the sparsity pattern of $\mathbf{W}_t$ is fixed, which means that we could compute the minor embedding[9], and re-use it throughout Q-FW. This ability of avoiding repetitive minor embeddings makes Q-FW a practically feasible algorithm.

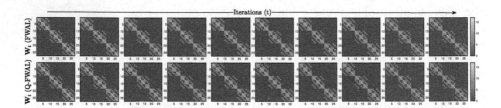

**Fig. 3.** Evolution of the gradient $\mathbf{W}_t$ for $0 < t < 100$ sampled in steps of 10: FWAL (top) and Q-FWAL (bottom).

---

[9] Requires solving a combinatorial optimization problem with heuristics.

# 6 Discussions and Conclusion

We have proposed Q-FW, a quantum computation backed, hybrid Frank Wolfe Augmented Lagrangian method. Thanks to the tight copositive relaxation and the QUBO formulation, our algorithm has successfully satisfied linear (in)equality constraints, such as permutation-ness, arising in many computer vision applications. We have solved the intermediary QUBO problems on a quantum computer to obtain high quality update directions and demonstrated the validity of Q-FW both on graph matching and permutation synchronization.

**Limitations.** The most obvious concern is the sub-linear convergence of our algorithm, which could sometimes require a large number of iterations particularly if high accuracy is needed. However, the rates of FWAL (hence, Q-FWAL) are optimal, *i.e.* they match the worst-case computational lower bounds for a generic class of linear optimization based convex programming algorithms [48]. Certain design variants of FW with stronger oracles [47] achieve faster rates. Such variants and their implications for Q-FWAL pose valuable questions for future study. We observed in practice a maximum of 300–400 iterations can be sufficient thanks to the high quality of the DWave solver. We are also limited by the small problem sizes, just likes the previous studies [7,67]. Yet, quantum computers evolve steadily and we are hopeful that the problems we could solve will only grow with time.

**Looking Forward.** Q-FWAL leaves ample room for future works. First, a plethora of QCV methods concerned with constraint satisfaction can benefit our approach. Using our algorithm to ensure constraints other than permutations (especially inequalities like partial permutations) is a future study. We would also like to deploy our algorithm in training vector-output RELU networks [64].

**Acknowledgment.** A.Y. received support from the Wallenberg AI, Autonomous Systems and Software Program (WASP) funded by the Knut and Alice Wallenberg Foundation.

# References

1. Albash, T., Lidar, D.A.: Adiabatic quantum computation. Rev. Mod. Phys. **90**(1), 015002 (2018)
2. Arrigoni, F., Ricci, E., Pajdla, T.: Multi-frame motion segmentation by combining two-frame results. Int. J. Comput. Vision **130**, 1–33 (2022)
3. Arthur, D., Pusey-Nazzaro, L., et al.: Qubo formulations for training machine learning models. Sci. Rep. **11**(1), 1–10 (2021)
4. Arute, F., et al.: Quantum supremacy using a programmable superconducting processor. Nature **574**(7779), 505–510 (2019)
5. Benkner, M.S., Lähner, Z., Golyanik, V., Wunderlich, C., Theobalt, C., Moeller, M.: Q-match: iterative shape matching via quantum annealing. In: Proceedings of the IEEE/CVF International Conference on Computer Vision, pp. 7586–7596 (2021)

6. Bernard, F., Theobalt, C., Moeller, M.: DS*: tighter lifting-free convex relaxations for quadratic matching problems. In: Proceedings of the IEEE Conference on Computer Vision and Pattern Recognition (CVPR), June 2018

7. Birdal, T., Golyanik, V., Theobalt, C., Guibas, L.J.: Quantum permutation synchronization. In: Proceedings of the IEEE/CVF Conference on Computer Vision and Pattern Recognition, pp. 13122–13133 (2021)

8. Birdal, T., Simsekli, U.: Probabilistic permutation synchronization using the riemannian structure of the birkhoff polytope. In: Proceedings of the IEEE/CVF Conference on Computer Vision and Pattern Recognition, pp. 11105–11116 (2019)

9. Birdal, T., Simsekli, U., Eken, M.O., Ilic, S.: Bayesian pose graph optimization via bingham distributions and tempered geodesic MCMC. In: Advances in Neural Information Processing Systems, vol. 31 (2018)

10. Bomze, I.M., Dür, M., De Klerk, E., Roos, C., Quist, A.J., Terlaky, T.: On copositive programming and standard quadratic optimization problems. J. Global Optim. **18**(4), 301–320 (2000)

11. Bomze, I.M., Rinaldi, F., Zeffiro, D.: Frank-wolfe and friends: a journey into projection-free first-order optimization methods. 4OR **19**(3), 313–345 (2021)

12. Born, M., Fock, V.: Beweis des adiabatensatzes. Zeitschrift für Physik **51**(3), 165–180 (1928)

13. Burer, S.: On the copositive representation of binary and continuous nonconvex quadratic programs. Math. Program. **120**(2), 479–495 (2009)

14. Caetano, T.S., McAuley, J.J., Cheng, L., Le, Q.V., Smola, A.J.: Learning graph matching. IEEE Trans. Pattern Anal. Mach. Intell. **31**(6), 1048–1058 (2009)

15. Cai, J., Macready, W.G., Roy, A.: A practical heuristic for finding graph minors. arXiv e-prints (2014)

16. Cavallaro, G., Willsch, D., Willsch, M., Michielsen, K., Riedel, M.: Approaching remote sensing image classification with ensembles of support vector machines on the d-wave quantum annealer. In: IEEE International Geoscience and Remote Sensing Symposium (IGARSS) (2020)

17. Chin, T.J., Suter, D., Chng, S.F., Quach, J.: Quantum robust fitting. arXiv preprint arXiv:2006.06986 (2020)

18. Cho, M., Alahari, K., Ponce, J.: Learning graphs to match. In: International Conference on Computer Vision (ICCV), pp. 25–32 (2013)

19. Clarkson, K.L.: Coresets, sparse greedy approximation, and the Frank-Wolfe algorithm. ACM Trans. Algorithms (TALG) **6**(4), 1–30 (2010)

20. D-Wave Systems Inc: dwave-system documentation (2022). https://docs.ocean.dwavesys.com/_/downloads/system/en/latest/pdf/. Accessed 05 Mar 2022

21. Dai, A., Nießner, M., Zollhöfer, M., Izadi, S., Theobalt, C.: Bundlefusion: real-time globally consistent 3D reconstruction using on-the-fly surface reintegration. ACM Trans. Graph. (TOG) **36**(4), 76a (2017)

22. Dattani, N., Szalay, S., Chancellor, N.: Pegasus: the second connectivity graph for large-scale quantum annealing hardware. arXiv e-prints (2019)

23. De Klerk, E., Pasechnik, D.V.: Approximation of the stability number of a graph via copositive programming. SIAM J. Optim. **12**(4), 875–892 (2002)

24. Deng, H., Birdal, T., Ilic, S.: PPF-FoldNet: unsupervised learning of rotation invariant 3D local descriptors. In: Proceedings of the European Conference on Computer Vision (ECCV), pp. 602–618 (2018)

25. Doan, A.D., Sasdelli, M., Chin, T.J., Suter, D.: A hybrid quantum-classical algorithm for robust fitting. arXiv preprint arXiv:2201.10110 (2022)

26. Dukanovic, I., Rendl, F.: Copositive programming motivated bounds on the stability and the chromatic numbers. Math. Program. **121**(2), 249–268 (2010)

27. Dür, M.: Copositive programming-a survey. In: Diehl, M., Glineur, F., Jarlebring, E., Michiels, W. (eds.) Recent Advances in Optimization and its Applications in Engineering, pp. 3–20. Springer, Heidelberg (2010). https://doi.org/10.1007/978-3-642-12598-0_1

28. Dür, M., Rendl, F.: Conic optimization: a survey with special focus on copositive optimization and binary quadratic problems. EURO J. Comput. Optim. **9**, 100021 (2021)

29. Farhi, E., Goldstone, J., Gutmann, S., Lapan, J., Lundgren, A., Preda, D.: A quantum adiabatic evolution algorithm applied to random instances of an np-complete problem. Science **292**(5516), 472–475 (2001)

30. Frank, M., Wolfe, P., et al.: An algorithm for quadratic programming. Nav. Res. Logist. Q. **3**(1–2), 95–110 (1956)

31. Gao, M., Lahner, Z., Thunberg, J., Cremers, D., Bernard, F.: Isometric multi-shape matching. In: Proceedings of the IEEE/CVF Conference on Computer Vision and Pattern Recognition, pp. 14183–14193 (2021)

32. Golyanik, V., Theobalt, C.: A quantum computational approach to correspondence problems on point sets. In: Computer Vision and Pattern Recognition (CVPR) (2020)

33. Govindu, V.M.: Lie-algebraic averaging for globally consistent motion estimation. In: Proceedings of the 2004 IEEE Computer Society Conference on Computer Vision and Pattern Recognition, CVPR 2004, vol. 1, p. I. IEEE (2004)

34. Grover, L.K.: A fast quantum mechanical algorithm for database search. In: Proceedings of the Twenty-Eighth Annual ACM Symposium on Theory of Computing, pp. 212–219 (1996)

35. Hazan, E.: Sparse approximate solutions to semidefinite programs. In: Laber, E.S., Bornstein, C., Nogueira, L.T., Faria, L. (eds.) LATIN 2008. LNCS, vol. 4957, pp. 306–316. Springer, Heidelberg (2008). https://doi.org/10.1007/978-3-540-78773-0_27

36. Hu, F., Wang, B.N., Wang, N., Wang, C.: Quantum machine learning with d-wave quantum computer. Quantum Eng. **1**(2), e12 (2019)

37. Huang, J., Birdal, T., Gojcic, Z., Guibas, L.J., Hu, S.M.: Multiway non-rigid point cloud registration via learned functional map synchronization. arXiv preprint arXiv:2111.12878 (2021)

38. Huang, J., et al.: Multibodysync: multi-body segmentation and motion estimation via 3D scan synchronization. In: Proceedings of the IEEE/CVF Conference on Computer Vision and Pattern Recognition, pp. 7108–7118 (2021)

39. Huang, Q.X., Guibas, L.: Consistent shape maps via semidefinite programming. In: Eurographics/ACM SIGGRAPH Symposium on Geometry Processing (SGP). Eurographics Association (2013)

40. Huber, D.F., Hebert, M.: Fully automatic registration of multiple 3D data sets. Image Vis. Comput. **21**(7), 637–650 (2003)

41. Jaggi, M.: Revisiting frank-wolfe: projection-free sparse convex optimization. In: International Conference on Machine Learning, pp. 427–435. PMLR (2013)

42. Kadowaki, T., Nishimori, H.: Quantum annealing in the transverse ising model. Phys. Rev. E **58**, 5355–5363 (1998)

43. Kezurer, I., Kovalsky, S.Z., Basri, R., Lipman, Y.: Tight relaxation of quadratic matching. In: Computer Graphics Forum, vol. 34, pp. 115–128. Wiley Online Library (2015)

44. Kirkpatrick, S., Gelatt, C.D., Vecchi, M.P.: Optimization by simulated annealing. Science **220**(4598), 671–680 (1983)

45. Krizhevsky, A., Sutskever, I., Hinton, G.E.: Imagenet classification with deep convolutional neural networks. In: Advances in Neural Information Processing Systems (NeurIPS), pp. 1097–1105 (2012)
46. Kuhn, H.W.: The Hungarian method for the assignment problem. Nav. Res. Logist. Q. **2**(1–2), 83–97 (1955)
47. Lacoste-Julien, S., Jaggi, M.: On the global linear convergence of frank-wolfe optimization variants. In: Advances in Neural Information Processing Systems, vol. 28 (2015)
48. Lan, G.: The complexity of large-scale convex programming under a linear optimization oracle. arXiv preprint arXiv:1309.5550
49. Levitin, E., Polyak, B.: Constrained minimization methods. USSR Comput. Math. Math. Phys. **6**(5), 1–50 (1966)
50. Li, J., Ghosh, S.: Quantum-soft QUBO suppression for accurate object detection. In: Vedaldi, A., Bischof, H., Brox, T., Frahm, J.-M. (eds.) ECCV 2020. LNCS, vol. 12374, pp. 158–173. Springer, Cham (2020). https://doi.org/10.1007/978-3-030-58526-6_10
51. Li, X., Larson, M., Hanjalic, A.: Pairwise geometric matching for large-scale object retrieval. In: Proceedings of the IEEE Conference on Computer Vision and Pattern Recognition, pp. 5153–5161 (2015)
52. Maset, E., Arrigoni, F., Fusiello, A.: Practical and efficient multi-view matching. In: International Conference on Computer Vision (ICCV) (2017)
53. McGeoch, C., Farré, P.: The advantage system: performance update. Technical report, Technical Report 14-1054A-A, D-Wave Systems Inc., Burnaby, Canada (2021)
54. Mirsky, L.: Symmetric gauge functions and unitarily invariant norms. Q. J. Math. **11**(1), 50–59 (1960)
55. Munkres, J.: Algorithms for the assignment and transportation problems. J. Soc. Ind. Appl. Math. **5**(1), 32–38 (1957)
56. Mur-Artal, R., Tardós, J.D.: ORB-SLAM2: an open-source SLAM system for monocular, stereo and RGB-D cameras. IEEE Trans. Rob. **33**(5), 1255–1262 (2017). https://doi.org/10.1109/TRO.2017.2705103
57. Neven, H., Denchev, V.S., Rose, G., Macready, W.G.: Qboost: large scale classifier training with adiabatic quantum optimization. In: Asian Conference on Machine Learning (ACML) (2012)
58. Neven, H., Rose, G., Macready, W.G.: Image recognition with an adiabatic quantum computer I. Mapping to quadratic unconstrained binary optimization. arXiv e-prints (2008)
59. Nguyen, N.T.T., Kenyon, G.T.: Image classification using quantum inference on the d-wave 2x. arXiv e-prints (2019)
60. Nielsen, M.A., Chuang, I.: Quantum computation and quantum information (2002)
61. Povh, J., Rendl, F.: Copositive and semidefinite relaxations of the quadratic assignment problem. Discret. Optim. **6**(3), 231–241 (2009)
62. Technical description of the d-wave quantum processing unit. https://docs.dwavesys.com/docs/latest/doc_qpu.html. Accessed 05 Mar 2022
63. Quist, A.J., de Klerk, E., Roos, C., Terlaky, T.: Copositive realxation for general quadratic programming. Optim. Methods Softw. **9**(1–3), 185–208 (1998)
64. Sahiner, A., Ergen, T., Pauly, J.M., Pilanci, M.: Vector-output relu neural network problems are copositive programs: convex analysis of two layer networks and polynomial-time algorithms. In: International Conference on Learning Representations (2020)

65. Sattler, T., Weyand, T., Leibe, B., Kobbelt, L.: Image retrieval for image-based localization revisited (2012)
66. Schonberger, J.L., Frahm, J.M.: Structure-from-motion revisited. In: Proceedings of the IEEE Conference on Computer Vision and Pattern Recognition, pp. 4104–4113 (2016)
67. Seelbach Benkner, M., Golyanik, V., Theobalt, C., Moeller, M.: Adiabatic quantum graph matching with permutation matrix constraints. In: International Conference on 3D Vision (3DV) (2020)
68. Shor, P.W.: Algorithms for quantum computation: discrete logarithms and factoring. In: Annual Symposium on Foundations of Computer Science (1994)
69. Systems, D.: D-wave details product expansion & cross platform roadmap (2021). https://tinyurl.com/yeyknn7y
70. Xiang, R., Lai, R., Zhao, H.: Efficient and robust shape correspondence via sparsity-enforced quadratic assignment. In: Proceedings of the IEEE/CVF Conference on Computer Vision and Pattern Recognition, pp. 9513–9522 (2020)
71. Yasuoka, H.: Computational complexity of quadratic unconstrained binary optimization. arXiv preprint arXiv:2109.10048 (2021)
72. Yurtsever, A., Fercoq, O., Cevher, V.: A conditional-gradient-based augmented lagrangian framework. In: International Conference on Machine Learning, pp. 7272–7281. PMLR (2019)
73. Yurtsever, A., Fercoq, O., Locatello, F., Cevher, V.: A conditional gradient framework for composite convex minimization with applications to semidefinite programming. In: International Conference on Machine Learning, pp. 5727–5736. PMLR (2018)
74. Yurtsever, A., Tropp, J.A., Fercoq, O., Udell, M., Cevher, V.: Scalable semidefinite programming. SIAM J. Math. Data Sci. **3**(1), 171–200 (2021)
75. Zaech, J.N., Liniger, A., Danelljan, M., Dai, D., Van Gool, L.: Adiabatic quantum computing for multi object tracking. arXiv preprint arXiv:2202.08837 (2022)
76. Zhou, X., Zhu, M., Daniilidis, K.: Multi-image matching via fast alternating minimization. In: International Conference on Computer Vision (ICCV), pp. 4032–4040 (2015)

# Self-supervised Learning of Visual Graph Matching

Chang Liu, Shaofeng Zhang, Xiaokang Yang, and Junchi Yan[✉]

MoE Key Lab of Artificial Intelligence, Shanghai Jiao Tong University,
Shanghai, China
{only-changer,sherrylone,xkyang,yanjunchi}@sjtu.edu.cn

**Abstract.** Despite the rapid progress made by existing graph matching methods, expensive or even unrealistic node-level correspondence labels are often required. Inspired by recent progress in self-supervised contrastive learning, we propose an end-to-end label-free self-supervised contrastive graph matching framework (SCGM). Unlike in vision tasks like classification and segmentation, where the backbone is often forced to extract object instance-level or pixel-level information, we design an extra objective function at node-level on graph data which also considers both the visual appearance and graph structure by node embedding. Further, we propose two-stage augmentation functions on both raw images and extracted graphs to increase the variance, which has been shown effective in self-supervised learning. We conduct experiments on standard graph matching benchmarks, where our method boosts previous state-of-the-arts under both label-free self-supervised and fine-tune settings. Without the ground truth labels for node matching nor the graph/image-level category information, our proposed framework SCGM outperforms several deep graph matching methods. By proper fine-tuning, SCGM can surpass the state-of-the-art supervised deep graph matching methods. Code is available at https://github.com/Thinklab-SJTU/ThinkMatch-SCGM.

**Keywords:** Self-supervise · Graph matching · Contrastive learning

## 1 Introduction

Graph matching (GM) has been a fundamental NP-hard problem, which has wide spectra of applications from computer vision, pattern recognition, to operational research. Traditional graph matching solvers either for two-graph matching [6,24,51] or multiple-graph matching [36,42,50] are mostly based on specific algorithms designed by human experts. Recently, machine learning-based approaches, especially deep network-based solvers are becoming more and more popular for their flexible data-driven nature and the easiness of making full use of the computing resource of the graphical processing unit (GPU). However,

---

C. Liu and S. Zhang—Equal Contribution.

© The Author(s), under exclusive license to Springer Nature Switzerland AG 2022
S. Avidan et al. (Eds.): ECCV 2022, LNCS 13683, pp. 370–388, 2022.
https://doi.org/10.1007/978-3-031-20050-2_22

most existing graph matching networks [10,29,32,37,53] as well as the shallow learning models [5] follow a supervised learning framework and thus call for ground truth node-level correspondences for training, which can be tedious or even impossible in practice.

In this paper, we resort to the **S**elf-supervised learning with **C**ontrastive learning and develop a learning network for visual **G**raph **M**atching without manually labeled node correspondence for supervision, called **SCGM**. In particular, we pursuit the most mild setting for label-free self-supervised learning of graph matching: even a single pair of matchable graphs is not required, let alone their node correspondences. In another word, we only assume there are multiple graphs (or images for graph extraction), which can be totally different and unmatchable to each other. In contrast, existing self-supervised GM model [38] requires access to the matchable pairs of graphs, and in fact often multiple such graphs to derive a global consistency or smooth loss. Moreover, existing graph matching methods need to assume that the matchable pairs of graphs always belong to the same category, which requires extra category information (normally only the same or very similar categories of objects can be matched) other than the node correspondences, while neither do we assume to require such category information. The essential difference of our approach is that we first perform data augmentation on the graph (with its visual appearance for images) to generate a set of its copies, such that **we can train neural networks to match any two of the copies from the same origin and the "ground truth" for this training can be easily calculated.** Besides, contrastive learning is performed by minimizing the distance of corresponding node features, that is, the node and its correspondences from the augmented graphs.

In particular, graph matching has been widely applied in computer vision ranging from image retrieval [40], object recognition [34], multi-object tracking [30] to action recognition [12], just to name a few. In this context as considered in this paper, it calls for effective learning of both visual appearances as well as graph structures. Based on this observation, we aim to incorporate both visual data augmentation as well as graph structure mixing to conduct self-supervised learning, and accordingly, both the convolutional neural networks and the graph neural networks are involved. Moreover, the node-level contrastive objective is proposed to help the encoder capture node-level information. In a nutshell, the main contributions are as follows:

1) To overcome the unrealistic labeling requirement for node correspondence bottleneck in existing supervised GM models, we propose a self-supervised based framework for label-free GM called SCGM. To the best of our knowledge, this is the first work for successfully learning a GM network without node correspondence labels (except for the finetuning stage), and even without the access to candidate matchable graphs[1]. In contrast, the (only) self-

---

[1] Typically matchable graphs are those falling into the same category, like the images of different cats, which is also the main setting of this paper. While it can be more general for graphs, e.g. there is partial matching between graphs.

supervised method GANN [38] assumes the access to matchable graphs. In other words, GANN needs extra category information while SCGM does not.

2) We propose a novel two-stage augmentation strategy on both raw images and constructed graphs to increase the variance of the views (copies) for self-supervised learning. Specifically for the graph augmentation, we propose a novel mixing strategy targeted to the previous arts, which helps reduce vicinal risk. To the best of our knowledge, we are the first to apply mixup in graph matching.

3) To better capture node-level information, we propose node-level contrastive objectives to auxiliarily train the encoder. In contrast, previous deep graph matching methods directly use a pretrained encoder (typically from ImageNet), which can be more focused on image-level information.

4) We evaluate our method in both label-free self-supervised and finetune settings in the common graph matching dataset. Results show that our method achieves promising performance. Specifically, our method outperforms GANN [38] with 10% accuracy under the label-free setting and more than 1% accuracy compared to BBGM [31] after finetuning in the Pascal VOC dataset.

## 2   Related Work

### 2.1   Graph Matching

Graph matching has been a standing problem in vision and pattern recognition, which attracted studies in developing both learning-free methods and learning-based models. For the latter which is the focus of this paper, most existing works assume that the node level correspondence is given, and this setting can be unrealistic due to the tedious labeling efforts. Readers are referred to the survey of deep graph matching [52].

We further briefly discuss the related GM works as follows. **1) Supervised models:** Most learning-based GM models fall into the supervised paradigm whereby the label information refers to the node correspondence among two graphs, which in fact require tedious human efforts. For pure graph matching, the graph neural network is introduced in the seminal work [29] without considering the visual information. In the context of GM with vision information as considered in this paper, the seminal work [54] for the first time shows how to end-to-end train a CNN to extract tailored visual features for GM. The subsequent works [19,37,53,57,58] further improve the performance for visual GM by introducing different techniques as well as the use of GNN. In particular, one recent competitive model [31] proposes to integrate classic combinatorial solvers with deep networks together. While NGMv2 [39] directly deals with the general Lawler's QAP form [26], which solves the problem via applying vertex classification on the association graph. **2) Label-free self-supervised models:** There also merge a few label-free self-supervised deep GM networks. In NGMv2 [39], a model is also devised by treating the smoothed matching outputs from pairwise matchings as the pseudo ground truth for self-supervised learning and in

GANN [38] the clustering and matching are jointly addressed with a side product of self-supervised GM network training, which achieves state-of-the-art performance and becomes the major competitor to our work.

## 2.2   Visual Correspondence Learning

Beyond deep graph matching, unsupervised learning has been an attractive paradigm for general visual correspondence problems including optical flow estimation, object tracking, stereo matching, and etc. **1) Optical flow:** Differing from the supervised flow network [8] that calls for dense pixel correspondence labels, concurrent work [18] propose unsupervised flow network by utilizing the classic photometric consistency over consecutive frames, with smoothness regularization, as the main metric for loss design. Along this direction, further, development is made in subsequent works either by better handling the occlusion (Unflow [27], OccAwareFlow [45]), and depth estimation [59] etc. Dense contrastive learning is also introduced in [44] for visual pre-training with shown benefits to downstream detection and segmentation tasks. While the self-supervising technique is also applied in registration with an explicit mapping function [46]. **2) Object tracking:** Spatio-temporal relevance and appearance consistency are often explored in tracker training as the self-supervision signal, which has shown promising performance in recent trackers [21,48]. In contrast, we focus on sparse correspondence problems with particular care on learning the graph structure.

## 2.3   Contrastive Learning

We generally divide the prior methods into two parts, i.e., task-irrelevant and task-relevant contrastive learning, where the former one aims to learn general information for better transferability. The latter one aims to learn backbone from the task-specific task, which can be used as a pre-trained model. **1) Task-irrelevant methods:** The classical objective of contrastive learning [3,13,16] is instance discrimination, which takes two views augmented from the same images as positives and others as negatives. Moco [16] proposes a memory bank module to store the negatives and they develop two tricks (stop-gradient and momentum update encoders) to prevent collapses [43]. SimCLR [3] proposes a simple, yet effective framework, which takes views of different images in one mini-batch as negatives. BYOL [11] directly discards the negative pairs. Correspondingly, a predictor module and EMA [22] update strategy are developed to prevent collapses. Recent work [4] is also devoted to exploring how to prevent collapses in SSL and hard negative mining by mixup [20,23]. These task-irrelevant methods [3,55] all show their strong transferability to other datasets or downstream tasks. **2) Task-relevant methods:** Task-relevant methods usually design pretext-tasks [7], which are similar to the target task. DenseCL [44] aims to improve the performance of detection and segmentation. Thus, they intuitively propose pixel-level contrastive learning, where for each query pixel in the feature map, they first find the corresponding closest pixel in the other view and maximize the agreement with them. Such a pretext task makes sense since, for segmentation and detection, pixel-wise information is required. PixPro [49] proposes to utilize the position information of each pixel before augmentation and maximize the agreement of the same pixel in the feature map of two views.

# 3 Preliminaries

**InfoNCE Based Contrastive Methods.** In general, the objective for InfoNCE [13] attracts representations of views from the same data sample e.g. image, and pushes the negative pairs away, which can be formulated as:

$$\mathcal{L}_{info} = -\mathbb{E}\left[\log \frac{\exp\left(\frac{\mathbf{z}_i^A \cdot \mathbf{z}_j^B}{\tau}\right)}{\sum_j \exp\left(\frac{\mathbf{z}_{j\neq i}^A \cdot \mathbf{z}_j^A}{\tau}\right) + \sum_j \exp\left(\frac{\mathbf{z}_i^A \cdot \mathbf{z}_j^B}{\tau}\right)}\right] \tag{1}$$

where $\mathbf{z}_i^A$ and $\mathbf{z}_i^B$ are the embedding of view $A$ and view $B$ of the $i$-th sample, respectively. $\tau$ is the temperature parameter [3,16]. The above objective function can be divided into two parts, i.e., **alignment** and **uniformity**, which can be expressed as:

$$\mathcal{L}_{info} = \underbrace{\mathbb{E}_{(x,x^+)\sim p_{pos}}\left[\frac{-f(x)^\top f(x^+)}{\tau}\right]}_{\text{alignment}}$$

$$+ \underbrace{\mathbb{E}_{\substack{(x,x^+)\sim p_{pos} \\ \{x_i^-\}_{i=1}^N \sim p_{data}}}\left[\log\left(e^{\frac{f(x)^\top f(x^+)}{\tau}} + \sum_i e^{\frac{f(x)^\top f(x_i^-)}{\tau}}\right)\right]}_{\text{uniformity}} \tag{2}$$

where $x^+$ and $x^-$ are positive samples and negative samples. Previous methods [4,43] have been devoted to exploring the effect of the two terms (alignment and uniformity), where the first term is the key to learning representations, while the second term can prevent collapses (all the data are mapped to a single point).

**Mixup in Supervised Learning.** Mixup [56] is an effective regularization with negligible computational overhead. It conducts a linear interpolation of two data instances in both input and label spaces and trains a model by minimizing the loss on the generated data and labels, which can be formulated as:

$$\mathcal{L}_{Mixup}((\mathbf{x}_i, \mathbf{y}_i), (\mathbf{x}_j, \mathbf{y}_j, \lambda)) = \mathcal{L}((1-\lambda)\cdot\mathbf{x}_i + \lambda\cdot\mathbf{x}_j, (1-\lambda)\cdot\mathbf{y}_i + \lambda\cdot\mathbf{y}_j) \tag{3}$$

where $\lambda$ is the pre-defined mixing rate. $\mathbf{x}_i$ and $\mathbf{y}_i$ mean the $i$-th data and label.

# 4 The Proposed SCGM

For matching of graphs extracted from visual images, we perform two-stage augmentation on both raw image data and the extracted graphs, as shown in Fig. 1.

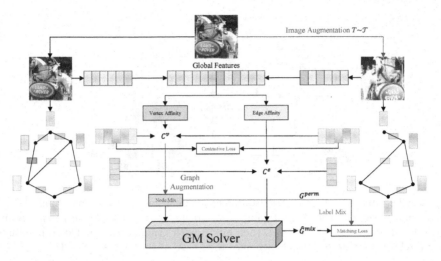

**Fig. 1.** Framework of the proposed SCGM (self-supervised contrastive graph matching framework). The proposed two-stage augmentation modules are highlighted in red. (Color figure online)

The objective is designated based on the resulting node information on augmented visual graphs. Note that previous self-supervised learning works either perform augmentation on image data [3,16], or on graph data alone [14,15]. While visual graph matching provides a pertinent test-bed for combing the two areas with new self-supervised learning approaches, which have not been studied in graph matching literature.

### 4.1 Two-Stage Augmentation with Label Mixing

Self-supervised learning methods often benefit from the variance of augmented views, where they force encoders to learn invariance over two views [43]. The intuition behind their success is maximizing the mutual information between two views $\mathcal{I}(\mathbf{Z}^A, \mathbf{Z}^B)$, where $\mathbf{Z}$ is the global semantic features. We do not directly follow the augmentation paradigm of existing methods [3,4,11]. Instead, we design two-stage augmentation on both raw images and constructed graphs to further increase the variance.

**Augmentation on Raw Images.** For the first-stage, to make sure each view can cover most of the node pixel in $\mathcal{P}$, we increase the crop size, which potentially increases the mutual information of two views $\mathcal{I}(\mathbf{X}^A, \mathbf{X}^B)$. Hence, we also increase the probability of other augmentations (gray-scale, Gaussian blur) to expand the variance of two views. The details (way and probability) of augmentations will be discussed in the experiment section about hyperparameters.

**Augmentations on Graph.** Augmentation on graph can be more subtle than on image. Many previous self-supervised methods in graph domain have tried

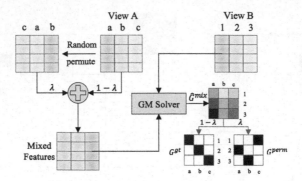

**Fig. 2.** Illustration of our mixing techniques for deep visual graph matching. Assume the pseudo ground truth of matching pairs are $[a \leftrightarrow 1]$, $[b \leftrightarrow 2]$, $[c \leftrightarrow 3]$, we first permute the node index of view $A$, then mix it with original feature. Correspondingly, the matching relation of $[a \leftrightarrow 1]$ becomes to $(1 - \lambda) \cdot [a \leftrightarrow 1] + \lambda \cdot [c \leftrightarrow 1]$.

different combinations of augmentations [14,15], e.g., edge/node dropping, add edge and re-weighting. However, node dropping and edge dropping are inappropriate for graph matching due to the lack of labeled nodes. Another approach is mixup [33], which not only helps classify data in decision boundary, but also reduces vicinal risk [2]. Given graph $\mathcal{G} = \{\mathbf{X}, \mathbf{A}\}$, where $\mathbf{X} \in \mathbb{R}^{N \times d}$ is the node sets. $N$ is the number of nodes and $d$ is the feature dimension. Then, for nodes in $i$-th graph, we generate new data by:

$$\mathbf{x}_i = (1 - \lambda) \cdot \mathbf{x}_i + \lambda \cdot \mathbf{x}_j \tag{4}$$

where $\mathbf{x}_i \in \mathbb{R}^{1 \times d}$ is the $i$-th node. $j \in [1, 2, \cdots, N]$ is a random value. Compared with the mixup in supervised learning, interpolating labels in graph matching calls for more non-trivial scheme design, which is detailed as follows.

**Mixing Labels.** Given two graphs with $N_1$ and $N_2$ nodes, we refer them to the number of nodes in view $A$ and view $B$ respectively. We denote the ground truth of node matching matrix as $\mathbf{G}^{gt} \in \mathbb{R}^{N_1 \times N_2}$, which can be easily calculated **without supervision** since view $A$ and view $B$ are from the same origin figure. Note that we only mix data of view $A$. Suppose one generated node $\hat{\mathbf{x}}_i^A = (1 - \lambda)\mathbf{x}_i^A + \lambda\mathbf{x}_j^A$, and $\mathbf{x}_i^A$, $\mathbf{x}_j^A$ should match with $\mathbf{x}_i^B$, $\mathbf{x}_j^B$, respectively. Then, the generated $\hat{\mathbf{x}}_i^A$ will match with both $\mathbf{x}_i^B$, $\mathbf{x}_j^B$ nodes with $(1 - \lambda)$ and $\lambda$ weights, respectively. Based on the random mixing index $(i \rightarrow j)$, we can construct a new matching matrix $\mathbf{G}^{perm}$. Finally, we formulate the weighted objective as: (see Fig. 2 as an illustration)

$$\mathcal{L}_{match} = (1 - \lambda) \cdot \mathcal{L}(\hat{\mathbf{G}}^{mix}, \mathbf{G}^{gt}) + \lambda \cdot \mathcal{L}(\hat{\mathbf{G}}^{mix}, \mathbf{G}^{perm}) \tag{5}$$

where $\hat{\mathbf{G}}^{mix}$ is the predicted matching matrix after the GM solver and $\mathcal{L}$ is the loss function of graph matching which is required to be compatible and the same with that used by the adopted deep GM backbone in SCGM, such as the permutation loss (for NGM [39]), and the Hamming loss (for BBGM [31]). Note that our method can be applied in both stat-of-the-art deep GM models in an out-of-box manner.

## 4.2 Node Level Contrastive Objective

A general paradigm of graph matching is to use the pre-trained encoder [17, 35] on ImageNet as backbone to obtain feature map, followed by some traditional algorithms [6] to construct graphs. However, this supervised pre-trained encoder only captures global information [31]. To enhance the ability of extracting finer-grained information of encoders, we design a node-level contrastive loss. Given a batch images $\mathbf{X} = \{\mathbf{x}_i\}_{i=1}^N$ and a set of node positions $\mathcal{P} = \{p_i\}_{i=1}^N$, we first generate two batch views $\mathbf{X}^A$ and $\mathbf{X}^B$ via a distribution of augmentation $\mathcal{T}$. Then, we feed the two batch views to encoder $f(\cdot, \theta)$ to get feature map $\mathbf{M}^A, \mathbf{M}^B \in \mathbb{R}^{C \times H \times W}$, respectively. In line with previous contrastive methods [3, 49], we add a pixel-level projection head after the encoder:

$$\mathbf{C}^A = \mathbf{W}_b(\sigma(\mathbf{W}_a \mathbf{M}^A)), \quad \mathbf{C}^B = \mathbf{W}_b(\sigma(\mathbf{W}_a \mathbf{M}^B)) \tag{6}$$

where $\sigma$ is the activation function. Instead of directly contrasting all the pixels in feature map like PixPro [49], which has been shown harmful to learn encoders [47], we utilize the prior of node positions. For each batch view, we select the node index by:

$$\mathcal{P}_i^{A(B)} = \{(i, h, w) | (h, w) \in p_i\} \tag{7}$$

where $\mathcal{P}_i^{A(B)}$ is the set of node index of the $i$-th image. Since view $A$ and view $B$ may cover different nodes (due to random cropping), we select the intersection set by:

$$\mathcal{S}_i^{A(B)} = \{(i, h, w) | (i, h, w) \in \mathcal{P}_i^A, (i, h, w) \in \mathcal{P}_i^B\} \tag{8}$$

Then, the node-level contrastive loss of view $A$ (similar for view $B$) is formulated as:

$$\mathcal{L}_{node}^A = -\mathbb{E}_{ihw} \log \frac{\exp(\mathbf{C}_{ihw}^A \cdot \mathbf{C}_{ihw}^B)}{\exp(\mathbf{C}_{ihw}^A \cdot \mathbf{C}_{ihw}^B) + \mathcal{N}} \tag{9}$$

where $(i, h, w) \in \mathcal{S}$ is the $h$-th row, $w$-th column pixel vector in feature map of $i$-th image. $\mathcal{N}$ is the negative part, which can be written as:

$$\mathcal{N} = \sum_{i'h'w'} \exp(\mathbf{C}_{ihw}^A \mathbf{C}_{i'h'w'}^B) + \exp(\mathbf{C}_{ihw}^A \mathbf{C}_{i'h'w'}^A) \tag{10}$$

where $(i', h', w') \in \mathcal{S}$ and $(i', h', w') \neq (i, h, w)$. The contrastive loss is the average of the two views:

$$\mathcal{L}_{node} = \mathcal{L}_{node}^A + \mathcal{L}_{node}^B \tag{11}$$

By the node-level contrastive loss, the encoder avoids contrasting each pixel, where some pixels are background (meaningless even harmful [47]). The overall objective function simply combines the contrastive loss and matching loss:

$$\mathcal{L} = \alpha \cdot \mathcal{L}_{node} + \mathcal{L}_{match} \tag{12}$$

where $\alpha$ is a pre-defined hyper-parameter about the ratio of contrastive loss.

# 5 Experiments

We conduct experiments on a popular open-source graph matching framework called ThinkMatch[2], which provides the implementation of many deep graph matching methods with protocol to popular datasets, for the purpose of better **reproducibility** and more fair comparison. We will release the code of our method and the configurations of all compared methods used in our experiments after publishing the paper. Experiments run on Intel(R) Xeon(R) E5-2678 v3 CPUs (2.50 GHz) and 8 GTX 2080 Ti GPUs.

## 5.1 Protocols

**Hyperparameters for Reproducibility.** The hyperparameters in our model can be basically divided into two parts: data augmentation and self-supervised learning. For the data augmentation part, the range of the cropping rate is $[0.3, 1.0]$, the range of the scale ratio is $[0.75, 1.33]$, the flip rate is $0.05$ for vertical and $0.25$ for horizontal, the color jitters parameters are $[0.4, 0.4, 0.4, 0.1]$ with the rate of $0.8$, the rate of gray-scale is $0.2$, the sigma of the Gaussian blur is $[0.1, 2.0]$ and the rate of Gaussian blur is $25$. For the self-supervised learning part, the mix rate $\lambda$ is set as $0.4$ and the contrastive loss ratio $\alpha$ is set as $0.2$. For the other hyperparameters of graph matching, we remain them as the same with the original backbone deep graph matching methods in ThinkMatch.

**Datasets.** We mainly use two real-world image datasets in our experiments:

1) **Pascal VOC dataset** [1] consists of 20 classes with keypoint labels on the natural images. The instances of this dataset vary by scale, pose, and illumination. The number of keypoints in each image ranges from 6 to 23, which is relatively large in the common GM dataset. We follow the standard data preparation procedure of [37]. Each object is cropped to its bounding box and scaled to 256 * 256 *px*.
2) **Willow Object dataset** [5] contains 256 images from 5 categories, of which each category is represented with at least 40 real-world images. Please note that the instances in the same class share 10 distinctive keypoints, which means there are no outliers. We follow the standard train-test split protocol in existing works [31, 39].

**Compared Methods.** We compare with various baselines, including learning-free, supervised learning, self-supervised learning graph matching methods. Please note SCGM is a pure label-free self-supervised learning framework, therefore, it is unfair to compare our method with existing supervised learning deep graph methods.

---

[2] https://github.com/Thinklab-SJTU/ThinkMatch.

**Learning-Free Methods: IFPF** [24] iteratively improves the solution via integer projection, given a continuous or discrete solution. **RRWM** [6] proposes a random walk view of the graph matching problem, with a re-weighted jump on graph matching. **PSM** [9] improves the spectral graph matching algorithm through a probabilistic view, which presents a probabilistic interpretation of the spectral relaxation scheme. **GNCCP** [25] follows the convex-concave path-following algorithm without involving the relaxation explicitly. **BPF** [41] designs a branch switching technique to deal with the singular point issue in the path following algorithms.

**Supervised Methods:** We compare our proposed method with existing popular deep graph matching methods: **GMN** [54], **PCA** [37], **NGM** [39], **IPCA** [37], **CIE** [53], **BBGM** [31], **NGMv2** [39], and the last two methods BBGM and NGMv2 are the state-of-the-art methods. Please note that the reported results of BBGM are slightly worse than the results in their paper since the protocol in ThinkMatch does not filter out keypoints out of the bounding box, as discussed in [39].

**Self-supervised Methods: GANN** [38] is the only self-supervised method of deep graph matching. We compare SCGM with the two-graph matching version of GANN. Please note that GANN still uses more information than SCGM, since GANN requires category information (two graphs belong to the same category) while SCGM does not. In fact, as discussed in the method section, learning of SCGM is still feasible even the graphs are all from different categories.

**Evaluation Metrics.** For testing, given the pair-wise images sampled from the dataset, graph matching methods predict a permutation matrix $\mathbf{X}^{pred} \in \mathbb{R}^{n_1 \times n_2}$. Based on $\mathbf{X}^{pred}$ and ground truth $\mathbf{X}^{gt} \in \mathbb{R}^{n_1 \times n_2}$ (note that $\sum \mathbf{X}^{gt}$ equals the number of inliers, since the rows and columns of outliers are always zeros.). Two popular evaluation metrics are used: accuracy and F1 score in the experiments on the real image datasets.

$$\mathbf{Precision} = \sum \left( \mathbf{X}^{pred} * \mathbf{X}^{gt} \right) / \sum \mathbf{X}^{pred}$$
$$\mathbf{Accuracy} \ (\ \mathrm{Recall}\ ) \ = \sum \left( \mathbf{X}^{pred} * \mathbf{X}^{gt} \right) / \sum \mathbf{X}^{gt} \qquad (13)$$
$$\mathbf{F1\ score} = (2 \cdot \mathrm{Recall} \cdot \mathrm{Precision}) / (\mathrm{Recall} + \mathrm{Precision})$$

where $*$ denotes element-wise multiplication. We use accuracy instead of F1 score in the non-outlier (intersection) settings since there is no need for calculating the F1 score.

**Table 1.** Average performance across all the objects w.r.t accuracy (%) on Pascal VOC with standard intersection filtering. The methods are grouped by supervised learning, learning-free, and self-supervised learning from top to bottom (see "Label").

| Method | Label | Aero | Bike | Bird | Boat | Bottle | Bus | Car | Cat | Chair | Cow | Table | Dog | Horse | Motor | Person | Plant | Sheep | Sofa | Train | Tv | Avg |
|---|---|---|---|---|---|---|---|---|---|---|---|---|---|---|---|---|---|---|---|---|---|---|
| GMN [54] | ✓ | 31.9 | 47.2 | 51.9 | 40.8 | 68.7 | 72.2 | 53.6 | 52.8 | 34.6 | 48.6 | 72.3 | 47.7 | 54.8 | 51.0 | 38.6 | 75.1 | 49.5 | 45.0 | 83.0 | 86.3 | 55.3 |
| PCA [37] | ✓ | 49.8 | 61.9 | 65.3 | 57.2 | 78.8 | 75.6 | 64.7 | 69.7 | 41.6 | 63.4 | 50.7 | 67.1 | 66.7 | 61.6 | 44.5 | 81.2 | 67.8 | 59.2 | 78.5 | 90.4 | 64.8 |
| NGM [39] | ✓ | 50.1 | 63.5 | 57.9 | 53.4 | 79.8 | 77.1 | 73.6 | 68.2 | 41.1 | 66.4 | 40.8 | 60.3 | 61.9 | 63.5 | 45.6 | 77.1 | 69.3 | 65.5 | 79.2 | 88.2 | 64.1 |
| IPCA [37] | ✓ | 53.8 | 66.2 | 67.1 | 61.2 | 80.4 | 75.3 | 72.6 | 72.5 | 44.6 | 65.2 | 54.3 | 67.2 | 67.9 | 64.2 | 47.9 | 84.4 | 70.8 | 64.0 | 83.8 | 90.8 | 67.7 |
| CIE [53] | ✓ | 52.5 | 68.6 | 70.2 | 57.1 | 82.1 | 77.0 | 70.7 | 73.1 | 43.8 | 69.9 | 62.4 | 70.2 | 70.3 | 66.4 | 47.6 | 85.3 | 71.7 | 64.0 | 83.8 | 91.7 | 68.9 |
| BBGM [31] | ✓ | 61.9 | 71.1 | 79.7 | 79.0 | 87.4 | 94.0 | 89.5 | 80.2 | 56.8 | 79.1 | 64.6 | 78.9 | 76.2 | 75.1 | 65.2 | 98.2 | 77.3 | 77.0 | 94.9 | 93.9 | 79.0 |
| NGMv2 [39] | ✓ | 61.8 | 71.2 | 77.6 | 78.8 | 87.3 | 93.6 | 87.7 | 79.8 | 55.4 | 77.8 | 89.5 | 78.8 | 80.1 | 79.2 | 62.6 | 97.7 | 77.7 | 75.7 | 96.7 | 93.2 | 80.1 |
| IPFP [24] | ✗ | 25.1 | 26.4 | 41.4 | 50.3 | 43.0 | 32.9 | 37.3 | 32.5 | 33.6 | 28.2 | 26.9 | 26.1 | 29.9 | 32.0 | 28.8 | 62.9 | 28.2 | 45.0 | 69.3 | 33.8 | 36.7 |
| RRWM [6] | ✗ | 30.9 | 40.0 | 46.4 | 54.1 | 52.3 | 35.6 | 47.4 | 37.3 | 36.3 | 34.1 | 28.8 | 35.0 | 39.1 | 36.2 | 39.5 | 67.8 | 38.6 | 48.4 | 70.5 | 41.3 | 43.0 |
| PSM [9] | ✗ | 32.6 | 37.5 | 49.9 | 53.2 | 47.8 | 34.6 | 50.1 | 35.5 | 37.2 | 36.3 | 23.1 | 32.7 | 42.4 | 37.1 | 38.5 | 62.3 | 41.7 | 54.3 | 72.6 | 40.8 | 43.0 |
| GNCCP [25] | ✗ | 28.9 | 37.1 | 46.2 | 53.1 | 48.0 | 36.3 | 45.5 | 34.7 | 36.3 | 34.2 | 25.2 | 35.3 | 39.8 | 39.6 | 40.7 | 61.9 | 37.4 | 50.5 | 67.0 | 34.8 | 41.6 |
| BPF [41] | ✗ | 30.9 | 40.4 | 47.3 | 54.5 | 50.8 | 35.1 | 46.7 | 36.3 | 40.9 | 38.9 | 16.3 | 34.8 | 39.8 | 39.6 | 39.3 | 63.2 | 37.9 | 50.2 | 70.5 | 41.3 | 42.7 |
| GANN [38] (two-graph) | ✗ | 19.2 | 20.5 | 24.1 | 27.9 | 30.8 | 50.9 | 36.4 | 22.3 | 24.4 | 23.2 | 39.8 | 21.7 | 20.5 | 23.9 | 15.8 | 42.2 | 29.8 | 17.1 | 61.8 | 78.0 | 31.5 |
| SCGM + BBGM [31] | ✗ | 37.6 | 49.9 | 54.8 | 54.5 | 65.6 | 56.4 | 60.6 | 52.3 | 36.8 | 51.4 | 50.4 | 47.2 | 59.4 | 51.2 | 38.3 | 91.3 | 59.3 | 52.7 | 83.1 | 88.4 | 57.1 |
| SCGM + NGMv2 [39] | ✗ | 34.3 | 48.2 | 51.0 | 52.2 | 63.3 | 56.0 | 62.0 | 50.1 | 38.5 | 49.9 | 39.9 | 46.2 | 54.8 | 52.1 | 37.4 | 82.3 | 56.8 | 51.4 | 80.2 | 78.8 | 54.3 |

**Table 2.** Average performance across all the objects w.r.t F1 score (%) (the higher the better) on Pascal VOC without filtering. It denotes that all graphs can contain outliers. The methods are grouped by supervised learning and self-supervised learning from top to bottom (see "Label").

| Method | Label | Aero | Bike | Bird | Boat | Bottle | Bus | Car | Cat | Chair | Cow | Table | Dog | Horse | Motor | Person | Plant | Sheep | Sofa | Train | Tv | Avg |
|---|---|---|---|---|---|---|---|---|---|---|---|---|---|---|---|---|---|---|---|---|---|---|
| GMN [54] | ✓ | 28.0 | 55.0 | 33.1 | 27.0 | 79.0 | 52.0 | 26.0 | 40.2 | 28.4 | 36.0 | 29.8 | 33.7 | 39.4 | 43.0 | 22.1 | 71.8 | 30.8 | 25.9 | 58.8 | 78.0 | 41.9 |
| PCA [37] | ✓ | 27.5 | 56.5 | 36.6 | 27.7 | 77.8 | 49.2 | 23.9 | 42.3 | 27.4 | 38.2 | 38.7 | 36.5 | 39.3 | 42.8 | 25.6 | 74.3 | 32.6 | 24.7 | 51.5 | 74.3 | 42.4 |
| BBGM [31] | ✓ | 37.0 | 65.0 | 50.1 | 34.8 | 86.7 | 67.1 | 25.4 | 56.1 | 41.6 | 58.0 | 38.3 | 52.9 | 55.0 | 66.6 | 30.7 | 96.5 | 49.5 | 36.4 | 76.4 | 83.1 | 55.4 |
| NGMv2 [39] | ✓ | 39.4 | 66.1 | 49.6 | 41.0 | 87.9 | 59.6 | 46.3 | 52.9 | 39.5 | 53.1 | 31.0 | 49.7 | 51.0 | 60.3 | 42.2 | 91.5 | 41.3 | 37.1 | 65.7 | 74.8 | 54.0 |
| GANN [38] (two-graph) | ✗ | 12.6 | 19.5 | 16.6 | 18.5 | 41.1 | 32.4 | 19.3 | 12.3 | 24.3 | 17.2 | 38.0 | 12.2 | 15.9 | 18.2 | 19.4 | 35.5 | 14.8 | 15.4 | 41.5 | 60.8 | 24.3 |
| SCGM + BBGM [31] | ✗ | 18.9 | 43.5 | 32.3 | 29.5 | 64.4 | 36.1 | 20.3 | 28.8 | 23.9 | 28.8 | 23.7 | 23.3 | 31.4 | 33.4 | 21.1 | 83.2 | 25.5 | 27.0 | 49.4 | 72.9 | 35.9 |
| SCGM + NGMv2 [39] | ✗ | 19.7 | 42.2 | 29.5 | 23.9 | 62.3 | 35.2 | 21.2 | 27.3 | 23.5 | 25.9 | 22.8 | 22.7 | 29.7 | 35.7 | 21.3 | 67.5 | 24.6 | 21.6 | 44.4 | 65.6 | 33.3 |

## 5.2  Experiments on the Pascal VOC Dataset

We first test our proposed self-supervised learning framework SCGM on the Pascal VOC dataset, which is a popular and relatively challenging dataset in the graph matching area. There are two common experiment settings in this dataset for pair-wise graph matching: 1) intersection ($\because \cap \therefore$) denotes the keypoints of each graph are filtered that only the keypoints present in both source and target image are preserved for the matching. 2) all keypoints ($\because \cup \therefore$) denote the keypoints are not filtered, which means there exist outliers in both the pair-wise graphs and the number of keypoints in two graphs may be different. In general, all-keypoints settings are harder than the intersection settings due to the outliers. We conduct the experiments on both intersection and all keypoints settings. The results are shown in Table 1 and Table 2. We adapt SCGM on BBGM and NGMv2, which are the two state-of-the-art deep graph matching methods.

In the intersection experiments, we compare our SCGM with supervised learning graph matching methods, traditional learning-free solvers, and self-supervised GANN. From the perspective of information required, SCGM uses

**Table 3.** Mean accuracy (%) across all the objects in the Willow Object dataset. The methods are grouped by supervised learning and self-supervised learning. Please note that our SCGM is trained in the Pascal VOC dataset and finetuned in Willow Object.

| Method | Label | Car | Duck | Face | Motorbike | Winebottle | Average |
|---|---|---|---|---|---|---|---|
| GMN [54] | ✓ | 67.9 | 76.7 | 99.8 | 69.2 | 83.1 | 79.3 |
| PCA [37] | ✓ | 87.6 | 83.6 | **100.0** | 77.6 | 88.4 | 87.4 |
| NGM [39] | ✓ | 84.2 | 77.6 | 99.4 | 76.8 | 88.3 | 85.3 |
| IPCA [37] | ✓ | 90.4 | 88.6 | **100.0** | 83.0 | 88.3 | 90.1 |
| CIE [53] | ✓ | 85.8 | 82.1 | 99.9 | 88.4 | 88.7 | 89.0 |
| BBGM [31] | ✓ | 96.8 | 89.9 | **100.0** | **99.8** | **99.4** | 97.2 |
| NGMv2 [39] | ✓ | **97.4** | **93.4** | **100.0** | 98.6 | 98.3 | **97.5** |
| GANN [38] (two-graph) | ✗ | 85.4 | **89.8** | **100.0** | 88.6 | 96.4 | **92.0** |
| SCGM + BBGM [31] | ✗ | **91.3** | 73.0 | **100.0** | 95.6 | **96.6** | 91.3 |
| SCGM + NGMv2 [39] | ✗ | 91.2 | 74.4 | 99.7 | **96.8** | 92.7 | 91.0 |

the same information as the learning-free solvers since we do not require any ground truth permutations. Please note that even GANN requires more information than SCGM since GANN needs to know two graphs belong to the same category while SCGM does not.

As shown in Table 1, our SCGM reaches the highest accuracy 57.1% among both the learning-free and self-supervised methods, which is even higher than the supervised learning GMN (55.3%). It is promising since SCGM does not require any ground truth matchings as labels, while GMN relies on such information for supervision.

In all keypoints experiments, we remove the traditional solvers since this setting is too hard for them and compare our SCGM with other deep graph matching baselines. As Table 2 shows, our SCGM surpasses GANN for more than 10%, with less information used than GANN. For illustration, we visualize some images from the data to show the matching results of SCGM in Fig. 5 (later in this section).

The experiments on Pascal VOC have verified SCGM. We notice that "SCGM + BBGM" is always better than "SCGM + NGMv2", but the performance of the original NGMv2 is better than BBGM. We think it is because NGMv2 uses a GNN as its back-end solver but BBGM uses a traditional one, making BBGM's training easier.

## 5.3 Experiments on the Willow Object Dataset

Then, we test SCGM on the Willow Object dataset, which is a traditional graph matching dataset. However, we have to face the issue that there are only 256 images in the Willow Object dataset, which is clearly not enough for our self-supervised training[3]. Therefore, we use the model trained by SCGM on the

---

[3] Unlike ours, GANN [38] utilizes another direction of self-supervised learning, which does not require the amount of data for pre-training.

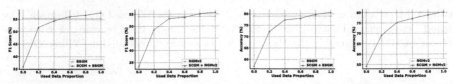

(a) BBGM; all keypoints (b) NGMv2; all keypoints  (c) BBGM; intersection  (d) NGMv2; intersection

**Fig. 3.** Results after finetuning with part of the data in the Pascal VOC dataset for our proposed self-supervised learning framework SCGM combined with BBGM and NGMv2. The settings of both intersection and all keypoints are reported.

**Table 4.** Ablation test about the sensitivity of hyper-parameters, as conducted on the Pascal VOC dataset with all keypoints. The backbone of SCGM is BBGM.

|          | 0.0   | 0.1   | 0.2       | 0.3   | 0.4       | 0.5   | 0.6   | 0.7   | 0.8   | 0.9   | 1.0   |
|----------|-------|-------|-----------|-------|-----------|-------|-------|-------|-------|-------|-------|
| $\alpha$ | 34.0% | 35.6% | **35.9%** | 35.1% | 33.8%     | 33.0% | 33.7% | 33.9% | 34.3% | 34.2% | 33.2% |
|          | 0.0   | 0.1   | 0.2       | 0.3   | 0.4       | 0.5   | 0.6   | 0.7   | 0.8   | 0.9   | 1.0   |
| $\lambda$| 33.7% | 35.0% | 35.7%     | 35.3% | **35.9%** | 35.4% | 25.8% | 24.0% | 21.8% | 22.8% | 21.6% |

Pascal VOC dataset as a prior and utilize few data from the Willow Object dataset to finetune the pre-trained model.

The results are shown in Table 3. We can see that SCGM outperforms many supervised learning methods including GMN, PCA, NGM, IPCA, and CIE. When compared with GANN, SCGM can reach better accuracy in the car, face, motorbike, and winebottle, except for the duck category. It is reasonable since **there are no duck images in the Pascal VOC dataset**, and it turns out SCGM is not trained well for the duck category. If we compare the other four categories, the average accuracy of "SCGM + BBGM" is 95.9%, which is 3% higher than GANN (92.6%).

To sum up, in the Willow Object dataset, our SCGM framework also reaches a competitive performance. It also shows that SCGM has some transferability and can generalize to other datasets to some extent.

### 5.4   Performance After Finetuning with Initialization

Except for pure self-supervised learning, our framework SCGM can also provide a better parameter initialization for existing graph matching methods. The self-supervised training procedure in SCGM can be regarded as finding a better-pretrained initialization. Therefore, we can finetune the model pretrained by SCGM in Table 1 and Table 2. To test initialization, we gradually add the amount of labeled data from 0% to 100%.

The results of finetuning in the intersection and all keypoints setting are shown in Fig. 3. We plot the results of normal training with all labeled data as a horizontal red line. The accuracy of finetuning with our initialization increases fast as more data is used. In all keypoints settings, finetuning with initialization can overhead the performance of the normal training with about 60%

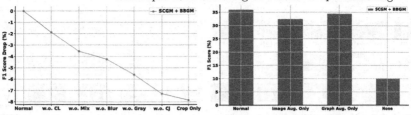

**Fig. 4.** F1 score drop by removing components from vanilla SCGM with BBGM as the backbone solver. **(left)**: Removing the components one by one; See x-axis from left to right by incrementally removing: contrastive loss, label mixing, Gaussian blur, gray-scale, color jitters, and finally, only crop remains. **(right)**: Removing the components categorized by graph augmentation and image augmentation. The x-axis denotes the normal SCGM, SCGM with only image augmentation, SCGM with only graph augmentation, and SCGM with no augmentation.

**Table 5.** Results after finetuning with part of the data from VOC. SCGM is pretrained on VOC and SPair-71k respectively, with BBGM as the backbone solver.

| Method | Pretrained dataset | Used data portion for finetuning | | | | |
|---|---|---|---|---|---|---|
| | | 20% | 40% | 60% | 80% | 100% |
| BBGM | – | – | – | – | – | 55.40% |
| SCGM + BBGM | Pascal VOC | **51.72%** | 54.45% | 56.21% | 56.79% | 57.76% |
| SCGM + BBGM | SPair-71k | 50.42% | **55.89%** | **56.57%** | **57.91%** | **59.52%** |

labeled data usage. Similar to previous experiments, SCGM is better combined with BBGM than with NGMv2. When finetune with all labeled data, our proposed framework can always reach the better accuracy: (a) 57.8% *vs.* 55.3%; (b) 55.9% *vs.* 54.0%; (c) 80.6% *vs.* 79.0%; (d) 80.2% *vs.* 80.1%; In the commonly used intersection settings, SCGM improves BBGM's accuracy by 1%.

We believe these results are promising since what we have done is only changing the initialization. It shows that our self-supervised framework SCGM can provide a better initialization for the graph matching problem.

## 5.5 Ablation Studies

The study focuses on two points: sensitivity of hyper-parameters used in SCGM, and impacts of different components of SCGM. First, we conduct the hyper-parameters experiments to show the impact of $\lambda$ (the mix rate) and $\alpha$ (the contrastive loss rate). The results are shown in Table 4. We keep one hyper-parameter unchanged and vary the value of the other one to see its sensitivity. In the normal setting of SCGM, we use $\alpha = 0.2$ and $\lambda = 0.4$ as the bold value in the table. We can see our proposed SCGM is not sensitive to $\alpha$, but sensitive to $\lambda$ when $\lambda > 0.5$. We conjecture it is because $\lambda > 0.5$ denotes that the original features are no longer the main component in the mixed features, which may cause the model to learn the wrong features. Then, we conduct experiments to see the

**Fig. 5.** Illustration of the matching results by SCGM combined with BBGM on the Pascal VOC. Green and red lines represent correct and incorrect node matchings respectively. The subtitle of each figure shows the correct matched/total keypoints count. (Color figure online)

effect of removing some components in SCGM. As Fig. 4 shows, we remove some of the key components of SCGM. In the left figure, we remove the components of SCGM one by one, from contrastive loss to label mixing, to Gaussian blur, to gray-scale, to color jitters, and at last only the crop of images remains. We can see that the removal of contrastive loss and label mixing lead to a relatively larger drop of performance. Therefore, the importance of contrastive loss and label mixing in SCGM is more significant to some extent, and the effectiveness of such design is proved. In the right figure, we divide the augmentations into graph augmentation and image augmentation, corresponding to our two-stage augmentation mentioned in Sect. 4. We can see that the performance of only using graph augmentation is better than the performance of only using image augmentation, and both are better than that with no augmentation. It turns out that the design of such two-stage augmentation in SCGM is necessary in better self-supervised learning in the graph matching area.

### 5.6  Ability of Transfer Learning

In the aforementioned experiments, we evaluate our method by the semi-supervised settings, which are also commonly used in BYOL [11]. In this subsection, we consider a new experiment scenario: pretraining SCGM on a larger dataset and then testing (transferring) on the Pascal VOC dataset. We think it is more useful to train the neural networks from a large-scale dataset and transfer the neural networks to downstream tasks, as a typical setting of self-supervised learning. Therefore, we conduct the experiments of transferring pretrained SCGM on Spair-71k [28] to the Pascal VOC dataset. Spair-71k is a large dataset in the graph matching area, which contains 70,958 images. We use the same training protocol as Sect. 4.4 and the results are shown in Table 5. The first two rows correspond to the results from Fig. 3(a), and the last row is the new experiments of pretraining from SPair-71k and testing (transferring) to VOC. It shows that pretrained on the larger dataset does improve the performance of our proposed SCGM, since SCGM performs much better when pretrained on the SPair-71k dataset.

# 6   Conclusion

In this paper, we have presented a self-supervised constrictive learning approach for visual graph matching, whereby neither node level correspondence label nor graph level class label is needed. The model involves contrastive learning with both convolution networks and graph neural networks. Moreover, we further generalize our model to the case that part of the graphs from the dataset are labeled by ground truth node correspondence. Comprehensive experimental results on natural images show the efficacy of our method, which outperforms the existing self-supervised graph matching methods. In the future, we aim to adapt SCGM to more complex settings, e.g. partial matching.

**Acknowledgements.** This work was supported in part by National Key Research and Development Program of China (2020AAA0107600), National Science of Foundation China (61972250, 72061127003), and Shanghai Municipal Science and Technology Major Project (2021SHZDZX0102).

# References

1. Bourdev, L., Malik, J.: Poselets: body part detectors trained using 3D human pose annotations. In: 2009 IEEE 12th International Conference on Computer Vision, pp. 1365–1372. IEEE (2009)
2. Chapelle, O., Weston, J., Bottou, L., Vapnik, V.: Vicinal risk minimization. In: Advances in Neural Information Processing Systems, pp. 416–422 (2001)
3. Chen, T., Kornblith, S., Norouzi, M., Hinton, G.: A simple framework for contrastive learning of visual representations. In: International Conference on Machine Learning, pp. 1597–1607. PMLR (2020)
4. Chen, X., He, K.: Exploring simple siamese representation learning. In: Proceedings of the IEEE/CVF Conference on Computer Vision and Pattern Recognition, pp. 15750–15758 (2021)
5. Cho, M., Alahari, K., Ponce, J.: Learning graphs to match. In: ICCV, pp. 25–32 (2013)
6. Cho, M., Lee, J., Lee, K.M.: Reweighted random walks for graph matching. In: Daniilidis, K., Maragos, P., Paragios, N. (eds.) ECCV 2010. LNCS, vol. 6315, pp. 492–505. Springer, Heidelberg (2010). https://doi.org/10.1007/978-3-642-15555-0_36
7. Doersch, C., Gupta, A., Efros, A.A.: Unsupervised visual representation learning by context prediction. In: ICCV, pp. 1422–1430 (2015)
8. Dosovitskiy, A., et al.: Flownet: learning optical flow with convolutional networks. In: ICCV, pp. 2758–2766 (2015)
9. Egozi, A., Keller, Y., Guterman, H.: A probabilistic approach to spectral graph matching. TPAMI **35**, 18–27 (2013)
10. Fey, M., Lenssen, J.E., Morris, C., Masci, J., Kriege, N.M.: Deep graph matching consensus. In: ICLR (2020)

11. Grill, J.B., et al.: Bootstrap your own latent: a new approach to self-supervised learning. arXiv preprint arXiv:2006.07733 (2020)
12. Guo, M., Chou, E., Huang, D.A., Song, S., Yeung, S., Fei-Fei, L.: Neural graph matching networks for fewshot 3D action recognition. In: Proceedings of the European Conference on Computer Vision (ECCV), pp. 653–669 (2018)
13. Hadsell, R., Chopra, S., LeCun, Y.: Dimensionality reduction by learning an invariant mapping. In: 2006 IEEE Computer Society Conference on Computer Vision and Pattern Recognition (CVPR 2006), vol. 2, pp. 1735–1742. IEEE (2006)
14. Hafidi, H., Ghogho, M., Ciblat, P., Swami, A.: Graphcl: contrastive self-supervised learning of graph representations. arXiv preprint arXiv:2007.08025 (2020)
15. Hassani, K., Khasahmadi, A.H.: Contrastive multi-view representation learning on graphs. In: International Conference on Machine Learning, pp. 4116–4126. PMLR (2020)
16. He, K., Fan, H., Wu, Y., Xie, S., Girshick, R.: Momentum contrast for unsupervised visual representation learning. In: Proceedings of the IEEE/CVF Conference on Computer Vision and Pattern Recognition, pp. 9729–9738 (2020)
17. He, K., Zhang, X., Ren, S., Sun, J.: Deep residual learning for image recognition. In: Proceedings of the IEEE Conference on Computer Vision and Pattern Recognition, pp. 770–778 (2016)
18. Yu, J.J., Harley, A.W., Derpanis, K.G.: Back to basics: unsupervised learning of optical flow via brightness constancy and motion smoothness. In: Hua, G., Jégou, H. (eds.) ECCV 2016. LNCS, vol. 9915, pp. 3–10. Springer, Cham (2016). https://doi.org/10.1007/978-3-319-49409-8_1
19. Jiang, B., Sun, P., Luo, B.: Glmnet: graph learning-matching convolutional networks for feature matching. Pattern Recogn. **121**, 108167 (2022)
20. Kalantidis, Y., Sariyildiz, M.B., Pion, N., Weinzaepfel, P., Larlus, D.: Hard negative mixing for contrastive learning. arXiv preprint arXiv:2010.01028 (2020)
21. Lai, Z., Lu, E., Xie, W.: Mast: a memory-augmented self-supervised tracker. In: CVPR (2020)
22. Lawrance, A., Lewis, P.: An exponential moving-average sequence and point process (EMA1). J. Appl. Probab. **14**(1), 98–113 (1977)
23. Lee, K., Zhu, Y., Sohn, K., Li, C.L., Shin, J., Lee, H.: I-mix: a domain-agnostic strategy for contrastive representation learning. arXiv preprint arXiv:2010.08887 (2020)
24. Leordeanu, M., Hebert, M., Sukthankar, R.: An integer projected fixed point method for graph matching and map inference. In: NIPS (2009)
25. Liu, Z.Y., Qiao, H., Xu, L.: An extended path following algorithm for graph-matching problem. TPAMI **34**(7), 1451–1456 (2012)
26. Loiola, E.M., de Abreu, N.M.M., Boaventura-Netto, P.O., Hahn, P., Querido, T.: A survey for the quadratic assignment problem. EJOR **176**, 657–90 (2007)
27. Meister, S., Hur, J., Roth, S.: Unflow: unsupervised learning of optical flow with a bidirectional census loss. arXiv preprint arXiv:1711.07837 (2017)
28. Min, J., Lee, J., Ponce, J., Cho, M.: Spair-71k: a large-scale benchmark for semantic correspondence. arXiv preprint arXiv:1908.10543 (2019)
29. Nowak, A., Villar, S., Bandeira, A., Bruna, J.: Revised note on learning quadratic assignment with graph neural networks. In: DSW (2018)
30. Pei, W.Y., Yang, C., Meng, L., Hou, J.B., Tian, S., Yin, X.C.: Scene video text tracking with graph matching. IEEE Access **6**, 19419–19426 (2018)
31. Rolínek, M., Swoboda, P., Zietlow, D., Paulus, A., Musil, V., Martius, G.: Deep graph matching via blackbox differentiation of combinatorial solvers. In: Vedaldi,

A., Bischof, H., Brox, T., Frahm, J.-M. (eds.) ECCV 2020. LNCS, vol. 12373, pp. 407–424. Springer, Cham (2020). https://doi.org/10.1007/978-3-030-58604-1_25

32. Sarlin, P.E., DeTone, D., Malisiewicz, T., Rabinovich, A.: Superglue: learning feature matching with graph neural networks. In: Proceedings of the IEEE/CVF Conference on Computer Vision and Pattern Recognition, pp. 4938–4947 (2020)

33. Shim, D., Kim, H.J.: Learning a domain-agnostic visual representation for autonomous driving via contrastive loss. arXiv preprint arXiv:2103.05902 (2021)

34. Shokoufandeh, A., Keselman, Y., Demirci, M.F., Macrini, D., Dickinson, S.: Many-to-many feature matching in object recognition: a review of three approaches. IET Comput. Vis. **6**(6), 500–513 (2012)

35. Simonyan, K., Zisserman, A.: Very deep convolutional networks for large-scale image recognition. arXiv preprint arXiv:1409.1556 (2014)

36. Solé-Ribalta, A., Serratosa, F.: Graduated assignment algorithm for multiple graph matching based on a common labeling. Int. J. Pattern Recognit. Artif. Intell. **27**(01), 1350001 (2013)

37. Wang, R., Yan, J., Yang, X.: Learning combinatorial embedding networks for deep graph matching. In: ICCV, pp. 3056–3065 (2019)

38. Wang, R., Yan, J., Yang, X.: Graduated assignment for joint multi-graph matching and clustering with application to unsupervised graph matching network learning. In: NeurIPS (2020)

39. Wang, R., Yan, J., Yang, X.: Neural graph matching network: learning lawler's quadratic assignment problem with extension to hypergraph and multiple-graph matching. TPAMI (2021)

40. Wang, S., Wang, R., Yao, Z., Shan, S., Chen, X.: Cross-modal scene graph matching for relationship-aware image-text retrieval. In: The IEEE Winter Conference on Applications of Computer Vision, pp. 1508–1517 (2020)

41. Wang, T., Ling, H., Lang, C., Feng, S.: Graph matching with adaptive and branching path following. IEEE TPAMI **40**(12), 2853–2867 (2017)

42. Wang, T., Jiang, Z., Yan, J.: Clustering-aware multiple graph matching via decayed pairwise matching composition. In: AAAI (2020)

43. Wang, T., Isola, P.: Understanding contrastive representation learning through alignment and uniformity on the hypersphere. In: International Conference on Machine Learning, pp. 9929–9939. PMLR (2020)

44. Wang, X., Zhang, R., Shen, C., Kong, T., Li, L.: Dense contrastive learning for self-supervised visual pre-training. In: ICCV (2021)

45. Wang, Y., Yang, Y., Yang, Z., Zhao, L., Xu, W.: Occlusion aware unsupervised learning of optical flow. In: CVPR, pp. 4884–4893 (2018)

46. Wang, Y., Solomon, J.M.: Prnet: self-supervised learning for partial-to-partial registration. arXiv preprint arXiv:1910.12240 (2019)

47. Wang, Z., et al.: Exploring set similarity for dense self-supervised representation learning. arXiv preprint arXiv:2107.08712 (2021)

48. Wu, Q., Wan, J., Chan, A.B.: Progressive unsupervised learning for visual object tracking. In: CVPR (2021)

49. Xie, Z., Lin, Y., Zhang, Z., Cao, Y., Lin, S., Hu, H.: Propagate yourself: exploring pixel-level consistency for unsupervised visual representation learning. In: Proceedings of the IEEE/CVF Conference on Computer Vision and Pattern Recognition, pp. 16684–16693 (2021)

50. Yan, J., Tian, Y., Zha, H., Yang, X., Zhang, Y., Chu, S.: Joint optimization for consistent multiple graph matching. In: ICCV (2013)

51. Yan, J., Zhang, C., Zha, H., Liu, W., Yang, X., Chu, S.: Discrete hyper-graph matching. In: CVPR (2015)

52. Yan, J., Yang, S., Hancock, E.: Learning graph matching and related combinatorial optimization problems. In: IJCAI (2020)
53. Yu, T., Wang, R., Yan, J., Li, B.: Learning deep graph matching with channel-independent embedding and Hungarian attention. In: ICLR (2019)
54. Zanfir, A., Sminchisescu, C.: Deep learning of graph matching. In: Proceedings of the IEEE Conference on Computer Vision and Pattern Recognition, pp. 2684–2693 (2018)
55. Zbontar, J., Jing, L., Misra, I., LeCun, Y., Deny, S.: Barlow twins: self-supervised learning via redundancy reduction. arXiv preprint arXiv:2103.03230 (2021)
56. Zhang, H., Cisse, M., Dauphin, Y.N., Lopez-Paz, D.: mixup: beyond empirical risk minimization. arXiv preprint arXiv:1710.09412 (2017)
57. Zhang, Z., Lee, W.S.: Deep graphical feature learning for the feature matching problem. In: ICCV, pp. 5087–5096 (2019)
58. Zhao, K., Tu, S., Xu, L.: IA-GM: a deep bidirectional learning method for graph matching. In: AAAI (2021)
59. Zou, Y., Luo, Z., Huang, J.-B.: DF-Net: unsupervised joint learning of depth and flow using cross-task consistency. In: Ferrari, V., Hebert, M., Sminchisescu, C., Weiss, Y. (eds.) ECCV 2018. LNCS, vol. 11209, pp. 38–55. Springer, Cham (2018). https://doi.org/10.1007/978-3-030-01228-1_3

# Scalable Learning to Optimize: A Learned Optimizer Can Train Big Models

Xuxi Chen[1]([✉]), Tianlong Chen[1], Yu Cheng[2], Weizhu Chen[2], Ahmed Awadallah[2], and Zhangyang Wang[1]

[1] The University of Texas at Austin, Austin, TX 78712, USA
{xxchen,tianlong.chen,atlaswang}@utexas.edu
[2] Microsoft Research, Redmond, USA
{yu.cheng,wzchen,hassanam}@microsoft.com

**Abstract.** Learning to optimize (**L2O**) has gained increasing attention since it demonstrates a promising path to automating and accelerating the optimization of complicated problems. Unlike manually crafted classical optimizers, L2O parameterizes and learns optimization rules in a data-driven fashion. However, the primary barrier, *scalability*, persists for this paradigm: as the typical L2O models create massive memory overhead due to unrolled computational graphs, it disables L2O's applicability to large-scale tasks. To overcome this core challenge, we propose a new scalable learning to optimize (**SL2O**) framework which (*i*) first constrains the network updates in a tiny subspace and (*ii*) then explores learning rules on top of it. Thanks to substantially reduced trainable parameters, learning optimizers for large-scale networks with a single GPU become feasible for the first time, showing that **the scalability roadblock of applying L2O to training large models is now removed**. Comprehensive experiments on various network architectures (i.e., ResNets, VGGs, ViTs) and datasets (i.e., CIFAR, ImageNet, E2E) across vision and language tasks, consistently validate that SL2O can achieve significantly faster convergence speed and competitive performance compared to analytical optimizers. For example, our approach converges 3.41~4.60 times faster on CIFAR-10/100 with ResNet-18, and 1.24 times faster on ViTs, at nearly no performance loss. Codes are in https://github.com/VITA-Group/Scalable-L2O.

## 1 Introduction

Gradient-based optimization methods are prevailing in the deep learning field, and over years dozens of gradient-based optimizers have been designed by researchers based on their expertise. Most of these optimizers apply specific

---

X. Chen and T. Chen—Equal Contribution.

---

**Supplementary Information** The online version contains supplementary material available at https://doi.org/10.1007/978-3-031-20050-2_23.

rules to calculate the update of parameters from their gradients, such as using momentum [33] or normalized gradients [12]. These manually crafted optimizers can mostly be expressed in a handful of analytical formulas, and they are often equipped with theoretical guarantees on some classes of optimization tasks [4].

However, recent works have pointed out that when focusing on a specific category of optimization tasks, one can pursue a different pathway to *learn* an optimizer instead of applying these hand-crafted optimizers to achieve better performance. This alternative paradigm, called Learning to Optimize (L2O) [27], aims at learning a more effective optimization algorithm from data. As depicted in Fig. 1, L2O normally takes the optimizee's training dynamic as input, and output optimization rules. Such learnable optimizers are capable of learning "shortcuts" that hand-crafted optimization algorithms fail to leverage [27], and they have demonstrated faster convergence speed and higher solution quality [4] and even save energy cost [24].

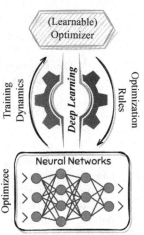

**Fig. 1.** The L2O pipeline.

L2O methods typically require a *meta-training* stage where a optimizer is learned with a set of *optimizees* sampled from a given *task distribution*. The learned optimizers are parameterized by neural networks, typically by recurrent neural networks [1,3,29,37]. However, L2O optimizers suffer from low *scalability*: the memory overhead due to the unrolled computational graphs required by training L2O optimizers limits the scales of optimization problems. For instance, [3] studied problems at matrix multiplication levels. [5] studied a three-layer multi-layer perceptron (MLP) ($\sim 10^4$ parameters) and a two-layer convolutional networks ($\sim 10^4$ parameters). [30,45] studied multi-layer MLPs for MNIST and CIFAR10 classification ($\sim 10^5$ parameters). [48] used the learned optimizer's weight to optimize Inception-V3 [40] but did not perform meta-training on it. [2] performed meta-training on Wide ResNet but they require thousands of CPU hours to parallelly train their RNN optimizers with multiple nodes. This main hurdle obstacles the more general application of L2O methods.

Our proposed solution, which aims at tackling the aforementioned obstacle, is a **subspace training framework for L2O**. Recent works [14,19,25,28] have suggested an alternative but effective way to train neural networks, *i.e.*, constraining the weight updates in tiny subspaces. The number of *independent* parameters is smaller in the subspace compared to full fine-tuning; therefore the corresponding subspace optimization problem is simplified. Motivated by these recent signs of progress on subspace training, we propose to reparameterize optimizee's weight updates inside a low dimensional subspace, making the optimization problem more memory-friendly for L2O. By reducing the number of independent parameters, the L2O models will track fewer intermediate representations for parameters, leading to smaller computational graphs and trimmed memory costs. For the first time, we enable the training of L2O models on giant models such as Vision Transformer [11] ($\sim 10^8$ parameters) and GPT-2 [34] ($\sim 10^8$ parameters) on a single GPU. Contributions are summarized as follows:

* We for the first time demonstrate that L2O can be scaled up to large-scale models such as ViT, removing the previous scalability roadblock of applying L2O methods. The keys behind scalability are simple subspace re-parameterization techniques.
* We propose a novel L2O training framework, **SL2O**, that seamlessly integrates subspace re-parameterization methods. We show that SL2O is applicable on a broad range of architectures like ResNets, VGG, and ViT[1], and can bring significantly better convergence and improved performance.
* Extensive experiments on vision (CIFAR-10, CIFAR-100, ImageNet) and language tasks (E2E) with large-scale networks validate the superiority of our proposals. For example, our learned optimizer obtains nearly unimpaired improvements with 29.3%/21.7% training iterations and 40 training parameters on ResNet-18 with CIFAR-10/CIFAR-100, which leads to impressive resource-efficiency compared to vanilla network training.

## 2    Related Work

*Low-Rank Structure in Training Neural Networks.* Literature [15, 25, 31, 52] point out that the intrinsic dimensionality of trained over-parameterized models is naturally low-rank. For example, [14, 25] perform optimization in a reduced subspace formed by random bases, leading to around 90% performance of regular SGD training. More works focus on imposing explicit low-rank constraints during training [20, 32, 36, 54, 55] and transferring [19, 46], which obtain considerable parameter efficiency. In the meantime, such low-rank structures enable more powerful optimization algorithms to address existing learning barriers like convergence speed. Specifically, thanks to largely reduced optimization variables, [28, 39, 43] exploit higher-order information and design delicate training approaches using curvature or Hessian, while maintaining overall computation efficiency and improving convergence. Different from previous works, we consider leveraging a superior learned optimizer to update within the tiny update subspace.

*Learning to Optimize.* Instead of hand-crafted optimization rules (e.g., SGD, Adam, and RMSprop), learning to optimize (L2O) leverages a data-driven learned model as the optimizer, which has achieved various successes in machine learning problems including black-box optimization [8], Bayesian swarm optimization [3], min-max optimization [37], domain adaptation [6, 24], adversarial training [21, 49], graph learning [51], and noisy label training [7]. [1] invents the first L2O pipeline parameterized by a long short-term memory (LSTM), which takes optimizee's gradients as input and outputs its update rules. It adopts a

---

[1] We also include GPT-2 results in the supplementary.

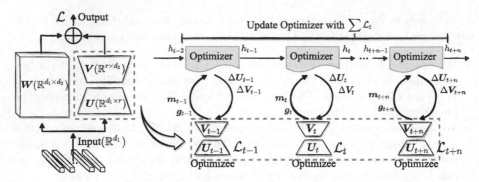

**Fig. 2.** The framework overview of our proposed scalable learning to optimize (SL2O). The network updates are constrained within certain intrinsic tiny subspaces, i.e., $U$ and $V$. Note that $W$ can be the concatenated weight matrix of CNN or a single transformer layer.

coordinate-wise manner that allows learned optimizers to be applicable for optimizees with different amounts of parameters. Another alternative reinforcement learning framework is proposed by [27], while it is limited in generalization to unseen optimizees. Latter, several efforts are made to empower the generalization ability of L2O. Specifically, [24,29] propose regularizers such as random scaling, objective convexifying, and Jacobian constraint; [48] designs a more sophisticated hierarchical recurrent neural networks (RNN) as an L2O; [5] utilizes advanced training techniques like curriculum learning and imitation learning; [30,46] constructs unbiased gradient estimators to learn enhanced optimizer. Recently, a survey paper of L2O [4] summarizes and benchmarks most of the achievements in this field.

## 3    Methods

### 3.1    Preliminaries

*Tiny Subspace of Network Updates.* The parameters inside a neural network are strongly correlated in multiple ways. For instance, the gradient back-propagation [17] process will relate gradients in different layers so that the parameters are also related. Therefore, it is possible to reduce the number of *independent* variables in a neural network. Recent studies [14,19,25] have pointed out that deep neural networks (DNN) can be trained in a tiny subspace. One can first identify a fixed number of "basis" vectors and then only optimize the *coefficient* of these basis vectors to get a sufficiently well-trained DNN. Generally speaking, a set of basis vectors $\{u_1, u_2, \ldots, u_N\}$ is calculated for a network (whose initialization is $W_0$), and the optimization goal is converted to learning a coefficient vector $w \in \mathbb{R}^N$ for weighing the bases. To derive the network's weights $W$ from $\{u_1, u_2, \ldots, u_N\}$ and $w$, a simple multiply-and-sum method would suffice: $W = W_0 - \sum_{i=1}^{N} w_i u_i$. Therefore, the network is updated in the subspace spanned by the bases $\{u_i\}_{i=1}^{N}$. Researchers have taken various methods to construct the bases and operate subspace training. [14,25] randomly generated these bases, and optimizing in the subspace spanned by these random bases can achieve surprisingly sufficient performance (over 90% of the full training accuracy). More recently, [28] sampled weights from the model training trajectory and performed spectral decomposition to derive orthogonal bases. Training in the subspace spanned by these orthogonal bases can match or even surpass the performance of optimizing all parameters in the model. [19] performed subspace training in a more refined layer-wise and efficient manner. The basis vectors are randomly initialized and can be optimized during training. This method has demonstrated its effectiveness on various language tasks, reaching on-par or even higher testing performance (Fig. 2).

*Learning to Optimize.* In Learning-to-Optimize (L2O), an *optimization task* is optimizing a network $f(\cdot; \theta)$, which we call *optimizee*, over a dataset. $\theta$ is the weights of the optimizee. The goal of L2O is to learn an *optimizer* for solving tasks from a *task distribution* $\mathcal{F}$, i.e., a set of similar optimization tasks. For example, $\mathcal{F}$ can be {Optimizing ResNet-20 on CIFAR-10}. Such a learned optimizer opt, parameterized by $\phi$, predicts the update for optimizee's weights as $\text{opt}(z_t; \phi)$. In literature, opt is usually modeled by a neural network. $z_t$ is a vector containing observations of historical training dynamics accessible at step $t$, such as the values and the gradients of $\theta_t$. The optimizee's weights $\theta$ are updated by $\theta_{t+1} := \theta_t - \text{opt}(z_t; \phi)$.

Learning an optimal update rule for an optimization task is equivalent to finding optimal optimizer weights $\phi$. A direct approach is to minimize the weighted sum of the optimizee's objectives over a time interval $T$ (i.e., *unroll length*):

$$\mathcal{L}(\phi) = \mathbb{E}\left[\sum_{t=1}^{T} \omega_t \mathcal{L}_t(f(x_t; \theta_t), y_t)\right], \quad \text{with } \theta_{t+1} = \theta_t - \text{opt}(z_t; \phi),$$

where $(x_t, y_t)$ are training samples and $\mathcal{L}_t(\cdot, \cdot)$ is the function for calculating the optimizee's objective, such as cross-entropy loss or mean-squared error. We set $\omega_t = 1, t = 1, 2, \ldots, T$ to assign equal importance to all training steps, and obtain $\phi$ by minimizing $\mathcal{L}$. Note that $\phi$ is correlated with $\mathcal{L}_t(f(x_t; \theta_t), y_t)$ since $\phi$ partially determines the optimizee's weights $\theta_t$.

Typically, the pipeline of L2O can be split into two stages: *meta-training* where $\phi$ is being optimized on tasks from the distribution $\mathcal{F}$, and *meta-testing* where $\phi$ is fixed and the learned optimizer $g$ is used to optimize a new optimization task. The meta-training stage is often done in an offline fashion since it requires time-consuming algorithms like truncated back-propagation through time [47]. However, the meta-training cost can be easily amortized at the meta-testing stage, which is expected to have a faster convergence speed.

## 3.2   Scalable Learning to Optimize

*Combining Subspace Training with L2O.* Previous L2O techniques directly predict updates for all the parameters, so most works can only perform meta-trainings on small-scale networks and require a large number of computational resources. In contrast, SL2O leverages the subspace training technique to reduce the number of independent parameters, and scale up to large models such as VGG-16 and ViT. For CNNs having $d$ parameters, we derive the orthogonal basis matrix $P \in \mathbb{R}^{r \times d}$ by performing SVD matrix decomposition and set $\boldsymbol{\theta} \in \mathbb{R}^{1 \times r}$ as the coefficients for $P$, where $r$ is the number of orthogonal basis vectors. Consequently, the weights of a CNN can be represented by $\boldsymbol{W} := \boldsymbol{W}_0 - \boldsymbol{\theta}P$. We do not directly embed $\boldsymbol{\theta}$ in CNNs and consider it as a *virtual* parameter. The gradient on $\boldsymbol{\theta}$ can be calculated by the following formula:

$$\frac{\partial \mathcal{L}_t}{\partial \boldsymbol{\theta}} = \nabla_{\boldsymbol{W}} \mathcal{L}_t \frac{\partial \boldsymbol{W}}{\partial \boldsymbol{\theta}} = (\nabla_{\boldsymbol{W}} \mathcal{L}_t) P^T,$$

suggesting that we only need a projection operation to construct the gradients. The predicted update for $\boldsymbol{\theta}$ from SL2O will also be projected back to update $\boldsymbol{W}$. By using such an indirect interacting method, we need not to store the value of $\boldsymbol{\theta}_t$ and save more memory. By default we set the number of independent trainable variables $r$ to 40, which is negligible compared to $d$.

For transformer-based models (ViT, DeiT, and GPT-2), we use a slightly different subspace method for transformer-based models since performing SVD decomposition at such scales requires enormous memory. Alternatively, we seek a more refined layerwise we decompose the update of weights $\Delta \boldsymbol{W} \in \mathbb{R}^{d_1 \times d_2}$ into two matrices $\boldsymbol{U} \in \mathbb{R}^{d_1 \times r}$ and $\boldsymbol{V} \in \mathbb{R}^{r \times d_2}$, and constrain $\Delta \boldsymbol{W} = \boldsymbol{U}\boldsymbol{V}$. $\boldsymbol{V}$ can be seen as a learnable and **shared** basis vectors since different rows in $\Delta \boldsymbol{W}$ are all linear combinations of row vectors in $\boldsymbol{V}$. For different layers in a network, we learn different decomposition matrices so that the subspace structures are more fine-grained. We explicitly embed $\boldsymbol{U}$ and $\boldsymbol{V}$ in the optimizee, and let $\boldsymbol{\theta} = \{\boldsymbol{U}, \boldsymbol{V}\}$ so that they would be the target parameters of SL2O. In this case we set $r$ to be 16; the number of trainable parameters in $\boldsymbol{U}$ and $\boldsymbol{V}$ is $(d_1 + d_2) \times r$, which is significantly smaller than $d_1 \times d_2$ if $r$ is small. We follow [19] to only apply the re-parameterization on attention weights.

*The Meta-training and Meta-testing Stage of SL2O Optimizers.* To train our SL2O optimizer, we sample multiple optimization tasks from a task distribution and train the optimizer on each task for a certain number of iterations. Previous works [3,5,45] also followed the same pipeline. For each task, the orders of training data are different so that the optimizer will not memorize the data order [50]. Following [29], we use the scaled gradients and their momentum as the observations of training dynamics. We limit the number of training steps to be $N$ for each optimization task, and we split the whole training sequence ($N$ training steps) into sub-sequences of length $T$. The value of $N$ is set as 1000 so the effort of training an L2O optimizer is small and can be easily amortized. The unroll length $T$ is fixed to be 10, and we will demonstrate that the choice of $T$

**Algorithm 1.** The general training pipeline of SL2O.

---

**Input:** optimizee $f(\cdot;\cdot)$, optimizer $opt(\cdot;\cdot)$, current training step $t$, initial optimizee weights $\boldsymbol{\theta}_0$, optimizer weights $\boldsymbol{\phi}_t$, optimizee's objective $\mathcal{L}_t(\cdot,\cdot)$, a training set $\mathcal{D}_{\text{train}}$, a testing set $\mathcal{D}_{\text{test}}$, coefficients $\beta_1$ and $\beta_2$, unroll length $T$, training steps $N$ for each epoch, and number of epochs $E$
**Output:** Optimal optimizer weights $\phi$
**for** epoch $< E$ **do**
   Initialize $\boldsymbol{m} = \boldsymbol{0}$ and $\boldsymbol{v} = \boldsymbol{0}$
   **for** i=0, $T$, $2T$ ..., $([N/T]-1) \times T$ **do**           $\triangleright$ $[N/T]$ sub-sequences
      Set $\mathcal{L} \leftarrow 0$
      **for** j=0, 1, 2 ..., $T-1$ **do**
         $t := i + j$
         Sample a batch $\mathcal{B}$ from the training set $\mathcal{D}_{\text{train}}$
         Calculate the training loss on $\mathcal{B}$ : $\mathbb{E}_{(x,y) \in \mathcal{B}} \mathcal{L}_t(f(\boldsymbol{x}; \boldsymbol{\theta}_t), y)$ and the gradient
on $\boldsymbol{\theta}_t$: $\boldsymbol{g}_t = \nabla_\theta \mathbb{E}_{(x,y) \in \mathcal{B}} \mathcal{L}_t(f(\boldsymbol{x}; \boldsymbol{\theta}_t), y)$
         Update $\boldsymbol{m} \leftarrow \beta_1 \boldsymbol{m} + (1-\beta_1)\boldsymbol{g}_t$ and $\boldsymbol{v} \leftarrow \beta_2 \boldsymbol{v} + (1-\beta_2)\boldsymbol{g}_t^2$
         Calculate $\hat{\boldsymbol{m}} \leftarrow \boldsymbol{m}/(1-\beta_1^{t+1})$, $\hat{\boldsymbol{v}} \leftarrow \boldsymbol{v}/(1-\beta_2^{t+1})$
         Calculate $\tilde{\boldsymbol{g}} \leftarrow \boldsymbol{g}_t/\sqrt{\hat{\boldsymbol{v}}+\epsilon}$, $\tilde{\boldsymbol{m}} \leftarrow \hat{\boldsymbol{m}}/\sqrt{\hat{\boldsymbol{v}}+\epsilon}$       $\triangleright$ features calculation
         Construct $\boldsymbol{z}_t$ from $\boldsymbol{z}_t$ from $\tilde{\boldsymbol{g}}$ and $\tilde{\boldsymbol{m}}$
         Update $\boldsymbol{\theta}_{t+1} \leftarrow \boldsymbol{\theta}_t - \text{opt}(\boldsymbol{z}_t; \boldsymbol{\phi})$     $\triangleright$ Update the optimizee's weights
         $\mathcal{L} \leftarrow \mathcal{L} + \mathbb{E}_{(x,y) \in \mathcal{B}} \mathcal{L}_t(f(\boldsymbol{x}; \boldsymbol{\theta}_t), y)$       $\triangleright$ Loss calculation
      Update $\phi$ by minimizing $\mathcal{L}$ using gradient descent-based methods for one step
   Evaluate $f(\cdot; \boldsymbol{\theta}_N)$ on $\mathcal{D}_{\text{test}}$ and find the optimal $\phi$

---

does not have a dominating effect in Sect. 4.5. We evaluate the model with the updated parameters $\boldsymbol{\theta}_N$ on the testing set $\mathcal{D}_{\text{valid}}$, and choose the best optimizer parameters according to the testing performance. A detailed algorithm for the meta-training stage is shown in Algorithm 1.

After we obtain the best parameters of the learned optimizers, we switch to the meta-testing stage and use the learned optimizer to train a new optimization task. Note that during this meta-testing stage we will fix $\phi$. The learned optimizer receives the same set of observations of the optimizee's training dynamics and predicts updates for $\boldsymbol{\theta}$ at every training step $t$.

# 4 Experiments

## 4.1 Implementation Details

*Architectures and Datasets.* We study two sets of networks: (*i*) CNNs, including ResNet-20 [16], ResNet-18 [16], and VGG-16 [38]; (*ii*) Transformer-based models [44], including ViT [11], DeiT [42] (and in supplementary, GPT-2 [34]). We study four datasets: CIFAR-10 [23], CIFAR-100 [23], and ImageNet [10], and E2E [13] dataset for the GPT-2 experiments. We also study a small network ResNet-8 (results deferred to the supplementary files).

*Baseline Optimizers.* We choose several widely used optimizers as the baselines for comparison: Stochastic Gradient Descent (SGD) [35], Momentum [33],

**Table 1.** Comparison of testing accuracy using different optimizers with four network architectures on CIFAR-10. We report both the average and the confidence interval of the best testing accuracy. The superscription $^\dagger$ means that the model is updated in a tiny subspace.

| Optimizer | Testing Accuracy | | | Convergence Steps | | |
|---|---|---|---|---|---|---|
| | ResNet-20 | ResNet-18 | VGG-16 | ResNet-20 | ResNet-18 | VGG-16 |
| SGD | $88.72_{\pm 0.09}\%$ | $93.48_{\pm 0.15}\%$ | $92.81_{\pm 0.22}\%$ | 5073.8 | 2351.2 | 1250.4 |
| Momentum | $91.27_{\pm 0.30}\%$ | $93.90_{\pm 0.37}\%$ | $92.96_{\pm 0.13}\%$ | 3280.8 | 4316.8 | 2972.0 |
| Adam | $90.19_{\pm 0.21}\%$ | $93.54_{\pm 0.13}\%$ | $92.06_{\pm 0.29}\%$ | 3554.0 | 2688.0 | 6767.0 |
| RMSProp | $90.16_{\pm 0.20}\%$ | $93.01_{\pm 0.22}\%$ | $86.26_{\pm 0.29}\%$ | 1776.2 | 1856.4 | 13189.4 |
| SGD$^\dagger$ | $90.61_{\pm 0.08}\%$ | $92.99_{\pm 0.08}\%$ | $89.03_{\pm 0.26}\%$ | 1468.0 | 1318.2 | 2315.8 |
| Momentum$^\dagger$ | $90.97_{\pm 0.03}\%$ | $93.70_{\pm 0.01}\%$ | $92.77_{\pm 0.05}\%$ | 333.0 | 216.8 | 383.4 |
| SL2O | $91.00_{\pm 0.05}\%$ | $93.61_{\pm 0.02}\%$ | $92.74_{\pm 0.03}\%$ | 90.2 | 63.6 | 57.4 |

Adam [22], and RMSProp [41]. The optimizer settings are reported in Table 1 in the supplementary file. We also apply two of them (SGD and Momentum) with the subspace training techniques, which we call "SGD$^a$" and "Momentum$^a$" (the $^a$superscription means subspace training).

*Metrics.* On image datasets (CIFAR-10, CIFAR-100, and ImageNet), we use the accuracy on testing set and the first convergence step of training as our metrics. We say the training is converged at step $t$ if $\text{std}(\mathcal{L}_{t-19}, \ldots, \mathcal{L}_t) < 0.1$ and $\mathcal{L}_t < \mathcal{L}^* + 0.1$, where $\text{std}(\cdot)$ is the standard deviation, $\mathcal{L}_t$ is the training loss at step $t$ and $\mathcal{L}^*$ is the globally minimal training loss. On the language dataset E2E, we report the validation loss. Note that most existing works on L2O evaluate their methods **only by reporting training losses**; we take one more step and also take the testing loss/accuracy into consideration.

*Meta-training and Meta-testing Settings.* We meta-train the optimizer on 20 sampled optimization tasks (i.e., 20 epochs) from every task distribution. We use Adam with a learning rate of 0.01 to train our optimizer, and maintain the same learning rate across the whole meta-training process. For the meta-testing stage, the numbers of training epochs for (ResNets, VGGs, ViT, DeiT) are by default (100, 100, 20, 20) respectively, and the training batch sizes are 128 for all experiments. For baseline optimizers, we share the same training epochs and batch sizes with our SL2O optimizer. The structure of our SL2O optimizer is based on an LSTM [18], and we will show the details of the architecture of our SL2O optimizer in the supplementary files. SL2O operates in a coordinate-wise fashion [8], which enables SL2O to optimizees with distinctive numbers of parameters. To be specific, for each parameter in the subspace, SL2O takes its observation vector as input and produces its update.

## 4.2   Superior Performance on ResNets

We first conduct experiments on CIFAR-10, and report the testing accuracy and the convergence steps in Table 1. We can draw several conclusions from

**Table 2.** Comparison of testing accuracy using different optimizers with four network architectures on CIFAR-100. We report both the average and the confidence interval of the best testing accuracy. The superscription $^\dagger$ means that the model is updated in a tiny subspace.

| Optimizer | Testing accuracy | | | Convergence steps | | |
|---|---|---|---|---|---|---|
| | ResNet-20 | ResNet-18 | VGG-16 | ResNet-20 | ResNet-18 | VGG-16 |
| SGD | $63.18_{\pm0.40}\%$ | $73.96_{\pm0.10}\%$ | $70.43_{\pm0.14}\%$ | 20286.6 | 6353.0 | 11558.6 |
| Momentum | $67.29_{\pm0.36}\%$ | $73.92_{\pm0.41}\%$ | $70.61_{\pm0.28}\%$ | 26242.2 | 6860.6 | 19693.4 |
| Adam | $64.59_{\pm0.39}\%$ | $73.76_{\pm0.23}\%$ | $66.05_{\pm0.20}\%$ | 18397.6 | 7947.0 | 19828.8 |
| RMSProp | $63.53_{\pm0.56}\%$ | $65.91_{\pm0.57}\%$ | $14.62_{\pm6.84}\%$ | 15459.6 | 6707.8 | 15589.0 |
| SGD$^\dagger$ | $66.64_{\pm0.18}\%$ | $74.74_{\pm0.05}\%$ | $59.96_{\pm0.95}\%$ | 4420.4 | 1787.2 | 10198.8 |
| Momentum$^\dagger$ | $66.89_{\pm0.04}\%$ | $74.76_{\pm0.06}\%$ | $70.98_{\pm0.04}\%$ | 636.2 | 283.2 | 2104.8 |
| SL2O | $67.04_{\pm0.07}\%$ | $74.67_{\pm0.14}\%$ | $71.02_{\pm0.09}\%$ | 105.4 | 61.6 | 168.2 |

these tables: 1) On CIFAR-10, Momentum is the overall best optimizer for all architectures regarding the testing accuracy. However, it needs over 1000 training steps to reach convergence; 2) Momentum$^\dagger$ and SL2O achieve nearly the same level of testing accuracy, and their performances are both comparable with the performance of Momentum; 3) The convergence speeds of SL2O are significantly faster than all other baselines. On {ResNet-20, ResNet-18, VGG-16}, our method can achieve convergence with {90.2,63.6,57.4} training steps on average, while the best analytical baseline optimizer Momentum$^\dagger$ needs {333.0,216.8,383.4} training steps for convergence on average, which is {3.69,3.41,6.68} times slower. We further show the training loss and testing accuracy in the first 10000 steps in Fig. 3. The convergence speeds of the L2O optimizer surpass the convergence speeds of other baselines: SL2O achieves nearly full accuracy after hundreds of training iterations, and the speed of training loss decreasing is the highest among all baseline methods. Moreover, the advantage on convergence speed of SL2O compared to other methods on CIFAR-10 seems to be bigger as the number of parameters gets larger, manifested by the enlarging spaces between early training loss curves collected from ResNet-20 to VGG-16 models.

We continue to test our method on CIFAR-100 with ResNet-20, ResNet-18, and VGG-16, and we have drawn a similar conclusion from the experiments. The testing accuracy and the convergence steps are shown in Table 2. We can see that: 1) Among all optimization methods, our L2O optimizer has the fastest convergence speed: on {ResNet-20,ResNet-18,VGG-16}, SL2O can achieve convergence with only {105.4, 61.6, 168.2} steps on average, while the most competitive baseline Momentum$^\dagger$ needs {636.2, 283.2, 2104.8} steps, which is {6.04, 4.60, 12.51} times more, respectively; 2) Compared to CIFAR-10, SL2O performs much better on CIFAR-100 in terms of testing accuracy, achieving superior performance on some cases compared to other analytical optimizers, with or without the subspace reparameterization technique. Specifically, we achieve higher testing accuracy on ResNet-20 and VGG-16 compared to Momentum$^\dagger$, although the confidence intervals overlap. From Fig. 4 we can further validate the superiority

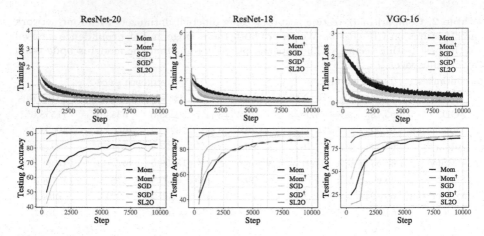

**Fig. 3.** Comparison of training loss and testing accuracy on CIFAR-10 with various optimizers. Results of the first 10,000 training steps are presented. The superscription † means that the model is updated in a tiny subspace.

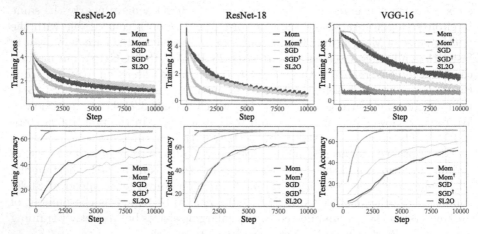

**Fig. 4.** Comparison of training loss and testing accuracy on CIFAR-10 with various optimizers. Results of the first 10,000 training steps are presented. The superscription † means that the model is updated in a tiny subspace.

of our SL2O method. SL2O achieves high accuracy with only hundreds of training steps, and the gaps between early training loss curves are more significant as the model sizes get larger.

Finally, we validate our SL2O optimizer on a large-scale dataset, *i.e.*, ImageNet, with ResNet-18. We present the training loss in the first 11000 steps and the best testing accuracy after training for 40 epochs in Fig. 5. We can see from the figure that SL2O significantly outperforms other methods regarding the convergence speed since the loss curve for SL2O becomes stable in less than 1000 training steps while the most competitive baseline (Mom†) needs around

5000 training steps, which is approximately 5 times faster. After training for 40 epochs, the testing accuracy of ResNet-18 optimized with SL2O (68.78%) is comparable to SGD† (68.86%) and Momentum† (68.83%), only with slight accuracy loss. In summary, our SL2O optimizer is capable of achieving convergence faster than all analytical baseline optimizers and comparable performance (testing accuracy) on various CNN optimizees.

### 4.3  Superior Performance on Transformer-Based Models

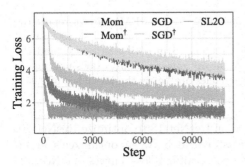

**Fig. 5.** Training loss on ImageNet with ResNet-18.

We deploy the SL2O optimizer to finetune two transformer-based vision models, ViT and DeiT, on CIFAR-10. To be more concrete, we use the official ViT-B/16 (~83M parameters) pretrained on ImageNet and the DeiT-tiny-distilled (~8M parameters) pretrained as the starting points for fine-tuning. The number of the fine-tuning epoch is set to 10 since we observe no improvement afterward. Figure 6 shows the performance of optimizing with Mom, Mom† with different learning rates, and the performance of SL2O on ViT-B/16. We can see from the figure that SL2O achieves lower training loss and fastest convergence while preserving high testing accuracy. Numerically, SL2O hits a testing accuracy of 98.5% with only two epochs and consistently outperforms other baselines with subspace training. Training by using SL2O converges at the 484-th step while Mom$^†_{0.04}$ needs 602 steps, which is 1.24 times longer. SL2O eventually gets surpassed by the analytical optimizer Momentum; however, it is still an efficient optimizer and demonstrates the effectiveness of SL2O on optimizees at the level of $10^8$ parameters. It is noteworthy that almost all existing L2O approaches benefit more at the early stage rather than the final performance [29], which is a fundamental yet unsolved problem in L2O, i.e., meta-testing with a "longer horizon" [29]. Note that the previous best L2O is capable of maintaining superior meta-testing performance for ~ 4k iterations on small MLPs, while our SL2O enables an improved "horizon" like 5k iterations in the ViT training. Lastly, we offer a simple remedy to this challenging problem - leveraging both learned and analytical optimizers: (i) apply SL2O in the early stage such as the first 5k steps then (ii) switch to the analytical optimizer, and we obtain an extra 0.12% accuracy boost and match Mom in the late stage. We have observed similar results and validness on DeiT; therefore, we defer these results to the supplementary files.

### 4.4  The Transferability of SL2O

We conduct two experiments to study the transferability of SL2O between different task distributions $\mathcal{F}$: using an SL2O optimizer meta-trained on ResNet-20 to

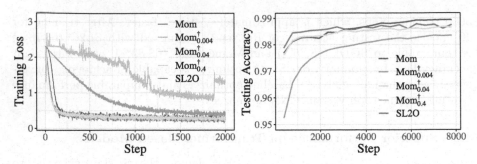

**Fig. 6.** Training loss and testing accuracy of ViT-B/16 on CIFAR-10. We report the training loss in the first 2000 steps and the testing accuracy in the first 8000 steps. The superscription $^{\dagger}$ means that the model is updated in a tiny subspace, and the subscription means the initial learning rate of the optimizers. $\text{Mom}^{\dagger}_{0.4}$ does not appear in the figure of testing accuracy since the accuracies are below the lower bar of 0.95.

optimize ResNet-18, and one meta-trained on ResNet-18 to optimize ResNet-20. We empirically prove that SL2O is **transferable** between optimizee's architectures in Fig. 7. The left figure shows the training loss curves on ResNet-18, and the right figure shows the curves on ResNet-20. ResNet-20→ResNet-18 means that the transferred SL2O optimizer is trained on ResNet-20, ResNet-18→ResNet-20 means the opposite. We can see from the figures that: 1) SL2O meta-trained on ResNet-18 can optimize ResNet-20 well, and vice versa; 2) When optimizing ResNet-20, the SL2O optimizer meta-trained on ResNet-18 can even out-perform the optimizer meta-trained on ResNet-20 at the early training stage. This may suggest that the L2O models meta-trained on more complicated problems (e.g., ResNet-18) can solve the easier problems (e.g., ResNet-20) more efficiently. Table 3 shows the average best testing accuracy of different combinations of meta-training/meta-testing schemes. We can see that meta-training and meta-testing on the same task distribution yield the best performance while transferring the trained optimizers only brings slight performance loss. These promising results show that the meta-training cost of SL2O can potentially be further amortized by training fewer optimizers and sharing between different optimization optimizees.

We also demonstrate the transferability of SL2O between various datasets in the supplementary file, which suggests the SL2O trained on one dataset can be seamlessly generalized across multiple datasets.

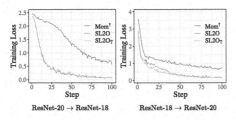

**Fig. 7.** Training loss of optimizing ResNet-18 (left) and ResNet-20 (right) on CIFAR-10. SL2O$_T$ means the optimizer is meta-trained on another architecture.

**Table 3.** The average of best testing accuracy with different combinations of meta-training and meta-testing datasets.

| Train on \ Test on | ResNet-20 | ResNet-18 |
| --- | --- | --- |
| ResNet-20 | 91.00% | 93.59% |
| ResNet-18 | 90.96% | 93.61% |

## 4.5  Ablation Study and Visualizations

*The Effects of Unroll Length and Different Training Iterations.* We study the effects of different unroll lengths $T$ and training iterations $N$ in the supplementary files. We have validated: 1) the unroll length $T$ does not have a dominating effect; 2) longer unroll lengths do not bring extra performance gain, while a smaller unroll length would result in slightly weak performance; 3) shorter training iterations probably make SL2O overfit to shorter training horizons. Detailed analysis are provided in the supplementary files.

*Learned Update Rules.* To understand how our L2O models generate update rules for models, we provide two sets of visualizations on ResNet-20. The first visualization is the training trajectory and the loss landscapes [26] of models trained by different optimizers. We use three optimizers, *i.e.* Momentum, Momentum$^\dagger$ and SL2O, to train ResNet-20 on CIFAR-10 from the same initialization weights. We focus on the first 100 training steps to demonstrate how optimizers behave at the early training stage. The endpoints of the training trajectory are set to be $(0,0)$. The three landscapes are presented in Fig. 8. We can draw multiple conclusions from these figures: 1) The training trajectories are similar for the three optimizers. We interpret such a similarity as a successful sanity check demonstrating the SL2O optimizer has learned valid optimization rules since it shares a similar optimization pathway with Momentum and Momentum$^\dagger$; 2) SL2O arrives at a lower loss region compared to Momentum$^\dagger$ and Momentum after 100 training steps, again showing that SL2O can be more efficient at reducing training loss; 3) SL2O reaches a region where the loss landscape is flatter, manifested by sparser contour lines around the endpoint $(0,0)$ in the loss landscape of SL2O. The flatness of loss landscapes is believed to measure the generalization ability of neural networks [53]; therefore, the model optimized by SL2O has potentially higher generalization ability and better quality compared to the Momentum$^\dagger$ optimized model after 100 training steps. The second visualization is what SL2O outputs. We provide the visualization of Momentum$^\dagger$ and SL2O on ResNet-20 in the supplementary files, showing that SL2O learns sophisticated update rules rather than always optimizing in the largest principal direction.

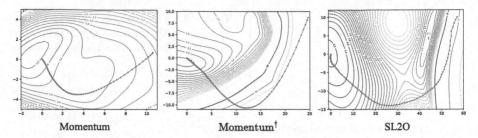

**Fig. 8.** The visualization of loss landscapes and training trajectories of ResNet-20 models optimized by Momentum, Momentum$^\dagger$, and SL2O, respectively.

*Explainability.* We use a classical tool, symbolic regression [9], to uncover a mathematical formula from the fitted optimizers. The symbolic regression (SR) will search within a space of mathematical formulas, and find one that best describes the numerical rules learned by SL2O. Different from normal regression techniques, the symbolic regression does not need pre-defined regression structures (e.g., $y = ax + b$) but finds reasonable structures automatically from the space. Such a property makes SR more flexible and explainable. The results are deferred to the supplementary files due to space constraints.

## 5    Discussion and Conclusions

In this paper, we challenge the "common experience" that learnable optimizers can only be meta-trained on extremely shallow networks without massive computation resources, which severely limits their piratical usage in real-world scenarios. We remove this primary barrier, scalability, for L2O by first projecting the network updates in a tiny subspace and then learning optimization rules on top of it. In this way, we for the first time enable the L2O training on large-scale models including Vision Transformer and GPT. Meanwhile, our scalable L2O has demonstrated superior convergence and comparable or even better testing performance. In future work, we would be interested in examining more about the transferability of SL2O to better amortize the meta-training cost of SL2O optimizers. We would be interested in combining L2O optimizers with analytical optimizers to see if we can further improve the convergence speed and testing performance. Exploring more efficient reparameterization techniques is also one of our future goals. As for the social impact, we see our proposals substantially reduce the computation cost of data-driven L2O training, which offers energy- and financial-saving solution.

## References

1. Andrychowicz, M., et al.: Learning to learn by gradient descent by gradient descent. In: Advances in Neural Information Processing Systems (NeurIPS) (2016)

2. Bello, I., Zoph, B., Vasudevan, V., Le, Q.V.: Neural optimizer search with reinforcement learning. In: Precup, D., Teh, Y.W. (eds.) Proceedings of the 34th International Conference on Machine Learning. Proceedings of Machine Learning Research, vol. 70, pp. 459–468. PMLR, 06–11 Aug 2017. https://proceedings.mlr.press/v70/bello17a.html

3. Cao, Y., Chen, T., Wang, Z., Shen, Y.: Learning to optimize in swarms. In: Advances in Neural Information Processing Systems (NeurIPS), pp. 15018–15028 (2019)

4. Chen, T., Chen, X., Chen, W., Heaton, H., Liu, J., Wang, Z., Yin, W.: Learning to optimize: a primer and a benchmark. arXiv preprint arXiv:2103.12828 (2021)

5. Chen, T., Zhang, W., Zhou, J., Chang, S., Liu, S., Amini, L., Wang, Z.: Training stronger baselines for learning to optimize. arXiv preprint arXiv:2010.09089 (2020)

6. Chen, W., Yu, Z., Wang, Z., Anandkumar, A.: Automated synthetic-to-real generalization. In: International Conference on Machine Learning (ICML). pp. 1746–1756 (2020)

7. Chen, X., et al.: Self-PU: self boosted and calibrated positive-unlabeled training. In: International Conference on Machine Learning (ICML), pp. 1510–1519 (2020)

8. Chen, Y., et al.: Learning to learn without gradient descent by gradient descent. In: International Conference on Machine Learning (ICML), pp. 748–756 (2017)

9. Cranmer, M.: PYSR: Fast & parallelized symbolic regression in python/Julia (2020)

10. Deng, J., Dong, W., Socher, R., Li, L.J., Li, K., Fei-Fei, L.: ImageNet: a large-scale hierarchical image database. In: 2009 IEEE Conference on Computer Vision and Pattern Recognition, pp. 248–255 (2009). https://doi.org/10.1109/CVPR.2009.5206848

11. Dosovitskiy, A., et al.: An image is worth 16×16 words: Transformers for image recognition at scale. arXiv preprint arXiv:2010.11929 (2020)

12. Duchi, J., Hazan, E., Singer, Y.: Adaptive subgradient methods for online learning and stochastic optimization. J. Mach. Learn. Res. $\mathbf{12}$(7), 1–39 (2011)

13. Dušek, O., Howcroft, D.M., Rieser, V.: Semantic noise matters for neural natural language generation. In: Proceedings of the 12th International Conference on Natural Language Generation, pp. 421–426. Association for Computational Linguistics, Tokyo, Japan, October–November 2019. https://doi.org/10.18653/v1/W19-8652, https://www.aclweb.org/anthology/W19-8652

14. Gressmann, F., Eaton-Rosen, Z., Luschi, C.: Improving neural network training in low dimensional random bases. arXiv preprint arXiv:2011.04720 (2020)

15. Gur-Ari, G., Roberts, D.A., Dyer, E.: Gradient descent happens in a tiny subspace. arXiv preprint arXiv:1812.04754 (2018)

16. He, K., Zhang, X., Ren, S., Sun, J.: Deep residual learning for image recognition. In: Proceedings of the IEEE Conference on Computer Vision and Pattern Recognition, pp. 770–778 (2016)

17. Hecht-Nielsen, R.: Theory of the backpropagation neural network. In: Neural Networks For Perception, pp. 65–93. Elsevier (1992)

18. Hochreiter, S., Schmidhuber, J.: Long short-term memory. Neural Comput. $\mathbf{9}$(8), 1735–1780 (1997)

19. Hu, E.J., Shen, Y., Wallis, P., Allen-Zhu, Z., Li, Y., Wang, S., Chen, W.: Lora: low-rank adaptation of large language models. arXiv preprint arXiv:2106.09685 (2021)

20. Jaderberg, M., Vedaldi, A., Zisserman, A.: Speeding up convolutional neural networks with low rank expansions. In: Proceedings of the British Machine Vision Conference. BMVA Press (2014)

21. Jiang, H., Chen, Z., Shi, Y., Dai, B., Zhao, T.: Learning to defense by learning to attack. arXiv preprint arXiv:1811.01213 (2018)

22. Kingma, D.P., Ba, J.: Adam: a method for stochastic optimization. arXiv preprint arXiv:1412.6980 (2014)

23. Krizhevsky, A., et al.: Learning multiple layers of features from tiny images (2009)

24. Li, C., Chen, T., You, H., Wang, Z., Lin, Y.: HALO: hardware-aware learning to optimize. In: Vedaldi, A., Bischof, H., Brox, T., Frahm, J.-M. (eds.) ECCV 2020. LNCS, vol. 12354, pp. 500–518. Springer, Cham (2020). https://doi.org/10.1007/978-3-030-58545-7_29

25. Li, C., Farkhoor, H., Liu, R., Yosinski, J.: Measuring the intrinsic dimension of objective landscapes. arXiv preprint arXiv:1804.08838 (2018)

26. Li, H., Xu, Z., Taylor, G., Studer, C., Goldstein, T.: Visualizing the loss landscape of neural nets. Adv. Neural. Inf. Process. Syst. **31**, 1–11 (2018)

27. Li, K., Malik, J.: Learning to optimize. arXiv preprint arXiv:1606.01885 (2016)

28. Li, T., Tan, L., Tao, Q., Liu, Y., Huang, X.: Low dimensional landscape hypothesis is true: DNNs can be trained in tiny subspaces (2021)

29. Lv, K., Jiang, S., Li, J.: Learning gradient descent: better generalization and longer horizons. In: International Conference on Machine Learning (ICML), pp. 2247–2255 (2017)

30. Metz, L., Maheswaranathan, N., Nixon, J., Freeman, D., Sohl-Dickstein, J.: Understanding and correcting pathologies in the training of learned optimizers. In: International Conference on Machine Learning, pp. 4556–4565. PMLR (2019)

31. Oymak, S., Fabian, Z., Li, M., Soltanolkotabi, M.: Generalization guarantees for neural networks via harnessing the low-rank structure of the Jacobean. arXiv preprint arXiv:1906.05392 (2019)

32. Povey, D., et al.: Semi-orthogonal low-rank matrix factorization for deep neural networks. In: Interspeech, pp. 3743–3747 (2018)

33. Qian, N.: On the momentum term in gradient descent learning algorithms. Neural Netw. **12**(1), 145–151 (1999)

34. Radford, A., Wu, J., Child, R., Luan, D., Amodei, D., Sutskever, I.: Language models are unsupervised multitask learners. OpenAI blog. **8**, 9 (2019)

35. Robbins, H.E.: A stochastic approximation method. Ann. Math. Stat. **22**, 400–407 (2007)

36. Sainath, T.N., Kingsbury, B., Sindhwani, V., Arisoy, E., Ramabhadran, B.: Low-rank matrix factorization for deep neural network training with high-dimensional output targets. In: 2013 IEEE International Conference on Acoustics, Speech and Signal Processing, pp. 6655–6659. IEEE (2013)

37. Shen, J., Chen, X., Heaton, H., Chen, T., Liu, J., Yin, W., Wang, Z.: Learning a minimax optimizer: a pilot study. In: International Conference on Learning Representations (ICLR) (2021)

38. Simonyan, K., Zisserman, A.: Very deep convolutional networks for large-scale image recognition. arXiv preprint arXiv:1409.1556 (2014)

39. Sohl-Dickstein, J., Poole, B., Ganguli, S.: Fast large-scale optimization by unifying stochastic gradient and quasi-newton methods. In: International Conference on Machine Learning, pp. 604–612. PMLR (2014)

40. Szegedy, C., Vanhoucke, V., Ioffe, S., Shlens, J., Wojna, Z.: Rethinking the inception architecture for computer vision. In: Proceedings of the IEEE Conference on Computer Vision and Pattern Recognition, pp. 2818–2826 (2016)

41. Tieleman, T., Hinton, G.: Lecture 6.5-RMSProp: divide the gradient by a running average of its recent magnitude. COURSERA: Neural Networks for Machine Learning (2012)

42. Touvron, H., Cord, M., Douze, M., Massa, F., Sablayrolles, A., Jégou, H.: Training data-efficient image transformers & distillation through attention. In: International Conference on Machine Learning, pp. 10347–10357. PMLR (2021)

43. Tuddenham, M., Prügel-Bennett, A., Hare, J.: Quasi-newton's method in the class gradient defined high-curvature subspace. arXiv preprint arXiv:2012.01938 (2020)

44. Vaswani, A., et al.: Attention is all you need. In: Advances in Neural Information Processing Systems, vol. 30 (2017)

45. Vicol, P., Metz, L., Sohl-Dickstein, J.: Unbiased gradient estimation in unrolled computation graphs with persistent evolution strategies. In: Meila, M., Zhang, T. (eds.) Proceedings of the 38th International Conference on Machine Learning. Proceedings of Machine Learning Research, vol. 139, pp. 10553–10563. PMLR, 18–24 July 2021. https://proceedings.mlr.press/v139/vicol21a.html

46. Wang, Z., Wohlwend, J., Lei, T.: Structured pruning of large language models. In: Proceedings of the 2020 Conference on Empirical Methods in Natural Language Processing (EMNLP), pp. 6151–6162 (2020)

47. Werbos, P.J.: Backpropagation through time: what it does and how to do it. Proc. IEEE **78**(10), 1550–1560 (1990)

48. Wichrowska, O., et al.: Learned optimizers that scale and generalize. In: International Conference on Machine Learning (ICML) (2017)

49. Xiong, Y., Hsieh, C.-J.: Improved adversarial training via learned optimizer. In: Vedaldi, A., Bischof, H., Brox, T., Frahm, J.-M. (eds.) ECCV 2020. LNCS, vol. 12353, pp. 85–100. Springer, Cham (2020). https://doi.org/10.1007/978-3-030-58598-3_6

50. Yin, M., Tucker, G., Zhou, M., Levine, S., Finn, C.: Meta-learning without memorization. arXiv preprint arXiv:1912.03820 (2019)

51. You, Y., Chen, T., Wang, Z., Shen, Y.: L2-GCN: layer-wise and learned efficient training of graph convolutional networks. In: Proceedings of the IEEE/CVF Conference on Computer Vision and Pattern Recognition (CVPR), pp. 2127–2135 (2020)

52. Yu, X., Liu, T., Wang, X., Tao, D.: On compressing deep models by low rank and sparse decomposition. In: Proceedings of the IEEE Conference on Computer Vision and Pattern Recognition, pp. 7370–7379 (2017)

53. Zhang, S., Wang, M., Liu, S., Chen, P.Y., Xiong, J.: Why lottery ticket wins? A theoretical perspective of sample complexity on sparse neural networks. Adv. Neural. Inf. Process. Syst. **34**, 2707–2720 (2021)

54. Zhang, Y., Chuangsuwanich, E., Glass, J.: Extracting deep neural network bottleneck features using low-rank matrix factorization. In: 2014 IEEE international conference on acoustics, speech and signal processing (ICASSP), pp. 185–189. IEEE (2014)

55. Zhao, Y., Li, J., Gong, Y.: Low-rank plus diagonal adaptation for deep neural networks. In: 2016 IEEE International Conference on Acoustics, Speech and Signal Processing (ICASSP), pp. 5005–5009. IEEE (2016)

# QISTA-ImageNet: A Deep Compressive Image Sensing Framework Solving $\ell_q$-Norm Optimization Problem

Gang-Xuan Lin[1], Shih-Wei Hu[1], and Chun-Shien Lu[1,2]( )

[1] Institute of Information Science, Academia Sinica, Taipei, Taiwan, ROC
lcs@iis.sinica.edu.tw
[2] Research Center for Information Technology Innovation, Academia Sinica,
Taipei, Taiwan, ROC

**Abstract.** In this paper, we study how to reconstruct the original images from the given sensed samples/measurements by proposing a so-called deep compressive image sensing framework. This framework, dubbed QISTA-ImageNet, is built upon a deep neural network to realize our optimization algorithm QISTA ($\ell_q$-ISTA) in solving image recovery problem. The unique characteristics of QISTA-ImageNet are that we (1) introduce a generalized proximal operator and present learning-based proximal gradient descent (PGD) together with an iterative algorithm in reconstructing images, (2) analyze how QISTA-ImageNet can exhibit better solutions compared to state-of-the-art methods and interpret clearly the insight of proposed method, and (3) conduct empirical comparisons with state-of-the-art methods to demonstrate that QISTA-ImageNet exhibits the best performance in terms of image reconstruction quality to solve the $\ell_q$-norm optimization problem.

## 1 Introduction

### 1.1 Problem Definition and Motivation

In sparse signal recovery such as compressive sensing (CS) [8,16], we typically let $x_0 \in \mathbb{R}^n$ denote a $k$-sparse signal to be sensed, let $A \in \mathbb{R}^{m \times n}$ represent a sensing/sampling matrix, and let $y \in \mathbb{R}^m$ be the measurement vector defined as $y = Ax_0$, where $k < m < n$ and $\frac{m}{n}$ is the measurement rate (MR), and $x_0$ can be either a 1D signal or obtained from reshaping a 2D image. At the decoder, $x_0$ can be recovered based on its sparsity by solving the $\ell_1$-norm regularization problem, which is known as "LASSO" [14,33]:

$$\text{(LASSO)} \quad \min_x \frac{1}{2} \|y - Ax\|_2^2 + \lambda \|x\|_1, \tag{1}$$

where $\lambda > 0$ is a regularization parameter.

---

**Supplementary Information** The online version contains supplementary material available at https://doi.org/10.1007/978-3-031-20050-2_24.

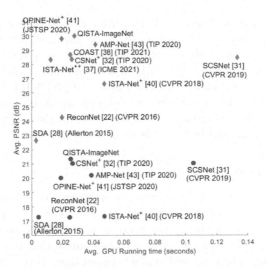

**Fig. 1.** Comparison of the reconstruction quality in terms of PSNR (dB) and GPU running time (in seconds) between QISTA-ImageNet and state-of-the-art methods. The average PSNR values are reconstruction results from dataset Set11 under measurement rates of 1% (in blue circle) and 10% (in red diamond), respectively. The average GPU running time is the time of reconstructing a $256 \times 256$ gray-scale image. Please note that since current learning-based CS algorithms have already achieved real-time recovery and the time actually depends on the used hardwares and programming languages, the running time results provided here were excerpted from the literautre for reference purpose only. The AMP-Net denotes the AMP-Net-9-BM version (with best results). We can see that, under the harsh environment of measurement rate 1%, QISTA-ImageNet surpass all the methods in reconstruction quality (in dB). Overall, all these methods exhibit similar tendencies under different datasets and measurement rates (see Sect. 4). (Color figure online)

Nevertheless, considering that LASSO cannot recover the original sparse signal under low MRs [11], $\ell_q$-norm regularization has been suggested [11,12]. The (non-convex) $\ell_q$-norm regularization problem has the form

$$(\ell_q): \quad \min_x \frac{1}{2} \|y - Ax\|_2^2 + \lambda \|x\|_q^q, \tag{2}$$

where $0 < q < 1$ and $\|x\|_q = \sum_{i=1}^n \left(|x_i|^q\right)^{1/q}$ is the $\ell_q$-quasi-norm (which is usually called $\ell_q$-norm).

It is noted that the discussions regarding an $(\ell_q)$-problem or effective algorithms for finding its optimal solution are very rare in the literature. In [23], we reformulated the non-convex $\ell_q$-norm minimization problem into a 2-step problem with $q \in (0,1)$ that is composed of one convex and one non-convex subproblems, and proposed an iterative algorithm, called QISTA ($\ell_q$-ISTA), to solve 1D signal recovery from the given incomplete samples.

In this paper, we further study how to reconstruct the original images from the given sensed data (samples/measurements) by proposing a so-called deep compressive image sensing framework. Our framework is built upon and extended from QISTA that aims at 1D signal recovery [23]. Although QISTA is not designed for image recovery that is often treated as an $(\ell_1)$-problem, we propose a new 2D image recovery algorithm, which is formulated as an $(\ell_q)$-problem and unfolded into a new network architecture, dubbed QISTA-ImageNet, for natural image reconstruction. For image recovery from incomplete samples, Fig. 1 shows that QISTA-ImageNet, compared with the state-of-the-art methods, achieves the relatively better results in terms of reconstruction quality.

## 1.2    Related Works

To learn signal reconstruction, the network architecture is generated by a technique called *algorithm unfolding* [27], which unfolds specific parameters of an iterative algorithm to be learning parameters. The network architectures for 2D image reconstruction can be classified into two categories: heuristic design and algorithm unfolding. The main difference between them is that algorithm unfolding connects the network architecture with the traditional iterative algorithm, which implies the trained network is interpretable [9,17].

For the first category, Mousavi *et al.* [28] first proposed to apply a stacked denoising auto-encoder (SDA) to learn the representation and to reconstruct natural images from their CS measurements. Kulkarni *et al.* [22] further developed a CNN-based method, dubbed ReconNet, to reconstruct the natural images. Similar to [22,28], all network architectures in MS-CSNet [30], DR$^2$-Net [19], MSRNet [24], CSNet$^+$ [32], and SCSNet [31] are heuristic designs for solving CS. For the second category, Yang *et al.* designed a network architecture called ADMM-Net [36], where the structure of each layer is obtained by unfolding the specific parameters in the traditional iterative algorithm, ADMM [7,35]. Zhang *et al.* designed ISTA-Net and ISTA-Net$^+$ [40] by unfolding the traditional iterative algorithm ISTA [4,14]. The authors further proposed two extensions, called COAST [38] and ISTA-Net$^{++}$ [37]. Different from ISTA-Net$^+$, COAST further designed a controllable proximal mapping module and a plug-and-play deblocking strategy to dynamically modulate the network features and effectively eliminate the blocking artifacts, respectively. Zhang *et al.* proposed a so-called OPINE-Net [41], which adopts the framework of ISTA-Net$^+$ [40] with an additional learning parameter in that it is a convolutional operator unfolded by the sampling matrix $A$. Zhang *et al.* proposed AMP-Net [43] inspired by two iterative algorithms, DIT and AMP [26], with an additional noise estimation. We also note that there is a branch of studies in (image) inverse problem that merges the iterative algorithm and DNN, which is the so-called plug-and-play (PnP) framework, including PnP-ADMM [10,29] and PnP proximal gradient method (PnP-PGM) [34]. However, the PnP framework is different from the framework of unfolding a traditional iterative algorithm in a DNN model in that the latter requires the traditional iterative algorithm to be presented explicitly, whereas the former does not seek to define an explicit regularization term because solving the proximal operator associated with the regularization term is impractical. Instead, both PnP-ADMM and PnP-PGM replace the proximal operator with

**Table 1.** Comparisons with state-of-the-art methods. FC and Conv. represent fully connected and convolutional oeprators, respectively.

| Methods | Interpretable | Sampling matrix training | Initialization | Deblocking strategy | Regularization |
|---|---|---|---|---|---|
| ReconNet [22] | – | ✓ | FC | ✓ | – |
| DR$^2$-Net [19] | – | ✓ | Least square | – | – |
| CSNet$^+$ [32] | – | ✓ | Conv. | ✓ | – |
| SCSNet [31] | – | ✓ | Conv. | ✓ | – |
| AMP-Net [43] | ✓ | ✓ | FC | ✓ | – |
| ADMM-Net [36] | ✓ | – | follow ADMM | – | Data-driven |
| ISTA-Net$^+$ [40] | ✓ | – | Least square | – | Convex |
| OPINE-Net [41] | ✓ | ✓ | Conv. | – | Convex |
| OPINE-Net$^+$ [41] | ✓ | ✓ | Conv. | ✓ | Convex |
| COAST [38] | ✓ | – | naive solution | ✓ | Data-driven |
| QISTA-ImageNet | ✓ | ✓ | FC | ✓ | Non-convex |

a trained denoiser and iterate the algorithm (ADMM or PGM) until it converges. Table 1 shows the characteristics of state-of-the-art learning-based image recovery algorithms.

### 1.3  Contributions

The contributions in QISTA-ImageNet include:

1. Different from its 1D counterpart [23], QISTA-ImageNet is proposed to get approximated instead of exact solution (Sect. 3). This enables us to interpret clearly the insight of the proposed iterative method (Eq. (15)) in each iterative step.
2. By introducing a generalized proximal operator, the learning-based proximal gradient descent (PGD) together with an iterative algorithm in reconstructing images are proposed (Sect. 3.1 and Sect. 3.2).
3. Benefited from considering the $\ell_q$-norm regularization problem in Eq. (8), we analyze how QISTA-ImageNet can exhibit better performances compared to state-of-the-art methods (Sect. 3.3).
4. In reconstructing the natural images, QISTA-ImageNet is empirically verified to be better than or comparable with state-of-the-art methods (Sect. 4).

## 2   Preliminary: $(\ell_q)$-ISTA for 1D Sparse Signal Reconstruction

In sparse signal reconstruction, to achieve the same reconstruction performance, the requirement of the measurement rate of $(\ell_q)$-based problem is lesser than that of $(\ell_1)$-based problem. Unfortunately, because $(\ell_q)$-based problem is non-convex, the algorithms that can achieve an acceptable solution are very rare in the literature. In [23], we proposed a new algorithm to solve the $(\ell_q)$-problem (2). We first approximated the $(\ell_q)$-problem into

$$\min_x F(x) = \frac{1}{2} \|y - Ax\|_2^2 + \lambda \sum_{i=1}^{n} \frac{|x_i|}{(|x_i| + \varepsilon_i)^{1-q}}, \tag{3}$$

where $\varepsilon_i > 0$ for all $i \in [1:n]$, then relaxed problem (3) (associated with the dimension of feasible domain) into

$$\min_{x,c} H(x,c) = \frac{1}{2} \|y - Ax\|_2^2 + \lambda \sum_{i=1}^{n} \frac{|x_i|}{(|c_i| + \varepsilon_i)^{1-q}}, \tag{4}$$

and reformulated problem (4) as a two-step problem:

$$\min_x \ H(x, \bar{c}), \tag{5a}$$

$$\min_c \ |H(\bar{x}, c) - H(\bar{x}, \bar{x}), |, \tag{5b}$$

where $\bar{x}$ and $\bar{c}$ are optimal solutions to problems (5a) and (5b), respectively. One can see that problem (4) is equivalent to problem (3) if $c = x$, and both the two problems (4) and (5) have the same optimal solution. On the one hand, since the problem (5a) is in the weighted-LASSO form (each component $|x_i|$ in the regularization term $\|x\|_1$ has weight $\frac{1}{(|c_i|+\varepsilon_i)^{1-q}}$), ISTA (iterative shrinkage-thresholding algorithm) was adopted to approach the optimal solution. On the other hand, the problem (5b) has a trivial optimal solution $c^* = \bar{x}$, even if the problem is non-convex. Thus, the $(\ell_q)$-ISTA algorithm is derived by adopting one iterative step of ISTA (Eqs. (6b) and (6c)) and alternatively iterating with the optimal solution to problem (5b) (Eq. (6a)) as follows:

$$c^t = x^{t-1}, \tag{6a}$$

$$r^t = x^{t-1} + \beta A^T \left(y - Ax^{t-1}\right), \tag{6b}$$

$$x_i^t = \eta \left(r_i^t; \frac{\beta\lambda}{(|c_i^t| + \varepsilon_i)^{1-q}}\right), \ \forall i, \tag{6c}$$

where $\eta(\cdot;\cdot)$ is a component-wise soft-thresholding operator, defined as:

$$\eta(r_i; w_i) = sign(r_i) \cdot \max\{0, |r_i| - w_i\}. \tag{7}$$

In comparison with the traditional $\ell_q$-norm minimization, the $(\ell_q)$-ISTA algorithm is also found to be relatively stable for $q$'s.

## 3   QISTA-ImageNet: Learning-Based Method for Reconstructing Natural Images

We describe a new method, QISTA-ImageNet, to reconstruct natural images. The image is, in general, a non-sparse signal in the space domain and exhibits a sparse representation in a transform domain (Fourier, STFT, wavelet, etc.). Let $x_0 \in \mathbb{R}^n$ be the vector representation of image $X_0 \in \mathbb{R}^{n_1 \times n_2}$, where $n = n_1 \cdot n_2$. Different from its 1D counterpart in problem (1), the traditional optimization method typically reconstructs the original image $x_0$ by solving the $\ell_1$-norm regularization problem in LASSO form as: $\min_x \frac{1}{2} \|y - Ax\|_2^2 + \lambda \|\Psi x\|_1$, where $A \in \mathbb{R}^{m \times n}$ is the sensing matrix and $\Psi \in \mathbb{R}^{n \times n}$ is the dictionary that allows $x_0$ to be sparsely represented.

In our method, we consider the $\ell_q$-norm regularization problem in the form

$$\min_x \frac{1}{2} \|y - Ax\|_2^2 + \lambda \|\Psi x\|_q^q, \tag{8}$$

where $0 < q < 1$. Similar to the process in deriving QISTA in Sect. 2, we can reformulate the problem (8) as a two-step problem:

$$\min_x \ H(x, \bar{c}), \tag{9a}$$

$$\min_c \ |H(\bar{x}, c) - H(\bar{x}, \Psi \bar{x})|, \tag{9b}$$

where $H(x, c) = \frac{1}{2} \|y - Ax\|_2^2 + \lambda \sum_{i=1}^n \frac{|(\Psi x)_i|}{(|c_i| + \varepsilon_i)^{1-q}}$, $\varepsilon_i > 0$ for all $i \in [1 : n]$, and $\bar{x}$ and $\bar{c}$ are the optimal solutions to the $x$-subproblem (9a) and $c$-subproblem (9b), respectively. In the following, we describe how to solve these two sub-problems in (9) for natural image recovery.

To solve the optimal solution pair $(\bar{x}, \bar{c})$ to problem (9), first we can see that the optimal value of problem (9b) is obviously zero with the optimal solution $\bar{c} = \Psi \bar{x}$. Second, if $\Psi(\cdot)$ is a linear operator, then problem (9a) is convex, and the optimal solution can be approached via the PGD algorithm [3]. Unfortunately, the iterative process of PGD algorithm cannot be represented explicitly due to the composite function $|\Psi(x)|$. This implies the PGD algorithm cannot be implemented directly. Nevertheless, together with the proximal operator for composition with an affine mapping (Theorem 6.15 in [3]), we derive the explicit formula approaching the optimal solution to problem (9a) in Sect. 3.1.

## 3.1   Proximal Operator for Composite Function

In this subsection, we aim to design an explicit iterative process that solves problem (9a). In problem (9a), we can observe that the regularization term of the objective function is in the form of the composite function $\|\Psi(x)\|_{1,w} = \left( \|\cdot\|_{1,w} \circ \Psi \right)(x)$, where $\|x\|_{1,w} = \sum_{i=1}^n w_i |x_i|$ and $w_i = \frac{\lambda}{(|\bar{c}_i| + \varepsilon_i)^{1-q}}$. Therefore, the PGD algorithm [3] for solving problem (9a) has the form

$$r^t = x^{t-1} + \beta A^T \left( y - Ax^{t-1} \right), \tag{10a}$$

$$x^t = \text{prox}_{\|\Psi(\cdot)\|_{1,w}} \left( r^t \right). \tag{10b}$$

Remark that the proximal operator in Eq. (10b) is the soft-thresholding operator (Eq. (7)) provided the dictionary $\Psi$ is an identity function [3,4]. However, since there is no useful calculus rule for computing the proximal operator of a composite function $\|\Psi(\cdot)\|_{1,w}$ for a general $\Psi$, Eq. (10b) cannot be written in an explicit function. To address this issue, we introduce the generalized proximal operator using the following theorem.

**Theorem 31** [3]. *Let $g : \mathbb{R}^n \to (-\infty, \infty]$ be a proper closed convex function, and let $f(x) = g(\mathcal{A}(x)+b)$, where $b \in \mathbb{R}^n$ and $\mathcal{A} : \mathbb{R}^{\hat{n}} \to \mathbb{R}^n$ is a linear transformation satisfying $\mathcal{A} \circ \mathcal{A}^T = \gamma \cdot I_n$ for some constant $\gamma > 0$. Then, for any $x \in \mathbb{R}^{\hat{n}}$,*

$$\mathrm{prox}_f(x) = x + \frac{1}{\gamma}\mathcal{A}^T \left(\mathrm{prox}_{\gamma g}(\mathcal{A}(x) + b) - (\mathcal{A}(x) + b)\right). \tag{11}$$

As described in Theorem 31, we can observe that if the dictionary $\Psi$ is linear and satisfies a certain orthogonality condition, the solution to the proximal operator of $\|\Psi(\cdot)\|_{1,w}$ in Eq. (10b) can be found.

Hence, we propose to replace $g(x)$ and $\mathcal{A}(x)$ in Theorem 31 by $\|\cdot\|_{1,w}$ and $\Psi(x)$, respectively, to get

$$\mathrm{prox}_{\|\Psi(\cdot)\|_{1,w}}\left(r^t\right) = r^t + \frac{1}{\gamma_{\bar{c}}}\Psi^T \left(\eta\left(\Psi\left(r^t\right); \gamma_{\bar{c}}\right) - \Psi(r^t)\right), \tag{12}$$

where $(\gamma_{\bar{c}})_i = \frac{\lambda}{(|\bar{c}_i|+\varepsilon_i)^{1-q}}$ for all $i \in [1:n]$ and $\frac{1}{\gamma_{\bar{c}}}$ is the component-wise reciprocal of $\gamma_{\bar{c}}$. Thus, Eq. (10) can be written as

$$r^t = x^{t-1} + \beta A^T \left(y - Ax^{t-1}\right) \tag{13a}$$

$$x^t = r^t + \frac{1}{\gamma_{\bar{c}}}\Psi^T \left(\eta\left(\Psi\left(r^t\right); \gamma_{\bar{c}}\right) - \Psi(r^t)\right). \tag{13b}$$

## 3.2   The Iterative Algorithm

To derive an iterative algorithm to solve problem (9), we know that the optimal solution to problem (9b) is $\bar{c} = \Psi(\bar{x})$ and the optimal solution to problem (9a) can be approached via Eq. (13). Similar to 1D signal recovery described in Eq. (6) in Sect. 2, we can design an iterative algorithm solving 2D image recovery problem (9) by replacing Eq. (6a) and Eq. (6c) with $c^t = \Psi\left(x^{t-1}\right)$ and Eq. (13b), respectively.

Moreover, since the dictionary $\Psi$ plays the key role of sparsely representing a natural image, together with the fact that

$$\bar{x} \approx \bar{r} \tag{14}$$

provided $\Psi$ is a linear operator satisfying a certain orthogonality condition, the optimal solution to problem (9b) is modified as $\bar{c} \approx \Psi(\bar{r})$. Remark that the validity of Eq. (14) is further illustrated in Appendix 6.1. Finally, the iterative algorithm is designed by iterating $c^t = \Psi(r^t)$ with Eq. (13) alternatively. More specifically, the iterative process at $t$-th iteration has the form

$$r^t = x^{t-1} + \beta A^T \left(y - Ax^{t-1}\right), \tag{15a}$$

$$c^t = \Psi\left(r^t\right), \tag{15b}$$

$$x^t = r^t + \frac{1}{\gamma_{c^t}}\Psi^T\left(\eta\left(\Psi\left(r^t\right);\gamma_{c^t}\right) - \Psi(r^t)\right), \tag{15c}$$

which is equivalent to

$$r^t = x^{t-1} + \beta A^T\left(y - Ax^{t-1}\right), \tag{16a}$$

$$x^t = r^t + \frac{1}{\hat{\gamma}}\Psi^T\left(\eta\left(\Psi\left(r^t\right);\hat{\gamma}\right) - \Psi(r^t)\right), \tag{16b}$$

where $\hat{\gamma}_i = \frac{\lambda}{\left(\left|(\Psi(r^t))_i\right| + \varepsilon_i\right)^{1-q}}$ for all $i \in [1:n]$.

### 3.3   Why Our Method Can Get Better Reconstructions?

We analyze the reason why the solution obtained by the iterative process (16) is closer to the original signal than $\ell_1$-based method. The algorithm (16) solving the problem (9) consists of two steps, the gradient descent step (Eq. (16a)) and the truncation (shrinkage) step (Eq. (16b)).

The gradient descent step updates the point by moving the current iterative point $x^{t-1}$ along the direction $A^T\left(y - Ax^{t-1}\right)$, which is perpendicular to the null space $\mathcal{N}(A)$ of $A$, with the step size $\beta$, to the updated point $r^t$, as shown in Fig. 2 (Left). Indeed, Eq. (16a) can be written as

$$\Psi\left(r^t\right) = \Psi\left(x^{t-1}\right) + \beta\Psi\left(A^T\left(y - Ax^{t-1}\right)\right), \tag{17}$$

in the dictionary domain (i.e., the space $\{\Psi\left(x\right);x\in\mathbb{R}^n\}$) provided $\Psi$ is a linear operator. That is, in the dictionary domain, the gradient descent step makes updates by moving the current iterative point $\Psi\left(x^{t-1}\right)$ along the direction $\Psi\left[A^T\left(y - Ax^{t-1}\right)\right]$, which is perpendicular to $\{\Psi(x) : x \in \mathcal{N}(A)\}$, with the step size $\beta$ to the updated point $\Psi\left(r^t\right)$, as shown in Fig. 2 (Right).

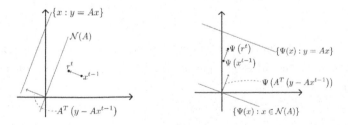

**Fig. 2.** Left: The gradient descent step (Eq. (16a)) in the space $\mathbb{R}^n$. Right: The gradient descent step (Eq. (17)) in the space $\{\Psi(x) : x \in \mathbb{R}^n\}$.

In the truncation step, Eq. (16b) is indeed the proximal operator of $\|\Psi\left(\cdot\right)\|_{1,w}$ in Eq. (12) with $\bar{c} = \Psi\left(r^t\right)$. As Theorem 31 indicates, $\Psi$ is a linear operator satisfying $\Psi \circ \Psi^T = \gamma_{\bar{c}} \cdot I_n$. Thus, Eq. (16b) can be written as

$$\Psi\left(x^t\right) = \Psi\left(r^t\right) + \frac{1}{\gamma_{\Psi(r^t)}} \Psi\left(\Psi^T\left(\eta\left(\Psi\left(r^t\right);\gamma_{\Psi(r^t)}\right) - \Psi(r^t)\right)\right) \tag{18a}$$

$$= \Psi\left(r^t\right) + \frac{\gamma_{\bar{c}}}{\gamma_{\Psi(r^t)}}\left(\eta\left(\Psi\left(r^t\right);\gamma_{\Psi(r^t)}\right) - \Psi(r^t)\right) \tag{18b}$$

$$= \Psi\left(r^t\right) + \left(\eta\left(\Psi\left(r^t\right);\gamma_{\Psi(r^t)}\right) - \Psi(r^t)\right) \tag{18c}$$

$$= \eta\left(\Psi\left(r^t\right);\gamma_{\Psi(r^t)}\right). \tag{18d}$$

Equation (18) is indeed the component-wise soft-thresholding operator operating at the point $\Psi\left(r^t\right)$ with the shrinkage parameter $\gamma_{\Psi(r^t)}$.

Moreover, in Eq. (18), the parameter $\left(\gamma_{\Psi(r^t)}\right)_i$, is determined by $|(\Psi\left(r^t\right))_i|$. We can observe that if $|(\Psi\left(r^t\right))_i|$ is non-zero or larger than the other components $\left|(\Psi\left(r^t\right))_j\right|$ (which indicates that the index $i$ should in the support set of $\Psi\left(r^t\right)$), then $\left(\gamma_{\Psi(r^t)}\right)_i$ is relatively small and the operator $\eta\left((\Psi\left(r^t\right))_i;\left(\gamma_{\Psi(r^t)}\right)_i\right)$ will preserve the value of $(\Psi\left(r^t\right))_i$. Conversely, if $|(\Psi\left(r^t\right))_i|$ is zero or is relatively small (which indicates that the $i^{\text{th}}$ component of $\Psi\left(r^t\right)$ should be zero), then $\left(\gamma_{\Psi(r^t)}\right)_i$ is relatively large and the operator $\eta\left((\Psi\left(r^t\right))_i;\left(\gamma_{\Psi(r^t)}\right)_i\right)$ will decrease the value of $|(\Psi\left(r^t\right))_i|$. As shown in Fig. 3, Eq. (18) updates the point $\Psi\left(r^t\right)$ by moving it, along the direction perpendicular to the curve $\{x : \|x\|_q = \|\Psi\left(r^t\right)\|_q\}$ (which is a contour line $\left\{x : \|x\|_q = s\right\}$ for some constant $s$) approximately, to approach the point $\Psi\left(x^t\right)$.

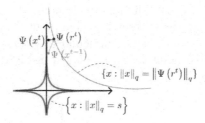

**Fig. 3.** The truncation step (Eq. (18)) aims at moving the point $\Psi\left(r^t\right)$ along the direction perpendicular to the curve $\left\{x : \|x\|_q = \|\Psi\left(r^t\right)\|_q\right\}$ approximately to approach the point $\Psi\left(x^t\right)$.

The above exploration reveals the insight into the iterative process (16) that gradually approaches the optimal solution to problem (8), as shown in Fig. 4. It should be noted that the parameter $\gamma_{\Psi(r^t)}$ adapts to the value of $\Psi\left(r^t\right)$ in a component-wise manner, instead of applying the same threshold to every component, as in $\ell_1$-based methods such as ISTA [3,4], ISTA-Net [40], and OPINE-Net

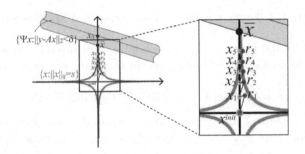

**Fig. 4.** The iterative process (16). The water-colored region is the set $\{\Psi(x) : \|y - Ax\|_2 < \delta\}$, where $\delta$ is a constant related to $\lambda$. The red curve is the contour line $\{x : \|x\|_q = s\}$ for a constant $s$. $x_0$ is the ground-truth and $\bar{x}$ is the optimal solution to the problem (8). (Color figure online)

[41]. This may explain why the solution obtained by the iterative process (16) is closer to the original signal than $\ell_1$-based methods.

### 3.4 Design of Dictionary in QISTA-ImageNet Is Non-trivial

Notably, $\Psi$ in both problem (8) and iterative algorithm (16) plays the role of a dictionary that provides an image a sparse representation. $\Psi$ is generally treated as an over-complete dictionary (*i.e.*, $\Psi \in \mathbb{R}^{N \times n}$ with $N > n$) to achieve better representation. However, its design is not trivial, since, as $N > n$, the assumption $\Psi \circ \Psi^T = \hat{\gamma} I_N$ in Theorem 31 is not satisfied at all. Thus, it is necessary to choose a $\Psi^\dagger$ satisfying $\Psi \circ \Psi^\dagger \approx \hat{\gamma} I_N$ to replace $\Psi^T$. We can observe that the left-inverse of $\Psi$ always exists, that is, $\tilde{\Psi} = \left(\Psi^T \circ \Psi\right)^{-1} \circ \Psi^T$ satisfies $\tilde{\Psi} \circ \Psi = I_n$, because $N > n$. Then, we have

$$\Psi^\dagger = I_n \circ \Psi^\dagger = \left(\tilde{\Psi} \circ \Psi\right) \circ \Psi^\dagger = \tilde{\Psi} \circ \left(\Psi \circ \Psi^\dagger\right) \approx \tilde{\Psi} \circ \hat{\gamma} I_N = \hat{\gamma} \tilde{\Psi}. \qquad (19)$$

Therefore, we relax the assumption in Theorem 31 as $\frac{1}{\hat{\gamma}} \Psi^T = \bar{\gamma} \tilde{\Psi}$, where $\bar{\gamma}$ is a constant to ensure that the solution to the proximal operator in Eq. (10b) can be approximated as

$$x^t = r^t + \bar{\gamma} \tilde{\Psi} \left(\eta(\Psi(r^t); \hat{\gamma}) - \Psi(r^t)\right). \qquad (20)$$

By replacing Eq. (16b) with Eq. (20), the iterative process becomes

$$r^t = x^{t-1} + \beta A^T \left(y - Ax^{t-1}\right), \qquad (21a)$$

$$x^t = r^t + \bar{\gamma} \tilde{\Psi} \left(\eta \left(\Psi \left(r^t\right); \hat{\gamma}\right) - \Psi(r^t)\right). \qquad (21b)$$

After imposing the above constraint of $\Psi$, inspired by the representation power of CNN [15] and the design of NN architecture in [40], the dictionary $\Psi$ is adopted in the form

$$\Psi = \mathcal{C}_3 \circ \text{ReLU} \circ \mathcal{C}_2 \circ \text{ReLU} \circ \mathcal{C}_1 \circ \text{ReLU} \circ \mathcal{C}_0 \qquad (22)$$

where $C_i$'s, $i = 0, 1, 2, 3$ are convolutional operators and ReLU is a rectified linear unit.

It should be noted that in order to exhibit a "left-inverse" structure of $\Psi$, in our design the $\tilde{\Psi}$ in Eq. (21b) is adopted in the same structure as that in Eq. (22) as

$$\tilde{\Psi} = C_7 \circ \text{ReLU} \circ C_6 \circ \text{ReLU} \circ C_5 \circ \text{ReLU} \circ C_4 \tag{23}$$

where $C_j$'s, $j = 4, 5, 6, 7$ are convolutional operators. Based on the aforementioned relaxation that $\frac{1}{\gamma_c}\Psi^T = \bar{\gamma}\tilde{\Psi}$, we will present a suitable loss function in Sect. 3.5 to ensure the left-inverse relation between $\Psi$ and $\tilde{\Psi}$. In Appendix 6.5, we provide an ablation study on the dictionary design.

## 3.5   Loss Function of QISTA-ImageNet

The MSE loss

$$\mathcal{L}_{\text{MSE}} = \frac{1}{n} \left\| x_0 - x^T \right\|_2^2, \tag{24}$$

where $x_0$ represents the ground-truth and $x^T$ is the output of the network architecture, is typically considered in learning-based models. However, because we have relaxed $\frac{1}{\gamma_c}\Psi^T \approx \bar{\gamma}\tilde{\Psi}$, we have to impose a constraint on the left-inverse relation between $\Psi$ and $\tilde{\Psi}$ at each layer $t$ as

$$\mathcal{L}_{\text{aux}} = \sum_{t=1}^{T} \left\| \tilde{\Psi}^t \left( \Psi^t \left( r^t \right) \right) - r^t \right\|_2^2. \tag{25}$$

Combining Eqs. (24) and (25), the loss function is designed as:

$$\mathcal{L} = \mathcal{L}_{\text{MSE}} + \delta\mathcal{L}_{\text{aux}}, \delta > 0 \text{ is a constant.} \tag{26}$$

## 3.6   The Network Architecture

We construct a network architecture based on the iterative algorithm (21). Let $T$ be the number of layers. At $t^{\text{th}}$ layer, $t = 1, 2, \cdots, T$, with the input $x^{t-1}$, the output $x^t$ is obtained by (QISTA-ImageNet):

$$r^t = x^{t-1} + \beta^t \mathcal{B} \left( y - \mathcal{A}x^{t-1} \right) \tag{27a}$$

$$x^t = r^t + \alpha^t \tilde{\Psi}^t \left( \eta(\Psi^t(r^t); \gamma^t) - \Psi^t(r^t) \right), \tag{27b}$$

where $\gamma_i^t = \frac{\lambda^t}{\left( \left| (\Psi^t(r^t))_i \right| + \varepsilon_i \right)^{1-q}}$ for all $i \in [1 : n]$, and $\beta^t$, $\mathcal{B}$, $\mathcal{A}$, $\alpha^t$, $\tilde{\Psi}^t$, $\Psi^t$ and $\lambda^t$ are learning parameters, which are unfolded by $\beta$, $A^T$, $A$, $\bar{\gamma}$, $\tilde{\Psi}$, $\Psi$, and $\lambda$, respectively. In Appendix 6.2, Fig. 5 illustrates the structure of QISTA-ImageNet.

More specifically, both $\mathcal{A}$ and $\mathcal{B}$ are fully connected operators, with the shape $m \times n$ and $n \times m$, respectively. Moreover, $\Psi^t$ and $\tilde{\Psi}^t$ follow the structures in Eqs. (22) and (23), respectively. That is, the training parameters represented by $\Psi^t$

and $\tilde{\Psi}^t$ are $\mathcal{C}_i^t$, $i = 0, 1, \cdots, 7$, where $\mathcal{C}_i^t$ is a convolutional operator. In summary, the learning parameters of QISTA-ImageNet are $\{\beta^t, \mathcal{B}, \mathcal{A}, \alpha^t, \lambda^t, \text{ and } \mathcal{C}_i^t\}_{t=1}^{T}$. Note that both the two learning parameters $\mathcal{A}$ and $\mathcal{B}$, which play the roles of $A$ and $A^T$, respectively, in the iterative algorithm are commonly used at each layer, whereas $\beta^t$, $\alpha^t$, $\lambda^t$, and $C_i^t$ are learning parameters dependent on each layer.

Given a measurement vector $y$ and a trained measurement matrix $\mathcal{A}$, a 2D image can be reconstructed via QISTA-ImageNet. The initial input to QISTA-ImageNet is commonly determined as

$$x^0 = \mathcal{B}y, \tag{28}$$

which plays the role of a naive initialization $A^T y$ in the iterative algorithm. In QISTA-ImageNet, instead of adopting $\mathcal{A}^T y$, the initial input is generated with the fully connected operator $\mathcal{B}$, which is independent of $\mathcal{A}$.

## 4  Experiments

We examine the performance of QISTA-ImageNet[1] in reconstructing the natural images and conduct comparison with state-of-the-art methods.

### 4.1  Parameters and Training Setting

The constant parameter in QISTA-ImageNet was $\varepsilon_i = 0.1$ for $i \in [1:n]$. The training parameters of QISTA-ImageNet were initialized as $\beta^t = 0.1$, $\lambda^t = 10^{-5}$, and $\alpha^t = 1$, and $\{\mathcal{B}, \mathcal{A}, \text{ and } \mathcal{C}_i^t, i = 0, 1, \cdots, 7\}$ were initialized using Xavier initializer [18]. All the convolutional operators $\mathcal{C}_i^t$ were set to $3 \times 3$, and the numbers of input features and output features of $\mathcal{C}_0 \sim \mathcal{C}_7$ were 32 except the numbers of input of $\mathcal{C}_0$ and output of $\mathcal{C}_7$ were set to 1. On the other hand, because $0 < q < 1$ and natural images are usually not sparse, we adopted $q = 0.5$ here Training details will be described in Appendix 6.3.

### 4.2  Datasets for Training and Testing

In the experiments, we follow CSNet[+] [32] and SCSNet [31] to use the 200 training images and 200 test images from the BSD500 database [2] as the training data. In addition, the datasets, including Set11 (11 images) [22], BSD68 (68 images) [25], Set5 (5 images) [5], Set14 (14 images) [39], and BSD100 (100 images) [25], were used for testing.

The training data were generated by cropping the gray-scale images into patches of size $64 \times 64$ with a stride of 24, and collected as a set of $91,200$ patches. Moreover, the training data were further generated by augmentation

---

[1] Our code can be downloaded from https://github.com/anonymous-deep-learning/QISTA-ImageNet/.

via flipping, rotation 90°, rotation 90° plus flipping, rotation 180°, rotation 180° plus flipping, rotation 270°, and rotation 270° plus flipping on each patch to yield a total of 729, 600 patches.

### 4.3  Performance Comparison of Natural Image Reconstruction

The experiments in this subsection were conducted on a PC with Intel Core i7-7700K CPU, a NVIDIA GeForce GTX 1080 Ti GPU, and Python with TensorFlow version 1.14.0. We compared QISTA-ImageNet with state-of-the-art learning-based methods, including SDA [28], ReconNet [22], ISTA-Net$^+$ [40], MS-CSNet [30], DR$^2$-Net [19], $\{0, 1\}$-BCSNet [32], $\{-1, +1\}$-BCSNet [32], CSNet$^+$ [32], SCSNet [31], MSRNet [24], OPINE-Net [41], AMP-Net [43], ISTA-Net$^{++}$ [37], COAST [38], and other methods [1, 20, 42]. The comparison results are shown in Table 2, Table 3, Table 4, Table 5, and Table 6, which correspond to datasets Set11, BSD68, Set5, Set14, and BSD100, respectively.

Note that the reconstruction results in Tables 2 and 3 were measured in terms of PSNR, whereas the results in Tables 4–6 of Appendix 6.4 were measured in terms of both the PSNR and SSIM [31]. This is because some prior works did not provide results for some datasets. Therefore, the "dash" mark in the tables implies that the results were not provided. In each table, the best reconstruction results are marked in bold red and the second ones are marked in bold blue. The reconstruction results in Table 2 and Table 3 indicate that QISTA-ImageNet outperforms the other methods in terms of PSNR in reconstructing Set11 and BSD68, respectively. Moreover, we can observe from Table 4, Table 5, and Table 6 that the reconstruction performance of QISTA-ImageNet in terms of PSNR outperforms the other methods in all measurement rates except for 1%. We conjecture that this is because SCSNet adopts sub-images with the size of 96 × 96 pixels as the input to the NN architecture, and this leads SCSNet to produce fewer blocking artifact effects. Overall, the reconstruction performance of QISTA-ImageNet in terms of SSIM is superior among all the results obtained.

In Appendix 6.4, Fig. 6, Fig. 7, and Fig. 8 show the visual comparison between the ground-truth and reconstruction results of CSNet$^+$ [32], SCSNet [31], AMP-Net-9-BM [43], OPINE-Net [41], and QISTA-ImageNet. Some methods were not selected for visual comparison as either the authors did not provide the implementation codes or [31] already offered those comparison results. As shown in Fig. 6, QISTA-ImageNet generates a relatively less blurring effect at the texture in front of the eyes of Parrot. Figure 7 demonstrates that QISTA-ImageNet is able to reconstruct the striped texture better than other methods. Finally, Fig. 8 shows that the words "multimedia" and "presentations" are relatively recognizable in the reconstruction from QISTA-ImageNet.

**Table 2.** Average PSNR (dB) comparisons of different methods with various measurement rates on Set11.

| Measurement rate | 50% | 40% | 30% | 25% | 10% | 4% | 1% |
|---|---|---|---|---|---|---|---|
| SDA [28] | 28.95 | 27.79 | 26.63 | 25.34 | 22.65 | 20.12 | 17.29 |
| ReconNet [22] | 31.50 | 30.58 | 28.74 | 25.60 | 24.28 | 20.63 | 17.27 |
| [42] | 36.23 | 34.06 | 31.18 | 30.07 | 24.02 | 17.56 | 7.70 |
| LISTA-CPSS [13] | 34.60 | 32.87 | 30.54 | – | – | – | – |
| ISTA-Net$^+$ [40] | 38.07 | 36.06 | 33.82 | 32.57 | 26.64 | 21.31 | 17.34 |
| DR$^2$-Net [19] | – | – | – | 29.06 | 24.71 | 21.29 | 17.80 |
| $\{0,1\}$-BCSNet [32] | 35.05 | 34.61 | 32.57 | – | 26.39 | – | 20.62 |
| $\{-1,+1\}$-BCSNet [32] | 35.57 | 34.94 | 33.42 | – | 28.03 | – | 20.93 |
| CSNet$^+$ [32] | 38.52 | 36.48 | 34.30 | – | 28.37 | – | 21.03 |
| SCSNet [31] | 39.01 | 36.92 | 34.62 | – | 28.48 | – | **21.04** |
| MSRNet [24] | – | – | – | 33.36 | 28.07 | 24.23 | 20.08 |
| [20] | – | – | – | 32.81 | 26.97 | – | 18.83 |
| AMP-Net-9-BM [43] | **40.34** | **38.28** | **36.03** | 34.63 | 29.40 | 25.26 | 20.20 |
| OPINE-Net$^+$ [41] | 40.19 | 38.11 | 35.96 | **34.81** | **29.81** | **25.52** | 20.02 |
| ISTA-Net$^{++}$ [37] | 38.73 | 36.94 | 34.86 | – | 28.34 | – | – |
| COAST [38] | 38.94 | 37.13 | 35.04 | – | 28.69 | – | – |
| QISTA-ImageNet | 40.87 | 38.84 | 36.64 | 35.41 | 30.01 | 26.07 | 21.34 |

**Table 3.** Average PSNR (dB) comparisons of different methods with various measurement rates on BSD68.

| Measurement rate | 50% | 40% | 30% | 25% | 10% | 4% | 1% |
|---|---|---|---|---|---|---|---|
| SDA [28] | 28.35 | 27.41 | 26.38 | – | 23.12 | 21.32 | – |
| ReconNet [22] | 29.86 | 29.08 | 27.53 | – | 24.15 | 21.66 | – |
| ISTA-Net$^+$ [40] | 34.01 | 32.21 | 30.34 | – | 25.33 | 22.17 | – |
| CSNet [32] | 34.89 | 32.53 | 31.45 | – | 27.10 | – | 22.34 |
| SCSNet [31] | 35.77 | 33.86 | 31.87 | – | 27.28 | – | **22.37** |
| AMP-Net-9-BM [43] | **36.82** | **34.86** | **32.84** | 31.74 | **27.86** | **25.26** | 22.28 |
| OPINE-Net$^+$ [41] | 36.32 | 34.33 | 32.46 | 31.50 | 27.81 | 25.16 | 21.88 |
| ISTA-Net$^{++}$ [37] | 34.85 | 33.00 | 31.10 | – | 26.25 | – | – |
| COAST [38] | 34.74 | 32.93 | 31.06 | – | 26.28 | – | – |
| QISTA-ImageNet | 37.19 | 35.15 | 33.08 | 32.03 | 28.06 | 25.43 | 22.39 |

# 5   Conclusion

We studied how to reconstruct the original images from the given sensed samples/measurements by proposing a so-called deep image sensing framework, dubbed QISTA-ImageNet. Its effectivenss has been verified through both analytic and empirical results.

**Acknowledgments.** This work was supported by Ministry of Science and Technology, Taiwan, ROC, under grants MOST 110-2221-E-001-020-MY2 and 109-2221-E-001-023.

# References

1. Adler, A., Boublil, D., Zibulevsky, M.: Block-based compressed sensing of images via deep learning. In: Proceedings of International on Workshop on Multimedia Signal Process (MMSP) (2017)
2. Arbelaez, P., Maire, M., Fowlkes, C., Malik, J.: Contour detection and hierarchical image segmentation. IEEE Trans. Pattern Anal. Mach. Intell. **33**(5), 898–916 (2011)
3. Beck, A.: First-order methods in optimization. MOS-SIAM Ser. Optim. (2017)
4. Beck, A., Teboulle, M.: A fast iterative shrinkage-thresholding algorithm for linear inverse problems. SIAM J. Imag. Sci. **2**(1), 183–202 (2009)
5. Bevilacqua, M., Roumy, A., Guillemot, C., Alberi-Morel, M.L.: Low-complexity single-image super-resolution based on nonnegative neighbor embedding. In: Proceedings of British Machine Vision Conference, pp. 135-1–135-10 (2012)
6. Borgerding, M., Schniter, P., Rangan, S.: AMP-inspired deep networks for sparse linear inverse problems. IEEE Trans. Signal Process. **65**(16), 4293–4308 (2017)
7. Boyd, S., Parikh, N., Chu, E., Peleato, B., Eckstein, J.: Distributed optimization and statistical learning via the alternating direction method of multipliers. Found. Trends Mach. Learn. **3**(1), 1–122 (2011)
8. Candès, E.J., Romberg, J., Tao, T.: Robust uncertainty principles: exact signal reconstruction from highly incomplete frequency information. IEEE Trans. Inf. Theory **52**(2), 489–509 (2006)
9. Chakraborty, S., et al.: Interpretability of deep learning models: a survey of results. In: IEEE SmartWorld, Ubiquitous Intelligence & Computing, Advanced & Trusted Computed, Scalable Computing & Communications, Cloud & Big Data Computing, Internet of People and Smart City Innovation (SmartWorld/SCALCOM/UIC/ATC/CBDCom/IOP/SCI), pp. 1–6 (2017)
10. Chan, S.H., Wang, X., Elgendy, O.A.: Plug-and-play ADMM for image restoration: fixed-point convergence and applications. IEEE Trans. Comput. Imaging **3**, 84–98 (2017)
11. Chartrand, R.: Exact reconstruction of sparse signals via nonconvex minimization. IEEE Signal Process. Lett. **14**(10), 707–710 (2007)
12. Chartrand, R., Yin, W.: Iteratively reweighted algorithms for compressive sensing. In: Proceedings of International Conference on Acoustics, Speech and Signal Processing (ICASSP) (2008)
13. Chen, X., Liu, J., Wang, Z., Yin, W.: Theoretical linear convergence of unfolded ISTA and its practical weights and thresholds. In: Advances in Neural Information Processing Systems (NeurIPS) (2018)

14. Daubechies, I., Defrise, M., Mol, C.D.: An iterative thresholding algorithm for linear inverse problems with a sparsity constraint. Commun. Pure Appl. Math. **57**(11), 1413–1457 (2004)

15. Dong, C., Loy, C.C., He, K., Tang, X.: Learning a deep convolutional network for image super-resolution. In: Fleet, D., Pajdla, T., Schiele, B., Tuytelaars, T. (eds.) ECCV 2014. LNCS, vol. 8692, pp. 184–199. Springer, Cham (2014). https://doi.org/10.1007/978-3-319-10593-2_13

16. Donoho, D.L.: Compressed sensing. IEEE Trans. Inf. Theory **52**(4), 1289–1306 (2006)

17. Fan, F.L., Xiong, J., Li, M., Wang, G.: On interpretability of artificial neural networks: a survey. IEEE Trans. Radiat. Plasma Med. Sci. **5**, 741–760 (2021)

18. Glorot, X., Bengio, Y.: Understanding the difficulty of training deep feedforward neural networks. In: Proceedings of International Conference on Artificial Intelligence and Statistics (AISTATS) (2010)

19. Yao, H., Dai, F., Zhang, S., Zhang, Y., Tian, Q., Xu, C.: DR$^2$-Net: deep residual reconstruction network for image compressive sensing. Neurocomputing **359**, 483–493 (2019)

20. Pavan Kumar Reddy, K., Chaudhury, K.N.: Learning iteration-dependent denoisers for model-consistent compressive sensing. In: Proceedings of International Conference on Image Processing (ICIP) (2019)

21. Kingma, D.P., Ba, J.L.: Adam: a method for stochastic optimization. arXiv:1412.6980 (2014)

22. Kulkarni, K., Lohit, S., Turaga, P., Kerviche, R., Ashok, A.: ReconNet: non-iterative reconstruction of images from compressively sensed measurements. In: Proceedings of the Conference on Computer Vision and Pattern Recognition (CVPR) (2016)

23. Lin, G.X., Lu, C.S.: QISTA-Net: DNN architecture to solve $\ell_q$-norm minimization problem. In: Proceedings of International Workshop on Machine Learning and Signal Processing (MLSP) (2020)

24. Liu, R., Li, S., Hou, C.: An end-to-end multi-scale residual reconstruction network for image compressive sensing. In: Proceedings of International Conference on Image Processing (ICIP) (2019)

25. Martin, D., Fowlkes, C., Tal, D., Malik, J.: A database of human segmented natural images and its application to evaluating segmentation algorithms and measuring ecological statistics. In: Proceedings of IEEE International Conference on Computer Vision (ICCV), pp. 416–423 (2001)

26. Metzler, C.A., Mousavi, A., Baraniuk, R.G.: Learned D-AMP: principled neural network based compressive image recovery. In: Advances in Neural Information Processing Systems (NeurIPS) (2017)

27. Monga, V., Li, Y., Eldar, Y.C.: Algorithm unrolling: interpretable, efficient deep learning for signal and image processing. IEEE Signal Process. Mag. **38**(2), 18–44 (2021)

28. Mousavi, A., Patel, A.B., Baraniuk, R.G.: A deep learning approach to structured signal recovery. In: Proceedings of the Annual Allerton Conference on Communication, Control, and Computing (Allerton) (2015)

29. Ryu, E., Liu, J., Wang, S., Chen, X., Wang, Z., Yin, W.: Plug-and-play methods provably converge with properly trained denoisers. In: Proceedings of International Conference on Machine Learning (ICML) (2019)

30. Shi, W., Jiang, F., Liu, S., Zhao, D.: Multi-scale deep networks for image compressed sensing. In: Proceedings of International Conference on Image Processing (ICIP) (2018)

31. Shi, W., Jiang, F., Liu, S., Zhao, D.: Scalable convolutional neural network for image compressed sensing. In: Proceedings of Conference on Computer Vision Pattern Recognition (CVPR) (2019)

32. Shi, W., Jiang, F., Liu, S., Zhao, D.: Image compressed sensing using convolutional neural network. IEEE Trans. Image Process. **29**, 375–388 (2020)

33. Starck, J.L., Donoho, D.L., Candès, E.J.: Astronomical image representation by the curvelet transform. Astron. Astrophys. **398**(2), 785–800 (2003)

34. Sun, Y., Wohlberg, B., Kamilov, U.S.: An online plug-and-play algorithm for regularized image reconstruction. IEEE Trans. Comput. Imaging **5**, 395–408 (2019)

35. Yang, J., Zhang, Y., Yin, W.: A fast alternating direction method for TVL1-L2 signal reconstruction from partial Fourier data. IEEE J. Sel. Top. Signal Process. **4**(2), 288–297 (2010)

36. Yang, Y., Sun, J., Li, H., Xu, Z.: Deep ADMM-net for compressive sensing MRI. In: Advances in Neural Information Processing Systems (NeurIPS) (2016)

37. You, D., Xie, J., Zhang, J.: ISTA-NET++: flexible deep unfolding network for compressive sensing. In: Proceedings of IEEE International Conference on Multimedia and Expo (ICME) (2021)

38. You, D., Zhang, J., Xie, J., Chen, B., Ma, S.: COAST: COntrollable arbitrary-sampling neTwork for compressive sensing. IEEE Trans. Image Process. **30**, 6066–6080 (2021)

39. Zeyde, R., Elad, M., Protter, M.: On single image scale-up using sparse-representations. In Proceedings of International Conference on Curves and Surfaces, pp. 711–730 (2010)

40. Zhang, J., Ghanem, B.: ISTA-Net: interpretable optimization-inspired deep network for image compressive sensing. In Proceedings of Conference on Computer Vision Pattern Recognition (CVPR) (2018)

41. Zhang, J., Zhao, C., Gao, W.: Optimization-inspired compact deep compressive sensing. IEEE J. Sel. Top. Signal Process. **14**, 765–774 (2020)

42. Zhang, K., Zuo, W., Gu, S., Zhang, L.: Learning deep CNN denoiser prior for image restoration. In: Proceedings of Conference on Computer Vision Pattern Recognition (CVPR) (2017)

43. Zhang, Z., Liu, Y., Liu, J., Wen, F., Zhu, C.: AMP-net: denoising-based deep unfolding for compressive image sensing. IEEE Trans. Image Process. **30**, 1487–1500 (2020)

# R-DFCIL: Relation-Guided Representation Learning for Data-Free Class Incremental Learning

Qiankun Gao[1], Chen Zhao[2], Bernard Ghanem[2], and Jian Zhang[1(✉)]

[1] Peking University Shenzhen Graduate School, Shenzhen, China
gqk@stu.pku.edu.cn, zhangjian.sz@pku.edu.cn
[2] King Abdullah University of Science and Technology (KAUST),
Thuwal, Saudi Arabia
{chen.zhao,bernard.ghanem}@kaust.edu.sa

**Abstract.** Class-Incremental Learning (CIL) struggles with catastrophic forgetting when learning new knowledge, and Data-Free CIL (DFCIL) is even more challenging without access to the training data of previously learned classes. Though recent DFCIL works introduce techniques such as model inversion to synthesize data for previous classes, they fail to overcome forgetting due to the severe domain gap between the synthetic and real data. To address this issue, this paper proposes relation-guided representation learning (RRL) for DFCIL, dubbed R-DFCIL. In RRL, we introduce relational knowledge distillation to flexibly transfer the structural relation of new data from the old model to the current model. Our RRL-boosted DFCIL can guide the current model to learn representations of new classes better compatible with representations of previous classes, which greatly reduces forgetting while improving plasticity. To avoid the mutual interference between representation and classifier learning, we employ local rather than global classification loss during RRL. After RRL, the classification head is refined with global class-balanced classification loss to address the data imbalance issue as well as learn the decision boundaries between new and previous classes. Extensive experiments on CIFAR100, Tiny-ImageNet200, and ImageNet100 demonstrate that our R-DFCIL significantly surpasses previous approaches and achieves a new state-of-the-art performance for DFCIL. Code is available at https://github.com/jianzhangcs/R-DFCIL.

**Keywords:** Incremental learning · Data-free · Representation learning

## 1 Introduction

Class-Incremental Learning (CIL) is a learning paradigm in which a model (referred to as a solver model) continually learns a sequence of classification

---

**Supplementary Information** The online version contains supplementary material available at https://doi.org/10.1007/978-3-031-20050-2_25.

tasks. The model suffers from catastrophic forgetting [5,21] since its access to data of previous tasks is restricted when learning a new task. Existing CIL works [2,4,8,15,20] try to overcome the challenge mainly through saving a small proportion of previous training data in memory. Despite their success of mitigating catastrophic forgetting, these approaches may bring issues such as violation of data legality and explosion of storage space. Instead, some works [3,9,24] simultaneously train the solver model and a data generator, which is used to generate data for previous classes at a new task. This usually performs poorly and still causes data privacy concerns because the generator may remember sensitive information in the real data. To address these concerns, researchers start to consider Data-Free CIL (DFCIL) [14,25,31], in which the model incrementally incorporates new information without storing data or generator of previous tasks.

Early DFCIL works, *e.g.*, LwF [14], are often ineffective in overcoming catastrophic forgetting without data of previous tasks [27]. More recently, Yin *et al.* introduce model inversion [31] to DFCIL to synthesize data for previous tasks when learning a new task, the forgetting of previous classes can be mitigated by performing knowledge distillation on these synthetic data. However, the synthetic data have a severe domain gap with the real data, misleading the decision boundaries between new and previous classes. These approaches may come through the first few tasks (*i.e.*, short-term CIL), but they lose the stability-plasticity balance when learning many tasks (*i.e.*, long-term CIL). It is still a great challenge to train a model with both good stability (*i.e.*, not forgetting previous knowledge) and plasticity (*i.e.*, learning new knowledge) in DFCIL.

After a thorough study on DFCIL with synthetic data of previous classes, we identify bottlenecks in prior approaches as follows: **1)** with the existence of domain gap between synthetic and real data, the global classification loss (*i.e.*, the cross-entropy between the model's prediction among all seen classes and the ground truth) leads classifiers to separate new and previous classes by domain features rather than semantic features, which also causes the model to learn more domain features of synthetic data than semantic features of previous classes; **2)** to overcome forgetting, prior works perform the same knowledge distillation method on the synthetic data and the data of new classes, ignoring the difference between them, which actually hurts the model's plasticity and is not helpful in alleviating the conflict between improving plasticity and maintaining stability. Please refer to the supplementary material for more details.

To address the above bottlenecks, we propose **1)** relation-guided representation learning (RRL) with hard knowledge distillation (HKD) for synthetic old data together with the relational knowledge distillation (RKD) for data of new task; **2)** local classification loss (*i.e.*, the cross-entropy between the model's prediction among new classes and ground truth) in place of global classification loss during representation learning, following classification head refinement with global class-balanced classification loss using a small learning rate.

Specifically, our novel approach R-DFCIL consists of three stages: **1)** before learning a new task, we **train an image synthesizer** by inverting the old model through model inversion technique [31], which is used to synthesize image during learning new task; **2)** we design three components to encourage the model to learn the representations of new classes without forgetting learned classes, in which **local classification loss** improves model's plasticity, **hard knowledge distillation** maintains model's stability, and **relational knowledge distillation** mitigates the conflict between them; **3)** after representation learning, we refine the classification head to address the data imbalance between classes as well as learn the decision boundaries between new and previous classes, in which a **global class-balanced classification loss** is adopted, and the weights of classes are computed by their number of training samples.

We summarize our contributions as follows:

- We propose a novel DFCIL approach R-DFCIL, which strikes a better stability-plasticity balance by relation-guided representation learning (RRL) and classification head refinement (CHR).
- To the best of our knowledge, we are the first to introduce relational knowledge distillation (RKD) to DFCIL, which is critical to mitigate the conflict between learning the representations for new classes and preserving the representations of previously learned classes.
- We conduct extensive experiments on CIFAR100 [10], Tiny-ImageNet200 [11], and ImageNet100 [8] datasets, on all of which, our R-DFCIL surpasses the previous state-of-the-art ABD [25] with accuracy gains of 8.46%, 9.23%, and 9.88%, respectively, and achieves a new record for DFCIL.

## 2 Related Work

**Class-Incremental Learning (CIL).** To overcome catastrophic forgetting, successful approaches [1,2,4,8,15,19,20,32] store representative training data for previously learned classes and replay them when updating the model with the data from new task. Knowledge distillation (KD) [7] techniques are widely used in these approaches to further alleviate forgetting of learned information, *e.g.*, iCaRL [20] conducts KD on the pre-softmax output of the old and new data, UCIR [8] designs a novel feature distillation loss, and PODNet [4] proposes to distill from not only the final embedding output but also the pooled output of the model's intermediate layers. However, these methods are not suitable for synthetic data, so we adopt a hard KD, which directly distills the knowledge from the model's output. PODNet requires another stage to fine-tune the classifier with balanced data, our approach also has a classification head refinement stage, in which the model addresses the data imbalance issue and learns decision boundaries between new and previous classes with a global class-balanced classification loss. The classification head also impacts the incremental performance: iCaRL works better with NME than CNN classifier, UCIR is more compatible with cosine classifier, and PODNet depends on LSC classifier. We remove the bias parameter of the linear classifier to adapt our approach better.

**Data-Free Class-Incremental Learning (DFCIL).** The earliest DFCIL work is LwF [14], which first introduces knowledge distillation (KD) to incremental learning. Unfortunately, KD has limited effectiveness in overcoming forgetting when using only new data. Some prior works [3,9,24,28,30] train a large generator simultaneously with the training of the solver model, which helps the solver model remember the knowledge of previous tasks through replaying the generated data. These approaches usually perform poorly [27] due to the domain gap between generated and real data, and they also cause data privacy concerns because the generator may remember sensitive information in the real data [16]. Recent works [25,31] introduce model inversion technique to synthesize data of previous tasks. Although the visual quality is very different from the real images, the synthetic images generally match the statistical distribution of the real data from previous tasks. The synthetic images often mix features from multiple classes, which confuse the decision boundaries between classes, the prior approaches that overcome forgetting with real data may fail with synthetic data. Our approach follows ABD [25] to synthesize data for previous classes by model inversion technique, but we further propose a training framework that separates representation and classifier learning to avoid the mutual interference caused by domain gap between synthetic and real data.

**Knowledge Distillation (KD)** was first introduced to Deep Learning by Hinton *et al.* [7] to transfer knowledge from a teacher model to a small student model. Since then, various KD methods [13,18,22,26] have been developed. Conventional KD methods extract knowledge from individual data, *i.e.*, keep the hidden activation or the final output of the student model consistent with those of the teacher model for individual training samples. In contrast, Park *et al.* [17] propose Relational KD (RKD) to transfer structural knowledge using mutual relations of data examples in the teacher's output presentation. Their experimental results demonstrate that RKD is superior to conventional individual KD (IKD) methods. KD techniques are also widely used in incremental learning to overcome catastrophic forgetting, but most of them are IKD methods. These IKD methods can improve the model's stability when applied to old data but may hurt the model's plasticity when applied to new data. Inspired by RKD, we propose relation-guided representation learning to address DFCIL problem.

## 3   Methodology

### 3.1   Problem Formulation and R-DFCIL Architecture

**Problem Formulation.** In the problem of Data-Free Class-Incremental Learning (DFCIL), a model sequentially learns a series of tasks, in which the $i^{th}$ task introduces a set of classes $\mathcal{T}_i$ that do not overlap with those in previous tasks. We use $\mathcal{T}_i$ and the $i^{th}$ task interchangeably in this paper, and denote the number of classes in $\mathcal{T}_i$ as $|\mathcal{T}_i|$. At learning phase $i$, the model can only access the training data of the current task $\mathcal{T}_i$, and predicts for all the data of the tasks $\mathcal{T}_{1:i}$ (*i.e.*, from $\mathcal{T}_1$ to $\mathcal{T}_i$) for inference after the learning is finished. We denote the

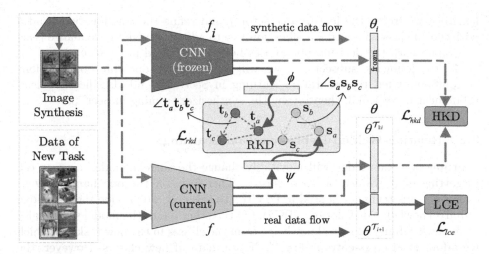

**Fig. 1.** Overview of our R-DFCIL. The model $\theta \circ f$ is learning the current task $\mathcal{T}_{i+1}$. The hard knowledge distillation loss $\mathcal{L}_{hkd}$ is applied on synthetic data to alleviate forgetting. The local classification loss $\mathcal{L}_{lce}$ is employed on new data to learn new knowledge. The relation knowledge distillation loss $\mathcal{L}_{rkd}$ transfers the structural relation of new data $\mathcal{D}_{i+1}^{train}$ from the previous model $\theta_i \circ f_i$ to the current model $\theta \circ f$. $\phi$ and $\psi$ are two linear transform functions.

feature extractor with stacks of convolutional layers as $f : \mathbb{R}^{h \times w \times 3} \rightarrow \mathbb{R}^d$, and the classification head with $c$ linear classifiers as $\theta : \mathbb{R}^d \rightarrow \mathbb{R}^c$, then the model $\theta \circ f$ predicts the class $y$ of input $\mathbf{x}$ via $\hat{y} = \arg\max_{j \in \{0,\ldots,c-1\}} \theta^{(j)}(f(\mathbf{x}))$. For simplicity, we denote the frozen snapshot of $\theta \circ f$ at the end of learning phase $i$ as $\theta_i \circ f_i$, which means $\theta_i \circ f_i$ has learned $\mathcal{T}_{1:i}$. The training data and test data of $\mathcal{T}_i$ are described by $\mathcal{D}_i^{train}$ and $\mathcal{D}_i^{test}$, respectively. We also refer $\mathcal{D}_{1:i}^{train}$ and $\mathcal{D}_{1:i}^{test}$ to the training and test data of $\mathcal{T}_{1:i}$ for convenience.

**R-DFCIL Architecture.** Figure 1 illustrates the architecture of our relation-guided representation learning for DFCIL (R-DFCIL). Our R-DFCIL is based on the framework that synthesizes old data when learning a new task, and contains the following three stages: **First**, at the beginning of the learning phase $i+1$, we train a synthesizer by inverting the old model $\theta_i \circ f_i$ through model inversion technique [31] following ABD [25]. **Then**, the model starts to learn new task $\mathcal{T}_{i+1}$ once the synthesizer training is completed. We temporarily keep the snapshot $\theta_i \circ f_i$ (old model) in memory, and add $|\mathcal{T}_{i+1}|$ new linear classifiers (denoted as $\theta^{\mathcal{T}_{i+1}}$) to $\theta$ (the original $\theta$ is denoted as $\theta^{\mathcal{T}_{1:i}}$). Then, we randomly sample a batch of training data $(X^{new}, Y^{new})$ from the new training data $\mathcal{D}_{i+1}^{train}$, and synthesize the same number of data $(X^{old}, Y^{old})$ by the synthesizer for previous classes, which are passed to the model to learn the representations of new classes without forgetting previous classes by integrating the hard knowledge distillation, local classification loss and relational knowledge distillation. **Last**, after representation learning, we freeze the feature extractor $f$ and refine the classification head $\theta$ with global class-balanced classification loss to address the data imbalance issue as well as learn the decision boundaries between new and previous classes.

In the following subsections, we will first describe our core contributions of relation-guided representation learning in Sect. 3.2 and classification head refinement in Sect. 3.3, then review the synthesizer training in Sect. 3.4.

### 3.2   Relation-Guided Representation Learning

Learning new knowledge will inevitably change the current model, causing the forgetting of previously learned classes. Therefore, on the one hand, how to overcome forgetting is essential in DFCIL. To this end, we provide the technique of hard knowledge distillation (HKD). On the other hand, the model should also have the flexibility to learn knowledge from the classes in the new task, for which we adopt local cross-entropy loss (LCE) on data of new classes. However, the conflict between overcoming forgetting by HKD and learning new knowledge by LCE still can not be well resolved, which motivates us to propose relation-guided representation learning (RRL) via relational knowledge distillation (RKD).

**Hard Knowledge Distillation (HKD).** Prior works usually take the following knowledge distillation method to keep the model from forgetting previous $1 : i$ tasks when learning the $i+1^{\text{th}}$ task:

$$\mathcal{L}_{kd} = \frac{1}{|X|} \sum_{\mathbf{x} \in X} \mathcal{D}_{KL} \left( \text{softmax} \left( \theta_i \left( f_i \left( \mathbf{x} \right) \right) / \tau \right), \text{softmax} \left( \theta^{\mathcal{T}_{1:i}} \left( f \left( \mathbf{x} \right) / \tau \right) \right) \right), \quad (1)$$

where $\tau$ is a temperature parameter, $\mathcal{D}_{KL}$ is KL divergence, and $X$ is one of $X^{new}$, $X^{old}$ and $X^{new} \cup X^{old}$. However, we find that it is not hard enough when applied to synthetic data. Instead, we use a harder variant of $\mathcal{L}_{kd}$ and **only apply it on synthetic data** without freezing $\theta^{\mathcal{T}_{1:i}}$. We formulate our HKD as:

$$\mathcal{L}_{hkd} = \frac{1}{|X^{old}| \times |\mathcal{T}_{1:i}|} \sum_{\mathbf{x} \in X^{old}} \| \theta_i \left( f_i \left( \mathbf{x} \right) \right) - \theta^{\mathcal{T}_{1:i}} \left( f \left( \mathbf{x} \right) \right) \|_1. \quad (2)$$

With this hard knowledge distillation, the outputs of old model $\theta_i \circ f_i$ and current model $\theta \circ f$ for the synthetic old data tend to be the same, but the model remains flexible inside to adapt to new knowledge. Next, we focus on learning representations of new classes, which requires the model to learn as many features from new task $\mathcal{T}_{i+1}$ as possible.

**Local Classification Loss.** In CIL, it's common to use *global* cross-entropy as the base loss that is applied on all available training data at the same time. However, when we use synthetic data to replace the real old data in DFCIL, the domain gap between synthetic and real data leads the model to separate new and old classes by the difference of domain rather than semantics, as pointed out in ABD [25]. We also observe that the decision boundaries within synthetic data are different from the ones within the real data. For instance, a synthetic fish image may mix a lot of features of a bird, which might confuse the old classifiers. Therefore, we adopt a *local* classification loss, which is the cross-entropy loss computed on the new data and the new classifiers (*i.e.*, $\theta^{\mathcal{T}_{i+1}}$), formulated as:

$$\mathcal{L}_{lce} = \frac{1}{|X^{new}|} \sum_{(\mathbf{x},y) \in (X^{new}, Y^{new})} \mathcal{L}_{CE} \left( \mathrm{softmax} \left( \theta^{\mathcal{T}_{i+1}} \left( f(\mathbf{x}) \right) \right), y \right). \quad (3)$$

This local classification loss does not directly affect classifiers of previous classes $\theta^{\mathcal{T}_{1:i}}$, but it changes $f$ to adapt to new task, which may corrupt the representations of previous learned classes.

The conflict between learning representations of new classes and maintaining representations of previously learned classes can only be mitigated by sacrificing one for the other if the representation learning is not properly guided, and finally they compromise each other to achieve a coarse balance. Therefore, we propose to guide the current model to learn representations of new classes by the structural relation of their data in the old model's feature space.

**Relational Knowledge Distillation (RKD).** The HKD applied on synthetic data prevents changes in the representation of previous classes, since it strictly forces the representation of a single sample to be consistent on the new and old models. However, it limits the model's plasticity when employed on data of new classes. In contrast to HKD, RKD [17] transfers structural information among a set of samples from teacher model to student model, endowing the student model more flexibility to learn new knowledge. The angle-wise RKD defines the relation on a triplet of samples $(\mathbf{x}_a, \mathbf{x}_b, \mathbf{x}_c)$ as the following cosine value:

$$\cos \angle \mathbf{r}_a \mathbf{r}_b \mathbf{r}_c = \left\langle \mathbf{e}^{ab}, \mathbf{e}^{cb} \right\rangle \quad \text{where} \quad \mathbf{e}^{ij} = \frac{\mathbf{r}_i - \mathbf{r}_j}{\|\mathbf{r}_i - \mathbf{r}_j\|_2}. \quad (4)$$

Here $\mathbf{r}_*$ is sample $\mathbf{x}_*$'s feature representation on the teacher or student model.

We incorporate RKD into our DFCIL framework, transferring the *structural information of the new data* in the feature space of *the old model* $\theta_i \circ f_i$ to current model $\theta \circ f$. Therefore, it can build a bridge between learning representations of new classes and maintaining representations of previously learned classes.

When applying RKD, instead of directly using the data representations from the model to construct the relation, we first transform the representations via a $d \times 2d$ linear layer denoted as $\phi$, considering the following. The new classes may not be effectively distinguished by their representations on old model $\theta_i \circ f_i$, and therefore, the structural relation built directly from the old representations may not help improving model's plasticity. The representations of the new classes on current model $\theta \circ f$ are transformed by another linear layer $\psi$ to align to the transformed old representations. Then, we apply the following angle-wise relational knowledge distillation to a triplet $(\mathbf{x}_a, \mathbf{x}_b, \mathbf{x}_c)$ of the new data:

$$\mathcal{L}_{rkd} = \frac{1}{|X^{new}|^3} \sum_{\mathbf{x}_a, \mathbf{x}_b, \mathbf{x}_c \in X^{new}} \| \cos \angle \mathbf{t}_a \mathbf{t}_b \mathbf{t}_c - \cos \angle \mathbf{s}_a \mathbf{s}_b \mathbf{s}_c \|_1, \quad (5)$$

where $\mathbf{t}_k = \phi \left( f_i(\mathbf{x}_k) \right), \mathbf{s}_k = \psi \left( f(\mathbf{x}_k) \right).$

By minimizing this loss, we limit the cases when the relation built from the transformed old representations hinders the improvement of plasticity or when the representation change hurts the model's stability. The two learnable transformation functions $\phi$ and $\psi$ are optimized with the representation learning to minimize this loss, making the relation distillation flexible. Using this relational knowledge distillation, we mitigate the conflict between improving plasticity by local classification loss and maintaining stability by hard knowledge distillation.

**RRL Loss.** The above three components form the relation-guided representation learning (RRL). The loss of the RRL at phase $i+1$ is formulated as:

$$\mathcal{L}_{rrl} = \lambda_{lce}^{i+1}\mathcal{L}_{lce} + \lambda_{hkd}^{i+1}\mathcal{L}_{hkd} + \lambda_{rkd}^{i+1}\mathcal{L}_{rkd}, \tag{6}$$

where lambdas are corresponding scale factors. Considering the amount of new knowledge increases with the number of new classes, and the difficulty of preserving previous knowledge grows as the ratio of previous classes to new classes gets larger, scale factors at learning phase $i+1$ are adaptively set as follows:

$$\lambda_{lce}^{i+1} = \frac{1 + 1/\alpha}{\beta}\lambda_{lce}, \quad \lambda_{hkd}^{i+1} = \alpha\beta\lambda_{hkd}, \quad \lambda_{rkd}^{i+1} = \alpha\beta\lambda_{rkd} \tag{7}$$

$$\text{where} \quad \alpha = \log_2(\frac{|\mathcal{T}_{i+1}|}{2} + 1), \quad \beta = \sqrt{\frac{|\mathcal{T}_{1:i}|}{|\mathcal{T}_{i+1}|}}, \tag{8}$$

in which $\lambda_{lce}$, $\lambda_{hkd}$ and $\lambda_{rkd}$ are base scale factors that can be configurable, $\alpha$ and $\beta$ denote the amount of new knowledge and the difficulty of preserving previous knowledge, respectively. We appropriately increase the local classification loss to compensate for its weakening as the number of new classes decreases. The overall loss of the RRL at learning phase $i+1$ is finally defined as:

$$\mathcal{L}_{rrl} = \frac{1 + 1/\alpha}{\beta}\lambda_{lce}\mathcal{L}_{lce} + \alpha\beta\lambda_{hkd}\mathcal{L}_{hkd} + \alpha\beta\lambda_{rkd}\mathcal{L}_{rkd}. \tag{9}$$

### 3.3   Classification Head Refinement

We achieve better stability-plasticity balance in feature extractor by relation-guided representation learning, but there are still two issues in classification head to address. One is that the decision boundaries between new and previous classes have not been learned by the model, and the other is that the imbalanced training data may cause biased classifiers. ABD attacks these problems concurrently with representation learning by a global task-balanced classification loss [12,24,29]. However, we find that the global classification loss is not beneficial to the representation learning due to the domain gap between synthetic and real data. In addition to the data imbalance between new and previous classes, the data imbalance also exists within previous classes because the label of synthetic images are random. Inspired by prior works [4,29], we fine-tune the classification head with *the feature extractor frozen* after representation learning, in which the $\mathcal{L}_{lce}$ is replaced with the following global class-balanced classification loss:

$$\mathcal{L}_{gce} = \frac{1}{|X|} \sum_{(\mathbf{x},y)\in(X,Y)} \frac{w_y}{\sum_{j=0}^{|\mathcal{T}_{1:i+1}|-1} w_j} \mathcal{L}_{CE}\left(\text{softmax}\left(\theta\left(f\left(\mathbf{x}\right)\right)\right), y\right),$$

(10)

$$\text{where} \quad (X,Y) = (X^{new} \cup X^{old}, Y^{new} \cup Y^{old}).$$

The weight $w_y$ of class $y$ is the reciprocal of it's number of samples (*i.e.*, synthetic for previous classes and real for new classes) passed to the model during training.

### 3.4 Image Synthesis

The model inversion technique was first introduced to DFCIL in DeepInversion [31] to synthesize data for previous classes. DeepInversion iteratively optimizes random noises to images of given classes together with training the classification model, which is time consuming. Instead, ABD [25] trains a synthesizer before learning new task, speeding up the learning process. Therefore, we follow ABD [25] to train our synthesizer using the following four optimization objectives. **The label diversity loss** forces the synthesizer to produce balanced data for previous classes. **The data content loss** is the cross-entropy loss with a large temperature parameter to scale down the difference between the model's output, so that the synthetic images can be predicted as a certain class with high confidence. **The stat alignment loss** minimizes the KL divergence between the distribution of synthetic data and the distribution in BatchNorm layers of $f_i$, which record the statistics of the real data during the previous training. **The image prior loss** encourages the synthesizer to produce more realistic images.

By this means, we can obtain synthetic data that mimic the old real data. However, there are still the following issues with the synthetic data, and different techniques of our R-DFCIL addresses these issues accordingly. **1) Class imbalance** is attacked by class-balanced classification loss defined in Sect. 3.3. **2) The domain gap** between synthetic and real data, which misleads classifiers to learn wrong decision boundaries between new and previous classes, is attacked by separating the learning process into representation learning (Sect. 3.2) and classifier learning (Sect. 3.3). **3) The conflict between model's plasticity and stability** is alleviated by relational knowledge distillation (Sect. 3.2), and catastrophic forgetting is effectively overcome by hard knowledge distillation.

## 4 Experiment

### 4.1 Datasets and Evaluation Protocol

**Datasets.** We chose three representative classification datasets CIFAR100 [10], Tiny-ImageNet200 [11] and ImageNet100 [8], in which CIFAR100 and ImageNet100 are two extensively used datasets in CIL, and Tiny-ImageNet200 is considered as a challenging dataset for DFCIL [25]. CIFAR100 contains 100 classes, each class with 500 training images of size $32 \times 32 \times 3$ and 100 test images in the same size. ImageNet100 is a subset of ImageNet1000 [23], with 100 randomly sampled classes. It has about 1300 training and 50 test images per class, and the spatial size of images vary. Tiny-ImageNet200 is an ImageNet-like dataset with smaller ($64 \times 64 \times 3$) images than ImageNet. It has 200 classes in total, with 500 training and 50 test images for each class.

**Evaluation Protocol.** In the CIL literature, there are two commonly used protocols. The first protocol splits the classes equally into $N = 5, 10, 20$ tasks for simulating short-term and large task incremental learning scenarios, in which $|\mathcal{T}_{1:i}|/|\mathcal{T}_{i+1}|$ is relatively small and the number of classes per task are relatively large. The other protocol introduced by Hou *et al.* [8] takes a half of classes as the first task, and equally divides the rest classes into 5, 10 or 25 tasks (*i.e.*, $N = 6, 11, 26$), which matches the situation of long-term and small task incremental learning. We follow prior works [4,8,20,25] to evaluate approaches by the typical incremental metrics: last incremental accuracy $A_N$ and average incremental accuracy $\bar{A}_N = \frac{1}{N}\sum_{i=1}^{N} A_i$, in which the incremental accuracy $A_i$ is formally defined as:

$$A_i = \frac{1}{|\mathcal{D}_{1:i}^{test}|} \sum_{(\mathbf{x},y)\in\mathcal{D}_{1:i}^{test}} \mathbb{1}\,(\hat{y} = y)\,, \text{ where } \hat{y} = \underset{0\leq j<|\mathcal{T}_{1:i}|}{\arg\max}\,\theta_i^{(j)}(f_i(\mathbf{x})), \qquad (11)$$

in which $\mathbb{1}(\cdot)$ is the indicator function that maps the boolean value to $\{0,1\}$.

**Table 1.** Evaluation on CIFAR100 with protocol that equally split 100 classes into $N$ tasks. The means and standard deviations are reported of three runs with random class orders. Approaches with * are reported directly from ABD paper.

| Approach | $N = 5$ | 10 | 20 |
|---|---|---|---|
| | $A_N$ (%) | $A_N$ (%) | $A_N$ (%) |
| Upper bound | $70.67 \pm 0.16$ | $70.67 \pm 0.16$ | $70.67 \pm 0.16$ |
| DGR* [24] | $14.40 \pm 0.40$ | $8.10 \pm 0.10$ | $4.10 \pm 0.30$ |
| LwF* [14] | $17.00 \pm 0.10$ | $9.20 \pm 0.00$ | $4.70 \pm 0.10$ |
| DeepInversion* [31] | $18.80 \pm 0.30$ | $10.90 \pm 0.60$ | $5.70 \pm 0.30$ |
| ABD* [25] | $43.90 \pm 0.90$ | $33.70 \pm 1.20$ | $20.00 \pm 1.40$ |
| ABD [25] | $47.36 \pm 0.48$ | $36.19 \pm 0.93$ | $22.29 \pm 0.65$ |
| **R-DFCIL (ours)** | $\mathbf{50.47 \pm 0.43}$ | $\mathbf{42.37 \pm 0.72}$ | $\mathbf{30.75 \pm 0.12}$ |
| | $\bar{A}_N$ (%) | $\bar{A}_N$ (%) | $\bar{A}_N$ (%) |
| ABD [25] | $63.23 \pm 1.49$ | $56.61 \pm 1.93$ | $45.10 \pm 2.01$ |
| **R-DFCIL (ours)** | $\mathbf{64.85 \pm 1.78}$ | $\mathbf{59.41 \pm 1.76}$ | $\mathbf{48.47 \pm 1.90}$ |

## 4.2   Implementation Details

All approaches are implemented within the same code base written in PyTorch. We reproduce the current SOTA DFCIL approach ABD [25], and two popular replay-based CIL approaches UCIR [8], PODNet [4]. To fairly comparision, we implement the UCIR-DF and PODNet-DF by replacing the real old data with the synthetic data that used by ABD and our R-DFCIL. For CIFAR100, we follow the prior works [4,8,20] to adopt a modified 32-layer ResNet [6] backbone and train the model with SGD optimizer for 160 epochs, the learning rate is initially set to 0.1 and is divided by 10 after 80 and 120 epochs, the weight decay is set to 0.0005 and batch size is 128. We change the weight decay to 0.0002 for Tiny-ImageNet200 and keep other settings same as CIFAR100. For ImageNet100, we employ a ResNet18 [6] backbone and train the model with SGD optimizer for 90 epochs, the learning rate starts from 0.1 and is divided by 10 after 30 and 60 epochs, the weight decay is set to 0.0001 and batch size is 64. Our R-DFCIL fine-tunes the classification head with a small constant learning rate 0.005 for another 40 epochs for CIFAR100, Tiny-ImageNet200, and 30 epochs for ImageNet100. The hyper parameters of our R-DFCIL are set to $\lambda_{lce} = 0.5$, $\lambda_{hkd} = 0.15$, $\lambda_{rkd} = 0.5$ in all experiments. Please see supplementary material for more details on hyper-parameter tuning.

**Table 2.** Evaluation on CIFAR100 with the protocol introduced by Hou *et al.* [8]. The results of UCIR, PODNet and their Data-Free implementation UCIR-DF, PODNet-DF (all with CNN classifier) are present here for clearly comparison.

| Approach | Data free | $N = 6$ | 11 | 26 |
|---|---|---|---|---|
| | | $A_N$ (%) | $A_N$ (%) | $A_N$ (%) |
| UCIR (CNN) [8] | ✗ | $55.73 \pm 0.89$ | $53.22 \pm 0.71$ | $50.08 \pm 0.35$ |
| PODNet (CNN) [4] | ✗ | $56.19 \pm 1.00$ | $52.53 \pm 0.55$ | $49.14 \pm 0.25$ |
| UCIR-DF (CNN) [8] | ✓ | $39.49 \pm 0.81$ | $25.54 \pm 1.51$ | $9.62 \pm 0.73$ |
| PODNet-DF (CNN) [4] | ✓ | $40.54 \pm 1.68$ | $33.57 \pm 2.48$ | $20.18 \pm 0.76$ |
| ABD [25] | ✓ | $50.55 \pm 1.14$ | $43.65 \pm 2.40$ | $25.27 \pm 1.09$ |
| **R-DFCIL (ours)** | ✓ | $\mathbf{54.76 \pm 0.76}$ | $\mathbf{49.70 \pm 0.61}$ | $\mathbf{30.01 \pm 0.56}$ |
| | | $\bar{A}_N$ (%) | $\bar{A}_N$ (%) | $\bar{A}_N$ (%) |
| UCIR (CNN) [8] | ✗ | $65.58 \pm 1.00$ | $63.54 \pm 1.12$ | $60.32 \pm 1.09$ |
| PODNet (CNN) [4] | ✗ | $66.82 \pm 1.25$ | $63.91 \pm 1.07$ | $61.56 \pm 1.02$ |
| UCIR-DF (CNN) [8] | ✓ | $57.82 \pm 0.86$ | $48.69 \pm 1.16$ | $33.33 \pm 1.18$ |
| PODNet-DF (CNN) [4] | ✓ | $56.85 \pm 1.40$ | $52.61 \pm 1.72$ | $43.23 \pm 1.70$ |
| ABD [25] | ✓ | $62.40 \pm 1.17$ | $58.97 \pm 1.87$ | $48.91 \pm 1.88$ |
| **R-DFCIL (ours)** | ✓ | $\mathbf{64.78 \pm 1.58}$ | $\mathbf{61.71 \pm 1.17}$ | $\mathbf{49.95 \pm 0.76}$ |

## 4.3    Results and Analysis

**CIFAR100.** We follow ABD [25] to conduct five-, ten-, and twenty-tasks class-incremental experiments, with respectively 20, 10 and 5 classes per task. We run all approaches on three random class orders with the seeds 0, 1, 2 (*i.e.*, consistent with the official ABD code) and report the means and standard deviations of these three runs. In Table 1, we report the results of ABD implemented by us and present the original data reported by ABD paper. Our R-DFCIL surpasses ABD by $3.11/1.62$ $(A_N/\bar{A}_N)$, $6.18/2.80$ and $8.46/3.37$ percent points on five-, ten-, and twenty-tasks settings, respectively. Table 2 shows results of the experiments with the protocol introduced by Hou *et al.* [8], in which the first task has 50 classes and 10, 5, 2 classes per incremental task for $N = 6, 11, 26$, respectively. From the comparison between UCIR/PODNet and UCIR-DF/PODNet-DF, we can see a great performance degradation of the popular replay-based approaches when replacing the real old data with synthetic old data. Prior CIL works believe that more tasks imply stronger forgetting. But we find that the initially learned knowledge and the number of classes in incremental tasks also impact forgetting, since both ABD and our R-DFCIL perform better with the second protocol than with the first protocol despite more tasks (Table 2 *vs.* 1).

**Tiny-ImageNet200.** We compare our R-DFCIL with ABD in the more challenging dataset Tiny-ImageNet200, in which we can observe similar results to the experiments on CIFAR100. From the data presented in Table 3, 4, we can see that there are more performance gains of our R-DFCIL over ABD as the total number of tasks increases (*e.g.*, $N = 5 \rightarrow 20$, $6 \rightarrow 26$). We plot the task-by-task incremental accuracy in Fig. 2, in which we can see the ABD drops faster than our R-DFCIL as the number of learned classes increases. We can conclude from the above observations that our R-DFCIL solves the forgetting of previously learned classes better than ABD.

**Table 3.** Evaluation on Tiny-ImageNet200 with the protocol that equally divides classes into $N$ tasks. The means and standard deviations are reported of three runs with random class orders. ABD* indicates data reported from ABD paper.

| Approach | $N = 5$ | 10 | 20 |
|---|---|---|---|
| | $A_N$ (%) | $A_N$ (%) | $A_N$ (%) |
| Upper bound | $55.39 \pm 0.33$ | $55.39 \pm 0.33$ | $55.39 \pm 0.33$ |
| ABD* [25] | – | – | 12.1 |
| ABD [25] | $30.56 \pm 0.22$ | $22.87 \pm 0.67$ | $15.20 \pm 1.01$ |
| **R-DFCIL (ours)** | $\mathbf{35.89 \pm 0.75}$ | $\mathbf{29.58 \pm 0.51}$ | $\mathbf{24.43 \pm 0.82}$ |
| | $\bar{A}_N$ (%) | $\bar{A}_N$ (%) | $\bar{A}_N$ (%) |
| ABD [25] | $45.30 \pm 0.50$ | $41.05 \pm 0.54$ | $34.74 \pm 0.91$ |
| **R-DFCIL (ours)** | $\mathbf{48.96 \pm 0.40}$ | $\mathbf{44.36 \pm 0.18}$ | $\mathbf{39.34 \pm 0.18}$ |

**Table 4.** Evaluation on Tiny-ImageNet200 with the protocol introduced by Hou *et al.* [8]. The means and standard deviations are reported of three runs with random class orders. The best values are in bold font.

| Approach | $N = 6$ | 11 | 26 |
|---|---|---|---|
| | $A_N$ (%) | $A_N$ (%) | $A_N$ (%) |
| ABD [25] | $33.18 \pm 0.46$ | $27.34 \pm 0.44$ | $16.46 \pm 0.34$ |
| **R-DFCIL (ours)** | $\mathbf{40.44 \pm 0.11}$ | $\mathbf{38.19 \pm 0.08}$ | $\mathbf{27.29 \pm 0.24}$ |
| | $\bar{A}_N$ (%) | $\bar{A}_N$ (%) | $\bar{A}_N$ (%) |
| ABD [25] | $44.55 \pm 0.13$ | $41.64 \pm 0.46$ | $34.47 \pm 0.29$ |
| **R-DFCIL (ours)** | $\mathbf{48.91 \pm 0.29}$ | $\mathbf{47.60 \pm 0.50}$ | $\mathbf{40.85 \pm 0.28}$ |

**ImageNet100.** We report the experimental results on ImageNet100 in Table 5. In these experiments, the model is less prone to forgetting than experiments on CIFAR100 and Tiny-ImageNet200 due to the large model capacity (11.0 *vs.* 0.4 million parameters). Although the performance of ABD is close to our R-DFCIL when $N = 5$, the difference becomes significant when $N$ increases to 20.

**Ablation Study.** We ablate three main components of our R-DFCIL, and display the results in Table 6. The experiments are conducted on CIFAR100 with total $N = 20$ tasks and 5 classes per task. All three components contribute greatly to our R-DFCIL, the last incremental accuracy drops by 9.21, 25.38, 7.00 percent point without relational knowledge distillation (RKD), hard knowledge distillation (HKD), classification head refinement (CHR), respectively. From Fig. 3, we

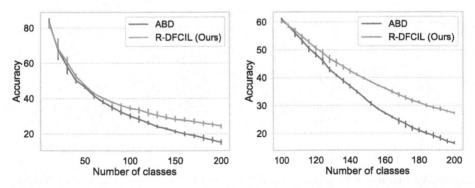

(a) 20 tasks, 10 classes / incremental task    (b) 26 tasks, 4 classes / incremental task

**Fig. 2. Incremental accuracy on Tiny-ImageNet200.** The lines show the phase-by-phase evaluation results of ABD [25] and our F-DFCIL. The means and standard deviations are reported of three runs with random class orders.

**Table 5.** Evaluation on ImageNet100 with the protocol that equally split 100 classes into $N$ tasks. We report the evaluation results of a single run.

| Approach | $N = 5$ | 10 | 20 |
|---|---|---|---|
| | $A_N$ (%) | $A_N$ (%) | $A_N$ (%) |
| Upper bound | 77.46 | 77.46 | 77.46 |
| ABD [25] | 51.46 | 35.96 | 22.40 |
| **R-DFCIL (ours)** | **53.10** | **42.28** | **30.28** |
| | $\bar{A}_N$ (%) | $\bar{A}_N$ (%) | $\bar{A}_N$ (%) |
| ABD [25] | 67.42 | 57.76 | 44.89 |
| **R-DFCIL (ours)** | **68.15** | **59.10** | **47.33** |

can clearly see that the HKD is necessary for reducing the forgetting of learned classes. We also observe that the RKD boost both plasticity and stability, demonstrating the success of our relation-guided representation learning in alleviating the conflict between improving plasticity and maintaining stability. In fact, our R-DFCIL achieves better plasticity as well as stability than previous approaches, the details are present in supplementary material. It is worth emphasizing that our adaptive design (*i.e.*, introduction of linear transformation functions) contributes about 2% gain in the last incremental accuracy. We also investigated some newer relational KD methods, please see supplementary material.

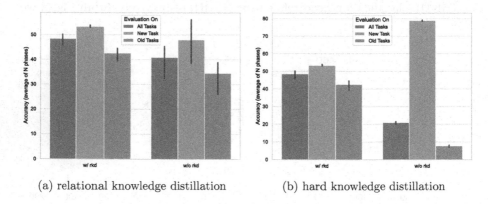

(a) relational knowledge distillation          (b) hard knowledge distillation

**Fig. 3. Ablation study about stability-plasticity balance.** The left (a) shows a better balance with RKD (w/ rkd), and the right show the importance of the HKD to mitigate forgetting.

**Table 6.** Abalation Study on CIFAR100 with $N = 20$. The results show the comparison between our R-DFCIL with all components and without relation knowledege distillation (RKD), hard knowledge distillation (HKD), classification head refinement (CHR, *i.e.*, training process ends with representation learning).

| RKD | HKD | CHR | $A_N$ (%) | $\bar{A}_N$ (%) |
|-----|-----|-----|-----------|-----------------|
| ✗ | ✓ | ✓ | $21.63 \pm 5.60$ | $40.86 \pm 5.98$ |
| ✓ | ✗ | ✓ | $5.37 \pm 0.35$ | $20.96 \pm 0.69$ |
| ✓ | ✓ | ✗ | $23.75 \pm 0.81$ | $43.09 \pm 1.53$ |
| ✓ | ✓ | ✓ | $\mathbf{30.75 \pm 0.12}$ | $\mathbf{48.47 \pm 1.90}$ |

## 5  Conclusion

This paper studies the problem of Data-Free Class-Incremental Learning (DFCIL). We propose relation-guided representation learning (RRL) for DFCIL (R-DFCIL) to address the catastrophic forgetting caused by the severe domain gap between synthetic and real data. In RRL, the model overcomes forgetting of previous classes by hard knowledge distillation on synthetic data, and learns new knowledge by the local classification loss on new data. The relational knowledge distillation (RKD) can mitigate the conflict between improving plasticity and maintaining stability by transferring structural relation of new data from the old to the current model. After RRL, the classification head is refined with global class-balanced classification loss to address data imbalance issue and learn the decision boundaries between classes. Our R-DFCIL surpasses previous SOTA approach on CIFAR100, Tiny-ImageNet200 and ImageNet100 with 8.46%, 9.23%, and 9.88% accuracy gain, respectively. Our R-DFCIL learns representation and classifier independently in two stages, which constructs a basic framework for future studies to address the domain gap between synthetic and real data in DFCIL. We introduce RKD to DFCIL for the first time, providing a reference for future works to overcome forgetting using structural information.

**Acknowledgments.** This work was supported by the King Abdullah University of Science and Technology (KAUST) Office of Sponsored Research (OSR) under Award No. OSR-CRG2021-4648 and the Shenzhen General Research Project (JCYJ20190808182805919).

## References

1. Bang, J., Kim, H., Yoo, Y., Ha, J., Choi, J.: Rainbow memory: continual learning with a memory of diverse samples. In: Proceedings of the IEEE/CVF Conference on Computer Vision and Pattern Recognition (CVPR) (2021)
2. Castro, F.M., Marín-Jiménez, M.J., Guil, N., Schmid, C., Alahari, K.: End-to-end incremental learning. In: Ferrari, V., Hebert, M., Sminchisescu, C., Weiss, Y. (eds.) ECCV 2018. LNCS, vol. 11216, pp. 241–257. Springer, Cham (2018). https://doi.org/10.1007/978-3-030-01258-8_15

3. Cong, Y., Zhao, M., Li, J., Wang, S., Carin, L.: GAN memory with no forgetting. In: Proceedings of the Advances in Neural Information Processing Systems (NeurIPS) (2020)
4. Douillard, A., Cord, M., Ollion, C., Robert, T., Valle, E.: PODNet: pooled outputs distillation for small-tasks incremental learning. In: Vedaldi, A., Bischof, H., Brox, T., Frahm, J.-M. (eds.) ECCV 2020. LNCS, vol. 12365, pp. 86–102. Springer, Cham (2020). https://doi.org/10.1007/978-3-030-58565-5_6
5. Goodfellow, I.J., Mirza, M., Xiao, D., Courville, A., Bengio, Y.: An empirical investigation of catastrophic forgetting in gradient-based neural networks. arXiv preprint arXiv:1312.6211 (2013)
6. He, K., Zhang, X., Ren, S., Sun, J.: Deep residual learning for image recognition. In: Proceedings of the IEEE/CVF Conference on Computer Vision and Pattern Recognition (CVPR) (2016)
7. Hinton, G., Vinyals, O., Dean, J.: Distilling the knowledge in a neural network. In: Proceedings of the Advances in Neural Information Processing Systems (NeurIPS), Deep Learning and Representation Learning Workshop (2015)
8. Hou, S., Pan, X., Loy, C.C., Wang, Z., Lin, D.: Learning a unified classifier incrementally via rebalancing. In: Proceedings of the IEEE/CVF Conference on Computer Vision and Pattern Recognition (CVPR) (2019)
9. Kemker, R., Kanan, C.: FearNet: brain-inspired model for incremental learning. In: Proceedings of the International Conference on Learning Representations (ICLR) (2018)
10. Krizhevsky, A., Hinton, G., et al.: Learning multiple layers of features from tiny images. Technical report (2009)
11. Le, Y., Yang, X.: Tiny ImageNet visual recognition challenge. CS 231N (2015)
12. Lee, K., Lee, K., Shin, J., Lee, H.: Overcoming catastrophic forgetting with unlabeled data in the wild. In: Proceedings of the IEEE/CVF International Conference on Computer Vision (ICCV) (2019)
13. Lee, S.H., Kim, D.H., Song, B.C.: Self-supervised knowledge distillation using singular value decomposition. In: Ferrari, V., Hebert, M., Sminchisescu, C., Weiss, Y. (eds.) ECCV 2018. LNCS, vol. 11210, pp. 339–354. Springer, Cham (2018). https://doi.org/10.1007/978-3-030-01231-1_21
14. Li, Z., Hoiem, D.: Learning without forgetting. IEEE Trans. Pattern Anal. Mach. Intell. (TPAMI) 40, 2935–2947 (2017)
15. Liu, Y., Schiele, B., Sun, Q.: Adaptive aggregation networks for class-incremental learning. In: Proceedings of the IEEE/CVF Conference on Computer Vision and Pattern Recognition (CVPR) (2021)
16. Nagarajan, V., Raffel, C., Goodfellow, I.J.: Theoretical insights into memorization in GANs. In: Proceedings of the Advances in Neural Information Processing Systems (NeurIPS) Workshop (2018)
17. Park, W., Kim, D., Lu, Y., Cho, M.: Relational knowledge distillation. In: Proceedings of the IEEE/CVF Conference on Computer Vision and Pattern Recognition (CVPR) (2019)
18. Passalis, N., Tefas, A.: Learning deep representations with probabilistic knowledge transfer. In: Ferrari, V., Hebert, M., Sminchisescu, C., Weiss, Y. (eds.) ECCV 2018. LNCS, vol. 11215, pp. 283–299. Springer, Cham (2018). https://doi.org/10.1007/978-3-030-01252-6_17
19. Prabhu, A., Torr, P.H.S., Dokania, P.K.: GDumb: a simple approach that questions our progress in continual learning. In: Vedaldi, A., Bischof, H., Brox, T., Frahm, J.-M. (eds.) ECCV 2020. LNCS, vol. 12347, pp. 524–540. Springer, Cham (2020). https://doi.org/10.1007/978-3-030-58536-5_31

20. Rebuffi, S.A., Kolesnikov, A., Sperl, G., Lampert, C.H.: iCaRL: incremental classifier and representation learning. In: Proceedings of the IEEE/CVF Conference on Computer Vision and Pattern Recognition (CVPR) (2017)
21. Robins, A.V.: Catastrophic forgetting, rehearsal and pseudorehearsal. Connect Sci. **7**, 123–146 (1995)
22. Romero, A., Ballas, N., Kahou, S.E., Chassang, A., Gatta, C., Bengio, Y.: FitNets: hints for thin deep nets. In: Proceedings of the International Conference on Learning Representations (ICLR) (2015)
23. Russakovsky, O., et al.: ImageNet large scale visual recognition challenge. Int. J. Comput. Vis. (IJCV) **115**, 211–252 (2015)
24. Shin, H., Lee, J.K., Kim, J., Kim, J.: Continual learning with deep generative replay. In: Guyon, I., et al. (eds.) Proceedings of the Advances in Neural Information Processing Systems (NeurIPS) (2017)
25. Smith, J., Hsu, Y.C., Balloch, J., Shen, Y., Jin, H., Kira, Z.: Always be dreaming: a new approach for data-free class-incremental learning. In: Proceedings of the IEEE/CVF International Conference on Computer Vision (ICCV) (2021)
26. Srinivas, S., Fleuret, F.: Knowledge transfer with Jacobian matching. In: Proceedings of the International Conference on Machine Learning (ICML) (2018)
27. van de Ven, G.M., Siegelmann, H.T., Tolias, A.S.: Brain-inspired replay for continual learning with artificial neural networks. Nat. Commun. **11**, 1–14 (2020)
28. Wu, C., Herranz, L., Liu, X., van de Weijer, J., Raducanu, B., et al.: Memory replay GANs: Learning to generate new categories without forgetting. In: Proceedings of the Advances in Neural Information Processing Systems (NeurIPS) (2018)
29. Wu, Y., et al.: Large scale incremental learning. In: Proceedings of the IEEE/CVF Conference on Computer Vision and Pattern Recognition (CVPR) (2019)
30. Ye, F., Bors, A.G.: Learning latent representations across multiple data domains using lifelong VAEGAN. In: Vedaldi, A., Bischof, H., Brox, T., Frahm, J.-M. (eds.) ECCV 2020. LNCS, vol. 12365, pp. 777–795. Springer, Cham (2020). https://doi.org/10.1007/978-3-030-58565-5_46
31. Yin, H., et al.: Dreaming to distill: data-free knowledge transfer via DeepInversion. In: Proceedings of the IEEE/CVF Conference on Computer Vision and Pattern Recognition (CVPR) (2020)
32. Yu, L., et al.: Semantic drift compensation for class-incremental learning. In: Proceedings of the IEEE/CVF Conference on Computer Vision and Pattern Recognition (CVPR) (2020)

# Domain Generalization
# by Mutual-Information Regularization
# with Pre-trained Models

Junbum Cha[1](✉), Kyungjae Lee[2], Sungrae Park[3], and Sanghyuk Chun[4]

[1] Kakao Brain, Seongnam, South Korea
junbum.cha@kakaobrain.com
[2] Chung-Ang University, Seoul, South Korea
kyungjae.lee@ai.cau.ac.kr
[3] Upstage AI Research, Seoul, South Korea
sungrae.park@upstage.ai
[4] NAVER AI Lab, Seoul, South Korea
sanghyuk.c@navercorp.com

**Abstract.** Domain generalization (DG) aims to learn a generalized model to an unseen target domain using only limited source domains. Previous attempts to DG fail to learn domain-invariant representations only from the source domains due to the significant domain shifts between training and test domains. Instead, we re-formulate the DG objective using mutual information with the oracle model, a model generalized to any possible domain. We derive a tractable variational lower bound via approximating the oracle model by a pre-trained model, called Mutual Information Regularization with Oracle (MIRO). Our extensive experiments show that MIRO significantly improves the out-of-distribution performance. Furthermore, our scaling experiments show that the larger the scale of the pre-trained model, the greater the performance improvement of MIRO. Code is available at https://github.com/kakaobrain/miro.

## 1 Introduction

Emerging studies on the generalizability of deep neural networks have revealed that the existing models, which assume independent and identically distributed (i.i.d.) training and test distribution, are not robust to significant distribution shifts between training and test distribution, *e.g.*, backgrounds [60], geographic distribution [57], demographic statistics [50,65], textures [3,23], or day-to-night shifts [17,40]. Domain generalization (DG) aims to learn robust representations against distribution shifts from multiple source domains during training. The trained model is evaluated on an unseen domain to measure the robustness. The

---

**Supplementary Information** The online version contains supplementary material available at https://doi.org/10.1007/978-3-031-20050-2_26.

existing DG approaches have tried to learn invariant features across multiple domains [2,11,13,22,32,53,70]. However, recent studies [24,29] have shown that simple baselines without learning invariant features are comparable to or even outperform the existing DG methods on the diverse DG benchmarks with a fair evaluation protocol in realistic settings (e.g., using ResNet-50 instead of ResNet-18 [25]). We presume that it is because training and test distributions differ too significantly to learn domain-invariant features by the training distribution only.

Instead of learning domain-invariant features, we let a model learn similar features to "oracle" representations, i.e., an optimal model generalized to *any* domain. In particular, we re-formulate the DG problem by maximizing the mutual information (MI) between the oracle model representations and the target model representations while preserving the training loss on source domains. However, the oracle model is not achievable in practice. Hence, we use a large pre-trained model (e.g., ImageNet pre-trained ResNet-50 [25]) as an approximation. With this approximation, we derive a tractable variational lower bound of the proposed maximization problem, named Mutual Information Regularization with Oracle (MIRO). At a high level, our MIRO objective consists of two objectives: an original target task (i.e., an ERM objective) and a regularization term between the pre-trained model and the current target model. Note that the standard DomainBed benchmark [24] uses the ImageNet pre-trained ResNet-50 as the initialization of a DG method, thus, we use the pre-trained ResNet as the initialization and the approximation of the oracle model at the same time.

While a naive fine-tuning approach of a large pre-trained model can harm the robustness against distribution shifts [31,59], our proposed algorithm remarkably improves the robustness against unseen domains during fine-tuning in a plug-and-play manner to any scale of the backbone model and datasets.

In our experiment, we observe that the naive fine-tuning of a larger pre-trained model can fail to provide better performances, even though the larger pre-trained model is trained with more data and domains. For example, ERM with the ResNet pre-trained on ImageNet (trained with 1.3M images) shows 64.2% of averaged accuracy, while ERM with the ViT pre-trained on CLIP (trained with 400M image-caption pairs) shows 61.1%. On the other hand, we show that our method can significantly improve the average DG performances with backbone models at different scales, e.g., ImageNet pre-trained ResNet (64.2% → 65.9%), 400M image-text pre-trained ViT (CLIP) [45] (61.1% → 73.7%) and Instagram 3.6B pre-trained RegNet (SWAG) [52] (68.0% → 74.1%). Especially, we observe that the pre-trained knowledge by larger pre-trained models, such as SWAG and CLIP, is more effective to learn domain generalized features than the ImageNet pre-trained model: MIRO with the ViT pre-trained on CLIP outperforms MIRO with the ResNet pre-trained on ImageNet in contrast to the naive fine-tuning. Furthermore, our feature-level regularization method is easily combined with the existing parameter space ensemble methods [13,59] (74.1% → **77.3%** average DG accuracy by combining with SWAD [13] and pre-trained RegNet).

Our contribution is as follows: (1) We re-formulate the DG objective by mutual information with the oracle model. Then, we approximate the oracle by a large pre-trained model to derive a tractable approximation of the target objective. We propose Mutual Information Regularization with Oracle (MIRO) to solve our objective. (2) We analyze the pre-trained models in terms of the MI with the oracle model. Our analysis shows that naive fine-tuning of pre-trained models can harm the MI with the oracle, on the other hand, MIRO shows high MI with the oracle. (3) We compare MIRO with state-of-the-art DG methods on DomainBed. MIRO outperforms all methods in all settings, including varying optimizers and pre-trained models. We also provide extensive analysis to understand MIRO. For example, we observe that MIRO shows stronger DG performances with larger pre-trained models, such as SWAG [52] or CLIP [45].

## 2    Related Works

**Domain Generalization.** Learning domain-invariant features from source domains has been a major branch in the DG field. The main idea is discarding biased knowledge to a specific domain while preserving invariant features over source domains, by minimizing feature divergences between the source domains [22,35,37,39,41,53,68], simulating domain shifts based on meta-learning [5,11,19,32,34,67], robust optimization [2,13,30,49,51], or augmenting source domain examples [4,12,42,43,47,64,69,70]. However, even if the model learns invariant representation to source domains, it can still be biased toward the source domains which causes limited performance on unseen target domains. That is, learning invariant representation across source domains is not enough to achieve the underlying objective of domain generalization [11,14,15]. To compensate for the issue, this paper employs pre-trained models, which provide general representations across various domains including unseen target domains.

**Exploiting Pre-trained Models** There have been numerous attempts to exploit pre-trained models in various fields. Transfer learning [36,62] and knowledge distillation [1,54] employ pre-trained models to improve in-domain performance when dataset or architecture shift occurs between pre-training and fine-tuning. Continual learning utilizes the pre-trained model to maintain old task performance when learning new tasks [38]. Recently, several studies targeting the out-of-distribution generalization are emerging [31,59]. Kumar et al. [31] show that naive fine-tuning distorts the pre-trained features and propose a simple baseline, named LP-FT, to alleviate the distortion. WiSE-FT [59] focuses on zero-shot models. It combines pre-trained and fine-tuned weights to preserve the generalizability of the pre-trained zero-shot models. In this paper, we propose a MI-based regularization method, MIRO, to exploit the generalizability of the pre-trained representation in the training process.

# 3   Methods

In this section, we first re-formulate the objective for the out-of-domain generalization by introducing an oracle model. Then, we derive a tractable variational bound of the objective by approximating the oracle model to the pre-trained model. The final form consists of the empirical risk and the mutual information (MI) regularization by querying the approximated oracle, named Mutual Information Regularization with Oracle (MIRO). We empirically validate our approximation by MI between the oracle model and large pre-trained models.

## 3.1   Mutual Information Regularization with Oracle

The main idea of the proposed method is to guide the learning process using oracle representations of training datasets. In general, the problem of domain generalization (DG) is to find a model that minimizes an expected loss of *any* domain by using training datasets from only partial domains, which are called source domains. Many existing methods minimize an empirical loss averaged over source domains. More specifically, suppose that training samples $\{\mathcal{S}_d\}_{d=1}^m$ are given in $m$ domains and we consider a hypothesis set $\mathcal{H}$ for optimization. Then, many existing DG frameworks can be formulated as follows:

$$\bar{h} = \arg\min_{h \in \mathcal{H}} \sum_{d=1}^m \mathcal{E}_{\mathcal{S}_d}(h), \qquad (1)$$

where $d$ indicates an individual source domain and $\mathcal{E}_{\mathcal{S}_d}$ is an empirical loss over the source domain $d$. Note that majority of existing DG methods can be interpreted as the variant of Eq. (1). For example, if we choose a simple cross-entropy loss for $\mathcal{E}_{\mathcal{S}_d}$, then Eq. (1) becomes "ERM" baseline used in [24][1]. Otherwise, $\mathcal{E}_{\mathcal{S}_d}$ can be formulated as a regularized ERM, such as IRM [2] or CORAL [53]. However, the formulation (1) still suffers from learning domain-invariant representations using only partial domains when the target distribution differs significantly from the training distribution. For example, CORAL, the state-of-the-art method, shows inconsistent out-of-domain accuracies across domains in Domain-Net [44]. While CORAL achieves ≈50% top-1 accuracy on four *easy* domains (59.2% for Clipart, 46.6% for Painting, 59.8% for Real, 50.1% for Sketches), it only shows 13.4% for QuickDraw and 19.7% for Infographics where the domains show the significant distribution shift comparing to others.

To alleviate this issue, we re-formulate the DG problem by employing *oracle* representations of source domains. Here, we define an oracle model as a model that can be generalized to *any* possible domain, not only for the source domains.

---

[1] Note that the terminology ERM can be unfair because other methods also minimize "empirical risk" but with different loss designs. We use the terminology "ERM" to indicate the cross-entropy baseline as suggested by Gulrajani and Lopez-Paz [24].

We define a model as a composition of a feature extractor $f$ and a classifier $g$ on the feature space where the whole classifier $h$ can be written as $h = f \circ g$. Then, let $f^*$ be a feature extractor of the oracle model. We first start from a strong assumption: we may assume that $f^*$ is accessible during the training phase. Then, we can obtain additional information from $f^*$ by querying the oracle representations of training samples in the source domains. By using the oracle representations, we can guide the learning process of a target model by maximizing MI between oracle representations and target ones. We formulate the proposed oracle-guided DG framework as follows:

$$\max_{h} \quad I(Z_{f^*}; Z_f)$$
$$\text{s.t.} \quad \mathcal{E}_{\mathcal{S}}(h) - \mathcal{E}_{\mathcal{S}}(\bar{h}) \leq \epsilon, \tag{2}$$

where $Z_{f^*}$ is a random feature extracted by $f^*$ and $Z_f$ is a random feature extracted by a target model $f$. $I(Z_{f^*}; Z_f)$ is MI between $Z_{f^*}$ and $Z_f$, and $\mathcal{E}_{\mathcal{S}}(\cdot) = \sum_{d=1}^{m} \mathcal{E}_{\mathcal{S}_d}(\cdot)$. The inequality constraint ensures the performance of the target model on the source domains. Maximizing the MI will inhibit the target model from overfitting domain-specific features in the limited source domains. Because we assume that the "oracle" is generalized well to *any* possible domain, the MI constraints (2) will be beneficial to learning robust representations.

Unfortunately, the oracle feature extractor $f^*$ is not accessible in practice. Instead, we approximate the oracle feature extractor by using a pre-trained model $f^0$. Our assumption is that a model pre-trained on large-scale diverse datasets, such as ImageNet [48], contains information on diverse domains. In practice, we choose $f^0$ as the ImageNet pre-trained ResNet-50 [25], the standard initialization choice for evaluating DG algorithms [24]. We also consider models trained by larger diverse datasets, such as CLIP [45] (trained with 400M web crawled image-text pairs) and SWAG [52] (trained with 3.6B noisy image-hashtag pairs crawled from Instagram). Although using CLIP and SWAG is not a fair comparison to the existing DG benchmark, here, we emphasize that naive fine-tuning of large pre-trained models leads to inferior generalizability to extreme distribution shifts at test time [31,59]. In our experiments, we also observe a similar observation: naive fine-tuning of CLIP shows an inferior DG performance (61.1%) than ERM (64.2%).

Through the approximation of the oracle model, we derive a tractable variational bound of our objective (2). We assume a pre-trained model $f^0$ is located near $f^*$ in terms of distance equipped on the hypothesis set of the feature extractors and it can provide approximated representation of $f^*$. Under this assumption, we can obtain a tractable objective by deriving an approximated lower bound of the MI. We first derive the variational lower bound of the MI as follows:

$$I(Z_{f^*}; Z_f) = \mathbb{E}_{Z_{f^*}, Z_f} \left[ \log \frac{q(Z_{f^*} \mid Z_f)}{p(Z_{f^*})} \right] + KL(p(Z_{f^*} \mid Z_f) \| q(Z_{f^*} \mid Z_f))$$

$$\geq \mathbb{E}_{Z_{f^*}, Z_f} [\log q(Z_{f^*} \mid Z_f)] + H(Z_{f^*}), \tag{3}$$

where $q$ is the variational distribution with a mild regularity condition. More detailed derivation can be found in Barber and Agakov [7]. Then, we approximate the expectation in Eq. (3) by using $f^0$.

$$I(Z_{f^*}; Z_f) \geq \mathbb{E}_{Z_{f^*}, Z_f} [\log q(Z_{f^*} \mid Z_f)] + H(Z_{f^*})$$

$$\geq \mathbb{E}_{Z_{f^0}, Z_f} [\log q(Z_{f^0} \mid Z_f)] - C d_{2,\infty}(f^*, f^0) + H(Z_{f^*}), \tag{4}$$

where $C$ is a constant and $d_{2,\infty}(f^*, f^0) := \sup_x \|f^*(x) - f^0(x)\|_2$. Note that $d_{2,\infty}$ is a proper metric on the hypothesis set of feature extractor. The last inequality of Equation (4) is derived by using the first-order Taylor expansion and assuming the regularity condition of $q$ (See Appendix). We would like to note that the inequality is tight enough due to Taylor's theorem. In other words, equality condition of the last inequality of Eq. (4) is $d_{2,\infty}(f^*, f^0) = 0$. Hence, $d_{2,\infty}(f^*, f^0)$ represents the effect of the pre-trained model $f^0$ on the approximation of the lower bound. Intuitively speaking, the lower bound shows that the smaller $d_{2,\infty}(f^*, f^0)$ is, the tighter the gap between the true lower bound and approximated one is. In summary, the MI between $Z_{f^*}$ and $Z_f$ can be maximized by maximizing the term $\mathbb{E}_{Z_{f^0}, Z_f}[\log q(Z_{f^0} \mid Z_f)]$.

---

**Algorithm 1:** Mutual Information Regularization with Oracle (MIRO)

---

**Input**: feature extractor $f$, classifier $g$, mean encoder $\mu$, variance encoder $\Sigma$,
　　　　regularization coefficient $\lambda$, batch size $N$.
**Init**: initialize $f$ to pre-trained feature extractor $f^0$.
**Output**: learned feature extractor $f$ and learned classifier $g$.
**for** sampled mini-batch $(\mathbf{x}, \mathbf{y})$ **do**

$\quad \mathbf{z}_f = f(\mathbf{x})$
$\quad \mathbf{z}_{f^0} = f^0(\mathbf{x})$
$\quad \mathcal{L} =$
$\quad \frac{1}{N} \sum_i^N \left[ \texttt{CrossEntropy}\left(g(z_f^i), y^i\right) + \lambda \left( \log |\Sigma(z_f^i)| + \|z_{f^0}^i - \mu(z_f^i)\|^2_{\Sigma(z_f^i)^{-1}} \right) \right]$
$\quad$ update $f, g, \mu, \Sigma$ to minimize $\mathcal{L}$

**end**

---

Finally, to consider the constraint term, we introduce the Lagrangian method to Eq. (2), then we can derive an objective function from Equation (4):

$$R(h) = \mathbb{E}_{Z_{f^0}, Z_f}[\log q(Z_{f^0} \mid Z_f)] - \beta \mathcal{E}_S(h), \tag{5}$$

where $\beta$ indicates the Lagrangian multiplier. Note that the entropy of $Z_{f^*}$ and $d_{2,\infty}(f^*, f^0)$ are omitted, since they are independent to our optimization target $h = f \circ g$. In the implementation, we model the variational distribution as a

Gaussian distribution with mean vector $\mu(Z_f)$ and covariance matrix $\Sigma(Z_f)$ and replace the multiplier $\beta$ with the regularization coefficient $\lambda$. Then, our final loss function becomes:

$$\textbf{(MIRO)} \quad \mathcal{L}(h) = \mathcal{E}_\mathcal{S}(h) + \lambda \mathbb{E}_{Z_{f^0}, Z_f} \left[ \log |\Sigma(Z_f)| + \|Z_{f^0} - \mu(Z_f)\|^2_{\Sigma(Z_f)^{-1}} \right], \tag{6}$$

where $\|x\|_A = \sqrt{x^\mathsf{T} A x}$ and constants independent on $h$ are omitted. Then, we optimize the loss function using a stochastic gradient method. The entire learning process is summarized in Algorithm 1. In the following sections, we empirically justify our approximation of $f^*$ and explain implementation details for the mean and variance encoders of the Gaussian distribution $q$.

### 3.2    Mutual Information Analysis with the Oracle Model

Here, we empirically show how our approximation by pre-trained models is close to the oracle model and how our algorithm is effective to learn representations having high mutual information (MI) to the underlying oracle model. More specifically, we compare MI between the candidate models and the oracle model on the PACS dataset. Since the *true* oracle model is not achievable in practice, we train an oracle model by directly optimizing a model on the entire domains. We train two oracle models with ResNet-50 and RegNetY-16GF backbones, where the average validation accuracies across all domains are 97.2% and 98.4%, respectively. We estimate MI between models by mutual information neural estimation (MINE) [9]. We describe the full details in Appendix.

Figure 1 illustrates the empirical MI between the candidate models and the oracle model. In the figures, we first observe that the larger and more powerful

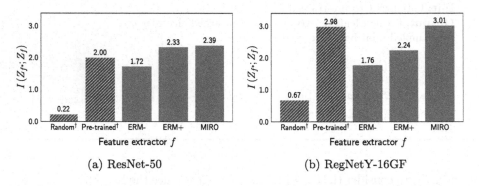

(a) ResNet-50                    (b) RegNetY-16GF

**Fig. 1. Mutual information $I(Z_{f^*}; Z_f)$ with oracle model.** The mutual information is estimated by MINE [9] in PACS. Oracle model is trained using all of the four domains. *Random* and *Pre-trained* indicate random and pre-trained model initialization, respectively. *ERM-* and *ERM+* are trained from random and pre-trained model initialization, respectively. † indicates models without fine-tuning. The experiments are repeated with two pre-trained models: ImageNet 1.3M pre-trained ResNet-50 and Instagram 3.6B pre-trained RegNetY-16GF.

pre-trained backbone ("Pre-trained" in Fig. 1b) shows higher MI than the smaller backbone ("Pre-trained" in Fig. 1a). Both pre-trained models consistently outperform "Random" in MI regardless of the backbone models. Our observations imply that a larger and stronger model is closer to the oracle model in terms of MI. Similarly, we observe that ERM+ always shows high MI than ERM−. However, interestingly, in Fig. 1b, we observe that fine-tuning significantly harms MI of the pre-trained model ("Pre-trained" vs. "ERM+") when the pre-trained model becomes larger and more powerful. Our observation is aligned in the same line as the previous studies on fine-tuning of large models [31,59]. Lastly, in both scenarios of ImageNet pre-trained ResNet (Fig. 1a) and SWAG pre-trained Reg-Net (Fig. 1b), our MIRO shows the highest MI with the oracle model. Note that MI with the oracle model may not be completely aligned with the DG performance, but in practice, we observed that the evaluation ranking of the candidates is the same as the MI ranking; MIRO scores the best, followed by ERM+ and ERM−. Detailed results are provided in Appendix.

### 3.3 Features and Encoders Design

**Multi-scale Features.** One can only use the last-level features for our regularization. However, high-level features can include pre-training task-related information, often irrelevant to the target task. Instead, we use the intermediate outputs by each model block, *i.e.*, stem output, blocks 1, 2, 3, and 4 for ResNet [25] and RegNet [46], and stem output, blocks 3, 6, 9, and 12 for ViT-B.

**Design of the Mean and Variance Encoders.** The multi-level structure increases the feature size, resulting in a computational cost increase. We alleviate the issue by employing simple yet effective architectures, identity function for the mean encoder and a bias-only model with diagonal covariance for the variance encoder. We also tested more complicated architectures, but only computational cost was increased without performance improvement.

## 4 Experiments

### 4.1 Experiment Setups and Implementation Details

**Evaluation Protocols and Datasets.** We employ DomainBed evaluation protocols [13,24] for a fair comparison. The five benchmark datasets are used: PACS [33] (4 domains, 7 classes, and 9,991 images), VLCS [21] (4 domains, 5 classes, and 10,729 images), OfficeHome [56] (4 domains, 65 classes, and 15,588 images), TerraIncognita [8] (4 domains, 10 classes, and 24,788 images), and DomainNet [44] (6 domains, 345 classes, and 586,575 images). All performance scores are evaluated by *leave-one-out cross-validation*, where averaging all cases that use a single domain as the target (test) domain and the others as the source (training) domains. Every experiment is repeated three times. We leave 20% of source domain data for validation. We use training-domain validation for the model selection and the hyperparameter search following DomainBed [24].

**Implementation Details.** We use ResNet-50 [25] pre-trained in the ImageNet [48] as default. The model is optimized using Adam [28] optimizer. A mini-batch contains all domains and 32 examples per domain. The regularization coefficient $\lambda$ is tuned in [1.0, 0.1, 0.01, 0.001]. The other hyperparameters, such as batch size, learning rate, dropout rate, and weight decay, are tuned in the similar search space proposed in Cha et al. [13]. We provide full details in Appendix.

## 4.2  Main Results

**Comparison with Domain Generalization Methods.** We provide exhaustive out-of-domain performance comparisons on five DG benchmarks in Table 1. Compared to ERM, the proposed MI regularization significantly improves performance on every benchmark dataset, resulting in +1.7pp average improvement. Compared with the state-of-the-art methods, MIRO achieves the best performances in all benchmarks, except PACS. Especially, MIRO remarkably outperforms previous methods: +1.3pp in OfficeHome (mDSDI [11]; 69.2% → 70.5%) and +1.8pp in TerraIncognita (SagNet [42]; 48.6% → 50.4%). Considering the extensive experiment setup with 5 datasets and 22 target domains, the results demonstrate the effectiveness of MIRO to the diverse visual data types.

The second part of Table 1 shows the performance with stochastic weight averaging densely (SWAD) [13], a state-of-the-art optimizer for DG by seeking flat minima. Since SWAD is an orthogonal direction to MIRO, we also evaluate the combination of MIRO and SWAD. As shown in the table, the combination of MIRO and SWAD achieves the best performance in all datasets, resulting in +0.8pp average improvement compared to the previous best results.

In the last part of Table 1, we push the limits of the out-of-domain performance by employing a large-scale backbone, RegNetY-16GF pre-trained by SWAG [52]; a weakly-supervised pre-trained model using 3.6 billion noisy Instagram images and hashtags. As shown in our previous study on MI with the oracle model, the pre-trained RegNet has higher MI than ImageNet pre-trained ResNet (Fig. 1). In the experiments, we first observe that the improvement gap by MIRO becomes remarkably large compared to the ResNet pre-trained model (from +1.7pp to +6.1pp). We presume that this significantly large gap originated from the negative effect of naive fine-tuning as observed by previous works [31,59] and our study (Fig. 1b). As shown in Fig. 1b, MIRO keeps MI with the oracle model high, resulting in remarkable performance gains on large-scale models. We further explore the effect of the scalability of pre-trained models in the later section. Finally, by combining MIRO with RegNet backbone and SWAD, we achieve the best domain generalization results (77.3%) on our evaluation benchmark.

**MIRO with Various Pre-trained Models.** In this subsection, we investigate the robustness of the proposed method to the choice of pre-trained models. In Table 2, we explore the performance changes of MIRO by varying pre-training datasets, methods, and backbones. From the pre-training method perspective,

**Table 1. Comparison with domain generalization methods.** Out-of-domain accuracies on five domain generalization benchmarks are shown. We highlight the **best results** in bold. The results marked by †, ‡ are the reported numbers from Gulrajani and Lopez-Paz [24] and Cha et al. [13], respectively. The results of Fish, SelfReg, and mDSDI are the reported ones from each paper. Average accuracies and standard errors are reported from three trials.

| Algorithm | PACS | VLCS | OfficeHome | TerraInc | DomainNet | Avg. |
|---|---|---|---|---|---|---|
| MMD† [35] | 84.7 ± 0.5 | 77.5 ± 0.9 | 66.3±0.1 | 42.2 ± 1.6 | 23.4 ± 9.5 | 58.8 |
| Mixstyle‡ [70] | 85.2 ± 0.3 | 77.9 ± 0.5 | 60.4 ± 0.3 | 44.0 ± 0.7 | 34.0 ± 0.1 | 60.3 |
| GroupDRO† [49] | 84.4 ± 0.8 | 76.7 ± 0.6 | 66.0 ± 0.7 | 43.2 ± 1.1 | 33.3 ± 0.2 | 60.7 |
| IRM† [2] | 83.5 ± 0.8 | 78.5 ± 0.5 | 64.3 ± 2.2 | 47.6 ± 0.8 | 33.9 ± 2.8 | 61.6 |
| ARM† [67] | 85.1 ± 0.4 | 77.6 ± 0.3 | 64.8 ± 0.3 | 45.5 ± 0.3 | 35.5 ± 0.2 | 61.7 |
| VREx† [30] | 84.9 ± 0.6 | 78.3 ± 0.2 | 66.4 ± 0.6 | 46.4 ± 0.6 | 33.6 ± 2.9 | 61.9 |
| CDANN† [37] | 82.6 ± 0.9 | 77.5 ± 0.1 | 65.8 ± 1.3 | 45.8 ± 1.6 | 38.3 ± 0.3 | 62.0 |
| DANN† [22] | 83.6 ± 0.4 | 78.6 ± 0.4 | 65.9 ± 0.6 | 46.7 ± 0.5 | 38.3 ± 0.1 | 62.6 |
| RSC† [26] | 85.2 ± 0.9 | 77.1 ± 0.5 | 65.5 ± 0.9 | 46.6 ± 1.0 | 38.9 ± 0.5 | 62.7 |
| MTL† [10] | 84.6 ± 0.5 | 77.2 ± 0.4 | 66.4 ± 0.5 | 45.6 ± 1.2 | 40.6 ± 0.1 | 62.9 |
| Mixup† [58, 61, 63] | 84.6 ± 0.6 | 77.4 ± 0.6 | 68.1 ± 0.3 | 47.9 ± 0.8 | 39.2 ± 0.1 | 63.4 |
| MLDG† [32] | 84.9 ± 1.0 | 77.2 ± 0.4 | 66.8 ± 0.6 | 47.7 ± 0.9 | 41.2 ± 0.1 | 63.6 |
| Fish [51] | 85.5 ± 0.3 | 77.8 ± 0.3 | 68.6 ± 0.4 | 45.1 ± 1.3 | 42.7 ± 0.2 | 63.9 |
| ERM‡ [55] | 84.2 ± 0.1 | 77.3 ± 0.1 | 67.6 ± 0.2 | 47.8 ± 0.6 | 44.0 ± 0.1 | 64.2 |
| SagNet† [42] | **86.3 ± 0.2** | 77.8 ± 0.5 | 68.1 ± 0.1 | 48.6 ± 1.0 | 40.3 ± 0.1 | 64.2 |
| SelfReg [27] | 85.6 ± 0.4 | 77.8 ± 0.9 | 67.9 ± 0.7 | 47.0 ± 0.3 | 42.8 ± 0.0 | 64.2 |
| CORAL† [53] | 86.2 ± 0.3 | 78.8 ± 0.6 | 68.7 ± 0.3 | 47.6 ± 1.0 | 41.5 ± 0.1 | 64.5 |
| mDSDI [11] | 86.2 ± 0.2 | **79.0 ± 0.3** | 69.2 ± 0.4 | 48.1 ± 1.4 | 42.8 ± 0.1 | 65.1 |
| **MIRO** | 85.4 ± 0.4 | **79.0 ± 0.0** | **70.5 ± 0.4** | **50.4 ± 1.1** | **44.3 ± 0.2** | **65.9** |
| *Combined with SWAD [13]* | | | | | | |
| ERM + SWAD‡ | 88.1 ± 0.1 | 79.1 ± 0.1 | 70.6 ± 0.2 | 50.0 ± 0.3 | 46.5 ± 0.1 | 66.9 |
| CORAL + SWAD‡ | 88.3 ± 0.1 | 78.9 ± 0.1 | 71.3 ± 0.1 | 51.0 ± 0.1 | 46.8 ± 0.0 | 67.3 |
| **MIRO + SWAD** | **88.4 ± 0.1** | **79.6 ± 0.2** | **72.4 ± 0.1** | **52.9 ± 0.2** | **47.0 ± 0.0** | **68.1** |
| *Using RegNetY-16GF backbone with SWAG pre-training [52]* | | | | | | |
| ERM | 89.6 ± 0.4 | 78.6 ± 0.3 | 71.9 ± 0.6 | 51.4 ± 1.8 | 48.5 ± 0.6 | 68.0 |
| **MIRO** | **97.4 ± 0.2** | **79.9 ± 0.6** | **80.4 ± 0.2** | **58.9 ± 1.3** | **53.8 ± 0.1** | **74.1** |
| ERM + SWAD | 94.7 ± 0.2 | 79.7 ± 0.2 | 80.0 ± 0.1 | 57.9 ± 0.7 | 53.6 ± 0.6 | 73.2 |
| **MIRO + SWAD** | 96.8 ± 0.2 | **81.7 ± 0.1** | **83.3 ± 0.1** | **64.3 ± 0.3** | **60.7 ± 0.0** | **77.3** |

we examine two image self-supervised pre-training methods (Barlow Twins [66] and MoCo v3 [16]), one image-language self-supervised pre-training method (CLIP [45]), and one weakly-supervised pre-training method (SWAG [52]), as well as ImageNet supervised pre-training baseline (ImageNet ERM). From the pre-training scale perspective, we employ the ImageNet [48] dataset of 1.3 million examples, the CLIP dataset of 400 million examples, and the Instagram

**Table 2. Comparison with various pre-training datasets, methods, and backbones.** We compare the performance changes according to the scale of the dataset, the method, and the backbone architecture of pre-training. ResNet-50 architecture is used as default. `OH`, `TI`, and `DN` indicate `OfficeHome`, `TerraIncognita`, and `DomainNet`, respectively. Every accuracy is averaged over three trials.

| Dataset (size) | Pre-training | Alg. | PACS | VLCS | OH | TI | DN | Avg. |
|---|---|---|---|---|---|---|---|---|
| ImageNet (1.3M) | ERM | ERM | 84.2 | 77.3 | 67.6 | 47.8 | 44.0 | 64.2 |
| | | MIRO | 85.4 | 79.0 | 70.5 | 50.4 | 44.3 | 65.9 (+1.7) |
| | Barlow Twins | ERM | 78.7 | 77.3 | 57.6 | 36.9 | 41.7 | 58.4 |
| | | MIRO | 80.7 | 79.4 | 63.7 | 43.2 | 42.6 | 61.9 (+3.5) |
| | MoCo v3 | ERM | 86.7 | 77.3 | 61.8 | 49.1 | 43.8 | 63.7 |
| | | MIRO | 86.3 | 78.5 | 66.8 | 48.4 | 44.7 | 65.0 (+ 1.3) |
| CLIP (400M) | CLIP (ResNet) | ERM | 64.3 | 69.8 | 28.2 | 32.9 | 29.5 | 44.9 |
| | | MIRO | 76.6 | 78.9 | 59.5 | 49.0 | 42.0 | 61.2 (+ 16.3) |
| | CLIP (ViT) | ERM | 83.4 | 75.9 | 66.4 | 35.3 | 44.4 | 61.1 |
| | | MIRO | 95.6 | 82.2 | 82.5 | 54.3 | 54.0 | 73.7 (+12.6) |
| Instagram (3.6B) | SWAG (RegNet) | ERM | 89.6 | 78.6 | 71.9 | 51.4 | 48.5 | 68.0 |
| | | MIRO | 97.4 | 79.9 | 80.4 | 58.9 | 53.8 | 74.1 (+6.1) |

dataset of 3.6 billion examples. We use ResNet-50 [25] backbone architecture as default, but a bigger model is also used for the large-scale pre-training, such as ViT-B [18] for CLIP or RegNetY-16GF [46] for SWAG.

As shown in the table, MIRO improves performances compared with the baseline ERM in all experiments. For the ImageNet pre-training, applying MIRO results in performance improvements of +1.7pp, +3.5pp, and +1.3pp for ERM (supervised learning), Barlow Twins, and MoCo v3, respectively. For the large-scale pre-training, such as CLIP and SWAG, MIRO brings larger performance improvements of +16.3pp, +12.6pp, and +6.1pp for CLIP, CLIP-ViT, and SWAG, respectively. These experiments demonstrate the robustness of the proposed method to the pre-training methods, datasets, and backbone architectures.

Notably, performance improvements of MIRO are remarkable with large-scale pre-trained models, such as CLIP, CLIP-ViT, and SWAG. This is consistent with our observation in Sect. 3.2. Our method helps large-scale pre-trained models (in terms of the pre-training dataset size) not to be biased to the training source domains compared to naive fine-tuning. Especially, naive fine-tuning of CLIP-ViT (61.1%) shows worse out-of-domain performance than fine-tuning ImageNet pre-trained model (64.2%). In contrast, MIRO can leverage the pre-trained knowledge from CLIP-ViT, resulting in superior performance (73.7%) compared with the ImageNet pre-trained model (65.9%). In our later analysis, we show that the knowledge of large-scale pre-trained models is more beneficial to domain generalization than the knowledge of ImageNet pre-trained models.

**Table 3. Comparison with methods exploiting pre-trained models.** Out-of-domain accuracies on five domain generalization benchmarks are shown. Average accuracies and standard errors are reported from three trials.

| Algorithm | PACS | VLCS | OfficeHome | TerraInc | DomainNet | Avg. |
|---|---|---|---|---|---|---|
| CRD [54] | $82.3 \pm 1.0$ | $76.6 \pm 0.9$ | $67.6 \pm 0.4$ | $44.0 \pm 1.9$ | $42.1 \pm 0.1$ | 62.5 |
| VID [1] | $84.9 \pm 0.3$ | $76.2 \pm 0.2$ | $64.6 \pm 0.5$ | $48.3 \pm 1.3$ | $42.5 \pm 0.1$ | 63.3 |
| LP-FT [31] | $84.6 \pm 0.8$ | $76.7 \pm 1.5$ | $65.0 \pm 0.2$ | $47.1 \pm 0.7$ | $43.0 \pm 0.1$ | 63.3 |
| $L^2$-SP [62] | $83.6 \pm 0.3$ | $78.8 \pm 0.4$ | $65.0 \pm 0.3$ | $47.9 \pm 2.1$ | $42.5 \pm 0.2$ | 63.6 |
| DELTA [36] | $83.1 \pm 1.1$ | $77.7 \pm 0.4$ | $68.5 \pm 0.3$ | $45.7 \pm 0.9$ | $42.8 \pm 0.1$ | 63.6 |
| LwF [38] | $83.1 \pm 0.8$ | $77.2 \pm 0.7$ | $70.0 \pm 0.2$ | $49.2 \pm 1.2$ | $42.7 \pm 0.1$ | 64.5 |
| **MIRO** | $\mathbf{85.4} \pm 0.4$ | $\mathbf{79.0} \pm 0.0$ | $\mathbf{70.5} \pm 0.4$ | $\mathbf{50.4} \pm 1.1$ | $\mathbf{44.3} \pm 0.2$ | **65.9** |

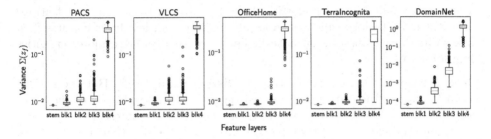

**Fig. 2. Distribution of $\Sigma(z_f)$.** We plot the estimated variances, $\Sigma(z_f)$, for each layer. X-axis indicates the feature layer where the features $z_f$ are collected. In all datasets, the variances increase as the layer is closer to the output

**Comparison with Methods Exploiting Pre-trained Models.** Other DG methods simply employ pre-trained models as weight initialization, while MIRO additionally exploits it in the training process. This is the first approach to exploit pre-trained models in domain generalization, but there are several studies in other fields for different purposes. Table 3 provides a comparison of the methods applicable to our DG settings. We exclude the methods that require additional information other than pre-trained models (*e.g.*, pre-training datasets) or are restricted to a specific model. As shown in the table, MIRO outperforms the comparison methods with large margins. These results demonstrate the effectiveness of our method design for the out-of-domain generalization.

## 4.3   Analysis of MIRO

**Loss Function Interpretation: $\Sigma$ Distribution Analysis.** We can interpret the variance term of MIRO, $\Sigma(z_f)$ in Eq. (6), as control variables of the distance loss between pre-trained features $z_{f^0}$ and current learning features $z_f$. During the training phase, if the variance values become smaller then the model will preserve MI with the pre-trained model. On the contrary, when the model needs to learn new information, the variance will increase. We illustrate the learned

**Table 4. Performance improvements in** `Camelyon17` **medical dataset.** Even in the large distribution shift setup between pre-training and target datasets, MIRO consistently outperforms ERM. Every accuracy is averaged over three trials.

| Pretrain | Algorithm | 1 | 2 | 3 | 4 | 5 | Avg. |
|---|---|---|---|---|---|---|---|
| ImageNet ERM | ERM | 97.1 | 94.7 | 95.7 | 96.4 | 90.7 | 94.9 |
| | MIRO | 97.5 | 94.5 | 95.6 | 96.7 | 93.7 | 95.6 (+0.7) |
| SWAG | ERM | 97.0 | 94.1 | 95.3 | 96.0 | 89.5 | 94.4 |
| | MIRO | 97.4 | 95.5 | 96.5 | 96.1 | 90.9 | 95.3 (+0.9) |

variances in Fig. 2. The figure shows that pre-trained information is preserved well in lower layers, while task-specific new information is learned in higher layers. This result is consistent with the interpretation that high layer features represent more task-specific semantic information than low layer features [20]; task shifts during fine-tuning make higher layer features learn more semantics than lower layers.

**Case Study on** `Camelyon17`**: Large Distribution Shift Between Pre-training and Fine-Tuning.** As shown in Eq. (4), the tightness of the lower bound is directly connected to the divergence between the representations of oracle and pre-trained models. Therefore, we investigate the case that there is a large shift between pre-trained and target datasets using the medical dataset [6,29], `Camelyon17`. This dataset consists of whole-slide images of histological lymph node sections from the five hospitals, where each hospital corresponds to each domain. The task is to predict whether the image contains tumor tissue of breast cancer. There is a large gap between the pre-training distribution (ImageNet or Instagram-3.6B) and the fine-tuning distribution (`Camelyon17`). Detailed visual examples are provided in Appendix. The results in Table 4 demonstrate MIRO

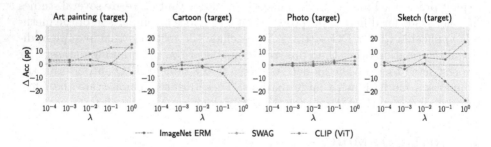

**Fig. 3. Comparison of three pre-trained models according to** $\lambda$. Y-axis indicates the performance difference of MIRO to ERM. $\lambda$ is the intensity of the mutual information regularization. We compare three models: ResNet-50 pre-trained in ImageNet [25], RegNetY-16GF pre-trained by SWAG [52], and ViT-B pre-trained by CLIP [45]

leads the model to learn robust representations even in the large distribution shift setup between pre-training and fine-tuning.

**Relationship Between the Pre-training Scale and the Intensity of the MI Regularization.** Our method has a control parameter $\lambda$, which controls the balance between the cross-entropy loss and the MI regularization loss. If $\lambda$ becomes larger, it implies that the strength of MI regularization becomes stronger, while it weakens the strength of the ERM objective. Intuitively, if the pre-trained knowledge is informative enough to the target task, larger $\lambda$ will improve the performances, while if the pre-trained knowledge is uninformative to the target task, then larger $\lambda$ can harm the performances, because of the penalty on the ERM objective. We compare three pre-trained models (ImageNet pre-trained model, SWAG, and CLIP-ViT) by varying $\lambda$. Figure 3 shows how the out-of-domain performance of MIRO with different pre-trained backbones changes by $\lambda$. The additional results on different datasets are given in Appendix.

First, we observe that the ImageNet pre-trained backbone has a negative correlation between the performance difference and $\lambda$ in target domains. When distribution shifts significantly differ, such as cartoon and sketch domains, we can observe an apparent negative correlation. We presume that it is because the ImageNet samples barely contain non-photo images, such as art painting or sketch images. On the other hand, we observe that MIRO with SWAG and CLIP-ViT backbones make significant performance improvements by choosing larger $\lambda$. In other words, SWAG and CLIP-ViT pre-trained knowledge are helpful to learn robust features for various target domains compared to the ImageNet pre-trained model. Furthermore, it implies that larger pre-trained models trained with massive diverse domain images show less sensitivity to the choice of $\lambda$, not only bringing remarkable performance improvements as shown in Table 2.

## 5    Conclusion

Traditional domain generalization (DG) approaches focus to learn a robust representation using multiple source domains. However, in the recent trends of scaling up pre-training, the use of a large-scale pre-trained model becomes more important than the use of DG algorithms for the real-world DG. In line with this trend, we propose Mutual Information Regularization with Oracle (MIRO) to robustly exploit the pre-trained model by approximating an oracle model. To do this, we first re-formulate the domain generalization objective by introducing a concept of an oracle model. Then, we derive a tractable variational bound of the objective by approximating the oracle model with the pre-trained model. Our experimental results demonstrate both the effectiveness and the potential of the proposed method. MIRO achieves state-of-the-art performance in the DomainBed benchmarks. Furthermore, when combining MIRO with large-scale pre-trained backbones, such as CLIP [45] or SWAG [52], the performance improvements remarkably increases. We hope that this study promotes a new research direction of exploiting pre-trained backbones to learn robust representations for domain generalization.

**Acknowledgments.** This work was supported by IITP grant funded by the Korea government (MSIT) (No. 2021-0-01341, AI Graduate School Program, CAU).

# References

1. Ahn, S., Hu, S.X., Damianou, A., Lawrence, N.D., Dai, Z.: Variational information distillation for knowledge transfer. In: Computer Vision and Pattern Recognition (2019)
2. Arjovsky, M., Bottou, L., Gulrajani, I., Lopez-Paz, D.: Invariant risk minimization. arXiv preprint arXiv:1907.02893 (2019)
3. Bahng, H., Chun, S., Yun, S., Choo, J., Oh, S.J.: Learning de-biased representations with biased representations. In: International Conference on Machine Learning (2020)
4. Bai, H., et al.: Decaug: Out-of-distribution generalization via decomposed feature representation and semantic augmentation. In: AAAI Conference on Artificial Intelligence (2021)
5. Balaji, Y., Sankaranarayanan, S., Chellappa, R.: Metareg: Towards domain generalization using meta-regularization. In: Neural Information Processing Systems (2018)
6. Bandi, P., et al.: From detection of individual metastases to classification of lymph node status at the patient level: the camelyon17 challenge. IEEE Trans. Med. Imaging **38**(2), 550–560 (2018)
7. Barber, D., Agakov, F.: The im algorithm: a variational approach to information maximization. In: Neural Information Processing Systems (2004)
8. Beery, S., Van Horn, G., Perona, P.: Recognition in Terra incognita. In: Ferrari, V., Hebert, M., Sminchisescu, C., Weiss, Y. (eds.) ECCV 2018. LNCS, vol. 11220, pp. 472–489. Springer, Cham (2018). https://doi.org/10.1007/978-3-030-01270-0_28
9. Belghazi, M.I., et al.: Mutual information neural estimation. In: International Conference on Machine Learning (2018)
10. Blanchard, G., Deshmukh, A.A., Dogan, U., Lee, G., Scott, C.: Domain generalization by marginal transfer learning. J. Mach. Learn. Res. **22**(2), 1–55 (2021)
11. Bui, M.H., Tran, T., Tran, A., Phung, D.: Exploiting domain-specific features to enhance domain generalization. In: Neural Information Processing Systems (2021)
12. Carlucci, F.M., D'Innocente, A., Bucci, S., Caputo, B., Tommasi, T.: Domain generalization by solving jigsaw puzzles. In: Computer Vision and Pattern Recognition (2019)
13. Cha, J., et al.: Swad: Domain generalization by seeking flat minima. In: Neural Information Processing Systems (2021)
14. Chattopadhyay, P., Balaji, Y., Hoffman, J.: Learning to balance specificity and invariance for in and out of domain generalization. In: Vedaldi, A., Bischof, H., Brox, T., Frahm, J.-M. (eds.) ECCV 2020. LNCS, vol. 12354, pp. 301–318. Springer, Cham (2020). https://doi.org/10.1007/978-3-030-58545-7_18
15. Chen, J., Wang, J., Lin, W., Zhang, K., de Silva, C.W.: Preserving domain private representation via mutual information maximization. arXiv preprint arXiv:2201.03102 (2022)

16. Chen, X., Xie, S., He, K.: An empirical study of training self-supervised vision transformers. In: International Conference on Computer Vision (2021)
17. Dai, D., Van Gool, L.: Dark model adaptation: Semantic image segmentation from daytime to nighttime. In: International Conference on Intelligent Transportation Systems (2018)
18. Dosovitskiy, A., Beyer, L., Kolesnikov, A., Weissenborn, D., Zhai, X., Unterthiner, T., Dehghani, M., Minderer, M., Heigold, G., Gelly, S., et al.: An image is worth 16x16 words: Transformers for image recognition at scale. In: International Conference on Learning Representations (2021)
19. Dou, Q., Castro, D.C., Kamnitsas, K., Glocker, B.: Domain generalization via model-agnostic learning of semantic features. In: Neural Information Processing System (2019)
20. Erhan, D., Bengio, Y., Courville, A., Vincent, P.: Visualizing higher-layer features of a deep network. University of Montreal **1341**(3), 1 (2009)
21. Fang, C., Xu, Y., Rockmore, D.N.: Unbiased metric learning: On the utilization of multiple datasets and web images for softening bias. In: International Conference on Computer Vision (2013)
22. Ganin, Y., et al.: Domain-adversarial training of neural networks. J. Mach. Learn. Res. **17**(1), 2030–2096 (2016)
23. Geirhos, R., Rubisch, P., Michaelis, C., Bethge, M., Wichmann, F.A., Brendel, W.: Imagenet-trained cnns are biased towards texture; increasing shape bias improves accuracy and robustness. In: International Conference on Learning Representations (2019)
24. Gulrajani, I., Lopez-Paz, D.: In search of lost domain generalization. In: International Conference on Learning Representations (2021)
25. He, K., Zhang, X., Ren, S., Sun, J.: Deep residual learning for image recognition. In: Computer Vision and Pattern Recognition (2016)
26. Huang, Z., Wang, H., Xing, E.P., Huang, D.: Self-challenging improves cross-domain generalization. In: Vedaldi, A., Bischof, H., Brox, T., Frahm, J.-M. (eds.) ECCV 2020. LNCS, vol. 12347, pp. 124–140. Springer, Cham (2020). https://doi.org/10.1007/978-3-030-58536-5_8
27. Kim, D., Yoo, Y., Park, S., Kim, J., Lee, J.: Selfreg: Self-supervised contrastive regularization for domain generalization. In: International Conference on Computer Vision (2021)
28. Kingma, D.P., Ba, J.: Adam: A method for stochastic optimization. In: International Conference on Learning Representations (2015)
29. Koh, P.W., et al.: Wilds: A benchmark of in-the-wild distribution shifts. In: International Conference on Machine Learning (2021)
30. Krueger, D., et al.: Out-of-distribution generalization via risk extrapolation (rex). arXiv preprint arXiv:2003.00688 (2020)
31. Kumar, A., Raghunathan, A., Jones, R., Ma, T., Liang, P.: Fine-tuning can distort pretrained features and underperform out-of-distribution. In: International Conference on Learning Representations (2022)
32. Li, D., Yang, Y., Song, Y.Z., Hospedales, T.: Learning to generalize: Meta-learning for domain generalization. In: AAAI Conference on Artificial Intelligence (2018)
33. Li, D., Yang, Y., Song, Y.Z., Hospedales, T.M.: Deeper, broader and artier domain generalization. In: International Conference on Computer Vision (2017)
34. Li, D., Zhang, J., Yang, Y., Liu, C., Song, Y.Z., Hospedales, T.M.: Episodic training for domain generalization. In: International Conference on Computer Vision (2019)
35. Li, H., Pan, S.J., Wang, S., Kot, A.C.: Domain generalization with adversarial feature learning. In: Computer Vision and Pattern Recognition (2018)

36. Li, X., Xiong, H., Wang, H., Rao, Y., Liu, L., Huan, J.: Delta: Deep learning transfer using feature map with attention for convolutional networks. In: International Conference on Learning Representations (2019)
37. Li, Y., Gong, M., Tian, X., Liu, T., Tao, D.: Domain generalization via conditional invariant representations. In: AAAI Conference on Artificial Intelligence (2018)
38. Li, Z., Hoiem, D.: Learning without forgetting. IEEE Trans. Pattern Anal. Mach. Intell. **40**(12), 2935–2947 (2017)
39. Matsuura, T., Harada, T.: Domain generalization using a mixture of multiple latent domains. In: AAAI Conference on Artificial Intelligence (2020)
40. Michaelis, C., et al.: Benchmarking robustness in object detection: Autonomous driving when winter is coming. arXiv preprint arXiv:1907.07484 (2019)
41. Muandet, K., Balduzzi, D., Schölkopf, B.: Domain generalization via invariant feature representation. In: International Conference on Machine Learning (2013)
42. Nam, H., Lee, H., Park, J., Yoon, W., Yoo, D.: Reducing domain gap by reducing style bias. In: Computer Vision and Pattern Recognition (2021)
43. Nuriel, O., Benaim, S., Wolf, L.: Permuted adain: Reducing the bias towards global statistics in image classification. In: Computer Vision and Pattern Recognition (2021)
44. Peng, X., Bai, Q., Xia, X., Huang, Z., Saenko, K., Wang, B.: Moment matching for multi-source domain adaptation. In: International Conference on Computer Vision (2019)
45. Radford, A., et al.: Learning transferable visual models from natural language supervision. In: International Conference on Machine Learning (2021)
46. Radosavovic, I., Kosaraju, R.P., Girshick, R., He, K., Dollár, P.: Designing network design spaces. In: Computer Vision and Pattern Recognition (2020)
47. Robey, A., Pappas, G.J., Hassani, H.: Model-based domain generalization. In: Neural Information Processing Systems (2021)
48. Russakovsky, O., et al.: Imagenet large scale visual recognition challenge. Int. J. Comput. Vision **115**(3), 211–252 (2015)
49. Sagawa*, S., Koh*, P.W., Hashimoto, T.B., Liang, P.: Distributionally robust neural networks. In: International Conference on Learning Representations (2020)
50. Scimeca, L., Oh, S.J., Chun, S., Poli, M., Yun, S.: Which shortcut cues will dnns choose? a study from the parameter-space perspective. In: International Conference on Learning Representations (2022)
51. Shi, Y., et al.: Gradient matching for domain generalization. In: International Conference on Learning Representations (2022)
52. Singh, M., et al.: Revisiting weakly supervised pre-training of visual perception models. In: Computer Vision and Pattern Recognition (2022)
53. Sun, B., Saenko, K.: Deep CORAL: Correlation alignment for deep domain adaptation. In: Hua, G., Jégou, H. (eds.) ECCV 2016. LNCS, vol. 9915, pp. 443–450. Springer, Cham (2016). https://doi.org/10.1007/978-3-319-49409-8_35
54. Tian, Y., Krishnan, D., Isola, P.: Contrastive representation distillation. In: International Conference on Learning Representations (2019)
55. Vapnik, V.: Statistical learning theory. Wiley, NY (1998)
56. Venkateswara, H., Eusebio, J., Chakraborty, S., Panchanathan, S.: Deep hashing network for unsupervised domain adaptation. In: Computer Vision and Pattern Recognition (2017)
57. de Vries, T., Misra, I., Wang, C., van der Maaten, L.: Does object recognition work for everyone? In: Computer Vision and Pattern Recognition Workshops (2019)

58. Wang, Y., Li, H., Kot, A.C.: Heterogeneous domain generalization via domain mixup. In: International Conference on Acoustics, Speech and Signal Processing (2020)
59. Wortsman, M., et al.: Robust fine-tuning of zero-shot models. In: Computer Vision and Pattern Recognition (2022)
60. Xiao, K.Y., Engstrom, L., Ilyas, A., Madry, A.: Noise or signal: The role of image backgrounds in object recognition. In: International Conference on Learning Representations (2020)
61. Xu, M., et al.: Adversarial domain adaptation with domain mixup. In: AAAI Conference on Artificial Intelligence (2020)
62. Xuhong, L., Grandvalet, Y., Davoine, F.: Explicit inductive bias for transfer learning with convolutional networks. In: International Conference on Machine Learning (2018)
63. Yan, S., Song, H., Li, N., Zou, L., Ren, L.: Improve unsupervised domain adaptation with mixup training. arXiv preprint arXiv:2001.00677 (2020)
64. Yang, F.E., Cheng, Y.C., Shiau, Z.Y., Wang, Y.C.F.: Adversarial teacher-student representation learning for domain generalization. In: Neural Information Processing Systems (2021)
65. Yang, K., Qinami, K., Fei-Fei, L., Deng, J., Russakovsky, O.: Towards fairer datasets: Filtering and balancing the distribution of the people subtree in the imagenet hierarchy. In: Conference on Fairness, Accountability, and Transparency (2020)
66. Zbontar, J., Jing, L., Misra, I., LeCun, Y., Deny, S.: Barlow twins: Self-supervised learning via redundancy reduction. In: International Conference on Machine Learning (2021)
67. Zhang, M., Marklund, H., Gupta, A., Levine, S., Finn, C.: Adaptive risk minimization: Learning to adapt to domain shift. In: Neural Information Processing Systems (2021)
68. Zhao, S., Gong, M., Liu, T., Fu, H., Tao, D.: Domain generalization via entropy regularization. In: Neural Information Processing Systems (2020)
69. Zhou, K., Yang, Y., Hospedales, T., Xiang, T.: Learning to generate novel domains for domain generalization. In: Vedaldi, A., Bischof, H., Brox, T., Frahm, J.-M. (eds.) ECCV 2020. LNCS, vol. 12361, pp. 561–578. Springer, Cham (2020). https://doi.org/10.1007/978-3-030-58517-4_33
70. Zhou, K., Yang, Y., Qiao, Y., Xiang, T.: Domain generalization with mixstyle. In: International Conference on Learning Representations (2021)

# Predicting Is Not Understanding: Recognizing and Addressing Underspecification in Machine Learning

Damien Teney[1,3(✉)], Maxime Peyrard[2], and Ehsan Abbasnejad[3]

[1] Idiap Research Institute, Martigny, Switzerland
damien.teney@idiap.ch
[2] EPFL, Vaud, Switzerland
maxime.peyrar@epfl.ch
[3] Australian Institute for Machine Learning, Adelaide, Australia
ehsan.abbasnejad@adelaide.edu.au

**Abstract.** Machine learning (ML) models are typically optimized for their accuracy on a given dataset. However, this predictive criterion rarely captures all desirable properties of a model, in particular how well it matches a domain expert's *understanding* of a task. Underspecification [6] refers to the existence of multiple models that are indistinguishable in their in-domain accuracy, even though they differ in other desirable properties such as out-of-distribution (OOD) performance. Identifying these situations is critical for assessing the reliability of ML models. We formalize the concept of underspecification and propose a method to identify and partially address it. We train multiple models with an independence constraint that forces them to implement different functions. They discover predictive features that are otherwise ignored by standard empirical risk minimization (ERM), which we then distill into a global model with superior OOD performance. Importantly, we constrain the models to align with the data manifold to ensure that they discover meaningful features. We demonstrate the method on multiple datasets in computer vision (collages, WILDS-Camelyon17, GQA) and discuss general implications of underspecification. Most notably, in-domain performance cannot serve for OOD model selection without additional assumptions (See https://arxiv.org/abs/2207.02598 for the full-length version of this work).

## 1 Introduction

**Is Data All You Need?** A finite set of i.i.d. examples is almost never sufficient to learn a task. Inductive biases have long been known to be necessary for

**Supplementary Information** The online version contains supplementary material available at https://doi.org/10.1007/978-3-031-20050-2_27.

in-domain generalization [32,54]. OOD[1] generalization complicates things further since one also needs to determine which predictive patterns of the training data will remain relevant at test time. Correlations between inputs and labels that are important for the task may be indistinguishable from spurious ones that result from dataset-specific artefacts such as selection biases.

**An Example in Image Recognition.** Image labels are often correlated with objects and the backgrounds they appear in (*e.g.* cars in cities, birds in nature). Recognizing either often suffice to predict correct labels. However, robust OOD generalization (*e.g.* correctly labeling images of birds in street scenes) requires to rely on shapes and to ignore the background. When this requirement cannot be deduced from the data (because both features leave a similar signature in the joint training distribution), the task is said to be underspecified. In this example, the task requires the additional knowledge that labels refer to object shapes rather than background textures [12]. Such knowledge is often task-specific. For example, the opposite choice of prioritizing color or texture over shape would be sensible for recognizing traffic signs or segmenting medical images.

---

**Underspecification gap**: the difference between the information provided in a dataset and the information required to perform *as desired* on a task.

---

The qualifier "*as desired*" captures the fact that different use cases require different properties such as adversarial robustness, interpretability, fairness, or OOD generalization. The latter is the focus of this paper. Underspecification arises because these properties do not necessarily correlate with the ERM objective [50] typically used to train models.

This paper argues that **identifying underspecification** is important for assessing the reliability of ML models, their reliance on hidden assumptions, and for identifying the information missing for OOD robustness. We identify underspecification by **discovering multiple understandings** of the data. We learn multiple predictive models compatible with a given dataset and hypothesis class (low in-domain risk). We force them to rely on different predictive features by encouraging orthogonality of their input gradients. We also ensure that these features remain semantically meaningful by constraining the input gradients to the data manifold. Training multiple models stands in contrast with the standard practice of optimizing a single solution to a learning problem – which hides the existence of underspecification. With our method, we discover predictive features otherwise ignored by standard ERM. This alone produces candidate models with superior OOD performance. In addition, we show how to distill selected features from multiple candidate models into one that is robust across a wider range of distribution shifts. In all cases, a selection strategy must be provided such as an OOD validation set, domain expertise, task-specific heuristics, etc.

**Experiments.** We apply the method to controlled data (collages [43,48]) and computer vision benchmarks (WILDS-Camelyon17 [27], GQA [20,24]). On visual

---

[1] In this paper, OOD means there is a covariate shift between training and test data [44].

question answering, we show that multiple models can produce similar answers while relying on different visual features (Fig. 1).

**Implications.** Our work complements other studies [6,30] in formalizing underspecification as a root cause of multiple challenges in ML including shortcut learning, distribution shifts, and even adversarial vulnerabilities (an extreme case of OOD inputs). Our formalization of underspecification makes it obvious that ID and OOD performance are not necessarily coupled. Therefore, without further assumptions, in-domain validation performance is not a reliable model selection strategy for OOD performance despite contradictory suggestions made in the literature [16,31]. The prevalence of underspecification [6] also suggests that task-specific knowledge and assumptions are often necessary to build robust ML models, since they cannot emerge from simply scaling up data and architectures. We summarize our contributions as follows. See the supp. mat. for related work.

Is the man to the right of the hammer wearing eye glasses? No.

Predictions: yes, yes, yes.

**Fig. 1.** Example of underspecification in visual question answering. Our method trains multiple models that each discover different predictive features. We obtain three models producing identical answers on most training and validation data, even though they rely on different visual clues (evidenced by grad-CAM visualizations over object proposals [41]). Each model reflects a **different understanding of the task** compatible with the data (possibly incomprehensible to humans) which reveals ambiguity in its specification.

1. We propose a mathematical framework for quantifying and addressing underspecification.
2. We derive a method to learn a set of models compatible with a given dataset that exhibit distinct OOD behaviour. We force the models to rely on different features (independence objective) that are nonetheless semantically meaningful (on-manifold constraint).
3. We use the method for (1) highlighting underspecification in given dataset/architecture pairs, and (2) building models with superior OOD performance on collages [43,48], WILDS-Camelyon17 [27], and GQA [20,24].

## 2   Formalizing Underspecification

Let us focus on binary classification tasks. A dataset provides **labeled examples** $\mathcal{D}_{\mathrm{tr}} = \{(\boldsymbol{x}_i, y_i)\}_i$ with $\boldsymbol{x} \in \mathbb{R}^{d_{\mathrm{in}}}$, $y_i \in \{0,1\}$. The goal of a learning algorithm is to identify a **predictor** $f : \mathbb{R}^{d_{in}} \rightarrow \mathbb{R}$ to estimate labels[2] of examples from a test set $\mathcal{D}_{\text{test}} = \{x_i\}_i$. While the input data $x$ is typically high-dimensional (*e.g.* vectorized images), natural data (*e.g.* photographs) occupies only a fraction of the input space assumed to form a low-dimensional **manifold** [53] $\mathcal{M} \subset \mathbb{R}^{d_{in}}$. The dimensionality $d_{\text{manifold}}$ ($< d_{\text{in}}$) is known as the **intrinsic dimensionality** of the data. Training and test data are drawn from a distribution on this manifold $P_{\text{ID}}$ (in-domain examples) while unbiased natural data (free of dataset-specific selection biases) is drawn from a distribution $P_{\text{OOD}}$ of typically broader support.

**Inductive Biases.** are the properties of a learning algorithm that determine what model $f_{\theta^*}$ is returned for a dataset $\mathcal{D}$ from a hypothesis class $\mathcal{H} = \{f_\theta, \forall \theta\}$ where $f_\theta$ is a model with free parameters $\theta$. Inductive biases enable generalization from finite data [32] by encoding assumptions on the relation between $\mathcal{D}$ and $\mathcal{D}_{\text{test}}$. In particular, classical learning theory assumes that $\mathcal{D}$ and $\mathcal{D}_{\text{test}}$ contain i.i.d. samples from the same distribution. For completeness, we summarize a standard training workflow.

---

1. Randomly split the data into training and validation sets: $\mathcal{D} = \mathcal{D}_{\text{tr}} \cup \mathcal{D}_{\text{val}}$.
2. A **hypothesis class** $\mathcal{H} = \{f_\theta, \forall \theta\}$ is chosen *e.g.* by defining a neural architecture $f$.
3. **Empirical risk minimization** serves to optimize the free parameters of $f$ as $\theta^* = \text{argmin}_\theta \, \mathcal{R}\left(f_\theta, \mathcal{D}_{\text{tr}}\right)$ where the empirical risk is defined as $\mathcal{R}(f, \mathcal{D}) = \Sigma_{(x,y) \in \mathcal{D}} \, \mathcal{L}_{\text{pred}}\left(y, \sigma\left(f(x)\right)\right) / |\mathcal{D}|$, $\mathcal{L}_{\text{pred}}$ is a predictive loss such as binary cross-entropy.
4. **Validation performance** serves to refine various choices (architecture, regularizers, …) by trial and error, *i.e.* loosely solving $f'_{\theta^{*'}} = \text{argmin}_{f, \dots} \, \mathcal{R}(f_{\theta^*}, \mathcal{D}_{\text{val}})$ where $\mathcal{R}$ is often substituted with a task-specific metric such as the error rate.

---

There is often a multitude of models satisfying the above procedure, not all are equally desirable because they differ in properties that the procedure does not constrain. The degree of underspecification indicates the importance of arbitrary and stochastic factors in the outcome of the learning process.

This paper focuses on **differences in OOD performance** among predictive models. OOD performance is the predictive performance of a model (in terms of risk, accuracy, or another task-specific metric) on test data drawn from a distribution $P_{\text{OOD}} \neq P_{\text{ID}}$. On OOD data, features that were predictive in the training data may become irrelevant or misleading, causing a drop in performance of a model that relies on them. By definition, OOD performance is underspecified by the ERM objective, since the empirical risk is estimated on in-domain data.

To capture variability in OOD performance, we propose a definition of underspecification based on the number of ways to fit the data with the above procedure and produce different OOD predictions.[3]

---

[2] We define $f$ to output logits. A binary prediction $\hat{y}$ is obtained as $\hat{y} = \text{round}\left(\sigma\left(f(x)\right)\right)$.

[3] Previously, [19,42] used volumes of hypothesis spaces to define Rashomon sets.

---

**Definition 1.** The **degree of underspecification** of a dataset $\mathcal{D} = \mathcal{D}_{tr} \cup \mathcal{D}_{val}$, input manifold $\mathcal{M}$, and hypothesis class $\mathcal{H} = \{f_\theta, \forall \theta\}$ is the ratio of volumes $\text{vol}(\mathcal{H}')/\text{vol}(\mathcal{H})$ of the largest subset of models $\mathcal{H}' \subset \mathcal{H}$ such that its elements $\{f_{\theta_m}\}_m$ all have, for small constants $\epsilon_{tr}, \epsilon_{val}$:

- A low training risk: $\mathcal{R}(f_{\theta_m}, \mathcal{D}_{tr}) < \epsilon_{tr}, \ \forall f_\theta \in \mathcal{H}'$,
- A low validation risk: $\mathcal{R}(f_{\theta_m}, \mathcal{D}_{val}) < \epsilon_{val}, \ \forall f_\theta \in \mathcal{H}'$,
- Distinct OOD predictions:  $\text{P}\big(\text{round}(\sigma(f_{\theta 1}(x)) \neq \text{round}(\sigma(f_{\theta 2}(x)))\big) \approx 1, \ f_{\theta 1}, f_{\theta 2} \in \mathcal{H}', \ f_{\theta 1} \neq f_{\theta 2}, \ x \sim \text{P}_{OOD}$.

---

The next section derives a method to learn a set of models with these properties.

# 3   Proposed Method

**Overview.** We train multiple models with the same architecture and data while enforcing them to represent different functions and use different features. The models use different initializations, but this does not always suffice to produce significantly-different models. We add two regularizers that enforce (1) independence of the models (mutually-orthogonal input gradients) and (2) alignment with the data manifold such that the models learn meaningful features.

Since the constraints follow from Definition 1, the number of models trainable to satisfy them indicates the degree of underspecification. The only existence of multiple such models thus highlights cases of underspecification. The models also discover some predictive features missed by standard ERM, which can be combined by distillation into a predictor with superior OOD performance. In the next sections, we implement the two constraints as differentiable regularizers.

## 3.1   Independent Models

To optimize for distinct OOD predictions, we turn the criteria of Definition 1 into a differentiable objective using the concept of independent models [39,40].

---

**Definition 2.** A pair of predictors $f_{\theta_1}, f_{\theta_2}$ are **locally independent** at $x$ iff their predictions are statistically independent for Gaussian perturbations around $x$: $f_{\theta_1}(\tilde{x}) \perp f_{\theta_2}(\tilde{x})$, $\tilde{x} \sim \mathcal{N}(x, \sigma I)$.

**Definition 3.** A set of predictors $\{f_{\theta_1}, ..., f_{\theta_M}\}$ are **globally independent** on a dataset $\mathcal{D}$ iff every pair of them are locally independent at every $x \in \mathcal{D}$.

---

This formalizes the notion that models can rely on different features. In our case, we seek a set of models globally independent from one another. We obtain a tractable objective using the relation between statistical independence and geometric orthogonality developed in [40].

**Proposition 1.** *A pair of predictors $f_{\theta_1}$, $f_{\theta_2}$ are locally independent at $x$ iff the mutual information $MI(f_{\theta_1}(\tilde{x}), f_{\theta_2}(\tilde{x})) = 0$ with $\tilde{x} \sim \mathcal{N}(x, \sigma I)$.*

For infinitesimally small perturbations ($\sigma \to 0$), samples $\tilde{x}$ can be approximated through linearization by the input gradients $\nabla_x f$. These are 1D Gaussian random variables whose correlation is given by $\cos\left(\nabla_x f_{\theta_1}(x), \nabla_x f_{\theta_2} x\right)$. Their mutual information [15] is $-\frac{1}{2}\ln\left(1 - \cos^2\left(\nabla_x f_{\theta_1}(x), \nabla_x f_{\theta_2}(x)\right)\right)$. Therefore, the statistical independence between the models' outputs as their inputs are perturbed by small Gaussian variations can be enforced by making their input gradients orthogonal. Our **local independence loss** for a pair of models is:

$$\mathcal{L}_{\text{indep}}\left(\nabla_x f_{\theta_{m_1}}(x), \nabla_x f_{\theta_{m_2}}(x)\right) = \cos^2\left(\nabla_x f_{\theta_{m_1}}(x), \nabla_x f_{\theta_{m_2}}(x)\right) \quad (1)$$

with $\cos^2(v, w) = (v^\mathsf{T} w)^2 / (v^\mathsf{T} v)(w^\mathsf{T} w)$. To enforce *global* independence, this loss will be applied to all training points and pairs of models in Eq. (3).

### 3.2   On-Manifold Constraint

The independence constraint (1) makes models' input gradients orthogonal to one another. The number of models satisfying it grows exponentially with the input dimension ($d_{\text{in}}$) but many are practically irrelevant because the natural data manifold usually occupies much fewer dimensions. Intuitively, when the constraint affects a model's gradients in dimensions pointing outward the manifold, it does not affect its predictions on natural data.

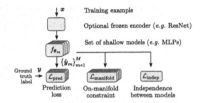

**Fig. 2.** Method overview during training

Consequently, the independence constraint could be satisfied by models that produce identical predictions on every natural input (thus defeating its purpose) because their decision boundaries are identical when projected on the manifold. The issue stems from the *isotropic* perturbations in Eq. (1). Only perturbations *on* the manifold are meaningful.

One straightforward solution would be to enforce independence after projecting the data on a learned approximation of the manifold. This approach, proposed in [39,40] failed in our early experiments because of the difficulty of optimizing the independence objective under such a strict on-manifold constraint. Instead, we implement a soft constraint as a regularizer that proved easy to train and resilient to imperfect models of the manifold.

To learn the data manifold $\mathcal{M}$, we need unlabeled examples, ideally containing the type of OOD data expected at test time *e.g.* a broad collection of natural images: $\mathcal{D}_{\text{OOD}} = \{x_i\} \sim \text{P}_{\text{OOD}}$. We use this data off-line to prepare a function $\text{proj}_{\mathcal{M}}(x, v)$ that projects an arbitrary vector $v$ at $x$ in the input space onto the manifold (Fig. 3). During training, we penalize each model with the distance between its input gradients and their projection on the manifold. The **on-manifold loss** is defined as

$$\mathcal{L}_{\text{manifold}}\big(\nabla f(\boldsymbol{x})\big) = \big\|\text{proj}_{\mathcal{M}}\big(\boldsymbol{x}, \nabla_{\boldsymbol{x}} f(\boldsymbol{x})\big) - \nabla_{\boldsymbol{x}} f(\boldsymbol{x})\big\|_2^2. \tag{2}$$

We describe possible implementations of $\text{proj}_{\mathcal{M}}(\cdot)$ in the supp. mat. with a variational auto-encoder (VAE) or a simple PCA. In summary, the on-manifold loss encourages a model to be sensitive to variations in the input that are likely to be encountered in natural test data. It typically has no effect on in-domain performance (Fig. 6c) since it only removes a model's sensitivity to unnatural inputs such as variations of isolated pixels unlikely to appear in natural images.

The overall learning objective combines the predictive, independence, and on-manifold losses:

$$\mathcal{L}(\mathcal{D}_{\text{tr}}, \boldsymbol{\theta}_1 \dots \boldsymbol{\theta}_M) = \Sigma_{\boldsymbol{x} \in \mathcal{D}_{\text{tr}}} \Big[ \; (1/M) \; \Sigma_{m=1}^M \mathcal{L}_{\text{pred}}\big(y, \sigma(f_{\boldsymbol{\theta}_m}(\boldsymbol{x}))\big)$$

$$+ \, (1/M^2) \, \Sigma_{m_1=1}^M \Sigma_{m_2=1}^M \lambda_{\text{indep}} \; \mathcal{L}_{\text{indep}}\big(\nabla_{\boldsymbol{x}} f_{\boldsymbol{\theta}_{m_1}}(\boldsymbol{x}), \nabla_{\boldsymbol{x}} f_{\boldsymbol{\theta}_{m_2}}(\boldsymbol{x})\big)$$

$$+ \, (1/M) \; \Sigma_{m=1}^M \lambda_{\text{manifold}} \; \mathcal{L}_{\text{manifold}}\big(\nabla_{\boldsymbol{x}} f_{\boldsymbol{\theta}_m}(\boldsymbol{x})\big) \Big]. \tag{3}$$

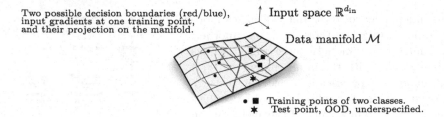

Two possible decision boundaries (red/blue), input gradients at one training point, and their projection on the manifold.

Input space $\mathbb{R}^{d_{\text{in}}}$

Data manifold $\mathcal{M}$

● ■ Training points of two classes.
★ Test point, OOD, underspecified.

**Fig. 3.** Effect of the proposed method in input space. Data such as natural images is assumed to lie on a low-dimensional manifold. The training set covers a subset of this manifold (gray ellipse). OOD test data (★) lies outside this subset. In this example, our method discovers two models (*red* and *blue* decision boundaries) whose input gradients are orthogonal (shown at one training point, in colors matching the boundary). Even though a third model (*green* vector) could satisfy the orthogonality constraint, its input gradient would point outside the manifold. This would violate the *on-manifold* constraint, which requires gradients to closely match their projection on the manifold (Color figure online)

### 3.3 Fine-Tuning

After training a set of models with (3), we propose to relax the independence and on-manifold constraints ($\lambda_{\text{indep}} \leftarrow 0$, $\lambda_{\text{manifold}} \leftarrow 0$) then fine-tune the models. This eases the optimization and typically allows the models to reach a higher predictive accuracy. Concretely, we apply binary masks on the data such that each model is fine-tuned only on the elements most relevant to itself: [4]

$$\mathcal{D}_{\text{tr}}^m = \{(\boldsymbol{x}_i \odot \textbf{mask}_i^m, y_i) : (\boldsymbol{x}_i, y_i) \in \mathcal{D}_{\text{tr}}\} \tag{4}$$

---

[4] In our implementation, masked elements are not replaced with zeros, but rater with random values from other instances in the current mini-batch.

with $\mathbf{mask}_i^m \in \{0,1\}^{d_{in}}$. They are computed before starting the fine-tuning to highlight the data most relevant to each model. Each element (pixel, channel) is unmasked only for the model with the largest corresponding gradient magnitude:

$$\mathbf{mask}_i^m = \mathbb{1}\left(m = \underset{1 \leq m \leq M}{\arg\max} \nabla f_{\boldsymbol{\theta}_m}(\boldsymbol{x}_i)\right) \quad \forall (\boldsymbol{x}_i, \cdot) \in \mathcal{D}_{\mathrm{tr}}. \tag{5}$$

We fine-tune each model on its own masked version of the data.[5] This ensures that the models remain distinct despite disabling the regularizers ($\lambda_{\mathrm{indep}} \leftarrow 0$, $\lambda_{\mathrm{manifold}} \leftarrow 0$). See Algorithm 1 for a summary.

### 3.4   Distilling Multiple Models into One

Finally, after training/fine-tuning a set of models, we propose to combine the best of them into a global one that uses all of the most relevant features. We train this global model from scratch, without regularizers, on masked data as described above, using masks from *multiple* selected models combined with a logical OR. In our experiments, we combine the two models with the highest accuracies on an OOD validation set. We repeat this pairwise combination as long the accuracy of the global model increases, usually for 2–3 iterations (as formalized in the supp. mat.).

---

**Algorithm 1:** Training and fine-tuning models.

---

**Inputs:** Labeled examples $\mathcal{D}_{\mathrm{tr}}$. Unlabeled examples $\mathcal{D}_{\mathrm{OOD}}$ (typically $\mathcal{D}_{\mathrm{tr}} \subset \mathcal{D}_{\mathrm{OOD}}$). Architecture $f$.
**Result:** Set of independent models $\{f_{\boldsymbol{\theta}_1} ... f_{\boldsymbol{\theta}_M}\}$.
**Method:**
With $\mathcal{D}_{\mathrm{OOD}}$, estimate dimensionality $d_{\mathrm{manifold}}$ [37] and set the number of models $M \leftarrow d_{\mathrm{manifold}}$.
With $\mathcal{D}_{\mathrm{OOD}}$, prepare function proj($\cdot$) by PCA decomp. or by training a VAE.
With $\mathcal{D}_{\mathrm{tr}}$, train $M$ instances of $f$ in parallel (Eq. 3):
$\{\boldsymbol{\theta}_1 ... \boldsymbol{\theta}_M\} \leftarrow \arg\min \mathcal{L}(\mathcal{D}_{\mathrm{tr}}, \boldsymbol{\theta}_1 ... \boldsymbol{\theta}_M)$.
Determine masks on input data (Eq. 5): $\{\mathbf{mask}_i^m\}_{i,m}$
**foreach** $m$ **do**    Optional fine-tuning on masked data
 | $\mathcal{D}_{\mathrm{tr}}^m \leftarrow \{(\boldsymbol{x}_i \odot \mathbf{mask}_i^m, y_i)\}_i$   Prepare masked data
 | $\lambda_{\mathrm{indep}} \leftarrow 0$, $\lambda_{\mathrm{manifold}} \leftarrow 0$   Use only predictive loss
 | $\boldsymbol{\theta}_m \leftarrow \arg\min \mathcal{L}(\mathcal{D}_{\mathrm{tr}}^m, \boldsymbol{\theta}_m)$   Fine-tune

---

## 4   Experiments

We first present experiments that validate the method on controlled data with multiple known features (collages, Sect. 4.1). We then demonstrate applications to existing datasets: WILDS-Camelyon17 (Sect. 4.2) and GQA (see the supp. mat.).

---

[5] We obtain very similar results between fine-tuning and retraining models from scratch on the masked data.

## 4.1    Experiments on Controlled Data: Collages

This diagnostic dataset contains images with binary labels that are constructed to contain multiple predictive features [43,48]. Each image contains four tiles representing one of two classes respectively from MNIST (0/1), CIFAR-10 (automobile/truck), Fashion-MNIST (pullover/coat), and SVHN (0/1).

– At **training time**, the labels are perfectly correlated with the four tiles (0/1 respectively for the first/second possible class in each tile). There are (at least) four equally-valid ways of understanding the task (*i.e.* relying on any of the four tiles).
– At **test time**, we evaluate a model on four test sets that represent different OOD conditions. In each, only one tile is correlated with the correct label while others tiles are randomized. By examining the performance on the four test sets, we can identify which tile(s) the model relies on

**Task Difficulty.** This dataset is surprisingly challenging because the tiles vary greatly in learning difficulty (*e.g.* MNIST 0s/1s are very distinct while Fashion-MNIST pullovers/coats look extremely similar). It would be reasonable to learn a model that relies on all four tiles. However, an ERM-trained baseline surprisingly uses only a few MNIST pixels (achieving ∼99% accuracy on the MNIST test set and ∼50% on the others), as shown in previous work on the simplicity bias of neural networks [48].

**Class 0**
Zero, pullover
automobile, zero.

**Class 1**
One, coat
truck, one.

**Fig. 4.** Examples of collages [48]. Tr. labels are correlated with all four tiles

We follow [48] and use our method to learn multiple models compatible with the data. We then report the accuracy of the best model on each test set, *i.e.* the best accuracy assuming perfect model selection. This avoids confounding the performance of the learning algorithm and with that of the selection strategy.

**Applying the Proposed Method.** We follow Algorithm 1. We prepare unlabeled data to defines the data manifold as the union of the training and test sets, thus covering all combinations of contents of the four tiles. With this data, we estimate the dimensionality of the manifold with [37] as about 23.8 ($\sigma = 0.16$ over 10 runs). We prepare two generative models of the manifold: a PCA with 24 components (capturing ∼85% of the variance) and a VAE with 24 latent dimensions (details in the supp. mat.). We define a simple architecture (2-layer MLPs) and train multiple instances in parallel with the proposed objective. The only hyperparameters are the number of models and weights of independence/on-manifold constraints. We plot a range of values in the supp. mat.

**Results.** Our method learns models that focus on different parts of the images. Remarkably, learning as few as 4 models is sufficient to obtain models with high accuracy on all of four test sets. Let us examine several ablations.

– The baseline ($\lambda_{indep} = \lambda_{manifold} = 0$) only learns about MNIST.
– The independence constraint ($\lambda_{indep} >$, $\lambda_{manifold} = 0$) is crucial for learning distinct models. On its own, it requires training a very large number of models ($\gg 32$) before picking up features outside the MNIST tiles. Visualizations of input gradients (Fig. 6) reveal that these models each rely only on a single or a few pixels. These trivial solutions to the independence constraint, akin to adversarial examples, are avoided with the on-manifold constraint.
– In the full method ($\lambda_{indep} > 0$, $\lambda_{manifold} > 0$) the models discover distinct features that align with the semantic contents of images. The effect of the on-manifold constraint on input gradients is striking (Fig. 6). It forces models to be sensitive to natural variations of the data – rather than unlikely single-pixel patterns. Remarkably, **image regions emerge as meaningful features without inductive bias for spatial locality** (*e.g.* no convolutions).

**Hyperparameters.** A number of models between 4 and 24 give excellent results. As expected, the larger this number, the more granular the features these models learn (Fig. 6). The effect breaks down for >24 models, matching theoretical expectations since the dimensionality of the manifold was estimated at ∼24. The method is stable over a range of regularizer weights. Additional comparisons in Table 1 show that a VAE is better than PCA to represent the manifold. This agrees with the general expectation that natural images form a non-linear manifold in pixel space. We also found overall results to be robust to variations in architecture and hyperparameters of the VAE.

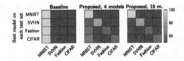

**Fig. 5.** Collages dataset: accuracy on the four test sets (columns) of models with best accuracy on each set (rows). Diagonal patterns indicate that **models specialize and learn different, non-overlapping features**. The baseline only learns features relevant to MNIST

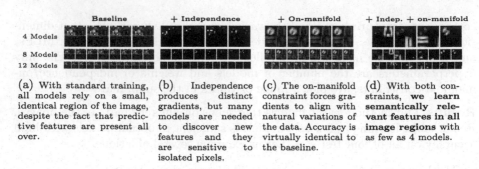

(a) With standard training, all models rely on a small, identical region of the image, despite the fact that predictive features are present all over.

(b) Independence produces distinct gradients, but many models are needed to discover new features and they are sensitive to isolated pixels.

(c) The on-manifold constraint forces gradients to align with natural variations of the data. Accuracy is virtually identical to the baseline.

(d) With both constraints, **we learn semantically relevant features in all image regions** with as few as 4 models.

**Fig. 6.** Input gradients for a random test image from the collages dataset. It is remarkable that, with the proposed method (d) **image regions emerge as meaningful features without any inductive bias for spatial locality** such as convolutions (models in these experiments are fully-connected MLPs)

**Fine-Tuning.** We report the accuracy of models fine-tuned on masked inputs as proposed in Sect. 3.3. This optional step relaxes the independence constraint to maximize each model's predictive performance. The accuracy jumps significantly and almost reaches the upper-bound on each test set (Table 1). We experimented with relaxing both the independence and on-manifold constraints. Disabling the former has a significant effect. But the latter has no significant effect on accuracy on its own as expected and discussed in Sect. 3.2.

**Distilling Multiple Models into One.** We report the performance of combinations of features described in Sect. 3.4. This procedure is most effective after training a large number of models (24 here). This is unsurprising since models then discover finer-grained features. Each combination selects features relevant to only one specific tile to achieve near-maximal accuracy on the test set of that tile. Simple traditional ensembling of models completely failed in our experiments.

**Comparison with Existing Methods.** No other method reported in Table 1 performed well on this dataset. The method of Teney *et al.* [48] is technically the most similar to ours, but it requires training a much larger number of models and still achieves much lower accuracy. While all experiments of this section used a model taking raw pixels as input, we repeated the whole evaluation using a shared, frozen ResNet to extract features in the supp. mat. This implementation is computationally appealing for larger-scale applications, and gave essentially similar findings with higher overall accuracy thanks to the deeper architecture.

**Table 1.** Accuracy on *collages* of existing and proposed methods (8 models per method unless specified). The 4 test sets simulate different OOD conditions: only one tile in each set is correlated with the labels. **Standard training only learns a fraction of predictive features.** Existing methods cannot do better than chance except on MNIST, or they require training a large number of models. Ours learns a variety of features and give near-optimal predictions on every test set (last row)

| Collages (accuracy in %) | Best model on | | | | |
|---|---|---|---|---|---|
| | MNIST | SVHN | Fashion | CIFAR-10 | Average |
| Upper bound | 99.9 | 92.4 | 80.8 | 68.6 | 85.5 |
| (training on test-domain data) | | | | | |
| ERM Baseline | 99.8 | 50.0 | 50.0 | 50.0 | 62.5 |
| Spectral decoupling [35] | 99.9 | 49.8 | 50.6 | 49.9 | 62.5 |
| Penalty: gradients' L1 norm | 98.5 | 49.6 | 50.5 | 50.0 | 62.1 |
| Penalty: g. L2 norm [18] | 96.6 | 52.1 | 52.3 | 54.3 | 63.8 |
| Input dropout (ratio 0.9) | 97.4 | 50.7 | 56.1 | 52.1 | 64.1 |
| Indep. loss (cos. sim.) [39] | 99.7 | 50.4 | 51.5 | 50.2 | 63.0 |
| Indep. loss (dot prod.) [48] | 99.5 | 53.5 | 53.3 | 50.5 | 64.2 |
| With many more models | | | | | |
| Indep. (cos. sim.), <u>1024</u> models | 99.5 | 58.1 | 66.8 | 63.0 | 71.9 |
| Indep. (dot prod.), <u>128</u> models | 98.7 | 84.9 | 71.6 | 61.5 | 79.2 |
| Proposed method (8 models) | | | | | |
| Indep. + on-manifold PCA | 97.3 | 69.8 | 62.2 | 60.0 | 72.3 |
| Indep. + on-manifold VAE* | 96.5 | 85.1 | 61.1 | 62.1 | 76.2 |
| (*) + FT  (fine-tuning) | 99.7 | 90.9 | 81.4 | 67.4 | 84.8 |
| (*) + FT + combi. (1×) | 99.9 | 92.2 | 79.3 | 66.3 | 84.4 |
| (*) + FT + combi. (2×) | 99.9 | 92.5 | 80.2 | 67.5 | 85.0 |
| (*) + **FT + combi. (3×)** | **99.9** | **92.3** | **80.8** | **68.5** | **85.4** |

## 4.2  Experiments on Real Data: WILDS-Camelyon17

**Dataset.** The WILDS-Camelyon17 benchmark [26] provides histopathology images to classify as *"tumor"* or *"normal"*. The images come from different sets of hospitals in the training, validation (val-OOD), and test splits (test-OOD). The challenge is to learn a model that generalizes from the training hospitals to those of the test set. The original authors [26] trained a Densenet-121 model from scratch on this data with 10 random seeds. They showed that the performance on val-OOD and test-OOD varies wildly across seeds, demonstrating that the task is severely underspecified with only the standard training images (the dataset provides additional hospital labels that could enable generalization; neither ERM nor our method uses them).

**Implementation of Our Method.** We use frozen features (last-layer activations) from one of the pretrained models from [26] as input. We will show that we can recover even more variability in performance than the complete

**Table 2.** Accuracy on WILDS-Camelyon17 while training 12 models. Each proposed component improves the accuracy of the best model from each run. The data appears simple enough that a PCA approximates the manifold well enough. This allows implementing the on-manifold constraint as a hard projection instead of a soft regularizer.

| WILDS-Camelyon17 | Best accuracy (%) on | |
|---|---|---|
| | val-OOD | test-OOD |
| Pseudo-Label [29] | – | 67.7 ± 8.2 |
| DANN [9] | – | 68.4 ± 9.2 |
| FixMatch [45] | – | 71.0 ± 4.9 |
| CORAL [46] | – | 77.9 ± 6.6 |
| NoisyStudent [56] | – | **86.7** ± 1.7 |
| ERM Baseline | 84.9 ± 0.1 | 68.4 ± 0.1 |
| + Independence constraint | 85.3 ± 0.5 | 74.6 ± 0.9 |
| + On-manifold soft regularizer, VAE | 85.4 ± 0.4 | 80.3 ± 1.7 |
| + On-manifold hard projection, VAE | 88.2 ± 2.1 | 76.3 ± 2.8 |
| + On-manifold soft regularizer, PCA | 87.8 ± 0.3 | 79.0 ± 2.9 |
| + On-manifold hard projection, PCA* | **88.4** ± 0.7 | 81.6 ± 1.4 |
| (*) + Fine-tuning & distillation | **88.4** ± 0.7 | **82.5** ± 2.4 |

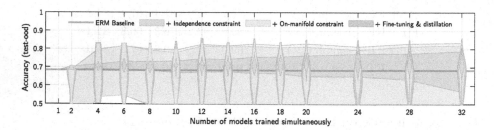

**Fig. 7.** Spread of accuracies on WILDS-Camelyon17 of models trained with different ablations of our method. The upper/lower bounds of the **shaded areas** show the highest/lowest accuracy of any model from one run, averaged over 6 seeds. The **violins** show distributions of accuracies over *all* seeds (hence some values outside the shaded areas). The independence constraint (**gray**) produces a wide variety of models, as opposed to the baseline (**red** line). However, the highest accuracy in each run grows slowly with the number of models. With the on-manifold constraint (**blue**), the improvement is larger and requires fewer models. Fine-tuning/distillation (**green**) bring additional marginal improvements (Color figure online)

models trained on different random seeds, even while keeping the model frozen (*i.e.* retraining only a classifier). We first determined that the best ERM-trained classifier on frozen features is a simple linear one, rather than an MLP. Our method simplifies in two ways with a linear classifier. First, input gradients are equal to the classifier weights, and the proposed regularizers do not require second-order derivatives anymore during back-propagation. Second, we found empirically that the soft on-manifold regularizer can be replaced with a hard constraint: we explicit project the input gradients onto the manifold and apply the independence regularizer on these projections, as proposed in [39]. As noted in Sect. 3.2, this option completely failed in our early experiments with MLPs, but it seems viable with linear classifiers. This further simplifies the implementation.

**Results.** We plot in Fig. 7 the spread of accuracies of models trained with different methods (using features from the first pretrained model from [26], see the supp. mat. for similar results with the others). The **ERM baseline** simply recovers the accuracy of the original complete Densenet, with essentially no variation across random seeds. With our **independence constraint**, the spread of accuracies significantly widens, both below and above the baseline. In the supp. mat. we show that the models span various trade-offs in accuracy on val-OOD and on test-OOD, neither of which is correlated with the accuracy on in-domain data (val-ID), thus showing evidence of underspecification. Back to Fig. 7, with our additional **on-manifold constraint**, the best models reach higher accuracies. This also tops out when training a handful of models (about 10–14, near the intrinsic dimensionality of the data estimated at 12 with [37]). Keeping in mind that we use frozen features, these results show that the ERM-pretrained model extracts features useful for OOD performance but that are ignored by the pretrained classifier. Similar findings were recently reported in [25, 38]. Our method recovers these features and produces alternative classifiers with a variety of trade-offs in performance across various OOD conditions.

**Ablations.** In Table 2, we compare additional ablations of our method, using a fixed number of 10 models. The **essential components are the independence and on-manifold constraints**. The fine-tuning and distillation steps contribute to a marginal improvement. We report similar *relative* improvements in the supp. mat. with other pretrained models, but the absolute performance is very much **dependent on a "good" pretrained model**.

**Model Selection.** Our method brings similar relative improvements on either val-OOD or test-OOD but typically with different models for each (see Fig. 7) despite both being OOD relative to the training data. **Model selection absent labelled target-domain data therefore remains an issue** on this dataset. Fortunately, only little such data may be sufficient. We repeated a few experiments while holding out 1% of test-OOD (less than 1,000 instances) and we observed a 99.87% correlation coefficient between the accuracy on test-OOD and this held-out data. While all our results assume perfect "oracle" model selection, it seems reasonable that real applications could provide a small amount of labelled test data to achieve similar results.

## 5    Discussion

We presented a method that highlights cases of underspecification by training multiple models with similar in-domain performance yet different OOD behaviour. This method offers a partial solution to building robust models since it discovers features that are otherwise missed by standard ERM due to shortcut learning or other implicit inductive biases [33,43].

**What do We Gain from Identifying Cases of Underspecification?** The level of underspecification (indicated by the number of models that can be trained with the proposed constraints) shows how far from unique a solution to a learning problem is. Diagnosing underspecification is not a pass-or-fail test: all but the simplest tasks and models are underspecified to some extent. Measuring underspecification should help determining the level of trust attributed to an ML model. Our constructive approach has the added advantage of exposing the range of predictive features present in the data.

**Importance to Both Engineering and Science.** There is a continuing source of research questions in the apparent mismatch between empirical practices in ML and some hard limitations of learning methods. The concept of underspecification has the potential to unify phenomena including shortcut learning, distribution shifts, and adversarial robustness. These are important for ML as an engineering discipline (improving reliability and applicability of ML methods) as well as a scientific endeavour (understanding the structure of real-world data and how/why existing methods work).

**A First Implication** of underspecification is that ERM is insufficient to guarantee OOD generalization. Identified cases of underspecification point at the need for additional task-specific information in the design of reliable learning methods. If such information cannot be integrated, learned models are at risk of unexpected behaviour when deployed on OOD data, because the depend on stochastic or arbitrary factors (*e.g.* texture *vs.* shape in image classification [12]).

**A Second Implication** is that ID and OOD performance are not necessarily coupled. Without further assumptions, in-domain validation is not a reliable model selection strategy for OOD performance despite some suggestions *e.g.* in [16,31]. It might be useful as a heuristic owing to some inherent structure in real-world data, but its limits of applicability are yet to be understood.

**A Third Implication** is that high OOD performance of a model is no guarantee for its reliability. High apparent performance might happen by accident in an underspecified setting. In such cases, the model behaviour depends on hidden assumptions and it could still fail unexpectedly. Identifying underspecification remains important to identify these hidden assumptions, which is particularly important for high-stakes applications such as medical imaging [3,13].

The proposed analysis also corroborates existing explanations for techniques that successfully improve generalization, such as data augmentation and contrastive learning. Both were indeed shown to depend on the injection of additional knowledge, respectively in the design of the augmentations [4,21,28] and pair selection strategy [57]. And this extra knowledge is often task-specific [55]. For example, augmenting images with rotations may help in identifying flowers but not traffic signs. Injecting task-specific knowledge is sometimes vilified in a "data-driven" culture. This study suggests that we would rather benefit from highlighting this practice and making assumptions more explicit, thus helping one to identify the limits of applicability of various methods.

**Conclusion.** This paper made theoretical and methodological steps on the study of underspecification. It complements an observational study [6] with a method to diagnose and address the problem.

**Limitations.** The proposed method for building models with better generalization is only a partial solution since it requires an external model selection procedure. New methods for model selection [8,11,22,52], robust evaluation [10,23], and explainability [14,49] are all suitable to implement this selection. Interactive approaches [7] are another option that injects expert knowledge. Another possible extension is to apply the method to the end-to-end training of larger models. Finally, this work focused on i.i.d. training data. We hope to extend the analysis to forms of data known to be valuable for OOD generalization such as multiple environments [2,5,34], counterfactual examples [23,47], and non-stationary data [1,17,36,51]. The analysis of multi-environment training as used for domain generalization may elucidate why these methods often fail in practice [16].

# References

1. Alesiani, F., Yu, S., Yu, X.: Gated information bottleneck for generalization in sequential environments. arXiv preprint arXiv:2110.06057 (2021)
2. Arjovsky, M., Bottou, L., Gulrajani, I., Lopez-Paz, D.: Invariant risk minimization. arXiv preprint arXiv:1907.02893 (2019)
3. Banerjee, I., et al.: Reading race: Ai recognises patient's racial identity in medical images. arXiv preprint arXiv:2107.10356 (2021)
4. Cubuk, E.D., Dyer, E.S., Lopes, R.G., Smullin, S.: Tradeoffs in data augmentation: An empirical study. In: Proceedings of the International Conference on Learning Representations (2021)
5. Teney, D., Ehsan Abbasnejad, A.v.d.H.: Unshuffling data for improved generalization. arXiv preprint arXiv:2002.11894 (2020)
6. D'Amour, A., et al.: Underspecification presents challenges for credibility in modern machine learning. arXiv preprint arXiv:2011.03395 (2020)
7. Das, S., Cashman, D., Chang, R., Endert, A.: Beames: Interactive multimodel steering, selection, and inspection for regression tasks. IEEE Comput. Graphics Appl. **39**(5), 20–32 (2019)
8. Deng, W., Gould, S., Zheng, L.: What does rotation prediction tell us about classifier accuracy under varying testing environments? arXiv preprint arXiv:2106.05961 (2021)

9. Ganin, Y., et al.: Domain-adversarial training of neural networks. J. Mach. Learn. Res. **17**, 1–35 (2016)

10. Gardner, M., et al.: Evaluating NLP models via contrast sets. arXiv preprint arXiv:2004.02709 (2020)

11. Garg, S., Balakrishnan, S., Kolter, J.Z., Lipton, Z.C.: Ratt: Leveraging unlabeled data to guarantee generalization. arXiv preprint arXiv:2105.00303 (2021)

12. Geirhos, R., Rubisch, P., Michaelis, C., Bethge, M., Wichmann, F.A., Brendel, W.: Imagenet-trained cnns are biased towards texture; increasing shape bias improves accuracy and robustness. arXiv preprint arXiv:1811.12231 (2018)

13. Ghimire, S., Kashyap, S., Wu, J.T., Karargyris, A., Moradi, M.: Learning invariant feature representation to improve generalization across chest x-ray datasets. In: International Workshop on Machine Learning in Medical Imaging (2020)

14. Goyal, Y., Wu, Z., Ernst, J., Batra, D., Parikh, D., Lee, S.: Counterfactual visual explanations. In: International Conference on Machine Learning, pp. 2376–2384. PMLR (2019)

15. Gretton, A., Herbrich, R., Smola, A.J.: The kernel mutual information. In: 2003 IEEE International Conference on Acoustics, Speech, and Signal Processing, 2003. Proceedings. (ICASSP 2003), vol. 4, pp. IV-880. IEEE (2003)

16. Gulrajani, I., Lopez-Paz, D.: In search of lost domain generalization. In: Proceedings of the International Conference on Learning (2021)

17. Hälvä, H., Hyvarinen, A.: Hidden markov nonlinear ica: Unsupervised learning from nonstationary time series. In: Conference on Uncertainty in Artificial Intelligence, pp. 939–948. PMLR (2020)

18. Hoffman, J., Roberts, D.A., Yaida, S.: Robust learning with jacobian regularization. arXiv preprint arXiv:1908.02729 (2019)

19. Hsu, H., Calmon, F.d.P.: Rashomon capacity: A metric for predictive multiplicity in probabilistic classification. arXiv preprint arXiv:2206.01295 (2022)

20. Hudson, D.A., Manning, C.D.: GQA: A new dataset for real-world visual reasoning and compositional question answering. In: Proceedings of the IEEE Conference on Computer Vision and Pattern Recognition (2019)

21. Ilse, M., Tomczak, J.M., Forré, P.: Designing data augmentation for simulating interventions. In: Proceedings of the International Conference on Machine Learning (2021)

22. Immer, A., Bauer, M., Fortuin, V., Rätsch, G., Khan, M.E.: Scalable marginal likelihood estimation for model selection in deep learning. arXiv preprint arXiv:2104.04975 (2021)

23. Kaushik, D., Hovy, E., Lipton, Z.C.: Learning the difference that makes a difference with counterfactually-augmented data. arXiv preprint arXiv:1909.12434 (2019)

24. Kervadec, C., Antipov, G., Baccouche, M., Wolf, C.: Roses are red, violets are blue... but should VQA expect them to? In: Proceedings of the IEEE Conference on Computer Vision and Pattern Recognition (2021)

25. Kirichenko, P., Izmailov, P., Wilson, A.G.: Last layer re-training is sufficient for robustness to spurious correlations. arXiv preprint arXiv:2204.02937 (2022)

26. Koh, P.W., et al.: Wilds: A benchmark of in-the-wild distribution shifts. arXiv preprint arXiv:2012.07421 (2020)

27. Koh, P.W., et al.: Wilds: A benchmark of in-the-wild distribution shifts. In: Proceedings of the International Conference on Machine Learning (2021)

28. von Kügelgen, J., et al.: Self-supervised learning with data augmentations provably isolates content from style. arXiv preprint arXiv:2106.04619 (2021)

29. Lee, D.H., et al.: Pseudo-label: The simple and efficient semi-supervised learning method for deep neural networks. In: Workshop on Challenges in Representation Learning, ICML (2013)

30. Mehrer, J., Spoerer, C.J., Kriegeskorte, N., Kietzmann, T.C.: Individual differences among deep neural network models. Nat. Commun. **11**(1), 1–12 (2020)

31. Miller, J.P., et al.: Accuracy on the line: on the strong correlation between out-of-distribution and in-distribution generalization. In: Proceedings of the International Conference on Machine Learning (2021)

32. Mitchell, T.M.: The need for biases in learning generalizations. Rutgers University (1980)

33. Ortiz-Jimenez, G., Salazar-Reque, I.F., Modas, A., Moosavi-Dezfooli, S.M., Frossard, P.: A neural anisotropic view of underspecification in deep learning. In: Proceedings of the International Conference on Learning Representations (2021)

34. Peters, J., Bühlmann, P., Meinshausen, N.: Causal inference by using invariant prediction: identification and confidence intervals. J. Royal Stat. Soc. Ser. B (Stat. Methodol.) **78**, 947–1012 (2016)

35. Pezeshki, M., Kaba, S.O., Bengio, Y., Courville, A., Precup, D., Lajoie, G.: Gradient starvation: A learning proclivity in neural networks. arXiv preprint arXiv:2011.09468 (2020)

36. Pfister, N., Bühlmann, P., Peters, J.: Invariant causal prediction for sequential data. J. Am. Stat. Assoc. **114**(527), 1264–1276 (2019)

37. Pope, P., Zhu, C., Abdelkader, A., Goldblum, M., Goldstein, T.: The intrinsic dimension of images and its impact on learning. arXiv preprint arXiv:2104.08894 (2021)

38. Rosenfeld, E., Ravikumar, P., Risteski, A.: Domain-adjusted regression or: Erm may already learn features sufficient for out-of-distribution generalization. arXiv preprint arXiv:2202.06856 (2022)

39. Ross, A., Pan, W., Celi, L., Doshi-Velez, F.: Ensembles of locally independent prediction models. In: Proceedings of the Conference on AAAI (2020)

40. Ross, A.S., Pan, W., Doshi-Velez, F.: Learning qualitatively diverse and interpretable rules for classification. arXiv preprint arXiv:1806.08716 (2018)

41. Selvaraju, R.R., et al.: Taking a hint: Leveraging explanations to make vision and language models more grounded. In: Proceedings of the IEEE International Conference on Computer Vision (2019)

42. Semenova, L., Rudin, C., Parr, R.: A study in rashomon curves and volumes: A new perspective on generalization and model simplicity in machine learning. arXiv preprint arXiv:1908.01755 (2019)

43. Shah, H., Tamuly, K., Raghunathan, A., Jain, P., Netrapalli, P.: The pitfalls of simplicity bias in neural networks. arXiv preprint arXiv:2006.07710 (2020)

44. Shimodaira, H.: Improving predictive inference under covariate shift by weighting the log-likelihood function. J. Statist. Planning Inference **90**(2), 227–244 (2000)

45. Sohn, K., et al.: Fixmatch: Simplifying semi-supervised learning with consistency and confidence. In: Proceedings of the Advances in Neural Information Processing Systems (2020)

46. Sun, B., Feng, J., Saenko, K.: Correlation alignment for unsupervised domain adaptation. In: Csurka, G. (ed.) Domain Adaptation in Computer Vision Applications. ACVPR, pp. 153–171. Springer, Cham (2017). https://doi.org/10.1007/978-3-319-58347-1_8

47. Teney, D., Abbasnedjad, E., van den Hengel, A.: Learning what makes a difference from counterfactual examples and gradient supervision. arXiv preprint arXiv:2004.09034 (2020)

48. Teney, D., Abbasnejad, E., Lucey, S., van den Hengel, A.: Evading the simplicity bias: Training a diverse set of models discovers solutions with superior OOD generalization. In: Proceedings of the IEEE Conference on Computer Vision and Pattern Recognition (2022)
49. Thiagarajan, J., Narayanaswamy, V.S., Rajan, D., Liang, J., Chaudhari, A., Spanias, A.: Designing counterfactual generators using deep model inversion. In: Proceedings of the Advances in Neural Information Processing Systems (2021)
50. Vapnik, V.: Statistical learning theory. john wiley&sons. Inc., New York (1998)
51. Venkateswaran, P., Muthusamy, V., Isahagian, V., Venkatasubramanian, N.: Environment agnostic invariant risk minimization for classification of sequential datasets. In: Proceedings of the 27th ACM SIGKDD Conference on Knowledge Discovery & Data Mining, pp. 1615–1624 (2021)
52. Wald, Y., Feder, A., Greenfeld, D., Shalit, U.: On calibration and out-of-domain generalization. arXiv preprint arXiv:2102.10395 (2021)
53. Weinberger, K.Q., Saul, L.K.: Unsupervised learning of image manifolds by semidefinite programming. Int. J. Comput. Vision **70**, 77–90 (2006)
54. Wolpert, D.H.: The lack of a priori distinctions between learning algorithms. Neural Comput. **8**(7), 1341–1390 (1996)
55. Xiao, T., Wang, X., Efros, A.A., Darrell, T.: What should not be contrastive in contrastive learning. arXiv preprint arXiv:2008.05659 (2020)
56. Xie, Q., Luong, M.T., Hovy, E., Le, Q.V.: Self-training with noisy student improves ImageNet classification. In: Proceedings of the IEEE Computer Society Conference on Computer Vision and Pattern Recognition (2020)
57. Zimmermann, R.S., Sharma, Y., Schneider, S., Bethge, M., Brendel, W.: Contrastive learning inverts the data generating process. arXiv preprint arXiv:2102.08850 (2021)

# Neural-Sim: Learning to Generate Training Data with NeRF

Yunhao Ge[1]([⊠]), Harkirat Behl[2], Jiashu Xu[1], Suriya Gunasekar[2], Neel Joshi[2], Yale Song[2], Xin Wang[2], Laurent Itti[1], and Vibhav Vineet[2]

[1] University of Southern California, California, USA
yunhaoge@usc.edu
[2] Microsoft Research, Washington, USA

**Abstract.** Training computer vision models usually requires collecting and labeling vast amounts of imagery under a diverse set of scene configurations and properties. This process is incredibly time-consuming, and it is challenging to ensure that the captured data distribution maps well to the target domain of an application scenario. Recently, synthetic data has emerged as a way to address both of these issues. However, existing approaches either require human experts to manually tune each scene property or use automatic methods that provide little to no control; this requires rendering large amounts of random data variations, which is slow and is often suboptimal for the target domain. We present the first fully differentiable synthetic data pipeline that uses Neural Radiance Fields (NeRFs) in a closed-loop with a target application's loss function. Our approach generates data on-demand, with no human labor, to maximize accuracy for a target task. We illustrate the effectiveness of our method on synthetic and real-world object detection tasks. We also introduce a new "YCB-in-the-Wild" dataset and benchmark that provides a test scenario for object detection with varied poses in real-world environments. Code and data could be found at https://github.com/gyhandy/Neural-Sim-NeRF.

**Keywords:** Synthetic data · NeRF · Bilevel optimization · Detection

## 1 Introduction

The traditional pipeline for building computer vision models involves collecting and labelling vast amounts of data, training models with different configurations, and deploying it to test environments [24,37,42]. Key to achieving good performance is collecting training data that mimics the test environment with

---

H. Behl and J. Xu—Equal contribution as second author.

**Supplementary Information** The online version contains supplementary material available at https://doi.org/10.1007/978-3-031-20050-2_28.

S. Avidan et al. (Eds.): ECCV 2022, LNCS 13683, pp. 477–493, 2022.
https://doi.org/10.1007/978-3-031-20050-2_28

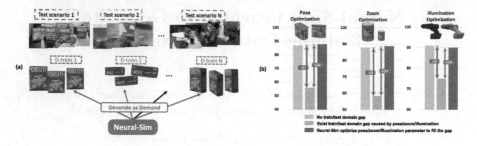

**Fig. 1.** (a) On-demand synthetic data generation: Given a target task and a test dataset, our approach "Neural-sim" generates data on-demand using a fully differentiable synthetic data generation pipeline which maximises accuracy for the target task. (b) Train/test domain gap causes significant detection accuracy drop (yellow bar to gray bar). We dynamically optimize the render parameters (pose/zoom/illumination) to generate the best data to fill the gap (blue bar). (Color figure online)

similar properties relating to the object (pose, geometry, appearance), camera (pose and angle), and scene (illumination, semantic structures) [2].

However, the traditional pipeline does not work very well in many real-world applications as collecting large amounts of training data which captures all variations of objects and environments is quite challenging. Furthermore, in many applications, users may want to learn models for unique objects with novel structures, textures, or other such properties. Such scenarios are very common particularly in business scenarios where there is desire to create object detectors for new products introduced in the market.

Recent advances in rendering, such as photo-realistic renderers [10,21] and generative models (GANs [6], VAEs [12,25]), have brought the promise of generating high-quality images of complex scenes. This has motivated the field to explore synthetic data as source of training data [13,14,18,19,23,27,28,38,40, 44,51]. However, doing so in an offline fashion has similar issues as the traditional pipeline. While it alleviates certain difficulties, e.g., capturing camera/lighting variations, it create dependency on 3D asset creation, which is time-consuming.

Recently, a new image generation technique called the Neural Radiance Field (NeRF) [34] was introduced as a way to replace the traditional rasterization and ray-tracing graphics pipelines with a neural-network based renderer. This approach can generate high-quality novel views of scenes without requiring explicit 3D understanding. More recent advancements in NeRFs allow to control other rendering parameters, like illumination, material, albedo, appearance, etc. [5,29,33,43,50]. As a result, they have attracted significant attention and have been widely adopted in various graphics and vision tasks [5,16,36,43]. NeRF and their variants possess some alluring properties: (i) differentiable rendering, (ii) control over scene properties unlike GANs and VAEs, and (iii) they are data-driven in contrast to traditional renderers which require carefully crafting 3D models and scenes. These properties make them suitable for generating the optimal data on-demand for a given target task.

To this end, we propose a bilevel optimization process to jointly optimize neural rendering parameters for data generation and model training. Further, we also propose a reparameterization trick, sample approximation, and patch-wise optimization methods for developing a memory efficient optimization algorithm.

To demonstrate the efficacy of the proposed algorithm, we evaluate the algorithm on three settings: controlled settings in simulation, on the YCB-video dataset [46], and in controlled settings on YCB objects captured in the wild. This third setting is with our newly created "YCB-in-the-wild" dataset, which involves capturing YCB objects in real environments with control over object pose and scale. Finally, we also provide results showing the interpretability of the method in achieving high performance on downstream tasks. Our key contributions are as follows:

(1) To the best of our knowledge, for the first time, we show that NeRF can substitute the traditional graphics pipeline and synthesize useful images to train downstream tasks (object detection).

(2) We propose a novel bilevel optimization algorithm to automatically optimize rendering parameters (pose, zoom, illumination) to generate optimal data for downstream tasks using NeRF and its variants.

(3) We demonstrate the performance of our approach on controlled settings in simulation, controlled settings in YCB-in-wild and YCB-video datasets. We release YCB-in-wild dataset for future research.

## 2   Related Work

**Traditional Graphics Rendering Methods** can synthesize high-quality images with controllable image properties, such as object pose, geometry, texture, camera parameters, and illumination [10,21,27,38,39]. Interestingly, NeRF has some important benefits over the traditional graphics pipelines, which make it more suitable for learning to generate synthetic datasets. First, NeRF learns to generate data from new views based only on image data and camera pose information. In contrast, the traditional graphics pipeline requires 3D models of objects as input. Getting accurate 3D models with correct geometry, material, and texture properties generally requires human experts (i.e. an artist or modeler). This, in turn, limits the scalability of the traditional graphics pipeline in large-scale rendering for many new objects or scenes. Second, NeRF is a differentiable renderer, thus allowing backpropagation through the rendering pipeline for learning how to control data generation in a model and scene-centric way.

**Deep Generative Models**, such as GANs [6,22], VAEs [12,25] and normalizing flows [9] are differentiable and require less human involvement. However, most of them do not provide direct control of rendering parameters. While some recent GAN approaches allow some control [1,20,47] over parameters, it is not as explicit and can mostly only change the 2D properties of images. Further, most generative models need a relatively large dataset to train. In comparison, NeRF can generate parameter-controllable high-quality images and requires a lesser number of images to train. Moreover, advancements in NeRF now allow the control of illumination, materials, and object shape alongside camera pose and scale [5,29,33,43,50]. We use NeRF and their variants (NeRF-in-the-wild [33]) to optimize pose, zoom and illumination as representative rendering parameters.

**Learning Simulator Parameters.** Related works in this space focus on learning non-differentiable simulator parameters for e.g., learning-to-simulate (LTS) [41], Meta-Sim [30], Meta-Sim2 [11], Auto-Sim [4], and others [17,32,48]. Our work in contrast has two differences: (i) a difference in the renderer used (NeRF vs traditional rendering engines), and (ii) a difference in the optimization approach. We discuss the different renderers and their suitability for this task in the previous subsection.

LTS [41] proposed a bilevel optimization algorithm to learn simulator parameters that maximized accuracy on downstream tasks. It assumed both data-generation and model-training as a black-box optimization process and used REINFORCE-based [45] gradient estimation to optimize parameters. This requires many intermediate data generation steps. Meta-sim [30] is also a REIN-FORCE based approach, which requires a grammar of scene graphs. Our approach does not use scene grammar. Most similar to our work is the work of Auto-Simulate [4] that proposed a local approximation of the bilevel optimization to efficiently solve the problem. However, since they optimized non-differentiable simulators like Blender [10] and Arnold [21], they used REINFORCE-based [45] gradient update. Further, they have not shown optimization of pose parameter whose search space is very large. In comparison, our proposed Neural-Sim approach can learn to optimize over pose parameters as well.

## 3   Neural-Sim

The goal of our method is to automatically synthesize optimal training data to maximize accuracy for a target task. In this work, we consider object detection as our target task. Furthermore, in recent times, NeRF and its variants (NeRFs) have been used to synthesize high-resolution photorealistic images for complex scenes [5,29,33,43,50]. This motivates us to explore NeRFs as potential sources of generating training data for computer vision models. We propose a technique to optimize rendering parameters of NeRFs to generate the *optimal set* of images for training object detection models.

**NeRF Model:** NeRF [34,49] takes as input the viewing direction (or camera pose) denoted as $V = (\phi, \rho)$, and renders an image $x = \text{NeRF}(V)$ of a scene as viewed along $V$. Note that our proposed technique is broadly applicable to differentiable renderers in general. In this work, we also optimize NeRF-in-the-wild (NeRF-w) [33] as it allows for appearance and illumination variations alongside pose variation. We first discuss our framework for optimizing the original NeRF model and later we discuss optimization of NeRF-w in Sect. 3.2.

**Synthetic Training Data Generation:** Consider a parametric probability distribution $p_\psi$ over rendering parameters $V$, where $\psi$ denotes the parameters of the distribution. It should be noted that $\psi$ corresponds to all rendering parameters

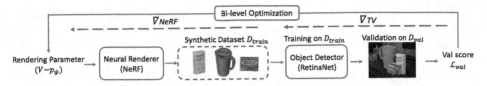

**Fig. 2.** Neural-Sim pipeline: Our pipeline finds the optimal parameters for generating views from a trained neural renderer (NeRF) to use as training data for object detection. The objective is to find the optimal NeRF rendering parameters $\psi$ that can generate synthetic training data $D_{train}$, such that the model (RetinaNet, in our experiments) trained on $D_{train}$, maximizes accuracy on a downstream task represented by the validation set $D_{val}$.

including pose/zoom/illumination, here, for simplicity, we consider $\psi$ to denote pose variable. To generate the synthetic training data, we first sample rendering parameters $V_1, V_2, ..., V_N \sim p_\psi$. We then use NeRF to generate synthetic training images $x_i = \text{NeRF}(V_i)$ with respective rendering parameters $V_i$. We use an off-the-shelf foreground extractor to obtain labels $y_1, y_2, \ldots, y_N$. the training dataset thus generated is denoted as $D_{train} = \{(x_1, y_1), (x_2, y_2), \ldots, (x_N, y_N)\}$.

**Optimizing Synthetic Data Generation.** Our goal is to optimize over the rendering distribution $p_\psi$ such that training an object detection model on $D_{train}$ leads to good performance on $D_{val}$. We formulate this problem as a bi-level optimization [4,8,15] as below:

$$\min_{\psi} \mathcal{L}_{val}(\hat{\theta}(\psi)); \quad s.t. \ \hat{\theta}(\psi) \in \arg\min_{\theta} \mathcal{L}_{train}(\theta, \psi), \tag{1a}$$

where $\theta$ denotes the parameters of the object detection model, $\mathcal{L}_{train}(\theta, \psi) = \mathbb{E}_{V \sim p_\psi} l(x, \theta) \approx \frac{1}{N} \sum_{i=1}^{N} l(x_i, \theta)$ is the training loss over the synthetic dataset from NeRF,[1] and $\mathcal{L}_{val}$ is the loss on the task-specific validation set $D_{val}$.

The bi-level optimization problem in (1) is challenging to solve; for example, any gradient based algorithm would need access to an efficient approximation of $\nabla_\psi \hat{\theta}(\psi)$, which in turn requires propagating gradients through the entire training trajectory of a neural network. Thus, we look to numerical approximations to solve this problem. Recently, Behl et al. [4] developed a technique for numerical gradient computation based on local approximation of the bi-level optimization. Without going into their derivation, we borrow the gradient term for the outer update, which at time step $t$ takes the form:

$$\frac{\partial \mathcal{L}_{val}(\hat{\theta}(\psi))}{\partial \psi}\bigg|_{\psi=\psi_t} \approx - \overbrace{\frac{\partial}{\partial \psi}\left[\frac{\partial \mathcal{L}_{train}(\hat{\theta}(\psi_t), \psi)}{\partial \theta}\right]^T}^{\nabla_{NeRF}}\bigg|_{\psi=\psi_t} \underbrace{\mathcal{H}(\hat{\theta}(\psi_t), \psi)^{-1}\frac{d\mathcal{L}_{val}(\hat{\theta}(\psi_t))}{d\theta}}_{\nabla_{TV}}.$$

$$\tag{2}$$

---

[1] For simplicity, we have dropped the dependence of loss $\ell$ on labels $y$.

We have divided the gradient term into two parts: $\nabla_{NeRF}$ corresponds to backpropagation through the dataset generation from NeRF, and $\nabla_{TV}$ corresponds to approximate backpropagation through training and validation (Fig. 2). $\nabla_{TV}$ is computed using the conjugate gradient method [4]. However, [4] treated the data generation as a black box and used REINFORCE [45] to compute the approximate gradient because they used non-differentiable renderers for data generation. However, REINFORCE is considered noisy process and is known to lead to high-variance estimates of gradients. In contrast, NeRF is differentiable, which gives us tools to obtain more accurate gradients. We propose an efficient technique for computing $\nabla_{NeRF}$, which we discuss in the next section.

### 3.1　Backprop Through Data Generation from NeRF

A good gradient estimation should possess the following properties: (i) high accuracy and low noise (ii) computational efficiency (iii) low memory footprint. We leverage different properties of NeRF, i.e., its differentiability and pixel-wise rendering, to design a customized technique which satisfies the above properties.

In computation of $\nabla_{NeRF}$ in (2), we approximate $\mathcal{L}_{train}(\theta, \psi)$ using samples in $D_{train}$ as $\mathcal{L}_{train}(\theta, \psi) \approx \frac{1}{N} \sum_{i=1}^{N} l(x_i, \theta)$. Using chain rule we then have partial derivative computation over $l(x, \theta)$ as follows:

$$
\frac{\partial}{\partial \psi} \left[ \frac{\partial l(x_i, \hat{\theta}(\psi_t))}{\partial \theta} \right] = \left[ \frac{\partial \left( \frac{\partial l(x_i, \hat{\theta}(\psi_t))}{\partial \theta} \right)}{\partial x_i} \right] \left[ \frac{\partial x_i}{\partial V_i} \right] \left[ \frac{dV_i}{d\psi} \right] \tag{3}
$$

The first term is the second order derivative through a detection network and can be computed analytically for each image $x_i$. The second term is the gradient of the rendered image w.r.t NeRF inputs, which can be obtained by backpropagating through the differentiable NeRF rendering $x_i = \text{NeRF}(V_i)$. While both these terms have exact analytical expressions, naively computing and using them in (2) becomes impractical even for small problems (see below in Tool2 and Tool3 for details and proposed solutions). Finally the third term $\frac{dV_i}{d\psi}$ requires gradient computation over probabilistic sampling $V_i \sim p_\psi$. We consider $p_\psi$ over discretized bins of pose parameters. For such discrete distributions $\frac{dV_i}{d\psi}$ is not well defined. Instead, we approximate this term using a reparameterization technique described below in Tool1. We summarize our technical tools below:

- For distributions $p_\psi$ over a discrete bins of pose parameters, we propose a reparametrization of $\psi$ that provides efficient approximation of $\frac{dV_i}{d\psi}$ (Tool1).
- We dramatically reduce memory and computation overhead of implementing the gradient approximation in (2) using a new *twice-forward-once-backward* approach (Tool2). Without this new technique the implementation would require high computation involving large matrices and computational graphs.
- Even with the above technique, the computation of first and second terms in (3) has a large overhead on GPU memory that depends on image size. We overcome this using a patch-wise gradient computation approach (Tool 3).

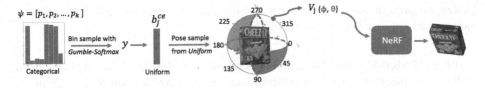

**Fig. 3.** A concrete example to one time sample, starting form a particular value of $\psi$, we can follow reparametrization sampling and obtain a pose. Each sample represents a pose that is input in NeRF to render one image.

**Tool 1: Reparametrization of Pose Sampling.** NeRF renders images $x_j$ using camera pose $V_j = (\phi_i, \rho_j)$, where $\phi_j \in [0, 360], \rho_j \in [0, 360]$. For simplicity we describe our method for optimizing over $\phi$, while keeping $\rho$ fixed to be uniform.

We discretize the pose into $k$ equal sized bins over the range of $\phi$ as $B_1 = \left[0, \frac{360}{k}\right), B_2 = \left[\frac{360}{k}, \frac{360 \times 2}{k}\right), \ldots$ and define the distribution over $\phi$ as the categorical distribution with $p_i$ as the probability of $\phi$ belonging to $B_i$. This distribution is thus parametrized by $\psi \equiv p = [p_1, ..., p_k]$. To back propagate through the sampling process, we approximate the sample from the categorical distribution by using Gumble-softmax "reparameterization trick" with parameters $y \in \mathbb{R}^k$, where $y_i$ are given as follows: $y_i = \mathrm{GS}_i(p) = \exp[(G_i + log(p_i))/\tau]/\sum_j \exp[(G_j + log(p_j))/\tau]$. Where $G_i \sim Gumbel(0, 1)$ are i.i.d. samples from the standard Gumbel distribution and $\tau$ is temperature parameter. The random vector $y$ defined as above satisfies the property that the coordinate (index) of the largest element in $y \in \mathbb{R}^k$ follows the categorical distribution with parameter $p$.

We now approximate sampling from the categorical distribution (see Fig. 3 for depiction). Denote the bin center of $B_i$ as $\bar{B}_i^{ce} = 360(i - 0.5)/k$; and the bin range as $\bar{b}^{ra} = 360/k$. We generate $V_j = (\phi_j, \rho_j) \sim p_\psi$ as below:

- Generate $y_i$'s for $i = 1, 2, \ldots k$
- Define $b_j^{ce} = \sum_i y_i \bar{B}_i^{ce}$ as the approximate bin center.
- Define the bin for the $j^{\text{th}}$ sample centered around $b_j^{ce}$ as $[b_j^{st}, b_j^{en}] = [b_j^{ce} - \bar{b}^{ra}/2, b_j^{ce} + \bar{b}^{ra}/2]$
- We sample $\phi_j$ from uniform distribution over $[b_j^{st}, b_j^{en}]$ which has a reparametrization for diffentiability: $\mathcal{U}(b_j^{st}, b_j^{en}) \equiv (1 - \epsilon)b_j^{st} + \epsilon b_j^{en}$ s.t. $\epsilon \sim \mathcal{U}(0, 1)$.
- $\rho_j \sim \mathcal{U}[0, 360]$, or can follow same process as $\phi_j$.

Note that in general the approximate bin centers $b_j^{ce}$ need not be aligned with original categorical distribution, however we can control the approximation using the temperature parameter $\tau$. We now have the full expression for approximate gradient of $\nabla_{NeRF}$ using (3) and reparametrization as follows:

$$\nabla_{NeRF} \approx \frac{1}{N} \sum_{j=1}^{N} \frac{\partial \left(\frac{\partial l(x_j, \hat{\theta}(\psi_t))}{\partial \theta}\right)}{\partial x_j} \frac{\partial x_j}{\partial V_j} \frac{\partial V_j}{\partial (b_j^{st}, b_j^{en})} \frac{\partial (b_i^{st}, b_i^{en})}{\partial y} \frac{\partial y}{\partial p}. \tag{4}$$

Below we present tools that drastically improve the compute and memory efficiency and are crucial for our pipeline.

**Tool 2: Twice-Forward-Once-Backward.** The full gradient update of our bi-level optimization problem involves using the approximation of $\nabla_{NeRF}$ in (4) and back in (2). This computation has three terms with the following dimensions:
$[(1)] \quad \frac{\partial(\frac{\partial l(x_j, \hat{\theta}(\psi_t))}{\partial \theta})}{\partial x_j} \in \mathbb{R}^{m \times d}, \quad [(2)] \quad \frac{\partial x_j}{\partial \psi} \in \mathbb{R}^{d \times k}, \quad [(3)] \quad \nabla_{TV} = \mathcal{H}(\hat{\theta}(\psi_t), \psi)^{-1} \frac{d\mathcal{L}_{val}(\hat{\theta}(\psi_t))}{d\theta} \in \mathbb{R}^{m \times 1}$, where $m = |\theta|$ is the # of parameters in object detection model, $d$ is the # of pixels in $x$, and $k$ is # of pose bins.

Implementing Eq. (2) with the naive sequence of (1)-(2)-(3) involves computing and multiplying large matrices of sizes $m \times d$ and $d \times k$. Further, this sequence also generates a huge computation graph. These would lead to prohibitive memory and compute requirements as $m$ is often in many millions. On the other hand, if we could follow the sequence of (3)-(1)-(2), then we can use the produce of $1 \times m$ output of (3) to do a weighted autograd which leads computing and storing only vectors rather than matrices. However, the computation of (3) needs the rendered image involving forward pass of (2) (more details in appendix.).

To take advantage of the efficient sequence, we propose a twice-forward-once backward method where we do two forward passes over NeRF rendering. In the first forward path, we do not compute the gradients, we only render images to form $D_{train}$ and save random samples of $y, \phi_j$ used for rendering. We then compute (3) by turning on gradients. In the second pass through NeRF, we keep the same samples and this time compute the gradient (1) and (2).

**Tool 3: Patch-Wise Gradient Computation.** Even though we have optimized the computation dependence on $m = |\theta|$ with the tool described above, computing (1)-(2) sequence in the above description still scales with the size of images $d$. This too can lead to large memory footprint for even moderate size images. To optimize the memory further, we propose patch-wise computation, where we divide the image into $S$ patches $x = (x^1, x^2, \ldots, x^S))$ and compute (3) as follows:

$$\frac{\partial}{\partial \psi} \frac{\partial l(x, \hat{\theta}(\psi_t))}{\partial \theta} = \sum_{c=1}^{S} \frac{\partial(\frac{\partial l(x^c, \hat{\theta}(\psi_t))}{\partial \theta})}{\partial x^c} \frac{\partial x^c}{\partial \psi}. \tag{5}$$

Since NeRF renders an image pixel by pixel, it is easy to compute the gradient of patch with respect to $\psi$ in the memory efficient patch-wise optimization.

## 3.2 Nerf-in-the-Wild

NeRF-in-the-wild (NeRF-w) extends NeRF model to allow image dependent appearance and illumination variations such that photometric discrepancies between images can be modeled explicitly. NeRF-w takes as input an appearance embedding denoted as $\ell$ alongside the viewing direction $V$ to render an image as

$x = \text{NeRF}(V, \ell)$. For NERF-w, the optimization of pose (V) remains the same as discussed above. For efficient optimization of lighting we exploit a noteworthy property of NeRF-w: it allows smooth interpolations between color and lighting. This enables us to optimize lighting as a continuous variable, where the lighting ($\ell$) can be written as an affine function of the available lighting embeddings ($\ell_i$) as $\ell = \sum_i \psi_i * \ell_i$ where $\sum_i \psi_i = 1$. To calculate the gradient from Eq. 3, $\frac{\partial x_i}{\partial \ell}$ is computed in the same way as described above utilizing our tools 2 and 3, and the term $\frac{d\ell}{d\psi}$ is straightforward and is optimized with projected gradient descent.

# 4    Experiments

We now evaluate the effectiveness of our proposed Neural-Sim approach in generating optimal training data on object detection task. We provide results under two variations of our Neural-Sim method. In the first case, we use Neural-Sim without using bi-level optimization steps. In this case, data from NeRF are always generated from the same initial distribution. The second case involves our complete Neural-Sim pipeline with bi-level optimization updates (Eq. 2). In the following sections, we use terms NS and NSO for Neural-Sim without and Neural-Sim with bi-level optimization respectively.

We first demonstrate that NeRF can successfully generate data for downstream tasks as a substitute for a traditional graphic pipeline (e.g., BlenderProc) (see appendix for results) with similar performance. Then we conduct experiments to demonstrate the efficacy of Neural-Sim in three different scenarios: controllable synthetic tasks on YCB-synthetic dataset (Sect. 4.1); controllable real-world tasks on YCB-in-the-wild dataset (Sect. 4.2); general real-world tasks on YCB-Video dataset (Sect. 4.3). We also show the interpretable properties of the Neural-Sim approach (NSO) during training data synthesis (Sect. 4.4). All three datasets are based on the objects from the YCB-video dataset [7,26,46]. It contains 21 objects and provides high-resolution RGBD images with ground truth annotation for object bounding boxes. The dataset consists of both digital and physical objects, which we use to create both real and synthetic datasets.

**Implementation Details:** We train one NeRF-w model for each YCB object using 100 images with different camera pose and zoom factors using Blender-Proc. We use RetinaNet [31] as our downstream object detector. To accelerate the optimization, we fix the backbone during training. During bi-level optimization steps, we use Gumble-softmax temperature $\tau = 0.1$. In each optimization iteration, we render 50 images for each object class and train RetinaNet for two epochs. More details are in the appendix.

**Baselines:** We compare our proposed approach against two state-of-the-art approaches that learn simulator parameters. First is Learning to simulate (LTS) [41] which proposed a REINFORCE-based simulator optimization approach. Also note that the meta-sim [30] is a REINFORCE-based approach. Next, we consider Auto-Sim [4] which proposed an efficient method to learn simulator parameters. We implemented LTS and received code from the authors of Auto-Sim.

## 4.1  YCB-synthetic Dataset

Next, we conduct experiments on a YCB-synthetic dataset to show how NSO helps to solve a drop in performance due to distribution shifts between the training and test data.

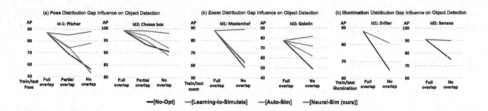

**Fig. 4.** Neural-Sim performance on YCB-Synthetic. When there are distribution gap between train and test sets ((a) pose (b) zoom (c) illumination gap), with the gap increase, object detection faces larger accuracy drop (black line). With the help of Neural-Sim (NSO) in blue line, the performance drop are filled. Observe improvement of NSO over LTS [41] (red line) and Auto-Sim [4] (green line). (Color figure online)

**Dataset Setting.** We select six objects that are easily confused with each other: *masterchef* and *pitcher* are both blue cylinders and *cheezit, gelatin, mug* and *driller* are all red colored objects. To conduct controlled experiments, we generate data with a gap in the distribution of poses between the training and test sets. For this, we divide the object pose space into $k = 8$ bins. For each objects $o_j$ and pose bin $i$ combination, we use BlenderProc [10] to synthesize 100 images. These images of the six selected objects with pose bin-labels form YCB-synthetic data.

**Train/Test Biasness.** We create controlled experiments by varying the degree of pose distribution overlap between the training and test sets. For each object (e.g. *pitcher*) we fix its pose distribution in the test set (e.g. images are generated with pose from bin 1) and change its pose distribution in training set in three ways. First, images are generated with pose with same distribution as test set (bin1 is dominant), uniform distribution (pose values uniformly selected from bin1 to bin 8) and totally different distribution from the test set (other bins are dominant except bin 1). We introduce such pose biasness in two of the six objects, *pitcher* and *driller*. For other four objects, test images are generated from an uniform distribution. The test set has 600 images (100 images per object).

**Results.** Quantitative results are shown in Fig. 4. First, we show the performance of our NS based training images rendered using three initial distributions described earlier. We observe that the object detection performance drops by almost 30% and 10% for *pitcher* and *driller* objects respectively when there is object pose gap between training and test distributions.

Our NSO is able to automatically find the optimal pose distribution of the test set. NeRF then uses the optimal distribution to synthesize training data. The object detection model trained on the optimal data helps improve performance significantly; average precision accuracy for the *pticher* and *driller* objects have been improved by almost 30% and 10%, respectively. The blue lines in Fig. 4 represent the performance of NSO which fill the gap caused by distribution mismatch. Note there is similar significant improvement in experiments where there is gap in camera zoom when using the proposed NSO approach.

We compare our NSO with LTS [41] and Auto-Sim [4] that use REINFORCE for non-differentiable simulator optimization (Fig. 4(a)(b)). We observe that on pose optimization, NSO achieves almost 34% and 11% improvement over LTS and Auto-Sim respectively on the pitcher object. We observe similar behaviour on zoom optimization. This highlights the gradients from differentiable NSO are more effective and generate better data than LTS and Auto-Sim.

**Experiments on Illumination Optimization.** To verify the effectiveness of Neural-Sim on illumination, we substitute vanilla NeRF model with NeRF-w. We conduct similar experiments as the pose and zoom experiments in Sect. 4.1 on illumination with YCB-synthetic dataset. The results show in Fig. 4(c). NSO has great performance on illumination optimization with 16% and 15% improvements on driller and banana objects respectively.

**Large scale YCB-Synthetic Dataset Experiments.** Here we highlight the results of our large-scale experiments on the YCB-synthetic dataset. Experiments demonstrate that our proposed NSO approach helps to solve a drop in performance due to distribution shifts between the train and test sets. We use the same setting as previous experiment except we conduct object detection on all 21 objects on the YCB-Synthetic dataset. The test set has 2100 images (100 images per object). The experiment results are shown in Table 1. Note that our proposed NSO achieves improvements of almost 14% and 13% points over NS and Auto-Sim baselines respectively.

**Table 1.** Large scale YCB-synthetic experiments

| Objects | mAP | Master chef can | Cracker box | Sugar box | Tomato soup can | Mustard bottle | Tuna fish can | Pudding box | Gelatin box | Potted meat can | Banana |
|---|---|---|---|---|---|---|---|---|---|---|---|
| NS | 68.4 | 93.5 | 96.6 | 58.3 | 83.9 | 78.4 | 44.3 | 78.0 | 65.2 | 55.3 | 89.4 |
| Auto-Sim | 69.3 | 96.0 | 82.5 | 92.3 | 37.4 | 81.3 | 52.0 | 80.6 | **79.4** | 74.4 | 83.4 |
| NSO | **82.1** | **98.5** | **98.4** | **98.2** | **81.8** | **90.5** | **64.6** | **84.1** | 57.6 | **92.2** | **91.6** |
| Objects | Pitcher base | Bleach cleanser | Bowl | Mug | Power drill | Wood block | Scissor | Large marker | Large clamp | Extra large clamp | Foam brick |
| NS | 29.0 | 49.9 | 78.7 | 46.8 | 89.3 | 97.8 | **67.9** | 42.9 | 47.8 | 72.7 | **69.6** |
| Auto-Sim | 7.7 | 81.5 | 78.3 | 60.0 | 83.2 | 95.6 | 64.1 | 41.5 | 46.6 | **79.0** | 57.9 |
| NSO | **83.5** | **93.4** | **98.5** | **87.9** | **93.6** | **98.7** | 55.3 | **56.9** | **50.8** | 78.6 | 68.2 |

## 4.2   YCB-in-the-Wild Dataset

To evaluate the performance of the proposed NS and NSO approaches on a real world dataset, we have created a real world *YCB-in-the-wild* dataset. The dataset has 6 YCB objects in it, which are same as in the *YCB-synthetic* dataset: *masterchef, cheezit, gelatin, pitcher, mug* and *driller*. We manually labelled both the object bounding box and the object pose. (More details in the appendix.)

To explore the performance of the NS and NSO under the training and test distribution gap on the *YCB-in-the-wild*, we use the same experiment setup as in Sect. 4.1. The test images are selected from *YCB-in-the-wild* and training images are synthesized by NeRF. The training data is generated under two categorical distributions: uniform distribution and a random bin as dominant bin.

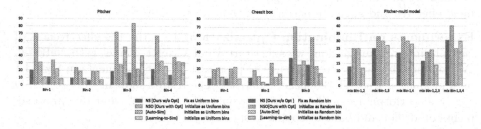

**Fig. 5.** Performance of Neural-Sim on the YCB-in-the-wild dataset. We observe that the Neural-Sim optimization (NSO) can consistently achieve 20% to 60% improvement in accuracy over our method without optimization (NS) case and large improvements over LTS (up to 58%) and Auto-Sim (up to 60%). Here each bin on $x-$axis represents bin from which test data is generated. We observe large improvement in both single-modal and multi-modal test data.

Quantitative results are provided in the Fig. 5. First we highlight the performance achieved by our NS approach to generate data according two different initial pose distributions. We observe that NS generated data helps achieve up to 30% in object detection accuracy on different objects starting from two different initial distributions. Moreover, our NSO approach achieves remarkable improvement in every experimental setup. For example, on *pitcher*, starting from uniform and random distributions, our optimization improve performance by almost 60%. Compared with other optimization methods LTS and Auto-Sim, we observe large improvement upto 58% improvement over LTS and 60% improvement over Auto-Sim on the pitcher object. This highlights three points. First, NeRF can be used to generate good data to solve object detection task in the wild; far more importantly, our Neural-Sim with bi-level optimization (NSO) approach can automatically find the optimal data that can help achieve remarkable improvements in accuracy on images captured in the wild. Third, the gradients from NSO are more effective and generate better data than LTS and Auto-Sim.

## 4.3   YCB Video Dataset

To show the performance of the proposed NS and NSO approaches on a general real world dataset, we also conduct experiments on the YCB-Video dataset [26, 46]. Each image in this dataset consists of multiple YCB objects (usually 3 to 6 different objects) in a real world scene. After sampling frames from 80 videos, $YCBV_{train}$ consists of over 2200 images, YCB-Video testset contains 900 images. Both train and test sets have all 21 YCB objects. In order to show the benefit of synthetic data, we create two different training scenarios (1) **Few-shot setting**, where we randomly select 10 and 25 images from ($YCBV_{train}$) to form different few shot training sets. (2) **Limited dataset setting**, where we randomly select 1%, 5%, 10% images from ($YCBV_{train}$) to form limited training sets.

Using a similar setting as in Sect. 4.2, we demonstrate performance of NS and NSO approaches starting from uniform distributions and compare with four baselines. First baseline-1 involves training RetinaNet using few-shot or limited training images from $YCBV_{train}$ data, and baseline-2 involves training RetinaNet using the images that were used to train NeRF. Baseline-3 is LTS and baseline-4 is Auto-Sim. Further, we combine the real-world few-shot or limited training images along with NeRF synthesized images during our Neural-Sim optimization steps. This *Combined* setting reduces the domain gap between synthetic and real data. All the models have been evaluated on YCB-Video testset.

**Table 2.** YCB-Video performance. Observe large improvement of the proposed Neural-Sim approaches before and after optimization over the baselines.

| Few-shot setting | 0-shot | 10-shot | 25-shot |
|---|---|---|---|
| Only YCBV-train | N/A | 0.45 | 0.49 |
| train(pre)+ours (w/o opt) | 2.3 | 3.9 | 4.6 |
| train(pre)+ours (with opt) | 4.5 | 4.9 | 4.9 |
| Learning-to-sim (com) | N/A | 12.4 | 22.5 |
| Auto-Sim (com) | N/A | 12.9 | 22.2 |
| train(com)+ours (w/o opt) | N/A | 12.2 | 21.0 |
| train(com)+ours (with opt) | N/A | **13.1** | **23.0** |

| Percent of $YCBV_{train}$ | 0.01 | 0.05 | 0.1 |
|---|---|---|---|
| Only YCBV-train | 5.77 | 8.88 | 12.5 |
| Only images to train NeRF | 3.9 | 3.9 | 3.9 |
| train(pre)+ours (w/o opt) | 7.9 | 11.8 | 14.4 |
| train(pre)+ours (with opt) | 8.9 | 12.4 | 14.5 |
| Learning-to-sim (com) | 36.9 | 44.1 | 48.2 |
| Auto-Sim (com) | 37.1 | 43.7 | 48.3 |
| train(com)+ours (w/o opt) | 36.7 | 43.6 | 47.9 |
| train(com)+ours (with opt) | **37.4** | **44.9** | **48.9** |

(a) Zero and few-shot setting (YCB-Video).

(b) limited data setting (YCB-Video)

For the normal Few-shot setting (rows 2, 3, 4 in Table 2(a)), NS starting from the uniform distribution achieves almost 3.45 and 4.11% improvement over the baseline-1 in 10 and 25 shots settings, respectively. Further, when we use NSO, we observe improvements of $4.45, 4.41\%$ over the baseline-1 and $1.0, 0.3\%$ improvements over the NS case in $10, 25$ shot settings respectively. We also observe almost 1.8% improvement in the zero-shot case. In addition, for the *Combined* Few-shot setting (rows 5,6,7,8 in Table 2(a)), we observe similar large improvements in accuracy. We observe similar large performance improvements in the limited data settings (Table 2(b)). Please refer to the appendix for more results and discussion including the results on ObjectNet [3] dataset.

#### 4.4   Interpretability of Neural-Sim

We raise a question: does the Neural-Sim optimization provide interpretable results? In order to demonstrate this behavior, we conduct experiment on *YCB-in-the-wild* dataset illustrated in Fig. 6. Generally, we find that no matter what the starting distributions the Neural-Sim approach used, the learned optimal $\psi^*$ is always aligned with the test distribution. More visualizations in the appendix.

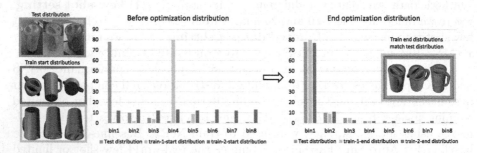

**Fig. 6.** NSO generates interpretable outputs. In the shown example, test images are sampled from distribution bin 1 as dominant bin. For Neural-Sim optimization (NSO), initial training pose distributions are uniform and bin 4 as dominant bin. Observe the bin distribution at the optimization - the final bin distribution at the end of Neural-Sim training matches with the test bin distribution.

## 5   Discussion and Future Work

It has been said that "Data is food for AI" [35]. While computer vision has made wondrous progress in neural network models in the last decade, the data side has seen much less advancement. There has been an explosion in the number and scale of datasets, but the **process** has evolved little, still requiring a painstaking amount of labor. Synthetic data is one of the most promising directions for transforming the data component of AI. While it has been used to show some impressive results, its wide-spread use has been limited, as creating good synthetic data still requires a large investment and specialized expertise.

We believe we have taken a big step towards making synthetic data easier to use for a broader population. By optimizing for how to synthesize data for training a neural network, we have shown big benefits over current synthetic data approaches. We have shown through extensive experiment that the data found by our system is better for training models. We have removed the need for any 3D modeling and for an expert to hand-tune the rendering parameters. This brings the promise of synthetic data closer for those that don't have the resources to use the current approaches.

We have handled camera pose, zoom and illumination; and our approach can be extended to other parameters (such as materials, etc.), by incorporating new advances in neural rendering. For future work, we hope to improve the ease of use of our approach, such as performing our optimization using lower quality, faster rendering using a smaller network for the neural rendering component, and then using the learned parameters to generate high quality data to train the final model. We hope that our work in this space will inspire future research.

**Acknowledgments.** We thank Yen-Chen Lin for help on using the nerf-pytorch code. This work was supported in part by C-BRIC (one of six centers in JUMP, a Semi-conductor Research Corporation (SRC) program sponsored by DARPA), DARPA (HR00112190134) and the Army Research Office (W911NF2020053). The authors affirm that the views expressed herein are solely their own, and do not represent the views of the United States government or any agency thereof.

# References

1. Jahanian, A., Lucy Chai, P.I.: On the "steerability" of generative adversarial networks. CoRR (2019)
2. Barbu, A., et al.: Objectnet: A large-scale bias-controlled dataset for pushing the limits of object recognition models. In: Wallach, H., Larochelle, H., Beygelzimer, A., d'Alché-Buc, F., Fox, E., Garnett, R. (eds.) Advances in Neural Information Processing Systems. vol. 32. Curran Associates, Inc. (2019), https://proceedings.neurips.cc/paper/2019/file/97af07a14cacba681feacf3012730892-Paper.pdf
3. Barbu, A., et al.: Objectnet: A large-scale bias-controlled dataset for pushing the limits of object recognition models. In: Advances in Neural Information Processing Systems, vol. 32 (2019)
4. Behl, H.S., Baydin, A.G., Gal, R., Torr, P.H.S., Vineet, V.: Autosimulate: (quickly) learning synthetic data generation. In: Vedaldi, A., Bischof, H., Brox, T., Frahm, J.-M. (eds.) ECCV 2020. LNCS, vol. 12367, pp. 255–271. Springer, Cham (2020). https://doi.org/10.1007/978-3-030-58542-6_16
5. Bi, S., et al.: Neural reflectance fields for appearance acquisition. arXiv preprint arXiv:2008.03824 (2020)
6. Brock, A., Donahue, J., Simonyan, K.: Large scale GAN training for high fidelity natural image synthesis. In: International Conference on Learning Representations (2019). https://openreview.net/forum?id=B1xsqj09Fm
7. Calli, B., Walsman, A., Singh, A., Srinivasa, S., Abbeel, P., Dollar, A.M.: Benchmarking in manipulation research: The ycb object and model set and benchmarking protocols. arXiv preprint arXiv:1502.03143 (2015)
8. Colson, B., Marcotte, P., Savard, G.: An overview of bilevel optimization. Ann. Oper. Res. **153**(1), 235–256 (2007)
9. Danilo Jimenez Rezende, S.M.: Variational inference with normalizing flows. In: ICML (2015)
10. Denninger, M., et al.: Blenderproc. arXiv preprint arXiv:1911.01911 (2019)
11. Devaranjan, J., Kar, A., Fidler, S.: Meta-Sim2: Unsupervised learning of scene structure for synthetic data generation. In: Vedaldi, A., Bischof, H., Brox, T., Frahm, J.-M. (eds.) ECCV 2020. LNCS, vol. 12362, pp. 715–733. Springer, Cham (2020). https://doi.org/10.1007/978-3-030-58520-4_42
12. Diederik Kingma, M.W.: Autoencoding variational bayes. In: ICLR (2014)
13. Doersch, C., Zisserman, A.: Sim2real transfer learning for 3d human pose estimation: motion to the rescue. In: NeurIPS (2019)

14. Dwibedi, D., Misra, I., Hebert, M.: Cut, paste and learn: Surprisingly easy synthesis for instance detection. In: ICCV (2017)
15. Franceschi, L., Frasconi, P., Salzo, S., Grazzi, R., Pontil, M.: Bilevel programming for hyperparameter optimization and meta-learning. In: International Conference on Machine Learning, pp. 1568–1577. PMLR (2018)
16. Gafni, G., Thies, J., Zollhofer, M., Nießner, M.: Dynamic neural radiance fields for monocular 4d facial avatar reconstruction. In: Proceedings of the IEEE/CVF Conference on Computer Vision and Pattern Recognition, pp. 8649–8658 (2021)
17. Ganin, Y., Kulkarni, T., Babuschkin, I., Eslami, S.M.A., Vinyals, O.: Synthesizing programs for images using reinforced adversarial learning. In: ICML (2018)
18. Ge, Y., Abu-El-Haija, S., Xin, G., Itti, L.: Zero-shot synthesis with group-supervised learning. arXiv preprint arXiv:2009.06586 (2020)
19. Ge, Y., Xu, J., Zhao, B.N., Itti, L., Vineet, V.: Dall-e for detection: Language-driven context image synthesis for object detection. arXiv preprint arXiv:2206.09592 (2022)
20. Ge, Y., Zhao, J., Itti, L.: Pose augmentation: Class-agnostic object pose transformation for object recognition. In: Vedaldi, A., Bischof, H., Brox, T., Frahm, J.-M. (eds.) ECCV 2020. LNCS, vol. 12373, pp. 138–155. Springer, Cham (2020). https://doi.org/10.1007/978-3-030-58604-1_9
21. Georgiev, I., et al.: Arnold: A brute-force production path tracer. TOG **37**, 1–12 (2018)
22. Goodfellow, I., et al.: Generative adversarial nets. In: Advances in neural information processing systems, pp. 2672–2680 (2014)
23. Handa, A., Patraucean, V., Badrinarayanan, V., Stent, S., Cipolla, R.: Understanding real world indoor scenes with synthetic data. In: CVPR (2016)
24. He, K., Gkioxari, G., Dollár, P., Girshick, R.: Mask r-cnn. In: ICCV (2017)
25. Higgins, I., et al.: beta-vae: Learning basic visual concepts with a constrained variational framework. In: 5th International Conference on Learning Representations, ICLR 2017, Toulon, France (2017)
26. Hodaň, T., et al.: BOP: Benchmark for 6d object pose estimation. In: Ferrari, V., Hebert, M., Sminchisescu, C., Weiss, Y. (eds.) ECCV 2018. LNCS, vol. 11214, pp. 19–35. Springer, Cham (2018). https://doi.org/10.1007/978-3-030-01249-6_2
27. Hodaň, T., et al.: Photorealistic image synthesis for object instance detection. In: ICIP (2019)
28. Ilg, E., Mayer, N., Saikia, T., Keuper, M., Dosovitskiy, A., Brox, T.: Flownet 2.0: Evolution of optical flow estimation with deep networks. In: 2017 IEEE Conference on Computer Vision and Pattern Recognition, CVPR 2017, Honolulu, HI, USA, 21–26 July 2017, pp. 1647–1655 (2017). https://doi.org/10.1109/CVPR.2017.179
29. Jang, W., Agapito, L.: Codenerf: Disentangled neural radiance fields for object categories. In: Proceedings of the IEEE/CVF International Conference on Computer Vision, pp. 12949–12958 (2021)
30. Kar, A., et al.: Meta-sim: Learning to generate synthetic datasets. In: ICCV (2019)
31. Lin, T.Y., Goyal, P., Girshick, R., He, K., Dollár, P.: Focal loss for dense object detection. In: Proceedings of the IEEE International Conference on Computer Vision, pp. 2980–2988 (2017)
32. Louppe, G., Cranmer, K.: Adversarial variational optimization of non-differentiable simulators. In: AISTATS (2019)
33. Martin-Brualla, R., Radwan, N., Sajjadi, M.S., Barron, J.T., Dosovitskiy, A., Duckworth, D.: Nerf in the wild: Neural radiance fields for unconstrained photo collections. In: Proceedings of the IEEE/CVF Conference on Computer Vision and Pattern Recognition, pp. 7210–7219 (2021)

34. Mildenhall, B., Srinivasan, P.P., Tancik, M., Barron, J.T., Ramamoorthi, R., Ng, R.: NeRF: Representing scenes as neural radiance fields for view synthesis. In: Vedaldi, A., Bischof, H., Brox, T., Frahm, J.-M. (eds.) ECCV 2020. LNCS, vol. 12346, pp. 405–421. Springer, Cham (2020). https://doi.org/10.1007/978-3-030-58452-8_24

35. Ng, A.: Mlops: From model-centric to data-centric ai. https://www.deeplearning.ai/wp-content/uploads/2021/06/MLOps-From-Model-centric-to-Data-centric-AI.pdf

36. Park, K., et al.: Nerfies: Deformable neural radiance fields. In: ICCV (2021)

37. Ren, S., He, K., Girshick, R., Sun, J.: Faster r-cnn: towards real-time object detection with region proposal networks. In: PAMI (2017)

38. Richter, S.R., Hayder, Z., Koltun, V.: Playing for benchmarks. In: ICCV (2017)

39. Richter, S.R., Vineet, V., Roth, S., Koltun, V.: Playing for data: Ground truth from computer games. In: Leibe, B., Matas, J., Sebe, N., Welling, M. (eds.) ECCV 2016. LNCS, vol. 9906, pp. 102–118. Springer, Cham (2016). https://doi.org/10.1007/978-3-319-46475-6_7

40. Ros, G., Sellart, L., Materzynska, J., Vázquez, D., López, A.M.: The SYNTHIA dataset: A large collection of synthetic images for semantic segmentation of urban scenes. In: CVPR (2016)

41. Ruiz, N., Schulter, S., Chandraker, M.: Learning to simulate. In: ICLR (2019)

42. Shelhamer, E., Long, J., Darrell, T.: Fully convolutional networks for semantic segmentation. In: PAMI (2017)

43. Srinivasan, P.P., Deng, B., Zhang, X., Tancik, M., Mildenhall, B., Barron, J.T.: Nerv: Neural reflectance and visibility fields for relighting and view synthesis. In: CVPR (2021)

44. Tremblay, J., To, T., Birchfield, S.: Falling things: A synthetic dataset for 3d object detection and pose estimation. In: CVPR (2018)

45. Williams, R.J.: Simple statistical gradient-following algorithms for connectionist reinforcement learning. Mach. Learn. **8**, 229–256 (1992)

46. Xiang, Y., Schmidt, T., Narayanan, V., Fox, D.: Posecnn: A convolutional neural network for 6d object pose estimation in cluttered scenes. arXiv preprint arXiv:1711.00199 (2017)

47. Xiaogang, X.u., Ying-Cong Chen, J.J.: View independent generative adversarial network for novel view synthesis. In: ICCV (2019)

48. Yang, D., Deng, J.: Learning to generate synthetic 3d training data through hybrid gradient. In: CVPR (2020)

49. Yen-Chen, L.: Nerf-pytorch. https://github.com/yenchenlin/nerf-pytorch/ (2020)

50. Zhang, X., Srinivasan, P.P., Deng, B., Debevec, P., Freeman, W.T., Barron, J.T.: Nerfactor: Neural factorization of shape and reflectance under an unknown illumination. ACM Trans. Graph. (TOG) **40**(6), 1–18 (2021)

51. Zhang, Y., et al.: Physically-based rendering for indoor scene understanding using convolutional neural networks. In: CVPR (2017)

# Bayesian Optimization with Clustering and Rollback for CNN Auto Pruning

Hanwei Fan[1,2] , Jiandong Mu[2] , and Wei Zhang[2(✉)]

[1] The Hong Kong University of Science and Technology (Guangzhou), Guangzhou, China
hfanah@connect.ust.hk
[2] The Hong Kong University of Science and Technology, Hong Kong, China
jmu@connect.ust.hk, wei.zhang@ust.hk

**Abstract.** Pruning is an effective technique for convolutional neural networks (CNNs) model compression, but it is difficult to find the optimal pruning policy due to the large design space. To improve the usability of pruning, many auto pruning methods have been developed. Recently, Bayesian optimization (BO) has been considered to be a competitive algorithm for auto pruning due to its solid theoretical foundation and high sampling efficiency. However, BO suffers from the curse of dimensionality. The performance of BO deteriorates when pruning deep CNNs, since the dimension of the design spaces increase. We propose a novel clustering algorithm that reduces the dimension of the design space to speed up the searching process. Subsequently, a rollback algorithm is proposed to recover the high-dimensional design space so that higher pruning accuracy can be obtained. We validate our proposed method on ResNet, MobileNetV1, and MobileNetV2 models. Experiments show that the proposed method significantly improves the convergence rate of BO when pruning deep CNNs with no increase in running time. The source code is available at https://github.com/fanhanwei/BOCR.

**Keywords:** CNN · Pruning · Bayesian optimization

## 1 Introduction

Convolutional neural networks (CNNs) are becoming popular due to their high performance and universality. There is a growing trend to apply CNNs in different scenarios such as object detection, speech recognition, *etc.* However, the high performance of CNNs is at the expense of their large model size and high computing complexity, which have prevented them from having broader usage. To solve this problem, network pruning [5] has been proposed to reduce the model size with little accuracy loss. Many works, *e.g.*, [4,8,20,42,47], have been

**Supplementary Information** The online version contains supplementary material available at https://doi.org/10.1007/978-3-031-20050-2_29.

proposed to prune CNNs with different granularity. Among these works, channel pruning [8,42], which reduces the model size and computing complexity by removing the redundant channels on the feature map, is widely adopted due to its high efficiency in hardware implementation.

As the depth of CNNs rapidly increases, the design space of the pruning policies, which indicates the preservation ratio of each layer of the CNN model, becomes too large to be fully explored by handcrafted efforts. To reduce the manpower overhead introduced by the pruning process while exploring the design space of pruning, reinforcement learning (RL) [9,45] and general probabilistic algorithms [18,19,46] are utilized to automate the channel pruning process. However, the above methods lead to a large time overhead as they need massive data and training trials to converge. To increase the practicality of auto pruning, a better algorithm is expected to search the design space more efficiently.

Bayesian optimization (BO) [25] is an effective method for tuning the hyper-parameters for the black-box function with high sample efficiency. Therefore, BO is considered to be a competitive candidate algorithm for building the automatic pruning agent [3,22,35]. However, BO suffers from a fatal drawback that the sampling efficiency of BO drops significantly when dealing with high-dimensional problems. Thus, it would be challenging to prune very deep networks with the BO agent. Currently, the BO-based pruning framework is usually used to deal with shallow networks to maintain high efficiency, and an enhanced BO agent is needed to provide better results when dealing with modern CNN models. Although many algorithms [14,21,29,39,40] have been proposed to mitigate the performance degradation of high-dimensional BO, these works only provide general solutions based on theoretical analysis, which might not be practical for specific applications. When applying BO to CNN pruning, specialized methods can be developed based on our prior knowledge about CNN pruning.

In this work, observing that some CNN layers have similar redundancy, we propose to cluster the layers by exploiting the similarity of their intrinsic properties and train the BO agent in a low-dimensional space. However, the dimensionality reduction risks missing the optimal pruning policy since the low-dimensional BO does not explore the whole design space. To achieve optimum, we propose a rollback algorithm in which we recover the original high-dimensional searching space for the BO agent and perform a fine-grained search with the low-dimensional data as the prior knowledge. In addition, to fully utilize the information collected during the policy searching in a low-dimensional space, we propose an adaptive searching domain scaling scheme to reduce the workload of the BO agent after rollback so that a faster fine-grained search can be achieved. Our proposed methods not only improve the performance of the BO agent significantly but enjoys simple implementation.

In summary, we make the following contributions:

1. We propose to solve the high-dimensional problem with a clustering-based dimension reduction scheme so that the BO agent can prune CNNs efficiently.

2. A rollback algorithm is used to recover the high-dimensional space so that the optimal pruning policy will not be missed, and the accuracy of the pruned model can be further improved.
3. Experiments show that our methods explore the design space with a considerable improvement in accuracy than naive BO with no increase in running time. When pruning ResNet56, our method delivers a 2.2% higher accuracy. For challenging tasks like pruning MobileNetV1 and MobileNetV2 on ImageNet, our method achieves a 2.0% and 1.9% higher accuracy, respectively.

## 2    Related Work

### 2.1    CNN Pruning

CNN model pruning has become a heated topic as CNNs are widely used in resource-constrained devices. A significant number of research works have been proposed to prune CNNs by removing the unimportant weights [5,11,26,34]. Recently, many research works focused on layer-wise channel pruning as it can achieve competitive performance while being hardware-friendly [8,42]. However, determining the optimal preservation ratio of each layer for the input models is challenging even for experts. In [9], the authors employed a deep deterministic policy gradient (DDPG) agent [17], which is one of the most popular RL algorithms for continuous action spaces, to automatically generate the optimal pruning policy for channel pruning so that human efforts can be released from the tedious handcrafted work. In [36], this RL-based auto pruning scheme was further extended to model quantization for the first time. In the recent work [45], the graph encoder and decoder were applied to generate the states for the RL, which further improved the learning outcome. Other works utilized probabilistic algorithms e.g., simulated annealing [18], evolutionary [19] and MCMC [46], to sample the pruning policy. Both RL and probabilistic algorithms need massive iterations to converge, causing the pruning process to be time-consuming. Therefore, it is of great interest to develop a better auto pruning agent to improve the convergence speed.

### 2.2    BO-based Auto Pruning and High-Dimensional BO

BO is an optimization framework that employs a continuously updated probabilistic model to predict the performance and variation of the design space so that sampling efficiency can be maximized. Nowadays, BO is widely used to tune hyperparameters, and it has become a natural thought to apply BO to CNN pruning. A few works [3,22,35] on automatically pruning CNN based on a BO agent are introduced here. In [35], the author proposed a fine-pruning method, which applied a BO agent to automatically adapt the layer-wise pruning parameters over time as the network changes. The work in [3] further improved this framework by setting constraints on BO and designing a cooling scheme to prune the CNN model to a user-specified preservation ratio gradually. However, these works dismissed the curse of high dimensionality of BO as they only conducted experiments on shallow networks such as AlexNet [15]. In [22], the authors successfully applied BO to prune deeper networks with an efficient acquisition function and a fast quality measure of the sampled network. However, the high-dimensional problem of the BO agent was not fundamentally solved. As an open problem, high-dimensional BO has attracted the attention of many researchers. [29] found that the length scale, a hyperparameter of Gaussian kernel that controls the smoothness, significantly impacts the performance of high-dimensional BO. Therefore, the author proposed an algorithm to tune the length scale in each iteration. However, the algorithm was only validated on squared exponential (SE) kernel, which is known to be unrealistic for modeling many physical processes [30]. Besides, there are two mainstream solutions for high-dimensional BO. One of them is additive-GP [14,21,31,38], which assumes an additive structure of the target function, making it not applicable to layer-wise pruning. The other is the random embedding approach [16,28,39,40], which maps the high-dimensional problem to an efficient subspace with the assumption that the unimportant dimensions can be replaced by the combinations of the important dimensions. Although the recent research [37] showed that the important layers might exist, obtaining the proper embedding is very difficult for random embedding methods.

Considering the above research gaps, we propose a novel clustering algorithm to reduce the dimensionality based on a moderate assumption that similar layers can share the same preservation ratios. Then, a rollback algorithm is followed to further boost the accuracy.

## 3   Methodology

In this section, we introduce our methodology by forming the auto pruning task as a BO process. The frequently used variables are shown in Table 1.

### 3.1   Channel Pruning with BO

In this work, we mainly focus on channel pruning as it can achieve a good trade-off between model size and accuracy while being hardware-friendly. We adopt the magnitude-based channel pruning scheme along with the weight reconstruction method proposed in [8] to prune the neural network. However, our proposed framework also can be applied to other pruning schemes. In channel pruning, a weights tensor with the shape of $n \times c \times k \times k$ is pruned into $n \times c' \times k \times k$, so the preservation ratio $p$ is $c'/c$. Then, the problem becomes determining the optimal $p_i$ for layer $i$ to maximize the accuracy of the pruned network while satisfying the constraints, which can be formulated as the following optimization problem:

**Table 1.** Variables in this work.

| Variable | Meaning |
|----------|---------|
| $i$ | Index of layer |
| $n$ | Number of input channels for layer |
| $k$ | Kernel size |
| $c, c'$ | Number of output channels before/after pruning |
| $t$ | The $t^{th}$ iteration of BO process |
| $\Theta, \Theta'$ | Network model before/after pruning |
| $p_i$ | Preservation ratio for layer $i$ |
| $p_{target}$ | Target preservation ratio |
| $N$ | Number of layers of the network |
| $\mathbf{P}$ | Pruning policy for the model |

$$
\max_{\mathbf{P}} f(\Theta')
$$
$$
s.t. p_f \leq p_{target}
$$
$$
\Theta' = Pruning(\Theta, \mathbf{P}) \tag{1}
$$
$$
p_f = Flops(\Theta')/Flops(\Theta),
$$

where the *Pruning* and *Flops* functions are well-defined and can be implemented explicitly in the program. $f$ is the target function, which is usually a black-box function. In our case, it is the accuracy of the pruned network and can be measured by conducting inferences on the images in the validation set.

This problem is hard to solve since there is no explicit form of $f$ due to the complex relationship between channel pruning policy and the corresponding accuracy. An alternative method is to build a fast model to approximate the black box function $f$ by iteratively interacting with the channel pruner, and the optimal pruning policy $\mathbf{P}^*$ can be achieved by finding the maximum of the model. BO, which models the black-box function with a continually updated probabilistic model, *e.g.* Gaussian Process (GP) model [23], becomes promising for optimizing expensive black-box functions due to its high sample efficiency.

During the BO process, we note the sampled policy in the $t$th iteration as $\mathbf{P}_t \in \mathbb{R}^N$, where $N$ is the depth of the network. Similarly, the pruning policies for time 1 to $t$ can be noted as $\mathbf{P}_{1:t}$. As we have mentioned before, we assume that the pruning samples can be modeled as a GP model, and therefore we have

$$
f(\Theta, \mathbf{P}_{1:t}) \sim \mathcal{N}\left(\mathbf{m}(\mathbf{P}_{1:t}), \mathbf{K}\left(\mathbf{P}_{1:t}, \mathbf{P}_{1:t}\right)\right), \tag{2}
$$

where $\mathbf{m}$ is the mean function, and $\mathbf{K}(\mathbf{P}_{1:t}, \mathbf{P}_{1:t})$ is the variance matrix. In the following discussion, we denote $f(\Theta, \mathbf{P}_{1:t})$ by $f(\mathbf{P}_{1:t})$ for simplicity. Then, the joint distribution of the previous samples together with the next sample can be represented by

$$
\begin{bmatrix} f(\mathbf{P}_{1:t}) \\ f(\mathbf{P}_{t+1}) \end{bmatrix} \sim \mathcal{N}\left( \begin{matrix} \mathbf{m}(\mathbf{P}_{1:t}) \\ \mathbf{m}(\mathbf{P}_{t+1}) \end{matrix}, \begin{bmatrix} \mathbf{K}(\mathbf{P}_{1:t}, \mathbf{P}_{1:t}), & \mathbf{k}(\mathbf{P}_{1:t}, \mathbf{P}_{t+1}) \\ \mathbf{k}(\mathbf{P}_{t+1}, \mathbf{P}_{1:t}), & k(\mathbf{P}_{t+1}, \mathbf{P}_{t+1}) \end{bmatrix} \right) \tag{3}
$$

and the probabilistic prediction of the next sample can be obtained by

$$
\begin{aligned}
f(\mathbf{P}_{t+1}) &\sim \mathcal{N}\left(\mu(\mathbf{P}_{t+1}), \sigma(\mathbf{P}_{t+1})\right) \\
\mu(\mathbf{P}_{t+1}) &= \mathbf{k}(\mathbf{P}_{t+1}, \mathbf{P}_{1:t})\mathbf{K}(\mathbf{P}_{1:t}, \mathbf{P}_{1:t})^{-1} f(\mathbf{P}_{1:t}) \\
\sigma(\mathbf{P_{t+1}}) &= k(\mathbf{P_{t+1}}, \mathbf{P}_{t+1}) \\
&\quad - \mathbf{k}(\mathbf{P}_{t+1}, \mathbf{P}_{1:t})\mathbf{K}(\mathbf{P}_{1:t}, \mathbf{P}_{1:t})\mathbf{k}(\mathbf{P}_{1:t}, \mathbf{P}_{t+1})
\end{aligned}
\tag{4}
$$

This means that the mean for the unexplored pruning policy $\mathbf{P}_{t+1}$ can be predicted via the history samples, and the corresponding variance of the prediction can also be obtained.

To enhance the sampling efficiency, a cheap surrogate function, which is called the acquisition function, is built to recommend the next sample point with the highest potential to maximize the objective function. Expected Improvement (EI) [1,24], which is defined by $\mathbb{E}[\max(f(\mathbf{P}) - f(\mathbf{P}^+), 0)]$, aims to find the sampling point that has the highest expected improvement over the current optimal policy $\mathbf{P}^+$, and has become one of the most popular acquisition functions over the past years. In this work, we utilize EI to sample the pruning policies. The framework for the BO-based auto pruning scenario thus can be illustrated by Fig. 1. We first evaluate the randomly generated policies as the initial samples. The initial policies are sampled according to the Sobol sequence [12,13] to make the BO process more stable as Sobol is an evenly distributed quasi-random low dependency sequence and has an overwhelming advantage in providing stable and evenly distributed samples. Then, we build the GP model to estimate the policies' mean and variance at unobserved locations according to Eq. 4. Next, the EI-based acquisition function is computed to indicate the potential benefits of each unexplored policy. Finally, the recommended policy, which shows the

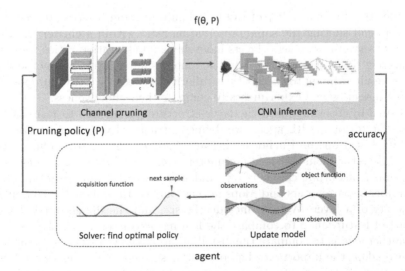

**Fig. 1.** Solving the auto pruning problem by BO.

highest potential of obtaining a better-pruned network, will be given by solving the maximum value of the acquisition functions and will serve as the next sample to update the GP model. By iterating this process, the recommended policy can keep improving until convergence. Based on the theoretical research of [2], the simple regret of BO, which defines as $f(\mathbf{P}^*) - f(\mathbf{P}_t)$, is upper bounded by $O(t^{-1/N})$, showing that the convergence rate of BO will significantly decrease as the CNN models get deeper. Therefore, we propose a layer clustering algorithm to solve this problem.

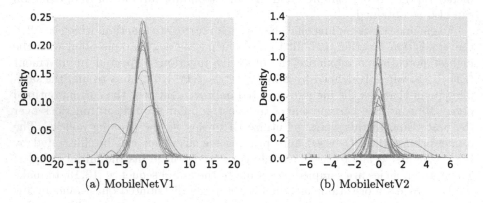

(a) MobileNetV1                    (b) MobileNetV2

**Fig. 2.** The distributions of the channel importance of the layers.

### 3.2   Layer Clustering

To reduce the dimensionality of BO-based auto pruning, we consider clustering the layers and sharing the same preservation ratio within a cluster. As we frequently observed that several layers have similar preservation ratios, we assume that sharing the same preservation ratio among similar layers will not affect the pruning result. Aiming to exploit the similarity between layers, we propose three different measures and experimentally compare their effectiveness.

Inspired by [9] which used the layer structure parameters to form the environment states of the RL agent, we define a structural vector and measure the similarity based on the Euclidean distance between the vectors. Our proposed structural vector includes basic parameters *e.g.*, the number of input channels ($n$), number of output channels ($c$), and kernel size ($k$). In addition, we take the number of parameters and Flops into account as they show the computation complexity of a layer. We also include the size and the dimensional change of the output feature map to compare the features extracted by the layers.

Another idea is to compare the distributions of the weights inside the layers. Since we adopt the importance-based pruning scheme that removes the less significant part of the weights, layers with similar distributions are more likely to have close preservation ratios. Note that, although we choose magnitude as the importance in this work, our method can also apply to another kind of importance *e.g.*, gradient-based [6], Nisp [44], *etc.* We utilize Gaussian kernel-density estimation (GKde) to fit the Gaussian distribution of each layer's channel importance. The distributions of the layers usually have different biases and do not overlap. Considering whether a channel is redundant depends on its position in the layer it belongs to, layers with different biases can have similar percentages of redundancy. Thus we relocate the distributions by subtracting their medians to make different distributions comparable. Figure 2 shows the distributions of different layers in MobilenetV1 and MobilenetV2, and it is obvious that some layers have similar channel importance distributions. Next, we compare two different methods to measure the similarity between distributions. One of them is Jensen-Shannon divergence (JSD), known as the symmetric version of KL divergence, which focuses on the information gap. The other is the Euclidean distance which focuses on shape. To find the best approach to measure the similarity of the layers, a set of experiments is conducted and will be shown in the experiment section.

Taking the similarity measures as the distance between the layers, the hierarchical agglomerative clustering (HAC) [41] can be adopted to cluster the layers as it has no limitation on the measure of distance while other methods may require the observations of the data. To minimize the total within-cluster variance, we update the distance between clusters with the Ward linkage method, whose details can be found in [27]. Another characteristic of HAC is that the existing clusters will not split when we decrease the number of clusters $C$, and results of different $C$ are stored after one single run. This characteristic is useful to the rollback algorithm, which will be introduced in the next subsection.

After dividing the layers into $C$ clusters, we only need to train a $C$-dimensional GP model instead of the high-dimensional model, improving the upper bound of the simple regret to $O(n^{-1/C})$. We assign the same preservation ratios for each cluster so that the $C$-dimensional vector generated by the low-dimensional model can be extended to the $N$-dimensional pruning policy $\mathbf{P}$.

## 3.3    Rollback for Higher Accuracy

With the layer clustering algorithm, we can efficiently obtain high-quality pruning policies. However, the possibility exists that we miss the optimal pruning policy since the low-dimensional BO does not explore the whole design space. Therefore, we propose to recover the original dimensionality after the low-dimensional model converges so that the whole design space can be reached and the optimal will not be missed. It is difficult for BO to find the peaks of the acquisition function in high-dimensional space [29], leading to random-like searching. However, with the data collected in the low-dimensional space, BO can easily locate the peaks and exploit better results when returning to the high-dimensional space as sufficient prior knowledge about the peaks is provided. To achieve this, we propose a rollback algorithm that rebuilds the GP model to search the whole design space with plenty of prior knowledge, which is presented in Algorithm 1.

**Direct Rollback.** A simple way to rollback is to build a $D$-dimensional model directly. To achieve this, we record the pruning policy $\mathbf{P}$ every iteration. Recall that $\mathbf{P}$ is extended from the low-dimensional sample of BO based on the clustering, thus we can recover the dimensionality of BO by rebuilding the GP model with $\mathbf{P}_{1:t}$. Since BO updates by fitting a new GP model every iteration, rebuilding the GP model causes no extra time overhead. Our experiments show that our rollback algorithm can further improve the results by discovering better pruning policies that the clustering-based BO can not reach.

**Gradual Rollback.** A more sophisticated way is to gradually rollback to reduce the learning gap between the low and high-dimensional space. To be detailed, a cluster number $C^*$, which satisfies $C < C^* < N$, can be chosen as the bridge stage so that we can first rollback to $C^*$-dimensional space and then rollback to the original dimensionality. As we mentioned in the last subsection, a nice feature of HAC is the consistency of results among different cluster numbers. Therefore, there is no mismatch between the corresponding dimensions after rollback. In addition, as all results of HAC are saved after one single run, we can obtain the clustering result of $C^*$ clusters without extra computation. To build the $C^*$-dimensional GP model, we only need to remove the dimensions that remain in clusters from $\mathbf{P}_{1:t}$. The effectiveness of gradual rollback is shown in the experiment section, and a detailed analysis of different choices of $C^*$ is shown in the supplementary material.

---

**Algorithm 1:** Rollback the Clustered BO

---

**Input**: $C$-dimensional GP model $M_C$, Original dimensionality $D$,
Max iteration $T$

**Result**: D-dimensional GP model

1  converge counter $= 0$;
2  **while** $t < T/2$ **do**
3  | Obtain $\mathbf{P}_t$ from $M_C$ and Record $\mathbf{P}_t$;
4  | **if** $f(\mathbf{P}_t) > f(\mathbf{P}^+)$ **then**
5  | | Push $\mathbf{P}_t$ to the Best Queue;
6  | | converge counter $= 0$;
7  | **if** converge counter $\geq 20$ **then**
8  | | break;
9  | update $M_C$;
10 | converge counter $++$;
11 Obtain the $D$-dimensional clustering result;
12 Reform $\mathbf{P}_{1:t}$ based on the $D$-dimensional clustering;
13 Perform adaptive searching domain scaling;
14 Generate the D-dimensional GP model;

---

**Adaptive Searching Domain Scaling.** To boost the efficiency of BO in high-dimensional space, we propose an adaptive searching domain scaling scheme, where we shrink the searching domain according to the history data collected during the low-dimensional BO process. We store the pruning policies with the highest accuracy in the Best Queue, which has ten entities, as we observe that ten entities can decrease the searching domain to a reasonable extent. Then, the searching domain of the high-dimensional BO process can be formulated as

$$\mathcal{D} = \left[ \min_{i,j} \mathbf{P}_j^{*i}, \max_{i,j} \mathbf{P}_j^{*i} \right]^C , \tag{5}$$

where $i$ ranges from 1 to 10, indicating the index of the high-performance samples in the queue. $j$ ranges from 1 to $C$, indicating the index of the clusters.

## 4 Experiments

In our experiments, we use GpyOpt [33] as the naive BO agent and implement the proposed methods based on it. We adopt Matern5/2 as the GP kernel as recommended in [30]. The hyperparameters of the kernel are decided by maximum likelihood estimation. RL agent in [9] is chosen as a baseline. To make a fair comparison, we adopt the same channel pruning scheme for all the methods. The accuracy is estimated based on a random subset of the training set, whose sizes are 5000 and 3000 for Cifar10 and ImageNet, respectively. We conduct our experiments on several representative CNN model architectures, including ResNet56 trained on Cifar10 [7], MobileNetV1 [10] and MobileNetV2 [32] both trained on ImageNet. We run each experiment for 200 epochs and report the mean ($m$) and the standard deviation ($\sigma$) of 10 different seeds. Note that our research focuses on the optimization process of auto pruning. Therefore, we perform a detailed analysis of the convergence process and all the experiment results are obtained before finetuning.

### 4.1 Analysis of Similarity Measures

To analyze the three proposed similarity measures, we perform layer clustering based on each of them and compare the searching results. Table 2 shows the cluster number $C$ and the mean of top-1 accuracy along with the variance. As shown in Table 2, the structure-based measure provides the best result for ResNet56, while Euclidean distance of distributions performs the best for the other two models.

We believe that significant architectural differences between the models lead to this result. ResNet56 has a plain architecture, as it is composed of repeated layers of only three different structures. Therefore, when the dimensionality reduces to three, the structure-based measure can achieve high accuracy while others suffer a considerable loss. Similarly, the structure-based measure achieves high accuracy for MobileNetV1 as it has five layers that share the same structure. However, the other layers of MobileNetV1 have different structures, which limits the effectiveness of the structure-based measure. For MobileNetV2, the distribution-based measure outperforms the structure-based measure by a large margin, showing its superiority in dealing with complex CNN models.

Except for ResNet56, which is unsuitable for distribution-based measures, Euclidean distance provides higher accuracy and lower variance than JSD. We explain this result in terms of the meaning of Euclidean distance and JSD. Euclidean distance focuses on the relative position of the weights, which has a significant impact on the importance-based pruning method. JSD measures the difference in information, which is not closely related to the importance-based pruning. Thus, Euclidean distance better measures the similarity among layers.

To summarize, the structure-based measure is suitable for simple models with repeated layers while the Euclidean distance of distributions is effective for complex models. Therefore, we adopt the structure-based measure for ResNet56 and adopt the Euclidean distance of distributions for MobileNetV1 and MobileNetV2 in the following experiments.

**Table 2.** Comparison of Similarity Measures.

|  | ResNet56 | MobileNetV1 | MobileNetV2 |
|---|---|---|---|
| $C$ | 3 | 6 | 6 |
| Structure | **91.68 (0.43)** | 48.46 (1.39) | 50.31 (0.71) |
| JS | 90.78 (0.27) | 47.99 (1.98) | 52.49 (1.27) |
| Euclidean | 88.95 (0.55) | **48.50 (1.20)** | **52.57 (0.98)** |

**Table 3.** Performance for ResNet56.

| Method | Top-1 $m$ | Top-1 $\sigma$ | Top-5 $m$ | Top-5 $\sigma$ |
|---|---|---|---|---|
| RL | 87.69 | 3.39 | 99.42 | 0.33 |
| Naive BO | 90.29 | 1.63 | 99.72 | 0.11 |
| Layer clustering | 91.68 | 0.43 | 99.77 | 0.06 |
| Rollback | **92.53** | 0.56 | **99.86** | 0.05 |

## 4.2    Experiments on ResNet56

ResNet56 is a representative model architecture trained on Cifar10 and it has a considerably large depth, leading to very high dimensions for layer-wise pruning tasks. Although the first layers of the residual branches are not prunable because the input feature maps are shared with the shortcut branches, there remain 28 layers to be pruned, which will cause the curse of dimensionality problem for the naive BO agent. While with layer clustering, there are only three parameters left for the BO agent to optimize.

In Table 3, we list the mean value $m$ and the standard deviation $\sigma$ of both top-1 and top-5 accuracy achieved by different methods when pruning 50% Flops for ResNet56. Our proposed layer clustering method improves BO's performance with 1.4% higher top-1 accuracy. The rollback scheme further improves the accuracy by 0.9%. Note that in [9], the author shows that AMC can achieve a 90.2% top-1 accuracy in 400 epochs. Our proposed rollback method can achieve 93.14 % within 200 epochs, which is significantly better than [9].

Table 3 also shows that the BO agent outperforms RL in efficiency by a large margin. It can be observed that the BO-based searching scheme is more stable than the RL-based counterpart and converges much faster, as the $\sigma$ of the RL agent is much higher than our proposed layer clustering and the rollback algorithm. In Fig. 3a, we show the effectiveness of the proposed methods in detail. The solid lines in the figure refer to the means, and the shaded areas refer to the corresponding $\sigma$. The layer clustering method can significantly boost the convergence of the BO agent. After its convergence, the rollback scheme turns the design space back into a high-dimensional space and can further improve the accuracy of the pruned network.

Note that all methods take around 800 s to finish 200 epochs in our device, which indicates the time spent for each trial in BO and RL is close and the time overhead of rollback is ignorable. Thus, our method is also much more efficient from the perspective of wall clock time.

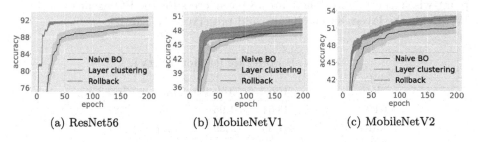

(a) ResNet56          (b) MobileNetV1          (c) MobileNetV2

**Fig. 3.** Comparison of BO-based methods.

### 4.3   Experiments on MobileNetV1

MobileNetV1 is a popular single-branch network trained on ImageNet and it is known to be challenging to prune due to its compact design. As the layers of MobileNet consist of pairs of depth-wise convolution and point-wise convolution layers, we only consider the point-wise convolution layers when searching for the pruning policy, and the corresponding channels in the depth-wise layer will be removed accordingly. We also note that the first layer is not prunable as its channel should be in line with the input images, and similarly for the final linear. As a result, there are 13 parameters for BO to optimize. We prune 50% Flops and we divide the layers into 6 clusters.

In Table 4, we show the accuracy and corresponding $\sigma$ for the proposed methods on MobileNetV1. Similar to the result of ResNet56, BO-based methods achieve significantly better results than the RL agent. Our rollback-based BO can achieve the best top-1 accuracy of 52.7%, while the best top-1 accuracy of the RL counterparts is 50.2%. Additionally, the layer clustering-based BO outperforms the original BO agent by 1.1% and 0.9% in top-1 and top-5 accuracy. The rollback scheme further improves the accuracy by 0.9% and 0.5% in top-1 and top-5 accuracy, respectively. Note that it is normal that the $\sigma$ gets higher after rollback as the simple regret increases in high-dimensional space.

In Fig. 3b, we compare the three BO-based methods in detail. The layer clustering method speeds up the convergence of the BO agent significantly, based on which rollback scheme further improves the accuracy.

### 4.4   Experiments on MobileNetV2

We also validate our method on the modern efficient network MobileNetV2, which is trained on ImageNet. As an improved version of MobileNetV1, MobileNetV2 is even more compact than MobileNetV1, making it challenging to prune. It adopts an inverted residual structure while keeping the depth-wise and point-wise design, leading to complex architecture. We use the same experimental setting as in Sect. 4.2 and 4.3 for the residual structure and the depth & point-wise structure, and there are 18 parameters for the BO agent to optimize. We divide the layers into 6 clusters and preserve 60% Flops.

**Table 4.** Performance for MobileNetV1.

| Method | Top-1 $m$ | Top-1 $\sigma$ | Top-5 $m$ | Top-5 $\sigma$ |
|---|---|---|---|---|
| RL | 45.61 | 1.95 | 71.88 | 1.87 |
| Naive BO | 47.39 | 1.39 | 73.11 | 1.47 |
| Layer Clustering | 48.49 | 1.20 | 74.03 | 0.87 |
| Rollback | **49.34** | 2.01 | **74.52** | 1.66 |

**Table 5.** Performance for MobileNetV2.

| Method | Top-1 $m$ | Top-1 $\sigma$ | Top-5 $m$ | Top-5 $\sigma$ |
|---|---|---|---|---|
| RL | 43.15 | 5.45 | 69.84 | 5.01 |
| Naive BO | 51.09 | 1.97 | 77.13 | 1.33 |
| Layer Clustering | 52.57 | 0.98 | 78.45 | 1.12 |
| Rollback | **52.86** | 0.61 | **78.57** | 0.70 |

As shown in Fig. 3c, the layer clustering algorithm successfully boosts the convergence of BO, which is consistent with previous experiments. Table 5 shows that our layer clustering algorithm can raise the top-1 accuracy over the naive BO agent by 1.5% while achieving a much lower $\sigma$. Moreover, our method outperforms the RL-based counterpart by a large margin as RL can not converge within the same iterations for this challenging task.

However, the rollback method only improves the top-1 accuracy of layer clustering by 0.29% which is 3× lower than the previous experiments. The reason is that the original dimensionality of MobileNetV2 is higher than MobileNetV1, resulting in a learning gap after performing the direct rollback. This motivates us to develop the gradual rollback algorithm. Note that since the image size of Cifar10 is much smaller than ImageNet, the design space of ResNet56 is also smaller. Therefore, the learning gap is alleviated for ResNet56.

### 4.5   Gradual Rollback for Higher Dimensionality

In this section, we demonstrate the effectiveness of the gradual rollback scheme with experiments on MobileNetV2. Both the structure-based measure and Euclidean distance of distributions are included for the layer clustering phase. To be fair, the bridge stage $C^*$ is 15 for both experiments. Table 6 shows the top-1 accuracy achieved by the layer clustering algorithm and compares the improvement provided by rollback and gradual rollback. Results show that gradual rollback successfully mitigates the learning gap and outperforms direct rollback. Additionally, when an inferior measure is chosen for the layer clustering, gradual rollback can make up for it by significantly increasing the accuracy.

**Table 6.** Comparison between direct and gradual rollback.

| Models | Layer clustering | Direct Rollback | Gradual rollback |
| --- | --- | --- | --- |
| Structure | 51.06 | +0.41 | +1.60 |
| Euclidean | 52.57 | +0.29 | +0.44 |

**Table 7.** Comparison of different cluster numbers. In parentheses is the $\sigma$.

| Top1 | 4 | 5 | 6 | 7 | 8 | 9 |
| --- | --- | --- | --- | --- | --- | --- |
| MobiletNetV1 | 47.65 | 47.12 | **47.7 (0.65)** | 47.7 (2.19) | 45.82 | 46.27 |
| MobiletNetV2 | 49.48 | 50.6 | **52.11** | 50.93 | 50.95 | 50.43 |

### 4.6   Choice of the Cluster Number

The choice of the cluster number $C$ is a common problem for clustering algorithms. In this work, if $C$ is large, the sampling efficiency of BO will decrease. When $C$ is small, good pruning policies are more likely to be excluded from the searching space. For models with plain architecture like ResNet56, the number of different layers they contain is a good choice for $C$. However, there is no obvious choice of $C$ for complex models. To analyze the effect of $C$, we set $C$ to different values and test them on MobileNetV1 and MobileNetV2. As shown in Table 7, choices around 6 lead to the best results. Note that the architecture of MobileNetV1 and MobileNetV2 are quite different, showing the generality of this result. Therefore, cluster numbers around 6 are reasonable choices.

## 5    Conclusion

We have analyzed the similarity between the CNN layers and proposed a novel layer clustering algorithm to boost the sampling efficiency of BO for CNN pruning. To further improve the accuracy of the output pruning policy, we developed a rollback algorithm to recover high-dimensional design space and perform a fine-grained search with the data collected in the low-dimensional space as the prior knowledge. Our experiments have validated the effectiveness of the proposed algorithms. In the future, we intend to extend our work to other layer-wise pruning methods that measure the importance of channels with different metrics. We are also interested in the theoretical proof for the rollback algorithm.

**Acknowledgment.** We would like to thank the anonymous reviewers for their valuable comments. We also thank the Turing AI Computing Cloud (TACC) [43] and HKUST iSING Lab for providing us computation resources on their platform. This research was supported in part by Hong Kong Research Grants Council General Research Fund (Grant No. 16215319).

## References

1. Brochu, E., Cora, V.M., De Freitas, N.: A tutorial on Bayesian optimization of expensive cost functions, with application to active user modeling and hierarchical reinforcement learning. arXiv preprint arXiv:1012.2599 (2010)
2. Bull, A.D.: Convergence rates of efficient global optimization algorithms. J. Mach. Learn. Res. **12**(10), 2879–2904 (2011)
3. Chen, C., Tung, F., Vedula, N., Mori, G.: Constraint-aware deep neural network compression. In: Ferrari, V., Hebert, M., Sminchisescu, C., Weiss, Y. (eds.) ECCV 2018. LNCS, vol. 11212, pp. 409–424. Springer, Cham (2018). https://doi.org/10.1007/978-3-030-01237-3_25
4. Guo, Y., Yao, A., Chen, Y.: Dynamic network surgery for efficient DNNs. Advances in Neural Information Processing Systems, vol. 29 (2016)
5. Han, S., et al.: Learning both weights and connections for efficient neural network. In: Advances in Neural Information Processing Systems (2015)
6. Hayou, S., Ton, J.F., Doucet, A., Teh, Y.W.: Robust pruning at initialization. arXiv preprint arXiv:2002.08797 (2020)
7. He, K., Zhang, X., Ren, S., Sun, J.: Deep residual learning for image recognition. In: Proceedings of the IEEE Conference on Computer Vision and Pattern Recognition, pp. 770–778 (2016)

8. He, Y., et al.: Channel pruning for accelerating very deep neural networks. In: Proceedings of the IEEE ICCV (2017)
9. He, Y., Lin, J., Liu, Z., Wang, H., Li, L.-J., Han, S.: AMC: autoML for model compression and acceleration on mobile devices. In: Ferrari, V., Hebert, M., Sminchisescu, C., Weiss, Y. (eds.) ECCV 2018. LNCS, vol. 11211, pp. 815–832. Springer, Cham (2018). https://doi.org/10.1007/978-3-030-01234-2_48
10. Howard, A.G., et al.: MobileNets: efficient convolutional neural networks for mobile vision applications. arXiv preprint arXiv:1704.04861 (2017)
11. Hu, H., Peng, R., Tai, Y.W., Tang, C.K.: Network trimming: a data-driven neuron pruning approach towards efficient deep architectures. arXiv preprint arXiv:1607.03250 (2016)
12. Joe, S., Kuo, F.Y.: Remark on algorithm 659: implementing Sobol's quasirandom sequence generator. ACM Trans. Math. Soft. (TOMS) **29**(1), 49–57 (2003)
13. Joe, S., Kuo, F.Y.: Constructing Sobol sequences with better two-dimensional projections. SIAM J. Sci. Comput. **30**(5), 2635–2654 (2008)
14. Kandasamy, K., Schneider, J., Póczos, B.: High dimensional bayesian optimisation and bandits via additive models. In: International Conference on Machine Learning, pp. 295–304. PMLR (2015)
15. Krizhevsky, A., Sutskever, I., Hinton, G.E.: Imagenet classification with deep convolutional neural networks. Adv. Neural. Inf. Process. Syst. **25**, 1097–1105 (2012)
16. Letham, B., Calandra, R., Rai, A., Bakshy, E.: Re-examining linear embeddings for high-dimensional bayesian optimization. Adv. Neural. Inf. Process. Syst. **33**, 1546–1558 (2020)
17. Lillicrap, T.P., et al.: Continuous control with deep reinforcement learning. arXiv preprint arXiv:1509.02971 (2015)
18. Liu, N., Ma, X., Xu, Z., Wang, Y., Tang, J., Ye, J.: Autocompress: an automatic DNN structured pruning framework for ultra-high compression rates. In: Proceedings of the AAAI Conference on Artificial Intelligence, vol. 34, pp. 4876–4883 (2020)
19. Liu, Z., Mu, H., Zhang, X., Guo, Z., Yang, X., Cheng, K.T., Sun, J.: Metapruning: meta learning for automatic neural network channel pruning. In: Proceedings of the IEEE/CVF International Conference on Computer Vision, pp. 3296–3305 (2019)
20. Louizos, C., et al.: Learning sparse neural networks through $L_0$ regularization. arXiv preprint arXiv:1712.01312 (2017)
21. Ma, X., Blaschko, M.B.: Additive tree-structured conditional parameter spaces in Bayesian optimization: a novel covariance function and a fast implementation. IEEE Trans. Pattern Anal. Mach. Intell. **43**, 3024–3036 (2020)
22. Ma, X., Triki, A.R., Berman, M., Sagonas, C., Cali, J., Blaschko, M.B.: A bayesian optimization framework for neural network compression. In: Proceedings of the IEEE/CVF International Conference on Computer Vision, pp. 10274–10283 (2019)
23. Mockus, J., Mockus, L.: Bayesian approach to global optimization and application to multiobjective and constrained problems. J. Optim. Theory Appl. **70**(1), 157–172 (1991)
24. Mockus, J.: Application of bayesian approach to numerical methods of global and stochastic optimization. J. Global Optim. **4**(4), 347–365 (1994)
25. Mockus, J., Tiesis, V., Zilinskas, A.: The application of Bayesian methods for seeking the extremum. Towards Global Opt. **2**(117–129), 2 (1978)
26. Molchanov, P., Tyree, S., Karras, T., Aila, T., Kautz, J.: Pruning convolutional neural networks for resource efficient inference. arXiv preprint arXiv:1611.06440 (2016)
27. Müllner, D.: Modern hierarchical, agglomerative clustering algorithms. arXiv preprint arXiv:1109.2378 (2011)

28. Qian, H., Hu, Y.Q., Yu, Y.: Derivative-free optimization of high-dimensional non-convex functions by sequential random embeddings. In: IJCAI, pp. 1946–1952 (2016)
29. Rana, S., Li, C., Gupta, S., Nguyen, V., Venkatesh, S.: High dimensional Bayesian optimization with elastic gaussian process. In: International Conference on Machine Learning, pp. 2883–2891. PMLR (2017)
30. Rasmussen, C.E.: Gaussian processes in machine learning. In: Bousquet, O., von Luxburg, U., Rätsch, G. (eds.) ML -2003. LNCS (LNAI), vol. 3176, pp. 63–71. Springer, Heidelberg (2004). https://doi.org/10.1007/978-3-540-28650-9_4
31. Rolland, P., Scarlett, J., Bogunovic, I., Cevher, V.: High-dimensional bayesian optimization via additive models with overlapping groups. In: International Conference on Artificial Intelligence and Statistics, pp. 298–307. PMLR (2018)
32. Sandler, M., Howard, A., Zhu, M., Zhmoginov, A., Chen, L.C.: Mobilenetv 2: inverted residuals and linear bottlenecks. In: Proceedings of the IEEE Conference on Computer Vision and Pattern Recognition, pp. 4510–4520 (2018)
33. SheffieldML: Gpyopt: a Bayesian optimization framework in python. GuitHub (2016). https://github.com/SheffieldML/GPyOpt
34. Srinivas, S., Babu, R.V.: Data-free parameter pruning for deep neural networks. arXiv preprint arXiv:1507.06149 (2015)
35. Tung, F., Muralidharan, S., Mori, G.: Fine-pruning: joint fine-tuning and compression of a convolutional network with bayesian optimization. arXiv preprint arXiv:1707.09102 (2017)
36. Wang, K., et al.: HAQ: hardware-aware automated quantization with mixed precision. In: Proceedings of the IEEE Conference on CVPR, pp. 8612–8620 (2019)
37. Wang, Z., Li, C., Wang, X.: Convolutional neural network pruning with structural redundancy reduction. In: Proceedings of the IEEE/CVF Conference on Computer Vision and Pattern Recognition (CVPR), pp. 14913–14922 (2021)
38. Wang, Z., Li, C., Jegelka, S., Kohli, P.: Batched high-dimensional bayesian optimization via structural kernel learning. In: International Conference on Machine Learning, pp. 3656–3664. PMLR (2017)
39. Wang, Z., Hutter, F., Zoghi, M., Matheson, D., de Feitas, N.: Bayesian optimization in a billion dimensions via random embeddings. J. Artif. Intell. Res. **55**, 361–387 (2016)
40. Wang, Z., Zoghi, M., Hutter, F., Matheson, D., De Freitas, N., et al.: Bayesian optimization in high dimensions via random embeddings. In: IJCAI, pp. 1778–1784 (2013)
41. Ward, J.H., Jr.: Hierarchical grouping to optimize an objective function. J. Am. Stat. Assoc. **58**(301), 236–244 (1963)
42. Wen, W., Wu, C., Wang, Y., Chen, Y., Li, H.: Learning structured sparsity in deep neural networks. Advances in Neural Information Processing Systems, vol. 29 (2016)
43. Xu, K., et al.: TACC: a full-stack cloud computing infrastructure for machine learning tasks (2021)
44. Yu, R., et al.: NISP: pruning networks using neuron importance score propagation. In: Proceedings of the IEEE Conference on Computer Vision and Pattern Recognition, pp. 9194–9203 (2018)
45. Yu, S., Mazaheri, A., Jannesari, A.: Auto graph encoder-decoder for neural network pruning. In: Proceedings of the IEEE/CVF International Conference on Computer Vision, pp. 6362–6372 (2021)

46. Zhang, Y., Gao, S., Huang, H.: Exploration and estimation for model compression. In: Proceedings of the IEEE/CVF International Conference on Computer Vision (ICCV), pp. 487–496 (2021)
47. Zhuang, Z., et al.: Discrimination-aware channel pruning for deep neural networks. In: Advances in Neural Information Processing Systems (2018)

# Learned Variational Video Color Propagation

Markus Hofinger[1]([✉]) [iD], Erich Kobler[2] [iD], Alexander Effland[3] [iD],
and Thomas Pock[1] [iD]

[1] Institute of Computer Graphics and Vision, Graz University of Technology,
Graz, Austria
{markus.hofinger,pock}@icg.tugraz.at
[2] Institute of Computer Graphics, University of Linz, Linz, Austria
[3] Institute for Applied Mathematics, University of Bonn, Bonn, Germany

**Abstract.** In this paper, we propose a novel method for color propagation that is used to recolor gray-scale videos (e.g. historic movies). Our energy-based model combines deep learning with a variational formulation. At its core, the method optimizes over a set of plausible color proposals that are extracted from motion and semantic feature matches, together with a learned regularizer that resolves color ambiguities by enforcing spatial color smoothness. Our approach allows interpreting intermediate results and to incorporate extensions like using multiple reference frames even after training. We achieve state-of-the-art results on a number of standard benchmark datasets with multiple metrics and also provide convincing results on real historical videos – even though such types of video are not present during training. Moreover, a user evaluation shows that our method propagates initial colors more faithfully and temporally consistent.

**Keywords:** Video color propagation · Learned variational refinement

## 1 Introduction

Interestingly, adding color to monochromatic images is as old as photography itself [18]. Lately, even entire movies have been meticulously colorized [20], e.g. *They Shall Not Grow Old – Peter Jackson*, to make historic movies more accessible to audiences used to the high-quality imagery of today's cinema. An enormous manual effort has been spent to get the color of, for instance, gear or

---

Markus Hofinger and Erich Kobler are shared co-first authors. Source code can be found on https://github.com/VLOGroup/LVVCP.

---

**Supplementary Information** The online version contains supplementary material available at https://doi.org/10.1007/978-3-031-20050-2_30.

S. Avidan et al. (Eds.): ECCV 2022, LNCS 13683, pp. 512–530, 2022.
https://doi.org/10.1007/978-3-031-20050-2_30

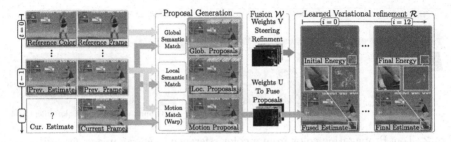

**Fig. 1.** Method overview: Video color propagation using color proposals from motion and semantic feature matching (to reference and prev. frame) are fused and then refined using a learned variational refinement. For details see page 516. Best viewed on screen.

uniforms correct from a historical perspective [31], which goes far beyond rough color guesses from pure fully automatic colorization.

One way of still keeping the colorization effort low is to avoid manual colorization of each frame but instead propagating the color from a single high quality manually colorized reference frame to subsequent frames. However, this also comes along with its own challenges, as can be seen at the top of Fig. 2. Here, a tree occludes parts of a car and simply propagating the color, as traditionally done using optical flow, leads to color artifacts at non-matched regions. Therefore, refinement is needed to keep results faithful over multiple frames.

Classical methods propose to solve this problem by setting up energy-based optimization problems [32] which assume that similar gray regions exhibit the same color, while at the same time enforcing color smoothness by using *hand-crafted* edge-aware regularizers [43]. Iteratively solving these optimization problems leads to smooth results with inpainted occlusions. Recent works demonstrate that a *deep learning* inspired total deep variation (TDV) regularizer $\mathcal{R}$ can outperform *hand-crafted* regularizers on various image restoration tasks [26,44]. Indeed, a TDV regularizer can be taught to inpaint color in an edge-aware fashion, as shown in a proof of concept in Fig. 2 (second row). Recently, deep learning-based approaches were proposed that transfer colors without optimization but rather use CNNs to regress colors based on color proposals from deep feature matches to the reference [38,60], or use CNNs for temporal smoothing [30].

In this work, we therefore propose a novel method that combines the benefits of deep learning and optimization based methods. We use colors warped by motion together with alternative plausible color proposals. These are generated via deep feature matches to the global reference frame and to the previous colorized frame, which is more local in time and therefore more similar. All these estimates are subsequently fused in a data-driven manner and further refined in an unrolled optimization scheme using a learned modified TDV regularizer. Moreover, the whole optimization process is steered by image-dependent data-driven weights, which are independently estimated for each image by a CNN termed WeightNet. Thus, our energy-based model learns to refine the color estimates and to resolve color ambiguities among the different color proposals. In

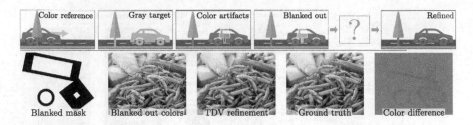

**Fig. 2.** Top: Propagating color from a color reference to a gray image according to the object motion (optical flow) leads to artifacts. These need to be detected and filled. Bottom: Proof of concept. A learned TDV is able to restore missing colors edge-aware. (Color figure online)

particular, the mathematical structure leads to interpretable and user overrideable intermediate results. Overall, the main contributions are as follows:

- Generation of multiple plausible color proposals of different types (global/local) by a sophisticated feature-matching process as well as motion.
- Learned color proposal fusion and guiding of the subsequently learned variational refinement to resolve ambiguities among numerous color proposals.
- Variational structure improves mathematical controllability and interpretable intermediate results allowing extensions to the method even after training.
- State-of-the-art results on several video color propagation datasets, metrics and promising qualitative results also validated by a user evaluation.

## 2    Related Work

Video color propagation is closely related to image colorization. While classic image colorization propagates color information spatially within one image, video color propagation additionally has to incorporate multiple frames. In literature, diverse colorization approaches exist that can be roughly classified into interactive [32,59,63], reference or exemplar-based [17,23,25,38,40,53,57], and fully automatic methods [11,22,48,61]. Our method is reference-based.

*Interactive* methods rely on some kind of user input, e.g. scribbles, defining the color for selected image pixels. Classically, the color of the remaining pixels is determined by diffusing color over the image or between frames using a locally adaptive distance, based on handcrafted similarity measures such as luminance [4,32], geodesic distance [59], or texture features [1,35,46]. Later, the amount of required user interaction was reduced by learning image-specific similarity measures using, for instance, local linear embeddings [10], iterative feature discrimination [58], or CNNs [14]. Motivated by the success of deep learning [29] and the availability of large-scale image datasets [34,49], Zhang et al. [63] learned a deep CNN that colorizes an image given either scribbles or a color histogram.

In contrast to the aforementioned approaches, *reference-based* methods utilize a reference image to transfer its colors to similar regions within a destination frame. Initial approaches transferred the color from the reference image solely based on luminance [47] and texture similarity [57], which often lead to spatially varying colors within an image region. Thus, optimization-based spatial regularization techniques were introduced to refine a coarse colorization based on correspondences [5,9,23,40,43]. Charpiat et al. [9] rephrased the colorization problem as a discrete labeling problem and resolved local ambiguities by minimizing a Markov random field (MRF) energy, which resulted in a spatially consistent image with discrete colors with a final variational refinement. Pierre et al. [40,43] advocated a variational method utilizing a hand-crafted regularizer favoring spatially consistent colors, and a dataterm for plausible pixel color proposals. They further extended this explicitly to video [41] by integrating motion-based color proposals from PatchMatch [3] and TV-$\ell_1$ optical flow [7]. Soon after, VPN [25] used a completely different deep learning-based approach using learnable bilateral filters to propagate color in videos. Other deep learning approaches tailored to videos followed [21,38,60]. These methods computed correspondences based on deep features [16,51] of the gray-scale images. Interestingly, Vondrick et al. [56] showed that networks learned tracking when trained on color propagation. DeepRemaster [21] utilized a temporal attention mechanism to colorize historic videos for a given example image. Deep image analogy [33] developed a PatchMatch for deep features, bridging larger domain gaps. He et al. [17] extended this approach for exemplar-based image colorization, filling non-matched regions using a CNN trained on a large database. The video extension DEB [60] focused on automatic exemplar-based video colorization by using not necessarily related exemplar images as references, allowing color deviations from the reference. In contrast, DVCP [38] payed close attention to staying close to the reference by combining motion estimation and feature-based matching to the global reference frame to avoid color drifts. Our method also focuses on staying faithful to the colors from a provided high quality reference.

*Fully automatic* colorization approaches predict reasonable colors without user input by learning on large-scale image datasets [34,49]. While classical methods are based on, e.g., conditional Gaussian random fields [13], more recent approaches [28,48,52,61] proposed different CNN architectures to address the multi-modality of colorization and introduced semantics from different perspectives. These colorization techniques relied on, e.g. semantic features [22], the prediction of a color histogram for each pixel of a gray-scale image [28,61], variational refinement [39], autoregressive neural networks [48], conditional variational autoencoders [12], conditional GANs [6,24], a color diversity loss [30], or conditional autoregressive transformers [27]. In contrast to automatic colorization, we focus on faithful propagation of high-quality references.

For further details on colorization and color propagation, we recommend the surveys [2,15,42], for (learnable) variational refinement [8,26].

## 3   Method

*Overview.* As shown in detail in Fig 1, our method propagates color from a given color reference frame sequentially to the following gray-scale frames. To avoid the aforementioned motion artifacts, our model fuses and refines diverse color proposals of various sources to a final color estimate. In detail, we extract multiple color proposals with confidences, for each pixel of a frame based on semantic matches to the Global reference frame and the already colorized previous (Local) frame. Further, we also use the Motion-compensated previous frame as color proposal. All these different color proposals are fused into an initial color estimate via a learned WeightNet $\mathcal{W}$. Then, this estimate is refined by unrolling an energy-based optimization algorithm that facilitates the learned edge-aware total deep variation (TDV [26]) regularizer $\mathcal{R}$. The optimization is further guided by pixel-wise weights, provided by $\mathcal{W}$ for each frame. Further details on proposal generation, fusion, and refinement are given in Sects. 3.1, 3.2 and 3.3, respectively.

*Setup and Notation.* We primarily operate in the CIE-Lab color space $\Omega^{lab}$ as it mimicks the human color perception. *Color images* like the ground truth $y$, the color estimate $x$, or the color proposals $c$ always refer to $ab$ channels, if no other channel subscript is given like in $y_g$ (original gray-scale), $y_l$ (CIE-Lab luminance) or $y_{lab}$. The *numbers of* pixels is denoted by $N_P$, pyramid levels by $N_J$, color proposals by $N_M/N_G/N_L$ and training frame augmentations by $N_A$ and we frequently use corresponding subscripts $(p, j, \ldots)$ as indices. Further, to index the *color proposal types* (Motion, Global, Local) we use $\gamma \in \{M, G, L\}$, i.e. $c_M$ denotes a motion color proposal, while $c_\gamma$ is a generic placeholder for any color proposal type. In addition, we indicate the pixel-wise product using broadcasting over color channels by $\odot$. To ease notation, we frequently omit the frame superscript $t$ if clear from the context.

### 3.1   Color Proposal Generation and Matching

In this section, we describe, how we generate our three color proposal *types* (see Fig. 1). In a nutshell, we bilinearly interpolate colors from matched positions in either the global reference $t = 0$ (G), or the previously colorized frame $t-1$ (L,M). On the previous (Local) frame we extract proposals via feature matching $C_L$ and via Motion $C_M$. We also use feature matching to the Global reference $C_G$. Each feature matching yields multiple proposals per pixel along with a confidence. The following paragraphs elaborate on the details.

For our color proposals based on *motion* $C_M$, we use RAFT [54] to estimate motion $m_M$ between the current frame $y_g^t$ and its previous frame $y_g^{t-1}$. We further compute the forward-backward motion difference $\delta_M$ for occlusion reasoning (following [19, suppl. Equation 10]), and also use it as a confidence, as motion provides wrong colors for occluded areas. To provide plausible colors for such areas, we use semantic feature matching, described next.

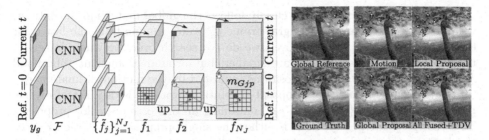

**Fig. 3.** Left: Global matching procedure for gray-scale images $y_g^t$ and $y_g^0$ using a feature pyramid $\{\tilde{f}_j^t\}_{j=1}^{N_J}$ with $N_J$-levels of features $\tilde{f}_j^t$. Right: Results of colorizing multiple frames with a single color proposal type (noisy) vs. our learned fusion $\mathcal{W}$ and TDV refinement; Mind the errors on the fast moving background. (Color figure online)

Our *global semantic matching* to the reference $y_g^0$, finds and refines $N_G$ best matches using a CNN feature encoder $\mathcal{F}$. In detail, we convert each gray frame to a pyramid of semantic features $\{f_j^t\}_{j=1}^{N_J} = \mathcal{F}(y_g^t)$ with different spatial resolutions on $N_J$ levels, as seen on the left in Fig. 3. Ablation experiments (see suppl.) revealed that VGG16 with batchnorm pre-trained for classification works best. We use instance normalization [55] yielding features $\tilde{f}$ of similar magnitude. For each pixel location $p$ within $\tilde{f}_j^t$, we search in locations $q$ around a neighborhood $\mathcal{N}(p)$ in the corresponding features $\tilde{f}_j^0$ of the reference image $y_g^0$, i.e.

$$\hat{k}_{Gjp}^t = \max_{q \in \mathcal{N}(p)} \left\{ \text{ReLU} \left( \left\langle \frac{\tilde{f}_{jp}^t}{\|\tilde{f}_{jp}^t\|_2}, \frac{\tilde{f}_{jq}^0}{\|\tilde{f}_{jq}^0\|_2} \right\rangle \right) \right\}. \tag{1}$$

Here, $\hat{k}_{Gjp}$ is the best global confidence for each pixel $p$ of the current level $j$, using a truncated normalized cross correlation. We define $m_{Gjp}$ as the according match (2D offset: $q - p$) that maximized $\hat{k}_{Gjp}$. The search process is repeated on the next finer level, centered around the position indicated by the upsampled $m_{Gjp}$. We use nearest neighbor upsampling and rescale to compensate the larger pixel spacing. Repeating this for all pixels and levels leads to a field of dense matches $m_G$ on the final level. While we use the whole image as the search neighborhood $\mathcal{N}(p)$ on the coarsest level, we restrict $\mathcal{N}(p)$ to $\pm 2$ pixels for refinement on the finer levels (see Fig 3). On the finest level we compute a final confidence by multiplying all confidences, using nearest neighbor upsampling ($\uparrow$), i.e.

$$k_G = \prod_{j=1}^{N_j} \uparrow^{N_j} (\hat{k}_{Gj}). \tag{2}$$

The corresponding Global color proposal $c_G$ for each match and pixel is computed by sampling from the color reference $y^0$ using the matched positions $m_G$. The global matching and refinement process is repeated $N_G$ times, using the $N_G$ most confident matches on the coarsest level. This yields a set of $C_G = \{c_G^n\}_{n=1}^{N_G}$ color proposal images, with a corresponding set of final confidences $K_G$.

The *Local matching* process closely follows the global matching. In contrast, we match against the *previous* gray frame $y_g^{t-1}$ and sample from the last color estimate $x^{t-1}$ to get $C_L$. Moreover, we do not search over the whole image on the coarsest level, as motions are smaller, but around a small neighborhood $\mathcal{N}(p) = \pm 8$ pixels around the positions indicated by the motion estimate $m_M$.

To summarize, our color proposal generation process yields a set of diverse proposal types $C = \{C_M, C_G, C_L\}$, containing all one or more color proposals. The *best proposal* per type $\hat{c}_\gamma$, is either the single proposal for motion $\hat{c}_M$, or the best via the pixel-wise confidence, yielding $\hat{c}_G$ or $\hat{c}_L$. To compare the differences of the proposal types, we propagate colors using each type's best proposal separately over many frames, see Fig. 3. While motion color proposals bleed into occluded areas, local proposals have less accumulated errors. Global proposals allow fixing objects that were occluded for multiple frames, like the leaves on the right, but at the cost of higher base noise. Fusing the color proposals in each step together with our learned refinement yields the best result as described next.

### 3.2   Initial Fusion with Weight Network

Since the color proposal types have very different properties (see Fig. 3), we use a CNN based UNet termed WeightNet $\mathcal{W}$ (details in suppl.) to fuse the initial best color proposals $(\hat{c}_M, \hat{c}_L, \hat{c}_G)$ using pixel-wise weights $U = \{u_M, u_G, u_L, u_0\}$. Moreover, we use $\mathcal{W}$ to predict an additional set of pixel-wise weights $V = \{v_M, v_G, v_L, v_0, v_\mathcal{R}\}$ to locally guide the subsequent variational refinement. To enable a propagation of weights across multiple frames, we also feed the (motion compensated) $U^{t-1}$ and $V^{t-1}$ from the previous frame into $\mathcal{W}$, i.e.

$$(U^t, V^t) = \mathcal{W}_\theta(y_l^t, \widehat{Z}^t, U^{t-1}, V^{t-1}). \tag{3}$$

Here, $y_l^t$ is the current frame's luminance, $\widehat{Z}^t$ concatenates the best color proposal per pixel for each proposal type, together with its associated confidence or motion delta $\delta_M$ and absolute luminance difference. All weights $U^t$ and $V^t$ have a pixel value in $[0, 1]$. Using the fusion weights $U^t$, the initial color estimate reads as

$$x^{t,0} = \sum\nolimits_{\gamma \in \{M,G,L\}} u_\gamma^t \odot \hat{c}_\gamma^t, \tag{4}$$

which essentially implements a pixel-wise soft-selection of the best type of color proposals $\hat{c}_\gamma^t$ or no proposal at all, since we enforce for each pixel that

$$\sum\nolimits_{\gamma \in \{M,G,L\}} u_{\gamma,p}^t \le 1, \qquad \sum\nolimits_{\gamma \in \{M,G,L\}} v_{\gamma,p}^t \le 1. \tag{5}$$

This is implemented via a pixelwise softmax using $u_0$ and $v_0$ allowing inequality.

Hence, $\mathcal{W}$ can blend colors or fade them out if all matches seem implausible. Recall that the best color proposal of each type $\hat{c}_\gamma^t$ is defined as the one whose associated pixel-wise confidence is maximal. Since only the best color proposal of each type $\hat{c}_\gamma^t$ is fed into the WeightNet, we can adapt the number of proposal per pixel individually for each type without any retraining. This also holds true for the subsequent learned variational refinement, which even uses the full set of proposals $C$, allowing it to undo initial wrong choices, as we will elaborate next.

## 3.3    Learned Variational Refinement

This section describes the details of our learned variational refinement, which we perform independently for each frame. In a nutshell, our model uses an unrolled optimization algorithm, to decrease an energy $\mathcal{E}$ consisting of a dataterm energy $\mathcal{D}$ that models coherence to the color proposals, and a total deep variation regularizer (TDV [26]) $\mathcal{R}$ that learns to model spatial color smoothness. The whole process is steered by pixel-wise weights provided by WeightNet $\mathcal{W}$, and automatically picks the best reference, as we will explain in the following.

In detail, we combine and extend the approaches [26,43] and let

$$\mathcal{E}(x) = \mathcal{D}(x, \mathrm{C}) + \mathcal{R}_\theta(x, y_l) \tag{6}$$

be our learnable energy, which is a function of the current color estimate $x$. Here, $y_l$ is the current frames luminance, and $\mathrm{C} = \{\mathrm{C}_M, \mathrm{C}_G, \mathrm{C}_L\}$ the set of all color proposal types. For example, $\mathrm{C}_G = \{c_G^n\}_{n=1}^{N_G}$ denotes the global color proposal, which already provides $N_G$ different proposals per pixel. The regularizer

$$\mathcal{R}_\theta(x, y_l) = \sum_{p=1}^{N_P} \mathrm{v}_{\mathcal{R},p} \cdot r_\theta(x, y_l)_p. \tag{7}$$

is weighted per pixel $p$ with a scalar weight $\mathrm{v}_{\mathcal{R},p} \in [0, 1]$ generated by Weight-Net $\mathcal{W}$. Therefore, $\mathcal{W}$ can allow to preserve high frequency textures in regions of high confidence and rely on the regularizer in uncertain regions. The regularizer itself, is a special twice differentiable UNet, detailed in TDV [26], with learnable parameters $\theta$. Similar to the regularizer, the dataterm

$$\mathcal{D}(x, \mathrm{C}) = \sum_{\gamma \in \{M,L,G\}} \lambda_\gamma \sum_{p=1}^{N_P} \mathrm{v}_{\gamma,p} \cdot d(x_p, \mathrm{C}_{\gamma,p}) \tag{8}$$

also consists of a weighted combination of the pixel-wise dataterms $d$ of each proposal type (M,L,G). The learned scalars $\lambda_\gamma \in \mathbb{R}^+$ balance the different dataterm types based on dataset statistics, and the scalar fields $\mathrm{v}_\gamma$ are again predicted by WeightNet $\mathcal{W}$. This allows $\mathcal{W}$ to shift attention between the dataterms of the proposal types, focusing on the most trusted type for each pixel.

While a standard $\ell_2$ dataterm uses a single fixed reference, we use a multi-well dataterm which automatically chooses the best reference from the $N_\gamma$ proposals per pixel. This means for each pixel $p$ we use the dataterm

$$d(x_p, \{c_{\gamma,p}^n\}_{n=1}^{N_\gamma}) = \min_{\tilde{c}_p \in \{c_{\gamma,p}^n\}_{n=1}^{N_\gamma}} \|x_p - \tilde{c}_p\|_2^2. \tag{9}$$

Hence, although the color proposal fusion only used the *best* proposal based on confidences, this multi-well dataterm can still choose from *all* proposals per pixel and type. Therefore, the optimization scheme does not only refine $x$ but also cleans the dataterm reference from initial color noise as illustrated in Fig. 4.

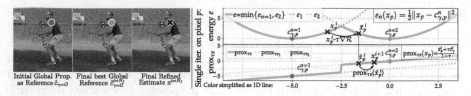

**Fig. 4.** Auto-selection of closest dataterm reference: Left shows how initial noisy ref. updates to a better option per pixel, easing TDV refinement of $x$. Right, details on the marked pixel's iterative update: Multi-well dataterm energy $e$ is a simplification of (9) for single pixel $x_p$. A step on $\nabla\mathcal{R}$ improves colors of estimate $x_p^i \to \bar{x}_p^i$, away from wrong blue ref. $c_{\gamma,p}^{n=1}$. The dataterm energy $e_2$ of proposal $c_{\gamma,p}^{n=2}$ is now lower than $e_1$, leading to the reference update. Hence, $\mathrm{prox}_{\tau e}$ now uses the better orange ref. $c_{\gamma,p}^{n=2}$ for $\tilde{c}_\gamma^i$.

Given the overall energy (6), our model refines the initial fused $x^0$ using $N_I$ unrolled iterations of a proximal gradient scheme [8]. A step on $\nabla\mathcal{R}$ for spatial color smoothness, is followed by a proximal dataterm step, updating $x^i$ to

$$x^{i+1} = \mathrm{prox}_{\tau\mathcal{D}}\left(\bar{x}^i\right) = \mathrm{prox}_{\tau\mathcal{D}}\left(x^i - \tau\nabla_1\mathcal{R}_\theta(x^i, y_l)\right) \tag{10}$$

in each iteration $i$. We use the proximal map

$$\mathrm{prox}_{\tau\mathcal{D}}\left(\bar{x}^i\right) = \frac{\bar{x}^i + \tau\sum_{\gamma\in\{M,G,L\}}\lambda_\gamma\mathrm{v}_\gamma\odot\tilde{c}_\gamma^i}{1 + \tau\sum_{\gamma\in\{M,G,L\}}\lambda_\gamma\mathrm{v}_\gamma}, \tag{11}$$

where $\mathrm{prox}_{\tau\mathcal{D}}$ is basically a convex combination of the intermediate estimate $\bar{x}^i$ and its currently closest color proposal per proposal type $\tilde{c}_\gamma^i$, with $\odot$ being the pixel-wise product with broadcasting along color channels (derivation in suppl.).

To summarize, our iterative approach refines the initial fused most confident color proposals, and enables an automatic adaption of the dataterm references in each iteration. Hence, if a regularizer update changes noisy pixels to favor color smoothness, the dataterms can change their pixel-wise color references $\hat{c}_{\gamma,p}$ from an initial most confident but noisy value to the best in the set of all proposals per type $C_{\gamma,p}$ for each pixel $p$. Finally, the interplay of all parts is shown in Fig. 5, where $\tilde{M}_O^t$ indicates occluded regions as explained in the supplementary.

### 3.4    Training

For training, we use an MSE loss in the $ab$ space, in combination with online-hard-example-mining (OHEM [50]) to focus on the 25% most difficult pixels per image, as most regions soon work very well. We train on a batch of frame pairs. In addition, we use the estimated result as augmented input (gradient-stopped) for the next frame and repeat this $N_A$ times to simulate realistic artifact accumulation. Although this teaches our model real artifacts, extreme cases can occur in the initial training phase, which would require a heuristic increase of the number of propagated frames with training duration. To avoid this, we rescale

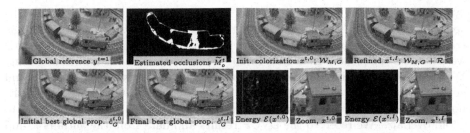

**Fig. 5.** Color refinement example; The backside of the train is initially occluded $(\tilde{M}_O^t)$; $\mathcal{W}$ fuses the initially most confident color proposals, which can contain noise; An unrolled optimization $(I = 12)$ with learned TDV further refines results for smooth colors.

the loss of each frame pair based on an oracle estimating the best currently possible initial proposal $\hat{c}_o^{t,0}$ from all proposals via

$$\hat{c}_{p,o}^{t,0} = \underset{c \in \{c_M^t, c_{G1}^t, \dots, c_{GN_k}^t, c_{L1}^t, \dots, c_{LN_k}^t\}}{\mathrm{argmin}} \|c_p - y_p^t\|_2, \tag{12}$$

$$\mathcal{L}_o(x,y) = \sum_{t=1}^{N_A} \frac{\mathcal{L}(x^t, y^t)}{\varepsilon_o + \mathcal{L}\left(\hat{c}_o^{t,0}, y^t\right)}, \tag{13}$$

where we set $\varepsilon_o$ to roughly 1% of the loss the model generates without loss rescaling and use $N_A = 5$ as default. To speed-up training, we pre-compute the gray-scale matches and train only $\mathcal{W}$ and $\mathcal{R}$. However, our method allows for full end-to-end training. Further details on training can be found in the supplementary material.

*Multimodel Training.* Using more proposal *types* for $\mathcal{W}$ typically provides better initial estimates. However, this also means that fewer errors remain for the TDV regularizer to train on. Hence, we propose to train a *shared regularizer* $\mathcal{R}$ with $\mathcal{W}$ using different color proposal types e.g. $\mathcal{W}_{M,G}$ and $\mathcal{W}_{M,G,L}$ at the same time. This allows to train $\mathcal{R}$ with a much wider variety of hard and easy cases.

## 4    Experiments

In this section, we show various quantitative and qualitative experimental results. Further ablation results, interactive experiments, and a discussion of limitations can be found in the supplementary material. The source code is on github.

*Baselines and datasets.* As baselines we use three color propagation methods VPN [25], DeepRemaster [21] and DVCP [38], as well as the exemplar-based colorization method DEB [60]. As DeepRemaster and DEB require image sizes to be a multiple of 32, we zero-pad the inputs and crop the results for them.

We report results on multiple datasets. For training and evaluation, we use the splits of DAVIS 2017 [45] as defined in the VPN [25] codebase. It consists of 35 training and 15 evaluation sequences of 25 consecutive frames each. For testing we use the 27 sequences from DAVIS-2017-test that are at least 45 frames long. We resample the original high-resolution sources to remove JPG artifacts and get highest quality ground-truth. Furthermore, we report results on NDVCP, the non-DAVIS subset from the test-set of [38] (55 videos of 45+ frames; Fig. 7) to avoid overlaps. We received the DVCP results and data from the authors[1] , and re-ran all open source methods. For datasets where we did not receive DVCP results (e.g. DAVIS-2017-test), we picked the next best open source method.

*Metrics.* In literature, metrics are computed quite differently, e.g. PSNR with different color spaces and normalizations [25,38], or showing averages over the first t frames [38] vs. reporting each step t [60], which prevents direct comparisons. Hence, to ensure fairness, we identically compute all metrics on the results of all methods. We compute PSNR over the CIE-Lab *ab* color channels ($PSNR_{ab}$), as the luminance is fixed (details in suppl.). Furthermore, we report CIDE2000 [36] in the supplementary. Finally, we compute the open source LPIPS metric [62], which corresponds well to human perception on patch level.

*Comparison on DAVIS.* Fig. 6 shows our results and ablations on DAVIS-2017-val [25]. Using our fused proposal generation ($N_G = N_L = 8$) alone already outperforms some baselines such as VPN or Levin. From the color proposals, $\hat{c}_L^{t,0}$ works best up to roughly 11 frames, when global color proposals perform better as they do not accumulate errors. Fusing motion and global color proposals ($\mathcal{W}_{M,G}$) already outperforms all baselines, and adding regularization ($\mathcal{W}_{M,G} + \mathcal{R}$) yields further improvement. Adding local color proposals further enhances results on initial frames. Training with frame propagation augmentation over 9 frames ($\mathcal{W}_{M,G,L} + \mathcal{R} + N_A = 9$) improves the long-range quality, without adding additional inference time. Using $N_G = N_L = 3$ ('fast') reduces inference time at similar performance. Performance improves further with multimodel training 'mm'. Hence, we use these two models for all further comparisons.

*Comparison on NDVCP and DAVIS-2017-test Dataset.*
Using the previously best methods, we computed results also on larger and longer datasets. Figure 7 shows results for $PSNR_{ab}$ (higher is better) of all pixels as well as on occluded areas for both datasets separately. The occlusions are estimated using the heuristic from [37] (see supplementary for details). Even though we train only on the 35 DAVIS sequences, we greatly outperform the baselines on both datasets also in occlusions. In addition, we compute the perceptual metric LPIPS (v0.1 VGG) [62], and also there our method outperformes the baselines by a clear margin (Fig. 8).

---

[1]  We thank DVCP authors for the data. As their results exclude the DAVIS-2017-val video *mallard-water*, we also omit it for fair comparison resulting in 14 sequences.

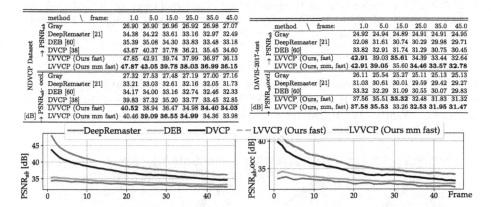

| method \ frame: | 1.0 | 5.0 | 10.0 | 15.0 | 20.0 | 24.0 |
|---|---|---|---|---|---|---|
| Gray | 25.30 | 25.40 | 25.49 | 25.46 | 25.59 | 25.60 |
| VPN | 29.74 | 28.65 | 27.84 | 27.69 | 27.51 | 26.99 |
| Levin | 39.35 | 33.76 | 30.94 | 29.27 | 28.40 | 27.78 |
| DeepRemaster | 32.30 | 31.88 | 31.52 | 31.22 | 31.03 | 30.71 |
| DEB | 34.67 | 33.57 | 32.80 | 31.93 | 31.86 | 31.58 |
| DVCP | 39.40 | 35.88 | 34.57 | 33.43 | 33.09 | 32.89 |
| $c_M^{t,0}$ Motion Cand. | 40.52 | 35.42 | 32.78 | 31.20 | 30.27 | 29.46 |
| $c_L^{t,0}$ Local Cand. | 42.06 | 36.87 | 34.29 | 32.59 | 31.69 | 30.90 |
| $c_G^{t,0}$ Global Cand. | 41.00 | 35.70 | 33.88 | 32.83 | 32.15 | 31.52 |
| $\mathcal{W}_{M,G}$ | 43.46 | 39.10 | 36.81 | 35.35 | 34.83 | 34.20 |
| $\mathcal{W}_{M,G}+\mathcal{R}$ | 44.05 | 39.90 | 37.60 | 36.21 | 35.69 | 35.01 |
| $\mathcal{W}_{M,G,L}+\mathcal{R}$ | **44.27** | 40.19 | 37.91 | 36.38 | 35.76 | 35.05 |
| $\mathcal{W}_{M,G,L}+\mathcal{R}+N_A$=9 | 44.25 | 40.18 | 37.94 | **36.44** | 35.86 | 35.16 |
| $\mathcal{W}_{M,G,L}+\mathcal{R}+N_A$=9, fast, mm | 44.19 | 40.15 | 37.92 | 36.37 | 35.87 | 35.20 |
| $\mathcal{W}_{M,G,L}+\mathcal{R}+N_A$=9, fast, mm | 44.17 | **40.20** | **37.97** | 36.42 | **35.91** | **35.23** |

**Fig. 6.** $\text{PSNR}_{ab}$ on DAVIS-2017-val Dataset; Already our weakest model $\mathcal{W}_{MG}$, outperforms all baselines. Adding refinement ($\mathcal{W}_{MG} + \mathcal{R}$), adds further improvements.

| method \ frame: | 1.0 | 5.0 | 15.0 | 25.0 | 35.0 | 45.0 |
|---|---|---|---|---|---|---|
| Gray | 26.90 | 26.90 | 26.96 | 26.92 | 26.98 | 27.07 |
| DeepRemaster [21] | 34.38 | 34.22 | 33.61 | 33.16 | 32.97 | 32.49 |
| DEB [60] | 35.39 | 35.08 | 34.30 | 33.83 | 33.48 | 33.18 |
| DVCP [38] | 43.67 | 40.37 | 37.78 | 36.21 | 35.45 | 34.60 |
| LVVCP (Ours fast) | 47.85 | 42.91 | 39.74 | 37.99 | 36.97 | 36.13 |
| LVVCP (Ours mm fast) | **47.87** | **43.05** | **39.78** | **38.03** | **36.99** | **36.15** |
| Gray | 27.32 | 27.53 | 27.48 | 27.19 | 27.00 | 27.16 |
| DeepRemaster [21] | 33.21 | 33.03 | 32.61 | 32.16 | 32.05 | 31.73 |
| DEB [60] | 34.17 | 34.00 | 33.16 | 32.74 | 32.46 | 32.33 |
| DVCP [38] | 39.83 | 37.32 | 35.20 | 33.77 | 33.45 | 32.85 |
| LVVCP (Ours fast) | **40.52** | 38.94 | 36.47 | 34.98 | **34.40** | **34.03** |
| LVVCP (Ours mm fast) | 40.46 | **39.09** | **36.55** | **34.99** | 34.36 | 33.98 |

| method \ frame: | 1.0 | 5.0 | 15.0 | 25.0 | 35.0 | 45.0 |
|---|---|---|---|---|---|---|
| Gray | 24.92 | 24.94 | 24.89 | 24.91 | 24.91 | 24.95 |
| DeepRemaster [21] | 32.08 | 31.61 | 30.74 | 30.29 | 29.98 | 29.71 |
| DEB [60] | 33.82 | 32.91 | 31.74 | 31.29 | 30.75 | 30.45 |
| LVVCP (Ours, fast) | **42.91** | 39.03 | **35.61** | 34.39 | 33.44 | 32.64 |
| LVVCP (Ours, mm, fast) | 42.91 | **39.05** | 35.60 | **34.46** | **33.57** | **32.78** |
| Gray | 26.11 | 25.54 | 25.27 | 25.11 | 25.13 | 25.13 |
| DeepRemaster [21] | 31.03 | 30.61 | 30.01 | 29.59 | 29.42 | 29.27 |
| DEB [60] | 33.32 | 32.29 | 31.09 | 30.55 | 30.07 | 29.83 |
| LVVCP (Ours, mm, fast) | **37.56** | **35.51** | **33.32** | 32.48 | 31.83 | 31.32 |
| LVVCP (Ours, mm, fast) | **37.58** | **35.53** | 33.26 | **32.53** | **31.95** | **31.47** |

**Fig. 7.** $\text{PSNR}_{ab}(\uparrow)$ on NDVCP and DAVIS-2017-test datasets. Top of each table = all pixels; Bottom = occluded regions only; Graph shows results on NDVCP subset. Performance in occluded regions is lower for all methods; We still outperform all baselines.

| method \ frame: | 1.0 | 5.0 | 15.0 | 25.0 | 35.0 | 45.0 |
|---|---|---|---|---|---|---|
| Gray | 0.1216 | 0.1220 | 0.1219 | 0.1227 | 0.1230 | 0.1216 |
| DeepRemaster [21] | 0.0723 | 0.0734 | 0.0773 | 0.0795 | 0.0820 | 0.0839 |
| DEB [60] | 0.0568 | 0.0585 | 0.0628 | 0.0656 | 0.0687 | 0.0710 |
| DVCP [38] | 0.0127 | 0.0246 | 0.0361 | 0.0445 | 0.0505 | 0.0559 |
| LVVCP (Ours fast) | 0.0067 | 0.0162 | 0.0274 | 0.0351 | 0.0418 | 0.0465 |
| LVVCP (Ours mm fast) | **0.0065** | **0.0155** | **0.0267** | **0.0344** | **0.0410** | **0.0455** |

| method \ frame: | 1.0 | 5.0 | 15.0 | 25.0 | 35.0 | 45.0 |
|---|---|---|---|---|---|---|
| Gray | 0.1569 | 0.1569 | 0.1575 | 0.1551 | 0.1553 | 0.1534 |
| DeepRemaster | 0.0872 | 0.0908 | 0.0979 | 0.1001 | 0.1019 | 0.1036 |
| DEB | 0.0635 | 0.0705 | 0.0775 | 0.0803 | 0.0814 | 0.0854 |
| LVVCP (Ours, fast) | **0.0161** | 0.0310 | 0.0470 | 0.0544 | 0.0612 | 0.0677 |
| LVVCP (Ours, mm, fast) | **0.0161** | **0.0305** | **0.0463** | **0.0525** | **0.0585** | **0.0649** |

**Fig. 8.** LPIPS [62] ($\downarrow$ lower is better ) on NDVCP (Left) and DAVIS-2017-test (Right); Both our models with and without multimodel training show lowest perceptual errors.

*User Evaluation.* To better asses the quality of the models for our task of faithful video color propagation, we asked 30 users to rate the models on the DAVIS-2017-val and DAVIS-2017-test sets Fig. 9. Each video was converted to grayscale and recolored by different methods given the ground-truth colored first frame. In particular, we asked the users which method propagates the colors from the still image reference most faithfully and consistent over time. The users then had to rank the methods from best to worst for each video sequence independently. Figure 9 shows how often each method ranked from best (green) to worst (red). As can be seen the users clearly prefer our method with a consistent large gap.

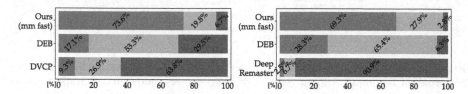

**Fig. 9.** User evaluation; Our method ranks best more than twice as the baselines; Left = DAVIS 2017 val, Right = DAVIS 2017 test; green = best, orange = 2nd , red = worst. (Color figure online)

*Qualitative Comparison.* Figure 10 shows a qualitative comparisons to the best performing baselines DEB [60] and DVCP [38] on a complex scene to reveal error patterns.　While DVCP lost most of the color of the soapbox and the drivers

**Fig. 10.** Qualitative results on DAVIS soapbox shows we keep realistic colors details for longer compared to DEB [60] and DVCP [38]. (Best viewed in color on screen) (Color figure online)

after 30 frames, DEB shows color drifts [60, Fig. 16 arXiv] and oversmoothing even on the background clearly visible in the reference, and over-saturates the heads to red. In contrast, our model manages to keep the details – even after occlusion (e.g. crowd in frame 30, was occluded in frame 15), while at the same time keeping the soapbox driver colorized, with some minimal color bleeding on the shirt, despite the drastic appearance and size changes. More qualitative results including a discussion on limiting cases can be found in the supplementary.

*Historic Western - 2 References.* Figure 11 demonstrates the extensibility of our method without re-training, on a historic scene from 1925. In frame 15, large

**Fig. 11.** Colorization of a historic sequence with FilmGrain - out of training domain; Without re-training our model can be extended to use multiple keyframe references.

portions of the arm and the jacket are occluded and are later visible with very different and new appearance. Therefore the matching to the global reference frame can be reduced and local feature matches take over. As a result, close-by similar textures dominate leading to wrong colorization. However, our flexible framework allows to add a slightly reworked frame as a second global reference. With the initial confidences and the multiwell dataterm, our method automatically selects best color proposal from *both* reference images. Using both also improves intermediate results, even though our method was never trained to work with two global references. An example on how to users can override the fusion of the color proposals can be found in the supplementary.

*Historic Theater.* Figure 12 compares our method to DEB [60] and DeepRemaster [21] – the best competitors with available source code – on a historic video of a theater play in 1902, with a manually colorized reference frame. While DeepRemaster looses colors, DEB over saturates them like on the floor, and shows a color drift on the wall. Both fail to keep details intact like the yellow sash.

**Fig. 12.** Colorized historic sequence from 1902; Mind details like the yellow sash, face, or color drift. Our method keeps colors more faithful to the manually colored reference. (Color figure online)

## 5    Conclusion

In this work, we proposed a method that successfully combines classical energy-based methods with deep learning to propagate colors in videos. Our method advanced the state-of-the-art – both quantitatively and qualitatively on multiple datasets and metrics as well as user ranking – even with much less training data. Further, our flexible mathematical structure allows for extensions like integrating additional references without retraining. Future work includes extension of user input capabilities and elaboration of loss functions such as adversarial losses.

**Acknowledgement.** This work was supported by the FFG-Program BRIDGE with short title RE:Color (No. 877161). Alexander Effland was also supported by the German Research Foundation under Germany's Excellence Strategy EXC-2047/1–390685813 and EXC2151-390873048.

## References

1. An, X., Pellacini, F.: Appprop: all-pairs appearance-space edit propagation. In: ACM SIGGRAPH, pp. 1–9 (2008)
2. Anwar, S., Tahir, M., Li, C., Mian, A., Khan, F.S., Muzaffar, A.W.: Image colorization: a survey and dataset. arXiv:2008.10774 (2020)
3. Barnes, C., Shechtman, E., Finkelstein, A., Goldman, D.B.: PatchMatch: a randomized correspondence algorithm for structural image editing. ACM Trans. Graph. **28**(3), 24 (2009)
4. Barron, J.T., Poole, B.: The fast bilateral solver. In: Leibe, B., Matas, J., Sebe, N., Welling, M. (eds.) ECCV 2016. LNCS, vol. 9907, pp. 617–632. Springer, Cham (2016). https://doi.org/10.1007/978-3-319-46487-9_38

5. Bugeau, A., Ta, V.T., Papadakis, N.: Variational exemplar-based image colorization. IEEE Trans. Image Process. **23**(1), 298–307 (2013)
6. Cao, Y., Zhou, Z., Zhang, W., Yu, Y.: Unsupervised diverse colorization via generative adversarial networks. In: Joint European Conference on Machine Learning and Knowledge Discovery in Databases, pp. 151–166 (2017)
7. Chambolle, A., Pock, T.: A first-order primal-dual algorithm for convex problems with applications to imaging. J. Math. Imaging Vis. **40**, 120–145 (2011)
8. Chambolle, A., Pock, T.: An introduction to continuous optimization for imaging. Acta Numer **25**, 161–319 (2016). https://doi.org/10.1017/S096249291600009X
9. Charpiat, G., Hofmann, M., Schölkopf, B.: Automatic image colorization via multimodal predictions. In: Forsyth, D., Torr, P., Zisserman, A. (eds.) ECCV 2008. LNCS, vol. 5304, pp. 126–139. Springer, Heidelberg (2008). https://doi.org/10.1007/978-3-540-88690-7_10
10. Chen, X., Zou, D., Zhao, Q., Tan, P.: Manifold preserving edit propagation. ACM Trans. Graph. **31**(6), 1–7 (2012)
11. Cheng, Z., Yang, Q., Sheng, B.: Deep colorization. In: International Conference on Computer Vision, pp. 415–423 (2015)
12. Deshpande, A., Lu, J., Yeh, M.C., Jin Chong, M., Forsyth, D.: Learning diverse image colorization. In: Conference on Computer Vision and Pattern Recognition (2017)
13. Deshpande, A., Rock, J., Forsyth, D.: Learning large-scale automatic image colorization. In: International Conference on Computer Vision, pp. 567–575 (2015)
14. Endo, Y., Iizuka, S., Kanamori, Y., Mitani, J.: Deepprop: extracting deep features from a single image for edit propagation. In: Computer Graphics Forum, pp. 189–201 (2016)
15. Faridul, H.S., Pouli, T., Chamaret, C., Stauder, J., Trémeau, A., Reinhard, E., et al.: A survey of color mapping and its applications. In: Eurographics (State of the Art Reports), vol. 3 (2014)
16. He, K., Zhang, X., Ren, S., Sun, J.: Deep residual learning for image recognition. In: IEEE Conference on Computer Vision and Pattern Recognition, pp. 770–778 (2016)
17. He, M., Chen, D., Liao, J., Sander, P.V., Yuan, L.: Deep exemplar-based colorization. ACM Trans. Graph. **37**(4), 47 (2018)
18. Henisch, H.K., Henisch, B.A.: The Painted photograph, 1839–1914: Origins, Techniques, Aspirations. Pennsylvania State University Press University Park (1996)
19. Hofinger, M., Bulò, S.R., Porzi, L., Knapitsch, A., Pock, T., Kontschieder, P.: Improving optical flow on a pyramid level. In: Vedaldi, A., Bischof, H., Brox, T., Frahm, J.-M. (eds.) ECCV 2020. LNCS, vol. 12373, pp. 770–786. Springer, Cham (2020). https://doi.org/10.1007/978-3-030-58604-1_46
20. Hurwitz, M.: Real war: how Peter Jackson's they shall not grow old breathed life into 100-year-old archival footage (2019). https://www.studiodaily.com/2019/05/real-war-peter-jacksons-shall-not-grow-old-breathed-life-100-year-old-archival-footage/
21. Iizuka, S., Simo-Serra, E.: Deepremaster: temporal source-reference attention networks for comprehensive video enhancement. ACM Trans. Graph. **38**(6), 1–13 (2019)
22. Iizuka, S., Simo-Serra, E., Ishikawa, H.: Let there be color! joint end-to-end learning of global and local image priors for automatic image colorization with simultaneous classification. ACM Trans. Graph. **35**(4), 1–11 (2016)
23. Irony, R., Cohen-Or, D., Lischinski, D.: Colorization by example. In: Eurographics Symposium on Rendering, pp. 201–210 (2005)

24. Isola, P., Zhu, J.Y., Zhou, T., Efros, A.A.: Image-to-image translation with conditional adversarial networks. In: Conference on Computer Vision and Pattern Recognition, pp. 1125–1134 (2017)
25. Jampani, V., Gadde, R., Gehler, P.V.: Video propagation networks. In: Conference on Computer Vision and Pattern Recognition, pp. 451–461 (2017)
26. Kobler, E., Effland, A., Kunisch, K., Pock, T.: Total deep variation for linear inverse problems. In: IEEE Conference on Computer Vision and Pattern Recognition (2020)
27. Kumar, M., Weissenborn, D., Kalchbrenner, N.: Colorization transformer. In: International Conference on Learning Representations (2021)
28. Larsson, G., Maire, M., Shakhnarovich, G.: Learning representations for automatic colorization. In: Leibe, B., Matas, J., Sebe, N., Welling, M. (eds.) ECCV 2016. LNCS, vol. 9908, pp. 577–593. Springer, Cham (2016). https://doi.org/10.1007/978-3-319-46493-0_35
29. LeCun, Y., Bengio, Y., Hinton, G.: Deep learning. Nature 521(7553), 436–444 (2015)
30. Lei, C., Chen, Q.: Fully automatic video colorization with self-regularization and diversity. In: Proceedings of the IEEE/CVF Conference on Computer Vision and Pattern Recognition, pp. 3753–3761 (2019)
31. Leitner, D.: The documentary masterpiece that is Peter Jackson's they shall not grow old (2018). https://filmmakermagazine.com/106589-the-documentary-masterpiece-that-is-peter-jacksons-they-shall-not-grow-old
32. Levin, A., Lischinski, D., Weiss, Y.: Colorization using optimization. In: ACM SIGGRAPH 2004 Papers, pp. 689–694 (2004)
33. Liao, J., Yao, Y., Yuan, L., Hua, G., Kang, S.B.: Visual attribute transfer through deep image analogy. arXiv preprint arXiv:1705.01088 (2017)
34. Lin, T.-S.: Microsoft COCO: common objects in context. In: Fleet, D., Pajdla, T., Schiele, B., Tuytelaars, T. (eds.) ECCV 2014. LNCS, vol. 8693, pp. 740–755. Springer, Cham (2014). https://doi.org/10.1007/978-3-319-10602-1_48
35. Luan, Q., Wen, F., Cohen-Or, D., Liang, L., Xu, Y.Q., Shum, H.Y.: Natural image colorization. In: Eurographics Conference on Rendering Techniques, pp. 309–320 (2007)
36. Luo, M., Cui, G., Rigg, B.: The development of the CIE 2000 colour-difference formula: Ciede 2000. Color Res. Appl. 26, 340–350 (2001). https://doi.org/10.1002/col.1049
37. Meister, S., Hur, J., Roth, S.: Unflow: unsupervised learning of optical flow with a bidirectional census loss. In: AAAI (2018)
38. Meyer, S., Cornillère, V., Djelouah, A., Schroers, C., Gross, M.: Deep video color propagation. In: British Machine Vision Conference (2018)
39. Mouzon, T., Pierre, F., Berger, M.O.: Joint CNN and variational model for fully-automatic image colorization. In: International Conference on Scale Space and Variational Methods in Computer Vision, pp. 535–546 (2019)
40. Pierre, F., Aujol, J.F., Bugeau, A., Papadakis, N., Ta, V.T.: Luminance-chrominance model for image colorization. SIAM J. Imaging Sci. 8(1), 536–563 (2015)
41. Pierre, F., Aujol, J.F., Bugeau, A., Ta, V.T.: Interactive video colorization within a variational framework. SIAM J. Imaging Sci. 10(4), 2293–2325 (2017)
42. Pierre, F., Aujol, J.F.: Recent Approaches for Image Colorization (2020). https://hal.archives-ouvertes.fr/hal-02965137

43. Pierre, F., Aujol, J.-F., Bugeau, A., Ta, V.-T.: A unified model for image colorization. In: Agapito, L., Bronstein, M.M., Rother, C. (eds.) ECCV 2014. LNCS, vol. 8927, pp. 297–308. Springer, Cham (2015). https://doi.org/10.1007/978-3-319-16199-0_21

44. Pinetz, T., Kobler, E., Pock, T., Effland, A.: Shared prior learning of energy-based models for image reconstruction. arXiv:2011.06539 (2020)

45. Pont-Tuset, J., et al.: The 2017 davis challenge on video object segmentation. arXiv:1704.00675 (2017)

46. Qu, Y., Wong, T.T., Heng, P.A.: Manga colorization. ACM Trans. Graph. **25**(3), 1214–1220 (2006)

47. Reinhard, E., Adhikhmin, M., Gooch, B., Shirley, P.: Color transfer between images. IEEE Comput. Graphics Appl. **21**(5), 34–41 (2001)

48. Royer, A., Kolesnikov, A., Lampert, C.H.: Probabilistic image colorization. In: British Machine Vision Conference (2018)

49. Russakovsky, O., et al.: Imagenet large scale visual recognition challenge. Int. J. Comput. Vision **115**(3), 211–252 (2015)

50. Shrivastava, A., Gupta, A., Girshick, R.: Training region-based object detectors with online hard example mining. In: IEEE Conference on Computer Vision and Pattern Recognition, pp. 761–769 (2016)

51. Simonyan, K., Zisserman, A.: Very deep convolutional networks for large-scale image recognition. In: International Conference on Learning Representations (2015)

52. Su, J.W., Chu, H.K., Huang, J.B.: Instance-aware image colorization. In: Conference on Computer Vision and Pattern Recognition, pp. 7968–7977 (2020)

53. Sỳkora, D., Buriánek, J., Žára, J.: Unsupervised colorization of black-and-white cartoons. In: International Symposium on Non-photorealistic Animation and Rendering, pp. 121–127 (2004)

54. Teed, Z., Deng, J.: RAFT: recurrent all-pairs field transforms for optical flow. In: Vedaldi, A., Bischof, H., Brox, T., Frahm, J.-M. (eds.) ECCV 2020. LNCS, vol. 12347, pp. 402–419. Springer, Cham (2020). https://doi.org/10.1007/978-3-030-58536-5_24

55. Ulyanov, D., Vedaldi, A., Lempitsky, V.S.: Instance normalization: the missing ingredient for fast stylization. arXiv:1607.08022 (2016)

56. Vondrick, C., Shrivastava, A., Fathi, A., Guadarrama, S., Murphy, K.: Tracking emerges by colorizing videos. In: Ferrari, V., Hebert, M., Sminchisescu, C., Weiss, Y. (eds.) ECCV 2018. LNCS, vol. 11217, pp. 402–419. Springer, Cham (2018). https://doi.org/10.1007/978-3-030-01261-8_24

57. Welsh, T., Ashikhmin, M., Mueller, K.: Transferring color to greyscale images. In: Conference on Computer Graphics and Interactive Techniques, pp. 277–280 (2002)

58. Xu, L., Yan, Q., Jia, J.: A sparse control model for image and video editing. ACM Trans. Graph. **32**(6), 1–10 (2013)

59. Yatziv, L., Sapiro, G.: Fast image and video colorization using chrominance blending. IEEE Trans. Image Process. **15**(5), 1120–1129 (2006)

60. Zhang, B., et al.: Deep exemplar-based video colorization. In: Conference on Computer Vision and Pattern Recognition, pp. 8052–8061 (2019)

61. Zhang, R., Isola, P., Efros, A.A.: Colorful image colorization. In: Leibe, B., Matas, J., Sebe, N., Welling, M. (eds.) ECCV 2016. LNCS, vol. 9907, pp. 649–666. Springer, Cham (2016). https://doi.org/10.1007/978-3-319-46487-9_40

62. Zhang, R., Isola, P., Efros, A.A., Shechtman, E., Wang, O.: The unreasonable effectiveness of deep features as a perceptual metric. In: Proceedings of the IEEE Conference on Computer Vision and pattern Recognition, pp. 586–595 (2018)
63. Zhang, R., et al.: Real-time user-guided image colorization with learned deep priors. ACM Trans. Graph. **36**(4), 1–11 (2017)

# Continual Variational Autoencoder Learning via Online Cooperative Memorization

Fei Ye and Adrian G. Bors[✉]

Department of Computer Science, University of York, York YO10 5GH, UK
{fy689,adrian.bors}@york.ac.uk

**Abstract.** Due to their inference, data representation and reconstruction properties, Variational Autoencoders (VAE) have been successfully used in continual learning classification tasks. However, their ability to generate images with specifications corresponding to the classes and databases learned during Continual Learning (CL) is not well understood and catastrophic forgetting remains a significant challenge. In this paper, we firstly analyze the forgetting behaviour of VAEs by developing a new theoretical framework that formulates CL as a dynamic optimal transport problem. This framework proves approximate bounds to the data likelihood without requiring the task information and explains how the prior knowledge is lost during the training process. We then propose a novel memory buffering approach, namely the Online Cooperative Memorization (OCM) framework, which consists of a Short-Term Memory (STM) that continually stores recent samples to provide future information for the model, and a Long-Term Memory (LTM) aiming to preserve a wide diversity of samples. The proposed OCM transfers certain samples from STM to LTM according to the information diversity selection criterion without requiring any supervised signals. The OCM framework is then combined with a dynamic VAE expansion mixture network for further enhancing its performance.

**Keywords:** VAE · Continual learning · Lifelong generative modelling

## 1 Introduction

One desired capability for an artificial intelligence system is to continually learn novel concepts without forgetting the knowledge learnt in the past. However, existing artificial systems are far away from such capabilities, characteristic of living organisms. A deep learning model which can recover the training data from a low-dimensional latent code space is the Variational Autoencoder (VAE) [25]. VAEs have been widely used in image synthesis [60,62], semi-supervised learning [1,63] and for image-to-image translation [38]. However, similar to other deep

**Supplementary Information** The online version contains supplementary material available at https://doi.org/10.1007/978-3-031-20050-2_31.

learning systems, VAEs suffer from degenerated performance when it is trained successively with new tasks, which is a result of catastrophic forgetting [42].

Existing works to relieve VAE's forgetting can be summarized as two categories. The first would usually train a generator [2,44,49], or store a few past learnt samples [39] in a memory buffer which replays old samples together with learning new tasks to optimize the model. The methods from the second category would focus on dynamically adding new VAE components into a mixture model to adapt to the data distribution shift [35,45] in which prior knowledge is preserved in the frozen network parameters and structures. These approaches have been extended for the case when the model is trained on non-stationary data streams without knowing the task information, a mechanism called Task Free Continual Learning (TFCL) [4,5]. However, the theoretical analysis for VAE's forgetting behaviour under TFCL has not been studied before.

In recent years, some studies have provided the theoretical analysis for continual learning from different perspectives including the NP-hard problem [27], risk bound [58,64], Teacher-Student framework [34,57] and game theory [43]. However, all these approaches require strong assumptions such as clearly defining the task identities, which is not applicable when the task information is missing. In this paper, we bridge this gap by developing a new theoretical framework which formulates TFCL as a dynamic optimal transport (OT) problem, and derives the approximate bounds on the data likelihood. The motivation behind OT is twofold : 1) OT models evaluate distances between pairs of probability density functions [8] and can be used for deriving the approximate bound to the data likelihood (See Sect. 4); 2) OT can be estimated by employing sampling [18], which is suitable for analysis and verification. The proposed theoretical analysis also highlights that the sample diversity in the memory used for training is crucial for overcoming forgetting and would not require the category information.

Another contribution of this study, inspired by the above mentioned theoretical analysis, is to develop a new memorization approach aiming to store diverse samples for training a VAE through the TFCL. Other approaches have proposed diversifying the information for memorization by evaluating the similarity on the gradient information [3] or by assigning balanced samples to memory buffers according to their categories' information [6,13]. However, most of these prior approaches require to access supervised signals, which are not available in unsupervised learning. Additionally, these approaches do not have theoretical guarantees and also ignore the data stream future information in the sample selection. Knowing both the past and future information was shown to improve time series prediction [22] and would be helpful for the sample selection.

In this paper, we address the aforementioned problems by : 1) Proposing a new learning paradigm called Online Cooperative Memorization (OCM) which consists of three components: a Long-Term Memory (LTM), a Short-Term Memory (STM) and a model (Learner). OCM implements a memorization mechanism which transfers the temporary information from the STM to LTM, according to a certain criterion. 2) A kernel-based information importance criterion for evaluating the similarity among the data stored in the STM for selecting diverse characteristic samples for LTM, without requiring a class label. The kernel evaluation of the similarity of a pair of data samples [15], defined as an inner product of the latent representations of each pair of the data stored in the memory, is shown to be efficient. This procedure ensures achieving an appropriate diversification among the samples stored in the LTM. We summarize our contributions as follows : 1) Our work is the first to provide theory insights for the forgetting behaviour of VAE under TFCL. 2) We propose the Online Cooperative Memorization (OCM) that can be used in any VAE variant with minimal modification and can also be extended to a dynamic expansion mixture approach to further enhance performance. 3) We propose a new sample selection approach for dynamically transferring selected samples from the STM to LTM without requiring any supervised signal. To our best knowledge, this is the first work to explore the kernel-based distance for the sample selection under TFCL. 4) The proposed sample selection approach can be used in both supervised and unsupervised learning without modifying the selection strategy.

## 2   Related Work

**Continual Learning.** One of the most popular approaches is to use a regularization loss within the optimization procedure [14,21,23,26,36,41,47,52,56], where the network parameters which are important to the past learnt data are re-weighted when learning a new task, in order to attempt to preserve past knowledge. Other approaches would employ a small buffer to store a few past data [3,10,53] or would train a generator as a generative replay network that provides pseudo data samples for the future task learning [2,44,45,49,57–59,66,69]. However, these approaches can not guarantee the optimal performance on the past task since stored or generated samples can not represent the true underlying data distributions [64]. This issue can be solved by storing the information of past samples into the network's parameters which are then frozen when learning novel tasks [35,64,65,67,68].

**Task Free Continual Learning.** Recent works have driven the attention to a more challenging scenario where task boundaries are unknown. Most approaches would focus on the sample selection approach that stores certain samples into a buffer to train the model. This approach was firstly investigated in [5] for training a classifier under TFCL and for training both classifiers and VAEs [4] using a new retrieving mechanism selecting called the Maximal Interfered Retrieval (MIR). The Gradient Sample Selection (GSS) [3] formulates the sample selection as a constrained optimization reduction. More recently, a Learner-Evaluator framework, called the Continual Prototype Evolution (CoPE) [13] stores the same number of samples for each class in the memory to enforce the balance replay. Different from these approaches, the proposed OCM does not require any supervised signals for the sample selection in both supervised and unsupervised learning.

Another approach for TFCL is based on the dynamic expansion mechanism [35], called the Continual Neural Dirichlet Process Mixture (CN-DPM), which introduces Dirichlet processes for the expansion of VAE components. This expansion mechanism was combined with the generative replay into the Continual

Unsupervised Representation Learning (CURL) [45], for learning the shared and task-specific representations, befitting on the clustering task.

**Optimal Transport (OT).** The OT aims to search for a minimal effort solution to transfer the mass from one distribution to another. OT has been recently applied in the domain adaptation problems [12,16] and was also used in auto-encoders to provide a flexible training loss for the VAE [54]. However, these models require to fully access all samples at all times, and are failing to capture the underlying data distributions under TFCL. In this paper, we formulate TFCL as the dynamic optimal transport problem which provides a new perspective for the forgetting behaviour of VAEs. To our best knowledge, this paper is the first work to employ OT for forgetting analysis under TFCL.

## 3   Preliminary

In this section, we firstly introduce the background of VAEs. Then we explain how TFCL can be seen as a dynamic optimal transport problem.

### 3.1   The Variational Autoencoder

The VAE [25] aims to jointly optimize the observed variable $\mathbf{x}$ and their corresponding encoded latent variables $\mathbf{z}$ within an unified optimization framework by maximizing the marginal log-likelihood $\log p_\theta(\mathbf{x}) = \int p_\theta(\mathbf{x} \mid \mathbf{z}) p(\mathbf{z}) \, d\mathbf{z}$. This integral involves the Normal prior distribution $p(\mathbf{z})$, which is intractable to optimize since it requires access to all $\mathbf{z}$. The VAE maximizes the Evidence Lower Bound (ELBO) on $\log p_\theta(\mathbf{x})$, while the distribution $p_\theta(\mathbf{z} \mid \mathbf{x})$ is approximated by a variational distribution $q_\omega(\mathbf{z} \mid \mathbf{x})$ :

$$\mathcal{L}_{ELBO}(\mathbf{x}; \theta, \omega) := \mathbb{E}_{z \sim q_\omega(\mathbf{z} \mid \mathbf{x})} \left[ \log p_\theta(\mathbf{x} \mid \mathbf{z}) \right] - KL \left[ q_\omega(\mathbf{z} \mid \mathbf{x}) \,\|\, p(\mathbf{z}) \right], \tag{1}$$

where $p_\theta(\mathbf{x} \mid \mathbf{z})$ is the decoder parameterized by $\theta$ and $\mathcal{L}_{ELBO}(\mathbf{x}; \theta, \omega)$ is a lower bound to $\log p_\theta(\mathbf{x})$. $KL(\cdot)$ represents the Kullback-Leibler (KL) divergence. Equation (1) can be further extended when considering multiple samples, as the Importance Weighted Autoencoder (IWVAE) [9] :

$$\mathcal{L}_{IW}^m(\mathbf{x}; \theta, \omega) := \mathbb{E}_{z_1, \cdots, z_m \sim q_\omega(\mathbf{z} \mid \mathbf{x})} \left[ \log \frac{1}{m} \sum_{i=1}^m w_i \right], \tag{2}$$

where $w_i = p_\theta(\mathbf{x}, \mathbf{z}_i) / q_\omega(\mathbf{z}_i \mid \mathbf{x})$ and $m$ is the number of importance samples. Since we have $\mathcal{L}_{IW}^m(\mathbf{x}; \theta, \omega) > \mathcal{L}_{ELBO}(\mathbf{x}; \theta, \omega)$ for $m > 1$ [9], Eq. (2) can be used as the estimator for the data likelihood [50].

### 3.2   Formulate TFCL as a Dynamic OT Problem

**Learning Setting.** Let $\mathcal{D}^S$ be a training set over the image space $\mathcal{X} \in \mathbb{R}^d$ with $d$ dimensions, we assume that there are $N$ training steps $\{t_1, \cdots, t_N\}$, for the part-by-part learning of $\mathcal{D}^S$, defined as $\mathcal{D}^S = \bigcup_{i=1}^{t_N} \mathbf{X}_b^i$, where $\mathbf{X}_b^i \cap \mathbf{X}_b^j = \varnothing$ for $i \neq j$. In each training step $t_i$, a model only observes a small batch of images $\mathbf{X}_b^i$ drawn from $\mathcal{D}^S$, without accessing all the prior batches $\{\mathbf{X}_b^1, \cdots, \mathbf{X}_b^{i-1}\}$. Once all training steps are finished, we evaluate the model on a testing dataset $\mathcal{D}^T$ by using two main criteria (negative log-likelihood estimation and reconstruction quality). In the following, we introduce several definitions and notations.

**Definition 1.** *(Memory.)* Let $\mathcal{M}_i$ represent a memory data buffer updated at the step $t_i$ and $\mathbb{P}_{m_i}$ represent the probabilistic representation of the samples drawn from $\mathcal{M}_i$. Let $\mathbb{P}_\mathbf{x}$ represent the probabilistic measure defined by the samples drawn from $\mathcal{D}^S$.

**Definition 2.** *(Model.)* Let $h^i$ be a VAE model trained on $\mathcal{M}_i$ at $t_i$. Let $\mathbb{P}_\mathbf{z}$ be a prior distribution (Normal distribution) on the latent variable space $\mathcal{Z}$.

**Definition 3.** *(Decoder.)* Let $\mathrm{G}_i \colon \mathcal{Z} \to \mathcal{X}$ be a generator (decoder in the $h^i$ model trained at $t_i$). $\mathrm{G}_i(\mathbf{z}) = p_\theta(\mathbf{x} \mid \mathbf{z})$ in $h^i$ is implemented as the Gaussian decoder $\mathcal{N}(\mathrm{G}_i^\star(\mathbf{z}), \sigma^2 \mathbf{I}_d)$, where $\mathrm{G}_i^\star$ is a deterministic generator, $\sigma > 0$ represents a small random variation for ensuring randomness, and $\mathbf{I}_d$ is the unit vector of dimension $d$. Let $\mathbb{P}_{\mathrm{G}_i}$ represent the probabilistic measure formed by samples drawn through the sampling process, $\mathbf{x} \sim p_\theta(\mathbf{x} \mid \mathbf{z}), \mathbf{z} \sim \mathbb{P}_\mathbf{z}$ of $h^i$.

In the generative modelling, we usually consider two probabilistic measures $\mathbb{P}_\mathbf{x}$ and $\mathbb{P}_{\mathrm{G}_i}$ over two distinct spaces, denoted as $\Omega_\mathbf{x}$ and $\Omega_{\mathrm{G}_i}$, respectively. Let $\mathbf{T} \colon \Omega_{\mathrm{G}_i} \to \Omega_\mathbf{x}$ be a transport map if satisfying $\mathbf{T}\#\mathbb{P}_{\mathrm{G}_i} = \mathbb{P}_\mathbf{x}$ that transforms $\mathbb{P}_{\mathrm{G}_i}$ into $\mathbb{P}_\mathbf{x}$. For a given arbitrary measurable cost function $\mathcal{L}$, the optimal transportation problem can be defined by Monge's formulation, expressed by :

$$\mathbf{T}^* = \arg\min_\mathbf{T} \int_{\Omega_{\mathrm{G}_i}} \mathcal{L}(\mathbf{x}, \mathbf{T}(\mathbf{x})) \, d\mathbb{P}_{\mathrm{G}_i}(\mathbf{x}) \, , \, s.t. \, \mathbf{T}\#\mathbb{P}_{\mathrm{G}_i} = \mathbb{P}_\mathbf{x} \, . \tag{3}$$

According to the optimal transport theory [12], the above problem is solved by the Kantorovitch formulation [24] :

$$\mathrm{W}_\mathcal{L}^\star(\mathbb{P}_\mathbf{x}, \mathbb{P}_{\mathrm{G}_i}) = \inf_{\mathbb{P}_{\mathbf{x} \times \mathrm{G}_i}} \mathbb{E}_{(\mathbf{x}^r, \mathbf{x}^g) \sim \mathbb{P}_{\mathbf{x} \times \mathrm{G}_i}} [\mathcal{L}(\mathbf{x}^r, \mathbf{x}^g)] \, , \tag{4}$$

where $\mathbb{P}_{\mathbf{x} \times \mathrm{G}_i}$ represents the set of all probabilistic couplings on $\Omega_\mathbf{x} \times \Omega_{\mathrm{G}_i}$ with marginals $\mathbb{P}_\mathbf{x}$ and $\mathbb{P}_{\mathrm{G}_i}$. $\mathbf{X}^r$ and $\mathbf{X}^g$ are the samples drawn from $\mathbb{P}_{\mathbf{x} \times \mathrm{G}_i}$. Different from the traditional OT problem, $\mathrm{W}_\mathcal{L}(\mathbb{P}_\mathbf{x}, \mathbb{P}_{\mathrm{G}_i})$ would be changed over time (when $i$ increases) because the model is trained on the dynamically evolved memory $\mathcal{M}_i$. We call Eq. (4) as the dynamic OT problem where the optimal solution is evolved each training time $t_i$. Equation (4) has an upper bound when $\mathrm{G}_i$ is the Gaussian decoder [8,54] :

$$\mathrm{W}_\mathcal{L}^\star(\mathbb{P}_\mathbf{x}, \mathbb{P}_{\mathrm{G}_i}) \leq \inf_{q_\omega(\mathbf{z})} \mathbb{E}_{\mathbb{P}_\mathbf{x}} \mathbb{E}_{q_\omega(\mathbf{z} \mid \mathbf{x})} [\mathcal{L}(\mathbf{x}, \mathrm{G}_i(\mathbf{z}))] \, , \tag{5}$$

where $q_\omega(\mathbf{z})$ is the marginal distribution of $q_\omega(\mathbf{z} \mid \mathbf{x})$ satisfying $q_\omega(\mathbf{z}) = p(\mathbf{z})$. We implement $\mathcal{L}(\mathbf{x}, \mathrm{G}_i(\mathbf{z})) = \|\mathbf{x} - \mathrm{G}_i(\mathbf{z})\|^2$ as the squared Euclidean cost function in which $\mathrm{W}_\mathcal{L}(\cdot)$ is the squared 2-Wasserstein distance [8].

# 4  Theoretical Framework

ELBO is an important indicator of the VAE's performance and is used as its main optimization function [11]. In the following, we provide a new perspective for analyzing the forgetfulness behaviour of VAEs during the continuous learning of several batches of data by formulating the ELBO's variation as a learning and forgetting process. The code and Supplemental Materials (SM) are available at https://github.com/dtuzi123/OVAE.

## 4.1  Analysis of Forgetting in a Single Model

Firstly, we derive an upper bound to ELBO of the target domain $\mathbb{P}_\mathbf{x}$, based on the dynamic OT problem (Eq. (5)).

**Theorem 1.** *For a VAE model $h^i$ trained at $t_i$, where $p_\theta(\mathbf{x}\,|\,\mathbf{z}) = \mathcal{N}(G_i(\mathbf{z}), \sigma^2 \mathbf{I}_d)$ is the Gaussian decoder and $\sigma = 1/\sqrt{2}$, we have :*

$$\inf_{q_\omega(\mathbf{z}) = p(\mathbf{z})} \mathbb{E}_{\mathbb{P}_\mathbf{x}}[\mathcal{L}_{ELBO}(\mathbf{x}; \theta, \omega)] \le -\frac{1}{2}\log\pi - W^\star_\mathcal{L}(\mathbb{P}_\mathbf{x}, \mathbb{P}_{G_i}), \tag{6}$$

The detailed proof is provided in Appendix-A from Supplemental Materials (SM). Based on the results from Theorem 1, we derive a bound that explains the forgetting process of VAEs.

**Theorem 2.** *Let $\mathbb{P}_{m_i}$ and $\mathbb{P}_\mathbf{x}$ be the source and target domains. From Eq. (6), we derive the bound on the ELBO between $\mathbb{P}_{m_i}$ and $\mathbb{P}_\mathbf{x}$ at the training step $t_i$ :*

$$\begin{aligned} \mathbb{E}_{\mathbb{P}_\mathbf{x}}[\mathcal{L}_{ELBO}(\mathbf{x}; \theta, \omega)] \le\ & \mathbb{E}_{\mathbb{P}_{m_i}}[\mathcal{L}_{ELBO}(\mathbf{x}; \theta, \omega)] \\ & + 2W^\star_\mathcal{L}(\mathbb{P}_{m_i}, \mathbb{P}_{G_i}) - W^\star_\mathcal{L}(\mathbb{P}_\mathbf{x}, \mathbb{P}_{m_i}) + \widetilde{F}(\mathbb{P}_{G_i}, \mathbb{P}_{m_i}), \end{aligned} \tag{7}$$

*where $\widetilde{F}(\mathbb{P}_{G_i}, \mathbb{P}_{m_i})$ is expressed as :*

$$\begin{aligned} \widetilde{F}(\mathbb{P}_{G_i}, \mathbb{P}_{m_i}) =\ & \mathbb{E}_{\mathbb{P}_{m_i}}[D_{KL}(q_\omega(\mathbf{z}\,|\,\mathbf{x})\,\|\,p(\mathbf{z}))] \\ & + \left| \mathbb{E}_{\mathbb{P}_{m_i}} \mathbb{E}_{q_\omega(\mathbf{z}\,|\,\mathbf{x})}[-\mathcal{L}(\mathbf{x}, G_i(\mathbf{z}))] - W^\star_\mathcal{L}(\mathbb{P}_{m_i}, \mathbb{P}_{G_i}) \right|. \end{aligned} \tag{8}$$

**Remark.** The detailed proof is provided in Appendix-B from SM. We have several observations from Theorem 2 : 1) Improving the performance on the source domain (ELBO on $\mathbb{P}_{m_i}$) would not lead to increasing ELBO on the target domain $\mathbb{P}_\mathbf{x}$ because the right hand side (RHS) of Eq. (7) involves the negative term, $-W^\star_\mathcal{L}(\mathbb{P}_\mathbf{x}, \mathbb{P}_{m_i})$. 2) Since RHS of Eq. (7) is upper bounded to ELBO on $\mathbb{P}_\mathbf{x}$, a large $W^\star_\mathcal{L}(\mathbb{P}_\mathbf{x}, \mathbb{P}_{m_i})$ decreases RHS of Eq. (7) and therefore leads to the degenerated performance, measured by ELBO, on $\mathbb{P}_\mathbf{x}$, corresponding to forgetting the knowledge at the training step $t_i$. This is usually caused by the memory $\mathcal{M}_i$ that fails to capture all information of $\mathbb{P}_\mathbf{x}$ during the initial training process (when $i$ is small) or after the training ($i = t_N$).

**The Effect of the Memory Diversity.** In practice, $\mathbb{P}_{\mathbf{x}}$ is divided into several separate distributions (target domains) $\{\mathbb{P}_{\mathbf{x}^1}, \cdots, \mathbb{P}_{\mathbf{x}^n}\}$ where each $\mathbb{P}_{\mathbf{x}^j}$ is the characteristic distribution of a data category. Under this setting we analyze the forgetting behaviour in the class-incremental scenario.

**Lemma 1.** *Let* $\{\mathbb{P}_{\mathbf{x}^1}, \cdots, \mathbb{P}_{\mathbf{x}^n}\}$ *and* $\mathbb{P}_{m_i}$ *be the target domains and source domain, respectively. The bound on ELBO between the source and target domain is derived as :*

$$\sum_{j=1}^{n} \mathbb{E}_{\mathbb{P}_{\mathbf{x}^j}}[\mathcal{L}_{ELBO}(\mathbf{x}; \theta, \omega)] \leq \sum_{j=1}^{n} \left\{ 2W_{\mathcal{L}}^{\star}(\mathbb{P}_{m_i}, \mathbb{P}_{G_i}) \right.$$
$$\left. + \mathbb{E}_{\mathbb{P}_{m_i}}[\mathcal{L}_{ELBO}(\mathbf{x}; \theta, \omega)] - W_{\mathcal{L}}^{\star}(\mathbb{P}_{\mathbf{x}^j}, \mathbb{P}_{m_i}) \right\} + n\widetilde{F}(\mathbb{P}_{G_i}, \mathbb{P}_{m_i}). \tag{9}$$

**Proof.** We sum up the bounds between $\mathbb{P}_{\mathbf{x}^j}$ and $\mathbb{P}_{m_i}$, where $j = 1, \cdots, n$ and prove Lemma 1.

**Remark.** We have several observations from Lemma 1 : 1) To maximize ELBO on target domains $\{\mathbb{P}_{\mathbf{x}^1}, \cdots, \mathbb{P}_{\mathbf{x}^n}\}$, $W_{\mathcal{L}}^{\star}(\mathbb{P}_{\mathbf{x}^j}, \mathbb{P}_{m_i}), j = 1, \cdots, n$ must be minimized, corresponding to the diverse samples replayed from $\mathbb{P}_{m_i}$. 2) We also provide new insights into the backward transfer [39] by using Eq. (9). When a memory $\mathcal{M}_i$ prefers to store samples from a few recent data distributions $\{\mathbb{P}_{\mathbf{x}^{n-1}}, \mathbb{P}_{\mathbf{x}^n}\}$, the model would lead to negative backward transfer on past target domains $\{\mathbb{P}_{\mathbf{x}^1}, \cdots, \mathbb{P}_{\mathbf{x}^{n-2}}\}$. Data diversity in memory can relieve this negative effect.

## 4.2   Forgetting Analysis of the Expanding VAE Mixture Model

In this section, we extend the forgetting analysis from a single VAE model to the Dynamic Expansion Model (DEM).

**Definition 4.** *Let* $\mathbf{H} = \{h_1, \cdots, h_k\}$ *be a dynamic expansion model trained at* $t_i$, *which has built* $k$ *components during the learning, where each* $h_i$ *is a VAE model. Let* $\mathbf{q} = \{q_1, \cdots, q_k\}$ *represent the training steps that each component converged on. For instance,* $h_i$ *converged on* $\mathcal{M}_{q_i}$ *at* $t_{q_i}$, *is not updated in the following training steps. Then* $\mathbb{P}_{G_{q_i}}$ *and* $\mathbb{P}_{m_{q_i}}$ *represent the generator distribution and the distribution of samples drawn from* $\mathcal{M}_{q_i}$.

**Lemma 2.** *Let* $\{\mathbb{P}_{\mathbf{x}^1}, \cdots, \mathbb{P}_{\mathbf{x}^n}\}$ *be a set of* $n$ *target domains. From Definition 4, the bound on the ELBO for the dynamic expansion model is derived as :*

$$\sum_{j=1}^{n} \mathbb{E}_{\mathbb{P}_{\mathbf{x}^j}}[\mathcal{L}_{ELBO}(\mathbf{x}; \theta, \omega)] \leq \sum_{i=1}^{n} F^{\star}(\mathbb{P}_{\mathbf{x}^i}), \tag{10}$$

*where* $F^{\star}(\mathbb{P}_{\mathbf{x}^i})$ *is the selection function, defined as :*

$$F^{\star}(\mathbb{P}_{\mathbf{x}^i}) = \max_{j=1, \cdots, k} \left\{ \mathbb{E}_{\mathbb{P}_{m_{q_j}}}[\mathcal{L}_{ELBO}(\mathbf{x}; \theta, \omega)] \right.$$
$$\left. + 2W_{\mathcal{L}}^{\star}(\mathbb{P}_{m_{q_j}}, \mathbb{P}_{G_{q_j}}) - W_{\mathcal{L}}^{\star}(\mathbb{P}_{\mathbf{x}^i}, \mathbb{P}_{m_{q_j}}) + \widetilde{F}(\mathbb{P}_{G_{q_j}}, \mathbb{P}_{m_{q_j}}) \right\}. \tag{11}$$

The proof is provided in Appendix-C from SM. To compare with a single model (Lemma 1), DEM would provide a maximum upper bound to the Left Hand Side (LHS) of Eq. (10) due to the selection process, Eq. (11). Additionally, DEM can relieve the negative backward transfer by preserving prior knowledge into the frozen components.

### 4.3  Mixture Expansion with the Task Information

Although the proposed theoretical framework is only used for TFCL, it can be extended for the case where task labels are known. We also apply the proposed theoretical framework for analyzing the forgetting behaviour of existing approaches (See details in Appendix-F from SM).

**Definition 5.** ( *Learning setting.*) Let $\mathcal{T} = \{\mathcal{T}_1, \cdots, \mathcal{T}_c\}$ represent a set of task labels where $c$ is the number of tasks and we consider that each $i$-th task is associated with a testing dataset $\mathcal{D}_i^T$ and a training dataset $\mathcal{D}_i^S$. Let $\mathbb{P}_{\mathbf{x}^i}$ and $\mathbb{P}_{\widetilde{\mathbf{x}}^i}$ represent the empirical distributions for $\mathcal{D}_i^S$ and $\mathcal{D}_i^T$, respectively. Since the task label is given, a mixture model starts to learn the first task and then either builds a new component or selects an existing component to learn a new task after the task switch. When a certain component is selected to learn a new task, the Generative Replay Mechanism (GRM) is used to relieve forgetting.

**Definition 6.** *(Generative replay.)* Let $\mathbb{P}_{\widetilde{\mathbf{x}}}^j$ represent the distribution of samples drawn from the generating process of $h_j$. Let $f_t : \mathcal{X} \to \mathcal{T}$ be the true labelling function that returns the task label for the data sample. If the $i$-th task is trained by $h_j$, let $\mathbb{P}_{\widetilde{\mathbf{x}}(i,m)}$ be the distribution of samples drawn from the process $\mathbf{x} \sim \mathbb{P}_{\widetilde{\mathbf{x}}}^j$ if $f_t(\mathbf{x}) = i$, where $m$ represents that $\mathbb{P}_{\widetilde{\mathbf{x}}(i,0)}$ is evolved to $\mathbb{P}_{\widetilde{\mathbf{x}}(i,m)}$ through $m$ generative replay processes [58]. Let $\mathbb{P}_{\widetilde{\mathbf{x}}(i,0)}$ and $\mathbb{P}_{\widetilde{\mathbf{x}}(i,-1)}$ represent $\mathbb{P}_{\mathbf{x}^i}$ and $\mathbb{P}_{\widetilde{\mathbf{x}}^i}$ for simplicity.

**Theorem 3.** *Let $\mathcal{A} = \{a_1, \cdots, a_n\}$ be a set where each $a_i$ represents the index of the component that has trained only once. Let $\widetilde{\mathcal{A}} = \{\widetilde{a}_1, \cdots, \widetilde{a}_n\}$ be a set of task labels where each $\widetilde{a}_i$ represents the index of the task learned by the $a_i$-th component. Let $\mathcal{B} = \{b_1, \cdots, b_{k-n}\}$ be a set where each $b_i$ represents the index of the component that is trained more than once. Let $\widetilde{b}_i = \{\widetilde{b}_i^1, \cdots, \widetilde{b}_i^m\}$ be a set of task labels for the $b_i$-th component. Let $c_i^j$ represent the number of generative replay processes for the $\widetilde{b}_i^j$-th task, achieved by the $b_i$-th component. Let $\mathbb{P}_{\mathrm{G}^i}$ represent the generator distribution of the $i$-th component. We derive the bound for a mixture model with $k$ components trained on $c$ tasks as :*

$$\sum_{i=1}^{|\mathcal{A}|} \left\{ \mathbb{E}_{\mathbb{P}_{\widetilde{\mathbf{x}}^{\widetilde{a}_i}}} [\mathcal{L}_{ELBO}(\mathbf{x}; \theta, \omega)] \right\} + \sum_{i=1}^{|\mathcal{B}|} \left\{ \sum_{q=1}^{|\widetilde{b}_i|} \{ \mathbb{E}_{\mathbb{P}_{\widetilde{\mathbf{x}}^{\widetilde{b}_i^q}}} [\mathcal{L}_{ELBO}(\mathbf{x}; \theta, \omega)] \} \right\} \le \mathcal{R}_S + \mathcal{R}_M \quad (12)$$

*where $|\cdot|$ denotes the cardinal of a set. $\mathcal{R}_S$ is estimated by components that are trained only once, defined as :*

$$\mathcal{R}_S = \sum_{i=1}^{|\mathcal{A}|} \left\{ 2\mathrm{W}_{\mathcal{L}}^{\star}(\mathbb{P}_{\mathbf{x}^{\widetilde{a}_i}}, \mathbb{P}_{\mathrm{G}^{a_i}}) + +\widetilde{\mathrm{F}}(\mathbb{P}_{\mathrm{G}^{a_i}} \mathbb{P}_{\mathbf{x}^{\widetilde{a}_i}}) \right.$$
$$\left. + \mathbb{E}_{\mathbb{P}_{\mathbf{x}^{\widetilde{a}_i}}} [\mathcal{L}_{ELBO}(\mathbf{x}; \theta, \omega)] - \mathrm{W}_{\mathcal{L}}^{\star}(\mathbb{P}_{\widetilde{\mathbf{x}}^{\widetilde{a}_i}}, \mathbb{P}_{\mathbf{x}^{\widetilde{a}_i}}) \right\}. \quad (13)$$

$\mathcal{R}_M$ is estimated by components that are trained on more than one task, as :

$$\mathcal{R}_M = \sum_{i=1}^{|\mathcal{B}|} \left\{ \sum_{q=1}^{|\widetilde{b}_i|} \left\{ \mathbb{E}_{\mathbb{P}_{\widetilde{\mathbf{x}}^{(\widetilde{b}_i^q, c_i^q)}}} [\mathcal{L}_{ELBO}(\mathbf{x}; \theta, \omega)] + \sum_{s=0}^{c_i^q} \left\{ 2\mathrm{W}_{\mathcal{L}}^{\star}(\mathbb{P}_{\widetilde{\mathbf{x}}^{(\widetilde{b}_i^q, s)}}, \mathbb{P}_{\mathrm{G}^{b_i}}) \right. \right. \right.$$
$$\left. \left. \left. + \widetilde{\mathrm{F}}(\mathbb{P}_{\mathrm{G}^{b_i}}, \mathbb{P}_{\widetilde{\mathbf{x}}^{(\widetilde{b}_i^q, s)}}) - \mathrm{W}_{\mathcal{L}}^{\star}(\mathbb{P}_{\widetilde{\mathbf{x}}^{(\widetilde{b}_i^q, s-1)}}, \mathbb{P}_{\widetilde{\mathbf{x}}^{(\widetilde{b}_i^q, s)}}) \right\} \right\} \right\}. \tag{14}$$

**Remark.** The detailed proof is provided in Appendix-D from SM. Theorem 3 has the following observations : 1) If the number of components $k$ is equal to the number of tasks, then $\mathcal{R}_M = 0$ and there is no forgetting. When the number of components decreases, forgetting happens because the last term in the RHS of Eq. (14) is increased, leading to a decrease in the RHS of Eq. (12) (corresponding to the decrease of ELBO on all target domains). 2) If $k = 1$, then $\mathcal{R}_S$ is about only the last task, then $\mathcal{R}_M$ is increased significantly since the accumulated errors $\sum_{s=0}^{c_i^q} \{ \mathrm{W}_{\mathcal{L}}^{\star}(\mathbb{P}_{\widetilde{\mathbf{x}}^{(\widetilde{b}_i^q, s-1)}}, \mathbb{P}_{\widetilde{\mathbf{x}}^{(\widetilde{b}_i^q, s)}}) \}$ in Eq. (14) increases. Learning early tasks would lead to more forgetting than when learning the recent tasks for $k = 1$ because early tasks would have more accumulated errors ($c_i^q$ in $\mathcal{R}_M$ is large as $i$ increases (See Appendix-D from SM)).

## 5   Methodology

Previous approaches have proposed to learn a diverse memory according to the category information. However, these approaches do not provide a theoretical guarantee for the accumulated memory's diversity. To our best knowledge, this paper is the first to provide a theoretical forgetting analysis and guarantees for existing TFCL models (See details in Appendix-F of SM). Additionally, the proposed theoretical framework demonstrates that the diversity of memory content can be achieved without knowing the category information (Lemma 1). Based on the conclusion of Lemma 1, we introduce a new memory approach which consists of three modules: LTM, STM and the Learner. The proposed approach does not require any task information or supervised signals for unsupervised learning. Firstly, we introduce the proposed OCM with the Learner implemented as a single VAE, and then we extend this into a dynamic expansion mechanism.

### 5.1   Online Cooperative Memorization (OCM)

**Notations.** Let $\mathcal{M}_i^l = \{\mathbf{x}_{i,j}^l\}_{j=1}^{n_i^l}$ and $\mathcal{M}_i^e = \{\mathbf{x}_{i,u}^e\}_{u=1}^{n_i^e}$ represent the samples stored in the LTM and STM, respectively, at the training step $t_i$ while $n_i^l$ and $n_i^e$ represent the number of samples. Let $\mathcal{M}_{Max}^e$ represent the maximum number of samples which can be stored in $\mathcal{M}_i^e$.

The training procedure, presented in Fig. 1, consists of three main stages, as described in the following.

**Stage 1 : Learning.** At the training step $t_i$, STM stores a new batch of samples $\mathbf{X}_i^b$ into $\mathcal{M}_i^e$, while the model, consisting of a single VAE, is trained to update both $\mathcal{M}_i^e$ and $\mathcal{M}_i^l$ using Eq. (1). Once the training is finished, we perform the next step.

**Stage 2: Evaluation.** We perform this step if and only if $n_i^e \geq \mathcal{M}_{Max}^e$ in order to reduce the computational cost. The main goal of this stage is to evaluate the correlation between stored samples from STM and LTM. Firstly, we treat each stored sample as a node and introduce a graph relationship matrix $\mathbf{S}_i \in \mathbb{R}^{n_i^e \times n_i^l}$, whose elements $\mathbf{S}_i(j, u)$ represent the correlation between two samples $\mathbf{x}_{i,j}^e$ and $\mathbf{x}_{i,u}^l$, from STM and LTM respectively. Directly evaluating each $\mathbf{S}_i(j, u)$ in the high-dimensional data space is intractable since it would require overloaded computations [17] and auxiliary training [7,37]. Since the model has been trained on both past samples from LTM and the current samples from STM, it can be used as a discriminator. We then evaluate the distance between two samples based

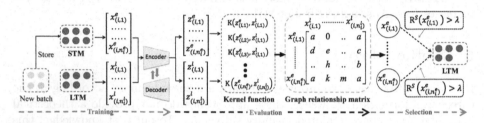

**Fig. 1.** The training of OCM consists of three stages : **(Learning.)** STM continually stores recent samples while the model is trained to adapt both LTM and STM; If STM is full, we perform the evaluation and selection stages, otherwise, we continually perform the learning stage. **(Evaluation.)** We obtain the feature vectors $\{\mathbf{z}_{(i,1)}^e, \cdots, \mathbf{z}_{(i,n_i^l)}^l\}$ from inputs $\{\mathbf{x}_{(i,1)}^e, \cdots, \mathbf{x}_{(i,n_i^l)}^l\}$ by using a VAE encoder, which is used for the evaluation of the sample similarity using the kernel from Eq. (15). This similarity information is preserved in the graph relationship matrix $\mathbf{S}_i$. **(Selection.)** We transfer the samples from STM to LTM using the proposed criterion Eq. (18) by means of $\mathbf{S}_i$ from (16).

| (a) Real testing samples. | (b) VAE-ELBO-Random. | (c) VAE-ELBO-OCM. |

**Fig. 2.** Image reconstruction compared to real images.

on the perceptual feature space of the learned model by using the Radial Basis Function (RBF) kernel :

$$K(\mathbf{x}_{i,j}^e, \mathbf{x}_{i,u}^l) = \exp\left(-\frac{\|\mathbf{z}_{i,j}^e - \mathbf{z}_{i,u}^l\|^2}{2\alpha^2}\right), \tag{15}$$

where $\mathbf{z}_{i,j}^e$ and $\mathbf{z}_{i,u}^l$ are feature vectors extracted from $\mathbf{x}_{i,j}^e$ and $\mathbf{x}_{i,u}^l$ using the feature extractor implemented by the output layer of the encoder $q_\omega(\mathbf{z} \mid \mathbf{x})$ of the VAE model, as illustrated in Fig. 1. $\mathbf{S}_i(j, u) = K(\mathbf{x}_{i,j}^e, \mathbf{x}_{i,u}^l)$ and $\|\cdot\|^2$ is the squared Euclidean distance. $\alpha$ is the scale hyperparameter for the kernel and we set $\alpha = 10$ to ensure that the output of $K(\cdot, \cdot)$ is within $[0, 1]$. Equation (15) can be further accelerated by the matrix operation, expressed as :

$$\mathbf{S}_i = F_{\exp}\left(-(\mathbf{Z}_i^e(-\mathbf{Z}_i^l)^{\mathrm{T}}) \odot (\mathbf{Z}_i^e(-\mathbf{Z}_i^l)^{\mathrm{T}})/2\alpha^2\right), \tag{16}$$

where $\mathbf{Z}_i^e \in \mathbb{R}^{n_i^e \times d_z}$ and $\mathbf{Z}_i^l \in \mathbb{R}^{n_i^l \times d_z}$ are the feature matrices corresponding to $\mathcal{M}_i^e$ and $\mathcal{M}_i^l$, where each row is a feature vector of dimension $d_z$. $(\cdot)^{\mathrm{T}}$ and $\odot$ are the transpose operation and Hadamard product, respectively. $F_{exp}(\cdot)$ is the exponential function for each element in a matrix.

**Stage 3: Sample Selection.** This stage also require satisfying $N_i^e \geq \mathcal{M}_{Max}^e$ to avoid excessive LTM growing. The main goal of this stage is to choose samples that are very different from those already stored in LTM. We achieve this by calculating the average similarity scores using kernels between each candidate sample $\mathbf{x}_{i,j}^e$ and each sample from LTM using $\mathbf{S}_i$ from Eq. (16) :

**Table 1.** The estimation of log-likelihood on all testing samples by using the IWVAE bound with 1000 importance samples.

| Methods | Split MNIST | | | Split Fashion | | | Split MNIST-Fashion | | |
|---|---|---|---|---|---|---|---|---|---|
| | Log | Memory | N | Log | Memory | N | Log | Memory | N |
| VAE-ELBO-Random | -150.79 | 3.0 K | 1 | -280.54 | 3.0 K | 1 | -247.46 | 3.0 K | 1 |
| LIMix [64] | -146.23 | 2.0 K | 30 | -262.52 | 2.0 K | 30 | -238.63 | 2.0 K | 30 |
| CNDPM [35] | -120.71 | 2.0 K | 30 | -257.56 | 2.0 K | 30 | -236.79 | 2.0 K | 30 |
| VAE-ELBO-OCM | -132.07 | 1.6 K | 1 | -250.74 | 1.6 K | 1 | -215.62 | 2.0 K | 1 |
| VAE-IWVAE50-OCM | -127.11 | 1.6 K | 1 | -247.90 | 1.6 K | 1 | -224.34 | 2.0 K | 1 |
| Dynamic-ELBO-OCM | **-115.89** | 1.1 K | 5 | **-237.69** | 1.3 K | 10 | **-187.49** | 1.4 K | 10 |

$$R^S(\mathbf{x}_{i,j}^e) = \frac{1}{n_i^l} \sum_{k=1}^{n_i^l} \mathbf{S}_i(j, k). \tag{17}$$

Equation (17) refers to the distance between $\mathbf{x}_{i,j}^e$ and all samples contained in the LTM. In order to control the size of LTM, we introduce a threshold $\lambda$ for the sample selection :

$$R^S(\mathbf{x}_{i,j}^e) > \lambda \Rightarrow \mathcal{M}_i^l = \mathcal{M}_i^l \cup \mathbf{x}_{i,j}^e. \tag{18}$$

The choice for $\lambda$ influences the diversity and memory size of LTM. Empirically, according to the ablation study in Appendix H.4 from SM, $\lambda \in [0.2, 0.5]$ can achieve the best performance resulting in a reasonable LTM size for most datasets. Once the selection is finished, $\mathcal{M}_i^e$ is cleared for storing novel samples during the next training step $t_{i+1}$.

**Table 2.** IS and FID scores under Split CIFAR10.

| Methods | IS | FID | Memory | N |
|---|---|---|---|---|
| VAE-ELBO-Random | 3.84 | 116.26 | 1.0 K | 1 |
| CNDPM [35] | 4.12 | 95.23 | 1.0 K | 30 |
| LIMix [64] | 3.02 | 156.46 | 1.0 K | 30 |
| VAE-ELBO-OCM | 4.13 | 98.76 | 0.5 K | 1 |
| Dynamic-ELBO-OCM | **4.16** | **92.99** | 0.4 K | 3 |

**Table 3.** The estimation of log-likelihood on "Cross domain"

| Methods | Log | Memory | N |
|---|---|---|---|
| VAE-ELBO-Random | -239.71 | 3.0 K | 1 |
| LIMix [64] | -226.63 | 2.0 K | 30 |
| CNDPM [35] | -218.15 | 2.0 K | 30 |
| VAE-ELBO-OCM | -201.31 | 2.0 K | 1 |
| VAE-IWVAE50-OCM | -204.35 | 2.0 K | 1 |
| Dynamic-ELBO-OCM | **-177.29** | 1.5 K | 11 |

## 5.2 Combining OCM with Expansion Mechanism

According to Lemma 2 and Sect. 4.3, by dynamically expanding the model with new components would lead to better performance. Moreover, the extension mechanism reduces negative transfer when each component learns different underlying data distributions (see detailed analysis in Appendix-C of SM). This analysis inspires us to implement the extension mechanism from two aspects. First, we introduce an expansion criterion to detect the data distribution shift by comparing the loss value between the previously learned and newly seen samples, which ensures a suitable network architecture. Second, to encourage each component to learn different underlying data distributions, we clear STM and LTM when we dynamically add a new component to the mixture model.

The newly added component can be an independent VAE or one that shares its parameters with existing components. In the following, we describe the latter setting. Let $f_{\omega_s}^e : \mathcal{X} \to \mathcal{Z}'$ and $f_{\omega_i}^e : \mathcal{Z}' \to \mathcal{Z}$ be the shared module and the component-specific module for the encoding process, where $i$ represents the component index and $\mathcal{Z}'$ is the feature space. Similar to the encoding process, we have two modules for the decoding process, $f_{\theta_s}^d : \mathcal{Z} \to \mathcal{X}'$ and $f_{\theta_i}^d : \mathcal{X}' \to \mathcal{X}$, where $\mathcal{X}'$ is the feature space. The encoding and decoding processes for the $i$-th component can be implemented by $q_{\theta_{s,i}}(\mathbf{z}\,|\,\mathbf{x}) = f_{\omega_s}^e \odot f_{\omega_i}^e(\mathbf{x})$ and $p_{\theta_{s,i}}(\mathbf{x}\,|\,\mathbf{z}) = f_{\theta_s}^e \odot f_{\theta_i}^e(\mathbf{z})$, respectively, where $f_{\omega_s}^e \odot f_{\omega_i}^e : \mathcal{X} \to \mathcal{Z}' \to \mathcal{Z}$ is the encoding process. The optimization for the $i$-th component corresponds to maximizing ELBO :

$$\mathcal{L}_{ELBO}^i(\mathbf{x}; \theta, \omega) := \mathbb{E}_{q_{\omega_{s,i}}(\mathbf{z}\,|\,\mathbf{x})}\left[\log p_{\theta_{s,i}}(\mathbf{x}\,|\,\mathbf{z})\right] - KL\left[q_{\omega_{s,i}}(\mathbf{z}\,|\,\mathbf{x})\,\|\,p(\mathbf{z})\right] \quad (19)$$

where $\mathbf{z} \sim q_{\omega_{s,i}}(\mathbf{z}\,|\,\mathbf{x})$ and the shared modules are only updated by using Eq. (19) for $i > 1$ in order to avoid forgetting.

**Criterion for Dynamic Expansion.** When a mixture model has multiple components, we evaluate the sample similarity from Eq. (15) by using an augmented feature extractor that concentrates features from each component. The training process for the new components from the dynamic expansion model is the same as the one described in Sect. 5.1 where we incorporate a criterion for the model expansion in

**Step 3 : (Sample Selection)** :

$$|\mathrm{R}_i - \mathrm{R}_{last}| > \lambda_2 \,, \mathrm{R}_i = \frac{1}{N'} \sum\nolimits_{j=1}^{N'} \left\{ \frac{1}{K} \sum\nolimits_{c=1}^{K} \{ \mathcal{L}_{ELBO}^c(\mathbf{x}_j; \theta, \omega) \} \right\}, \qquad (20)$$

where $\mathbf{x}_j$ is the $j$-th sample from the joint memory $\mathcal{M}_i^e \cup \mathcal{M}_i^l$. $N' = n_i^e + n_i^l$ and $\mathrm{R}_i$ is the loss evaluated on all memorized samples using the mixture model at the training step $t_i$. $\mathrm{R}_{last}$ is the most recent loss value. The pseudocode of the algorithm is provided in Appendix-H from SM.

## 6   Experiments

### 6.1   Experiment Setting and Datasets

**Datasets.** For the Log-likelihood evaluation, we have the following settings: 1) **Split MNIST/Fashion.** Split MNIST [33] into ten parts according to the category information and create a data stream by collecting these parts in a class-incremental way. This is also done for Fashion database; 2) **Split MNIST-Fashion.** Combine Split MNIST and Split Fashion into a data stream; 3) **Cross-Domain.** Combine Split MNIST-Fashion and unsorted samples from OMNIGLOT [31]. We adapt CIFAR10 [28] and Tiny-ImageNet [32] for the generative modelling task. Similar to Split MNIST, we divide CIFAR10 and Tiny-ImageNet into ten parts, namely Split CIFAR10 and Split Tiny-ImageNet, respectively. The details of dataset, hyperparameter and network architecture are provided in Appendix-H.1 of SM.

**Evaluation Criteria.** We use the Inception Score (IS) [48] and Fréchet Inception Distance (FID) [19] for the evaluation of reconstruction quality. For the density estimation task, we estimate the real sample log-likelihood by using IWVAE bound [9], as in Eq. (2), considering 5000 importance samples.

**Baseline.** We introduce several baselines used in experiments: 1) VAE-ELBO-OCM : We train a single VAE model with ELBO using the proposed OCM. 2) VAE-IWVAE50-OCM : We train a single VAE model with IWVAE using the proposed OCM where the number of importance samples is 50. 3) VAE-ELBO-Random : We train a single VAE model with a memory that randomly removes samples when it reaches the maximum memory size. 4) Dynamic-ELBO-OCM : We train a mixture model with ELBO using the proposed OCM. 5) CNDPM

[35] : CNDPM uses Dirichlet process for the expansion of the mixture system; 6) LIMix [64] : We assign an episodic memory with a fixed buffer size for the LIMix model used for TFCL. The maximum number of components for various models is set to 30 to avoid memory overload.

**Table 4.** The classification accuracy of five indepdnent runs for various models on three datasets.

**Table 5.** IS and FID on ImageNet database.

| Methods | Split MNIST | Split CIFAR10 | Split CIFAR100 |
|---|---|---|---|
| Finetune* | 19.75 ± 0.05 | 18.55 ± 0.34 | 3.53 ± 0.04 |
| GEM* [39] | 93.25 ± 0.36 | 24.13 ± 2.46 | 11.12 ± 2.48 |
| iCARL* [46] | 83.95 ± 0.21 | 37.32 ± 2.66 | 10.80 ± 0.37 |
| Reservoir* [55] | 92.16 ± 0.75 | 42.48 ± 3.04 | 19.57 ± 1.79 |
| MIR* [4] | 93.20 ± 0.36 | 42.80 ± 2.22 | 20.00 ± 0.57 |
| GSS* [3] | 92.47 ± 0.92 | 38.45 ± 1.41 | 13.10 ± 0.94 |
| CoPE-CE* [13] | 91.77 ± 0.87 | 39.73 ± 2.26 | 18.33 ± 1.52 |
| CoPE* [13] | 93.94 ± 0.20 | 48.92 ± 1.32 | 21.62 ± 0.69 |
| CURL* [45] | 92.59 ± 0.66 | - | - |
| CNDPM* [35] | 93.23 ± 0.09 | 45.21 ± 0.18 | 20.10 ± 0.12 |
| Dynamic-OCM | **94.02 ± 0.23** | **49.16 ± 1.52** | **21.79 ± 0.68** |

| Model | IS | FID |
|---|---|---|
| MVAE-Gau [61] | **6.84** | / |
| MVAE-Gau fixed [61] | 6.30 | / |
| MVAE-GS [61] | 6.52 | / |
| MSVI [30] | 6.12 | / |
| InfoVAE [70] | 6.14 | / |
| $\beta$-VAE [20] | 5.05 | / |
| VAE [25] | 5.46 | / |
| MAE [40] | 5.87 | / |
| VAE-ELBO-Random | 3.15 | 145.36 |
| VAE-ELBO-OCM | 3.36 | 133.23 |

## 6.2 Log-Likelihood Evaluation

In this section, we implement each VAE model or component by using the Bernoulli decoder. All datasets are binarized according to the setting from [9]. The results for Split MNIST, Split Fashion, Split MNIST-Fashion and Cross-domain are provided in Tables 1 and 3, where "Memory" represents the number of samples $N^l$ in LTM. The proposed OCM can improve the performance on the density estimation tasks even when using a small memory size compared to the random selection approach. Additionally, the expansion mechanism combined with the proposed OCM can further improve the performance with a reasonable memory use, especially when learning multiple datasets (Split MNIST-Fashion and Cross-Domain). We also find that the use of IWVAE bound (Eq. (2)) into the proposed OCM can also improve the performance on a single dataset. To compare with the expansion models, such as LIMix and CNDPM, a single model with OCM outperforms these models by using a few more stored samples such as 2.0 K for LTM and 0.5 K for STM vs 2.0 K for LIMix and CNDPM, in Cross-Domain experiments. However, OCM with the expansion mechanism outperforms LIMix and CNDPM by using fewer mixture components.

## 6.3 Evaluation of the Reconstruction Quality

To evaluate the reconstruction quality, we use $\beta$-VAE loss [20] where $\beta = 0.01$ for all models in order to avoid the over-regularization issue [51]. We report the IS and FID scores for the reconstruction quality in Table 2. We can observe that the proposed OCM with the expansion mechanism outperforms other baselines. The IS and FID for Tiny-ImageNet are reported in Appendix-H.3 from SM.

We also explore training a single VAE with OCM for learning ImageNet [29] under TFCL where the batch size is 64. The maximum size for STM and LTM is set to 512 and 2048, respectively, to avoid increasing the computational cost. We follow the settings from [61], as described in Appendix-H.3 from SM, after resizing all images to 64 × 64 pixels. The FID and IS results are provided in Table 5 and the results of all baselines (training on a single dataset) are cited from [61]. The visual results are shown in Fig. 2 where we can observe that the reconstruction of VAE-ELBO-Random is blurred when compared with VAE-ELBO-OCM. These results show that the proposed OCM outperforms the random selection approach in the large-scale dataset under TFCL.

### 6.4  Classification Task

The proposed approach is mainly used in unsupervised learning. We also show that OCM can be used in classification tasks when we train a classifier with OCM on the labelled dataset. We adapt the setting and network architecture from [13] with a batch size of 10 and the memory size for Split MNIST, Split CIFAR10 and Split CIFAR100 is limited to 2 K, 1 K and 5 K, respectively. We report the results in Table 4 where '*' means that the result is cited from [13]. The additional information about baselines and the proposed Dynamic-OCM is provided in Appendix-H.2 of SM. The number of required parameters is provided in Appendix-H.6 of SM. These results show that the proposed OCM outperforms the state-of-the-art methods in the classification task using fewer parameters.

### 6.5  Ablation Study and Theoretical Results

A full ablation study is performed including testing the configuration for the threshold $\lambda$ from Eq (18), STM memory size, batch size and $\lambda_2$ from Eq. (20). We also provide the empirical results for the theoretical analysis. These ablation results and their analysis are provided in Appendix-H.4 from SM.

## 7  Conclusion

We introduce a new theoretical framework for providing insights into the forgetting behaviour of deep models based on VAEs under TFCL. The theoretical analysis demonstrates that ensuring a diversity of data in the pre-training memory is crucial for relieving forgetting in continuous learning systems. Inspired by this result, we propose the Online Cooperative Memorization (OCM) that does not require any supervised signals and therefore can be used in an unsupervised fashion. The empirical results demonstrate the effectiveness of the proposed OCM method.

# References

1. Abbasnejad, E., Dick, M., van der Hengel, A.: Infinite variational autoencoder for semi-supervised learning. In: Proceedings of IEEE Conference on Computer Vision and Pattern Recognition (CVPR), pp. 5888–5897 (2017)
2. Achille, A., et al.: Life-long disentangled representation learning with cross-domain latent homologies. In: Proceedings Advances in Neural Information Processing Systems (NeurIPS), pp. 9873–9883 (2018)
3. Aljundi, R., Lin, M., Goujaud, B., Bengio, Y.: Gradient based sample selection for online continual learning. In: Advances Neural Information Processing Systems (NeurIPS), vol. 33, pp. 11817–11826 (2019)
4. Aljundi, R., et al.: Online continual learning with maximal interfered retrieval. In: Advances in Neural Information Processing Systems (NeurIPS), vol. 33, pp. 11872–11883 (2019)
5. Aljundi, R., Kelchtermans, K., Tuytelaars, T.: Task-free continual learning. In: Proceedings of IEEE/CVF Conference on Computer Vision and Pattern Recognition, pp. 11254–11263 (2019)
6. Bang, J., Kim, H., Yoo, Y., Ha, J.W., Choi, J.: Rainbow memory: continual learning with a memory of diverse samples. In: Proceedings of the IEEE/CVF Conference on Computer Vision and Pattern Recognition, pp. 8218–8227 (2021)
7. Belghazi, M.I., et al.: Mutual information neural estimation. In: Proceedings International Conference on Machine Learning (ICML), vol. PMLR 80, pp. 531–540 (2018)
8. Bousquet, O., Gelly, S., Tolstikhin, I., Simon-Gabriel, C.J., Schoelkopf, B.: From optimal transport to generative modeling: the VEGAN cookbook. arXiv preprint arXiv:1705.07642 (2017)
9. Burda, Y., Grosse, R., Salakhutdinov, R.: Importance weighted autoencoders. arXiv preprint arXiv:1509.00519 (2015)
10. Chaudhry, A., et al.: On tiny episodic memories in continual learning. arXiv preprint arXiv:1902.10486 (2019)
11. Chen, L., Dai, S., Pu, Y., Li, C., Su, Q., Carin, L.: Symmetric variational autoencoder and connections to adversarial learning. In: Proceedings International Conference on Artificial Intelligence and Statistics (AISTATS) 2018, vol. PMLR 84, pp. 661–669 (2018)
12. Courty, N., Flamary, R., Tuia, D., Rakotomamonjy, A.: Optimal transport for domain adaptation. IEEE Trans. Pattern Anal. Mach. Intell. **39**(9), 1853–1865 (2016)
13. De Lange, M., Tuytelaars, T.: Continual prototype evolution: learning online from non-stationary data streams. In: Proceedings of the IEEE/CVF International Conference on Computer Vision (ICCV), pp. 8250–8259 (2021)
14. Egorov, E., Kuzina, A., Burnaev, E.: BooVAE: boosting approach for continual learning of VAE. Adv. Neural Inf. Process. Syst. (NeurIPS) **35**, 17889–17901 (2021)
15. Fang, P., Harandi, M., Petersson, L.: Kernel methods in hyperbolic spaces. In: Proceedings of the IEEE/CVF International Conference on Computer Vision (ICCV), pp. 10665–10674 (2021)
16. Fatras, K., Séjourné, T., Flamary, R., Courty, N.: Unbalanced minibatch optimal transport; applications to domain adaptation. In: International Conference on Machine Learning (ICML), vol. PMLR 139. pp. 3186–3197 (2021)

17. Goldberger, J., Gordon, S., Greenspan, H., et al.: An efficient image similarity measure based on approximations of kl-divergence between two gaussian mixtures. In: Proceedings IEEE International Conference on Computer Vision (ICCV), vol. 3, pp. 487–493 (2003)
18. Goodfellow, I., et al.: Generative adversarial nets. In: Proceedings Advances in Neural Information Proceedings Systems (NIPS), pp. 2672–2680 (2014)
19. Heusel, M., Ramsauer, H., Unterthiner, T., Nessler, B., Hochreiter, S.: GANs trained by a two time-scale update rule converge to a local Nash equilibrium. In: Proceedings Advances in Neural Information Processing Systems (NIPS), pp. 6626–6637 (2017)
20. Higgins, I., et al.: $\beta$-VAE: learning basic visual concepts with a constrained variational framework. In: Proceedings International Conference on Learning Representations (ICLR) (2017)
21. Hinton, G., Vinyals, O., Dean, J.: Distilling the knowledge in a neural network. In: Proceedings NIPS Deep Learning Workshop. arXiv preprint arXiv:1503.02531 (2014)
22. Hua, Y., Zhao, Z., Li, R., Chen, X., Liu, Z., Zhang, H.: Deep learning with long short-term memory for time series prediction. IEEE Commun. Mag. **57**(6), 114–119 (2019)
23. Jung, H., Ju, J., Jung, M., Kim, J.: Less-forgetting learning in deep neural networks. arXiv preprint arXiv:1607.00122 (2016)
24. Kantorovitch, L.: On the translocation of masses. Manag. Sci. **5**(1), 1–4 (1958)
25. Kingma, D.P., Welling, M.: Auto-encoding variational Bayes. arXiv preprint arXiv:1312.6114 (2013)
26. Kirkpatrick, J., et al.: Overcoming catastrophic forgetting in neural networks. Proc. Nat. Acad. Sci. (PNAS) **114**(13), 3521–3526 (2017)
27. Knoblauch, J., Husain, H., Diethe, T.: Optimal continual learning has perfect memory and is NP-hard. In: Proceedings International Conference on Machine Learning (ICML), vol PMLR 119. pp. 5327–5337 (2020)
28. Krizhevsky, A., Hinton, G.: Learning multiple layers of features from tiny images. Technical report (2009)
29. Krizhevsky, A., Sutskever, I., Hinton, G.E.: ImageNet classification with deep convolutional neural networks. In: Advances in Neural Information Processing Systems (NIPS), pp. 1097–1105 (2012)
30. Kurle, R., Günnemann, S., van der Smagt, P.: Multi-source neural variational inference. In: Proceedings of AAAI Conference on Artificial Intelligence, vol. 33, pp. 4114–4121 (2019)
31. Lake, B.M., Salakhutdinov, R., Tenenbaum, J.B.: Human-level concept learning through probabilistic program induction. Science **350**(6266), 1332–1338 (2015)
32. Le, Y., Yang, X.: Tiny imagenet visual recognition challenge. CS 231N **7**(7), 3 (2015)
33. LeCun, Y., Bottou, L., Bengio, Y., Haffner, P.: Gradient-based learning applied to document recognition. Proc. IEEE **86**(11), 2278–2324 (1998)
34. Lee, S., Goldt, S., Saxe, A.: Continual learning in the teacher-student setup: impact of task similarity. In: International Conference on Machine Learning (ICML), vol. PMLR 139. pp. 6109–6119 (2021)
35. Lee, S., Ha, J., Zhang, D., Kim, G.: A neural Dirichlet process mixture model for task-free continual learning. In: Proceedings International Conference on Learning Representations (ICLR), arXiv preprint arXiv:2001.00689 (2020)
36. Li, Z., Hoiem, D.: Learning without forgetting. IEEE Trans. Pattern Anal. Mach. Intell. **40**(12), 2935–2947 (2017)

37. Liu, H., Gu, X., Samaras, D.: Wasserstein GAN with quadratic transport cost. In: Proceedings of the IEEE/CVF International Conference on Computer Vision (ICCV), pp. 4832–4841 (2019)

38. Liu, M.Y., Breuel, T., Kautz, J.: Unsupervised image-to-image translation networks. In: Advances in Neural Information Processing Systems, pp. 700–708 (2017)

39. Lopez-Paz, D., Ranzato, M.: Gradient episodic memory for continual learning. In: Advances in Neural Information Processing Systems, pp. 6467–6476 (2017)

40. Ma, X., Zhou, C., Hovy, E.: MAE: mutual posterior-divergence regularization for variational autoencoders. In: Proceedings International Conference on Learning Representations (ICLR), arXiv preprint arXiv:1901.01498 (2019)

41. Nguyen, C.V., Li, Y., Bui, T.D., Turner, R.E.: Variational continual learning. In: Proceedings of International Conference on Learning Representations (ICLR), arXiv preprint arXiv:1710.10628 (2018)

42. Parisi, G.I., Kemker, R., Part, J.L., Kanan, C., Wermter, S.: Continual lifelong learning with neural networks: a review. Neural Netw. **113**, 54–71 (2019)

43. Raghavan, K., Balaprakash, P.: Formalizing the generalization-forgetting trade-off in continual learning. In: Advances in Neural Information Processing Systems, vol. 34 (2021)

44. Ramapuram, J., Gregorova, M., Kalousis, A.: Lifelong generative modeling. In: Proceedings International Conference on Learning Representations (ICLR), arXiv preprint arXiv:1705.09847 (2017)

45. Rao, D., Visin, F., Rusu, A.A., Teh, Y.W., Pascanu, R., Hadsell, R.: Continual unsupervised representation learning. In: Advances Neural Information Processing Systems (NeurIPS), pp. 7645–7655 (2019)

46. Rebuffi, S.A., Kolesnikov, A., Sperl, G., Lampert, C.H.: iCaRL: incremental classifier and representation learning. In: Proceedings of the IEEE Conference on Computer Vision and Pattern Recognition (CVPR), pp. 2001–2010 (2017)

47. Ren, B., Wang, H., Li, J., Gao, H.: Life-long learning based on dynamic combination model. Appl. Soft Comput. **56**, 398–404 (2017)

48. Salimans, T., Goodfellow, I., Zaremba, W., Cheung, V., Radford, A., Chen, X.: Improved techniques for training GANs. In: Proceedings Advances in Neural Information Processing Systems (NIPS), pp. 2234–2242 (2016)

49. Shin, H., Lee, J.K., Kim, J., Kim, J.: Continual learning with deep generative replay. In: Advances in Neural Information Processing Systems (NIPS), pp. 2990–2999 (2017)

50. Sobolev, A., Vetrov, D.: Importance weighted hierarchical variational inference. In: Advances in Neural Information Processing Systems (NeurIPS), vol. 33 (2019)

51. Takahashi, H., Iwata, T., Yamanaka, Y., Yamada, M., Yagi, S.: Variational autoencoder with implicit optimal priors. In: Proceedings of the AAAI Conference on Artificial Intelligence, vol. 33, pp. 5066–5073 (2019)

52. Tang, S., Chen, D., Zhu, J., Yu, S., Ouyang, W.: Layerwise optimization by gradient decomposition for continual learning. In: Proceedings of the IEEE/CVF Conference on Computer Vision and Pattern Recognition (CVPR), pp. 9634–9643 (2021)

53. Titsias, M.K., Schwarz, J., Matthews, A.G.D.G., Pascanu, R., Teh, Y.W.: Functional regularisation for continual learning with Gaussian processes. In: Proceedings International Conference on Learning Represenations (ICLR), arXiv preprint arXiv:1901.11356 (2019)

54. Tolstikhin, I., Bousquet, O., Gelly, S., Schoelkopf, B.: Wasserstein auto-encoders. In: International Conference on Learning Representations (ICLR), arXiv preprint arXiv:1711.01558 (2018)

55. Vitter, J.S.: Random sampling with a reservoir. ACM Trans. Math. Softw. (TOMS) **11**(1), 37–57 (1985)
56. Wang, S., Li, X., Sun, J., Xu, Z.: Training networks in null space of feature covariance for continual learning. In: Proceedings of the IEEE/CVF Conference on Computer Vision and Pattern Recognition (CVPR), pp. 184–193 (2021)
57. Ye, F., Bors, A.: Lifelong teacher-student network learning. IEEE Trans. Pattern Anal. Mach. Intell. (2021). https://doi.org/10.1109/TPAMI.2021.3092677
58. Ye, F., Bors, A.G.: Learning latent representations across multiple data domains using lifelong VAEGAN. In: Vedaldi, A., Bischof, H., Brox, T., Frahm, J.-M. (eds.) ECCV 2020. LNCS, vol. 12365, pp. 777–795. Springer, Cham (2020). https://doi.org/10.1007/978-3-030-58565-5_46
59. Ye, F., Bors, A.G.: Lifelong learning of interpretable image representations. In: Proceedings International Conference on Image Processing Theory, Tools and Applications (IPTA), pp. 1–6 (2020)
60. Ye, F., Bors, A.G.: Mixtures of variational autoencoders. In: 2020 Tenth International Conference on Image Processing Theory, Tools and Applications (IPTA), pp. 1–6 (2020)
61. Ye, F., Bors, A.G.: Deep mixture generative autoencoders. IEEE Trans. Neural Netw. Learn. Syst. **33**, 1–15 (2021). https://doi.org/10.1109/TNNLS.2021.3071401
62. Ye, F., Bors, A.G.: Infovaegan: learning joint interpretable representations by information maximization and maximum likelihood. In: Proceedings IEEE International Conference on Image Processing (ICIP), pp. 749–753 (2021). https://doi.org/10.1109/ICIP42928.2021.9506169
63. Ye, F., Bors, A.G.: Learning joint latent representations based on information maximization. Inform. Sci. **567**, 216–236 (2021)
64. Ye, F., Bors, A.G.: Lifelong infinite mixture model based on knowledge-driven Dirichlet process. In: Proceedings of the IEEE International Conference on Computer Vision (ICCV) (2021)
65. Ye, F., Bors, A.G.: Lifelong mixture of variational autoencoders. IEEE Trans. Neural Netw. Learn. Syst. 1–14 (2021). https://doi.org/10.1109/TNNLS.2021.3096457
66. Ye, F., Bors, A.G.: Lifelong twin generative adversarial networks. In: Proceedings IEEE International Conference on Image Processing (ICIP), pp. 1289–1293 (2021)
67. Ye, F., Bors, A.G.: Learning an evolved mixture model for task-free continual learning (2022)
68. Ye, F., Bors, A.G.: Lifelong generative modelling using dynamic expansion graph model. In: AAAI on Artificial Intelligence. AAAI Press (2022)
69. Zhai, M., Chen, L., Tung, F., He, J., Nawhal, M., Mori, G.: Lifelong GAN: continual learning for conditional image generation. In: Proceedings of the IEEE/CVF International Conference on Computer Vision (ICCV), pp. 2759–2768 (2019)
70. Zhao, S., Song, J., Ermon, S.: InfoVAE: balancing learning and inference in variational autoencoders. In: Proceedings AAAI Conference on Artificial Intelligence, vol. 33, pp. 5885–5892 (2019)

# Learning to Learn with Smooth Regularization

Yuanhao Xiong$^{(\boxtimes)}$ and Cho-Jui Hsieh

University of California, Los Angeles, CA 90095, USA
{yhxiong,chohsieh}@cs.ucla.edu

**Abstract.** Recent decades have witnessed great advances of deep learning in tackling various problems such as classification and decision making. The rapid development gave rise to a novel framework, Learning-to-Learn (L2L), in which an automatic optimization algorithm (optimizer) modeled by neural networks is expected to learn rules for updating the target objective function (optimizee). Despite its advantages for specific problems, L2L still cannot replace classic methods due to its instability. Unlike hand-engineered algorithms, neural optimizers may suffer from the instability issue—under distinct but similar states, the same neural optimizer can produce quite different updates. Motivated by the stability property that should be satisfied by an ideal optimizer, we propose a regularization term that can enforce the smoothness and stability of the learned optimizers. Comprehensive experiments on the neural network training tasks demonstrate that the proposed regularization consistently improve the learned neural optimizers even when transferring to tasks with different architectures and datasets. Furthermore, we show that our smoothness-inducing regularizer can improve the performance of neural optimizers on few-shot learning tasks. Code can be found at https://github.com/xyh97/SmoothedOptimizer.

**Keywords:** Learning to Learn · Smoothness-inducing regularizer

## 1 Introduction

Optimization is always regarded as one of the most important foundations for deep learning, and its development has pushed forward tremendous breakthroughs in various domains including computer vision and natural language processing [3, 16]. Effective algorithms such as SGD [22], Adam [12] and AdaBound [15] have been proposed to work well on a variety of tasks. In parallel to this line of hand-designed methods, Learning-to-Learn (L2L) [1,3,16,18,28], a novel framework aimed at an automatic optimization algorithm (optimizer), provides a new direction to performance improvement in updating a target function (optimizee). Typically, the optimizer, modeled as a neural network, takes as

**Supplementary Information** The online version contains supplementary material available at https://doi.org/10.1007/978-3-031-20050-2_32.

input a certain state representation of the optimizee and outputs corresponding updates for parameters. Then such a neural optimizer can be trained like any other network based on specific objective functions.

Empirical results have demonstrated that these learned optimizers can perform better optimization in terms of the final loss and convergence rate than general hand-engineered ones [1,3,16,18,28]. In addition, such advantages in faster training make the learned optimizer a great fit for few-shot learning (FSL) [11,20], where only a limited number of labelled examples per class are available for generalizing a classifier to a new task.

However, instability concealed behind the algorithm impedes its development significantly. There are some unsolved issues challenging the promotion of neural optimizers such as gradient explosion in unrolled optimization [18] and short-horizon bias [29]. One of the most essential problems is that contrary to traditional optimizers, the learned ones modeled as neural networks cannot guarantee smoothness with respect to input data. Specifically, an ideal optimizer is expected to conduct similar updates given similar states of the target optimizee. For instance, SGD updates a parameter by a magnitude proportional to its original gradient. However, current meta learners neglect this property and suffer from the issue that they would produce a quite different output while merely adding a small perturbation to the input state.

Such a phenomenon has been widely observed in other machine learning problems like image classification [7], where the perturbed image can fool the classifier to make a wrong prediction. Inspired by the progress in adversarial training [17] where the worst-case loss is minimized, we propose an algorithm that takes the smoothness of the learned optimizer into account. Through penalizing the non-smoothness by a regularization term, the neural optimizer is trained to capture a smooth update rule with better performance.

In summary, we are the first to consider the smoothness of neural optimizers, and our main contributions include:

- A smoothness-inducing regularizer is proposed to improve the existing training of learned optimizers. This term, representing the maximal distance of updates from the current state to the other in the neighborhood, is minimized to narrow the output gap for similar states.
- We evaluate our proposed regularization term on various classification problems using neural networks and the learned optimizer outperforms hand-engineered methods even if transferring to tasks with different architectures and datasets.
- In addition to generic neural network training, we also conduct experiments on few-shot learning based on a Meta-LSTM optimizer [20] and SIB [11]. Results show that our regularizer consistently improves the accuracy on FSL benchmark datasets for 5-way few shot learning problems.

## 2  Related Work

Gradient-based optimization has drawn extensive attention due to its significance to deep learning. There are various algorithms that have been proposed to improve training of deep neural networks, including SGD [22], Adam [12], RMSProp [10], and the like. On the other hand, a profound thought of updating the optimizee automatically rather than using hand-engineered algorithms has broken the routine and shown great potentials in improving performance for specific problems. Early attempts can be dated back to 1990s s when [5] leveraged recurrent neural networks to model adaptive optimization algorithms. The idea was further developed in [31] where neural optimizers were trained to tackle fundamental convex optimization problems. Recently in the era of deep learning, a seminal work of [1] designed a learning-to-learn framework with an LSTM optimizer, which obtained better performance than some traditional optimizers for training neural networks. Follow-up work in [16] and [28] have improved the generalization and scalability of learned optimizers. L2L framework is easier to train and can adaptively determine the step size and update direction in the meanwhile. L2L has also been extended to various applications such as few-shot learning [20], zeroth-order optimization [23] and adversarial training [30].

This paper is the first to investigate the smoothness of neural optimizers. It is related to the notion of adversarial robustness in classification models. As observed in [7], neural network based models are vulnerable to malicious perturbations. In particular, for image classification the classifier would be fooled by adversarial examples to make a wrong prediction [7], while for reinforcement learning the agent is likely to act differently under perturbed states [25]. Our learned optimizers might be affected by this issue as well. In other domains some algorithms have been proposed to mitigate the non-smooth property of neural networks such as adversarial training [17], and $SR^2L$ [25]. In this paper, our method utilizes the idea of minimizing the worst-case loss to regularize training of neural optimizers towards smoothness. In contrast to previous algorithms targeted at classification, we design a specific regularizer to neural optimizers.

## 3    Background on the L2L Framework

In this section, we present the framework of learning to learn with neural optimizers for tackling problems of general optimization for classification and few-shot learning.

### 3.1    Optimization

As shown in Fig. 1, like any traditional optimization methods, we can apply the learned optimizer in following steps:

(a) At each time step $t$, feed a batch of training examples $\{(x, y)\}$ from the distribution $\mathcal{D}$ into the target classifier $f$ parameterized by $\theta$, and the state of the optimizee $s_t$ can be described by several values. In the paper, we use $s_t = (\theta_t, \nabla_{\theta_t}\ell, \mu_t, \nu_t)$. $\mu_t$ and $\nu_t$ are first and second moment respectively.
(b) Given the current state $s_t$ and the hidden state $h_t$, the neural optimizer $m$ parameterized by $\phi$ accordingly outputs the increment of the parameter and the next hidden state by $u_t, h_{t+1} = m(s_t, h_t)$.

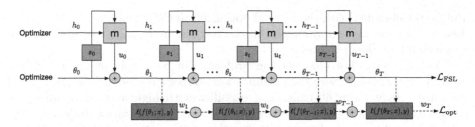

**Fig. 1.** The framework of learning-to-learn. The dashed line shows the computation graph of the objective function $\mathcal{L}_{\text{opt}}$ for training the optimizer to learn a general update rule while the horizontal full line is the one for few-shot learning. Note that $m$ is the neural optimizer parameterized by $\phi$, and $s_t$ is the state of the optimizee taking the form of $s_t = (\theta_t, \ldots, \nabla_\theta \ell)^T$.

(c) Then the optimizer just updates the parameter by $\theta_{t+1} = \theta_t + u_t$.

Note that all operations are coordinate-wise, which means the parameters of the optimizee are updated by a shared neural optimizer independently and maintain their individual hidden states.

The exploitation of the learned optimizer is straightforward but how can we train it? Following [1], since parameters of the optimizee depend implicitly on the optimizer, which can be written as $\theta_t(\phi)$, the quality of the optimizer can be reflected by performance of the optimizee for some horizon $T$, leading to the objective function below to evaluate the optimizer:

$$\mathcal{L}_{\text{opt}}(\phi) = \mathbb{E}_{(x,y)\sim\mathcal{D}} \left[ \sum_{t=1}^{T} w_t \ell(f(\theta_t(\phi); x), y) \right]. \tag{1}$$

$\ell(\cdot, \cdot)$ represents cross-entropy and $w_t$ is the weight assigned for each time step.

### 3.2 Few-Shot Learning

Apart from optimization, the superiority of learned optimizers is a natural fit for few-shot learning. Generally, FSL is a type of machine learning problems with only a limited number of labeled examples for a specific task [27]. In this paper, we mainly focus on FSL targeted at image classification, specifically $N$-way-$K$-shot classification. We deal with a group of meta-sets $\mathcal{D}_{\text{meta}}$ in this task. Each element in $\mathcal{D}_{\text{meta}}$ is a meta-set $D = (D_{\text{train}}, D_{\text{test}})$, where $D_{\text{train}}$ is composed of $K$ images for each of the $N$ classes (thus $K \cdot N$ images in total) and $D_{\text{test}}$ contains a number of examples for evaluation. The goal is to find an optimization strategy that trains a classifier leveraging $D_{\text{train}}$ with only a few labeled examples to achieve good learning performance on $D_{\text{test}}$. All meta-sets are further divided into three separate sets: meta-training set $\mathcal{D}_{\text{meta-train}}$, meta-validation set $\mathcal{D}_{\text{meta-val}}$, and meta-testing set $\mathcal{D}_{\text{meta-test}}$. More concretely, $\mathcal{D}_{\text{meta-train}}$ is utilized to learn an optimizer and $\mathcal{D}_{\text{meta-val}}$ is for hyperparameter optimization. After the optimizer is determined, we conduct evaluation on $\mathcal{D}_{\text{meta-test}}$: we first update the classifier with the learned optimizer on the training-set in $\mathcal{D}_{\text{meta-test}}$; then we use the average accuracy on the test set in $\mathcal{D}_{\text{meta-test}}$ to evaluate the performance of the optimizer.

The $N$-way-$K$-shot classification problem can be simply incorporated into the L2L framework, where the optimization strategy is modeled by the learned optimizer. As we aim at training a classifier with high average performance on the testing set, instead of harnessing the whole optimization trajectory, the objective can be modified to attach attention only to the final testing loss:

$$\mathcal{L}_{\text{FSL}} = \mathbb{E}_{D\sim\mathcal{D}_{\text{meta}}}\mathbb{E}_{(x,y)\sim D_{\text{test}}}\left[\ell\left(f\left(\theta_T(\phi); x\right), y\right)\right], \tag{2}$$

where $\theta_T$ is updated based on a procedure described in Sect. 3.1 under examples from $D_{\text{train}}$.

## 4   Method

### 4.1   Motivation

Despite great potentials of neural optimizers in improving traditional optimization and few-shot learning, there exists a significant problem impeding the development of L2L. In contrast to classical hand-engineered optimization methods, those learned ones cannot guarantee a smooth update of parameters, i.e., producing similar outputs for similar states, where by state we mean the gradient or parameters of the optimizee. In Fig. 2, we demonstrate the non-smoothness of the learned optimizer explicitly. This is a typical phenomenon in various neural-network-based algorithms such as image classification and reinforcement learning. [8] and [25] have pointed out advantages of smoothness of a function to mitigate overfitting, improve sample efficiency and stabilize the overall training procedure. Thus, enforcing the smoothness of the learned optimier can be crucial to improve its performance and stability.

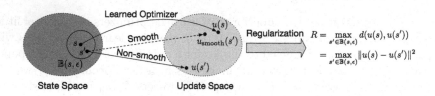

**Fig. 2.** An illustration of non-smoothness in the neural optimizer.

### 4.2   Smoothness Regularization

Some techniques, such as $L_2$ regularization and gradient clipping, have been developed and utilized in training neural optimizers to enforce smoothness but they are shown insufficient to reduce non-smoothness [1,16,18]. We propose to robustify the learned optimizer through a smoothness-inducing training procedure where a regularization term is introduced to narrow the gap between outputs of two similar input states. It is also known as an effective method to constrain the Lipschitz constant of neural networks to boost smoothness.

To describe our method clearly, we first denote two states before updating the optimizee at the time step $t+1$ by $s_t$ and $s_t'$. Note that $s_t$ and $s_t'$ are distinct but similar states, i.e., $s_t' \in \mathbb{B}(s_t, \epsilon)$, where $\mathbb{B}(s_t, \epsilon)$ represents the neighborhood of $s$ within the $\epsilon$-radius ball in a certain norm and $\epsilon$ is perturbation strength. In this paper, we just use $\ell_\infty$ norm without loss of generality. Fix the hidden state $h_t$, then $u_t$ and $u_t'$, which are the corresponding parameter increments of $s_t$ and $s_t'$, can be written as functions of the state $u(s_t)$ and $u(s_t')$ explicitly. An ideal optimizer is expected to produce similar updates and thus to attain such an optimizer, our goal is to minimize the discrepancy $d(\cdot, \cdot)$ between $u(s_t)$ and $u(s_t')$. Inspired by adversarial training [17], it is intuitive to find the gap under the worst-case as the targeted difference that takes the form of $\max d(u(s_t), u(s_t'))$ and minimize this term directly. However, the optimizer that takes the state of optimizee as input and the update as output, is different from the classifier whose input is an image and output is a vector of softmax logits. There is no classification for the optimizer so distance metrics such as cross-entropy and KL-divergence are not applicable to our problem. Since the output is a scalar value, we measure the distance with the squared difference and the desired gap at the time step $t+1$ becomes

$$R_{t+1}(\phi) = \max_{s_t' \in \mathbb{B}(s_t,\epsilon)} d(u(s_t), u(s_t')) = \max_{s_t' \in \mathbb{B}(s_t,\epsilon)} \|u(s_t) - u(s_t')\|^2. \tag{3}$$

After the regularization term is determined, we can then add it to the original objective function of L2L as a regularizer. For each time step, we have the following training objective:

$$\ell_t(\phi) = \ell(f(\theta_t(\phi); x), y) + \lambda R_t(\phi), \tag{4}$$

where $\lambda$ is the regularization coefficient and the parameters $\phi$ of the optimizer is updated by

$$\min_\phi \mathcal{L}_{\text{opt}}(\phi) = \mathbb{E}_{(x,y)\sim D} \left[ \sum_{t=1}^{T} w_t \ell_t(\phi) \right]. \tag{5}$$

For few-shot learning, we store regularization terms during the training procedure with $D_{\text{train}}$ and simply add the accumulation of them to Eq. 2, leading to the training of the learned optimizer as

$$\min_\phi \mathcal{L}_{\text{FSL}}(\phi) = \mathbb{E}_{D\sim\mathcal{D}_{\text{meta}}} \left[ \mathbb{E}_{(x,y)\sim D_{\text{test}}} \ell \left( f(\theta_T(\phi); x), y \right) \right.$$

$$\left. + \mathbb{E}_{(x,y)\sim D_{\text{train}}} \lambda \sum_{t=1}^{T} R_t(\phi) \right]. \tag{6}$$

It should be emphasized that our proposed regularizer can be applied to any neural optimizer-based algorithms in meta-learning, such as methods in [1,11, 16].

### 4.3  Training the Optimizer

The key component for training the optimizer is the calculation of the regularization term in Eq. 3. As stated in [25], in practice we can effectively approximate the solution of the inner maximization by a fixed number of Projected Gradient Descent (PGD) steps:

$$s' = \Pi_{\mathbb{B}(s,\epsilon)}(\eta \operatorname{sign}(\nabla_{s'} d(u(s), u(s'))) + s'), \tag{7}$$

where $\Pi$ is the projection operator to control the state located within the given radius of the neighborhood. Note that we use truncated Backpropagation Through Time (BPTT) to update our RNN optimizer in case of a too long horizon. For the predefined weight in Eq. 5, to make best use of the optimization trajectory and concentrate more on the loss of the last step at the same time [3], we adopt a linearly-increasing schedule that $w_t = t \bmod (T + 1)$ where $T$ is the number of step in each truncation. We present the whole training procedure in Algorithm 1 below.

---

**Algorithm 1** Learning-to-Learn with Smooth-inducing regularization

---

1: **Input:** training data $\{(x, y)\}$, step sizes $\eta_1$ and $\eta_2$, inner steps $K$, total steps $T_{\text{total}}$, truncated steps $T$, classifier parameterized by $\theta$, optimizer parameterized by $\phi$
2: **repeat**
3:     Initialize $\theta$ randomly, reset RNN hidden state
4:     $\mathcal{L} \leftarrow 0$
5:     **for** $t = 0, \dots, T_{\text{total}} - 1$ **do**
6:         Sample a batch of data $(x, y)$, feed it to the classifier, obtain state $s_t$
7:         Update $\theta$ as demonstrated in Sect. 3.1
8:         $s'_t \leftarrow s_t + 0.05 * \mathcal{N}(\mathbf{0}, \mathbf{I})$
9:         **for** $k = 1, \dots, K$ **do**                                          ▷ Find the perturbed state
10:             $s'_t \leftarrow \Pi_{\mathbb{B}(s_t, \epsilon)}(\eta_1 \operatorname{sign}(\nabla_{s'_t} d(u(s_t), u(s'_t))) + s'_t)$
11:         **end for**
12:         $R_{t+1} \leftarrow \|u(s_t) - u(s'_t)\|^2$                                ▷ Regularization term
13:         $\mathcal{L} \leftarrow \mathcal{L} + w_{t+1} \ell_{t+1}$                            ▷ $\ell_{t+1}$ is computed by Eq. 4
14:         **if** $t \bmod T - 1 == 0$ **then**
15:             Update $\phi$ by $\mathcal{L}$ using Adam with $\eta_2$
16:             $\mathcal{L} \leftarrow 0$
17:         **end if**
18:     **end for**
19: **until** converged

---

Specifically, since our aim is to find a perturbed state in the neighborhood of the original state, we can obtain it as follows: a) Starting from the original state $s$, we add an imperceptible noise to initialize $s'$; b) Compute the current value of $d(u(s), u(s'))$, backpropagate the gradient back to $s'$ to calculate $\nabla_{s'} d(u(s), u(s'))$, and then adjust the desired state by a small step $\eta$ in the direction, i.e., $\text{sign}(\nabla_{s'} d(u(s), u(s')))$, that maximizes the difference; (c) Run $K$ steps in Eq. 7 to approximate the regularization term in Eq. 3.

## 5  Experimental Results

We are implementing comprehensive experiments for evaluation of our proposed regularizer. Detailed results are presented in Sect. 5.1 for neural network training and Sect. 5.2 for few-shot learning. All algorithms are implemented in PyTorch-1.2.0 with one NVIDIA 1080Ti GPU.

### 5.1  L2L for Neural Network Training

In this part, we evaluate our method through the task of learning the general update rule for training neural networks. The performance of different optimization algorithms is primarily displayed in learning curves of both training and testing loss, as suggested in previous studies [1, 4, 16, 18]. As loss and accuracy do not necessarily correlate, we also report accuracy curves for thoroughness.

**Experiment Settings.** We consider image classification on two popular datasets, MNIST [14] and CIFAR10 [13]. Our learned optimizer with regularization is compared with hand-designed methods including SGD, SGD with momentum (SGDM), Adam, AMSGrad, and RMSProp, as well as neural optimizers including DMOptimizer [1] and SimpleOptimizer [3]. For hand-designed optimizers, we tune the learning rate with grid search over a logarithmically spaced range $[10^{-4}, 1]$ and report the performance with the best hyperparameters. As to baseline neural optimizers, we use recommended hyperparameters, optimizer structures, and state definitions in [1] and [3] respectively. We have tried different hyperparameters for baselines and found that recommended ones are the best in our experiments. Our smoothed optimizers adopt original settings, except for two extra hyperparemeters for training, the perturbation strength $\epsilon$ and the regularization coefficient $\lambda$. In particular, $\epsilon$ and $\lambda$ in our method are also determined by a logarithmic grid search with the range $\epsilon \in [10^{-2}, 10]$ and $\lambda \in [10^{-1}, 10^2]$. Neural optimizers are learned with Adam of the learning rate $10^{-4}$ with the number of total steps $T_{\text{total}} = 200$ and truncated steps $T = 20$. Note that for all neural optimizers we only tune the hyperparameters during training and directly apply them to a new optimization problem, while for hand-engineered algorithms, the learning rate is always tuned for the specific task. Experiments for each task are conducted five times with different seeds and the batch size used for following problems is 128. More implementation details are presented in Appendix C.

**Compatibility of the Proposed Regularizer.** First of all, we conduct an experiment to demonstrate that the proposed regularization term can be combined with various L2L structures. We demonstrate the performance of learned optimizers including training loss and testing loss for training a 2-layer MLP on MNIST. As can be seen in Fig. 3a and 3d, two L2L architectures, DMOptimizer [1] and SimpleOptimizer [3], are compared. With the regularizer, the smoothed version of both optimizers make an improvement in the final training and testing loss, and obtain a faster convergence rate at the same time. In addition, since SimpleOptimizer performs better than DMOptimizer, which is consistent with the observation in [3], we will apply it as our base optimizer in the later experiments.

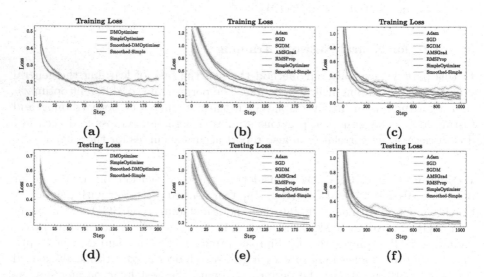

**Fig. 3.** Learning curves of classification on MNIST. Training loss is shown in the first row and testing loss in the second row. (a) and (d) are results of two neural optimizer structures to show the compatibility of our proposed regularizer; (b) and (e) demonstrate performance of different optimizers for training LeNet of 200 steps, while (c) and (f) extend the optimization to 1000 steps.

**Training on MNIST.** In this experiment, we conduct experiments to train the neural optimizers for a 200-step optimization of LeNet on MNIST. We observe its performance under two scenarios:

**(a) Training LeNet with different initializations.** As the learned optimizer is originally trained to update parameters of LeNet, we directly apply it to optimize networks with the same architecture but distinct initializations. Performances of various optimizers in training and testing loss are presented in Fig. 3b and 3e. We can see that our proposed smoothed optimizer outperforms all other baselines including hand-designed methods and the original SimpleOptimizer.

**(b) Generalization to longer steps.** Following [1], we also make an evaluation on optimization for more steps. Although the neural optimizer is only trained within 200 steps, it is capable of updating the optimizee until 1000 steps with faster convergence rate and better final loss consistently, as shown in Fig. 3c and 3f.

**Training on CIFAR-10.** It is insufficient to merely test different optimizers on MNIST, whose size is relatively small. Therefore, we add to the difficulty of the targeted task and focus on image classification on CIFAR-10. The classifier of interest is a 3-layer convolutional neural network with 32 units per layer and the learned optimizer is employed to update the optimizee for 10000 steps. It should be pointed out that the neural optimizer is still trained within 200 steps and the optimization step for evaluation is 50 times larger than what it has explored during training. Figure 4a and 4b demonstrate its great generalization ability: the smooth version of the learned optimizer can converge faster and better than hand-engineered algorithms such as SGD and Adam, even though it only observes the optimization trajectory in the limited steps at the very beginning. Our smoothed variant also outperforms the original learned optimizer.

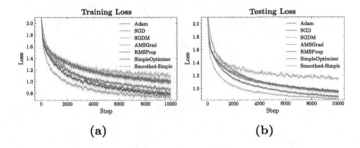

**Fig. 4.** Performance of training a 3-layer CNN for 10000 steps on CIFAR10.

**Transferrablity to Different Settings.** After obtaining a neural optimizer trained on CIFAR-10 with a 3-layer CNN, we evaluate its transferrability in multiple aspects. Specifically, we first transfer the optimizer to training another network structure, ResNet-18 [9] for 10000 steps. In Fig. 5a and 5d, Smoothed-Simple without finetuning can still beat all hand-designed methods. Besides, it should be emphasized that SimpleOptimizer oscillates violently at the end of training and loses its advantages over traditional methods for this transferring task, while the performance of our Smoothed-Simple is consistent and robust.

Moreover, since we have shown that our neural optimizer can generalize to longer training horizon and different network architectures on optimizees with the same dataset, this naturally leads to the following question: can our neural optimizer learn the intrinsic update rule so that it can generalize to unseen data? To answer this question, we modify the experimental setting to evaluate our proposed optimizer on unseen data. We split the original CIFAR-10 dataset into three different sets: a training set containing 6 classes, a validation set and a testing set with 2 classes respectively. When training the optimizer, we sample 2 classes from training set and minimize the objective function for a binary classification problem. Images in the validation set are exploited to select the optimizer which achieves best final testing loss in the 200-step optimization. A comparison of learning curves among our smoothed optimizer, SimpleOptimizer, and the rest hand-designed methods for updating the classifier on two unseen classes is shown in Fig. 5b and 5e. We can observe that the smoothed optimizer learns more quickly and better than other algorithms.

Finally, we test the performance of our optimizer in the most difficult setting: training a ResNet-18 on CIFAR-100, where both the network structure and the dataset are modified. It can be observed in Fig. 5c and 5f that Smoothed-Simple has comparable performance with fine-tuned hand-engineered optimizers in terms of testing loss. On the contrary, SimpleOptimizer is incapable of dealing with this scenario with a large dataset and a complicated network.

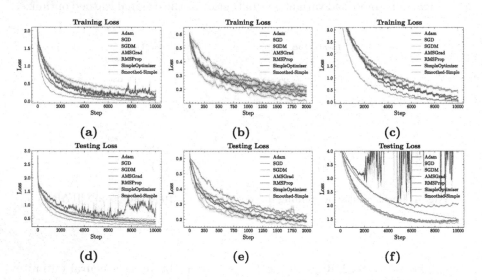

**Fig. 5.** Performance under transferred settings. (a) and (d) are results of 10000-step optimization of ResNet-18. Results of a designed binary classification are reported in (b) and (e). (c) and (f) are results of a transferring task to train a ResNet-18 on CIFAR100.

**Comparison with Other Regularization Methods.** As the proposed method serves as a novel regularization term, for the completeness of experiments, we compare our adversarial regularization with three representative techniques: $\ell_2$ regularization [24], orthogonal regularization [2], and spectral normalization [19]. In detail, we train a 3-layer CNN on CIFAR-10 for 10000 steps, following the setting in Sect. 5.1. Results of training and testing loss can be found in Fig. 6, and we also report the test accuracy for reference in Table 1. It can be observed that orthogonal regularization even worsens the learned optimizer, which cannot provide meaningful updates and only leads to a random-guess classifier with 10.00% on test accuracy. While $\ell_2$ regularization and spectral normalization can improve the SimpleOptimizer to 69.69% and 69.35% respectively, our proposed Smoothed-Simple still outperforms them significantly with 72.50%. This experiment shows that the smoothness-inducing regularization obtained by PGD can achieve performance gain against other popular regularization techniques and is more suitable in training a neural optimizer.

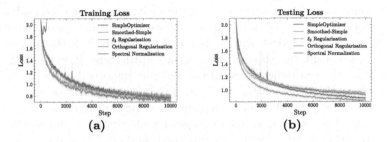

**Fig. 6.** Performance of neural optimizers with different regularization methods.

**Table 1.** Test accuracy of different regularizers.

| Regularizer | Test accuracy |
| --- | --- |
| SimpleOptimizer | 69.02 ± 0.58% |
| Simple-Smoothed | **72.50 ± 0.49%** |
| $\ell_2$ Regularization | 69.69 ± 0.56% |
| Orthogonal Regularization | 10.00 ± 0.04% |
| Spectral Normalization | 69.35 ± 1.23% |

**Smoothness with Perturbation.** In this section, we analyze the optimizer's smoothness property with perturbation. Detailedly, we sample 1000 points from $\mathcal{N}(0, 0.1)$ to form a set of perturbed states around 0. Then these states are fed into the simple and smoothed optimizer respectively, and corresponding outputs are shown in Fig. 7 (x-axis in (a) is the state number while (b) sorts the specific state values.) Around the zero state with zero gradient, the update with a small magnitude is expected for an ideal optimizer. We can see that the smooth version can produce much more stable updates around zero state, while SimpleOptimizer suffers from non-smoothness.

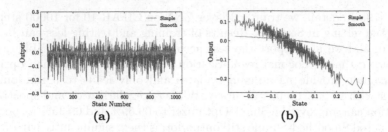

**Fig. 7.** A comparison of smoothness between simple and smoothed optimizer.

**Additional Evaluation.** Besides the metric of loss, we explore classification accuracy which is another important performance indicator, to show advantages of our smoothed neural optimizer. In Fig. 8, we present curves of training and testing accuracy, for MNIST with LeNet and CIFAR10 with the 3-layer CNN. We can observe that the relative ranks of all optimizers do not change if the evaluation metric is switched to accuracy, and our smoothed optimizer still outperforms other algorithms with best final training and testing accuracy as well as convergence rate. Furthermore, we conduct experiments on a comparatively large-scale dataset, tiny-ImageNet in Appendix D. Similar performance on this dataset shows the effectiveness of our proposed method. We also include preliminary experimental results on a sentiment analysis task in Appendix D.

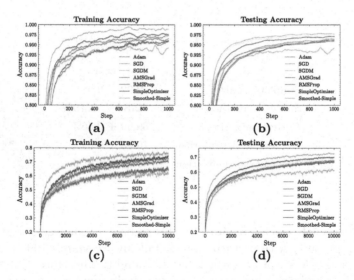

**Fig. 8.** Performance of different optimizers in training and testing accuracy. (a)-(b) for MNIST with LeNet and (c)-(d) for CIFAR-10 with a 3-layer CNN.

Furthermore, we conduct experiments on a comparatively large-scale dataset, tiny-ImageNet in Appendix D.3. Similar performance on this dataset shows the effectiveness of our proposed method.

## 5.2 Few-Shot Learning with LSTM

Apart from improving the training procedures, L2L can be applied to few-shot learning as well. Therefore, in this part we primarily explore the effectiveness of our smoothed neural optimizer in FSL, in particular, $N$-way-$K$-shot learning. We consider 5-way-1-shot and 5-way-5-shot problems on two benchmark datasets, miniImageNet [26] and tieredImageNet [21]. The base structure we utilize is Meta-LSTM, proposed in [20] to train an LSTM-based meta learner to learn the optimization rule in the few-shot regime. We compare it with our smoothed version. We keep all hyperparameters the same as reported in [20] and only tune $\epsilon$ and $\lambda$ in a manner introduced in Sect. 5.1. Statistical results of 5 experiments with different random seeds are reported in Table 2. Our smoothed Meta-LSTM attains 2% percents improvement over all scenarios against the baseline. It should be emphasized that the performance boost is purely credited to the regularizer since we apply our regularization term to the exactly same structure as Meta-LSTM. Since the official code for Meta-LSTM is written in lua and is out-of-date, we use the latest PyTorch implementation in [6]. Thus, our results might lead to inconsistency with the original paper but do not affect the conclusion.

**Table 2.** Average accuracy of 5-way few shot learning on miniImageNet and tieredIamgeNet.

| Model | miniImageNet | | tieredImageNet | |
|---|---|---|---|---|
| | 1-shot | 5-shot | 1-shot | 5-shot |
| Meta-LSTM | $38.20 \pm 0.73\%$ | $56.56 \pm 0.65\%$ | $36.43 \pm 0.65\%$ | $53.45 \pm 0.61\%$ |
| Smoothed Meta-LSTM | $\mathbf{40.42 \pm 0.68\%}$ | $\mathbf{58.90 \pm 0.61\%}$ | $\mathbf{36.74 \pm 0.76\%}$ | $\mathbf{55.14 \pm 0.60\%}$ |

In addition, we integrate our proposed regularizer into one of the most recent methods involving a neural optimizer, SIB [11] on miniImageNet and CIFAR-FS. Results are presented in Table 3 and with regularization, SIB performs consistently better especially for 5-shot tasks.

**Table 3.** Average accuracy of 5-way few shot learning problems on miniImageNet and CIFAR-FS.

| Model | Backbone | miniImageNet | | CIFAR-FS | |
|---|---|---|---|---|---|
| | | 1-shot | 5-shot | 1-shot | 5-shot |
| SIB($\eta = 1e^{-3}$, $K = 3$) | WRN-28-10 | $69.6 \pm 0.6\%$ | $78.9 \pm 0.4\%$ | $78.4 \pm 0.6\%$ | $85.3 \pm 0.4\%$ |
| Smoothed SIB | WRN-28-10 | $\mathbf{70.0 \pm 0.5\%}$ | $\mathbf{80.8 \pm 0.3\%}$ | $\mathbf{79.2 \pm 0.4\%}$ | $\mathbf{86.1 \pm 0.4\%}$ |

# 6    Conclusion and Discussion

This paper first investigates the smoothness of learned optimizers and leverage it to achieve performance improvement. Specifically, we propose a regularization term for neural optimizers to enforce similar parameter updates given similar input states. Extensive experiments show that the regularizer can be combined with different L2L structures involving neural optimizers, and verify its effectiveness of consistently improving current algorithms for various tasks in classification and few-shot learning. Despite promising results, currently the learned optimizer is constrained to a group of problems with a moderate number of optimization steps and cannot replace hand-crafted ones in such settings. Training a powerful optimizer that can generalize to longer horizon still remains a challenge and can be a potential future direction. Besides, how to design a neural optimizer to deal with language tasks with RNNs or even more complex models like Transformers is also an interesting problem to be explored.

**Acknowledgements.** This work is supported by NSF IIS-2008173, IIS-2048280 and Google.

# References

1. Andrychowicz, M., et al.: Learning to learn by gradient descent by gradient descent. In: Advances in Neural Information Processing Systems, pp. 3981–3989 (2016)
2. Bansal, N., Chen, X., Wang, Z.: Can we gain more from orthogonality regularizations in training deep CNNs? arXiv preprint arXiv:1810.09102 (2018)
3. Chen, P.H., Reddi, S., Kumar, S., Hsieh, C.J.: Learning to learn with better convergence (2020). https://openreview.net/forum?id=S1xGCAVKvr
4. Chen, T., et al.: Training stronger baselines for learning to optimize. In: Advances in Neural Information Processing Systems 33 (2020)
5. Cotter, N.E., Conwell, P.R.: Fixed-weight networks can learn. In: 1990 IJCNN International Joint Conference on Neural Networks, pp. 553–559. IEEE (1990)
6. Dong, M.: PyTorch implementation of optimization as a model for few-shot learning. https://github.com/markdtw/meta-learning-lstm-pytorch (2019)
7. Goodfellow, I.J., Shlens, J., Szegedy, C.: Explaining and harnessing adversarial examples. arXiv preprint arXiv:1412.6572 (2014)
8. Hampel, F.R.: The influence curve and its role in robust estimation. J. Am. Stat. Assoc. **69**(346), 383–393 (1974)
9. He, K., Zhang, X., Ren, S., Sun, J.: Deep residual learning for image recognition. In: Proceedings of the IEEE Conference on Computer Vision and Pattern Recognition, pp. 770–778 (2016)
10. Hinton, G., Srivastava, N., Swersky, K.: Neural networks for machine learning lecture 6a overview of mini-batch gradient descent (2012)
11. Hu, S.X., et al.: Empirical bayes transductive meta-learning with synthetic gradients. arXiv preprint arXiv:2004.12696 (2020)
12. Kingma, D.P., Ba, J.: Adam: a method for stochastic optimization. arXiv preprint arXiv:1412.6980 (2014)
13. Krizhevsky, A., Nair, V., Hinton, G.: The CIFAR-10 dataset. https://www.cs.toronto.edu/kriz/cifar.htmlwww.cs.toronto.edu/kriz/cifar.html 55 (2014)

14. LeCun, Y.: The mnist database of handwritten digits. https://yann.lecun.com/exdb/mnist/yann.lecun.com/exdb/mnist/ (1998)

15. Luo, L., Xiong, Y., Liu, Y., Sun, X.: Adaptive gradient methods with dynamic bound of learning rate. arXiv preprint arXiv:1902.09843 (2019)

16. Lv, K., Jiang, S., Li, J.: Learning gradient descent: better generalization and longer horizons. In: Proceedings of the 34th International Conference on Machine Learning-Volume 70, pp. 2247–2255. JMLR.org (2017)

17. Madry, A., Makelov, A., Schmidt, L., Tsipras, D., Vladu, A.: Towards deep learning models resistant to adversarial attacks. arXiv preprint arXiv:1706.06083 (2017)

18. Metz, L., Maheswaranathan, N., Nixon, J., Freeman, C.D., Sohl-Dickstein, J.: Understanding and correcting pathologies in the training of learned optimizers. arXiv preprint arXiv:1810.10180 (2018)

19. Miyato, T., Kataoka, T., Koyama, M., Yoshida, Y.: Spectral normalization for generative adversarial networks. In: International Conference on Learning Representations (2018)

20. Ravi, S., Larochelle, H.: Optimization as a model for few-shot learning. In: ICLR (2017)

21. Ren, M., et al.: Meta-learning for semi-supervised few-shot classification. arXiv preprint arXiv:1803.00676 (2018)

22. Robbins, H., Monro, S.: A stochastic approximation method. The annals of mathematical statistics, pp. 400–407 (1951)

23. Ruan, Y., Xiong, Y., Reddi, S., Kumar, S., Hsieh, C.J.: Learning to learn by zeroth-order oracle. arXiv preprint arXiv:1910.09464 (2019)

24. Schmidhuber, J.: Deep learning in neural networks: an overview. Neural Netw. **61**, 85–117 (2015)

25. Shen, Q., Li, Y., Jiang, H., Wang, Z., Zhao, T.: Deep reinforcement learning with smooth policy. arXiv preprint arXiv:2003.09534 (2020)

26. Vinyals, O., Blundell, C., Lillicrap, T., Wierstra, D., et al.: Matching networks for one shot learning. In: Advances in Neural Information Processing Systems, pp. 3630–3638 (2016)

27. Wang, Y., Yao, Q., Kwok, J., Ni, L.M.: Generalizing from a few examples: a survey on few-shot learning. arXiv preprint arXiv: 1904.05046 (2019)

28. Wichrowska, O., et al.: Learned optimizers that scale and generalize. In: Proceedings of the 34th International Conference on Machine Learning-Volume 70, pp. 3751–3760. JMLR. org (2017)

29. Wu, Y., Ren, M., Liao, R., Grosse, R.: Understanding short-horizon bias in stochastic meta-optimization. arXiv preprint arXiv:1803.02021 (2018)

30. Xiong, Y., Hsieh, C.J.: Improved adversarial training via learned optimizer. arXiv preprint arXiv:2004.12227 (2020)

31. Younger, A.S., Hochreiter, S., Conwell, P.R.: Meta-learning with backpropagation. In: IJCNN'01. International Joint Conference on Neural Networks. Proceedings (Cat. No. 01CH37222), vol. 3. IEEE (2001)

# Incremental Task Learning
# with Incremental Rank Updates

Rakib Hyder[1], Ken Shao[1], Boyu Hou[1], Panos Markopoulos[2],
Ashley Prater-Bennette[3], and M. Salman Asif[1]

[1] University of California Riverside, California, USA
sasif@ucr.edu
[2] Rochester Institute of Technology, New York, USA
[3] Air Force Research Laboratory, New York, USA

**Abstract.** Incremental Task learning (ITL) is a category of continual
learning that seeks to train a single network for multiple tasks (one after
another), where training data for each task is only available during the
training of that task. Neural networks tend to forget older tasks when
they are trained for the newer tasks; this property is often known as
catastrophic forgetting. To address this issue, ITL methods use episodic
memory, parameter regularization, masking and pruning, or extensible
network structures. In this paper, we propose a new incremental task
learning framework based on low-rank factorization. In particular, we
represent the network weights for each layer as a linear combination
of several rank-1 matrices. To update the network for a new task, we
learn a rank-1 (or low-rank) matrix and add that to the weights of every
layer. We also introduce an additional selector vector that assigns different weights to the low-rank matrices learned for the previous tasks. We
show that our approach performs better than the current state-of-the-
art methods in terms of accuracy and forgetting. Our method also offers
better memory efficiency compared to episodic memory- and mask-based
approaches. Our code will be available at https://github.com/CSIPlab/
task-increment-rank-update.git

## 1    Introduction

Deep neural networks have been extremely successful for a variety of learning and
representation tasks (e.g., image classification, object detection/segmentation,
reinforcement learning, generative models). A typical network is trained to learn
a function that maps input to the desired output. The input-output relation is
assumed to be fixed and input-output data samples are drawn from a stationary
distribution [25]. If the input-output relations or data distributions change, the
network can be retrained using a new set of input-output data samples. Since the
storage, computing, and network capacity are limited, we may need to replace

---

**Supplementary Information** The online version contains supplementary material
available at https://doi.org/10.1007/978-3-031-20050-2_33.

old data samples with new samples. Furthermore, privacy concerns may also force data samples to be available for a limited time [10,25]. In such a training process, a network often forgets the previously learned tasks; this effect is termed *catastrophic forgetting* [21,26].

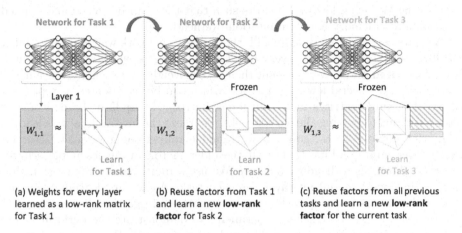

(a) Weights for every layer learned as a low-rank matrix for Task 1

(b) Reuse factors from Task 1 and learn a new **low-rank factor** for Task 2

(c) Reuse factors from all previous tasks and learn a new **low-rank factor** for the current task

**Fig. 1.** An overview of our proposed method for continual learning via low-rank network updates. We first represent (and learn) the weight matrix (or tensor) for each layer as a product of low-rank matrices. To train a network for new tasks without forgetting the earlier tasks, we reuse the factors from the earlier tasks and add a new set of factors for the new task. Our experiments suggest that a rank-1 update is often sufficient for successful continual learning.

Incremental task learning is a subcategory of continual learning or lifelong learning approaches aim to address the problem of catastrophic forgetting by adapting the network or training process to learn new tasks without forgetting the previously learned ones [2–4,6,12,16,23,28,29]. In this paper, we focus on task-incremental continual learning in which data for every task are provided in a sequential manner to train/update the network [8]. It has been a popular continual learning setup even in the very recent literature [7,11,14,31,36,40]. ITL finds its application in setups where task id is available during inference; for instance, tasks performed under different weather/light/background conditions and we know the changes, or tasks learned on different data/classes where we know the task id.

Let us denote the network function that maps input $x$ to output for task $t$ as $f(x; \mathcal{W}_t)$, where $\mathcal{W}_t$ denotes the network weights for task $t$. We seek to update the $\mathcal{W}_t$ for all $t$ as we sequentially receive dataset for one task at a time. Suppose the training dataset for task $t$ is given as $(\mathcal{X}_t, \mathcal{Y}_t)$ drawn from a distribution $\mathcal{P}_t$, where $\mathcal{X}_t$ denotes the set of input samples and $\mathcal{Y}_t$ denotes the corresponding ground-truth outputs. Our goal is to update network weights from the previous task $(\mathcal{W}_{t-1})$ to $\mathcal{W}_t$ such that

$$y \approx f(x; \mathcal{W}_t), \quad \text{for all } (x, y) \sim \mathcal{P}_t. \tag{1}$$

ITL setup above assumes that the task identity of test samples is known at the test time and the corresponding network weights are used for inference. Dynamic architecture approaches have the potential to achieve *zero forgetting*, using $\mathcal{W}_t$ for testing data for task $t$; however, this also requires storing the $\mathcal{W}_t$ for all the tasks. One of the main contributions of this paper is to represent, learn, and update the $\mathcal{W}_t$ using low-rank factors such that they can be stored and applied with minimal memory and computation overhead.

We propose a new method for ITL that updates network weights using rank-1 (or low-rank) increments for every new task. Figure 1 provides an illustration of our proposed method. We represent the network weights for each layer as a linear combination of several low-rank factors (which can be represented as a product of two low-rank matrices and a diagonal matrix). To update the network for task $t$ without forgetting the earlier tasks, we freeze the low-rank factors learned from the previous tasks, add a new trainable rank-1 (or low-rank) factor for every layer, and combine that with the older factors using learnable *selector weights* (shown as a diagonal matrix). We use a multi-head configuration that has an independent output layer for each task. As we are learning separate diagonal matrices for every task, we can achieve zero forgetting during inference. We present an extensive set of experiments to demonstrate the performance of our proposed method for different benchmark datasets. We observe that our proposed method outperforms the current state-of-the-art methods in terms of accuracy with small memory overhead.

The main contributions of this paper are as follows.

1. **Represent layers as low-rank matrices:** We represent and learn network weights for each layer as a low-rank structure. We show that low-rank structure is sufficient to represent all the tasks in continual learning setup.
2. **Reuse old factors for better performance with a small memory overhead:** We limit the number of parameters required for network update by reusing the factors learned from previous tasks. We demonstrate that a rank-1 increment suffices to outperform the existing techniques.
3. **Zero forgetting without replay buffer:** Our method has zero forgetting that is achieved using incremental rank update or network weights. In contrast, most of the existing continual learning techniques require replay buffer or large memory overhead to achieve zero forgetting.

**Limitations.** Our method shares same inherent limitation of ITL (i.e. the requirement of task-id during inference). In addition, since we use all the previously learned factors for inference, the later tasks require more memory and computation for inference. Nevertheless, we show that using low-rank structure, our total memory requirement is significantly lower than a single network. Furthermore, as we learn separate diagonal matrices for each task, we can maintain high performance even if the network reaches full rank with a large number of tasks.

## 2    Background and Related Work

Incremental task learning (ITL) [10,34] aims to train a single model on a sequence of different tasks and perform well on all the trained tasks once the training is finished. While training on new tasks, the old data from previous tasks will not be provided to the model. This scenario mimics the human learning process where they have the ability to acquire new knowledge and skills throughout their lifespan. However, this setting is still challenging to neural network models as a common phenomenon called "catastrophic forgetting [21]" is observed during this learning process. Catastrophic forgetting occurs when the data from the new tasks interfere with the data seen in the previous tasks and thus deteriorating model performance on preceding tasks. To overcome this issue, different approaches have been proposed so far which can be divided into three main categories: regularization-based approaches, memory and replay-based approaches, and dynamic network architecture-based approaches. Some of these approaches are especially designed for ITL whereas others are designed for more general continual learning setup.

**Regularization-Based Approaches.** [15,16,23] update the whole model in each task but a regularization term $\ell_{reg}$ is added to the total loss $\mathcal{L} = \ell_{current} + \lambda\ell_{reg}$ to penalize changes in the parameters important to preceding tasks thus preserving the performance on previous learned tasks. For example, Elastic Weight Consolidation (EWC) [15] estimates the importance of parameters using Fisher Information matrix; Variational Continual Learning (VCL) [23] approximates the posterior distribution of the parameters using variational inference; Learning without Forgetting (LwF) [16] regularizes the current loss with soft targets taken from previous tasks using knowledge distillation [13]. GCL [5] mixes rehearsal with knowledge distillation and regularization to mitigate catastrophic forgetting. A number of recently proposed methods force weight updates to belong to the null space of the feature covariance [35,37].

**Memory-Based Approaches.** [8,9,27,28,35] usually use memory and replay/rehearsal mechanism to recall a small episodic memory of previous tasks while training new tasks thus reduce the loss in the previous tasks. For example, iCaRL [27] is the first replay method, which learns in a class-incremental way by selecting and storing exemplars closest to the feature mean of each class; Meta-Experience Replay (MER) [28] combines experience replay with optimization-based meta-learning to optimize the symmetric trade-off between transfer and interference by enforcing gradient alignment across examples; AGEM [8] projects the gradient on the current minibatch by using an external episodic memory of patterns from previous experiences as an optimization constraint; ER-Ring [9] jointly trains new task data with that of the previous tasks.

**Dynamic Network Architectures.** [7,19,30,33,38,39,41] try to add new neurons to the model at additional new tasks, thus the performances on previous tasks are preserved by freezing the old parameters and only updating the newly added parameters. For example, Progressive neural networks (PNNs) [30] leverage prior knowledge via lateral connections to previously learned features; Pack-Net [19] iteratively assigns parameter subsets to consecutive tasks by constituting binary masks. SupSup [39] also finds masks in order to assign different subsets of the weights for different tasks. BatchEnsemble [38] learns on separate rank-1 scaling matrices for each task which are then used to scale weights of the shared network. HAT [33] incorporates task-specific embeddings for attention masking. [24] also proposes task-conditioned hypernetworks for continual learning. [20] proposes nonoverlapping sets of units being active for each task. Piggyback [18] learns binary masks on an existing network to provide good performance on new tasks. [1] proposes task specific convolutional filter selection for continual learning. The mask-based methods listed above provide excellent results for continual learning, but they require a significantly large number of parameters to represent the masks for each task. A factorization-based approach was proposed in [22] that performs automatic rank selection per task for variational inference using Indian Buffet process. The method requires significantly large rank increments per task to achieve high accuracy; in contrast, our method uses a learning-based approach to find rank-1 increments and reuse old factors with the learned selector weights. ORTHOG-SUBSPACE [7] learns tasks in different (low-rank) vector sub-spaces that are kept orthogonal to each other in order to minimize interference.

Our proposed method falls under the category of dynamic network architecture approaches. Note that we can represent a low-rank weight matrix using two smaller fully-connected layers and increasing the rank of the weight matrix is equivalent to adding new nodes in the two smaller fully-connected layers.

## 3    Incremental Task Learning via Rank Increment

We focus on the incremental task learning setup in which we seek to train a network for $T$ tasks. The main difference between incremental task learning and regular learning is that the training data for every task is only available while training the network for that task. The main challenge in incremental task learning is to not forget the previous tasks as we learn new tasks. Learning each task entails training weights for the network to learn the task-specific input-output relationship using the task-specific training data.

We seek to develop an ITL framework in which we represent the weights of any layer using a small number of low-rank factors. We initialize the network with a base architecture in which weights for each layer can be represented using a low-rank matrix. We then add new low-rank factors to each layer as we learn new tasks.

Let us assume the network has $K$ layers and the weights for the $k$th layer and task $t$ can be represented as $W_{k,t}$. Let us further assume that the weights for the $k$th layer and task $t = 1$ can be represented as a low-rank matrix

$$W_{k,1} = U_{k,1}S_{k,1,1}V_{k,1}^{\top}, \qquad (2)$$

where $U_{k,1}, V_{k,1}$ represent two low-rank matrices and $S_{k,1,1}$ represents a diagonal matrix. To learn the network for task 1, we learn $U_{k,1}, V_{k,1}, S_{k,1,1}$ for all $k$. For task 2, we represent the weights for $k$th layer as

$$W_{k,2} = U_{k,1}S_{k,1,2}V_{k,1}^{\top} + U_{k,2}S_{k,2,2}V_{k,2}^{\top}.$$

$U_{k,1}, V_{k,1}$ represent the two low-rank matrices learned for task 1 and frozen afterwards. $U_{k,2}, V_{k,2}$ represent two low-rank matrices that are added to update the weights, and these will be learned for task 2. $S_{k,1,2}, S_{k,2,2}$ represent the diagonal matrices, which will be learned for task 2. We learn $S_{k,1,2}$, which is a diagonal matrix that assigns weights to factors corresponding to task 1, to include/exclude or favor/suppress frozen factors from previous tasks for the new tasks. We can represent the weights for the $k$th layer and task $t$ as

$$W_{layer,task} = W_{k,t} = \sum_{i \leq t} U_{k,i}S_{k,i,t}V_{k,i}^{\top}$$

$$= \sum_{i < t} \underbrace{U_{k,i}}_{\text{frozen}} S_{k,i,t} \underbrace{V_{k,i}^{\top}}_{\text{frozen}} + U_{k,t}S_{k,t,t}V_{k,t}^{\top}, \qquad (3)$$

where $U_{k,i}, V_{k,i}$ are frozen for all $i < t$ and $U_{k,t}, V_{k,t}$ and all the $S_{k,i,t}$ are learned for task $t$. The entire network for task $t$ can be represented as $\mathcal{W}_t = \{U_{k,i}, S_{k,i,t}, V_{k,i}\}_{i \leq t}$. To update the trainable network parameters for task $t$, we solve the following optimization problem:

$$\min_{U_{k,t}, S_{k,i,t}, V_{k,t}} \sum_{(x,y) \in (\mathcal{X}_t, \mathcal{Y}_t)} \text{loss}(f(x; \mathcal{W}_t[U_{k,t}, S_{k,i,t}, V_{k,t}]), y)$$

$$\text{for all } k \leq K \text{ and } i \leq t, \qquad (4)$$

where we use $\text{loss}(\cdot, \cdot)$ to denote the loss function and $\mathcal{W}_t[U_{k,t}, S_{k,i,t}, V_{k,t}]$ to indicate the trainable parameters in $\mathcal{W}_t$, while the rest are frozen. We sometimes call $S_{k,i,t}$ a *selector weight matrix/vector* to indicate that its diagonal entries determine the contribution of each factor toward each task/layer weights.

Our proposed ITL algorithm works as follows. We train the low-rank factors for the given task using the respective training samples. Then we freeze the factors corresponding to the older tasks and only update the new factors and the diagonal matrices. In this manner, the total number of parameters we add in our model is linearly proportional to the rank of the new factors. To keep the network complexity small, we seek to achieve good accuracy using small rank for each task update and layer. We summarize our approach in Algorithms 1 and 2.

Note that we do not need to create the weight matrix $W_{k,t}$ for any layer explicitly since we can compute all the steps in forward and backward propagation efficiently using the factorized form of each layer. The size of each layer is determined by the choice of the network architecture. The rank of each layer for every task is a hyper-parameter that we can select according to the tasks at hand. To keep the memory overhead small, we need to use small values for rank increment. Let us denote the rank for $U_{k,t}$ as $r_{k,t}$, which represents the

---

**Algorithm 1** ITL with rank-1 increments (Training)

---

**Input:** Data ($\mathcal{X}_1$ and $\mathcal{Y}_1$) for the $1^{st}$ task.
Set initial rank, $r_1$.
Initialize weight factors $U_{k,1}, V_{k,1}$ at random and $S_{k,1,1}$ as an identity marix.
Learn $U_{k,1}, V_{k,1}$ and $S_{k,1,1}$.                                    ▷ Optimization in (4)
**for** $t = 2, 3, ..., T$ **do**
    **Input:** Training data ($\mathcal{X}_t$ and $\mathcal{Y}_t$) for $t^{th}$ task.
    Initialize low-rank update factors $U_{k,t}, V_{k,t}$.
    Freeze the previous factors $\{U_{k,i}, V_{k,i}\}_{i<t}$.
    Initialize the diagonal entries of $\{S_{k,i,t}\}$ as 1
        for $i = t$ and 0 for $i < t$.
    Learn $U_{k,t}, V_{k,t}$ and $S_{k,i,t}$
        for $i < t$.                                    ▷ Optimization in (4)
**end for**

---

**Algorithm 2** ITL with rank-1 increments (Inference)

---

**Input:** Test data $x$ with task identity $t$.
**Retrieve trained weights:** $\mathcal{W}_t = \{U_{k,i}, V_{k,i}, S_{k,i,t}\}$ for all $k$ and $i \leq t$.
**Output:** Calculate the network output as $f(x, \mathcal{W}_t)$.

---

increment rank for $k$th layer and task $t$. At the time of test, we can use an appropriate number of factors depending on the task. For instance, if we want to predict output for task 1 then we use first $r_{k,1}$ factors and for task 2 we use $r_{k,1} + r_{k,2}$ factors. We can add new factors in an incremental manner as we add new tasks in the ITL setup. In the extreme case of rank-1 increments, $r_{k,t} = 1$. In our experiments, we observed that rank-1 updates compete or exceed the performance of existing ITL methods (see Table 1) and the performance of our method improves further as we increase the rank (see Table 5). Any increase in the rank comes at the expense of an increased memory overhead.

## 4   Experiments and Results

We used different classification tasks on well known continual learning benchmarks to show the significance of our proposed approach.

### 4.1   Datasets and Task Description

Experiments are conducted on four datasets: Split CIFAR100, Permuted MNIST, Rotated MNIST, and Split MiniImageNet.

**P-MNIST** creates new tasks by applying a certain random permutation on the pixels of all images in the original dataset. In our experiment, we generate 20 different tasks, each of which corresponds to a certain but different permutation.
**R-MNIST** is similar to Permuted MNIST, but instead of applying a certain random permutation on the pixels, it applies a certain random rotation to the images in the same tasks. We create 20 different tasks, each corresponds to a certain but different version of rotation from $[0, 180]$ degree interval.

**S-CIFAR100** splits the original CIFAR-100 dataset into 20 disjoint sets, each of which, containing 5 classes, is considered as a separate task. The 5 classes in each task is randomly chosen without replacement from the total 100 classes. **S-miniImageNet** splits a subset of Imagenet dataset into 20 disjoint sets, each of which, containing 5 classes, is considered as a separate task. The 5 classes in each task is randomly chosen without replacement from the total 100 classes.

## 4.2   Training Details

**Network.** In the first set of experiments, we used a three layer (fully-connected) multilayer perceptron (MLP) with 256-node hidden layers, similar to the network in [7]. We flattened multi-dimensional input image to a 1D vector input. We used ReLU activation for all the layers except the last one. We used Softmax for the muticlass classification tasks. We used the same network for all the tasks with necessary modifications for input and output sizes. Our approach can be used in convolutional networks as well. We report the results using ResNet18 with our approach on S-CIFAR100 and S-miniImageNet dataset in Table 6.

**Factorization and Rank Selection.** We used the matrix factorization defined in (3) in all our experiments. We empirically selected the rank for the first task,$r_{k,1}$ as 11 based on the experiments on a sample Rotated MNIST task and kept the same value for all the experiments. We then performed rank-1 increment ($r_{k,t}$) for each additional task. We would like to point that AGEM and Orthog Subspace use first 3 tasks for hyperparameter tuning. We did not tune our hyperparameters on the test data, rather we choose the parameters which provides better convergence during training. We increment the weight matrices by rank-1 per task; therefore, learning rate and the number of epochs are the only hyperparameters in our experiments.

**Optimization.** We used orthogonal initialization for the low-rank factors, as described in [32]. We used all one initialization for the additional factors of the selector matrices $S_{k,t,t}$. We used Adam optimization to update the factors. We used the batch size of 128 for each task.

**Performance Metrics.** We use *accuracy* and *forgetting* per task, which are two commonly used metrics in the continual learning literature [6,7], to evaluate the performance of the described methods. Let $a_{t,j}$ be the test accuracy of task $j < t$ after the model has finished learning task $t \in \{1, ..., T\}$ in a incremental manner. The average accuracy $A_t$ after the model has learned task $t$ is defined as $A_t = \frac{1}{t} \sum_{j=1}^{t} a_{t,j}$. On the other hand, *forgetting* is the decrease in the accuracy of a task after its training, and after one or several tasks are learned incrementally. We define the average forgetting $F_t$ as $F_t = \frac{1}{t-1} \sum_{j=1}^{t-1} (a_{j,j} - a_{t,j})$.

In Fig. 2, we show the evolution of average accuracy $A_t$ as $t$ increases. We also show the evolution of task-wise accuracy $a_{t,j}$ in Fig. 3, where $(t, j)$ pixel intensity reflects $a_{t,j}$. We report the average accuracy $A_T$, the average accuracy after the model has learnt every tasks incrementally, in Table 1. We report the forgetting $F_T$ after the model has learnt all the tasks incrementally in Table 2. Note that our method performs incremental task learning without forgetting.

### 4.3   Comparing Techniques

We compare our method against different state-of-the-art ITL methods. **EWC** [15] is a regularization-based method that uses the Fisher Information matrix to estimate posterior of previous tasks to preserve important parameters. **ICARL** [27] is a memory-based method that uses exemplars and knowledge distillation [13] to retain previous knowledge. **AGEM** [8] is a memory-based method built upon [17] that uses episodic memory to solve an constrained optimization problem. **ER-Ring** [9] is another memory-based method that jointly trains on new task data with that of the previous tasks. **Orth. sub.** [7] learn tasks in different (low-rank) vector subspaces that are kept orthogonal to each other in order to minimize interference. Other than the above mentioned approaches, we compared with masked based approaches which, like our approach, also fall under dynamic architecture category. **HAT** [33] that incorporates task-specific embeddings for attention masking. **PackNet** [19] that iteratively assigns subsets of a single binary mask to each task. The mask-based approaches utilize the redundancy of the network parameters to represent different tasks with different masked versions of the same network weights. We also present comparisons with some recent methods: **IBP-WF** [22], **DER** [5] and **Adam-NSCL** [37], in terms of average accuracy for one experiment on two datasets.

In addition, we report results for two *non-continual* baseline methods: **Parallel learning** and **Multitask learning**. **Parallel learning** trains independent (smaller) low-rank networks of same size for each task. We report results for three such networks. **Parallel 2** uses rank-2 layers, **Parallel 4** uses rank-4 layers, and **Parallel full** uses a full-rank MLP. Parallel 2 requires approximately the same number of parameters as the rank-1 ITL network that we use in our experiments; Parallel 4 provides higher network capacity, while requiring fewer parameters than the full-rank network. We can treat the performance of the **Parallel full** approach as the upper limit that we can achieve using ITL methods. Finally, **Multitask learning** has been used as a baseline in [7,8]. In multitask learning, we have access to all data to optimize a single network.

### 4.4   Results with Three-Layer MLP

**Classification Performance and Comparison.**   We report classification results for P-MNIST, R-MNIST, S-CIFAR100, and S-miniImageNet tasks in Table 1. We also show the results for the comparing techniques. We observe that our method with rank-1 update perform better than all the comparing methods (EWC, ICARL, AGEM, HAT, PackNet, Orthog Subspace) on R-MNIST, S-CIFAR100 and S-miniImageNet tasks using significantly fewer number of parameters. Our method performs close to Orthog Subspace on P-MNIST tasks.

We also observe that the proposed rank-1 update outperforms non-continual Parallel 2 baseline that has similar number of parameters compared to our approach. We perform similar to Parallel 4 baseline that uses nearly twice the number of parameters as our approach. Parallel full acts as an upper limit with the network structure of our choice as it trains independent full rank networks for every task. Multitask learning is another non-continual baseline that uses all the data from all the tasks simultaneously. Table 1 suggests that our ITL method can learn complex tasks such as CIFAR100 and miniImageNet classification with a three layer MLP, whereas multitask learning (which is solving 100-class classification problem) fails with such a simple network. We also tested Resnet18 network, which has significantly more parameters than the network used in Table 1. The results for Resnet18 are presented in Table 6.

**Table 1.** Average test accuracy of ITL for P-MNIST, R-MNIST, S-CIFAR100, and S-miniImageNet with three layer MLP. Standard deviation of test accuracy over five runs is shown in parenthesis for some of the experiments.
* Orthog subspace does not use replay buffer for MNIST variations.

| Method | Replay buffer | P-MNIST | R-MNIST | S-CIFAR100 | S-miniImageNet |
|---|---|---|---|---|---|
| EWC [15] | No | 67.9 ($\pm$ 0.68) | 44.5 ($\pm$ 1.09) | 52.7 ($\pm$ 0.81) | 29.3 ($\pm$ 1.08) |
| ICARL [27] | Yes | 85.4 ($\pm$ 0.01) | 51.2 ($\pm$ 2.41) | 56.9($\pm$ 0.31) | 39.9($\pm$ 0.27) |
| AGEM [8] | Yes | 73.9 ($\pm$ 0.52) | 53.4 ($\pm$ 1.80) | 51.3($\pm$ 1.54) | 31.3($\pm$ 0.89) |
| HAT [33] | No | **90.1**($\pm$ 1.60) | 89.1($\pm$ 2.51) | 64.8 ($\pm$ 0.32) | 47.0 ($\pm$ 0.88) |
| PackNet [19] | No | 90.0($\pm$ 0.24) | 88.4($\pm$ 0.37) | 63.7($\pm$ 0.41) | 45.1($\pm$ 1.05) |
| Orth sub [7] | Yes* | 86.6 ($\pm$ 0.79) | 80.2 ($\pm$ 0.41) | 57.8 ($\pm$ 1.03) | 38.1 ($\pm$ 0.67) |
| DER [5] | Yes | – | – | 48.21 | 33.19 |
| Adam-NSCL[37] | No | – | – | 64.26 | 47.32 |
| IBP-WF [22] | No | – | – | 53.22 | 40.52 |
| Ours | No | 85.6 ($\pm$ 0.15) | **91.1** ($\pm$ 0.12) | **65.9** ($\pm$ 2.16) | **54.7** ($\pm$ 2.87) |
| Parallel 2 (r = 2) | – | 65.3 | 65.5 | 62.8 | 55.4 |
| Parallel 4 (r = 4) | – | 86.3 | 87.4 | 65.6 | 58.6 |
| Parallel fullrank | – | 95.9 | 97.3 | 73.1 | 63.1 |
| Multitask | – | 96.8 | 97.7 | 16.4 | 4.21 |

We present the task-wise test performance for some of the comparing approaches on P-MNIST, R-MNIST, S-CIFAR100 and S-miniImageNet datasets in Fig. 2. We observe that as we train new tasks, task-wise performance drops for the comparing approaches, especially for P-MNIST and R-MNIST.

ICARL and AGEM require replay buffer (episodic memory) for each task. Although Orthog Subspace did not use replay buffer for MNIST experiments, it requires replay buffer in their algorithm and used it for S-CIFAR100 and S-miniImageNet experiments. EWC does not require any replay buffer, but it suffers from high forgetting as shown in Fig. 3. Our proposed approach does not require a replay buffer, and it outperforms other approaches in Table 1.

**Accuracy vs Forgetting.** We report the average forgetting of different comparing approaches in Table 2. Our method, mask-based approaches (HAT and PackNet) and parallel baselines have zero forgetting, whereas all other comparing methods exhibit some level of forgetting. To better demonstrate the forgetting, in Fig. 3, we show the accuracy for the tasks along the entire training procedure. $i^{th}$ row (top-bottom) of the diagram denotes the performance of $i$ tasks on the test sets when we train the $i^{th}$ task. As expected, we can observe that the training performance for the previously learned tasks usually drops with the gradual training of the subsequent tasks specially for the regularization based approach, EWC. However, our algorithm maintains the same performance for the past tasks as we do not change any previously learned factors. Even orthogonal subspace approach observes such forgetting over some tasks.

**Table 2.** Average forgetting results corresponding to Table 1 for different datasets using different approaches. We report the forgetting in percentage unit (%). We also report the standard deviation over 5 experiments for some methods.

| | EWC | AGEM | Orthog subspace | DER | Adam-NSCL | Parallel fullrank, HAT, PackNet **Ours**, IBP-WF |
|---|---|---|---|---|---|---|
| P-MNIST | 25.8 (± 0.70) | 19.6 (± 0.64) | 4.49 (± 0.93) | – | – | 0 |
| R-MNIST | 52.9 (± 1.17) | 44.2 (± 1.85) | 14.7 (± 0.39) | – | – | 0 |
| S-CIFAR100 | 6.96 (± 0.80) | 21.5 (± 2.89) | 6.30 (± 0.38) | 10.6 | 8.5 | 0 |
| S-miniImageNet | 17.3 (± 1.81) | 18.8 (± 1.40) | 9.98 (± 0.31) | 20.11 | 11.23 | 0 |

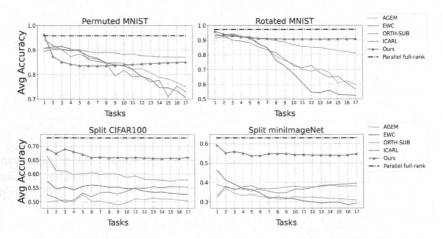

**Fig. 2.** Average test accuracy for different datasets (Permuted MNIST, Rotated MNIST, Split CIFAR100, Split miniImageNet) along different tasks using different algorithms (AGEM,EWC, Orthog. Subspace, ICARL and our approach). We use three layer MLP here. Parallel full-rank results corresponds to the case when we train every task on separate full rank networks independently (serves as an upper limit for ITL methods). We showed the average of 20 tasks.

**Memory Complexity.** Our method increments the rank of each layer for each task; therefore, we compare the total number of parameters in the incrementally trained network and the Parallel baselines. Note that if the number of parameters in two approaches is same, we can train one small network per task independently. We report total number of parameters and replay buffer size for different methods in Table 3. Since we used similar fully connected network structure for all the tasks, we report results for Split CIFAR100 experiments. Although we increase the rank for every task, the increment is small enough that even after 20 tasks our total parameter count remains smaller than all other methods.

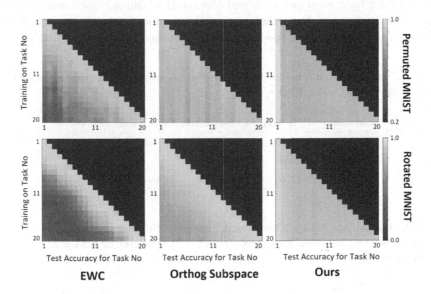

**Fig. 3.** Evolution of task-wise test accuracy on P-MNIST (first row) and R-MNIST (second row) datasets for EWC, Orthogonal Subspace, and Our approach. We can observe from the decrease in the test accuracy that EWC and Orthogonal Subspace forget the previous tasks as they learn new tasks. Our approach does not show any forgetting as we learn new tasks.

**Table 3.** Number of parameters and buffer size in ITL methods with 3-layer MLP.

|  | Ours | IBP-WF | EWC | AGEM | Ortho Sub | DER | Adam-NSCL | Para. Full |
|---|---|---|---|---|---|---|---|---|
| # params. | **0.17 M** | 0.23 M | 0.93 M | 1.76 M | 2.82 M | 0.88 M | 0.88 M | 19.7 M |
| Buffer size | 0 | 0 | 1.71 M | 7.90 M | 9.01 M | 6.14 M | 0 | 0 |

We also report the number of parameters used by mask-based zero forgetting algorithms (HAT and PackNet) to learn 20 different tasks on different datasets in Table 4. We can observe that our approach outperforms HAT and PackNet for R-MNIST, S-CIAR100 and S-miniImageNet with a significantly smaller number of parameters. Even though all the approaches use the same network, our approach uses rank-1 factors that require a significantly smaller number of parameters for incremental learning of tasks. Note that P-MNIST and R-MNIST experiments require the same number of parameters.

**Effect of Rank.** In Table 5, we evaluate the effect of different rank selection for different MNIST datasets using our ITL approach. We tested the initial rank (rank for the first task) of 1, 6, and 11, keeping the rank increment to 1. We observed that the accuracy increase as the initial rank increases, and we achieve nearly 90% accuracy with initial rank of 11. We also tested different values of rank increment per task and observe that the accuracy increases with larger rank increment. Nevertheless, rank-1 increment provides us comparable or better performance than the comparing techniques as shown in Table 1.

**Table 4.** Number of parameters used by different zero-forgetting algorithms (HAT, PackNet, and Ours) using 3-layer MLP.

| Method | P/R-MNIST | S-CIFAR100 | S-miniImageNet |
|--------|-----------|------------|----------------|
| HAT | 0.33 M | 0.89 M | 5.51 M |
| PackNet | 0.26M | 0.83M | 5.50 M |
| Ours | 0.11 M | 0.17 M | 0.72 M |

**Table 5.** Test accuracy for different rank choices of the proposed ITL approach and multi-task baseline networks for P-MNIST and R-MNIST. Initial rank is $r_{k,1}$ and rank increment/task is $r_{k,t}$.

| Setup | 1 | 2 | 3 | 4 | 5 |
|-------|-----|-----|-----|-----|-----|
| $(r_{k,1}, r_{k,t})$ | (1,1) | (6,1) | (11,1) | (11,2) | (11,4) |
| P-MNIST | 74.23 | 82.21 | 85.61 | 90.51 | 93.84 |
| R-MNIST | 81.57 | 89.39 | 91.09 | 92.76 | 94.12 |
| # parameters | 0.09 M | 0.1 M | 0.11 M | 0.14 M | 0.2 M |

## 4.5   Results with ResNet18

The proposed low-rank increments approach can be generalized to other type of networks and layers as well. For example, convolutional kernels have four-dimensional weight tensors as opposed to the two-dimensional weight matrices of fully connected layers. They are usually formulated as a tensor of output and input channel $(C_{out}, C_{in})$, and the two dimensions of the convolutional filters $(H, W)$. We reshape the convolutional weight tensors into matrices of size $C_{out} \times C_{in}HW$ and perform similar low-rank updates per task as we described for the MLP in the main paper. We report the results for S-CIFAR-100 and S-miniImageNet datasets with Resnet18 architecture. For each convolutional layers, we reshaped and decomposed the convolution weight tensors into the same low-rank factors described in (3) and performed low-rank updates per tasks. We report the results in Table 6. For most of the comparing techniques, results from [7] are reported since we use the same architecture and dataset. For missing comparisons, we trained the models using same procedure as outlined in [7].

Instead of using a fixed value for rank at each layer as we did in the MLP setup, we used rank size that is proportional to the size of $C_{out,i}$ at $i^{th}$ convolutional layer because the weights for different layers of ResNet18 are different in size. We select initial rank = $0.1\,C_{out,i}$ for the first task and incremental rank = $0.02\,C_{out,i}$ for the subsequent incremental tasks.

The results in Table 6 show that the performance of every method improves with the convolutional ResNet18 structure over the 3-layer MLP. Nevertheless, our method outperforms the comparing approaches for both datasets. Adam-NSCL [37] gets better results on CIFAR100, but it requires 11.21 M parameters (compared to 1.33 M parameters required by our method).

**Table 6.** Comparison of test accuracy and forgetting for split CIFAR-100 and split miniImageNet datasets using ResNet18 architecture.

| Method | S-CIFAR-100 | | S-miniImageNet | |
|---|---|---|---|---|
| | Accuracy | Forgetting | Accuracy | Forgetting |
| EWC [15] | 43.2 (± 2.77) | 26 (± 2) | 34.8 (± 2.34) | 24 (± 4) |
| ICARL [27] | 46.4 (± 1.21) | 16 (± 1) | 44.2 | 24.64 |
| AGEM [8] | 60.34 (± 2.05) | 11.0 (± 2.88) | 42.3 (± 1.42) | 17 (± 1) |
| ER-Ring [9] | 59.6 (± 1.19) | 14 (± 1) | 49.8 (± 2.92) | 12 (± 1) |
| Ortho sub [7] | 63.42 (± 1.82) | 8.37 (± 0.71) | 51.4 (± 1.44) | 10 (± 1) |
| DER [5] | 67.16 | 8.95 | 57.81 | 14.70 |
| Adam-NSCL [37] | **74.31** | 9.47 | 57.92 | 13.42 |
| IBP-WF [22] | 68.25 | 0 | 55.84 | 0 |
| Ours | 68.46 (± 2.52) | **0** | **59.26** (± 1.15) | **0** |
| Parallel full-rank | 92.7 | 0 | 94.5 | 0 |
| Multitask learning | 70.2 | 0 | 65.1 | 0 |

**Effect of Updating Last Few Layers.** We performed an experiment on S-CIFAR-100 where we factorize last $L$ layers of the ResNet18 architecture keeping the rest of the network fixed at trained weights on Task 1. Updating last $L = \{1, 2, 3, 4, 5\}$ layers provide average accuracy of $\{34.38, 34.99, 53.41, 57.08, 65.03\}$, respectively. This result suggests that updating last few layers may suffice since the initial layers merely work as a feature extractor.

## 5  Conclusion

We proposed a new incremental task learning method in which we update the network weights using low rank increments as we learn new tasks. Network layers are represented as a linear combination of low-rank factors. To update the network for a new task, we freeze the factors learned for previous tasks, add a new low-rank (or rank-1) factor, and combine that with the previous factors using a learned combination. The proposed method offered considerable improvement in performance compared to the state-of-the-art methods for ITL in image classification tasks. In addition, the proposed low-rank ITL circumvents the use of memory buffer or large memory overhead while achieving zero forgetting.

The need for task ID knowledge is a general limitation of our and other ITL methods. Such methods can be useful for incremental multitask learning where task ID is available during inference but training data is only available in a short window. Extending this method to class incremental learning (which does not require task ID) is an important problem for future work.

**Acknowledgments.** This material is based upon work supported in part by Air Force Office of Scientific Research (AFOSR) awards FA9550-21-1-0330, FA9550-20-1-0039, Office of Naval Research (ONR) award N00014-19-1-2264, and National Science Foundation (NSF) award CCF-2046293. Approved for Public Release by AFRL; Distribution Unlimited: Case Number AFRL-2021-4063

## References

1. Abati, D., Tomczak, J., Blankevoort, T., Calderara, S., Cucchiara, R., Bejnordi, B.E.: Conditional channel gated networks for task-aware continual learning. In: Proceedings of the IEEE/CVF Conference on Computer Vision and Pattern Recognition, pp. 3930–3939 (2020)
2. Aljundi, R., Babiloni, F., Elhoseiny, M., Rohrbach, M., Tuytelaars, T.: Memory aware synapses: Learning what (not) to forget. In: Ferrari, V., Hebert, M., Sminchisescu, C., Weiss, Y. (eds.) ECCV 2018. LNCS, vol. 11207, pp. 144–161. Springer, Cham (2018). https://doi.org/10.1007/978-3-030-01219-9_9
3. Aljundi, R., Chakravarty, P., Tuytelaars, T.: Expert gate: Lifelong learning with a network of experts. In: Proceedings of the IEEE Conference on Computer Vision and Pattern Recognition, pp. 3366–3375 (2017)
4. Aljundi, R., Lin, M., Goujaud, B., Bengio, Y.: Gradient based sample selection for online continual learning. Adv. Neural. Inf. Process. Syst. **32**, 11816–11825 (2019)
5. Buzzega, P., Boschini, M., Porrello, A., Abati, D., Calderara, S.: Dark experience for general continual learning: a strong, simple baseline. Adv. Neural. Inf. Process. Syst. **33**, 15920–15930 (2020)
6. Chaudhry, A., Dokania, P.K., Ajanthan, T., Torr, P.H.S.: Riemannian walk for incremental learning: Understanding forgetting and intransigence. In: Ferrari, V., Hebert, M., Sminchisescu, C., Weiss, Y. (eds.) ECCV 2018. LNCS, vol. 11215, pp. 556–572. Springer, Cham (2018). https://doi.org/10.1007/978-3-030-01252-6_33
7. Chaudhry, A., Khan, N., Dokania, P., Torr, P.: Continual learning in low-rank orthogonal subspaces. In: Advances in Neural Information Processing Systems, vol. 33 (2020)

8. Chaudhry, A., Marc'Aurelio, R., Rohrbach, M., Elhoseiny, M.: Efficient lifelong learning with a-gem. In: International Conference on Learning Representations, ICLR (2019)
9. Chaudhry, A., et al.: On tiny episodic memories in continual learning. arXiv preprint arXiv:1902.10486 (2019)
10. Delange, M., et al.: A continual learning survey: Defying forgetting in classification tasks. IEEE Trans. Pattern Anal. Mach. Intell. **44**, 3366–3385 (2021)
11. Deng, D., Chen, G., Hao, J., Wang, Q., Heng, P.A.: Flattening sharpness for dynamic gradient projection memory benefits continual learning. In: Advances in Neural Information Processing Systems, vol. 34 (2021)
12. Farajtabar, M., Azizan, N., Mott, A., Li, A.: Orthogonal gradient descent for continual learning. In: International Conference on Artificial Intelligence and Statistics, pp. 3762–3773. PMLR (2020)
13. Hinton, G., Vinyals, O., Dean, J.: Distilling the knowledge in a neural network. In: NeurIPS (2014)
14. Hurtado, J., Raymond-Saez, A., Soto, A.: Optimizing reusable knowledge for continual learning via metalearning. In: Advances in Neural Information Processing Systems, vol. 34 (2021)
15. Kirkpatrick, J., et al.: Overcoming catastrophic forgetting in neural networks. Proc. Natl. Acad. Sci. **114**(13), 3521–3526 (2017)
16. Li, Z., Hoiem, D.: Learning without forgetting. IEEE Trans. Pattern Anal. Mach. Intell. **40**(12), 2935–2947 (2017)
17. Lopez-Paz, D., Ranzato, M.: Gradient episodic memory for continual learning. Adv. Neural. Inf. Process. Syst. **30**, 6467–6476 (2017)
18. Mallya, A., Davis, D., Lazebnik, S.: Piggyback: Adapting a single network to multiple tasks by learning to mask weights. In: Ferrari, V., Hebert, M., Sminchisescu, C., Weiss, Y. (eds.) ECCV 2018. LNCS, vol. 11208, pp. 72–88. Springer, Cham (2018). https://doi.org/10.1007/978-3-030-01225-0_5
19. Mallya, A., Lazebnik, S.: Packnet: Adding multiple tasks to a single network by iterative pruning. In: Proceedings of the IEEE Conference on Computer Vision and Pattern Recognition, pp. 7765–7773 (2018)
20. Masse, N.Y., Grant, G.D., Freedman, D.J.: Alleviating catastrophic forgetting using context-dependent gating and synaptic stabilization. Proc. Natl. Acad. Sci. **115**(44), E10467–E10475 (2018)
21. McCloskey, M., Cohen, N.J.: Catastrophic interference in connectionist networks: The sequential learning problem. In: Psychology of learning and motivation, vol. 24, pp. 109–165. Elsevier (1989)
22. Mehta, N., Liang, K., Verma, V.K., Carin, L.: Continual learning using a bayesian nonparametric dictionary of weight factors. In: International Conference on Artificial Intelligence and Statistics, pp. 100–108. PMLR (2021)
23. Nguyen, C.V., Li, Y., Bui, T.D., Turner, R.E.: Variational continual learning. In: International Conference on Learning Representations (2018)
24. von Oswald, J., Henning, C., Sacramento, J., Grewe, B.F.: Continual learning with hypernetworks. In: International Conference on Learning Representations (2019)
25. Parisi, G.I., Kemker, R., Part, J.L., Kanan, C., Wermter, S.: Continual lifelong learning with neural networks: A review. Neural Netw. **113**, 54–71 (2019)
26. Ratcliff, R.: Connectionist models of recognition memory: constraints imposed by learning and forgetting functions. Psychol. Rev. **97**(2), 285 (1990)
27. Rebuffi, S.A., Kolesnikov, A., Sperl, G., Lampert, C.H.: icarl: Incremental classifier and representation learning. In: Proceedings of the IEEE conference on Computer Vision and Pattern Recognition, pp. 2001–2010 (2017)

28. Riemer, M., et al.: Learning to learn without forgetting by maximizing transfer and minimizing interference. In: International Conference on Learning Representations (2019)
29. Rolnick, D., Ahuja, A., Schwarz, J., Lillicrap, T., Wayne, G.: Experience replay for continual learning. Adv. Neural. Inf. Process. Syst. **32**, 350–360 (2019)
30. Rusu, A.A., et al.: Progressive neural networks. arXiv preprint arXiv:1606.04671 (2016)
31. Saha, G., Garg, I., Roy, K.: Gradient projection memory for continual learning. In: International Conference on Learning Representations (2021)
32. Saxe, A.M., McClelland, J.L., Ganguli, S.: Exact solutions to the nonlinear dynamics of learning in deep linear neural networks. arXiv preprint arXiv:1312.6120 (2013)
33. Serra, J., Suris, D., Miron, M., Karatzoglou, A.: Overcoming catastrophic forgetting with hard attention to the task. In: International Conference on Machine Learning, pp. 4548–4557. PMLR (2018)
34. Silver, D.L., Mercer, R.E.: The task rehearsal method of life-long learning: Overcoming impoverished data. In: Cohen, R., Spencer, B. (eds.) AI 2002. LNCS (LNAI), vol. 2338, pp. 90–101. Springer, Heidelberg (2002). https://doi.org/10.1007/3-540-47922-8_8
35. Tang, S., Chen, D., Zhu, J., Yu, S., Ouyang, W.: Layerwise optimization by gradient decomposition for continual learning. In: Proceedings of the IEEE/CVF Conference on Computer Vision and Pattern Recognition, pp. 9634–9643 (2021)
36. Veniat, T., Denoyer, L., Ranzato, M.: Efficient continual learning with modular networks and task-driven priors. In: International Conference on Learning Representations (2021)
37. Wang, S., Li, X., Sun, J., Xu, Z.: Training networks in null space of feature covariance for continual learning. In: Proceedings of the IEEE/CVF Conference on Computer Vision and Pattern Recognition, pp. 184–193 (2021)
38. Wen, Y., Tran, D., Ba, J.: Batchensemble: an alternative approach to efficient ensemble and lifelong learning. In: International Conference on Learning Representations (2020)
39. Wortsman, M., et al.: Supermasks in superposition. In: Advances in Neural Information Processing Systems, vol. 33 (2020)
40. Yin, H., Li, P., et al.: Mitigating forgetting in online continual learning with neuron calibration. In: Advances in Neural Information Processing Systems, vol. 34 (2021)
41. Yoon, J., Yang, E., Lee, J., Hwang, S.J.: Lifelong learning with dynamically expandable networks. In: International Conference on Learning Representations (2018)

# Batch-Efficient EigenDecomposition for Small and Medium Matrices

Yue Song$^{(\boxtimes)}$ , Nicu Sebe, and Wei Wang

DISI, University of Trento, 38123 Trento, Italy
yue.song@unitn.it
https://github.com/KingJamesSong/BatchED

**Abstract.** EigenDecomposition (ED) is at the heart of many computer vision algorithms and applications. One crucial bottleneck limiting its usage is the expensive computation cost, particularly for a mini-batch of matrices in the deep neural networks. In this paper, we propose a QR-based ED method dedicated to the application scenarios of computer vision. Our proposed method performs the ED entirely by batched matrix/vector multiplication, which processes all the matrices simultaneously and thus fully utilizes the power of GPUs. Our technique is based on the explicit QR iterations by Givens rotation with double Wilkinson shifts. With several acceleration techniques, the time complexity of QR iterations is reduced from $O(n^5)$ to $O(n^3)$. The numerical test shows that for small and medium batched matrices (*e.g.*, *dim*<32) our method can be much faster than the Pytorch SVD function. Experimental results on visual recognition and image generation demonstrate that our methods also achieve competitive performances.

**Keywords:** Differentiable SVD · Global covariance pooling · Universal style transfer · Vision transformer

## 1 Introduction

The EigenDecomposition (ED) or the Singular Value Decomposition (SVD) explicitly factorize a matrix into the eigenvalue and eigenvector matrix, which serves as a fundamental tool in computer vision and deep learning. Recently, many algorithms integrated the SVD as a meta-layer into their models to perform some desired spectral transformations [5,8,9,13,22,23,30,32,33,37,44–46]. The applications vary in global covariance pooling [30,37,43], decorrelated Batch Normalization (BN) [22,23,38,44], Perspective-n-Points (PnP) problems [5,8,13], and Whitening and Coloring Transform (WCT) [9,31,46].

The problem setup of the ED in computer vision is quite different from other fields. In other communities such as scientific computing, batched matrices rarely arise and the ED is usually used to process a single matrix. However, in deep

---

**Supplementary Information** The online version contains supplementary material available at https://doi.org/10.1007/978-3-031-20050-2_34.

S. Avidan et al. (Eds.): ECCV 2022, LNCS 13683, pp. 583–599, 2022.
https://doi.org/10.1007/978-3-031-20050-2_34

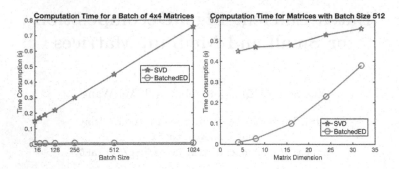

**Fig. 1.** The speed comparison of our Batched ED against the TORCH.SVD. (*Left*) Time consumption for a mini-batch of 4×4 matrices with different batch sizes. (*Right*) Time consumption for matrices with batch size 512 but in different matrix dimensions.

learning and computer vision, the model takes a mini-batch of matrices as the input, which raises the requirement for an ED solver that works for batched matrices efficiently. Moreover, the differentiable ED works as a building block and needs to process batched matrices millions of times during the training and inference. This poses a great challenge to the efficiency of the ED solver and could even stop people from adding the ED meta-layer in their models due to the huge time consumption (see Fig. 1).

In the current deep learning frameworks such as Pytorch [36] or Tensor-flow [1], the ED solvers mainly adopt the SVD implementation from the linear algebra libraries (*e.g.*, LAPACK [3] and Intel MKL [42]). These solvers can efficiently process a single matrix but do not support batched matrices on GPUs well. Most of the implementations are based on the Divide-and-Conquer (DC) algorithm [11,20]. This algorithm partitions a matrix into multiple small sub-matrices and performs the ED simultaneously for each sub-matrix. Aided by the power of parallel and distributed computing, its speed is only mildly influenced by the matrix dimension and can be very fast for a single matrix. The core of the DC algorithm is the characteristic polynomials $\det(\lambda\mathbf{I}-\mathbf{A})=0$, which can be solved by various methods, such as secular equations [20] and spectral division [34]. However, solving the polynomial requires simultaneously localizing all the eigenvalue intervals for each individual matrix. Despite the high efficiency for a single matrix, these DC algorithms do not scale to batched matrices.

Except for the DC algorithm, some ED solvers would use the QR iteration. The QR iteration has many implementation methods and one particular batch-efficient choice is by Givens rotation. The Givens rotation can be implemented via matrix-matrix multiplications, which naturally extends to batched matrices. During the QR iterations, the Givens rotation is applied successively to annihilate the off-diagonal entries until the matrix becomes diagonal. The major drawback limiting the usage of QR iterations is the $O(n^5)$ time cost, which makes this method only applicable to tiny matrices (*e.g.*, *dim*<9). To alleviate this issue, modern QR-based ED implementations apply the technique of *deflation* [2,6,7], *i.e.*, partition the matrix into many sub-matrices. The deflation technique can greatly improve the speed of the QR iterations but only works for an individual matrix. For the QR iteration, the convergence speed is related with the adjacent eigenvalue ratio $\frac{\lambda_{i+1}}{\lambda_i}$. For multiple matrices within a mini-batch, the off-diagonal entries of each matrix converge to zero with inconsistent speed and where each matrix can be partitioned is different. Consequently, the deflation technique does not apply to batched matrices either. To give a concrete example, consider 2 matrices of sizes 8×8 in a mini-batch. Suppose that the deflation would split one into two 3×3 and 5×5 matrices, while the other matrix might be partitioned into two 4×4 matrices. In this case, the partitioned matrices cannot be efficiently processed as a mini-batch due to the inconsistent matrix sizes.

To attain a batch-friendly and GPU-efficient ED method dedicated to computer vision field, we propose a QR-based ED algorithm that performs the ED via batched matrix/vector multiplication. Each step of the ED algorithm is carefully motivated for the best batch-efficient and computation-cheap consideration. We first perform a series of batched Householder reflectors to tri-diagonalize the matrix by the batched matrix-vector multiplication. Afterward, the explicit QR iteration by matrix rotation with double Wilkinson shifts [47] is conducted to diagonalize the matrix. The proposed shifts make the last two diagonal entries of the batched matrices have consistent convergence speed. Thereby the convergence is accelerated and the matrix dimension can be progressively shrunk during the QR iterations. Besides the dimension reduction, we also propose some economic computation methods based on the complexity analysis. The time complexity of QR is thus reduced from $O(n^5)$ to $O(n^3)$. The numerical tests demonstrate that, for matrices whose dimensions are smaller than 24, our Pytorch implementation is consistently much faster than the default SVD routine for any batch size. For matrices with larger dimensions (*e.g., dim*=32 or 36), our method could also have an advantage when the batch size is accordingly large (see also Fig. 1). We validate the effectiveness of our method in several applications of differentiable SVD, including decorrelated BN, covariance pooling for vision transformers, and neural style transfer. Our Batched ED achieves competitive performances against the SVD.

The contributions of the paper are summarized threefold:

- We propose an ED algorithm for a mini-batch of small and medium matrices which is dedicated to many application scenarios of computer vision. Each step of ED is carefully motivated and designed for the best batch efficiency.
- We propose dedicated acceleration techniques for our Batched ED algorithm. The progressive dimension shrinkage is proposed to reduce the matrix size during the iterations, while some economic computation methods grounded on the complexity analysis are also developed.
- Our batch-efficient ED algorithm is validated in several applications of differentiable SVD. The experiments on visual recognition and image generation demonstrate that our method achieves very competitive performances against the SVD encapsuled in the current deep learning platforms.

## 2    Related Work

In this section, we discuss the related work in computing the differentiable ED and its applications.

### 2.1    Computing the Differentiable ED

To perform the ED, modern deep learning frameworks (*e.g.*, Pytorch and Tensorflow) call the LAPACK's SVD routine by default. The routine uses the Divide-and-Conquer algorithm [11,20] to conduct the ED. Assisted by the power of parallel and distributed computing, the divide-and-conquer-based ED can simultaneously process each sub-matrix and achieve high efficiency for a single matrix regardless of the matrix size. However, solving the core characteristic polynomials requires simultaneously finding all the eigenvalue intervals for each individual matrix, which causes this algorithm unable to scale to batched matrices well. There are also some routines that use QR iterations with deflation for performing the ED [6,7]. Equipped with the deflation technique to partition the matrices, the QR iteration can also have a fast calculation speed. When it comes to a mini-batch of matrices, the off-diagonal entries of each matrix converge to zero with different speeds, and where each matrix can be partitioned is inconsistent. Hence, the deflation technique cannot be applied to batched matrices.

For the back-propagation of the ED, it suffers from the numerical instability caused by the close and repeated eigenvalues. Recently, several methods have been proposed to solve the instability issue [37,44,45]. Wei *et al.* [44] propose to use Power Iteration (PI) to approximate the SVD gradients. Song *et al.* [37] propose to use Padé approximants to closely estimate the gradients. Despite the applicability of these methods, a more practical approach is to divide the features $\mathbf{X} \in \mathbb{R}^{C \times BHW}$ into groups $\mathbf{X} \in \mathbb{R}^{G \times \frac{C}{G} \times BHW}$ in the channel dimension and attain a mini-batch of small covariance matrices $\mathbf{X}\mathbf{X}^T \in \mathbb{R}^{G \times \frac{C}{G} \times \frac{C}{G}}$ [22,35], which can keep more channel statistics and naturally avoid the gradient explosion issue caused by the rank-deficiency. This also raises the need of such an ED solver that works for batched matrices efficiently.

To attain the batch-efficient ED algorithm dedicated to computer vision field, we propose our QR-based algorithm for small and medium batched matrices. We motivate each step of our ED algorithm for the best batch efficiency. Our ED solver integrates double Wilkinson shifts [47] to guarantee that the last two diagonal entries have consistent convergence speed within the mini-batch, and consequently the matrix dimension can be progressively reduced. With several other acceleration technique grounded on the complexity analysis, our solver can be much faster than Pytorch SVD for a mini-batch of small matrices.

### 2.2    Applications of the Differentiable ED

The need for differentiable ED arises in numerous applications of computer vision. Some methods adopt the end-to-end ED to compute the matrix square root of the global covariance feature before the fully-connected layer [16,29,30, 33,37,39,40,43,48]. Such approaches are termed as Global Covariance Pooling

**Householder Tridiagonalization**

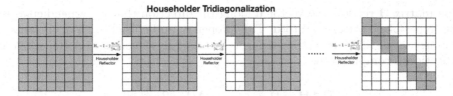

**Fig. 2.** Visual illustration of our batched Householder tri-diagonalization. After $(n-2)$ designed reflections, the symmetric matrix $\mathbf{A}$ is reduced to a tri-diagonal matrix $\mathbf{T}$.

(GCP) methods, and they have achieved state-of-the-art performances on both generic and fine-grained visual recognition. Another line of research uses the ED to perform the decorrelated batch normalization (BN) [22–25,35,38,38]. The process resembles the ZCA whitening transform to compute the inverse square root for eliminating the correlation between features. The differentiable ED can be also applied in the area of neural style transfer. As pointed out in [17,18], the feature covariance naturally embeds the style information. Some methods use the differentiable ED to perform successive WCT on the feature covariance for the universal style transfer [9,10,31]. In the geometric vision, the ED is often applied to solve the PnP problem and estimate the camera pose [5,8,13,28]. Besides the main usages above, there are some other minor applications [12,41].

## 3    Methodology

In this section, we present our method that performs the Batched ED. Our algorithm is implemented via the sequential batched Householder reflectors to tri-diagonalize the matrix and the batched QR iteration to diagonalize the tri-diagonal matrix. Both processes are GPU-friendly and batch-efficient. Now we illustrate each process in detail. Notice that every step is applied on batched matrices for the best efficiency.

### 3.1    Batched Tri-diagonalization Based on Householder Reflection

Given the Hermitian matrix $\mathbf{A}$, the tri-diagonalization process is defined as:

$$\mathbf{A} = \mathbf{PTP}^T \tag{1}$$

where $\mathbf{T}$ is a tri-diagonal matrix, and $\mathbf{P}$ is an orthogonal matrix. To perform such an orthogonal similarity transform, we can decompose $\mathbf{P}$ into $n-2$ Householder reflectors. This leads to the re-formulation:

$$\mathbf{T} = \mathbf{P}^T\mathbf{A}\mathbf{P} = (\mathbf{H}_n \ldots \mathbf{H}_4\mathbf{H}_3)^T\mathbf{A}(\mathbf{H}_n \ldots \mathbf{H}_4\mathbf{H}_3) \tag{2}$$

Each reflector is both orthogonal ($\mathbf{HH}^T=\mathbf{I}$) and unitary ($\mathbf{H}=\mathbf{H}^T$). The reflector is constructed using an vector:

$$\mathbf{H} = \mathbf{I} - 2\frac{\mathbf{uu}^T}{||\mathbf{u}||_{\mathrm{F}}^2} \tag{3}$$

The matrix $\mathbf{H}$ reflects the vector $\mathbf{u}$ along the direction that is perpendicular to the hyper-plane orthogonal to $\mathbf{u}$. This property can be used to tri-diagonalize a symmetric matrix by reflecting each row and column sequentially. A Householder reflection is computed by:

$$
\begin{aligned}
\mathbf{HAH} &= (\mathbf{I} - 2\frac{\mathbf{uu}^T}{||\mathbf{u}||_{\mathrm{F}}^2})\mathbf{A}(\mathbf{I} - 2\frac{\mathbf{uu}^T}{||\mathbf{u}||_{\mathrm{F}}^2}) \\
&= \mathbf{A} - \mathbf{pu}^T - \mathbf{uq}^T
\end{aligned}
\tag{4}
$$

where the temporary variables $\mathbf{q}$, $\mathbf{p}$, and $K$ are defined as:

$$
\mathbf{q} = \mathbf{p} - K\mathbf{u}, \mathbf{p} = \frac{2\mathbf{Au}}{||\mathbf{u}||_{\mathrm{F}}^2}, K = \frac{\mathbf{u}^T\mathbf{p}}{||\mathbf{u}||_{\mathrm{F}}^2}
\tag{5}
$$

As can be seen, Eq. 4 actually defines a symmetric rank-2 update on $\mathbf{A}$. By some deductions on Eq. 4, each Householder reflector can be designed to introduce zero entries to a row and a column (see Fig. 2). We omit the derivation of the vector for conciseness and give the result here:

$$
\begin{aligned}
\mathbf{u}_i &= [0, \ldots, a_{i,i}, a_{i,i+1}, \ldots, a_{i,n-1}, \sigma], \\
\sigma &= \pm\sqrt{a_{i,i}^2 + a_{i,i+1}^2 + \cdots + a_{i,n-1}^2}
\end{aligned}
\tag{6}
$$

where $a_{i,j}$ denotes the entry of $\mathbf{A}$ at $i$-th row and $j$-th column, and the sign of $\sigma$ is usually chosen as $\mathrm{sign}(a_{i,n})$ to reduce the round-off error. By such a construction, only $n-2$ reflections are needed to transform the symmetric matrix into the tri-diagonal form. Each householder reflection needs 2 matrix-matrix multiplication, which takes $O(2n^3)$ complexity. However, as indicated in Eq. 4 and Eq. 5, the calculation can be reduced to one matrix-matrix multiplication and two matrix-vector multiplication, which needs the complexity of $O(n^3+2n^2)$.

When the eigenvector is required, we can calculate $\mathbf{P}$ by accumulating the Householder reflectors:

$$
\mathbf{P} = \mathbf{H}_n \ldots \mathbf{H}_4\mathbf{H}_3
\tag{7}
$$

The computation needs $(n-2)$ matrix multiplication where the complexity of each multiplication is $O(n^3)$. We note this step can be further accelerated by:

**Theorem 1. (WY representation [4])** For any accumulation of $m$ Householder matrices $\mathbf{H}_1 \ldots \mathbf{H}_m$, there exists $\mathbf{W}, \mathbf{Y} \in \mathbb{R}^{(n-2) \times m}$ such that we have the relation $\mathbf{I} - 2\mathbf{WY}^T = \mathbf{H}_1 \ldots \mathbf{H}_m$. Computing $\mathbf{W}$ and $\mathbf{Y}$ takes $O((n-2)m)$ time and $(m-1)$ sequential Householder multiplications.

Relying on this theorem, we can divide the accumulation $\mathbf{H}_n \ldots \mathbf{H}_4\mathbf{H}_3$ into $(n-2)/m$ sub-sequences and compute them in parallel. Each sub-sequence takes $O((m-1)n^3+(n-2)m)$ time to compute the WY representation and $O((n-2)^2m)$ time to compute $\mathbf{I} - 2\mathbf{WY}^T$. Combining all the sub-sequence needs extra time of $O((n-2)^3/m)$. This can further reduce the complexity of computing $\mathbf{P}$ from $O((n-3)n^3)$ to $O((m-1)n^3+(n-2)m+(n-2)^2m+(n-2)^3/m)$. The computation saving would be huge when $n$ is large.

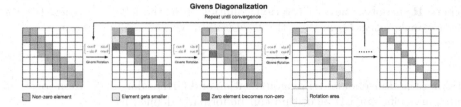

**Fig. 3.** Visual illustration of the batched Givens diagonalization. For each QR iteration, the Givens rotation is applied from the left top corner to the bottom right corner to reduce the magnitude of the off-diagonal elements. The iteration continues till the off-diagonal entries become zero or below a certain tolerance.

## 3.2  Batched Diagonalization Based on QR Iteration

After obtaining the tri-diagonal matrix $\mathbf{T}$, we use the Givens rotation to perform the QR iterations, which can be implemented efficiently via batched matrix multiplication. Based on the ordinary QR iteration, we further apply several techniques to speed up the convergence and save the computational budget.

**Basic QR Iteration by Givens Rotation.** Given the tri-diagonal matrix $\mathbf{T}$, the QR iteration takes the following iterative update:

$$\mathbf{T}_k = \mathbf{Q}_k \mathbf{R}_k, \ \mathbf{T}_{k+1} = \mathbf{R}_k \mathbf{Q}_k \tag{8}$$

where $\mathbf{Q}_k$ denotes the orthogonal matrix, and $\mathbf{R}_k$ is the upper-triangular matrix. Replacing $\mathbf{R}_k$ with $\mathbf{Q}_k^T \mathbf{T}_k$ leads to the re-formulation of Eq. 8 :

$$\mathbf{T}_{k+1} = \mathbf{Q}_k^T \mathbf{T}_k \mathbf{Q}_k \tag{9}$$

As can be seen, a single QR iteration is equivalent to performing an orthogonal similarity transform. By performing the iterations, the sub-diagonal and super-diagonal entries are gradually reduced till the matrix becomes diagonal.

For each QR iteration, we construct the orthogonal transform using successive Givens rotations moving from the left top corner to the right bottom corner. The 2×2 Givens Rotation and its $n{\times}n$ extension are defined by:

$$\mathbf{R}_{2\times 2} = \begin{bmatrix} \cos\theta & -\sin\theta \\ \sin\theta & \cos\theta \end{bmatrix}, \mathbf{R}_{n\times n} = \begin{bmatrix} \mathbf{I} & \mathbf{0} & \mathbf{0} \\ \mathbf{0} & \mathbf{R}_{2\times 2} & \mathbf{0} \\ \mathbf{0} & \mathbf{0} & \mathbf{I} \end{bmatrix} \tag{10}$$

where $\theta$ is the rotation angle, and the rotation matrix is orthogonal but not symmetric (*i.e.,* $\mathbf{R}^T\mathbf{R}{=}\mathbf{I}$ and $\mathbf{R}^T{\neq}\mathbf{R}$). As shown in Fig. 3, by design of the rotation angle, the successive Givens Rotation applied on $\mathbf{T}$ can keep the tri-diagonal form but reduce the magnitude of off-diagonal elements. For the derivation of Givens rotation, please refer to the supplementary material for detail. The sequential Givens rotations moving along the diagonal form one single QR iteration:

$$\mathbf{T}_{k+1} = (\mathbf{R}_{n-2}^T \dots \mathbf{R}_0^T)\mathbf{T}_k(\mathbf{R}_0 \dots \mathbf{R}_{n-2}) \tag{11}$$

where $\mathbf{R}_i$ denotes the $i$-th rotation counting from the left top corner. For the orthogonal matrix $\mathbf{Q}_i$ in the $i$-th QR iteration, we can easily find out

$$\mathbf{Q}_k = \mathbf{R}_0 \dots \mathbf{R}_{n-2} \tag{12}$$

Taking the Householder tri-diagonalization and Givens diagonalization together, our batch-efficient ED algorithm can be formally defined by:

$$\mathbf{A} = (\mathbf{PQ}_0 \dots \mathbf{Q}_k)\mathbf{\Lambda}(\mathbf{PQ}_0 \dots \mathbf{Q}_k)^T \tag{13}$$

where $k$ is the iteration times of the QR iteration, $\mathbf{\Lambda}$ is the eigenvalue matrix, and $\mathbf{PQ}_0 \dots \mathbf{Q}_k$ is the eigenvector matrix. For the convergence, we have:

**Theorem 2. (Convergence of QR iteration)** *Let* $\mathbf{T}$ *be the positive definite tri-diagonal matrix with the eigendecomposition* $\mathbf{Q\Lambda Q}^T$ *and assume* $\mathbf{Q}^T$ *can be LU decomposed. Then the QR iteration of* $\mathbf{T}$ *will converge to* $\mathbf{\Lambda}$.

We defer the proof to the Supplementary Material. The key results of this theorem is that the convergence speed depends on the adjacent eigenvalue ratio $\frac{\lambda_i}{\lambda_j}$ for $i>j$. The QR iterations usually take $2n$ iterations to make the resultant matrix diagonal [15]. Consider the fact that each iteration takes $(n-1)$ Givens rotation. The computation overhead would be huge. For deriving the eigenvalues, we need $4n(n-1)n^3$ time, while it takes the complexity of $2n(n-2)n^3+(2n-1)n^3$ to compute the eigenvector. The time complexity of the QR iteration is quintic to the matrix dimension $n$, which would make this method only applicable to the tiny matrices ($<9$). Existing deflation techniques [6,7] to accelerate the computation cannot be applied to our batched matrices. To resolve this issue, we propose the following techniques:

**Double Wilkinson Shift.** As indicated in Theorem 2, the convergence speed of QR iteration depends on the ratio $\frac{\lambda_i}{\lambda_j}$, where $i>j$. A natural approach to accelerate the convergence is to shift the matrix by $\mathbf{T} - \mu\mathbf{I}$ such that the convergence speed becomes $\frac{\lambda_i-\mu}{\lambda_j-\mu}$. A preferable shift coefficient should be $u=\lambda_j$, as this can help the matrices to converge quickly: $\frac{\lambda_i-\mu}{\lambda_j-\mu}=\infty$. This is particularly useful for matrices in a mini-batch as the speed can be made consistent by shifting.

Since each Givens rotation will affect the area rotated by the previous one, only the last $2\times2$ Givens rotation will not be influenced, $i.e.$, the two eigenvalues of the last block can be locally estimated. Thus, we propose to extract the shift coefficients from the $2\times2$ block on the right bottom corner:

$$\mu_{n-2}, \mu_{n-1} = Wilkinson(\mathbf{T}_k[n - 2 : n]) \tag{14}$$

where $\mathbf{T}_k[n-2{:}n]$ denotes the last $2\times2$ block of $\mathbf{T}_k$, and $\mu_{n-2}$ and $\mu_{n-1}$ are the two eigenvalues computed from this block. These shifting coefficients are referred to as the Wilkinson shift [47], and we give the derivation in the supplementary material. After attaining the shifts, we can reformulate the QR iterations with double shifts:

$$\mathbf{T}_{k+1/2} = \mathbf{Q}_k^T(\mathbf{T}_k - \mu_{n-1}\mathbf{I})\mathbf{Q}_k + \mu_{n-1}\mathbf{I}$$
$$\mathbf{T}_{k+1} = \mathbf{Q}_k^T(\mathbf{T}_{k+1/2} - \mu_{n-2}\mathbf{I})\mathbf{Q}_k + \mu_{n-2}\mathbf{I} \tag{15}$$

With the shifts, the integrated iteration consists of two sequential QR iterations shifted by the eigenvalues $\mu_{n-2}$ and $\mu_{n-1}$, respectively.

**Progressive Dimension Shrinkage.**
One direct benefit brought by the Wilkinson shift is that, for all the matrices in a mini-batch, the last two diagonal entries can quickly converge to the corresponding eigenvalues and the off-diagonal elements can converge to zero:

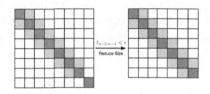

$$t_{n-2,n-2}{\rightarrow}\lambda_{n-2}, \; t_{n-2,n-3}=t_{n-3,n-2}{\rightarrow}0$$
$$t_{n-1,n-1}{\rightarrow}\lambda_{n-1}, \; t_{n-2,n-1}=t_{n-1,n-2}{\rightarrow}0 \tag{16}$$

We can use this property to speed up the computation by gradually reducing the matrix dimension, *i.e.*, shrinking the

**Fig. 4.** Illustration of the progressive dimension reduction in the QR iterations. After one iteration, if the last sub-diagonal entry is below a small threshold $\epsilon$, we can remove the last row and column.

matrix by $\mathbf{T}{\in}\mathbb{R}^{n \times n}{\rightarrow}\mathbf{T}{\in}\mathbb{R}^{(n-1)\times(n-1)}$ after one iteration. As shown in Fig. 4, when the last sub-diagonal entry is below a given small threshold (*e.g.*, 1e−5), we could shrink the matrix by removing the last row and column. In doing so, the matrix size is progressively reduced during the QR iterations. With the dimension reduction, one QR iteration would take $(n-1-r)$ Givens rotations, where $r$ is the reduction times.

**Economic Eigenvalue Calculation.** For a Givens rotation, it only affects the adjacent 4×4 block. We can save the computation budget by applying the matrix multiplication on the 4×4 rotation region in the neighborhood. This reduces the time of a rotation from $O(2n^3)$ to $O(2 \times 4^3)=O(128)$, which makes each rotation consume a constant time cost. Taking the above dimension reduction into account, the QR iterations need $O(256n(n-1-r))$ time to derive the eigenvalues.

**Economic Eigenvector Calculation.** Equipped with the progressive dimension reduction, the orthogonal transform $\mathbf{Q}_k$ in a QR iteration is defined by:

$$\mathbf{Q}_k = \mathbf{R}_0\mathbf{R}_1\dots\mathbf{R}_{n-2-r} \tag{17}$$

where we need $(n-2-r)$ rotations for each iteration. The computation can be potentially simplified by the theorem:

**Theorem 3. (Implicit Q Theorem** [19]**)** Let $\mathbf{B}$ be an upper Hessenberg and only have positive elements on its first sub-diagonal. Assume there exists a unitary transform $\mathbf{Q}^H\mathbf{A}\mathbf{Q}{=}\mathbf{B}$. Then $\mathbf{Q}$ and $\mathbf{B}$ are uniquely determined by $\mathbf{A}$ and the first column of $\mathbf{Q}$.

We give the proof and some discussion in the supplementary document. This theorem implies that, without the need of explicit QR iteration, the orthogonal transform $\mathbf{Q}$ and the transformed matrix $\mathbf{B}$ can be both implicit calculated. However, it assumes that the sub-diagonal elements of $\mathbf{B}$ are positive. In our case, the Givens rotation can easily zero out the last two sub-diagonal entries. Consequently, directly using the theorem would cause large round-off errors and data overflow.

Although the theorem cannot be directly applied, it allows us to simplify the eigenvector calculation. As indicated by the theorem, the $i$-th rotation would only affect the orthogonal matrix $\mathbf{Q}$ on the area after the $i$-th row and column. We can reduce the computation by involving only part of the matrix and simplify the calculation in Eq. 17 as:

$$\mathbf{Q}_k = \mathbf{R}_0[1\!:]\mathbf{R}_1[2\!:]\ldots\mathbf{R}_{n-2-r}[n-2-r\!:] \tag{18}$$

where $[i\!:]$ denotes part of the matrix that excludes the first $i$ rows and columns. By doing so, the time complexity of calculating $\mathbf{Q}_k$ can be reduced to:

$$(n-2-r)^2 n + (n-3-r)^2 n + \ldots + 1^2 n$$
$$= \sum_{i=1}^{n-2-r} i^2 n = \frac{(n-2-r)(n-1-r)(2n-3-2r)}{6} n \tag{19}$$

Compared with the original time cost $O((n-2-r)n^3)$, the saving would be considerable for large $n$ and $r$.

### 3.3  Computation Complexity Summary

**Table 1.** Comparison of time complexity of the basic QR-based ED solver and our ED solver dedicated for batched matrices. Here $n$ denotes the matrix size and $r$ represents the average reduction times during the QR iterations.

| Time | Basic QR-based ED solver | |
|---|---|---|
| | Eigenvalue | Eigenvector |
| Tri-diag. | $2n^3$ | $(n-3)n^3$ |
| QR | $4n(n-1)n^3$ | $2n(n-2)n^3+(2n-1)n^3$ |
| Sum | $(4n^2-4n+2)n^3$ | $(2n^2-n-4)n^3$ |
| Time | Our Batched ED solver | |
| | Eigenvalue | Eigenvector |
| Tri-diag. | $n^3+2n^2$ | $(m-1)n^3+(n-2)m+(n-2)^2m+\frac{(n-2)^3}{m}$ |
| QR | $256(n-1-r)n$ | $\frac{(n-2-r)(n-1-r)(2n-3-2r)}{6}2n^2+(2n-1)n^3$ |
| Sum | $n^3+258n^2-256n(1+r)$ | $\frac{2}{3}n^5-(2r+1)n^4+(2r^2+6r+\frac{7}{3}+m)n^3$ |
| | | $-(\frac{3}{2}r^3+3r^2+\frac{13}{3}r+2-m)n^2-(3m-\frac{3}{m})n+2m-\frac{6}{m}$ |

Table 1 summarizes the time complexity of the basic QR-based ED solver and our proposed ED solver dedicated for batched matrices. Taking the highest-order term for simpler analysis, our ED solver reduces the time from $O(4n^5)$ to $O(n^3)$ for computing the eigenvalues, and saves the time from $O(2n^5)$ to $O(\frac{2}{3}n^5)$ for eigenvectors. Moreover, depending on the reduction times $r$, the complexity can be further reduced with the term $-256(1+r)n$ for eigenvalues and $-(2r+1)n^4$ for eigenvectors.

### 3.4  Convergence and Error Bounds

For the tri-diagonalization process, the convergence is guaranteed with $n-2$ Householder reflectors. The error is only related to the machine precision and data precision, which can be sufficiently neglected. For the QR iterations, the convergence mainly depends on the adjacent eigenvalue ratio $\frac{\lambda_{i+1}}{\lambda_i}$ and the shift $\mu$. In certain cases when the two eigenvalue are close ($\frac{\lambda_{i+1}}{\lambda_i} \approx 1$), the convergence speed is slow and the residual term $(\frac{\lambda_{i+1}-\mu}{\lambda_i-\mu})^{2n}$ becomes the error. Another error source comes from the tolerance $\epsilon$ for the dimension reduction. Let $\bar{\Lambda}$ represent the exact eigenvalues and $\Lambda$ denote the eigenvalues calculated by our ED solver. Then the error is bounded by:

$$||\bar{\Lambda} - \Lambda||_F \leq \max_i (( \frac{\lambda_{i+1} - \mu}{\lambda_i - \mu})^{2n}|l_{i+1,i}|) + \epsilon \qquad (20)$$

where $l_{i+1,i}$ is the entry of $\mathbf{L}$ computed by $\mathbf{Q}^T = \mathbf{L}\mathbf{U}$, and the shift $\mu$ changes every QR iteration. Since $\mathbf{Q}$ is orthogonal, the magnitude of $l_{i+1,i}$ is often quite small. Considering the small magnitude of $l_{i+1,i}$ and the additional shifting technique, the accuracy of our method will not get affected.

## 4  Experiments

In this section, we first perform a numerical test to compare our method with SVD for matrices in different dimensions and batch sizes. Subsequently, we evaluate the effectiveness of the proposed methods in three computer vision applications: decorrelated BN, second-order vision transformer, and neural style transfer. The implementations details are referred to supplementary material.

### 4.1  Numerical Test

Figure 5 depicts the computational time of our Batched ED against the SVD for different matrix dimensions and batch sizes. The time cost of the SVD grows almost linearly with the batch size, while the time consumption of our Batched ED only has slight or mild changes against varying batch sizes. For matrices whose dimensions are smaller than 24, our Batched ED is consistently faster than the SVD for any batch size. When the matrix dimension is 32, our method is faster than the SVD from batch size 256 on. The speed of our Batched ED is more advantageous for smaller matrix dimensions and larger batch sizes.

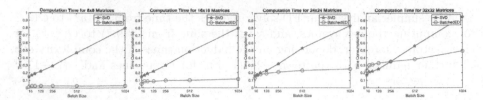

**Fig. 5.** The speed comparison of our Batched ED against TORCH.SVD for different batch sizes and matrix dimensions. Our implementation is more batch-friendly and the time cost does not vary much against different batch sizes. For matrices in small and moderate sizes, our method can be significantly faster than the Pytorch SVD.

**Table 2.** Validation error of decorrelated BN on ResNet-18 [21]. The results are reported based on 5 runs, and we measure the time of the forward ED in a single step.

| Solver | Group | Size | Time (s) | CIFAR10 | | CIFAR100 | |
|---|---|---|---|---|---|---|---|
| | | | | Mean $\pm$ std | min | Mean $\pm$ std | min |
| SVD | 16 | $16 \times 4 \times 4$ | 0.172 | $4.52 \pm 0.09$ | 4.33 | $\mathbf{21.24 \pm 0.17}$ | 20.99 |
| Batched ED | | | 0.006 | $\mathbf{4.37 \pm 0.11}$ | **4.29** | $21.25 \pm 0.20$ | **20.90** |
| SVD | 8 | $8 \times 8 \times 8$ | 0.170 | $4.55 \pm 0.13$ | 4.34 | $21.32 \pm 0.31$ | 20.88 |
| Batched ED | | | 0.016 | $\mathbf{4.36 \pm 0.11}$ | **4.25** | $\mathbf{20.97 \pm 0.27}$ | **20.62** |
| SVD | 4 | $4 \times 16 \times 16$ | 0.165 | $4.52 \pm 0.14$ | 4.33 | $21.30 \pm 0.33$ | **20.86** |
| Batched ED | | | 0.075 | $\mathbf{4.45 \pm 0.11}$ | **4.32** | $\mathbf{21.19 \pm 0.21}$ | 20.98 |

### 4.2 Decorrelated BN

Following [38], we first conduct an experiment on the task of ZCA whitening. In the whitening process, the inverse square root of the covraince is multiplied with the feature as $(\mathbf{XX}^T)^{-\frac{1}{2}}\mathbf{X}$ to eliminate the correlation between each dimension. We insert the ZCA whitening meta-layer into the ResNet-18 [21] architecture and evaluate the validation error on CIFAR10 and CIFAR100 [27]. Table 2 compares the performance of our Batched ED against the SVD. Depending on the number of groups, our method can be 2X faster, 10X faster, and even 28X faster than the SVD. Furthermore, our method outperforms the SVD across all the metrics on CIFAR10. With CIFAR100, the performance is also on par.

### 4.3 Second-Order Vision Transformer

We turn to the experiment on the task of global covariance pooling for the Second-order Vision Transformer (So-ViT) [48]. To leverage the rich semantics embedded in the visual tokens, the covariance square root of the visual tokens $(\mathbf{XX}^T)^{\frac{1}{2}}$ are used to assist the classification task. Since the global covariance matrices are typically very ill-conditioned [37], this task poses a huge challenge to the stability of the ED algorithm. We choose the So-ViT architecture with different depths and validate the performance on ImageNet [14]. As observed from

Table 3, our Batched ED has the competitive performance against the standard SVD. Moreover, our method is about 44% and 27% faster than the SVD for covariance in different sizes.

**Table 3.** Validation accuracy on ImageNet [14] for the second-order vision transformer with different depths. Here 32 and 36 denote the spatial dimension of visual tokens. We report the time consumption of the forward ED in a single step.

| Solver | Size | Time (s) | Architecture | |
|---|---|---|---|---|
| | | | So-ViT-7 | So-ViT-10 |
| SVD | $768 \times 32 \times 32$ | 0.767 | 76.01/**93.10** | **77.97/94.10** |
| Batched ED | | 0.431 | **76.04**/93.05 | 77.91/94.08 |
| SVD | $768 \times 36 \times 36$ | 0.835 | **76.10/93.14** | 78.09/94.13 |
| Batched ED | | 0.612 | 76.07/93.10 | **78.11/94.19** |

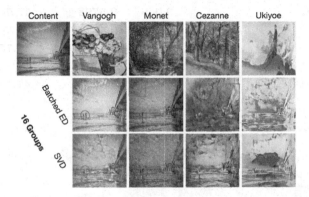

**Fig. 6.** Exemplary visual comparison. The red circle/rectangular indicates the region with subtle details. In this example, our method generates sharper images with more coherent style information and less artifacts. Zoom in for a better view. (Color figure online)

### 4.4   Universal Style Transfer

Now we apply our Batched ED in the WCT for neural style transfer. Given the content feature $\mathbf{X}_c$ and the style feature $\mathbf{X}_s$, the WCT performs successive whitening $((\mathbf{X}_c\mathbf{X}_c)^{-\frac{1}{2}}\mathbf{X}_c)$ and coloring $((\mathbf{X}_s\mathbf{X}_s)^{\frac{1}{2}}\mathbf{X}_c)$ to transfer the target style. We follow [31,46] to use the LPIPS distance and the user preference as the evaluation metrics. Table 4 presents the quantitative comparison with different groups. Our Batched ED achieves very competitive performance and predominates the speed. To give a concrete example, when the group number is 64, our method is about 35X faster than the default SVD. Figure 6 displays the exemplary visual comparison. In this specific example, our Batched ED generates images with better visual appeal.

Similar to the finding in [9], we also observe that the number of groups has an impact on the extent of transferred style. As shown in Fig. 7, when more groups are used, the style in the transferred image becomes more distinguishable and the details are better preserved. Since the number of groups determines the number of divided channels and the covariance size, more groups correspond to smaller covariance and this might help to better capture the local structure. Despite this superficial conjecture, giving a more comprehensive and rigorous analysis is worth further research.

**Table 4.** The LPIPS distance between the transferred image and the content image and the user preference (%) on the Artworks [26] dataset. We report the time consumption of the forward ED that is conducted 10 times to exchange the style and content feature at different network depths. The batch size is set to 4.

| Solver | Group | Size | Time (s) | LPIPS [49] (↑) | Preference (↑) |
|---|---|---|---|---|---|
| SVD | 64 | $256 \times 4 \times 4$ | 3.146 | 0.5776 | **48.25** |
| Batched ED | | | 0.089 | **0.5798** | 47.75 |
| SVD | 32 | $128 \times 8 \times 8$ | 2.306 | **0.5722** | 47.75 |
| Batched ED | | | 0.257 | 0.5700 | **48.75** |
| SVD | 16 | $64 \times 16 \times 16$ | 1.973 | 0.5614 | 46.25 |
| Batched ED | | | 0.876 | **0.5694** | **47.75** |

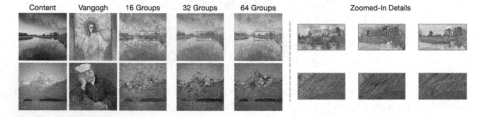

**Fig. 7.** Visual illustration of the impact of groups. When more groups are used, the strength of the target style is increased and the details are better preserved.

To sum up, our ED solver has demonstrated the superior batch efficiency for small matrices in various real-world experiments and numerical tests. The limitation on large matrices indicates the key difference: *our method is more batch-efficient, while* TORCH.EIG/SVD *is more dimension-efficient.*

## 5    Conclusion

In this paper, we propose a batch-efficient QR-based ED algorithm dedicated for batched matrices which are common in the context of computer vision and deep learning. Aided by the proposed acceleration techniques, our solver is much faster than Pytorch SVD function for a mini-batch of small and medium matrices. Our method can directly benefit a wide range of computer vision applications and we showcase this merit in several applications of differentiable ED. Extensive experiments on visual recognition and image generation demonstrate that our method can also achieve very competitive performances.

**Acknowledgement.** This research was supported by the EU H2020 projects AI4Media (No. 951911) and SPRING (No. 871245).

# References

1. Abadi, M., et al.: {TensorFlow}: A system for {Large-Scale} machine learning. In: 12th USENIX Symposium on Operating Systems Design and Implementation (OSDI 2016), pp. 265–283 (2016)
2. Ahues, M., Tisseur, F.: A new deflation criterion for the qr algorithm. LAPACK Working Note 122 (1997)
3. Anderson, E., et al.: LAPACK Users' guide. SIAM (1999)
4. Bischof, C., Van Loan, C.: The wy representation for products of householder matrices. SIAM J. Sci. Stat. Comput. **8**(1), s2–s13 (1987)
5. Brachmann, E., et al.: Dsac-differentiable ransac for camera localization. In: CVPR (2017)
6. Braman, K., Byers, R., Mathias, R.: The multishift qr algorithm. part i: Maintaining well-focused shifts and level 3 performance. SIAM J. Matrix Anal. Appli. **23**(4), 929–947 (2002)
7. Braman, K., Byers, R., Mathias, R.: The multishift qr algorithm. part ii: Aggressive early deflation. SIAM J. Matrix Anal. Appli. **23**(4), 948–973 (2002)
8. Campbell, D., Liu, L., Gould, S.: Solving the blind perspective-n-point problem end-to-end with robust differentiable geometric optimization. In: Vedaldi, A., Bischof, H., Brox, T., Frahm, J.-M. (eds.) ECCV 2020. LNCS, vol. 12347, pp. 244–261. Springer, Cham (2020). https://doi.org/10.1007/978-3-030-58536-5_15
9. Cho, W., Choi, S., Park, D.K., Shin, I., Choo, J.: Image-to-image translation via group-wise deep whitening-and-coloring transformation. In: CVPR (2019)
10. Choi, S., Jung, S., Yun, H., Kim, J.T., Kim, S., Choo, J.: Robustnet: Improving domain generalization in urban-scene segmentation via instance selective whitening. In: CVPR (2021)
11. Cuppen, J.J.: A divide and conquer method for the symmetric tridiagonal eigenproblem. Numer. Math. **36**(2), 177–195 (1980)
12. Dai, T., Cai, J., Zhang, Y., Xia, S.T., Zhang, L.: Second-order attention network for single image super-resolution. In: CVPR (2019)
13. Dang, Z., Yi, K.M., Hu, Y., Wang, F., Fua, P., Salzmann, M.: Eigendecomposition-free training of deep networks for linear least-square problems. In: TPAMI (2020)
14. Deng, J., Dong, W., Socher, R., Li, L.J., Li, K., Fei-Fei, L.: Imagenet: A large-scale hierarchical image database. In: CVPR (2009)
15. Francis, J.G.: The qr transformation-part 2. Comput. J. **4**(4), 332–345 (1962)
16. Gao, Z., Wang, Q., Zhang, B., Hu, Q., Li, P.: Temporal-attentive covariance pooling networks for video recognition. In: NeurIPS (2021)
17. Gatys, L., Ecker, A.S., Bethge, M.: Texture synthesis using convolutional neural networks. In: NeurIPS (2015)

18. Gatys, L.A., Ecker, A.S., Bethge, M.: Image style transfer using convolutional neural networks. In: CVPR (2016)
19. Golub, G.H., Van Loan, C.F.: Matrix computations. edition (1996)
20. Gu, M., Eisenstat, S.C.: A divide-and-conquer algorithm for the symmetric tridiagonal eigenproblem. SIAM J. Matrix Anal. Appl. **16**(1), 172–191 (1995)
21. He, K., Zhang, X., Ren, S., Sun, J.: Deep residual learning for image recognition. In: CVPR (2016)
22. Huang, L., Yang, D., Lang, B., Deng, J.: Decorrelated batch normalization. In: CVPR (2018)
23. Huang, L., Zhao, L., Zhou, Y., Zhu, F., Liu, L., Shao, L.: An investigation into the stochasticity of batch whitening. In: CVPR (2020)
24. Huang, L., Zhou, Y., Liu, L., Zhu, F., Shao, L.: Group whitening: Balancing learning efficiency and representational capacity. In: CVPR (2021)
25. Huang, L., Zhou, Y., Zhu, F., Liu, L., Shao, L.: Iterative normalization: Beyond standardization towards efficient whitening. In: CVPR (2019)
26. Isola, P., Zhu, J.Y., Zhou, T., Efros, A.A.: Image-to-image translation with conditional adversarial networks. In: CVPR (2017)
27. Krizhevsky, A.: Learning multiple layers of features from tiny images. Master's thesis, University of Tront (2009)
28. Lepetit, V., Moreno-Noguer, F., Fua, P.: Epnp: An accurate o (n) solution to the pnp problem. In: IJCV (2009)
29. Li, P., Xie, J., Wang, Q., Gao, Z.: Towards faster training of global covariance pooling networks by iterative matrix square root normalization. In: CVPR (2018)
30. Li, P., Xie, J., Wang, Q., Zuo, W.: Is second-order information helpful for large-scale visual recognition? In: ICCV (2017)
31. Li, Y., Fang, C., Yang, J., Wang, Z., Lu, X., Yang, M.H.: Universal style transfer via feature transforms. In: NeurIPS (2017)
32. Lin, T.Y., Maji, S.: Improved bilinear pooling with cnns. arXiv preprint arXiv:1707.06772 (2017)
33. Lin, T.Y., RoyChowdhury, A., Maji, S.: Bilinear cnn models for fine-grained visual recognition. In: ICCV (2015)
34. Nakatsukasa, Y., Higham, N.J.: Stable and efficient spectral divide and conquer algorithms for the symmetric eigenvalue decomposition and the svd. SIAM J. Sci. Comput. **35**(3), A1325–A1349 (2013)
35. Pan, X., Zhan, X., Shi, J., Tang, X., Luo, P.: Switchable whitening for deep representation learning. In: ICCV (2019)
36. Paszke, A., et al.: Pytorch: An imperative style, high-performance deep learning library. In: NeurIPS (2019)
37. Song, Y., Sebe, N., Wang, W.: Why approximate matrix square root outperforms accurate svd in global covariance pooling? In: ICCV (2021)
38. Song, Y., Sebe, N., Wang, W.: Fast differentiable matrix square root. In: ICLR (2022)
39. Song, Y., Sebe, N., Wang, W.: Fast differentiable matrix square root and inverse square root. arXiv preprint arXiv:2201.12543 (2022)
40. Song, Y., Sebe, N., Wang, W.: On the eigenvalues of global covariance pooling for fine-grained visual recognition. In: IEEE TPAMI (2022)
41. Sun, Q., Zhang, Z., Li, P.: Second-order encoding networks for semantic segmentation. Neurocomputing (2021)
42. Wang, E., et al.: Intel math Kernel Library. In: High-Performance Computing on the Intel® Xeon Phi™, pp. 167–188. Springer, Cham (2014). https://doi.org/10.1007/978-3-319-06486-4_7

43. Wang, Q., Xie, J., Zuo, W., Zhang, L., Li, P.: Deep cnns meet global covariance pooling: Better representation and generalization. In: TPAMI (2020)
44. Wang, W., Dang, Z., Hu, Y., Fua, P., Salzmann, M.: Backpropagation-friendly eigendecomposition. In: NeurIPS (2019)
45. Wang, W., Dang, Z., Hu, Y., Fua, P., Salzmann, M.: Robust differentiable svd. In: TPAMI (2021)
46. Wang, Z., et al.: Diversified arbitrary style transfer via deep feature perturbation. In: CVPR (2020)
47. Wilkinson, J.: The algebraic eigenvalue problem. In: Handbook for Automatic Computation, Volume II, Linear Algebra. Springer-Verlag, New York (1971)
48. Xie, J., Zeng, R., Wang, Q., Zhou, Z., Li, P.: So-vit: Mind visual tokens for vision transformer. arXiv preprint arXiv:2104.10935 (2021)
49. Zhang, R., Isola, P., Efros, A.A., Shechtman, E., Wang, O.: The unreasonable effectiveness of deep features as a perceptual metric. In: CVPR (2018)

# Ensemble Learning Priors Driven Deep Unfolding for Scalable Video Snapshot Compressive Imaging

Chengshuai Yang, Shiyu Zhang, and Xin Yuan(✉)

School of Engineering, Westlake University, Hangzhou 310030, Zhejiang, China
{zhangshiyu,xyuan}@westlake.edu.cn

**Abstract.** Snapshot compressive imaging (SCI) can record a 3D datacube by a 2D measurement and algorithmically reconstruct the desired 3D information from that 2D measurement. The reconstruction algorithm thus plays a vital role in SCI. Recently, deep learning (DL) has demonstrated outstanding performance in reconstruction, leading to better results than conventional optimization-based methods. Therefore, it is desirable to improve DL reconstruction performance for SCI. Existing DL algorithms are limited by two bottlenecks: 1) a high-accuracy network is usually large and requires a long running time; 2) DL algorithms are limited by scalability, *i.e.*, a well-trained network cannot generally be applied to new systems. To this end, this paper proposes to use **ensemble learning priors** in DL to achieve high reconstruction speed and accuracy in a single network. Furthermore, we develop the scalable learning approach during training to empower DL to handle data of different sizes without additional training. Extensive results on both simulation and real datasets demonstrate the superiority of our proposed algorithm. The code and model can be accessed at https://github.com/integritynoble/ELP-Unfolding/tree/master.

**Keywords:** Deep unfolding · Ensemble · Snapshot compressive imaging · Scalable learning

## 1 Introduction

Recently, video snapshot compressive imaging (SCI) [7,30,60] has attracted much attention because it can improve imaging speed by capturing three-dimensional (3D) information from 2D measurement. When video SCI works, multiple frames are first modulated by different masks (in the optical domain), and these modulated frames are mapped into a single measurement. After this, the reconstruction algorithm recovers these multiple frames from single measurement [56]. At present, the mask can easily be adjusted with a higher speed

---

**Supplementary Information** The online version contains supplementary material available at https://doi.org/10.1007/978-3-031-20050-2_35.

than the capture rate of the camera [20,38,41]. Thus, SCI enjoys the advantages of high speed, low memory, low bandwidth, low power and potentially low cost [58,59].

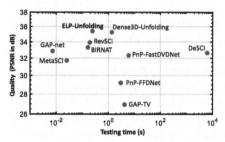

**Fig. 1.** Trade-off between quality and testing-time of various algorithms for SCI reconstruction. Our proposed Ensemble Learning Priors (ELP) unfolding achieves the state-of-the-art results in a short testing time. Besides, after scalable learning, our ELP-Unfolding can be used in different masks and different compression ratios and thus can be applied to various scenes by a single trained model.

How to recover the original multiple frames from the single measurement always plays a vital role in SCI. Recently, deep learning reconstruction methods have outperformed traditional iterative reconstruction methods not only in reconstruction accuracy but also in test time [8–10,24, 34,43,50,51]. But most deep learning methods lack interpretability. To increase interpretability, deep unfolding method has been developed, which simulates the iterative algorithm [17,31,51,63]. Deep unfolding method adopts iterative framework but replaces traditional denoiser (such as total variation [4,26] and nonlocal self-similarity [12,29]) with the trained neural network denoiser. So far, the deep unfolding method has achieved the best result for SCI. Among deep unfolding algorithms, GAP-net [31] can use the shortest time (0.0072 s s) to achieve 32 dB for PSNR for benchmark dataset. Dense3D-Unfolding [46] achieved the best result (35 dB), though it costs a long time (1.35 s) due to the use of complex 3D convolutional neural networks (CNNs). Thus, *the speed and accuracy have not coexisted in one algorithm yet.* What's worse, most of these deep learning algorithms are limited by scalability. To apply the trained model to new systems, the model usually should be trained again. Although MetaSCI [45] can be quickly applied to new SCI modulations (in spatial but not in temporal dimension), it still requires adaptation (retraining).

Bearing the above concerns in mind, in order to achieve a higher reconstruction accuracy with a high computing speed, we develop the Ensemble Learning Priors (ELP) unfolding based on 2D-CNN for SCI. Specifically, 2D-CNN can retain fast processing and ensemble learning can increase reconstruction accuracy. Ensemble learning is powerful in achieving reconstruction accuracy and has also achieved state-of-the-art (SOTA) results in a number of models on other tasks [36,65,68], due to the fact that mutiple models/priors have complementary advantages over a single model/prior. Fortunately, the deep unfolding algorithm can include many neural network priors, even if these priors stay at different (iteration) stages. In this paper, we first propose to gather multiple neural network priors in one stage to realize **ensemble learning** for SCI without increasing training time. To further increase the reconstruction accuracy, dense connection is employed in our network, which can help the latter (stage) models learn some useful information from the previous (stage) models. In this manner, our ELP-unfolding can achieve SOTA result, outperform Dense3D-Unfolding [46], and use a shorter running time.

Furthermore, to realize the scalability, we develop a scalable learning procedure for SCI. Our method *not only has scalability in the spatial dimensions but also in the temporal dimension*. Considering the spatial scalability, we set our ELP-unfolding to be fully convolutional without the multilayer perception (MLP) structure. For temporal dimension scalability, the input of neural network priors is set to have the same channels even for different temporal dimensional scenes. Based on this, our scalable learning method can have the same capability as traditional iteration algorithms, to be applied to different systems. Specific contributions of our paper are listed as follows:

- We develop the **ensemble learning prior unfolding** for SCI. ELP unfolding is a general method for inverse algorithms, which can also be applied to other fields, such as single pixel camera [16,19,40], MRI [2,28], lensless imaging [3,57,61], spectral compressive imaging [6,18,21,27,32,66], and tomography imaging [11,39,52].
- We first propose the **scalable learning for SCI**. After training once, our model can be used in new systems with different modulations or different compression ratios. Besides, scalable learning can achieve better results than PnP algorithm with a fast inference speed.
- We adopt skip connection techniques in unfolding. In our ELP-unfolding, the skip connection only uses the simple adding and concatenating. By contrast, the Dense3D-Unfolding [46] adopts complex methods such as DFMA (dense feature map adaption) to realize connection.
- Our method **achieves SOTA results** for SCI in benchmark dataset based on 2D-CNN, outperforming the 3D-CNN method at a faster inference speed [46] as shown in Fig. 1.

In a nutshell, our ensemble learning priors unfolding has two periods. In the first period, i.e. a single prior period, each stage contains one neural network prior. Afterwards, in the second (ensemble priors) period, each stage contains all previous stage priors in the ensemble manner.

## 2   Related Work

SCI is related to compressive sensing (CS) [22,67], where reconstruction is significantly important as it provides the desired signals (such as images) from the compressed measurements. For CS [22,24,31,34,43], there are two kinds of reconstruction methods: traditional iterative method and deep learning method. The traditional iteration method contains a lot of iterations and each iteration contains the projection operation and denoising operation (and optionally some other steps). The denoising operation generally determines the performance of one algorithm. For example, total variation [4,26] denoiser has a fast speed but usually can only provide blurry images while the nonlocal self-similarity based denoiser [12,29] can achieve a clearer image but take a long time. Recently, deep learning has shown strong power in reconstructing images [24,34,43,50,51]. At first, deep learning was regarded as a black box and the trained model can get the better images than traditional iterative method at a fast speed. As a black box to train, the trained model will contain measurement matrix (masks) information. Thus, the training model usually can not be applied to new masks (such as a new hardware system). To address this problem, the deep unfolding method for CS has be developed. Deep unfolding method simulates traditional iterative method using a few iterations (stages), each of which has projection operation and denoising operation. Different from traditional methods, deep unfolding uses a trained neural network as a denoising prior. Therefore, deep learning mainly contributes to denoising in deep unfolding method with little dependence on mask information. The mask information is mainly processed by the projection operation. Thus, deep unfolding algorithms has a strong robustness to a variety of masks [31,63]. Besides, Dense3D-Unfolding [46] obtained SOTA for SCI by combining deep unfolding method and 3D-CNN, but at the cost of slow computation. Though the unfolding method can solve the scalability problem of various masks, the scalability problem of various sizes (both spatial size and temporal size, a.k.a., the compression ratio) still remains in unfolding method. Deep unfolding method still does not have the same scalability as the traditional iterative method.

To address these challenges, in this paper, we develop the ensemble learning priors unfolding for scalable SCI. We use ensemble learning and 2D-CNN to realize high reconstruction accuracy and speed, and develop scalable learning to realize scalability.

## 3   Preliminary: Video SCI System

As depicted in Fig. 2, let $\{\mathbf{X}_1, \ldots, \mathbf{X}_B\}$ denote the discretized video frames at timestamps $\{t_1, \ldots, t_B\}$. These video frames are modulated by dynamic coded aperture, a.k.a., the masks $\{\mathbf{C}_1, \ldots, \mathbf{C}_B\}$, respectively. The modulated frames are then integrated into a single coded measurement (a compressed image) $\mathbf{Y}$. Here, $\{\mathbf{X}_b\}_{b=1}^{B} \in \mathbb{R}^{n_x \times n_y \times B}$, $\{\mathbf{C}_b\}_{b=1}^{B} \in \mathbb{R}^{n_x \times n_y \times B}$ and $\mathbf{Y} \in \mathbb{R}^{n_x \times n_y}$. This forward model can be written as

$$\mathbf{Y} = \sum_{b=1}^{B} \mathbf{C}_b \odot \mathbf{X}_b + \mathbf{Z}, \tag{1}$$

where $\odot$ and $\mathbf{Z} \in \mathbb{R}^{n_x \times n_y}$ denote the matrix element-wise product and noise, respectively. Equation (1) is equivalent to the following linear form

$$y = \mathbf{H}x + z, \tag{2}$$

where $y = \mathrm{Vec}(\mathbf{Y}) \in \mathbb{R}^{n_x n_y}, z = \mathrm{Vec}(\mathbf{Z}) \in \mathbb{R}^{n_x n_y}$ and $x = \mathrm{Vec}(\mathbf{X}) = [\mathrm{Vec}(\mathbf{X}_1), \ldots, \mathrm{Vec}(\mathbf{X}_B)] \in \mathbb{R}^{n_x n_y B}$. Different from traditional compressive sensing [13–15], the sensing matrix $\mathbf{H}$ in (2) has a very special structure and can be written as

$$\mathbf{H} = [\mathbf{D}_1, \ldots, \mathbf{D}_B], \tag{3}$$

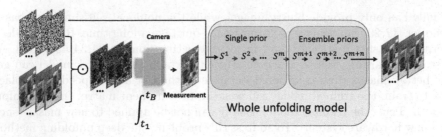

**Fig. 2.** Principle of Video SCI (left) and our ELP-unfolding (right). **Left**: the high speed dynamic scene at timestamps $t_1$ to $t_B$, encoded by high-speed variant masks (dynamic coded apertures) and then integrated to a single coded measurement (a compressed image) **Y**. **Right**: our whole ELP-unfolding reconstructs the original dynamic scene from the masks $\{\mathbf{C}_1, \ldots, \mathbf{C}_B\}$ and the compressed image **Y**, which includes the single prior period in Fig. 3(a) and ensemble priors period in Fig. 3(b). $S^m$ represents the $m^{th}$ stage.

where $\{\mathbf{D}_b = diag(\text{Vec}(\mathbf{C}_b)) \in \mathbb{R}^{n_x n_y \times n_x n_y}\}_{b=1}^B$ are diagonal matrices of masks. Therefore, the compressive sampling rate in SCI is equal to $1/B$. The reconstruction error of SCI is bounded even when $B > 1$ [22].

## 4   Our Proposed Methods

### 4.1   Ensemble Learning Priors Unfolding for SCI

Given the compressed measurement **Y** and coding pattern $\{\mathbf{C}_b\}_{b=1}^B$ captured by the SCI system, there exist two optimization frameworks to predict the desired high speed frames $\{\mathbf{X}_b\}_{b=1}^B$: penalty function method and augmented Lagrangian (AL) method. The performance of AL method is better than that of the penalty function method, which has been proved in previous work [1,25,48]. Therefore the AL method is adopted here, which is formulated as follows:

$$x = \text{argmin}_x \, \varPhi(x) - \boldsymbol{\lambda}_1^T (y - \mathbf{H}x) + \tfrac{\gamma_1}{2} \|y - \mathbf{H}x\|_2^2, \qquad (4)$$

where $\varPhi(x), \boldsymbol{\lambda}_1$ and $\gamma_1$ denote the prior regularization, Lagrangian multiplier and penalty parameter, respectively. For convenience, Eq. (4) is further written as

$$x = \text{argmin}_x \, \varPhi(x) + \tfrac{\gamma_1}{2} \left\| y - \mathbf{H}x - \tfrac{\lambda_1}{\gamma_1} \right\|_2^2. \qquad (5)$$

**Single Prior.** To solve Eq. (5), an auxiliary variable $v$ is introduced. Then Eq. (5) is further written as

$$x = \text{argmin}_x \, \varPhi(v) + \tfrac{\gamma_1}{2} \left\| y - \mathbf{H}x - \tfrac{\lambda_1}{\gamma_1} \right\|_2^2 \text{ subject to } \, v = x. \qquad (6)$$

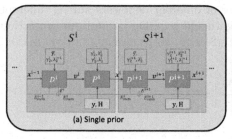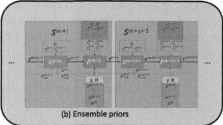

(a) Single prior                                      (b) Ensemble priors

**Fig. 3.** (a) Principle of the single prior period. Here, $D^i$ represents the $i^{th}$ denoising operation, as in Eq. (11) while $P^i$ represents the $i^{th}$ projection operation, as in Eq. (10). (b) Principle of ensemble priors period. Here, several denoising results $v^m...v^{m+1}$ are gathered together projection operation.

By adopting alternating direction method of multipliers (ADMM) method [5,49], Eq. (6) is further written as

$$x, v = \operatorname{argmin}_{x,v} \Phi(v) + \frac{\gamma_2}{2} \left\| x - v - \frac{\lambda_2}{\gamma_2} \right\|_2^2 + \frac{\gamma_1}{2} \left\| y - Hx - \frac{\lambda_1}{\gamma_1} \right\|_2^2. \quad (7)$$

According to ADMM, Eq. (7) can be divided into the two subproblems and solved iteratively, as shown in Fig. 3(a)

$$v^i = \operatorname{argmin}_v \Phi(v) + \frac{\gamma_2^i}{2} \left\| x^{i-1} - v - \frac{\lambda_2^i}{\gamma_2^i} \right\|_2^2, \quad (8)$$

$$x^i = \operatorname{argmin}_x \frac{\gamma_2^i}{2} \left\| x - v^i - \frac{\lambda_2^i}{\gamma_2^i} \right\|_2^2 + \frac{\gamma_1^i}{2} \left\| y - Hx - \frac{\lambda_1^i}{\gamma_1^i} \right\|_2^2, \quad (9)$$

where the superscript $i$ denotes the iteration index.

For subproblem $x_i$, there exists a closed-form solution, which is called projection operation

$$x^i = (\gamma_2^i I + \gamma_1^i H^T H)^{-1} \left[ \lambda_2^i + \gamma_2^i v^i + H^T \gamma_1^i (y - \frac{\lambda_1^i}{\gamma_1^i}) \right]. \quad (10)$$

Due to the special structure of $H$, this can be solved in one shot [29].

For subproblem $v_i$, Eq. (8) can be rewritten as

$$v^i = \operatorname{argmin}_v \Phi(v) + \frac{\gamma_2^i}{2} \left\| u^{i-1} - v \right\|_2^2, \quad (11)$$

where $u^{i-1} = x^{i-1} - \frac{\lambda_2^{i-1}}{\gamma_2^i}$. Equation (11) is a classical denoising problem, which can be solved by denoising prior such as TV, wavelet transformation, denoising network, *etc.*. In this paper, denoising network prior is adopted as shown in Fig. 4.

**Ensemble Priors.** In every stage of unfolding, the denoising prior has different parameters and thus plays different roles in removing noise, even these priors have the same structure. To take full use of different denoisers among different stages, these priors after $m$ stages are gathered together to perform projection operation to produce $x$. Therefore, Eqs. (8) and (9) in ensemble priors period, as shown in Fig. 3(b), becomes

$$v^{m+j} = \text{argmin}_v \, \Phi(v_1) + \frac{\gamma_2^{m+j}}{2} \left\| x^{m+j-1} - v - \frac{\lambda_2^{m+j-1}}{\gamma_2^{m+j}} \right\|_2^2, \tag{12}$$

and

$$x^{m+j} = \text{argmin}_x \, \frac{\gamma_2^m}{2} \left\| x - v^m - \frac{\lambda_2^m}{\gamma_2^m} \right\|_2^2 + \frac{\gamma_2^{m+1}}{2} \left\| x - v^{m+1} - \frac{\lambda_2^{m+1}}{\gamma_2^{m+1}} \right\|_2^2 + \cdots$$
$$+ \frac{\gamma_1^{m+j}}{2} \left\| y - Hx - \frac{\lambda_1^{m+j}}{\gamma_1^{m+j}} \right\|_2^2. \tag{13}$$

For subproblem $v_i$, Eq. (12) can still adopt the same denoising prior form as in single-prior period. For subproblem $x_i$, there is a slightly difference because of ensemble

$$x^{m+j} = [(\gamma_2^m + \gamma_2^{m+1} + \cdots + \gamma_2^{m+j})I + H^T \gamma_1^{m+j} H]^{-1}$$
$$\left[ \lambda_2^m + \gamma_2^m v^m + \cdots + \lambda_2^{m+j} + \gamma_2^{m+j} v^{m+j} + H^T \gamma_1^{m+j} (y - \frac{\lambda_1^{m+j}}{\gamma_1^{m+j}}) \right]. \tag{14}$$

Last but not least, the Lagrangian multipliers $\lambda_1^i$ and $\lambda_2^i$ are updated by

$$\lambda_1^i = \lambda_1^{i-1} - \gamma_1^i (y - Hx^{i-1}), \tag{15}$$
$$\lambda_2^i = \lambda_2^{i-1} - \gamma_2^i (x - v^{i-1}). \tag{16}$$

Besides, the $\gamma_1^i$ and $\gamma_2^i$ are trained with the denoising prior parameters at every stage.

In our method, the whole algorithm body should be divided into two parts: a single prior period and an ensemble priors period, because the first several stages can only provide rough estimates. If the priors in the first several stages are coupled to the latter stages, the poor performance of the first several priors will worsen the whole algorithm performance. There are 13 stages in our algorithm, the first 8 stages are single prior periods and latter 5 stages are ensemble priors periods. It is noted that there are 6 priors in last stage. As we can see in Eq. (13) and Eq. (14), there exist six $v$'s if $j = 5$.

**Denoising Prior Structure.** As shown in Fig. 4, U-net [42] is used as the backbone for denoising prior, which we adopt from FastDVDnet [44], but here we remove batch normalization and quadruple the depth; this means that the channels for three different features are 128, 256 and 512, respectively. Thus, the training parameters of our proposed ELP-unfolding mainly consists of these 13 U-net structures. More details can be found in the supplementary materials (SM). Following [44,64], the penalty parameter $\gamma_2^i$ is expanded to a noise map as part of the input. To help denoising, the normalized measurement $\overline{\mathbf{Y}}$ is also added to the input [8,45,46], which is defined as

$$\overline{\mathbf{Y}} = \mathbf{Y} \oslash \sum_{b=1}^{B} \mathbf{C}_b, \qquad (17)$$

where $\oslash$ represents the matrix element-wise division. Therefore, the input consists of noise map $\gamma_2^i$, normalized measurement $\overline{\mathbf{Y}}$ and $x^{i-1} - \frac{\lambda_2^{i-1}}{\gamma_2^i}$, and the output is $v^i$. Besides, dense connection is employed in the denoising prior network design.

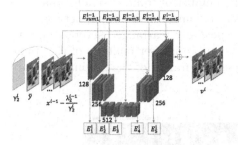

**Fig. 4.** Denoising prior structure based on U-net [42]. To realize connection, sum feature $\mathbf{E}_{sumj}^{i-1}$ from previous priors is coupled into current prior and current feature $\mathbf{E}_j^i$ is used to help form next sum feature $\mathbf{E}_{sumj}^i$.

**Algorithm 1.** ELP-unfolding for SCI Reconstruction

---

**Require: H,** $y$, $\overline{\mathbf{Y}}$, $\{\gamma_1^0, \ldots, \gamma_1^{m+n}\}$, $\{\gamma_2^0, \ldots, \gamma_2^{m+n}\}$.
1: Initial $v^0 = 0$, $\lambda_1^0 = 0$, $\lambda_2^0 = 0$.
2: Update $x^0$ by Eq. (10)
3: % *single prior period*
4: **for** i = 1, ..., m **do**
5:    Update $v^i$ by Eq. (11), $\lambda_2^i$ by Eq. (16).
6:    Update $\lambda_1^i$ by Eq. (15), $x^i$ by Eq. (10).
7: **end for**
8: % *ensemble priors period*
9: **for** k = m+1, ..., m+n **do**
10:    Update $v^k$ by Eq. (11), $\lambda_2^k$ by Eq. (16).
11:    Update $\lambda_1^k$ by Eq. (15), $x^k$ by Eq. (14).
12: **end for**

---

**Dense Connection for Unfolding.** In traditional unfolding method, the connection between two stages are $v$ and $u$, that is $x^{i-1} - \frac{\lambda_2^{i-1}}{\gamma_2^i}$, which have a small number of temporal dimensions. Therefore, most latent information in U-net structure cannot be transferred between different priors. To break this bottleneck, the skip connection technique is used here. As shown in Fig. 4, in the $i^{th}$ prior, the feature $\mathbf{E}_j^i$ and feature $\mathbf{E}_{sumj}^{i-1}$ operate in the latent space of U-net structure as a whole feature. Besides, the feature $\mathbf{E}_j^i$ will add to $\mathbf{E}_{sumj}^{i-1}$ to form $\mathbf{E}_{sumj}^i$, that is, $\mathbf{E}_{sumj}^i = \mathbf{E}_{sumj}^{i-1} + \mathbf{E}_j^i$.

By re-ordering the updating equations, we summarize the entire algorithm in Algorithm 1.

### 4.2   Scalable Learning for SCI

Existing deep learning methods usually have limited scalability, *i.e.*, one trained model can only be applied to one system with specific masks and compression ratio $B$. When the scene data size changes, the new corresponding model usually needs to be trained again. The most recent MetaSCI [45] can quickly be applied to a new model but also demands new adaptation process. In addition, MetaSCI adaptation is limited in space but not suitable for time (compression ratio). Even some deep learning methods that are independent of multi-layer perception, such as Dense3D-Unfolding, can be applied to different spatial size cases, but they have no temporal scalability. They must be trained again for new applications with different temporal dimensions $B$.

To address this problem, we develop scalable learning for SCI. This scalable learning has scalability not only in the spatial dimension but also in the temporal dimension. Specifically, to ensure spatial scalability, we only employ the convolutional neural network, ignoring MLP; to ensure temporal scalability, we train a scalable frames model within a certain number of frames, which is the maximum frames $M$. During training, the number of frames (smaller than $M$) is randomly chosen; $M$ is also the number of channel in denoising networks. In most cases, the original data should be repeatedly rearranged several times to satisfy the frames number $M$. When $M$ is not an integer multiple of the frame number of dynamic scene, only the first several frames of the original data are used in the last arranging process.

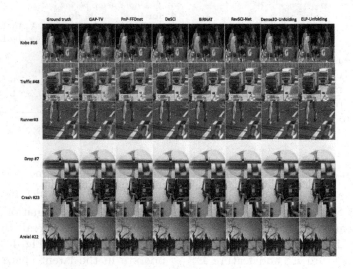

**Fig. 5.** Selected reconstruction results of benchmark dataset by GAP-TV [55], DeSCI [29], PnP-FFDNet [58], RevSCI [8] and the proposed ELP-unfolding (Please zoom-in to see details).

Even though the maximum temporal size needs to be pre-set, the new maximum temporal model can conveniently use the previous different maximum temporal models as the pre-trained model to speed up the training process.

### 4.3 Training

Given the measurement $\mathbf{Y}$ and masks $\{\mathbf{C}_b\}_{b=1}^B$, our ELP-unfolding can generate $\{\hat{\mathbf{X}}_b\}_{b=1}^B \in \mathbb{R}^{n_x \times n_y \times B}$. The mean square error (MSE) is selected as our loss function, expressed as

$$\ell_{MSE} = \frac{1}{SBn_x n_y} \sum_{s=1}^{S} \sum_{b=1}^{B} \left\| \mathbf{X}_b - \hat{\mathbf{X}}_b \right\|_2^2, \tag{18}$$

where $\mathbf{X}_b$ is ground truth and $S$ is batchsize.

We use PyTorch [35] to train our model on an NVIDIA A40 GPU. For all training processes, we adopt the Adam optimizer [23] with a mini-batch size of 3 and a spatial size of $256 \times 256$. We also adopt a pre-training strategy. The whole training process has two periods. Firstly, 8 stages with a single prior model are trained as pretrained parameters. Secondly, the whole ELP-unfolding with the pretrained parameters, is then trained, with 13 stages, 6 ensemble-priors in the last stage. And the first 8 stages just contains a single prior in each stage. Besides, the former 8 stages in the entire ELP-unfolding match the pretrained model very well, completely adopting the pretrained parameters. The latter 5 stages priors adopt the same last stage parameters in the pretrained model.

**Table 1.** Benchmark datasets: the average results of PSNR in dB (left entry in each cell) and SSIM (right entry in each cell) and run time per measurement in seconds by different algorithms on 6 benchmark datasets.

| Algorithm | Kobe | Traffic | Runner | Drop | Crash | Aerial | Average | Run time (s) |
|---|---|---|---|---|---|---|---|---|
| GAP-TV [55] | 26.92, 0.838 | 20.66, 0.691 | 29.81, 0.895 | 34.95, 0.966 | 24.48, 0.799 | 24.81, 0.811 | 26.94, 0.833 | 4.2 (CPU) |
| DeSCI [29] | 33.25, 0.952 | 28.71, 0.925 | 38.48, 0.969 | 43.10, 0.992 | 27.04, 0.909 | 25.33, 0.860 | 32.65, 0.934 | 6180 (CPU) |
| PnP-FFDNet [58] | 30.33, 0.925 | 24.01, 0.835 | 32.44, 0.931 | 39.68, 0.986 | 24.67, 0.833 | 24.29, 0.820 | 29.21, 0.888 | 3.0 (GPU) |
| PnP-FastDVDnet [59] | 32.73, 0.947 | 27.95, 0.932 | 36.29, 0.962 | 41.82, 0.989 | 27.32, 0.925 | 27.98, 0.897 | 32.35, 0.942 | 6 (GPU) |
| BIRNAT [10] | 32.71, 0.950 | 29.33, 0.942 | 38.70, 0.976 | 42.28, 0.992 | 27.84, 0.927 | 28.99, 0.927 | 33.31, 0.951 | 0.16 (GPU) |
| GAP-Unet-S12 [31] | 32.09, 0.944 | 28.19, 0.929 | 38.12, 0.975 | 42.02, 0.992 | 27.83, 0.931 | 28.88, 0.914 | 32.86, 0.947 | **0.0072 (GPU)** |
| Meta-SCI [45] | 30.12, 0.907 | 26.95, 0.888 | 37.02, 0.967 | 40.61, 0.985 | 27.33, 0.906 | 28.31, 0.904 | 31.72, 0.926 | 0.025 (GPU) |
| RevSCI [8] | 33.72, 0.957 | 30.02, 0.949 | 39.40, 0.977 | 42.93, 0.992 | 28.12, 0.937 | 29.35, 0.924 | 33.92, 0.956 | 0.19 (GPU) |
| Dense3D-Unfolding [46] | **35.00, 0.969** | **31.76, 0.966** | 40.03, 0.980 | 44.96, **0.995** | 29.33, 0.956 | 30.46, 0.943 | 35.26, 0.968 | 1.35 (GPU) |
| ELP-Unfolding (Ours) | 34.41, 0.966 | 31.58, 0.962 | **41.16, 0.986** | **44.99, 0.995** | **29.65, 0.960** | **30.68, 0.943** | **35.41, 0.969** | 0.24 (GPU) |

Regarding the learning rate, we adopt the same strategy for these two training periods. The difference lies in the initial learning rate. For the first (pretrained) period, the initial learning rate is set to $1 \times 10^{-4}$. For the second (ELP-unfolding) period, the initial learning rate is set to $2 \times 10^{-5}$. After the first five epochs, the learning rate decays a factor of 0.9 every 15 epochs. Besides, for the first (pretrained) period, the total number of epoch is 200 and training time is about 8 days. For the second period, the total number of epoch is 320 and training time is about 13 days.

In this paper we used above training strategies to train three models, namely benchmark model, scalable model and real data model.

## 5 Experiment

### 5.1 Training Dataset

We used DAVIS2017 [37] dataset with a resolution of $480 \times 894$ (480p) as our training dataset for all experiments. Video clips with spatial size of $256 \times 256$ are randomly cropped from this training dataset.

## 5.2    Benchmark Datasets for SCI

Kobe, Traffic, Runner, Drop, Crash, and Aerial are the Benchmark datasets for SCI [59], where the data-size is $256 \times 256 \times 8$, $i.e.n_x=n_y=256$, $B=8$. Based on these datasets, we compare our ELP-unfolding with a special temporal size of 8 to other SOTA algorithms, including GAP-TV [55], DeSCI [29], PnP-FFDNet [58], PnP-FastDVDnet [59], BIRNAT [10], GAP-Unet-S12 [31], Meta-SCI [45], RevSCI [8], Dense3D-Unfolding [46]. The results are summarized in Table 1. As we can see, iterative algorithms including PnP based algorithms (GAP-TV, DeSCI, PnP-FFDNet, PnP-FastDVDnet) provide inferior results at a slow speed (more than one second). Deep learning algorithms can achieve better result in a short running time (usually less than 1 s).

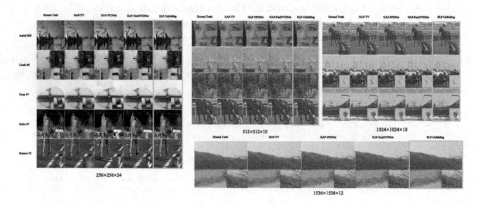

**Fig. 6.** Scalability: Selected results by GAP-TV, PnP-FFDNet, PnP-FastDVDnet and our ELP-unfolding with various spatial sizes and compression ratios.

For direct comparison of deep learning algorithms, Table 2 shows the results of top three algorithms, namely, RevSCI, Dense3D-Unfolding and ours. Although Dense3D-Unfolding has achieved the best results before, it costs a long time to test (1.35 s). Our ELP-unfolding algorithm not only achieves better result than Dense3D-Unfolding, but also saves test time (costing 0.24 s). For visualization purpose, we also present some images in Fig. 5, from the zoom areas we can see that our ELP-unfolding provides much clearer images with sharper edges and more abundant details than other algorithms, even the Dense3D-Unfolding (Crash). We also believe that by adopting 3D-CCN, ELP-unfolding can achieve even better results.

**Table 2.** The comparison of top three algorithms: time, memory for training one batch and reconstruction accuracy (PSNR).

|                    | Time    | Memory   | PSNR     |
|--------------------|---------|----------|----------|
| RevSCI             | 0.19 s  | Flexible | 33.92 dB |
| Dense3D-Unfolding  | 1.35 s  | 28.7 G   | 35.26 dB |
| Our method         | 0.24 s  | 12.5 G   | 35.41 dB |

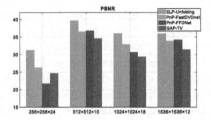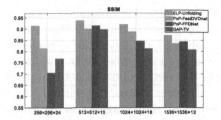

**Fig. 7.** Scalability: Reconstruction results by GAP-TV, PnP-FFDNet, PnP-FastDVDnet and the proposed ELP-unfolding with various spatial sizes and compression ratios.

### 5.3 Scalable Datasets for SCI

To verify the scalability of our ELP-unfolding method, we trained one model to test four different size datasets: $256 \times 256 \times 24$, $512 \times 512 \times 10$, $1024 \times 1024 \times 18$ and $1536 \times 1536 \times 12$. The latter three datasets are cropped from the Ultra Video Group (UVG) dataset [33] in the same way as in Meta-SCI [45]. The former dataset is also the benchmark. but the compression ratio $B$ is now set to 24. Because previous deep learning algorithms (including Meta-SCI) cannot scale for different compression ratios, traditional iteration algorithms including GAP-TV, PnP-FFDNet and PnP-FastDVDnet are chosen as baselines.

It can be noticed from Fig. 7 that these algorithms yield worse results than ELP-unfolding meanwhile cost a longer time (details in SM). In the case of $1536 \times 1536 \times 12$, PnP-FFDNet is able to get good results as ELP-unfolding. However, it is unstable and gets the worst results in the case of $256 \times 256 \times 24$. Figure 6 shows some selected images with much sharper boundaries and fewer artifacts reconstructed by ELP-unfolding than other algorithms. Please refer to the reconstructed videos in SM.

### 5.4 Ablation Study

In our ELP-unfolding model, the single prior period contains 8 stages, ensemble priors period contains 5 stages and thus the whole model contains 13 stages. Stage 9 has two priors to deal with projection operation while stage 10 has three priors and so on and so forth. In the end, in stage 13, there are six priors.

Focusing on the number of stages in Table 3b, we can see that the more stages one model has, the better result the model can achieve. But when the number of stages reaches 13, the reconstruction accuracy can not be improved any more. Regarding the priors, by adopting ensemble learning priors strategy, the 6 priors (with 13 stages) model can still improve reconstruction accuracy. Besides, the ensemble learning model always behaves better than its single prior counterpart in the same number of stage case. For instance, in the 9-stage model, two priors in the last stage always leads to better results than the single prior counterpart.

Next, we consider a more complicated structure. Specifically, we use 2 priors in stage 2 and 3 priors in stage 3 and so on and so forth. For a fair comparison, we also use a 13stage model. The result of this complicated model is called 'Ensemble all' in Table 3c. We can observe that even though the model is more complicated, it cannot lead to better results than our proposed structure, because the first several stages only provides rough estimates and the poor performance of first several priors can deteriorate the whole algorithm performance if coupled to the latter stages. In addition, the 'Ensemble no' in Table 3c denotes a single prior used in all stages, and the same for the 13 stages in Table 3b. This model can lead to decent results but not as good as ensemble priors structure. After comparison, we set the 6 priors model as our final ELP-unfolding, the results of which are also shown in 'Integrating all' in Table 3c.

**Table 3.** Ablations. Average PSNR and SSIM for different setups in simulation.

(a) 'm-n' means m stages model has n priors in the last stage.

| 6 single stages | | 7 single stages | | 8 single stages | |
|---|---|---|---|---|---|
| '7-2' 32.69 | '7-1' 30.71 | '8-2' 32.82 | '8-1' 30.98 | '9-2' 33.24 | '9-1' 31.25 |
| '9-4' 32.92 | '9-1' 31.25 | '9-3' 33.03 | '9-1' 31.25 | '11-4' 33.33 | '11-1' 31.45 |
| '11-6' 33.06 | '11-1' 31.45 | '11-5' 33.19 | '11-1' 31.45 | '13-6' 33.46 | '13-1' 31.75 |
| 'aver' 32.89 | 'aver' 31.14 | 'aver' 33.13 | 'aver' 31.23 | 'aver' 33.34 | 'aver' 31.48 |

(b) Different stages and ensemble priors in the last stage

| 1 stage | 3 stages | 5 stages | 7 stages | 8 stages | 9 stages | 11 stages | 13 stages | 1 prior | 2 priors | 4 priors | 6 priors | 8 priors |
|---|---|---|---|---|---|---|---|---|---|---|---|---|
| 31.21, 0.926 | 33.29, 0.953 | 34.33, 0.964 | 34.50, 0.965 | 34.83, 0.966 | 34.92, 0.967 | 35.11, 0.968 | 35.07, 0.968 | 34.83, 0.966 | 34.98, 0.967 | 35.15, 0.968 | 35.41, 0.969 | 35.34, 0.969 |

(c) Running 13 stages in different situations.

| Ensemble all | Ensemble no | Part training-set | Removing connection | Integrating all |
|---|---|---|---|---|
| 34.97, 0.967 | 35.09, 0.968 | 34.73, 0.966 | 34.77, 0.966 | 35.41, 0.969 |

(d) '7-1' means 7 stages 1 prior while '13-6'means 13 stages 6 priors.

| 7-1 w/o connection | 7-1 w/ connection | 13-6 w/o connection | 13-6 w/connection |
|---|---|---|---|
| 34.23, 0.961 | 34.85, 0.967 | 34.77, 0.966 | 35.41, 0.969 |

**Effect of Dense Connection.** To verify the effect of the dense connection in ELP-unfolding, we make the comparisons with and without dense connection in the 7 stages model ('7-1') and 6 priors model ('13-6'). The 7 stages model has seven stages but each stage contains only one prior, while the 6-prior model is the full model in our paper that achieves SOTA results. As shown in Table 3d, removing the dense connection will lower the performance of unfolding algorithms including the single prior model and the ensemble prior model, because the information transmitted between priors is limited. It should be noticed that our dense connection operation is simple, only consisting of adding and concatenating, instead of complex operations such as the dense feature map adaption in Dense3D-Unfolding [46]. Thus our ELP-unfolding provides a simple strategy (dense connection) to improve the performance of deep unfolding.

**Effect of Ensemble Priors.** Table 3b can't completely reflect the effect of ensemble priors, because we adopt a large model by using connection technique

and wide channels (512 channels in unet middle layer) to get SOTA accuracy
to outperform Dense3D-Unfolding, which leaves little room for ensemble priors
improvement. In most circumstances, it is unnecessary to use such big models. Thus, we use the normal 128 channels and remove connection technique to
display the effect of ensemble priors, as shown in Table 3a. As we can see, the
ensemble priors method can improve the reconstruction accuracy of PNSR by
more than 1.75 dB on average. Besides, ensemble priors method doesn't increase
memory to train and time to test. Thus, ensemble priors have a huge advantage
in the field of deep unfolding.

**Effect of Training Dataset.** Training dataset plays a key role in performance
of deep learning algorithms, and ELP-unfolding is no exception. We verify this
by using part of the training dataset, *i.e.* the dataset in DAVIS2017 that only
trains on 480p videos, but does not include the test dataset and test challenge
dataset. The results are shown in 'Part training-set' in Table 3c. By comparing
'Part training-set' and 'Integrating all', we find that reducing the amount of
training set hurts the performance of ELP-unfolding.

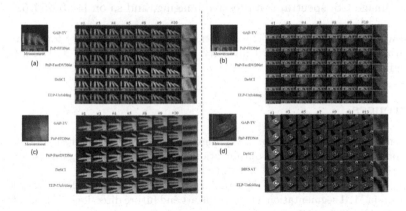

**Fig. 8.** Real data `duomino` (a, 512×512×10), `waterballon` (b, 512×512×10), `hand` (c,
512×512×10) and `chop` (d, 256×256×14) reconstructed from a compressed measurement.

## 6   Real Datasets for SCI

We now apply the proposed ELP-unfolding to real datasets, namely chopwheel [30], waterBalloon [38], duomino [38] and hand [56]. Because of the
unavoidable measurement noise, it is more challenging to reconstruct real measurements. The size of the Chopwheel data is $256 \times 256 \times 14$, while the size of the
other three datasets is $512 \times 512 \times 10$. From Fig. 8, we can see that our method
can generate more apparent contours while reducing artifacts and ghosting.
What's more, previous deep learning algorithms didn't succeed in reconstructing
hand because of the big noise in this data. Our ELP-unfolding firstly obtains

614 C. Yang et al.

the hand reconstruction by deep learning. Thus, we can only show the comparison with traditional iteration algorithms such as GAP-TV, PnP-FFDNet and DeSCI. Therefore, we can conclude that in practical applications, our method is powerful in reconstructing high-speed scenes. The relative videos can be seen in SM.

## 7 Conclusions and Future Work

Inspired by ensemble learning and iterative based optimization algorithm, we develop ensemble learning priors unfolding for scalable snapshot compressive imaging. Our ELP-unfolding algorithm has achieved state-of-the-art results in a short running time. Besides, we have firstly proposed the scalable function for SCI, not only in the spatial dimension but also in the temporal dimension.

To further improve the reconstruction accuracy, we will consider combining 3D-CNN with ELP-unfolding. Besides, to reduce the testing time and the parameters of neural network, a distilling method will be employed. We believe that our proposed ELP-unfolding framework can also be used for other inverse problems such as image CS, spectral compressive imaging, and so on [47,53,54,62].

**Acknowledgements.** We would like to thank the Research Center for Industries of the Future (RCIF) at Westlake University, Westlake Foundation (2021B1501-2) and the funding from Lochn Optics.

## References

1. Afonso, M.V., Bioucas-Dias, J.M., Figueiredo, M.A.: An augmented Lagrangian approach to the constrained optimization formulation of imaging inverse problems. IEEE Trans. Image Process. **20**(3), 681–695 (2010)
2. Akkus, Z., Galimzianova, A., Hoogi, A., Rubin, D.L., Erickson, B.J.: Deep learning for brain MRI segmentation: state of the art and future directions. J. Digit. Imaging **30**(4), 449–459 (2017)
3. Antipa, N., Oare, P., Bostan, E., Ng, R., Waller, L.: Video from stills: lensless imaging with rolling shutter. In: 2019 IEEE International Conference on Computational Photography (ICCP), pp. 1–8. IEEE (2019)
4. Bioucas-Dias, J.M., Figueiredo, M.A.: A new twist: two-step iterative shrinkage/thresholding algorithms for image restoration. IEEE Trans. Image Process. **16**(12), 2992–3004 (2007)
5. Boyd, S., Parikh, N., Chu, E., Peleato, B., Eckstein, J.: Distributed optimization and statistical learning via the alternating direction method of multipliers. Found. Trends Mach. Learn. **3**(1), 1–122 (2011)
6. Cai, Y., et al.: Mask-guided spectral-wise transformer for efficient hyperspectral image reconstruction. In: Proceedings of the IEEE/CVF Conference on Computer Vision and Pattern Recognition (2022)
7. Chen, Z., Zheng, S., Tong, Z., Yuan, X.: Physics-driven deep learning enables temporal compressive coherent diffraction imaging. Optica **9**(6), 677–680 (2022)

8. Cheng, Z., Chen, B., Liu, G., Zhang, H., Lu, R., Wang, Z., Yuan, X.: Memory-efficient network for large-scale video compressive sensing. In: Proceedings of the IEEE/CVF Conference on Computer Vision and Pattern Recognition, pp. 16246–16255 (2021)

9. Cheng, Z., Chen, B., Lu, R., Wang, Z., Zhang, H., Meng, Z., Yuan, X.: Recurrent neural networks for snapshot compressive imaging. In: IEEE Transactions on Pattern Analysis and Machine Intelligence (2022)

10. Cheng, Z., Lu, R., Wang, Z., Zhang, H., Chen, B., Meng, Z., Yuan, X.: BIRNAT: bidirectional recurrent neural networks with adversarial training for video snapshot compressive imaging. In: Vedaldi, A., Bischof, H., Brox, T., Frahm, J.-M. (eds.) ECCV 2020. LNCS, vol. 12369, pp. 258–275. Springer, Cham (2020). https://doi.org/10.1007/978-3-030-58586-0_16

11. Dong, J., Fu, J., He, Z.: A deep learning reconstruction framework for x-ray computed tomography with incomplete data. PLoS ONE 14(11), e0224426 (2019)

12. Dong, W., Shi, G., Li, X., Ma, Y., Huang, F.: Compressive sensing via nonlocal low-rank regularization. IEEE Trans. Image Process. 23(8), 3618–3632 (2014)

13. Donoho, D.L.: Compressed sensing. IEEE Trans. Inf. Theory 52(4), 1289–1306 (2006)

14. Duarte, M.F., et al.: Single-pixel imaging via compressive sampling. IEEE Signal Process. Mag. 25(2), 83–91 (2008)

15. Emmanuel, C., Romberg, J., Tao, T.: Robust uncertainty principles: exact signal reconstruction from highly incomplete frequency information. IEEE Trans. Inf. Theory 52(2), 489–509 (2006)

16. Gibson, G.M., et al.: Real-time imaging of methane gas leaks using a single-pixel camera. Opt. Express 25(4), 2998–3005 (2017)

17. Gregor, K., LeCun, Y.: Learning fast approximations of sparse coding. In: Proceedings of the 27th International Conference on Machine Learning, pp. 399–406 (2010)

18. He, W., Yokoya, N., Yuan, X.: Fast hyperspectral image recovery via non-iterative fusion of dual-camera compressive hyperspectral imaging. IEEE Trans. Image Process. 30, 1–12 (2021)

19. Higham, C.F., Murray-Smith, R., Padgett, M.J., Edgar, M.P.: Deep learning for real-time single-pixel video. Sci. Rep. 8(1), 1–9 (2018)

20. Hitomi, Y., Gu, J., Gupta, M., Mitsunaga, T., Nayar, S.K.: Video from a single coded exposure photograph using a learned over-complete dictionary. In: 2011 International Conference on Computer Vision, pp. 287–294. IEEE (2011)

21. Hu, X., Cai, Y., Lin, J., Wang, H., Yuan, X., Zhang, Y., Timofte, R., Van Gool, L.: Hdnet: High-resolution dual-domain learning for spectral compressive imaging. In: Proceedings of the IEEE/CVF Conference on Computer Vision and Pattern Recognition (2022)

22. Jalali, S., Yuan, X.: Snapshot compressed sensing: performance bounds and algorithms. IEEE Trans. Inf. Theory 65(12), 8005–8024 (2019)

23. Kingma, D.P., Ba, J.: Adam: a method for stochastic optimization. In: 3rd International Conference on Learning Representations, ICLR 2015, San Diego, CA, USA, 7–9 May 2015, Conference Track Proceedings (2015)

24. Kulkarni, K., Lohit, S., Turaga, P., Kerviche, R., Ashok, A.: Reconnet: Non-iterative reconstruction of images from compressively sensed measurements. In: Proceedings of the IEEE Conference on Computer Vision and Pattern Recognition, pp. 449–458 (2016)

25. Li, C.: An Efficient Algorithm For Total Variation Regularization with Applications to the Single Pixel Camera and Compressive Sensing. Rice University (2010)

26. Li, C., Yin, W., Jiang, H., Zhang, Y.: An efficient augmented Lagrangian method with applications to total variation minimization. Comput. Optim. Appl. **56**(3), 507–530 (2013)
27. Lin, J., et al.: Coarse-to-fine sparse transformer for hyperspectral image reconstruction. arXiv preprint arXiv:2203.04845 (2022)
28. Liu, J., et al.: Applications of deep learning to MRI images: a survey. Big Data Mining Anal. **1**(1), 1–18 (2018)
29. Liu, Y., Yuan, X., Suo, J., Brady, D.J., Dai, Q.: Rank minimization for snapshot compressive imaging. IEEE Trans. Pattern Anal. Mach. Intell. **41**(12), 2990–3006 (2018)
30. Llull, P., Liao, X., Yuan, X., Yang, J., Kittle, D., Carin, L., Sapiro, G., Brady, D.J.: Coded aperture compressive temporal imaging. Opt. Express **21**(9), 10526–10545 (2013)
31. Meng, Z., Jalali, S., Yuan, X.: Gap-net for snapshot compressive imaging. arXiv preprint arXiv:2012.08364 (2020)
32. Meng, Z., Ma, J., Yuan, X.: End-to-end low cost compressive spectral imaging with spatial-spectral self-attention. In: Vedaldi, A., Bischof, H., Brox, T., Frahm, J.-M. (eds.) ECCV 2020. LNCS, vol. 12368, pp. 187–204. Springer, Cham (2020). https://doi.org/10.1007/978-3-030-58592-1_12
33. Mercat, A., Viitanen, M., Vanne, J.: Uvg dataset: 50/120fps 4k sequences for video codec analysis and development. In: Proceedings of the 11th ACM Multimedia Systems Conference, pp. 297–302 (2020)
34. Mousavi, A., Patel, A.B., Baraniuk, R.G.: A deep learning approach to structured signal recovery. In: 2015 53rd Annual Allerton Conference on Communication, Control, and Computing (Allerton), pp. 1336–1343. IEEE (2015)
35. Paszke, A., et al.: Pytorch: an imperative style, high-performance deep learning library. Adv. Neural. Inf. Process. Syst. **32**, 8026–8037 (2019)
36. Pintelas, P., Livieris, I.E.: Special issue on ensemble learning and applications. Algorithms **13**(6), 140 (2020)
37. Pont-Tuset, J., Perazzi, F., Caelles, S., Arbeláez, P., Sorkine-Hornung, A., Van Gool, L.: The 2017 Davis challenge on video object segmentation. arXiv preprint arXiv:1704.00675 (2017)
38. Qiao, M., Meng, Z., Ma, J., Yuan, X.: Deep learning for video compressive sensing. APL Photon. **5**(3), 030801 (2020)
39. Qiao, M., Sun, Y., Ma, J., Meng, Z., Liu, X., Yuan, X.: Snapshot coherence tomographic imaging. IEEE Trans. Comput. Imaging **7**, 624–637 (2021)
40. Radwell, N., et al.: Deep learning optimized single-pixel lidar. Appl. Phys. Lett. **115**(23), 231101 (2019)
41. Reddy, D., Veeraraghavan, A., Chellappa, R.: P2c2: programmable pixel compressive camera for high speed imaging. In: Proceedings of the IEEE Conference on Computer Vision and Pattern Recognition (CVPR), pp. 329–336 (2011)
42. Ronneberger, O., Fischer, P., Brox, T.: U-Net: convolutional networks for biomedical image segmentation. In: Navab, N., Hornegger, J., Wells, W.M., Frangi, A.F. (eds.) MICCAI 2015. LNCS, vol. 9351, pp. 234–241. Springer, Cham (2015). https://doi.org/10.1007/978-3-319-24574-4_28
43. Shi, W., Jiang, F., Zhang, S., Zhao, D.: Deep networks for compressed image sensing. In: 2017 IEEE International Conference on Multimedia and Expo (ICME), pp. 877–882. IEEE (2017)
44. Tassano, M., Delon, J., Veit, T.: FastDVDNet: towards real-time deep video denoising without flow estimation. In: Proceedings of the IEEE/CVF Conference on Computer Vision and Pattern Recognition, pp. 1354–1363 (2020)

45. Wang, Z., Zhang, H., Cheng, Z., Chen, B., Yuan, X.: MetaSci: scalable and adaptive reconstruction for video compressive sensing. In: Proceedings of the IEEE/CVF Conference on Computer Vision and Pattern Recognition, pp. 2083–2092 (2021)
46. Wu, Z., Zhang, J., Mou, C.: Dense deep unfolding network with 3d-CNN prior for snapshot compressive imaging. In: IEEE International Conference on Computer Vision (ICCV) (2021)
47. Xue, Y., et al.: Block modulating video compression: an ultra low complexity image compression encoder for resource limited platforms. CoRR (2022)
48. Yang, C., et al.: Improving the image reconstruction quality of compressed ultrafast photography via an augmented Lagrangian algorithm. J. Opt. **21**(3), 035703 (2019)
49. Yang, C., et al.: High-fidelity image reconstruction for compressed ultrafast photography via an augmented-Lagrangian and deep-learning hybrid algorithm. Photon. Res. **9**(2), B30–B37 (2021)
50. Yang, Y., Sun, J., Li, H., Xu, Z.: Deep ADMM-net for compressive sensing MRI. In: Proceedings of the 30th International Conference on Neural Information Processing Systems, pp. 10–18 (2016)
51. Yang, Y., Sun, J., Li, H., Xu, Z.: ADMM-CSNET: a deep learning approach for image compressive sensing. IEEE Trans. Pattern Anal. Mach. Intell. **42**(3), 521–538 (2018)
52. Yoo, J., Sabir, S., Heo, D., Kim, K.H., Wahab, A., Choi, Y., Lee, S.I., Chae, E.Y., Kim, H.H., Bae, Y.M., et al.: Deep learning diffuse optical tomography. IEEE Trans. Med. Imaging **39**(4), 877–887 (2019)
53. Yuan, X.: Compressive dynamic range imaging via Bayesian shrinkage dictionary learning. Opt. Eng. **55**(12), 123110 (2016)
54. Yuan, X., Liao, X., Llull, P., Brady, D., Carin, L.: Efficient patch-based approach for compressive depth imaging. Appl. Opt. **55**(27), 7556–7564 (2016)
55. Yuan, X.: Generalized alternating projection based total variation minimization for compressive sensing. In: 2016 IEEE International Conference on Image Processing (ICIP), pp. 2539–2543 (2016)
56. Yuan, X., Brady, D.J., Katsaggelos, A.K.: Snapshot compressive imaging: theory, algorithms, and applications. IEEE Signal Process. Mag. **38**(2), 65–88 (2021)
57. Yuan, X., Jiang, H., Huang, G., Wilford, P.A.: Slope: shrinkage of local overlapping patches estimator for lensless compressive imaging. IEEE Sens. J. **16**(22), 8091–8102 (2016)
58. Yuan, X., Liu, Y., Suo, J., Dai, Q.: Plug-and-play algorithms for large-scale snapshot compressive imaging. In: Proceedings of the IEEE/CVF Conference on Computer Vision and Pattern Recognition (CVPR), pp. 1447–1457 (2020)
59. Yuan, X., Liu, Y., Suo, J., Durand, F., Dai, Q.: Plug-and-play algorithms for video snapshot compressive imaging. In: IEEE Transactions on Pattern Analysis and Machine Intelligence (2021)
60. Yuan, X., et al.: Low-cost compressive sensing for color video and depth. In: IEEE Conference on Computer Vision and Pattern Recognition (CVPR), pp. 3318–3325 (2014)
61. Yuan, X., Pu, Y.: Parallel lensless compressive imaging via deep convolutional neural networks. Opt. Express **26**(2), 1962–1977 (2018)
62. Zhang, B., Yuan, X., Deng, C., Zhang, Z., Suo, J., Dai, Q.: End-to-end snapshot compressed super-resolution imaging with deep optics. Optica **9**(4), 451–454 (2022)
63. Zhang, J., Ghanem, B.: ISTA-Net: interpretable optimization-inspired deep network for image compressive sensing. In: Proceedings of the IEEE Conference on Computer Vision and Pattern Recognition, pp. 1828–1837 (2018)

64. Zhang, K., Zuo, W., Zhang, L.: FFDNet: toward a fast and flexible solution for CNN-based image denoising. IEEE Trans. Image Process. **27**(9), 4608–4622 (2018)
65. Zheng, H., et al.: A new ensemble learning framework for 3d biomedical image segmentation. In: Proceedings of the AAAI Conference on Artificial Intelligence, vol. 33, pp. 5909–5916 (2019)
66. Zheng, S., et al.: Deep plug-and-play priors for spectral snapshot compressive imaging. Photon. Res. **9**(2), B18–B29 (2021)
67. Zheng, S., Wang, C., Yuan, X., Xin, H.L.: Super-compression of large electron microscopy time series by deep compressive sensing learning. Patterns **2**(7), 100292 (2021)
68. Zhou, K., Yang, Y., Qiao, Y., Xiang, T.: Domain adaptive ensemble learning. IEEE Trans. Image Process. **30**, 8008–8018 (2021)

# Approximate Discrete Optimal Transport Plan with Auxiliary Measure Method

Dongsheng An[1], Na Lei[2(✉)], and Xianfeng Gu[1]

[1] Stony Brook University, Stony Brook, USA
{doan,gu}@cs.stonybrook.edu
[2] Dalian University of Technology, Dalian, China
nalei@dlut.edu.cn

**Abstract.** Optimal transport (OT) between two measures plays an essential role in many fields, ranging from economy, biology to machine learning and artificial intelligence. Conventional discrete OT problem can be solved using linear programming (LP). Unfortunately, due to the large scale and the intrinsic non-linearity, achieving discrete OT plan with adequate accuracy and efficiency is challenging. Generally speaking, the OT plan is highly sparse. This work proposes an auxiliary measure method to use the semi-discrete OT maps to estimate the sparsity of the discrete OT plan with squared Euclidean cost. Although obtaining the accurate semi-discrete OT maps is difficult, we can find the sparsity information through computing the approximate semi-discrete OT maps by convex optimization. The sparsity information can be further incorporated into the downstream LP optimization to greatly reduce the computational complexity and improve the accuracy. We also give a theoretic error bound between the estimated transport plan and the OT plan in terms of Wasserstein distance. Experiments on both synthetic data and color transfer tasks demonstrate the accuracy and efficiency of the proposed method.

**Keywords:** Optimal transport · Convex optimization · Linear programming · Auxiliary measure

## 1 Introduction

Optimal transport (OT) is a powerful tool to compute the Wasserstein distance between probability measures, which are widely used to model various natural phenomena, including those observed in economics [12], optics [14], biology [27], differential equations [16] and other domains. Recently, OT has been successfully applied in the areas of machine learning, such as parameter estimation in Bayesian nonparametric models [24], computer vision [3,9,31], natural language processing [20,33] etc. In these applications, the complex probability measures are approximated by Dirac measures supported on their samples. To compute

**Supplementary Information** The online version contains supplementary material available at https://doi.org/10.1007/978-3-031-20050-2_36.

Wasserstein distances among Dirac measures, we have to solve the discrete OT problems. Unfortunately, solving large scale discrete OT problem with high accuracy still remains a great challenge. To tackle this problem, we propose a novel method to improve the accuracy by utilizing the sparsity of discrete OT plan.

**Semi-discrete OT Problem.** The origin of the optimal transport problem can be traced back to 1781, when Monge asked if there existed an OT map between two measures with the given cost function. Depending on the cost function and the measures, the OT map may not exist. In 1950's, Kantorovich relaxed the OT map to OT plan, and showed the existence and the uniqueness of the plan under mild conditions [32]. In 1980's, Brenier [6] discovered that when the density of the source measure is absolutely continuous and the cost function is the squared Euclidean distance, the OT map is given by the gradient of a convex function, the so-called Brenier potential.

Recently, the equivalence between the Brenier potential and Alexandrov's convex polytope has been rigours proved in [15], both of them can be obtained by solving the non-linear Monge-Ampère equation. This connection leads to a practical algorithm to solve the semi-discrete OT problem using convex geometry. According to Theorem 2 in this paper, the Brenier potential can be represented as the upper envelope of a set of hyperplanes, and its projection induces a power diagram of the source domain, which gives the semi-discrete OT map. Moreover, the power diagram can be estimated efficiently using Monte Carlo based method in high dimensional space [2].

**Discrete OT Problem** In this work, we focus on computing the OT plan between two discrete measures. Suppose the source and target discrete distributions are represented by $\nu_1 = \sum_{i=1}^{m} \nu_i^1 \delta(x - x_i)$ and $\nu_2 = \sum_{j=1}^{n} \nu_j^2 \delta(y - y_j)$, respectively. The transport plan is denoted as $\pi : \nu_1 \rightarrow \nu_2$, and $\pi = \{\pi_{ij} | \sum_i \pi_{ij} = \nu_j^2, \sum_j \pi_{ij} = \nu_i^1, \pi_{ij} \geq 0\}$, where $\pi_{ij}$ represents the total mass transported from $x_i$ to $y_j$. For the Kantorovich problem (Eq. (5)), there are $mn$ unknowns in total and $m + n$ constraints. We can solve it using the conventional linear programming (LP) method, whose time complexity is $O(n^{2.5})$ with Vaidya's algorithm [7]. For large scale problems, this is prohibitively high.

**The Proposed Method.** In this paper, to compute the optimal transport plan between two discrete measures, we propose the auxiliary measure method. Basically, we construct an auxiliary measure $\mu$ with absolutely continuous density function defined on a convex domain $\Omega$. Then we compute two semi-discrete OT maps $T_k : \mu \rightarrow \nu_k$, $k = 1, 2$. Each $T_k$ induces a cell decomposition (power diagram) of $\Omega$:

$$\Omega = \bigcup_{i=1}^{m} W_i^1 = \bigcup_{j=1}^{n} W_j^2, T_1 : W_i^1 \rightarrow x_i, T_2 : W_j^2 \rightarrow y_j.$$

The overlap of the two cell decomposition induces a refined cell decomposition:

$$\Omega = \bigcup_{i=1}^{m} \bigcup_{j=1}^{n} W_i^1 \cap W_j^2 = \bigcup_{i=1}^{m} \bigcup_{j=1}^{n} W_{ij}$$

where $W_{ij} := W_i^1 \cap W_j^2$. If we treat $T_1 : W_i^1 \rightarrow x_i$ as invertible, its inverse will be a set-valued map $T_1^{-1} : x_i \rightarrow W_i^1$, then the following diagram commutes,

The composition $\tilde{\pi} = T_2 \circ T_1^{-1}$ is a transport plan from $\nu_1$ to $\nu_2$, where $\tilde{\pi}_{ij} = \mu(W_{ij})$. Algorithms for finding a transport plan $\tilde{\pi}$ need to solve two semi-discrete OT problems with $m+n$ unknowns in total, which is much simpler than the LP method with $mn$ unknowns. Both $T_1$ and $T_2$ are OT maps, but $\tilde{\pi}$ may not be optimal. Even so, $\tilde{\pi}$ is a transport plan with explicit sparsity. Namely, if $W_{ij}$ is

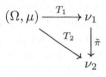

empty, then $\tilde{\pi}_{ij}$ is 0. Suppose the OT plan is $\hat{\pi} : \nu_1 \to \nu_2$, we can use the sparsity of $\tilde{\pi}$ to predict the sparsity of $\hat{\pi}$. Thus, by carefully choosing the auxiliary measure $\mu$, we can make $\tilde{\pi}$ a good approximation of $\hat{\pi}$, and $\tilde{\pi}$ tells which $\hat{\pi}_{ij}$'s are zeros beforehand.

However, computing the accurate semi-discrete OT map for general OT problems is difficult [30]. In our settings, we only need the overlap information of $\{W_i^1\}$ and $\{W_j^2\}$, namely if $W_{ij} = \emptyset$ or not. To achieve this, there is no need to accurately compute the semi-discrete OT map. With the SDOT algorithm [2], we can obtain good estimations of the semi-discrete OT maps $T_1, T_2$, and thus get a coarse approximation of $\{W_{ij}\}$. Then by extending the coarse cell decomposition with nearest neighbour, we finally obtain the sparsity information of $\tilde{\pi}$, or equivalently $\{W_{ij}\}$. This greatly improves the efficiency of finding $\hat{\pi}$.

**Contribution.** The contribution of the paper includes: **(i)** We propose an auxiliary measure method to solve the discrete OT problem by computing two approximate semi-discrete OT maps with $O(m+n)$ unknowns in total. With the auxiliary measure, we can greatly reduce the storage complexity of the discrete OT problem. **(ii)** The sparsity of the transport plan obtained by the auxiliary measure is used to estimate the sparsity of the discrete OT plan. The sparsity information is incorporated into the downstream LP to reduce the computational complexity and improve the accuracy of the computed OT cost. **(iii)** We give a theoretic error bound for the estimated transport plan and the OT plan in terms of Wasserstein distance. Experiments demonstrate the accuracy and efficiency of the proposed auxiliary measure method.

## 2   Related Work

OT plays an important role in various kinds of fields, and there is huge of research in this area. For detailed overview, we refer the readers to [25].

The semi-discrete OT problem computes the OT map between continuous and Dirac measures. Kitagawa et al. [18] use the damped Newton's method to solve such a problem. Genevay et al. [13] propose a semi-dual approach to solve the OT problems under discrete, semi-discrete or continuous settings. However, this method does not give an explicit form of the transport map. Arjovsky et al. [3] propose an approach that specializes to 1-Wasserstein distance, where the Lipschitz constraints are replaced by weight clipping at each iteration. This restricts the approximation accuracy of Wasserstein distance. By approximating the Alexandrov potential with DNN, Seguy et al. [29] solve a relaxed OT problem, and the resulting OT map can be obtained. However, their approximation using DNN is not globally convex and thus is not guaranteed to achieve global optimum. Earlier, Gu et al. [15] propose to minimize a convex energy through the connection between the OT problem and convex geometry. In [21] the authors link the convex geometry viewed optimal transport with Kantorovich duality by Legendre dual theory. Recently, An et al. [2] extend the method to solve high dimensional semi-discrete OT problems by Monte Carlo Sampling.

When both the source and target measures are discrete, the OT problem can be treated as a standard LP task. To extend the problem into large dataset, Cuturi [10] adds an entropic regularizer into the prime OT problem. As a result, the regularized problem can be quickly solved with the Sinkhorn algorithm. Later, other entropy regularization based methods are proposed [1,8,11,22]. The problem of the Sinkhorn based methods is that they lose the sparse information of the OT plan. To solve this problem, Blondel et al. [4] incorporate structural information directly into the OT problem and keep the sparsity of the solution. However, the result, which is only an approximation of the OT plan, is not a transport plan. Schmitzer [28] then proposes a coarse-to-fine scheme to find the sparse plan for the entropy regularized problem.

Another genre to approximate the Wasserstein distance is the sliced Wasserstein distance [5], which projects the high-dimensional distribution into infinitely many one-dimensional spaces and then computes the average of the Wasserstein distance between these one-dimensional distributions. Then Kolouri et al. [19] generalize the sliced Wasserstein distance by the generalization of the Radon Transform. By selecting the most informative projection directions, Meng et al. [23] proposed the projection pursuit Monge map, which accelerates the computation of the original sliced optimal transport problem. But this kind of methods cannot give the OT plan.

## 3   Optimal Transport Theory

In this section, we will introduce some basic concepts and theorems in classic OT theory, focusing on the Brenier's approach and its generalization to the discrete settings. The details can be found in Villani's book [32].

*Optimal Transport Problem.* Suppose $X, Y$ are both subsets of $d$-dimensional Euclidean space $\mathbb{R}^d$, $\mu$ and $\nu$ are two probability measures defined on $X$ and $Y$, respectively, with equal total measure $\mu(X) = \nu(Y)$.

**Definition 1 (Measure-Preserving Map).** *A map $T : X \to Y$ is measure preserving if, for any measurable set $B \subset Y$, the set $T^{-1}(B)$ is $\mu$-measurable and $\mu(T^{-1}(B)) = \nu(B)$. The measure-preserving condition is denoted as $T_{\#}\mu = \nu$.*

Given the cost function $c(x,y) : X \times Y \to \mathbb{R}_{\geq 0}$, which indicates the cost of moving each unit mass from $x$ to $y$, the total *transport cost* of the map $T : X \to Y$ is defined to be $\int_X c(x, T(x))d\mu(x)$.

The Monge's OT problem aims to find the measure-preserving map that minimizes the total transport cost.

*Problem 1* **Monge Problem.** Given the cost function $c : X \times Y \to \mathbb{R}_{\geq 0}$, find the measure preserving map $T : X \to Y$ that minimizes the total transport cost

$$(MP)\mathcal{M}_c(\mu, \nu) := \min_{T_\# \mu = \nu} \int_X c(x, T(x)) d\mu(x). \tag{1}$$

The solution to the Monge's problem is called the *optimal transport map*, whose total transport cost is called the *optimal transport cost* between $\mu$ and $\nu$, denoted as $\mathcal{M}_c(\mu, \nu)$.

**Kantorovich's Approach.** Depending on the cost functions and the measures, the OT map between $(X, \mu)$ and $(Y, \nu)$ may not exist. Kantorovich relaxed the OT maps to OT plans, and defined the joint probability measure $\pi : X \times Y \to \mathbb{R}_{\geq 0}$, such that the marginal probability of $\pi$ equals to $\mu$ and $\nu$, respectively. Formally, let the projection maps be $\rho_x(x, y) = x$, $\rho_y(x, y) = y$, then we define

$$\Pi(\mu, \nu) := \{\pi : X \times Y \to \mathbb{R}_{\geq 0} : (\rho_x)_\# \pi = \mu, (\rho_y)_\# \pi = \nu\}$$

*Problem 2* **Kantorovich Problem.** Given the cost function $c : X \times Y \to \mathbb{R}_{\geq 0}$, find the joint probability measure $\pi : X \to Y$ that minimizes the total transport cost

$$(KP)\mathcal{M}_c(\mu, \nu) = \min_{\pi \in \Pi(\mu, \nu)} \int_{X \times Y} c(x, y) d\pi(x, y). \tag{2}$$

**Brenier's Approach.** For the quadratic Euclidean distance cost, the existence, uniqueness and the intrinsic structure of the OT map were proven by Brenier [6].

**Theorem 1 (Brenier Theorem).** *Suppose $X$ and $Y$ are the subsets of the Euclidean space $\mathbb{R}^d$ and the transport cost is given by the quadratic Euclidean distance $c(x, y) = \|x - y\|^2$. Furthermore, $\mu$ is absolutely continuous, both $\mu$ and $\nu$ have finite second order moments. Then there exists a convex function $u : X \to \mathbb{R}$, the so-called the Briener potential, and its gradient map $\nabla u$ gives the solution to the Monge's problem. The Brenier potential is unique up to adding a constant, hence the optimal transport map is unique.*

*Semi-discrete OT Problem.* Suppose the source measure $\mu$ is absolutely continuous and defined on a convex domain $\Omega \subset \mathbb{R}^d$, the target measure is a Dirac measure $\nu = \sum_{i=1}^n \nu_i \delta(y - y_i), i \in [n]$ and $y_i \in \mathbb{R}^d$. Also, we assume $\mu(\Omega) = \sum_{i=1}^n \nu_i$. The semi-discrete OT map is the measure-preserving map that minimizes the transport cost, $T^* := \arg \min_{T_\# \mu = \nu} \int_\Omega c(x, T(x)) d\mu(x)$.

When the cost function is set to be the quadratic Euclidean distance $c(x, y) = \|x - y\|^2$, the Brenier potential can be expressed as $u_h(x) = \max_i\{\langle x, y_i \rangle + h_i, \forall i \in [n]\}$. The induced OT map pushing forward $\mu$ to $\nu$ is $T^* : W_i \to y_i$, where $W_i = \{x | \langle x, y_i \rangle + h_i \geq \langle x, y_k \rangle + h_k, \forall k \in [n]\}$.

Under the semi-discrete OT map $T^* : \Omega \to Y$, a cell decomposition (also a power diagram) is induced $\Omega = \bigcup_{i=1}^n W_i$, such that every $x$ in the cell $W_i$

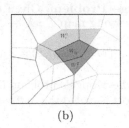

(a)    (b)

**Fig. 1.** (a) Brenier potential and the corresponding power diagram. Each cell $W_i$ is mapped to the corresponding $y_i$, and $\mu(W_i) = \nu_i$. (b) The illustration of the sparsity of $\hat{\pi}$. $\{W_i^1\}$ and $\{W_j^2\}$ are two cell decomposition induced by the semi-discrete OT maps from $\mu$ to $\nu_1$ and $\nu_2$. The refined cell decomposition $\{W_{ij}\}$ with $W_{ij} = W_i^1 \cap W_j^2$ not only gives the solution of $\hat{\pi}$, but also gives a good approximation of the sparsity of the OT plan between $\nu_1$ and $\nu_2$.

is mapped to the target $y_i$, $T : x \in W_i \mapsto y_i$, and $\mu(W_i) = \nu_i$. As shown in Fig. 1(a), the cell $W_i$ is mapped to the corresponding $y_i$, which corresponds to the hyperplane $\langle x, y_i \rangle + h_i$. The total cost of $T$ is given by $\int_\Omega c(x, T(x))d\mu(x) = \sum_{i=1}^n \int_{W_i} c(x, y_i)d\mu(x)$.

The following gives the generalization of the Brenier theorem to compute the semi-discrete OT map [15].

**Theorem 2.** *Let $\mu$ be a probability measure defined on a compact convex domain $\Omega$ in $\mathbb{R}^d$, $\nu = \sum_{i=1}^n \nu_i \delta(y - y_i)$ with $y_i \in \mathbb{R}^d$. If $\sum_{i=1}^n \nu_i = \mu(\Omega)$ and $c(x,y) = \|x - y\|^2$, then there exists $h = (h_1, h_2, \ldots, h_n) \in \mathbb{R}^n$, unique up to adding a constant $(k, k, \ldots, k)$, so that $w_i(h) = \nu_i \ \forall i \in [n]$, where $w_i(h) = \mu(W_i(h))$ with $W_i(h) = \{x| \ \langle x, y_i \rangle + h_i \geq \langle x, y_k \rangle + h_k, \ \forall k \in [n]\}$. The vector $h$ is the unique minimum of the convex energy*

$$E(h) = \int_0^h \sum_{i=1}^n w_i(\eta)d\eta_i - \sum_{i=1}^n h_i \nu_i, \tag{3}$$

*defined on an open convex set $\mathcal{H} = \{h \in \mathbb{R}^n : \sum_{i=1}^n h_i = 0\}$. Furthermore, if we define $u_h(x) = \max_i\{\langle x, y_i \rangle + h_i, \ \forall i \in [n]\}$, the map $\nabla u_h(x) : W_i(h) \to y_i \ \forall i \in [n]$ minimizes $\int_\Omega \|x - T(x)\|^2 d\mu(x)$ among all measure preserving maps $T_{\#}\mu = \nu$.*

Now, the gradient of the above energy is given by:

$$\nabla E(h) = (w_1(h) - \nu_1, w_2(h) - \nu_2, \ldots, w_n(h) - \nu_n)^T \tag{4}$$

*Discrete OT Problem.* Given both the source measure $\nu_1 = \sum_{i=1}^m \nu_i^1 \delta(x - x_i)$ and the target measure $\nu_2 = \sum_{j=1}^n \nu_j^2 \delta(y - y_j)$, with the supports defined by

$X = \{x_i\}_{i=1}^m$ and $Y = \{y_j\}_{j=1}^n$, there may not exist an OT map $T : X \to Y$, but the OT plan always exists, which is the solution of the Kantorovich problem:

$$\mathcal{M}_c(\nu_1, \nu_2) = \min_{\pi \geq 0} \sum_{i=1}^m \sum_{j=1}^n c_{ij} \pi_{ij}$$

$$s.t. \quad \sum_{i=1}^m \pi_{ij} = \nu_j^2, \quad \sum_{j=1}^n \pi_{ij} = \nu_i^1 \tag{5}$$

where $c_{ij} = c(x_i, y_j)$ and $\pi \in R^{m \times n}$ is the transport plan. And the problem of Eqn. (5) can be solved by classical LP.

*Sparse Discrete OT Problem.* It requires $mn$ unknown variables of $\pi_{ij}$ to solve the discrete OT problem with LP. But in general cases, the discrete optimal transport plans are highly sparse. For example, if the OT problem is an assignment problem, that is $m = n$ and $\nu_i^1 = \nu_j^2 = 1/n \ \forall \ i, j \in [n]$, then the OT plan degenerates to an OT map, and among the $n^2 \ \pi_{ij}$'s, only $n$ of them are non-zeros. If the $\pi_{ij}$s that are zeros can be determined beforehand, we will only need to consider the non-zero ones during the optimization, and this will greatly improve the computational accuracy and efficiency of the Kantorovich problem of Eq. (5).

In the following, we give some theoretical analysis to estimate the approximation error bound for the auxiliary measure method. Suppose the discrete measures $\nu_1$ and $\nu_2$ are given, both of them are defined in a Euclidean space $\mathbb{R}^d$. All the probability measures defined in $\mathbb{R}^d$ form an infinite dimensional metric space $\mathcal{P}(\mathbb{R}^d)$, with the Wasserstein distance $\mathcal{W}_c$ as the metric, where $c$ is the squared Euclidean distance. Then there is a unique geodesic $\gamma$ in $\mathcal{P}(\mathbb{R}^d)$ connecting $\nu_1$ and $\nu_2$. Let $\mu \in \mathcal{P}(\mathbb{R}^d)$ be the auxiliary measure, the closest point on $\gamma$ to $\mu$ is $\mu^* := \arg\min_{\nu \in \gamma} \mathcal{W}_c(\mu, \nu)$, and the distance from $\mu$ to the geodesic is $d = \mathcal{W}_c(\mu, \mu^*)$.

**Theorem 3.** *Given $\nu_1, \nu_2 \in \mathcal{P}(\mathbb{R}^d)$, the auxiliary measure $\mu$, $T_k : \mu \to \nu_k, k = 1, 2$ are the OT maps. Suppose the distance from $\mu$ to the geodesic connecting $\nu_1$ and $\nu_2$ is $d$, then $T_2 \circ T_1^{-1} : \nu_1 \to \nu_2$ is measure preserving and its transport cost $\mathcal{C}$ is bounded by*

$$\mathcal{W}_c(\nu_1, \nu_2) \leq \mathcal{C}^{\frac{1}{2}}(T_2 \circ T_1^{-1}) \leq \mathcal{W}_c(\nu_1, \nu_2) + 2d \tag{6}$$

The proof of the theorem can be found in the supplement. From the inequality of Eq. (6), it is obvious that the quality of the approximate transport map $T_2 \circ T_1^{-1}$ is determined by the Wasserstein distance $d = \mathcal{W}_c(\mu, \mu^*)$. If $\mu$ is on the geodesic, then $\tilde{\pi} = T_2 \circ T_1^{-1}$ is the desired OT plan between $\nu_1$ and $\nu_2$. If $d$ is relatively small, then the approximated transport plan is close to the OT plan, therefore the sparsity of $\tilde{\pi}$ is similar to that of the OT plan. In practice, we use the sparsity of the approximate plan $\tilde{\pi}$ as the constraints to compute the OT plan between $\nu_1$ and $\nu_2$ and obtain $\hat{\pi}$. It can be seen that

$$\mathcal{W}_c^2(\nu_1, \nu_2) \leq \mathcal{C}(\hat{\pi}) \leq \mathcal{C}(T_2 \circ T_1^{-1})$$

therefore $\hat{\pi}$ is a better approximation than $T_2 \circ T_1^{-1}$, but with the same sparsity.

Assume $\{W_i^1\}$ and $\{W_j^2\}$ are the cell decomposition induced by $T_1$ and $T_2$, respectively, the newly refined cell decomposition $\{W_{ij}|W_{ij} = W_i^1 \cap W_j^2\}$ (shown in Fig. 1(b)) gives $\tilde{\pi}_{i,j} = \mu(W_{ij})$. With the cost function between $\nu_1$ and $\nu_2$ being $c_{ij} = \|x_i - y_j\|^2$, define $\Phi = \{(i,j)|W_i^1 \cap W_j^2 \neq \emptyset\}$, Kantorovich problem of Eq. (5) can be approximated by:

$$\mathcal{M}_c(\nu_1, \nu_2) = \min_{\pi \geq 0} \sum_{i=1}^{m} \sum_{j=1}^{n} c_{ij} \pi_{ij}$$

$$s.t. \quad \sum_{i=1}^{m} \pi_{ij} = \nu_j^2, \quad \sum_{j=1}^{n} \pi_{ij} = \nu_i^1 \tag{7}$$

$$\pi_{ij} = 0 \quad \forall (i,j) \notin \Phi$$

## 4    Computational Algorithms

This section explains the computational algorithms for the auxiliary measure method in detail.

### 4.1    Semi-discrete OT Algorithm

Based on Theorem 2, finding the semi-discrete OT map from the given absolutely continuous measure $\mu$ to the discrete measure $\nu = \sum_{i=1}^{n} \nu_i \delta(x - x_i)$ is equivalent to optimizing the convex energy in Eq. (3) with respect to the height vector $h$. The optimization can be carried out using the gradient descend method. In the gradient formula of Eq. (4), we need to estimate the $\mu$-volume $w_i(h)$ for each cell $W_i(h)$ with the Monte Carlo method proposed in [2]: $N$ random samples $\{z_j\}_{j=1}^{n}$ are drawn from $\mu$, then the $\mu$-volume of the cell $W_i(h)$ is estimated by $\hat{w}_i(h) = \#\{z_j \mid z_j \in W_i(h)\}/N$. Given a random sample $z_j$, let $i = \arg\max_k \{\langle z_j, x_k \rangle + h_k, k \in [n]\}$, then $z_j \in W_i(h)$. When $N$ goes to infinity, $\hat{w}_i(h)$ converges to $w_i(h)$. Hence the gradient of the energy can be approximated by $\nabla E \approx (\hat{w}_i(h) - \nu_i)^T$. Once the gradient is estimated, we can use the Adam algorithm [17] to minimize the energy.

When $N$ is small, the estimated $\mu$-volume is coarse but the computation is fast; when $N$ is large, the estimated $\mu$-volume is accurate but the computation is slow. To balance the efficiency and accuracy, we first use a small $N$ to coarsely estimate $h$, when the energy $E(h)$ stops decreasing, we increase $N$ to improve the accuracy of the estimation. The predefined total $\mu$-volume distortion $\theta$ gives the stop condition, namely the algorithm stops when $\|\nabla E(h)\|_1 \leq \theta$. The sampling of $z_j$s is independent of each other and the cell location estimation for each $z_j$ can be paralleled, therefore the whole algorithm can be accelerated by GPUs. The algorithm is called SDOT and its details can be found in Alg. S1 of the supplement.

## 4.2    Discrete OT Plan with Auxiliary Measure

With the cell decompositions induced by the approximate OT maps computed by the SDOT algorithm, we firstly use a sparse matrix $S$ to represent the overlap information. Then $S$ is extended by nearest neighbours. Finally, we give two strategies for the choice of the auxiliary measure $\mu$.

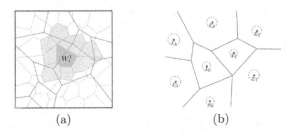

(a)                                    (b)

**Fig. 2.** (a) The orange cells and the purple cells represent the power diagrams induced by the computed semi-discrete OT maps $T_1, T_2$ from $\mu$ to $\nu_1$ and $\nu_2$ with $\mu$-volume accuracy $\theta$. When computing the overlap information of $W_i^1$, we take both $W_i^1$ (the dark orange cell) and its neighbours (the light orange cells) into consideration. (b) The cell decomposition of $\nu_1 = \sum_{i=1}^m \nu_i^1 \delta(x - x_i)$ when $\mu = \sum_{i=1}^m \nu_i^1 N(x_i, \sigma I)$ with small $\sigma$. The cell $W_i^1$ that is mapped to $x_i$ by the semi-discrete OT map $T_1$ covers $x_i$. (Color figure online)

**Estimate the Sparsity Matrix.** Given two discrete measures $\nu_1 = \sum_{i=1}^m \nu_i^1 \delta(x - x_i)$ and $\nu_2 = \sum_{j=1}^n \nu_j^2 \delta(y - y_j)$, and an auxiliary measure $\mu$ defined on a convex support $\Omega$, we use the SDOT algorithm with $\mu$-volume distortion parameter $\theta$ to compute the semi-discrete OT maps $T_k : \mu \to \nu_k$, $k = 1, 2$. Each map induces a cell decomposition $\{W_i^1\}$ and $\{W_j^2\}$.

We use an $m \times n$ matrix $S = (s_{ij})$ to represent the overlapping relation among the cells of the two power diagrams, and call the matrix as the sparsity matrix. The sparsity matrix is defined as

$$s_{ij} = \begin{cases} 1 & W_i^1 \cap W_j^2 \neq \emptyset \\ 0 & W_i^1 \cap W_j^2 = \emptyset \end{cases}$$

The sparsity matrix can be estimated by random sampling. We randomly sample $z_k \sim \mu$, then compute the cells containing $z_k$. If both $W_i^1$ and $W_j^2$ contain $z_k$, then we set $s_{ij}$ to be 1. The procedure keeps running until the sparsity matrix $S$ converges to the steady state. The algorithm for computing the sparsity matrix is given in Alg. S2 of the supplement.

Note that the above $\{W_i^1\}$ and $\{W_j^2\}$, which are computed by the SDOT algorithm under the $\mu$-volume distortion parameter $\theta$, are just approximations of the groundtruth power diagrams induced by the groundtruth semi-discrete OT maps. To make $S$ better represent the sparse information of the groundtruth OT plan, we then not only use the computed $\{W_i^1\}$ and $\{W_j^2\}$ to compute $S$, the neighborhoods of each cell is also used to extend $S$. As shown in Fig. 2(a), to find the cells in $\{W_j^2\}$ that overlapping with the real $\hat{W}_i^1$ of the groundtruth semi-discrete OT map, we not only use the cell $W_i^1$ (the dark orange cell) to compute $S$, but also use the cells around $W_i^1$ (the light orange cells) to extend $S$. Based on the property of the semi-discrete OT map, the cells around $W_i^1$ corresponds to the neighbours of $x_i$ in $X$. Therefore, we can use neighbours of $x_i$ to update $S$.

Specifically, we extend $S$ so that it includes the overlap information of the neighbours of each $W_i^1$ and $W_j^2$. For each sample $x_i$ of $\nu_1$, we find the $k$ nearest neighbours of it, namely $x_{i1}, x_{i2}, \ldots, x_{ik}$. Then the rows of $i1, i2, \ldots, ik$ of $S$ are added to the $i$th row of $S$. Thus, the $i$th row of $S$ includes the overlap information of both $W_i^1$ and its neighbour cells. Similarly, for each $y_j$, the $k$ nearest neighbours of it are also found, marked as $y_{j1}, y_{j2}, \ldots, y_{jk}$. Then columns $j1, j2, \ldots, jk$ of $S$ are added to its $j$th column. By replacing $\Phi$ with the new sparse matrix $S$, which represents the sparsity of the OT plan, the problem of Eq. (7) can be solved effectively through LP.

**Auxiliary Measure $\mu$.** In theory, the auxiliary measure $\mu$ should locate at the geodesic from the source measure $\nu_1$ to the target measure $\nu_2$, which will make the bound tight in Theorem 3 and the computed transport plan be the OT plan. However, given two general distributions, it is hard to compute the geodesic between them without computing the OT plan first. Thus, in practice we make the distance $d$ from the auxiliary measure $\mu$ to the geodesic between $\nu_1$ and $\nu_2$ small enough, then the computed transport cost should approximate the OT cost well according to Theorem 3. To achieve this, we can utilize the information inherited in the source distribution $\nu_1$. If we can find a continuous $\mu$ that is close to $\nu_1$, namely $\mathcal{W}_c(\mu, \nu_1)$ is small, that we can deduce that the distance $d$ from $\mu$ to the geodesic between $\nu_1$ and $\nu_2$ is smaller than $\mathcal{W}_c(\mu, \nu_1)$ accordingly.

**Strategy 1:** If we know the continuous distribution $\hat{\nu}_1$ where $\nu_1$ is sampled from, it is reasonable to set $\mu$ to be $\hat{\nu}_1$. In such a situation, $\mathcal{W}_c(\mu, \nu_1)$ should be reasonably small (See Alg. S3 in the supplement).

**Strategy 2:** Alternatively, we can set $\mu$ to be a Gaussian mixture model based on $\nu_1$, i.e. $\mu = \sum_{i=1}^m \nu_i^1 N(x_i, \sigma I_d)$, where $\sigma \ll \min d(x_i, x_k) \ \forall \ i, k \in [m]$ and $i \neq k$, and $I_d$ represents the $d$-dimensional identity matrix. In such case, we have the following proposition (proof in the supplement):

**Proposition 1.** *Given $\mu = \sum_{i=1}^m \nu_i^1 N(x_i, \sigma I_d)$ and $\nu_1 = \sum_{i=1}^m \nu_i^1 \delta(x - x_i)$, then we have $\mathcal{W}_c(\mu, \nu_1) \leq \sigma$ under the quadratic Euclidean cost. Moreover, if $\sigma$ is small enough, then the cell $W_i$ of the cell decomposition induced by the semi-discrete OT map from $\mu$ to $\nu_1$ should cover $x_i$ itself.*

Then Eq. (6) can be written as:

$$\mathcal{W}_c(\nu_1, \nu_2) \leq \mathcal{C}^{\frac{1}{2}}(T_2 \circ T_1^{-1}) \leq \mathcal{W}_c(\nu_1, \nu_2) + 2\sigma \qquad (8)$$

Figure 2(b) illustrates the relationship of the cell decomposition $\{W_i\}$ and $\{x_i\}$. Then we only need to compute the semi-discrete OT map $T_2 : \mu \to \nu_2$.

The sparse matrix $S$ can be estimated as follows: firstly we set $s_{ij}$ to be 1 if and only if $x_i \in W_j^2$, then the sparse matrix $S$ is extended with the neighbourhood information. This method (see Algorithm S4 in the supplement) is more applicable and makes the computation much faster.

## 5  Experiments

This section reports our experimental results. All of our experiments are conducted on Intel Core i7-9800X CPU with 32GB RAM and NVIDIA GeForce RTX 2080 Ti GPU. We investigate the influence of different parameters, including the auxiliary measure $\mu$, the $\mu$-volume distortion parameter $\theta$ for the SDOT algorithm, and the number $k$ of the nearest neighbours to extend the sparsity matrix $S$. We first test our algorithm on synthetic tasks, and then apply it to the color transfer problem. Experimental results demonstrate that the proposed method outperforms the state-of-the-arts.

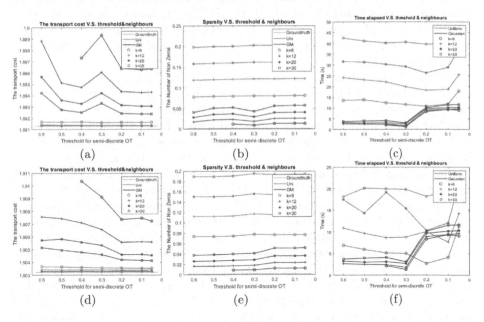

**Fig. 3.** The performances of the proposed algorithm on synthetic data with different parameters $\theta$, $\mu$ and $k$.

### 5.1  Performance on Synthetic Dataset

We test the proposed method on two synthetic tasks with different parameters.

*Two Tasks.* We set $\nu_1 = \sum_{i=1}^{m} \nu_i^1 \delta(x - x_i)$, where $x_i$s are randomly sampled from the $d$-dimensional uniform distribution $[0, 1]^d$; $\nu_2 = \sum_{j=1}^{n} \nu_j^2 \delta(y - y_j)$, where $y_j$'s are sampled from $d$-dimensional Gaussian distribution $N(0, I_d)$. We conduct two tasks with $d = 5$: **(i)** compute the OT plan from $\nu_1$ to $\nu_2$, where $m = 1000$, $n = 2000$, the weights $\nu_i^1, i \in [m]$ and $\nu_j^2, j \in [n]$ are randomly sampled from the uniform distribution and then normalized by $\nu_i^1 = \nu_i^1 / \sum_{k=1}^{m} \nu_k^1$ and $\nu_j^2 = \nu_j^2 / \sum_{k=1}^{n} \nu_k^2$; and **(ii)** the assignment problem with $m = n = 1500$ and $\nu_i^1 = \nu_j^2 = 1/n \; \forall \; i, j \in [n]$.

*Choice of Parameters.* We use different parameters for the testing, including **(i)** the $\mu$-volume accuracy threshold $\theta$ for computing the semi-discrete OT map between $\mu$ and $\nu_1$, $\nu_2$; **(ii)** the number $k$ of the nearest neighbors to extend the sparsity matrix $S$; and **(iii)** the auxiliary measure $\mu$, one is the 5-dimensional uniform distribution where $\nu_1$ is sampled from; the other is the Gaussian mixture distribution with $\sigma = 0.1 \min_{i \neq j} d(x_i, x_j)$.

*Comparison Results.* We compare the computational results obtained with different parameters using three indicators: **(i)** The transport cost $\mathcal{C}$ of the computed transport plan; **(ii)** The sparsity, represented by $|S|/mn$, where $|S|$ is the number of nonzero entries in the sparsity matrix $S$; and **(iii)** The running time of the whole pipeline.

Figure 3 summarizes the comparison results. Figure 3(a–c) show the statistics of the first task and Fig. 3(d–f) show results for the second task. In Fig. 3(a–f), the green curves correspond to the results of the real OT plan computed by LP. The red curves show the results computed with $\mu$ being the uniform distribution, and the blue curves are the results of $\mu$ as Gaussian mixture distribution. Different blue (or red) curves are with different $k$s (number of neighbors).

In Fig. 3(a), the horizontal axis represents the threshold $\theta$; the vertical axis is the computed transport cost. Since the OT cost between $\nu_1$ and $\nu_2$ is independent of $\theta$, the green curve is a horizontal line. It can be observed that the transport cost decreases when $\theta$ decreases; the cost decreases when $k$ increases; and the costs for uniform $\mu$, where $\nu_1$ is sampled from, are smaller than those for Gaussian mixture $\mu$. In Fig. 3(b), the horizontal axis represents $\theta$, the vertical axis represents the sparsity. It is easy to see that the real OT plan is with the minimal sparsity; the Gaussian mixture $\mu$ induces better sparsity than the uniformly distributed $\mu$; and the sparsity decreases when $k$ increases. In Fig. 3(c), the horizontal axis is $\theta$, the vertical axis is the running time. The green curve is not shown, because the LP method is far slower than our method. It is obvious that the method using Gaussian mixture $\mu$ is faster than that using uniform $\mu$; when $k$ decreases, the computation is faster. Figure 3(d–f) show the statistics for the second task, i.e., the assignment problem. The comparison results are similar to those obtained from the first task.

In summary, comparing with the Gaussian mixture auxiliary measure $\mu$ constructed through the source measure $\nu_1$, the known $\mu$ where $\nu_1$ is sampled from, gives more accurate transport plan (with less transport cost), but less sparsity and slower computation speed.

## 5.2    Comparison with State-of-the-Art Techniques

We compare our algorithm with the state-of-the-art methods, including the Sinkhorn method [10], SOT [4], and PPMM [23].

To demonstrate that our method can compute accurate transport plans in different dimensions, we choose the dimension parameter $d$ to be 2, 5 and 20. The nearest neighbor parameter $k$ is set to be 10, the $\mu$-volume accuracy threshold $\theta$ is 0.3. For Gaussian-mixture auxiliary measure $\mu$, we set $\sigma = 0.1 \min_{i \neq j} d(x_i, x_j)$.

Figure 4 shows the comparisons. The horizontal axis shows the sizes of the data sets, represented as $m \times n \times d$, meaning $\nu_1$ has $m$ points in $\mathbb{R}^d$ and $\nu_2$ $n$ points in $\mathbb{R}^d$. The vertical axis illustrates *the difference between the computed transport cost and the OT cost*, both using the squared Euclidean distance as the cost function. The green circles are the OT cost obtained by LP. The red crosses, yellow triangles, blue stars, black squares and Cyan diamonds denote the results obtain by our method with uniform $\mu$ where $\nu_1$ is sampled from, our method with Gaussian mixture $\mu$, Sinkhorn, SOT with L-BFGS solver for the smoothed semi-dual formula and PPMM, respectively.

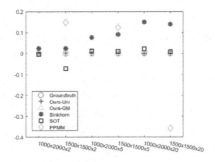

**Fig. 4.** Comparison among our proposed method and others.

From Fig. 4, we can see that our proposed method with auxiliary measures always obtains the minimal discrepancy in terms of OT cost. SOT method gives accurate result in general, but sometimes it leads to invalid transport plan (TP), as shown by the negative result in the second test. Similarly, the sixth result of PPMM method is negative. Furthermore, the figure shows that the results of the Sinkhorn method tends to become inaccurate when $d$ is large.

## 5.3    Application to Color Transfer

Given a color image, its color distribution can be represented by the histogram in the RGB color space. Assume there are $m$ colors represented by $x_1, x_2, \ldots, x_m$, each $x_i = (r_i, g_i, b_i)$ is a point in $\mathbb{R}^3$, and the corresponding normalized frequencies are $\nu_1, \nu_2, \ldots, \nu_m$, then the image color distribution is represented by a discrete distribution in $\mathbb{R}^3$ [26]: $\nu = \sum_{i=1}^{m} \nu_i \delta(x - x_i)$. Given two images, the source image color distribution is $\nu_1 = \sum_{i=1}^{m} \nu_i^1 \delta(x - x_i)$ and the target is $\nu_2 = \sum_{j=1}^{n} \nu_j^2 \delta(y - y_j)$. We can find the OT plan $\pi : \nu_1 \rightarrow \nu_2$. For each color $x_i$, we apply the barycentric interpolation to get the mapping $T(x_i) = \frac{\sum_{j=1}^{n} \pi_{ij} y_j}{\sum_{j=1}^{n} \pi_{ij}}$. By replacing the color $x_i$ of the source image with $T(x_i)$, we obtain a new image with content coming from the source and color distribution from the target.

(a) Source          (b) Target          (c) Sinkhorn          (d) SOT          (e) Ours.

**Fig. 5.** Comparison of the results on color transfer tasks. (Zoom in/out for better visualization.)

**Table 1.** The comparison between our method, Sinkhorn [10] and SOT [4] on the color transfer tasks.

| | Sinkhorn | | | SOT | | | Ours | | |
|---|---|---|---|---|---|---|---|---|---|
| | Cost | TP | Sparse | Cost | TP | Sparse | Cost | TP | Sparse |
| Autumn → comunion | 88.7535 | ✓ | ✗ | 69.5143 | ✗ | ✓ | 87.4280 | ✓ | ✓ |
| Graffiti → rainbow | 84.5362 | ✓ | ✗ | 74.0894 | ✗ | ✓ | 84.3785 | ✓ | ✓ |
| Autumn → graffiti | 131.0952 | ✓ | ✗ | 86.3683 | ✗ | ✓ | 129.6989 | ✓ | ✓ |
| Autumn → rainbow | 83.1778 | ✓ | ✗ | 55.2500 | ✗ | ✓ | 81.9912 | ✓ | ✓ |
| Comunion → graffiti | 70.7658 | ✓ | ✗ | 41.9410 | ✗ | ✓ | 70.1804 | ✓ | ✓ |
| Comunion → rainbow | 39.7300 | ✓ | ✗ | 27.0912 | ✗ | ✓ | 39.4653 | ✓ | ✓ |

Here we use four different images. The number of samples in the color space $\mathbb{R}^3$ for each input image is 13892 for 'autumn', 18103 for 'comunion', 17820 for 'graffiti' and 15129 for 'rainbow-bridge'. Figure 5 shows the color transfer results from 'graffiti' to 'rainbow-bridge' using our proposed method and other state-of-the-art methods (please see the supplement for more experiments). Figure 5(a) shows the source image and the second column the target image. Figure 5(c) shows the result of the Sinkhorn algorithm [10], which is blurry due to the dense transport plan. Figure 5(d) illustrates the results of SOT [4]. Figure 5(e) shows the result of our method, which have consistent color distribution with the target image, and is much sharper than those generated by Sinkhorn. This shows our method obtains more accurate transport plan with higher sparsity.

We also estimate the OT cost among the color distributions of the 4 input images, using the Sinkhorn method [10], SOT [4] and our method. The results are reported in Table 1. In the table, 'TP' represents 'valid transport plan'. From the table, we can find that both the results of the Sinkhorn algorithm and the proposed method are valid transport plans, and our method outperforms Sinkhorn both in the estimated OT cost and the sparsity. Though the solutions of SOT are sparse, they are not even valid transport plans. In conclusion, the proposed method gives more accurate OT plan with higher sparsity.

## 6    Conclusions

This work proposes an auxiliary measure method using semi-discrete OT maps to estimate the discrete OT plan by reducing the number of unknowns from $O(mn)$ to $O(m + n)$. The sparsity information of the transport plan obtained by the auxiliary measure is used to estimate the sparsity of the discrete OT plan. And the sparsity of the OT plan is incorporated into the downstream LP optimization to greatly reduce the computational complexity of the discrete Kantorovich problem and improve the accuracy. We also give a theoretic error bound for the estimated transport plan and the OT plan in terms of Wasserstein distance. Experiments on synthetic data and color transfer of real images demonstrate the accuracy and efficiency our method. In the future, we will explore to find much better auxiliary measures to further improve the accuracy of the method.

**Acknowledgement.** Lei was supported by the National Natural Science Foundation of China No. 61936002 and the National Key R&D Program of China 2021YFA1003003. Gu is partially supported by NSF 2115095, NSF 1762287, NIH 92025 and NIH R01LM012434.

## References

1. Altschuler, J., Niles-Weed, J., Rigollet, P.: Near-linear time approximation algorithms for optimal transport via sinkhorn iteration. In: Advances in Neural Information Processing Systems 30 (2017)
2. An, D., Guo, Y., Lei, N., Luo, Z., Yau, S.T., Gu, X.: Ae-ot: A new generative model based on extended semi-discrete optimal transport. In: International Conference on Learning Representations (2020)
3. Arjovsky, M., Chintala, S., Bottou, L.: Wasserstein generative adversarial networks. In: ICML, pp. 214–223 (2017)
4. Blondel, M., Seguy, V., Rolet, A.: Smooth and sparse optimal transport. In: Proceedings of the Twenty-First International Conference on Artificial Intelligence and Statistics, pp. 880–889 (2018)
5. Bonneel, N., Rabin, J., Peyre, G., Pfister, H.: Sliced and radon wasserstein barycenters of measures. Journal of Mathematical Imaging and Vision (2014)
6. Brenier, Y.: Polar factorization and monotone rearrangement of vector-valued functions. Comm. Pure Appl. Math. **44**(4), 375–417 (1991)
7. Bubeck, S.: Convex Optimization: Algorithms and Complexity, vol. 8. Foundations and Trends in Machine Learning (2015)
8. Chakrabarty, D., Khanna, S.: Better and simpler error analysis of the sinkhorn-knopp algorithm for matrix scaling. Math. Program. **188**(1), 395–407 (2021)

9. Courty, N., Flamary, R., Tuia, D., Rakotomamonjy, A.: Optimal transport for domain adaptation. IEEE Trans. Pattern Anal. Mach. Intell. **39**(9), 1853–1865 (2017)
10. Cuturi, M.: Sinkhorn distances: Lightspeed computation of optimal transportation distances. In: International Conference on Neural Information Processing Systems, vol. 26, pp. 2292–2300 (2013)
11. Dvurechensky, P., Gasnikov, A., Kroshnin, A.: Computational optimal transport: Complexity by accelerated gradient descent is better than by Sinkhorn's algorithm. In: International Conference on Machine Learning, pp. 1367–1376 (2018)
12. Galichon, A.: Optimal Transport Methods in Economics. Princeton University Press (2016)
13. Genevay, A., Cuturi, M., Peyré, G., Bach, F.: Stochastic optimization for large-scale optimal transport. In: Advances in Neural Information Processing Systems, pp. 3440–3448 (2016)
14. Glimm, T., Oliker, V.: Optical design of single reflector systems and the Monge-Kantorovich mass transfer problem. J. Math. Sci. **117**(3), 4096–4108 (2003)
15. Gu, D.X., Luo, F., Sun, J., Yau, S.T.: Variational principles for minkowski type problems, discrete optimal transport, and discrete monge-ampère equations. Asian Journal of Mathematics (2016)
16. Jordan, R., Kinderlehrer, D., Otto, F.: The variational formulation of the fokker-planck equation. SIAM J. Math. Anal. **29**(1), 1–17 (1998)
17. Kingma, D.P., Ba, J.: Adam: A method for stochastic optimization. arXiv preprint arXiv:1412.6980 (2014)
18. Kitagawa, J., Mérigot, Q., Thibert, B.: Convergence of a newton algorithm for semi-discrete optimal transport. J. Eur. Math. Soc. **21**(9), 2603–2651 (2019)
19. Kolouri, S., Nadjahi, K., Simsekli, U., Badeau, R., Rohde, G.: Generalized sliced wasserstein distances. In: Advances in Neural Information Processing Systems 32 (2019)
20. Kusner, M., Sun, Y., Kolkin, N., Weinberger, K.: From word embeddings to document distances. In: Proceedings of the 32nd International Conference on Machine Learning. pp. 957–966 (2015)
21. Lei, N., Su, K., Cui, L., Yau, S.T., Gu, D.X.: A geometric view of optimal transportation and generative mode. Computer Aided Geometric Design **68**, 1–21 (2019)
22. Lin, T., Ho, N., Jordan, M.I.: On efficient optimal transport: An analysis of greedy and accelerated mirror descent algorithms. In: International Conference on Machine Learning. pp. 3982–3991 (2019)
23. Meng, C., Ke, Y., Zhang, J., Zhang, M., Zhong, W., Ma, P.: Large-scale optimal transport map estimation using projection pursuit. In: Advances in Neural Information Processing Systems 32 (2019)
24. Nguyen, X.: Convergence of latent mixing measures in finite and infinite mixture models. Ann. Statist **41**, 370–400 (2013)
25. Peyré, G., Cuturi, M.: Computational Optimal Transport. arXiv:1803.00567 (2018)
26. Pitie, F., Kokaram, A.C., Dahyot, R.: Automated colour grading using colour distribution transfer. Computer Vision and Image Understanding (2007)
27. Schiebinger, G., Shu, J., Tabaka, M., Cleary, B., Subramanian, V., Solomon, A., Gould, J., Liu, S., Lin, S., Berube, P., Lee, L., Chen, J., Brumbaugh, J., Rigollet, P., Hochedlinger, K., Jaenisch, R., Regev, A., Lander, E.: Optimal-transport analysis of single-cell gene expression identifies developmental trajectories in reprogramming. Cell **176**(4), 928–943 (2019)
28. Schmitzer, B.: Stabilized sparse scaling algorithms for entropy regularized transport problems. SIAM J. Sci. Comput. **41**(3), A1443–A1481 (2019)

29. Seguy, V., Damodaran, B.B., Flamary, R., Courty, N., Rolet, A., Blondel, M.: Large-scale optimal transport and mapping estimation. Stat **1050**, 26 (2018)
30. Taskesen, B., Shafieezadeh-Abadeh, S., Kuhn, D.: Semi-discrete optimal transport: Hardness, regularization and numerical solution. arXiv preprint arXiv:2103.06263 (2021)
31. Tolstikhin, I., Bousquet, O., Gelly, S., Schoelkopf, B.: Wasserstein auto-encoders. In: ICLR (2018)
32. Villani, C.: Optimal transport: old and new, vol. 338. Springer Science & Business Media (2008)
33. Yurochkin, M., Claici, S., Chien, E., Mirzazadeh, F., Solomon, J.M.: Hierarchical optimal transport for document representation. In: Advances in Neural Information Processing Systems 32 (2019)

# A Comparative Study of Graph Matching Algorithms in Computer Vision

Stefan Haller[1]([✉])(iD), Lorenz Feineis[1], Lisa Hutschenreiter[1], Florian Bernard[2],
Carsten Rother[1], Dagmar Kainmüller[3](iD), Paul Swoboda[4](iD),
and Bogdan Savchynskyy[1]

[1] Heidelberg University, Heidelberg, Germany
stefan.haller@iwr.uni-heidelberg.de
[2] University of Bonn, Bonn, Germany
[3] MDC Berlin, Berlin, Germany
[4] MPI-INF Saarbrücken, Saarbrücken, Germany

**Abstract.** The graph matching optimization problem is an essential component for many tasks in computer vision, such as bringing two deformable objects in correspondence. Naturally, a wide range of applicable algorithms have been proposed in the last decades. Since a common standard benchmark has not been developed, their performance claims are often hard to verify as evaluation on differing problem instances and criteria make the results incomparable. To address these shortcomings, we present a comparative study of graph matching algorithms. We create a uniform benchmark where we collect and categorize a large set of existing and publicly available computer vision graph matching problems in a common format. At the same time we collect and categorize the most popular open-source implementations of graph matching algorithms. Their performance is evaluated in a way that is in line with the best practices for comparing optimization algorithms. The study is designed to be reproducible and extensible to serve as a valuable resource in the future.

Our study provides three notable insights: **(i)** popular problem instances are exactly solvable in substantially less than 1 s, and, therefore, are insufficient for future empirical evaluations; **(ii)** the most popular baseline methods are highly inferior to the best available methods; **(iii)** despite the NP-hardness of the problem, instances coming from vision applications are often solvable in a few seconds even for graphs with more than 500 vertices.

**Keywords:** Graph matching · Optimization · Benchmark

## 1 Introduction

Finding correspondences between elements of two discrete sets, such as keypoints in images or vertices of 3D meshes, is a fundamental problem in computer

**Supplementary Information** The online version contains supplementary material available at https://doi.org/10.1007/978-3-031-20050-2_37.

vision and as such highly relevant for numerous vision tasks, including 3D reconstruction [49], tracking [64], shape model learning [29], and image alignment [7],
among others. Graph matching [24,55,63] is a standard way to address such
problems. In graph matching, vertices of the matched graphs correspond to the
elements of the discrete sets to be matched. Graph edges define the cost structure of the problem: pairs of matched vertices are penalized in addition to the
vertex-to-vertex matchings. This allows to take, e.g., the underlying geometri-
cal relationship between vertices into account, but also makes the optimization
problem NP-hard.

Deep graph matching [51] is a modern learning-based approach, that combines neural networks for computing matching costs with combinatorial graph
matching algorithms to find a matching. The graph matching algorithm plays a
crucial role in this context, as it has to provide high-quality solutions within
a limited time budget. The high demand on run-time is also due to backpropagation learning and graph matching minimization being interleaved and
executed together many times during training.

Hense, our work focuses on the *optimization* part of the graph matching
pipeline. The modeling and learning aspects are beyond its scope. We evaluate a
range of existing *open-source* algorithms. Our study compares their performance
on a diverse set of computer vision problems. The focus of the evaluation lies on
both, speed and objective value of the solution.

**Why Do We Require a Benchmark?**     Dozens of algorithms addressing
the graph matching problem have been proposed in the computer vision literature, see, e.g., the surveys [24,55,63], and references therein. Most works promise
state-of-the-art performance, which is persuasively demonstrated by experimental evaluation. However, (i) results from one article are often incomparable to
results from another, since different problem instances with different costs are
used, even if these instances are based on the same image data; (ii) not every
existing method is evaluated on all available problem instances, even if open-
source code is available. Some methods, especially those with poor performance
on many instances, are very popular as baselines, whereas better performing
techniques are hardly considered in comparisons; (iii) new algorithms are often
only evaluated on easy, small-scale problems. This does not provide any information on how these algorithms perform on larger, more difficult problem instances.

For these reasons, the field of graph matching has, in our view, not developed
as well as it could have done. By providing a reproducible and extensible benchmark we hope to change this in the future. Such a benchmark is of particular
importance for the fast-moving field of *deep graph matching*, as it helps to select
an appropriate, fast solver for the combinatorial part of the learning pipeline.

**Graph Matching Problem.**     Let $\mathcal{V}$ and $\mathcal{L}$ be the two finite sets, whose
elements we want to match to each other. For each pair $i, j \in \mathcal{V}$ and each pair
$s, l \in \mathcal{L}$ a cost $c_{is,jl} \in \mathbb{R}$ is given. Each pair can be interpreted as an *edge* between
a pair of *vertices* of an underlying graph. This is where the term *graph matching*
comes from. Note that direct *vertex-i-to-vertex-s* matching costs are defined by
the *diagonal* elements $c_{is,is}$ of the resulting *cost* (or *affinity*) *matrix* $C = (c_{is,jl})$

with $is = (i, s) \in \mathcal{V} \times \mathcal{L}$, $jl = (j, l) \in \mathcal{V} \times \mathcal{L}$. The diagonal elements are referred to as *unary costs*, in contrast to the *pairwise costs* defined by non-diagonal entries. The goal of graph matching is to find a *matching*, or mutual *assignment*, between elements of the sets $\mathcal{V}$ and $\mathcal{L}$ that minimizes the total cost for all pairs of assignments. It can be formulated as the following integer quadratic problem[1]:

$$\min_{x \in \{0,1\}^{\mathcal{V} \times \mathcal{L}}} \sum_{i,j \in \mathcal{V}} \sum_{s,l \in \mathcal{L}} c_{is,jl}\, x_{is}\, x_{jl} \quad \text{s.t.} \quad \begin{cases} \forall i \in \mathcal{V}: \sum_{s \in \mathcal{L}} x_{is} \leq 1, \text{ and} \\ \forall s \in \mathcal{L}: \sum_{i \in \mathcal{V}} x_{is} \leq 1. \end{cases}$$

(1)

The vector $x$ defines the matching as $x_{is} = 1$ corresponds to assigning $i$ to $s$. The inequalities in (1) allow for this assignment to be *incomplete*, i.e., some elements of both sets may remain unassigned. This is in contrast to *complete* assignments, where each element of $\mathcal{V}$ is matched to *exactly one* element of $\mathcal{L}$ and vice versa. Note that complete assignments require $|\mathcal{V}| = |\mathcal{L}|$.

**Relation to the Quadratic Assignment Problem.** The graph matching problem (1) is closely related to the NP-hard [50] *quadratic assignment problem (QAP)* [12], which is well-studied in operations research [12,15,48]. The QAP only considers *complete* assignments, i.e., $|\mathcal{V}| = |\mathcal{L}|$ and equality is required in the constraints in (1). In contrast, in the field of computer vision incomplete assignments are often required in the model to allow for, e.g., outliers or matching of images with different numbers of features. Still, graph matching and the QAP are polynomially reducible to each other, see supplement for a proof.

The most famous QAP benchmark is the QAPLIB [11] containing 136 problem instances. However, the benchmark problems in computer vision (CV) substantially differ from those in QAPLIB both by the feasible set that includes incomplete assignments, as well as by the structure of the cost matrix $C$: **(i)** CV problems are usually of a general, more expressive *Lawler* form [42], whereas QAPLIB considers factorizable costs $c_{is,jl} = f_{ij}d_{sl}$ known as *Koopmans-Beckmann* form. The latter allows for more efficient specialized algorithms. **(ii)** the cost matrix $C$ in QAPLIB is often dense, whereas in CV problems it is typically sparse, i.e., a large number of entries in $C$ are 0; **(iii)** for CV problem instances the cost matrix $C$ may contain *infinite* costs on the diagonal to prohibit certain vertex-to-vertex mappings; **(iv)** QAPLIB problems are different from an optimization point of view. For instance, while the classical LP relaxation [1] is often quite loose for QAPLIB problem instances, it is tight or nearly tight for typical instances considered in CV.

Consequently, comparison results on QAPLIB and CV instances differ significantly. It is also typical for NP-hard problems that instances coming from different applied areas require different optimization techniques. Therefore, a dedicated benchmarking on the CV datasets is required.

**Contributions.** Our contribution is three-fold: **(i)** Based on open source data, we collected, categorized and generated 451 *existing* graph matching instances

---

[1] For sets $A$ and $B$ the notation $x \in A^B$ denotes a vector $x$ whose coordinates take on values from the set $A$ and are indexed by elements of $B$, i.e., each element of $B$ corresponds to a value from $A$.

grouped into 11 datasets in a common format. Most graph matching papers use only a small subset of these datasets for evaluation. Our format provides a *ready-to-use* cost matrix $C$ and does not require any image analysis to extract the costs. **(ii)** We collected and categorized 20 open-source graph matching algorithms and evaluated them on the above datasets. During that we adapted the cost matrix to requirements of particular algorithms where needed. For each method we provide a brief technical description. We did not consider algorithms with no publicly available open source code. **(iii)** To allow our benchmark to grow further, we set up a web site[2] with all results. Our benchmark is reproducible, extensible and follows the best practices of [6]. We will maintain its web-page in the future and welcome scientists to add problem instances as well as algorithms.

Our work significantly excels evaluations in *all* the papers introducing the algorithms we study. This implies also to the largest existing comparison [31] so far. The latter considers only 8 out of the 11 datasets and evaluates 6 algorithms out of our 20.

## 2    Background to Algorithms

In this section we briefly review the main theoretical concepts and building blocks of the considered approaches.

**Linearization.** In case all pairwise costs are zero, the objective in (1) linearizes to $\sum_{i \in \mathcal{V}, s \in \mathcal{L}} c_{is,is} x_{is}$, turning (1) into the *incomplete linear assignment problem (iLAP)*. A typical way of how the iLAP is obtained in existing algorithms is by considering the Taylor expansion of the objective (1) in the vicinity of a given point $x$. The linear term of this expansion forms the iLAP objective. The iLAP can be reduced to a complete linear assignment problem (LAP) [10], see supplement, and addressed by, e.g., Hungarian [41] or auction [8] algorithms. Below, when we refer to LAP this includes both LAP and iLAP problems.

**Birkhoff Polytope and Permutation Matrices.**    For $|\mathcal{V}| = |\mathcal{L}|$ and $x \in [0,1]^{\mathcal{V} \times \mathcal{L}}$, where $[0,1]$ denotes the closed interval from 0 to 1, the constraints $\sum_{s \in \mathcal{L}} x_{is} = 1, \forall i \in \mathcal{V}$, and $\sum_{i \in \mathcal{V}} x_{is} = 1, \forall s \in \mathcal{L}$, define the set of *doubly-stochastic matrices* also known as *Birkhoff polytope*. Its restriction to binary vectors $x \in \{0,1\}^{\mathcal{V} \times \mathcal{L}}$ is called the *set of permutations* or *permutation matrices*.

**Inequality to Equality Transformation.**    By adding *slack* or *dummy* variables, indexed by $\#$, with zero cost in the objective in (1), the uniqueness constraints in (1) can be rewritten as equalities for $\mathcal{V}^{\#} := \mathcal{V} \dot{\cup} \{\#\}$, $\mathcal{L}^{\#} := \mathcal{L} \dot{\cup} \{\#\}$, and $x \in [0,1]^{\mathcal{V}^{\#} \times \mathcal{L}^{\#}}$, where $\dot{\cup}$ is the disjoint union:

$$\mathcal{B} := \left\{ x \mid \forall i \in \mathcal{V} \colon \sum_{s \in \mathcal{L}^{\#}} x_{is} = 1 \quad \text{and} \quad \forall s \in \mathcal{L} \colon \sum_{i \in \mathcal{V}^{\#}} x_{is} = 1 \right\}. \quad (2)$$

Here, $x_{i\#} = 1$ (or $x_{\#s} = 1$) means that the node $i$ (or label $s$) is unassigned. Following [65], we refer to the elements of $\mathcal{B}$ as *doubly-semi-stochastic matrices*.

---

[2] The web site for the benchmark is available at https://vislearn.github.io/gmbench/.

**Doubly-Stochastic Relaxation.** Replacing the *integrality constraints* $x \in \{0,1\}^{\mathcal{V} \times \mathcal{L}}$ in (1) with the respective *box constraints* $x \in [0,1]^{\mathcal{V} \times \mathcal{L}}$ leads to a *doubly-stochastic relaxation* of the graph matching problem.[3]. Despite the convexity of its feasible set, the doubly-stochastic relaxation is NP-hard because of the non-convexity of its quadratic objective in general [53].

**Probabilistic Interpretation.** Doubly-stochastic relaxations are often motivated from a probabilistic perspective, where the individual matrix entries represent matching probabilities. An alternative probabilistic interpretation is to consider the *product graph* between $\mathcal{V}$ and $\mathcal{L}$, in which the edge weights directly depend on the cost matrix $C$. This way, graph matching can be understood as selecting reliable nodes in the product graph, e.g., by random walks [17].

**Injective and Bijective Formulations.** Assume $|\mathcal{V}| \leq |\mathcal{L}|$. A number of existing approaches consider an asymmetric formulation of the graph matching problem (1), where the uppermost constraint in (1) is exchanged for equality, i.e., $\forall i \in \mathcal{V}: \sum_{s \in \mathcal{L}} x_{is} = 1$. We call this formulation *injective*. The strict inequality case $|\mathcal{V}| < |\mathcal{L}|$ is also referred to as an *unbalanced QAP* in the literature. Note that to address problems of the general form (1) by such algorithms, it is necessary to extend the set $\mathcal{L}$ with $|\mathcal{V}|$ dummy elements. This is similar to the reduction from graph matching to QAP described in the supplement. Since availiable implementations of multiple considered algorithms are additionally restricted to the case $|\mathcal{V}| = |\mathcal{L}|$, i.e. to the classical QAP as introduced in Sect. 1, we adopt the term *bijective* to describe the corresponding algorithms and datasets.

**Spectral Relaxation.** The graph matching objective in (1) can be compactly written as $x^{\top} C x$. Instead of the uniqueness constraints in (1) the *spectral relaxation* considers the non-convex constraint $x^{\top} x = n$. This constraint includes all matchings with exactly $n$ assignments, which is of interest when the total number of assignments $n$ is known, e.g., for the injective formulation where $n = |\mathcal{V}|$. The minimization of $x^{\top} C x$ subject to $x^{\top} x = n$ reduces to an *eigenvector problem*, i.e., finding a vector $x$ corresponding to the smallest eigenvalue of the matrix $C$. The latter amounts to minimizing a Rayleigh quotient [30].

**Path Following.** Another way to deal with the non-convexity of the graph matching problem is *path-following*, represented by [69] in our study. The idea is to solve a sequence of optimization problems with objective $f_{\alpha^t}(x) = (1 - \alpha^t) f_{\mathrm{cvx}}(x) + \alpha^t f_{cav}(x)$ for $\alpha^t$, $t \in 1, \ldots, N$, gradually growing from 0 to 1. The (approximate) solution of each problem in the sequence is used as a starting point for the next. The hope is that this iterative process, referred to as *following the convex-to-concave path*, leads to a solution with low objective value for the whole problem. The objective for $\alpha^1 = 0$ is equal to $f_{\mathrm{cvx}}(x)$ and is convex, therefore it can be solved to global optimality. The objective for $\alpha^N = 1$ is equal to $f_{cav}(x)$ and is concave. Its local optima over the set of doubly-stochastic matrices are

---

[3] Strictly speaking, the term *doubly-stochastic* corresponds to the case when equality constraints are considered in (1). In [65] the inequality variant is called *doubly semi-stochastic* but we use *doubly-stochastic* in both cases

guaranteed to be binary, and, therefore, *feasible assignments*, i.e., they satisfy all constraints of (1).

**Graphical Model Representation.**    The graph matching problem can be represented in the form of a *maximum a posteriori (MAP) inference* problem for discrete graphical models [54], known also as *Markov random field (MRF) energy minimization* and closely related to *valued and weighted constraint satisfaction* problems. As several graph matching works in computer vision [31,57,67], use this representation, we provide it below in more detail.

Let $(\mathcal{V}, \mathcal{E})$ be an undirected graph, with the finite set $\mathcal{V}$ introduced above being the *set of nodes* and $\mathcal{E} \subseteq \binom{\mathcal{V}}{2}$ being the set of *edges*. For convenience we denote edges $\{i, j\} \in \mathcal{E}$ simply by $ij$. Let the finite set $\mathcal{L}$ introduced above be the set of *labels*. We associate with each node $i \in \mathcal{V}$ a set $\mathcal{L}_i^\# = \mathcal{L}_i \dot\cup \{\#\}$ with $\mathcal{L}_i \subseteq \mathcal{L}$. Like above, # stands for the *dummy label* distinct from all labels in $\mathcal{L}$ to encode that *no label* is selected. With each label $s \in \mathcal{L}_i^\#$ in each node $i \in \mathcal{V}$ the *unary cost* $\theta_{is} := c_{is,is}$ (0 for $s = \#$) is associated. The case $|\mathcal{L}_i| < |\mathcal{L}|$ corresponds to infinite unary costs $c_{is,is} = \infty$, $s \in \mathcal{L} \backslash \mathcal{L}_i$, as the respective assignments can be excluded from the very beginning. Likewise, with each edge $ij \in \mathcal{E}$ and each label pair $sl \in \mathcal{L}_i^\# \times \mathcal{L}_j^\#$, the pairwise cost $\theta_{is,jl} = c_{is,jl} + c_{jl,is}$ (0 for $s$ or $l = \#$) is associated. The graph $(\mathcal{V}, \mathcal{E})$ being undirected implies $ij = ji$ and $\theta_{is,jl} = \theta_{jl,is}$. An edge $ij$ belongs to $\mathcal{E}$ only if there is a label pair $sl \in \mathcal{L}_i \times \mathcal{L}_j$ such that $\theta_{is,jl} \neq 0$. In this way a sparse cost matrix $C$ may translate into a sparse graph $(\mathcal{V}, \mathcal{E})$.

The problem of finding an optimal assignment of labels to nodes, equivalent to the *graph matching* problem (1), can thus be stated as

$$\min_{y \in \mathcal{Y}} \left[ E(y) := \sum_{i \in \mathcal{V}} \theta_{iy_i} + \sum_{ij \in \mathcal{E}} \theta_{iy_i, jy_j} \right] \text{ s.t. } \forall i, j \in \mathcal{V}, i \neq j : y_i \neq y_j \text{ or } y_i = \# \quad (3)$$

where $\mathcal{Y}$ stands for the Cartesian product $\times_{i \in \mathcal{V}} \mathcal{L}_i^\#$, and $y_i = s$, $s \in \mathcal{L}_i$, is equivalent to $x_{is} = 1$ in terms of (1). Essentially, (3) corresponds to a *MAP inference problem for discrete graphical models* [54] with additional uniqueness constraints for the labels.

**ILP Representation and LP Relaxations.**    Based on (3) the graph matching problem can be expressed by a linear objective subject to linear and integrality constraints by introducing variables $x_{is,jl} = x_{jl,is}$ for each pair of labels $sl \in \mathcal{L}_i^\# \times \mathcal{L}_j^\#$ in neighboring nodes $ij \in \mathcal{E}$, and enforcing the equality $x_{is,jl} = x_{is}x_{jl}$ with suitable linear constraints. An *integer linear program (ILP)* formulation of the graph matching problem (1) can then be written as:

$$\min_{x \in \{0,1\}^{\mathcal{J}}} \sum_{i \in \mathcal{V}, s \in \mathcal{L}_i^\#} c_{is} x_{is} + \sum_{ij \in \mathcal{E}, sl \in \mathcal{L}_i^\# \times \mathcal{L}_j^\#} (c_{is,jl} + c_{jl,is}) x_{is,jl} \quad (4)$$

$$\forall i \in \mathcal{V} : \sum_{s \in \mathcal{L}_i^\#} x_{is} = 1, \forall s \in \mathcal{L} : \sum_{i \in \mathcal{V}} x_{is} \leq 1, \quad (5)$$

$$\forall ij \in \mathcal{E}, \ l \in \mathcal{L}_j^{\#}: \ \sum_{s \in \mathcal{L}_i^{\#}} x_{is,jl} = x_{jl}. \tag{6}$$

Here $\mathcal{J} = \{(i,s): i \in \mathcal{V}, \ s \in \mathcal{L}_i^{\#}\} \cup \{(is,jl): ij \in \mathcal{E}, sl \in \mathcal{L}_i^{\#} \times \mathcal{L}_j^{\#}\}$ denotes the set of coordinates of the vector $x$. The formulation (4)–(6) differs from the standard ILP representation for discrete graphical models by the label uniqueness constraints (5, rightmost). Substitution of the integrality constraints $x \in \{0,1\}^{\mathcal{J}}$ in (4) with the box constraints $x \in [0,1]^{\mathcal{J}}$ results in the respective *LP relaxation*.

**Table 1. Method properties.** Purely primal heuristics are separated from the dual methods by a horizontal line.

| method | IQP | ILP | bijective | non-pos. | 0-unary | lineariz. | norm | doubly | spectral | discret. | path fol. | fusion | duality | SGA | BCA | Matlab | C++ |
|---|---|---|---|---|---|---|---|---|---|---|---|---|---|---|---|---|---|
| fgmd [69] | + | | + | | | | | | | | + | | | | | [68] | |
| fm [31] | | + | | | | | | + | | | | | | | | | [32] |
| fw [62] | + | | | | + | + | | | | | | | | | | | [56] |
| ga [27] | + | | + | | + | + | + | | | | | | | | | [20] | |
| ipfps [46] | + | | + | + | + | + | | | | + | | | | | | [44] | |
| ipfpu [46] | + | | + | | + | + | | | | + | | | | | | [44] | |
| lsm [33] | + | | + | + | | | | + | | + | | | | | | [66] | |
| mpm [18] | + | | + | + | | | | + | | + | | | | | | [19] | |
| pm [65] | + | | + | + | + | | | | + | + | | | | | | [68] | |
| rrwm [17] | + | | + | | | | + | | + | + | | | | | | [16] | |
| smac [21] | + | | + | + | | | | + | | + | | + | | | | [20] | |
| sm [43] | + | | + | + | | | | + | | + | | + | | | | [44] | |
| dd-ls(0/3/4) [59] | | + | | | | | | | | | | | | + | + | | [38] |
| fm-bca [31] | | + | | | | | | | | | | + | + | | + | | [32] |
| hbp [67] | | + | + | | | | | | | | | | + | | | + | [66] |
| mp(-mcf/-fw) [57] | | + | | | | | | | | | | | + | | + | | [56] |

**Meaning of properties** ('+' indicates presence): *IQP*: addresses IQP formulation; *ILP*: addresses ILP formulation; *bijective*: addresses bijective formulation; *non-pos.*: requires non-positive costs, see Remark 1; *0-unary*: requires zero unary costs; *lineariz.*: linearization-based method; *norm*: imposes norm-constraints; *doubly*: addresses doubly-stochastic relaxation; *spectral*: solves spectral relaxation; *discret.*: discretization as in Remark 2; *path fol.*: path following method; *fusion*: utilizes fusion; *duality*: Lagrange duality-based; *SGA*: uses dual sub-gradient ascent; *BCA*: uses dual block-coordinate ascent; *Matlab/C++*: implemented in Matlab/C++ [reference to code]

# 3   Graph Matching Algorithms

Below we summarize the graph matching methods that we consider in our comparison, see Table 1 for an overview of their characteristics and references.

## 3.1   Primal Heuristics

**Linearization Based.** These methods are based on iterative linearizations of the quadratic objective (1) derived from its Taylor expansion.

*Iterated projected fixed point* (ipfp) [46] solves on each iteration the LAP obtained through linearization in the vicinity of a current, in general non-integer, assignment. Between iterations the quadratic objective is optimized along the direction to the obtained LAP solution, which yields a new, in general non-integer assignment. We evaluate two versions of ipfp which differ by their initialization: ipfpu is initialized with $x^0 \in [0,1]^{\mathcal{V} \times \mathcal{L}}$, where $x_{is}^0 = 1/\sqrt{N}$ if $c_{is,is} < \infty$, and $x_{is}^0 = 0$ otherwise. Here, $N := |\{is \in \mathcal{V} \times \mathcal{L} \mid c_{is,is} < \infty\}|$. ipfps starts from the result of the spectral matching sm [43] described below.

*Graduated assignment* (**ga**) [27] optimizes the doubly-stochastic relaxation. On each iteration it approximately solves the LAP obtained through linearization in the vicinity of a current, in general non-integer, assignment utilizing the Sinkhorn algorithm [40] for a given fixed temperature. The obtained approximate solution is used afterwards as the new assignment. The temperature is decreased over iterations to gradually make the solutions closer to integral.

*Fast approximate quadratic programming* (**fw**) [62] considers the Frank-Wolfe method [25] for optimizing over the set $\mathcal{B}$, c.f. (2). Each iteration first solves a LAP to find the optimum of the linearization at the current solution, followed by a line search in order to find the best convex combination of the current and the new solution. To obtain an integer solution, the objective of the LAP solution is evaluated in each iteration, and the lowest one among all solutions is kept. The initial LAP is based on the unary costs only. The implementation [56] we evaluate is applicable to the general Lawler form of the problem (1), in contrast to the Koopmans-Beckmann form addressed in [62].

**Norm Constraints Based.** *Spectral matching* (**sm**) [43] uses a spectral relaxation that amounts to a Rayleigh quotient problem [30] which can be optimized by the power iteration method. Here, each update comprises of a simple matrix multiplication and a subsequent normalization, so that $x^t$ is iteratively updated via $x^{t+1} = -Cx^t/\|Cx^t\|_2$.

*Spectral matching with affine constraints* (**smac**) [21] is similar to **sm**, but additionally takes into account affine equality constraints that enforce one-to-one matchings. The resulting formulation amounts to a Rayleigh quotient problem under affine constraints, that can efficiently be computed in terms of the eigenvalue decomposition.

*Max-pooling matching* (**mpm**) [18] resembles **sm**, but it replaces the sum-pooling implemented in terms of the matrix multiplication $-Cx$ in the power iteration update of **SM** by a max-pooling operation. With that, only candidate matches with the smallest costs are taken into account.

*Local sparse model* (**lsm**) [33] solves the relaxation $\max_x x^\top Cx$, s.t. $\|x\|_{1,2}^2 = \sum_{i=1}^{|\mathcal{V}|} \left(\sum_{k=1}^{|\mathcal{L}|} |x_{ik}|\right)^2 = 1$, $x \geq 0$. The $l_{1,2}$-norm $\|x\|_{1,2}$ should encourage the solution of the above relaxation to be sparse in each row when treating $x$ as a matrix. This resembles the sparsity property of permutation matrices, which satisfy $\|x\|_{1,2} = |\mathcal{V}|$.

*Remark 1.* All of the norm constraints based algorithms described above require non-positive[4] costs in order to guarantee convergence of the underlying iterative techniques. This condition can be w.l.o.g. assumed for any graph matching problem. The corresponding cost transformation is described in the supplement.

**Probabilistic Interpretation Based.** *Reweighted Random Walks Matching* (**rrwm**) [17] interprets graph matching as the problem of selecting reliable nodes in an *association graph*, whose weighted adjacency matrix is given by $-C$.

---

[4] Non-negative in original maximization formulations.

Nodes are selected through a random walk that starts from one node and randomly visits nodes according to a Markov transition matrix derived from the edge weights of the association graph. In order to take into account matching constraints, the authors of [17] consider a reweighted random walk strategy.

*Probabilistic Matching* (pm) [65] considers a probabilistic formulation of graph matching in which the quadratic objective is replaced by a relative entropy objective. It is shown that by doing so one can obtain a convex problem formulation via marginalization, which is optimized in terms of an iterative successive projection algorithm.

*Remark 2.* Most of the primal heuristics considered above aim to optimize the quadratic objective (1) over a continuous set such as, e.g., the Birkhoff polytope. The resulting assignment $x \in \mathbb{R}^{\mathcal{V} \times \mathcal{L}}$ is, therefore, not guaranteed to be integer. As suggested in [17], to obtain an integer assignment we solve a LAP with $(-x)$ treated as the cost matrix. We apply this procedure as a postprocessing step for ipfp, ga, sm, smac, mpm, lsm, rrwm, and pm. Note that this postprocessing does not change an integer assignment.

**Path Following Based.** *Factorized graph matching* (fgmd) [69] proposes an efficient factorization of the cost matrix to speed-up computations, and is based on the convex-concave path following strategy, see Sect. 2. Individual problems from the path are solved with the Frank-Wolfe method [25].

**Randomized Generation and Fusion Based.** *Fusion moves with a greedy heuristic* (fm) [31] is based on the graphical model representation and consists of two parts: A randomized greedy assignment generation, and *fusion* of the assignments. The randomized generator greedily fixes labels in the nodes in a way that minimizes the objective value restricted to the already fixed labels. The fusion procedure merges the current assignment with the next generated one by approximately solving an auxiliary *binary* MAP inference problem utilizing QPBO-I [52]. The merged solution is guaranteed to be at least as good as the two input assignments. This property guarantees monotonic improvement of the objective value.

## 3.2   Lagrange Duality-Based Techniques

The methods below consider the Lagrange decompositions [28] of the graph matching problem (1) [59], or its graphical model representation (3) [31,57,67], and optimize the corresponding dual. The methods differ in the dual optimization and chosen primal solution reconstruction algorithms.

**Block-Coordinate Methods (hbp, mp-\*, fm-bca).** The works [31,57,67] employ a block-coordinate ascent (BCA) technique to optimize the dual problem obtained by relaxing the coupling (6) and label uniqueness constraints (5, rightmost). Since the dual is piece-wise linear, BCA algorithms may not attain the dual optimum, but may get stuck in a sub-optimal fixed point [9,54].

Although the elementary operations performed by these algorithms are very similar, their convergence speed and attained fixed points differ drastically. In a nutshell, these methods decompose the problem (3) into the graphical model without uniqueness constraints, and the LAP problem, as described, e.g., in [31]. Dual algorithms reparametrize the problem making it more amenable to primal techniques [54]. Table 2 gives an overview of the evaluated combinations for **(i)** optimizing the dual of the graphical model, **(ii)** optimizing the LAP, and **(iii)** obtaining the primal solution from the reparametrized costs[5], which influence the practical performance of BCA solvers. Additionally, mp-mcf and mp-fw tighten the relaxation by considering triples of graph nodes as subproblems.

**Subgradient Method (dd-ls*).** The algorithms denoted as dd-ls* with * being 0, 3 or 4 represent different variants of a dual subgradient optimization method [59]. The variant dd-ls0 addresses the relaxation equivalent to a symmetrized graphical model formulation, see supplement for a description. This is achieved by considering the Lagrange decomposition of the problem into two graphical models, with $\mathcal{V}$ and $\mathcal{L}$ being the set of nodes, respectively, and a LAP subproblem. The graphical models are further decomposed into acyclic ones, i.e. trees, solvable by dynamic programming, see, e.g., [54, Ch.9]. The *tree decomposition* is not described in [59], and we reconstructed it based on the source code [38] and communication with the authors. As we observed it to be more efficient than the *max-flow subproblems* suggested in the paper [59] the latter were not used in our evaluation.

**Table 2.** Characterization of dual BCA algorithms.

| | (i) graphical model | (ii) LAP | (iii) primal | Algorithms used for optimizing the *graphical model* and *LAP* part, as well as technique used to obtain a *primal* solution. For *LAP* in the *primal* column the solution of the LAP subproblem is reused as feasible assignment. Instead of solving the LAP subproblem, fm-bca performs a series of *BCA* steps wrt. the LAP dual variables. |
|---|---|---|---|---|
| hbp | MPLP [26] | Hungarian [41] | branch & bound | |
| mp(-mcf) | } anisotropic | } network | LAP | |
| mp-fw | } diffusion [54] | } simplex [2] | fw | |
| fm-bca | MPLP++ [60] | BCA | fm | |

Variants dd-ls3 and dd-ls4 tighten the relaxation of dd-ls0 by considering *local subproblems* of both graphical models in the decomposition. These are obtained by reducing the node sets $\mathcal{V}$ and $\mathcal{L}$ to 3 or respectively 4 elements inducing a connected subgraph of the graphical model, see [59] for details.

## 4  Benchmark

**Datasets.** The 11 datasets we collected for evaluation of the graph matching algorithms stem from applications in computer vision and bio-imaging. All existing graph matching papers use only a subset of these datasets for evaluation purposes. Together these datasets contain 451 problem instances. Table 3 gives an overview of their characteristics. We modified costs in several datasets to make them amenable to some algorithms, see supplement. Our modification

---

[5] *Reparametrized* costs are also known as *reduced* costs, e.g., in the simplex tableau.

results in a constant shift of the objective value for each feasible assignment, and, therefore, does not influence the quality of the solution.

Below we give a brief description of each dataset. Along with the standard computer vision datasets with small-sized problems, hotel, house-dense/sparse, car, motor and opengm with $|\mathcal{V}|$ up to 52, our collection contains the middle-sized problems flow, with $|\mathcal{V}|$ up to 126, and the large-scale worms and pairs problems with $|\mathcal{V}|$ up to 565.

*Wide baseline matching* (hotel, house-dense/sparse) is based on a series of images of the same synthetic object with manually selected landmarks from different viewing angles based on the work by [14]. For hotel and house-dense we use the same models as in [57] published in [58]. house-sparse consists of the same image pairs as house-dense, but the cost structure is derived following the approach of [67] that results in significantly sparser problem instances. Graphs with the landmarks as nodes are obtained by Delaunay triangulation. The costs are set to $c_{is,jl} = -\exp(-(d_{ij} - d_{sl})^2/2500)A_{ij}^1 A_{sl}^2$ where $d_{ij}, d_{sl}$ are Euclidean distances between two landmarks and $A^1 \in \{0,1\}^{\mathcal{V} \times \mathcal{V}}$, $A^2 \in \{0,1\}^{\mathcal{L} \times \mathcal{L}}$ are adjacency matrices of the corresponding graphs. The unary costs are zero.

**Table 3. Dataset properties.** A '+' indicates that all problem instances of the dataset have the respective property.

| dataset | #inst. | #opt. | bijective | injective | non-pos. | 0-unary | $|\mathcal{V}|$ | $|\mathcal{L}|/|\mathcal{V}|$ | density (%) | diagonal dens. (%) | data |
|---|---|---|---|---|---|---|---|---|---|---|---|
| caltech-large [17] | 9 | 1 | + | + | + | | 36-219 | 0.4-2.3 | 0.55 | 18.1 | [16] |
| caltech-small [17] | 21 | 12 | + | + | + | | 9-117 | 0.4-3 | 0.99 | 26.8 | [16] |
| car [23,47] | 30 | 30 | + | | + | | 19-49 | 1 | 2.9 | 100 | [45] |
| flow [3,57] | 6 | 6 | | | | | 48-126 | ≈ 1 | 0.39 | 15.8 | [4,5] |
| hotel [14,59] | 105 | 105 | + | | | | 30 | 1 | 12.8 | 100 | [13,58] |
| house-dense [14,59] | 105 | 105 | + | | | | 30 | 1 | 12.6 | 100 | [13,58] |
| house-sparse [14,67] | 105 | 105 | + | | + | + | 30 | 1 | 1.5 | 100 | [13] |
| motor [23,47] | 20 | 20 | + | | + | | 15-52 | 1 | 3.8 | 100 | [45] |
| opengm [36,39] | 4 | 4 | + | | | | 19-20 | 1 | 74.8 | 100 | [37] |
| pairs [31,34] | 16 | 0 | | | | | 511-565 | ≈ 1 | 0.0019 | 3.7 | [32] |
| worms [34] | 30 | 28 | | | | | 558 | ≈ 2.4 | 0.00038 | 1.6 | [35] |

**Meaning of properties:**
*#inst.*: number of problem instances; *#opt.*: number of known optima; *bijective/injective*: bi-/injective assignment is assumed; *non-pos.*: all costs are non-positive; *0-unary*: datasets with zero unary costs; $|\mathcal{V}|$: number of elements in $\mathcal{V}$; $|\mathcal{L}|/|\mathcal{V}|$: ratio of the number of elements in $\mathcal{L}$ to the number of elements in $\mathcal{V}$; *density (%)*: percentage of non-zero elements in the cost matrix $C$; *diag. dens. (%)*: percentage of non-infinite elements on the diagonal of $C$; *data*: [references] to problem instances, images, feature coordinates or ground truth.

*Keypoint matching* (car, motor) contains *car* and *motor*bike images from the PASCAL VOC 2007 Challenge [23] with the features and costs from [47]. We use the instances available from [32].

*Large displacement flow* (flow) was introduced by [3] for key point matching on scenes with large motion. We use the instances from [32] which use keypoints and costs as in [57].

*OpenGM matching* (opengm) is a set of non-rigid point matching problems by [39], now part of the *OpenGM* Benchmark [36]. We use the instances from [32].

The caltech dataset was proposed in [17]. The data available at the project page [16] contains the *mutual projection error* matrix $D = (d_{is,jl})$, lists of possible assignments, and partial ground truth. We reconstructed the dataset from this data. Unary costs are set to zero. Pairwise costs for pairs of possible assignments are set to $c_{is,jl} = -\max(50 - d_{is,jl}, 0)$. We divided the dataset into caltech-small and caltech-large, where all instances with more than 40000 non-zero pairwise costs are considered as large.

*Worm atlas matching* (worms) has the goal to annotate nuclei of *C. elegans*, a famous model organism used in developmental biology, by assigning nuclei names from a known atlas of the organism. A detailed description can be found in [34]. We use the instances obtained from [32] which are originally from [35].

*Worm-to-worm matching* (pairs) directly matches the cell nuclei of individual *C. elegans* worms to each other. The resulting models are much coarser than those of the worms dataset. We consider the same 16 problem instances as [31] using the models from [32].

**Evaluation metrics.** For *fixed-time* performance evaluation [6] we restrict run-time (1, 10, 100 s) and evaluate attained objective values $E$, lower bound $D$ and, for datasets with ground truth available, accuracy *acc*. We also report the number of optimally solved instances per dataset.

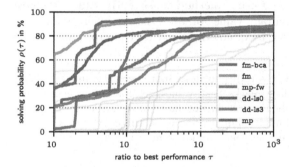

Methods solving the largest number of instances, see $\rho(\tau = 10^3)$, are highlighted in color. Other methods are shown as "ghosts", i.e., unlabeled in gray. fm is the best solver in 65% of all cases, see $\rho(\tau = 1)$. fm-bca outperforms fm when the allowed performance ratio is increased to $\tau \geq 3.7$. Overall, fm-bca solves ≈97% and fm solves ≈95% of all instances. Following are duality-based methods like mp-fw and dd-ls0.

**Fig. 1. Run-time performance profile** [22] across all 451 instances.

For *fixed-target* performance evaluation [6] we measure the time $t_s(p)$ until each solver $s$ solves the problem $p$ within an optimality tolerance of 0.1%. For instances with unknown optimum, we consider the best achieved objective value across all methods as optimum as suggested in [6]. The performance ratio to the best solver is computed by $r_s(p) = \frac{t_s(p)}{\min\{t_s(p):\forall s\}}$. We create a performance profile [6,22] by computing $\rho_s(\tau) = \frac{1}{|P|} \cdot |\{r_s(p) \leq \tau : \forall p\}|$ for each solver $s$ where $|P|$ denotes the total number of problem instances. Intuitively, $\rho_s(\tau)$ is the probability of solver $s$ being at most $\tau$ times slower than the fastest solver.

## 5   Empirical Results

Fixed-time evaluation presented in Table 4 addresses small problem instances, whereas Table 5 addresses mid-size and large problem instances. The performance profile for fixed-target evaluation is presented in Fig. 1. More detailed results are available in the supplement. Results have been obtained by taking the minimum run-time across five trials on an AMD EPYC 7702 2.0 GHz processor. Randomized algorithms were made deterministic by fixing their random seed (fm and fm-bca). We equally treat Matlab and C++ implementations, in spite of the apparent efficiency considerations, because the solution quality of *all* Matlab algorithms is inferior to the C++ techniques, even if run-time is ignored.

For **small problems** we show results for 1 second in Table 4, as the best methods already solve almost all instances to optimality within this time. The best methods on these datasets are fm, fm-bca and dd-ls0. dd-ls3/4 have higher costs per iteration, and require more than 1 s to arrive at the solution quality of dd-ls0. The other dual BCA-based methods perform almost as good on all but the opengm dataset, which seems to be the most difficult dataset amongs the one in Table 4. Apart from fm pure primal heuristics are unable to compete with duality-based techniques. The comparison of the results for house-dense and house-sparse shows that most of the primal heuristics perform much better on sparse problems.

For **larger problems** the most representative times shown in Table 5 are 1, 10 and 100 s, depending on the dataset. Again, the duality-based methods and the fm heuristic lead the table. The fm-bca method consistently attains the best or close to best objective and accuracy values on all datasets, whereas its lower bound is often worse than the lower bounds obtained by the mp-* and dd-ls*

**Table 4. Fixed-time evaluation of small problem instances.** Maximal run-time per problem instance is 1 s. Boldface marks best values, except for accuracy since algorithms do not optimize it explicitly and do not have access to a ground truth. Horizontal line separates purely primal from duality-based methods. Accuracy omitted for opengm as no ground truth available. Dual bounds omitted as most problems are solved optimally.

| | hotel (1s) | | | house-dense (1s) | | | house-sparse (1s) | | | car (1s) | | | motor (1s) | | | opengm (1s) | | caltech-small (1s) | | |
|---|---|---|---|---|---|---|---|---|---|---|---|---|---|---|---|---|---|---|---|---|
| | opt | E | acc | opt | E | acc | opt | E | acc | opt | E | acc | opt | E | acc | opt | E | opt | E | acc |
| fgmd | 0 | —* | | 0 | —* | | 0 | —* | | 0 | —* | | 0 | —* | | 0 | —* | 0 | —* | |
| fm | 97 | -4292 | 100 | **100** | **-3778** | 100 | **100** | **-67** | 100 | 77 | **-69** | 88 | 90 | **-63** | 93 | **100** | -171 | 52 | -8906 | 58 |
| fw | 97 | -4288 | 99 | **100** | **-3778** | 100 | 0 | 0 | 0 | 7 | -63 | 63 | 20 | -58 | 70 | 0 | -152 | 0 | 0 | 0 |
| ga | 0 | 947 | 15 | 0 | 3491 | 8 | **100** | **-67** | 100 | 57 | -68 | 84 | 55 | -62 | 90 | 50 | -167 | 0 | —* | |
| ipfps | 0 | 1051 | 14 | 0 | 3654 | 8 | **100** | **-67** | 100 | 10 | -65 | 80 | 25 | -61 | 85 | 0 | -95 | 19 | **-8983** | 67 |
| ipfpu | 0 | 1062 | 15 | 0 | 3659 | 8 | **100** | **-67** | 100 | 7 | -60 | 69 | 15 | -58 | 77 | 0 | -86 | 10 | -8829 | 62 |
| lsm | 0 | —* | | 0 | —* | | 46 | -65 | 96 | 0 | -51 | 52 | 10 | -52 | 64 | 0 | -67 | 0 | —* | |
| mpm | 43 | -2585 | 78 | 0 | 1260 | 53 | 0 | -60 | 90 | 7 | —* | | 5 | —* | | 0 | -94 | 0 | —* | |
| pm | 0 | 775 | 33 | 0 | 3262 | 18 | 0 | -54 | 83 | 0 | -35 | 23 | 0 | -35 | 32 | 0 | -83 | 0 | -6510 | 51 |
| rrwm | 0 | 744 | 15 | 0 | 2895 | 10 | **100** | **-67** | 100 | 37 | -68 | 82 | 50 | -62 | 89 | 0 | -154 | 5 | —* | |
| sm | 0 | 1086 | 13 | 0 | 3789 | 9 | 96 | **-67** | 100 | 0 | -63 | 76 | 40 | -60 | 87 | 0 | -101 | 0 | -3932 | 36 |
| smac | 1 | -1571 | 61 | 0 | 2817 | 31 | 37 | -44 | 63 | 0 | -52 | 52 | 10 | -52 | 66 | 0 | -84 | 0 | -6196 | 42 |
| dd-ls0 | **100** | **-4293** | 100 | **100** | **-3778** | 100 | **100** | **-67** | 100 | 97 | **-69** | 91 | **100** | **-63** | 97 | 50 | -160 | 43 | -7414 | 58 |
| dd-ls3 | **100** | **-4293** | 100 | **100** | **-3778** | 100 | 96 | -66 | 100 | 47 | -57 | 74 | 65 | -57 | 87 | 0 | -118 | 33 | -6842 | 57 |
| dd-ls4 | 98 | -4291 | 100 | 92 | -3763 | 99 | 18 | -56 | 86 | 3 | -49 | 59 | 30 | -52 | 78 | 0 | -105 | 24 | -6332 | 54 |
| fm-bca | **100** | **-4293** | 100 | **100** | **-3778** | 100 | **100** | **-67** | 100 | 93 | **-69** | 92 | **100** | **-63** | 97 | 75 | -170 | 38 | -8927 | 62 |
| hbp | 97 | —* | | 98 | —* | | **100** | **-67** | 100 | 77 | —* | | 95 | —* | | 0 | —* | 0 | —* | |
| mp | 93 | -4280 | 99 | 99 | -3777 | 100 | **100** | **-67** | 100 | 80 | **-69** | 92 | 90 | **-63** | 96 | 0 | -57 | 14 | -7967 | 59 |
| mp-fw | 99 | -4292 | 100 | **100** | **-3778** | 100 | **100** | **-67** | 100 | 90 | **-69** | 91 | 95 | **-63** | 98 | 0 | -150 | 33 | -8886 | 60 |
| mp-mcf | 90 | -4245 | 98 | 31 | -3542 | 89 | **100** | **-67** | 100 | 87 | **-69** | 91 | 90 | **-63** | 98 | 0 | -57 | 5 | -7882 | 60 |

**opt:** optimally solved instances (%); **E:** average best objective value; **acc:** average accuracy corresponding to best objective (%)
**—*:** method yields no solution for at least one problem instance within the given time interval.

methods. In contrast, most of the primal heuristics as well as hbp fail, and, for brevity, are omitted in Table 5.

Algorithms dd-ls3/4 consider tighter relaxations than dd-ls0, but are slower, therefore lose in the competition on short time intervals. However, they have the ability to attain the best lower bounds given longer runs ($\gg 100$ s).

There is a significant performance gap between the closely related hbp, mp-* and fm-bca methods. Foremost, this is explained by the method for reconstructing the primal solution: The fm algorithm used in the fm-bca solver is solid also as a stand-alone technique, and significantly outperforms the fw and LAP heuristics used in the mp-* algorithms. The branch-and-bound solver used in hbp is quite slow and does not scale well. The second reason for different performance of these methods is the specific BCA algorithm used for the underlying discrete graphical model, c.f. Table 2. According to the recent study [61], which provides a unified treatment of the dual BCA methods for dense[6] graphical models, MPLP ++ performs best, followed by anisotropic diffusion and MPLP as the slowest method. Table 5 shows that there is no solution suitable for every purpose: The speed of fm-bca comes at the price of a looser lower bound. Nonetheless, combining a primal heuristic with a dual optimizer consistently improves upon the results obtained by the heuristic alone. This holds for fm, but the effect is even more pronounced for the fw and LAP heuristics.

**Table 5. Fixed-time evaluation of mid-size and large problem instances.** Only the best performing algorithms are shown. Notation is the same as in Table 4. For each dataset the maximum allowed run-time per instance is given in parentheses. For flow no ground truth is available, so the column *acc* is omitted. For caltech-large and pairs no global optima are known, and the column *opt* is omitted.

| | hotel (1s) | | | house-dense (1s) | | | house-sparse (1s) | | | car (1s) | | | motor (1s) | | | opengm (1s) | | caltech-small (1s) | | |
|---|---|---|---|---|---|---|---|---|---|---|---|---|---|---|---|---|---|---|---|---|
| | opt | E | acc | opt | E | acc | opt | E | acc | opt | E | acc | opt | E | acc | opt | E | opt | E | acc |
| fgmd | 0 | —* | | 0 | —* | | 0 | —* | | 0 | —* | | 0 | —* | | 0 | —* | 0 | —* | |
| fm | 97 | -4292 | 100 | 100 | -3778 | 100 | 100 | -67 | 100 | 77 | -69 | 88 | 90 | -63 | 93 | 100 | -171 | 52 | -8906 | 58 |
| fw | 97 | -4288 | 99 | 100 | -3778 | 100 | 0 | 0 | 0 | 7 | -63 | 63 | 20 | -58 | 70 | 0 | -152 | 0 | 0 | 0 |
| ga | 0 | 947 | 15 | 0 | 3491 | 8 | 100 | -67 | 100 | 57 | -68 | 84 | 55 | -62 | 90 | 50 | -167 | 0 | —* | |
| ipfps | 0 | 1051 | 14 | 0 | 3654 | 8 | 100 | -67 | 100 | 10 | -65 | 80 | 25 | -61 | 85 | 0 | -95 | 19 | **-8983** | 67 |
| ipfpu | 0 | 1062 | 15 | 0 | 3659 | 8 | 100 | -67 | 100 | 7 | -60 | 69 | 15 | -58 | 77 | 0 | -86 | 10 | -8829 | 62 |
| lsm | 0 | —* | | 0 | —* | | 46 | -65 | 96 | 0 | -51 | 52 | 10 | -52 | 64 | 0 | -67 | 0 | —* | |
| mpm | 43 | -2585 | 78 | 0 | 1260 | 53 | 0 | -60 | 90 | 7 | —* | | 5 | —* | | 0 | -94 | 0 | —* | |
| pm | 0 | 775 | 33 | 0 | 3262 | 18 | 0 | -54 | 83 | 0 | -35 | 23 | 0 | -35 | 32 | 0 | -83 | 0 | -6510 | 51 |
| rrwm | 0 | 744 | 15 | 0 | 2895 | 10 | 100 | -67 | 100 | 37 | -68 | 87 | 50 | -62 | 89 | 0 | -154 | 5 | —* | |
| sm | 0 | 1086 | 13 | 0 | 3789 | 9 | 96 | -67 | 100 | 7 | -63 | 76 | 40 | -60 | 87 | 0 | -101 | 0 | -3932 | 36 |
| smac | 1 | -1571 | 61 | 0 | 2817 | 31 | 37 | -44 | 63 | 0 | -52 | 52 | 10 | -52 | 66 | 0 | -84 | 0 | -6196 | 42 |
| dd-ls0 | 100 | -4293 | 100 | 100 | -3778 | 100 | 100 | -67 | 100 | 97 | -69 | 91 | 100 | -63 | 97 | 50 | -160 | 43 | -7414 | 58 |
| dd-ls3 | 100 | -4293 | 100 | 100 | -3778 | 100 | 96 | -66 | 100 | 47 | -57 | 74 | 65 | -57 | 87 | 0 | -118 | 33 | -6842 | 57 |
| dd-ls4 | 98 | -4291 | 100 | 92 | -3763 | 99 | 18 | -56 | 86 | 3 | -49 | 59 | 30 | -52 | 78 | 0 | -105 | 24 | -6332 | 54 |
| fm-bca | 100 | -4293 | 100 | 100 | -3778 | 100 | 100 | -67 | 100 | 93 | -69 | 92 | 100 | -63 | 97 | 75 | -170 | 38 | -8927 | 62 |
| hbp | 97 | —* | | 98 | —* | | 100 | -67 | 100 | 77 | —* | | 95 | —* | | 0 | —* | 0 | —* | |
| mp | 93 | -4280 | 99 | 99 | -3777 | 100 | 100 | -67 | 100 | 80 | -69 | 92 | 90 | -63 | 96 | 0 | -57 | 14 | -7967 | 59 |
| mp-fw | 99 | -4292 | 100 | 100 | -3778 | 100 | 100 | -67 | 100 | 90 | -69 | 91 | 95 | -63 | 98 | 0 | -150 | 33 | -8886 | 60 |
| mp-mcf | 100 | -4245 | 98 | 31 | -3542 | 89 | 100 | -67 | 100 | 87 | -69 | 91 | 90 | -63 | 98 | 0 | -57 | 5 | -7882 | 60 |

opt: optimally solved instances (%); E: average best objective value; acc: average accuracy corresponding to best objective (%)
—*: method yields no solution for at least one problem instance within the given time interval.

---

[6] Most of the considered graphical models are dense in terms of [61].

The fixed-target evaluation in Fig. 1 confirms that the fm and fm-bca method are amongst the best performing solvers. While fm-bca uses fm as primal heuristics with additional dual BCA updates, the overhead of the latter is visible. After increasing the allowed performance ratio for fm-bca to a factor of 3.7, we can expect better solutions than fm alone. Other top performers are duality-based algorithms with mp-fw and dd-ls0 being the closest followers.

## 6    Conclusions

Our evaluation shows that: **(i)** Most instances from the popular datasets hotel, house, car and motor can be solved to optimality in well below a second by several optimization techniques. opengm can also be solved to optimality in under a second, although it turns out to be hard for many methods. Therefore, we argue that *these datasets alone are not sufficient anymore to empirically show efficiency of new algorithms.* The most difficult in our collection are the datasets caltech-* and pairs. For a comprehensive evaluation of new methods more datasets are required. **(ii)** The most popular comparison baselines like ipfp, ga, rrwm, pm, sm, smac, lsm, mpm and fgmd are not competitive, and, therefore, *comparison to these alone should not anymore be considered as sufficient.* **(iii)** The most efficient methods are duality-based techniques equipped with efficient primal heuristics. In particular, the fm/fm-bca method currently attains the best or nearly best objective values for most problem instances in the shortest time. **(iv)** Although being NP-hard in general, the graph matching problem can be often efficiently solved in computer vision practice. For many of the considered datasets, including those with $|\mathcal{L}| > 1000$ and $|\mathcal{V}| > 500$, a reasonable approximate solution can be attained in less than a second.

**Acknowledgements.** This work was supported by the DFG grant SA 2640/2-1 and the Helmholtz Information & Data Science School for Health. We thank the ZIH at TU Dresden for providing high performance computing resources.

## References

1. Adams, W.P., Johnson, T.A.: Improved linear programming-based lower bounds for the quadratic assignment problem. Discrete Math. Theor. Comput. Sci. **16**, 43–77 (1994)
2. Ahuja, R.K., Magnanti, T.L., Orlin, J.B.: Network Flows: Theory. Prentice Hall, Algorithms and Applications (1993)
3. Alhaija, H.A., Sellent, A., Kondermann, D., Rother, C.: GraphFlow - 6D large displacement scene flow via graph matching. In: Proceedings of the DAGM German Conference on Pattern Recognition (2015)
4. Alhaija, H.A., Sellent, A., Kondermann, D., Rother, C.: Graph Matching Problems for GraphFlow - 6D Large Displacement Scene Flow Problem Instances (2018), https://research-explorer.app.ist.ac.at/record/5573
5. Alhaija, H.A., Sellent, A., Kondermann, D., Rother, C.: Project GraphFlow - 6D Large Displacement Scene Flow Images (2018). https://hci.iwr.uni-heidelberg.de/vislearn/research/image-matching/graphflow/

6. Beiranvand, V., Hare, W., Lucet, Y.: Best practices for comparing optimization algorithms. Optimization and Engineering (2017)
7. Bernard, F., Thunberg, J., Gemmar, P., Hertel, F., Husch, A., Goncalves, J.: A solution for multi-alignment by transformation synchronisation. In: Proceedings of the IEEE Conference on Computer Vision and Pattern Recognition (2015)
8. Bertsekas, D.P.: A distributed algorithm for the assignment problem. Lab. for Information and Decision Systems Working Paper, MIT (1979)
9. Bertsekas, D.P.: Nonlinear programming, second edition. Athena scientific (1999)
10. Burkard, R., Dell'Amico, M., Martello, S.: Assignment Problems. SIAM (2009)
11. Burkard, R., Karisch, S., Rendl, F.: QAPLIB - a quadratic assignment problem library. J. Global Optim. **10**, 391–403 (1997)
12. Drezner, Z.: The quadratic assignment problem. In: Laporte, G., Nickel, S., da Gama, F.S. (eds.) Location Science, pp. 345–363. Springer, Cham (2015). https://doi.org/10.1007/978-3-319-13111-5_13
13. Caetano, T.: Data for Learning Graph Matching (2011). https://www.tiberiocaetano.com/data/
14. Caetano, T.S., McAuley, J.J., Cheng, L., Le, Q.V., Smola, A.J.: Learning Graph Matching. IEEE Trans. Pattern Anal. Mach. Intell. **31**, 1048–1058 (2009)
15. Cela, E.: The Quadratic Assignment Problem: Theory and Algorithms, vol. 1. Springer Science & Business Media (2013)
16. Cho, M., Jungmin, L., Kyoung, M.L.: Reweighted Random Walks for Graph Matching: Project Page (2010). https://cv.snu.ac.kr/research/~RRWM/
17. Cho, M., Lee, J., Lee, K.M.: Reweighted random walks for graph matching. In: Daniilidis, K., Maragos, P., Paragios, N. (eds.) ECCV 2010. LNCS, vol. 6315, pp. 492–505. Springer, Heidelberg (2010). https://doi.org/10.1007/978-3-642-15555-0_36
18. Cho, M., Sun, J., Duchenne, O., Ponce, J.: Finding matches in a haystack: a max-pooling strategy for graph matching in the presence of outliers. In: Proceedings of the IEEE Conference on Computer Vision and Pattern Recognition (2014)
19. Cho, M., Sun, J., Duchenne, O., Ponce, J.: Finding matches in a haystack source code (2014). https://www.di.ens.fr/willow/research/maxpoolingmatching/
20. Cour, T.: Graph Matching Toolbox in MATLAB (2010). http://www.timotheecour.com/software/graph_matching/graph_matching.html
21. Cour, T., Srinivasan, P., Shi, J.: Balanced graph matching. In: Advances in Neural Information Processing Systems (2007)
22. Dolan, E.D., Moré, J.J.: Benchmarking optimization software with performance profiles. Mathematical Programming (2002)
23. Everingham, M., Van Gool, L., Williams, C.K., Winn, J., Zisserman, A.: The PASCAL visual object classes challenge 2007 results (2007). http://www.pascal-network.org/challenges/VOC/voc2007/workshop/index.html
24. Foggia, P., Percannella, G., Vento, M.: Graph matching and learning in pattern recognition in the last 10 years. Int. J. Pattern Recogn. Artif. Intelli. **28**, 1450001 (2014)
25. Frank, M., Wolfe, P., et al.: An Algorithm for Quadratic Programming. Naval Research Logistics Quarterly (1956)
26. Globerson, A., Jaakkola, T.S.: Fixing max-product: convergent message passing algorithms for MAP LP-relaxations. In: Advances in Neural Information Processing Systems (2008)
27. Gold, S., Rangarajan, A.: A graduated assignment algorithm for graph matching. IEEE Trans. Pattern Anal. Mach. Intell. **28**, 1450001 (1996)

28. Guignard, M., Kim, S.: Lagrangean decomposition: a model yielding stronger lagrangean bounds. Mathematical Programming (1987)
29. Heimann, T., Meinzer, H.P.: Statistical shape models for 3D medical image segmentation: a review. Med. Image Anal. **13**, 543–563 (2009)
30. Horn, R.A., Johnson, C.R.: Matrix Analysis. Cambridge University Press (2012)
31. Hutschenreiter, L., Haller, S., Feineis, L., Rother, C., Kainmüller, D., Savchynskyy, B.: Fusion moves for graph matching. In: Proceedings of the IEEE International Conference on Computer Vision (2021)
32. Hutschenreiter, L., Haller, S., Feineis, L., Rother, C., Kainmüller, D., Savchynskyy, B.: Fusion moves for graph matching website (2021). https://vislearn.github.io/libmpopt/iccv2021/
33. Jiang, B., Tang, J., Ding, C., Luo, B.: A local sparse model for matching problem. In: Proceedings of the AAAI Conference on Artificial Intelligence (2015)
34. Kainmueller, D., Jug, F., Rother, C., Myers, G.: Active graph matching for automatic joint segmentation and annotation of C. elegans. In: Proceedings of the International Conference on Medical Image Computing and Computer Assisted Intervention (2014)
35. Kainmueller, D., Jug, F., Rother, C., Myers, G.: Graph matching problems for annotating C. elegans (2017). https://doi.org/10.15479/AT:ISTA:57
36. Kappes, J.H., et al.: A comparative study of modern inference techniques for structured discrete energy minimization problems. Int. J. Comput. Vis. **115**, 155–184 (2015)
37. Kappes, J.H., et al.: OpenGM Benchmark (2015). http://hciweb2.iwr.uni-heidelberg.de/opengm/index.php?l0=benchmark
38. Kolmogorov, V.: Feature Correspondence via Graph Matching Source Code (2015). https://pub.ist.ac.at/~vnk/software.html#GRAPH-MATCHING
39. Komodakis, N., Paragios, N.: Beyond Loose LP-Relaxations: Optimizing MRFs by Repairing Cycles. In: Proceedings of the European Conference on Computer Vision (2008)
40. Kosowsky, J., Yuille, A.: The invisible hand algorithm: solving the assignment problem with statistical physics. Neural Networks (1994)
41. Kuhn, H.W.: The Hungarian Method for the Assignment Problem. Naval Research Logistics Quarterly (1955)
42. Lawler, E.L.: The quadratic assignment problem. Manage. Sci. **9**, 586–599 (1963)
43. Leordeanu, M., Hebert, M.: A Spectral Technique for Correspondence Problems Using Pairwise Constraints. In: Proceedings of the IEEE International Conference on Computer Vision (2005)
44. Leordeanu, M.: Efficient methods for graph matching and MAP inference (2013). https://sites.google.com/site/graphmatchingmethods/
45. Leordeanu, M., Hebert, M.: Cars and Motor Models. https://datasets.d2.mpi-inf.mpg.de/discrete-cv-problems/car_motor_graph_matching.zip
46. Leordeanu, M., Hebert, M., Sukthankar, R.: An Integer projected fixed point method for graph matching and MAP inference. In: Advances in Neural Information Processing Systems (2009)
47. Leordeanu, M., Sukthankar, R., Hebert, M.: Unsupervised Learning for Graph Matching. International Journal of Computer Vision (2012)
48. Loiola, E.M., Maia de Abreu, N.M., Boaventura-Netto, P.O., Hahn, P., Querido, T.: An analytical survey for the quadratic assignment problem. Eur. J. Oper. Res. (2007)
49. Ma, J., Jiang, X., Fan, A., Jiang, J., Yan, J.: Image matching from handcrafted to deep features: a survey. Int. J. Comput. Vis. **129**, 23–79 (2021)

50. Pardalos, P.M., Rendl, F., Wolkowicz, H.: The Quadratic Assignment Problem - A Survey and Recent Developments. Quadratic Assignment and Related Problems (1993)
51. Rolínek, M., Swoboda, P., Zietlow, D., Paulus, A., Musil, V., Martius, G.: Deep Graph Matching via Blackbox Differentiation of Combinatorial Solvers. In: Proceedings of the European Conference on Computer Vision (2020)
52. Rother, C., Kolmogorov, V., Lempitsky, V.S., Szummer, M.: Optimizing binary MRFs via extended roof duality. In: Proceedings of the IEEE Conference on Computer Vision and Pattern Recognition (2007)
53. Sahni, S.: Computationally related problems. SIAM J. Comput. **3**, 262–279 (1974)
54. Savchynskyy, B.: Discrete graphical models - an optimization perspective. In: Foundations and Trends in Computer Graphics and Vision (2019)
55. Sun, H., Zhou, W., Fei, M.: A survey on graph matching in computer vision. In: International Congress on Image and Signal Processing. BioMedical Engineering and Informatics (2020)
56. Swoboda, P.: LPMP Source Code (2021). https://github.com/LPMP/LPMP
57. Swoboda, P., Rother, C., Abu Alhaija, H., Kainmuller, D., Savchynskyy, B.: A study of lagrangean decompositions and dual ascent solvers for graph matching. In: Proceedings of the IEEE Conference on Computer Vision and Pattern Recognition (2017)
58. Torresani, L., Kolmogorov, V., Rother, C.: Hotel and House-sparse Models. https://datasets.d2.mpi-inf.mpg.de/discrete_cv_problems/graph_matching_hotel_house.zip
59. Torresani, L., Kolmogorov, V., Rother, C.: A dual decomposition approach to feature correspondence. IEEE Trans. Pattern Anal. Mach. Intell. **35**, 259–271 (2013)
60. Tourani, S., Shekhovtsov, A., Rother, C., Savchynskyy, B.: MPLP++: fast, parallel dual block-coordinate ascent for dense graphical models. In: Ferrari, V., Hebert, M., Sminchisescu, C., Weiss, Y. (eds.) ECCV 2018. LNCS, vol. 11208, pp. 264–281. Springer, Cham (2018). https://doi.org/10.1007/978-3-030-01225-0_16
61. Tourani, S., Shekhovtsov, A., Rother, C., Savchynskyy, B.: Taxonomy of dual block-coordinate ascent methods for discrete energy minimization. In: Proceedings of the Conference on Artifical Intelligence and Statistics (2020)
62. Vogelstein, J.T., et al.: Fast approximate quadratic programming for graph matching. PLOS ONE (2015)
63. Yan, J., Yin, X.C., Lin, W., Deng, C., Zha, H., Yang, X.: A short survey of recent advances in graph matching. In: Proceedings of the ACM International Conference on Multimedia Retrieval (2016)
64. Yilmaz, A., Javed, O., Shah, M.: Object tracking: a survey. ACM Comput. **38**, 13-es (2006)
65. Zass, R., Shashua, A.: Probabilistic graph and hypergraph matching. In: Proceedings of the IEEE Conference on Computer Vision and Pattern Recognition (2008)
66. Zhang, Z.: HungarianBP: pairwise matching through max-weight bipartite belief propagation source code (2016). https://github.com/zzhang1987/HungarianBP
67. Zhang, Z., Shi, Q., McAuley, J., Wei, W., Zhang, Y., van den Hengel, A.: Pairwise matching through max-weight bipartite belief propagation. In: Proceedings of the IEEE Conference on Computer Vision and Pattern Recognition (2016)
68. Zhou, F.: Implementation of Factorized Graph Matching (2018). https://github.com/zhfe99/fgm
69. Zhou, F., la Torre, F.D.: Factorized graph matching. IEEE Trans. Pattern Anal. Mach. Intell. **38**, 1774–1789 (2016)

# Improving Generalization in Federated Learning by Seeking Flat Minima

Debora Caldarola[1(✉)], Barbara Caputo[1,2], and Marco Ciccone[1]

[1] Politecnico di Torino, Turin, Italy
{debora.caldarola,barbara.caputo,marco.ciccone}@polito.it
[2] CINI, Rome, Italy

**Abstract.** Models trained in federated settings often suffer from degraded performances and fail at generalizing, especially when facing heterogeneous scenarios. In this work, we investigate such behavior through the lens of geometry of the loss and Hessian eigenspectrum, linking the model's lack of generalization capacity to the sharpness of the solution. Motivated by prior studies connecting the sharpness of the loss surface and the generalization gap, we show that i) training clients locally with Sharpness-Aware Minimization (SAM) or its adaptive version (ASAM) and ii) averaging stochastic weights (SWA) on the server-side can substantially improve generalization in Federated Learning and help bridging the gap with centralized models. By seeking parameters in neighborhoods having uniform low loss, the model converges towards flatter minima and its generalization significantly improves in both homogeneous and heterogeneous scenarios. Empirical results demonstrate the effectiveness of those optimizers across a variety of benchmark vision datasets (e.g. CIFAR10/100, Landmarks-User-160k, IDDA) and tasks (large scale classification, semantic segmentation, domain generalization).

## 1 Introduction

Federated Learning (FL) [51] is a machine learning framework enabling the training of a prediction model across distributed clients while maintaining their privacy, never disclosing local data. In recent years it has had a notable resonance in the world of computer vision, with applications ranging from large-scale classification [27] to medical imaging [22] to domain generalization [49] and many others [21,43,66,72]. The learning paradigm is based on communication rounds where a sub-sample of clients trains the global model independently on their local datasets, and the produced updates are later aggregated on the server-side. The heterogeneous distribution of clients' data, which is usually non-i.i.d. and unbalanced, poses a major challenge in realistic federated scenarios, leading to degraded

---

D. Caldarola and M. Ciccone—Equal contribution.
Official code: https://github.com/debcaldarola/fedsam.

---

**Supplementary Information** The online version contains supplementary material available at https://doi.org/10.1007/978-3-031-20050-2_38.

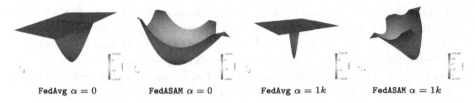

**FedAvg** $\alpha = 0$    **FedASAM** $\alpha = 0$    **FedAvg** $\alpha = 1k$    **FedASAM** $\alpha = 1k$

**Fig. 1.** Cross-entropy loss landscapes of the global model in heterogeneous ($\alpha = 0$) and homogeneous ($\alpha = 1k$) federated scenarios on CIFAR100. When trained with FedAvg, the global model converges towards sharp minima. The sharpness-aware optimizer ASAM significantly smooths the surfaces.

convergence performances [26,45,73]. Locally, the model has only access to a small portion of the data failing to generalize to the rest of the underlying distribution. That contrasts with the standard centralized training, where the learner can uniformly sample from the whole distribution. While many promising works in the literature focus on regularizing the local objective to align the global and local solutions, thus reducing the client drift [1,34,45], less attention has been given to the explicit optimization of the loss function for finding better minima. Several works studied the connection between the sharpness of the loss surface and model's generalization [12,25,30,35,38,41,59], and proposed effective solutions based on the minimization of the derived generalization bound [18,40,69] or on averaging the network's parameters along the trajectory of SGD [29].

In this work, we first analyze the heterogeneous federated scenario to highlight the causes behind the poor generalization of the federated algorithms. We hypothesize during local training the model overfits the current distribution, and the resulting average of the updates is strayed apart from local minima. Thus, the global model is not able to generalize to the overall underlying distribution and has a much slower convergence rate, *i.e.* it needs a much larger number of rounds to reach the performance of the homogeneous setting. To speed up training and reduce the performance gap in the case of non-i.i.d. data, we look at improving the generalization ability of the model. Motivated by recent findings relating the geometry of the loss and the generalization gap [16,32,35,41] and by the achievements in the field of Vision Transformers [12], we analyze the loss landscape in the federated scenario and find out that models converge to sharp minima (Fig. 1), hence the poor generalization. As a solution, we introduce methods of the current literature that explicitly look for flat minima: i) Sharpness-Aware Minimization (SAM) [18] and its adaptive version (ASAM) [40] on the client-side and ii) Stochastic Weight Averaging (SWA) [29] on the server-side. These modifications, albeit simple, surprisingly lead to significant improvements. Their use is already effective if taken individually, but the best performance is obtained when combined. The resultant models exhibit smoother loss surfaces and improved final performance consistently across several vision tasks. To summarize, our main contributions are:

- We analyze the behavior of models trained in heterogeneous and homogeneous federated scenarios by looking at their convergence points, loss surfaces and Hessian eigenvalues, linking the lack in generalization to sharp minima.

- To encourage convergence towards flatter minima, we introduce SAM and ASAM in the local client-side training and SWA in the aggregation of the updates on the server-side. The resultant models show smoother loss landscapes and lower Hessian eigenvalues, with improved generalization capacities.
- We test our approach on multiple vision tasks, *i.e.* small and large scale classification [27], domain generalization [7] and semantic segmentation [11,50].
- We compare our method with strong data augmentations techniques and state-of-the-art FL algorithms, further validating its effectiveness.

## 2    Related Works

We describe here the existing approaches closely related to our work. For a comprehensive analysis of the state of the art in FL, we refer to [33,44,70].

### 2.1    Statistical Heterogeneity in Federated Learning

Federated Learning is a topic in continuous growth and evolution. Aiming at a real-world scenario, the non-i.i.d. and unbalanced distribution of users' data poses a significant challenge. The *statistical heterogeneity* of local datasets leads to unstable and slow convergence, suboptimal performance and poor generalization of the global model [26,27,73]. FedAvg [51] defines the standard optimization method and is based on multiple local SGD [56] steps per round. The server-side aggregation is a weighted average of the clients' updates. This simple approach is effective in homogeneous scenarios. Still, it fails to achieve comparable performance against non-i.i.d. data due to local models straying from each other and leading the central model away from the global optimum [34]. To mitigate the effect of the *client drift*, many works enforce regularization in local optimization so that the local model is not led too far apart from the global one [1,27,34,43,45]. Indeed, averaging models/gradients collected from clients having access to a limited subset of tasks may translate into oscillations of the global model and suboptimal performance on the global distribution [48]. Therefore, other lines of research look at improving the aggregation stage using server-side momentum [26] and adaptive optimizers [55], or aggregating task-specific parameters [8,9,59].

In this work, we attempt to explain the behavior of the model in federated scenarios by looking at the loss surface and convergence minima, which is, in our opinion, a fundamental perspective to fully understand the reasons behind the degradation of heterogeneous performance relative to centralized and homogeneous settings. To this end, *we focus on explicitly seeking parameters in uniformly low-loss neighborhoods, without any additional communication cost*. By encouraging local convergence towards flatter minima, we show that the generalization capacity of the global model is consequently improved. Moreover, thanks to the cyclical average of stochastic weights - accumulated along the trajectory of SGD during rounds on the server-side - broader regions of the weight space are explored, and wider optima are reached. Referring to the terminology introduced by [68], we aim at bridging the *participation gap* introduced by unseen clients distributions. Concurrently, [54] provide a theoretical analysis of SAM in FL, matching the convergence rates of the existing methods. Unlike our work, they do not explicitly focus on the issue of statistical heterogeneity in vision tasks.

## 2.2 Real-World Vision Scenarios in Federated Learning

Research on FL has mainly focused on algorithmic aspects, often overlooking its application to real scenarios and vision tasks. Here, we perform an analysis of the following real-world settings.

*Large-Scale Classification.* Synthetic federated datasets for classification tasks are usually limited in size and do not offer a faithful representation of reality in the data distribution across clients [27]. [27] addresses such issue by adapting the large-scale Google Landmarks v2 [64] to the federated context, using authorship information. We employ the resulting *Landmarks-User-160k* in our experiments.

*Semantic Segmentation.* A crucial task for real-world applications [19,53], *e.g.*autonomous driving [58,61], is Semantic Segmentation (SS), which assigns each image pixel to a known category. Most studies of SS in FL focus on medical imaging applications and propose ad hoc techniques to safeguard the patients' privacy [6,46,57,67]. Differently, [52] focuses on object segmentation using prototypical representations. A recently studied application is FL in autonomous driving, motivated by the large amount of privacy-protected data collected by self-driving cars: the authors of [17] propose a new benchmark for analyzing such a scenario, FedDrive. None of those works study the relation between loss landscape and convergence minima of the proposed solution. We apply our approach to the FedDrive benchmark and prove its efficacy in addressing the federated SS task.

*Domain Generalization.* When it comes to image data collected from devices around the world, it is realistic to assume there may be different *domains* resulting from the several acquisition devices, light, weather conditions, noise, or viewpoints. With the rising development of FL and the privacy concerns, the problem of Domain Generalization (DG) [7] in a federated setting becomes crucial. DG aims to learn a domain-agnostic model capable of satisfying performances on unseen domains, and its application to federated scenarios is still poorly studied. For instance, [49,62] focus on domain shifts deriving from equipment in the medical field, while [17] analyzes the effects of changing landscapes and weather conditions in the setting of autonomous driving. We show that our approach improves generalization to unseen domains both in classification and SS tasks.

## 2.3 Flat Minima and Generalization

To understand neural networks' generalization, several theoretical and empirical studies analyze its relationship with the geometry of the loss surface [16,25,32,35,41], connecting sharp minima with poor generalization. *"Flatness"* [25] is defined as the dimension of the region connected around the minimum in which the training loss remains low. Interestingly, it has been shown [32] that sharpness-based measures highly correlate with generalization performance. The above studies lead to the introduction of Sharpness-Aware Minimization (SAM) [18] which explicitly seeks flatter minima and smoother loss surfaces through a simultaneous minimization of loss sharpness and value during training. As highlighted by [40], SAM is sensitive to parameter re-scaling, weakening the connection between loss sharpness and generalization gap. ASAM [40] solves such issue introducing the concept of adaptive sharpness. Encouraged by their effectiveness across a variety of architectures and tasks [4,12], we ask whether SAM and ASAM can improve generalization in FL as well and find it effective even in the most difficult scenarios. In addition, [15,20] show that local optima found by SGD are connected through a path of near constant loss and that ensambling those points in the weight space leads to high performing networks. Building upon these insights, [29] proposes to average the points traversed by SGD to improve generalization and indeed show the model converges towards wider optima. We modify this approach for FL and use it to cyclically ensemble the models obtained with FedAvg on the server side.

## 3    Behind the Curtain of Heterogeneous FL

### 3.1    Federated Learning: Overview

The standard federated framework is based on a central server exchanging messages with $K$ distributed clients. Each device $k$ has access to a privacy-protected dataset $\mathcal{D}_k$ made of $N_k$ images belonging to the input space $\mathcal{X}$. The goal is to learn a global model $f_\theta$ parametrized by $\theta \in \mathcal{W} \subseteq \mathbb{R}^d$, where $f_\theta : \mathcal{X} \to \mathcal{Y}$ when solving the classification task and $f_\theta : \mathcal{X} \to \mathcal{Y}^{N_p}$ in semantic segmentation, with $\mathcal{Y}$ being the output space and $N_p$ the total number of pixels of each image. We assume the structure of $\theta$ to be identical across all devices. The learning procedure spans over $T$ communications rounds, during which a subset of clients $\mathcal{C}$ receives the current model parameters $\theta^t$ with $t \in [T]$ and trains it on $\mathcal{D}_k \forall k \in \mathcal{C}$, minimizing a local loss function $\mathcal{L}_k(\theta^t) : \mathcal{W} \times \mathcal{X} \times \mathcal{Y} \to \mathbb{R}_+$. In FedAvg [51], the global model is updated as a weighted average of the clients' updates $\theta_k^t$, aiming at solving the global objective $\arg\min_{\theta \in \mathbb{R}^d} \frac{1}{N} \sum_{k \in \mathcal{C}} N_k \mathcal{L}_k(\theta)$, with $N = \sum_{k \in \mathcal{C}} N_k$ being the total training images. In particular, from the generalization perspective - defined $\mathcal{D} \triangleq \bigcup_{k \in [K]} \mathcal{D}_k$ the overall clients' data, $\mathfrak{D}$ its distribution and $\mathcal{L}_\mathcal{D} = 1/\sum_k N_k \sum_{k \in [K]} N_k \mathcal{L}_k(\theta)$ the training loss - we aim at learning a model having low population loss $\mathcal{L}_\mathfrak{D}(\theta) \triangleq \mathbb{E}_{(x,y) \sim \mathfrak{D}} [\mathbb{E}_\mathfrak{D}[\mathcal{L}_k(y, f(x, \theta))]]$ [68]. The difference between the population and training losses defines the *generalization gap*, *i.e.* the ability of the model to generalize to unseen data [18].

In realistic scenarios, given two clients $i$ and $j$, $\mathcal{D}_i$ likely follows a different distribution than $\mathcal{D}_j$, *i.e.* $\mathfrak{D}_i \neq \mathfrak{D}_j$, and the loss $\mathcal{L}_i(\theta) \forall i \in [K]$ is typically non-convex in $\theta$. The loss landscape comprehends a multiplicity of local minima leading to models with different generalization performance, *i.e.* significantly different values of $\mathcal{L}_\mathfrak{D}(\theta)$ [18]. Moreover, at each round, the model is likely not to see the entire distribution, further widening the generalization gap [23,24].

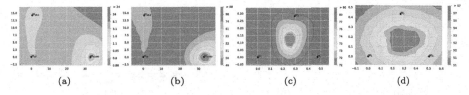

(a)    (b)    (c)    (d)

**Fig. 2. Left**: CNN convergence points in distinct federated scenarios with $\alpha \in [0, 0.5, 1k]$ on CIFAR100. Please refer to Appendix C for implementation details. **(a)** Train loss surface showing the weights obtained at convergence. **(b)** Test error surface of the same models. **Right**: Test error surfaces computed on CIFAR100 using three distinct local models after training. **(c)** When $\alpha = 0$, the local models are not able to generalize to the overall data distribution, being too specialized on the local data. **(d)** When $\alpha = 1k$, the resulting models are connected through a low-loss region.

## 3.2 Where Heterogeneous FL Fails at Generalizing

In order to fully understand the behavior of a model trained in a heterogeneous federated scenario, we perform a thorough empirical analysis from different perspectives. Our experimental setup replicates that proposed by [27] both as regards the dataset and the network. The CIFAR100 dataset [39], widely used as benchmark in FL, is split between 100 clients, following a Dirichlet distribution with concentration parameter $\alpha$. To replicate a heterogeneous scenario, we choose $\alpha \in \{0, 0.5\}$, while $\alpha$ is set to 1000 for the homogeneous one. The model is trained over $20k$ rounds. Fore more details, please refer to Appendix C.

*Model Behavior in Heterogeneous and Homogeneous Scenarios.* In Fig. 3, we compare the training trends in centralized, homogeneous and heterogeneous federated settings: in the latter, not only is the trend much noisier and more unstable, but the performance gap is considerable. Consequently, we question the causes of such behavior. First of all, we wonder if the heterogeneous distribution of the data totally inhibits the model from achieving comparable performances: we find it is only a matter of rounds, *i.e.* with a much larger round budget - 10 times larger in our case - the model reaches convergence (Fig. 3). So it becomes obvious the training is somehow slowed down and there is room for improvement. This hypothesis is further validated by the convergence points of the models trained in different settings (Fig. 2): when $\alpha = 1k$ a low-loss region is reached at the end of training, while the same does not happen with lower values of $\alpha$, meaning that local minima are still to be found. Moreover, the shift between the train and test surfaces suggests us the model trained in the heterogeneous setting ($\alpha = 0$) is unable to generalize well to unseen data, finding itself in a high-loss region [29]. By analyzing the model behavior, we discover that shifts in client data distribution lead to numerous fluctuations in learning, *i.e.* at each round the model focuses on a subset of the just seen tasks and is unable to generalize to the previously learned ones. This phenomenon is also known as *catastrophic interference* of neural networks [37] and is typical of the world of multitask learning [10,60]. Figure 3 highlights this by comparing the accuracy of the global model on the clients' data and the test set when $\alpha = 0$ and $\alpha = 1k$. In the first case, at each round the model achieves very high performances on one

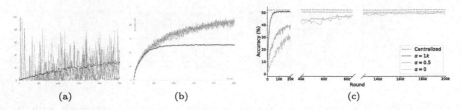

(a)                    (b)                              (c)

**Fig. 3.** CIFAR100 Accuracy trends. **Left**: Global model on local distributions with **(a)** $\alpha = 0$ and **(b)** $1k$ @ $20k$ rounds. Each color represents a local distribution (*i.e.* one class for $\alpha = 0$). **(c)**: $\alpha \in \{0, 0.5, 1k\}$ with necessary rounds to reach convergence.

class but forgets about the others and this behavior is only slightly attenuated as the training continues. In the homogeneous scenario, on the other hand, the model behaves very similarly on each client and convergence is easily reached, giving way to overfitting as the number of rounds increases.

We analyze the clients' local training for further insights from the characteristics of the updated models. By plotting the position of the weights in the loss landscape after training, we find the models easily overfit the local data distribution (Fig. 2): when tested on the test set, the clients' updates are positioned in very high-error regions and as a result the global model moves away from the minimum, meaning the clients specialize too much on their own data and are not able to generalize to the overall underlying distribution. Moreover, Fig. 2 highlights another relevant issue: models trained on homogeneous distributions are connected through a path of low error and can therefore be ensambled to obtain a more meaningful representation [20], but the same does not hold when $\alpha = 0$, where the models are situated in different loss-value regions. Therefore, FedAvg averages models that are too far apart to lead to a meaningful result.

***Federated Training Converges to Sharp Minima.*** Many works tried to account for this difficulty arising in federated scenarios by enforcing regularization in local optimization not to lead the local model too far apart from the global one [1,27,34,43,45], or by using momentum on the server-side [26], or learning task-specific parameters keeping distinct models on the server-side [8,9,59]. To the best of our knowledge, this is the first work addressing such behavior by looking at the loss landscape. Inspired by a recent trend in Deep Learning connecting the geometry of the loss and the generalization gap [16,29,32,35,40,41], we investigate the geometry of the loss surface of models trained in non-i.i.d. scenarios with the intention of understanding whether sharp minima may cause the lack of generalization in FL. Following [41], we plot the loss surfaces obtained with models trained in a heterogeneous and in a homogeneous scenario (Fig. 1) showing that both converge to sharp regions, providing a plausible explanation for the highlighted lack of generalization. Additionally, [35] characterizes flatness through the eigenvalues of the Hessian: the dominant eigenvalue $\lambda_{max}$ evaluates the worst-case landscape curvature, *i.e.* the larger $\lambda_{max}$ the greater the change in loss in that direction and the steeper the minimum. Hence, we compute the Hessian eigenspectrum (first 50 eigenvalues) using the power iteration mode and analyze it both from the global and local perspectives (Fig. 4 and 5). Table 1

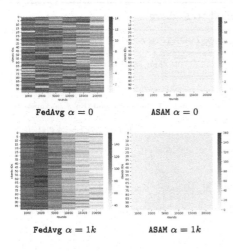

**Fig. 4.** $\lambda^k_{max}$ for each client $k$ as rounds pass.

**Table 1.** CIFAR100 Hessian eigenvalues.

| Algorithm | $\lambda_{max}$ | | $\lambda_{max}/\lambda_5$ | |
|---|---|---|---|---|
| | $\alpha = 0$ | $\alpha = 1k$ | $\alpha = 0$ | $\alpha = 1k$ |
| FedAvg E=1 | 93.46 | 106.14 | 2.00 | 1.31 |
| FedAvg E=2 | 110.62 | 118.35 | 2.32 | 1.30 |
| FedSAM | 70.29 | 51.28 | **1.79** | 1.48 |
| FedASAM | **30.11** | **20.19** | 1.80 | **1.27** |
| FedAvg + SWA | 97.24 | 120.02 | 1.49 | 1.39 |
| FedSAM + SWA | 73.16 | 54.20 | 1.56 | 1.61 |
| FedASAM + SWA | **24.57** | 20.49 | **1.51** | **1.30** |

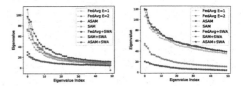

**Fig. 5.** Hessian eigenspectra of the global model with $\alpha \in \{0, 1k\}$.

reports the values of $\lambda_{max}$ and the ratio $\lambda_{max}/\lambda_5$, commonly used as a proxy for sharpness [31], as the heterogeneity varies. As expected, $\lambda_{max}$ is large in all settings when using `FedAvg`, implying that such method leads the model towards sharp minima regardless of the data distribution, confirming what was noted in the loss landscapes. As for the client-side analysis, we compute the value of $\lambda^k_{max}$ using the locally updated parameters $\theta^t_k$ on the $k$-th device's data $\mathcal{D}_k \forall t \in [T]$. Comparing the i.i.d. and non-i.i.d. settings, we note i) the local values of $\lambda_{max}$ are much lower if $\alpha = 0$, *i.e.*the clients locally reach wide minima (low Hessian maximum eigenvalue, $\lambda^k_{max} \leq 14$) due to the simplicity of the learned task, *i.e.*a narrow subset of the classes, but the average of the distinct updates drives the model towards sharper minima (high Hessian eigenvalues of the global model, $\lambda_{max} \simeq 94$). ii) When $\alpha \in \{0.5, 1k\}$, $\lambda_{max}$ decreases as the rounds pass, *i.e.*the global model is moving towards regions with lower curvature, while this is not as evident in the heterogeneous setting. Motivated by these results, we believe that introducing an explicit search for flatter minima can help the model generalize.

## 4   Seeking Flat Minima in Federated Learning

Common first-order optimizers (*e.g.* SGD [56], Adam [36]) are usually non-robust to unseen data distributions [12], since they only aim at minimizing the training loss $\mathcal{L}_\mathcal{D}$, without looking at higher-order information correlating with generalization (*e.g.* curvature). The federated scenario exacerbates such behavior due to its inherent statistical heterogeneity, resulting in sharp minima and poor generalization. We hypothesize that encouraging the local model to converge towards flatter neighborhoods may help bridging the generalization gap. To this end, we introduce sharpness-aware minimizers, namely `SAM` [18] and `ASAM` [40], on the

---

**Algorithm 1.** `SAM/ASAM` and `SWA` applied to `FedAvg`

---

**Require:** Initial random model $f_\theta^0$, $K$ clients, $T$ rounds, learning rates $\gamma_1, \gamma_2$, neighborhood size $\rho > 0$, $\eta > 0$, batch size $|\mathcal{B}|$, local epochs $E$, cycle length $c$

1: **for** each round $t = 0$ to $T - 1$ **do**
2:    **if** $t = 0.75 * T$ **then**                   ▷ Apply `SWA` from 75% of training onwards
3:       $\theta_{\text{SWA}} \leftarrow \theta^t$                               ▷ Initialize `SWA` model
4:    **end if**
5:    **if** $t \geq 0.75 * T$ **then**
6:       $\gamma = \gamma(t)$                       ▷ Compute LR for the round (Eq. 7 in Appendix)
7:    **end if**
8:    Subsample a set $\mathcal{C}$ of clients
9:    **for** each client $k$ in $\mathcal{C}$ in parallel **do**          ▷ Iterate over subset $\mathcal{C}$ of clients
10:       $\theta_{k,0}^{t+1} \leftarrow \theta^t$
11:       **for** $e = 0$ to $E - 1$ **do**
12:          **for** $i = 0$ to $N_k/|\mathcal{B}|$ **do**
13:             Compute gradient $\nabla_\theta \mathcal{L}_\mathcal{B}(\theta_{k,i}^{t+1})$ on batch $\mathcal{B}$ from $\mathcal{D}_k$
14:             Compute $\hat\epsilon(\theta_{k,i}^{t+1}) = \rho \nabla_\theta \mathcal{L}_\mathcal{B}(\theta_{k,i}^{t+1})/||\nabla_\theta \mathcal{L}_\mathcal{B}(\theta_{k,i}^{t+1})||_2 =: \hat\epsilon(\theta)$   ▷ Solve local maximization (Eq. 3)
15:             $\theta_{k,i+1}^{t+1} \leftarrow \theta_{k,i}^{t+1} - \gamma\left(\nabla_\theta \mathcal{L}_\mathcal{B}(\theta_{k,i}^{t+1})\big|_{\theta+\hat\epsilon(\theta)}\right)$   ▷ Local update with sharpness-aware gradient (Eq. 4)
16:          **end for**
17:       **end for**
18:       Send $\theta_k^{t+1}$ to the server
19:    **end for**
20:    $\theta^{t+1} \leftarrow \frac{1}{\sum_{k\in\mathcal{C}} N_k} \sum_{k\in\mathcal{C}} N_k \theta_k^{t+1}$                   ▷ `FedAvg`
21:    **if** $t \geq 0.75 * T$ and $\text{mod}(t, c) = 0$ **then**             ▷ End of cycle
22:       $n_{\text{models}} \leftarrow t/c$
23:       $\theta_{\text{SWA}} \leftarrow \frac{\theta_{\text{SWA}} \cdot n_{\text{models}} + \theta^{t+1}}{n_{\text{models}} + 1}$                  ▷ Update `SWA` average (Eq. 8)
24:    **end if**
25: **end for**

---

client-side during local training, and Stochastic Weight Averaging [29] on the server-side after the aggregation, adapting the scenario of [29] to FL. By minimizing the sharpness of the loss surface and the generalization gap, the local models are more robust towards unseen data distributions and, when averaged, build a more solid central model. Defined the *sharpness* of a training loss $\mathcal{L}_\mathcal{D}$ as $\max_{||\epsilon||_p \leq \rho} \mathcal{L}_\mathcal{D}(\theta + \epsilon) - \mathcal{L}_\mathcal{D}(\theta)$, with $\rho$ being the neighborhood size and $p \in [1, \infty)$, SAM aims at minimizing it by solving $\min_{\theta\in\mathbb{R}^d} \max_{||\epsilon||_p \leq \rho} \mathcal{L}_\mathcal{D}(\theta + \epsilon) + \lambda ||\theta||_2^2$. SWA averages weights proposed by SGD, while using a learning rate schedule to explore regions of the weight space corresponding to high performing networks. For a detailed explanation of SAM, ASAM and SWA we refer the reader to Appendix A. Algorithm 1 sums up the details of our approach.

## 5 Experiments

In this Section, we show the effectiveness of SAM, ASAM and SWA in federated scenarios when addressing tasks of image classification (Sect. 5.1), large-scale classification, SS and DG (Sect. 5.2). Their strength indeed lies in finding flatter minima (Sect. 5.1), which consequently help the model to generalize especially in the heterogeneous scenario. We compare our method with algorithms proper of the FL literature and strong data augmentations (Sect. 5.1), commonly used to improve generalization in DL, further validating the efficacy of our proposal. We refer to App. C for implementation details and App. E for the ablation studies.

**Table 2.** FedSAM, FedASAM and SWA on CIFAR100 and CIFAR10.

| Algorithm | $\alpha = 0$ | | | $\alpha = 0.5/0.05$ | | | $\alpha = 1000/100$ | | |
|---|---|---|---|---|---|---|---|---|---|
| | 5cl | 10cl | 20cl | 5cl | 10cl | 20cl | 5cl | 10cl | 20cl |
| **CIFAR100** | | | | | | | | | |
| FedAvg E=1 | 30.25 | 36.74 | 38.59 | 40.43 | 41.27 | 42.17 | 49.92 | 50.25 | 50.66 |
| FedAvg E=2 | 24.94 | 31.81 | 35.18 | 38.21 | 39.59 | 40.94 | 48.72 | 48.64 | 48.45 |
| FedSAM | 31.04 | 36.93 | 38.56 | 44.73 | 44.84 | 46.05 | 54.01 | 53.39 | 53.97 |
| FedASAM | 36.04 | 39.76 | 40.81 | 45.61 | 46.58 | 47.78 | **54.81** | **54.97** | **54.50** |
| FedAvg + SWA | 39.34 | 39.74 | 39.85 | 43.90 | 44.02 | 42.09 | 50.98 | 50.87 | 50.92 |
| FedSAM + SWA | 39.30 | 39.51 | 39.24 | 47.96 | 46.76 | 46.47 | **53.90** | 53.67 | **54.36** |
| FedASAM + SWA | **42.01** | **42.64** | **41.62** | **49.17** | **48.72** | **48.27** | 53.86 | **54.79** | 54.10 |
| **CIFAR10** | | | | | | | | | |
| FedAvg E=1 | 65.00 | 65.54 | 68.52 | 69.24 | 72.50 | 73.07 | 84.46 | 84.50 | 84.59 |
| FedAvg E=2 | 61.49 | 62.22 | 66.36 | 69.23 | 69.77 | 73.48 | 83.93 | 84.10 | 84.21 |
| FedSAM | 70.16 | 71.09 | 72.90 | 73.52 | 74.81 | 76.04 | 84.58 | 84.67 | **84.82** |
| FedASAM | **73.66** | **74.10** | **76.09** | 75.61 | 76.22 | **76.98** | 84.77 | 84.72 | 84.75 |
| FedAvg + SWA | 69.71 | 69.54 | 70.19 | 73.48 | 72.80 | 73.81 | 84.35 | 84.32 | 84.47 |
| FedSAM + SWA | 74.97 | 73.73 | 73.06 | **76.61** | 75.84 | 76.22 | 84.23 | 84.37 | 84.63 |
| FedASAM + SWA | **76.44** | **75.51** | **76.36** | 76.12 | **76.16** | 76.86 | **84.88** | **84.80** | 84.79 |

## 5.1 The Effectiveness of the Search for Flat Minima in FL

In Sect. 3.2, we have shown that, given a fixed number of rounds, FL models trained in heterogeneous settings present a considerable performance gap compared to their homogeneous counterparts. Indeed, the gap between the two scenarios can be significant with a difference of up to 20% points (Table 2). We identify the clients' overspecialization on local data as one of the causes of the poor generalization of the global model to the underlying training distribution. We confirm this by showing the model converges to sharp minima, correlated to a poor generalization capacity. In Table 2, we show that explicitly optimizing for flat minima in both the local training and the server-side aggregation does help improving performances, with evident benefits especially in heterogeneous scenarios. We test SAM, ASAM and their combination with SWA on the federated CIFAR10 and CIFAR100 [26,27,39] with several levels of heterogeneity ($\alpha \in \{0, 0.05, 100\}$ for CIFAR10 and $\alpha \in \{0, 0.5, 1k\}$ for CIFAR100) and clients participation ($K \in \{5, 10, 20\}$, i.e. 5%, 10%, 20%). As for CIFAR100, we additionally test our approach on the setting proposed by [55], later referred to as CIFAR100-PAM, where the splits reflect the "coarse" and "fine" label structure proper of the dataset. Since both SAM and ASAM perform a step of gradient ascent and one of gradient descent for each iteration, they should be compared with FedAvg with 2 local epochs. However, the results show FedAvg with $E = 2$ suffers even more from statistical heterogeneity, so we will compare our baseline with the better-performing FedAvg with $E = 1$. Our experiments reveal that applying ASAM to FedAvg leads to the best accuracies with a gain of $+6\%$ and $+8\%$ points respectively on CIFAR100 and CIFAR10 in the most challenging scenario, i.e. $\alpha = 0$ and 5 clients per round. This gain is further improved by FedASAM + SWA with a corresponding increase of $+12\%$ and $+11.5\%$. The stability introduced by SWA especially helps with lower clients participation, where the trend is noisier. Our ablation studies (Appendix E.3) prove the boost given by SWA is mainly related to the average of the stochastic weights, rather than the cycling learning rate. Table 3 shows the results on CIFAR100-PAM with ResNet18: here SAM and SAM + SWA help more than ASAM.

**Table 3.** Accuracy results on Cifar100-PAM with ResNet18.

| Algorithm | Aug | E = 1 | | | | | | E = 2 | | | | | |
|---|---|---|---|---|---|---|---|---|---|---|---|---|---|
| | | 10 clients | | | 20 clients | | | 10 clients | | | 20 clients | | |
| | | @5k | @10k | w/ SWA | @5k | @10k | w/ SWA | @5k | @10k | w/ SWA | @5k | @10k | w/ SWA |
| FedAvg | | 46.60 | 47.03 | 52.70 | 46.51 | 45.83 | 50.28 | 44.58 | 43.90 | 51.10 | 43.31 | 42.88 | 47.95 |
| FedSAM | | 50.71 | **53.10** | **55.44** | 52.96 | 53.41 | **54.67** | **52.36** | 52.04 | 55.23 | 51.41 | 51.35 | 53.41 |
| FedASAM | | 49.31 | 51.10 | 54.25 | 47.21 | **53.50** | 54.29 | 49.03 | 49.33 | 53.01 | **53.88** | 52.94 | 54.18 |
| FedAvg | Mixup | 43.47 | 49.25 | 56.71 | 50.33 | 49.89 | 55.74 | **44.76** | 46.44 | 57.15 | 47.10 | 47.59 | 54.40 |
| FedSAM | Mixup | 42.83 | **51.92** | 53.96 | 49.66 | **55.77** | 57.70 | 42.17 | 51.04 | 56.54 | **53.50** | 54.75 | **58.88** |
| FedASAM | Mixup | 43.13 | 51.09 | 56.31 | 50.51 | 52.62 | 56.89 | **44.74** | 50.14 | **58.31** | 49.87 | 50.87 | 55.86 |
| FedAvg | Cutout | 48.64 | 48.59 | 55.40 | 47.00 | 46.96 | 51.70 | 45.19 | 45.46 | 55.40 | 44.68 | 44.25 | 49.39 |
| FedSAM | Cutout | 48.28 | 53.53 | 57.25 | 52.06 | **54.37** | **56.70** | **49.39** | 51.88 | **57.32** | **52.16** | 52.37 | 55.45 |
| FedASAM | Cutout | 47.52 | **52.13** | 57.01 | 50.01 | 50.66 | 53.54 | 48.99 | 50.09 | 55.77 | 48.48 | 48.77 | 52.00 |

*ASAM and SWA Lead to Flatter Minima in FL.* We extend the analysis on the loss landscape and the Hessian eigenspectrum to the models trained with FedSAM, FedASAM and SWA. As expected, both the loss surfaces (Fig. 1) and the Hessian spectra (Fig. 5) indicate us those methods indeed help converging towards flatter minima. The value of $\lambda_{max}$ goes from 93.5 with FedAvg to 70.3 with FedSAM to 30.1 with FedASAM in the most heterogeneous setting (Table 1). The result is further improved by FedASAM + SWA, obtaining $\lambda_{max} = 24.6$. We notice there is a strict correspondence between the best $\lambda_{max}$ and the best ratio $\lambda_{max}/\lambda_5$. Even if the maximum eigenvalue resulting with FedAvg + SWA and FedSAM + SWA is higher than the respective one without SWA, the corresponding lower ratio $\lambda_{max}/\lambda_5$ actually tells us the bulk of the spectrum lies in a lower curvature region [18], proving the effectiveness of SWA. Looking at ASAM's behavior from each client's perspective (Fig. 4), flat minima are achieved from the very beginning of the training and that reflects positively on the model's performance.

*ASAM and SWA Enable Strong Data Augmentations in FL.* Data augmentations usually play a key role in the performance of a neural network and its ability to generalize [5, 65, 71], but their design often requires domain expertise and greater computational capabilities, two elements not necessarily present in a federated context. In Table 3 and 4, we distinctly apply Mixup [71] and Cutout [14] on Cifar100-PAM and Cifar100 (Cifar10 in Appendix F.2). Surprisingly, both lead to worse performances across all algorithms, so instead of helping the model to generalize, they further slow down training. When combined with our methods, the performance improves in the heterogeneous scenarios w.r.t. the corresponding baseline (FedAvg + data augmentation) and SWA brings a significant boost, enabling the use of data augmentation techniques in FL.

*Heterogeneous FL Benefits Even More from Flat Minima.* Given the marked improvement brought by SAM, ASAM and their combination with SWA, one might wonder if this simply reflects the gains achieved in the centralized scenario. In Table 5, we prove the positive gap obtained in the heterogeneous federated scenario is larger than the centralized one, showing those approaches are actually helping the training. We also note that while Cutout and Mixup improve the performances in the centralized setting, they do not help in FL, where they achieve a final accuracy worse than FedAvg (Appendix F.1 for $\alpha \in \{0.5, 1k\}$).

**Table 4.** FedAvg, SAM, ASAM and SWA w/ strong data augmentations (Mixup, Cutout).

|  | Algorithm | SWA | Aug | $\alpha = 0$ | | | $\alpha = 0.5/0.05$ | | | $\alpha = 1000/100$ | | |
|---|---|---|---|---|---|---|---|---|---|---|---|---|
|  |  |  |  | 5cl | 10cl | 20cl | 5cl | 10cl | 20cl | 5cl | 10cl | 20cl |
| CIFAR100 | FedAvg | ✗ | Mixup | 29.91 | 33.67 | 35.67 | 35.10 | 37.80 | 39.34 | 55.34 | **55.81** | **55.98** |
|  | FedSAM | ✗ |  | 30.46 | 34.10 | 35.89 | 38.76 | 40.31 | 42.03 | 54.21 | 54.94 | 55.24 |
|  | FedASAM | ✗ |  | 34.04 | 36.82 | 36.97 | 40.71 | 42.24 | **44.45** | 49.75 | 49.87 | 49.68 |
|  | FedAvg | ✓ |  | 35.56 | 36.07 | 36.08 | 39.21 | 39.22 | 38.31 | **55.43** | 55.37 | 55.39 |
|  | FedSAM | ✓ |  | 35.62 | 36.25 | 35.66 | 42.13 | 41.95 | 42.03 | 52.9 | 53.14 | 53.48 |
|  | FedASAM | ✓ |  | **40.08** | **38.74** | **37.47** | **44.53** | **43.97** | 44.22 | 46.97 | 47.24 | 46.93 |
|  | FedAvg | ✗ | Cutout | 24.24 | 31.55 | 32.44 | 37.72 | 38.45 | 39.48 | 53.48 | 53.83 | 52.90 |
|  | FedSAM | ✗ |  | 23.51 | 30.92 | 33.12 | 40.33 | 40.31 | 42.58 | **54.27** | **54.75** | **54.76** |
|  | FedASAM | ✗ |  | 30.05 | 33.62 | 34.51 | 41.86 | 41.84 | 43.33 | 51.88 | 51.78 | 53.03 |
|  | FedAvg | ✓ |  | 33.65 | 34.40 | 35.03 | 40.43 | 40.12 | 39.32 | 53.87 | 54.09 | 52.75 |
|  | FedSAM | ✓ |  | 34.00 | 34.08 | 34.26 | 43.09 | 42.81 | 42.85 | 53.78 | 54.28 | 53.93 |
|  | FedASAM | ✓ |  | **39.30** | **37.46** | **36.27** | **44.76** | **43.48** | **43.95** | 50.00 | 49.65 | 50.81 |

**Table 5.** Comparison of improvements (%) in centralized and heterogeneous federated scenarios ($\alpha = 0$, 5 clients) on CIFAR100, computed w.r.t. the reference at the bottom.

| Algorithm | Accuracy | | Absolute Improvement | | Relative Improvement | |
|---|---|---|---|---|---|---|
|  | Centr. | $\alpha = 0$ | Centr. | $\alpha = 0$ | Centr. | $\alpha = 0$ |
| SAM | 55.22 | 31.04 | +3.02 | +0.79 | +5.79 | +2.61 |
| ASAM | 55.66 | 36.04 | +3.46 | +5.79 | +6.63 | +19.14 |
| SWA | 52.72 | 39.34 | +0.52 | +9.09 | +1.00 | +30.05 |
| SAM + SWA | 55.75 | 39.30 | +0.55 | +9.05 | +1.06 | +29.92 |
| ASAM + SWA | 55.96 | 42.01 | +3.76 | +11.76 | +7.20 | +38.88 |
| Mixup | 58.01 | 29.91 | +5.81 | -0.34 | +11.13 | -1.12 |
| Cutout | 55.30 | 24.24 | +3.10 | -6.01 | +5.94 | -19.87 |

Centralized: **52.20** - FedAvg: **30.25**

*Comparison with FL SOTA.* We compare our method with FedProx [45], SCAFFOLD [34], FedAvgM [26], FedDyn [1] and AdaBest [63], both on their own and combined with SAM, ASAM and SWA (Table 6). FedProx adds a proximal term to the local objective and, as expected [42,63], does not bring any notable improvement. SCAFFOLD uses control variates to reduce the client drift, exchanging twice the parameters at each round. While performing on par with FedAvg in the homogeneous scenario (84.5% on CIFAR10 and 51.9% on CIFAR100), its performance is heavily affected by the data statistical heterogeneity. The same happens for FedAvgM. FedDyn dynamically aligns global and local stationary points and, as highlighted by [63], is prone to parameters explosion: while it achieves good results on the simpler CIFAR10, it requires heavy gradient clipping and is unable to reach the end of training on CIFAR100. As a solution, AdaBest is proposed, exceeding FedAvg by a few points. Our results demonstrate the consistent effectiveness of FedASAM w.r.t. the SOTA baselines, improving the accuracy by $\approx$ 6% points on the best SOTA on both datasets. Moreover, by adding ASAM, all FL algorithms notably increase their performance. In particular i) we enable FedAvgM and SCAFFOLD to train in most of the settings with highest heterogeneity, ii) even if limited by the necessary gradient clipping, the results reached by FedDyn on CIFAR100 are almost doubled. Lastly, the best results are obtained with ASAM + SWA which stabilizes the noisy learning trends and enables models to converge close to centralized performance with $\alpha = 0$.

**Table 6.** SOTA comparison on CIFAR10 and CIFAR100 (centralized performance).

| | Algorithm | w/o SWA | | | | w/ SWA | | | |
|---|---|---|---|---|---|---|---|---|---|
| | | $\alpha = 0$ | | $\alpha = 0.05/0.5$ | | $\alpha = 0$ | | $\alpha = 0.05/0.5$ | |
| | | 5cl | 20cl | 5cl | 20cl | 5cl | 20cl | 5cl | 20cl |
| CIFAR10 | FedAvg | 65.00 | 68.52 | 69.24 | 73.07 | 69.71 | 70.19 | 73.48 | 73.81 |
| | FedSAM | 70.16 | 72.90 | 73.52 | 76.04 | 74.97 | 73.06 | 76.61 | 76.22 |
| | FedASAM | **73.66** | **76.09** | **75.61** | 76.98 | 76.44 | **76.36** | 76.12 | 76.86 |
| | FedAvgM | 10.00 | 10.00 | 10.00 | **78.51** | 10.00 | 10.00 | 10.00 | **84.00** |
| | FedProx | 62.72 | 68.44 | 68.38 | 73.02 | 70.56 | 70.08 | 74.27 | 73.67 |
| | SCAFFOLD | 32.25 | 15.56 | 54.46 | 44.76 | 11.98 | 10.00 | 33.25 | 24.11 |
| | FedDyn | 67.69 | 73.81 | 71.36 | 75.20 | 77.00 | 74.00 | 77.99 | 75.12 |
| | AdaBest | 66.77 | 72.29 | 69.84 | 75.89 | **78.94** | 76.12 | **80.35** | 79.35 |
| | FedAvgM + ASAM | 77.30 | **84.89** | 77.06 | **84.92** | 80.88 | **85.98** | 78.29 | **86.03** |
| | FedProx + ASAM | 73.74 | 75.76 | 75.32 | 77.03 | 76.89 | 75.92 | 76.65 | 76.95 |
| | SCAFFOLD + ASAM | **77.78** | 77.93 | 77.59 | 77.80 | 75.66 | 75.30 | 75.32 | 75.29 |
| | FedDyn + SAM | 77.38 | 81.00 | **79.18** | 81.70 | **83.81** | **86.07** | 83.18 | **85.57** |
| | AdaBest + ASAM | 77.48 | 78.43 | 78.41 | 79.72 | 82.00 | 80.80 | 81.87 | 80.81 |
| CIFAR100 | FedAvg | 30.25 | 38.59 | 40.43 | 42.17 | 39.34 | 39.85 | 43.90 | 42.09 |
| | FedSAM | 31.04 | 38.56 | 44.73 | 46.05 | 39.30 | 39.24 | 47.96 | 46.47 |
| | FedASAM | **36.04** | 40.81 | 45.61 | 47.78 | 42.01 | 41.62 | **49.17** | 48.27 |
| | FedAvgM | 1.00 | 40.64 | 4.60 | **47.88** | 1.00 | **53.50** | 4.60 | **53.69** |
| | FedProx | 31.20 | 38.59 | 39.53 | 42.17 | 39.06 | 39.68 | 43.98 | 41.84 |
| | SCAFFOLD | 1.00 | 1.00 | 33.26 | 1.00 | 1.00 | 1.00 | 5.76 | 1.00 |
| | FedDyn | 1.00 | 1.40 | 22.03 | 24.75 | 1.00 | 1.40 | 8.27 | 35.15 |
| | AdaBest | 29.90 | 39.11 | 36.93 | 43.25 | **44.48** | 44.21 | 48.20 | 44.51 |
| | FedAvgM + ASAM | 1.00 | 39.61 | 4.60 | **51.65** | 1.00 | **51.58** | 4.60 | **56.19** |
| | FedProx + ASAM | 36.10 | 40.91 | 44.81 | 48.17 | 43.90 | 42.06 | 48.66 | 48.19 |
| | SCAFFOLD + ASAM | **43.65** | 42.61 | **46.50** | 46.76 | 40.63 | 39.07 | 44.87 | 44.28 |
| | FedDyn + ASAM | 22.16 | 23.51 | 38.43 | 38.60 | 17.51 | 19.22 | 38.60 | 31.06 |
| | AdaBest + ASAM | 39.75 | **45.00** | 45.25 | 49.56 | **51.75** | 47.42 | **51.89** | **51.47** |

## 5.2 ASAM and SWA in Real World Vision Scenarios

In this Section, we analyze our method in real world scenarios, *i.e.* large scale classification, Semantic Segmentation (SS) for autonomous driving [17] and Domain Generalization (DG) applied to both classification and SS.

***Large-Scale Classification.*** We extend our analysis on visual classification tasks to Landmarks-User-160k [27] to validate the effectiveness of SAM, ASAM, and SWA in the presence of real-world challenges such as *Non-Identical Class Distribution* (different distribution of classes per device), and *Imbalanced Client Sizes* (varying number of training data per device). Results confirm the benefits of applying client-side sharpness-aware optimizers, especially in combination with server-side weight averaging with an improvement in final accuracy of up to 7%.

***Semantic Segmentation for Autonomous Driving.*** SS is a fundamental task for applications of autonomous driving. Due to the private nature of the data collected by self-driving cars, it is reasonable to study this task within a federated scenario. We refer to FedDrive [17] - a new benchmark for autonomous driving in FL - for both settings and baselines. The employed datasets are Cityscapes [13] and IDDA [2] with both uniform and heterogeneous settings. To test the generalization capabilities of the model when facing both semantic and appearance shift, the test domain of IDDA either contains pictures taken in the countryside, or in rainy conditions. The model is tested on both previously seen and unseen domains. As shown in Table 8, ASAM performs best both on Cityscapes and heterogeneous IDDA. The best performance is obtained combining ASAM + SWA with SiloBN [3], keeping the BatchNorm [28] statistics local to each client [47] while sharing the learnable parameters across domains.

**Table 7.** Accuracy Results (%) on Landmarks-User-160k.

| | @5k rounds | w/ SWA 75 | w/ SWA 100 |
|---|---|---|---|
| FedAvg | 61.91 | 66.05 | 67.52 |
| FedSAM | 63.72 | 67.11 | 68.12 |
| FedASAM | 64.23 | 67.17 | **68.32** |
| Centralized | | 74.03 | |

**Table 8.** Federated SS on Cityscapes and IDDA. Results in mIoU (%) @ 1.5k rounds.

| Algorithm | Uniform | Country seen | Country unseen | Rainy seen | Rainy unseen | mIoU | |
|---|---|---|---|---|---|---|---|
| FedAvg | ✓ | 63.31 | 48.60 | **65.16** | 27.38 | 43.61 | |
| FedSAM | ✓ | **64.22** | **49.74** | 64.81 | 30.00 | 44.58 | |
| FedASAM | ✓ | 62.74 | 48.73 | 64.74 | **31.32** | **45.86** | |
| FedAvg + SWA | ✓ | **63.91** | 43.28 | 63.24 | 47.72 | 45.64 | |
| FedSAM + SWA | ✓ | 62.26 | **46.26** | **63.69** | 48.40 | 45.29 | |
| FedASAM + SWA | ✓ | 60.78 | 44.23 | 63.18 | **51.76** | **45.69** | CITYSCAPES |
| FedAvg | ✗ | 42.06 | 36.04 | 39.50 | 24.59 | 38.65 | IDDA |
| FedSAM | ✗ | 43.28 | **37.83** | 39.65 | 29.27 | 41.22 | |
| FedASAM | ✗ | **43.67** | 36.11 | **41.68** | **30.07** | **42.27** | |
| FedAvg + SWA | ✗ | 37.16 | 37.48 | 37.06 | 42.33 | 42.48 | |
| FedSAM + SWA | ✗ | 44.26 | **40.45** | 38.15 | 45.25 | **43.42** | |
| FedASAM + SWA | ✗ | **45.23** | 39.72 | **42.09** | **45.40** | 43.02 | |
| SiloBN | ✗ | 45.86 | 32.77 | 48.09 | 39.67 | 45.96 | |
| SiloBN + SAM | ✗ | **46.88** | 33.71 | 48.22 | 40.08 | 49.10 | |
| SiloBN + ASAM | ✗ | 46.57 | **35.22** | **48.33** | 40.76 | **49.75** | |

*Domain Generalization.* To further show the generalization performance acquired by the model trained with SAM, ASAM and SWA, we test it on the corrupted CIFAR datasets [24]. The test images are altered by 19 corruptions each with 5 levels of severity. Figure 6 shows the results on the highest severity and once again validate the efficacy of seeking flat minima in FL (complete results in App. D).

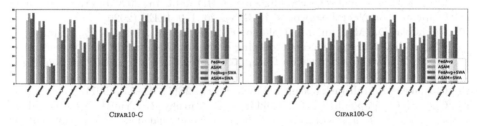

CIFAR10-C                                    CIFAR100-C

**Fig. 6.** Domain generalization in FL. Results with $\alpha = 0$, 20 clients, severity level 5.

## 6   Conclusions

Heterogeneous Federated Learning suffers from degraded performances and slow-down in training due to the poor generalization of the learned global model. Inspired by recent trends in deep learning connecting the loss landscape and the generalization gap, we analyzed the behavior of the model through the lens of the geometry of the loss surface and linked the lack of generalization to convergence towards sharp minima. As a solution, we introduced Sharpness-Aware Minimization, its adaptive version and Stochastic Weight Averaging in FL for encouraging convergence towards flatter minima. We showed the effectiveness of this approach in several vision tasks and datasets.

**Acknowledgments.** We thank L. Fantauzzo for her help with the SS experiments. We acknowledge the CINECA HPC infrastructure. Work funded by CINI.

# References

1. Acar, D.A.E., Zhao, Y., Navarro, R.M., Mattina, M., Whatmough, P.N., Saligrama, V.: Federated learning based on dynamic regularization. In: International Conference on Learning Representations (2021)
2. Alberti, E., Tavera, A., Masone, C., Caputo, B.: IDDA: a large-scale multi-domain dataset for autonomous driving. IEEE Robot. Autom. Lett. **5**(4), 5526–5533 (2020)
3. Andreux, M., du Terrail, J.O., Beguier, C., Tramel, E.W.: Siloed federated learning for multi-centric histopathology datasets. In: Albarqouni, S., et al. (eds.) DART/DCL -2020. LNCS, vol. 12444, pp. 129–139. Springer, Cham (2020). https://doi.org/10.1007/978-3-030-60548-3_13
4. Bahri, D., Mobahi, H., Tay, Y.: Sharpness-aware minimization improves language model generalization. arXiv preprint arXiv:2110.08529 (2021)
5. Bello, I., et al.: Revisiting resNets: improved training and scaling strategies. In: Advances in Neural Information Processing Systems 34 (2021)
6. Bercea, C.I., Wiestler, B., Rueckert, D., Albarqouni, S.: FedDis: disentangled federated learning for unsupervised brain pathology segmentation. arXiv preprint arXiv:2103.03705 (2021)
7. Blanchard, G., Lee, G., Scott, C.: Generalizing from several related classification tasks to a new unlabeled sample. In: Advances in Neural Information Processing Systems 24 (2011)
8. Briggs, C., Fan, Z., Andras, P.: Federated learning with hierarchical clustering of local updates to improve training on non-IID data. In: 2020 International Joint Conference on Neural Networks (IJCNN), pp. 1–9. IEEE (2020)
9. Caldarola, D., Mancini, M., Galasso, F., Ciccone, M., Rodolà, E., Caputo, B.: Cluster-driven graph federated learning over multiple domains. In: Proceedings of the IEEE/CVF Conference on Computer Vision and Pattern Recognition Workshop, pp. 2749–2758 (2021)
10. Caruana, R.: Multitask learning. Mach. Learn. **28**(1), 41–75 (1997)
11. Chen, L.C., Papandreou, G., Kokkinos, I., Murphy, K., Yuille, A.L.: DeepLab: semantic image segmentation with deep convolutional nets, atrous convolution, and fully connected CRFs. IEEE Trans. Pattern Anal. Mach. Intell. **40**(4), 834–848 (2017)
12. Chen, X., Hsieh, C.J., Gong, B.: When vision transformers outperform resNets without pre-training or strong data augmentations. In: International Conference on Learning Representations (2022)
13. Cordts, M., et al.: The cityscapes dataset for semantic urban scene understanding. In: Proceedings of the IEEE Conference on Computer Vision and Pattern Recognition, pp. 3213–3223 (2016)
14. DeVries, T., Taylor, G.W.: Improved regularization of convolutional neural networks with cutout. arXiv preprint arXiv:1708.04552 (2017)
15. Draxler, F., Veschgini, K., Salmhofer, M., Hamprecht, F.: Essentially no barriers in neural network energy landscape. In: International conference on machine learning, pp. 1309–1318. PMLR (2018)
16. Dziugaite, G.K., Roy, D.M.: Computing nonvacuous generalization bounds for deep (stochastic) neural networks with many more parameters than training data. arXiv preprint arXiv:1703.11008 (2017)
17. Fantauzzo, L., et al.: FedDrive: generalizing federated learning to semantic segmentation in autonomous driving. In: IEEE/RSJ International Conference on Intelligent Robots and Systems (2022)

18. Foret, P., Kleiner, A., Mobahi, H., Neyshabur, B.: Sharpness-aware minimization for efficiently improving generalization. In: International Conference on Learning Representations (2021)
19. Garcia-Garcia, A., Orts-Escolano, S., Oprea, S., Villena-Martinez, V., Garcia-Rodriguez, J.: A review on deep learning techniques applied to semantic segmentation. arXiv preprint arXiv:1704.06857 (2017)
20. Garipov, T., Izmailov, P., Podoprikhin, D., Vetrov, D.P., Wilson, A.G.: Loss surfaces, mode connectivity, and fast ensembling of DNNs. In: Advances in neural information processing systems 31 (2018)
21. Gong, X., et al.: Ensemble attention distillation for privacy-preserving federated learning. In: Proceedings of the IEEE/CVF International Conference on Computer Vision (ICCV), pp. 15076–15086 (2021)
22. Guo, P., Wang, P., Zhou, J., Jiang, S., Patel, V.M.: Multi-institutional collaborations for improving deep learning-based magnetic resonance image reconstruction using federated learning. In: Proceedings of the IEEE/CVF Conference on Computer Vision and Pattern Recognition (CVPR), pp. 2423–2432 (June 2021)
23. Hendrycks, D., et al.: The many faces of robustness: a critical analysis of out-of-distribution generalization. In: Proceedings of the IEEE/CVF International Conference on Computer Vision, pp. 8340–8349 (2021)
24. Hendrycks, D., Dietterich, T.: Benchmarking neural network robustness to common corruptions and perturbations. In: International Conference on Learning Representations (2019)
25. Hochreiter, S., Schmidhuber, J.: Flat minima. Neural Comput. $9(1)$, 1–42 (1997)
26. Hsu, T.M.H., Qi, H., Brown, M.: Measuring the effects of non-identical data distribution for federated visual classification. In: NeurIPS Workshop (2019)
27. Hsu, T.-M.H., Qi, H., Brown, M.: Federated visual classification with real-world data distribution. In: Vedaldi, A., Bischof, H., Brox, T., Frahm, J.-M. (eds.) ECCV 2020. LNCS, vol. 12355, pp. 76–92. Springer, Cham (2020). https://doi.org/10.1007/978-3-030-58607-2_5
28. Ioffe, S., Szegedy, C.: Batch normalization: accelerating deep network training by reducing internal covariate shift. In: International conference on machine learning, pp. 448–456. PMLR (2015)
29. Izmailov, P., Podoprikhin, D., Garipov, T., Vetrov, D., Wilson, A.G.: Averaging weights leads to wider optima and better generalization. In: Uncertainty in Artificial Intelligence (UAI) (2018)
30. Jastrzebski, S., Kenton, Z., Ballas, N., Fischer, A., Bengio, Y., Storkey, A.: On the relation between the sharpest directions of DNN loss and the SGD step length. In: International Conference on Learning Representations (2019)
31. Jastrzebski, S., Szymczak, M., Fort, S., Arpit, D., Tabor, J., Cho, K., Geras, K.: The break-even point on optimization trajectories of deep neural networks. arXiv preprint arXiv:2002.09572 (2020)
32. Jiang, Y., Neyshabur, B., Mobahi, H., Krishnan, D., Bengio, S.: Fantastic generalization measures and where to find them. arXiv preprint arXiv:1912.02178 (2019)
33. Kairouz, P., et al.: Advances and open problems in federated learning. arXiv preprint arXiv:1912.04977 (2019)
34. Karimireddy, S.P., Kale, S., Mohri, M., Reddi, S., Stich, S., Suresh, A.T.: Scaffold: stochastic controlled averaging for federated learning. In: International Conference on Machine Learning, pp. 5132–5143. PMLR (2020)
35. Keskar, N.S., Mudigere, D., Nocedal, J., Smelyanskiy, M., Tang, P.T.P.: On large-batch training for deep learning: Generalization gap and sharp minima. In: International Conference on Learning Representations (2017)

36. Kingma, D.P., Ba, J.: Adam: a method for stochastic optimization. ICLR (2015)
37. Kirkpatrick, J., et al.: Overcoming catastrophic forgetting in neural networks. Proc. Natl. Acad. Sci. **114**(13), 3521–3526 (2017)
38. Kleinberg, B., Li, Y., Yuan, Y.: An alternative view: when does SGD escape local minima? In: International Conference on Machine Learning, pp. 2698–2707. PMLR (2018)
39. Krizhevsky, A., et al.: Learning multiple layers of features from tiny images (2009)
40. Kwon, J., Kim, J., Park, H., Choi, I.K.: Asam: adaptive sharpness-aware minimization for scale-invariant learning of deep neural networks. In: International Conference on Machine Learning (2021)
41. Li, H., Xu, Z., Taylor, G., Studer, C., Goldstein, T.: Visualizing the loss landscape of neural nets. In: Neural Information Processing Systems (2018)
42. Li, Q., Diao, Y., Chen, Q., He, B.: Federated learning on non-IID data silos: an experimental study. arXiv preprint arXiv:2102.02079 (2021)
43. Li, Q., He, B., Song, D.: Model-contrastive federated learning. In: Proceedings of the IEEE/CVF Conference on Computer Vision and Pattern Recognition, pp. 10713–10722 (2021)
44. Li, T., Sahu, A.K., Talwalkar, A., Smith, V.: Federated learning: challenges, methods, and future directions. IEEE Signal Process. Mag. **37**(3), 50–60 (2020)
45. Li, T., Sahu, A.K., Zaheer, M., Sanjabi, M., Talwalkar, A., Smith, V.: Federated optimization in heterogeneous networks. Proceed. Mach. Learn. Syst. **2**, 429–450 (2020)
46. Li, W., et al.: Privacy-preserving federated brain tumour segmentation. In: Suk, H.-I., Liu, M., Yan, P., Lian, C. (eds.) MLMI 2019. LNCS, vol. 11861, pp. 133–141. Springer, Cham (2019). https://doi.org/10.1007/978-3-030-32692-0_16
47. Li, Y., Wang, N., Shi, J., Liu, J., Hou, X.: Revisiting batch normalization for practical domain adaptation. In: ICLR Workshop (2017)
48. Lin, T., Kong, L., Stich, S.U., Jaggi, M.: Ensemble distillation for robust model fusion in federated learning. arXiv preprint arXiv:2006.07242 (2020)
49. Liu, Q., Chen, C., Qin, J., Dou, Q., Heng, P.A.: FedDG: federated domain generalization on medical image segmentation via episodic learning in continuous frequency space. In: Proceedings of the IEEE/CVF Conference on Computer Vision and Pattern Recognition, pp. 1013–1023 (2021)
50. Long, J., Shelhamer, E., Darrell, T.: Fully convolutional networks for semantic segmentation. In: Proceedings of the IEEE Conference on Computer Vision and Pattern Recognition, pp. 3431–3440 (2015)
51. McMahan, B., Moore, E., Ramage, D., Hampson, S., y Arcas, B.A.: Communication-efficient learning of deep networks from decentralized data. In: Artificial intelligence and statistics, pp. 1273–1282. PMLR (2017)
52. Michieli, U., Ozay, M.: Prototype guided federated learning of visual feature representations. arXiv preprint arXiv:2105.08982 (2021)
53. Ouahabi, A., Taleb-Ahmed, A.: Deep learning for real-time semantic segmentation: application in ultrasound imaging. Pattern Recogn. Lett. **144**, 27–34 (2021)
54. Qu, Z., Li, X., Duan, R., Liu, Y., Tang, B., Lu, Z.: Generalized federated learning via sharpness aware minimization. In: Chaudhuri, K., Jegelka, S., Song, L., Szepesvari, C., Niu, G., Sabato, S. (eds.) Proceedings of the 39th International Conference on Machine Learning. Proceedings of Machine Learning Research, vol. 162, pp. 18250–18280. PMLR (17–23 July 2022)
55. Reddi, S., et al.: Adaptive federated optimization. In: International Conference on Learning Representations (2021)
56. Ruder, S.: An overview of gradient descent optimization algorithms. arXiv preprint arXiv:1609.04747 (2016)

57. Sheller, M.J., Reina, G.A., Edwards, B., Martin, J., Bakas, S.: Multi-institutional deep learning modeling without sharing patient data: a feasibility study on brain tumor segmentation. In: Crimi, A., Bakas, S., Kuijf, H., Keyvan, F., Reyes, M., van Walsum, T. (eds.) BrainLes 2018. LNCS, vol. 11383, pp. 92–104. Springer, Cham (2019). https://doi.org/10.1007/978-3-030-11723-8_9

58. Siam, M., Gamal, M., Abdel-Razek, M., Yogamani, S., Jagersand, M., Zhang, H.: A comparative study of real-time semantic segmentation for autonomous driving. In: Proceedings of the IEEE conference on computer vision and pattern recognition workshops, pp. 587–597 (2018)

59. Smith, S.L., Le, Q.V.: A bayesian perspective on generalization and stochastic gradient descent. In: International Conference on Learning Representations (2018)

60. Smith, V., Chiang, C.K., Sanjabi, M., Talwalkar, A.S.: Federated multi-task learning. In: Advances in Neural Information Processing systems 30 (2017)

61. Tavera, A., Cermelli, F., Masone, C., Caputo, B.: Pixel-by-pixel cross-domain alignment for few-shot semantic segmentation. In: Proceedings of the IEEE/CVF Winter Conference on Applications of Computer Vision, pp. 1626–1635 (2022)

62. Tian, C.X., Li, H., Wang, Y., Wang, S.: Privacy-preserving constrained domain generalization for medical image classification. arXiv preprint arXiv:2105.08511 (2021)

63. Varno, F., Saghayi, M., Rafiee, L., Gupta, S., Matwin, S., Havaei, M.: Minimizing client drift in federated learning via adaptive bias estimation. arXiv preprint arXiv:2204.13170 (2022)

64. Weyand, T., Araujo, A., Cao, B., Sim, J.: Google landmarks dataset v2-a large-scale benchmark for instance-level recognition and retrieval. In: Proceedings of the IEEE/CVF Conference on Computer Vision and Pattern Recognition, pp. 2575–2584 (2020)

65. Xie, C., Tan, M., Gong, B., Wang, J., Yuille, A.L., Le, Q.V.: Adversarial examples improve image recognition. In: Proceedings of the IEEE/CVF Conference on Computer Vision and Pattern Recognition, pp. 819–828 (2020)

66. Yao, C.H., Gong, B., Qi, H., Cui, Y., Zhu, Y., Yang, M.H.: Federated multi-target domain adaptation. In: Proceedings of the IEEE/CVF Winter Conference on Applications of Computer Vision, pp. 1424–1433 (2022)

67. Yi, L., Zhang, J., Zhang, R., Shi, J., Wang, G., Liu, X.: SU-Net: an efficient encoder-decoder model of federated learning for brain tumor segmentation. In: Farkaš, I., Masulli, P., Wermter, S. (eds.) ICANN 2020. LNCS, vol. 12396, pp. 761–773. Springer, Cham (2020). https://doi.org/10.1007/978-3-030-61609-0_60

68. Yuan, H., Morningstar, W., Ning, L., Singhal, K.: What do we mean by generalization in federated learning? In: NeurIPS Workshop (2021)

69. Yue, X., Nouiehed, M., Kontar, R.A.: SALR: sharpness-aware learning rates for improved generalization. arXiv preprint arXiv:2011.05348 (2020)

70. Zhang, C., Xie, Y., Bai, H., Yu, B., Li, W., Gao, Y.: A survey on federated learning. Knowl.-Based Syst. **216**, 106775 (2021)

71. Zhang, H., Cisse, M., Dauphin, Y.N., Lopez-Paz, D.: mixup: beyond empirical risk minimization. In: International Conference on Learning Representations (2018)

72. Zhang, L., Luo, Y., Bai, Y., Du, B., Duan, L.Y.: Federated learning for non-IID data via unified feature learning and optimization objective alignment. In: Proceedings of the IEEE/CVF International Conference on Computer Vision (ICCV), pp. 4420–4428 (2021)
73. Zhao, Y., Li, M., Lai, L., Suda, N., Civin, D., Chandra, V.: Federated learning with non-IID data. arXiv preprint arXiv:1806.00582 (2018)

# Semidefinite Relaxations of Truncated Least-Squares in Robust Rotation Search: Tight or Not

Liangzu Peng[1,2(✉)], Mahyar Fazlyab[1,2], and René Vidal[2,3]

[1] Department of Electrical and Computer Engineering, Johns Hopkins University,
Baltimore, USA
{lpeng25,mahyarfazlyab}@jhu.edu
[2] Mathematical Institute for Data Science, Johns Hopkins University,
Baltimore, USA
rvidal@jhu.edu
[3] Department of Biomedical Engineering, Johns Hopkins University, Baltimore, USA

**Abstract.** The rotation search problem aims to find a 3D rotation that best aligns a given number of point pairs. To induce robustness against outliers for rotation search, prior work considers truncated least-squares (TLS), which is a non-convex optimization problem, and its semidefinite relaxation (SDR) as a tractable alternative. Whether or not this SDR is theoretically tight in the presence of noise, outliers, or both has remained largely unexplored. We derive conditions that characterize the tightness of this SDR, showing that the tightness depends on the noise level, the truncation parameters of TLS, and the outlier distribution (random or clustered). In particular, we give a short proof for the tightness in the noiseless and outlier-free case, as opposed to the lengthy analysis of prior work.

## 1 Introduction

Robust geometric estimation problems in computer vision have been studied for decades [28,40]. However, the analysis of their computational complexity is not sufficiently well understood [51]: There are fast algorithms that run in real time [21,43,46,56], and there are computational complexity theorems that negate the existence of efficient algorithms [4,51].[1] For example, the commonly used *consensus maximization* formulation (for *robust fitting*) is shown to be NP hard in general [51], and its closely related *truncated least-squares* formulation is not *approximable* [4], even though they are both highly robust to noise and outliers. Between these "optimistic" algorithms and "pessimistic" theorems, semidefinite relaxations of truncated least-squares [35,57,58] strike a favorable balance between efficiency (as they are typically solvable in polynomial time) and robustness (which is inherited to some extent from the original formulation).

---

[1] The catch is that the fast methods might not always be correct (e.g., at extreme outlier rates).

© The Author(s), under exclusive license to Springer Nature Switzerland AG 2022
S. Avidan et al. (Eds.): ECCV 2022, LNCS 13683, pp. 673–691, 2022.
https://doi.org/10.1007/978-3-031-20050-2_39

Even though noise and outliers are ubiquitous in geometric vision, and non-convex formulations and their semidefinite relaxations have been widely used in a large body of papers [1–3, 7–9, 14, 15, 18, 24–27, 33, 34, 37, 41, 47, 49, 61], much fewer works [16, 23, 30, 38, 42, 48, 52, 55, 60][2] provide theoretical insights on the robustness of semidefinite relaxations to noise, a few semidefinite relaxations [13, 35, 57, 58] are empirically robust to outliers, and only one paper on *rotation synchronization* [54] gives theoretical guarantees for noise, outliers, and both. Complementary to the story of [51] and inheriting the spirit of [54], in this paper we consider the question of *whether "a specific semidefinite relaxation" for "robust rotation search" is "tight" or not*, and provide tightness characterizations that account for the presence of noise, outliers, and both.

More formally, in this paper we consider the following problem (see [43, 44, 57] for what has motivated this problem):

**Problem 1.** (*Robust Rotation Search*). Let $\{(\boldsymbol{y}_i, \boldsymbol{x}_i)\}_{i=1}^{\ell}$ be a collection of $\ell$ 3D point pairs. Assume that a subset $\mathcal{I}^* \subseteq \{1, \ldots, \ell\}$ of these pairs are related by a 3D rotation $\boldsymbol{R}_0^* \in \mathrm{SO}(3)$ up to bounded noise $\{\boldsymbol{\epsilon}_i : \|\boldsymbol{\epsilon}_i\|_2 \leq \delta\}_{i=1}^{\ell} \subset \mathbb{R}^3$ with $\delta \geq 0$, i.e.,

$$\begin{cases} \boldsymbol{y}_i = \boldsymbol{R}_0^* \boldsymbol{x}_i + \boldsymbol{\epsilon}_i, & i \in \mathcal{I}^* \\ \boldsymbol{y}_i \text{ and } \boldsymbol{x}_i \text{ are arbitrary} & i \notin \mathcal{I}^*. \end{cases} \tag{1}$$

Here, $\mathcal{I}^*$ is called the *inlier* index set. If $i \in \mathcal{I}^*$ then $\boldsymbol{x}_i$, $\boldsymbol{y}_i$, or $(\boldsymbol{y}_i, \boldsymbol{x}_i)$ is called an *inlier*, otherwise it is called an *outlier*. The goal is to find $\boldsymbol{R}_0^*$ and $\mathcal{I}^*$ from $\{(\boldsymbol{y}_i, \boldsymbol{x}_i)\}_{i=1}^{\ell}$.

To solve this problem, we consider the *truncated least-squares* formulation (rotation version), where the hyper-parameter $c_i^2 \geq 0$ is called the *truncation parameter*:

$$\min_{\boldsymbol{R}_0 \in \mathrm{SO}(3)} \sum_{i=1}^{\ell} \min \left\{ \|\boldsymbol{y}_i - \boldsymbol{R}_0 \boldsymbol{x}_i\|_2^2, \ c_i^2 \right\}. \tag{TLS-R}$$

While (TLS-R) is highly robust to outliers and noise [58], it is non-convex and hard to solve. Via a remarkable sequence of algebraic manipulations, [57] showed that (TLS-R) is equivalent to some non-convex *quadratically constrained quadratic program* (QCQP), which can be relaxed to a *semidefinite program* (SDR) via the standard *lifting* technique. The exact forms of (QCQP) and (SDR) will be shown in Sect. 2. One approach to study how much robustness (SDR) inherits from (TLS-R) or (QCQP) is to verify if the solution of (SDR) leads to a global minimizer to (QCQP). Informally, if this is true, then we say that (SDR) is *tight* (cf. Definition 1). Here, we make the following contributions:

- For noiseless point sets without outliers ($\boldsymbol{\epsilon}_i = 0, \mathcal{I}^* = \{1, \ldots, \ell\}$ in Problem 1), we prove that (SDR) is always tight (Theorem 1). While this result had already been proven in [57, Section E.3], our proof is simpler and shorter.

---

[2] [5, 12, 39, 62] analyzed SDRs under noise but they are not for geometric vision problems.

- For noiseless point sets with outliers, Theorem 2 states that (SDR) is tight for sufficiently small truncation parameters $c_i^2$ and *random* outliers (regardless of the number of outliers), but it is not tight if $c_i^2$ is set too large. Theorem 3 reveals that (SDR) is vulnerable to (e.g., not tight in the presence of) *clustered* outlier point pairs that are defined by a rotation different from $R_0^*$. Different from Theorem 1, outliers and improper choices of $c_i^2$ might actually undermine the tightness of (SDR).
- For noisy point sets without outliers, Theorems 4 and 5 show that (SDR) is tight for sufficiently small noise and for sufficiently large $c_i^2$. Theorem 4 is not hard to prove within our analysis framework, while Theorem 5 improves over Theorem 4 by giving a better bound on $c_i^2$ through non-trivial constructive arguments.
- The case of noisy data with outliers is the most challenging, but from our analysis of the two previous cases, a tightness characterization for this difficult case follows (Theorem 6). Thus, we will discuss this case only sparingly.

**Paper Organization.** In Sect. 2 we review the derivations of (SDR) from (TLS-R) [57], while we also provide new insights. In Sect. 3, we discuss our main results. In Sect. 4, we present limitations of our work and potential avenues for future research. The proofs of our results can be found in our full paper [45].

**Notations and Basics.** We employ the MATLAB notation $[a_1; \ldots; a_\ell]$ to denote concatenation into a column vector. Given a $4(\ell+1) \times 4(\ell+1)$ matrix $\mathcal{A}$, we employ the bracket notation $[\mathcal{A}]_{ij}$ of [57] to denote the $4 \times 4$ submatrix of $\mathcal{A}$ whose rows are indexed by $\{4i+1, \ldots, 4i+4\}$ and columns by $\{4j+1, \ldots, 4j+4\}$. Following our previous work on robust rotation search [46], we treat *unit quaternions* as unit vectors on the 3-sphere $\mathbb{S}^3$. Each $R \in SO(3)$ can be equivalently written as

$$R = \begin{bmatrix} w_1^2 + w_2^2 - w_3^2 - w_4^2 & 2(w_2 w_3 - w_1 w_4) & 2(w_2 w_4 + w_1 w_3) \\ 2(w_2 w_3 + w_1 w_4) & w_1^2 + w_3^2 - w_2^2 - w_4^2 & 2(w_3 w_4 - w_1 w_2) \\ 2(w_2 w_4 - w_1 w_3) & 2(w_3 w_4 + w_1 w_2) & w_1^2 + w_4^2 - w_2^2 - w_3^2 \end{bmatrix}, \quad (2)$$

where $w = [w_1; w_2; w_3; w_4] \in \mathbb{S}^3$ and $-w$ are unit quaternions. Conversely, every $3 \times 3$ matrix of the form (2) with $[w_1; w_2; w_3; w_4] \in \mathbb{S}^3$ is a 3D rotation. This means a two-to-one correspondence between unit quaternions ($\mathbb{S}^3$) and 3D rotations ($SO(3)$).

## 2 (TLS-R) and Its Relaxation: Review and New Insights

In Sect. 2.1 we derive a semidefinite relaxation (SDR) from (TLS-R). More specifically, we show that (TLS-R) is equivalent to a truncated least-squares problem named (TLS-Q), with the optimization variable being a unit quaternion. We further show that (TLS-Q) can be equivalently written as a quadratically constrained quadratic program, labeled as (QCQP). Thus, we obtain the semidefinite relaxation (SDR) of (QCQP), as a result of *lifting*, and their dual program (D). See Table 1 for an overview.

While Sect. 2.1 follows the development of [57] in spirit, our derivation is simpler. For example, we dispensed with the use of *quaternion product* [29] in [57], which is a sophisticated algebraic operation. That said, it is safe to treat our (SDR) as equivalent to the *naive relaxation* of [57]; see the full paper [45] for a detailed discussion.

In Sect. 2.2 we discuss the KKT optimality conditions that are essential for studying the interplay among (QCQP), (SDR), and (D), and thus the tightness of (SDR).

**Table 1.** Descriptions of different programs. TLS means Truncated Least-Squares.

| Programs | Description |
|---|---|
| (TLS-R) | The TLS problem with the optimization variable being a 3D rotation |
| (TLS-Q) | TLS with the optimization variable being a unit quaternion, equivalent to (TLS-R) |
| (QCQP) | A quadratically constrained quadratic program, equivalent to (TLS-Q) |
| (SDR) | The semidefinite relaxation of (QCQP), obtained via *lifting* |
| (D) | The dual program of (SDR) and (QCQP) |

### 2.1 Derivation

Notice that the term $\|\boldsymbol{y}_i - \boldsymbol{R}_0 \boldsymbol{x}_i\|_2^2 = \|\boldsymbol{y}_i\|_2^2 + \|\boldsymbol{x}_i\|_2^2 - 2\boldsymbol{y}_i^\top \boldsymbol{R}_0 \boldsymbol{x}_i$ of (TLS-R) depends linearly on the rotation $\boldsymbol{R}_0$. Moreover, each entry of a 3D rotation $\boldsymbol{R}_0$ depends quadratically on its *unit quaternion* representation $\boldsymbol{w}_0 \in \mathbb{S}^3$; recall (2). One then naturally asks whether $\|\boldsymbol{y}_i - \boldsymbol{R}_0 \boldsymbol{x}_i\|_2^2$ is a quadratic form in $\boldsymbol{w}_0$; the answer is affirmative:

**Lemma 1. (Rotations and Unit Quaternions).** *Let $\boldsymbol{R}_0$ be a 3D rotation, then we have*

$$\left\|\boldsymbol{y}_i - \boldsymbol{R}_0 \boldsymbol{x}_i\right\|_2^2 = \boldsymbol{w}_0^\top \boldsymbol{Q}_i \boldsymbol{w}_0, \tag{3}$$

*where $\boldsymbol{Q}_i$ is a $4 \times 4$ positive semidefinite matrix, and $\boldsymbol{w}_0 \in \mathbb{S}^3$ is the unit quaternion representation of $\boldsymbol{R}_0$. Moreover, the eigenvalues of $\boldsymbol{Q}_i$ are respectively*

$$\left(\|\boldsymbol{y}_i\|_2 + \|\boldsymbol{x}_i\|_2\right)^2, \left(\|\boldsymbol{y}_i\|_2 + \|\boldsymbol{x}_i\|_2\right)^2, \left(\|\boldsymbol{y}_i\|_2 - \|\boldsymbol{x}_i\|_2\right)^2, \left(\|\boldsymbol{y}_i\|_2 - \|\boldsymbol{x}_i\|_2\right)^2. \tag{4}$$

While the exact form of $\boldsymbol{Q}_i$ is complicated, Lemma 1 provides a characterization of the eigenvalues of $\boldsymbol{Q}_i$, which is much easier to work with. Note that, while the relationship between 3D rotations and unit quaternions is well known (see, e.g., [29]), we have not found (4) in the literature, except in the appendix of our prior work [46].

From Lemma 1, we now see that (TLS-R) is equivalent to

$$\min_{\boldsymbol{w}_0 \in \mathbb{S}^3} \sum_{i=1}^{\ell} \min \left\{ \boldsymbol{w}_0^\top \boldsymbol{Q}_i \boldsymbol{w}_0, \ c_i^2 \right\}. \tag{TLS-Q}$$

Using the following simple equality ($\theta \in \{-1, 1\}$ in [35,57]; see also [31])

$$\min\{a, b\} = \min_{\theta \in \{0,1\}} \theta a + (1 - \theta)b = \min_{\theta^2 = \theta} \theta a + (1 - \theta)b, \tag{5}$$

problem (TLS-Q) can be equivalently written as

$$\min_{w_0 \in \mathbb{S}^3, \theta_i^2 = \theta_i} \sum_{i=1}^{\ell} \left(\theta_i w_0^\top Q_i w_0 - \theta_i c_i^2\right) + \sum_{i=1}^{\ell} c_i^2. \tag{6}$$

Note that, while the constant $\sum_{i=1}^{\ell} c_i^2$ in (6) can be ignored, keeping it there will simplify matters. Even though the objective of (6) is a cubic polynomial in the entries of the unknowns $w_0$ and $\theta_i$'s, problem (6) is equivalent to a quadratic program. Indeed, let $w_i := \theta_i w_0$, which implies $\theta_i = w_0^\top w_i$. Then (6) becomes

$$\min_{w_0 \in \mathbb{S}^3, w_i \in \{w_0, 0\}} \sum_{i=1}^{\ell} \left(w_0^\top (Q_i - c_i^2 I_4) w_i\right) + \sum_{i=1}^{\ell} c_i^2 \tag{7}$$

The objective function of problem (7) is now quadratic. Moreover, the constraints are also quadratic. To see this, one easily verifies that the binary constraint $w_i \in \{w_0, 0\}$ can be equivalently written quadratically as $w_i w_0^\top = w_i w_i^\top$. Collecting all vectors of variables into a $4(\ell + 1)$ dimensional column vector $w = [w_0; \ldots; w_\ell]$, we have

$$\begin{cases} w_0 \in \mathbb{S}^3 \\ w_i \in \{w_0, 0\} \end{cases} \Leftrightarrow \begin{cases} \mathrm{tr}(w_0 w_0^\top) = 1 \\ w_i w_0^\top = w_i w_i^\top \end{cases} \Leftrightarrow \begin{cases} \mathrm{tr}\left([ww^\top]_{00}\right) = 1 \\ [ww^\top]_{0i} = [ww^\top]_{ii}. \end{cases} \tag{8}$$

In the last equivalence of (8) we used the notation $[\cdot]_{ij}$ of Sect. 1. Having confirmed (8), we can now equivalently transform (7) into the following (QCQP):

$$\min_{w \in \mathbb{R}^{4(\ell+1)}} \mathrm{tr}\left(Qww^\top\right) + \sum_{i=1}^{\ell} c_i^2 \tag{QCQP}$$

$$\text{s.t. } [ww^\top]_{0i} = [ww^\top]_{ii}, \quad \forall i \in \{1, \ldots, \ell\} \tag{9}$$

$$\mathrm{tr}\left([ww^\top]_{00}\right) = 1 \tag{10}$$

In (QCQP), $Q$ is our $4(\ell + 1) \times 4(\ell + 1)$ data matrix, symmetric and satisfying

$$\begin{cases} [Q]_{0i} = [Q]_{i0} = \frac{1}{2}(Q_i - c_i^2 I_4), \quad \forall i \in \{1, \ldots, \ell\} \\ \text{all other entries of } Q \text{ are zero.} \end{cases} \tag{11}$$

It is now not hard to derive the semidefinite relaxation (SDR) and dual program (D) from (QCQP) via lifting and standard Lagrangian calculation respectively:

**Lemma 2.** ((SDR) and (D)). *The dual and semidefinite relaxation of* (QCQP) *are*

$$\max_{\mu, \mathcal{D}} \quad \mu + \sum_{i=1}^{\ell} c_i^2 \quad s.t. \quad Q - \mu \mathcal{B} - \mathcal{D} \succeq 0 \tag{D}$$

$$\min_{\mathcal{W} \succeq 0} \quad \mathrm{tr}\left(Q\mathcal{W}\right) + \sum_{i=1}^{\ell} c_i^2 \tag{SDR}$$

$$s.t. \quad [\mathcal{W}]_{0i} = [\mathcal{W}]_{ii}, \quad \forall \, i \in \{1, \ldots, \ell\} \tag{12}$$

$$\mathrm{tr}\left([\mathcal{W}]_{00}\right) = 1 \tag{13}$$

*In the dual* (D), $\mathcal{B}$ *is a matrix of zeros except* $[\mathcal{B}]_{00} = I_4$, *while* $\mathcal{D} \in \mathbb{R}^{4(\ell+1) \times 4(\ell+1)}$ *is a matrix of dual variables accounting for the $\ell$ constraints of* (9), *i.e.,* $\mathcal{D}$ *satisfies*

$$\begin{cases} \mathcal{D} \text{ is symmetric,} \quad [\mathcal{D}]_{ii} + 2[\mathcal{D}]_{0i} = 0, \quad \forall \, i \in \{1, \ldots, \ell\} \\ \text{all other entries of } \mathcal{D} \text{ are zero.} \end{cases} \tag{14}$$

In (D), we omitted constraint (14) on $\mathcal{D}$ for simplicity, but we will keep it in mind.

### 2.2 The Tightness and KKT Optimality Conditions

Studying the interplay among (D), (SDR), and (QCQP) is the main theme of the paper, which will be discussed in more detail in Sect. 3. Here we give some basic results, to begin with. Note that weak duality between (QCQP) and (D) holds as a result of Lagrangian calculation. Also, with $\mathcal{D}$ of the form (14) satisfying $[\mathcal{D}]_{0i} := \frac{1}{2}(Q_i + c_i^2 I_4)$ and with $\mu$ sufficiently small, it is not hard to show that $Q - \mu \mathcal{B} - \mathcal{D} \succ 0$ (cf. the proof of Theorem 1), thus $(\mu, \mathcal{D})$ is a strictly feasible point of (D) and the Slater's condition is satisfied, hence strong duality between (D) and (SDR) holds. In summary, we have

$$\hat{\mu} + \sum_{i=1}^{\ell} c_i^2 = \hat{g}_{\mathrm{D}} = \hat{g}_{\mathrm{SDR}} \leq \hat{g}_{\mathrm{QCQP}}, \tag{15}$$

where the last three terms of (15) are the optimal objective values of (D), (SDR), and (QCQP), respectively. The next question is whether there are conditions under which the last inequality becomes an equality, i.e., $\hat{g}_{\mathrm{SDR}} = \hat{g}_{\mathrm{QCQP}}$. A (seemingly) stronger version of this objective value equality is the following notion of tightness:

**Definition 1 (Tightness).** (SDR) *is said to be tight if it admits* $\hat{w}(\hat{w})^{\top}$ *as a global minimizer, where* $\hat{w} \in \mathbb{R}^{4(\ell+1)}$ *globally minimizes* (QCQP).

The following proposition provides a starting point for tightness analysis whose proof follows from a standard duality argument:

**Proposition 1 (Optimality Conditions).** *Recall that $\mathcal{B}$ is defined in Lemma 2 and $\hat{w}$ denotes a global minimizer of (QCQP). Let $\hat{\mu}$ be such that $\hat{\mu} + \sum_{i=1}^{\ell} c_i^2$ globally minimizes (D). (SDR) is tight if and only if there is a matrix $\hat{\mathcal{D}}$ of the form (14) that satisfies*

*(i) $(Q - \hat{\mu}\mathcal{B} - \hat{\mathcal{D}})\hat{w} = 0$*
*(ii) $Q - \hat{\mu}\mathcal{B} - \hat{\mathcal{D}} \succeq 0$*
*(iii) The minimum $\hat{\mu} + \sum_{i=1}^{\ell} c_i^2$ of (SDR) is also the minimum of (QCQP).*

Next, we simplify the above optimality conditions to ease the use.

**Proposition 2 (Simplified Optimality Conditions).** *Let $Q_1, \ldots, Q_{k^*}$ be inliers and $Q_{k^*+1}, \ldots, Q_\ell$ outliers. Let $\hat{w}_0$ globally minimize (TLS-Q). Assume (TLS-Q) preserves all inliers and rejects all outliers. Then the $4(\ell+1)$ dimensional vector $\hat{w} = [\hat{w}_0; \ldots; \hat{w}_0; 0; \ldots, 0]$, where $\hat{w}_0$ appeared $k^* + 1$ times, is a global minimizer of (QCQP), and the optimality conditions of Proposition 1 can be simplified as follows:*

- *If $\hat{\mu} = \sum_{i=1}^{k^*} \left( \hat{w}_0^\top Q_i \hat{w}_0 - c_i^2 \right)$, condition (i) of Proposition 1 is equivalent to*

$$\begin{cases} (2[\hat{\mathcal{D}}]_{0i} + Q_i - c_i^2 I_4)\hat{w}_0 = 0, & \forall i \in \{1, \ldots, k^*\} \\ (2[\hat{\mathcal{D}}]_{0j} + c_j^2 I_4 - Q_j)\hat{w}_0 = 0, & \forall j \in \{k^*+1, \ldots, \ell\}. \end{cases} \tag{O1}$$

- *Condition (ii) of Proposition 1 is equivalent to ($\forall z_i \in \mathbb{R}^4$)*

$$-\hat{\mu}\|z_0\|_2^2 + 2\sum_{i=1}^{\ell} z_i^\top [\hat{\mathcal{D}}]_{0i} z_i - \sum_{i=1}^{\ell} z_0^\top \left(2[\hat{\mathcal{D}}]_{0i} - Q_i + c_i^2 I_4\right) z_i \geq 0. \tag{O2}$$

- *Condition (iii) of Proposition 1 is equivalent to*

$$\hat{\mu} = \sum_{i=1}^{k^*} \left( \hat{w}_0^\top Q_i \hat{w}_0 - c_i^2 \right). \tag{O3}$$

Thanks to Propositions 1 and 2, establishing whether (SDR) is tight or not reduces to finding *dual certificates* $[\hat{\mathcal{D}}]_{0i}$'s (and $\hat{\mu}$) that fulfill the (simplified) optimality conditions. Identifying eligible $[\hat{\mathcal{D}}]_{0i}$'s or showing that such $[\hat{\mathcal{D}}]_{0i}$'s do not exist is a core idea in proving our Theorems 1–6, which we discuss in greater detail in the next section.

## 3 Main Results

In this section we present our main results regarding the tightness of (SDR). Our results are naturally categorized into four subsections. Section 3.1 treats the simplest noiseless + outlier-free case (Theorem 1). Sections 3.2 and 3.3 consider the case where the data is corrupted by outliers (Theorems 2 and 3) and noise (Theorems 4 and 5), respectively, and Sect. 3.4 brings them together for the noisy + outliers case (Theorem 6).

## 3.1   The Noiseless + Outlier-Free Case

**Theorem 1 (Noiseless and Outlier-Free Point Sets).** *In the absence of noise and outliers, (SDR) is tight, meaning that $w^*(w^*)^\top$ globally minimizes (SDR), where $w^* = [w_0^*; \ldots; w_0^*] \in \mathbb{R}^{4(\ell+1)}$ is a global minimizer of (QCQP).*

*Proof.* Note that $w^* = [w_0^*; \ldots; w_0^*]$ is a global minimizer of (QCQP) that results in the optimal value 0. Let $\hat{\mathcal{D}}$ satisfy the constraint (14) with $[\hat{\mathcal{D}}]_{0i} := \frac{1}{2}(Q_i + c_i^2 I_4)$ for every $i = 1, \ldots, \ell$ and let $\hat{\mu} := -\sum_{i=1}^{\ell} c_i^2$. Then, with $Q_i w_0^* = 0$ (Lemma 1), one easily verifies that optimality conditions (O1) and (O3) of Proposition 2 hold. It remains to prove condition (O2). Substitute the values of $[\hat{\mathcal{D}}]_{0i}$, $\hat{\mu}$ into (O2) and it simplifies:

$$\sum_{i=1}^{\ell} c_i^2 \|z_0\|_2^2 + \sum_{i=1}^{\ell} z_i^\top (Q_i + c_i^2 I_4) z_i - 2 \sum_{i=1}^{\ell} c_i^2 z_i^\top z_0 \geq 0, \quad \forall z_i \in \mathbb{R}^4 \quad (16)$$

$$\Leftrightarrow \sum_{i=1}^{\ell} \left( c_i^2 \|z_0 - z_i\|_2^2 + z_i^\top Q_i z_i \right) \geq 0, \quad \forall z_i \in \mathbb{R}^4 \quad (17)$$

Thus (O2) holds, as every $Q_i$ is positive semidefinite (Lemma 1). One also observes that the equality is attained if and only if $z_0 = \cdots = z_\ell = w_0^*$ or $z_0 = \cdots = z_\ell = 0$.

Our contribution here is a shorter proof for Theorem 1 than that in [57]. Besides Lemma 1, another key idea that shortens the proof is our construction of the dual certificate $\hat{\mathcal{D}}$ (or $[\hat{\mathcal{D}}]_{0i}$'s). While constructing dual certificates might be an art as there might not exist general approaches for doing so, our experience is to (1) start with the *simplest* case (e.g., noiseless + outlier-free), (2) make *observations*: observe the optimality conditions (cf. Proposition 1), inspect the first and second order Riemannian optimality conditions (cf. [6]), discover some properties of data (e.g., Lemma 1), (3) *repeatedly try* different choices of certificates. In what follows, due to space limitations, we not always provide full proofs of our theorems, but we always provide a sketch of the dual certificate.

## 3.2   The Noiseless + Outliers Case

Different from Theorem 1, in this case the tightness of (SDR) depends on both the data and truncation parameter $c_i^2$, as stated in the following result.

**Theorem 2 (Noiseless Point Sets with Outliers).** *Suppose there is no noise. Consider (TLS-Q) with outliers $Q_{k^*+1}, \ldots, Q_\ell$ ($k^* < \ell$). Recall $w_0^*$ denotes the unit quaternion that represents the ground-truth rotation $R_0^*$. Let $w^* := [w_0^*; \ldots; w_0^*; 0; \ldots; 0] \in \mathbb{R}^{4(\ell+1)}$, where $w_0^*$ appears $k^* + 1$ times, and let $W^* := w^*(w^*)^\top$. Then we have:*

- *If $0 < c_j^2 < \lambda_{min}(Q_j)$, for all $j = k^*+1, \ldots, \ell$, then (SDR) is tight, admitting $W^*$ as a global minimizer.*

– If $c_j^2 > (\boldsymbol{w}_0^*)^\top \boldsymbol{Q}_j \boldsymbol{w}_0^*$ for some $j \in \{k^* + 1, \ldots, \ell\}$, then $\mathcal{W}^*$ is not a global minimizer of (SDR).

*Proof (Sketch).* For the first part, note that $c_j^2 < \lambda_{\min}(\boldsymbol{Q}_j)$, $\forall j = k^* + 1, \ldots, \ell$, so (TLS-Q) rejects all outliers and preserves all inliers, $\boldsymbol{w}_0^*$ globally minimizes (TLS-Q), and $w^*$ globally minimizes (QCQP) with the minimum value $\sum_{j=k^*+1}^\ell c_j^2$. Let $[\hat{\mathcal{D}}]_{0i} := \frac{1}{2}(\boldsymbol{Q}_i + c_i^2 \boldsymbol{I}_4)$ ($\forall i = 1, \ldots, k^*$), $[\hat{\mathcal{D}}]_{0j} := \frac{1}{2}(\boldsymbol{Q}_j - c_j^2 \boldsymbol{I}_4)$ ($\forall j = k^* + 1, \ldots, \ell$), and $\hat{\mu} := -\sum_{i=1}^{k^*} c_i^2$. With $\boldsymbol{Q}_i \boldsymbol{w}_0^* = 0$, $\forall i = 1, \ldots, k^*$, (Lemma 1), one easily verifies conditions (O1) and (O3) of Proposition 2 hold. Condition (O2) is the same as

$$\sum_{i=1}^{k^*} \left( c_i^2 \|\boldsymbol{z}_0 - \boldsymbol{z}_i\|_2^2 + \boldsymbol{z}_i^\top \boldsymbol{Q}_i \boldsymbol{z}_i \right) + \sum_{j=k^*+1}^\ell \boldsymbol{z}_j^\top (\boldsymbol{Q}_j - c_j^2 \boldsymbol{I}_4) \boldsymbol{z}_j \geq 0, \quad \forall \boldsymbol{z}_i \in \mathbb{R}^4, \quad (18)$$

which holds true because $\boldsymbol{Q}_i$' are positive semidefinite as per Lemma 1 and $\boldsymbol{Q}_j \succeq c_j^2 \boldsymbol{I}_4$. This proves the first part. For the second part, it suffices to prove that, given $c_\ell^2 > (\boldsymbol{w}_0^*)^\top \boldsymbol{Q}_\ell \boldsymbol{w}_0^*$, the three conditions of Proposition 1 (or Proposition 2) can not be simultaneously satisfied by $w^*$ and any $\hat{\mu}$ and $\hat{\mathcal{D}}$, where $\hat{\mathcal{D}}$ is of the form (14). This is proved by constructing a specific counterexample; see our full paper [45] for details.

*Remark 1 (Noiseless Point Sets with Random Outliers).* If outlier $(\boldsymbol{y}_j, \boldsymbol{x}_j)$ is randomly drawn from $\mathbb{R}^3 \times \mathbb{R}^3$ according to some continuous probability distribution, then with probability 1 we have $\|\boldsymbol{y}_j\|_2 \neq \|\boldsymbol{x}_j\|_2$ (Lemma 2 of [53]), which implies $\lambda_{\min}(\boldsymbol{Q}_j) > 0$. Thus, (SDR) is always tight to such random outliers, if $c_j^2 \to 0$. Note that this discussion is theoretical and does not apply to the case where $|\|\boldsymbol{y}_j\|_2 - \|\boldsymbol{x}_j\|_2|$ is nonzero but is below machine accuracy, as $c_j^2$ can not be set even smaller (the case $c_j^2 = 0$ is trivial).

If the condition $c_j^2 < \lambda_{\min}(\boldsymbol{Q}_j)$ of the first statement in Theorem 2 holds then $\boldsymbol{Q}_j$ will always be rejected by (TLS-Q) as an outlier. In fact, since $\lambda_{\min}(\boldsymbol{Q}_j)$ can be easily computed (Lemma 1), in practice one usually throws away the point pairs $(\boldsymbol{y}_j, \boldsymbol{x}_j)$'s for which $c_j^2 < \lambda_{\min}(\boldsymbol{Q}_j)$ as a means of preprocessing (cf. [11, 46]), and these point pairs might not enter into the semidefinite optimization. Thus, Theorem 2 suggests that (SDR) can distinguish this type of "simple" outliers, as long as $c_j^2$ is properly chosen.

In the second statement of Theorem 2, if the condition $c_\ell^2 > (\boldsymbol{w}_0^*)^\top \boldsymbol{Q}_\ell \boldsymbol{w}_0^*$ holds true for outlier $\boldsymbol{Q}_\ell$, then (TLS-Q) would attempt to minimize $\boldsymbol{w}_0^\top \boldsymbol{Q}_\ell \boldsymbol{w}_0 + \sum_{i=1}^{k^*} \boldsymbol{w}_0^\top \boldsymbol{Q}_i \boldsymbol{w}_0$ over $\boldsymbol{w}_0 \in \mathbb{S}^3$ at least—an outlier showed up in the eigenvalue optimization—thus the global minimizer of (TLS-Q) is unlikely to be $\boldsymbol{w}_0^*$. This is why we do not expect $\mathcal{W}^*$ to globally minimize (SDR); our theorem confirms this.

Admittedly, Theorem 2 leaves a gap: What if $c_j^2$ is sandwiched between $\lambda_{\min}(\boldsymbol{Q}_j)$ and $(\boldsymbol{w}_0^*)^\top \boldsymbol{Q}_j \boldsymbol{w}_0^*$? Or what can we say about the tightness of (SDR) if

$$\lambda_{\min}(\boldsymbol{Q}_j) < c_j^2 < (\boldsymbol{w}_0^*)^\top \boldsymbol{Q}_j \boldsymbol{w}_0^* \ ? \tag{19}$$

While our empirical observation suggests that $\mathcal{W}^*$ does not globally minimize (SDR) if (19) holds (with $k^* < \ell$), the analysis of this case without further assumptions on the outliers appears hard. The difficulty is that the outliers $\boldsymbol{Q}_j$'s could be so adversarial that $(\boldsymbol{w}_0^*)^\top \boldsymbol{Q}_j \boldsymbol{w}_0^*$ is arbitrarily close[3] to 0 while $\lambda_{\min}(\boldsymbol{Q}_j) = 0$ for every $j > k^*$. Thus, the value of Theorem 2 is in that it shows that (SDR) can only handle "simple" outliers that can be filtered out, and thus reveals a fundamental limit on the performance of (SDR).

Next, we consider the situation where outliers $\boldsymbol{Q}_j$'s can not be simply removed by preprocessing, e.g., $\lambda_{\min}(\boldsymbol{Q}_j) = 0$. In particular, we assume the outliers are *clustered* and show that the (SDR) under investigation is even more vulnerable:

**Theorem 3 (Noiseless Point Sets with Clustered Outliers).** *With the notation of Theorem 2, further suppose outliers $\boldsymbol{Q}_{k^*+1}, \ldots, \boldsymbol{Q}_\ell$ are "clustered" in the sense that*

$$\boldsymbol{Q}_{k^*+1} \boldsymbol{w}_0^{cl} = \cdots = \boldsymbol{Q}_\ell \boldsymbol{w}_0^{cl} = 0 \tag{20}$$

*with $\boldsymbol{w}_0^{cl} \in \mathbb{S}^3$ some unit quaternion that is different from $\pm \boldsymbol{w}_0^*$. If*

$$1 - \frac{\sum_{j=k^*+1}^{\ell} c_j^2}{2 \sum_{i=1}^{k^*} c_i^2} < \left| (\boldsymbol{w}_0^{cl})^\top \boldsymbol{w}_0^* \right|, \tag{21}$$

*then $\mathcal{W}^*$ does not globally minimize (SDR).*

*Proof (Sketch).* The proof uses the same idea as in proving the second statement of Theorem 2: Prove via counterexamples that the three conditions of Proposition 2 can no hold simultaneously. They differ though, in how the counterexamples are constructed.

The *clustered* outliers of Theorem 3 defined in the sense of (20) mean that the outlier pairs $(\boldsymbol{y}_j, \boldsymbol{x}_j)$ $(j > k^*)$ are related by the same 3D rotation $\boldsymbol{R}_0^{cl}$ that correspond to $\boldsymbol{w}_0^{cl}$, that is $\boldsymbol{y}_j = \boldsymbol{R}_0^{cl} \boldsymbol{x}_j$, $\forall j > k^*$ (Lemma 1). Clustered outliers can be thought of as a special type of *adversarial* outliers, the latter usually used to study the robustness of algorithms in the worse case; it should be distinguished from data clustering [22,32].

To understand condition (21) of Theorem 3, consider a situation where all truncation parameters are equal, $c_1^2 = \cdots = c_\ell^2$. Then (21) simplifies to $1 - (\ell - k^*)/(2k^*) < \left| (\boldsymbol{w}_0^{cl})^\top \boldsymbol{w}_0^* \right|$; also note that $\left| (\boldsymbol{w}_0^{cl})^\top \boldsymbol{w}_0^* \right| \in [0, 1)$. Thus, if $\ell - k^* > 2k^*$, then (21) always holds, and so $\mathcal{W}^*$ never globally minimizes (SDR), which is forgivable as in this case $\boldsymbol{w}_0^*$ neither globally minimizes (TLS-Q). However, even if the number of outliers is only half the number of inliers, i.e., $\ell - k^* = k^*/2$, Theorem 3 implies that $\mathcal{W}^*$ would still fail to globally minimize (SDR) as long

---

[3] Alternatively, if $(\boldsymbol{w}_0^*)^\top \boldsymbol{Q}_j \boldsymbol{w}_0^*$ is small, then $\boldsymbol{Q}_j$ might be treated as noisy data rather than an outlier. We consider such noisy case in Sects. 3.3 (without outliers) and 3.4 (with outliers).

as $\left|(\boldsymbol{w}_0^{\text{cl}})^\top \boldsymbol{w}_0^*\right| > 3/4$, but $\boldsymbol{w}_0^*$ would *in general* globally minimize (TLS-Q) with suitable $c_j^2$ (cf. [59]). Then one might conclude that (SDR) is *strictly* less robust to outliers than (TLS-Q).

Finally, we note that Theorem 3 might be overly pessimistic. In fact, experiments show that (SDR) is robust to 40%–50% outliers $(\boldsymbol{y}_j, \boldsymbol{x}_j)$'s, where $\boldsymbol{y}_j$ and $\boldsymbol{x}_j$ are sampled uniformly at random from $\mathbb{S}^2$ (so $\lambda_{\min}(\boldsymbol{Q}_j) = 0$ by Lemma 1). Two factors account for this empirically better behavior: i) Such random outliers are less adversarial than clustered ones, ii) the extra projection step that converts the global minimizer of (SDR) to a unit quaternion alleviates to some extent the issue of $\mathcal{W}^*$ not minimizing (SDR). In retrospect, there are two downsides in our analysis of Theorems 2 and 3: (1) We have not taken such extra projection step into account, and (2) we only showed that $\mathcal{W}^*$ might not minimize (SDR) but have not proved how far the global minimizers of (SDR) can be from $\mathcal{W}^*$, the latter being much more challenging though, in our opinion.

## 3.3   The Noisy + Outlier-Free Case

The noisy case, even without outliers, is more difficult to penetrate than previous cases. A general reason for this is that the global minimizers of (QCQP) and (SDR) are now complicated functions of noise. Since we already have Theorem 1, one might wonder whether it can be extended to the noisy + outlier-free case using some continuity argument. In fact, [20] shows that, under certain conditions, if the noiseless version of the Schor relaxation of some QCQP is tight, then its noisy version is also tight. While this result is quite general, its conditions are abstract and hard to verify. In fact, it is not applicable to our case directly, as in our problem the truncation parameters $c_i^2$ also have impacts on the tightness, and the approach of [20] does not model, and thus could not control the values of $c_i^2$. Instead, our analysis must take both $c_i^2$ and noise into account.

We begin by decomposing $\boldsymbol{Q}_i$ of (TLS-Q) into the pure data part and noise part:

**Lemma 3.** *Let* $\boldsymbol{R}_0 \in \mathrm{SO}(3)$. *If* $(\boldsymbol{y}_i, \boldsymbol{x}_i)$ *is an inlier that obeys* (1), *then we have*

$$\left\|\boldsymbol{y}_i - \boldsymbol{R}_0\boldsymbol{x}_i\right\|_2^2 = \boldsymbol{w}_0^\top \boldsymbol{Q}_i \boldsymbol{w}_0, \quad \boldsymbol{Q}_i = \boldsymbol{P}_i + \boldsymbol{E}_i + \left\|\boldsymbol{\epsilon}_i\right\|_2^2 \boldsymbol{I}_4, \tag{22}$$

*where* $\boldsymbol{w}_0 \in \mathbb{S}^3$ *is the unit quaternion representation of* $\boldsymbol{R}_0$, *and* $\boldsymbol{P}_i$ *and* $\boldsymbol{E}_i$ *are* $4 \times 4$ *symmetric matrices that repsectively satisfy the following properties:*

- $\boldsymbol{P}_i$ *is positive semidefinite with its entries depending on* $\boldsymbol{y}_i$ *and* $\boldsymbol{x}_i$, *and it has two different eigenvalues* $4\|\boldsymbol{x}_i\|_2^2$ *and* 0, *each of multiplicity* 2. *The ground-truth unit quaternion* $\boldsymbol{w}_0^*$ *is an eigenvector of* $\boldsymbol{P}_i$ *corresponding to eigenvalue* 0, *i.e.,* $\boldsymbol{P}_i\boldsymbol{w}_0^* = 0$. *In particular, we have* $\boldsymbol{Q}_i\boldsymbol{w}_0^* = \boldsymbol{P}_i\boldsymbol{w}_0^* = 0$ *in the noiseless case.*
- $\boldsymbol{E}_i$ *has entries depending on* $\boldsymbol{y}_i$, $\boldsymbol{x}_i$, *and noise* $\boldsymbol{\epsilon}_i$, *and has two different eigenvalues* $2\boldsymbol{\epsilon}_i^\top \boldsymbol{R}_0^* \boldsymbol{x}_i + 2\|\boldsymbol{\epsilon}_i\|_2\|\boldsymbol{x}_i\|_2$ *and* $2\boldsymbol{\epsilon}_i^\top \boldsymbol{R}_0^* \boldsymbol{x}_i - 2\|\boldsymbol{\epsilon}_i\|_2\|\boldsymbol{x}_i\|_2$, *each of multiplicity* 2. *We have* $\boldsymbol{w}_0^\top \boldsymbol{E}_i \boldsymbol{w}_0 = 2\boldsymbol{\epsilon}_i^\top(\boldsymbol{R}_0^* \boldsymbol{x}_i - \boldsymbol{R}_0\boldsymbol{x}_i)$ *and in particular* $(\boldsymbol{w}_0^*)^\top \boldsymbol{E}_i \boldsymbol{w}_0^* = 0$.

**A Warm-Up Result.** We first consider a simple case where $c_i^2$ is sufficiently large:

**Theorem 4 (Noisy and Outlier-Free Point Sets $\{(\boldsymbol{y}_i, \boldsymbol{x}_i)\}_{i=1}^\ell$).** *Consider* (TLS-Q) *with noisy inliers $\{\boldsymbol{Q}_i\}_{i=1}^\ell$ and $\hat{\boldsymbol{w}}_0 \in \mathbb{S}^3$ its global minimizer. Let $\hat{w} := [\hat{\boldsymbol{w}}_0; \ldots; \hat{\boldsymbol{w}}_0]$. If $c_i^2 > \lambda_{max}(\boldsymbol{Q}_i)$ for every $i = 1, \ldots, \ell$, then* (SDR) *is tight as it admits $\hat{w}(\hat{w})^\top$ as a global minimizer, and, moreover, the angle $\hat{\tau}_0^*$ between $\hat{\boldsymbol{w}}_0$ and the ground-truth unit quaternion $\boldsymbol{w}_0^* \in \mathbb{S}^3$ grows proportionally with the magnitude of noise $\epsilon_i$:*

$$\sin^2(\hat{\tau}_0^*) \leq \frac{4\sum_{i=1}^\ell \|\epsilon_i\|_2 \|\boldsymbol{x}_i\|_2}{\lambda_{min2}\left(\sum_{i=1}^\ell \boldsymbol{P}_i\right)}, \qquad \sin^2(\hat{\tau}_0^*) := 1 - (\hat{\boldsymbol{w}}_0^\top \boldsymbol{w}_0^*)^2 \qquad (23)$$

*In* (23), *each $\boldsymbol{P}_i$ corresponds to the "pure data" part of $\boldsymbol{Q}_i$ that satisfies $\boldsymbol{P}_i \boldsymbol{w}_0^* = 0, \boldsymbol{P}_i \succeq 0$ (Lemma 3), and $\lambda_{min2}(\cdot)$ denotes the second smallest eigenvalue of a matrix.*

*Proof (Sketch).* Let $\hat{\mathcal{D}}$ satisfy (14) with $[\hat{\mathcal{D}}]_{0i} = \frac{1}{2}(c_i^2 \boldsymbol{I}_4 - \boldsymbol{Q}_i), \forall i = 1, \ldots, \ell$, and let $\hat{\mu} = \sum_{i=1}^\ell (\hat{\boldsymbol{w}}_0^\top \boldsymbol{Q}_i \hat{\boldsymbol{w}}_0 - c_i^2)$. Since $c_i^2 > \lambda_{max}(\boldsymbol{Q}_i)$, the minimum of (QCQP) is $\sum_{i=1}^\ell \hat{\boldsymbol{w}}_0^\top \boldsymbol{Q}_i \hat{\boldsymbol{w}}_0$. Again, one easily verifies conditions (O1) and (O3) of Proposition 2 hold. Moreover, condition (O2) of Proposition 2 is equivalent to ($\forall \boldsymbol{z}_i \in \mathbb{R}^4$)

$$\sum_{i=1}^\ell \left( (\boldsymbol{z}_i - \boldsymbol{z}_0)^\top (c_i^2 \boldsymbol{I}_4 - \boldsymbol{Q}_i)(\boldsymbol{z}_i - \boldsymbol{z}_0) + \boldsymbol{z}_0^\top \left( \boldsymbol{Q}_i - (\hat{\boldsymbol{w}}_0^\top \boldsymbol{Q}_i \hat{\boldsymbol{w}}_0) \boldsymbol{I}_4 \right) \boldsymbol{z}_0 \right) \geq 0,$$

which holds, as $c_i^2 \boldsymbol{I}_4 - \boldsymbol{Q}_i \succeq 0$ and $\hat{\boldsymbol{w}}_0^\top \left( \sum_{i=1}^\ell \boldsymbol{Q}_i \right) \hat{\boldsymbol{w}}_0$ is the minimum eigenvalue of $\sum_{i=1}^\ell \boldsymbol{Q}_i$. This proves the tightness. For the proof of bound (23), see our full paper [45].

First we note that the error bound (23) becomes zero as $\epsilon_i \to 0$ and thus $\hat{\boldsymbol{w}}_0 = \boldsymbol{w}_0^*$, provided that $\|\boldsymbol{x}_i\|_2 / \lambda_{min2}\left( \sum_{i=1}^\ell \boldsymbol{P}_i \right)$ is not too large. The denominator $\lambda_{min2}\left( \sum_{i=1}^\ell \boldsymbol{P}_i \right)$ seems inevitable, as it usually determines the stability of solving a minimum eigenvalue problem: If $\lambda_{min2}\left( \sum_{i=1}^\ell \boldsymbol{P}_i \right) \to 0 = \lambda_{min}\left( \sum_{i=1}^\ell \boldsymbol{P}_i \right)$, then $\hat{\boldsymbol{w}}_0$ can be arbitrarily far from $\boldsymbol{w}_0^*$ even in the slightest presence of noise. Similarly, the bound can be trivial if $\|\boldsymbol{x}_i\|_2$ is too large. However, one can show that, for $\ell$ large enough, if the entries of each $\boldsymbol{x}_i$ are i.i.d. Gaussian, then $\lambda_{min2}\left( \sum_{i=1}^\ell \boldsymbol{Q}_i \right)$ is a positive multiple of $\sum_{i=1}^\ell \|\boldsymbol{x}_i\|_2^2$ with high probability; see our paper [45] for rigorous statements. In other words, for random Gaussian data, $\|\boldsymbol{x}_i\|_2 / \lambda_{min2}\left( \sum_{i=1}^\ell \boldsymbol{P}_i \right)$ is small and the bound (23) is well-behaved.

Condition $c_i^2 > \lambda_{max}(\boldsymbol{Q}_i)$ guarantees that no $\boldsymbol{Q}_i$ will get rejected as an outlier. In fact, it implies that the inner minimization of (TLS-Q) always "chooses" the quadratic term $\boldsymbol{w}_0^\top \boldsymbol{Q}_i \boldsymbol{w}_0$ for any unit quaternion $\boldsymbol{w}_0$. While (SDR) "is aware of" $c_i^2 > \lambda_{max}(\boldsymbol{Q}_i)$ (e.g., when it holds, (SDR) is tight), this condition presents a gap from Theorem 1: $\lambda_{max}(\boldsymbol{Q}_i) \neq 0$ even in the absence of noise but Theorem 1 holds for every $c_i^2 > 0$. Thus, while Theorem 4 promises the tightness if $c_i^2$ is large enough, it leads us to the task of finding the smallest possible $c_i^2$ for which (SDR) remains tight. This turns out to be very challenging. In what follows, we give our efforts to this task, which we hope will provide further insights into the noisy and outlier-free case.

**Smaller Truncation Parameters for the Tightness.** The smaller truncation parameters $c_i^2$ that we find are tightly related to the *eigengap* $\zeta$, defined as the ratio between the second smallest eigenvalue $\lambda_{\min 2}(\cdot)$ of $\sum_{i=1}^{\ell} \boldsymbol{Q}_i$ and its minimum eigenvalue:

$$\zeta := \frac{\lambda_{\min 2}\left(\sum_{i=1}^{\ell} \boldsymbol{Q}_i\right)}{\lambda_{\min}\left(\sum_{i=1}^{\ell} \boldsymbol{Q}_i\right)} \tag{24}$$

In analysis of eigenvalue algorithms (cf. [17]), the eigengap is typically defined as the *difference* between two consecutive eigenvalues of some matrix. Our eigengap (24) that takes the *division* of two smallest eigenvalues is not standard, but it will be convenient for our purpose. Also note that, $\boldsymbol{Q}_i$ is a perturbed version of $\boldsymbol{P}_i$ by noise $\epsilon_i$ (Lemma 3), so $\lambda_{\min}\left(\sum_{i=1}^{\ell} \boldsymbol{Q}_i\right)$ is in general nonzero, while it indeed approaches zero if $\epsilon_i \to 0$. Clearly $\zeta \geq 1$. Moreover, we have the following immediate observation:

*Remark 2.* If (TLS-Q) has a unique solution and if $c_i^2 > \hat{\boldsymbol{w}}_0^\top \boldsymbol{Q}_i \hat{\boldsymbol{w}}_0$ ($\forall i$), then $\zeta > 1$.

We are now ready to state the following result:

**Theorem 5 (Noisy and Outlier-Free Point Sets, Version 2).** *Suppose* $\zeta \geq \ell/(\ell-1)$. *The same conclusion of Theorem 4 holds true if*

$$c_i^2 > \hat{\boldsymbol{w}}_0^\top \boldsymbol{Q}_i \hat{\boldsymbol{w}}_0 + \|\boldsymbol{Q}_i \hat{\boldsymbol{w}}_0\|_2 + \frac{|d_i| + d_i}{2}, \quad \forall i = 1, \ldots, \ell \tag{25}$$

$$\text{with} \quad d_i := \frac{\sum_{i=1}^{\ell} \hat{\boldsymbol{w}}_0^\top \boldsymbol{Q}_i \hat{\boldsymbol{w}}_0}{\ell} - \hat{\boldsymbol{w}}_0^\top \boldsymbol{Q}_i \hat{\boldsymbol{w}}_0 + \frac{\lambda_{max}\left(\sum_{j \neq i}(\boldsymbol{Q}_i - \boldsymbol{Q}_j)\right)}{\zeta(\ell-1)}. \tag{26}$$

*Proof (Sketch).* Let $\widehat{\boldsymbol{V}} := [\widehat{\boldsymbol{V}}_0, \ \hat{\boldsymbol{w}}_0] \in \mathbb{R}^{4 \times 4}$ form an orthonormal basis of $\mathbb{R}^4$; $\widehat{\boldsymbol{V}}_0 \in \mathbb{R}^{4 \times 3}$ satisfies $\widehat{\boldsymbol{V}}_0^\top \hat{\boldsymbol{w}}_0 = 0$ and $\widehat{\boldsymbol{V}}_0^\top \widehat{\boldsymbol{V}}_0 = \boldsymbol{I}_3$. Let $\hat{\mu} := \sum_{i=1}^{\ell}\left(\hat{\boldsymbol{w}}_0^\top \boldsymbol{Q}_i \hat{\boldsymbol{w}}_0 - c_i^2\right)$ and

$$[\widehat{\mathcal{D}}]_{0i} := \widehat{\boldsymbol{V}} \begin{bmatrix} \widehat{\boldsymbol{T}}_i & 0 \\ 0 & 0 \end{bmatrix} \widehat{\boldsymbol{V}}^\top - \frac{1}{2}\left(\boldsymbol{Q}_i - c_i^2 \boldsymbol{I}_4\right), \quad \forall i = 1, \ldots, \ell \tag{27}$$

where $\widehat{\boldsymbol{T}}_i$ is a $3 \times 3$ symmetric matrix defined as

$$\widehat{\boldsymbol{T}}_i := \frac{\zeta - \frac{\ell}{\ell-1}}{\zeta} \widehat{\boldsymbol{V}}_0^\top \boldsymbol{Q}_i \widehat{\boldsymbol{V}}_0 + \frac{\sum_{j=1}^{\ell} \widehat{\boldsymbol{V}}_0^\top \boldsymbol{Q}_j \widehat{\boldsymbol{V}}_0}{\zeta(\ell-1)} - \frac{\left(\sum_{i=1}^{\ell} \hat{\boldsymbol{w}}_0^\top \boldsymbol{Q}_i \hat{\boldsymbol{w}}_0\right) \boldsymbol{I}_3}{\ell}. \tag{28}$$

Then, similarly to the proof sketch of Theorem 4, it is not hard to show that conditions (O1) and (O3) of Proposition 2 are satisfied. Yet, proving (O2) under assumptions (25) and $\zeta \geq \ell/(\ell - 1)$ is not that obvious, and we omit it here in interest of space.                                                                     $\square$

Theorem 5 is better understood via numerics. We take randomly generated $\ell = 100$ point pairs $(\boldsymbol{y}_i, \boldsymbol{x}_i)$'s with $\boldsymbol{x}_i \sim \mathcal{N}(0, \boldsymbol{I}_3)$, and add different levels of Gaussian noise $\epsilon_i \sim \mathcal{N}(0, \sigma^2 \boldsymbol{I}_3)$, where $\sigma$ ranges from 1% to 10%. The values of $\lambda_{\min}\left(\sum_{i=1}^{\ell} \boldsymbol{Q}_i\right)$ and $\lambda_{\min 2}\left(\sum_{i=1}^{\ell} \boldsymbol{Q}_i\right)$, and thus $\zeta$, are shown in Fig. 1a, where one might observe that $\zeta \approx 250$ for 10% noise, $\zeta \approx 25000$ for 1% noise, and, in general, $\zeta = \infty$ for the noiseless case. This empirically validates the assumption $\zeta \geq \ell/(\ell - 1) = 100/99$.

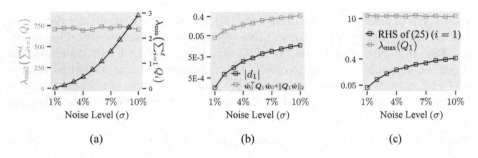

(a)                                     (b)                                     (c)

**Fig. 1.** Numerical illustration of condition (25) of Theorem 5 (500 trials, $\ell = 100$).

We then elaborate the more complicated condition (25). First we recall that $c_i^2 > \hat{\boldsymbol{w}}_0^\top \boldsymbol{Q}_i \hat{\boldsymbol{w}}_0$ is essential for (TLS-Q) to preserve all inliers. Second, we argue that the term $\|\boldsymbol{Q}_i \hat{\boldsymbol{w}}\|_2$ in (25) is also essential, as it accounts for the fact that noise destroys the inequality $\lambda_{\min}(\boldsymbol{Q}_i) - \hat{\boldsymbol{w}}_0^\top \boldsymbol{Q}_i \hat{\boldsymbol{w}}_0 \geq 0$ which holds in the noiseless case (where $\lambda_{\min}(\boldsymbol{Q}_i) = \hat{\boldsymbol{w}}_0^\top \boldsymbol{Q}_i \hat{\boldsymbol{w}}_0 = 0$) but gets violated (in general) in the presence of noise. Finally, (25) also incurs a curious term $(|d_i| + d_i)/2$, with $d_i$ defined in a sophisticated way (26). If $d_i < 0$ then this term is 0. Thus it remains to understand the values of $|d_i|$. In particular, we plotted the values of $|d_1|$ in Fig. 1b in comparison to $\hat{\boldsymbol{w}}_0^\top \boldsymbol{Q}_1 \hat{\boldsymbol{w}}_0 + \|\boldsymbol{Q}_1 \hat{\boldsymbol{w}}\|_2$, and observed that $|d_1|$ is two orders of magnitude smaller (there is nothing special about the choice of index 1). In fact, as noise approaches zero, we have $\boldsymbol{Q}_i \hat{\boldsymbol{w}}_0 \to 0$ and (in general) $\zeta \to \infty$, hence $d_i \to 0$ by definition (26). Overall, condition (25) degenerates into $c_i^2 > 0$ in the noiseless case. Thus one might conclude that condition (25) is tighter than $c_i^2 > \lambda_{\max}(\boldsymbol{Q}_i)$ of Theorem 4, as Lemma 1 implies $\lambda_{\max}(\boldsymbol{Q}_i) \neq 0$ even without noise. Indeed, this is further numerically evidenced by Fig. 1 where the lower bound of (25) with $i = 1$ ranges from 0.04 to 0.4, while the counterpart $\lambda_{\max}(\boldsymbol{Q}_1)$ of Theorem 4 is roughly 12, arguably much larger.

While the term $(|d_i| + d_i)/2$ is quite small (Fig. 1b) and sometimes harmless (e.g., when $d_i < 0$), it appears as an artifact of our analysis, and we expect an ideal condition for the noisy + outlier-free case to be $c_i^2 > \hat{\boldsymbol{w}}_0^\top \boldsymbol{Q}_i \hat{\boldsymbol{w}}_0 + \|\boldsymbol{Q}_i \hat{\boldsymbol{w}}_0\|_2$.

However, proof under this alternative condition demands showing some matrix inequality that involves a sum of matrix inverses always holds; we were not able to prove it.

## 3.4   The Noisy + Outliers Case

Combine the proof ideas of Theorems 2 and 5, and we obtain:

**Theorem 6 (Noisy Point Sets with Outliers).** *Let* $Q_1, \ldots, Q_{k^*}$ *be inliers, the rest* $Q_j$*'s outliers, and* $\hat{w}_0$ *a global minimizer of* (TLS-Q). *Define*

$$\zeta_{in} := \frac{\lambda_{\min2}\left(\sum_{i=1}^{k^*} Q_i\right)}{\lambda_{\min}\left(\sum_{i=1}^{k^*} Q_i\right)}. \tag{29}$$

*Assume (1)* $\zeta_{in} \geq k^*/(k^* - 1)$, *(2) for every* $j = k^* + 1, \ldots, \ell$, *we have* $0 < c_j^2 < \lambda_{min}(Q_j)$, *(3) for every* $i = 1, \ldots, k^*$, *(25) holds with* $d_i$ *now defined as*

$$d_i := \frac{\sum_{i=1}^{k^*} \hat{w}_0^\top Q_i \hat{w}_0}{k^*} - \hat{w}_0^\top Q_i \hat{w}_0 + \frac{\lambda_{\max}\left(\sum_{j \neq i} (Q_i - Q_j)\right)}{\zeta(k^* - 1)}. \tag{30}$$

*Then* (SDR) *is tight and, similarly to* (23) *we have*

$$\sin^2(\hat{\tau}_0^*) \leq \frac{4\sum_{i=1}^{k^*} \|\epsilon_i\|_2 \|x_i\|_2}{\lambda_{\min2}\left(\sum_{i=1}^{k^*} P_i\right)}, \qquad \sin^2(\hat{\tau}_0^*) := 1 - (\hat{w}_0^\top w_0^*)^2 \tag{31}$$

*Here we recall that* $w_0^* \in \mathbb{S}^3$ *is the ground-truth unit quaternion, and each* $P_i$ *is the "pure data" part of* $Q_i$ *that satisfies* $P_i w_0^* = 0, P_i \succeq 0$ *(Lemma 3).*

*Proof.* The given assumptions ensure that (TLS-Q) rejects all outliers and admit all inliers, and the minimum of (TLS-Q) is $\sum_{i=1}^{k^*} \hat{w}_0^\top Q_i \hat{w}_0 + \sum_{j=k^*+1}^{\ell} c_j^2$. For $i = 1, \ldots, k^*$ let $\mathcal{D}_{0i}$ be defined as in (27), and for $j = k^* + 1, \ldots, \ell$ let $[\hat{D}]_{0j} := \frac{1}{2}(Q_j - c_j^2 I_4)$. Let $\hat{\mu} := \sum_{i=1}^{k^*} (\hat{w}_0^\top Q_i \hat{w}_0 - c_i^2)$. One then verifies the optimality conditions (O1) and (O3) of Proposition 2 are satisfied. (O2) is equivalent to $(\forall z_i \in \mathbb{R}^4)$

$$\underbrace{-\hat{\mu}\|z_0\|_2^2 + \sum_{i=1}^{k^*} \left(2z_i^\top [\hat{D}]_{0i} z_i - z_0^\top \left(2[\hat{D}]_{0i} - Q_i + c_i^2 I_4\right) z_i\right)}_{\text{Inlier Term}} + \underbrace{\sum_{j=k^*+1}^{\ell} O_j}_{\text{Outlier Term}} \geq 0,$$

where $O_j := z_j(Q_j - c_j^2 I_4)z_j$. Since $Q_j \succeq c_j^2 I_4$, $O_j$ is non-negative. Under the given assumptions, one can replace $\ell$ by $k^*$ in the proof of Theorem 5 and then find the inlier term is also non-negative. This finishes proving (O2) and thus the tightness of (SDR). The error bound (31) follows from the proof of Theorem 4 with $\ell$ replaced by $k^*$.

Note that all assumptions of Theorem 6 have their counterparts in previous results (e.g., Theorems 2 and 5), so we omitted further explanations.

# 4   Discussion and Future Work

We have investigated the tightness of a semidefinite relaxation (SDR) of truncated least-squares for robust rotation search in four different cases, and in each case we either showed improvements over prior work or proved new theoretical results. Our investigation can potentially be borrowed to understand semidefinite relaxations of many other geometric vision tasks; see [58] for 6 examples of truncated least-squares and see also [3,10,20].

As is common in the optimization literature, the relaxation we analyzed is at the first (i.e., lowest) relaxation order of the *Lasserre* hierarchy [36], or otherwise known as the *Shor relaxation* [50]. A tighter relaxation that has quadratically more constraints than (SDR) exists (cf. [57]). However, analyzing this tighter relaxation is significantly harder, as one needs to either (1) construct quadratically more dual certificates during the proof, or (2) use more abstract optimality conditions (cf. [19,20]). Therefore, we leave this challenging question to future work.

**Acknowledgments.** This work was supported by grants NSF 1704458, NSF 1934979 and ONR MURI 503405-78051.

# References

1. Agostinho, S., Gomes, J., Del Bue, A.: CvxPnPL: a unified convex solution to the absolute pose estimation problem from point and line correspondences. Technical report. arXiv:1907.10545v2 [cs.CV] (2019)
2. Aholt, C., Agarwal, S., Thomas, R.: A QCQP approach to triangulation. In: Fitzgibbon, A., Lazebnik, S., Perona, P., Sato, Y., Schmid, C. (eds.) ECCV 2012. LNCS, vol. 7572, pp. 654–667. Springer, Heidelberg (2012). https://doi.org/10.1007/978-3-642-33718-5_47
3. Alfassi, Y., Keren, D., Reznick, B.: The non-tightness of a convex relaxation to rotation recovery. Sensors **21**(21), 7358 (2021)
4. Antonante, P., Tzoumas, V., Yang, H., Carlone, L.: Outlier-robust estimation: hardness, minimally tuned algorithms, and applications. IEEE Trans. Robot. (2021)
5. Bandeira, A.S., Boumal, N., Singer, A.: Tightness of the maximum likelihood semidefinite relaxation for angular synchronization. Math. Program. **163**(1–2), 145–167 (2017)
6. Boumal, N.: An introduction to optimization on smooth manifolds. Available online (2020). http://www.nicolasboumal.net/book
7. Briales, J., Gonzalez-Jimenez, J.: Fast global optimality verification in 3D SLAM. In: IEEE/RSJ International Conference on Intelligent Robots and Systems, pp. 4630–4636 (2016)
8. Briales, J., Gonzalez-Jimenez, J.: Convex global 3D registration with lagrangian duality. In: IEEE Conference on Computer Vision and Pattern Recognition, pp. 4960–4969 (2017)
9. Briales, J., Kneip, L., Gonzalez-Jimenez, J.: A certifiably globally optimal solution to the non-minimal relative pose problem. In: IEEE Conference on Computer Vision and Pattern Recognition, pp. 145–154 (2018)

10. Brynte, L., Larsson, V., Iglesias, J.P., Olsson, C., Kahl, F.: On the tightness of semidefinite relaxations for rotation estimation. J. Math. Imaging Vision **64**(1), 57–67 (2022)
11. Bustos, A.P., Chin, T.J.: Guaranteed outlier removal for rotation search. In: IEEE International Conference on Computer Vision, pp. 2165–2173 (2015)
12. Candes, E.J., Strohmer, T., Voroninski, V.: Phaselift: exact and stable signal recovery from magnitude measurements via convex programming. Commun. Pure Appl. Math. **66**(8), 1241–1274 (2013)
13. Carlone, L., Calafiore, G.C.: Convex relaxations for pose graph optimization with outliers. IEEE Robot. Automation Lett. **3**(2), 1160–1167 (2018)
14. Carlone, L., Calafiore, G.C., Tommolillo, C., Dellaert, F.: Planar pose graph optimization: duality, optimal solutions, and verification. IEEE Trans. Rob. **32**(3), 545–565 (2016)
15. Carlone, L., Rosen, D.M., Calafiore, G., Leonard, J.J., Dellaert, F.: Lagrangian duality in 3D SLAM: verification techniques and optimal solutions. In: IEEE/RSJ International Conference on Intelligent Robots and Systems, pp. 125–132 (2015)
16. Chaudhury, K.N., Khoo, Y., Singer, A.: Global registration of multiple point clouds using semidefinite programming. SIAM J. Optim. **25**(1), 468–501 (2015)
17. Chen, Y., Chi, Y., Fan, J., Ma, C., et al.: Spectral methods for data science: a statistical perspective. Found. Trends Mach. Learn. **14**(5), 566–806 (2021)
18. Cheng, Y., Lopez, J.A., Camps, O., Sznaier, M.: A convex optimization approach to robust fundamental matrix estimation. In: Proceedings of the IEEE Conference on Computer Vision and Pattern Recognition, pp. 2170–2178 (2015)
19. Cifuentes, D.: A convex relaxation to compute the nearest structured rank deficient matrix. SIAM J. Matrix Anal. Appl. **42**(2), 708–729 (2021)
20. Cifuentes, D., Agarwal, S., Parrilo, P.A., Thomas, R.R.: On the local stability of semidefinite relaxations. Mathematical Programming, pp. 1–35 (2021)
21. Ding, T., et al.: Robust homography estimation via dual principal component pursuit. In: IEEE Conference on Computer Vision and Pattern Recognition, pp. 6080–6089 (2020)
22. Elhamifar, E., Vidal, R.: Sparse subspace clustering: algorithm, theory, and applications. IEEE Trans. Pattern Anal. Mach. Intell. **35**(11), 2765–2781 (2013)
23. Eriksson, A., Olsson, C., Kahl, F., Chin, T.J.: Rotation averaging and strong duality. In: Conference on Computer Vision and Pattern Recognition, pp. 127–135 (2018)
24. Fredriksson, J., Olsson, C.: Simultaneous multiple rotation averaging using lagrangian duality. In: Lee, K.M., Matsushita, Y., Rehg, J.M., Hu, Z. (eds.) ACCV 2012. LNCS, vol. 7726, pp. 245–258. Springer, Heidelberg (2013). https://doi.org/10.1007/978-3-642-37431-9_19
25. Garcia-Salguero, M., Briales, J., Gonzalez-Jimenez, J.: Certifiable relative pose estimation. Image Vis. Comput. **109**, 104142 (2021)
26. Garcia-Salguero, M., Gonzalez-Jimenez, J.: Fast and robust certifiable estimation of the relative pose between two calibrated cameras. J. Math. Imaging Vis. **63**(8), 1036–1056 (2021)
27. Giamou, M., Ma, Z., Peretroukhin, V., Kelly, J.: Certifiably globally optimal extrinsic calibration from per-sensor egomotion. IEEE Robot. Automation Lett. **4**(2), 367–374 (2019)
28. Hartley, R., Zisserman, A.: Multiple View Geometry in Computer Vision. Cambridge University Press (2004)
29. Horn, B.K.: Closed-form solution of absolute orientation using unit quaternions. J. Opt. Soc. Am. A **4**(4), 629–642 (1987)

30. Iglesias, J.P., Olsson, C., Kahl, F.: Global optimality for point set registration using semidefinite programming. In: IEEE Conference on Computer Vision and Pattern Recognition (2020)
31. Ikami, D., Yamasaki, T., Aizawa, K.: Fast and robust estimation for unit-norm constrained linear fitting problems. In: IEEE Conference on Computer Vision and Pattern Recognition, pp. 8147–8155 (2018)
32. Jain, A.K., Murty, M.N., Flynn, P.J.: Data clustering: a review. ACM Comput. Surv. **31**(3), 264–323 (1999)
33. Kahl, F., Henrion, D.: Globally optimal estimates for geometric reconstruction problems. Int. J. Comput. Vision **74**(1), 3–15 (2007)
34. Khoo, Y., Kapoor, A.: Non-iterative rigid 2D/3D point-set registration using semidefinite programming. IEEE Trans. Image Process. **25**(7), 2956–2970 (2016)
35. Lajoie, P.Y., Hu, S., Beltrame, G., Carlone, L.: Modeling perceptual aliasing in SLAM via discrete-continuous graphical models. IEEE Robot. Automation Lett. **4**(2), 1232–1239 (2019)
36. Lasserre, J.B.: Global optimization with polynomials and the problem of moments. SIAM J. Optim. **11**(3), 796–817 (2001)
37. Li, M., Liang, G., Luo, H., Qian, H., Lam, T.L.: Robot-to-robot relative pose estimation based on semidefinite relaxation optimization. In: IEEE/RSJ International Conference on Intelligent Robots and Systems, pp. 4491–4498 (2020)
38. Ling, S.: Near-optimal bounds for generalized orthogonal procrustes problem via generalized power method. arXiv:2112.13725 [cs.IT] (2021)
39. Lu, C., Liu, Y.F., Zhang, W.Q., Zhang, S.: Tightness of a new and enhanced semidefinite relaxation for MIMO detection. SIAM J. Optim. **29**(1), 719–742 (2019)
40. Ma, Y., Soatto, S., Košecká, J., Sastry, S.: An Invitation to 3D Vision: From Images to Geometric Models, vol. 26. Springer (2004)
41. Maron, H., Dym, N., Kezurer, I., Kovalsky, S., Lipman, Y.: Point registration via efficient convex relaxation. ACM Trans. Graph. **35**(4) (2016)
42. Ozyesil, O., Singer, A., Basri, R.: Stable camera motion estimation using convex programming. SIAM J. Imag. Sci. **8**(2), 1220–1262 (2015)
43. Parra Bustos, A., Chin, T.J.: Guaranteed outlier removal for point cloud registration with correspondences. IEEE Trans. Pattern Anal. Mach. Intell. **40**(12), 2868–2882 (2018)
44. Parra Bustos, A., Chin, T.J., Eriksson, A., Li, H., Suter, D.: Fast rotation search with stereographic projections for 3D registration. IEEE Trans. Pattern Anal. Mach. Intell. **38**(11), 2227–2240 (2016)
45. Peng, L., Fazlyab, M., Vidal, R.: Towards understanding the semidefinite relaxations of truncated least-squares in robust rotation search. Technical report, arXiv:2207.08350 [math.OC] (2022)
46. Peng, L., Tsakiris, M.C., Vidal, R.: ARCS: accurate rotation and correspondences search. In: IEEE/CVF Conference on Computer Vision and Pattern Recognition, pp. 11153–11163 (2022)
47. Probst, T., Paudel, D.P., Chhatkuli, A., Gool, L.V.: Convex relaxations for consensus and non-minimal problems in 3D vision. In: IEEE/CVF International Conference on Computer Vision, pp. 10233–10242 (2019)
48. Rosen, D.M., Carlone, L., Bandeira, A.S., Leonard, J.J.: SE-Sync: a certifiably correct algorithm for synchronization over the special euclidean group. Int. J. Robot. Res. **38**(2–3), 95–125 (2019)
49. Shi, J., Heng, Y., Carlone, L.: Optimal pose and shape estimation for category-level 3d object perception. In: Robotics: Science and Systems (2021)

50. Shor, N.Z.: Dual quadratic estimates in polynomial and boolean programming. Ann. Oper. Res. **25**(1), 163–168 (1990)

51. Tat-Jun, C., Zhipeng, C., Neumann, F.: Robust fitting in computer vision: Easy or hard? Int. J. Comput. Vision **128**(3), 575–587 (2020)

52. Tian, Y., Khosoussi, K., Rosen, D.M., How, J.P.: Distributed certifiably correct pose-graph optimization. IEEE Trans. Rob. **37**(6), 2137–2156 (2021)

53. Unnikrishnan, J., Haghighatshoar, S., Vetterli, M.: Unlabeled sensing with random linear measurements. IEEE Trans. Inf. Theory **64**(5), 3237–3253 (2018)

54. Wang, L., Singer, A.: Exact and stable recovery of rotations for robust synchronization. Inf. Inference J. IMA **2**(2), 145–193 (2013)

55. Wise, E., Giamou, M., Khoubyarian, S., Grover, A., Kelly, J.: Certifiably optimal monocular hand-eye calibration. In: IEEE International Conference on Multisensor Fusion and Integration for Intelligent Systems, pp. 271–278. IEEE (2020)

56. Yang, H., Antonante, P., Tzoumas, V., Carlone, L.: Graduated non-convexity for robust spatial perception: From non-minimal solvers to global outlier rejection. IEEE Robot. Automation Lett. **5**(2), 1127–1134 (2020)

57. Yang, H., Carlone, L.: A quaternion-based certifiably optimal solution to the Wahba problem with outliers. In: IEEE International Conference on Computer Vision, pp. 1665–1674 (2019)

58. Yang, H., Carlone, L.: Certifiable outlier-robust geometric perception: Exact semidefinite relaxations and scalable global optimization. Technical report, arXiv:2109.03349 [cs.CV] (2021)

59. Yang, H., Shi, J., Carlone, L.: TEASER: fast and certifiable point cloud registration. IEEE Trans. Rob. **37**(2), 314–333 (2021)

60. Zhao, J.: An efficient solution to non-minimal case essential matrix estimation. IEEE Trans. Pattern Anal. Mach. Intell. (2020)

61. Zhao, J., Xu, W., Kneip, L.: A certifiably globally optimal solution to generalized essential matrix estimation. In: IEEE Conference on Computer Vision and Pattern Recognition (2020)

62. Zhong, Y., Boumal, N.: Near-optimal bounds for phase synchronization. SIAM J. Optim. **28**(2), 989–1016 (2018)

# Transfer Without Forgetting

Matteo Boschini[1]([envelope]) [iD], Lorenzo Bonicelli[1] [iD], Angelo Porrello[1] [iD],
Giovanni Bellitto[2] [iD], Matteo Pennisi[2] [iD], Simone Palazzo[2] [iD],
Concetto Spampinato[2] [iD], and Simone Calderara[1] [iD]

[1] AImageLab, University of Modena and Reggio Emilia, Modena, Italy
{matteo.boschini,lorenzo.bonicelli,angelo.porrello,
simone.calderara}@unimore.it
[2] PeRCeiVe Lab, University of Catania, Catania, Italy
{giovanni.bellitto,matteo.pennisi,simone.palazzo,
concetto.spampinato}@unict.it

**Abstract.** This work investigates the entanglement between Continual
Learning (CL) and Transfer Learning (TL). In particular, we shed light
on the widespread application of network pretraining, highlighting that
it is itself subject to catastrophic forgetting. Unfortunately, this issue
leads to the under-exploitation of knowledge transfer during later tasks.
On this ground, we propose Transfer without Forgetting (TwF), a hybrid
approach building upon a fixed pretrained sibling network, which continuously propagates the knowledge inherent in the source domain through a
layer-wise loss term. Our experiments indicate that TwF steadily outperforms other CL methods across a variety of settings, averaging a 4.81%
gain in Class-Incremental accuracy over a variety of datasets and different buffer sizes. Our code is available at https://github.com/mbosc/
twf.

**Keywords:** Continual learning · Lifelong learning · Experience
replay · Transfer learning · Pretraining · Attention

## 1 Introduction

Thanks to the enthusiastic development carried out by the scientific community,
there exist myriad widely available deep learning models that can be either readily deployed or easily adapted to perform complex tasks [4,24,48,60,64]. However, the desiderata of practical applications [59] often overstep the boundaries of
the typical *i.i.d.* paradigm, fostering the study of different learning approaches.

In contrast with the natural tendency of biological intelligence to seamlessly
acquire new skills and notions, deep models are prone to an issue known as
*catastrophic forgetting* [39], *i.e.*, they fit the current input data distribution to

**Supplementary Information** The online version contains supplementary material
available at https://doi.org/10.1007/978-3-031-20050-2_40.

the detriment of previously acquired knowledge. In light of this limitation, the sub-field of Continual Learning (CL) [16,46,63] aspires to train models capable of adaptation and lifelong learning when facing a sequence of changing tasks, either through appositely designed architectures [38,56,57], targeted regularization [31, 34,70] or by storing and replaying previous data points [8,14,50,52].

On a similar note, human intelligence is especially versatile in that it excels in contrasting and incorporating knowledge coming from multiple domains. Instead, the application of deep supervised learning algorithms typically demands large annotated datasets, whose collection has significant costs and may be impractical. To address this issue, Transfer Learning (TL) techniques are typically applied with the purpose of transferring and re-using knowledge across different data domains. In this setting, the simplest technique is to pre-train the model on a huge labeled dataset (*i.e.* the source) and then finetune it on the *target* task [19,23,51]. Such a simple schema has been recently overcome by more sophisticated domain adaptation algorithms [15,35,36] mainly based on the concept of *feature alignment*: here, the goal is to reduce the shift between the feature distributions of target and source domains. Unfortunately, these approaches often require the availability of the source dataset during training, which clashes with the usual constraints imposed in the CL scenarios.

In this work, we explore the interactions between pretraining and CL and highlight a blind spot of continual learners. Previous work underlined that naive pretraining is beneficial as it leads the learner to reduced forgetting [40]. However, we detect that the pretraining task itself is swiftly and catastrophically forgotten as the model veers towards the newly introduced stream of data. This matter is not really detrimental if all target classes are available at once (*i.e.*, joint training): as their exemplars can be accessed simultaneously, the learner can discover a joint feature alignment that works well for all of them while leaving its pretraining initialization. However, if classes are shown in a sequential manner, we argue that transfer mostly concerns the early encountered tasks: as a consequence, pretraining ends up being fully beneficial only for the former classes. For the later ones, since pretraining features are swiftly overwritten, the benefit of pretraining is instead lowered, thus undermining the advantages of the source knowledge. In support of this argument, this work reports several experimental analyses (Sect. 3.1) revealing that state-of-the-art CL methods do not take full advantage of pretraining knowledge.

To account for such a disparity and let all tasks profit equally from pretraining, this work sets up a framework based on Transfer Learning techniques. We show that the Continual Learning setting requires specific and *ad-hoc* strategies to fully exploit the source knowledge without incurring its forgetting. Consequently, we propose an approach termed **Transfer without Forgetting (TwF)** that equips the base model with a pretrained and fixed sibling network, which continuously propagates its internal representations to the former network through a per-layer strategy based on *knowledge distillation* [27]. We show that our proposal is more effective than alternative approaches (*i.e.*, extending anti-forgetting regularization to the pretraining initialization) and beneficial even if the data used for pretraining is strongly dissimilar w.r.t. to the target task.

## 2  Related Work

Continual Learning (CL) [16,46] is an increasingly popular field of machine learning that deals with the mitigation of catastrophic forgetting [39]. CL methods are usually grouped as follows, according to the approach they take.

*Regularization-based* methods [12,13,31,37] typically identify subsets of weights that are highly functional for the representations of previous tasks, with the purpose to prevent their drastic modification through apposite optimization constraints. Alternatively, they consolidate the previous knowledge by using past models as soft teachers while learning the current task [34].

*Architectural* approaches dedicate distinct sets of parameters to each task, often resorting to network expansion as new tasks arrive [38,56,58]. While capable of high performance, they are mostly limited to the Task-IL scenario (described in Sect. 4.1) as they require task-identifiers at inference time.

*Rehearsal-based* methods employ a fixed-size buffer to store a fraction of the old data. ER [49,53] interleaves training samples from the current task with previous samples: notably, several works [8,20] point out that such a simple strategy can effectively mitigate forgetting and achieve superior performance. This method has hence inspired several works: DER [8] and its extension X-DER [6] also store past model responses and pin them as an additional teaching signal. MER [52] combines replay and meta-learning [21,44] to maximize transfer from the past while minimizing interference. Other works [3,9] propose different sample-selection strategies to include in the buffer, while GEM [37] and its relaxation A-GEM [13] employ old training data to minimize interference. On a final note, recent works [7,61] exploit the memory buffer to address semi-supervised settings where examples can be either labeled or not.

**Transfer Learning (TL)** [45] is a machine learning methodology aiming at using the knowledge acquired on a prior task to solve a distinct target task. In its classical formulation [68], a model is trained on the source dataset and then finetuned on the (possibly much smaller) target dataset to adapt the previously learned features. Alternatively, transfer can be induced via multi-level Knowledge Distillation, guided by meta-learning [30], attention [66] or higher-level descriptions of the flow of information within the model [67].

## 3  Method

**Setting.** In CL, a classification model $f_{(\theta,\phi)}$ (composed of a multilayered feature extractor $h_\theta = h_{\theta_l}^{(l)} \circ h_{\theta_{l-1}}^{(l-1)} \circ \cdots \circ h_{\theta_1}^{(1)}$ and a classifier $g_\phi$, $f_{(\theta,\phi)} = g_\phi \circ h_\theta$) is trained on a sequence of $N$ tasks $\mathcal{T}_i = \{(x_j^i, y_j^i)\}_{j=1}^{|\mathcal{T}_i|}$. The objective of $f_{(\theta,\phi)}$ is minimizing the classification error across all seen tasks:

$$\min_{\theta,\phi} \mathcal{L} = \mathbb{E}_i \left[ \mathbb{E}_{(x,y) \sim \mathcal{T}_i} \left[ \ell(y, f_{(\theta,\phi)}(x)) \right] \right], \tag{1}$$

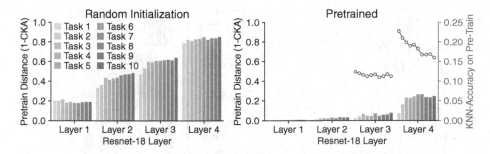

**Fig. 1.** Forgetting of the initialization, measured as the distance from the pretrain $(1-\mathrm{CKA}$ [32]) (lower is better) and $k$NN accuracy (higher is better). Features extracted by a pretrained model remain closer to the initialization w.r.t. a randomly initialized model. Furthermore, the steady decrease in $k$NN accuracy as training progresses reveals that features become less specific for past tasks.

where $\ell$ is a suitable loss function. Unfortunately, the problem framed by Eq. 1 cannot be directly optimized due to the following key assumptions: *i)* while learning the current task $\mathcal{T}_c$, examples and labels of previous tasks are inaccessible; *ii)* the label space of distinct tasks is disjoint $(y_m^i \neq y_n^j \ \forall i \neq j)$ *i.e.*, classes learned previously cannot recur in later phases. Therefore, Eq. 1 can only be approximated, seeking adequate performance on previously seen tasks (*stability*), while remaining flexible enough to adapt to upcoming data (*plasticity*).

### 3.1   Pretraining Incurs Catastrophic Forgetting

*Mehta et al.* [40] have investigated the entanglement between continual learning and pretraining, highlighting that the latter leads the optimization towards wider minima of the loss landscape. As deeply discussed in [6,8], such property is strictly linked to a reduced tendency in incurring forgetting.

On this latter point, we therefore provide an alternate experimental proof of the benefits deriving from pretraining initialization. In particular, we focus on ResNet-18 trained with ER [53] on Split CIFAR-100[1] and measure how each individual layer differs from its initialization. It can be observed that a randomly initialized backbone (Fig. 1, *left*) significantly alters its parameters at all layers while tasks progress, resulting in a very low Centered Kernel Alignment [32] similarity score already at the first CL task. On the contrary, a backbone pretrained on Tiny ImageNet (Fig. 1, *right*) undergoes limited parameter variations in its layers, with the exception of the last residual layer (although to a lesser extent w.r.t. random init.). This latter finding indicates that its pretraining parametrization requires relevant modifications to fit the current training data. This leads to the *catastrophic forgetting* of the source pretraining task: namely, the latter is swiftly forgotten as the network focuses on the initial CL tasks.

---

[1] This preliminary experiment follows the same setting presented in Sect. 4.1.

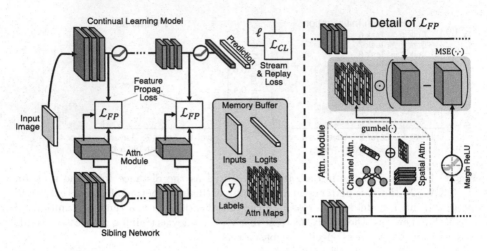

**Fig. 2.** Overview of TwF and detail of $\mathcal{L}_{FP}$: Given a batch of samples from the current task or from $\mathcal{B}$, we *i)* extract intermediate features from both the student and fixed sibling backbones at multiple layers; *ii)* compute the corresponding binarized attention maps $\mathbb{M}(\cdot)$; *iii)* pull the attention-masked representations of the two models closer.

This is corroborated by the decreasing accuracy for pretraining data of a $k$NN classifier trained on top of *Layer 3* and *Layer 4* representations in Fig. 1 (*right*).

To sum up, while pretraining is certainly beneficial, the model drifts away from it one task after the other. Hence, only the first task takes full advantage of it; the optimization of later tasks, instead, starts from an initialization that increasingly differs from the one attained by pretraining. This is detrimental, as classes introduced later might be likewise advantaged by the reuse of different pieces of the initial knowledge.

### 3.2   Transfer without Forgetting

To mitigate the issue above, we propose a strategy that enables a continuous transfer between the source task and the incrementally learned target problem.

**Feature Propagation.** As the training progresses, the input stream introduces new classes that might benefit from the adaptation of specific features of the pretrained model. To enable feature transfer without incurring pretraining forgetting, we maintain a copy of it (the *sibling* model) and adopt an intermediate feature knowledge distillation [2,26,41,55,66] objective. Considering a subset of $L$ layers, we seek to minimize the distance between the activations of the base network $h_\theta^{(l)} \triangleq h_\theta^{(l)}(x)$ and those from its pretrained sibling $\widehat{h}^{(l)} \triangleq h_{\theta^t}^{(l)}(x)$:

$$\mathop{\mathbb{E}}_{x \sim \mathcal{T}_c} \left[ \sum_{l=1}^{L} ||h_\theta^{(l)} - \text{ReLU}_{\text{m}}(\widehat{h}^{(l)})||_2^2 \right], \tag{2}$$

where $c$ is the current task and $\text{ReLU}_m(\cdot)$ indicates the application of a margin ReLU activation [26]. It is noted that the objective outlined by Eq. 2 leads the CL model to focus on mirroring the internal representations of the pretrained teacher and maximizing transfer. However, focusing on the latter solely can lead to excessive rigidity, thus preventing the model from fitting the data from the current task altogether. On these grounds, we take inspiration from [66] and use a weighted version of Eq. 2. In particular, an apposite learnable module computes a gating attention map $\text{M}(\cdot)$ over the feature maps of the sibling, which serves as a binary mask selecting which spatial regions have to be aligned. The resulting objective is consequently updated as follows:

$$\mathop{\mathbb{E}}_{x \sim \mathcal{T}_c} \left[ \sum_{l=1}^{L} ||\text{M}(\widehat{h}^{(l)}) \odot \left( h_\theta^{(l)} - \text{ReLU}_m(\widehat{h}^{(l)}) \right)||_2^2 \right], \tag{3}$$

where $\odot$ indicates the Hadamard product between two tensors of the same dimensions. The attention maps $\text{M}(\cdot)$ are computed through specific layers, whose architectural design follows the insights provided in [47]. Specifically, they forward the input activation maps into two parallel branches, producing respectively a Channel Attention $\text{M}_{\text{Ch}}(\cdot)$ map and a Spatial Attention $\text{M}_{\text{Sp}}(\cdot)$ map. These two intermediate results are summed and then activated through a binary Gumbel-Softmax sampling [29], which allows us to model discrete *on-off* decisions regarding which information we want to propagate. In formal terms:

$$\text{M}(\widehat{h}^{(l)}) \triangleq \text{gumbel}(\text{M}_{\text{Ch}}(\widehat{h}^{(l)}) + \text{M}_{\text{Sp}}(\widehat{h}^{(l)})). \tag{4}$$

The Spatial Attention $\text{M}_{\text{Sp}}(\widehat{h}^{(l)})$ regulates the propagation of spatially localized information and is obtained by stacking four convolutional layers [47] with different configurations (*i.e.*, the kernel sizes and dilation rates – please refer to supplementary materials for additional details):

$$\text{M}_{\text{Sp}}(\widehat{h}^{(l)}) \triangleq \text{C}_{1\times1} \circ \text{C}_{3\times3} \circ \text{C}_{3\times3} \circ \text{C}_{1\times1}(\widehat{h}^{(l)}), \tag{5}$$

where C denotes a sequence of convolutional, batch normalization, and ReLU activation layers. On the other hand, the Channel Attention $\text{M}_{\text{Ch}}(\widehat{h}^{(l)})$ estimates the information across the channels of $\widehat{h}^{(l)}$; in its design, we draw inspiration from the formulation proposed in [28]. Formally, considering the result $\widehat{h}^{(l)}_{\text{GAP}}$ of the Global Average Pooling (GAP) applied on top of $\widehat{h}^{(l)}$, we have:

$$\text{M}_{\text{Ch}}(\widehat{h}^{(l)}) \triangleq \tanh(\text{BN}(W_1^\mathsf{T} \widehat{h}^{(l)}_{\text{GAP}})) \cdot \sigma(\text{BN}(W_2^\mathsf{T} \widehat{h}^{(l)}_{\text{GAP}})) + W_3^\mathsf{T} \widehat{h}^{(l)}_{\text{GAP}}, \tag{6}$$

where $W_1$, $W_2$, and $W_3$ are the weights of three fully connected layers organized in parallel and BN indicates the application of batch normalization.

**Diversity Loss.** Without a specific loss term supervising the attention maps, we could incur in useless behaviors, *e.g.*, all binary gates being either on or off, or some channels being always propagated and some others not. While recent works provide a target expected activation ratio [1,58] as a countermeasure, we encourage the auxiliary modules to assign different propagation gating masks to different examples. The intuition is that each example has its own preferred subset of channels to be forwarded from the sibling. To do so, we include an additional auxiliary loss term [42] as follows:

$$\mathcal{L}_{\text{AUX}} \triangleq -\lambda \sum_{l=1}^{L} \mathbb{E}_{x_1,\dots,x_n \sim \mathcal{T}_c} \left[ \sum_{j=1}^{n} \log \frac{e^{g_{ij}^{\text{T}} g_{ij}/T}}{\frac{1}{n} \sum_{k=1}^{n} e^{g_{ij}^{\text{T}} g_{ik}/T}} \right], \tag{7}$$

$$g_{ij} \triangleq \text{NORM}(\text{GAP}(\text{M}(\widehat{h}^{(l)}(x_j)))),$$

where $n$ indicates the batch size, NORM a normalization layer, $T$ a temperature and finally $\lambda$ is a scalar weighting the contribution of this loss term to the overall objective. In practice, we ask each vector containing channel-wise average activity to have a low dot product with vectors of other examples.

### 3.3 Knowledge Replay

The training objective of Eq. 3 is devised to facilitate selective feature transfer between the in-training model and the immutable sibling. However, to prevent forgetting tied to previous CL tasks to the greatest extent, the model should also be provided with a targeted strategy. We thus equip the continual learner with a small memory buffer $\mathcal{B}$ (populated with examples from the input stream via *reservoir sampling* [65]) and adopt the simple labels and logits replay strategy proposed in [8]:

$$\mathcal{L}_{\text{CL}} \triangleq \mathbb{E}_{(x,y,l)\sim\mathcal{B}} \left[ \alpha \cdot ||f_{(\theta,\phi)}(x) - l||_2^2 + \beta \cdot \ell(y, f_{(\theta,\phi)}(x)) \right], \tag{8}$$

where $(x, y, l)$ is a triplet of example, label and original network responses $l = f(x)$ recorded at the time of sampling and $\alpha$, $\beta$ are scalar hyperparameters. Although extremely beneficial, we remark that the model need not optimize $\mathcal{L}_{\text{CL}}$ to achieve basic robustness against catastrophic forgetting (as shown in Sect. 5): preserving pretraining features already serves this purpose.

**Replaying Past Propagation Masks.** With the purpose of protecting the feature propagation formulated in Eq. 3 from forgetting, we also extend it to replay examples stored in memory. It must be noted that doing so requires taking additional steps to prevent cross-task interference; indeed, simply applying Eq. 3 to replay items would apply the feature propagation procedure unchanged to all tasks, regardless of the classes thereby included. For this reason, we take an extra step and make all batch normalization and fully connected layers in Eqs. 4, 5 and 6 conditioned [17] w.r.t. the CL task. Consequently, we add to $\mathcal{B}$ for each example $x$ both its task label $t$ and its corresponding set of binary attention maps $m = (m^1, ..., m^l)$ generated at the time of sampling. Equation 3 is finally updated as:

$$\mathcal{L}_{\text{FP}} \triangleq \mathop{\mathbb{E}}_{\substack{(x,t=c)\sim\mathcal{T}_c \\ (x;t)\sim\mathcal{B}}} \left[ \sum_{l=1}^{L} ||\text{M}(\widehat{h}^{(l)}; t) \odot \left( h^{(l)} - \text{ReLU}_{\text{m}}(\widehat{h}^{(l)}) \right) ||_2^2 \right]$$

$$+ \mathop{\mathbb{E}}_{\substack{(x,t,m)\sim\mathcal{B} \\ l=1,...,L}} \left[ \text{BCE}\left( \text{M}(\widehat{h}^{(l)}; t), m^{(l)} \right) \right], \quad (9)$$

where the second term is an additional replay contribution distilling past attention maps, with BCE indicating the binary cross entropy criterion.

**Overall Objective.** Our proposal – dubbed **Transfer without Forgetting (TwF)** – optimizes the following training objective, also summarized in Fig. 2:

$$\min_{\theta,\phi} \mathop{\mathbb{E}}_{(x,y)\sim\mathcal{T}_c} \left[ \ell(y_j^i, f_{(\theta,\phi)}(x_j^i)) \right] + \mathcal{L}_{\text{CL}} + \mathcal{L}_{\text{FP}} + \mathcal{L}_{\text{AUX}}. \quad (10)$$

We remark that: *i)* while TwF requires keeping a copy of the pretrained model during training, this does not hold at inference time; *ii)* similarly, task labels $t$ are not needed during inference but only while training, which makes TwF capable of operating under both the Task-IL and Class-IL CL settings [63]; *iii)* the addition of $t$ and $m$ in $\mathcal{B}$ induces a limited memory overhead: $t$ can be obtained from the stored labels $y$ for typical classification tasks with a fixed number of classes per task, while $m$ is a set of Boolean maps that is robust to moderate re-scaling (as we demonstrate by storing $m$ at half resolution for our experiments in Sect. 4). We finally point out that, as maps $m$ take discrete binary values, one could profit from lossless compression algorithms (such as Run-Length Encoding [54] or LZ77 [71]) and thus store a compressed representation into the memory buffer. We leave the comprehensive investigation of this application to future works.

## 4 Experiments

### 4.1 Experimental Setting

**Metrics.** We assess the overall performance of the models in terms of *Final Average Accuracy* (FAA), defined as the average accuracy on all seen classes after learning the last task, and *Final Forgetting* [12] (FF), defined as:

$$\text{FF} \triangleq \frac{1}{T-1} \sum_{i=0}^{T-2} \max_{t\in\{0,...,T-2\}} \{a_i^t - a_i^{T-1}\}, \quad (11)$$

where $a_i^t$ denotes the accuracy on task $\tau_i$ after training on the $t^{\text{th}}$ task.

**Settings.** We report results on two common protocols [63]: *Task-Incremental Learning* (Task-IL), where the model must learn to classify samples only from within each task, and *Class-Incremental Learning* (Class-IL), where the model must gradually learn the overall classification problem. The former scenario is a relaxation of the latter, as it provides the model with the task identifier of each sample at test time; for this reason, we focus our evaluation mainly on the Class-IL protocol, highlighted as a more realistic and challenging benchmark [3,20].

**Datasets.** We initially describe a scenario where the transfer of knowledge from the pretrain is facilitated by the similarity between the two distributions. Precisely, we use **CIFAR-100** [33] as the pretrain dataset and then evaluate the models on **Split CIFAR-10** [70] (5 binary tasks) (see Table 1). In Table 2 we envision a second and more challenging benchmark, which relies on **Split CIFAR-100** [70] with the opportunity to benefit from the knowledge previously learned on **Tiny ImageNet** [62]. Due to the size mismatch between CIFAR-100 and the samples from Tiny ImageNet, we resize the latter to $32 \times 32$ during pretraining. The last scenario (Table 3) involves pretraining on ImageNet [18] and learning incrementally **Split CUB-200** [13,69], split into 10 tasks of 20 classes each. With an average of only 29.97 images per class and the use of higher-resolution input samples (resized to $224 \times 224$), this benchmark is the most challenging. We use ResNet18 [25] for all experiments involving Split CIFAR-10 and Split CIFAR-100, as in [8,50], while opting for ResNet50 on Split CUB-200. The supplementary materials report other details on the experimental protocols.

**Competitors.** We focus our comparison on state-of-the-art rehearsal algorithms, as they prevail on most benchmarks in literature [8,14,63].

- **Experience Replay (ER)** [49,53] is the first embodiment of a rehearsal strategy that features a small memory buffer containing an *i.i.d.* view of all the tasks seen so far. During training, data from the stream is complemented with data sampled from the buffer. While this represents the most straightforward use of a memory in a CL scenario, ER remains a strong baseline, albeit with a non-negligible memory footprint.
- **Dark Experience Replay (DER)** [8] envisions a self-distillation [22] constraint on data stored in the memory buffer and represents a simple extension to the basic rehearsal strategy of ER. In this work, we compare against DER++, which includes both ER and DER objectives.
- **Incremental Classifier and Representation Learning (iCaRL)** [50] tackle catastrophic forgetting by distilling the responses of the model at the previous task boundary and storing samples that better represent the current task. In addition to simple replay, those *exemplars* are used to compute class-mean prototypes for nearest-neighbor classification.
- **ER with Asymmetric Cross-Entropy (ER-ACE)** [10] recently introduced a method to alleviate class imbalances to ER. The authors obtain a major gain in accuracy by simply separating the cross-entropy contribution of the classes in the current batch and that of the ones in the memory buffer.

- **Contrastive Continual Learning (CO$^2$L)** [11] proposes to facilitate knowledge transfer from samples stored in the buffer by optimizing a contrastive learning objective, avoiding any potential bias introduced by a cross-entropy objective. To perform classification, a linear classifier needs to be first trained on the exemplars stored in the buffer.

In addition, we also include results from two popular regularization methods. **Online Elastic Weight Consolidation (oEWC)** [31] penalizes changes on the most important parameters by means of an online estimate of the Fisher Information Matrix evaluated at task boundaries. **Learning without Forgetting (LwF)** [34] includes a distillation target similar to iCaRL but does not store any exemplars. We remark that **all competitors undergo an initial pretraining phase** prior to CL, thus ensuring a fair comparison.

**Table 1.** Final Average Accuracy (FAA) [↑] and Final Forgetting (FF) [↓] on Split CIFAR-10 w. pretrain on CIFAR-100.

| FAA (FF) | Split CIFAR-10 (*pretr. CIFAR-100*) | | | |
|---|---|---|---|---|
| Method | Class-IL | | Task-IL | |
| Joint (UB) | 92.89 (−) | | 98.38 (−) | |
| Finetune | 19.76 (98.11) | | 84.05 (17.75) | |
| oEwC [57] | 26.10 (88.85) | | 81.84 (19.50) | |
| LwF [34] | 19.80 (97.96) | | 86.41 (14.35) | |
| **Buffer size** | 500 | 5120 | 500 | 5120 |
| ER [53] | 67.24 (38.24) | 86.27 (13.68) | 96.27 (2.23) | 97.89 (0.55) |
| CO$^2$L [11] | 75.47 (21.80) | 87.59 (9.61) | 96.77 (1.23) | 97.82 (0.53) |
| iCaRL [50] | 76.73 (14.70) | 77.95 (12.90) | 97.25 (0.74) | 97.52 (0.15) |
| DER++ [8] | 78.42 (20.18) | 87.88 (8.02) | 94.25 (4.46) | 96.42 (1.99) |
| ER-ACE [10] | 77.83 (10.63) | 86.20 (5.58) | 96.41 (2.11) | 97.60 (0.66) |
| **TwF (ours)** | **83.65 (11.59)** | **89.55 (6.85)** | **97.49 (0.86)** | **98.35 (0.17)** |

To gain a clearer understanding of the results, all the experiments include the performance of the upper bound (**Joint**), obtained by jointly training on all classes in a non-continua fashion. We also report the results of the model obtained by training sequentially on each task (**Finetune**), *i.e.*, without any countermeasure to forgetting.

## 4.2 Comparison with State-of-the-Art

**Regularization Methods.** Across the board, non-rehearsal methods (oEWC and LwF) manifest a profound inability to effectively use the features learned during the pretrain. As those methods are not designed to extract and reuse any

**Table 2.** Accuracy (forgetting) on Split CIFAR-100 w. pretrain on Tiny ImageNet.

| FAA (FF) | Split CIFAR-100 (*pretr. Tiny ImageNet*) | | | |
|---|---|---|---|---|
| Method | Class-IL | | Task-IL | |
| Joint (UB) | 75.20 (−) | | 93.40 (−) | |
| Finetune | 09.52 (92.31) | | 73.50 (20.53) | |
| oEwC [57] | 10.95 (81.71) | | 65.56 (21.33) | |
| LwF [34] | 10.83 (90.87) | | 86.19 (4.77) | |
| Buffer size | 500 | 2000 | 500 | 2000 |
| ER [53] | 31.30 (65.40) | 46.80 (46.95) | 85.98 (6.14) | 87.59 (4.85) |
| CO$^2$L [11] | 33.40 (45.21) | 50.95 (31.20) | 68.51 (21.51) | 82.96 (8.53) |
| iCaRL [50] | 56.00 (19.27) | 58.10 (16.89) | **89.99 (2.32)** | 90.75 (1.68) |
| DER++ [8] | 43.65 (48.72) | 58.05 (29.65) | 73.86 (20.08) | 86.63 (6.86) |
| ER-ACE [10] | 53.38 (21.63) | 57.73 (17.12) | 87.21 (3.33) | 88.46 (2.46) |
| TwF (ours) | **56.83 (23.89)** | **64.46 (15.23)** | 89.82 (3.06) | **91.11 (2.24)** |

useful features from the initialization, the latter is rapidly forgotten, thus negating any knowledge transfer in later tasks. This is particularly true for oEWC, whose objective proves to be both too strict to effectively learn the current task and insufficient to retain the initialization. Most notably, on Split CUB-200 oEWC shows performance lower than Finetune on both Task- and Class-IL.

**Rehearsal Methods.** In contrast, rehearsal models that feature some form of distillation (DER++ and iCaRL) manage to be competitive on all benchmarks. In particular, iCaRL proves especially effective on Split CIFAR-100, where it reaches the second highest FAA even when equipped with a small memory thanks to its *herding* buffer construction strategy. However, this effect is less pronounced on Split CIFAR-10 and Split CUB-200, where the role of pretraining is far more essential due to the similarity of the two distributions for the former and the higher difficulty of the latter. In these settings, we see iCaRL fall short of DER++, which better manages to maintain and reuse the features available from its initialization. Moreover, we remark that iCaRL and DER++ show ranging Class-IL performance in different tasks, whereas our method is much less sensitive to the specific task at hand.

While it proves effective on the easier Split CIFAR-10 benchmark, CO$^2$L does not reach satisfactory results on either Split CIFAR-100 or Split CUB-200. We ascribe this result to the high sensitivity of this model to the specifics of its training process (*e.g.*, to the applied transforms and the number of epochs required to effectively train the feature extractor with a contrastive loss). Remarkably, while we extended the size of the batch in all experiments with CO$^2$L to 256 to provide a large enough pool of negative samples, it still shows off only a minor improvement on non-rehearsal methods for Split CUB-200.

**Table 3.** Accuracy (forgetting) on Split CUB-200 w. pretrain on ImageNet.

| FAA (FF) | Split CUB-200 (*pretr. ImageNet*) | |
| --- | --- | --- |
| Method | Class-IL | Task-IL |
| Joint (UB) | 78.54 (−) | 86.48 (−) |
| Finetune | 8.56 (82.38) | 36.84 (50.95) |
| oEwC [57] | 8.20 (71.46) | 33.94 (40.36) |
| LwF [34] | 8.59 (82.14) | 22.17 (67.08) |

| Buffer size | 400 | 1000 | 400 | 1000 |
| --- | --- | --- | --- | --- |
| ER [53] | 45.82 (40.76) | 59.88 (25.65) | 75.26 (9.82) | 80.19 (4.52) |
| CO$^2$L [11] | 8.96 (32.04) | 16.53 (20.99) | 22.91 (26.42) | 35.79 (16.61) |
| iCaRL [50] | 46.55 (12.48) | 49.07 (11.24) | 68.90 (3.14) | 70.57 (3.03) |
| DER++ [8] | 56.38 (26.59) | 67.35 (13.47) | 77.16 (7.74) | 82.00 (3.25) |
| ER-ACE [10] | 48.18 (25.79) | 58.19 (16.56) | 74.34 (9.78) | 78.27 (6.09) |
| **TwF (ours)** | **57.78 (18.32)** | **68.32 (6.74)** | **79.35 (5.77)** | **82.81 (2.14)** |

**Table 4.** Impact of each loss term and of using no memory buffer on TwF. Results given in the Class-IL scenario following the same experimental settings as Tables 1, 2 and 3.

| $\mathcal{L}_{CL}$ | $\mathcal{L}_{FP}$ | $\mathcal{L}_{AUX}$ | Split CIFAR-10 | | | Split CIFAR-100 | | | Split CUB-200 | | |
| --- | --- | --- | --- | --- | --- | --- | --- | --- | --- | --- | --- |
| Buffer size | | | w/o/*buf.* | 500 | 5120 | w/o/*buf.* | 500 | 2000 | w/o/*buf.* | 400 | 1000 |
| ✓ | ✓ | ✓ | − | **83.65** | **89.55** | − | **56.83** | **64.46** | − | **59.67** | **68.32** |
| ✓ | ✗ | ✗ | − | 75.79 | 87.54 | − | 44.01 | 57.84 | − | 56.53 | 67.29 |
| ✓ | ✓ | ✗ | − | <u>83.29</u> | <u>89.53</u> | − | <u>55.50</u> | <u>63.53</u> | − | <u>59.06</u> | <u>67.83</u> |
| ✗ | ✓ | ✗ | 60.07 | 62.63 | 62.75 | 49.14 | 50.20 | 50.22 | 37.57 | 38.43 | 38.93 |
| ✗ | ✓ | ✓ | 60.90 | 63.19 | 63.79 | 49.74 | 50.88 | 50.52 | 37.99 | 39.20 | 39.31 |

Interestingly, while both ER and ER-ACE do not feature distillation, we find their performance to be competitive for large enough buffers. In particular, the asymmetric objective of ER-ACE appears less sensitive to a small memory buffer but always falls short of DER++ when this constraint is less severe.

**Transfer without Forgetting.** Finally, results across all proposed benchmarks depict our method (TwF) as consistently outperforming all the competitors, with an average gain of 4.81% for the Class-IL setting and 2.77% for the Task-IL setting, w.r.t. the second-best performer across all datasets (DER++ and ER-ACE, respectively). This effect is especially pronounced for smaller buffers on Split CIFAR-10 and Split CUB-200, for which the pretrain provides a valuable source of knowledge to be transferred. We argue that this proves the efficacy of our proposal to retain and adapt features available from initialization through distillation. Moreover, we remark that its performance gain is consistent in all settings, further attesting to the resilience of the proposed approach.

## 5    Ablation Studies

**Breakdown of the Individual Terms of TwF.** To better understand the importance of the distinct loss terms in Eq. 10 and their connection, we explore their individual contribution to the final accuracy of TwF in Table 4. Based on these results, we make the following observations: *i)* $\mathcal{L}_{\mathrm{CL}}$ is the most influential loss term and it is indispensable to achieve results in line with the SOTA; *ii)* $\mathcal{L}_{\mathrm{FP}}$ applied on top of $\mathcal{L}_{\mathrm{CL}}$ induces better handling of pretraining transfer, as testified by the increased accuracy; *iii)* $\mathcal{L}_{\mathrm{AUX}}$ on top of $\mathcal{L}_{\mathrm{FP}}$ reduces activation overlapping and brings a small but consistent improvement.

Further, in the columns labeled as w/o/buf., we consider what happens if TwF is allowed **no replay example at all** and only optimizes $\mathcal{L}_{\mathrm{FP}}$ and $\mathcal{L}_{\mathrm{AUX}}$ on current task examples. Compared to oEwC in Tables 1, 2 and 3 – the best non-replay method in our experiments – we clearly see preserving pretraining features is in itself a much more effective approach, even with rehearsal is out of the picture.

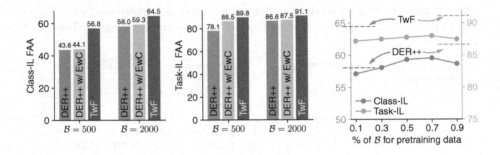

**Fig. 3.** Class-IL (left) and Task-IL (center) FAA performance comparison of our proposal with different possible methods to retain knowledge from pretrain. (Right) Influence of different allocation rates of pretrain examples in $\mathcal{B}$ for DER++, $|\mathcal{B}| = 2000$.

**Alternatives for the Preservation of Pretraining Knowledge.** TwF is designed to both preserve pretraining knowledge and facilitate its transfer. However, other approaches could be envisioned for the same purpose. Hence, we compare here TwF with two alternative baselines for pretraining preservation.

**Pretraining Preservation with EwC.** We complement a strong approach such as DER++ with an additional regularization term based on EwC:

$$\mathcal{L}_{\mathrm{EwC}} = \lambda(\theta - \theta^t)^T \mathrm{diag}(F)(\theta - \theta^t), \tag{12}$$

where $\mathrm{diag}(F)$ indicates the diagonal of the empirical Fisher Information Matrix, estimated on the pretraining data at the optimum $\theta^t$. When equipped with this additional loss term, DER++ is anchored to its initialization and prevented from changing its pretraining weights significantly, while its replay-based loss term prevents forgetting of knowledge acquired in previous tasks. As shown by Fig. 3 (left, center), the EwC loss allows DER++ to improve its accuracy on Split CIFAR-100 with Tiny ImageNet pretraining (especially in the Task-IL setting). However, this improvement is not actively incentivizing feature reuse and thus falls short of TwF. We finally remark that TwF and DER++ w/ EwC have a comparable memory footprint (both retain the initialization checkpoint).

**Pretraining Preservation Through Rehearsal.** An alternative for preserving the source knowledge is to assume that pretraining data is available and can be treated as an auxiliary data stream [5]. To evaluate this strategy with a bounded memory footprint, we test our baseline method (DER++) on Split CIFAR-100 with different percentages of the buffer dedicated to pretraining images (from Tiny ImageNet). The results shown in Fig. 3 (right) confirm our main claim: DER++ coupled with pretraining rehearsal improves over DER++ with only pretraining. This finding proves that, if pretraining is available, it is beneficial to guard it against catastrophic forgetting.

**Table 5.** Dissimilar pretrain tasks: accuracy on CIFAR-100 pretrained on SVHN.

| FAA (FF) | Class-IL | | Task-IL | |
|---|---|---|---|---|
| Buffer size | 500 | 2000 | 500 | 2000 |
| iCaRL [50] | 39.59 (21.81) | 42.02 (18.78) | 78.89 (4.04) | 80.65 (2.24) |
| DER++ [8] | 36.46 (53.47) | 52.29 (24.04) | 75.05 (16.22) | 83.36 (8.04) |
| **TwF (ours)** | **43.56 (40.02)** | **56.15 (21.51)** | **80.89 (10.12)** | **87.30 (3.12)** |

Furthermore, we highlight that TwF outperforms the baseline introduced here. When replaying pretraining data, indeed, the model has to maintain its predictive capabilities on the classes of the source task, *i.e.*, we enforce both backward and forward transfer. TwF, instead, allows the model to disregard the classes of the source dataset, as long as the transfer of its internal representations favors the learning of new tasks ($\Rightarrow$ **it only enforces forward transfer**). This substantial distinction helps to understand the merits of TwF: namely, a full but still functional exploitation of the pretraining knowledge.

**Role of Pretraining Datasets.** Here, we seek to gain further proof of our claim about the ability of TwF to adapt features from the pretrain. Specifically, we study a scenario where the source data distribution and the target one are highly dissimilar: namely, we first pretrain a ResNet18 backbone on SVHN [43] and then follow with Split CIFAR-100. We compare our model with the second-best performer from Table 2, *i.e.*, iCaRL, and DER++. The results, reported in Table 5, suggest that our method outranks the competitors not only when pretrained on a similar dataset – as in Table 2 – but also when the tasks are very dissimilar. We argue that this result further shows the ability of TwF to identify which pretraining features are really advantageous to transfer.

## 6    Conclusions

We introduced Transfer without Forgetting, a hybrid method combining Rehearsal and Feature transfer, designed to exploit pretrained weights in an incremental scenario. It encourages feature sharing throughout all tasks, yielding a stable performance gain across multiple settings. We also show that TwF outperforms other hybrid methods based on rehearsal and regularization and that it is able to profit even from pretraining on a largely dissimilar dataset.

**Acknowledgments.** This paper has been supported from Italian Ministerial grant PRIN 2020 "LEGO.AI: LEarning the Geometry of knOwledge in AI systems", n. 2020TA3K9N. Matteo Pennisi is a PhD student enrolled in the National PhD in Artificial Intelligence, XXXVII cycle, course on Health and life sciences, organized by Università Campus Bio-Medico di Roma.

## References

1. Abati, D., Tomczak, J., Blankevoort, T., Calderara, S., Cucchiara, R., Bejnordi, B.E.: Conditional channel gated networks for task-aware continual learning. In: Proceedings of the IEEE conference on Computer Vision and Pattern Recognition (2020)
2. Aguilar, G., Ling, Y., Zhang, Y., Yao, B., Fan, X., Guo, C.: Knowledge distillation from internal representations. In: Proceedings of the AAAI Conference on Artificial Intelligence (2020)
3. Aljundi, R., Lin, M., Goujaud, B., Bengio, Y.: Gradient based sample selection for online continual learning. In: Advances in Neural Information Processing Systems (2019)
4. Allegretti, S., Bolelli, F., Pollastri, F., Longhitano, S., Pellacani, G., Grana, C.: Supporting skin lesion diagnosis with content-based image retrieval. In: International Conference on Pattern Recognition (2021)
5. Bellitto, G., et al.: Effects of auxiliary knowledge on continual learning. In: International Conference on Pattern Recognition (2022)
6. Boschini, M., Bonicelli, L., Buzzega, P., Porrello, A., Calderara, S.: Class-incremental continual learning into the extended der-verse. arXiv preprint arXiv:2201.00766 (2022)
7. Boschini, M., Buzzega, P., Bonicelli, L., Porrello, A., Calderara, S.: Continual semi-supervised learning through contrastive interpolation consistency. arXiv preprint arXiv:2108.06552 (2021)
8. Buzzega, P., Boschini, M., Porrello, A., Abati, D., Calderara, S.: Dark experience for general continual learning: a strong, simple baseline. In: Advances in Neural Information Processing Systems (2020)

9. Buzzega, P., Boschini, M., Porrello, A., Calderara, S.: Rethinking experience replay: a bag of tricks for continual learning. In: International Conference on Pattern Recognition (2020)
10. Caccia, L., Aljundi, R., Asadi, N., Tuytelaars, T., Pineau, J., Belilovsky, E.: New insights on reducing abrupt representation change in online continual learning. In: International Conference on Learning Representations (2022)
11. Cha, H., Lee, J., Shin, J.: Co2l: Contrastive continual learning. In: IEEE International Conference on Computer Vision (2021)
12. Chaudhry, A., Dokania, P.K., Ajanthan, T., Torr, P.H.: Riemannian walk for incremental learning: Understanding forgetting and intransigence. In: Proceedings of the European Conference on Computer Vision (2018)
13. Chaudhry, A., Ranzato, M., Rohrbach, M., Elhoseiny, M.: Efficient lifelong learning with A-GEM. In: International Conference on Learning Representations (2019)
14. Chaudhry, A., et al.: On tiny episodic memories in continual learning. In: International Conference on Machine Learning Workshop (2019)
15. Chen, T., Kornblith, S., Norouzi, M., Hinton, G.: A simple framework for contrastive learning of visual representations. In: International Conference on Machine Learning (2020)
16. De Lange, M., et al.: A continual learning survey: defying forgetting in classification tasks. IEEE Trans. Pattern Anal. Mach. Intell. **44**, 3366–3385 (2021)
17. De Vries, H., Strub, F., Mary, J., Larochelle, H., Pietquin, O., Courville, A.C.: Modulating early visual processing by language. In: Advances in Neural Information Processing Systems (2017)
18. Deng, J., Dong, W., Socher, R., Li, L.J., Li, K., Fei-Fei, L.: Imagenet: A large-scale hierarchical image database. In: Proceedings of the IEEE conference on Computer Vision and Pattern Recognition (2009)
19. Devlin, J., Chang, M.W., Lee, K., Toutanova, K.: Bert: Pre-training of deep bidirectional transformers for language understanding. In: Proceedings of the Conference of the North American Chapter of the Association for Computational Linguistics (2019)
20. Farquhar, S., Gal, Y.: Towards robust evaluations of continual learning. In: International Conference on Machine Learning Workshop (2018)
21. Finn, C., Abbeel, P., Levine, S.: Model-agnostic meta-learning for fast adaptation of deep networks. In: International Conference on Machine Learning (2017)
22. Furlanello, T., Lipton, Z.C., Tschannen, M., Itti, L., Anandkumar, A.: Born again neural networks. In: International Conference on Machine Learning (2018)
23. He, K., Gkioxari, G., Dollár, P., Girshick, R.: Mask r-cnn. In: IEEE International Conference on Computer Vision (2017)
24. He, K., Zhang, X., Ren, S., Sun, J.: Delving deep into rectifiers: Surpassing human-level performance on imagenet classification. In: IEEE International Conference on Computer Vision (2015)
25. He, K., Zhang, X., Ren, S., Sun, J.: Deep residual learning for image recognition. In: Proceedings of the IEEE Conference on Computer Vision and Pattern Recognition (2016)
26. Heo, B., Kim, J., Yun, S., Park, H., Kwak, N., Choi, J.Y.: A comprehensive overhaul of feature distillation. In: IEEE International Conference on Computer Vision (2019)
27. Hinton, G., Vinyals, O., Dean, J.: Distilling the knowledge in a neural network. In: Neural Information Processing Systems Workshops (2015)
28. Ilse, M., Tomczak, J., Welling, M.: Attention-based deep multiple instance learning. In: International Conference on Machine Learning (2018)

29. Jang, E., Gu, S., Poole, B.: Categorical reparameterization with gumbel-softmax. In: International Conference on Learning Representations (2017)
30. Jang, Y., Lee, H., Hwang, S.J., Shin, J.: Learning what and where to transfer. In: International Conference on Machine Learning (2019)
31. Kirkpatrick, J., et al.: Overcoming catastrophic forgetting in neural networks. In: Proceedings of the National Academy of Sciences (2017)
32. Kornblith, S., Norouzi, M., Lee, H., Hinton, G.: Similarity of neural network representations revisited. In: International Conference on Machine Learning (2019)
33. Krizhevsky, A., et al.: Learning multiple layers of features from tiny images. Technical report, Citeseer (2009)
34. Li, Z., Hoiem, D.: Learning without forgetting. IEEE Trans. Pattern Anal. Mach. Intell. 40, 2935–2947 (2017)
35. Long, M., Cao, Z., Wang, J., Jordan, M.I.: Conditional adversarial domain adaptation. In: Advances in Neural Information Processing Systems (2018)
36. Long, M., Zhu, H., Wang, J., Jordan, M.I.: Deep transfer learning with joint adaptation networks. In: International Conference on Machine Learning (2017)
37. Lopez-Paz, D., Ranzato, M.: Gradient episodic memory for continual learning. In: Advances in Neural Information Processing Systems (2017)
38. Mallya, A., Lazebnik, S.: Packnet: adding multiple tasks to a single network by iterative pruning. In: Proceedings of the IEEE Conference on Computer Vision and Pattern Recognition (2018)
39. McCloskey, M., Cohen, N.J.: Catastrophic interference in connectionist networks: the sequential learning problem. Psychology of learning and motivation (1989)
40. Mehta, S.V., Patil, D., Chandar, S., Strubell, E.: An empirical investigation of the role of pre-training in lifelong learning. In: International Conference on Machine Learning (2021)
41. Monti, A., Porrello, A., Calderara, S., Coscia, P., Ballan, L., Cucchiara, R.: How many observations are enough? knowledge distillation for trajectory forecasting. In: Proceedings of the IEEE conference on Computer Vision and Pattern Recognition (2022)
42. Müller, R., Kornblith, S., Hinton, G.: Subclass distillation. arXiv preprint arXiv:2002.03936 (2020)
43. Netzer, Y., Wang, T., Coates, A., Bissacco, A., Wu, B., Ng, A.Y.: Reading digits in natural images with unsupervised feature learning. In: Advances in Neural Information Processing Systems (2011)
44. Nichol, A., Schulman, J.: On first-order meta-learning algorithms. arXiv preprint arXiv:1803.02999 (2018)
45. Pan, S.J., Yang, Q.: A survey on transfer learning. IEEE Trans. Knowl. Data Eng. 3, 1–40 (2009)
46. Parisi, G.I., Kemker, R., Part, J.L., Kanan, C., Wermter, S.: Continual lifelong learning with neural networks: a review. Neural Networks (2019)
47. Park, J., Woo, S., Lee, J.Y., Kweon, I.S.: Bam: bottleneck attention module. In: British Machine Vision Conference (2018)
48. Porrello, A., et al.: Spotting insects from satellites: modeling the presence of culicoides imicola through deep cnns. In: International Conference on Signal-Image Technology & Internet-Based Systems (2019)
49. Ratcliff, R.: Connectionist models of recognition memory: constraints imposed by learning and forgetting functions. Psychological Review (1990)
50. Rebuffi, S.A., Kolesnikov, A., Sperl, G., Lampert, C.H.: icarl: incremental classifier and representation learning. In: Proceedings of the IEEE Conference on Computer Vision and Pattern Recognition (2017)

51. Ren, S., He, K., Girshick, R., Sun, J.: Faster R-CNN: towards real-time object detection with region proposal networks. In: Advances in Neural Information Processing Systems (2015)
52. Riemer, M., et al.: Learning to learn without forgetting by maximizing transfer and minimizing interference. In: International Conference on Learning Representations (2019)
53. Robins, A.: Catastrophic forgetting, rehearsal and pseudorehearsal. Connection Science (1995)
54. Robinson, A.H., Cherry, C.: Results of a prototype television bandwidth compression scheme. In: Proceedings of the IEEE (1967)
55. Romero, A., Ballas, N., Kahou, S.E., Chassang, A., Gatta, C., Bengio, Y.: Fitnets: Hints for thin deep nets. In: International Conference on Learning Representations (2015)
56. Rusu, A.A., et al.: Progressive neural networks. arXiv preprint arXiv:1606.04671 (2016)
57. Schwarz, J., et al.: Progress & compress: a scalable framework for continual learning. In: International Conference on Machine Learning (2018)
58. Serra, J., Suris, D., Miron, M., Karatzoglou, A.: Overcoming catastrophic forgetting with hard attention to the task. In: International Conference on Machine Learning (2018)
59. Shaheen, K., Hanif, M.A., Hasan, O., Shafique, M.: Continual learning for real-world autonomous systems: algorithms, challenges and frameworks. Journal of Intelligent & Robotic Systems (2022)
60. Silver, D., et al.: Mastering the game of go with deep neural networks and tree search. Nature (2016)
61. Smith, J., Balloch, J., Hsu, Y.C., Kira, Z.: Memory-efficient semi-supervised continual learning: the world is its own replay buffer. In: International Joint Conference on Neural Networks (2021)
62. Stanford: Tiny ImageNet Challenge (CS231n) (2015). https://www.kaggle.com/c/tiny-imagenet
63. van de Ven, G.M., Tolias, A.S.: Three continual learning scenarios. In: Neural Information Processing Systems Workshops (2018)
64. Vinyals, O., et al.: Grandmaster level in starcraft ii using multi-agent reinforcement learning. Nature (2019)
65. Vitter, J.S.: Random sampling with a reservoir. ACM Trans. Math. Softw. **11**, 37–57 (1985)
66. Wang, K., Gao, X., Zhao, Y., Li, X., Dou, D., Xu, C.Z.: Pay attention to features, transfer learn faster CNNs. In: International Conference on Learning Representations (2019)
67. Yim, J., Joo, D., Bae, J., Kim, J.: A gift from knowledge distillation: Fast optimization, network minimization and transfer learning. In: Proceedings of the IEEE Conference on Computer Vision and Pattern Recognition (2017)
68. Yosinski, J., Clune, J., Bengio, Y., Lipson, H.: How transferable are features in deep neural networks? In: Advances in Neural Information Processing Systems (2014)
69. Yu, L., et al.: Semantic drift compensation for class-incremental learning. In: Proceedings of the IEEE Conference on Computer Vision and Pattern Recognition (2020)
70. Zenke, F., Poole, B., Ganguli, S.: Continual learning through synaptic intelligence. In: International Conference on Machine Learning (2017)
71. Ziv, J., Lempel, A.: A universal algorithm for sequential data compression. IEEE Trans. Inf. Theory **23**, 337–343 (1977)

# AdaBest: Minimizing Client Drift in Federated Learning via Adaptive Bias Estimation

Farshid Varno[1,2]($\boxtimes$) (iD), Marzie Saghayi[1] (iD), Laya Rafiee Sevyeri[2,3] (iD),
Sharut Gupta[2,4] (iD), Stan Matwin[1,5] (iD), and Mohammad Havaei[2] (iD)

[1] Dalhousie University, Halifax, Canada
{f.varno,m.saghayi}@dal.ca, stan@cs.dal.ca
[2] Imagia Cybernetics Inc., Montreal, Canada
[3] Concordia University, Montreal, Canada
[4] Indian Institute of Technology Delhi, New Delhi, India
[5] Polish Academy of Sciences, Warsaw, Poland

**Abstract.** In Federated Learning (FL), a number of clients or devices collaborate to train a model without sharing their data. Models are optimized locally at each client and further communicated to a central hub for aggregation. While FL is an appealing decentralized training paradigm, heterogeneity among data from different clients can cause the local optimization to *drift* away from the global objective. In order to estimate and therefore remove this drift, variance reduction techniques have been incorporated into FL optimization recently. However, these approaches inaccurately estimate the clients' drift and ultimately fail to remove it properly. In this work, we propose an adaptive algorithm that accurately estimates drift across clients. In comparison to previous works, our approach necessitates less storage and communication bandwidth, as well as lower compute costs. Additionally, our proposed methodology induces stability by constraining the norm of estimates for client drift, making it more practical for large scale FL. Experimental findings demonstrate that the proposed algorithm converges significantly faster and achieves higher accuracy than the baselines across various FL benchmarks.

**Keywords:** Federated Learning · Distributed learning · Client drift · Biased gradients · Variance reduction

## 1 Introduction

In Federated Learning (FL), multiple sites with data often known as *clients* collaborate to train a model by communicating parameters through a central hub called *server*. At each round, the server broadcasts a set of model parameters

**Supplementary Information** The online version contains supplementary material available at https://doi.org/10.1007/978-3-031-20050-2_41.

to a number of clients. Selected clients separately optimize towards their local objective. The locally trained parameters are sent back to the server, where they are aggregated to form a new set of parameters for the next round. A well-known aggregation is to simply average the parameters received from the participating clients in each round. This method is known as FEDAVG [17] or LOCALSGD [25].

In order to reduce the communication costs as well as privacy concerns [32], multiple local optimization steps are often preferable and sometimes inevitable [17]. Unfortunately, multiple local updates subject the parameters to *client drift* [7]. While SGD is an unbiased gradient descent estimator, LOCALSGD is biased due to the existence of client drift. As a result, LOCALSGD converges to a neighborhood around the optimal solution with a distance proportionate to the magnitude of the bias [2]. The amount of this bias itself depends on the heterogeneity among the clients' data distribution, causing LOCALSGD to perform poorly on non-iid benchmarks [31].

One effective way of reducing client drift is by adapting Reduced Variance SGD (RV-SGD) methods [6,19,22,23] to LOCALSGD. The general strategy is to regularize the local updates with an estimate of gradients of inaccessible training samples (i.e., data of other clients). In other words, the optimization direction of a client is modified using the estimated optimization direction of other clients. These complementary gradients could be found for each client $i$ by subtracting an estimate of the local gradients from an estimate of the oracle's[1] full gradients. In this paper, we refer to these two estimates with $h_i$ and $h$, respectively. Therefore, a reduced variance local gradient for client $i$ would be in general form of $\nabla L_i + (h - h_i)$ where $\nabla L_i$ corresponds to the true gradients of the local objective for client $i$.

The majority of existing research works on adapting RV-SGD to distributed learning do not meet the requirement to be applied to FL. Some proposed algorithms require full participation of clients [15,21,24], and thus are not scalable to *cross-device* FL[2]. Another group of algorithms require communicating the true gradients [14,18] and, as a result, completely undermine the FL privacy concerns such as attacks to retrieve data from true gradients [32].

SCAFFOLD [7] is an algorithm that supports partial participation of clients and does not require the true gradients at the server. While SCAFFOLD shows superiority in performance and convergence rate compared to its baselines, it consumes twice as much bandwidth. To construct the complementary gradients, it computes and communicates $h$ as an extra set of parameters to each client along with the model parameters. FEDDYN [1] proposed to apply $h$ in a single step prior to applying any local update, and practically found better performance and convergence speed compared to SCAFFOLD. Since applying $h$ uses the same operation in all participating clients, [1] moved it to the server instead of applying on each client. This led to large savings of local computation, and more

---

[1] Oracle dataset refers to the hypothetical dataset formed by stacking all clients' data. Oracle gradients are the full-batch gradients of the Oracle dataset.

[2] In contrast to *cross-silo* FL, cross-device FL is referred to a large-scale (in terms of number of clients) setting in which clients are devices such as smart-phones.

importantly to use the same amount of communication bandwidth as vanilla LOCALSGD (i.e., FEDAVG), which is half of what SCAFFOLD uses.

FEDDYN make several assumptions that are often not satisfied in large-scale FL. These assumptions include having prior knowledge about the total number of clients, a high rate of re-sampling clients, and drawing clients uniformly from a stationary set. Even with these assumptions, we show that $h$ in FEDDYN is pruned to explosion, especially in large-scale setting. This hurts the performance and holds the optimization back from converging to a stationary point.

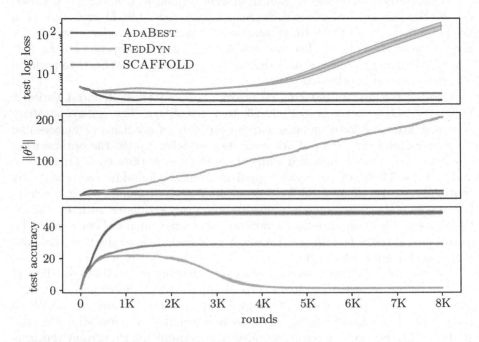

**Fig. 1.** Asymptotic instability of FEDDYN as a results of unbounded increase of $\|h^t\|$. From top to bottom test loss (log scale), norm of cloud parameters, and test accuracy are shown in subplots. The shared horizontal axis shows the number of communication rounds. Each experiment is repeated 5 times with different random seed of data partitioning. Solid lines and shades represent mean and standard deviation respectively

This paper proposes ADABEST, a Reduced Variance LocalSGD (RV-LSGD) solution to minimize the client drift in FL. Compared to the baselines, we define a simpler yet more elegant method of incorporating previous observations into estimates of complementary gradients. Our solution alleviates the instability of the norm of $h$ in FEDDYN (see Fig. 1 for empirical evaluation) while consuming the same order of storage and communication bandwidth, and even reducing the compute cost (see supplementary material for quantitative comparison). Unlike previous works, our algorithm provides a mechanism for adapting to changes in the distribution of client sampling and does not require prior knowledge of the entire set of clients. These characteristics of ADABEST, combined with its stability, provide a practical solution for large-scale cross-device FL. Our main contributions are as follows:

- We show that the existing RV-LSGD approaches for cross-device FL fail to efficiently converge to a stationary point. In particular, the norm of the parameters in FEDDYN is pruned to explosion (see Sect. 3.4 for discussion).
- We formulate a novel arithmetic approach for implicit accumulation of previous observations into the estimates of oracle full gradients ($h$).
- Using the new formulation, we present ADABEST, a novel algorithm that can be thought as a generalization of both FEDAVG and FEDDYN. We introduce a new factor $\beta$ that stabilizes our algorithm through controlling the norm of $h$. As a result, the optimization algorithm converges to a stationary point (see Sects. 3.4 for detailed discussion). Unlike baselines, ADABEST does not assume that the set of training clients are stationary nor it requires a prior knowledge about its cardinality.
- We conduct various experiments under different settings of number of clients, balance among partitions, and heterogeneity. Our results indicate superior performance of ADABEST in nearly all benchmarks (up to 94% improvement in test accuracy compared to the second best candidate; almost twice better), in addition to significant improvements in stability and convergence rate.

## 2    Related Work

A major challenge in FL is data heterogeneity across clients where the local optima in the parameter space at each client may be far from that of the global optima. This causes a *drift* in the local parameter updates with respect to the server aggregated parameters. Recent research has shown that in such heterogeneous settings, FEDAVG is highly pruned to client drift [31].

To improve the performance of FL with heterogeneous data, some previous works use knowledge distillation to learn the cloud model from an ensemble of client models. This approach has been shown to be more effective than simple parameter averaging in reducing bias of the local gradients [12, 16, 33].

Another group of methods can be categorized as *gradient based* in which the gradients are explicitly constrained on the clients or sever for bias removal. FEDPROX [13] penalizes the distance between the local and cloud parameters whereas [26] normalizes the client gradients prior to aggregation. Inspired by momentum SGD, [29] uses a local buffer to accumulate gradients from previous rounds at each client and communicate the momentum buffer with the server as well as the local parameters which doubles the consumption of communication bandwidth. Instead of applying momentum on the client level, [5, 27] implement a server momentum approach which avoids increasing communication costs.

Inspired by Stochastic Variance Reduction Gradients (SVRG) [6], some works incorporate variance reduction into local-SGD [1, 7, 9, 14, 15, 18, 19, 30]. DANE [24], AIDE [21], and VRL-SGD [15] incorporated RV-SGD in distributed learning for full client participation. FEDDANE [14] is an attempt to adapt DANE to FL setting[3], though it still undermines the privacy concerns such as attacks to retrieve data from true gradients [32]. Different from our work, most methods in this category such as VRL-SGD [15], FSVRG [9], FEDSPLIT [20] and FEDPD [30] require full participation of clients which makes them less suitable for cross-device setting where only a fraction of clients participate in training at each round. While FEDDANE [14] works in partial participation, empirical results show it performs worse than Federated Averaging [1]. More comparable to our method are those capable of learning in partial participation setting. In particular, SCAFFOLD [7] uses control variates on both the server and clients to reduce the variance in local updates. In addition to the model parameters, the control variates are also learned and are communicated between the server and the clients which take up additional bandwidth. [18] also reduces local variance by estimating the local bias at each client and using an SVRG-like approach to reduce the drift. While SCAFFOLD applied variance reduction on clients, FEDDYN [1] applies it partly on the server and partly on the clients. Our proposed method, is probably closer to FEDDYN than to others; however, they differ in the way gradients are estimated. See Sect. 3.4 for detailed comparison of ADABEST with FEDDYN and SCAFFOLD.

## 3   Method

In this section, we present an overview of the general FL setup and further introduce our notation to formulate the problem statement. Next we detail the proposed algorithm and how to apply it. Finally, we demonstrate the efficacy of our technique by comparing it with the most closely related approaches.

### 3.1   Federated Learning

We assume a standard FL setup in which a central server communicates parameters to a number of clients. The goal is to find an optimal point in the parameter space that solves a particular task while clients keep their data privately on their devices during the whole learning process.

Let $S^t$ be the set of all registered clients at round $t$ and $\mathcal{P}^t$ be a subset of it drawn from a distribution $P(S^\tau; \tau = t)$. The server broadcasts the *cloud model* $\theta^{t-1}$ to all the selected clients. Each client $i \in \mathcal{P}^t$, optimizes the cloud model based on its local objective and transmits the optimized *client model*, $\theta_i^t$ back to the server. The server aggregates the received parameters and prepares a new cloud model for the next round. Table 1 lists the most frequently used symbols in this paper along with their meanings. Note that the *aggregate model* (client gradients) is an average of *client model* (client gradients) over values of $i \in \mathcal{P}^t$.

---

[3] Recall that Federated Learning is a sub-branch of distributed learning with specific characteristics geared towards practicality [17].

## 3.2 Adaptive Bias Estimation

Upon receiving the client models of round $t$ ($\{\forall i \in \mathcal{P}^t : \boldsymbol{\theta}_i^t\}$) on the server, the aggregate model, $\bar{\boldsymbol{\theta}}^t$ is computed by averaging them out.

**Definition 1.** *Pseudo-gradient of a variable $u$ at round $t$ is $u^{t-1} - u^t$.*

*Remark 1.* Aggregating client models by averaging is equivalent to applying a gradient step of size 1 from the previous round's cloud model using average of client pseudo-gradients or mathematically it is $\bar{\boldsymbol{\theta}}^t \leftarrow \frac{1}{|S^t|} \sum_{i \in S^t} \boldsymbol{\theta}_i^t = \boldsymbol{\theta}^{t-1} - \bar{\boldsymbol{g}}^t$.

**Table 1.** Summary of notion used in this paper

| | |
|---|---|
| $u^t, u_i^t, u_i^{t,\tau}$ | **Variable** $u$ at {round $t$, and client $i$, and local step $\tau$} |
| $\lvert \cdot \rvert, \langle \cdot, \cdot \rangle, u^{(v)}$ | **cardinality, inner product, power** |
| $\lVert \cdot \rVert^2, \angle(\cdot, \cdot)$ | **2-norm squared, angle** |
| $S^t, \mathcal{P}^t$ | Set of {all, round} **clients** |
| $\boldsymbol{\theta}^t, \bar{\boldsymbol{\theta}}^t, \boldsymbol{\theta}_i^t, \boldsymbol{\theta}_i^{t,\tau}$ | {cloud, aggregate, client, local} **model** |
| $\boldsymbol{g}^t, \bar{\boldsymbol{g}}^t, \boldsymbol{g}_i^t, \boldsymbol{g}_i^{t,\tau}$ | {oracle, aggregate, client, local} **gradients** |
| $\boldsymbol{h}^t, \boldsymbol{h}_i^t$ | {full, client} **gradients estimates** |

Next, the server finds the *cloud model* $\boldsymbol{\theta}^t$ by applying the estimate of the oracle gradients $\boldsymbol{h}^t$; that is

$$\boldsymbol{\theta}^t \leftarrow \bar{\boldsymbol{\theta}}^t - \boldsymbol{h}^t, \tag{1}$$

where $\boldsymbol{h}^t$ is found as follows

$$\boldsymbol{h}^t = \beta(\bar{\boldsymbol{\theta}}^{t-1} - \bar{\boldsymbol{\theta}}^t). \tag{2}$$

In Sect. 3.5, we further discuss the criteria for chosen $\beta$ which leads to a fast convergence. The described cycle continues by sending the cloud model to the clients sampled for the next round ($t + 1$) while the aggregate model ($\bar{\boldsymbol{\theta}}^t$) is retained on the server to be used in calculation of $\boldsymbol{h}^{t+1}$ or deployment. A schematic of the geometric interpretation of the additional drift removal step taken at the server is shown in Fig. 2.

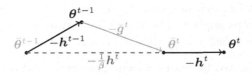

**Fig. 2.** Geometric interpretation of AdaBest's correction applied to the server updates. Server moves the aggregate parameters in the direction of $\bar{\boldsymbol{\theta}}^{t-1} - \bar{\boldsymbol{\theta}}t$ before sending the models to the next round's clients

After receiving the cloud model, each client $i \in \mathcal{P}^t$, optimizes its own copy of the model towards its local objective, during which the drift in the local optimization steps is reduced using the client's pseudo-gradients stored from the previous rounds (see Algorithm 1). The modified client objective is $\arg\min_\theta \mathfrak{R}_i(\boldsymbol{\theta}^t)$ where $\mathfrak{R}_i(\boldsymbol{\theta}^t) = L_i(\boldsymbol{\theta}^t) - \mu\langle\boldsymbol{\theta}^t, \boldsymbol{h}_i^{t_i'}\rangle$, where $L_i$ is the local empirical risk defined by the task and data accessible by the client $i$, and $t_i'$ is the last round that client $i$ participated in the training. Accordingly, the local updates with step size $\eta$ becomes

$$\boldsymbol{\theta}_i^{t,\tau} \leftarrow \boldsymbol{\theta}_i^{t,\tau-1} - \eta(\nabla L_i(\boldsymbol{\theta}_i^{t,\tau-1}) - \mu\boldsymbol{h}_i^{t_i'}), \tag{3}$$

where $\mu$ is the *regularization factor* (FEDDYN has a similar factor; see supplementary material for further discussion on the choice of optimal value for $\mu$).

After the last local optimization step, each sampled client updates the estimate for its own local gradients and stores it locally to be used in the future rounds that the client participate in the training. This update is equivalent to $\boldsymbol{h}_i^t = \frac{1}{t-t_i'}\boldsymbol{h}^{t_i'} + \boldsymbol{g}_i^t$ where $\boldsymbol{g}_i^t = \boldsymbol{\theta}^{t-1} - \boldsymbol{\theta}_i^t$. Finally, the participating clients send the optimized model $\boldsymbol{\theta}_i^t$ back to the server. Our method along with SCAFFOLD and FEDDYN is presented in Algorithm 1.

### 3.3    Relation to RV-SGD

Stochastic Variance Reduction Gradients (SVRG) [6] and its variants [3,4,8,19, 28] are of the most recent and popular RV-SGD algorithms. Given parameters $\boldsymbol{w}$ and an objective function $\ell$ to minimize it modifies SGD update from $\boldsymbol{w}^k \leftarrow \boldsymbol{w}^{k-1} - \eta\nabla\ell(\boldsymbol{w}^{k-1}, \boldsymbol{x}_k)$ to

$$\boldsymbol{w}^k \leftarrow \boldsymbol{w}^{k-1} - \eta(\nabla\ell(\boldsymbol{w}^{t-1}, \boldsymbol{x}_k) + \mathcal{G}(\tilde{\boldsymbol{w}}) - \ell(\tilde{\boldsymbol{w}}, \boldsymbol{x}_k)), \tag{4}$$

where $\boldsymbol{x}_k$ is a sample of data, $\tilde{\boldsymbol{w}}$ is a snapshot of $\boldsymbol{w}$ in the past and $\mathcal{G}(\tilde{\boldsymbol{w}})$ is full batch gradients at $\tilde{\boldsymbol{w}}$. The analytic result of this unbiased modification is that if empirical risk is strongly convex and the risk function over individual samples are both convex and L-smooth then the error in estimating gradients of $\mathcal{G}(\tilde{\boldsymbol{w}})$ is not only bounded but also linearly converges to zero (refer to [6] for proof). Under some conditions, [3] showed that this convergence rate is not largely impacted if a noisier estimate than original $\mathcal{G}(\tilde{\boldsymbol{w}})$ proposed by SVRG is chosen for full batch gradients. [4] investigated applying SVRG in non-convex problems and [8] generalized it for mini-batch SGD. [19] proposed SARAH, a biased version of SVRG that progressively updates the estimate for full gradients for optimizations steps applied in between taking two snapshots. Our algorithm could be thought as a distributed variant of SARAH where

1. $\mathcal{G}(\tilde{\boldsymbol{w}})$ is approximated by biased pseudo-gradients (and renamed to $\boldsymbol{h}$).
2. The outer loop for taking the snapshot is flattened using an exponential weighted average.

**Algorithm 1.** SCAFFOLD/m , FEDDYN , and ADABEST

---

**Input:** $T, \theta^0, \mu, \beta$
**for** $t = 1$ **to** $T$ **do**
    Sample clients $\mathcal{P}^t \subseteq S^t$.
    Transmit $\theta^{t-1}$ to each client in $\mathcal{P}^t$
    Transmit $h^{t-1}$ to each client in $\mathcal{P}^t$ (SCAFFOLD/m)
    **for** each client $i \in \mathcal{P}^t$ **in parallel do**
        /* receive cloud model */
        $\theta_i^{t,0} \leftarrow \theta^{t-1}$
        /* locally optimize for $K$ local steps */
        **for** $k = 1$ **to** $K$ **do**
            Compute mini-batch gradients $L_i(\theta_i^{t,k-1})$
            $g_i^{t,k-1} \leftarrow \nabla L_i(\theta_i^{t,k-1}) - h_i^{t_i'} + h^t$ (SCAFFOLD/m)
            $g_i^{t,k-1} \leftarrow \nabla L_i(\theta_i^{t,k-1}) - h_i^{t_i'} - \mu(\theta^{t-1} - \theta_i^{t,k-1})$ (FEDDYN)
            $g_i^{t,k-1} \leftarrow \nabla L_i(\theta_i^{t,k-1}) - h_i^{t_i'}$ (ADABEST)
            $\theta_i^{t,k} \leftarrow \theta_i^{t,k-1} - \eta g_i^{t,k-1}$
        **end for**
        /* update local gradient estimates */
        $g_i^t \leftarrow \theta^{t-1} - \theta_i^{t,K}$
        $h_i^t \leftarrow \frac{|S^t|-1}{|S^t|} h_i^{t-1} + \frac{|\mathcal{P}^t|}{K\eta|S^t|}(\theta^{t-1} - \bar{\theta}^t)$ (SCAFFOLD/m)
        $h_i^t \leftarrow h_i^{t_i'} + \mu g_i^t$ (FEDDYN)
        $h_i^t \leftarrow \frac{1}{t-t_i'} h_i^{t_i'} + \mu g_i^t$ (ADABEST)
        $t_i' \leftarrow t$
        Transmit client model $\theta_i^t := \theta_i^{t,K}$.
    **end for**
    /* aggregate received models */
    $\bar{\theta}^t \leftarrow \frac{1}{|\mathcal{P}^t|} \sum_{i \in \mathcal{P}^t} \theta_i^t$
    /* update oracle gradient estimates */
    $h^t \leftarrow \frac{|S^t|-1}{|S^t|} h^{t-1} + \frac{|\mathcal{P}^t|}{K\eta|S^t|}(\theta^{t-1} - \bar{\theta}^t)$ (SCAFFOLD/m)
    $h^t \leftarrow h^{t-1} + \frac{|\mathcal{P}^t|}{|S^t|}(\theta^{t-1} - \bar{\theta}^t)$ (FEDDYN)
    $h^t \leftarrow \beta(\bar{\theta}^{t-1} - \bar{\theta}^t)$ (ADABEST)
    /* update cloud model */
    $\theta^t \leftarrow \bar{\theta}^t$ (SCAFFOLD/m)
    $\theta^t \leftarrow \bar{\theta}^t - h^t$ (FEDDYN)
    $\theta^t \leftarrow \bar{\theta}^t - h^t$ (ADABEST)
**end for**

---

## 3.4   Relation to FL Baselines

Algorithm 1 demonstrates where our method differs from the baselines by color codes. Compared to the original SCAFFOLD, we made a slight modification in the way communication to the server occurs, preserving a quarter of the communication bandwidth usage. We refer to this modified version as SCAF-FOLD/m. In the rest of this section, we will discuss the key similarities and differences between our algorithm, FEDDYN and SCAFFOLD in terms of cost, robustness and functionality.

**Cost.** SCAFFOLD consumes twice as much communication bandwidth as FEDDYN and ADABEST. This should be taken into account when comparing the experimental performance and convergence rate of these algorithms. All of these three algorithms require the same amount of storage on the server and on each client. Finally, ADABEST has a lower compute cost compared to FEDDYN, SCAFFOLD both locally (on clients) and on the server. We provide quantitative comparison of these costs in supplementary material.

**Robustness.** According to the definition of cross-device FL, the number of devices could even exceed the number of examples per each device [17]. In such a massive pool of devices, if the participating devices are drawn randomly at uniform (which our baselines premised upon), there is a small chance for a client to be sampled multiple times in a short period of time. In FEDDYN, however, $h^t = \sum_{\tau=1}^{t} \frac{|\mathcal{P}^t|}{|S^t|} \bar{g}^t$, making it difficult for the norm of $h$ to decrease if pseudo-gradients in different rounds are not negatively correlated with each other (see Theorem 1 and its proof in supplementary material). In case clients are not re-sampled with a high rate then this negative correlation is unlikely to occur due to changes made to the state of the parameters and so the followup pseudo-gradients (see Sect. 3.5 for detailed discussion). A large norm of $h^t$ leads to a large norm of $\theta^t$ and in turn a large $\|\bar{\theta}^{t+1}\|^2$. This process is exacerbated during training and eventually leads to exploding norm of the parameters (see Fig. 1). In Sect. 3.5, we intuitively justify the robustness of ADABEST for various scale and distribution of client sampling.

**Theorem 1.** *In* FEDDYN, $\|h^t\|^2 \leq \|h^{t-1}\|^2$ *requires*

$$\cos(\angle(h^{t-1}, \bar{g}^t)) \leq -\frac{|\mathcal{P}^t|}{2\,S^t|} \frac{\|\bar{g}^t\|}{\|h^{t-1}\|}. \tag{5}$$

**Functionality.** ADABEST allows to control how far to look back through the previous rounds for effective estimation of full and local gradients compared to existing RV-LSGD baselines. To update the local gradient estimates, we dynamically scale the previous values down because the period between computing and using $h_i^{t_i'}$ on client $i$ (the period between two participation, i.e., $t - t_i'$) can be long during which the error of estimation may notable increase. See Algorithm 1 for comparing our updates on local gradients estimation compared to that of the baselines. Furthermore, at the server, $h^t$ is calculated as the weighted difference of two consecutive aggregate models. Note that, if expanded as a power series, this difference by itself is equivalent to accumulating pseudo-gradients across previous rounds with an exponentially weighted factor. This series is presented in Remark 3 for which the proof is provided in the supplementary material. Unlike previous works, proposed pseudo-gradients' accumulation does not necessitate any additional effort to explicitly maintain information about the previous rounds. Additionally, it reduces the compute cost as quantitatively shown in the supplementary material. It is a general arithmetic; therefore, could be adapted to work with our baselines as well.

*Remark 2.* $\bar{\theta}^{t-1} - \bar{\theta}^t$ is equivalent to $h^{t-1} + \bar{g}^t$ in ADABEST.

*Remark 3.* Cloud pseudo-gradients of ADABEST form a power series of $h^t = \sum_{\tau=1}^{t} \beta^{(t-\tau)} \bar{g}^t$, given that superscript in parenthesis means power.

## 3.5 Adaptability

As indicated earlier, the error in estimation of oracle full gradients in FEDDYN is only supposed to be eliminated by using pseudo-gradients. A difficult learning task, both in terms of optimization and heterogeneity results in a higher variance of pseudo-gradients when accompanies with a low rate of client participation. The outcome of constructing a naive estimator by accumulating these pseudo-gradients is sever. This is shown in Fig. 1, where, on average, there is a long wait time between client re-samples due to the large number of participating clients. The results of this experiment empirically validates that $\|\theta^t\|^2$ in FEDDYN grows more rapidly and to a much higher value than ADABEST. SCAFFOLD is prune to the same type of failure; however, because it scales down previous values of $h$ in its accumulation, the outcomes are less severe than that of FEDDYN. In the supplementary material, we present, similar analysis, for a much simpler task (classification on EMNIST-L). It is important not to confuse the source of FEDDYN's instability with overfitting (see supplementary material for overfitting analysis). However, our observations imply that the stability of FEDDYN decreases with the difficulty of the task.

Our parameter $\beta$ solves the previously mentioned problem with norm of $h$. It is a scalar values between 0 and 1 that acts as a slider knob to determine the trade-off between the amount of information maintained from the previous estimate of full gradient and the estimation that a new round provides. On an intuitive level, a smaller $\beta$ is better to be chosen for a more difficult task (both in terms of optimization and heterogeneity) and lower level participation–and correspondingly higher round to round variance among pseudo-gradients and vice versa. We provide an experimental analysis of $\beta$ in the supplementary material; however, in a practical engineering level, $\beta$ could be dynamically adjusted based on the variance of the pseudo-gradients. The goal of this paper is rather showing the impact of using $\beta$. Therefore, we tune it like other hyper-parameters in our experiments. We leave further automation for finding an optimal $\beta$ to be an open question for the future works.

*Remark 4.* FEDAVG is a special case of ADABEST where $\beta = \mu = 0$.

*Remark 5.* Server update of FEDDYN is a special case of ADABEST where $\beta = 1$ except that **an extra $\frac{|\mathcal{P}|}{|S|}$ scalar is applied which also adversely makes FedDyn require prior knowledge about the number of clients.**

**Theorem 2.** *If $S$ be a fixed set of clients, $\bar{\theta}$ does not converge to a stationary point unless $h \to 0$.*

As mentioned in Sect. 3.4 and more particular with Theorem 1, FEDDYN is only able to decrease norm of $h$ if pseudo-gradients are negatively correlated with oracle gradient estimates which could be likely only if the rate of client re-sampling is high. Therefore, with these conditions often being not true in large-scale FL and partial-participation, it struggles to converge to an optimal point. SCAFFOLD has a weighting factor that eventually could decrease $\|h\|$ but it is not controllable. Our algorithm enables a direct decay of $h$ through decaying $\beta$. We apply this decay in our experiments when norm of $h$ plateaus (see Sect. 4.4). This is consistent with Theorem 2 which states that converging to a stationary point require $h \to 0$.

## 4    Experiments

### 4.1    Setup

We evaluate performance and speed of convergence of our algorithm against state-of-the-art baselines. We concentrate on FL classification tasks defined using three well-known datasets. These datasets are, the letters classification task of EMNIST-L [11] for an easy task, CIFAR10 [10] for a moderate task and CIFAR100 [10] for a challenging task. The training split of the dataset is partitioned randomly into a predetermined number of clients, for each task. 10% of these clients are set aside as validation clients and only used for evaluating the performance of the models during hyper-parameter tuning. The remaining 90% is dedicated to training. The entire test split of each dataset is used to evaluate and compare the performance of each model. Our assumption throughout the experiments is that, test dataset, oracle dataset, and collective data of validations clients have the same underlying distribution.

To ensure consistency with previous works, we follow [1] to control heterogeneity and sample balance among client data splits. For heterogeneity, we evaluate algorithms in three modes: IID, $\alpha = 0.3$ and $\alpha = 0.03$. The first mode corresponds to data partitions (clients' data) with equal class probabilities. For the second and third modes, we draw the skew in each client's labels from a Dirichlet distribution with a concentration parameter $\alpha$. For testing against balance of sample number, we have two modes: *balanced* and *unbalanced* such that in the latter, the number of samples for each client is sampled from a log-normal distribution with concentration parameter equal to 0.3.

Throughout the experiments we consistently keep the local learning rate, number of local epochs and batch size as 0.1, 5 and 45 respectively. Local learning rate is decayed with a factor of 0.998 at each round. As tuned by [1], the local optimizer uses a weight decay of $10^{-4}$ for the experiments on EMNIST-L and $10^{-3}$ for the experiment on CIFAR10 and CIFAR100. Further details about the optimization is provided in supplementary material.

To tune the hyper-parameters we first launch each experiment for 500 rounds. $\mu$ of FEDDYN is chosen from $[0.002, 0.02, 0.2]$, with 0.02 performing best in all cases except EMNIST-L, where 0.2 also worked well. For the sake of consistency, we kept $\mu = 0.02$ for ADABEST as well. We found the rate of client participation to be an important factor for choosing a good value for $\beta$. Therefore, for 1% client participation experiments we search $\beta$ in $[0.2, 0.4, 0.6]$. For higher rates of client participation, we use the search range of $[0.94, 0.96, 0.98, 1.0]$. For all these cases, 0.96 and 0.98 are selected for 10% and 100% client participation rates, respectively (both balanced and unbalanced). We follow [1] for choosing the inference model by averaging client models though the rounds. Experiments are repeated 5 times, each with a different random seed of data partitioning. The reported mean and standard deviation of the performance are calculated based on the the last round of these 5 instance for each setting.

## 4.2   Model Architecture

We use the same model architectures as [17] and [1]. For EMNIST-L, the architecture comprises of two fully-connected layers, each with 100 hidden units. For CIFAR10 and CIFAR100, there are two convolutional layers with $5 \times 5$ kernel size and 64 kernels each, followed by two fully-connected layers with 394 and 192 hidden units, respectively.

## 4.3   Baselines

We compare the performance of ADABEST against FEDAVG [17], SCAFFOLD [7] and FEDDYN [1]. These baselines are consistent with the ones that the closest work to us [1], has experimented with[4]. However, we avoided their choice of tuning the number of local epochs since we believe it does not comply with a fair comparison in terms of computation complexity and privacy loss.

---

[4] FEDDYN additionally compares with FEDPROX [13]; however, as shown in their benchmarks it performs closer to FEDAVG than the other baselines.

## 4.4   Evaluation

Table 2 compare the performance of our model to all the baselines in various settings with 100 clients. The results show that our algorithm is effective in all settings. The 1000-device experiments confirm our arguments about the large-scale cross-device setting and practicality of ADABEST in comparison to the baselines. Our algorithm has notable gain both in the speed of convergence and the generalization performance. This gain is only reduced for some benchmarks in full client participation settings (CP = 100%) where the best $\beta$ is chosen close to one. According to Remark 5, and the fact that in full participation $\frac{|\mathcal{P}^t|}{|S^t|} = 1$ and $t_i = t'_i + 1$ for all feasible $i$ and $t$, FEDDYN and ADABEST become nearly identical in these settings. In Fig. 3, we show the impact of scaling the number of clients in both balanced and imbalanced settings for the same dataset and the same number of clients sampled per round (10 clients). During the hyper-parameter tuning we noticed that the sensitivity of FEDDYN and ADABEST to their $\mu$ is small specially for the cases with larger number of clients.

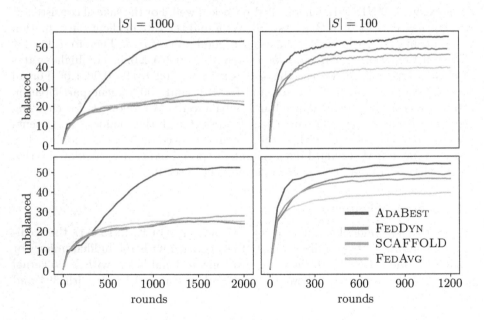

**Fig. 3.** Test accuracy on balanced (top) and unbalanced (bottom) settings for training on 1000 (left) and 100 (right) clients. The training dataset is CIFAR100 and $|\mathcal{P}|=10$

**Table 2.** Mean and standard deviation of test accuracy for various settings. The results are based on 5 random data partitioning seeds. Models are trained for 1k, 1.2k, and 2k rounds, for 1%, 10% and 100% client participation settings, respectively. A *smaller* $\alpha$ indicates *higher* heterogeneity. *CP stands for rate of client participation ($\frac{|\mathcal{P}|}{|\mathcal{S}|}$)

| CP* | Dataset | Setting | Top-1 Test accuracy | | | |
|---|---|---|---|---|---|---|
| | | | FEDAVG | FEDDYN | SCAFFOLD | ADABEST |
| 1% | EMNIST-L | $\alpha = 0.03$ | $94.28 \pm 0.07$ | $92.42 \pm 0.14$ | $93.99 \pm 0.16$ | $\mathbf{94.49 \pm 0.07}$ |
| | | $\alpha = 0.3$ | $94.47 \pm 0.10$ | $92.64 \pm 0.31$ | $94.34 \pm 0.23$ | $\mathbf{94.72 \pm 0.22}$ |
| | | IID | $94.04 \pm 1.37$ | $92.89 \pm 0.14$ | $94.48 \pm 0.11$ | $\mathbf{94.81 \pm 0.08}$ |
| | CIFAR10 | $\alpha = 0.03$ | $78.18 \pm 0.80$ | $77.91 \pm 0.79$ | $75.83 \pm 2.36$ | $\mathbf{78.44 \pm 1.12}$ |
| | | $\alpha = 0.3$ | $82.21 \pm 0.36$ | $82.06 \pm 0.17$ | $82.96 \pm 0.42$ | $\mathbf{83.09 \pm 0.76}$ |
| | | IID | $83.84 \pm 0.17$ | $83.36 \pm 0.39$ | $84.18 \pm 0.26$ | $\mathbf{85.05 \pm 0.31}$ |
| | CIFAR100 | $\alpha = 0.03$ | $47.56 \pm 0.59$ | $46.27 \pm 0.65$ | $47.29 \pm 0.95$ | $\mathbf{47.91 \pm 0.83}$ |
| | | $\alpha = 0.3$ | $49.63 \pm 0.47$ | $50.53 \pm 0.36$ | $52.87 \pm 0.61$ | $\mathbf{53.62 \pm 0.23}$ |
| | | IID | $49.93 \pm 0.36$ | $50.85 \pm 0.38$ | $53.43 \pm 0.44$ | $\mathbf{55.33 \pm 0.44}$ |
| 10% | EMNIST-L | $\alpha = 0.03$ | $93.58 \pm 0.25$ | $93.57 \pm 0.20$ | $94.29 \pm 0.11$ | $\mathbf{94.62 \pm 0.17}$ |
| | | $\alpha = 0.3$ | $94.04 \pm 0.04$ | $93.54 \pm 0.22$ | $94.54 \pm 0.11$ | $\mathbf{94.64 \pm 0.11}$ |
| | | IID | $94.32 \pm 0.10$ | $93.60 \pm 0.35$ | $94.62 \pm 0.16$ | $\mathbf{94.70 \pm 0.24}$ |
| | CIFAR10 | $\alpha = 0.03$ | $74.04 \pm 0.88$ | $76.85 \pm 0.91$ | $77.19 \pm 1.10$ | $\mathbf{79.64 \pm 0.58}$ |
| | | $\alpha = 0.3$ | $79.74 \pm 0.07$ | $81.91 \pm 0.19$ | $82.26 \pm 0.38$ | $\mathbf{84.15 \pm 0.36}$ |
| | | IID | $81.35 \pm 0.23$ | $83.56 \pm 0.31$ | $83.50 \pm 0.15$ | $\mathbf{85.78 \pm 0.14}$ |
| | CIFAR100 | $\alpha = 0.03$ | $39.18 \pm 0.56$ | $44.24 \pm 0.66$ | $45.80 \pm 0.36$ | $\mathbf{48.56 \pm 0.45}$ |
| | | $\alpha = 0.3$ | $38.78 \pm 0.35$ | $48.92 \pm 0.37$ | $46.34 \pm 0.43$ | $\mathbf{54.51 \pm 0.35}$ |
| | | IID | $37.45 \pm 0.57$ | $49.60 \pm 0.24$ | $44.30 \pm 0.22$ | $\mathbf{55.58 \pm 0.14}$ |
| 100% | EMNIST-L | $\alpha = 0.03$ | $93.36 \pm 0.15$ | $94.18 \pm 0.21$ | $\mathbf{94.38 \pm 0.20}$ | $94.06 \pm 0.11$ |
| | | $\alpha = 0.3$ | $93.99 \pm 0.19$ | $94.23 \pm 0.14$ | $\mathbf{94.53 \pm 0.16}$ | $94.40 \pm 0.21$ |
| | | IID | $94.06 \pm 0.33$ | $94.37 \pm 0.15$ | $94.63 \pm 0.10$ | $\mathbf{94.69 \pm 0.14}$ |
| | CIFAR10 | $\alpha = 0.03$ | $72.97 \pm 1.09$ | $\mathbf{78.24 \pm 0.77}$ | $77.64 \pm 0.25$ | $78.07 \pm 0.71$ |
| | | $\alpha = 0.3$ | $79.12 \pm 0.15$ | $83.19 \pm 0.18$ | $82.26 \pm 0.23$ | $\mathbf{83.20 \pm 0.25}$ |
| | | IID | $80.72 \pm 0.33$ | $84.39 \pm 0.20$ | $83.55 \pm 0.25$ | $\mathbf{84.75 \pm 0.17}$ |
| | CIFAR100 | $\alpha = 0.03$ | $38.24 \pm 0.63$ | $46.00 \pm 0.42$ | $\mathbf{46.51 \pm 0.50}$ | $46.16 \pm 0.79$ |
| | | $\alpha = 0.3$ | $37.03 \pm 0.35$ | $50.42 \pm 0.29$ | $45.48 \pm 0.38$ | $\mathbf{50.90 \pm 0.42}$ |
| | | IID | $35.92 \pm 0.48$ | $50.61 \pm 0.25$ | $43.73 \pm 0.23$ | $\mathbf{51.33 \pm 0.41}$ |

## 5   Conclusions

In this paper, we introduce ADABEST, an adaptive approach for tackling client drift in Federated Learning. Unlike the existing solutions, our approach is robust to low rates of clients re-sampling, which makes it practical for large-scale cross-device Federated Learning. Our performance and empirical convergence rates demonstrate the efficacy of our technique compared to all the baselines across various benchmarks. We have a gain of up to 0.94% in test accuracy with respect to the second best candidate which is nearly twice as good. Our algorithm consumes no more communication bandwidth or storage than the baselines, and it even has a lower compute cost. ADABEST addresses the instability of norm of gradient estimates used in FEDDYN by adapting to the most relevant information about the direction of the client drift. Furthermore, we formulated the general estimate of oracle gradients in a much elegant arithmetic that eliminates the need for the explicit, recursive form used in the previous algorithms.

Future work for this study includes deriving theoretical bounds for our proposed algorithm. Furthermore, in the current paper, the parameter $\beta$ is manually tuned to account for the trade-off between the amount of information retained from the previous estimations of oracle's gradients and the estimation provided by a new round. Developing a method for automatically tuning $\beta$ is an important direction for improving the proposed algorithm.

**Acknowledgments.** The first author wishes to express gratitude for the financial support provided by *MITACS* and *Research Nova Scotia*. In addition, the fifth author acknowledges Natural Sciences and Engineering research Council of Canada, CHIST-ERA grant CHIST-ERA-19-XAI-0 and the Polish NCN Agency NCN(grant No. 2020/02/Y/ST6/00064). We are grateful to Sai Praneeth Karimireddy, the first author of [7], for enlightening us on the proper implementation of SCAFFOLD. William Taylor-Melanson is also acknowledged for reviewing this paper and providing numerous helpful comments.

# References

1. Acar, D.A.E., Zhao, Y., Matas, R., Mattina, M., Whatmough, P., Saligrama, V.: Federated learning based on dynamic regularization. In: International Conference on Learning Representations (2020)
2. Ajalloeian, A., Stich, S.U.: On the convergence of SGD with biased gradients. arXiv preprint arXiv:2008.00051 (2020)
3. Harikandeh, R.B., Ahmed, M.O., Virani, A., Schmidt, M., Konečný, J., Sallinen, S.: Stopwasting my gradients: practical svrg. Adv. Neural Inf. Process. Syst. **28** (2015)
4. Bi, J., Gunn, S.R.: A variance controlled stochastic method with biased estimation for faster non-convex optimization. In: Oliver, N., Pérez-Cruz, F., Kramer, S., Read, J., Lozano, J.A. (eds.) ECML PKDD 2021. LNCS (LNAI), vol. 12977, pp. 135–150. Springer, Cham (2021). https://doi.org/10.1007/978-3-030-86523-8_9
5. Hsu, T.M.H., Qi, H., Brown, M.: Measuring the effects of non-identical data distribution for federated visual classification. arXiv preprint arXiv:1909.06335 (2019)
6. Johnson, R., Zhang, T.: Accelerating stochastic gradient descent using predictive variance reduction. Adv. Neural. Inf. Process. Syst. **26**, 315–323 (2013)
7. Karimireddy, S.P., Kale, S., Mohri, M., Reddi, S., Stich, S., Suresh, A.T.: SCAFFOLD: stochastic controlled averaging for federated learning. In: International Conference on Machine Learning, pp. 5132–5143. PMLR (2020)
8. Konečný, J., Liu, J., Richtárik, P., Takáč, M.: Mini-batch semi-stochastic gradient descent in the proximal setting. IEEE J. Sel. Top. Signal Process. **10**(2), 242–255 (2015)
9. Konečný, J., McMahan, H.B., Ramage, D., Richtárik, P.: Federated optimization: distributed machine learning for on-device intelligence. arXiv preprint arXiv:1610.02527 (2016)
10. Krizhevsky, A., Hinton, G., et al.: Learning multiple layers of features from tiny images. University of Toronto, Technical report (2009)
11. LeCun, Y., Bottou, L., Bengio, Y., Haffner, P.: Gradient-based learning applied to document recognition. Proc. IEEE **86**(11), 2278–2324 (1998)
12. Li, D., Wang, J.: FedMD: heterogenous federated learning via model distillation. arXiv preprint arXiv:1910.03581 (2019)

13. Li, T., Sahu, A.K., Zaheer, M., Sanjabi, M., Talwalkar, A., Smith, V.: Federated optimization in heterogeneous networks. Proc. Mach. Learn. Syst. **2**, 429–450 (2020)
14. Li, T., Sahu, A.K., Zaheer, M., Sanjabi, M., Talwalkar, A., Smithy, V.: FedDANE: a federated newton-type method. In: 2019 53rd Asilomar Conference on Signals, Systems, and Computers, pp. 1227–1231. IEEE (2019)
15. Liang, X., Shen, S., Liu, J., Pan, Z., Chen, E., Cheng, Y.: Variance reduced local SGD with lower communication complexity. arXiv preprint arXiv:1912.12844 (2019)
16. Lin, T., Kong, L., Stich, S.U., Jaggi, M.: Ensemble distillation for robust model fusion in federated learning. Adv. Neural. Inf. Process. Syst. **33**, 2351–2363 (2020)
17. McMahan, B., Moore, E., Ramage, D., Hampson, S., Arcas, B.A.: Communication-efficient learning of deep networks from decentralized data. In: Artificial Intelligence and Statistics, pp. 1273–1282. PMLR (2017)
18. Murata, T., Suzuki, T.: Bias-variance reduced local SGD for less heterogeneous federated learning. In: International Conference on Machine Learning, pp. 7872–7881. PMLR (2021)
19. Nguyen, L.M., Liu, J., Scheinberg, K., Takáč, M.: SARAH: a novel method for machine learning problems using stochastic recursive gradient. In: International Conference on Machine Learning, pp. 2613–2621. PMLR (2017)
20. Pathak, R., Wainwright, M.J.: FedSplit: an algorithmic framework for fast federated optimization. Adv. Neural. Inf. Process. Syst. **33**, 7057–7066 (2020)
21. Reddi, S.J., Konečnỳ, J., Richtárik, P., Póczós, B., Smola, A.: AIDE: fast and communication efficient distributed optimization. arXiv preprint arXiv:1608.06879 (2016)
22. Roux, N., Schmidt, M., Bach, F.: A stochastic gradient method with an exponential convergence _rate for finite training sets. Adv. Neural Inf. Process. Syst. **25** (2012)
23. Shalev-Shwartz, S., Zhang, T.: Stochastic dual coordinate ascent methods for regularized loss minimization. J. Mach. Learn. Res. **14**(2) (2013)
24. Shamir, O., Srebro, N., Zhang, T.: Communication-efficient distributed optimization using an approximate newton-type method. In: International Conference on Machine Learning, pp. 1000–1008. PMLR (2014)
25. Stich, S.U.: Local SGD converges fast and communicates little. In: International Conference on Learning Representations (2018)
26. Wang, J., Liu, Q., Liang, H., Joshi, G., Poor, H.V.: Tackling the objective inconsistency problem in heterogeneous federated optimization. Adv. Neural. Inf. Process. Syst. **33**, 7611–7623 (2020)
27. Wang, J., Tantia, V., Ballas, N., Rabbat, M.: SlowMo: improving communication-efficient distributed SGD with slow momentum. arXiv preprint arXiv:1910.00643 (2019)
28. Xiao, L., Zhang, T.: A proximal stochastic gradient method with progressive variance reduction. SIAM J. Optim. **24**(4), 2057–2075 (2014)
29. Yu, H., Jin, R., Yang, S.: On the linear speedup analysis of communication efficient momentum SGD for distributed non-convex optimization. In: International Conference on Machine Learning, pp. 7184–7193. PMLR (2019)
30. Zhang, X., Hong, M., Dhople, S., Yin, W., Liu, Y.: FedPD: a federated learning framework with optimal rates and adaptivity to Non-IID data. arXiv preprint arXiv:2005.11418 (2020)
31. Zhao, Y., Li, M., Lai, L., Suda, N., Civin, D., Chandra, V.: Federated learning with Non-IID data. arXiv preprint arXiv:1806.00582 (2018)

32. Zhu, L., Han, S.: Deep leakage from gradients. In: Federated Learning, pp. 17–31. Springer (2020)
33. Zhu, Z., Hong, J., Zhou, J.: Data-free knowledge distillation for heterogeneous federated learning. In: International Conference on Machine Learning, pp. 12878–12889. PMLR (2021)

# Tackling Long-Tailed Category Distribution Under Domain Shifts

Xiao Gu[1], Yao Guo[2], Zeju Li[1], Jianing Qiu[1], Qi Dou[3],
Yuxuan Liu[2], Benny Lo[1(✉)], and Guang-Zhong Yang[2(✉)]

[1] Imperial College London, London, England
{xiao.gu17,zeju.li18,jianing.qiu17,benny.lo}@imperial.ac.uk
[2] Shanghai Jiao Tong University, Shanghai, China
{yao.guo,200009051yx,gzyang}@sjtu.edu.cn
[3] The Chinese University of Hong Kong, Hong Kong, China
{qidou@cuhk.edu.hk}

**Abstract.** Machine learning models fail to perform well on real-world applications when 1) the category distribution $P(Y)$ of the training dataset suffers from long-tailed distribution and 2) the test data is drawn from different conditional distributions $P(X|Y)$. Existing approaches cannot handle the scenario where both issues exist, which however is common for real-world applications. In this study, we took a step forward and looked into the problem of long-tailed classification under domain shifts. We designed three novel core functional blocks including Distribution Calibrated Classification Loss, Visual-Semantic Mapping and Semantic-Similarity Guided Augmentation. Furthermore, we adopted a meta-learning framework which integrates these three blocks to improve domain generalization on unseen target domains. Two new datasets were proposed for this problem, named AWA2-LTS and ImageNet-LTS. We evaluated our method on the two datasets and extensive experimental results demonstrate that our proposed method can achieve superior performance over state-of-the-art long-tailed/domain generalization approaches and the combinations. Source codes and datasets can be found at our project page https://xiaogu.site/LTDS.

**Keywords:** Long tail · Domain generalization · Cross-modal representation learning · Meta learning

## 1 Introduction

Deep learning has made unprecedented achievements on various applications ranging from self-driving [2], service robots [8], to health and wellbeing [26]. The model would perform well with the assumption that training and testing data are independent identically distributed (*i.i.d.*); however it seldomly holds

**Supplementary Information** The online version contains supplementary material available at https://doi.org/10.1007/978-3-031-20050-2_42.

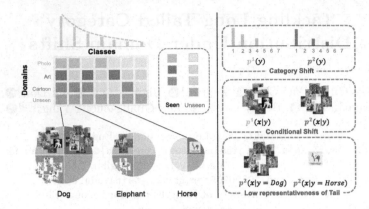

**Fig. 1.** Visual illustrations of the issues complicated with long-tailed category distribution and conditional distribution shifts across domains. The overall dataset (Images are adopted from PACS [15]. Its distribution originally is not long-tailed. Here just for intuitive explanation of our focused problem) is long-tailed distributed over classes. Meanwhile, with data collected from multiple domains (e.g., different styles), head classes (e.g., *Dog*) can be observed in most domains, whereas tail classes (e.g., *Horse*) only contain a few samples in certain specific domains.

for real-world applications. The violation of *i.i.d.* assumption could hinder the performance of deep learning models upon practical deployment. Without loss of generality, we denote the data and label as $X$ and $Y$, the joint distribution as $P(X, Y)$, the latter of which can be formulated by $P(Y)P(X|Y)$. We argue that the reason why current models fail to generalize well in real-world applications is rooted in both the categorical distribution $P(Y)$ and class conditional distribution $P(X|Y)$.

On one hand, real-world data exhibits long-tailed distribution over categories, with only a few classes (*head*) accounting for the major proportions, whilst many more classes (*tail*) presenting extremely limited samples [43]. For instance, in action recognition, the case of "*open door*" is common in daily activities, whereas some actions such as "*repair door*" occur much less frequently. This leads to a long-tailed label distribution of $P(Y)$, where conventional training strategies that apply common classification losses (mostly cross-entropy) on instance-level sampled batches would fail. In this case, the trained model would gain high performance on the head classes but behave poorly on tail classes, failing to achieve consistently good performance across all categories. On the other hand, the conditional distribution $P(X|Y)$ is also prone to changes in the real world [35]. Different styles of image recognition data, camera viewpoints of action recognition data, acquisition protocols of medical images, etc., would alter the distribution of $P(X|Y)$, leading to diversified distributions, a.k.a. domain shifts.

In this regard, long-tailed categorical distribution (**LT**) [43] and domain shifts (**DS**) [35] have been two major issues concerned with real-world datasets. Although increasing research efforts have been made, these two issues are so far tackled individually, with their complex co-existence situation not being considered yet. Existing solutions cannot deal with the entanglement of **LT** and **DS**, since a balanced distribution $P(Y)$ or identical $P(X|Y)$ are their prior assumptions of those **DS** [6,35] and **LT** [13,17,27] solutions, respectively. As we know, in real-world scenarios, these two issues often come together. Take medical image data as an example, the conditional distribution varies across different hospitals, and, there are a large population of patients with common diseases whilst some patients with rare diseases. In addition, the low prevalence of those rare diseases may lead to the inclusion of corresponding patients only by certain hospitals. This also similarly applies to many other applications [4] where the head classes are common in most domains, whilst tail classes only appear in certain domains due to the low-frequency. Such combination of $<$ and **DS** leads to a more challenging, yet more practical scenario where $P(Y)$ of each individual domain is not only imbalanced, but also partial. Ideally a reasonable model should be robust across classes and generalize across domains, simultaneously.

We argue that there are three main challenges posed by the problem of **LT-DS** (cf. Fig. 1). **1)** Because of the existence of multiple domains, the categorical distributions $P(Y)$ are different across domains. Given the relatively low frequency of non-head classes, their corresponding samples may be collected only in certain domains. As a result, the spurious correlation between non-head classes and domain-specific characteristics might be learned as biased shortcuts. **2)** The conditional distributions $P(X|Y)$ are varied significantly across domains. It is expected that the model can handle such shifts, with domains aligned and unbiased representations learned. **3)** It is hard to explicitly model the distribution of tail classes $P(X|Y = tail)$, as only a paucity of domain-specific samples exist. This poses challenges to avoiding overfitting on the tails. Hence, research is desperately needed to solve the co-occurrence of these issues in **LT-DS**.

In this work, we propose an effective solution to tackle all of the aforementioned challenges. First, a novel domain-specific distribution calibrated loss is introduced to address the infinite imbalance ratio of each domain. Subsequently, we leverage class distributional embeddings as unbiased semantic features, to align the derived visual representations to unbiased semantic space via the alignment between domain-specific visual prototypes and semantic embeddings. Furthermore, we propose a semantic-similarity guided module by leveraging the knowledge learned from head classes, for implicit augmentation of tail classes. In addition, to ensure the model is capable of handling out-of-distribution data in unseen domains, a meta-learning framework integrating the above three core modules is proposed to boost the generalization capability. To evaluate the effectiveness of the proposed method, we developed two datasets with **LT-DS** problems, namely **AWA2-LTS** and **ImageNet-LTS**, and conducted extensive comparison experiments on both datasets. Results demonstrate that our proposed method exceeds state-of-the-art **LT** or **DS** methods by a large margin.

## 2    Related Works

**Long-Tailed Category Distribution.** To learn from class imbalanced training data, one line of existing works aims to manipulate class-wise contributions by resampling [1,9], reweighting [11,19,38], logits adjustment [10,27], and two-stage training [14,32]. Another emerging line has made attempts at ensemble learning under long-tailed settings, such as contrastive learning [36], knowledge distillation [12], variance-bias calibration [37]. In particular, RIDE [37] indicates that the predictions of head classes would be of larger intra-class variances, whereas tail classes would exhibit larger biases. This becomes more serious in the **LT-DS** scenario, since the intra-class variances are related to not only semantics but also domains shifts; whereas the representations of non-head classes may easily be biased by domain-specific characteristics. Unfortunately, most of the existing methods do not take into account conditional-distribution-shift introduced biases, instead assuming identical in their work. Similar issues exist in recent meta-learning based approaches. To ensure good performance across all classes, recent works investigated the category shift between long-tailed and balanced distributions, and introduced meta-learning strategies to optimize parameters on a held-out balanced meta-test subset [13,17]. This is not applicable for **LT-DS**, since it is impossible to sample a held-out meta-test proportion with balanced category distribution without conditional distribution shifts.

**Model Generalization at Domain Shifts.** Domain generalization (DG) aims to develop computational models that are capable of handling data from unseen domains. Existing domain generalization solutions are varied, including aligning intra-class representations across domains [18], factoring out domain-specific information [7,34], simulating domain gaps via sophisticated training strategies [6,16], or performing data augmentation [22,44]. The shortcomings of most solutions become apparent when faced with **LT-DS**, as **LT-DS** poses imbalanced distribution over a large number of classes. For the methods benefiting from explicit categorical distribution alignment [18], it is computationally prohibitive to design class-specific aligning models, and impossible to align domain-specific tail classes. Furthermore, the large class number makes sampling classes from multiple domains intractable, thus being difficult to cover relatively large portions of the label set in a mini batch [6]. Even worse, for those tail classes, since they are only available in certain domains due to the low-frequency, some shortcuts of the classifier may be learned due to the spurious correlation between the domain-specific information and the occurrence of associated tail classes.

On the other hand, most current domain generalization approaches assume similar categorical distribution across domains, yet this can hardly hold true in the real world [20,29,42]. A similar issue has been raised in [29] referred to as open domain generalization, where the distribution and label sets of each source domain and target domain can be different. Shu *et al.* [29] introduced the domain-specific model in each individual source domain and applied a meta learning strategy to generalize each domain-specific model to other domains, by knowledge distillation from other domains. However, this framework cannot well apply to **LT-DS** settings. To be specific, the knowledge derived from each domain is easy to get biased due to the specific long-tailed and incomplete categorical distribution in each domain. Even worse, there is no guarantee that under such bias, the spurious correlation between non-semantic domain-specific characteristics and domain-specific classes can be avoided.

**Cross-Modal Representation Learning.** Leveraging information from multiple modalities is popular for related multi-modality applications [25, 30] to facilitate effective representation learning of each individual modality. One of the related applications is few/zero-shot learning, where one line of research aims to establish the relationship between semantic space and visual space [41]. Maniyar *et al.* [23] leveraged the semantic space to enable zero-shot domain generalization, and Mancini *et al.* [22] used the semantic embeddings as the classifier for zero-shot learning in unseen domains. These inspired our work; however as a different task setting, our goal is to derive unbiased predictor under long-tailed settings such that the missing classes in seen domains can be recognized as well.

Recently, Samuel *et al.* [28] leveraged class descriptors to facilitate long-tailed classification. It developed a dual network to derive both visual features and semantic features from the input image, and then fused these two together to boost the performance of long-tailed classification. Although it applied semantic embeddings similar to our work, our task aims to address a more challenging problem, where both imbalance and conditional distribution shifts exist.

## 3  Methodologies

### 3.1  Problem Setup and Preliminaries

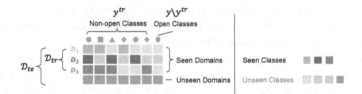

**Fig. 2.** Illustrations of domain splits, open/non-open classes, and seen/unseen classes.

We denote the input and label spaces as $\mathcal{X}$ and $\mathcal{Y}$, and the domain space as $\mathcal{D}$. $\mathcal{D}$ consists of totally $K$ domains $\{D_k\}_{k=1}^K$ and there are totally $C$ categories in the label space. Each sample is denoted as $\{x_i, y_i, d_i\}$, where $i$ indicates the sample index, $x_i$ the input sample, $y_i$ the ground truth label, and $d_i$ the domain index; $1 \le d_i \le K$. The training domains and testing domains are denoted as $\mathcal{D}_{tr}$ and $\mathcal{D}_{te}$, respectively, where $\mathcal{D}_{tr} \subset \mathcal{D}$ and $\mathcal{D}_{te} = \mathcal{D}$. The categorical distribution $p^k(y)$ of each training domain $k$ follows a long-tailed distribution, and the low prevalence of tail classes may lead to the failure of collecting training samples from rare classes, i.e., $\mathcal{Y}^k \subset \mathcal{Y}$. We denote the label set of all training data as $\mathcal{Y}^{tr} = \bigcup_{k=1}^{|\mathcal{D}_{tr}|} \mathcal{Y}^k$. To test the overall performance across all classes, test data is sampled under balanced distribution over all classes. Since there might be domain-specific non-head classes in each domain, open classes exist in the testing domains, namely $\mathcal{Y}^{tr} \subset \mathcal{Y}$, $\mathcal{Y}^{te} = \mathcal{Y}$. A visual illustration is presented in Fig. 2.

Our ultimate goal is to build a computational model that is able to recognize all the non-open classes across domains, as well as open classes belonging to $\mathcal{Y} \setminus \mathcal{Y}^{tr}$.

The computational model $g : \mathcal{X} \to \mathcal{Y}$ maps raw input to the final prediction. Following previous domain generalization works [6], it can be decoupled into a feature extractor $f$ and a head classifier $h$, where $f : \mathcal{X} \to \mathcal{Z}$, and $h : \mathcal{Z} \to \mathbb{R}^C$. The final prediction $\hat{y} = g(\boldsymbol{x}) = h \circ f(\boldsymbol{x})$. With the loss function denoted as $\mathcal{L}(h \circ f(\boldsymbol{x}), y)$, we derive the estimated error $\epsilon$ on test data as:

$$\begin{aligned} \epsilon &= \mathbb{E}_{m \sim P_{\mathcal{D}_{te}}} \mathbb{E}_{(\boldsymbol{x},y) \sim p^m(\boldsymbol{x},y)} \mathcal{L}(h \circ f(\boldsymbol{x}), y) \\ &= \mathbb{E}_{\substack{m \sim P_{\mathcal{D}_{te}} \\ n \sim P_{\mathcal{D}_{tr}}}} \mathbb{E}_{(\boldsymbol{x},y) \sim p^n(\boldsymbol{x},y)} \mathcal{L}(h \circ f(\boldsymbol{x}), y) \frac{p^m(f(\boldsymbol{x}), y)}{p^n(f(\boldsymbol{x}), y)} \\ &= \mathbb{E}_{\substack{m \sim P_{\mathcal{D}_{te}} \\ n \sim P_{\mathcal{D}_{tr}}}} \mathbb{E}_{(\boldsymbol{x},y) \sim p^n(\boldsymbol{x},y)} \mathcal{L}(h \circ f(\boldsymbol{x}), y) \frac{p^m(y) p^m(f(\boldsymbol{x})|y)}{p^n(y) p^n(f(\boldsymbol{x})|y)}, \end{aligned} \quad (1)$$

where $P_{\mathcal{D}_{tr}} \& P_{\mathcal{D}_{te}}$ denotes the probability of sampling data from training or testing domains.

To minimize $\epsilon$ as in Eq. (1), it is of paramount significance to model the term $\frac{p^{te}(y) p^{te}(f(\boldsymbol{x})|y)}{p^{tr}(y) p^{tr}(f(\boldsymbol{x})|y)}$ to ensure the robustness under **LT-DS**. However, there exist several issues that are challenging to resolve:

**1)** $p^n(y)$ of each individual training domain is imbalanced. Even through a balanced resampling on seen classes, those unseen classes of each individual domain still leads to "imbalance" with an infinite ratio.

**2)** It comes with challenges in aligning the distribution of $p^n(f(\boldsymbol{x})|y)$ to an unbiased and semantically meaningful space, since there are some classes unseen in each individual domain, especially for those tail classes.

**3)** The distributions of tail classes $p(f(\boldsymbol{x})|y)$ are difficult to model compared to head classes, as caused by the limited sample number in certain domains.

**4)** Since we aim to model and align $p^n(f(\boldsymbol{x})|y)$ rather than $p^n(\boldsymbol{x}|y)$, it is important to make sure that $f$ is able to handle out-of-distribution data itself, thus enabling extracting domain-invariant and discriminative features by $f(\boldsymbol{x})$.

It should be noted that Eq. (1) gets some inspirations from the recent work [13], while they are conceptually different. To be specific, Jamal *et al.* [13] considers the distribution shifts across long-tailed and balanced distributions; whereas the shifts of $P(X|Y)$ like style changes are not taken into consideration.

In the following, we first go through the core functional blocks to address aforementioned issues, followed by a meta-learning based framework to integrate these functional blocks.

## 3.2    Core Functional Blocks

***Distribution Calibrated Classification Loss***-Model $\frac{p^m(y)}{p^n(y)}$. Considering the term $\frac{p^m(y)}{p^n(y)}$, we aim to tackle the imbalance of training data $p^n(y)$ so as to work on balanced distribution $p^m(y)$ with distribution calibrated classification loss. In [27], Ren *et al.* proposed a variant version of softmax function to approximate

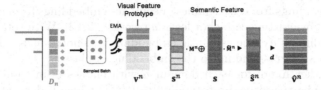

**Fig. 3.** Transformation between **semantic space s** and **visual feature prototypes** $\mathbf{v}^n$ of each domain $D_n$. **s** denotes semantic features based on word embeddings from class names or sentence embeddings from class descriptors. In each iteration, based on sampled batch from domain $D_n$, its visual prototype $\mathbf{v}^n$ is updated by exponential moving average (EMA). After transforming it to the semantic space $\mathbf{s}^n$ by $e$, the missing entries in $\mathbf{v}^n$ are filled by the corresponding semantic embeddings in **s** to derive the complete $\hat{\mathbf{s}}^n$ and then converted back to the visual space as $\hat{\mathbf{v}}^n$.

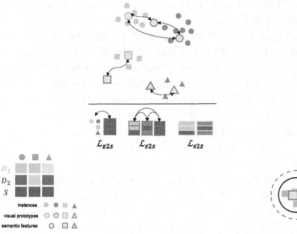

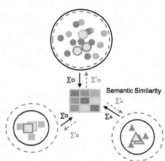

**Fig. 4.** Illustration of visual-semantic mapping to derive domain-invariant and unbiased $p^n(f(\boldsymbol{x})|y)$ across domains.

**Fig. 5.** Illustration of semantic-similarity guided augmentation to facilitate distribution modelling of tail classes by utilizing the semantic relationship between tail and head classes.

the discrepancy of the posterior distributions between training and testing data. Similar ideas have also been introduced in [10]. Based on [10,27], the distribution calibrated classification loss is formulated as:

$$\mathcal{L}_{dc}(\boldsymbol{x}_i, y_i, d_i; f, h) = -\log \frac{n_{y_i}^{d_i} \exp\left([h \circ f(\boldsymbol{x}_i)]_{y_i}\right)}{\sum_{c=1}^{C} n_c^{d_i} \exp([h \circ f(\boldsymbol{x}_i)]_c)}, \tag{2}$$

where $n_c^{d_i}$ denotes the sample number of class $c$ in the training domain $D_{d_i}$. Please see supplementary material for proof.

***Visual-Semantic Mapping*-**Align $p^n(f(\boldsymbol{x})|y)$. To ensure unbiased and semantically meaningful representations, we leverage the semantic embeddings based on word embeddings from class names or sentence embeddings from class descriptors, inspired by existing zero-shot learning works [22,23]. With totally $C$ classes and feature dim as $d_s$, the semantic embedding is denoted as $\mathbf{s} \in \mathbb{R}^{C \times d_s}$, with its $c$ element $\mathbf{s}_c$ corresponding to the embedding of class $c$.

On the other hand, for each domain $n$ with classes $C$ in total and feature dim as $d_v$, we have a visual prototype $\mathbf{v}^n \in \mathbb{R}^{C \times d_v}$, which is derived in an online manner by exponential moving average (EMA). Some entries of $\mathbf{v}^n$ are probably empty caused by the missing categories in each individual domain $n$. The index mask of valid entries is denoted as $\mathbf{M}^n$ for convenience.

To achieve the alignment between visual feature prototype $\{\mathbf{v}^n\}$ and $\mathbf{s}$, we introduce another two functions $e$ and $d$, where $e : \mathcal{Z} \to \mathcal{S}$ and $d : \mathcal{S} \to \mathcal{Z}$. $\{\mathbf{v}^n\}$ is firstly transformed to the semantic space by $e$ as $\mathbf{s}^n$ and subsequently, the missing entries of $\mathbf{s}^n$ are filled by the corresponding semantic features in $\mathbf{s}$ to $\hat{\mathbf{s}}^n$, by $e(\mathbf{v}^n) \cdot \mathbf{M}^n \oplus \mathbf{s} \cdot \tilde{\mathbf{M}}^n$. By the function $d$, $\hat{\mathbf{s}}^n$ is transformed back to visual space as $\hat{\mathbf{v}}^n$. The data flow is visualized in Fig. 3.

We introduce three typical losses to fulfill the goal of visual-semantic alignment, which are visually illustrated in Fig. 4. First of all, $\mathcal{L}_{z2s}$ of Eq. (3) is utilized to align each training sample to its corresponding semantic feature. In Eq. (3), we adopt margin contrastive loss on a unit-normalized embedding space, where the margin $\alpha$ is inspired by [33] as to encourage more tight distribution of intra-class embeddings, and $\tau$ is the temperature constant.

Furthermore, to avoid shifts across domains, we enforce a cross-prototype contrastive loss as in Eq. (4), which aims to decrease intra-class inter-domain discrepancies and enlarge inter-class distances. Additionally, to enforce the manifold constraint of our learned feature representation, we convert $\hat{\mathbf{s}}_v^n$ back to visual space $\hat{\mathbf{v}}^n$ and apply $\mathcal{L}_{s2s}$ as in Eq. (5). It applied the classification loss based on the visual classifier $h$, and also aims to align $\hat{\mathbf{v}}^n$ to semantic embeddings by $\mathcal{L}_{s2s}([e(\hat{\mathbf{v}}^n)], \mathbf{s})$ similar to a cycle loss [45]. To deal with the class imbalance in each batch, $\mathcal{L}_{z2s}$ is further integrated with the last module when calculating the loss.

$$\mathcal{L}_{z2s}(\boldsymbol{x}_i, y_i, \mathbf{s}; e, f) = -\log \frac{\exp(([e \circ f(\boldsymbol{x}_i)]^\mathsf{T} \mathbf{s}_{y_i} - \alpha)/\tau)}{\exp(([e \circ f(\boldsymbol{x}_i)]^\mathsf{T} \mathbf{s}_{y_i} - \alpha)/\tau) + \sum\limits_{j \neq y_i} \exp(([e \circ f(\boldsymbol{x}_i)]^\mathsf{T} \mathbf{s}_j)/\tau)},$$

$$\tag{3}$$

$$\mathcal{L}_{s2s}(\hat{\mathbf{s}}^m, \hat{\mathbf{s}}^n) = \mathbb{E}_c\left[ -\log \frac{\exp((\hat{\mathbf{s}}_c^{m\mathsf{T}} \hat{\mathbf{s}}_c^n - \alpha)/\tau)}{\underbrace{\exp((\hat{\mathbf{s}}_c^{m\mathsf{T}} \hat{\mathbf{s}}_c^n - \alpha)/\tau) + \sum\limits_{j \neq c} \exp(\hat{\mathbf{s}}_c^{m\mathsf{T}} \hat{\mathbf{s}}_j^n/\tau) + \sum\limits_{j \neq c} \exp(\hat{\mathbf{s}}_c^{m\mathsf{T}} \hat{\mathbf{s}}_j^m/\tau)}_{\text{enlarge inter-class inter-/intra-domain distance}}} \right],$$

$$\tag{4}$$

$$\mathcal{L}_{s2z}(\hat{\mathbf{v}}^n; e, h) = \mathbb{E}_i\left[ -\log \frac{\exp([h(\hat{\mathbf{v}}_i^n)]_i)}{\sum_{c=1}^C \exp([h(\hat{\mathbf{v}}_i^n)]_c)} \right] + \mathcal{L}_{s2s}([e(\hat{\mathbf{v}}^n)], \mathbf{s}). \tag{5}$$

***Semantic-Similarity Guided Augmentation***-Model $p(f(\boldsymbol{x})|y)$. Another troubling issue lies in the poor diversity of tail classes. In addition to achieving semantically meaningful and unbiased representations, it is also expected that overfitting on the tail classes can be avoided. It emphasizes the importance of adding to the diversity and richness of tail classes. Therefore, a semantic similarity guided feature augmentation method is proposed as below.

We define the conditional feature distribution (assumed as multi-variate Gaussian distribution, aggregated from all domains) as $p(f(\boldsymbol{x})|c) \sim \mathcal{N}(\boldsymbol{\mu}_c, \boldsymbol{\Sigma}_c)$. The classifier $h$ is composed of a weight matrix $[w_1, ..., w_C]^\mathsf{T}$ and biases $[b_1, ..., b_C]^\mathsf{T}$. Without loss of generality and for simplicity, we only consider the weight matrix in the following. The upper bound of softmax cross entropy loss [39] can therefore be derived as in Eq. (6), with proof in supplementary material.

$$
\begin{aligned}
\mathbb{E}_{f(\boldsymbol{x}_i)} & \left[ -\log \frac{\exp(w_{y_i}^\mathsf{T} f(\boldsymbol{x}_i))}{\sum_{c=1}^{C} \exp(w_c^\mathsf{T} f(\boldsymbol{x}_i))} \right] \\
& \leqslant \log \left[ \sum_{c=1}^{C} \exp((w_c^\mathsf{T} - w_{y_i}^\mathsf{T})\boldsymbol{\mu}_{y_i} + \frac{\lambda}{2}(w_c^\mathsf{T} - w_{y_i}^\mathsf{T})\boldsymbol{\Sigma}_{y_i}(w_c - w_{y_i})) \right].
\end{aligned}
\tag{6}
$$

This indicates that by adding the penalty of $\frac{\lambda}{2}(w_c^\mathsf{T} - w_{y_i}^\mathsf{T})\boldsymbol{\Sigma}_{y_i}(w_c - w_{y_i})$, the up-boundary of classification loss can be approximated by implicit augmentation, where $\lambda$ can be considered as a term to control the augmentation degree [39].

Thus far, we assume a nearly-identical visual space (i.e., similar $f(\boldsymbol{x}|y = c) \approx \boldsymbol{\mu}_c$ across domains) after visual-semantic mapping; however the estimation of $\boldsymbol{\Sigma}_c$ is hardly possible for tail classes. Guided by the semantic inter-class relationship from $\mathbf{s}$, we select the top $k$ classes that are most similar to the corresponding class $c$ (including $c$ itself). This stems from the observation that similar classes are supposed to have similar semantic variances. For example, *deer* and *antelope* may share similar characteristics of the variations of shape, color, etc. Motivated by this, we introduce a weighted covariance estimation strategy to leverage the knowledge learned from head classes,

$$
Sim_c = \{\mathbf{s}_c^\mathsf{T}\mathbf{s}_i | i = 1, 2, ..., C\}; \mathbf{k}_c = \{i | \mathbf{s}_c^\mathsf{T}\mathbf{s}_i \in topk(Sim_c)\},
$$
$$
\boldsymbol{\Sigma}_c' = \frac{\sum_{k \in \mathbf{k}_c} n_k \boldsymbol{\Sigma}_k}{\sum_{k \in \mathbf{k}_c} n_k}.
\tag{7}
$$

Afterwards, we applied an surrogate loss introduced in Eq. (6) to optimize the boundary of classification loss by adding implicit augmentation terms:

$$
\mathcal{L}_{aug}(\boldsymbol{x}_i, y_i; f, h) = -\log \frac{\exp(w_{y_i}^\mathsf{T} f(\boldsymbol{x}_i))}{\sum_{c=1}^{C} \exp(w_{y_i}^\mathsf{T} f(\boldsymbol{x}_i) + \frac{\lambda}{2}(w_c - w_{y_i})^\mathsf{T} \boldsymbol{\Sigma}_{y_i}'(w_c - w_{y_i}))}.
\tag{8}
$$

In practice, the covariance $\boldsymbol{\Sigma}$ is online calculated from $T_\Sigma$ steps onwards to avoid the effect of inter-domain variances.

### 3.3 Meta-learning Based Generalization

The objective of meta-learning is to ensure that the trained models are robust against domain shifts and perform well on all seen and unseen classes. If combining the functional blocks introduced above, we can obtain relatively good results by conventional training strategies. However, the generalization capability on unforeseen domains is not guaranteed. Thus, we apply meta-learning to simulate the domain distribution gaps in an episodic manner, inspired by previous DG works [6]. The optimization process is illustrated in Algorithm 1. For each iteration, the training domains are randomly divided into two splits, $\mathcal{D}_{mtr}$ and $\mathcal{D}_{mte}$. We make sure that data in $\mathcal{D}_{mte}$ always come from different domains from $\mathcal{D}_{mtr}$. After training on $\mathcal{D}_{mtr}$, the model is expected to perform well on unseen domains (especially for domain-unique tail classes) in $\mathcal{D}_{mte}$.

**Meta Train.** Over the course of meta-training, we make the model trained on $\mathcal{D}_{mtr}$ able to derive semantically meaningful and unbiased representations. With a batch data of size $B$ sampled from each domain in $\mathcal{D}_{mtr}$, i.e., $\{x_i, y_i, d_i\}_{i=1}^{B \times |\mathcal{D}_{mtr}|}$, we exert the following typical loss functions.

First of all, in order to calibrate the loss from imbalanced distributions to balanced ones, we apply the domain calibrated softmax loss with $\mathcal{L}_{Cls} = \frac{1}{B \times |\mathcal{D}_{mtr}|} \sum_i \mathcal{L}_{dc}(x_i, y_i, d_i; f, h)$. In this way, we can improve the performance over all classes and not propagating discouraging gradients to unseen classes. Subsequently, to build unbiased representations, the visual-semantic alignment loss $\mathcal{L}_{Z2S} = \frac{1}{B \times |\mathcal{D}_{mtr}|} \sum_i \mathcal{L}_{z2s}(f(x_i), y_i, \mathbf{s}; e)$ is adopted to align the embeddings in the semantic space. Furthermore, to enable domain-invariant feature learning as well as to avoid the prohibitive costs of sampling all classes in all domains when the class number is huge, a prototype alignment loss is utilized, $\mathcal{L}_{S2S} = \mathbb{E}_{m,n \in \mathcal{D}_{mtr}} \mathcal{L}_{s2s}(\hat{\mathbf{s}}^m, \hat{\mathbf{s}}^n) + \mathbb{E}_{n \in \mathcal{D}_{mtr}} \mathcal{L}_{s2s}(\hat{\mathbf{s}}^n, \mathbf{s})$. In addition, we apply $\mathcal{L}_{S2Z} = \mathbb{E}_{n \in \mathcal{D}_{mtr}} \mathcal{L}_{z2s}(\hat{\mathbf{v}}^n; e, h)$ to further constrain the semantic manifold.

With intra-class inter-domain distribution aligned, the intra-class variances would be more semantically relevant. We then track the covariance of $f(x)$ feature distribution from $T_\Sigma$ steps onwards, and apply the surrogate augmentation loss, $\mathcal{L}_{Aug} = \frac{1}{B \times |\mathcal{D}_{mtr}|} \sum_i \mathcal{L}_{aug}(x_i, y_i; f, h)$, to increase the diversity of feature distributions, especially for the tail classes. $\mathcal{L}_{Aug}$ is set to 0 before $T_\Sigma$.

The overall meta-training loss is formulated as $\mathcal{L}_{mtr} = \mathcal{L}_{Cls} + w_1 \mathcal{L}_{Z2S} + w_2 \mathcal{L}_{S2S} + w_3 \mathcal{L}_{S2Z} + w_4 \mathcal{L}_{Aug}$, where $w_1$, $w_2$, $w_3$, $w_4$ are weight hyperparameters. The model parameters $\theta\{f, h, e, d\}$ at step $t$ are firstly updated based on $\mathcal{L}_{mtr}$ with an optimization step with learning rate $\beta_1$:

$$\theta^t\{f', h', e', d'\} = \theta^t\{f, h, e, d\} - \beta_1 \nabla \mathcal{L}_{mtr}. \tag{9}$$

**Meta Test.** The model optimized on $\mathcal{D}_{mtr}$ is expected to perform well on held-out domains $\mathcal{D}_{mte}$. In other words, the optimized representations $\theta\{f', h', e', d'\}$ should be unbiased and semantically meaningful, generalizing well when faced with label distribution shifts and novel domain-specific classes. With samples $\{x_i, y_i, d_i\}_{i=1}^{B \times |\mathcal{D}_{mte}|}$ from $\mathcal{D}_{mte}$, the following losses are utilized. First comes the calibrated classification loss $\mathcal{L}_{MCls} = \frac{1}{B \times |\mathcal{D}_{mte}|} \sum_i \mathcal{L}_{dc}(x_i, y_i, d_i; f', h')$. Subsequently, with $\hat{\mathbf{s}}^n$ of meta training domains updated to $\hat{\mathbf{s}}^{n\prime}$, another loss $\mathcal{L}_{MZ2S} = \frac{1}{B \times |\mathcal{D}_{mte}|} \sum_i \mathcal{L}_{z2s}(f'(x_i), y_i, \mathbf{s}; e') + \mathbb{E}_{n \in \mathcal{D}_{mtr}} \mathcal{L}_{z2s}(f'(x_i), y_i, \hat{\mathbf{s}}^{n\prime}; e')$ aims to align the visual features to both the semantic embeddings $\mathbf{s}$ and the visual prototypes

---

**Algorithm 1.** Meta-learning for long-tailed domain generalization.

---

**Input:** Training set $\mathcal{D}^{tr}$; semantic embeddings $\mathbf{s}$; initialized visual prototype $\mathbf{v}^n$.
**Hyperparameters:** Steps $T_\Sigma, T_{max}$; Weights $w_1, w_2, w_3, w_4, w_{mte}$; LR $\beta_1, \beta_2$.
**Initialized model parameters:** Feature extractor $f$; classifier $h$; models $e$ and $d$.
**Output:** Optimized models $f$ and $h$.

1: **for** $t \leq T_{max}$ **do**
2:      Randomly split $\mathcal{D}_{tr}$ into $\mathcal{D}_{mtr}$ and $\mathcal{D}_{mte}$.
3:
4:      Sample $\{\mathbf{x}_i, y_i, d_i\}_{i=1}^{B \times |\mathcal{D}_{mtr}|}$ from $\mathcal{D}_{mtr}$.                     ▷ Meta Train.
5:      Calculate losses: $\mathcal{L}_{Cls}, \mathcal{L}_{Z2S}$.
6:      *Update* $\{\mathbf{v}^n | n \in \mathcal{D}_{mtr}\}$ based on $f(\mathbf{x}_i)$.
7:      Calculate new $\{\hat{\mathbf{s}}^n, \hat{\mathbf{v}}^n | n \in \mathcal{D}_{mtr}\}$ based on $e, d, \mathbf{v}$.
8:      *Update* $\mathbf{\Sigma}$ $\mathbf{\Sigma}'$ when $t \geq T_\Sigma$.
9:      Calculate losses: $\mathcal{L}_{S2S}, \mathcal{L}_{S2Z}$, and $\mathcal{L}_{Aug}$.
10:      Calculate meta-training loss: $\mathcal{L}_{mtr} = \mathcal{L}_{Cls} + w_1\mathcal{L}_{Z2S} + w_2\mathcal{L}_{S2S} + w_3\mathcal{L}_{S2Z} + w_4\mathcal{L}_{Aug}$.
11:      Calculate new $\theta^t\{f', h', e', d'\} = \theta^t\{f, h, e, d\} - \beta_1 \triangledown \mathcal{L}_{mtr}$.
12:
13:      Sample $\{\mathbf{x}_i, y_i, d_i\}_{i=1}^{B \times |\mathcal{D}_{mte}|}$ from $\mathcal{D}_{mte}$.                     ▷ Meta Test.
14:      Calculate losses: $\mathcal{L}_{MCls}, \mathcal{L}_{MZ2S}, \mathcal{L}_{MAug}$.
15:      Calculate new $\{\hat{\mathbf{s}}^{n\prime}, \hat{\mathbf{v}}^{n\prime} | n \in \mathcal{D}_{mtr}\}$ based on $e', d', \{\mathbf{v}^n\}$.
16:      Calculate meta-testing loss: $\mathcal{L}_{mte} = \mathcal{L}_{MCls} + w_1\mathcal{L}_{MZ2S} + w_4\mathcal{L}_{MAug}$.
17:      *Update* $\theta^{t+1}\{f, h, e, d\} = \theta^t\{f, h, e, d\} - \beta_2 \triangledown (\mathcal{L}_{mtr} + w_{mte}\mathcal{L}_{mte})$.
18: **end for**

---

of $\mathcal{D}_{mtr}$. This ensures that the knowledge extracted from meta-training steps are domain-invariant and semantically meaningful across all classes seen in $\mathcal{D}_{mte}$. In addition, the surrogate augmentation loss is enforced from $T_\Sigma$ onwards, to increase the feature diversity, $\mathcal{L}_{MAug} = \frac{1}{B \times |\mathcal{D}_{mtel}|} \sum \mathcal{L}_{aug}(\mathbf{x}_i, y_i; f', h')$.

The overall meta-test loss is $\mathcal{L}_{mte} = \mathcal{L}_{MCls} + w_1\mathcal{L}_{MZ2S} + w_4\mathcal{L}_{MAug}$, and we finally update the $\theta\{f, h, e, d\}$ based on $\mathcal{L}_{mtr} + w_{mte}\mathcal{L}_{mte}$ by learning rate $\beta_2$:

$$\theta^{t+1}\{f, h, e, d\} = \theta^t\{f, h, e, d\} - \beta_2 \triangledown (\mathcal{L}_{mtr} + w_{mte}\mathcal{L}_{mte}). \tag{10}$$

## 4   Experiments

### 4.1   Experimental Settings

**Datasets.** Two datasets were adopted to evaluate the effectiveness of our proposed methods. **AWA2** [40] and **ImageNet-LT** [21]. To benchmark our proposed task, **AWA2** was firstly randomly resampled to convert to a long-tailed version. Regarding **AWA2-LT** and **ImageNet-LT**, we applied off-the-shelf style transfer models (Hayao & Shinkai[1]; Vangogh & Ukiyoe[2]) to simulate domain shifts as shown in Fig. 6 and the generated new datasets are referred to

---

[1]  https://github.com/Yijunmaverick/CartoonGAN-Test-Pytorch-Torch.
[2]  https://github.com/junyanz/pytorch-CycleGAN-and-pix2pix.

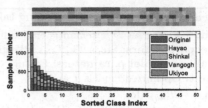

**Fig. 6.** Examples of simulated domain shifts by off-the-shelf style transfer models. Each original sample was randomly assigned a style to make up for the final dataset. Some samples of non-head classes in certain domains were randomly dropped out to simulate the practical **LT-DS** problem studied in this work.

**Fig. 7.** Data distribution of **AWA2-LTS**.

**Table 1.** Dataset details.

| Dataset | $|D|$ | $|C|$ | $|x|$ | Ratio* |
|---|---|---|---|---|
| AWA2-LTS | 5 | 50 | ~8k | ~78 |
| ImageNet-LTS | 5 | 1000 | ~100k | ~256 |

as **AWA2-LTS** and **ImageNet-LTS**, respectively. Some classes from certain domains were deliberately dropped out to simulate a more realistic settings with entangled long-tailed and shifted distributions. A visual explanation of **AWA2-LTS** training data distribution is given in Fig. 7. Please see Table 1 and refer to supplementary material for more details.

**Model Training Setup.** We deployed all models using Pytorch with NVIDIA RTX3090. For **AWA2-LTS** and **ImageNet-LTS**, ResNet10 was adopted as the backbone with random initialization. Regarding semantic features, Word2Vec embeddings [24] were adopted for **ImageNet-LT**. BERT embeddings [5] of class descriptors were utilized for **AWA2-LTS**. More details can be found in supplementary material and our project page https://xiaogu.site/LTDS.

**Evaluation Setup.** Following [29,42], a threshold was empirically set up to apply on the prediction confidence. Classes below the given threshold are defined as open classes, belonging to $\mathcal{Y} \setminus \mathcal{Y}^{tr}$. We applied leave-one-domain-out protocol for evaluation. We reported the **Acc-U** for the non-open classes in the held-out unseen domain. In addition, the domain-averaged accuracy of non-open classes in all the domains **Acc**, and harmonic score **H** of all the classes in all the domains are reported. The score **Acc** and **H** take into account those classes belonging to $\mathcal{Y}^{tr} \setminus \mathcal{Y}^{i}$ of each individual domain $i$. Therefore both metrics can to some extent reflect whether those domain-specific tail classes could lead to spurious correlations during training.

### 4.2 Long-Tail with Conditional Distribution Shifts

We evaluated the performance under **LT-DS** based on two benchmarks **AWA2-LTS** and **ImageNet-LTS** proposed in this work. For comparison, Agg Baseline,

¡ solutions (cRT [14], BSCE [27], Equal [31], Remix [3]), **DG** solutions (Epic-FCR [16], MixStyle [44], CuMix [22], DAML [29]) were implemented.

**Table 2.** Results on **AWA2-LTS** based on leave-one-domain-out evaluation.

| Method | | Original | | | Hayao | | | Shinkai | | | Vangogh | | | Ukiyoe | | |
|---|---|---|---|---|---|---|---|---|---|---|---|---|---|---|---|---|
| | | Acc-U | Acc | H | Acc-U | Acc | H | Acc-U | Acc | H | Acc-U | Acc | H | Acc-U | Acc | H |
| | Agg | 29.4 | 27.0 | 34.5 | 20.4 | 29.9 | 36.2 | 30.8 | 33.5 | 38.6 | 27.1 | 34.2 | 41.0 | 25.5 | 34.2 | 38.6 |
| LT | cRT [14] | 30.4 | 29.1 | 34.8 | 23.5 | 33.6 | 38.9 | **34.7** | 35.8 | 39.6 | 28.6 | 35.8 | 43.0 | 28.4 | 36.7 | 35.7 |
| | BSCE [27] | 41.8 | 35.9 | 41.7 | 24.7 | 36.1 | 41.7 | 30.2 | 35.8 | 40.7 | 29.0 | 37.7 | 43.2 | 25.9 | 33.6 | 35.1 |
| | Equal [31] | 34.1 | 32.9 | 36.6 | 24.3 | 35.3 | 42.7 | 33.5 | 36.2 | 40.5 | 28.8 | 35.8 | 42.4 | 27.3 | 34.7 | 34.0 |
| | Remix [3] | 32.7 | 30.3 | 35.9 | 16.9 | 30.7 | 33.3 | 27.6 | 32.0 | 37.5 | 26.9 | 31.8 | 41.2 | 26.5 | 32.0 | 34.9 |
| DG | Epi-FCR [16] | 34.0 | 33.1 | 40.5 | 23.3 | 34.0 | 40.6 | 29.7 | 35.5 | 39.1 | 27.5 | 36.1 | 42.0 | 27.0 | 35.7 | 38.0 |
| | MixStyle [44] | 36.7 | 34.0 | 41.2 | 27.1 | 36.2 | 41.7 | 32.0 | 36.2 | 40.6 | 28.4 | 36.0 | 41.9 | 28.8 | 36.2 | 38.3 |
| | CuMix [22] | 36.1 | 33.8 | 38.6 | 24.7 | 35.3 | 41.0 | 30.2 | 35.1 | 41.4 | 28.2 | 35.1 | 40.9 | 26.5 | 34.7 | 34.6 |
| | DAML [29] | 13.9 | 10.7 | 16.2 | 14.7 | 22.5 | 29.8 | 17.3 | 24.9 | 30.4 | 14.3 | 19.5 | 25.6 | 22.9 | 28.9 | 36.0 |
| | DAML [29]-Warmup | 42.2 | 35.3 | 42.5 | 25.7 | 35.2 | 39.5 | 31.2 | 36.8 | 44.0 | 29.4 | 37.5 | 45.3 | 28.6 | 36.0 | 41.4 |
| | MixStyle+BSCE | 40.0 | 36.8 | 41.8 | 28.8 | 39.7 | 43.5 | 32.4 | 38.3 | 44.2 | 30.8 | 38.2 | 43.3 | 29.8 | 38.9 | 39.3 |
| | Epi-FCR+BSCE | 41.3 | 36.9 | 42.0 | 24.0 | 35.9 | 41.2 | 32.0 | 39.2 | 42.5 | 30.1 | 38.5 | 41.7 | 26.6 | 35.9 | 38.7 |
| | Ours | **49.4** | **42.1** | **45.8** | **29.8** | **42.4** | **46.3** | 34.3 | **42.6** | **45.3** | **32.7** | **40.3** | **46.3** | **32.9** | **42.4** | 39.3 |

**Table 3.** Results on **ImageNet-LTS** based on leave-one-domain-out evaluation.

| Method | | Original | | | Hayao | | | Shinkai | | | Vangogh | | | Ukiyoe | | |
|---|---|---|---|---|---|---|---|---|---|---|---|---|---|---|---|---|
| | | Acc-U | Acc | H | Acc-U | Acc | H | Acc-U | Acc | H | Acc-U | Acc | H | Acc-U | Acc | H |
| | Agg | 19.5 | 18.1 | 23.5 | 13.0 | 18.2 | 24.4 | 15.2 | 18.0 | 24.2 | 13.2 | 17.5 | 23.7 | 12.5 | 17.9 | 24.1 |
| LT | cRT [14] | 20.7 | 18.7 | 24.8 | 13.8 | 19.0 | 24.3 | 16.2 | 18.8 | 24.8 | 14.0 | 18.4 | 25.5 | 13.6 | 18.7 | 25.3 |
| | BSCE [27] | 20.8 | 19.1 | 25.6 | 14.3 | 19.4 | 25.2 | 16.5 | 19.1 | 25.2 | 14.7 | 18.8 | 25.5 | 14.1 | 19.1 | 26.4 |
| | Equal [31] | 16.3 | 15.4 | 20.6 | 10.7 | 15.2 | 20.6 | 13.2 | 16.4 | 22.2 | 10.5 | 14.8 | 21.4 | 10.9 | 15.8 | 21.3 |
| | Remix [3] | 14.8 | 13.8 | 18.6 | 10.1 | 14.1 | 20.0 | 11.3 | 14.1 | 22.0 | 11.1 | 13.5 | 18.2 | 10.5 | 14.8 | 20.8 |
| DG | Epi-FCR [16] | 19.2 | 18.8 | 23.1 | 13.5 | 19.0 | 23.3 | 15.0 | 20.0 | 25.1 | 12.2 | 18.0 | 23.8 | 13.0 | 17.5 | 25.2 |
| | MixStyle [44] | 17.7 | 16.4 | 22.0 | 12.1 | 16.7 | 22.1 | 13.6 | 16.5 | 22.9 | 11.8 | 16.0 | 22.9 | 11.5 | 16.2 | 21.4 |
| | CuMix [22] | 18.2 | 17.2 | 23.7 | 13.2 | 17.5 | 22.7 | 14.2 | 17.1 | 22.4 | 12.1 | 16.8 | 22.3 | 12.1 | 17.1 | 23.7 |
| | DAML [29]-Warmup | 14.7 | 12.7 | 18.2 | 10.5 | 13.0 | 18.2 | 11.5 | 13.2 | 18.0 | 9.7 | 12.8 | 16.9 | 10.1 | 13.0 | 18.6 |
| | Ours | **24.3** | **20.8** | **25.9** | **16.3** | **21.3** | **25.4** | **17.4** | **20.9** | **25.8** | 14.3 | **20.3** | **26.6** | **15.4** | **20.3** | **26.7** |

**Quantitative Results.** As shown in Tables 2 & 3, our method achieves overall superior performance compared to other methods. In addition, two combinations MixStyle+BSCE and Epi-FCR+BSCE were applied on **AWA2-LTS** dataset for comparison. We noticed the extremely low performance of DAML [29] under **LT-DS**. Since it is based on the knowledge distillation from each domain-specific model, the knowledge learned from individual long-tailed distribution would be significantly biased towards the head classes. We simply moderated such bias by a warm-up pretraining, and the variant is referred to as DAML-Warmup. Although DAML-Warmup can alleviate the class imbalance issue when the imbalance ratio and class number is small, we observed its failure on **ImageNet-LTS**. It may indicate that it cannot handle the semantic information when a large proportion of classes are missing. Overall, our results demonstrate superior performance compared to existing methods.

**Qualitative Results.** We present the t-SNE visualizations of features from the test split of **AWA2-LTS** in Fig. 8 along with the results from the baseline Agg. Different colors indicate different domains on the upper row, whereas different categories ranging from head to tail on the bottom. It can be observed that the samples which are sampled from the same classes but from different domains (including the unseen domain) are better clustered. More qualitative analysis can be found in supplementary material.

**Table 4.** Ablation studies on **AWA2-LTS**. CE indicates cross-entropy loss.

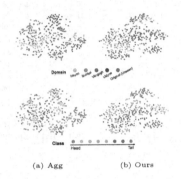

| Index | $\mathcal{L}_{dc}$ | CE | $\mathcal{L}_{Z2S}$ | $\mathcal{L}_{S2S}$ | $\mathcal{L}_{S2Z}$ | $\mathcal{L}_{Aug}$ | Meta | Avg Acc-U | Acc | H |
|---|---|---|---|---|---|---|---|---|---|---|
| a | – | ✓ | – | – | – | – | – | 26.6 | 31.8 | 37.8 |
| b | ✓ | – | – | – | – | – | – | 30.6 | 36.7 | 39.2 |
| c | – | ✓ | – | – | – | – | ✓ | 28.9 | 34.3 | 33.8 |
| d | ✓ | – | – | – | – | – | ✓ | 34.3 | 40.0 | 40.2 |
| e | ✓ | – | ✓ | – | – | – | – | 31.5 | <u>41.2</u> | 41.0 |
| f | ✓ | – | ✓ | ✓ | – | – | – | 32.0 | 40.8 | 41.2 |
| g | ✓ | – | ✓ | ✓ | ✓ | – | – | 32.5 | 40.8 | 42.8 |
| h | ✓ | – | – | – | – | ✓ | – | 26.2 | 30.0 | 36.8 |
| i | ✓ | – | ✓ | ✓ | ✓ | ✓ | – | 34.0 | 40.9 | 42.8 |
| j | ✓ | – | ✓ | ✓ | ✓ | ✓ | ✓ | **35.7** | **42.0** | **44.6** |
| k | Single prototype alignment | | | | | | | 32.5 | 41.0 | 41.6 |
| l | No-weight augmentation | | | | | | | <u>34.6</u> | 40.7 | <u>43.0</u> |

**Fig. 8.** t-SNE of **AWA2-LTS** test set. Left: Agg. Right: Ours.

**Ablation Studies.** We validate the performance of each proposed module and the whole meta learning framework by ablation studies as shown in Table 4 indicates the effectiveness of each individual modules. In particular, the ablated model indexed by d also presents relatively good performance, demonstrating that even without additional semantic features for alignment, it is still comparable to existing solutions. We also did two another ablation studies, with just single prototype for alignment and without weighted term in Eq. (8) for updating covariance matrix. Please see more detailed discussions in our supplementary material. Additional experiments on sample complexity, choices of embeddings, as well as results on open domain generalization datasets can also be found in supplementary materials.

## 5    Conclusions

Long-tailed category distribution and domain shifts have been two major issues concerned with real-world datasets, leading to degraded performance upon practical deployment. The combination of these two problems poses a significantly challenging scenario, where not only these two problems should be addressed, but the domain-specific non-head classes should also be paid attention to, to avoid shortcuts. We proposed a meta-learning framework to ensure that the model can perform well over all classes and all domains, including unseen novel domains. We evaluated two benchmarks proposed in this paper. The experimental results demonstrate that the proposed method can achieve superior performance, when compared to either long-tailed/domain-generalization solutions or the combinations. In the future, we are going to apply our method to more specific applications like behavioural analysis and health care.

# References

1. Buda, M., Maki, A., Mazurowski, M.A.: A systematic study of the class imbalance problem in convolutional neural networks. Neural Netw. **106**, 249–259 (2018)
2. Chen, Y., et al.: GeoSim: realistic video simulation via geometry-aware composition for self-driving. In: Proceedings of the IEEE/CVF Conference on Computer Vision and Pattern Recognition, pp. 7230–7240 (2021)
3. Chou, H.-P., Chang, S.-C., Pan, J.-Y., Wei, W., Juan, D.-C.: Remix: rebalanced mixup. In: Bartoli, A., Fusiello, A. (eds.) ECCV 2020. LNCS, vol. 12540, pp. 95–110. Springer, Cham (2020). https://doi.org/10.1007/978-3-030-65414-6_9
4. Damen, D., et al.: Rescaling egocentric vision. arXiv preprint arXiv:2006.13256 (2020)
5. Devlin, J., Chang, M.W., Lee, K., Toutanova, K.: BERT: pre-training of deep bidirectional transformers for language understanding. arXiv preprint arXiv:1810.04805 (2018)
6. Dou, Q., de Castro, D.C., Kamnitsas, K., Glocker, B.: Domain generalization via model-agnostic learning of semantic features. Adv. Neural Inf. Process. Syst. **32**, 6450–6461 (2019)
7. Gu, X., Guo, Y., Deligianni, F., Lo, B., Yang, G.Z.: Cross-subject and cross-modal transfer for generalized abnormal gait recognition. IEEE Trans. Neural Netw. Learn. Syst. **32**(2), 546–560 (2020)
8. Gupta, A., Savarese, S., Ganguli, S., Fei-Fei, L.: Embodied intelligence via learning and evolution. Nat. Commun. **12**(1), 1–12 (2021)
9. Han, H., Wang, W.-Y., Mao, B.-H.: Borderline-SMOTE: a new over-sampling method in imbalanced data sets learning. In: Huang, D.-S., Zhang, X.-P., Huang, G.-B. (eds.) ICIC 2005. LNCS, vol. 3644, pp. 878–887. Springer, Heidelberg (2005). https://doi.org/10.1007/11538059_91
10. Hong, Y., Han, S., Choi, K., Seo, S., Kim, B., Chang, B.: Disentangling label distribution for long-tailed visual recognition. In: Proceedings of the IEEE/CVF Conference on Computer Vision and Pattern Recognition, pp. 6626–6636 (2021)
11. Huang, C., Li, Y., Loy, C.C., Tang, X.: Learning deep representation for imbalanced classification. In: Proceedings of the IEEE Conference on Computer Vision and Pattern Recognition, pp. 5375–5384 (2016)
12. Iscen, A., Araujo, A., Gong, B., Schmid, C.: Class-balanced distillation for long-tailed visual recognition. In: Proceedings of the British Machine Vision Conference (BMVC). BMVA Press (2021)
13. Jamal, M.A., Brown, M., Yang, M.H., Wang, L., Gong, B.: Rethinking class-balanced methods for long-tailed visual recognition from a domain adaptation perspective. In: Proceedings of the IEEE/CVF Conference on Computer Vision and Pattern Recognition, pp. 7610–7619 (2020)
14. Kang, B., et al.: Decoupling representation and classifier for long-tailed recognition. arXiv preprint arXiv:1910.09217 (2019)

15. Li, D., Yang, Y., Song, Y.Z., Hospedales, T.M.: Deeper, broader and artier domain generalization. In: Proceedings of the IEEE International Conference on Computer Vision, pp. 5542–5550 (2017)
16. Li, D., Zhang, J., Yang, Y., Liu, C., Song, Y.Z., Hospedales, T.M.: Episodic training for domain generalization. In: Proceedings of the IEEE/CVF International Conference on Computer Vision, pp. 1446–1455 (2019)
17. Li, S., Gong, K., Liu, C.H., Wang, Y., Qiao, F., Cheng, X.: MetaSAug: meta semantic augmentation for long-tailed visual recognition. In: Proceedings of the IEEE/CVF Conference on Computer Vision and Pattern Recognition, pp. 5212–5221 (2021)
18. Li, Y., et al.: Deep domain generalization via conditional invariant adversarial networks. In: Proceedings of the European Conference on Computer Vision (ECCV), pp. 624–639 (2018)
19. Lin, T.Y., Goyal, P., Girshick, R., He, K., Dollár, P.: Focal loss for dense object detection. In: Proceedings of the IEEE International Conference on Computer Vision, pp. 2980–2988 (2017)
20. Liu, X., et al.: Domain generalization under conditional and label shifts via variational Bayesian inference. In: Proceedings of the Thirtieth International Joint Conference on Artificial Intelligence, IJCAI-21, pp. 881–887. International Joint Conferences on Artificial Intelligence Organization, August 2021
21. Liu, Z., Miao, Z., Zhan, X., Wang, J., Gong, B., Yu, S.X.: Large-scale long-tailed recognition in an open world. In: Proceedings of the IEEE/CVF Conference on Computer Vision and Pattern Recognition, pp. 2537–2546 (2019)
22. Mancini, M., Akata, Z., Ricci, E., Caputo, B.: Towards recognizing unseen categories in unseen domains. In: Vedaldi, A., Bischof, H., Brox, T., Frahm, J.-M. (eds.) ECCV 2020. LNCS, vol. 12368, pp. 466–483. Springer, Cham (2020). https://doi.org/10.1007/978-3-030-58592-1_28
23. Maniyar, U., Deshmukh, A.A., Dogan, U., Balasubramanian, V.N., et al.: Zero shot domain generalization. arXiv preprint arXiv:2008.07443 (2020)
24. Mikolov, T., Sutskever, I., Chen, K., Corrado, G.S., Dean, J.: Distributed representations of words and phrases and their compositionality. Adv. Neural Inf. Process. Syst. **26**, 3111–3119 (2013)
25. Radford, A., et al.: Learning transferable visual models from natural language supervision. arXiv preprint arXiv:2103.00020 (2021)
26. Ravì, D., Wong, C., Deligianni, F., Berthelot, M., Andreu-Perez, J., Lo, B., Yang, G.Z.: Deep learning for health informatics. IEEE J. Biomed. Health Inform. **21**(1), 4–21 (2016)
27. Ren, J., et al.: Balanced meta-softmax for long-tailed visual recognition. arXiv preprint arXiv:2007.10740 (2020)
28. Samuel, D., Atzmon, Y., Chechik, G.: From generalized zero-shot learning to long-tail with class descriptors. In: Proceedings of the IEEE/CVF Winter Conference on Applications of Computer Vision, pp. 286–295 (2021)
29. Shu, Y., Cao, Z., Wang, C., Wang, J., Long, M.: Open domain generalization with domain-augmented meta-learning. In: Proceedings of the IEEE/CVF Conference on Computer Vision and Pattern Recognition, pp. 9624–9633 (2021)
30. Socher, R., Ganjoo, M., Manning, C.D., Ng, A.: Zero-shot learning through cross-modal transfer. In: Advances in Neural Information Processing Systems, pp. 935–943 (2013)
31. Tan, J., et al.: Equalization loss for long-tailed object recognition. In: Proceedings of the IEEE/CVF Conference on Computer Vision and Pattern Recognition, pp. 11662–11671 (2020)

32. Tang, K., Huang, J., Zhang, H.: Long-tailed classification by keeping the good and removing the bad momentum causal effect. arXiv preprint arXiv:2009.12991 (2020)
33. Wang, F., Cheng, J., Liu, W., Liu, H.: Additive margin softmax for face verification. IEEE Signal Process. Lett. **25**(7), 926–930 (2018)
34. Wang, G., Han, H., Shan, S., Chen, X.: Cross-domain face presentation attack detection via multi-domain disentangled representation learning. In: Proceedings of the IEEE/CVF Conference on Computer Vision and Pattern Recognition, pp. 6678–6687 (2020)
35. Wang, J., Lan, C., Liu, C., Ouyang, Y., Zeng, W., Qin, T.: Generalizing to unseen domains: a survey on domain generalization. arXiv preprint arXiv:2103.03097 (2021)
36. Wang, P., Han, K., Wei, X.S., Zhang, L., Wang, L.: Contrastive learning based hybrid networks for long-tailed image classification. In: Proceedings of the IEEE/CVF Conference on Computer Vision and Pattern Recognition, pp. 943–952 (2021)
37. Wang, X., Lian, L., Miao, Z., Liu, Z., Yu, S.: Long-tailed recognition by routing diverse distribution-aware experts. In: International Conference on Learning Representations (2021). https://openreview.net/forum?id=D9I3drBz4UC
38. Wang, Y.X., Ramanan, D., Hebert, M.: Learning to model the tail. In: Proceedings of the 31st International Conference on Neural Information Processing Systems, pp. 7032–7042 (2017)
39. Wang, Y., Pan, X., Song, S., Zhang, H., Huang, G., Wu, C.: Implicit semantic data augmentation for deep networks. Adv. Neural. Inf. Process. Syst. **32**, 12635–12644 (2019)
40. Xian, Y., Lampert, C.H., Schiele, B., Akata, Z.: Zero-shot learning–a comprehensive evaluation of the good, the bad and the ugly. IEEE Trans. Pattern Anal. Mach. Intell. **41**(9), 2251–2265 (2018)
41. Xian, Y., Sharma, S., Schiele, B., Akata, Z.: F-VAEGAN-D2: a feature generating framework for any-shot learning. In: Proceedings of the IEEE/CVF Conference on Computer Vision and Pattern Recognition, pp. 10275–10284 (2019)
42. You, K., Long, M., Cao, Z., Wang, J., Jordan, M.I.: Universal domain adaptation. In: Proceedings of the IEEE/CVF Conference on Computer Vision and Pattern Recognition, pp. 2720–2729 (2019)
43. Zhang, Y., Kang, B., Hooi, B., Yan, S., Feng, J.: Deep long-tailed learning: a survey. arXiv preprint arXiv:2110.04596 (2021)
44. Zhou, K., Yang, Y., Qiao, Y., Xiang, T.: MixStyle neural networks for domain generalization and adaptation. arXiv preprint arXiv:2107.02053 (2021)
45. Zhu, J.Y., Park, T., Isola, P., Efros, A.A.: Unpaired image-to-image translation using cycle-consistent adversarial networks. In: Proceedings of the IEEE International Conference on Computer Vision, pp. 2223–2232 (2017)

# Doubly-Fused ViT: Fuse Information from Vision Transformer Doubly with Local Representation

Li Gao, Dong Nie, Bo Li, and Xiaofeng Ren[✉]

Alibaba Group, Hangzhou, China
{liangliang.gl,dong.nie,shize.lb,x.ren}@alibaba-inc.com

**Abstract.** Vision Transformer (ViT) has recently emerged as a new paradigm for computer vision tasks, but is not as efficient as convolutional neural networks (CNN). In this paper, we propose an efficient ViT architecture, named Doubly-Fused ViT (DFvT), where we feed low-resolution feature maps to self-attention (SA) to achieve larger context with efficiency (by moving downsampling prior to SA), and enhance it with fine-detailed spatial information. SA is a powerful mechanism that extracts rich context information, thus could and should operate at a low spatial resolution. To make up for the loss of details, convolutions are fused into the main ViT pipeline, without incurring high computational costs. In particular, a Context Module (CM), consisting of fused downsampling operator and subsequent SA, is introduced to effectively capture global features with high efficiency. A Spatial Module (SM) is proposed to preserve fine-grained spatial information. To fuse the heterogeneous features, we specially design a Dual AtteNtion Enhancement (DANE) module to selectively fuse low-level and high-level features. Experiments demonstrate that DFvT achieves state-of-the-art accuracy with much higher efficiency across a spectrum of different model sizes. Ablation study validates the effectiveness of our designed components.

**Keywords:** Vision transformer · Convolutional neural networks · Efficient network

## 1 Introduction

For quite some time now, convolutional neural networks (CNN) [24,29,43,45] have dominated computer vision (CV) tasks, such as image classification, object detection, semantic segmentation, and tracking. CNN extracts information hierarchically, and high-level feature representations are obtained by gradually processing features from the bottom to top layers. In addition, using weight sharing

---

Code is available at https://github.com/ginobilinie/DFvT.

---

**Supplementary Information** The online version contains supplementary material available at https://doi.org/10.1007/978-3-031-20050-2_43.

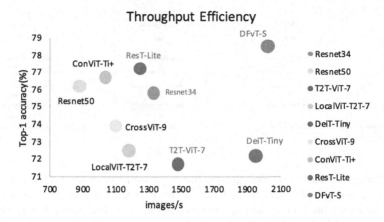

**Fig. 1.** Scatterplot of top-1 accuracy on ImageNet-1K validation set with respect to speed. The proposed Doubly-Fused ViT (DFvT) achieves state-of-the-art performance with high efficiency, outperforming popular convolution and transformer backbones.

and pooling, CNN has the nice property of (approximate) shift-invariance and equivariance. Nevertheless, the CNN architecture has its drawbacks. A convolution kernel is localized and has a fixed size, so local information is efficiently captured, but large receptive fields and long-range dependencies can only be represented by either increasing the depth of the network or utilizing large kernels, both with much higher computation cost. Also, the weights of the convolution kernels are fixed when training is over, and the filter weights cannot be adjusted when the input changes.

Transformer [50] was first proposed for Natural Language Processing (NLP) [10,23,61], showing to be superior in performance on machine translation tasks. Instead of localized convolution, transformer uses self-attention mechanisms to capture global contextual information and establishes long-range dependencies, proving a powerful paradigm for feature extraction. One pioneering work of transformer for computer vision tasks is ViT [11], which applies the encoder in the standard transformer to visual tasks by dividing an input image into patches and making an analogy between patches and tokens in NLP.

The ViT design and its follow-up show great promises in achieving higher performance on a variety of vision tasks, but they have disadvantages. Firstly, the patch stem of ViT greatly reduces the resolution of the input image and is not friendly to downstream tasks that require dense pixel prediction, such as semantic segmentation. Secondly, the computational complexity of the vanilla ViT is quadratic in the number of patches/tokens, which leads to a high amount of computation. Many researches has been undertaken to alleviate these two issues. Some efforts [15,25,34,44,64] introduced hierarchical constructions (commonly used in CNN) to build hierarchical transformers. Others [13,14,57] incorporated CNN to add inductive bias to transformers to help improve performance. There were also studies on reducing the computational costs of transformers

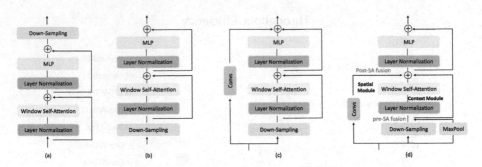

**Fig. 2.** Different transformer designs (we use a pyramid ViT with window SA as baseline.). (a) Baseline ViT (e.g., [28]). Token maps are (spatially) down-sampled at the end. (b) Downsampled ViT: placing down-sampling at the beginning, before the main transformer block. Computation and memory costs are greatly reduced, but there is a loss of information (and lower accuracy). (c) Parallel ViT: one way to compensate for information loss is to supplement transformer with a separate CNN path (e.g. [9]). Note that the input of CNN and transformer has the same resolution and dimension, which is computation demanding and memory consuming. (d) We propose Doubly-Fused ViT (DFvT), which opens up the transformer block and enhance it with convolution, both before and after self-attention. This design tightly integrates transformer and convolution with CM and SM complementing each other, achieving high accuracy and high speed. See ablation studies.

[4,12,32,49], such as decreasing the number of tokens or modifying the self-attention mechanism. So far, we do not yet have good designs that can make transformers achieves both high performance and high efficiency.

In this work, we propose a simple yet novel vision transformer architecture, named Doubly-Fused ViT (DFvT), which is efficient in both speed and memory comparable to CNN, while retaining ViT's high performance. This is achieved by opening up and redesigning the transformer block and tightly integrating it with convolutions. Specifically, our first change is proposing a Context Module (CM), which moves the downsampling operation (e.g., convolution with stride 2), usually at the end of the transformer block (in a hierarchical design e.g. [28]), to the beginning of the block. Our intuition is that self-attention in the transformer is powerful at capturing large contexts, and this can be done with a low spatial resolution. As a result, computation and memory costs of the transformer are substantially reduced. However, this downsampling operation in CM does result in a serious loss of information, that of spatial details, and a much lower performance. Our second change is to enhance the transformer with detailed spatial information through convolution, with two fusions at distinctive locations, both prior to and after self-attention (SA). The first fusion is in the CM to provide diversified and salient information as input to self-attention; for the second fusion, we introduce a Spatial Module (SM) to provide local details that can be easily missed by the downsampled self-attention which mainly focus on global information. Considering the heterogeneous nature of the two information paths, we designed a Dual AtteNtion Enhancement (DANE) module to fuse the features. It turns out that our design is effective: DFvT can achieve competitive accuracy with compelling efficiency, validated at multiple model sizes. A plot of speed-accuracy on the small version DFvT is shown in Fig. 1. Several design choices are outlined in Fig. 2, and their performances are compared in the ablation studies.

The contributions of our work are as follows:

- We proposed the Doubly-Fused ViT (DFvT), a general vision transformer backbone with high performance (comparable to standard ViT) and high efficiency (comparable to CNN). We regroup the downsampling operators and self-attention to formulate a Context Module (CM) which can efficiently and effectively capture global information. We also design a Spatial Module (SM) to preserve local details. The context features and fine details are fused with a DANE module.
- A Dual AtteNtion Enhancement (DANE) module is carefully designed to fuse spatial details and contextual features. In DANE, channel attention is adopted to cope with contextual features since no channel interaction in self-attention, and spatial attention is dedicated to local features. Then a automatically selective mechanism is introduced to finally fuse the two heterogeneous features so that we can capture features at different scales (for instance, local and contextual).
- The DFvT design can be instantiated at multiple model sizes (at the level of ResNet101, ResNet50-ResNet18, and MobileNet). We carry out a series of experiments to show that DFvT is flexible and can apply to varying computational demands, outperforming the state-of-the-art (of both transformer and CNN).

## 2   Related Work

### 2.1   CNNs

CNNs have achieved great success and dominated computer vision in the past decade [16,22,30,39,40,43,45]. The basic building block in CNNs is a standard convolutional layer, which does well in capturing local details but not in modeling long-range dependency due to limited receptive field. The network requires sufficient context information to perform strong recognition. Stacking convolutional layers is one way to learn context information. With batch normalization (BN) [42] and residual block [16], modern CNNs can go through as deep as 1,000 layers and achieve SoTA performance on many vision tasks. Efforts have been made to improve context modeling in CNN. [35] explored the role of large kernels in segmentation and concluded that large kernels work better than stacking small filters. [63] utilized dilated convolution to aggregate multi-scale features. [8] presented a novel convolution operation with learnable offsets to model long-range dependency and geometric shapes. [55] employed non-local blocks (i.e., self-attention) to increase the receptive field and learn better context.

## 2.2  Vision Transformer

The pioneering vision transformer (ViT) [11] has recently achieved competitive performance to CNNs, especially when using a large amount of data, which demonstrates the capability and potential of transformers in computer vision. Follow-up research to improve ViT can be roughly categorized into three directions. One is to improve building components of the vision transformer [2,20,48,58,65] under the isotropic structure (i.e., fixed token numbers and channels) like ViT, for example: T2T-ViT [65] developed a Tokens-to-Token (T2T) transformation to embed local structure for each token instead of using naive tokenization. CaiT [48] proposed a layer-scalar for training a deeper network to achieve better performance, and LV-ViT [20] improved the model training by applying CutMix [66]. CrossViT [2] proposed a dual-path architecture (each with a different scale) to learn multi-scale features. A second direction for improving vision transformer is to introduce pyramid structure [1,6,17,53,67]. PVT [53] and PiT [17] introduced the pyramid structure which is standard in most CNN models, making PVT and PiT more suitable for image recognition tasks due to the multi-scale features. Swin [28], ViL [67] and Twins [7] further constrained self-attention into a local region and then proposed different strategies to allow information interactions among local regions, leading to even higher recognition accuracy and less computational complexity. RegionViT [3] employed a novel regional-to-local attention within the pyramid structure to boost information communication. The third direction is to combine convolution with transformer. DeiT [47] proposed an efficient training scheme that allows vision transformer to achieve competitive performance with CNN models while training only on ImageNet-1K. LocalViT [26] and ConT [60] presented methods to mix convolutions with self-attention to encode locality information.

## 2.3  Efficient Architecture for CNNs and ViTs

Computational efficiency is critical for large-scale training, reducing cost, and deployment on edge devices. It is common to reduce the model size by redesigning the model architecture. In CNNs, scaling dimensions of depth/width/resolution [46] and designing efficient operations (e.g., separable convolution [41] and shuffle block [31]) are the widely adopted strategies to build efficient networks. In ViTs, pyramid structure (e.g. [28]) and token sparsification (e.g. [38]) are common ways to design efficient models. Besides, carefully combining CNNs and ViTs can also improve efficiency. For instance, ConViT [9] introduced a form of positional self-attention to control the balance between content-based self-attention and the convolutionally initialized positional self-attention. CvT [57] utilized convolution for token embedding and designed the convolutional transformer block in each stage to bring desirable properties of CNN to ViT and obtained a more efficient model than plain ViT. Mobile-Former [5] utilized a parallel structure with a two-way bridge in-between to combine MobileNet and Transformer, endowing the model with local processing and global interaction capabilities. MobileViT [32], another lightweight model

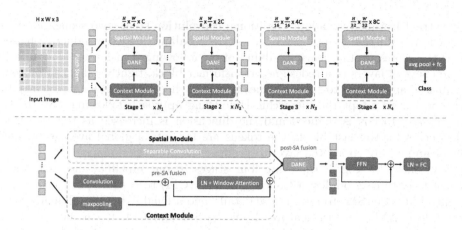

**Fig. 3.** The pipeline of the proposed Doubly-Fused ViT (DFvT) for image classification, where the number of tokens is reduced as the network goes deeper with a
hierarchical representation. We design our efficient transformer block (Spatial Module
(SM), Context Module (CM) and DANE). In the CM, we place the downsampling
prior to SA to reach larger context information and reduce computation and memory
costs simultaneously. Note we use convolved features to make up for the serious loss of
information in the CM. To further compensate for the loss of information, we design
the SM to retain local details. Moreover, we design a Dual AtteNtion (DANE) module
fusing local details and global contexts.

with transformer, introduced transformer as convolution to rebuild MobileNet,
achieving a lightweight and low-latency network on vision tasks. These designs
are efficient, but they typically result in a loss of performance, trading accuracy
for efficiency.

## 3    Method

The strength of transformer lies in its multi-head self-attention, which can
effectively capture context information (i.e., long-range information dependency
modeling) from shallow layers [37]. However, self-attention has a high computational cost which limits the efficiencies of the ViTs. Many works are conducted to
reduce the computational complexity in a theoretic aspect, e.g., from quadratic
to linear, however, performance drop usually comes together with them. Also,
these approaches cannot decrease the memory cost. We propose a simple yet
effective method, that is, we reduce the size of the features fed into self-attention
to achieve more context with high efficiency, set up a spatial path to retain the
detailed information, and specially design a module to fuse the features. The
overall framework of the proposed DFvT is presented in Fig. 3. Given an RGB
image with a shape of $H \times W \times 3$, it is first encoded into overlapped patches by two
consecutive convolutions. The patches can be viewed as tokens in NLP. Unlike
the patch stem in ViT [11], which uses large-kernel plus large-stride convolutions

to extract features, we adopt traditional convolution stem (two sequential convolutions with the kernel of $3 \times 3$ to strike a balance between inductive biases and the representation learning ability of the following transformer blocks [59]). Then several layers of a redesigned transformer block, tightly enhanced by convolution, are applied to these patches to extract higher-dimensional features. In this work, we adopt the hierarchical modeling approach following [28], so the number of tokens is reduced and the dimension is increased as the layers go deeper. After the last block, the tokens are fed into a global average pooling layer and a fully connected layer to produce the prediction maps.

As shown in Fig. 3, there are four stages in our pipeline, and each stage consists of three modules: a Context Module (CM) to capture large context, a Spatial Module (SM) to retain local details, and a Dual AtteNtion Enhancement module (DANE) to fuse features from the SM and CM. It can be seen that transformer and convolution blocks are tightly integrated, and both fusion steps take place before transformer's FFN step.

## 3.1   Context Module

We first adopt a convolution block for fast downsampling to obtain high-level semantic context information with three consecutive convolutions. Following the design in ResNet [16], there are a $1 \times 1$ convolution, a $3 \times 3$ separable convolution with stride 2 for downsampling, and a $1 \times 1$ projection convolution to integrate channel information. The convolution kernels extract low-resolution features and allow the following steps to have larger respective field.

Then we adopt $N$ window-based self-attention modules following Swin Transformer [28], which are responsible for extracting medium- and high-level (and long-distance) information. Note that the tokens fed into transformer are downsampled to reduce computational and memory costs and expand the receptive field.

The Context Module (CM) is designed to efficiently and effectively learn context information. The CM downsamples the feature maps and then feed them into self-attention, which ensures the self-attention mechanism has much smaller computational (also memory) costs, and can obtain larger receptive field to enlarge the context.

**Pre-SA Fusion.** We downsample the input feature map of the CM before computing W-MHSA to reduce the amount of computation (approximately a factor of 4 for window-based SA, 1/16 for regular self-attention). However, this reduction in resolution would result in a loss of information, especially salient features. We propose to compensate for this loss in a parameter-free way (i.e., maxpooling) before it is processed by self-attention. Features from the maxpooling steps could be used for such enrichment, as those features are notable ones and can provide translation/rotation for the following transformer.

To this end, we add the feature map from the maxpooling step to that of the convolutions in the transformer. The pre-SA fusion and the output of the

W-MHSA in CM can be expressed as:

$$\mathcal{F}_{CM} = W{-}MHSA(LN(maxpool(\mathcal{F}) + Conv(\mathcal{F})))$$
$$+ maxpool(\mathcal{F}) + Conv(\mathcal{F}) \tag{1}$$

where $\mathcal{F}$ represents the input feature maps to both CM and SM, and $Conv$ denotes three consecutive convolutions, respectively.

## 3.2  Spatial Module

It has been observed that preserving the detailed spatial information is crucial to high performance in recognition tasks [33,51,62]. However, the CM has seriously lost the fine-detailed features. To compensate the local details, we propose a spatial module (SM) which maintains the large spatial size of tokens. In particular, we adopt separable convolution with a $3 \times 3$ kernel to encode the local features. Since the spatial module does not involve any global operator, the spatial details are well preserved in this path.

## 3.3  DANE

The features of CM and SM represent different scales of information, i.e., SM means local features and CM represents global contexts, it is not a good idea to just simply add the heterogeneous features up. Instead, we design a fusion module called Dual AtteNtion Enhancement (DANE), which consists of a channel attention, a spatial attention and a automatic selective mechanism to allocate attentions to enhance context and spatial features respectively. The structure of the proposed module is shown in Fig. 4.

Since the features extracted by CM lack interaction between channels (self-attention has no inter-channel integration), we perform the channel-wise attention to enhance the useful features of the CM and suppress noise information. This generates a set of global dependencies on channel dimension by aggregating the feature maps in its spatial dimension. Let the token map output from the CM be $\mathcal{F}_{CM}$, we use a global average pooling operation, and two consecutive FC layers for squeeze and excitation [19], to get the channel-wise weights as described below:

$$\mathcal{W}_c = \boldsymbol{f}_{ex}(\boldsymbol{f}_{sq}(avgpool(\mathcal{F}_{CM}))) \tag{2}$$

The feature maps of the SM contain rich fine-grained spatial information, but lack global context information, so we use spatial-wise attention on SM features to learn spatial weighting, enhancing useful spatial areas and suppressing irrelevant ones. Let the SM output be $\mathcal{F}_{SM}$, the spatial-wise weights are generated by aggregating the feature maps in the channel dimension with a FC layer as follows:

$$\mathcal{W}_s = \boldsymbol{f}_{sq}(\mathcal{F}_{SM}) \tag{3}$$

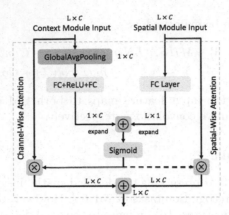

**Fig. 4.** The framework of the proposed DANE module, which fuses the information from SM and CM with both spatial and channel attention.

With the weight parameters learned, the tokens can learn high- and low-level features from both SM and CM simultaneously, which are calculated as:

$$\mathcal{W} = sigmoid(\mathcal{W}_c + \mathcal{W}_s),$$
$$\mathcal{F} = \mathcal{F}_{CM} * \mathcal{W} + \mathcal{F}_{SM} * (1 - \mathcal{W}) \tag{4}$$

After DANE being introduced, SM and CM are complementary to each other for higher performance. That is, each token in the feature map can obtain both high-level context information and low-level spatial information by adaptively adjusting the weight parameters balancing between SM and CM (sum to 1). This module introduces a small number of parameters but can effectively fuse different level of information representation from these paths.

With fully fusing information from SM and CM, the final output of the transformer block is:

$$\mathcal{F} = MLP(LN(\mathcal{F})) + \mathcal{F} \tag{5}$$

Finally, a standard layernorm operation and a fully connected layer are applied to the feature maps to increase the dimension. After all the basic blocks, the tokens go through global average pooling and a fully connected layer to obtain final predictions.

### 3.4 Model Scaling

By simply adjusting the dimension and the number of transformer blocks (also with minor adjustment of some other configurations), we can adapt our design to a range of model complexity (and computational cost), namely: Tiny (0.3 GFLOPs), Small (0.8 GFLOPs), and Base (2.5 GFLOPs). These models roughly correspond to MobileNet, ResNet and Swin-T, respectively. Their peformance on ImageNet-1K are shown in Sect. 4.1. Details of these models are listed in the supplementary material.

**Table 1.** Comparison of the model family of DFvT and state-of-the-art methods on the ImageNet-1K validation set. The memory cost is tested with a batch size 64, and when testing fps we turn up the batch size to the maximum on a single 2080 Ti GPU. For fair comparison, we don't adopt the mixed precision, and the results reported here are tested on the same platform.

| Results on ImageNet-1K validation set | | | | | | | |
|---|---|---|---|---|---|---|---|
| Group | Model | Image size | Params (M) | FLOPs (G) | Memory (GB) | Throughput (images/s) | Top-1 Acc. (%) |
| 0.2G FLOPs and More | MobileNetV1 [18] | 224 | 4.2 | 0.6 | 5.0 | 3247.5 | 70.6 |
| | MobileNetV2 [41] | 224 | 3.5 | 0.3 | 4.4 | 2780.6 | 72.0 |
| | ShffleNetV1 1.5x [69] | 224 | 3.4 | 0.3 | 3.3 | 3140.3 | 71.6 |
| | ShffleNetV2 1.0x [31] | 224 | 2.3 | 0.2 | 2.4 | 7285.2 | 69.4 |
| | MobileFormer-52M [5] | 224 | 3.5 | 0.6 | 1.8 | 3033.8 | 68.7 |
| | PvTv2-B0 [52] | 224 | 3.4 | 0.6 | 2.5 | 1624.3 | 70.5 |
| | **DFvT-T** | 224 | 4.0 | 0.3 | 1.5 | 4760.1 | **73.0** |
| 0.8G FLOPs and More | ResNet18 [16] | 224 | 11.7 | 1.8 | 1.0 | 2506.4 | 69.8 |
| | ResNet34 [16] | 224 | 21.8 | 3.7 | 1.5 | 1329.4 | 75.8 |
| | ResNet50 [16] | 224 | 25.6 | 4.1 | 3.2 | 879.0 | 76.2 |
| | MobileFormer-294M [5] | 224 | 11.8 | 3.2 | 6.2 | 857.7 | 77.9 |
| | T2T-ViT-7 [65] | 224 | 4.3 | 1.2 | 3.0 | 1483.4 | 71.7 |
| | LocalViT-T [26] | 224 | 5.3 | 1.3 | 4.2 | 1180.3 | 72.5 |
| | DeiT-Tiny [47] | 224 | 5.7 | 1.2 | 2.2 | 1950.7 | 72.2 |
| | CrossViT-9 [54] | 224 | 8.6 | 1.8 | 3.7 | 1098.9 | 73.9 |
| | PVT-Tiny [53] | 224 | 13.2 | 1.9 | 4.3 | 1087.8 | 75.1 |
| | ConViT-Ti+ [9] | 224 | 10.0 | 2.0 | 4.0 | 1034.4 | 76.7 |
| | ResT-Lite [68] | 224 | 10.5 | 1.4 | 3.4 | 1246.3 | 77.2 |
| | **DFvT-S** | 224 | 11.2 | 0.8 | 2.8 | 2202.3 | **78.3** |
| 2.5G FLOPs and More | ResNet101 [16] | 224 | 44.5 | 7.8 | 4.7 | 502.6 | 77.4 |
| | RegNetX-4G [36] | 224 | 22.1 | 4.0 | 7.7 | 789.8 | 78.6 |
| | ViT-Base [11] | 384 | 86.8 | 17.6 | OOM | 235.4 | 77.9 |
| | DeiT-Small [47] | 224 | 22.1 | 4.3 | 4.8 | 786.6 | 79.8 |
| | Swin-Tiny [28] | 224 | 28.3 | 4.5 | 8.0 | 536.8 | 81.3 |
| | CrossViT-S [54] | 224 | 26.7 | 5.6 | 7.0 | 533.9 | 81.0 |
| | PVT-Small [53] | 224 | 24.5 | 3.8 | 7.0 | 594.6 | 79.8 |
| | PVT-Medium [53] | 224 | 44.2 | 6.7 | 9.5 | 390.4 | 81.2 |
| | Conformer-Ti [13] | 224 | 23.5 | 5.2 | 7.1 | 515.1 | 81.3 |
| | CvT-13 [57] | 224 | 20.0 | 4.5 | 6.6 | 541.9 | 81.6 |
| | T2T-ViT-14 [65] | 224 | 21.5 | 5.2 | 6.8 | 610.7 | 81.5 |
| | CoTNet-50 [27] | 224 | 22.2 | 3.3 | OOM | 633.3 | 81.3 |
| | ConViT-S [9] | 224 | 27.8 | 5.4 | 7.9 | 462.0 | 81.3 |
| | ResT-Base [68] | 224 | 30.3 | 4.3 | 6.4 | 598.5 | 81.6 |
| | **DFvT-B** | 224 | 37.3 | 2.5 | 5.5 | 962.8 | **82.0** |

# 4   Experiments

We conduct experiments on image classification to evaluate and validate performance and efficiency of the proposed DFvT design.

## 4.1   Image Classification on ImageNet-1K

For the task of image classification, DFvT is trained on ImageNet-1K [22] training set, which contains 1.28 million images of 1k classes, and is tested on the validation set that includes 50k images. In the experiments, image size is set to $224 \times 224$, and top-1 accuracy on a single crop is reported. Efficiency is measured using FLOPs, actual throughput (images/sec), and memory usage. We use AdamW [21] as the optimizer with a cosine decay learning rate scheduler for 300 epochs and linear warm-up for 20 epochs. We set the batch size to 1024 for

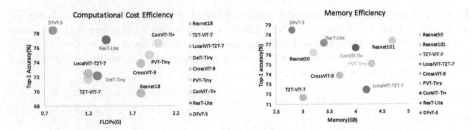

**Fig. 5.** Illustrations of top-1 accuracy in ImageNet-1K validation set with respect to memory and computational cost.

DFvT-T and DFvT-S, 512 for DFvT-B, the initial learning rate to $1e-3$, weight decay to 0.05. The data augmentation and regularization strategies follow [28]. The models are trained on 4 NVIDIA GeForce RTX 2080 Ti GPUs implemented using PyTorch.

The results are shown in Table 1. Our model, DFvT-S achieves 78.3% top-1 accuracy, which is higher than ResNet101 (77.4%) [16] in terms of accuracy, and is approximately 4 times faster with 90% less computational complexity (in FLOPs). Our model also costs 35% less memory. DFvT-S can even compare to small ResNet (i.e., ResNet18) in terms of computational cost and inference throughput, but our model provides a much better accuracy (i.e., 8.5 % higher for top-1 accuracy). Compared to the widely adopted ResNet50, DFvT-S outperforms it in all perspectives.

DFvT-S is also competitive with other ViTs. In the group of 0.8G FLOPs and more, our DFvT-S is among the top performers with respect to the accuracy, computational cost, and inference speed. For example, DFvT-S outperforms many recently developed ViT models, such as T2T-ViT-7, LocalVit-7, CrossViT-9, PVT-Tiny, ConViT-Ti+, and ResT-Lite, concerning the accuracy, FLOPs, inference throughput, and memory. As for MobileFormer-294M, our model achieves comparable accuracy with substantially lower memory and computational costs and higher throughput.

**Model Scaling.** Table 1 shows the experimental results of our scaled models on image classification (ImageNet-1K). Our tiny model (i.e., DFvT-T) can achieve a competitive accuracy (73.0%) compared to the SOTA lightweight models. More importantly, DFvT-T has advantages over the SOTA methods in terms of the FLOPs, memory costs as well as inference throughput except for ShuffleNetV2 (but note DFvT-T accuracy is 3.6% higher than ShuffleNetV2). For instance, the throughput of DFvT-T is approximately twice as much as MobileNetV2 [41] on a single NVIDIA 2080 Ti GPU while only using one-third of memory. As for the DFvT-B (large model), we also achieve competitive results with lower computational and memory costs. The scatterplots on computational/memory costs and accuracy are shown in Fig. 5.

## 4.2    Ablation Study

In this section, we conduct extensive ablation experiments to demonstrate the overall effectiveness of our design, the necessity of Context Module (CM), Spatial Module(SM) and DANE block.

**Transformer Design.** Table 2 presents the four options for model design depicted in Fig. 2. It can be observed that baseline ViT has presented decent top-1 accuracy with a small number of parameters, but the computational cost and inference speed are not ideal. If we directly downsampled the input size of the input feature map (Downsampled ViT), we can largely improve the throughput (2 times faster) and greatly reduce the computational complexity (2 times smaller) as well as the memory cost (45% smaller). However, the accuracy becomes much lower, which is assumed due to the information loss. The parallel ViT, which sets up a parallel convolution path to provide local information, can substantially improve the accuracy compared to Downsampled ViT (71.9% to 76.9%). Nevertheless, memory and inference speed become much worse. Our designed DFvT can not only save memory, computational cost, and accelerate the inference compared to baseline and parallel ViT, it can also achieve the best accuracy, which can attribute to the two paths design. The spatial information from SM can be efficiently integrated to CM. As a trade-off between efficiency and accuracy, decoupling design is the optimal choice.

**Table 2.** Experimental results of models with different designs corresponding to Fig. 2. Note that the ViT we use is a pyramid structure with window SA.

| Model | Params (M) | FLOPs (G) | FPS (imgs/s) | Memory (GB) | Top-1 Acc. (%) |
|---|---|---|---|---|---|
| a: Baseline ViT | 9.8 | 1.4 | 1168.2 | 3.2 | 74.7 |
| b: Downsampled ViT | 8.8 | 0.5 | 3091.5 | 1.8 | 71.9 |
| c: Parallel ViT | 13.1 | 1.1 | 1843.3 | 5.0 | 76.9 |
| d: DFvT-S | 11.2 | 0.8 | 2203.3 | 2.8 | 78.3 |

**Spatial Module and Context Module.** Table 3 shows the effectiveness of each components. The model gets a moderate performance of 77.0% with only CM, which can be explained that though suffering from the lost of detailed information, the CM has extracted enough global context information for classification. After introducing the detailed low-level information from SM, the performance is improved from 77.0% to 77.5%. It is because that the SM can supply the missing local spatial information of CM, which is helpful for higher performance.

**Table 3.** Detailed performance comparison of each component in DFvT-S.

| Model | Params (M) | FLOPs (G) | Top-1 Acc. (%) | Gains (%) |
|---|---|---|---|---|
| CM | 10.3 | 0.7 | 77.0 | – |
| CM + SM | 11.1 | 0.8 | 77.5 | +0.5 |
| CM + SM + DANE | 11.2 | 0.8 | 78.3 | +1.3 |

**Impact of Context Module (CM).** As introduced in Sect. 3.1, CM has two major components, pre-SA fusion and window-SA. Since window-SA is a necessity portion, we mainly consider the design of pre-SA.

Pre-SA has two input, max-pooling features and convolutional features. Table 4 demonstrates the importance of each factor for the pre-SA fusion. The accuracy will be significantly decreased by 6.1% if removing convolutional information flow for pre-SA fusion. Similarly, we also show that the information flow from the max-pooling operation is important because the accuracy will drop by 0.2%. Obviously, convolutional features are more important for the pre-SA fusion. The reason may lie in that the convolutions provide fine-grained and diversified information, while maxpooling only retains the maximum fired neurons. Nevertheless, we still keep the max-pooling operation as it can improve the diversity of the fused information and can also contribute to the accuracy with negligible cost.

**Table 4.** Ablation study of pre-SA fusion in Context Module in terms of the number of parameters, FLOPs and top-1 accuracy on ImageNet-1K.

| Model | Params (M) | FLOPs (G) | Top-1 Acc. (%) | Declines (%) |
|---|---|---|---|---|
| DFvT-S | 11.2 | 0.8 | 78.3 | – |
| w/o maxpooling info | 11.2 | 0.8 | 78.1 | −0.2 |
| w/o conv info | 9.6 | 0.5 | 72.2 | −6.1 |

**Impact of Spatial Module (SM).** Table 3 proves that the Spatial Module can improve the performance of 0.5% with little FLOPs introduced (i.e., 0.7G to 0.8G). The depthwise convolution in SM mainly focuses on encoding fine-detailed information, thus complementing the context information from CM well.

**Impact of DANE.** We have carefully designed the feature fusion block (i.e., DANE) for post-SA feature aggregation. To validate the designation, we compare DANE with some widely used feature fusion methods, namely, "SUM": element-wise addition, "SUM+MUL": element-wise addition and multiplication, "SE": use channel attention mechanism to fuse the features [19], "SPATIAL": use spatial attention to fuse the features [56], "rDANE": reverse version of DANE, that

**Table 5.** Different designs of the feature aggregation module to fuse the information from SM and CM.

| Model | Params (M) | FLOPs (G) | Top-1 Acc. (%) | Gains (%) |
|---|---|---|---|---|
| SUM | 11.1 | 0.8 | 77.5 | – |
| SUM+MUL | 11.1 | 0.8 | 77.6 | +0.1 |
| SE | 11.2 | 0.8 | 78.0 | +0.5 |
| SPATIAL | 11.2 | 0.8 | 77.8 | +0.3 |
| rDANE | 11.2 | 0.8 | 78.1 | +0.6 |
| DANE | 11.2 | 0.8 | 78.3 | +0.8 |

is, we use channel and spatial attention for inputs from CM and SM respectively. The difference is not obvious since the size of our model is not large enough. We believe that the difference will become apparent when the model size becomes larger. Note that we do not consider concatenation because it will vastly increase the parameters and computational cost. The experimental results are reported in Table 5. The attention-based fusion strategies perform better than the pure addition or multiplication since it is not suitable to directly fuse information with different level of information representation. Among the attention based fusion operators, DANE demonstrates the best performance. This confirms our assumption that features from CM and SM exhibit different characteristics and they are complementary to each other.

## 5 Conclusion

In this paper, we propose a new hybrid transformer and convolution backbone, Doubly-Fused ViT (DFvT), for image classification, which retains the high accuracy of ViT but is highly efficient in computational and memory costs. The features in a standard transformer block are fast downsampled to extract context information in Context Module (CM), and is enhanced with spatial information using convolution in Spatial Module (SM). Moreover, a Dual AtteNtion Enhancement (DANE) module is used for fusion by combining spatial-wise attention for SM and channel-wise attention for CM. We also conduct model scaling to further trade off accuracy and efficiency to provide more choices for various scenarios. Experiments on ImageNet-1K image classification demonstrate that DFvT outperforms the state of the art in either accuracy or speed, or both.

## 6 Social Impact and Limitations

Efficient algorithms, including efficient transformer designs, are appealing for practical applications. In a world that is increasingly conscious of carbon footprint, it is particularly important to be able to reduce computational cost and its associated environmental cost, hence making AI systems more feasible for adaption. In the meantime, efficient algorithms such as efficient transformers can also be potentially used in a wider range of scenarios and bring value to a wider range of users.

Due to computational resource constraints, we have not studied DFvT design on larger scale datasets. Because the DFvT design is general and performs well under multiple settings, and transformers tend to be more data-driven, we are optimistic about its learning ability on larger scale data.

# References

1. Chen, B., et al.: GLiT: neural architecture search for global and local image transformer. In: Proceedings of the IEEE International Conference on Computer Vision, pp. 12–21 (2021)
2. Chen, C.F., Fan, Q., Panda, R.: CrossViT: cross-attention multi-scale vision transformer for image classification. arXiv preprint arXiv:2103.14899 (2021)
3. Chen, C.F., Panda, R., Fan, Q.: RegionViT: regional-to-local attention for vision transformers. arXiv preprint arXiv:2106.02689 (2021)
4. Chen, P., Chen, Y., Liu, S., Yang, M., Jia, J.: Exploring and improving mobile level vision transformers. arXiv preprint arXiv:2108.13015 (2021)
5. Chen, Y., et al.: Mobile-former: Bridging MobileNet and transformer. arXiv preprint arXiv:2108.05895 (2021)
6. Chen, Z., Xie, L., Niu, J., Liu, X., Wei, L., Tian, Q.: Visformer: the vision-friendly transformer. arXiv preprint arXiv:2104.12533 (2021)
7. Chu, X., et al.: Twins: revisiting spatial attention design in vision transformers. arXiv preprint arXiv:2104.13840 (2021)
8. Dai, J., Qi, H., Xiong, Y., Li, Y., Zhang, G., Hu, H., Wei, Y.: Deformable convolutional networks. In: Proceedings of the IEEE International Conference on Computer Vision, pp. 764–773 (2017)
9. d'Ascoli, S., Touvron, H., Leavitt, M., Morcos, A., Biroli, G., Sagun, L.: ConViT: improving vision transformers with soft convolutional inductive biases. arXiv preprint arXiv:2103.10697 (2021)
10. Devlin, J., Chang, M.W., Lee, K., Toutanova, K.: BERT: pre-training of deep bidirectional transformers for language understanding. arXiv preprint arXiv:1810.04805 (2018)
11. Dosovitskiy, A., et al.: An image is worth 16 × 16 words: transformers for image recognition at scale. arXiv preprint arXiv:2010.11929 (2020)
12. El-Nouby, A., et al.: XCiT: cross-covariance image transformers. arXiv preprint arXiv:2106.09681 (2021)
13. Gulati, A., et al.: Conformer: convolution-augmented transformer for speech recognition. arXiv preprint arXiv:2005.08100 (2020)
14. Guo, J., et al.: CMT: convolutional neural networks meet vision transformers. arXiv preprint arXiv:2107.06263 (2021)
15. Han, K., Guo, J., Tang, Y., Wang, Y.: PyramidTNT: improved transformer-in-transformer baselines with pyramid architecture (2022)
16. He, K., Zhang, X., Ren, S., Sun, J.: Deep residual learning for image recognition. In: Proceedings of the IEEE Conference on Computer Vision and Pattern Recognition (2016)
17. Heo, B., Yun, S., Han, D., Chun, S., Choe, J., Oh, S.J.: Rethinking spatial dimensions of vision transformers. arXiv preprint arXiv:2103.16302 (2021)

18. Howard, A.G., et al.: MobileNets: efficient convolutional neural networks for mobile vision applications. arXiv preprint arXiv:1704.04861 (2017)

19. Hu, J., Shen, L., Sun, G.: Squeeze-and-excitation networks. In: Proceedings of the IEEE Conference on Computer Vision and Pattern Recognition, pp. 7132–7141 (2018)

20. Jiang, Z., et al.: Token labeling: Training a 85.5% top-1 accuracy vision transformer with 56 m parameters on ImageNet. arXiv preprint arXiv:2104.10858 (2021)

21. Kingma, D.P., Ba, J.: Adam: a method for stochastic optimization. arXiv preprint arXiv:1412.6980 (2014)

22. Krizhevsky, A., Sutskever, I., Hinton, G.E.: ImageNet classification with deep convolutional neural networks **25**, 1097–1105 (2012)

23. Lan, Z., Chen, M., Goodman, S., Gimpel, K., Sharma, P., Soricut, R.: ALBERT: a lite BERT for self-supervised learning of language representations. arXiv preprint arXiv:1909.11942 (2019)

24. Lecun, Y., Bottou, L., Bengio, Y., Haffner, P.: Gradient-based learning applied to document recognition. Proc. IEEE **86**(11), 2278–2324 (1998). https://doi.org/10.1109/5.726791

25. Li, K., et al.: UniFormer: unifying convolution and self-attention for visual recognition. arXiv preprint arXiv:2201.09450 (2022)

26. Li, Y., Zhang, K., Cao, J., Timofte, R., Van Gool, L.: LocalViT: bringing locality to vision transformers. arXiv preprint arXiv:2104.05707 (2021)

27. Li, Y., Yao, T., Pan, Y., Mei, T.: Contextual transformer networks for visual recognition. arXiv preprint arXiv:2107.12292 (2021)

28. Liu, Z., et al.: Swin transformer: hierarchical vision transformer using shifted windows. arXiv preprint arXiv:2103.14030 (2021)

29. Liu, Z., Mao, H., Wu, C.Y., Feichtenhofer, C., Darrell, T., Xie, S.: A convnet for the 2020s (2022)

30. Long, J., Shelhamer, E., Darrell, T.: Fully convolutional networks for semantic segmentation. In: Proceedings of the IEEE Conference on Computer Vision and Pattern Recognition, pp. 3431–3440 (2015)

31. Ma, N., Zhang, X., Zheng, H.T., Sun, J.: ShuffleNet v2: practical guidelines for efficient CNN architecture design. In: Proceedings of the European Conference on Computer Vision, pp. 116–131 (2018)

32. Mehta, S., Rastegari, M.: MobileViT: light-weight, general-purpose, and mobile-friendly vision transformer. arXiv preprint arXiv:2110.02178 (2021)

33. Nie, D., Xue, J., Ren, X.: Bidirectional pyramid networks for semantic segmentation. In: Proceedings of the Asian Conference on Computer Vision (2020)

34. Pan, Z., Zhuang, B., Liu, J., He, H., Cai, J.: Scalable vision transformers with hierarchical pooling. In: Proceedings of the IEEE International Conference on Computer Vision, pp. 377–386 (2021)

35. Peng, C., Zhang, X., Yu, G., Luo, G., Sun, J.: Large kernel matters-improve semantic segmentation by global convolutional network. In: Proceedings of the IEEE Conference on Computer Vision and Pattern Recognition, pp. 4353–4361 (2017)

36. Radosavovic, I., Kosaraju, R.P., Girshick, R., He, K., Dollár, P.: Designing network design spaces. In: Proceedings of the IEEE Conference on Computer Vision and Pattern Recognition, pp. 10428–10436 (2020)

37. Raghu, M., Unterthiner, T., Kornblith, S., Zhang, C., Dosovitskiy, A.: Do vision transformers see like convolutional neural networks? vol. 34 (2021)

38. Rao, Y., Zhao, W., Liu, B., Lu, J., Zhou, J., Hsieh, C.J.: DynamicViT: efficient vision transformers with dynamic token sparsification. arXiv preprint arXiv:2106.02034 (2021)

39. Ren, S., He, K., Girshick, R., Sun, J.: Faster R-CNN: towards real-time object detection with region proposal networks. **28**, 91–99 (2015)
40. Ronneberger, O., Fischer, P., Brox, T.: U-Net: convolutional networks for biomedical image segmentation. In: Navab, N., Hornegger, J., Wells, W.M., Frangi, A.F. (eds.) MICCAI 2015. LNCS, vol. 9351, pp. 234–241. Springer, Cham (2015). https://doi.org/10.1007/978-3-319-24574-4_28
41. Sandler, M., Howard, A., Zhu, M., Zhmoginov, A., Chen, L.C.: MobileNetV2: inverted residuals and linear bottlenecks. In: Proceedings of the IEEE Conference on Computer Vision and Pattern Recognition, pp. 4510–4520 (2018)
42. Santurkar, S., Tsipras, D., Ilyas, A., Madry, A.: How does batch normalization help optimization? In: Proceedings of the 32nd International Conference on Neural Information Processing Systems, pp. 2488–2498 (2018)
43. Simonyan, K., Zisserman, A.: Very deep convolutional networks for large-scale image recognition. arXiv preprint arXiv:1409.1556 (2014)
44. Srinivas, A., Lin, T.Y., Parmar, N., Shlens, J., Abbeel, P., Vaswani, A.: Bottleneck transformers for visual recognition. In: Proceedings of the IEEE Conference on Computer Vision and Pattern Recognition, pp. 16519–16529 (2021)
45. Szegedy, C., et al.: Going deeper with convolutions. In: Proceedings of the IEEE Conference on Computer Vision and Pattern Recognition (2015)
46. Tan, M., Le, Q.: EfficientNet: rethinking model scaling for convolutional neural networks. In: Proceedings of the International Conference on Machine Learning, pp. 6105–6114 (2019)
47. Touvron, H., Cord, M., Douze, M., Massa, F., Sablayrolles, A., Jégou, H.: Training data-efficient image transformers & distillation through attention. In: Proceedings of the International Conference on Machine Learning, pp. 10347–10357 (2021)
48. Touvron, H., Cord, M., Sablayrolles, A., Synnaeve, G., Jégou, H.: Going deeper with image transformers. arXiv preprint arXiv:2103.17239 (2021)
49. Vaswani, A., Ramachandran, P., Srinivas, A., Parmar, N., Hechtman, B., Shlens, J.: Scaling local self-attention for parameter efficient visual backbones. In: Proceedings of the IEEE Conference on Computer Vision and Pattern Recognition, pp. 12894–12904 (2021)
50. Vaswani, A., et al.: Attention is all you need. In: Proceedings of the Advances in Neural Information Processing Systems, pp. 5998–6008 (2017)
51. Wang, J., et al.: Deep high-resolution representation learning for visual recognition. TPAMI (2019)
52. Wang, W., et al.: PVT v2: improved baselines with pyramid vision transformer. arXiv preprint arXiv:2106.13797 (2021). https://doi.org/10.1007/s41095-022-0274-8
53. Wang, W., et al.: Pyramid vision transformer: a versatile backbone for dense prediction without convolutions. arXiv preprint arXiv:2102.12122 (2021)
54. Wang, W., Yao, L., Chen, L., Cai, D., He, X., Liu, W.: CrossFormer: a versatile vision transformer based on cross-scale attention. arXiv preprint arXiv:2108.00154 (2021)
55. Wang, X., Girshick, R., Gupta, A., He, K.: Non-local neural networks. In: Proceedings of the IEEE Conference on Computer Vision and Pattern Recognition, pp. 7794–7803 (2018)
56. Woo, S., Park, J., Lee, J.Y., Kweon, I.S.: CBAM: convolutional block attention module. In: Proceedings of the European Conference on Computer Vision, pp. 3–19 (2018)
57. Wu, H., et al.: CVT: introducing convolutions to vision transformers. arXiv preprint arXiv:2103.15808 (2021)

58. Wu, K., Peng, H., Chen, M., Fu, J., Chao, H.: Rethinking and improving relative position encoding for vision transformer. In: Proceedings of the IEEE International Conference on Computer Vision, pp. 10033–10041 (2021)
59. Xiao, T., Singh, M., Mintun, E., Darrell, T., Dollár, P., Girshick, R.: Early convolutions help transformers see better. arXiv preprint arXiv:2106.14881 (2021)
60. Yan, H., Li, Z., Li, W., Wang, C., Wu, M., Zhang, C.: ConTNet: why not use convolution and transformer at the same time? arXiv preprint arXiv:2104.13497 (2021)
61. Yang, Z., Dai, Z., Yang, Y., Carbonell, J., Salakhutdinov, R.R., Le, Q.V.: XLNet: generalized autoregressive pretraining for language understanding, vol. 32 (2019)
62. Yu, C., Wang, J., Peng, C., Gao, C., Yu, G., Sang, N.: BiSeNet: bilateral segmentation network for real-time semantic segmentation. In: Proceedings of the European Conference on Computer Vision (2018)
63. Yu, F., Koltun, V.: Multi-scale context aggregation by dilated convolutions. arXiv preprint arXiv:1511.07122 (2015)
64. Yu, W., et al.: MetaFormer is actually what you need for vision. arXiv preprint arXiv:2111.11418 (2021)
65. Yuan, L., et al.: Tokens-to-token ViT: training vision transformers from scratch on ImageNet. In: Proceedings of the IEEE International Conference on Computer Vision, pp. 558–567 (2021)
66. Yun, S., Han, D., Oh, S.J., Chun, S., Choe, J., Yoo, Y.: CutMix: regularization strategy to train strong classifiers with localizable features. In: Proceedings of the IEEE International Conference on Computer Vision, pp. 6023–6032 (2019)
67. Zhang, P., et al.: Multi-scale vision longformer: a new vision transformer for high-resolution image encoding. arXiv preprint arXiv:2103.15358 (2021)
68. Zhang, Q., Yang, Y.: ResT: an efficient transformer for visual recognition. arXiv preprint arXiv:2105.13677v3 (2021)
69. Zhang, X., Zhou, X., Lin, M., Sun, J.: ShuffleNet: an extremely efficient convolutional neural network for mobile devices. In: Proceedings of the IEEE Conference on Computer Vision and Pattern Recognition, pp. 6848–6856 (2018)

# Author Index

Printed in the United States
by Baker & Taylor Publisher Services